THE

WAR OF THE REBELLION:

A COMPILATION OF THE

OFFICIAL RECORDS

OF THE

UNION AND CONFEDERATE ARMIES.

PUBLISHED UNDER THE DIRECTION OF

The Hon. REDFIELD PROCTOR, Secretary of War.

BY

Maj. GEORGE B. DAVIS, U. S. A.,
Mr. LESLIE J. PERRY,
Mr. JOSEPH W. KIRKLEY,
Board of Publication.

SERIES I—VOLUME XXXVIII—IN FIVE PARTS.
PART V—CORRESPONDENCE, ETC.

WASHINGTON:
GOVERNMENT PRINTING OFFICE.
1891.

PART V.–VOL. XXXVIII.

CORRESPONDENCE, ORDERS, AND RETURNS RELATING TO OPERATIONS IN THE ATLANTA CAMPAIGN, FROM JULY 1, 1864, TO SEPTEMBER 8, 1864.*

UNION CORRESPONDENCE, ETC.

NEAR KENESAW, *July 1, 1864.*
(Received 1 p. m. 2d.)

Hon. E. M. STANTON,
    Secretary of War:

General Thomas offered General Crittenden a good division—Butterfield's, in Hooker's corps—but Crittenden declines, on the ground that he formerly commanded a corps in the same army. A division is the legitimate command of a major-general, and he having declined I am released of the promise made through you to give General Crittenden a command.

W. T. SHERMAN,
Major-General.

NEAR KENESAW, GA., *July 1, 1864—9.30 p. m.*
(Received 12 m. 2d.)

Maj. Gen. H. W. HALLECK,
    Washington, D. C.:

General Schofield is now south of Olley's Creek, and on the head of Nickajack. I have been hurrying down provisions and forage, and to-morrow night propose to move General McPherson from the left to the extreme right, back of General Thomas. This will bring my right within three miles of Chattahoochee and about five of the railroad. By this movement I think I can force Johnston to move his army down from Kenesaw, to defend his railroad crossing and the Chattahoochee, when I will, by the left flank, reach the railroad below Marietta; but I cut loose from the railroad with ten days' supplies in wagons. Johnston may come out of his intrenchments and attack General Thomas, which is what I want, for General Thomas is well intrenched, parallel with the enemy, south of Kenesaw. I think Allatoona and the line of the Etowah are strong enough for me to venture on this move. The movement is substantially down the Sandtown road, straight for Atlanta.

W. T. SHERMAN,
Major-General.

---

*For Correspondence, etc., from May 1 to June 30, 1864, see Part IV.

FRANKFORT, KY., *July 1, 1864.*

Major-General SHERMAN:

I have just been relieved from the command of a gallant division in the Army of the Potomac at my own request, because most of the corps commanders were my juniors. Gladly as I would serve under you, yet I do not desire the command of a division in an army where I have commanded a corps and where most of the corps commanders are my juniors.

T. L. CRITTENDEN,
Major-General.

HDQRS. MILITARY DIVISION OF THE MISSISSIPPI,
In the Field, near Kenesaw, July 1, 1864.

General CRITTENDEN,
Frankfort, Ky.:

I think you make a great mistake in declining a division, which is a major-general's command. You could not expect a corps commander to be removed to give place to you. Still, you had the offer of a good division, which is now withdrawn, and General Thomas says he has no other command to offer you.

W. T. SHERMAN,
Major-General, Commanding.

HDQRS. MILITARY DIVISION OF THE MISSISSIPPI,
In the Field, near Kenesaw, July 1, 1864.

A. ANDERSON,
General Supt. of Military Railroads, Nashville:

I hear Mr. Taylor, the new superintendent, spoken of very highly. Bear in mind that these are war times and all must incur some risk. We here will do our share, but if the road or wires to the rear are interrupted, the repair must come mostly from your end. Keep Colonel McCallum advised that he must be prepared to lose half a dozen or more trains every month by guerrillas and dashes at the road which cannot be prevented.

W. T. SHERMAN,
Major-General, Commanding.

NASHVILLE, *July 1, 1864.*

Major-General SHERMAN:

We have made and continue to make large preparations for contingencies, loss of trains, and the like. We receive five to eight new engines per week and average over thirty cars per week. In July the number of cars received will be much greater. No pains, effort, or expense will be spared on our part.

A. ANDERSON,
General Superintendent.

LOST MOUNTAIN SIGNAL STATION, GA.,
July 1, 1864—7.30 p. m.

Capt. C. R. CASE,
    Chief Signal Officer, Department of the Cumberland:

Have opened with Captain Daniels, chief signal officer, Twenty-third Army Corps, south 40 degrees east, seven miles distant. Had fair view of Atlanta this evening. See fires in Marietta. No other rebel fires in sight.

HOWGATE,
Lieutenant, Acting Signal Officer.

HDQRS. MILITARY DIVISION OF THE MISSISSIPPI,
In the Field, near Kenesaw, July 1, 1864.

General THOMAS:

Let your artillery and skirmishers stir up the enemy a little this evening and to-morrow morning. I fear they are getting too strong on General Schofield, who has gone farther toward Ruff's Mill than I contemplated.

W. T. SHERMAN,
Major-General, Commanding.

(Same to McPherson.)

HEADQUARTERS DEPARTMENT OF THE CUMBERLAND,
Near Kenesaw Mountain, Ga., July 1, 1864.

Maj. Gen. O. O. HOWARD,
    Commanding Fourth Army Corps:

GENERAL: Let your artillery stir up the enemy this evening and to-morrow morning. It is feared they are getting too strong on General Schofield.

By command of Major-General Thomas:

WM. D. WHIPPLE,
Assistant Adjutant-General.

(Same to Palmer and Hooker.)

HEADQUARTERS DEPARTMENT OF THE CUMBERLAND,
In the Field, July 1, 1864.

Maj. Gen. O. O. HOWARD,
    Commanding Fourth Army Corps:

GENERAL: In the directions given this evening to stir up the enemy with artillery I should have said skirmishers and artillery. I desire now to make that correction.

Very respectfully, your obedient servant,

WM. D. WHIPPLE,
Assistant Adjutant-General.

(Same to Palmer and Hooker.)

HEADQUARTERS FOURTH ARMY CORPS,
In the Field, near Kenesaw Mountain, Ga., July 1, 1864.

Major-General STANLEY,
First Division, Fourth Army Corps:

GENERAL: You will relieve General Newton's troops as soon as it is dark to-night, extending your line on the left as far as Sutermeister's battery.

By order of Major-General Howard:

> J. S. FULLERTON,
> *Assistant Adjutant-General.*

HEADQUARTERS FOURTEENTH ARMY CORPS,
In the Field, July 1, 1864.

Brig. Gen. W. D. WHIPPLE,
Chief of Staff, Department of the Cumberland:

I am informed by General Baird that he has already relieved not only General Geary but also a part of General Williams' command, and General Williams has notified him this morning that he is about to draw out the rest of his force. I do not understand this or upon what grounds it is expected that all the men of Baird's division are to be forced into the lines. If ordered by proper authority it will be done, but I will not allow of it otherwise.

Respectfully,

> JOHN M. PALMER,
> *Major-General.*

HEADQUARTERS DEPARTMENT OF THE CUMBERLAND,
Near Kenesaw Mountain, Ga., July 1, 1864.

Maj. Gen. J. M. PALMER,
Commanding Fourteenth Army Corps:

GENERAL: Major-General Thomas has seen your note of this a. m., and directs me to say that he has no objection to your relieving, by General Baird's division, one brigade of General Williams', but that you will do no more.

Very respectfully, your obedient servant,

> SOUTHARD HOFFMAN,
> *Assistant Adjutant-General.*

HEADQUARTERS DEPARTMENT OF THE CUMBERLAND,
Near Kenesaw Mountain, July 1, 1864.

Surg. G. E. COOPER,
Medical Director, Department of the Cumberland:

First. I recognize the authority of the Surgeon-General or Assistant Surgeon-General to assign to duty and relieve from duty officers of the medical department with this army, provided that they report to me that such officers are assigned to or relieved from duty in my army. The commander of an army cannot exercise the proper control over it unless he has authority to regulate all its details.

Second. I consider the general hospitals wherever established under the control of the Surgeon-General U. S. Army, but should he desire the services of any medical officer of this army with any of the general hospitals, he must procure such by proper application and orders through the army commander to which such medical officers belong. Any other proceeding is ruinous to discipline as well as an efficient working of the details of army administration.

Third. The Sanitary and Christian Commissions have done much good when we have been fortunate enough to deal with sensible and public spirited agents, but it has occurred to me that frequently complaints have been made when there has been no earthly necessity for them, and many obstacles to the efficient working of the medical department interposed, either absolutely or by insinuation, which has caused much embarrassment, and ultimately resulted in unnecessary suffering to the wounded and sick of our armies. Both institutions have done much good, but they would do much more if their agents confined themselves to their legitimate duties under the direction of the medical department of the army, the alleviation of the suffering of our sick and wounded soldiers, and not to pointing out whenever officers of the medical department have neglected their duties. It has been my experience to observe that when a new bureau or separate department of the military service has been or attempted to be established that the officers of that bureau make a point to decry all other departments which might interfere with its complete success. So with the Sanitary and Christian Commissions. They have caused much trouble and could be easily dispensed with for the good of the service, as their duties are legitimately those of and should be performed by the medical department.

Very respectfully,

GEO. H. THOMAS,
Major-General, U. S. Volunteers, Commanding.

HEADQUARTERS ARMY OF THE OHIO,
In the Field, July 1, 1864.

Major-General SHERMAN:

Stoneman reports the enemy's cavalry in strong force west of Sweet Water toward Villa Rica. He thinks it will not do to cross to the east of Sweet Water, leaving the enemy in his rear.

J. M. SCHOFIELD,
Major-General.

HEADQUARTERS ARMY OF THE OHIO,
July 1, 1864—9.30 a. m.

Major-General SHERMAN:

Stoneman crossed the Sweet Water just below the mouth of Powder Springs Creek at 7 o'clock, and is pushing toward Sweet Water Town. Hascall is progressing satisfactorily. Will be able to give you more definite information soon.

J. M. SCHOFIELD,
Major-General.

HDQRS. MILITARY DIVISION OF THE MISSISSIPPI,
[July 1, 1864.]

General SCHOFIELD:

It is not reasonable to suppose Joe Johnston will keep at Villa Rica anything more than a cavalry force of observation. If General Stoneman deems it impossible to occupy the position of Sweet Water Town, let him take position across Sweet Water Creek, below Powder Springs, and put a regiment in observation near Salt Springs, on the road between Villa Rica and Sweet Water Town. The enemy's cavalry force will then be divided, and that is what I want.

W. T. SHERMAN,
Major-General, Commanding.

HDQRS. MILITARY DIVISION OF THE MISSISSIPPI,
In the Field, near Kenesaw, July 1, 1864.

General SCHOFIELD:

I have ordered the telegraph wire to follow. To what point do you want it? Leave some person to show the road to the repair party. Is there a practicable road from Clark's across by Byrd's position to that of Reilly? I want Stoneman, if necessary, to fight hard for that position at Sweet Water. Did you get a fair proportion of the stores yesterday?

W. T. SHERMAN,
Major-General, Commanding.

SCHOFIELD'S HEADQUARTERS,
July 1, 1864.

Major-General SHERMAN:

I shall want the telegraph line to Cheney's or some point beyond. I will have a man show the way. There is a good road from Clark's to Byrd's position, and from there to Reilly's. I think Stoneman will get the position. He was here last evening and understands the importance of it. My trains were loaded last night. I have not heard what amount they got, but presume a fair share. My troops are moving. I am about starting to the front, and will keep you advised of our progress.

J. M. SCHOFIELD,
Major-General.

HEADQUARTERS ARMY OF THE OHIO,
In the Field, July 1, 1864—3 p. m.

Major-General SHERMAN:

We have advanced as far as the cross-roads, meeting with a stubborn resistance all the way. The enemy's force seems to be increasing. I am now trying to get the point where the Marietta and Ruff's Mill roads intersect, which is about half a mile to the left of the Sandtown road. My position will be very extended.

J. M. SCHOFIELD,
Major-General.

HDQRS. MILITARY DIVISION OF THE MISSISSIPPI,
In the Field, near Kenesaw Mountain, July 1, 1864.

General SCHOFIELD:

According to my maps, the position at Wade's was as far as I expected you to take. I intended to put McPherson at Ruff's and Daniels' Mills and at Widow Mitchell's; but hold fast all you make, and intrench. Let me be fully advised to-night.

W. T. SHERMAN,
Major-General, Commanding.

SCHOFIELD'S HEADQUARTERS,
July 1, 1864—9 p. m.

Major-General SHERMAN:

The line has been down, so that I could not communicate with you till now. I got your dispatches about the position you desired me to take and about Stoneman's movements. I found it necessary to go beyond Wade's about three-quarters of a mile to get control of the roads. I have got the desired position and am intrenching securely. The Powder Springs road comes in at Wade's; the Ruff's Mill road branches off one-quarter of a mile beyond Wade's, and intersects the Marietta road at Moss', only quarter of a mile from the Sandtown road, on which we moved. The Marietta road comes into the Sandtown road only half a mile from Moss', and three-quarters of a mile from Wade's. Hascall holds all those cross-roads, and his position is good. His artillery reaches the Nickajack, and his pickets are near it. The enemy seems to be in force beyond the creek. There is a cross-road leaving the Sandtown road about half a mile in front of Reilly and joining the Marietta road about half a mile to the left of Hascall. Cox has a brigade on that cross-road commanding the Marietta road. The rest of his troops are in their old position. I do not hear anything of Colonel Barter being relieved. I now need him very much. My two divisions are too far apart to support each other, but their positions are good. We will make them as strong as possible, and hold what we have if it is in our power. Stoneman reports this evening that he has found only a small rebel force west of the Sweet Water. He sent a detachment to Sweet Water Town and found the bridge there strongly guarded. I will send him your instructions. My loss to-day is not more than 50 killed and wounded, among them some valuable officers.

J. M. SCHOFIELD,
Major-General.

HDQRS. MILITARY DIVISION OF THE MISSISSIPPI,
In the Field, July 1, 1864.

General SCHOFIELD:

If you apprehend the want of help I can order McPherson to send a division at once. Your positions all seem good. The bridge at Sweet Water is held by cavalry, of course, who will quit as soon as McPherson reaches Mrs. Mitchell's. He will not get there till the day after to-morrow.

W. T. SHERMAN,
Major-General, Commanding.

HEADQUARTERS ARMY OF THE OHIO,
In the Field, July 1, 1864—9.45 p. m.

Major-General SHERMAN:

I think it would be well for McPherson to send a division to-night. My positions are too important to be hazarded. There appears no force in my front this evening that can drive me away, but of course I cannot tell what there may be in the morning.

J. M. SCHOFIELD,
Major-General.

JULY 1, 1864.

Major-General SCHOFIELD:

I have ordered General McPherson to send a division to you to start at 4 a. m., and have a copy of your dispatch to General Thomas.

W. T. SHERMAN,
Major-General.

HEADQUARTERS ARMY OF THE OHIO,
July 1, 1864.

Maj. Gen. GEORGE H. THOMAS:

General Geary is not able to relieve Colonel Barter's brigade, of General Cox's division, which is on this side of Olley's Creek. It is important for me to have that brigade beyond the creek, as at best my line will be quite extended; but it will probably suffice if the brigade be relieved at any time during the day.

J. M. SCHOFIELD,
Major-General.

(Copy sent to General Sherman.)

HEADQUARTERS ARMY OF THE OHIO,
In the Field, Ga., July 1, 1864—9 p. m.

Maj. Gen. GEORGE STONEMAN,
Commanding Cavalry Corps, Department of the Ohio:

GENERAL: I have just received your dispatch of 6.15 p. m. I inclose one from General Sherman, giving his views, &c.* Hascall has reached the cross-roads at Watson's and William Moss'. Butler connects with Hascall's right, but has not been able to advance his own right. It occurs to me that you might, according to General Sherman's plan, push a larger force down this side of Sweet Water, and press the enemy back from the bridge at Sweet Water Town. However, I leave this for you to judge. I have not yet heard what is to be done to-morrow; will let you know as soon as I learn. Please send me a man to carry a dispatch to you. I doubt whether one of mine could find you.

Very respectfully, your obedient servant,

J. M. SCHOFIELD,
Major-General, Commanding

HDQRS. THIRD DIVISION, TWENTY-THIRD ARMY CORPS,
Lynch's, Friday Evening, July 1, 1864.

Brigadier-General HASCALL,
Commanding Second Division:

GENERAL: My line of skirmishers connecting with Colonel Byrd's brigade is so long that I find it will be impossible for me to alter it to-night, and I must therefore request you to leave Colonel Hobson's line where it is till morning, as Colonel Cameron has already eleven companies on the skirmish line toward my center. My whole skirmish line is over three miles long, and you will appreciate my embarrassment in keeping it up, to say nothing of adding to it.

Truly, yours,

J. D. COX,
Brigadier-General, Commanding.

---

* See p. 7.

HEADQUARTERS ARMY OF THE OHIO,
In the Field, Ga., July 1, 1864—10.15 p. m.

Brig. Gen. M. S. HASCALL,
Commanding Second Division, Twenty-third Army Corps:

GENERAL: General McPherson is ordered to send a division to support us in the morning, to start at 4 a. m. I have directed General Cox if you are attacked in the morning to support you with all his available force, relying upon General McPherson's troops to hold his present position and give what additional support may be necessary. Make your defenses strong and extend them far enough to deploy your whole division if necessary. You can then hold in check anything the enemy may send until re-enforcements can reach you.

Very respectfully, your obedient servant,

J. M. SCHOFIELD,
Major-General, Commanding.

HEADQUARTERS ARMY OF THE OHIO,
In the Field, Ga., July 1, 1864—10.15 p. m.

Brig. Gen. J. D. COX,
Commanding Third Division, Twenty-third Army Corps:

GENERAL: I have not yet learned whether Barter will be relieved to-night. But General McPherson is to send a division to support us in the morning; it is to start at 4 a. m. Hence, if Hascall or Cameron should be attacked in the morning you can support them with all your available force, relying upon General McPherson's troops to hold your present position and give what additional support may be necessary.

Very respectfully, your obedient servant,

J. M. SCHOFIELD,
Major-General, Commanding.

HDQRS. MILITARY DIVISION OF THE MISSISSIPPI,
In the Field, near Kenesaw, July 1, 1864.

General McPHERSON:

General Schofield to-day had advanced farther than I contemplated. He has control of all the roads from Reed's to Maple's. You know his command is small, and though there is no force now that can disturb him, he thinks there may be in the morning. I want you to start one of your divisions down about 4 a. m., and to act in support of Schofield until your command gets there the next day.

W. T. SHERMAN,
Major-General, Commanding.

HEADQUARTERS CAVALRY DIVISION,
July 1, 1864.

Major-General McPHERSON,
Commanding Army of the Tennessee:

GENERAL: Within the last hour two of the cavalry pickets in my front, belonging to the Fifth Georgia, came into my line. They report Wheeler in his camp in my front, but that he has ordered four days' rations and forage to be issued, and that he intends to go to our rear. They spoke of Cartersville as one point. They say, as every one says to me, that Wheeler draws forage for 15,000 horses. If Wheeler goes he can take with him about 8,000 men, and their leave enough to picket the right of their army.

These deserters say the papers have been abusing Wheeler for his inactivity and want of success, and for his losses and failures when he has met me, and that he is now desirous of doing something to redeem his character. If Wheeler starts and I am to go after him, I should be ahead of him and across the Etowah before he gets there, somewhere in the neighborhood of Cartersville.

This story has the air of probability, and I think it true; still, something might prevent it.

The proper place for a force to prevent a raid is north of the Etowah. Where I am, or anywhere in this vicinity, it is impossible to counteract the movements of the enemy's cavalry, as it is so much more numerous, and it can move out of sight and reach of my scouts and pickets, and cross the Etowah east of Canton, and still keep a force in my front.

It seems large to say the enemy has 15,000 cavalry, but every one—deserters, prisoners, &c.—confirms it. Allow him 8,000, he then has two to my one and could spare 3,000 to make a raid. Wheeler is to start some time to-morrow or next day. If I can be spared would it not be well to have me move back to a position north of the Etowah, where I can interpose between him and his proposed raid?

Very respectfully, your obedient servant,
K. GARRARD,
Brigadier-General, Commanding Division.

(Forwarded to General Sherman.)

HDQRS. MILITARY DIVISION OF THE MISSISSIPPI,
In the Field, near Kenesaw, July 1, 1864.

General STEEDMAN,
Chattanooga, Tenn.:

To-morrow I propose to move in such a way that my communication with the railroad may be broken for some days, and great attention must be given to the line of the Etowah, especially Cartersville and Allatoona. Now that you have General John E. Smith's division, send to Allatoona and Rome the two regiments that belong there that have been detained along the road. You will now have all of Lowe's division of cavalry for guarding off to the east; it has heretofore been tied down to Kingston, but should now be over about Adairsville and Talking Rock, scouting all the time.

W. T. SHERMAN,
Major-General, Commanding.

JULY 1, 1864.

General STEEDMAN:

Don't fail to order Colonel Pugh to Allatoona, as he and his regiment will be needed there at once.

W. T. SHERMAN,
Major-General.

HDQRS. THIRD DIVISION, FIFTEENTH ARMY CORPS,
Kingston, Ga., July 1, 1864.
Col. GREEN B. RAUM,
    Commanding Second Brigade:

SIR: You will embark three regiments of your command on cars immediately and proceed by rail, leaving the Seventeenth Iowa Infantry at Tilton, the Tenth Missouri Infantry at Resaca, and the Fifty-sixth Illinois Infantry one-half at Calhoun and one-half at Adairsville, the Eightieth Ohio Infantry at this place, establishing brigade headquarters at Resaca. Relieve the troops stationed at these points, directing them to report to their commanding officer. You will patrol the road between the different stations garrisoned by your command, morning, evening, and once during the night. For additional instructions apply to the officers whom you relieve. The transportation belonging to your brigade will be stopped on its way out, under charge of Capt. Holly Skinner, assistant quartermaster.

By order of Brig. Gen. John E. Smith:

CARL. L. WHITE,
Captain and Assistant Adjutant-General.

HEADQUARTERS DISTRICT OF NORTHERN ALABAMA,
July 1, 1864.
Major POLK,
    Assistant Adjutant-General:

MAJOR: It gives me pleasure to call the attention of the general commanding to the activity of the troops in my district in carrying out my aggressive policy for the protection of the railroad. The following just received from Colonel Anderson, Twelfth Indiana Cavalry:

I have the guerrilla Parson Johnson and 4 of his men, mortally wounded, at Whitesburg, and shall have his entire gang to-night. I have Mead invested.

The enemy has been attacked on the south side of the river seven times in the last two weeks, and always with success, damaging him more or less every time, with the loss of only 1 man killed and 4 wounded on our side. Their loss will reach 50 in killed, wounded, and prisoners. On the north side of the river I have a scout out every other day, to be absent two days. They have disposed of a number of guerrillas.

Very respectfully,

R. S. GRANGER,
Brigadier-General.

CHATTANOOGA, *July 1, 1864.*
General SMITH:

The army will move to-morrow, and the greatest vigilance will be necessary, in the direction of Cartersville and Allatoona. Send at least half of Colonel Lowe's command to Adairsville to scout the country to Talking Rock.

JAMES B. STEEDMAN,
Major-General.

CAMP, KENESAW, GA.,
July 1, 1864—10 p. m.

Maj. THOMAS T. ECKERT,
   Assistant Superintendent U. S. Military Telegraph:

To-day Schofield pushed off toward Fulton, extending our right nearly eight miles, and beginning the movement which is expected to give us Marietta or a fight in open field. Johnston discovered the move, and massed on his left toward evening, threatening Schofield and calling out [*sic*], and making a demonstration along the whole line, which will be renewed in the morning. Supplies come up now rapidly, and the whole army will have ten days' on hand by to-morrow evening. Telegraph line followed Schofield, and he reports over it occurrences of to-day. No rain.

J. C. VAN DUZER.

SPECIAL FIELD ORDERS,   HDQRS. MIL. DIV. OF THE MISS.,
                In the Field, near Kenesaw Mountain, Ga.,
   No. 31.   *July 1, 1864.*

The object of the contemplated movement is to deprive the enemy of the great advantage he has in Kenesaw as a valuable watchtower from which to observe our every movement; to force him to come out of his intrenchments or move farther south. To obtain which end:

I. All army commanders will fill up their wagons at Big Shanty depot to the utmost capacity with provisions, ammunition, and forage. The chief quartermaster and commissary will give all necessary orders to clean out the depots in front of Allatoona, and so instruct that the locomotives and cars will come forward of Allatoona with great caution, and only when ordered by the chief quartermaster.

II. Major-General Thomas will hold the ground below Kenesaw as far as Olley's Creek near Mount Zion, Major-General Schofield that from Olley's Creek to the Nickajack, and General McPherson will move his train and troops rapidly in a single march and as little observed from Kenesaw as possible to the Sandtown road, and down it to the extreme right, with one corps near the Widow Mitchell's, another near Ruff's Mill, on the Nickajack, and the third in reserve near the forks of the road.

III. General Garrard's cavalry will cover the roads out of Marietta which pass north of Kenesaw, and General Stoneman's cavalry will occupy Sweet Water Old Town, coincident with the movement of McPherson. In case the enemy presses Garrard back by superior and overwhelming forces he will send one of his brigades to the flank of General Thomas and with the others fall back gradually toward Allatoona, disputing every foot of ground.

IV. Major-General McPherson will threaten the Chattahoochee River and also the railroad, and General Thomas will press the enemy close and at the very earliest possible moment break his lines and reach the railroad below Marietta. All movements must be vigorous and rapid, as the time allowed is limited by the supplies in our wagons.

By order of Maj. Gen. W. T. Sherman:

L. M. DAYTON,
Aide-de-Camp.

SPECIAL FIELD ORDERS, }   NEAR KENESAW MOUNTAIN,
      No. 56.   }   July 1, 1864.

*   *   *   *   *   *   *

X. In accordance with instructions just received in following telegram* from Major-General Sherman, Major-General Logan, commanding Fifteenth Army Corps, will direct the division of Brig. Gen. M. L. Smith to march to-morrow morning, 4 o'clock, by a road to the rear of General Sherman's headquarters until the Sandtown road is reached, upon which road the division will move to the support of Major-General Schofield, whose headquarters are at Cheney's Church, at the intersection of the Marietta, Powder Springs, and Sandtown roads.

*   *   *   *   *   *   *

By order of Maj. Gen. James B. McPherson:
                              WM. T. CLARK,
                                   Assistant Adjutant-General.

HEADQUARTERS DEPARTMENT OF THE CUMBERLAND,
                                        July 2, 1864.
Major-General SHERMAN:
    I am inclined to think they are about to fall back from Kenesaw. They are evidently watching us closely.
                              GEO. H. THOMAS,
                                   Major-General.

                                        JULY 2, 1864.
Major-General SHERMAN:
    The enemy is aware that our wagons are moving to his left.
                              GEO. H. THOMAS,
                                   Major-General.

HEADQUARTERS DEPARTMENT OF THE CUMBERLAND,
                                        July 2, 1864.
Major-General SHERMAN:
    Has General Garrard been ordered to connect with me; and where has he been directed to have his headquarters?
                              GEO. H. THOMAS,
                                   Major-General, &c.

HDQRS. MILITARY DIVISION OF THE MISSISSIPPI,
              In the Field, near Kenesaw, July 2, 1864.
General THOMAS:
    He was notified two days ago to study the roads and ground thoroughly. He will have his headquarters in the woods between Big Shanty and the north point of Kenesaw. I will direct him to report to you.
                              W. T. SHERMAN,
                                   Major-General, Commanding.

---

*See p. 11.

HDQRS. MILITARY DIVISION OF THE MISSISSIPPI,
In the Field, near Kenesaw, July 2, 1864.

General THOMAS:

General McPherson reports all ready to move to-night. Will you be ready for him to uncover the railroad by daylight to-morrow?

W. T. SHERMAN,
Major-General, Commanding.

———

HEADQUARTERS DEPARTMENT OF THE CUMBERLAND,
July 2, 1864.

Major-General SHERMAN:

General King will be in position to-night, and everything prepared.

GEO. H. THOMAS,
Major-General.

———

SHERMAN'S HEADQUARTERS,
July 2, 1864—9.20 p. m.

General THOMAS:

General Harrow, one of McPherson's division commanders, reports that as he was about to withdraw from his position according to orders, the enemy advanced in column from the mountain and are forming in line of battle at his picket-line at 8 p. m., but I hear no firing. Have telegraphed McPherson that you have reason to believe that the enemy are retiring, and that I regard their coming out this time of night with ostentation to be evidence of their retiring, and have ordered Harrow not to withdraw now, but to feel the enemy and ascertain what he is about. You had better instruct the enemy to be felt at two or three convenient points of your line between this and midnight. We must not attempt any night movements with large forces—because confusion would result—but must be prepared at break of day to act according to the very best information we can gather during the night. I have already re-enforced.*

W. T. SHERMAN,
Major-General.

———

HEADQUARTERS DEPARTMENT OF THE CUMBERLAND,
July 2, 1864.

Major-General SHERMAN:

Your dispatch of 9.20 p. m. received. The orders indicated will be given immediately. I have not learned that McCook has returned. He had orders to return when Stoneman had securely established his position. Lost Mountain has been signaled twice to-night, but he had not returned up to 9 p. m.

GEO. H. THOMAS,
Major-General.

———

SHERMAN'S HEADQUARTERS,
July 2, 1864.

Major-General THOMAS:

By the papers you sent me, I see Forrest is at Tupelo; that the enemy has detected the fact that a heavy force, under A. J. Smith, is

———

* Remainder of dispatch illegible. It probably referred to the re-enforcement of Schofield with Morgan L. Smith's division of the Fifteenth Corps.

moving out of Memphis, as they suppose, to re-enforce us. This will hold Forrest there. Now will be a good time for the raid from Decatur on Opelika. It should consist of not over 2,500 cavalry. No wagons or artillery, or at most a section, and should move first on Pillow, at Oxford or Talladega, and then pass him rapidly, cross the Tallapoosa, and break up the road. If you agree with me I will order it now.

W. T. SHERMAN,
Major-General.

HEADQUARTERS DEPARTMENT OF THE CUMBERLAND,
July 2, 1864.

Major-General SHERMAN:

I think now would be a good time for the expedition to Opelika if you have any good officers to place in command. I have heard that Roddey also had moved west of Tuscumbia, evidently attracted in that direction by the movements of Smith.

GEO. H. THOMAS,
Major-General.

HEADQUARTERS DEPARTMENT OF THE CUMBERLAND,
In the Field, near Kenesaw Mountain, July 2, 1864.

Maj. Gen. O. O. HOWARD,
Commanding Fourth Army Corps:

GENERAL: Brigadier-General King's division to-night moves into a position to be vacated by Major-General McPherson's troops. The major-general commanding directs that you to-night, after dark, take up the position indicated to you yesterday, now occupied by General King's division and a portion of General McPherson's troops, your left resting on the Dallas and Marietta road.

Very respectfully, your obedient servant,

WM. D. WHIPPLE,
Chief of Staff.

HEADQUARTERS DEPARTMENT OF THE CUMBERLAND,
In the Field, near Kenesaw Mountain, July 2, 1864.

Maj. Gen. J. M. PALMER,
Commanding Fourteenth Army Corps:

GENERAL: Major-General McPherson reports himself ready to move to-night. You will, therefore, please direct General King to move his troops this evening after dark and take up the position pointed out yesterday by the major-general commanding. Major-General Howard will be directed to relieve Brigadier-General King's division.

I am, sir, very respectfully, your obedient servant,

WM. D. WHIPPLE,
Assistant Adjutant-General.

2 R R—VOL XXXVIII, PT V

HEADQUARTERS DEPARTMENT OF THE CUMBERLAND,
  In the Field, July 2, 1864.   (Received 11.40 p. m.)
Maj. Gen. J. M. PALMER,
  Commanding Fourteenth Army Corps:

GENERAL: There is reason to believe that the enemy intends to withdraw to-night. The major-general commanding therefore directs that
you feel the enemy at some point of your line to-night and in the morning for the purpose of ascertaining whether he has done so. It will not
do to attempt any night movements with large forces, because confusion would result, but be prepared at break of day to act according to
the very best information we can gain to-night. General Schofield has
been re-enforced by one division from General McPherson. Brigadier-
General Harrow reports that as he was about to withdraw from his position, according to orders, the enemy advanced in column from the
mountain and formed line of battle at his picket-line at 8 p. m. This
is thought by General Sherman to be a blind to cover their retreat.
General Harrow has, however, been ordered not to withdraw now, but
to feel the enemy and ascertain what he is about. General Howard
will also be ordered to feel the enemy in his front between this and midnight, if it can be done so soon. Please do the same on your front
between now and midnight.
  Very respectfully, your obedient servant,
                            WM. D. WHIPPLE,
                                  Chief of Staff.
(Same to General Howard.)

HEADQUARTERS DEPARTMENT OF THE CUMBERLAND,
                          In the Field, July 2, 1864.
Major-General HOOKER,
  Commanding Twentieth Corps:

GENERAL: There is reason to believe that the enemy intends to withdraw to-night at least from his present position on Kenesaw and in front
of our left. The major-general commanding therefore directs that you
feel him to-night and in the morning at some point in front of your line
for the purpose of ascertaining his intentions, and be prepared at daylight to follow him up should he have moved.
  Yours, very respectfully,
                            WM. D. WHIPPLE,
                                  Assistant Adjutant-General.

[Indorsement.]

Colonel CARMAN:
  Please see that the picket-line feel repeatedly the rebel line, as directed last evening. If any indications of movement are observed,
report at once. Return this by bearer.
                            A. S. W[ILLIAMS],
                                  Brigadier-General.

HEADQUARTERS FOURTH ARMY CORPS,
                              July 2, 1864.
Major-General THOMAS, *Commanding Department:*

GENERAL: A vigorous demonstration was made by the artillery of
the corps, the skirmishers, and such portions of the main line as are in

sight of the enemy's works. The demonstration closed between 6 and 7. The enemy did not reply by artillery and kept his infantry pretty well concealed, though there was quite a return fire. Major Angle, of the Ninetieth Ohio, General Stanley's skirmish officer, was killed during the action.

Respectfully,

O. O. HOWARD,
Major-General.

HEADQUARTERS FOURTH ARMY CORPS,
Near Kenesaw Mountain, Ga., July 2, 1864—11.40 p. m.

Major-General STANLEY,
Commanding First Division:

In accordance with instructions just received from department headquarters you will at once feel the enemy at some point in your front for the purpose of discovering whether he is withdrawing. There is reason to believe that he is doing so either for the purpose of retreating or to attack General Schofield. If you find him still in our front and no change in his position again feel him very early in the morning. It will not do to attempt any night movements with a large force, but be prepared at daybreak to act according to such information as you may gain to-night.

By order of Major-General Howard:

J. S. FULLERTON,
Assistant Adjutant-General.

HEADQUARTERS FOURTH ARMY CORPS,
Near Kenesaw Mountain, July 2, 1864—11.40 p. m.

General NEWTON:

There is reason to believe that the enemy is retreating to-night. Major-General Stanley has just been instructed to feel him, for the purpose of discovering whether this supposition is correct. You will have your troops prepared at break of day to follow him (the enemy) if he has gone. Please report any movements that you may discover in your front.

By order of Major-General Howard:

J. S. FULLERTON,
Assistant Adjutant-General.

(Same to General Wood.)

HDQRS. MILITARY DIVISION OF THE MISSISSIPPI,
In the Field, near Kenesaw, July 2, 1864.

General ROUSSEAU,
Nashville, Tenn.:

Now is the time for the raid to Opelika. Telegraph me whether you go yourself or who will command. Forrest is in Mississippi, and Roddey has also gone there. All other rebel cavalry is here.

W. T. SHERMAN,
Major-General, Commanding.

HEADQUARTERS ARMY OF THE OHIO,
In the Field, July 2, 1864—4.30 a. m.

Major-General SHERMAN:

Yes. All right, so far. No indications of an attack yet.

J. M. SCHOFIELD,
Major-General.

HDQRS. MILITARY DIVISION OF THE MISSISSIPPI,
In the Field, near Kenesaw, July 2, 1864.

General SCHOFIELD:

General McPherson reports he will be ready to move to-night. Are you ready for him to uncover the railroad? Telegraph me any news on your flank, especially what Stoneman is about. Has General Morgan L. Smith's division come to you yet? I will move my headquarters to-morrow to Cheney's.

W. T. SHERMAN,
Major-General, Commanding.

HEADQUARTERS ARMY OF THE OHIO,
July 2, 1864—7.30 a. m.

Major-General SHERMAN:

Smith's division is here. I will put it in position on the Ruff's Mill and Sandtown road on which McPherson is to move, while I will hold the Marietta road and from there back to Olley's Creek.

J. M. SCHOFIELD,
Major-General.

HDQRS. MILITARY DIVISION OF THE MISSISSIPPI,
In the Field, near Kenesaw, July 2, 1864.

General SCHOFIELD:

General McPherson is now moving out. General Garrard will cover the depot; but one of the greatest probabilities is that Wheeler's cavalry will, the moment the disposition of the infantry is discovered, sweep round the flank of the cavalry and try to capture our depot, which should be cleared out to-night or very early in the morning. All were so instructed this morning.

W. T. SHERMAN,
Major-General, Commanding.

JULY 2, 1864.

General SCHOFIELD:

As your command will not probably move from the present position, you had better unload all wagons and send and bring something in the nature of provisions from the depot to-night. I understand there is an excess of sugar, coffee, and salt. These, with beef, are better than nothing. It may be you can also procure the full measure of bread. At all events, haul to Wade's all you can to-day and to-night, empty-ing your wagons, where they now are, on the ground.

W. T. SHERMAN,
Major-General.

HEADQUARTERS ARMY OF THE OHIO,
In the Field, July 2, 1864—8.30 a. m.

Major-General SHERMAN:

I have only three days' supplies, including a train not yet in. I send a train to-day which can bring three days' more, if they are at the depot. Possibly I may be able to make this last until the 10th. If you think this sufficient, I can get everything away from the railroad some time to-night. Some of my sick must go back to-day. I am not informed whether they can get railroad transportation to-night.

J. M. SCHOFIELD,
Major-General.

HEADQUARTERS ARMY OF THE OHIO,
In the Field, July 2, 1864—12.50 p. m.

Major-General SHERMAN:

The enemy is extremely quiet in my front and shows only a light skirmish line. At 10 o'clock Stoneman had possession of the bridge at Sweet Water Town and of the west bank of the creek as far down as the Factory, with a force moving toward Campbellton. He was repairing the bridge and would push out on all roads to the north and east as soon as his horses could be got across. Stoneman has met no enemy except small parties. He thinks the main body of Jones' and Wheeler's cavalry is near Campbellton. His scouts just returned so report.

J. M. SCHOFIELD,
Major-General.

HDQRS. MILITARY DIVISION OF THE MISSISSIPPI,
In the Field, near Kenesaw, July 2, 1864.

General SCHOFIELD:

Report to me the fullest news of General Stoneman to-night. I want to find out as soon as possible if the enemy has a bridge at Campbellton.

W. T. SHERMAN,
Major-General, Commanding.

HEADQUARTERS ARMY OF THE OHIO,
In the Field, July 2, 1864—6 p. m.

Major-General SHERMAN:

I have not heard from Stoneman since 10 a. m. Expect full report from him to-night, and will send it to you as soon as received. In his dispatch he says: "There is a ferry at Campbellton and one a few miles above." Also " a bridge at Franklin, sixty miles below Atlanta." He does not give the source of his information.

J. M. SCHOFIELD,
Major-General.

JULY 2, 1864.

General SCHOFIELD:

Is there any musketry or cannonading on your front now?

W. T. SHERMAN,
Major-General.

ARMY OF THE OHIO,
July 2, 1864—8.45 p. m.

General SHERMAN:

There is no firing on my front. I hear occasional reports like artillery in Stoneman's direction, but am not certain whether it is artillery or thunder, there is so much of the latter. I think there has been some firing in front of Hooker.

J. M. SCHOFIELD,
Major-General.

———

HEADQUARTERS ARMY OF THE OHIO,
In the Field, July 2, 1864—9.30 p. m.

Major-General SHERMAN:

I have nothing from Stoneman since noon to-day, at which time he had crossed the Sweet Water at Sweet Water Town and connected with his brigade on this side. He has not heard from the force sent toward Campbellton. Captain Twining, of my staff, was with Stoneman yesterday and until 12 o'clock. He is certain the enemy has no bridge at or near Campbellton. Their cavalry cross there on a ferry.

J. M. SCHOFIELD,
Major-General.

———

JULY 2, 1864.

General SCHOFIELD:

If the enemy's cavalry rely upon a ferry at Campbellton, there can be no force of any size in that neighborhood. Ask Captain Twining if McCook was still with Stoneman up to the time of his leaving.

W. T. SHERMAN,
Major-General.

———

HEADQUARTERS ARMY OF THE OHIO,
July 2, 1864—8 p. m.

General SHERMAN:

Have you decided when you will uncover the railroad? My trains are there to-night but it is uncertain when they can get away. I understand the bread for my command is expected to arrive to-night.

J. M. SCHOFIELD,
Major-General.

———

HEADQUARTERS ARMY OF THE OHIO,
In the Field, July 2, 1864—9 p. m.

Major-General SHERMAN:

My command is supplied with bread for only three days. The others, I am told, have ten days' supply. I have had trains waiting at the depot continually during the last six days. I will order back my empty trains early in the morning and do the best I can.

J. M. SCHOFIELD,
Major-General.

JULY 2, 1864.

General SCHOFIELD:

Don't order back your empty wagons, but have them loaded with bran, rice, hominy, sugar and coffee, and salt, and I will see, if the commissaries have slighted you in distribution of bread rations, that it be made good. I also think it will be safe for your wagons to remain at Big Shanty throughout to-morrow, as Garrard's cavalry (Thomas' left), rear McPherson's column, will cover the place all day. At all events, your teams will have plenty notice in case danger. Can soon gain the cover of Thomas' troops, which remain in position. The enemy evidently detected our movement, and therefore we must act quick. Johnston will either attack in the morning or draw his extreme right "back" to the Chattahoochee. I want his movements watched close to-night and early in the morning, and could form better opinion if I could hear from Stoneman. Do you know whether McCook is with Stoneman? McCook has artillery; Stoneman, none.

W. T. SHERMAN,
Major-General.

HEADQUARTERS ARMY OF THE OHIO,
In the Field, July 2, 1864—10 p. m.

Major-General SHERMAN:

McCook is with Stoneman and has his artillery. I have heard no reports since the thunder ceased, and presume it was all thunder. My signal officer at dusk reported the enemy's camp-fires in my front stronger than last evening, but at least a mile away. I will watch them closely to-night and in the morning. He also saw camp-fires along the railroad below Marietta. Very few railroad trains have been moving to-day. Yesterday they were very numerous.

J. M. SCHOFIELD,
Major-General.

TREE SIGNAL STATION, *July 2, 1864—sunrise.*

General SCHOFIELD:

No movements visible in front of your corps. Heavy cannonading can be seen extending from the left of the army around to Hascall's old position. Can see the shells burst on and all around this side of Kenesaw Mountain. Shelling appears to be mostly from our guns.

WM. REYNOLDS,
First Lieutenant, Signal Officer.

HEADQUARTERS ARMY OF THE OHIO,
In the Field, Ga., July 2, 1864—8.30 a. m.

Maj. Gen. GEORGE STONEMAN,
Commanding Cavalry Corps, Department of the Ohio:

GENERAL: There will be no farther advance of the infantry to-day. General Sherman desires you to do what you can in accordance with his directions, and to keep him advised of your progress. If you need supplies from the railroad they will have to be drawn to-day.

Very respectfully, your obedient servant,

J. M. SCHOFIELD,
Major-General, Commanding.

SWEET WATER BRIDGE, *July 2, 1864.*
(Received 2 p. m.)

General McCOOK:

We have a position that we can hold against the whole rebel army. Send up every thing you have in the way of transportation, and every-thing there that may be back at the bridge behind you belonging to my two brigades. Send and have the 100 men at the upper bridge and the 20 men at the ford below, where Adams crossed, relieved and sent to their regiments. After everything has passed by you send for Adams and come up yourself. I have opened up communication with Butler.

STONEMAN,
General.

Tell Adams to have 100 men to hold the cross-roads where you are now.

G. S.

———

HEADQUARTERS ARMY OF THE OHIO,
In the Field, Ga., July 2, 1864—12.30 p. m.

Maj. Gen. GEORGE STONEMAN,
Comdg. Cavalry Corps, Department of the Ohio:

GENERAL: I have your dispatches of 6.30 and 10 a. m. I sent you a dispatch last evening and one this morning, but fear you did not get either of them, as you say nothing about it. I do not deem it prudent to send you the plan of operations until I am sure it will reach you in safety. There is no movement of infantry to-day. Our right is where it was last evening. There is some cavalry in Hascall's front. I have heard nothing from Butler to-day. Your movement is good so far. If you will send in a party this evening I will give you full information.

Very respectfully, your obedient servant,

J. M. SCHOFIELD,
Major-General, Commanding.

———

HEADQUARTERS ARMY OF THE OHIO,
In the Field, Ga., July 2, 1864—10 p. m.

Brig. Gen. J. D. COX,
Comdg. Third Division, Twenty-third Army Corps:

GENERAL: General Sherman informs me that the enemy has evi-dently detected our movement, and is himself in motion. It seems certain that he will either retreat to-night or attack us in the morning. He appears now to be preparing to attack our extreme left (McPher-son's). Watch carefully all indications of the enemy's movement dur-ing the night and inform me of everything of importance. Especially give me a report of the condition of affairs in your front, at or a little before 4 o'clock. General Sherman desires a report at that time.

Very respectfully, your obedient servant,

J. M. SCHOFIELD,
Major-General, Commanding.

———

HDQRS. MILITARY DIVISION OF THE MISSISSIPPI,
In the Field, near Kenesaw, July 2, 1864.

General GARRARD, *Commanding Cavalry:*

Report by letter or a staff officer the disposition of your command under the orders of last night to General Thomas, who is to remain where he now is. I will go to Cheney's or Wade's, down the Sandtown road. General Stoneman has been down to the Sweet Water Town and Factory, and controls that region.

W. T. SHERMAN,
Major-General, Commanding.

HDQRS. MILITARY DIVISION OF THE MISSISSIPPI,
In the Field, near Kenesaw, July 2, 1864.

General MCPHERSON:

General Garrard's communication is secured. He will be required to cover your line during the movement. If Wheeler goes up to Centreville he will find more than he bargains for, and then will be time for Garrard to cut in behind.

W. T. SHERMAN,
Major-General, Commanding.

HDQRS. MILITARY DIVISION OF THE MISSISSIPPI,
In the Field, near Kenesaw, July 2, 1864.

General MCPHERSON:

Written orders have gone to you. Make orders for Garrard and the corps commanders. If there be any part not clear after you have the orders, let me know.

W. T. SHERMAN,
Major-General, Commanding.

HEADQUARTERS DEPARTMENT OF THE TENNESSEE,
July 2, 1864.

Major-General SHERMAN:

Following just received:

HEADQUARTERS FIFTEENTH ARMY CORPS.
Lieutenant-Colonel CLARK:

General Logan directs me to send you the information that one of General Harrow's aides reports that the enemy have advanced in column from the mountain in his front, and are forming in line of battle on the picket-line. This at 8 p. m.

R. R. TOWNES,
Assistant Adjutant-General.

JAS. B. MCPHERSON,
Major-General.

HDQRS. MILITARY DIVISION OF THE MISSISSIPPI,
In the Field, near Kenesaw, July 2, 1864.

General MCPHERSON:

Relieve your pickets and all detachments before daylight. General Thomas will occupy such ground as he prefers to accomplish the end. He is notified that you will withdraw during the night.

W. T. SHERMAN,
Major-General, Commanding.

CHATTANOOGA, *July 2, 1864.*

Brigadier-General SMITH:

Have you relieved the troops at Resaca and Tilton?

J. B. STEEDMAN,
Major-General.

HDQRS. THIRD DIVISION, FIFTEENTH ARMY CORPS,
Kingston, Ga., July 2, 1864.

Maj. Gen. JAMES B. STEEDMAN,
Chattanooga, Tenn.:

I have relieved the troops from Tilton to this place, placing Seventeenth Iowa at Tilton, Tenth Missouri at Resaca, Fifty-sixth Illinois at Calhoun and Adairsville. Train conveying these regiments left last evening.

JNO. E. SMITH.
Brigadier-General.

HDQRS. THIRD DIVISION, FIFTEENTH ARMY CORPS,
Kingston, Ga., July 2, 1864.

Lieut. Col. WILLIAM T. CLARK,
Asst. Adjt. Gen., Department and Army of the Tennessee:

In compliance with orders from your headquarters, I have the honor to report my arrival at this place with my command, excepting the Fifth Ohio Cavalry, Eighteenth Wisconsin Infantry, and pioneer corps, who are en route for this place with the wagon train of the division, and the Twenty-sixth Missouri Infantry, who are escorting cattle from Chattanooga here. The Tenth Iowa Veteran Volunteer Infantry are also absent from the command, on veteran furlough, by your order. By direction of Major-General Steedman, I have relieved the troops of Colonel Lowe, commanding cavalry, between Tilton and this place by placing the Seventeenth Iowa at Tilton, Tenth Missouri at Resaca, Fifty-sixth Illinois at Calhoun and Adairsville, and to-day I am relieving the troops guarding the Etowah River with the Third Brigade of this division. The disposal of the balance of my command will be duly reported.

I am, colonel, very respectfully, your obedient servant,

JNO. E. SMITH,
Brigadier-General.

HDQRS. THIRD DIVISION, FIFTEENTH ARMY CORPS,
Kingston, Ga., July 2, 1864.

Col. JABEZ BANBURY,
Comdg. Third Brig., Third Div., Fifteenth Army Corps:

COLONEL: The general commanding directs that you take charge and guard the Etowah River from Caldwell's Ford, two miles and a half above Gillem's Bridge, to Murchison's Ford below, and that you make preparations to move at once, placing the Fifth Iowa Veteran Volunteer Infantry at Wooley's Bridge, throwing out one small post at Murchison's Ford, one small post at Runnel's Ford, and one small post at Runnel's Ferry. The Ninety-third Illinois Infantry will be stationed at Gillem's Bridge, with one outpost of 100 men at Island Ford and one outpost of 50 men at Caldwell's Ford, with directions to commanding officers to communicate frequently between posts. By applying to Colonel Lowe, commanding cavalry division, at these headquarters, you will be furnished with the necessary transportation and guides for the disposition of your command. After having examined the line placed under your command with a view to a complete guard of the river, and the most suitable location for brigade headquarters, you will report to the general commanding, when the detachment of the Tenth Iowa will be assigned to duty on the same line.

By order of Brig. Gen. John E. Smith:

CARL. L. WHITE,
Captain and Assistant Adjutant-General.

ACWORTH, *July 2, 1864.*

ASSISTANT ADJUTANT-GENERAL,
MILITARY DIVISION OF THE MISSISSIPPI:

A company, undoubtedly fifty strong, of rebel guerrilla cavalry, approached this post from northwest, two roads, to within two miles of this place, and three-quarters of a mile of the first railroad bridge northerly, capturing about 5 stragglers from the dismounted cavalry, left here by Colonel Dorr's brigade, and, as is said, a major of Tennessee cavalry. One of Mr. Rossell's construction corps was captured and robbed. He afterward escaped when our men approached and drove off the rebels. I sent three companies in pursuit, but being dismounted accomplished only the driving them off and examining the road and bridge. I have sent one company to the bridge to remain until further orders. The railroad is undisturbed. I have frequently before heard of rebel cavalry having been seen and heard of from three to eight miles northwest from here.

SAMUEL ROSS,
Colonel Twentieth Connecticut Vol. Infantry, Comdg. Post.

HEADQUARTERS DEPARTMENT OF THE CUMBERLAND,
In the Field, July 2, 1864.

Col. SAMUEL ROSS,
Acworth:

Your dispatch to assistant adjutant-general, headquarters military division, received and referred here where it should have been sent. Occurrences like that you report are to be expected. You must guard your post and see that they do not destroy the railroad in your vicinity. If those guerrillas ever fall into your hands take no prisoners.

WM. D. WHIPPLE,
Chief of Staff.

GENERAL THOMAS' HEADQUARTERS,
Near Marietta, Ga., July 2, 1864—11.30 p. m.

Maj. THOMAS T. ECKERT,
Assistant Superintendent U. S. Military Telegraph:

Movement to turn Johnston's position made progress to-day, General Schofield getting in position better than was expected, and McPherson being ready to move at dark, when absence of enemy from

Schofield's front and threats against the left caused Sherman to stop McPherson. At this hour General Thomas is of the opinion that Johnston is falling back and covering his movement by feint against left. General Sherman agrees that he is correct, or that Johnston will attack at daylight, and is prepared for either contingency.

J. C. VAN DUZER.

SPECIAL FIELD ORDERS, } NEAR KENESAW MOUNTAIN, GA.,
No. 57. } *July 2, 1864.*

*   *   *   *   *   *   *

V. In order to carry out Special Field Orders, No. 31, headquarters Military Division of the Mississippi, a copy of which is inclosed herewith,* the following movements will be made:

1. The supply trains of the Army of the Tennessee, as fast as they are loaded with stores, will be moved to-day, under the direction of Lieut. Col. J. Condit Smith, acting chief quartermaster, by the most practicable route to the Sandtown road, thence south to Cheney's, at the intersection of the Sandtown and Powder Springs and Marietta roads, where they will be parked.

2. Maj. Gen. F. P. Blair, commanding Seventeenth Army Corps, will commence moving his command from the left at 9 p. m. this day, continuing successively to the right, and will march by the route selected by his staff officers to-day to the Sandtown road and thence down it to some good point near the Widow Mitchell's, indicated on the map.

3. Maj. Gen. G. M. Dodge, commanding Left Wing, Sixteenth Army Corps, will commence moving his command from the left as soon as Maj. Gen. F. P. Blair's troops have filed out, and will march by the most practicable route selected by his staff officers to-day to the Sandtown road and there follow Major-General Blair's command down it to where the road branches off to Ruff's Mill, on the Nickajack Creek, and take up a good position near Ruff's Mill.

4. Maj. Gen. John A. Logan, commanding Fifteenth Army Corps, will commence moving his command from the left as soon as Major-General Dodge's troops have filed out, and will march to the Sandtown road, thence down it, following Major-General Dodge's command to the forks of the road leading to Ruff's Mill and Widow Mitchell's, where he will halt and act as a reserve.

5. Brigadier-General Garrard, commanding cavalry division, will move his command at 9 p. m. to-day to the vicinity of Big Shanty to cover the rail and wagon roads leading north from Marietta and east of Kenesaw Mountain, availing himself of the defenses thrown up by our troops. He will establish and keep open communication with the left of General Thomas' command, and will send one good regiment for picket duty over this afternoon to report at these headquarters at 5 o'clock to relieve the pickets of Blair's and Dodge's commands.

6. These movements will be made with as much celerity as possible, and with the least amount of noise. All arrangements, except moving troops and artillery, should be made quietly before dark to avoid confusion.

7. Troops and trains will move as much under cover and screened from the view of the enemy as practicable.

---

* See p. 14.

8. One wagon with ammunition for each regiment and battery will follow each division as heretofore ordered; the remainder of the ordnance train of each division will go forward with the general supply train, in charge of ordnance officers.

*   *   *   *   *   *   *

By order of Maj. Gen. James B. McPherson:

WM. T. CLARK,
Assistant Adjutant-General.

MARIETTA, GA., *July 3, 1864—10 a. m.*
(Received 5 p. m.)

Maj. Gen. H. W. HALLECK,
    Washington, D. C.:

The movement on our right caused the enemy to evacuate. We occupied Kenesaw at daylight and Marietta at 8.30 a. m. Thomas is moving down the main road, toward the Chattahoochee; McPherson toward the mouth of Nickajack, on the Sandtown road. Our cavalry is on the extreme flank. Whether the enemy will halt this side of Chattahoochee or not will soon be known. Marietta is almost entirely abandoned by its inhabitants, and more than a mile of the railroad iron is removed between the town and the foot of Kenesaw. I propose to press the enemy close till he is across the Chattahoochee River, when I must accumulate stores and better guard my rear.

W. T. SHERMAN,
Major-General.

HEADQUARTERS DEPARTMENT OF THE CUMBERLAND,
July 3, 1864—2.45 a. m.

Major-General SHERMAN:

General Palmer reports that he felt for the enemy in Davis' front, between 12 and 1 o'clock, and found him gone. One prisoner captured gives it as his opinion that they have fallen back three miles to another line of works.

GEO. H. THOMAS,
Major-General.

SHERMAN'S HEADQUARTERS,
July 3, 1864—4 a. m.

Major-General THOMAS:

I will stop Logan on your left to make him feel up Little Kenesaw. Feel out and find where the enemy is as quick as possible.

W. T. SHERMAN,
Major-General.

HEADQUARTERS DEPARTMENT OF THE CUMBERLAND,
In the Field, July 3, 1864—5 a. m.

Major-General SHERMAN:

The enemy has gone from General Hooker's front, and he is advancing on the Powder Springs and Marietta road, and on lines parallel to it.

GEO. H. THOMAS,
Major-General.

JULY 3, 1864.

General THOMAS:

I can see our men on top both Big and Little Kenesaw.

W. T. SHERMAN,
Major-General.

(Same to General Schofield.)

HEADQUARTERS DEPARTMENT OF THE CUMBERLAND,
July 3, 1864.

Major-General SHERMAN:

The enemy has disappeared from my entire front, and my troops have been in pursuit since daylight.   Please direct Garrard to feel upon our left.

GEO. H. THOMAS,
Major-General.

HDQRS. MILITARY DIVISION OF THE MISSISSIPPI,
In the Field, near Kenesaw, July 3, 1864.

General THOMAS:

I will go to Marietta, to the south of Kenesaw, and will communicate to you from there.   Will expect to find you substantially on the rail-road, on the direct pursuit.   Garrard has already got orders which will carry him east of Marietta.

W. T. SHERMAN,
Major-General, Commanding.

SHERMAN'S HEADQUARTERS,
July 3, 1864.

General THOMAS:

I have sent Audenried to you, telling that Stoneman's cavalry has pursued the enemy across the Chattahoochee near Campbellton.   Scho-field reports all quiet in his front, and I have ordered him to cross Nick-ajack Creek.   I want you with your entire army to follow substantially the main army till he is across the Chattahoochee or makes a stand. McPherson will occupy Marietta and Kenesaw until further develop-ments, and Garrard's cavalry will feel over toward Roswell Factory.

W. T. SHERMAN,
Major-General.

HDQRS. MILITARY DIVISION OF THE MISSISSIPPI,
In the Field, Marietta, Ga., July 3, 1864—6.45 p. m.

General THOMAS:

The more I reflect the more I know Johnston's halt is to save time to cross his material and men.   No general, such as he, would invite bat-tle with the Chattahoochee behind him.   I have ordered McPherson and Schofield to cross Nickajack at any cost and work night and day to get the enemy started in confusion toward his bridges.   I know you appreciate the situation.   We will never have such a chance again, and I want you to impress on Hooker, Howard, and Palmer the importance of the most intense energy of attack to-night and in the morning and to press with vehemence at any cost of life and material. Every inch of his line should be felt and the moment there is a give, pursuit should be made—by day with lines, but by night with a single head of column and section of artillery to each corps, following a road. Hooker should communicate with McPherson by a circuit if necessary and act in concert. You know what loss would ensue to Johnston if he crosses his bridges at night in confusion with artillery thundering at random in his rear. I have reason to know that if our head of column had marched for Ruff's instead of Marietta we would have cut off 2,000 men and 300 wagons. But still we have now the best chance ever offered, of a large army fighting at a disadvantage with a river to his rear. Send copies of this to Hooker, Palmer, and Howard. I have instructed Schofield, McPherson, and Garrard.

Yours,

W. T. SHERMAN,
Major-General, Commanding.

———

HEADQUARTERS FOURTH ARMY CORPS,
July 3, 1864—3.40 a. m.
Major-General STANLEY:

GENERAL: In accordance with instructions received from department headquarters, you will at once organize your troops and be ready for pursuit of the enemy. Your division will lead, followed by General Newton, then Wood.

By order of Major-General Howard:

J. S. FULLERTON,
Assistant Adjutant-General.

———

HEADQUARTERS FOURTH ARMY CORPS,
Near Neal Dow Station, Ga., July 3, 1864—8 p. m.
Major-General THOMAS:

GENERAL: I have the honor to report that my command has taken 167 prisoners—164 enlisted men and 3 commissioned officers.

Very respectfully, your obedient servant,

O. O. HOWARD,
Major-General.

———

HEADQUARTERS TWENTIETH CORPS,
July 3, 1864—4 a. m.
Brigadier-General WHIPPLE,
Chief of Staff:

GENERAL: It is reported to me that the enemy have disappeared from my front. General Ward is in possession of their works. Until further developments I shall advance on the Powder Springs road, and on lines parallel to it, to the right and left.

Very respectfully, your obedient servant,

JOSEPH HOOKER,
Major-General, Commanding.

HDQRS. DEPARTMENT OF THE CUMBERLAND,
GEORGIA MILITARY INSTITUTE,
Marietta, Ga., July 3, 1864.

Maj. Gen. O. O. HOWARD,
Commanding Fourth Army Corps:

GENERAL: The major-general commanding directs that you occupy the attention of the enemy in your front to-night and to-morrow morning by skirmishing and artillery, so as to prevent his massing upon Major-Generals Schofield and McPherson, who are to attack his left flank. It is not intended that your operations shall amount in the aggregate to anything like a battle, but that you make use of any means that may occur to you as best calculated to accomplish the object intended without really attacking him.

Very respectfully, your obedient servant,
WM. D. WHIPPLE,
Chief of Staff.

(Same to Palmer and Hooker.)

HEADQUARTERS FOURTH ARMY CORPS,
Near Neal Dow Station, Ga., July 3, 1864—9.30 p. m.

Brigadier-General NEWTON,
Commanding Second Division:

It has been discovered that the enemy's right is nearer General Stanley's left than was supposed this afternoon. Also General Stanley will make a strong demonstration for the purpose of attracting the attention of the enemy at daybreak to-morrow. You will therefore move your division directly forward at daybreak to-morrow, close to Colonel Taylor's brigade (General Stanley's rear brigade). General Wood will be ordered to close up on you.

By order of Major-General Howard:
J. S. FULLERTON,
Assistant Adjutant-General.

[JULY 3, 1864.—For McCook to Elliott, reporting operations, &c., see Part II, p. 759.]

Statement of J. M. Glass (scout).

OFFICE PROVOST-MARSHAL-GENERAL,
DEPARTMENT OF THE CUMBERLAND,
Near Marietta, July 3, 1864.

Reports that he left the Federal lines 30th June. Had instructions to visit along the river between the bridge and Baker's Ferry and ascertain if the rebels had any pontoon across the same. The first day I reached Powder Springs, next day reached Marietta, crossing Sweet Water Creek at the mouth on the ferry. Reported to Colonel Hill, provost-marshal-general, rebel army; staid there till next morning, and then started for the river. When I got back as far as Ruff's Station, four miles below Marietta, I discovered they were running their train off, and the army was about to fall back. I concluded to come back and report the same. Started back immediately by way of Dobbins'

Mill, from there to Villa Rica and Atlanta road, and taking a left-hand road struck General Stoneman's pickets about 3 p. m. yesterday. Came on from there toward General Schofield's headquarters; when about one mile and a half this side of Noyes' Creek bridge I was stopped by a sergeant in charge of a squad of cavalry pickets on the road; he would not allow me to come in or send me in under guard. I was compelled to stay there all night. I explained to the sergeant my business, and that I had valuable information for the Federal army. The sergeant's name I cannot recollect nor his regiment; he belongs to Colonel Capron's command. Colonel Hill intimated to me that I would not find him in the same place when I came over again. At Marietta I discovered that all the wagons were being loaded and sent off toward the river. Trains were running rapidly all day; did not notice any troops on the cars. Friday night troops were moving toward the river; think it was a division; they came from the front near the mountain. J. C. Moore had been in Marietta on Thursday; left there that day. Did not see any fortifications as far back as I went, between Marietta and the river. A citizen living at the ferry, Baker's, informed me that they were fortifying at Campbellton; that they were going to mount cannon there. The cannon were to come from Fairburn. General Johnston has ordered out every negro to work on the fortifications. My opinion is that the army will not cross the river, making a stand on this side at the fortifications.

HEADQUARTERS ARMY OF THE OHIO,
July 3, 1864—4 a. m.

Major-General SHERMAN:

I have heard from Stoneman. The force sent toward Campbellton returned, finding no enemy this side of Chattahoochee. All had crossed the river or Sweet Water Creek near its mouth, where there is a ford. Stoneman now holds a line from the right of our infantry to Ferguson's Bridge, a little above Sweet Water Factory. McCook is at the bridge over Sweet Water on the Powder Springs and Campbellton road. All is quiet along my lines. I have no report of any movement of the enemy.

J. M. SCHOFIELD,
Major-General.

HEADQUARTERS ARMY OF THE OHIO,
July 3, 1864—7.30 a. m.

Major-General SHERMAN:

My signal officer on Byrd's hill sees a long column of wagons and artillery moving south along the railroad; also a column of cavalry. He sees rebel troops cooking their breakfast in the fields across the Nickajack.

J. M. SCHOFIELD,
Major-General.

HDQRS. MILITARY DIVISION OF THE MISSISSIPPI,
In the Field, Marietta, July 3, 1864—11.35 a. m.

General SCHOFIELD:

General Thomas is moving directly down the road hence to railroad bridge. Garrard's cavalry is off to the left between railroad and Chat-

tahoochee. I want you and McPherson to threaten the flank of the
enemy from Ruff's Mill; also in the direction of Turner's Ferry. We
have gathered in many prisoners, and by pushing them will get many
more. Send this to McPherson. Cross the Nickajack with a strong
head of column, so as to threaten the enemy and take advantage of any
confusion resulting from Thomas' pursuit.

W. T. SHERMAN,
Major-General, Commanding.

JULY 3, 1864—2.30 p. m.
General SHERMAN:

I have just received your dispatch of 11.35 and shown it to McPherson. He is moving out, and I will support him if necessary. Our signal
officers were informed from Lost Mountain that you had not taken
Marietta or I would have been some distance ahead.

Respectfully,

J. M. SCHOFIELD,
Major-General.

JULY 3, 1864.
General SCHOFIELD:

I will send McPherson according to former orders to Widow Mitchell's.
General Thomas with his whole army will follow the enemy's main
army, and in case he crosses the Chattahoochee, I propose to move you
again over to the left, but in mean time let your skirmishers fall down
to and across Nickajack. Let your wagons get provisions at Big
Shanty to-day.

W. T. SHERMAN,
Major-General.

HEADQUARTERS ARMY OF THE OHIO,
In the Field, Ga., July 3, 1864—5.30 a. m.
Brig. Gen. J. D. COX,
Comdg. Third Division, Twenty-third Army Corps:

GENERAL: Our troops have possession of Kenesaw. General Thomas
will follow the main army in its retreat. General McPherson moves to
the right according to the original programme. Our movements will
depend upon developments. Let your skirmishers well out, and find
what has become of the enemy; especially see if he is in position across
the Nickajack.

By order of Major-General Schofield:

J. A. CAMPBELL,
Major and Assistant Adjutant-General.

HDQRS. THIRD DIVISION, TWENTY-THIRD ARMY CORPS,
Lynch's, on Sandtown Road, Ga., July 3, 1864.
Major-General SCHOFIELD,
Commanding, &c.:

GENERAL: The reconnaissance from Colonel Byrd has proceeded
southeasterly over a mile, crossing the Marietta road and reaching

the Nickajack Creek. Its skirmishers are over the creek about half a mile. No enemy in their front, but they hear of a rebel force of infantry about a mile farther up the Marietta road. I have ordered them to hold a good position and examine their left in the direction indicated, by smaller scouting parties. The reconnaissance from Colonel Cameron has followed a cross-road toward Ruff's Mill, and advanced about one mile and a half, as they report. They find a mounted force just across the creek in their front, and the cannonade in front of General Smith is on their right rear. I have ordered them to hold a good position, communicate with Colonel Byrd's detachment on Marietta road, and watch carefully the effect of Hascall's and Smith's reconnaissance, advancing if practicable.

Very respectfully, your obedient servant,

J. D. COX,
Brigadier-General, Commanding.

Moss' House, *July 3, 1864—10.30 a. m.*

Major-General SCHOFIELD,
 Commanding Corps:

GENERAL: I have advanced a regiment in front of Colonels Strickland's and Hobson's brigades and General Smith has advanced two regiments on the road toward Watson's house, and two on the Ruff's Station road. My regiment in front of Colonel Strickland soon encountered the enemy's cavalry skirmishers, but drove them back to the vicinity of Nickajack Creek; Colonel Hobson's regiment not yet heard from. General Smith's two regiments on the Ruff's Station road encountered the enemy in considerable force, and found more difficulty in pressing him back. They have two or three pieces of artillery already operating on the Ruff's Station road. General Smith's regimental commanders report that a strong line of infantry skirmishers are advancing against them on the Ruff's Station road, backed by a line of infantry. This may be so, or it may be dismounted cavalry. If it is infantry, an attack here is not improbable. I am by no means certain that it is infantry. General Smith and myself thought we could not develop much by advancing our skirmishers simply, so left them where they were, and made the dispositions already described. General Smith's force on the Watson house road have encountered nothing but cavalry, and are now about a mile and a half in advance; skirmishing with the cavalry somewhat brisk. Artillery firing is heard in that direction, but it may be our artillery with General Stoneman. The enemy's earth-works are visible from our advanced position, and are probably beyond Nickajack Creek.

Yours, respectfully,

MILO S. HASCALL,
Brigadier-General of Volunteers, Commanding Division.

P. S.—The cavalry are advancing simultaneously with us. General Smith's force on the Ruff's Station road now reports that it is cavalry in their front, but that they discover an infantry force on a rise to their right. I give this for what it is worth.

Yours,

M. S. H.,
Brigadier-General.

HEADQUARTERS ARMY OF THE OHIO,
In the Field, July 3, 1864—6 a. m.

Maj.-Gen. GEORGE STONEMAN,
Comdg. Cavalry Corps, Department of the Ohio:

GENERAL: The enemy abandoned Kenesaw in the night and has fallen back along his entire line; how far does not yet appear. General Thomas is following. General McPherson is moving over onto our right, according to yesterday's orders. If the enemy cross the river we will resume our old place on the left. Garrard remains for the present on the left of Thomas and protecting the railroad. During the present keep up communication with whatever infantry may be on the right, and act in concert with it. I will write you more fully when I hear more from Sherman.

Very respectfully, your obedient servant,
J. M. SCHOFIELD,
Major-General, Commanding.

HDQRS. DEPARTMENT AND ARMY OF THE TENNESSEE,
In the Field, Moss' House, Ruff's Mill Road,
July 3, 1864—2.30 p. m.

Major-General SHERMAN,
Commanding, &c.:

GENERAL: Your dispatch of 11.35 to Major-General Schofield has just been shown me. General Blair's command is here, and General Dodge is following closely. Brig. Gen. Morgan L. Smith, with Lightburn's brigade, supported by Hascall's division, will make a strong demonstration at Ruff's Mill and, if possible, secure a good position on the east side of Nickajack Creek. Gresham's division is moving down to Widow Mitchell's, which is a little over a mile in front of Brig. Gen. Giles Smith's position. As soon as Gresham reaches Widow Mitchell's, two regiments of Giles Smith's brigade, which are there, will make a demonstration toward Turner's Ferry. Major-General Stoneman's cavalry, I understand, is on this side of Sweet Water, and is pushing east from Sweet Water Factory toward the Nickajack and Chattahoochee.

Very respectfully, your obedient servant,
JAS. B. McPHERSON,
Major-General.

HDQRS. MILITARY DIVISION OF THE MISSISSIPPI,
In the Field, Marietta, July 3, 1864—6.15 p. m.

General McPHERSON:

Thomas has Hooker on the road out of Marietta, which is called an Atlanta road, but runs to the Sandtown road, crossing Nickajack at Ruff and Daniels' Mill. He finds the enemy intrenched a mile this side the mill. Howard is on the main Atlanta road, which is on the left of the railroad, and Palmer intermediate, all finding the enemy near the line indicated by the cross-road from above Wade's to the main road about a mile and a half below Ruff's. Now, I am convinced the enemy left Marietta in haste and confusion this morning. All the columns have taken many prisoners, and had the pursuit been vigorous we would have secured 3,000 or 4,000 prisoners and many wagons. Now the halt is, of course, to save time. If you ever worked in your life, work at daybreak to-morrow on that flank, crossing Nickajack some-how, and the moment you discover confusion pour in your fire. You know what a retreating mass across pontoon bridges means. Feel strong to-night and make feints of pursuit with artillery. I know John-ston's withdrawal is not strategic, but for good reasons, after he crosses the Chattahoochee; but his situation with that river behind him is not comfortable at all. If you can get him once started, follow up and call on Schofield. Let him read this. You both see the whole game as well as I do. Let Stoneman threaten about Baker's and Howell's Ferries, and you secure, if you can, the ridge and crossing at Nickajack, opposite Turner's. I will send Logan to you to-morrow, but you have as many men as can operate in that pocket. I don't confine you to any crossing, but press the enemy all the time in flank till he is across Chattahoochee.

Yours,

W. T. SHERMAN,
Major-General.

HEADQUARTERS LEFT WING, SIXTEENTH ARMY CORPS,
Near Ruff's Mill, Ga., July 3, 1864.

Lieut. Col. WILLIAM T. CLARK,
Asst. Adjt. Gen., Department and Army of the Tennessee:

COLONEL: I have the honor to report the operations of this command for to-day (July 3): At daylight the Sixty-fourth Illinois Infantry, as skirmishers, advanced and took possession of Kenesaw Mountain. The command then moved to a point near Ruff's Mill, bivouacked, and the Second Division went into position, relieving General Lightburn's brigade, of General M. L. Smith's division, intrenching themselves on west side of Nickajack Creek, with two regiments intrenched on east side to hold cross-roads and the commanding ground. Between my present position and that held by General M. L. Smith is a dense wood. The enemy appear to be in greatest force south of this wood and west of creek, which, with my limited force and owing to the lateness of the hour, compelled me to make such dispositions as would best protect the troops in case of an attack. The ground on the east side of the creek is, I should judge, the best to occupy, but will require a larger force than I have on the line. It is generally believed that nothing but cav-alry is in our front. Large camp-fires are plainly visible two or three miles due east from our position, supposed to be the enemy's. I inclose herewith hurried sketch* of my position.

I am, colonel, very respectfully, your obedient servant,

G. M. DODGE,
Major-General.

HEADQUARTERS OF THE POST,
Chattanooga, July 3, 1864.

Col. W. B. McCREERY,
Commanding Engineer Brigade:

COLONEL: Information which is deemed reliable is that the enemy is again advancing in force against La Fayette, who or what force we do not know. It is probably desirable that you should notify your pickets and also the various camps to increased vigilance and to be ready. If you have vedettes would it not be well to have some of them

---

* To appear in the Atlas.

four to six miles in advance? I am instructed also by Major-General Steedman to say to you for your guidance now and hereafter that should you be attacked it will be expected of you to hold your position as long as you can without endangering your command, and should that be the case you will move all property that can be moved to this place and as a last resort fall back upon this post. Two guns from Fort Mihalotzy is the signal for alarm. Thirteen guns will be fired at sunrise as a Federal salute. Now, colonel, do you stay in your bed to-night unless attacked and send your officers to attend to picket duty. I will take the liberty of sending a line by the orderly to the company half way up the mountain directing them to have out three sentinels and to be watchful.

Very truly, your obedient servant,

T. R. STANLEY,
Colonel, Commanding Post.

SUGAR VALLEY, GA., *July 3, 1864—5 p. m.*

Major-General STEEDMAN:

I have just received dispatch from Watkins, stating enemy are advancing on him in force, and asking me to come to assistance; it is twenty miles, and I will leave as soon as possible, halting at Ship's Gap, five miles this side, until I learn more. If Watkins is confronted by a large force I recommend the evacuation of La Fayette in preference to attempting to get troops enough there to hold it. You must answer this dispatch at once, so that it will overtake me to-night, and I shall know definitely.

Respectfully,

JNO. T. CROXTON,
Colonel Fourth Kentucky Mounted Infantry.

HEADQUARTERS DISTRICT OF THE ETOWAH,
Chattanooga, Tenn., July 3, 1864.

Colonel CROXTON,
Resaca, Ga. :

I have received some information from Watkins and sent orders by him. You will hold Ship's Gap with a sufficient force, lending all the assistance you can to Watkins, and if confronted too strong fall back toward Ringgold, securing Gordon's Springs Gap, but using most of your force to check the advance of the enemy. There are 700 infantry and a section of artillery at Gordon's Mills; keep them advised. Leave your wagons at Resaca.

By command of Major-General Steedman:

S. B. MOE,
Captain and Assistant Adjutant-General.

HEADQUARTERS DISTRICT OF THE ETOWAH,
Chattanooga, Tenn., July 3, 1864—5.50 p. m.

Colonel CROXTON,
Fourth Kentucky Mounted Infantry :

COLONEL: In the event of an advance of the enemy, just reported to me by courier from Colonel Watkins, proving to be correct, you will hold

Ship's and Gordon's Springs Gaps, while Colonel Watkins holds Nicka-jack Gap, checking, as far as you can with safety, his advance toward the railroad in any direction, and sending me by courier all the information you can get. If attacked fight as long as you can without endangering your command, and if overwhelmed fall back in the direction of Dalton and Resaca.

Yours, truly,

J. B. STEEDMAN,
Major-General, Commanding.

HEADQUARTERS DISTRICT OF THE ETOWAH,
Chattanooga, Tenn., July 3, 1864—5.40 p. m.

Colonel WATKINS:

Your dispatch just received. If attacked you will fight as long as you can without endangering your command; if overpowered fall back if possible in the direction of this post, or Ringgold. Re-enforcements will be on the march in an hour, but before pushing infantry too far out it is necessary I should know what force the enemy has. It will not do to give the enemy an opportunity to cut us off in detail. If their force is a large one you will fall back on the infantry at Gordon's Mills, holding the enemy in check and sending couriers at once to this post, and informing the officer in command at Gordon's Mills.

Very truly,

J. B. STEEDMAN,
Major-General, Commanding.

HDQRS. SECOND BRIG., THIRD DIV., 15TH ARMY CORPS,
Resaca, Ga., July 3, 1864.

Capt. C. L. WHITE,
Assistant Adjutant-General:

CAPTAIN: I have information that Colonel Hart, Sixth Georgia Cavalry, with 300 men, is encamped near Jasper, in Pickens, where he is gathering up and feeding stock. I think that the force might be captured by sending a detachment of cavalry from Kingston to seize the mountain gaps south and east of Jasper, while an attack is made from the north by a cavalry force sent from here. Colonel Croxton, Fourth Kentucky Mounted Infantry, and Colonel Baldwin, Fifth Kentucky Cavalry, called on me this morning; their regiments, with a detachment of the Third Kentucky Cavalry, number, say, 1,100 or 1,200 men. Croxton and Baldwin are both intelligent men, and if you order the movement I have no doubt they will execute it vigorously. Do you propose to enter upon the immediate execution of General Steedman's order banishing citizens from the line of the railroad? If so copies should be distributed along the line. I have seen one copy, but have none.

Very respectfully, your obedient servant,

GREEN B. RAUM,
Colonel, Commanding Brigade.

RESACA, *July 3, 1864—7 p. m.*

Capt. C. L. WHITE:

Colonel Croxton, Fourth Kentucky, reports from Snake Creek Gap a dispatch from Colonel Watkins at La Fayette that the enemy is advancing upon him in force.   Colonel Croxton will move to Villanow to-night, and to Ship's Gap at daybreak.   I will direct Colonel Baldwin, Fifth Kentucky, to send a force to Snake Creek Gap, and another in the direction of Jasper.   Colonel Croxton requests that Colonel Lowe be informed of these facts.

GREEN B. RAUM,
Colonel, Commanding Brigade.

RESACA, July 3, 1864.

Capt. S. B. Moe,
    Assistant Adjutant-General:

Colonel Croxton, Fourth Kentucky, is at Snake Creek Gap.   He will move to-night to Villanow; at daylight in the morning to Ship's Gap to the relief of La Fayette, which is threatened by enemy.   Colonel Moore left here for Tunnel Hill yesterday evening.

G. B. RAUM,
Colonel, Commanding.

RESACA, July 3, 1864.

Capt. C. L. White,
    Assistant Adjutant-General:

Two train loads of ammunition are here to be stored.   If attacked my force is inadequate for the defense of the bridge and the ammunition.   Can you spare the Eightieth Ohio?

G. B. RAUM,
Colonel, Commanding.

CARTERSVILLE, July 3, 1864.

General J. E. Smith:

Colonel Murray is to-night near Calhoun, with one regiment on way to Resaca; will reach there to-morrow.   Colonel Baldwin with parts of two regiments is near Resaca.   Will telegraph him at once to do what he can to render assistance if needed.   He is out of forage, and has been for two days.

W. W. LOWE,
Colonel, Commanding.

HDQRS. THIRD DIVISION, FIFTEENTH ARMY CORPS,
Kingston, Ga., July 3, 1864.

Colonel Lowe,
    Cartersville, Ga.:

Colonel Raum says that Colonel Hart, Sixth Georgia (rebel), is near Jasper with 300 men.

JNO. E. SMITH,
Brigadier-General.

HDQRS. THIRD DIVISION, FIFTEENTH ARMY CORPS,
Kingston, Ga., July 3, 1864.
Col. GREEN B. RAUM,
Comdg. 2d Brig., 3d Div., 15th Army Corps, Resaca, Ga.:

Your dispatch relative to the movement of the enemy received. The general commanding directs that you give no orders to the cavalry force of Colonel Lowe, stationed at or near Resaca, as they have been concentrated to that point by order of Major-General Thomas for a specified purpose. I will notify Colonel Lowe of the information you have received. In the mean time keep me advised of all movements.

CARL. L. WHITE,
Captain and Assistant Adjutant-General.

———

HDQRS. THIRD DIVISION, FIFTEENTH ARMY CORPS,
Kingston, Ga., July 3, 1864.
Col. GREEN B. RAUM,
Commanding Second Brigade:

Colonel Lowe sends out his command by order of General Thomas to-morrow to scout the country from Cartersville to Canton, Jasper, and Talking Rock, &c. General Steedman's order, No. 2, has been sent you.*

CARL. L. WHITE,
Captain and Assistant Adjutant-General.

———

HDQRS. THIRD DIVISION, FIFTEENTH ARMY CORPS,
Kingston, Ga., July 3, 1864.
Col. GREEN B. RAUM,
Resaca, Ga.:

Colonel Lowe replies to my dispatch that Colonel Murray is to-night near Calhoun with one regiment on his way to Resaca, and will reach there to-morrow. Colonel Baldwin, with part of two regiments, is near Resaca, and will be directed at once to do what he can to render assistance if needed.

CARL. L. WHITE,
Captain and Assistant Adjutant-General.

———

NASHVILLE, *July 3, 1864.*
Major-General SHERMAN:

Your dispatch that this is the proper time is received. I shall go in person; shall leave General R. S. Granger to take care of the district. A little preparation will be required. I will announce to you when I am ready to go.

L. H. ROUSSEAU.

———

MARIETTA, GA., *July 3, 1864—6.30 p. m.*
Maj. T. T. ECKERT:

As was anticipated, Johnston retreated during last night and is now intrenched on line of Chattahoochee. His movement was effected in

———

* See Part IV, p. 634.

good order and without loss, except a few deserters. Two miles of railroad removed, and four of telegraph. My office is three miles out on railroad. Sherman's, Thomas', and McPherson's headquarters here. Schofield is on the right, some eight miles south. Will rest here for some time, and I can get to Nashville, perhaps.

J. C. VAN DUZER.

HEADQUARTERS TWENTIETH CORPS,
July 3, 1864.

Order of march for to-day:

The enemy having left, General Ward, with his division, will follow him with dispatch on the Powder Springs road. General Williams will advance from his left flank and follow on a line parallel with the Powder Springs road, in the same direction. General Geary will advance from his right flank. The pursuit to be made with the greatest possible vigor. In order that no delay may be caused by the trains they will be sent on to the Powder Springs road. Headquarters will be with the center column.

By command of Major-General Hooker:

H. W. PERKINS,
Assistant Adjutant-General.

HDQRS. MILITARY DIVISION OF THE MISSISSIPPI,
In the Field, July 4, 1864.

Major-General THOMAS:

I have no doubt that the enemy will attempt to molest our rear with his cavalry, and that he has reserved Roswell fortified for that very purpose. To counteract his designs I have ordered Garrard, with his whole cavalry, to proceed to Roswell, take the place if he can, otherwise hang near it, watching the river, opposing such a movement all he can and giving us and all points of the railroad timely notice. I wish you would so hold McCook as promptly to re-enforce Garrard, if need be. As soon as I understand the exact situation on the right, as to Turner's Ferry, and what progress McPherson has made, I will order Schofield round where Garrard now is.

I will go to-morrow, and in the mean time I wish you to hold strong the points now at Howard's and Palmer's head of column and merely picket light the road by which Garrard moved, as I feel sure the enemy will not attempt a sally there. Hooker need not hold the line from Palmer round to McPherson, but draw in to his left, save by a line of vedettes. I want you with your whole army to press steadily down on the enemy while McPherson cuts in on his flank. Schofield is to be held to re-enforce either part. Stoneman will threaten to cross the Chattahoochee and break the Atlanta and West Point Railroad, especially if the enemy send cavalry against our line of road. Instead of occupying Acworth, Big Shanty, and Marietta, I think we had better concentrate about the base of Kenesaw, near that water station, a point that could be defended against cavalry with great ease.

I am, &c.,

W. T. SHERMAN,
Major-General, Commanding.

HDQRS. MILITARY DIVISION OF THE MISSISSIPPI,
In the Field, Marietta, July 4, 1864.

Major-General THOMAS,
Commanding Army of the Cumberland:

GENERAL: I am directed by the general commanding to say the two divisions of the Fifteenth Corps now near here have been ordered to move about 9 o'clock and join General McPherson, and he desires you will relieve the provost guard of one regiment as soon as convenient, that they may also join their command. Let your command guard the place until such time as some arrangement for garrison may be made.

I am, general, with much respect, yours, &c.,

L. M. DAYTON,
Aide-de-Camp.

HEADQUARTERS FOURTH CORPS,
Near Neal Dow Station, July 4, 1864—8.20 p. m.

Major-General THOMAS:

GENERAL: In accordance with your instructions General Stanley strengthened his skirmish line and pushed it rapidly across the open corn-field in his front, taking the rebel rifle-pits, under a severe artillery and infantry fire. He immediately moved forward his main line and covered it by a barricade. Later in the day Generals Newton and Wood seized portions of the enemy's skirmish line, and have established their main line facing the same open field across which General Stanley advanced. The conduct of the troops in the charge to-day could not be surpassed. We have taken 88 prisoners, 3 of whom are officers. General King moved upon our right in conjunction with Stanley and intrenched important heights on the right. Our losses about 95 wounded according to hospital report this afternoon.

O. O. HOWARD.

HEADQUARTERS DEPARTMENT OF THE CUMBERLAND,
GEORGIA MILITARY INSTITUTE,
Marietta, July 4, 1864.

Maj. Gen. J. M. PALMER,
Commanding Fourteenth Army Corps:

GENERAL: The major-general commanding directs that in accordance with instructions from Major-General Sherman you detail one brigade of your corps to garrison the town of Marietta until other arrangements can be made. Give the commanding officer orders to preserve everything in and about the town as nearly in the same state as that in which he finds it upon his assuming command.

I am, general, very respectfully, your obedient servant,

WM. D. WHIPPLE,
Chief of Staff.

[Indorsement.]

General PALMER:

I have ordered the detail, as it is after 9 o'clock, from General Baird.

Very respectfully,

A. C. McCLURG.

HEADQUARTERS FIRST DIVISION CAVALRY,
July 4, 1864—3.30 p. m.

General W. L. ELLIOTT,
    Chief of Cavalry:

GENERAL: Yesterday after writing to you, and after General Stoneman had moved toward the right of our army, I took 300 men and a section of artillery and advanced on the Howell and Green's Ferry road to a point where it crosses the main Sandtown road. There I found breast-works occupied in part by the infantry of the enemy. I got my artillery within 300 yards of their works, and opened with good effect. I made no effort to take the breast-works, and withdrew at my leisure. Among our wounded was Lieutenant Hill, of my staff. I think that a column of infantry pushed down this road, or the Sandtown or Camp-bellton roads, could cross the Chattahoochee without much or any opposition now. I will move to Darby's this afternoon, and I feel satisfied that to-day these roads are occupied by nothing but a cavalry force.

E. M. McCOOK,
Brigadier-General, Commanding.

HDQRS. MILITARY DIVISION OF THE MISSISSIPPI,
    In the Field, on Marietta and Turner's Ferry Road,
        July 4, 1864—6 p. m.

Major-General SCHOFIELD,
    Commanding Army of the Ohio:

GENERAL: I am directed by the general commanding to say it was not his intention to move you to the left of the army until he succeeds in forcing Johnston across the Chattahoochee. In the mean time you will act in support and co-operate with General McPherson; General Hooker may be, by circumstances as they develop, moved toward General Palmer to concentrate General Thomas' army, in which case you will be required to act upon McPherson's flank. When Johnston is across the Chattahoochee then he will move you to the left.

I am, general, with much respect,

L. M. DAYTON,
Aide-de-Camp.

HEADQUARTERS ARMY OF THE OHIO,
        July 4, 1864—7.45 p. m.

Capt. L. M. DAYTON,
    Aide-de-Camp:

CAPTAIN: I have just received your letter dated 6 p. m. explaining General Sherman's intentions as to my movements. I understood the general's orders precisely as you explain them, and have been acting, or rather holding my troops ready to act, accordingly. From a map sent me by General Hooker, showing the position in which his "corps is being established," and from personal examination of the ground occupied by General Dodge, I judge that Hooker's right must be in rear of Dodge's left, and if advanced would overlap it. Perhaps there is some mistake as to positions. I will examine the ground myself in the morning and put in whatever force can be used between General Hooker and General McPherson's left. General McPherson has had to-day quite as many troops across the Nickajack, beyond Ruff's Mill, as could be used there. Please inform the general that Stoneman's cavalry has control of the country from McPherson's right, on the Turner's Ferry road, to the river, near Sandtown. He has beaten the enemy's cavalry in several small affairs and captured many prisoners and a large number of good horses and mules. I am just informed by Colonel Cameron, commanding a brigade of General Cox's division, which has been covering General Hooker's right during his advance, that at 5 p. m. to-day General Hooker united with General Dodge beyond Nickajack, and his (Colonel Cameron's) troops were thereby relieved.

Very respectfully,

J. M. SCHOFIELD,
Major-General.

HEADQUARTERS ARMY OF THE OHIO,
In the Field, Ga., July 4, 1864—7.30 p. m.

Maj. Gen. JOSEPH HOOKER,
Commanding Twentieth Army Corps:

GENERAL: I have just received Colonel Perkins' note inclosing a plat to indicate the position in which your corps is being established. If your maps are all right your right must be some distance in rear of General Dodge's left. General Dodge crossed the Nickajack at Ruff's Mill and his line crossed the road leading from that point toward Ruff's Station. I have also a brigade on his left with instructions to feel for your right. In the morning I will put in whatever additional force may be necessary.

Very respectfully, your obedient servant,

J. M. SCHOFIELD,
Major-General, Commanding.

SANDTOWN AND MARIETTA ROAD,
July 4, 1864.

Colonel CAPRON,
Commanding Brigade:

As soon as you reach this road or its immediate vicinity, in case you cannot strike it, try by all means to communicate with Colonel Butler on your left and on this road where the left-hand branch from the barricade strikes it, and send me word by the bearer of this when you have done so. Scout the country well to your front and right and try to communicate with McCook or Adams on your right. One or both of them ought to be between you and the Chattahoochee River on this road (the Sandtown and Marietta). I shall be on this road until further notice, and I hope you will be able to send me by this road direct.

Respectfully, &c.,

STONEMAN,
General, Commanding.

IN THE FIELD, GA., July 4, 1864—8 a. m.

Maj. Gen. W. T. SHERMAN,
Commanding Military Division of the Mississippi:

Your dispatch, per Lieutenant Vernay, was received last night. Lightburn's brigade, of Morgan L. Smith's division, secured a position across Nickajack Creek at Ruff's Mill yesterday afternoon and were relieved by a portion of Sweeny's division. Dodge is pushing forward his command in the direction of the railroad east of Nickajack Creek at Ruff's Mill. Blair is near Widow Mitchell's, and has sent two regiments of infantry and a section of artillery, in connection with a brigade of Stoneman's cavalry, on the road to Turner's Ferry, with orders to secure, if possible, the crossing of Nickajack Creek. Stoneman's cavalry hold the country from the Sandtown road west to Sweet Water, and most of his cavalry is along the Sandtown road. Your dispatch to me was shown to Major-General Schofield.

Very respectfully, your obedient servant,

JAS. B. McPHERSON,
Major-General.

HDQRS. MILITARY DIVISION OF THE MISSISSIPPI,
In the Field, at front, July 4, 1864.
General McPHERSON:

Howard charged across the field on his front and captured most of the advance line, but found the main line too strong with artillery. I have worked all along the line and shall continue to strengthen this point, where the Marietta and Sandtown road first crosses Nickajack. Davis has a brigade across and the others and Baird in close support. I will give my personal attention that if you have to fight on that line, you shall have the assistance of all of Thomas' army if they have to assault the parapet. Davis is here and can be relied on. Hooker is in communication with you, and if we have a fight will all fight together; you may pitch in strong. I doubt if the enemy will expect an attack by that line, for they seem to have prepared on their front. I think 1,000 prisoners have been taken on this line. I am disappointed so little has been done to-day, but think the causes are at work that will produce the direct result. Our whole line is in communication. I will camp on this road one mile and a half back of this point about five miles out of Marietta on the Sandtown road. Let me hear every chance.

W. T. SHERMAN,
Major-General.

JULY 4, 1864—4.45 p. m.
Major-General SHERMAN:

I had just got a position and directed artillery to be put in and open when your dispatch came.

McPHERSON,
Major-General.

HDQRS. DEPARTMENT AND ARMY OF THE TENNESSEE,
Near Ruff's Mill, Ga., July 4, 1864—8.45 p. m.
Major-General SHERMAN,
Commanding, &c.:

GENERAL: In pursuance of your instructions, at daybreak this morning I directed Major-General Dodge to take his entire command and push across Nickajack Creek at Ruff's Mill, General Blair to send two regiments and a section of artillery, supported by Stoneman's cavalry, from Widow Mitchell's down to Nickajack, near Turner's Ferry. Dodge moved across and ran against Stevenson's division, and as he developed his lines captured a few prisoners from each division of Hood's corps. I sent over Morgan L. Smith's division, and General Schofield sent in a brigade on Dodge's left to try and communicate with Hooker. As soon as the troops were over and in position, I directed Dodge to strengthen his skirmish line, so as to make it almost equivalent to a line of battle, especially over rough ground, and to assault the enemy's rifle-pits. The order was gallantly executed, the works taken, and some 50 prisoners captured; our loss not heavy; Colonel Noyes, Thirty-ninth Ohio, severely wounded. This gives Dodge a position about one mile and a quarter east of Nickajack Creek. He has one brigade of Schofield on his left, and Morgan L. Smith's division on his right and rear. The cavalry and infantry demonstration on the Turner's Ferry road reached a point, as they think, half a mile* from Nickajack, and found it tolerably well fortified, with four guns in position. This brought the infantry to a halt, and they have not advanced since. They will, however, hold all the ground they have gained, and be ready to try the strength of the enemy's works, if it is deemed desirable. I have about 15,000 men across the creek with Dodge, and Logan's two divisions (Osterhaus' and Harrow's) in reserve at the forks of the road. They got in late and completely worn out. I do not think more than half of the divisions arrived.

Very respectfully, your obedient servant,

JAS. B. McPHERSON,
Major-General.

HDQRS. MILITARY DIVISION OF THE MISSISSIPPI,
In the Field, Marietta, July 4, 1864.

Maj. Gen JOHN A. LOGAN,
Commanding Fifteenth Army Corps:

GENERAL: By direction of the general commanding, you will move your command, starting about 9 o'clock, and report with it to Major-General McPherson, by the way of Cheney's or Wade's. The regiment now doing provost duty will remain until relieved by Major-General Thomas.

I am, general, with respect, yours, &c.,

L. M. DAYTON,
Aide-de-Camp.

HDQRS. SECOND DIVISION, SIXTEENTH ARMY CORPS,
In the Field, near Ruff's Mill, Ga., July 4, 1864.

Col. E. W. RICE,
Commanding First Brigade:

COLONEL: You will deploy one company of your command as skirmishers, supported by two companies, on the left flank of the Sixty-sixth Illinois Infantry. They will move forward the distance of one mile, and discover if any of the enemy are in that locality. Should they meet with opposition they will immediately report the fact to these headquarters.

By order of T. W. Sweeny, brigadier-general, commanding:

JAMES DAVIDSON,
First Lieut., Fifty-second Illinois Infantry, and Aide-de-Camp.

---

* Reads a mile and a half in Howard's quotation. See Part III, p. 37.

HEADQUARTERS SEVENTEENTH ARMY CORPS,
In the Field, July 4, 1864—7.15 p. m.

Brigadier-General LEGGETT,
Commanding Third Division, Seventeenth Army Corps:

GENERAL: The major-general commanding desires you to withdraw General Force from his present position and move out toward the Fourth Division, camping on the ground indicated by Lieutenant Tompkins, aide-de-camp.

I have the honor to be, very respectfully, your obedient servant,
A. J. ALEXANDER,
Assistant Adjutant-General.

HEADQUARTERS SECOND CAVALRY DIVISION,
In front of Marietta, July 4, 1864.

Brig. Gen. W. L. ELLIOTT,
Chief of Cavalry, Department of the Cumberland:

GENERAL: I have the honor to report that I advanced on the Pace's Ferry road about a mile and a half, driving the enemy's pickets, crossing a creek and taking a range of hills on the south side. The enemy was strong, and, being in front of the infantry, while they did not advance, knowing that any farther progress would be impossible on my part, I connected late this afternoon my vedettes with General Howard's pickets. My dismounted men were half a mile in advance of where my vedettes now stand. The enemy's cavalry picket the Powers' Ferry road and on the Roswell Factory road; my pickets extend from the Powers' Ferry road to the Fourth Corps.

Are there any orders for me?

Very respectfully, your obedient servant,
K. GARRARD,
Brigadier-General, Commanding Division.

HDQRS. MILITARY DIVISION OF THE MISSISSIPPI,
In the Field, July 4, 1864.

General GARRARD,
Commanding Division of Cavalry:

GENERAL: I am satisfied the enemy will attempt with his cavalry to cross the Chattahoochee about Roswell and make an attempt on our communications. To counteract him you will move in that direction and watch close, taking some position on which to rally on infantry, a brigade of which is at Marietta, a strong brigade at Allatoona, and General Thomas, will be instructed to hold McCook's brigade ready to go to your assistance. You may draw out at once and go to Roswell, and if you can force your way to it, you may gain a secure position from which you can watch that point. In case the enemy's cavalry get across, you must hang to him, opposing him whenever opposition is possible, and send couriers rapidly to me, and to the points of the railroad threatened. In the mean time report to me frequently and use your cavalry as though you were preparing to cross yourself or were only waiting for the waters to subside and make the ford practicable. You now understand the geography so well that I have no doubt you can prevent Wheeler from doing much damage between Marietta and Allatoona. In case he passes round by Canton to go toward Cartersville, send notice and hang on his rear. We now have a full division of infantry at Kingston. Arrest every citizen in the country whom you find likely to prove a spy, and keep moving so that your force cannot be computed.

I am, &c.,

W. T. SHERMAN,
Major-General, Commanding.

HEADQUARTERS DISTRICT OF THE ETOWAH,
Chattanooga, July 4, 1864.

Brig. Gen. J. E. SMITH,
Kingston, Ga.:

GENERAL: I am instructed by the general commanding district to say that Colonel Watkins yesterday notified him that the rebels were moving down the Broomtown road toward La Fayette in considerable force. He desires that you will keep the stations at which your command are posted well advised of the whereabouts of these squads and forces, and caution them to be on the lookout all the time.

I am, general, respectfully, your obedient servant,

S. B. MOE,
Assistant Adjutant-General.

RESACA, *July 4, 1864.*

Capt. C. L. WHITE:

Your three dispatches of last night just received. Colonel Croxton moved toward La Fayette upon his own responsibility. Colonel Baldwin moved to Snake Creek Gap upon my order at 10.30 last night with 200 men. The balance of his command is here.

GREEN B. RAUM,
Colonel, Commanding Brigade.

ROME, GA., *July 4, 1864.*

Brig. Gen. JOHN E. SMITH:

The rebels it is reported are to cross the Etowah on the bridge three miles west of Kingston for the purpose of obstructing the road to Rome.

WM. VANDEVER,
Brigadier-General, Commanding.

GENERAL ORDERS, }   HDQRS. SEVENTEENTH ARMY CORPS,
No. 7.   }   *In the Field, near Ruff's Mill, July 4, 1864.*

Maj. J. T. Cheney is announced as chief of artillery on the staff of the major-general commanding. He will be obeyed and respected accordingly.

By command of Maj. Gen. Frank P. Blair:

A. J. ALEXANDER,
Assistant Adjutant-General.

NEAR CHATTAHOOCHEE RIVER, *July 5, 1864.*
Maj. Gen. H. W. HALLECK,
   Washington, D. C.:

On the 3d we pursued the enemy by all the roads south till we found him in an intrenched position which had been prepared in advance, its salient on the main Marietta and Atlanta road about five miles south of Marietta, and the wings behind the Nickajack and Rottenwood Creeks. During the 4th General Thomas pressed the salient, and McPherson and Schofield moved against Nickajack by pressing close and threatening the Chattahoochee at Sandtown and below. Johnston again retreated in the night and now has his main force and wagons across the Chattahoochee, with Hardee's corps on this side, strongly intrenched in a sort of tête-de-pont on a ridge of hills beginning at the railroad bridge and extending down the river to the mouth of the Nickajack. We have worked hard, and now Thomas' left is on the Chattahoochee, three miles above the railroad bridge at Pace's Ferry. Stoneman has been most active with the cavalry about Sweet Water, and is now on the Chattahoochee about Sandtown, and Garrard started this morning for Roswell Factory. I have no report from him yet. I am now far ahead of my railroad and telegraph, and want them to catch up, and may be here some days. Atlanta is in plain view, nine miles distant. We have had continual skirmishing, but our losses are small, while we have inflicted more to the enemy. Our prisoners taken in the last two days will not fall short of 2,000. The extent of the enemy's parallels already taken is wonderful, and much of the same sort confronts us yet, and is seen beyond the Chattahoochee.

       W. T. SHERMAN,
        Major-General.

       WAR DEPARTMENT,
      July 5, 1864—3.45 p. m.
Major-General SHERMAN,
   Marietta, Ga.:

The President has issued his proclamation declaring martial law in the State of Kentucky. News just received of a naval battle off Cherbourg between the pirate Alabama and the United States war steamer Kearsarge. After a close engagement of one hour and forty minutes the Alabama was sunk. Semmes and his officers and part of the crew found shelter in a British yacht. No one killed on the Kearsarge.

       EDWIN M. STANTON,
        Secretary of War.

  HEADQUARTERS DEPARTMENT OF THE CUMBERLAND,
      In the Field, July 5, 1864.
Maj. Gen. W. T. SHERMAN,
   Commanding Military Division of the Mississippi:

GENERAL: We discovered at daylight this morning that the enemy had gone from in front of us, and I immediately ordered the troops in pursuit.

  Very respectfully, your obedient servant,
       GEO. H. THOMAS,
        Major-General, Commanding.

HEADQUARTERS FOURTH ARMY CORPS,
July 5, 1864—9 p. m.

Brigadier-General WHIPPLE, *Chief of Staff:*

GENERAL: I have the honor to report that my command left camp at 5 this a. m. in pursuit of the enemy, and moved down the railroad, Brigadier-General Wood's division leading, followed by General Newton's, and then Major-General Stanley's.

General Wood met the enemy's dismounted cavalry, and commenced skirmishing with it about one mile and a half from camp. They delayed our advance as much as possible, making a stand at every advantageous position from that point to the place where I have gone into camp.

When about two miles from camp I learned from a report of one of my scouts that one of the trains of the enemy was moving toward the river on a road about two miles to our left. I directed General Newton to send a brigade of his division after it, but it had too much the start to be overtaken by infantry.

At 10 a. m. my head of column arrived at Vining's Station on the railroad, and at 11 a. m. I started down the road leading from there to Pace's Ferry. Very near the station the enemy's dismounted cavalry took up a position on a ridge behind rail barricades, and when General Wood's skirmishers came up they left their cover, and charging them, attempted to drive them back, but they were quickly repulsed, and from this point were slowly driven back to the river at the ferry. So closely were they followed that they had not an opportunity to destroy the pontoon bridge over which they crossed. They cut it on this side, however, and it swung over to the other side of the river.

I now hold this side of the crossing, and General Wood has gone into position on a ridge almost parallel with the river, and near thereto; General Newton in his rear, and extending to his left, and General Stanley on the left of General Newton.

The losses in this command to-day have been very small for the results. We have taken 101 enlisted men prisoners.

Very respectfully, your obedient servant,

O. O. HOWARD,
Major-General.

———

HEADQUARTERS FOURTH ARMY CORPS,
Near Neal Dow Station, Ga., July 5, 1864—4.20 a. m.

Brigadier-General WHIPPLE, *Chief of Staff:*

GENERAL: General Stanley reports that the enemy have gone from his front, and that he occupies their works.

O. O. HOWARD,
Major-General.

———

HEADQUARTERS FOURTH ARMY CORPS,
Near Neal Dow Station, July 5, 1864—4.25 a. m.

Major-General STANLEY,
Commanding First Division, Fourth Army Corps:

GENERAL: The enemy have retreated. Make every preparation to follow him as soon as possible. General Wood's division will lead, General Newton will follow, then yours.

By order of Major-General Howard:

J. S. FULLERTON,
Assistant Adjutant-General.

HEADQUARTERS FOURTH ARMY CORPS,
Pace's House, near Vining's Station, Ga., July 5, 1864—6.30 p. m.

Orders of the day for the Fourth Army Corps for July 6, 1864:

Brigadier-General Wood will force a crossing of the Chattahoochee River to-morrow morning at 5 o'clock. He will make the attempt to cross at Pace's Ferry, at the point where the enemy crossed on the pontoon bridge this morning, making use of the enemy's bridge now lying on the other side of the river, if he can obtain possession of the same. If he cannot cross at this point a pontoon bridge will be furnished him, and he will cross at such point as he may select. All of the artillery of the First and Second Divisions of this corps will co-operate with General Wood's artillery in this movement, and for this purpose will be placed in such position as Captain Bridges, acting chief of artillery of this corps, may designate.

By order of Major-General Howard:

J. S. FULLERTON,
Assistant Adjutant-General.

HEADQUARTERS FOURTH ARMY CORPS,
Near Vining's Station, Ga., July 5, 1864—9.20 p. m.

Major-General THOMAS,
Commanding Army of the Cumberland:

GENERAL: Please have the pontoon bridge at General Wood's by 5 a. m. to-morrow.

Very respectfully, your obedient servant,

O. O. HOWARD,
Major-General.

HDQRS. THIRD BRIG., SECOND DIV., 4TH ARMY CORPS,
July 5, 1864—2.15 a. m.

Brigadier-General NEWTON,
Commanding Second Division, Fourth Army Corps:

GENERAL: Colonel Opdycke and Lieutenant-Colonel Moore, of the One hundred and twenty-fifth Ohio Infantry, both report the enemy retreating. They report trains moving off—artillery, baggage and railroad trains. The enemy still keep up a slight firing from their skirmish line. Both Colonels Opdycke and Moore seem confident that the report they bring is correct.

Very respectfully, your obedient servant,

L. P. BRADLEY,
Colonel, Commanding.

HEADQUARTERS DEPARTMENT OF THE CUMBERLAND,
In the Field, July 5, 1864—4.40 a. m.

Maj. Gen. JOHN M. PALMER,
Commanding Fourteenth Army Corps:

GENERAL: The enemy has gone from General Howard's front. The major-general commanding directs that you push after him without a moment's delay, and, if possible, inflict some damage upon him before he gets entirely across the Chattahoochee.

Very respectfully, your obedient servant,

WM. D. WHIPPLE,
Assistant Adjutant-General.

HEADQUARTERS TWENTIETH CORPS,
July 5, 1864.

Brigadier-General WILLIAMS,
 Commanding First Division:

GENERAL: The major-general commanding directs that you examine the country in your front, and ascertain if you can move your division by any by-road due east. The enemy have gone and we must follow. If no road can be found which you can cross the creek and get onto, you will have to bring your division back here and march out on this road. Our scouts have been sent out to find roads, if possible, but the general wishes you to send also.

 Very respectfully, your obedient servant,
       H. W. PERKINS,
       Assistant Adjutant-General.

HEADQUARTERS TWENTIETH CORPS,
July 5, 1864.

Brigadier-General GEARY,
 Commanding Second Division:

GENERAL: The major-general commanding directs me to say that the indications are that the enemy will leave here to cross the river to-night. He wishes you to keep your pickets well pushed up to-night, and if they should leave to occupy their works at once. He would also like to have you get possession, if possible, this p. m. of that point of their works that Major Reynolds is now taking a battery down to shell. He will point it out to you. But this is not to be construed into an order to assault.

 Very respectfully, your obedient servant,
       H. W. PERKINS,
       Assistant Adjutant-General.

HDQRS. CHIEF OF CAVALRY, DEPT. OF THE CUMBERLAND,
Four miles below Marietta, July 5, 1864.

Brig. Gen. E. M. McCOOK,
 Commanding First Cavalry Division:

GENERAL : The general commanding directs that you march with your command to the left and rear of the Army of the Cumberland. General Howard's (Fourth) corps is on the left, with his right resting on the railroad. General Garrard's division is on the extreme left. Your position will be in rear of the left of General Howard, so as to be in readiness to support General Garrard.

 I am, general, very respectfully, your obedient servant,
       DAVID F. HOW,
  Lieutenant and Acting Assistant Adjutant-General.

HEADQUARTERS ARMY OF THE OHIO,
July 5, 1864—7 p. m.

Major-General SHERMAN,
 Commanding Military Division of the Mississippi:

GENERAL: I have had no opportunity to use my troops to-day. General McPherson's having been quite as many as could be brought into

action on this side of Nickajack, consequently I have not moved my
column beyond Watson's house. I will confer with General McPherson
to-night and see what can be done in the morning in case the enemy
remain on this side of the river. I understand he is behind strong
works along the Nickajack, covering Turner's Ferry, and presume
McPherson will not be able to force a crossing this evening. If I do
not hear from you to-night I will move down at daylight in the morning
and co-operate with McPherson.

Very respectfully,

J. M. SCHOFIELD,
Major-General.

HDQRS. MILITARY DIVISION OF THE MISSISSIPPI,
In the Field, near Chattahoochee, July 5, 1864.

Major-General SCHOFIELD:

Move your entire command, except Stoneman's cavalry, to Ruff's Station, en route for position on our left, which will be either about Roswell
Factory or the mouth of Rottenwood Creek. Ruff's Station is five
miles south of Marietta, on the railroad, and I think there is a plain
road from where you now are. Notify General McPherson of your departure and report to me by letter or in person on arrival.

Yours,

W. T. SHERMAN,
Major-General, Commanding.

HDQRS. THIRD DIVISION, TWENTY-THIRD ARMY CORPS,
Lynch's, on Sandtown Road, July 5, 1864—9.30 a. m.

Colonel BYRD,
Commanding Third Brigade:

SIR: You will, on receipt of this, move your command by the road
leading in this direction from the front of your works, and down the
Sandtown road from this point to the intersection of the road from Powder Springs to Ruff's Station with this road, at which place you will
receive further orders. The point you will reach is at or near Wade's
house, and at any convenient locality near there you will halt and mass
your troops, unless you receive other orders. The whole division is in
motion. The enemy are again in retreat.

J. D. COX,
Brigadier-General, Commanding.

HDQRS. THIRD DIVISION, TWENTY-THIRD ARMY CORPS,
In the Field, Ga., July 5, 1864.

Col. R. F. BARTER,
Comdg. First Brig., First Div., 23d Army Corps:

COLONEL: The general commanding directs that I inform you that
this division will move out upon the Sandtown road immediately. But
he desires that your command remain in its present position, guarding cross-roads, trains, &c., until further orders.

Very respectfully, your obedient servant,

THEO. COX,
Lieut. and Aide-de-Camp, Acting Assistant Adjutant-General.

HDQRS. THIRD DIVISION, TWENTY-THIRD ARMY CORPS,
                    In the Field, Ga., July 5, 1864.
Col. E. W. CRITTENDEN,
       Commanding Dismounted Cavalry Brigade:

COLONEL: The general commanding directs me to say that this division will move out upon the Sandtown road immediately, and he desires that your command move forward in the rear of the other brigades, and that you report to him in person upon the road when your command overtakes the others.

       Very respectfully, your obedient servant,
                              THEO. COX,
       Lieut. and Aide-de-Camp, Acting Assistant Adjutant-General.

                                        JULY 5, 1864.
Colonel CAPRON:

The infantry is close upon you; try to drive everything across the river, and then move your brigade down the bank to Baker's Ferry. Butler will go on your right at Sandtown. On your arrival at Baker's Ferry you can forage your horses and send for rations for your men, if you are in want of them.

                              STONEMAN,
                                        General.

                                JULY 5, 1864—7.30 a. m.
Major-General SHERMAN:

Dodge reports that enemy has evacuated main line of works in his front. His skirmishers are pushing forward.

                              McPHERSON,
                                        Major-General.

                                JULY 5, 1864—11.30 a. m.
Major-General SHERMAN:

A large portion of Dodge's command is across the Nickajack at Ruff's Mill, and has run against Stevenson's division, and possibly some other portion of Hood's corps, out about one mile; some little skirmishing.

                              McPHERSON,
                                        Major-General.

HDQRS. DEPARTMENT AND ARMY OF THE TENNESSEE,
            Near Gordon's, on Turner's Ferry Road, Ga.,
                              July 5, 1864—9 p. m.
Maj. Gen. W. T. SHERMAN,
       Commanding Military Division of the Mississippi:

GENERAL: I send you herewith sketch* of the position of the Army of the Tennessee to-night. Early this forenoon Gresham's division, of Blair's command, charged and carried a line of rebel rifle-pits on the Turner's Ferry road, and then pressed forward until about 6 p. m. they gained a position on Nickajack Creek, within about 500 yards of rebel

---

* Not found with this communication; but see McPherson to Schofield, following.

intrenchments on the Chattahoochee. Leggett's division moved down to Howell's Ferry, on the Chattahoochee; drove the enemy away on the opposite side of the river, where they were erecting rifle-pits; left a brigade there and four 24-pounder howitzers (brass), and then moved up the river toward the mouth of Nickajack Creek, and connected with Gresham. We have had some pretty lively skirmishing and a good deal of artillery firing. The enemy appear to have strong works north of the Chattahoochee, but if they remain where they are to-morrow I think we can punish them severely, as I am getting batteries into position to-night.

Very respectfully, your obedient servant,

JAS. B. McPHERSON,
Major-General.

HDQRS. DEPARTMENT AND ARMY OF THE TENNESSEE,
Near Gordon's, on Turner's Ferry Road, Ga., July 5, 1864.

Major-General SCHOFIELD,
Commanding Department of the Ohio :

GENERAL: I send you herewith sketches* of the position of the Army of the Tennessee to-night. Early this forenoon Gresham's division, of Blair's command, charged and carried a line of rebel rifle-pits on the Turner's Ferry road, and then pressed forward until about 6 p. m. they gained a position on Nickajack Creek, within about 500 yards of rebel intrenchments on the Chattahoochee. Leggett's division moved down to Howell's Ferry across the Chattahoochee; drove the enemy away on the opposite side of the river, where they were erecting rifle-pits; left a brigade there and four 24-pounder howitzers (brass), and then moved up the river toward the mouth of Nickajack Creek, and connected with Gresham. We have had some pretty lively skirmishing and a good deal of artillery firing. The rebels appeared to have strong works north of the Chattahoochee, but if they remain where they are to-morrow I think we can punish them severely, as I am getting batteries in position to-night. You can move up as soon as practicable toward Widow Mitchell's. In the mean time I expect to receive orders from Major-General Sherman. Hooker's train is on the Sandtown road, at least a portion of it; where his troops are I do not know, as I have not seen or heard any firing to my left to-day.

Yours, truly,

JAS. B. McPHERSON,
Major-General.

HDQRS. MILITARY DIVISION OF THE MISSISSIPPI,
In the Field, three miles from Railroad Bridge,
July 5, 1864—8 p. m.

Major-General MCPHERSON:

GENERAL: I have ordered Schofield over to this road, in rear of the center, preparatory to moving him over to about the mouth of Rottenwood or Roswell Factory according to reports I may receive from General Garrard. I was in hopes you would get control of the ridge commanding Turner's Ferry before the enemy could get across, but I think it is now too late unless you have gained the ridge described as lying along the Chattahoochee above the mouth of Nickajack. Do not

---

*See pp. 57, 58.

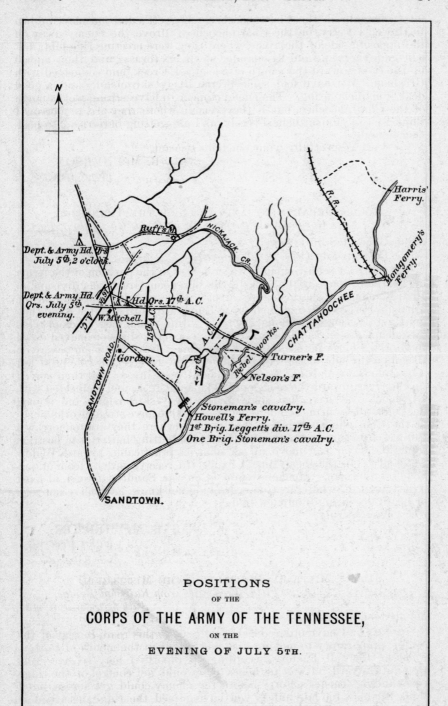

POSITIONS

OF THE

CORPS OF THE ARMY OF THE TENNESSEE,

ON THE

EVENING OF JULY 5TH.

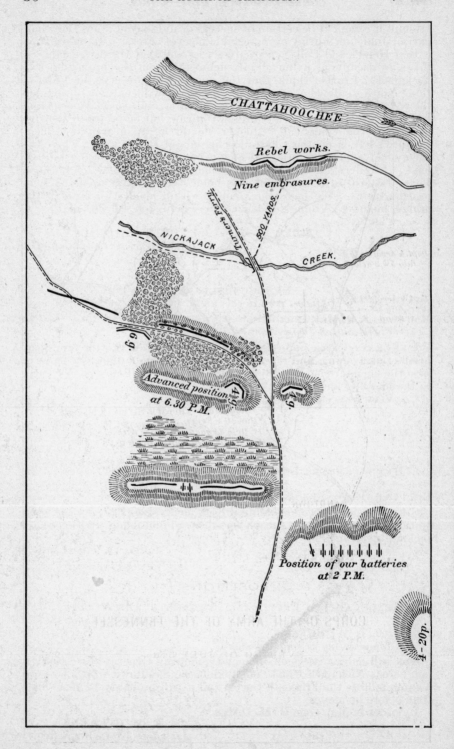

CHATTAHOOCHEE

Rebel works.

Nine embrasures.

NICKAJACK

Turner's Ferry

500 YARDS

CREEK.

6.9.

Advanced position
at 6.30 P.M.

4.9.

4.9.

Position of our batteries
at 2 P.M.

4 - 20p.

attempt it except it be certain of success or unless you know that some part of Johnston's army or material is not yet across. My information is that Hood's and Polk's corps are across and that Hardee remains on this side occupying a line of intrenchments from the bridge down to Nickajack. I rather think that the enemy will preserve this order of things until we develop our game. Stoneman will continue to threaten the river between Nickajack and Sweet Water, and you may co-operate and gain any substantial advantage you can, but be prepared to move wherever events may call. Hooker should be up nearer to Palmer. Howard's left is on the Chattahoochee about Pace's Ferry, where the enemy had a pontoon bridge, which is cut loose and is swung to their bank. I understand he has two pontoon bridges at the railroad bridge. That bridge is still good, and was being very actively used to-day in passing trains. We have the road to within about two miles of the bridge, including Vining's Station, where Johnston was last night.

I am, &c.,

W. T. SHERMAN,
Major-General, Commanding.

HEADQUARTERS ARMY OF THE OHIO,
In the Field, Ga., July 5, 1864—7 p. m.

Maj. Gen. J. B. McPHERSON,
Commanding Department of the Tennessee:

GENERAL: Please inform me what the situation is after your operations this evening, and report what you think can be done to-morrow in case the enemy remain on this side the river. I will move down early in the morning and co-operate with you.

Very respectfully, your obedient servant,

J. M. SCHOFIELD,
Major-General, Commanding.

HEADQUARTERS LEFT WING, SIXTEENTH ARMY CORPS,
July 5, 1864.

Brig. Gen. T. W. SWEENY:

SIR: The general commanding directs me to state that he wishes you to throw a strong line of skirmishers forward and follow up the enemy, picking up stragglers.

GEO. E. FORD,
Captain and Aide-de-Camp.

HEADQUARTERS LEFT WING, SIXTEENTH ARMY CORPS,
In the Field, July 5, 1864.

Brig. Gen. T. W. SWEENY,
Commanding Second Division:

You will move with your command, following General Veatch's division, across Nickajack Creek and taking the Sandtown road. General Veatch follows the Fifteenth Corps, and it will probably be some little time before he moves.

By order of Maj. Gen. G. M. Dodge:

J. W. BARNES,
Assistant Adjutant-General.

HEADQUARTERS SEVENTEENTH ARMY CORPS,
In the Field, July 5, 1864—8 p. m.

Brigadier-General LEGGETT,
    Commanding Third Division:

GENERAL: General Gresham succeeded in throwing skirmishers across the Nickajack this afternoon, and is ordered to attack the enemy's works to-morrow morning early. He will have to form his command under the fire of the fort after crossing the creek. The major-general commanding therefore desires you at daylight to-morrow morning to open vigorously from every gun you have upon the enemy's works to divert their attention from General Gresham's movements. Any other diversion you can make will be to the advantage of the command.

I have the honor to be, very respectfully, your obedient servant,

A. J. ALEXANDER,
Assistant Adjutant-General.

HEADQUARTERS CAVALRY DIVISION,
July 5, 1864.

Captain DAYTON,
    Acting Assistant Adjutant-General:

CAPTAIN: I have to report for the information of the major-general commanding that my command is camped on the Willeyo Creek near Roswell Factory. My advance is at the Factory. I will destroy all buildings. The bridge at this point over the river is burnt by the rebels. The ford is passable, so reported by citizens. I sent a regiment to the paper-mills, burnt the paper-mills, flouring-mills, and machine-shops. The citizens report the banks of the river high at Powers' Ferry and batteries in position on south bank. They had a pontoon bridge at Pace's Ferry, a few miles below, where a portion of their army crossed. There is a road running from Roswell Factory down the river below the paper-mills, and near the mills and above passes on the bank of river. As fast as possible I will send information of the roads, fords, ferries, &c.

Very respectfully, your obedient servant,

K. GARRARD,
Brigadier-General, Commanding Division.

SANDTOWN FERRY, GA., *July 5, 1864.*

Major-General SHERMAN:

GENERAL: I think, or at least hope, that during the past six or seven days we have accomplished all that was expected of us; if not, it has not been from [lack of] efforts to do so. We have worked day and night and covered a good deal of country. I was detained on the 1st by representations from General McCook to the effect that a few days before a large cavalry force had been in Villa Rica, and the correctness of which I was forced to ascertain by sending out strong scouting parties, and also to see where the force had gone to. I found that the force had been a good deal magnified, and that it had gone either south of the Chattahoochee River or across the Sweet Water near its mouth, where there is a good ford and the only one on the creek. As soon as we got to the

Chattahoochee River I kept one brigade acting along its north bank in hopes that it might induce the enemy to think it your intention to cross south of the railroad, and it seems from the inclosed dispatches this morning picked up on the road that it had its effect. We covered the river from Campbellton up as far as Sandtown, and had not General McCook been withdrawn by General Elliott yesterday, I think he would have been able to have helped us to get to Howell's Ferry yesterday. As it was we did not get there until 8 o'clock this morning. One division of General Blair's relieved one of my brigades yesterday, on the road crossing the Nickajack a few miles above its mouth, and another division of General Blair's has just now taken the place of my remaining brigade at Howell's Ferry. I have now one brigade at Baker's Ferry, one at and below Sandtown, and the third in reserve. Our horses are improving every day; we get plenty for them and a good deal for the men from the country. Our ration return has never equaled our effective strength, which I was not aware of until orders induced me to compare the ration and field returns. We are ready for anything except guarding communications in the rear.

If Barry has got a good four-gun battery, I could make use of it, as I have a lot of dismounted men I could make use of to support it. We have all the transportation we want and can move at any time, with twenty days' supply for the men. All we lack is some ammunition for some of our arms, and that I am told is not to be obtained. General McCook informs me that he is in the same fix. I wish I could get my regiment, or rather the regiment to which I belong (the Fourth), with us. Can't you manage it?

I inclose a sketch of this region.*

Very respectfully, &c.,

GEORGE STONEMAN,
Major-General, Commanding.

HDQRS. MILITARY DIVISION OF THE MISSISSIPPI,
In the Field, near Chattahoochee River, July 5, 1864.

Maj. Gen. GEORGE STONEMAN,
Commanding Cavalry:

DEAR STONEMAN: I have your note, which is very satisfactory. I have heard of your general success from other quarters. I will instruct General Barry to give you a good four-gun battery, if he can get one from some of the commands. Our left is now on the river above the railroad bridge. We find Hardee's corps intrenched on this side the river from the bridge down to the mouth of the Nickajack; we hear the other two corps and militia are across; we can see Atlanta plain, but it will require hard fighting and science to take it. It must be done. Garrard is gone up to Roswell, and I hope to hear from him to-night. I think Johnston will send all his effective cavalry round by the north, to strike our railroad, and must keep Garrard well on that flank and McCook to support him. I think you can whip anything that attempts to cross on that flank. Keep up the delusion of our crossing below Sandtown as long as possible, and I have reason to believe the enemy expects it. We have a nice game of war and must make no mistakes. We ought to have caught Johnston on his retreat, but he had prepared the way too well. We have killed and crippled a good

---

* To appear in the Atlas.

number and have a couple thousand prisoners, some taken in fair fight and some gathered up straggling behind. He can no longer look into our camps as he did from Kenesaw. Try and pick up as many of his scouts as you can, and gather in as prisoners every citizen of whom you entertain a suspicion. Schofield will move over to our left, up the Chattahoochee about Roswell or below it. Write often. My headquarters are on the main road about three miles back from the railroad bridge.

W. T. SHERMAN,
Major-General, Commanding.

NEAR GORDON'S, ON TURNER'S FERRY ROAD,
July 5, 1864—9 p. m.

Major-General STONEMAN,
    Commanding Cavalry:

The enemy are still reported in force in the works we were firing at yesterday. I inclose herewith a letter from General Sherman, which will give you his idea of matters.* Schofield goes over to the "left," and you are to go to-morrow on the right and continue to threaten the river. I am having Nickajack thoroughly examined to see if I cannot find some point or points where a crossing can be effected and a good position secured. You will continue to move your cavalry so as best to cover the country and threaten the river. I will send one division of Dodge's command to Howell's Ferry and one to the intersection of Howell's Ferry and Sandtown road. I will endeavor to keep you advised of any important movement along my front.

    Yours, truly,

JAS. B. McPHERSON,
Major-General.

HEADQUARTERS DEPARTMENT OF THE CUMBERLAND,
In the Field, near Ruff's Station, Ga., July 5, 1864.

Col. N. GLEASON,
    Commanding, Marietta:

COLONEL: The major-general commanding directs that you endeavor to preserve public and private property in Marietta as nearly as possible in the state in which you found it, and prevent plundering and pillaging. You will arrest all deserters and stragglers from all the armies and forward those belonging to the Army of the Cumberland to these headquarters by squads of from thirty to fifty. Those belonging to the Armies of the Tennessee and the Ohio you will send to the headquarters of their respective armies as opportunity offers. You will permit no officer to take quarters in Marietta, except by order of Major-General Sherman, and the topographical engineers of the Army of the Cumberland who have been sent there to establish a lithographic press for making maps. You will permit all Union people desiring to go north for the purpose of remaining there to do so, and order transportation for themselves, families, and baggage. You will arrest all resident rebels and report their names to these headquarters. You will seize all cotton belonging to the rebel Government, or which has been abandoned, and turn it over to the quartermaster's department for shipment north, taking receipts for the same, which receipts you will for-

* See p. 56.

ward to these headquarters. All cotton belonging to private individuals you will have nothing to do with any more than any other private property.

I am, colonel, very respectfully, your obedient servant,

WM. D. WHIPPLE,
Chief of Staff.

HEADQUARTERS DEPARTMENT OF THE CUMBERLAND,
July 5, 1864.

Major-General STEEDMAN:

A rebel officer, deserter, reports that the rebel cavalry have drawn eight days' rations and are to make a big raid, 10,000 strong, upon our railroad, passing by the left of the Federal army. Caution your commanders.

WM. D. WHIPPLE,
Assistant Adjutant-General.

RESACA, GA., *July 5, 1864.*

Capt. C. L. WHITE,
Assistant Adjutant-General:

A dispatch from Colonel Laiboldt (Dalton) says 100 to 200 rebel cavalry are scouting above here, east of the railroad, three miles south of this place. I have ordered Colonel Murray to send a strong force in the direction of Spring Place to try to intercept them. I think the force reported by General Vandever passed Villanow Sunday night and tore up the track south of Tunnel Hill. They may have formed a junction with the Sixth Georgia Cavalry, and comprise the force Colonel Laiboldt speaks of. I think half a regiment should be placed between Calhoun and Adairsville.

GREEN B. RAUM,
Colonel, Commanding Brigade.

RESACA, *July 5, 1864—12 p. m.*

Capt. C. L. WHITE,
Assistant Adjutant-General:

A train of sixteen cars has been captured and burned three miles and a half south of Dalton to-night. Colonel Murray sent 200 men out in that direction this evening. The enemy is reported to be 300 strong. I have advised Colonel Murray to send out an additional force.

GREEN B. RAUM,
Colonel, Commanding Brigade.

HDQRS. THIRD DIVISION, FIFTEENTH ARMY CORPS,
Kingston, Ga., July 5, 1864.

Brig. Gen. WILLIAM VANDEVER,
Rome, Ga.:

Do you know of any crossing on the Etowah between my outposts, three miles below here, and Rome? I have no cavalry here, and as yet have had but little time to explore the country adjoining my line. At last account Hart (Sixth Georgia) was at Jasper.

JNO. E. SMITH,
Brigadier-General.

ROME, GA., *July 5, 1864.*

Brigadier-General SMITH:

I have no information that any force has crossed the Etowah between Rome and Kingston.

WM. VANDEVER,
Brigadier-General.

ROME, *July, 5, 1864.*

Brig. Gen. J. E. SMITH:

A rebel soldier captured reports that Friday morning fifty of Wheeler's cavalry scouts left Cedartown destined to the railroad near Calhoun or Resaca; expects to form a junction with Hart's (Sixth Georgia) cavalry. He says this force is prepared with torpedoes to blow up trains; he reports also that Pillow is to act in concert with an additional force. This statement has come to me through two sources.

WM. VANDEVER,
Brigadier-General.

HEADQUARTERS DISTRICT OF THE ETOWAH,
Chattanooga, July 5, 1864.

General SMITH,
Kingston, Ga.:

Brigadier-General Whipple telegraphs that the rebel cavalry in considerable force have passed around the left of our army. Keep a sharp lookout for them.

JAMES B. STEEDMAN,
Major-General, Commanding.

(Same to commanding officer at Dalton.)

STEVENSON, *July 5, 1864.*

General STEEDMAN:

A deserter from the rebel lines this morning came into my camp and informed me that 5,000 or 6,000 rebels, under Forrest and Wheeler, are now encamped on Sand Mountain near mouth of Raccoon Creek. He was taken by a scouting party, and learned these facts while with them. Also that they are intending a dash on the road this side of Chattanooga somewhere.

SAM. C. VANCE,
Colonel, Commanding Post.

CHATTANOOGA, TENN., *July 5, 1864.*

Brig. Gen. W. D. WHIPPLE,
Chief of Staff:

A force of 5,000 or 6,000 strong is reported to be on Sand Mountain.

JAMES B. STEEDMAN,
Major-General.

HDQRS. THIRD DIVISION, FIFTEENTH ARMY CORPS,
Kingston, Ga., July 5, 1864.
Col. GREEN B. RAUM,
Resaca, Ga.:

General Vandever, at Rome, informs me that on Friday fifty of Wheeler's scouts left Cedartown, destined to the railroad near Calhoun or Resaca, expecting to form a junction with Hart's cavalry (Sixth Georgia). He states that this force is prepared with torpedoes to blow up trains. He also states that Pillow is to act in concert with an additional force.

CARL. L. WHITE,
Captain and Assistant Adjutant-General.

HDQRS. THIRD DIVISION, FIFTEENTH ARMY CORPS,
Kingston, Ga., July 5, 1864.
Brig. Gen. WILLIAM VANDEVER,
*Commanding at Rome, Ga.. *

GENERAL: For your information I would respectfully state that on the 2d instant the cavalry command of Colonel Lowe, then guarding the railroad and Etowah River, were relieved by my division from Tilton, Ga., to this place, and from Caldwell's Ford to Murchison's Ford, placing at Tilton the Seventeenth Iowa Infantry, Col. C. R. Wever commanding; Resaca, Tenth Missouri Volunteer Infantry, Col. F. C. Deimling, also Second Brigade headquarters, Col. Green B. Raum commanding; Calhoun, one-half Fifty-sixth Illinois Volunteer Infantry, Lieut. Col. John P. Hall commanding, and at Adairsville one-half Fifty-sixth Illinois, Captain ——— commanding. The river at and between the points mentioned above is strongly guarded by the Fifth Iowa and Ninety-third Illinois, under command of Col. Jabez Banbury, commanding Third Brigade. As my present force is composed entirely of infantry, which will not enable me to patrol the country as I should desire to do, rendering my line liable to attack without warning, I should be obliged for all information in regard to the movements of the enemy that may come to your knowledge.

I am, general, very respectfully, your obedient servant,

JNO. E. SMITH,
Brigadier-General.

ON CHATTAHOOCHEE, *July 6, 1864—7 p. m.*
(Received 7th.)
Maj. Gen. H. W. HALLECK,
Chief of Staff:

I have just received Secretary Stanton's dispatch, and do not understand how Semmes and crew were allowed to leave the sinking Alabama in an English yacht. I would have preferred the President had not proclaimed martial law in Kentucky, but simply allowed the military commanders to arrest and banish all malcontents, while the honest and industrious stay-at-homes were encouraged by the increase of security. Johnston made two breaks in the railroad, one above Marietta and one near Vining's Station. The former is already done, and Johnston's army has already heard the sound of our locomotives. The telegraph is done to Vining's, and the field wire is just at my bivouac, and will be ready to convey this to you as soon as translated into cipher. I propose to study the crossings of the Chattahoochee, and when all is ready to move quick. As a beginning I keep the wagons and troops well back from the river, and display to the enemy only the picket-line, with a few batteries along at random. Have moved General Schofield to a point whence he can in a single march reach the Chattahoochee, at a point above the railroad bridge, where there is a ford. At present the waters are turbid and swollen by the late rains; but if the present hot weather lasts the water will run down very fast. We have pontoons enough for four bridges, but, as our crossing will be resisted, we must maneuver some. All the regular crossing-places are covered by forts, apparently of long construction; but we shall cross in due time, and instead of attacking Atlanta direct, or any of its forts, I propose to make a circuit, destroying all its railroads. This is a delicate movement and must be done with caution. Our army is in good condition and full of confidence; but the weather is intensely hot, and a good many men have fallen with sunstroke. This is a high and healthy country, and the sanitary condition of the army is good.

W. T. SHERMAN,
Major-General.

HEADQUARTERS DEPARTMENT OF THE CUMBERLAND,
Near Vining's Station, Ga., July 6, 1864.

Maj. Gen. J. M. PALMER,
  Commanding Fourteenth Army Corps:

GENERAL: The major-general commanding directs that you only attempt to hold your present position by strong skirmish lines, and put your troops in camps where they will have shade and be convenient to water, and enjoy as much rest as possible during the few days that we are to remain here, and prepare roads so that they can with rapidity and without difficulty debouch upon the main roads leading through the country. Corps commanders will also make use of this opportunity to bring forward clothing to issue to the men.

Very respectfully, your obedient servant,

WM. D. WHIPPLE,
Chief of Staff.

(Same to Generals Howard and Hooker.)

HEADQUARTERS ARMY OF THE CUMBERLAND,
Vining's Station, July 6, 1864.

Major-General HOOKER:

I wish you to move your corps across Nickajack Creek, and take position either on the right of Davis' division, or if there is not room enough between his regiment and the creek, encamp in reserve behind Davis. Make as little show of your force as possible so as to conceal your position from the enemy. Keep nothing in his view except a strong skirmish line.

GEO. H. THOMAS,
Major-General, Commanding.

HEADQUARTERS TWENTIETH ARMY CORPS,
July 6, 1864.

Brigadier-General WHIPPLE, *Chief of Staff:*

GENERAL: I have the honor to report that the Twentieth Corps crossed the Nickajack this afternoon and two divisions of it established on a line indicated by your instructions of to-day. No news. My headquarters are in rear of the center of the corps.

Very respectfully, your obedient servant,

JOSEPH HOOKER,
Major-General, Commanding.

HDQRS. CHIEF OF CAVALRY, DEPT. OF THE CUMBERLAND,
In the Field, July 6, 1864.

Brig. Gen. E. M. McCOOK,
Commanding First Cavalry Division:

You will proceed with your command to Powers' Ferry and hold that position, communicating with General Garrard, who it is reported is at or near Howell's Factory (of linen map No. 3). Your supplies will be drawn from Marietta.

I am, general, very respectfully, your obedient servant,

W. L. ELLIOTT,
Brigadier-General and Chief of Cavalry.

HEADQUARTERS FIRST DIVISION CAVALRY,
July 6, 1864.

Lieut. D. F. HOW, *Acting Assistant Adjutant-General:*

I have the honor to report that, in compliance with orders received, and also with verbal directions from Major-General Sherman, I proceeded to this point (Hargrove's house), divided my force, sending one detachment to Powers' Ferry, and marching with the other to the mouth of Soap Creek, about six miles distant, where there is also a ferry and a bad ford, said by citizens to be almost impracticable. Artillery was opened from the other side of the river on my men at both points, one gun at the upper and two at the lower ferry, without any effect, however, except killing 3 horses. I found a bridge across Soap Creek, three-quarters of a mile from its mouth, burned; the bridge at Roswell Factory has also been burned. The distance between here and there is twelve miles. There is no difficulty in communicating with General Garrard, as there are no rebels on this side of the Chattahoochee. I find this country full of ravines and bridges, tolerably open and well watered, but there is neither grass, wheat, nor other forage on which to subsist stock. The little that was in the vicinity has been exhausted by Wheeler's force, who has been encamped here, until yesterday morning, for the last five days. I will furnish you with a map of the roads, &c., some time to-morrow. None of the enemy's trains had passed this way; they all crossed on bridges below. I forgot to mention that at Powers' Ferry there is a small boat and a wire stretched across. I can get my artillery in position within 500 yards of their battery. This ferry is well watched and guarded. I have pickets also at mouth of Soap Creek and at Johnson's Ferry, a mile and a half above that point.

I am, sir, very respectfully, your obedient servant,

E. M. McCOOK,
Brigadier-General, Commanding Division.

HEADQUARTERS CAVALRY DIVISION,
Near Roswell, July 6, 1864—7 p. m.

Major-General SHERMAN,
   Commanding Army:

GENERAL: Roswell was occupied by my command with but small opposition, the few hundred rebels on the roads falling back before my advance, and burning the bridge after crossing. There is a good ford at this place, so I am informed (the shallow ford), but as the opposite banks command this one, and pickets lie on the other side, I have not crossed any of my men. The approach to Roswell from Marietta can be made on two roads—one, as it approaches within two miles of Roswell, is by a crooked, hilly road that could be easily defended; the other, the river road, passes so close to the river as to come under the fire of the enemy's rifles. I had one man shot on this road from the other side. There are branch roads which lead into the Cummings road and the old Alabama road, and the approach on the latter is the best and safest in case the enemy is in this vicinity or secrecy is desirable. The position in rear of Roswell for me is not good, as roads come in from all directions, but by being on Soap Creek I can watch all this country, the fords, &c., and passing west of Sweat Mountain will have the short line on the enemy. There is a road leading over to the old Alabama road, a distance of about two miles. As fast as I can gain information I will send it to you.

My impression is that Johnston will make no attempt on this flank, but that his cavalry has gone to his left. He will try to keep his communications with the source of his supplies westward. All information from citizens and his acts in this vicinity lead to this belief. His cavalry instead of falling back to the fords and bridges in this locality crossed on the bridges, &c., with the infantry. Everything is taken out of this country; the grain cut by the rebel soldiers and hauled off. All citizens of property also have left. There were some fine factories here, one woolen factory, capacity 30,000 yards a month, and has furnished up to within a few weeks 15,000 yards per month to the rebel Government, the Government furnishing men and material. Capacity of cotton factory 216 looms, 191,086 yards per month, and 51,666 pounds of thread, and 4,229 pounds of cotton rope. This was worked exclusively for the rebel Government. The other cotton factory, one mile and a half from town, I have no data concerning. There was six months' supply of cotton on hand. Over the woolen factory the French flag was flying, but seeing no Federal flag above it I had the building burnt. All are burnt. The cotton factory was worked up to the time of its destruction, some 400 women being employed. There was some cloth which had been made since yesterday morning, which I will save for our hospitals (several thousand yards of cotton cloth), also some rope and thread. I have just learned that McCook is near the paper-mills, on Soap Creek, and I may not take up the position first proposed in this letter. I will try to disguise the strength of my command.

Very respectfully, your obedient servant,

K. GARRARD,
Brigadier-General, Commanding.

The machinery of the cotton factory cost before the war $400,000. The superintendent estimates that it alone was worth with its material, &c., when burnt over a million of our money.

K. GARRARD,
Brigadier-General, Commanding.

HDQRS. MILITARY DIVISION OF THE MISSISSIPPI,
In the Field, near Chattahoochee, July 6, 1864.

General GARRARD:

GENERAL: I have just received your note announcing that you have possession of Roswell. This is important; watch well the crossing there, but not in force; keep your main force concealed somewhat. General McCook has just started for some point between Rottenwood and Soap Creek, where he will be near you. I propose to throw Schofield over on that flank the moment I propose to attempt a crossing; fords are much better than bridges, and therefore have the river examined well as to fords. I am on the main road at the point where a branch goes to Vining's on the railroad. Howard is at Vining's and has possession at Pace's. McPherson's right is at Howell's Ferry, below Nickajack. The enemy holds this bank from the railroad bridge down to Nickajack, and seems to have it well fortified. Atlanta in plain view. Stoneman threatens the river down to Sweet Water. I will soon have a telegraph at Vining's and you can then communicate by Marietta. You will have rest for a few days and should take advantage of all grain fields.

Yours, truly,

W. T. SHERMAN,
Major-General, Commanding.

HEADQUARTERS ARMY OF THE OHIO,
In the Field, July 6, 1864.

Maj. Gen. J. B. MCPHERSON,
Commanding Department of the Tennessee:

GENERAL: By direction of Major-General Sherman I move this morning to position on the left. I start at 6 o'clock. General Stoneman will remain upon the right until further orders.

Very respectfully, your obedient servant,

J. M. SCHOFIELD,
Major-General, Commanding.

HEADQUARTERS ARMY OF THE OHIO,
In the Field, July 6, 1864—4 a. m.

Brig. Gen. J. D. COX,
Commanding Third Division, Twenty-third Army Corps:

GENERAL: The corps will move to position on the left this morning, near Ruff's Mill and Ruff's Station. The Second Division will move in advance and will start at 6 o'clock. Let Barter's brigade join you and the trains follow.

Very respectfully, your obedient servant,

J. M. SCHOFIELD,
Major-General, Commanding.

IN THE FIELD, GA., *July 6, 1864.*

Maj. Gen. GEORGE STONEMAN,
Commanding Cavalry:

In accordance with instructions from Major-General Sherman not to display any troops, I have directed the two regiments and battery belonging to General Leggett's division at Howell's Ferry to leave there and join their division, and have countermanded the order to Major-General Dodge to send a division to the ferry. This will leave the point without any troops except your cavalry scouts. General Dodge will, however, leave a brigade at the intersection of the Sandtown and Howell's Ferry roads. I am also directed to send you a battery of four 3-inch Rodman guns. Where will you have them report? Please notify General Blair, who is to furnish the guns.

Very truly, yours,

JAS. B. McPHERSON,
Major-General.

IN THE FIELD, GA., *July 6, 1864—5 p. m.*

Maj. Gen. GEORGE STONEMAN,
Commanding Cavalry:

Have your scouts and patrols along the river particularly vigilant. The enemy have been for the last two hours moving across the river south, and seem to come from the enemy's right or center, as seen from the hill where we were yesterday. They are too far off for any of our guns to reach them.

Yours, truly,

JAS. B. McPHERSON,
Major-General.

JULY 6, 1864—9.30 p. m.

General McPHERSON:

Your note of this 5 p. m. confirms my impression that there has been for the past forty-eight hours an extensive movement of the enemy down the river. Trains of wagons have been seen during the day and heard during the night-time moving rapidly down the river, and long columns of cavalry have been seen and heard. Every prominent point on the other side has a redoubt and rifle-pits which effectually prevent us from getting near the river. I however got close enough to-day to see it in three places, and found it not so wide as I expected. The bottoms are very narrow and the ground gently sloping down on each side. This side is much more open than the other, the woods approaching the stream only in a very few places, and we were shelled whenever we came out into the fields in any force, so that we have to stay with the animals a mile or two back from the river in the woods. They have all the scows and canoes on their own side, and well guarded by men behind rifle-pits, armed with guns of much longer range than our carbines. The negroes that came across the river last night say that Wheeler with "his company" passed down the river yesterday and last night, and the heavy smokes back from the river opposite the mouth of Sweet Water indicate no inconsiderable force in that region. The negroes say that the troops were going down to keep us from crossing at Campbellton, or in that vicinity, and that they are throwing up works all along the river. I have myself seen them at work in many places and at all the crossings. I am now covering upward of twelve miles of the river with pickets and scouts. I have not yet heard from the scout I sent down to Campbellton. I have also guards at all the crossings on the Sweet Water as far up as the crossing on the road from Powder Springs to Campbellton.

The country, with the exception of a skirt on the river and creek, is densely timbered and quite broken. Please transmit the information herein contained, or such portion as may be interesting to know, to General Sherman, as he desired me to keep him informed and advised.

Respectfully, &c.,

STONEMAN,
General.

I sleep to-night on the Sandtown road between the forks of the Howell's Ferry road and the old Alabama road, just in advance of where I was last night. I will try and see you in the morning.

G. S.

(Forwarded to General Sherman.)

HDQRS. MILITARY DIVISION OF THE MISSISSIPPI,
In the Field, Chattahoochee River, July 6, 1864.

General ROUSSEAU,
Nashville and Decatur:

That cavalry expedition must now be off, and must proceed with the utmost energy and confidence. Everything here is favorable, and I have official information that General A. J. Smith is out from Memphis with force enough to give Forrest full occupation. Expeditions inland are also out from Vicksburg and Baton Rouge, as well as against Mobile. If managed with secrecy and rapidity the expedition cannot fail of success and will accomplish much good.

W. T. SHERMAN,
Major-General, Commanding.

CHATTAHOOCHEE, *July 6, 1864.*

Maj. Gen. L. H. ROUSSEAU,
Nashville:

Has that expedition started?

W. T. SHERMAN,
Major-General.

DALTON, *July 6, 1864.*

Major-General STEEDMAN,
Commanding:

I have received information that rebel cavalry, in a line that took one hour in passing, went by Mr. Holland's house in the bend of Connesauga River, six miles southeast from here.

B. LAIBOLDT,
Colonel, Commanding Post.

DALTON, *July 6, 1864.*

Major-General STEEDMAN:

The same party of raiders that burned the train yesterday are reported to be from 300 to 500 strong at the bend of Connesauga River, near Holland's house, three miles from the railroad and six miles southeast of this place. I notified the commanding officer at Resaca yesterday at 2 p. m. of their presence, with the request to send up his cavalry, which appears not to have been done. I also endeavored to warn him again this morning.

                                    B. LAIBOLDT,
                                    Commanding Post.

                                    CHATTANOOGA, *July 6, 1864.*
General SMITH:

My dispatch yesterday should have said rebel cavalry reported passing round left of our army.

                                    J. B. STEEDMAN,
                                    Major-General.

                                    STEVENSON, *July 6, 1864.*
Brig. Gen. J. B. STEEDMAN:

From all information that I can gain, there is no large force at the mouth of Raccoon Creek, only some scouting parties.

                                    SAM. C. VANCE,
                                    Colonel, Commanding Post.

                                    MARIETTA, GA., *July 6, 1864—8 a. m.*
Maj. T. T. ECKERT:

Enemy's rear guard only on this side Chattahoochee, now holding strong intrenched position covering railroad and road bridges. Our flanks rest on river above and below, and cavalry holds right bank from Roswell to mouth of Sweet Water Creek, except just the bridge-head mentioned. Railroad will be repaired by 3 p. m., so that trains can go directly to front. Telegraph is working to General Sherman's headquarters, but is interrupted south of Dalton. Sherman expects to cross the Chattahoochee within three days. We hear nothing late from the East.

                                    J. C. VAN DUZER.

CAMP ON CHATTAHOOCHEE, GA., *July 6, 1864—9.30 p. m.*
                                    (Received 9.40 a. m. 7th.)
Maj. THOMAS T. ECKERT,
          War Department:

No material change in position of army since my cipher of this morning. Railroads and telegraph working to Vining's Bridge, and field-wire opened this evening. I suggest by letter a change in form of field insulators and instruments.

                                    J. C. VAN DUZER.

SPECIAL ⎫   HEADQUARTERS DEPARTMENT
FIELD ORDERS, ⎬   AND ARMY OF THE TENNESSEE,
  No. 60. ⎭ *Near Gordon's, on Turner's Ferry Road, July 6, 1864.*

Major-General Dodge, commanding Left Wing, Sixteenth Army Corps, will move one division of his command down to Howell's Ferry and relieve the brigade of General Leggett's division there stationed. The brigade, on being relieved, will join its command. Major-General Dodge will move his other division down to the junction of the Howell's Ferry and Sandtown roads, where it will take up position.

By order of Maj. Gen. James B. McPherson:

W. T. CLARK,
Assistant Adjutant-General.

NEAR CHATTAHOOCHEE, GA., *July 7, 1864—11 a. m.*
(Received 5 p. m.)

Maj. Gen. H. W. HALLECK,
Chief of Staff:

General Garrard reports to me that he is in possession of Roswell, where were several valuable cotton and woolen factories in full operation, also paper-mills, all of which, by my order, he destroyed by fire. They had been for years engaged exclusively at work for the Confederate Government, and the owner of the woolen factory displayed the French flag; but as he failed also to show the United States flag, General Garrard burned it also. The main cotton factory was valued at a million of United States dollars. The cloth on hand is reserved for use of United States hospitals, and I have ordered General Garrard to arrest for treason all owners and employés, foreign and native, and send them under guard to Marietta, whence I will send them North. Being exempt from conscription, they are as much governed by the rules of war as if in the ranks. The women can find employment in Indiana. This whole region was devoted to manufactories, but I will destroy every one of them. Johnston is maneuvering against my right, and I will try and pass the Chattahoochee by my left. Ask Mr. Stanton not to publish the substance of my dispatches, for they reach Richmond in a day, and are telegraphed at once to Atlanta. The Atlanta papers contain later news from Washington than I get from Nashville. Absolute silence in military matters is the only safe rule. Let our public learn patience and common sense.

W. T. SHERMAN,
Major-General.

HDQRS. MILITARY DIVISION OF THE MISSISSIPPI,
In the Field, near Chattahoochee, July 7, 1864.

Major-General THOMAS,
Commanding Army of the Cumberland:

GENERAL: By direction of the major-general commanding, you will please order your pontoon train party, with bridge, to report to General Schofield, near the mouth of Soap Creek, as early to-morrow as possible: also direct General Howard to send a regiment along up the river to connect with General Schofield, the bridge over Rottenwood Creek having been repaired.

I am, &c.,

L. M. DAYTON,
Aide-de-Camp.

[Indorsement.]

HEADQUARTERS DEPARTMENT OF THE CUMBERLAND,
July 7, 1864—1.05 a. m.

The inclosed copy of General Sherman's communication is respectfully forwarded for information of Major-General Howard.

SOUTHARD HOFFMAN,
Assistant Adjutant-General.

HEADQUARTERS DEPARTMENT OF THE CUMBERLAND,
July 7, 1864—4.30 p. m.

Major-General HOWARD,
Commanding Fourth Corps:

GENERAL: General Sherman has ordered Schofield to cross the river to-night at Roswell Factory, and secure a lodgment on the south side. To divert the enemy's attention as much as possible from him I wish you to display a force in front of Pace's Ferry, about sundown, as if you were making preparations to cross there. Open with your artillery on their batteries on the opposite side, and after getting the range cease firing until about 8 p. m. At that hour fire rapidly for fifteen minutes or half an hour, with the elevation necessary to reach the enemy's batteries, and have persons posted near the river, in some secure place, with instructions to give commands as if marching a strong column to the ferry to effect the laying of a bridge; at the same time keeping up a heavy fire from the skirmish line on the river-bank.

Respectfully,

GEO. H. THOMAS,
Major-General, U. S. Volunteers, Commanding.

HEADQUARTERS DEPARTMENT OF THE CUMBERLAND,
Near Vining's Station, Ga., July 7, 1864.

Maj. Gen. O. O. HOWARD,
Commanding Fourth Army Corps:

GENERAL: The major-general commanding directs that you send a regiment along up the river to connect with General Schofield, the bridge over Rottenwood Creek having been repaired.

I am, very respectfully,

SOUTHARD HOFFMAN,
Assistant Adjutant-General.

[Indorsement.]

HEADQUARTERS FOURTH ARMY CORPS,
In the Field, near Vining's Station, Ga.,
July 7, 1864—11.30 p. m.

Respectfully forwarded.

I have directed General Newton to comply with the within order; but I do not precisely understand it, since the bridge across Rottenwood Creek is reported uninjured, and the place for Schofield's crossing to-night is Roswell Factory, between fifteen and twenty miles distant. The hour of sending this dispatch is not named. Shall I dispatch the regiment at once to Roswell Factory? I have ordered it at daylight to-morrow.

O. O. HOWARD,
Major-General.

HEADQUARTERS FIRST DIVISION CAVALRY,
July 7, 1864.

Maj. J. C. McCOY,
    Aide-de-Camp:

Some of my men, four or five, got to the other bank of the river yesterday evening. This afternoon I sent a small party of the First Tennessee to attempt a crossing; the enemy permitted them to reach the middle of the river, when they opened so briskly with artillery and musketry that they could not get across. I have possession of an island near the middle of the river where everything they do on the opposite bank can be observed. A ford is reported some six or seven miles above here only knee-deep and practicable for infantry. I have sent officers up to examine it and report. So soon as they return I will send you the result.

Very respectfully, your obedient servant,

E. M. McCOOK,
Brigadier-General, Commanding.

HDQRS. FIRST BRIGADE, FIRST CAVALRY DIVISION,
July 7, 1864. (Received 2.30 p. m.)

Captain LE ROY:

Agreeably with the directions of the general commanding, I sent a small party to get possession of the island above Powers' Ferry, with the design of crossing the river. The party (from First Tennessee) was allowed to reach the middle of the stream, when the enemy opened upon them in such force that the officer in command returned. As the ford was ascertained to be very rocky, I did not think best to renew the attempt.

Respectfully, your obedient servant,

J. B. DORR,
Colonel, Commanding First Brigade.

HEADQUARTERS CAVALRY DIVISION,
July 7, 1864—5 p. m.

Major-General SHERMAN,
    Commanding Army:

GENERAL : I have nothing special to report. All day to-day I have been inspecting the country near here and find I can take position to advantage north of Roswell and about two miles from the town, and command all the roads between that place and the Etowah, which lead toward the railroad, leaving McCook's division to look after the part from the paper-mills to Pace's Ferry. I think I will move early to-morrow. I have [not] seen nor heard of any of the enemy this side of McAfee's Bridge, eight miles up the river. The only good ford I can hear of is just at this point. The Island Ford, three miles above, is good for footmen, but no roads lead to it or from it, and on the other side it is thick woods and very hilly and two miles over to the Atlanta road. This ford could be used to secure the lower one, but not for artillery, cavalry, or wagons until we hold the other bank and make a road. I can hear of no practicable fords except these within fifteen miles of this place. McAfee's Bridge is not burnt and the rebels hold it.

Very respectfully, your obedient servant,

K. GARRARD,
Brigadier-General, Commanding.

Hdqrs. Military Division of the Mississippi,
In the Field, near Chattahoochee, July 7, 1864.

General GARRARD,
Roswell, Ga.:

GENERAL: Your report is received and is most acceptable. I had no idea that the factories at Roswell remained in operation, but supposed the machinery had all been removed. Their utter destruction is right and meets my entire approval, and to make the matter complete you will arrest the owners and employés and send them, under guard, charged with treason, to Marietta, and I will see as to any man in America hoisting the French flag and then devoting his labor and capital in supplying armies in open hostility to our Government and claiming the benefit of his neutral flag. Should you, under the impulse of anger, natural at contemplating such perfidy, hang the wretch, I approve the act beforehand. I have sent General Schofield to reconnoiter over on that flank, and I want a lodgment made on the other bank as soon as possible anywhere from Roswell down to the vicinity of Soap Creek. I have no doubt the opposite bank is picketed, but, as you say, the main cavalry force of Wheeler has moved to the other flank, and we should take advantage of it. If you can make a lodgment on the south bank anywhere and secure it well, do so. General Schofield will be near to follow it up and enlarge the foothold. He had just started from Ruff's Station a few minutes before I received your dispatch, but I telegraphed the substance to be sent to overtake him. Keep a line of couriers back to Marietta and telegraph me very fully and often. I now have the wires to my bivouac. By selecting some one ford, say the second or third below the mouth of Willeyo Creek, on your sketch, and holding a force there concealed, say a brigade, with your battery, then have the heads of each your other two brigades close by above and below at the nearest fords, let detachments from these latter brigades cross at night at the nearest fords, and, without firing a gun, close in front of the brigade in position ready to cross with artillery. When across with artillery the best position on a commanding hill should be fortified. I will see that the cavalry is relieved by General Schofield at once. I merely suggest this plan and its execution about daylight to-morrow, and I prefer you should do it.

I assure you, spite of any little disappointment I may have expressed, I feel for you personally not only respect but affection, and wish for your unmeasured success and reputation, but I do wish to inspire all cavalry with my conviction that caution and prudence should be but a very small element in their characters.

I repeat my orders that you arrest all people, male and female, connected with those factories, no matter what the clamor, and let them foot it, under guard, to Marietta, whence I will send them by cars to the North. Destroy and make the same disposition of all mills save small flouring mills manifestly for local use, but all saw-mills and factories dispose of effectually, and useful laborers, excused by reason of their skill as manufacturers from conscription, are as much prisoners as if armed. The poor women will make a howl. Let them take along their children and clothing, providing they have the means of hauling or you can spare them. We will retain them until they can reach a country where they can live in peace and security.

In your next letter give me as much information as you can as to the size and dimensions of the burned bridge at Roswell across the Chattahoochee. We have plenty of pontoon bridging, but I much prefer fords for so large an army as we have.

I am, with respect, yours, truly,

> W. T. SHERMAN,
> *Major-General, Commanding.*

HDQRS. MILITARY DIVISION OF THE MISSISSIPPI,
July 7, 1864—9.50 a. m.

Major-General SCHOFIELD:

I have a letter from Garrard; he has possession of the factory at Roswell. I wish you to make an examination thereabouts and secure a foothold, fortified on the other side, anywhere about Roswell or mouth of Soap Creek. I also know that Johnston's cavalry has moved to the south flank. It is important to do this at once, for the fords are very important to us.

> W. T. SHERMAN,
> *Major-General.*

HEADQUARTERS ARMY OF THE OHIO,
In the Field, July 7, 1864—11.15 a. m.

Major-General SHERMAN:

I have just received your dispatch of 9.50 a. m. I will go at once to Roswell and examine the ground, and prepare to cross to-morrow.

> J. M. SCHOFIELD,
> *Major-General.*

HEADQUARTERS ARMY OF THE OHIO,
In the Field, July 7, 1864.

Major-General SHERMAN:

I am about starting to reconnoiter the river. Have you any additional information from Garrard which would be of service to me ?

> J. M. SCHOFIELD,
> *Major-General.*

HDQRS. MILITARY DIVISION OF THE MISSISSIPPI,
In the Field, near the Chattahoochee, July 7, 1864.

General SCHOFIELD:

Nothing new from General Garrard. General McCook is about Soap Creek. He drew fire from the enemy's artillery at two points between Rottenwood and Soap Creek, across the Chattahoochee.

> W. T. SHERMAN,
> *Major-General.*

HEADQUARTERS ARMY OF THE OHIO,
July 7, 1864—7.30 p. m.

Major-General SHERMAN:

I have not been able to reconnoiter as far as Roswell to-day. I find a pretty good crossing near mouth of Soap Creek. Half a mile above the creek is a shallow ford where infantry can cross easily, but there is no road leading to it and it would be difficult to make one. Isham's Ferry just below mouth of the creek is a good place for a bridge. About 400 yards from the river on east side is a commanding ridge very favorable for a bridge-head. The crossing would be very difficult if that ridge were held in force; but there appears at present only a squad of cavalry and one or two pieces of artillery. If there be no greater force to oppose it, the crossing can be effected very easily by crossing infantry at the ford above, to clear the ridge and cover the construction of the bridge. The ground on this side is favorable for our artillery. Johnston's cavalry being gone, I take it for granted that I can cross at Roswell without difficulty. The higher up the river the less probability of serious opposition; therefore I think we may choose whichever point you deem it most desirable to have. I propose to move at daylight and cross the river with as little delay as possible, and believe there is very little chance of failure, no matter which point you select.

J. M. SCHOFIELD,
Major-General.

———

HDQRS. MILITARY DIVISION OF THE MISSISSIPPI,
In the Field, near Chattahoochee, July 7, 1864.

General SCHOFIELD, *Ruff's Station:*

You may move to the neighborhood of the mouth of Soap Creek. Mask well your command and make a lodgment across the Chattahoochee, but do not attempt it until you have a ford near by by which to re-enforce the party first sent, or by which it may be necessary to retire. We can, after lodgment, make roads to the crossing and may add pontoon bridges, of which we have enough for four bridges. After securing a point opposite Soap Creek, Roswell will follow as a matter of course, and will be additional. The moment I hear that General Garrard has made a lodgment at Roswell, I will send a division of General McPherson to hold fast all he makes. With Roswell and mouth of Soap Creek, we have plenty of room, with Marietta as the depot. I will go down to General McPherson's and stir them up in the morning by way of diversion.

W. T. SHERMAN,
Major-General, Commanding.

———

HEADQUARTERS ARMY OF THE OHIO,
July 7, 1864.

Major-General SHERMAN:

The ford above the mouth of Soap Creek is an old fish-dam. I do not think it can be made practicable for wagons, though it may be. I deem it important to have a bridge to throw across as soon as I have effected a lodgment, so that I can, without delay, put over force enough with artillery to make my position secure.

J. M. SCHOFIELD,
Major-General.

HDQRS. MILITARY DIVISION OF THE MISSISSIPPI,
In the Field, near Chattahoochee River, July 7, 1864.

General SCHOFIELD,
  Ruff's Station:

I will order a pontoon train to report to you on the road.

W. T. SHERMAN,
Major-General, Commanding.

———

HEADQUARTERS ARMY OF THE OHIO,
In the Field, Smyrna Camp-Ground, July 7, 1864—9 p. m.

Brig. Gen. J. D. COX,
  Commanding Third Division, Twenty-third Army Corps:

GENERAL: Please have your division ready to move promptly at 4 o'clock to-morrow morning. I will send you further instructions as soon as practicable. Can you tell where and what the artillery firing is which I hear in your direction?

Very respectfully, your obedient servant,

J. M. SCHOFIELD,
Major-General, Commanding.

(Copy to General Hascall.)

———

HEADQUARTERS CAVALRY CORPS,
July 7, 1864—10.30 p. m.

Colonel CAPRON,
  Commanding Brigade:

I sent you an order by your staff officer to move down to Sandtown Ferry. Circumstances render it necessary to change your location, and I wish you would move by the Alabama road to-night in time to reach Sweet Water Town bridge (the point you occupied a few days ago) by daylight to-morrow morning. Your pickets along the river will be relieved by the infantry to-morrow morning, after which they can join you. Colonel Adams, who is a few miles below where you will be on Sweet Water Creek, thinks the enemy is in considerable force on this side of the Chattahoochee River, and west of Sweet Water Creek. I wish you would push scouting parties well out on the Alabama road toward Villa Rica, and at the same time to Powder Springs, going by the bridge over the Sweet Water Creek (the upper one) over which we passed, and returning via the bridge over Noyes' Creek over which we passed, and around to the right. Pick up all the scouting parties you can and arrest all suspicious persons. You and Colonel Adams act in concert, and have an understanding with each other in regard to all movements. I will try to be with you to-morrow, if I can get through with General Sherman in time. Keep me advised of what you see, hear, and do, and oblige,

Very respectfully, &c.,

STONEMAN,
General.

Hdqrs. Military Division of the Mississippi,
In the Field, July 7, 1864—8 a. m.

General McPherson:

Dear General: I send McCoy down to see you. I did intend to ride the lines to-day but have my mind so intent on a crossing-place that I want to be near. The cars now run into Marietta and down as far as a break that will be repaired to-day about four miles back of the bridge. The enemy hold as a tête-de-pont the hills from the Nickajack to a point about two miles above the bridge. I rather prefer this should be so, as he will have less on the other side. I wish you to display as much anxiety to cross as possible and as low down, but keep your masses ready to move to the real quarter when required. I wish you to use artillery pretty freely, and if, as I understand, you have a plunging fire on the extreme point of that range near Nickajack get plenty of guns, say thirty, to bear and give it thunder. I send you copy of an important dispatch from Canby,* in addition to which Rousseau will start from Decatur for Opelika. If you see Stoneman feel him and see how he would like to work down the river, say thirty miles, and also make a dash for Opelika, swinging back to us or to Rome for safety. A break of twenty miles from Opelika westward is perfectly practicable and would be a good blow. In the mean time we can improve our communications and get a sure crossing at some point above.

    Yours,

                        W. T. SHERMAN,
                        Major-General, Commanding.

In the Field, Ga., *July 7, 1864—12 m.*

Maj. Gen. G. M. Dodge,
    Commanding Left Wing, Sixteenth Army Corps:

Inclosed I send you copy of dispatch† just received from Major-General Sherman. From it you will see that he wants us to keep our troops well in hand for any movement, but at the same time make demonstrations as though we were trying to find a crossing on the Chattahoochee. The enemy have batteries of from one to four guns opposite all the ferries as near as I can learn, and are strengthening their defenses, and the banks on the opposite side from us are lined with sharpshooters. I wish you to take or cause a regiment of infantry and a section of artillery to go to each of the ferries (Howell's and Sandtown). Let a portion of each regiment be deployed as sharpshooters to disturb the enemy, and open on his batteries with your artillery or on any train or column of troops you may see moving. Major-General Stoneman reports that the enemy have been moving troops and trains down the river for the last twenty-four hours. I send Captain Reese down with this order, who will accompany the regiments and artillery as he is familiar with the roads, &c.

    Yours, truly,

                        JAS. B. McPHERSON,
                        Major-General.

---

* Of June 27 and relating to operations on the Mississippi, &c. See Vol. XLI.
† See next preceding.

HDQRS. DEPARTMENT AND ARMY OF THE TENNESSEE,
In the Field, near Chattahoochee River, Ga., July 7, 1864.

Maj. Gen. G. M. DODGE,
Commanding Left Wing, Sixteenth Army Corps:

GENERAL: In order to relieve a portion of Major-General Stoneman's cavalry, so that he can make a scout to the west of Sweet Water Creek, as well as to keep up appearances of trying to find a place to cross the Chattahoochee, you will send one brigade of your command at an early hour to-morrow morning down to the vicinity of Sandtown Ferry, where the Sixty-sixth Illinois is at present, and have them extend their pickets down the river about one mile to a hill just below Lawyer Edge's house.

Yours, respectfully,

JAS. B. McPHERSON,
Major-General, Commanding.

[Indorsement.]

HEADQUARTERS LEFT WING, SIXTEENTH ARMY CORPS,
In the Field, July 7, 1864.

Respectfully referred to Brig. Gen. T. W. Sweeny, commanding Second Division, who will move one brigade of his command at daylight to-morrow morning in compliance with these instructions.

By order of Maj. Gen. G. M. Dodge:

J. W. BARNES,
Assistant Adjutant-General.

HEADQUARTERS LEFT WING, SIXTEENTH ARMY CORPS,
In the Field, Ga., July 7, 1864.

Brig. Gen. T. W. SWEENY,
Commanding Second Division:

Send one regiment of infantry (sharpshooters) to the river at Sandtown Ferry. Have the infantry engage the rebel skirmishers on the opposite side of the river and gain the river if possible. Send one section of artillery with the regiment to co-operate with it. Captain Reese, of General McPherson's staff, will accompany them. Make a determined effort as though you were going to cross. Use artillery freely.

By order of Maj. Gen. G. M. Dodge:

J. W. BARNES,
Assistant Adjutant-General.

NASHVILLE, *July 7, 1864—10 a. m.*

Major-General SHERMAN:

Your telegram just received. Have had a good deal of trouble in organizing an efficient force. Shall go to Decatur to-morrow, and leave Decatur on the 9th at daylight.

L. H. ROUSSEAU,
Major-General.

NASHVILLE, *July 7, 1864—4 p. m.*

Major-General SHERMAN:

There is no railroad bridge at Ten Islands. There is one at Wilson-ville and plenty of supplies along below route; also pretty good ford just at that bridge.

> L. H. ROUSSEAU,
> *Major-General.*

HDQRS. MILITARY DIVISION OF THE MISSISSIPPI,
In the Field, near Chattahoochee, July 7, 1864.

General ROUSSEAU,
   Nashville, Tenn.:

My instructions were to cross the Coosa at the Ten Islands or the railroad bridge; these points are well apart and you can best choose between them after you are well out.

> W. T. SHERMAN,
> *Major-General, Commanding.*

NEAR CHATTAHOOCHEE, *July 7, 1864—9 p. m.*

Maj. Gen. L. H. ROUSSEAU,
   Nashville or Decatur:

I have no new instructions or information to convey to you, but expect you to leave Decatur on the 9th. If Roddey be about Tuscumbia, you might send a small infantry force down to Waterloo to amuse him by threatening to cross to burn the Bear Creek bridge, eight miles back from Eastport and about five miles east of Iuka. You may give out that you are going to Selma, but be sure to go to Opelika, and break up railroad between it and Montgomery. There is but a single road there which unites the Mississippi road with the Alabama roads. I am con-vinced General A. J. Smith will give full employment to Forrest, and I will keep Johnston fully employed, and Major-General Canby will look out for the Mobile garrison. When you reach the road do your work well; burn the ties in piles, heat the iron in the middle, and when red hot let the men pull the ends so as to give a twist to the rails. If sim-ply bent, the rails may be used, but if they are twisted or wrenched they cannot be used again. In returning you should take the back track, and, if pursued, turn for me or for Rome or Kingston or Alla-toona. Be sure to take no wagons, but pack some led horses. Travel early and late in the day, but rest at midday and midnight. Spare your horses for the first week, and keep the horses ready for the return trip. I think the only force in your route is Pillow's, about Oxford or Jacksonville or Gadsden. We are down to the Chattahoochee, and will soon be across. All is well with us.

> W. T. SHERMAN,
> *Major-General.*

HEADQUARTERS DEPARTMENT OF THE CUMBERLAND,
In the Field, July 7, 1864.

Maj. Gen. J. B. STEEDMAN,
   Chattanooga, Tenn.:

Yours received. The only point on the road at which the enemy can do any damage is at the Running Water bridge. A good reliable garrison should be kept there, which will fight until re-enforcements can reach them from Chattanooga. It will not do, however, to reduce the garrison of Chattanooga too much to strengthen that point, as an attack there might be a feint while the real attack is made upon Chattanooga. They cannot capture Bridgeport.

WM. D. WHIPPLE,
Assistant Adjutant-General.

DALTON, *July 7, 1864.*

Major-General STEEDMAN:

A force reported to be between 75 and 100 strong was seen this morning at 7 o'clock at Thompson's Mill, going north from the Spring Place road.

BERNARD LAIBOLDT,
Colonel, Commanding.

ADAIRSVILLE, *July 7, 1864.*

Major-General STEEDMAN:

I have this evening dispersed a party of rebels, fifty in number, within two miles of this place, capturing 7. Prisoners report that Captain Harvey with sixty men has gone up the railroad between Dalton and Cleveland, with intention of destroying it. One of my detachments captured 22 out in the country in the direction of Fairmount.

L. WOLFLEY,
Major Third Kentucky.

RESACA, GA., *July 7, 1864.*

Capt. C. L. WHITE:

The commanding officer at Dalton last evening reported the enemy between Dalton and Tilton, three miles east of the railroad. I sent Colonel Wever with 300 men to find him. Colonel Murray, commanding cavalry brigade, sent out 250 men east of the river, in addition to 200 men sent out the night before. At 10 p. m. Colonel Murray heard that the enemy was moving southeast in the direction of Ball Play Post-Office, his troops following him. Last night Colonel Croxton reported from Snake Creek Gap that the enemy, 300 strong, had passed north the day before.

G. B. RAUM,
Colonel, Commanding Brigade.

RESACA, GA., *July 7, 1864.*

Capt. C. L. WHITE,
    Assistant Adjutant-General:

There is a detachment of the Seventh Illinois two miles south of Dalton. The commanding officer at that place telegraphs that he has no men to relieve them; troops cannot well be spared from Tilton to do so. Is it intended that I should go so far north? If convenient, please answer to-night.

G. B. RAUM,
Colonel, Commanding Brigade.

RESACA, *July 7, 1864.*

Capt. C. L. WHITE,
    Assistant Adjutant-General:

There is no telegraph office at Tilton. The train was captured early in the night, before Colonel Murray sent the 200 cavalry in search of enemy, and I advised him immediately upon receipt of news from Dalton, so Colonel Wever could not have received information from here in time to save the train. There should be a small cavalry force at Tilton, Calhoun, and Adairsville. Can a portion of the Fifth Ohio Cavalry be stopped at those points? I think the intervals are too great between troops along the line.

G. B. RAUM,
Colonel, Commanding Brigade.

HEADQUARTERS U. S. FORCES,
    Pulaski, July 7, 1864.

Capt. C. T. GARDNER,
    Assistant Adjutant-General, Decatur:

My scouts who have been absent so long have just got in from Corinth, Bethel, &c. Col. William A. Johnson, commanding at Corinth, has three regiments and one battalion cavalry there. Forrest with his main force is at Tupelo. Roddey is with him. Roddey was to take command at Corinth and Johnson was to return up valley near Tuscumbia. State guard at Savannah had a skirmish with Burt Hays' guerrillas. Five companies of Roddey's command at or near Tuscumbia. Our gun-boats were up as high as Waterloo last week. Enemy have flat-boats at Eastport, mouth of Bear Creek. Enemy say that Nashville is the point they intend to aim for. Have taken four large droves of cattle out of the country and am continually collecting them. My scouts were captured by twenty-five of Forrest's command nine miles southwest of Lawrenceburg to-day. Have sent out a scout after the enemy.

JOHN C. STARKWEATHER,
Brigadier-General, Commanding.

(Copy to Major Polk, assistant adjutant-general, Nashville.)

HDQRS. MILITARY DIVISION OF THE MISSISSIPPI,
    In the Field, near Chattahoochee, July 7, 1864.

General E. R. S. CANBY,
    New Orleans:

Your dispatch of 27th of June* is received, and is very agreeable news. I think Generals Smith and Mower can take care of Forrest. We have fought Johnston steadily back for 100 miles over very difficult ground, fortified at immense labor. I don't think our loss exceeds that of the enemy. It has been one immense skirmish with small battles interspersed. This army remains strong in numbers and spirits, and has been wonderfully supplied. Though repeatedly broken, our railroad and telegraph are in good order to the rear, and I have depots of supplies accumulated at fortified points to my rear. Atlanta is in sight, and is defended by a well handled

---

* See Vol. XLI.

army, and a circle of finished redoubts, yet I shall not pause. The expeditions from Memphis, Vicksburg, and Baton Rouge are most important and will keep employed the forces of the enemy that might be mischievous to my rear; also the move on Mobile will be most opportune, no matter in what strength, even if confined to a feint. On the 9th I start a lightly equipped cavalry force of about 3,000, without wagons, from Decatur, Ala., to Opelika, to break up the single track from Montgomery eastward; the effect of which will be to separate Alabama from Georgia. This force may be compelled to go to Pensacola. Please let the commanding officer at Pensacola look out for them about the 20th to 25th of July. If they make Pensacola they will leave horses there, and come back to Tennessee by water. Major-General Rousseau will command.

W. T. SHERMAN,
Major-General, Commanding.

SPECIAL FIELD ORDERS, }   HDQRS. ARMY OF THE OHIO,
    No. 46.   }   *Smyrna Camp-Ground, Ga., July 7, 1864.*

*   *   *   *   *   *   *

II. The corps will endeavor to effect a crossing of the Chattahoochee to-morrow. The point selected for the crossing is near the mouth of Soap Creek. The troops will march at 4 a. m., the Third Division in advance. General Hascall's artillery will move near the head of his column, in order that it may be at hand to cover the crossing. The trains of both divisions will move in rear of the corps. One brigade of the Third Division will cross Soap Creek at the paper-factory, about a mile above its mouth, and move down the road toward the bank of the river, keeping out of view from the opposite bank. The brigade commander will deploy a strong line of skirmishers, with large reserves, behind the ridge near the river, and prepare a party of about fifty good men to lead the crossing and effect a lodgment on the opposite side. The men should be tall and strong, on account of the possible difficulty in fording. It is not necessary to select men from the Twenty-third Corps for their bravery. The brigade commander will keep his men out of sight, and not open fire unless the enemy's pickets be found on this side of the river, in which case he will drive them away without throwing any more force than necessary for the purpose. The point of crossing for the advance is an old fish-dam, constituting a practicable ford for infantry, about half a mile above the mouth of Soap Creek. The brigade commander will report the completion of the above preparations and await further orders. General Cox will mass the remainder of his division on the west side of Soap Creek and in rear of the ridges bordering the river, and reconnoiter for positions for his artillery. General Hascall will mass his division in a convenient position in rear of that of General Cox and send forward his artillery to report to the chief of artillery. General Cox will cause his skirmishers to be deployed, under cover, ready to advance to the river-bank. The artillery will be ready to move into position, and the troops will clear the road for the pontoon train, which will follow immediately after the infantry. Every precaution must be taken to avoid any display of force until the order is given to commence operations. Even groups of officers should not be seen by the enemy. This precaution is very important, since much delay may occur in perfecting the arrangements necessary to success, whereby the enemy, if warned of our intentions, might have time to bring up re-enforcements. The troops must make as little noise as practicable. Build no fires nor give any other indication of the presence of a large force. It is proposed to lay the pontoon bridge at Isham's Ferry, just below the mouth of Soap Creek, and to use the ford above to cross infantry enough to cover the laying of the bridge. The commanding general will be on the ground, and will give further orders, after full and careful reconnaissance.

By command of Major-General Schofield:

J. A. CAMPBELL,
Major and Assistant Adjutant-General.

HDQRS. MILITARY DIVISION OF THE MISSISSIPPI,
In the Field, near Chattahoochee, July 8, 1864.

General THOMAS:

I will go over to the right to-day. General Schofield will see as to making a lodgment about the mouth of Soap Creek, and General Garrard at Roswell Factory. I want you to stir up the enemy to-day, and this afternoon and to-night to send down rafts to break the pontoons. I think the railroad bridge was burned last night. Have you any reports to that effect?

W. T. SHERMAN,
Major-General, Commanding.

HEADQUARTERS DEPARTMENT OF THE CUMBERLAND,
July 8, 1864.

Major-General SHERMAN:

My people kept the enemy pretty well stirred up last night. Will have them occupy their attention to-day also. I will give orders about the rafts. Have received no reports about the bridge yet.

GEO. H. THOMAS,
Major-General.

HDQRS. MILITARY DIVISION OF THE MISSISSIPPI,
In the Field, near Chattahoochee, July 8, 1864.

General THOMAS:

I have an Atlanta paper of the 6th; I think its tone is changed and it apologizes for the necessity of civilians quitting the place. By it I see that General Slocum is at Jackson, Miss., and I have no doubt we will soon perceive other effects of General Smith's move in Mississippi, and General Canby's against Mobile. If General Howard could get a cable over to that pontoon bridge and haul it into place it would be a constant threat at that point.

W. T. SHERMAN,
Major-General, Commanding.

HEADQUARTERS DEPARTMENT OF THE CUMBERLAND,
July 8, 1864.

Major-General SHERMAN:

I caused Howard to make a demonstration last night at Pace's Ferry, which resulted in the capture of the pontoon bridge. It is now secure in our possession. I will direct Howard to make another demonstration to-morrow morning. I have been on the lines all day, and think I have found a hill on Baird's front from which the rebel rifle-pits can be enfiladed. I have also discovered the location of the railroad bridge, and saw three trains of cars pass over. I think the hill in Baird's front commands the bridge also.

GEO. H. THOMAS,
Major-General.

HDQRS. MILITARY DIVISION OF THE MISSISSIPPI,
In the Field, near Chattahoochee, July 8, 1864.

General THOMAS:

General Garrard will effect a lodgment to-morrow morning at Roswell, and General Schofield about the mouth of Soap Creek. The moment I hear that General Garrard is successful I will send one of General McPherson's corps up, but he is so far off that it may become necessary to re-enforce him (General Garrard) in the night to-morrow, in which case I will call for a division of General Howard nearest to Roswell, to be relieved by General McPherson as soon as he can get there. At daybreak to-morrow make some display to assist in covering the movements.

W. T. SHERMAN,
Major-General, Commanding.

SHERMAN'S HEADQUARTERS,
July 8, 1864.

General THOMAS:

All right. General Dodge is just here; is going up, and will be able to relieve that division to-morrow.

W. T. SHERMAN,
Major-General.

VINING'S HILL, *July 8, 1864.*
(Received 10 a. m.)

Captain CASE:

South two degrees east from this station and about five miles distant a pontoon train of fifteen or twenty wagons is parked. Rebel wagon trains moving both to right and left at the front, when railroad trains stop. In the large open field, through which the river runs, infantry, artillery, and wagons have been moving to the right, down the river, constantly since the fog raised.

HOWGATE,
Lieutenant and Acting Signal Officer.

VINING'S HILL, *July 8, 1864.*

General THOMAS:

I have had a good chance to count all the pontoons since I reported the fact to you. They were twenty-two in all. Could trace their movement some distance by the dust. See some of the enemy south ten degrees west some seven miles distant.

S. BACHTELL,
Lieutenant and Acting Signal Officer.

HEADQUARTERS FOURTH ARMY CORPS,
Near Vining's Station, Ga., July 8, 1864—7.30 p. m.

Brigadier-General WHIPPLE,
      Assistant Adjutant-General and Chief of Staff:

In accordance with instructions the Rottenwood Creek bridge was strengthened, and a regiment marched this a. m. to the vicinity of the mouth of Soap Creek. I accompanied the regiment. The distance from my left to General Schofield's right is about five miles in a direct line and as much as seven by the practicable roads. His preparations for throwing the bridge were nearly in readiness at 3 p. m. to-day when I left. General Hazen reports the rebel pontoon bridge near Pace's Ferry now on this side of the river. He will endeavor to secure it to-night.

Very respectfully, your obedient servant,
                                        O. O. HOWARD,
                                              Major-General.

P. S.—My scouts, two of whom I left with General Schofield, have just returned; they report that General S[chofield] crossed four regiments over the river and secured a lodgment on the other side about one hour before sundown; then the enemy fired but two guns—one discharge from each, and these canister—and two musket-shots at them, and that the pontoon bridge would be laid by sundown.

HDQRS. SECOND BRIG., THIRD DIV., FOURTH CORPS,
                                        July 8, 1864.

Capt. M. P. BESTOW,
      Assistant Adjutant-General:

The pontoon bridge of the enemy was cut loose last night, probably while the firing was going on, believing we were about to cross. It floated to our side the river, and is lodged opposite my second picket station from the right. At night I will be able to attach ropes and make it fast.

Very respectfully,

                                        W. B. HAZEN,
                                              Brigadier-General.

HEADQUARTERS DEPARTMENT OF THE CUMBERLAND,
                Near Vining's Station, Ga., July 8, 1864.

Maj. Gen. O. O. HOWARD,
      Commanding Fourth Army Corps:

GENERAL: Brigadier-General Garrard is to effect a lodgment at Roswell Factory to-morrow morning, and as soon as he reports himself successful General Sherman is to send a corps of the Army of the Tennessee to that point. General McPherson is, however, so far away that it may become necessary to re-enforce him before that corps could reach there. You will therefore hold the division of your corps nearest Roswell Factory in readiness to move to that point whenever called on by General Sherman, to return upon the arrival of General McPherson's troops. The major-general commanding directs also that you make a display at daybreak to-morrow morning to cover the movements up the river. If you could do something to make the rebels think that you intended to make use of the pontoon bridge to cross the river, it would serve as a continual threat to that point.

I am, general, very respectfully, your obedient servant,

WM. D. WHIPPLE,
Chief of Staff.

HDQRS. MILITARY DIVISION OF THE MISSISSIPPI,
In the Field, near Chattahoochee, July 8, 1864.

General SCHOFIELD, *Ruff's Station:*

It is all important I should know as soon as possible the general topography on the other side of the river, as to the practicability of the roads in every direction, especially toward Stone Mountain and Decatur. If you can catch a few people who ought to know all about it, send them to me. I will go to the extreme right to-day. General Rousseau will start from Decatur for Opelika to-morrow, and General Stoneman may feign down as far as Campbellton. I think the railroad bridge was burned last night. No other news.

W. T. SHERMAN,
Major-General, Commanding.

HEADQUARTERS ARMY OF THE OHIO,
Isham's Ferry, Chattahoochee, July 8, 1864—7 p. m.

Major-General SHERMAN,
Commanding Military Division of the Mississippi:

GENERAL: I have a division (General Cox's) across the river at this place. It has a good position, and is rapidly intrenching. Colonel Buell has laid one bridge and will have another across to-night. I spent most of the day in reconnoitering and perfecting arrangements to make success sure. All was done so quietly that the enemy was taken entirely by surprise, so that when my artillery and infantry opened from the west bank the enemy fled, leaving a piece of artillery, which fell into our hands. My men crossed by the ford and in boats at the same time without losing a single man. The enemy used his artillery upon our officers while reconnoitering during the day, but when we opened upon them they fired but a single shot and fled. I presume they were Brown's militia. We have gained the desired point, captured one piece of artillery and nobody hurt. I will give you information concerning roads, &c., beyond the river as soon as possible.

Very respectfully,

J. M. SCHOFIELD,
Major-General.

HDQRS. THIRD DIVISION, TWENTY-THIRD ARMY CORPS,
July 8, 1864—1.30 p. m.

Col. D. CAMERON,
Commanding Second Brigade:

SIR: You will make all your arrangements to commence crossing the river at 3.30 o'clock precisely, having your advance guard ready to enter the water at that time, and the brigade within easy supporting distance, but keeping all carefully hid till the last moment, when the movement must be made with dash and the men must be encouraged to overcome all obstacles. As soon as a regiment is over it will at once occupy defensible ground and feel down the river toward the point opposite the mouth of the creek, and as soon as the brigade is over it will boldly push for that point, with a view to occupy the ridge above, and cover the construction of the bridge. As a collateral movement, we shall ferry some troops across in the pontoons if possible at the same time. Your officers will be on the lookout for these. If Colonel Casement commands the demi-brigade in advance, let him carefully read this dispatch before beginning the movement. The object is first to get a lodgment on the other side of the Chattahoochee, and second to push immediately for the point a little below Soap Creek and opposite so as to protect the bridge building, and connect with any troops we may be able to ferry over. Stop for nothing but heavy infantry force and artillery. After the movement is begun it will probably be easiest to communicate with me along the river-bank to the mouth of the creek.

J. D. COX,
Brigadier-General, Commanding.

HDQRS. THIRD DIVISION, TWENTY-THIRD ARMY CORPS,
July 8, 1864—4.30 p. m.

Major-General SCHOFIELD:

Cameron is over with all his brigade but one regiment, which is left for reserve. Our skirmishers here have the river-banks, and we can progress as fast as Colonel Buell's pontoons are ready.

J. D. COX,
Brigadier-General.

HEADQUARTERS SEVENTEENTH ARMY CORPS,
Near Chattahoochee River, July 8, 1864.

Brigadier-General LEGGETT, *Commanding Third Division:*

GENERAL: In conversation with Generals Sherman and McPherson to-day they expressed a desire that a demonstration should be made upon the river by this corps. General Blair, therefore, desires you to change your front, if possible, so as to effect this object. With this view it would be desirable to erect your batteries on the most favorable points to cover the enemy's lines and batteries on the eastern bank of the river, and to make such disposition of your troops as will protect them from the fire of the enemy. The general would like this change made, if possible, to-night. This feint is to cover a real crossing on the extreme left of the army.

I have the honor to be, very respectfully, your obedient servant,

A. J. ALEXANDER,
Assistant Adjutant-General.

HEADQUARTERS SEVENTEENTH ARMY CORPS,
Near Chattahoochee River, July 8, 1864.

Lieut. Col. WILLIAM T. CLARK,
Asst. Adjt. Gen., Department and Army of the Tennessee:

COLONEL: I have the honor to report that the batteries of my command have almost entirely exhausted their supply of ammunition, particularly in the Fourth Division. I received a dispatch from the chief of ordnance of this corps, who is now at Marietta, saying that there is no suitable ammunition at that depot, and he cannot ascertain where he will be able to obtain any. Under these circumstances, I have the honor to request that the batteries of this command may be supplied with ammunition from some other source.

Very respectfully, your obedient servant,

FRANK P. BLAIR, JR.,
Major-General, Commanding.

SHERMAN'S HEADQUARTERS,
July 8, 1864.

General GARRARD, *Roswell:*

I have been to our extreme right and all well. Be active at daylight to-morrow to draw attention as far down the river as possible. The moment I hear you have made a lodgment on the south bank I will send a division up to re-enforce you, and it will be followed by one of McPherson's corps from the extreme right. From the nature of the ground I have no doubt you can hold the ground till re-enforced. It is better that no infantry should be seen there till you have made a good lodgment. Schofield will cross below you near the mouth of Soap Creek, and his lodgment will be as much a part of yours as possible, for he will be between you and the main enemy. Send word the instant you get a good foothold and the troops will start. Audenried can guide them.

W. T. SHERMAN,
Major-General.

HDQRS. MILITARY DIVISION OF THE MISSISSIPPI,
Near Chattahoochee, July 9, 1864.

Maj. Gen. H. W. HALLECK, *Washington, D. C.:*

GENERAL: I telegraph to you, and Mr. Secretary Stanton answers. Drop me a word now and then of advice and encouragement. I think I have done well to maintain such an army in such a country, fighting for sixty days, and yet my losses are made up by the natural increase. The assault I made was no mistake; I had to do it. The enemy and our own army and officers had settled down into the conviction that the assault of lines formed no part of my game, and the moment the enemy was found behind anything like a parapet, why everybody would deploy, throw up counter-works and take it easy, leaving it to the " old man" to turn the position. Had the assault been made with one-fourth more vigor, mathematically, I would have put the head of George Thomas' whole army right through Johnston's deployed lines on the best ground for go-ahead, while my entire forces were well in hand on roads converging to my then object, Marietta. Had Harker and McCook not been struck down so early the assault would have succeeded, and then the battle would have all been in our favor on account of our superiority of numbers, position, and initiative. Even as it was, Johnston has been much more cautious since, and gives ground more freely. His next fighting line, Smyrna Camp-Ground, he only held one day.

I have got General Schofield across the Chattahoochee with two good pontoon bridges, without loss, and momentarily wait the news of my cavalry being across at Roswell Factory, where is the best ford on the whole river, but before going ahead I will add there a good pier or trestle bridge and will at some point intermediate, convenient to roads, put down two more pontoon bridges, making five bridges and three fords, before I put the army across the Chattahoochee.

I call your attention to the inclosed paper* in reference to the Roswell factories. They were very valuable, and were burned by my orders. They have been engaged almost exclusively in manufacturing cloth for the Confederate Army, and you will observe they were transferred to the English and French flags for safety, but such nonsense cannot deceive me. They were tainted with treason, and such fictitious transfer was an aggravation. I will send all the owners, agents, and employés up to Indiana to get rid of them here. I take it a neutral is no better than one of our own citizens, and we would not respect the property of one of our own citizens engaged in supplying a hostile army.

Write me a note occasionally and suggest anything that may occur to you, as I am really in the wilderness down here, but I will fight any and all the time on anything like fair terms, and that is the best strategy, but it would not be fair to run up against such parapets as I find here.

            Your friend,
                        W. T. SHERMAN,
                        Major-General, Commanding.

                NEAR CHATTAHOOCHEE, *July 9, 1864.*
                            (Received 8 p. m.)
Maj. Gen. H. W. HALLECK, *Chief of Staff:*

General Schofield effected a lodgment across the Chattahoochee near the mouth of Soap Creek last night, and has two good pontoon bridges. He captured the single gun that guarded the passage, but the guard fled. General Garrard crossed at Roswell Factory, and has a secure lodgment at the shallow ford. General Dodge is moving to that point to take Garrard's place, and has orders to build a good bridge there. These crossings will be strongly covered with forts. I will then endeavor to break the railroad south of Atlanta by an expedition from Decatur under General Rousseau, and another from here. In the mean time will collect supplies and secure better my rear, and then cross over the main army and go ahead. Weather is very hot, but the country is high and healthy.

                        W. T. SHERMAN,
                        Major-General.

    HDQRS. MILITARY DIVISION OF THE MISSISSIPPI,
        In the Field, near Chattahoochee River, July 9, 1864.
General WEBSTER, *Nashville:*

I have ordered the arrest of the operators at the Confederate manufactories at Roswell and Sweet Water, to be sent North. When they reach Nashville have them sent across the Ohio River and turned loose to earn a living where they won't do us any harm. If any of the principals seem to you dangerous, you may order them imprisoned for a

---
* Not found as an inclosure.

time. The men were exempt from conscription by reason of their skill, but the women were simply laborers that must be removed from this district.

W. T. SHERMAN,
Major-General, Commanding.

Hdqrs. Military Division of the Mississippi,
In the Field, near Chattahoochee, Ga., July 9, 1864—12.30 a. m.
Major-General Thomas,
Commanding Army of the Cumberland:

General: I am directed by the general commanding to say that General Schofield has effected a crossing and lodgment, and has two bridges laid. He captured a gun and did not lose a man. The general commanding directs, also, that you will move one division at daylight in the morning to Roswell to support and make sure anything General Garrard may effect until they can be relieved by General McPherson's troops, who will march via Marietta. Let the division move without wagons and march by such roads as not to be seen by the enemy.

I am, general, very respectfully,

L. M. DAYTON,
Aide-de-Camp.

Sherman's Headquarters,
July 9, 1864—1.30 a. m.
General Thomas:

I think that inasmuch as General Schofield has made a lodgment that Johnston is forced in strategy to attack you or McPherson in the morning, or abandon this bank of the Chattahoochee altogether. He will not attempt to hold both shores after we have secured a crossing, which is already done. Indeed, the firing at this moment convinces me that he is withdrawing, and I have so instructed McPherson, and I wish you to do all that is possible to take advantage of the situation. Cannot Baird open with rifled artillery on the bridge, which will stampede the troops, and, it may be, force them to leave some artillery and stores? At daylight let your troops feel the enemy boldly, and, if not in force, endeavor to capture a part of them. This is not to interfere with sending a division, as before ordered, to Roswell Factory—a position of great importance to us, and to which I have ordered Dodge's corps, with strong pioneer parties, to fortify and rebuild the trestle bridge. If Howard could place the enemy's pontoons in position, it would be a bold stroke, and I refer to it only as a possibility.

W. T. SHERMAN,
Major-General.

Headquarters Department of the Cumberland,
July 9, 1864—1.45 a. m.
Major-General Sherman:

Your dispatch received. Howard has already been ordered to send a division to Roswell Factory and to make an attempt to lay the pontoon bridges. Orders will be immediately given to press the enemy at all points. I will have my heavy battery fire on them in the morning.

GEO. H. THOMAS,
Major-General.

Hdqrs. Military Division of the Mississippi,
In the Field, near Chattahoochee, July 9, 1864.

General Thomas:

I hear considerable firing on your front; is it anything more than the usual pickets?

W. T. SHERMAN,
Major-General, Commanding.

Headquarters Department of the Cumberland,
July 9, 1864.

Major-General Sherman:

It is the execution of your orders last night to push the enemy. I am trying to fit the hill in front of Baird to plant a battery to fire on their bridges, &c.

GEO. H. THOMAS,
Major-General.

Signal Station, *July 9, 1864—10 a. m.*

Major-General Sherman:

I can see heavy column of the enemy's infantry, with artillery and wagons, moving from behind their forts in my front, going toward Atlanta. Will keep watch and inform you if they turn off and go up river.

GEO. H. THOMAS,
Major-General.

Signal Hill, Ga., *July 9, 1864—9 a. m.*

Major-Generals Sherman and Thomas:

Heavy column of dust rising eight miles east, moving toward Stone Mountain; also column of troops and wagons moving toward our left in open field on river bottom near first heavy work.

A. S. COLE,
Captain and Signal Officer.

Signal Station, *July 9, 1864—10 a. m.*

General Sherman:

Column of dust eight miles distant east, moving north rapidly. Should say it was cavalry.

A. S. COLE,
Captain and Signal Officer.

Headquarters Department of the Cumberland,
In the Field, July 9, 1864—12.45 a. m.

Maj. Gen. O. O. Howard,
Commanding Fourth Army Corps:

General: The major-general commanding directs that at daylight you move a division for Roswell Factory to support and make sure of everything that may be gained by Garrard. Let it move without wagons and remain until relieved by General McPherson's troops, which will march via Marietta. This is in execution of the preparatory instructions sent you last evening. General Schofield has effected a crossing and lodgment; has two bridges laid. He captured a gun and did not lose a man.

Yours, very respectfully,

WM. D. WHIPPLE,
Chief of Staff.

HEADQUARTERS DEPARTMENT OF THE CUMBERLAND,
In the Field, July 9, 1864—1.30 a. m.
(Received 4 a. m.)

Maj. Gen. O. O. HOWARD, *Commanding Fourth Army Corps:*

GENERAL: It is the opinion of the major-general commanding the Military Division of the Mississippi that inasmuch as General Schofield has made a lodgment, that Johnston will be forced in strategy to attack us or General McPherson, or withdraw. The major-general commanding therefore directs that you do all you can to take advantage of his situation by feeling the enemy's skirmishers at daylight, if you have any in front of you not across the river, and if you could get [in position] the pontoon bridge of the enemy's which has fallen into our hands it would be a good stroke. This is mentioned as a possibility only, and this order is not to interfere with sending a division to Roswell Factory at daybreak in the morning, as directed in previous communication. The other corps will be directed to feel strongly the enemy's lines at daylight.

Yours, very respectfully,

WM. D. WHIPPLE,
Chief of Staff.

HEADQUARTERS FOURTH ARMY CORPS,
Near Vining's Station, Ga., July 9, 1864—11.10 a. m.

Major-General STANLEY, *First Division, Fourth Army Corps:*

GENERAL: The enemy has opened his artillery in our front, and he may be making a reconnaissance to discover our weak point. Please keep a strict lookout, and if you think he is doing so, push a regiment of infantry up to Powers' Ferry, and bring it back this evening (not near enough to the ferry to be exposed to artillery fire).

By order of Major-General Howard:

J. S. FULLERTON,
Assistant Adjutant-General.

HEADQUARTERS FOURTH ARMY CORPS,
Vining's Station, Ga., July 9, 1864.

Brigadier-General WHIPPLE, *Chief of Staff:*

GENERAL: I placed two regiments opposite General Baird's left in support of a battery which he will send up. This is on the ridge where you desired to have it, and is a good artillery position. I moved forward the skirmish line some 300 yards in front of that ridge to the edge of a corn-field and in full view of the river. Colonel Brownlow, commanding cavalry, crossed the river this p. m. just above Powers' Ferry, capturing 3 cavalrymen. They reported a post of twelve men and a reserve of fifty men farther back. The river was too high for wading, so that the men were compelled to swim part of the way.

Respectfully,

O. O. HOWARD,
Major-General.

NEAR VINING'S STATION, GA., *July 9, 1864—8.30 p. m.*

Major-General THOMAS:

Captain Kirlin, my aide-de-camp, has just returned from Roswell Ferry. General Newton arrived there at 2 p. m., and he has crossed two brigades over the river. General Garrard crossed at 6 a. m.; had but little opposition. Lost no men. Captured a few.

O. O. HOWARD,
Major-General.

HEADQUARTERS DEPARTMENT OF THE CUMBERLAND,
In the Field, July 9, 1864.

Maj. Gen. J. HOOKER, *Commanding Twentieth Corps:*

GENERAL: General Schofield has effected a crossing and lodgment, and has two bridges laid. He captured a general [gun] and lost not a man. The major-general commanding directs that you take advantage of the situation to gain as much as possible by feeling strongly with skirmishers at daylight, and if the enemy is not in force endeavor to capture some of them. The major-general commanding the military division is of the opinion that Johnston will be forced by the present situation either to attack or withdraw.

Yours, very respectfully,

WM. D. WHIPPLE,
Chief of Staff.

HEADQUARTERS DEPARTMENT OF THE CUMBERLAND,
In the Field, July 9, 1864.

Maj. Gen. J. HOOKER, *Commanding Twentieth Corps:*

GENERAL: The major-general commanding directs that to-morrow morning you close the gap which will be left between your corps and Brigadier General Davis' division, in consequence of the latter moving to his left. The gap to be closed will probably be equal to the front of a division. General Davis moves to-morrow morning.

Very respectfully, your obedient servant,

WM. D. WHIPPLE,
Assistant Adjutant-General.

HEADQUARTERS TWENTIETH ARMY CORPS,
July 9, 1864.

Brigadier-General WHIPPLE, *Chief of Staff:*

GENERAL: It is reported to me that the enemy in my front are in the same strength and position as heretofore. Their pickets were relieved this morning the same as usual on previous days.

Very respectfully, your obedient servant,

JOSEPH HOOKER,
Major-General.

HEADQUARTERS CHIEF OF CAVALRY,
July 9, 1864.

Col. W. W. LOWE,
    Cartersville, Ga.:

General Thomas says keep the party at work under guard of dismounted men.* Why did Major Wolfley capture guerrillas? There is another way of treating them. His energy in pursuit and capture of rebel soldiers is commendable.

W. L. ELLIOTT,
Brigadier-General and Chief of Cavalry.

HDQRS. MILITARY DIVISION OF THE MISSISSIPPI,
In the Field, near Chattahoochee, July 9, 1864.

Colonel LOWE,
    Cartersville:

That is very well, but why is the telegraph interrupted beyond Dalton? I now have a division across the Chattahoochee, and expect to have four by night, with two separate bridges and fords. Don't spare the rascals at work to destroy our road. I approve the severest measures.†

W. T. SHERMAN,
Major-General, Commanding.

CARTERSVILLE, *July 9, 1864.*

Col. E. H. MURRAY:

General Sherman says that's very well. Take no prisoners if it can be avoided. When it is evident they are railroad destroyers, he will approve the severest measures. Part of our army is across the Chattahoochee.

W. W. LOWE,
Colonel, Commanding.

CARTERSVILLE, *July 9, 1864.*

Major-General STEEDMAN:

I am informed by General Sherman that Colonel Garrard is on the way to the front with a brigade of cavalry. The general directs me to take command of any and all cavalry on the way to the front to enable [me] to clear the country of rebels. I have something in view for Colonel Garrard. Will you be kind enough to tell me how I can communicate with him most readily. We captured over 40 of the railroad destroyers yesterday; think I will get some more to-day.

W. W. LOWE,
Colonel, Comdg. Cavalry Division, Dept. of the Cumberland.

JULY 9, 1864.

General SCHOFIELD:

General Garrard is across at Roswell, and Dodge is moving to that point with orders to fortify a tête-de-pont and to build a good trestle

---

* See Lowe to Sherman. Part II, p. 866.
† In answer to Lowe, Part II, p. 866.

bridge. I want from you a minute description of your position and all information as to roads from it to the east of the Stone Mountain. I propose to operate some to the south, to accumulate stores, and then ahead.

SHERMAN,
General.

HEADQUARTERS ARMY OF THE OHIO,
July 9, 1864—11 a. m.

Major-General SHERMAN,
    Commanding Military Division of the Mississippi:

GENERAL: I have advanced my troops somewhat this morning to get more room and better position. We now occupy a very high and commanding ridge, rather more than a mile from the river, with flanks resting upon spurs running from the ridge toward the stream. The position is very strong, and I think perfectly secure. I have put over two of Hascall's brigades in addition to Cox's division, in order to fully occupy the position. I have two brigades still on this side of the river. Nothing appears in our front this morning but a small cavalry force. The ground beyond our position, as far as can be seen, is extremely rough and wooded. The hills we occupy are high and the roads difficult. I am having them improved, and new ones cut; will make them as good as I can. I have not been able to get any valuable information of the roads and country beyond our position in addition to what the maps give. I am making efforts to find somebody who knows more about it.

    Very respectfully,

J. M. SCHOFIELD,
Major-General.

HDQRS. MILITARY DIVISION OF THE MISSISSIPPI,
In the Field, July 9, 1864.

General MCPHERSON,
    Army of the Tennessee:

GENERAL: We now have a good lodgment on the other bank of the river, Schofield at the mouth of Soap Creek and Garrard opposite Roswell. I saw General Dodge to-day en route for Roswell and explained to him the importance of the place, and he understands it fully. He and Garrard can hold it secure whilst we maneuver a little more on our right and give time to collect stores at Marietta, and for Rousseau to get a good offing. We noticed a good deal of flutter in the enemy's camps to-day, troops and wagons moving rapidly east and north. Johnston sees I threaten Decatur and Stone Mountain, and now is a good time for Stoneman to strike south. I want him if possible to secure a point at Campbellton or below, and strike the West Point road. I do believe he can do it, for Johnston will spread his force so much that it will be weak at all points. I have told Stoneman that if he secures both banks at Campbellton, with its ferry-boats, he may call on you for a brigade to hold it whilst he strikes the railroad. Of course we do not intend to attack the tête-de-pont of the enemy, and unless Johnston supposes I have scattered my force too much he will not venture to sally, and if he does our position is as strong against him as his against us, and I have no apprehensions on that score; therefore, if Stoneman calls for a brigade send it. Keep hammering away all the time, and the moment he lets go of this bank occupy it; but if he holds on, as soon as the time comes we will let him stay on this side and we will go over. With Thomas things are in statu quo. Railroad and telegraph all right.

Yours,

W. T. SHERMAN,
Major-General, Commanding.

HDQRS. MILITARY DIVISION OF THE MISSISSIPPI,
Near Chattahoochee, July 9, 1864.

Major-General STONEMAN,
Commanding Division of Cavalry:

GENERAL: In pursuance of our conversation of this day, I have to request that you proceed with your command to Campbellton to-morrow night, appearing suddenly before the place and securing if possible the boats there, or forcing the enemy to destroy them. If you can possibly do it get possession of those boats and also of the other bank. I am very anxious that an attack or demonstration be made against the railroad below Atlanta, and will instruct General McPherson to have a brigade of infantry ready to come down and hold the river whilst you with your cavalry strike the railroad. I am satisfied that the crossing of Schofield and Garrard above will draw in that direction Johnston's chief army, and that what troops are left south of Atlanta will be strung out as far as West Point, where he will keep the chief force. The point where the road would be easiest reached will be, say, half way from Atlanta and West Point, but it would not be safe for you to pass Campbellton unless the ferry was well destroyed. The bridge at Franklin is almost too far down, but still it too might be reached by you and either used or destroyed. A ford but little known or used below Campbellton and this side of Franklin bridge will be the best if such exists, and you may incur any risk sure of my approval, for whether you make a break of the road or merely cause a diversion you will do good. Don't be absent more than four or five days, and keep me advised on all possible occasions.

Yours, truly,

W. T. SHERMAN,
Major-General, Commanding.

HDQRS. MILITARY DIVISION OF THE MISSISSIPPI,
In the Field, near Chattahoochee, July 9, 1864.

General GARRARD,
Roswell:

What news? Have you crossed? You know that Schofield is across.

W. T. SHERMAN,
Major-General, Commanding.

JULY 9, 1864—7 a. m.

Major-General SHERMAN:

I have the ridge on the south bank of the river. The infantry should come up at once. I see no reason why I cannot hold it, but cannot tell what may occur before long.

I am, very respectfully, your obedient servant,

K. GARRARD,
Brigadier-General, U. S. Volunteers.

SHERMAN'S HEADQUARTERS,
July 9, 1864—10 a. m.

Brig. Gen. K. GARRARD,
        Roswell:

Dispatch received. One division of Thomas' moved for Roswell last night by the river road. Two divisions of McPherson, Dodge's corps, are now moving for Roswell via Marietta. Hold fast all you have made, and fortify until re-enforced.

                    W. T. SHERMAN,
                        Major-General.

JULY 9, 1864—10 a. m.

Major-General SHERMAN:

GENERAL: At 7 o'clock I sent you word that I was over the river and had the ridge. I have now a good position, and hold the Roswell and Atlanta road, which passes over the bridge. The ford is a little rough, but not deep. All is quiet in my front; but the regiment I sent to take the bridge, eight miles above, failed, and find some considerable force there. They can keep the enemy from burning the bridge, but cannot get possession of it. Prisoners report Kelly's division, Wheeler's corps, near that bridge.

    Very respectfully, your obedient servant,
                    K. GARRARD,
                        Brigadier-General.

SHERMAN'S HEADQUARTERS,
July 9, 1864.

General GARRARD,
        Roswell:

I have your second dispatch. Dodge was here en route for Roswell, and will come to you to-morrow; but in the mean time a division of Thomas' should be near there now. When Dodge comes up see him and consult as to the necessity of taking the upper bridge, or forcing the enemy to destroy it. Dodge will rebuild the bridge at the Factory. All well here. The enemy has moved troops to the other side, northward, but toward Schofield, I think.

                    W. T. SHERMAN,
                        Major-General.

ROSWELL, *July 9, 1864—9 p. m.*

Major-General SHERMAN:

I have to report the arrival of General Newton with his division, Fourth Corps. All was quiet, and he relieved me about dark. My cavalry pickets are about two miles from the river, on the Atlanta road. There has been but slight opposition to-day, though my cavalry pickets stand opposite to those of the enemy, and have had some skirmishes. No sign of large force of the enemy's infantry. The ford is very rough and about belly deep. Wagons might be passed over, though it would be better to have the bridge built. Dimensions of old bridge: Length, 642 feet; 6 spans; good stone piers 14 feet from water.

                    K. GARRARD,
                Brigadier-General, Commanding Cavalry.

SHERMAN'S HEADQUARTERS,
July 9, 1864—9.40 p. m.

General GARRARD:

It is reported from Acworth that the road is threatened by a regiment of Texans, 500 strong. As soon as you are strengthened by infantry, increase your force above Roswell at the upper bridge, to interpose between it and the bridge. This is the reason why that bridge was held this morning by the division of Kelly.

W. T. SHERMAN,
Major-General.

RINGGOLD, *July 9, 1864.*

Capt. S. B. MOE,
Assistant Adjutant-General:

Party of rebel cavalry fired on and wounded a number of Michigan Engineers scattered in woods cutting timber between three and four miles south of here. Have sent out to ascertain facts; will telegraph again. These rebels scattered and hid in the woods; and without cavalry, of which I have none, nothing can be done with them. I do not think the rebel force large.

H. K. MILWARD,
Lieutenant-Colonel, Commanding.

RESACA, *July 9, 1864.*

Capt. S. B. MOE,
Assistant Adjutant-General:

I think it is of vital importance that a cavalry force be stationed at Snake Creek Gap. Scouting parties of the enemy may dash upon the railroad from that direction at any time unless our scouting parties keep a close watch. If the Fourth Kentucky is removed, I ask that one of Colonel Murray's regiments now here be ordered there.

G. B. RAUM,
Colonel, Commanding.

CHATTANOOGA, *July 9, 1864.*

Colonel MURRAY:

Send 150 cavalry with all possible dispatch to Tilton, to operate between Tilton and Dalton for the protection of the railroad.

JAMES B. STEEDMAN,
Major-General.

GENERAL SHERMAN'S HEADQUARTERS,
July 9, 1864. (Received 2 a. m. 10th.)

Maj. T. T. ECKERT:

Garrard's cavalry has effected a lodgment on south side Chattahoochee, and is moving. Schofield will cross and do the same. The Sixteenth Corps is moving to Roswell to-day, and will cross to-morrow. General Howard has captured one of the enemy's pontoons above Wilkins' Bridge. Heavy columns seen moving north and east to-day. Skirmishing all day.

J. C. VAN DUZER.

Orders.]   Headquarters Twentieth Corps,
                                July 9, 1864.

At daylight to-morrow morning Brigadier-General Ward, command-ing Third Division, will move his command to the left of General Will-iams' division and relieve the troops of General Davis' division, of the Fourteenth Corps, and hold the line now occupied by that command. At the same hour Brigadier-General Williams, commanding First Di-vision, and Brigadier-General Geary, commanding Second Division, will move their reserve brigades on to the line and occupy the position vacated by General Ward's division. If there should be any difficulty in relieving the pickets in the daylight, it can be postponed till night. General Ward will bring up his artillery and put in position on his new line.

By command of Major-General Hooker:

H. W. PERKINS,
Lieutenant-Colonel and Assistant Adjutant-General.

Near Chattahoochee, Ga., *July 10, 1864—6.30 a. m.*
                                (Received 2 p. m.)
Maj. Gen. H. W. Halleck, *Washington, D. C.:*

The enemy this morning burned his bridges across the Chattahoochee, the railroad bridge included. If General Grant has nothing particular for Hunter, Crook, and Averell to do, and if they be in the Kanawha Valley, as is represented, they could be well employed by going to Abingdon, smashing up things in that quarter, and then going over into North Carolina.

W. T. SHERMAN,
Major-General.

Signal Hill, *July 10, 1864.*
Major-General Sherman:

Rebels burning railroad bridge and wagon bridges over Chattahoo-chee River.

HOWGATE.

Hdqrs. Military Division of the Mississippi,
In the Field, near Chattahoochee, July 10, 1864.
General Thomas:

Signal officers report railroad and all other bridges burning. Of course if such be the case, the enemy has gone across, and yet I hear firing of pickets. Report to me the truth as soon as ascertained.

W. T. SHERMAN,
Major-General, Commanding.

Headquarters Department of the Cumberland,
July 10, 1864—4.45 a. m.
Major-General Sherman:

The enemy has left my front and burned the railroad and wagon bridge over the river. I have ordered the skirmishers to feel up and as-certain if they are still on this side. I presume the firing we hear is the pickets exchanging shots across the river.

GEO. H. THOMAS,
Major-General.

HDQRS. MILITARY DIVISION OF THE MISSISSIPPI,
In the Field, near Chattahoochee, July 10, 1864.

General THOMAS:

Let Howard move up to supporting distance of Schofield to assist him in case the enemy attempts to dislodge him. Detachments of Hooker and Palmer should occupy the redoubts this side, but keep your wagons and masses out of sight for the present.

W. T. SHERMAN,
Major-General, Commanding.

HEADQUARTERS DEPARTMENT OF THE CUMBERLAND,
July 10, 1864.

Major-General SHERMAN:

Hooker and Palmer occupy the enemy's works in their fronts, and have skirmishers on the river-bank. Their camps have not been moved. Howard has been ordered to move to supporting distance of Schofield.

GEO. H. THOMAS,
Major-General.

HDQRS. MILITARY DIVISION OF THE MISSISSIPPI,
In the Field, near Chattahoochee River, July 10, 1864.

General THOMAS:

Did you visit enemy's works on this side the Chattahoochee? Describe them to me that I may embrace the substance in my dispatch to-morrow to General Halleck.

W. T. SHERMAN,
Major-General, Commanding.

HEADQUARTERS DEPARTMENT OF THE CUMBERLAND,
July 10, 1864.

Major-General SHERMAN:

I visited the enemy's works on this side of the river. The works were in two strong lines similar to those we have had heretofore. At certain distances citadels were built for infantry covering the line about twelve feet, so as to give an enfilading fire on assaulting columns. The front was protected by abatis on open fields and by felled timber where the lines ran through woods; this for thirty or forty yards in their front. The entire front of the lines was covered by palisades of sharpened timbers. In rear of these lines were two strong works on either side of the bridge, connected with the river by lines of rifle-pits. Their left rested in a marsh on Nickajack Creek, their right on the river. From the works on this side I could see a strong work for artillery and several batteries on the other side, connected by lines of rifle-pits.

GEO. H. THOMAS,
Major-General.

HDQRS. MILITARY DIVISION OF THE MISSISSIPPI,
In the Field, near Chattahoochee River, July 10, 1864.

General THOMAS:

General Schofield has a good bridge and position, but the road up the hill is narrow, crooked, and steep. I think the road out from

Powers' Ferry is better and leads straight to Cross Keys, the first point common to the roads out from Roswell, McPherson's; Phillips', Schofield's; Powers' and Pace's, yours. General Dodge will make a good bridge at Roswell, General Schofield will make a bridge at Phillips', and you can have your own and McPherson's pontoons at Powers' and Pace's. General Howard is close up to General Schofield, and General Newton will join him as soon as General Dodge has made his bridge and works. I think it would be well for General Howard to secure the hill at Powers' Ferry, just below the crossing, and move the pontoons down as soon as General Schofield gets a trestle bridge done. I want General McPherson to feign strong at Turner's and cover General Stoneman's movements down the river, and I want you to make strong demonstrations at the railroad bridge, but keep in mind that you are to cross at Powers' and Pace's. All the roads back to Marietta are good, but the cross-roads are steep and hilly. The road from Powers' to Vining's is quite good; crosses Rottenwood at a mill-dam. All preparations should be made in three days.

W. T. SHERMAN,
Major-General, Commanding.

HEADQUARTERS DEPARTMENT OF THE CUMBERLAND,
July 10, 1864.

Major-General SHERMAN:

The Roswell Factory hands, 400 or 500 in number, have arrived at Marietta. The most of them are women. I can only order them transportation to Nashville, where it seems hard to turn them adrift. What had best be done with them?

GEO. H. THOMAS,
Major-General.

HDQRS. MILITARY DIVISION OF THE MISSISSIPPI,
In the Field, near Chattahoochee, July 10, 1864.

General THOMAS:

I have ordered General Webster, at Nashville, to dispose of them. They will be sent to Indiana.

W. T. SHERMAN,
Major-General, Commanding.

HDQRS. MILITARY DIVISION OF THE MISSISSIPPI,
In the Field, near Chattahoochee, July 10, 1864.

COMMANDING OFFICER,
Roswell:

By signal from signal station enemy has burned his bridge here, and is supposed to be all across the Chattahoochee. Dodge is supposed to be near you. Make a strong lodgment on the south bank and fortify. Let General Newton stay there till further orders.

W. T. SHERMAN,
Major-General, Commanding.

HDQRS. MILITARY DIVISION OF THE MISSISSIPPI,
In the Field, near Chattahoochee, July 10, 1864.

COMMANDING OFFICER,
Marietta:

The Eightieth Indiana should go to the mouth of Soap Creek and join its corps. General Schofield will need every man, if, as I suppose, the enemy will attempt to dislodge him.

W. T. SHERMAN,
Major-General, Commanding.

———

HDQRS. MILITARY DIVISION OF THE MISSISSIPPI,
In the Field, near Chattahoochee River, July 10, 1864.

COMMANDING OFFICER,
Marietta:

The officer at Acworth reports that a cavalry force of the enemy is near and that they threaten to burn a bridge between you and Acworth. Now that the main army of the enemy is across the Chattahoochee, Allatoona is safe, and you can safely detach one or more regiments forward to secure the road. See that the bridges are all well guarded as far as Acworth. Four companies are at Big Shanty.

W. T. SHERMAN,
Major-General, Commanding.

———

HDQRS. MILITARY DIVISION OF THE MISSISSIPPI,
In the Field, near Chattahoochee, July 10, 1864.

COMMANDING OFFICER,
Marietta:

The Twenty-third Corps is now across the Chattahoochee at the mouth of Soap Creek, and being exposed will need every regiment in it. It is my smallest army. The signal officer reports the enemy's bridge burning, in which case the enemy will, of course, abandon this side altogether. As soon as that is ascertained to be actual truth, I will arrange for permanent details to guard the road back as far as Allatoona.

W. T. SHERMAN,
Major-General, Commanding.

———

HDQRS. MILITARY DIVISION OF THE MISSISSIPPI,
In the Field, near Chattahoochee, July 10, 1864.

COMMANDING OFFICER,
Rome, Ga.:

Johnston's army is now driven across the Chattahoochee. You should now keep detachments well out toward Van's Valley, Villa Rica, and toward Gadsden, getting familiar with the country, getting grain and forage, and picking up prisoners. Instead of being passive, all should now be most active.

W. T. SHERMAN,
Major-General, Commanding.

HEADQUARTERS DEPARTMENT OF THE CUMBERLAND,
In the Field, July 10, 1864—7.30 a. m.

Maj. Gen. O. O. HOWARD,
Commanding Fourth Army Corps:

GENERAL: The major-general commanding directs that you move the two divisions now with you to within supporting distance of General Schofield, to assist him in case the enemy attempt to dislodge him. Let them move to-day.

Very respectfully, your obedient servant,
WM. D. WHIPPLE,
Assistant Adjutant-General.

HDQRS. SECOND DIVISION, FOURTEENTH ARMY CORPS,
July 10, 1864.

Captain McCLURG,
Assistant Adjutant-General, Fourteenth Army Corps:

CAPTAIN: I have just returned from the river. The enemy is all across the other side and the bridges burnt. I have two regiments on the bank of the river at the railroad crossing. The enemy skirmished pretty sharply from the opposite bank, but it is unnecessary to keep so large a force there; a small picket is sufficient. Please inform the general commanding of the above report and ask him for instructions.

Very respectfully,
JEF. C. DAVIS,
Brigadier-General, Commanding Division.

HEADQUARTERS DEPARTMENT OF THE CUMBERLAND,
In the Field, July 10, 1864—4.40 a. m.

Major-General HOOKER:

GENERAL: The enemy have left General Palmer's front, also burned the railroad and wagon bridge over the Chattahoochee. The major-general commanding directs that you feel up with your skirmishers and see if they have left your front.

Respectfully, your obedient servant,
WM. D. WHIPPLE,
Assistant Adjutant-General.

HDQRS. FIRST BRIGADE, FIRST DIVISION CAVALRY,
DEPARTMENT OF THE CUMBERLAND,
In the Field, July 10, 1864.

Captain LE ROY,
Assistant Adjutant-General, First Division:

My scouting party sent to Johnson's Ferry this morning returned to camp; report no picket at that point. It was withdrawn day before yesterday.

Respectfully, your obedient servant,
J. B. DORR,
Colonel, Commanding.

P. S.—I sent word by Lieutenant Belfield that the forces of General Schofield now hold the opposite side of the river from my outposts at Powers' Ferry and Cochran's Ford. They are fortifying the ridge upon which the rebel battery was planted at Powers' Ferry.

DORR.

Hdqrs. Department and Army of the Tennessee,
Near Turner's Ferry, July 10, 1864—12 m.

Major-General Sherman,
          Commanding, &c.:

General: My skirmishers are near the river and the enemy on the opposite side in rifle-pits, both above and below Turner's Ferry. The enemy also have a work on the opposite side within easy cannon-range of the bluffs on the north side, in which they have artillery. I am having a battery of 3-inch Rodmans and 20-pounder Parrotts put in position, and will try to develop what is in front of us. We have captured about 50 prisoners, principally from the enemy's skirmish line.

Colonel Scott, of Leggett's division, reports that the rebels burned their pontoon bridge after the main body crossed, and before their skirmishers were relieved.

Major-General Stoneman is here, and desires to know whether the retreat of the rebels across the Chattahoochee will make any change in the plans proposed for him yesterday. If he goes on the expedition, he wishes to start at 8 o'clock this evening. From the result of his reconnaissance last night in the vicinity of Campbellton, he finds there is no bridge or ford until he reaches Franklin, and no enemy on this side of the river. I send this by Captain Gile in order to get an answer quickly.

Very respectfully, your obedient servant,
          JAS. B. McPHERSON,
                    Major-General.

Hdqrs. Department and Army of the Tennessee,
Near Chattahoochee River, Ga., July 10, 1864—10 p. m.

Maj. Gen. W. T. Sherman,
          Commanding, &c.:

General: Major-General Stoneman has made all his arrangements and started on his expedition at 8 o'clock this evening, intending to go as far down as Campbellton to-night. I have sent a brigade of infantry down to the vicinity of Sandtown Ferry, with instructions to picket and patrol along the river between the mouth of Nickajack and Sweet Water. Early this morning my skirmishers moved forward and took up a position in advance of the rebel works and have been skirmishing with the enemy across the Chattahoochee all day. Seven regiments of infantry were moved up to the rebel works to support them (four from Gresham's division, one from Harrow's, one from Osterhaus', and one from Morgan L. Smith's), the balance being held ready for any emergency. I am also having batteries constructed; will get the guns in to-night and be able to open on the enemy to-morrow morning. I also directed Major-General Blair to send a brigade down as far as Howell's Ferry to make a demonstration and develop the position of the enemy if possible, and inclose herewith the report* of Brigadier-General Leggett, who accompanied the brigade. I have not attempted to cross the Chattahoochee River, which I think can be effected in the vicinity of Sandtown Ferry, as it would necessitate putting down our pontoon bridge, which, from the instructions I have received, I inferred you did

---

* Not found.

not wish done at present. Major-General Stoneman said that he did not care about the infantry covering the river any farther down than the mouth of Sweet Water. If he cannot effect a crossing in the vicinity of Campbellton, he will, after making a lively demonstration there to-morrow, push rapidly to-morrow night for Franklin bridge and try to cross there.

Very respectfully, your obedient servant,

JAS. B. McPHERSON,
Major-General.

HDQRS. MILITARY DIVISION OF THE MISSISSIPPI,
In the Field, near Chattahoochee, July 10, 1864.

Major-General McPHERSON,
Commanding Army of the Tennessee:

GENERAL: I have pretty much made up my mind as to the next move, but would be glad to hear any suggestion from you. I propose that General Stoneman shall attempt to break the road below Atlanta, to accumulate stores at Marietta and increase our guards to the rear, then suddenly to shift you to Roswell, General Dodge in the mean time to get you a good tête-de-pont and bridge. General Schofield is already at Phillips' Ferry, across and fortified. He too will make a good trestle bridge. General Thomas will group his [command] at Powers' and Pace's Ferries. But for the next three days, while these preparations are being made, I want you to demonstrate as though intending to cross at Turner's or below, and General Thomas the same at the railroad bridge. When General Stoneman is back, I will give you the word to shift rapidly to Roswell and cross, and in anticipation you can get your wagons back to Marietta, except such as you need. General Thomas will need yours and his pontoons to cross at Powers' and Pace's. At the right time I will leave Generals Stoneman and McCook to cover the front, and cross all the balance of the army and advance its right on or near Peach Tree Creek, and the left (you) swing toward Stone Mountain. Johnston will be found to occupy his redoubts about Atlanta and also Stone Mountain and Decatur. We can maneuver so as to compel him to weaken his center or one of his flanks, when we can act. If he neglect his right or center we get on his Augusta road. If he neglect Atlanta, we take it. If he assume the offensive, we cover our roads and base and can make as good use of Peach Tree Creek as he. If General Stoneman could break the road, so much the better, but if he cannot, I calculate that General Rousseau will do so within a week, quite as early as we can be at or near Cross Keys. The ground opposite still continues rough, but that we cannot help. I find all the roads leading back from Roswell, Phillips' and Powers' Ferries to Marietta are good, but the cross-roads are hilly and steep. The advantage of this plan over the one crossing to the south is, that we are all between the enemy and our base, and now that he has destroyed his own bridges he cannot get over without fighting us. Study your maps and be ready, but in the mean time stir up the enemy all you can on that flank and make feints as though designing to cross.

W. T. SHERMAN,
Major-General, Commanding.

HDQRS. MILITARY DIVISION OF THE MISSISSIPPI,
In the Field, near Chattahoochee, July 10, 1864.

General DODGE,
En route from Marietta:

The signal officer reports the railroad and other bridge burning. If this be so, the enemy will, of course, quit this sphere, and you should be duly vigilant at Roswell. Get there as quick as possible and fortify on the other side.

W. T. SHERMAN,
Major-General, Commanding.

HEADQUARTERS LEFT WING, SIXTEENTH ARMY CORPS,
Roswell, July 10, 1864—1.30 p. m.

Major-General SHERMAN:

My troops are arriving and crossing. I have been here three hours, and, in company with General Newton, have thoroughly examined the country. I will occupy and fortify to-night a tête-de-pont half a mile from the river, and extending up and down one mile, covering the entire ford, bridge, and roads leading to them. The ford is half a mile or more in extent, very rough, and impracticable except for troops. To bridge the stream I will have to build over 650 feet in length. I shall use the old piers, and trestle between. We have a strong picket out three miles covering the forks of road leading to McAfee's Bridge, eight miles up the river, and covering the forks of road that leads to Atlanta. It is too far out to take the command until the river is easily passed by artillery and trains.

G. M. DODGE,
Major-General.

ROSWELL, *July 10, 1864—8 p. m.*

Major-General SHERMAN:

Forces are all over river, hard at work fortifying. Have got batteries over also; have built a float bridge. The road bridge is a pretty big job, but will work hard on it. No force in my front that we can hear of.

G. M. DODGE,
Major-General.

HDQRS. MILITARY DIVISION OF THE MISSISSIPPI,
In the Field, near Chattahoochee River, July 10, 1864.

General DODGE, *Roswell:*

I have been out all day; am just back. Have received General Garrard's and your dispatches. I design that General McPherson's whole army shall come to that flank, and you are to prepare the way. General Newton will stay with you till you feel all safe, when he will rejoin his corps now in support of General Schofield, eight miles below you. General Garrard will picket the roads, and I want you to fortify a tête-de-pont and bridge. General McPherson will operate to the right and then when all is ready will come rapidly to your flank, therefore make all preparations to that end. General Schofield has a secure place opposite the mouth of Soap Creek. Keep me well advised by courier to Marietta, and telegraph.

W. T. SHERMAN,
Major-General, Commanding.

HEADQUARTERS SEVENTEENTH ARMY CORPS,
Near Chattahoochee River, Ga., July 10, 1864.

Lieut. Col. W. T. CLARK,
Asst. Adjt. Gen., Department and Army of the Tennessee:

COLONEL: In compliance with orders from your headquarters, I left one brigade and two batteries of artillery at Allatoona. As this brigade was small, and in order to carry out the spirit of the order, I left in addition two regiments detailed from other brigades. Since that time the Forty-first Illinois has reached Allatoona, and has been ordered to remain there. As my command is small, I have the honor to request the Fifty-third Illinois Infantry may be relieved from that post and ordered to report to me for duty in its proper division.

Very respectfully, your obedient servant,

FRANK P. BLAIR, Jr.,
Major-General.

———

HDQRS. FOURTH DIVISION, SEVENTEENTH ARMY CORPS,
July 10, 1864.

Lieut. Col. A. J. ALEXANDER,
Assistant Adjutant-General:

The enemy left their works last night, and deserters say they have fallen back across the river.

Very respectfully,

W. Q. GRESHAM,
Brigadier-General.

[Indorsement.]

HDQRS. DEPARTMENT AND ARMY OF THE TENNESSEE,
July 10, 1864—6.40 a. m.

Respectfully forwarded to Major-General Sherman.

Brigadier-General Gresham has four of his regiments in the enemy's works, and is now getting a battery in position to shell them on the other side of the river. The enemy's sharpshooters are still on the south bank.

Yours, truly,

JAS. B. McPHERSON,
Major-General.

———

HDQRS. DEPARTMENT AND ARMY OF THE TENNESSEE,
Near Chattahoochee, July 10, 1864—4.30 p. m.

Maj. Gen. F. P. BLAIR, Jr.,
Commanding Seventeenth Army Corps:

GENERAL: Major-General Sherman has directed General Stoneman with his cavalry to move down the river to Campbellton, or below, and, if possible, to get across the river and cut the railroad between Montgomery and Atlanta. To do this will require his whole force. You will, therefore, direct General Leggett to send one of his brigades down immediately to a point in the vicinity of Sandtown Ferry to picket and guard the river at Howell's, Baker's, Sandtown, and Adaholt's (sometimes called Dodge's) Ferries, taking the place of the cavalry pickets. The infantry will march light, and anything required for them can be sent down to-morrow. The infantry are to guard the line of the river down as far as the mouth of Sweet Water Creek until the return of the cavalry expedition.

Very respectfully, your obedient servant,

JAS. B. McPHERSON,
Major-General.

HEADQUARTERS SEVENTEENTH ARMY CORPS,
Near Chattahoochee River, July 10, 1864.

Brig. Gen. W. Q. GRESHAM,
Commanding Fourth Division:

GENERAL: I am directed to inform you that one brigade of the Third Division has been sent off to the extreme right to guard fords, &c. Should any attack be made on General Leggett, the major-general commanding desires you to hold a portion of your command in readiness to assist him if necessary.

Very respectfully, your obedient servant,

[A. J. ALEXANDER,]
Assistant Adjutant-General.

ROSWELL, *July 10, 1864.*

Major-General SHERMAN:

Your dispatch in regard to the reported force near Acworth has just been received. Communications, except by telegraph to Marietta, come very late; those by telegraph and my courier line in two hours. I will make full investigation to-day in regard to what force the enemy have north of the river. They come over in small parties, scatter, and then concentrate at some point inside our lines, and it is difficult to catch them, but I will take such precautions that no large organized force can get far without my knowledge. All is quiet, and I have directed my pickets south of the river to advance on the Atlanta road, if possible.

K. GARRARD,
Brigadier-General.

HDQRS. MILITARY DIVISION OF THE MISSISSIPPI,
In the Field, near Chattahoochee, July 10, 1864.

General GARRARD,
Roswell:

Signal officer reports the railroad and wagon road bridges burning. If this be so, of course the enemy is on the other side. The truth will be ascertained at once. In the mean time be watchful.

W. T. SHERMAN,
Major-General, Commanding.

HEADQUARTERS,
Roswell, July 10, 1864.

Major-General SHERMAN:

To-day I have sent patrols toward Canton, Loring's, Goodbridge, Cumming, and up the river, and I can learn of no large force of cavalry on this side of the river. There are small parties of five to ten scattered through the country, but no organized force. As well as I can judge, the cavalry have fallen back toward Cross Keys. The bridge to-day eight miles above was crossed by my troops and is in good order. Shall I send a force to keep it from being destroyed?

K. GARRARD,
Brigadier-General.

HDQRS. MILITARY DIVISION OF THE MISSISSIPPI,
In the Field, near Chattahoochee, July 10, 1864.
General STEEDMAN,
Chattanooga:

We have now driven Johnston's army across the Chattahoochee, and will continue to give full employment to his main forces, cavalry as well as infantry. I want General John E. Smith's reserve division moved to Cartersville and the Allatoona Pass, and the brigade now at Allatoona forward to Kenesaw Mountain; also the cavalry and all the garrisons to be most active in gathering in grain and forage and in picking up prisoners. The country behind us now should be cleaned out of all the elements out of which guerrillas and loafers are made up, and we should appropriate and put in store all forage and produce within reach. Whenever the people are in the way ship them to a new country north and west.

W. T. SHERMAN,
Major-General, Commanding.

CHATTANOOGA, *July 10, 1864.*
General J. E. SMITH:

You will move with that portion of your command stationed at Kingston to Cartersville, and relieve the Second Brigade, Fourth Division, Seventeenth Army Corps, stationed at Etowah and Allatoona. On being relieved, that brigade will proceed to Kenesaw Mountain.

By command of Major-General Steedman:

S. B. MOE,
Assistant Adjutant-Generel.

HDQRS. MILITARY DIVISION OF THE MISSISSIPPI,
In the Field, near Chattahoochee River, July 10, 1864.
General STEEDMAN,
Chattanooga, Tenn.:

I don't know that I told you that General Rousseau was to start on the 9th from Decatur, Ala., for the railroad between Montgomery and Opelika via Oxford. If Pillow be at Oxford he will have to quit. This move will check a repetition of Pillow's attempt. Still be watchful.

W. T. SHERMAN,
Major-General, Commanding.

CHATTANOOGA, *July 10, 1864.*
Brig. Gen. JOHN E. SMITH:

There will be no troops to relieve you; Colonel Lowe with what cavalry he has will have to take care of Kingston for the present.

JAMES B. STEEDMAN,
Major-General.

HEADQUARTERS DISTRICT OF THE ETOWAH,
Chattanooga, Tenn., July 10, 1864.

Brig. Gen. W. D. WHIPPLE,
Chief of Staff and Asst. Adjt. Gen., Dept. of the Cumberland:

GENERAL: The whole country between this post and the front is infested with guerrilla bands, who will and can constantly interrupt our line of communications unless they are broken up and driven out of the country. To do this requires a mounted force, and it will be accomplished in the shortest time and most effectually by men who are acquainted with the country and the character and associations of the leaders of these bands. Having learned that there is a probability of the First East Tennessee Cavalry, Colonel Brownlow, being mounted, I respectfully ask the major-general commanding the Department of the Cumberland to order this regiment, if mounted, to report to me, that I may use it to clear the country of the bands of thieves and marauders now organized and being organized to depredate upon our communications. Brownlow's regiment has in it men who know the country, every road and bridle path, and understand the political sentiments of the people, and hence would not be so readily imposed upon and misled by rebel sympathizers as troops who are strangers in the country.

Very respectfully,

JAMES B. STEEDMAN,
Major-General, Commanding.

SPECIAL FIELD ORDERS, }   HDQRS. MIL. DIV. OF THE MISS.,
                }   *In the Field, near Chattahoochee River,*
No. 32.   }   *July 10, 1864.*

I. The division of General John E. Smith will occupy the Allatoona Pass, with a detachment at Kingston and Cartersville, and the brigade now at the Allatoona Pass will occupy Kenesaw Mountain and Big Shanty. The District of the Etowah will be extended to embrace the Kenesaw Mountain.

II. Each of the three armies will have one regiment at Marietta, of the average strength of 330 men for fatigue duty, to unload cars; the commanding officers to report for orders to the chief commissary, Colonel Beckwith. Marietta will be the grand depot, but the chief quartermaster may arrange to deliver stores in bulk at Ruff's or Vining's Stations, according to the facilities of the railroad.

III. Commissaries and quartermasters must keep ten days' supplies on hand at all times, without special orders to that effect, and the army must be ready for quick, prompt movement, as our future plans depend on the enemy.

By order of Maj. Gen. W. T. Sherman:

L. M. DAYTON,
Aide-de-Camp.

NEAR CHATTAHOOCHEE RIVER, GA., *July 11, 1864—7 a. m.*
(Received 9.15 a. m. 13th.)

Maj. Gen. H. W. HALLECK,
Washington, D. C.:

The enemy is now all beyond the Chattahoochee, having destroyed all his bridges. We occupy the west bank for thirty miles, and have two heads of columns across; one at the shallow ford at Roswell, and the other at the mouth of Soap Creek (Phillips'). At these we are making good pier bridges. Water is shallow, rock bottom, but strong and rapid current. I propose to have another of pontoons lower down, about the mouth of Rottenwood or Island Creeks. The last works abandoned by the enemy were the strongest of all, embracing two detached redoubts and extending along the river hills for about five miles, having in its whole extent finished abatis and parapet, with glacis obstructed with chevaux-de-frise, and all manner of impediments. But the moment Johnston detected that I had ignored his forts, and had secured two good lodgments above him on the east bank, at Roswell Factory and at Phillips', he drew his forces across and burned all his bridges, viz, one railroad, one trestle, and three pontoons. We now commence the real game for Atlanta, and I expect pretty sharp practice, but I think we have the advantage, and propose to keep it.

W. T. SHERMAN,
Major-General.

WASHINGTON, *July 11, 1864—10.15 a. m.*

Maj. Gen. W. T. SHERMAN,
   Georgia:

Hunter, Crook, and Averell have their hands more than full, and cannot operate as you suggest.

H. W. HALLECK,
Major-General and Chief of Staff.

HDQRS. MILITARY DIVISION OF THE MISSISSIPPI,
In the Field, near Chattahoochee River, July 11, 1864.

General THOMAS:

I have ordered General McPherson to send his pontoons here to-morrow. I will order them to Powers' Ferry, and I will want you to effect a lodgment there to-morrow night and next day. There is no enemy of any size to our immediate front, and General Dodge reports the enemy's cavalry alone above Peach Tree Creek at Buck Head. He says he has an Atlanta paper of the 10th, that all the wealthy people are leaving, and that a council of war was held, when it was decided to fight for Atlanta. General Rousseau telegraphs from Decatur on the 8th that he started that day and would be on the Montgomery and Opelika road in eight or nine days. I think we should as soon as possible secure the opposite bank from Roswell down to Peach Tree Creek. I think the bridge across the Peach Tree near the railroad bridge is still standing. I watched it close to-day and think I saw half a dozen men pass it, but with that exception there was no life visible. There was no danger in standing in full view in the redoubt to-day. The signal officer reports the absence of all camps from the other side to-day. I suppose Johnston will group his army about Atlanta, and wait for us to develop our game. I only await news from Stoneman to put General McPherson in motion.

W. T. SHERMAN,
Major-General, Commanding.

HDQRS. MILITARY DIVISION OF THE MISSISSIPPI,
In the Field, near Chattahoochee, July 11, 1864.
General THOMAS:

Colonel Beckwith says the three regiments have reported at Marietta. You can order the brigade left there to join its proper command. The brigade of General McPherson at Kenesaw will be near enough to protect the depot.

W. T. SHERMAN,
Major-General, Commanding.

HEADQUARTERS DEPARTMENT OF THE CUMBERLAND,
Near Vining's Station, Ga., July 11, 1864.
(Received 4 p. m.)
Maj. Gen. O. O. HOWARD, *Commanding Fourth Army Corps:*

GENERAL: I have the honor, by direction of the major-general commanding, to acknowledge your communication of this day relative to the return of General Newton's division, and in reply to state that orders were given for General Newton's return as soon as relieved by General Dodge, and the major-general commanding thinks he should join you to-day.

I am, general, very respectfully, your obedient servant,

ROBT. H. RAMSEY,
Captain and Assistant Adjutant-General.

[JULY 11, 1864.]
Major-General SHERMAN:

General Howard will, to-morrow morning, move a brigade down the south bank of the river from Phillips' to Powers' Ferry, and move one of the pontoon bridges from the former point to the latter. The road at Phillips' is so narrow on each side that but one wagon can pass at a time, consequently there is use for but one bridge. The trestle bridge will not be completed for several days.

GEO. H. THOMAS,
Major-General.

[JULY 11, 1864.]
(Received 3 a. m. 12th.)
Major-General HOWARD, *Commanding Fourth Army Corps:*

GENERAL: The major-general commanding directs that when you get the bridge complete you move your whole corps to the south bank of the river.

Very respectfully, your obedient servant,

WM. D. WHIPPLE,
Assistant Adjutant-General.

HDQRS. THIRD DIVISION, FOURTH ARMY CORPS,
In the Field, Ga., July 11, 1864.
Lieut. Col. J. S. FULLERTON, *Assistant-Adjutant General:*

COLONEL: Moore, a scout whom I sent out on the 7th instant, has just returned, bringing the following information:

He left General Johnston's headquarters at 3 p. m. yesterday. General Johnston's headquarters are at a small white house three miles this side of Atlanta, on what is called the Atlanta and Marietta road. The railroad passes near it. General Stewart's headquarters are near General Johnston's. Stewart's corps, late Polk's, is still on the right of Johnston's army, with the right resting on the railroad, about two miles beyond Peach Tree Creek, going from here toward Atlanta. Moore says he heard the officers saying they were going to intrench a position with their right resting on the railroad and their left at Cedar Bluffs. He says he was told that the principal part of the rebel wagon train had been moved beyond Atlanta toward Augusta; that a good deal of machinery had been moved from Atlanta in the same direction, and that the refugees, in great numbers, taking the negroes, &c., are also going in the same direction. He heard officers say that they did not expect any general engagement would take place in the vicinity of Atlanta without they received re-enforcements. He heard a camp rumor that a part of Kirby Smith's force was on the way by rail to join Johnston's army, but he could not get this from any reliable source. He says the rumor was that this re-enforcement would be there to-day. Moore says his impression is that the left of the rebel army rests at present on the river. Moore says he heard yesterday a report in the rebel camp that two of their corps are at Harper's Ferry. Early's corps is one, and he does not remember the other corps. He also heard a report that there had been a fight between Forrest and General Washburn. Moore says he saw Colonel Sherman at a distance, but did not have an opportunity to speak to him. He says Colonel Sherman has been forwarded to Anderson[ville]. In returning Moore came back by the way of Buck Head, entering our lines through General Dodge's command. He reported there early this morning. Moore says Wheeler's rebel cavalry pickets are two miles from General Dodge's outposts. Wheeler's cavalry lies between there and Buck Head. Moore says the Georgia State Troops, under General G. W. Smith, are on the left, under the general direction of General Hood.

Respectfully, your obedient servant,

TH. J. WOOD,
Brigadier-General of Volunteers, Commanding.

P. S.—Moore says he saw Mrs. Johnston and other ladies at General Johnston's headquarters yesterday. They seem to be having a jollification.

W.

Moore brings rebel papers to yesterday.

HEADQUARTERS DEPARTMENT OF THE CUMBERLAND,
In the Field, near Vining's Station, Ga., July 11, 1864.
Brig. Gen. E. M. McCOOK,
Commanding First Cavalry Division:

GENERAL: The major-general commanding directs that you take a sufficient force of your command, proceed to Dallas, and arrest the following-named men, bring them to these headquarters, and turn them over to the provost-marshal-general of the Department of the Cumberland: Green B. Turner, who lives two miles and a half from Dallas; Nick Allen, who lives three miles west of Dallas; Stephen Allen, who lives three miles west of Dallas; Lem. Anderson, who lives in Dallas; John Hicks, who lives five miles west of Dallas; Aleck Bullock, who lives three miles west of Dallas. Be sure to arrest Lem. Anderson, the Allens, and Aleck Bullock. After you have made these arrests inform the men arrested that they are arrested for their past deeds under the Confederacy, for what they have done since our army was at Dallas, and because they are disturbers of the peace of the community in which they live. Inform the people of Dallas of the same, and, moreover, that so long as they conduct themselves properly they will not be disturbed, but if any of them choose to conduct themselves as these men have done they will be arrested in the same manner and banished from the United States as these men will be.

I am, general, very respectfully, your obedient servant,

WM. D. WHIPPLE,
Chief of Staff.

HDQRS. DEPARTMENT AND ARMY OF THE TENNESSEE,
In Field, July 11, 1864—7.45 p. m.

Maj. Gen. W. T. SHERMAN,
Commanding, &c.:

GENERAL: I have the honor to inclose herewith report just received from Major-General Dodge.   Everything along this part of the front has been very quiet to-day.   I am having batteries erected on this side of the river at Turner's Ferry, and will have sixteen guns in position to-morrow morning to open on the enemy's redoubt on the opposite side, distant about 900 yards.   Deserters state that the redoubt has six guns, two 20-pounder Parrotts and four 10-pounders.   One brigade of Leggett's division is near Sandtown Ferry picketing the river, and I have one brigade of Morgan L. Smith's division near Widow Mitchell's and the other brigade at the intersection of the Sandtown and Alabama roads.   To-morrow morning De Gress will take his battery of 20-pounder Parrotts and go down to Sandtown Ferry and try to knock a small battery of the enemy's on the south side of the river to pieces.   General Stoneman got off last night.   No news from him to-day.

Very respectfully, your obedient servant,

JAS. B. McPHERSON,
Major-General.

P. S.—Your dispatch received.   The pontoon train will report accordingly.

J. B. McP.

Also inclose communication from General Leggett, just received.

[Inclosure No. 1.]

HEADQUARTERS LEFT WING, SIXTEENTH ARMY CORPS,
Roswell, Ga., July 11, 1864.

Maj. Gen. J. B. McPHERSON,
Commanding Department and Army of the Tennessee:

GENERAL: I arrived here yesterday at noon, the command crossed and the troops were all in position before night, and now have intrenchments up.   I have over a mile of ford and bridges to cover, and cannot make a tête-de-pont very far out that will cover it.   I have taken and extended the line selected by General Newton.   Our trains are all on the north side of the river.   The ford is very rough, but shallow, and the bridge we will have to build is 650 feet long and 14 feet high.   I put a foot bridge across last night, so that troops can pass.   It is very difficult for them to wade, the water is swift and bottom full of holes.   The enemy's pickets are near Buck Head, and men out of Atlanta to-day say that there is no infantry after you get four miles this side of Atlanta, and that Stewart is on their right.   Johnston's headquarters are at a little house three miles this side of Atlanta, on the railroad.   Atlanta papers of the 10th instant say that a council of war was held that day, and that it is rumored that Johnston would make a fight for the city. This would tend to show that it is not their intention.   All trains belonging to the army have gone toward Augusta, and everybody fleeing. Eight miles up the river from here is a good bridge that is not destroyed. I will work hard on the bridge here and finish it as soon as possible. It is a big job as you will perceive from the length.   Everything was burned up here that we could use—houses, mills, lumber, and all.

I am, very respectfully, your obedient servant,

G. M. DODGE,
Major-General, Commanding.

[Inclosure No. 2.]

HDQRS. THIRD DIVISION, SEVENTEENTH ARMY CORPS,
Chattahoochee River, July 11, 1864.

Lieut. Col. A. J. ALEXANDER,
Assistant Adjutant-General:

COLONEL: In obedience to orders from the major-general commanding the army corps, I took one brigade of infantry and a section of artillery and went to Howell's Ferry, and made considerable display, opening artillery fire from two points, and a brisk fire from our sharpshooters, but failed to get any response, except from the rebel sharpshooters in rifle-pits close to the river.   These sharpshooters seem to be few in number, and I am unable to form an opinion as to whether they are supported by a reserve in the woods in the rear, and I cannot ascertain without means to attempt a crossing; hence have returned.

Very respectfully, your obedient servant,

M. D. LEGGETT,
Brigadier-General.

HDQRS. MILITARY DIVISION OF THE MISSISSIPPI,
In the Field, near Chattahoochee River, July 11, 1864.

General DODGE,
Roswell, Ga.:

I know you have a big job, but that is nothing new for you.   Tell General Newton that his corps is now up near General Schofield's crossing, and that all is quiet thereabouts.   He might send down and move his camp to the proximity of his corps; but I think Roswell and Shallow Ford so important that I prefer him to be near you, until you are well fortified.   If he needs rations tell him to get his wagons up, and I think you will be able to spare him day after to-morrow.   I know the bridge at Roswell is important and you may destroy all Georgia to make it good and strong.

W. T. SHERMAN,
Major-General, Commanding.

HEADQUARTERS LEFT WING, SIXTEENTH ARMY CORPS,
Roswell, July 11, 1864.
Maj. Gen. W. T. SHERMAN,
            Commanding:

All quiet this morning. I had no fear about being able to build the bridge, but thought you might expect it finished sooner than possible, as it was twice as long as I expected to find it, and twice as long as the river is wide down at Sandtown. I have over 1,000 men at work on it day and night, and it is already well under way. I have planking for floor now on the ground, and not one minute shall be lost in pushing it forward. Every man that can work on it shall be kept at it. Reports here show no force of the enemy's infantry this side of Peach Tree. Wheeler's cavalry advance is at Buck Head, with all of his force south of there. Last night Joe Johnston's headquarters were three miles this side of Atlanta on the railroad. Atlanta papers of the 10th instant say that at a council of war held that day it was decided to fight for Atlanta. All trains of the enemy are reported by citizens and deserters to have gone toward Augusta, and a general refugeeing is going on among the wealthy citizens.

G. M. DODGE,
Major-General.

HDQRS. MILITARY DIVISION OF THE MISSISSIPPI,
In the Field, near Chattahoochee River, July 11, 1864.
General DODGE,
            Roswell:

Your dispatch is received. Send me any Atlanta papers you get. I have no doubt you will have the bridge done in time. As soon as you can spare General Newton he should be relieved to join his corps where his camp equipage is. I rode along the river-bank to-day, and the force of the enemy seemed to be merely sharpshooters in small numbers in their forts. All well with us.

W. T. SHERMAN,
Major-General, Commanding.

HDQRS. MILITARY DIVISION OF THE MISSISSIPPI,
In the Field, near Chattahoochee River, July 11, 1864.
General GARRARD,
            Roswell:

Certainly, by all means save the bridge above Roswell, and get me information of the lay of the country from it toward Stone Mountain.

W. T. SHERMAN,
Major-General, Commanding.

ROSWELL, *July 11, 1864—8 p. m.*
Major-General SHERMAN:

I have nothing new to report. All is quiet to-day. Parties have been in every direction and no evidence of any considerable force on this side of the river.

Very respectfully,

K. GARRARD,
Brigadier-General.

Near Chattahoochee River, *July 11, 1864—7 a. m.*
Maj. Gen. John A. Logan,
   Commanding Fifteenth Army Corps:

   Major-General Stoneman having gone on an expedition with his cavalry, thus rendering it necessary to picket the river between the mouth of the Nickajack and Sweet Water with infantry, you will send one of your divisions to some point on the Sandtown road near Widow Mitchell's with instructions to the commanding officer to station one brigade at the intersection of the Sandtown and Howell's Ferry roads, sometimes called the "Alabama Cross-Roads." A portion of General Blair's command is picketing the river, and your division will be in the nature of a reserve to cover our trains, &c., until the cavalry returns. Instruct the officer in command of the brigade to be stationed at the cross-roads to communicate with Blair's troops near Sandtown Ferry.

   Yours, truly,

JAS. B. McPHERSON,
   Major-General.

Hdqrs. Military Division of the Mississippi,
   In the Field, near Chattahoochee, July 11, 1864.
Col. W. W. Wright,
   Superintendent Railroad Construction, Marietta:

   I will want an accumulation of stores in Allatoona Pass, and suggest you lay down a side track between the bridge and Allatoona depot about where the old foundry was. The quartermaster will erect temporary sheds.

W. T. SHERMAN,
   Major-General, Commanding.

Hdqrs. Military Division of the Mississippi,
   In the Field, near Chattahoochee River, July 11, 1864.
Major-General Steedman,
   Commanding District of the Etowah:

   General: The importance of your command to the success of my operations is, I know, already appreciated by you; but when I suggest any additional work or precaution, I beg you to consider it as resulting from my supposed large experience in the military art.

   In the first place, I fear that our infantry officers suppose if cavalry comes about, they are excused from doing anything but to defend their own posts. This is not so. Infantry can always whip cavalry, and in a wooded and mountainous country can actually thwart it, and even at times capture it. Of course, as a general rule, a footman cannot catch a horseman on a fair open road or country, but nothing is more awkward in a wooded and mountainous country than a command of cavalry forced to go through narrow defiles, across streams at particular fords or bridges, or up and down certain valleys which can be seen from the mountain tops and ambushed. I have not yet seen in this war a cavalry command of a thousand that was not afraid of the sight of a dozen infantry bayonets, for the reason that the cavalry, to be effective, has to have a road or smooth field; whereas the infantryman steps into the bushes and is safe, or can block a road in five minutes and laugh at the man on horseback.

The moral I wish to inculcate by these simple illustrations is, by knowing the country and thinking ahead, an infantry garrison can act against cavalry. Therefore, it is expected of the infantry guarding our road that they are not to sit down and let cavalry prance all around them, but that they ambush their roads, anticipate their passage at mountain passes and creek crossings, or even pursue them and catch them jammed in narrow roads or at bridges. Thus at Dalton a lookout should be kept all along Taylor's Ridge and give notice of horsemen in the far off valleys, and then they should be waylaid. Rewards should be offered and paid to faithful citizens and negroes who give notice of the presence of parties of the enemy, but they should always be waylaid and pursued.

Another matter I will draw your attention to: officers and men naturally slip into houses and establish headquarters, offices, &c., and are about as useless as if posted in Canada. Make a positive order that each garrison shall build anew a good stockade with earth-work, abatis, &c., not too strong, but to serve as a stronghold and rallying point, to hold a dash of cavalry in check, and more especially to allow a part of the garrison to hold the post while the greater portion goes forth to battle with the enemy. A fixed garrison is harmless and useless. Its only value is in its power of offense.

I think you had better embody some of these ideas, and such others as may suggest themselves to you, in a general order, and have it printed on pasteboard and hung up at every post, and then make your inspectors enforce it.

We are now in full possession of the country down to the Chattahoochee, and have two good crossings—one at Roswell, and the other at the mouth of Soap Creek, known as Phillips', and I only await a few developments to go ahead. General Vandever telegraphs from Rome that Pillow's force has gone toward Meridian. If another attempt is made from that quarter, it should be counteracted by moving behind it from Rome and Gunter's Landing.

W. T. SHERMAN,
Major-General, Commanding.

KINGSTON, *July 11, 1864.*

Major General SHERMAN:

Received orders to move yesterday to Cartersville and Allatoona with a portion of my command at this place. It can not be the intention to leave this point unprotected, and I am not advised that there are any troops ordered here to relieve me. There are two important bridges across the Etowah and several fords. Do you want the bridges destroyed?

JNO. E. SMITH,
Brigadier-General.

SHERMAN'S HEADQUARTERS,
July 11, 1864.

Brig. Gen. JOHN E. SMITH:

For the present leave two regiments at Kingston. Take up the planking, but do not disturb the frame work of the bridges.

W. T. SHERMAN,
Major-General.

Hdqrs. Military Division of the Mississippi,
In the Field, Chattahoochee River, July 11, 1864.

Commanding Officer,
Allatoona:

General J. E. Smith's division from Kingston will relieve you, and you will receive orders to move forward and occupy Kenesaw Mountain. Be prepared for the change.

W. T. SHERMAN,
Major-General, Commanding.

Sherman's Headquarters,
July 11, 1864.

General J. E. Smith:

In the next stage of progress you will move forward to Cartersville and the Allatoona Pass; orders are already issued. I give you this notice. I want a depot of supplies kept in Allatoona, and a side track to be made near where the old foundry was.

W. T. SHERMAN,
Major-General.

Chattanooga, Tenn., *July 11, 1864.*
(Received 11.30 p. m.)

Maj. T. T. Eckert:

Am here crossing to rebuild the line and add another wire between this and Atlanta. Line not working south in consequence of storm, though it has worked well all day. Rebels last night withdrew entirely from west bank Chattahoochee, and burned bridge. Said that Johnston is moving toward Stone Mountain, and will not oppose advance on Atlanta. Garrard and General Schofield across Chattahoochee, and intrenched to protect crossing of rest of army, which will cross on the 12th or 13th.

J. C. VAN DUZER.

SPECIAL FIELD ORDERS, } Hdqrs. Army of the Ohio,
                       In the Field, Isham's Ferry, Ga.,
No. 50.   } *July 11, 1864.*

I. Brigadier-General Hascall, commanding Second Division, Twenty-third Army Corps, will move his entire command across the river and put three brigades in line, keeping one in reserve on the right, in the position now occupied and intrenched. General Cox will correspondingly contract his line from the right, strengthen it if necessary, and put at least one brigade in reserve.

II. Supply trains will habitually be kept on the west bank of the river until the corps moves from its present position. They will cross the river to make issues, and return without unnecessary delay. A guard will be furnished from troops on duty at army headquarters.

*   *   *   *   *   *   *

By command of Major-General Schofield.

J. A. CAMPBELL,
Major and Assistant Adjutant-General.

HDQRS. MILITARY DIVISION OF THE MISSISSIPPI,
In the Field, near Chattahoochee River, July 12, 1864.

Lieutenant-General GRANT, *Near Petersburg, Va.:*

DEAR GENERAL: I have written you but once since the opening of the campaign, but I report by telegraph to Halleck daily, and he furnishes you copy. My progress was slower than I calculated, from two chief causes, an uninterrupted rain from June 2 to about the 22d, and the peculiar sub-mountainous character of the country from the Etowah to the Chattahoochee. But we have overcome all opposition and whipped Johnston in every fight where we were on anything like fair terms, and I think the army feels that way, that we can whip the enemy in anything like a fair fight, but he has uniformly taken shelter behind parallels of strong profile made in advance for him by negroes and militia.

I regarded an assault on the 27th of June necessary for two good reasons: first, because the enemy as well as my own army had settled down into the belief that flanking alone was my game; and second, that on that day and ground, had the assault succeeded, I could have broken Johnston's center and pushed his army back in confusion, and with great loss to his bridges over the Chattahoochee. We lost nothing in morale by the assault, for I followed it up on the extreme right and compelled him to quit the very strong lines of Kenesaw, Smyrna Camp, and the Chattahoochee in quick succession.

My railroad and telegraph are now up and we are rapidly accumulating stores in Marietta and Allatoona that will make us less timid about the roads to our rear.

We have been wonderfully supplied in provisions and ammunition; not a day has a regiment been without bread and essentials. Forage has been the hardest, and we have cleaned the country in a breadth of thirty miles of grain and grass. Now the corn is getting a size which makes a good fodder, and the railroad has brought us grain to the extent of four pounds per animal per day.

I have now fulfilled the first part of the grand plan. Our lines are up to the Chattahoochee, and the enemy is beyond. Morgan failed in his Kentucky raid, and we have kept Forrest employed in Mississippi. The defeat of Sturgis was unfortunate; still, he kept Forrest away from us; and now A. J. Smith is out with a force amply sufficient to whip him. I hear of Slocum at Jackson, Miss., and Canby telegraphs me of a trip from Baton Rouge and another against Mobile, so that I am well satisfied that all my people are well employed. At this moment I have Stoneman down the Chattahoochee, with orders, if possible, to cross and strike the West Point road; and Rousseau left Decatur the 8th instant, with about 3,000 cavalry and no wagons, with orders to make a bold push for the railroad between Montgomery and West Point and break it good; to return to the Tennessee, if possible, but if headed off to make for Pensacola. The moment I got Johnston to the Chattahoochee I sent Schofield to a ford above, and he effected a crossing without the loss of a man, and has two pontoon bridges. About the same time, Garrard's cavalry crossed, still above, at Roswell Factory, and has been relieved by Dodge's corps, so that I now cover the Chattahoochee and have two good crossings well secured; by to-night I will have a third.

As soon as I hear from Stoneman I will shift all of McPherson to Roswell and cross Thomas about three miles above the railroad bridge and move against Atlanta, my left well to the east, to get possession of the Augusta road about Decatur or Stone Mountain. I think all will be ready in three days. I will have nearly 100,000 men.

I feel certain we have killed and crippled for Johnston as many as we have sent to the rear. Have sent back about 6,000 or 7,000 prisoners, taken 11 guns of Johnston, and about 10 in Rome. Have destroyed immense iron, cotton, and wool mills, and have possession of all the niter country. My operations have been rather cautious than bold, but on the whole I trust are satisfactory to you. All of Polk's corps is still here; also Hardee's and Hood's, and the Georgia militia, under G. W. Smith.

Let us persevere and trust to the fortunes of war, leaving statesmen to work out the solution.

As ever, your friend,

W. T. SHERMAN.

NEAR CHATTAHOOCHEE RIVER, GA., *July 12, 1864—8.30 p. m.*
(Received 9.20 p. m. 13th.)
Maj. Gen. H. W. HALLECK,
Washington, D. C.:

Mark your maps Phillips' Ferry at mouth of Soap Creek; Powers' Ferry just above the mouth of the Rottenwood and Island Creeks; Pace's Ferry one mile below the mouth of Island Creek. General Dodge's corps is across at Roswell; General Schofield's corps at Phillips'; General Howard's corps at Powers'. All well.

W. T. SHERMAN,
Major-General, Commanding.

SHERMAN'S HEADQUARTERS,
July 12, 1864.
Major-General THOMAS:

McPherson's pontoon train is on its way here. Where do you want it?

W. T. SHERMAN,
Major-General.

THOMAS' HEADQUARTERS,
July 12, 1864.
Major-General SHERMAN:

Please have the pontoon train sent to Powers' Ferry.

GEO. H. THOMAS,
Major-General.

HDQRS. MILITARY DIVISION OF THE MISSISSIPPI,
In the Field, near Chattahoochee River, July 12, 1864.
General THOMAS:

Has anything been done with the pontoon bridge of the enemy at Pace's? We should either get full possession of it or destroy it altogether, for when we cross to the other side, leaving a mere guard of cavalry on this, the bridge might be most mischievous to us. Please order that it be got out at night, or the planking thrown off and boats scuttled.

W. T. SHERMAN,
Major-General, Commanding.

HEADQUARTERS DEPARTMENT OF THE CUMBERLAND,
July 12, 1864.

Major-General SHERMAN:

My intention is to use the enemy's pontoon bridge in connection with ours. If it is not used in that way I will have it destroyed.

GEO. H. THOMAS,
Major-General, U. S. Volunteers.

HDQRS. MILITARY DIVISION OF THE MISSISSIPPI,
In the Field, near Chattahoochee River, July 12, 1864.

General THOMAS:

General McPherson's pontoons will make two good bridges at Powers'. You have enough for two at Pace's. If we can save the rebel bridge it will do for one, and save us enough boats for a spare one, which I want very much, so that in leaving General Stoneman to watch at Turner's he will have a bridge and can threaten to cross at Turner's and below when we are engaged over about the neighborhood of Decatur. Try and manage to accomplish this result. General McPherson will have a good, permanent bridge at Roswell, and General Schofield a pier or trestle bridge at Phillips', so that you will have control of all the pontoons. I estimate we have enough for four bridges, and if we can secure that left by the rebels it will exactly fill our wants.

W. T. SHERMAN,
Major-General, Commanding.

HDQRS. MILITARY DIVISION OF THE MISSISSIPPI,
In the Field, near Chattahoochee River, July 12, 1864.

General THOMAS:

I have ordered the Fifteenth Corps to move this afternoon for Roswell, leaving General Blair's corps to watch Turner's Ferry and Sandtown till General Stoneman returns. Better notify Hooker, as it leaves a gap, but the gap is well covered by the river.

W. T. SHERMAN,
Major-General, Commanding.

HEADQUARTERS ARMY OF THE CUMBERLAND,
July 12, 1864.

Major-General SHERMAN:

General Howard reports two divisions of his command across the river and in position near Abernathy's house. Do you wish Palmer to cross at Pace's Ferry to-morrow or next day? I do not think Buell can reach there in time for him to cross to-morrow.

GEO. H. THOMAS,
Major-General, U. S. Volunteers, Commanding.

SHERMAN'S HEADQUARTERS,
July 12, 1864.

General THOMAS:

Where is Abernathy's house, in reference to Schofield's position?

W. T. SHERMAN,
Major-General.

HEADQUARTERS DEPARTMENT OF THE CUMBERLAND,
July 12, 1864.

Major-General SHERMAN:

Abernathy's house is about one-fourth of a mile in front of Schofield's right center; Howard's troops overlap Schofield's right. I have directed Howard to send a division down the river to Pace's Ferry at daylight Thursday morning to cover the laying of the bridges at that place.

GEO. H. THOMAS,
Major-General.

SHERMAN'S HEADQUARTERS,
July 12, 1864.

General THOMAS:

I understand that Howard has a pontoon bridge at Powers' Ferry

W. T. SHERMAN,
Major-General.

HEADQUARTERS ARMY OF THE CUMBERLAND,
July 12, 1864.

Major-General SHERMAN:

The road from Powers' Ferry to Abernathy's house is said to be good. Howard has one bridge at Powers' Ferry, but I want to replace that by McPherson's bridge, as it will be nearer to his position, and Buell's at Pace's Ferry will be nearer to mine.

GEO. H. THOMAS,
Major-General, U. S. Volunteers.

HDQRS. MILITARY DIVISION OF THE MISSISSIPPI,
In the Field, near Chattahoochee River, July 12, 1864.

General THOMAS:

You need not attempt the crossing at Pace's till I hear further of General Stoneman. The day after to-morrow will be soon enough. I heard of twenty men on foot armed, about four miles from Big Shanty, who questioned a negro as to the force at Marietta. Yet it is well that Colonel Gleason sent the regiment, as it will make it certain. The Fifteenth Corps will pass Marietta in the night for Roswell, and it seems impossible that any force should be near the place described. The brigade from Allatoona for Kenesaw should also be in position by to-morrow.

W. T. SHERMAN,
Major-General, Commanding.

HEADQUARTERS DEPARTMENT OF THE CUMBERLAND,
In the Field, near Vining's Station, Ga., July 12, 1864.

Col. G. P. BUELL,
Comdg. Fifty-eighth Regiment Indiana Vols. (Pontoniers):

COLONEL: The major-general commanding directs that as soon as Captain Kossak has laid a bridge at Powers' Ferry, that you take up your bridge, now at that place, and throw it across the river at Pace's

Ferry below. You will also turn over the work of building the trestle bridge at Phillips' entirely to the Army of the Ohio, or rather to Captain Twining, who commands the engineers of the Twenty-third Corps, and as soon as it is completed you will move your bridge, now at that place, and throw it across the river near the other at Pace's Ferry.

I am, colonel, very respectfully, your obedient servant,

WM. D. WHIPPLE,
Chief of Staff.

HEADQUARTERS DEPARTMENT OF THE CUMBERLAND,
Near Vining's Station, Ga., July 12, 1864.
(Received 1 p. m.)

Maj. Gen. O. O. HOWARD,
Commanding Fourth Army Corps:

GENERAL : General Sherman has ordered Captain Kossak to go with his pontoon to the saw-mill at Rottenwood, which is only a mile back of Powers' Ferry. You will use this bridge instead of Colonel Buell's. If Colonel Buell has a bridge down at Powers' Ferry, relieve it so soon as the trestle is completed at Phillips'. Order Colonel Buell to bridge Pace's.

By command of Major-General Thomas:

SOUTHARD HOFFMAN,
Assistant Adjutant-General.

HEADQUARTERS DEPARTMENT OF THE CUMBERLAND,
In the Field, July 12, 1864.

Maj. Gen. J. M. PALMER,
Commanding Fourteenth Army Corps:

GENERAL: The major-general commanding the department desires that you will make an explanation upon the following subject, thinking there must have been some mistake or misunderstanding: Last evening General Thomas directed General Brannan to cause artillery to be placed in the redoubts abandoned by the enemy near the railroad bridge over the Chattahoochee, for the purpose of firing upon the enemy's works upon the opposite side of the river. General Brannan communicated the order to Major Houghtaling, your chief of artillery, but for some reason the artillery was not placed in the position ordered, or anywhere else. The reason alleged by Major Houghtaling is that you countermanded the order of the major-general commanding, saying that if General Thomas had any order of the kind to communicate he could do so in writing. There was perhaps some misunderstanding.

Very respectfully, your obedient servant,

WM. D. WHIPPLE,
Assistant Adjutant-General.

HDQRS. MILITARY DIVISION OF THE MISSISSIPPI,
In the Field, near Chattahoochee, July 12, 1864—2 a. m.

Major-General McPHERSON,
Commanding Army of the Tennessee:

GENERAL: I have received your dispatches of last night. You may put in motion at once the Fifteenth Corps and trains for Roswell, leaving General Blair with such artillery and wagons as he may need to await the return of General Stoneman, and to make in the mean time the necessary demonstrations about Sandtown, Howell's, and Turner's. The enemy having destroyed his bridges, cannot come back on General Blair, and therefore he can strip light so as to follow you as little encumbered as possible when General Stoneman does get back or is heard from. Instruct General Blair fully on these points, and let him report to me direct while thus detached. Let your troops move in the cool of the evening and moonlight and in the morning, sparing men and animals as much as possible. You will then proceed in person to Roswell, and take control of matters on that flank, giving the necessary orders to your own troops and General Garrard's cavalry. I want everything done that is prudent and necessary at Roswell to make it a kind of secondary base for operations against Atlanta, and the roads east toward Augusta and Macon. As you know, the bridges are under progress and the telegraph will be there as soon as you. The ford there, though rough, is always practicable in case of accident to ourselves or the bridges, and constitutes one of the reasons for its use as a point of departure, and the roads to and from Roswell are all old and much used. The country thereabouts is also represented as abounding in grass, grain, and corn-fields, all of which will come into use. Your wagons and artillery should move by Marietta and fill up with provisions, forage, and ammunition, and, I think, that also is the best road for the troops, although a few miles could be saved by cutting across by Smyrna Camp-Ground. If convenient, you might ride by the Turner's Ferry road along the enemy's recent works by General Thomas' and my headquarters to confer and to compare maps.

I am, with respect, yours, &c.,

W. T. SHERMAN,
Major-General, Commanding.

HDQRS. MILITARY DIVISION OF THE MISSISSIPPI,
In the Field, near Chattahoochee River, July 12, 1864.

General DODGE,
Roswell, via Marietta:

The Fifteenth Corps will start this p. m. for Roswell via Marietta. General McPherson will follow in person to-morrow; the Seventeenth Corps will remain for a few days to await the return of General Stoneman. All quiet everywhere.

W. T. SHERMAN,
Major-General, Commanding.

HEADQUARTERS LEFT WING, SIXTEENTH ARMY CORPS,
Roswell, Ga., July 12, 1864.

Maj. Gen. WILLIAM T. SHERMAN,
Commanding Military Division of the Mississippi:

I send herewith a rough map* of the country south of here, taking in nearly all the roads. I got it up from surveys and from information received from different citizens, and I think generally it is as correct as such maps can be made. The roads, citizens living upon them, &c., are pretty reliable. You will see it is different from any of our maps. I pushed my mounted infantry down five miles to-day to the crossing of Nancy's Creek, where we found the enemy's cavalry in force, and they followed

---

* Not found.

us back. One-half mile above the bridge at this place is a ferry, and will be a good place to put in a pontoon bridge should you desire. The river is about 300 feet wide. I will have the bridge at this place finished to-morrow. All the bents are up to-night, stringers on, and planked one-third the distance across. When done it will take safely over any number of troops and their trains. All quiet here. River slowly rising.

I am, very respectfully, your obedient servant,

G. M. DODGE,
Major-General, Commanding.

HEADQUARTERS LEFT WING, SIXTEENTH ARMY CORPS,
Roswell, Ga., July 12, 1864.

Lieut. Col. WILLIAM T. CLARK,
Asst. Adjt. Gen., Department and Army of the Tennessee:

COLONEL: There is nothing new here; all quiet. We are progressing on the bridge, and work night and day. My mounted infantry has been down five miles south of here, where they strike the enemy's cavalry. All deserters and prisoners of war state that the enemy's works are from two to four miles north of Atlanta. None this side of that. A very intelligent man, who left Lee's army at Petersburg last Wednesday, came in. He says this is the first time that Lee's army was ever discouraged; that their losses have been enormous, and that every man in the country has gone to it. Ewell, with his corps, he says, has been sent on a raid to Pennsylvania. He also says that there are no guards on the railroads after getting twenty miles away from Atlanta, and that Johnston's trains have all gone to Augusta, Ga.

Very respectfully, your obedient servant,

G. M. DODGE,
Major-General, Commanding.

HEADQUARTERS SEVENTEENTH ARMY CORPS,
Near Chattahoochee River, Ga., July 12, 1864.

Brig. Gen. M. D. LEGGETT, *Commanding Third Division:*

GENERAL: Inclosed please find copy of Special Field Orders, No. 66, Department and Army of the Tennessee.*

The major-general commanding desires you to make such demonstrations as you may think best. Colonel Scott might throw one or two companies across the river and drive away their skirmishers, and the enemy might be driven across the river above Howell's, provided your men are not too much exposed in doing so. These are merely suggestions by which you are not to be governed unless supported by your judgment.

I am, general, very respectfully, your obedient servant,

A. J. ALEXANDER,
Assistant Adjutant-General.

HDQRS. THIRD DIVISION, SEVENTEENTH ARMY CORPS,
Turner's Ferry, July 12, 1864.

Lieut. Col. A. J. ALEXANDER, *Assistant Adjutant-General:*

COLONEL: During the day we have done all in our power to extend our information as to the character and number of the enemy in our

---

* See p. 130.

front. The Forty-first Mississippi is opposite us near the mouth of the Nickajack; the Thirty-second Georgia is opposite to us at Howell's Ferry, with what supports, if any, I do not know. Stewart's division, of Hood's corps, is opposed to us in the region of Sandtown Ferry. A band of guerrillas, consisting of Georgia State Troops, was on this side of the Chattahoochee, just beyond the Sweet Water, last night. Stoneman was near Campbellton this morning, not having effected a crossing. He reports the enemy, 8,000 strong, opposing him.

Very respectfully,

M. D. LEGGETT,
Brigadier-General.

CARTERSVILLE, *July 12, 1864.*

Lieut. DAVID F. HOW,
　　Actg. Asst. Adjt. Gen., Headquarters Cavalry:

Major Thayer, Tenth Ohio Cavalry, has returned from expedition. Eight miles above Canton he dispersed a band of rebels, driving them into the mountains. Captain Oglethorpe, commanding the band, was wounded. The major brought in 17 mules, 7 horses, and 15 deserters from rebel army, and 2 prisoners of war.

W. W. LOWE,
Colonel, Commanding.

SHERMAN'S HEADQUARTERS,
July 12, 1864. (Received 9.30 p. m. 13th.)

Major ECKERT:

Heads of two columns crossed. Howard has two divisions crossed; think all will be across by 15th. In the mean time supplies are being accumulated rapidly.

J. C. VAN DUZER.

SPECIAL ⎫　　HDQRS. MIL. DIV. OF THE MISS.,
FIELD ORDERS, ⎬　　*In the Field, near Chattahoochee River,*
No. 34. ⎭　　　　　　　　　　　*July 12, 1864.*

I. The Fifth Regiment Iowa Infantry is hereby transferred from the Department of the Tennessee to the Department of the Cumberland, and the commanding officer will report to Maj. Gen. George H. Thomas for instructions.

*　　　*　　　*　　　*　　　*　　　*　　　*

By order of Maj. Gen. W. T. Sherman:

L. M. DAYTON,
Aide-de-Camp.

SPECIAL FIELD ORDERS, ⎱　　HDQRS. DEPT. OF THE TENN.,
No. 66. ⎰　　*Near Chattahoochee River, July 12, 1864.*

*　　　*　　　*　　　*　　　*　　　*

II. Maj. Gen. John A. Logan, commanding Fifteenth Army Corps, will march his command at 5 o'clock this p. m. toward the bridge across the Chattahoochee near Roswell Factory, making a distance of about ten miles to-night if practicable. He will resume his march at an early hour to-morrow morning, thus protecting his men and animals from the heat of the day.

III. Maj. Gen. F. P. Blair, commanding Seventeenth Army Corps, will remain in his present position until the return of General Stoneman, or until further orders, making such demonstrations about Sandtown, Howell's, and Turner's as may be made necessary, communicating in the mean time with Major-General Sherman, and receiving from him instructions. Four days' rations will be issued to the men of the Seventeenth Corps, and the trains sent to Marietta with the general supply train.

IV. All the wagons and artillery will move by Marietta and fill up with provisions, forage, and ammunition.

By order of Maj. Gen. James B. McPherson:

WM. T. CLARK,
Assistant Adjutant-General.

HEADQUARTERS DEPARTMENT OF THE CUMBERLAND,
July 13, 1864.

Major-General SHERMAN:

I will try to save enough of the pontoon bridge to make one for Stoneman.

GEO. H. THOMAS,
Major-General, U. S. Volunteers.

HDQRS. MILITARY DIVISION OF THE MISSISSIPPI,
In the Field, near Chattahoochee River, July 13, 1864.

General THOMAS:

Get everything ready and wait till I hear of Stoneman. Blair must remain where he is till Stoneman comes, and will have a two days' march to reach Roswell, giving you ample time.

W. T. SHERMAN,
Major-General, Commanding.

HDQRS. MILITARY DIVISION OF THE MISSISSIPPI,
In the Field, near Chattahoochee River, July 13, 1864.

General THOMAS:

Do you propose to effect a crossing at Pace's to-morrow? If not ordered, better wait one more day. I have my orders ready, conditioned on Stoneman's return. Expected back the day after to-morrow. Did you see anything worth reporting to-day?

W. T. SHERMAN,
Major-General, Commanding.

HEADQUARTERS DEPARTMENT OF THE CUMBERLAND,
July 13, 1864.

Major-General SHERMAN:

I am ready to effect a crossing at Pace's Ferry to-morrow, but will wait if you think best until you hear from Stoneman. I have not seen anything worth reporting to-day.

GEO. H. THOMAS,
Major-General, U. S. Volunteers, Commanding.

SHERMAN'S HEADQUARTERS,
July 13, 1864.

Major-General THOMAS:

Telegraph office is now opened at Roswell.

W. T. SHERMAN,
Major-General.

HEADQUARTERS FOURTH ARMY CORPS,
July 13, 1864—8 p. m.

General WHIPPLE,
Chief of Staff:

GENERAL: I have reconnoitered for about a mile to my right and front. Met some rebel cavalry pickets, but no infantry, on the bluff just across Island Creek. General Wood will march for Pace's Ferry at 5 a. m. to-morrow. After examination, I concluded to start a trestle bridge, and will try to finish it by to-morrow night.

Respectfully,

O. O. HOWARD,
Major-General.

HEADQUARTERS DEPARTMENT OF THE CUMBERLAND,
In the Field, July 13, 1864—8.30 p. m.

Maj. Gen. O. O. HOWARD,
Commanding Fourth Army Corps:

GENERAL: In consequence of Major-General Sherman wishing to wait until he hears from General Stoneman before crossing the Fourteenth Corps, the major-general commanding directs me to write that you need not move your division down the river in the morning, as heretofore ordered, but await further orders in your present camp.

I am, general, very respectfully, your obedient servant,

WM. D. WHIPPLE,
Assistant Adjutant-General.

HEADQUARTERS DEPARTMENT OF THE CUMBERLAND,
In the Field, July 13, 1864.

Maj. Gen. J. M. PALMER,
Commanding Fourteenth Army Corps:

GENERAL: A pontoon bridge will be laid at Pace's Ferry to-morrow morning probably by 8 o'clock. The major-general commanding directs that as soon as the bridge is ready you commence crossing your corps, and continue until it is all over. Major-General Howard will to-morrow morning march a division from Powers' Ferry down the south bank of the river for the purpose of covering your crossing. As soon as you get one division across please relieve General Howard's division and permit it to return to its camp.

Very respectfully, your obedient servant,

WM. D. WHIPPLE,
Assistant Adjutant-General.

HEADQUARTERS ARMY OF THE OHIO,
July 13, 1864.

Major-General SHERMAN, *Comdg. Military Div. of the Mississippi:*

GENERAL: I have been reconnoitering to-day, and have got a little additional information about roads, &c., which I will send you to-morrow. In the morning I will move forward onto the ridge now occupied by General Howard, connecting with him, and refuse my left, so as to cover my bridge. I will then be able to reconnoiter farther.

Very respectfully,

J. M. SCHOFIELD,
Major-General.

———

HEADQUARTERS ARMY OF THE OHIO,
Isham's Ferry, Ga., July 13, 1864.

Maj. Gen. O. O. HOWARD, *Commanding Fourth Army Corps:*

GENERAL: I have reconnoitered the ridge, which you now occupy, about two miles beyond your left; also the ground about the head-waters of the creek which runs between my present position and yours. I can easily place my corps on good ground, so as to connect my present right with your left and form with you a continuous line, covering the two bridges. I will take that position in the morning if we do not get orders for a farther advance. I would do so this evening, but that my men are drawing clothing to-day, and there appears to be no considerable force of the enemy within several miles of us. If you get information of the enemy which seems to make it advisable for me to change my line to-night please inform me and I will act accordingly.

Very respectfully, your obedient servant,

J. M. SCHOFIELD,
Major-General, Commanding.

———

MOORE'S BRIDGE, GA., *July 13, 1864.*

Major-General SHERMAN:

GENERAL: By taking a roundabout way, and by unfrequented roads, our parties succeeded in capturing or cutting off every scout the enemy had out. We surprised the guard at the bridge (the First Tennessee Cavalry), and drove them from the bridge before they had time to set fire to the straw and pine-knots prepared for its conflagration. The Eleventh Kentucky Cavalry had the advance, under Colonel Adams, and did the thing handsomely. The bridge had been partially destroyed by tearing up the sleepers and planks, but we will have it repaired during the night. It is a covered structure, very well built, 480 feet long, on two main spans. One of the couriers we captured came down on this side of the river, bore a message to the commanding officer here that the Yankees were coming in large force, and that he must hold the bridge at all hazards, and that re-enforcements were on the way. This point is twenty-five miles from Campbellton. There is another bridge at Franklin, twenty-five miles lower down. Newnan, on the railroad, is ten miles from here, and I understand the road leads through dense woods. We will try what we can do to-morrow morning as soon as it is light. I can hear of no railroad bridge in this vicinity. The people, negroes and others, say the road runs on a ridge, but if we do nothing to the road it will create a diversion.

GEORGE STONEMAN,
Major-General.

ROSWELL, *July 13, 1864—3.30 p. m.*

Major-General SHERMAN:

Telegraph is finished here. Scouting parties went five miles south on Buck Head road. Found no enemy. Enemy is strong on Decatur road near Vance's Creek, and also on road one mile south of McAfee's Bridge. All quiet and everything progressing satisfactorily. Bridge will be finished to-day.

G. M. DODGE,
Major-General.

HDQRS. MILITARY DIVISION OF THE MISSISSIPPI,
In the Field, near Chattahoochee River, July 13, 1864.

General DODGE,
Roswell:

General McPherson left here about 10 a. m. for Marietta and Roswell. Report to me this evening his arrival and that of the Fifteenth Corps. All very quiet here.

W. T. SHERMAN,
Major-General, Commanding.

ROSWELL, *July 13, 1864—9 p. m.*

Major-General SHERMAN:

Advance of Fifteenth Army Corps is camped near Roswell. General McPherson has not arrived. Men who left Atlanta yesterday, employés in Government shops, say all machinery, stores, &c., have been packed up and are being sent to Augusta. They came by way of Decatur. Report no force of enemy in that direction, or works. They think most of infantry is west of railroad. They saw no works after leaving Atlanta. Bridge is built; is double track.

G. M. DODGE,
Major-General.

HEADQUARTERS SEVENTEENTH ARMY CORPS,
Near Chattahoochee River, July 13, 1864.

Major-General SHERMAN,
Commanding Military Division of the Mississippi:

GENERAL: In obedience to your order conveyed in the indorsement on General Stoneman's communication, I have directed General Leggett to picket the mouth of the Sweet Water Creek. General Leggett pickets now from the mouth of Nickajack Creek to the mouth of Sweet Water Creek, and General Gresham pickets from the mouth of Nickajack to General Hooker's right, a distance of about three miles, making a total distance picketed by this corps of about ten miles. This leaves me a reserve of only two regiments belonging to the Fourth Division, General Gresham's, and which will be placed in the most available position to act as a reserve.

The enemy have at various points along the river small boats in which parties can be conveyed across at night, making it necessary to have heavier pickets than would otherwise be required, which accounts for the fact the reserve is so small.

I have the honor to inclose for your information a report of Brigadier-General Force, commanding the brigade which pickets the extreme right.

Very respectfully, your obedient servant,

FRANK P. BLAIR, JR.,
Major-General, Commanding.

[Inclosure.]

HDQRS. FIRST BRIG., THIRD DIV., 17TH ARMY CORPS,
July 13, 1864.

Capt. J. C. DOUGLASS, *Assistant Adjutant-General:*

CAPTAIN: I have the honor to report that all remains quiet here. The rebels appear to have a continuous picket-line along the river; none on this side. At regular crossings and where ravines go down to the river they have earth-works. I have seen only two embrasures, and they are without guns. Yesterday afternoon one gun opened near Sandtown Ferry on men in a blackberry patch, and another on a reconnoitering party which went to Adaholt's Ferry, at the mouth of Sweet Water. They were brought up and taken away by the rebels; were not in position. About 2 o'clock yesterday afternoon a body of cavalry—some of the pickets call it one, some two regiments—accompanied by four or five wagons, went toward the interior from Sandtown Ferry. A body of infantry—they called it a brigade—accompanied by about thirty wagons, moved to the south of southwest from near the same point. They can be seen only a short distance from the river, however. Opposite Adaholt's, clothes hanging on bushes indicate a small camp. In a valley between Baker's and Sandtown Ferries, perhaps Utoy Creek, has appeared to be a larger camp, judging by smoke and the glimmer of fire. Nothing heard down the river, except two guns about dusk in direction of General Stoneman.

Very respectfully, your obedient servant,

M. F. FORCE,
Brigadier-General, Commanding Brigade.

HEADQUARTERS SEVENTEENTH ARMY CORPS,
Near Chattahoochee River, July 13, 1864.

Brig. Gen. M. D. LEGGETT,
Comdg. Third Division, Seventeenth Army Corps:

GENERAL: A report from General Stoneman to General Sherman says that he made an effort to cross at Campbellton, but from the condition of the river and the position of the enemy was unable to do so. He, however, left one brigade there, and has gone on to Franklin with the remainder of his command. In an indorsement upon this paper General Sherman directs that a picket be kept "at the ford across Sweet Water near its mouth, the same that is used by the cavalry." The major-general commanding desires you to carry this order into effect by placing a strong picket at the point indicated, keeping up your line along the river. As soon as the Fourth Division is allowed to contract its present extended front, should you think it necessary, a portion of it will be placed in such a position as to act in reserve. If the regiment detailed to guard the trains has not returned to you, you will please send a peremptory order for it to join you immediately. Please say by return messenger whether it has returned or not.

I have the honor to be, very respectfully, your obedient servant,

A. J. ALEXANDER,
Assistant Adjutant-General.

ROSWELL, GA., *July 13, 1864—8.30 p. m.*
(Received 3.25 a. m. 14th.)

Maj. T. T. ECKERT:

Line of telegraph opened to this place this morning. No material change in position of army since my last. Movement by left flank progressing steadily, and headquarters of Sherman, Thomas, and McPherson will be here to-morrow. Heat excessive, and men suffer.

J. C. VAN DUZER.

GENERAL ORDERS, }   HDQRS. MIL. DIV. OF THE MISSISSIPPI,
No. 20.   }   *Nashville, Tenn., July 13, 1864.*

I. The grain and hay raised in the State of Tennessee being required for the use of the army, its exportation from the State is positively prohibited.

II. The quartermaster's department will purchase the grain and hay required for consumption by the army.

By order of Maj. Gen. W. T. Sherman:

R. M. SAWYER,
Assistant Adjutant-General.

SPECIAL FIELD ORDERS, }   HDQRS. ARMY OF THE OHIO,
No. 52.   }   *Isham's Ferry, Ga., July 13, 1864.*

    *   *   *   *   *   *   *

VIII. To-morrow morning General Hascall will move his division forward on the ridge now occupied by General Howard's corps, connect with General Howard's left, and prolong his line along the crest of the main ridge until it reaches the dividing ridge between the creeks, in front and on the left of our present position. General Cox will swing forward his right so as to occupy the ridge last described, connect with General Hascall's left, and let his own left rest substantially where it now is. The troops will intrench the new position as soon as they are established upon it. Gaps will be left in the works wherever they may cross the roads which run along the ridges where the lines are to be established, as well as where cross-roads intersect the line. A staff officer will be sent to the division commanders about 7 a. m. to point out the positions referred to.

By command of Major-General Schofield:

J. A. CAMPBELL,
Major and Assistant Adjutant-General.

HDQRS. MILITARY DIVISION OF THE MISSISSIPPI,
In the Field, near Chattahoochee River, July 14, 1864.
(Received 6 p. m.)

Maj. Gen. H. W. HALLECK,
Washington, D. C.:

If State recruiting agents must come into the limits of my command under the law, I have the honor to request that the commanding officers or adjutants of regiments be constituted such agents, and that States be entitled to a credit for recruits they may enlist, who are accepted and mustered in by the regular mustering officer of their division and corps. This will obviate the difficulty I apprehend from civilian agents.

W. T. SHERMAN,
Major-General, Commanding.

Near Chattahoochee River, Ga., *July 14, 1864—10 p. m.*
(Received 3.45 a. m. 15th.)
Maj. Gen. H. W. Halleck,
Washington, D. C.:

All is well. I have now accumulated stores at Allatoona and Marietta, both fortified and garrisoned points. I have also three points at which to cross the Chattahoochee in my possession, and only await General Stoneman's return from a trip down the river to cross the army in force and move on Atlanta. Stoneman is now out two days, and had orders to be back on the fourth or fifth day, at farthest. Rousseau should reach Opelika about July 17. Before regulations are made for the States to send recruiting officers into the rebel States, I must express my opinion that it is the height of folly. I cannot permit it here, and I will not have a set of fellows here hanging about on any such pretenses. We have no means to transport and feed them. The Sanitary and Christian Commissions are enough to eradicate all traces of Christianity out of our minds, much less a set of unscrupulous State agents in search of recruits. All these dodges and make-shifts but render us ridiculous in our own estimation. I must protect my army, and I say beforehand, I have no means to transport recruiting parties south of Nashville, or to feed them, if they come here in spite of me.

W. T. SHERMAN,
Major-General, Commanding.

Hdqrs. Chief of Cavalry, Dept. of the Cumberland,
Near Vining's Station, July 14, 1864.
Brig. Gen. E. M. McCook,
Comdg. First Cavalry Division, Dept. of the Cumberland:

General: The general commanding directs that you move with your division to-morrow morning to this vicinity. When the Army of the Cumberland crosses the river or moves from its present position your division will patrol and picket the Chattahoochee from Pace's to Turner's Ferry. Lilly's battery will be posted by General Brannan in position on the left of and near the railroad crossing of the river. The work for it is now being made.

I am, general, very respectfully, your obedient servant,
DAVID F. HOW,
Lieutenant and Acting Assistant Adjutant-General.

Headquarters First Division Cavalry,
Hargrove's House, July 14, 1864.
Brig. Gen. W. D. Whipple,
Chief of Staff, Department of the Cumberland:

I have the honor to report that in compliance with your letter of instructions, dated July 11, I proceeded to Dallas, twenty-nine miles distant from my camp, on the morning of the 12th and reached there at 5 p. m. the same day. I succeeded in arresting Green B. Turner, Stephen Allen, and Aleck. Bullock. Nick Allen and Lem. Anderson, two of the other parties you instructed me to arrest, are across the Chattahoochee; John Hicks could not be found. No force of the enemy has been in that vicinity, but small scouting parties of from eight to ten pass through Dallas every few days and frequently return with prisoners.

My men captured 4 of their soldiers and 7 mules. As you desired, I endeavored to impress upon the minds of all the citizens remaining in Dallas the fact that they would meet with prompt and severe punishment if guilty of any acts in the future which would either disturb the peace of the community or give aid and comfort to the enemies of the Government. On my return I marched on a road leading into the Powder Springs and Lost Mountain road—one our army has not yet passed over. We found many of the enemy's dead buried along it; at one place over sixty graves, and at several others from twenty-five to thirty in each. I judge from this that their loss on our right was heavier than supposed.

Very respectfully, your obedient servant, •

EDWARD M. McCOOK,
Brigadier-General, Commanding Division.

HDQRS. THIRD DIVISION, FOURTH ARMY CORPS,
South of the Chattahoochee, July 14, 1864.

Col. J. S. FULLERTON,
Assistant Adjutant-General:

COLONEL: Moore, a scout whom I sent out on the 13th at daylight, has just returned, and makes the following statement: He left Atlanta at 3 p. m. yesterday. He came out of Atlanta, returning by the Peach Tree road. About a mile from the town on this road the rebels were busily engaged in constructing four separate forts on the separate hills. The inhabitants of Atlanta are still leaving, going farther south, and the town is pretty well cleaned out. All the valuable property, such as machinery and army stores, has been removed, and he heard toward Augusta. Moore says only a small supply of subsistence is kept in Atlanta, only so much as could be readily moved in case of a retreat. Moore says General Bragg arrived from Richmond on Tuesday evening and a brigade of four regiments from Pollard, Ala. Moore says that it was reported in the rebel camps that this brigade was from Kirby Smith, but that he talked with the men of the brigade, who told him they were from Pollard, Ala., and had never been with Kirby Smith. Moore says in returning he came out by the Peach Tree road till he struck the Turner's Ferry road, which he took and went to the extreme left of the rebel infantry line. This point is a small church in sight of the ferry. General Manigault's brigade is on the extreme left; thence to Campbellton the river is watched by squads of cavalry. From the left of the rebel line Moore returned to Buck Head, where he found Wheeler's cavalry, and thence into our lines through General Dodge's command, to whom he reported. Moore brings an Atlanta paper of yesterday.

Respectfully, &c.,

TH. J. WOOD,
Brigadier-General of Volunteers, Commanding.

P. S.—Moore says as he passed along the rebel lines yesterday afternoon, Hardee's corps, which has been in the center for some time, was breaking up its camp, and is, he understood, to take position to the right of Stewart's corps, which would place Hardee's corps on the extreme rebel right, and Moore says it would be entirely to the right or east of the railroad.

WOOD.

[Indorsement.]

HEADQUARTERS FOURTH ARMY CORPS,
Powers' Ferry, Chattahoochee River, Ga., July 14, 1864.

Respectfully forwarded for the information of the major-general commanding Department of the Cumberland.

O. O. HOWARD,
Major-General, Commanding.

ROSWELL BRIDGE, *July 14, 1864.*

Major-General SHERMAN,
        Commanding:

GENERAL: The bridge is finished, and the Fifteenth Army Corps will cross the river this afternoon and be in position by night, on the left and a little in advance of General Dodge.   Nothing new here.

JAS. B. McPHERSON,
Major-General.

HDQRS. MILITARY DIVISION OF THE MISSISSIPPI,
In the Field, near Chattahoochee River, July 14, 1864.

General McPHERSON,
        Roswell:

General Blair reports a movement of cavalry down the river on the other side all last night, drawn there doubtless by Stoneman's and Rousseau's movement.   Let General Garrard feel out strong and disturb those that are left.

W. T. SHERMAN,
Major-General, Commanding.

ROSWELL BRIDGE, *July 14, 1864—5 p. m.*

Major-General SHERMAN:

Would it not be a good move for Garrard to cross his division at McAfee's Bridge, push one of his brigades out toward Cross Keys, and engage the cavalry there; and send his other brigade rapidly via Lawrenceville down to Covington on the railroad, and burn the bridge across Yellow River and other streams in the vicinity, and do all the damage they can?   The distance is forty miles.

JAS. B. McPHERSON,
Major-General.

HDQRS. MILITARY DIVISION OF THE MISSISSIPPI,
In the Field, near Chattahoochee River, July 14, 1864.

General McPHERSON,
        Roswell:

The bridge over Yellow River is too well guarded by men and redoubts to be carried by our cavalry, but General Garrard might dash at the road east of the Stone Mountain.   See him, and it is useless to attempt anything unless he be willing, for until our infantry is out as far as the railroad he may encounter most of Wheeler's cavalry, but I have no doubt most of Johnston's cavalry is gone to the south toward West Point, drawn there by Generals Stoneman and Rousseau. A dash at the road would develop the truth, but to be certain, the infantry should be out as far as the head of Nancy's Creek. I hope to hear of General Stoneman to-night.

W. T. SHERMAN,
Major-General, Commanding.

HDQRS. DEPARTMENT AND ARMY OF THE TENNESSEE,
Near [Roswell] Bridge, July 14, 1864.

Maj. Gen. JOHN A. LOGAN,
Commanding Fifteenth Corps:

GENERAL: You will move your command across the Chattahoochee on the bridge just finished by Major-General Dodge's command and take up a position on the Roswell and Atlanta road in the vicinity of a man's house named Beaver, about two miles from the river. Captain Reese, of the Engineers, will indicate the position.

Very respectfully, your obedient servant,

JAS. B. McPHERSON,
Major-General.

HEADQUARTERS SEVENTEENTH ARMY CORPS,
July 14, 1864.

Brigadier-General LEGGETT,
Commanding Third Division, Seventeenth Army Corps:

GENERAL: General Sherman is very anxious to know at the very earliest moment of the return of Major-General Stoneman. The general therefore requests that you will direct the commanding officer of the troops on your extreme right, if possible, to communicate this to the commanding officers of the cavalry on your right with the request that they send an express to you, which please forward to these headquarters.

I have the honor to be, very respectfully, your obedient servant,

A. J. ALEXANDER,
Assistant Adjutant-General.

HDQRS. MILITARY DIVISION OF THE MISSISSIPPI,
In the Field, near Chattahoochee River, July 14, 1864.

Commanding Officer of the Troops ordered from Allatoona to Kenesaw:

The position at Kenesaw is selected on account of its peculiar strength. The main part of your force should be held at some good camp near its base, with a strong picket and lookout on the eastern hill and the one known as Brushy Hill, occupied by General Leggett, during our operations before Marietta. The point known as the tan-yard, or it may be the water station, appeared to me the best point for your camp. The chief object is to guard the railroad as far down as Marietta and to protect our stores in Marietta. There are three regiments in Marietta to load and unload cars and to guard the place, and, should the depot become threatened, you will make the proper disposition to cover it. I don't want troops quartered in a town because the universal experience is that they lose in discipline and efficiency. Keep your regiments in good camps, with regular guard mountings and evening

parades. When you send out patrols and expeditions give clear written instructions, and caution your men not to straggle about and get
picked up in detail. As long as our main army is here or in front no
enemy will threaten you but small squads of cavalry that are sent on
errands of mischief. Send frequent patrols down to Lost Mountain and
Powder Springs; also up toward Laughing Gal and Canton. Show no
mercy to guerrillas or persons threatening our road or telegraph. Remove to the rear all suspicious persons and families, and bear in mind
that the safety of this army is not to be imperiled by any citizens, no
matter how hard their friends may plead. I understand you have four
regiments besides the Fifty-third Indiana, which should join General
Blair as he passes Marietta en route for Roswell to-morrow or next day.
Instruct your men not to fear cavalry. Infantry can take to the bushes
and hills so quickly that they are safe against any odds of cavalry, and
by waylaying the road at known points can defeat cavalry by firing
from ambush.

W. T. SHERMAN,
Major-General, Commanding.

Sherman's Headquarters,
July 14, 1864.

Brig. Gen. John E. Smith:

I regard Allatoona of the first importance in our future plans. It is
a second Chattanooga; its front and rear are susceptible of easy defense
and its flanks are strong. The post properly extends from the Etowah
to Allatoona Depot, and flanks the Pumpkin Vine and Allatoona Creeks,
embracing a space wherein can be accumulated supplies that would
make a raid to our rear less to be feared, giving us the means of living
till repairs could be made. I want you to study it in all its bearings. As
long as our army is in front, in good order, of course nothing could
threaten Allatoona, and then its garrison should scour the country for
miles around, especially up the Pumpkin Vine and Euharlee Creeks
and in the direction of Noonday and Canton. Everything in the nature
of grain, forage, and vegetables should be collected. No suspicious
citizens should be allowed near the railroad or in the country. The
safety of this army must not be imperiled by citizens. If you entertain a bare suspicion against any family send it to the North. Any
loafer or suspicious person seen at any time should be imprisoned and
sent off. If guerrillas trouble the road or wires between Kingston and
Acworth, they should be shot without mercy. Rowland's Springs,
Laughing Gal, Canton, and Dallas should receive sudden and unexpected visits by night by parties about 200 strong. I will soon be in
motion again and will feel more confidence that I know you are at
Allatoona.

W. T. SHERMAN,
Major-General, Commanding.

Hdqrs. Military Division of the Mississippi,
In the Field, near Chattahoochee River, July 14, 1864.

Commanding Officer,
Marietta, Ga.:

I have ordered three regiments at Marietta and a brigade at Kenesaw.
This brigade will come to Marietta in case of danger to the depot, but

Kenesaw is selected on account of its security and proximity, and troops are more easily disciplined in camp than in a town. Although you are chiefly needed as a town guard and to handle stores, you should not neglect the military duties. Always be prepared for a dash of cavalry. Occupy the court-house and barricade and loophole the doors and windows; also make a good ladder to the roof, and make the balustrade bullet-proof, so that a party of men on its roof could sweep the streets. Other houses should also be selected and prepared near the railroad depot. A few hours' work will convert any good brick or stone house into a citadel. Arms and ammunition should always be kept handy, and pickets kept well out to give notice. All citizens of whom you entertain the least suspicion should be sent North, no matter the seeming hardships. The safety of our depot must not depend upon the pleasure and convenience of citizens. Should any one be caught molesting our road, telegraph wires, or our stores, he should be disposed of finally and summarily, especially if disguised in the garb of a citizen.

W. T. SHERMAN,
Major-General, Commanding.

SPECIAL FIELD ORDERS, }   HDQRS. MIL. DIV. OF THE MISS.,
                        }   In the Field, near Chattahoochee River,
No. 35.   }   July 14, 1864.

Preliminary steps having already begun, the following general plan will be observed and adhered to:

I. Major-General Thomas will prepare to cross his army at Powers' and Pace's Ferries, and take position out from the Chattahoochee River, until he controls the country from Island Creek to Kyle's Bridge, over Nancy's Creek, but will not move the whole of General Palmer's and General Hooker's corps across until he hears that General Stoneman is back from his present expedition. He will endeavor to provide General Stoneman enough pontoon boats, balks, and chesses to make one bridge. He will dispose of General McCook's cavalry and detachments of his own infantry to watch the Chattahoochee about the old railroad crossing.

II. As soon as General Stoneman returns he will dispose his cavalry to watch the Chattahoochee at Turner's Ferry and about the mouth of Nickajack, connecting by patrols with General McCook, and will, if possible, procure enough pontoons to make a bridge ready on the first chance to cross the river about Howell's or Sandtown, and break the Atlanta and West Point railroad and telegraph.

III. Major-General Schofield, after having well secured his crossing-place at Phillips', will move out toward Cross Keys until he controls the ridge between Island and Nancy's Creeks and the road represented as leading from Roswell to Buck Head.

IV. Major-General Blair will immediately, on the return of Major-General Stoneman, move rapidly to Roswell and join his army. Major-General McPherson will then move his command out, either by the Cross Keys road or the old Hightower trail, until he is abreast of Major-General Schofield, and General Garrard, with his cavalry, will scout from McAfee's Bridge toward Pinckneyville, and if no enemy is there in force will picket McAfee's Bridge and take post on General McPherson's left, about Buchanan's.

V. The whole army will thus form a concave line behind Nancy's Creek, extending from Kyle's Bridge to Buchanan's, but no attempt will

be made to form a line of battle.   Each army will form a unit and connect with its neighbor by a line of pickets.   Should the enemy assume
the offensive at any point, which is not expected until we reach below
Peach Tree Creek, the neighboring army will at once assist the one
attacked.   All preliminary steps may at once be made, but no corps
need move to any great distance from the river until advised that
General Stoneman is back.

VI. Major-General Thomas will study well the country toward Decatur
via Buck Head, Major-General Schofield to a point of the railroad four
miles northeast of Decatur, and Major-General McPherson and General
Garrard that toward Stone Mountain.   Each army should leave behind the Chattahoochee River, at its bridge or at Marietta, all wagons
or incumbrances not absolutely needed for battle.   A week's work
after crossing the Chattahoochee should determine the first object
aimed at, viz, the possession of the Atlanta and Augusta road east of
Decatur, or of Atlanta itself.

By order of Maj. Gen. W. T. Sherman:

L. M. DAYTON,
Aide-de-Camp.

CITY POINT, VA., *July 15, 1864.*

Major-General HALLECK,
Washington, D. C.:

In view of the possible recurrence of the late raid into Maryland, I
would suggest that the following precautions be taken: First. There
should be an immediate call for all the troops we are likely to require.
Second. Washington City, Baltimore, and Harper's Ferry should be
designated as schools of instruction, and all troops raised east of the
State of Ohio should be sent to one of these three places as fast as
raised.   Nashville, Decatur, and Stevenson should also be named as
schools of instruction, and all troops raised in Ohio and west of it
should be sent to those.   By doing this we always have the benefit of
our increased force, and they in turn improve more rapidly by contact
with veteran troops.   To supply Sherman, all the rolling-stock that can
possibly be got to him should be sent.   An effort ought to be made to
transfer a large portion of stores now at Nashville to Chattanooga.
This might be facilitated by withdrawing for awhile the rolling-stock
from the Nashville and Reynoldsburg Railroad, and a large part of the
stock upon the Kentucky roads.   There is every indication now, judging from the tone of the Southern press, that, unless Johnston is re-
enforced, Atlanta will not be defended.   They seem to calculate largely
upon driving Sherman out by keeping his lines of communication cut.
If he can supply himself once with ordnance and quartermaster's stores,
and partially with subsistence, he will find no difficulty in staying until
a permanent line can be opened with the south coast.   The road from
Chattanooga to Atlanta will be much more easily defended than that
north of the Tennessee.   With the supplies above indicated at Chattanooga, with, say, sixty days' provisions there, I think there will be no
doubt but that the country will supply the balance.   Sherman will,
once in Atlanta, devote himself to collecting the resources of the country.   He will take everything the people have, and will then issue from
the stores so collected to rich and poor alike.   As he will take all their
stock, they will have no use for grain further than is necessary for
bread.   If the enemy do not detach from here against Sherman, they
will, in case Atlanta falls, bring most of Johnston's army here with the

expectation of driving us out, and then unite against Sherman. They will fail if they attempt this programme. My greatest fear is of their sending troops to Johnston first. Sherman ought to be notified of the possibility of a corps going from here, and should be prepared to take up a good defensive position in case one is sent—one which he could hold against such increase. If Hunter cannot get to Gordonsville and Charlottesville to cut the railroad, he should make all the valley south of the Baltimore and Ohio road a desert as high up as possible. I do not mean that houses should be burned, but all provisions and stock should be removed, and the people notified to move out.

U. S. GRANT,
Lieutenant-General.

HDQRS. MILITARY DIVISION OF THE MISSISSIPPI,
In the Field, near Chattahoochee River, July 15, 1864.

General THOMAS:

A man came in last night from Columbus, Ga., with provost-marshal's pass of July 4, who had escaped from Anderson[ville], and was one who was captured the time I went to Meridian. He gives but little news, and says the guard at Columbus and West Point are not over 500 each. Heard nothing from Mobile or Montgomery on his way up. A scout in from Atlanta with dates to 3 p. m. 13th says Bragg and staff had arrived, and Kirby Smith, with 20,000, was expected from Meridian. All bosh of course. All newspapers have quit Atlanta except the Memphis Appeal. That, I suppose, is tired of moving, and wants to be let alone.

W. T. SHERMAN,
Major-General, Commanding.

HDQRS. MILITARY DIVISION OF THE MISSISSIPPI,
In the Field, near Chattahoochee River, July 15, 1864.

General THOMAS:

I have a letter from Major-General Stoneman, dated 13th, at Moore's Bridge, on the Chattahoochee. He had captured the scouts and drove off the bridge guard before he could burn it. This bridge is twenty-five miles below Campbellton, on the road from Carrollton to Newnan. General Stoneman said, at daylight next morning, viz, yesterday, he could make a demonstration on the railroad ten miles out. He captured a courier to the bridge guard, saying that a Yankee force was coming, but the bridge must be held at all hazards till the re-enforcements arrived.

W. T. SHERMAN,
Major-General, Commanding.

HDQRS. MILITARY DIVISION OF THE MISSISSIPPI,
In the Field, near Chattahoochee River, July 15, 1864.

General THOMAS:

I have heard from General Stoneman. He attempted to cross at Moore's Bridge, but encountered too much artillery, and thought it imprudent to attempt, lest he might not get back. He is now near

Villa Rica, and will move this evening to Sweet Water. I have ordered him to come on over to Turner's Ferry and relieve General Blair, whom I have ordered to draw out of sight of the enemy to-night and move to-morrow for Roswell. You may therefore make all preparations to cross at Pace's Ferry to-morrow night or next morning and move out to control the bridge over Nancy's Creek. I will move my headquarters to-morrow to Powers' Ferry. The redoubt from which General McCook is to control the lower bridge over Peach Tree Creek should be prepared for him to-night by infantry. Cavalry cannot work on parapets to-morrow.

W. T. SHERMAN,
Major-General, Commanding.

CAMP NEAR VILLA RICA, *July 15, 1864.*
Major-General SHERMAN:

GENERAL: As I indicated to you in my last note, we completed the bridge (Moore's), and were ready to cross at daybreak yesterday morning, but before we essayed it a report came from Major Buck, in command of a battalion seven miles above, that the enemy had been crossing above him on a boat or a bridge, and that his pickets had been cut off. I, of course, made preparations accordingly, and found that the report originated in the sound made by the enemy crossing a bridge over a creek on the other side of the river, and nearly opposite to Major Buck. On attempting to cross the bridge the enemy opened upon it with four pieces of artillery from the edge of the timbers on the opposite side and made an endeavor to retake their rifle-pits near the water's edge. Deeming it inexpedient to push our endeavors farther, and knowing that it was easier to retain the men long enough to burn the bridge than to get them back again after they had been driven off, I ordered the bridge to be burned and the boats that had been collected there for security destroyed. During the day I sent scouts down the river to within thirteen miles of Franklin, where there is another bridge, and found neither ford nor ferry-boats, and in the evening came to this point. We shall remain here and graze during the day, and in the evening move to the vicinity of Sweet Water Town, or within eight miles of it. Colonel Biddle, who was left with his brigade at Campbellton, reports the enemy quite strong at that point, with two guns of long range in each of the two redoubts on the opposite bluff, which are opened upon him whenever any of his men show themselves. We get plenty of forage for the horses, beef, and blackberries, and some bacon for the men, and are getting on finely. We want horseshoes and nails, and a little time where we can avail ourselves of a blacksmith shop to fit the shoes, to complete the cavalry and make it ready for any service. The artillery, however, want better horses and better ammunition, as the horses they have would be unable to make long consecutive marches, and the ammunition is but little better than solid-shot. I was very anxious to strike the railroad from personal as well as other considerations, but I became convinced that to attempt it would incur risks inadequate to the results, and unless we could hold the bridge, as well as penetrate into the country, the risk of capture or dispersion, with loss of animals (as I could hear of no ford), was almost certain. It is impossible to move without every step we take being known, women as well as men acting as scouts and messengers. I have sent to the rear about 40 prisoners, 1 of them the commander of the picket at the bridge on this side, and 16 or 17 of them pickets and scouts in the vicinity of the bridge. I am unable to say how much force is opposite to us, but from what can be seen and I can hear, I am convinced it is no inconsiderable one.

GEORGE STONEMAN,
Major-General, &c.

Hdqrs. Military Division of the Mississippi,
In the Field, near Chattahoochee River, July 15, 1864.

General Stoneman,
Commanding Cavalry Division:

General: I have just received your note of 15th and wish you to hasten to your old position to relieve General Blair. I want you to cover and watch Turner's Ferry and mouth of Nickajack whilst we cross above and move out. You will have plenty of time to shoe and fix up. General Blair has your orders.

I am, sir, very respectfully, &c.,

W. T. SHERMAN,
Major-General, Commanding.

Headquarters Army of the Ohio,
In the Field, July 15, 1864.

Maj. Gen. W. T. Sherman,
Commanding Military Division of the Mississippi:

General: I send you a map* of the country which I reconnoitered yesterday. Sandy Spring Camp-Ground is an important center of roads. It is situated just at the head of Island Creek. The main road from that point appears to lead toward Pinckneyville at McAfee's Bridge. No doubt the road to Cross Keys leaves it only a short distance beyond the camp-ground. There are no people left in the country except a few ignorant women and children. Hence, it is impossible to get accurate information except by actual reconnaissance. As soon as I receive information that the general movement is to commence as directed in your Field Orders, No. 35, I propose to move my command to the camp-ground, and then reconnoiter toward Pinckneyville, Cross Keys, and Buck Head until I find the ground you desire me to occupy, and its relation to that to be occupied by Generals Thomas and McPherson.

Very respectfully, your obedient servant,

J. M. SCHOFIELD,
Major-General, Commanding.

Hdqrs. Military Division of the Mississippi,
In the Field, near Chattahoochee River, July 15, 1864.

General McPherson,
Roswell:

One of our Meridian men came in last night, an escape from the prison at Anderson[ville]. He brings a provost-marshal's pass from Columbus, of July 4. He came by way of La Grange and Franklin; saw but few of the enemy. Says West Point and Columbus are defended chiefly by

---

* To appear in the Atlas.

enrolled militia. Heard nothing of General Stoneman, General Rousseau, or from Mobile. I expect General Stoneman back, and have ordered General Blair to start the moment General Stoneman gets up as far as Sandtown. Of course the report of Kirby Smith with his 20,000 is all nonsense. Bragg's arrival from Richmond must be to consult.

> W. T. SHERMAN,
> *Major-General, Commanding.*

HDQRS. MILITARY DIVISION OF THE MISSISSIPPI,
In the Field, near Chattahoochee River, July 15, 1864.

General McPHERSON,
Roswell:

I have heard from General Stoneman. He did not break the lower railroad, but burned a bridge over the Chattahoochee near Newnan. He will be in to-night, and I have ordered General Blair to move for Roswell to-morrow. You may, therefore, make all preparations to move out toward the Stone Mountain the day after to-morrow. Notify General Garrard to move in connection with you, sending his train to yours. That Augusta road must be destroyed and occupied between Decatur and Stone Mountain by you and General Garrard.

> W. T. SHERMAN,
> *Major-General, Commanding.*

HDQRS. MILITARY DIVISION OF THE MISSISSIPPI,
In the Field, near Chattahoochee River, July 15, 1864.

General McPHERSON,
Roswell:

What sort of a road do you find the Hightower trail? Do you find a road leading direct to Stone Mountain or to Decatur? If General Schofield moves straight on Cross Keys, and you so that your left is on Hightower trail, when across Nancy's Creek or the ridge between Nancy's and the Peach Tree, your centers should not be more than three miles apart. I would like you to find a road from about Buchanan's to the head of Snapfinger Creek.

> W. T. SHERMAN,
> *Major-General, Commanding.*

HDQRS. MILITARY DIVISION OF THE MISSISSIPPI,
In the Field, near Chattahoochee River, July 15, 1864.

General BLAIR,
Commanding Seventeenth Corps:

GENERAL: I have just heard from General Stoneman, who says he will be over at Sweet Water Town to-night. I have ordered him to hurry and relieve you. Haul out of sight all your guns to-night ready in the morning to move to Roswell. You can save much distance by coming by my headquarters and taking a road near the Chattahoochee, but the main Marietta road is plainer and easier for wagons and it may be is best. Choose for yourself. Do not go to Roswell town, but to the bridge or across where General McPherson is.

I am, sir, very respectfully, &c.,

> W. T. SHERMAN,
> *Major-General, Commanding.*

HEADQUARTERS SEVENTEENTH ARMY CORPS,
Near Chattahoochee River, July 15, 1864.

Brigadier-General LEGGETT,
Commanding Third Division, Seventeenth Army Corps:

GENERAL: Inclosed please find orders for the movement of this command to-morrow morning. As a portion of your command is so distant the entire corps will encamp just beyond the Nickajack, at the point where General Force crossed the first day of our arrival in this vicinity. A note from General Sherman says that General Stoneman is at Sweet Water Creek to-night and will commence relieving you early to-morrow morning. It is desirable that you leave your pickets on until relieved by Stoneman, in order to mask this movement as long as possible from the enemy. The bulk of your force can move out at any time you may select; the pickets being unencumbered can rapidly join them after being relieved. All necessary arrangements have been made to provide the men with rations at their camp to-morrow night. The general desires you to give the men the advantage of the cooler portions of the day as much as possible.

I have the honor to be, very respectfully, your obedient servant,

A. J. ALEXANDER,
Assistant Adjutant-General.

P. S.—Upon further reflection the general thinks you had better withdraw all your pickets up to Sandtown, leave a strong picket there, withdraw all from that point up to Howell's, and picket from there to Gresham's left until the remainder of your command is concentrated, when they will all be withdrawn.

Respectfully, &c.,

A. J. ALEXANDER,
Assistant Adjutant-General.

HEADQUARTERS DEPARTMENT OF THE CUMBERLAND,
July 15, 1864.

Major-General SHERMAN:

Granger reports about 2,800 of the enemy's cavalry across the Tennessee, near Claysville. I have telegraphed him he has force enough, and I shall expect him to whip any force the enemy can now get across the Tennessee.

GEO. H. THOMAS,
Major-General.

HEADQUARTERS DEPARTMENT OF THE CUMBERLAND,
In the Field, July 15, 1864.

Brigadier-General GRANGER,
Decatur, Ala.:

Your dispatches received. The major-general commanding says you have force enough to whip any force which may cross the river, and he expects you will do it; and after you have driven them off arrest all sympathizers with the rebellion in your district and send them to Brigadier-General Webster, at Nashville, to be banished from the United States.

WM. D. WHIPPLE,
Assistant Adjutant-General.

BRIDGEPORT, *July 15, 1864.*

Captain CIST,
        Assistant Adjutant-General:

I received a dispatch from Brigadier-General Granger and one from Major-General Milroy that 2,800 rebels, with artillery, were crossing the river at Claysville, but not stating under whose command and what direction they were moving. If I receive the arms and ammunition as soon as possible, I can hold this post. If I should need any re-enforcements I will telegraph.

W. KRZYZANOWSKI,
Colonel, Commanding Post.

HDQRS. MILITARY DIVISION OF THE MISSISSIPPI,
In the Field, near Chattahoochee River, July 15, 1864.

General JOHN E. SMITH,
        Allatoona:

The general will move forward some little distance to-morrow, but will be glad to see you. Your telegram has not been received, but that by courier came this noon.

L. M. DAYTON,
Aide-de-Camp.

SPECIAL FIELD ORDERS, ⎞ HDQRS. FIFTEENTH ARMY CORPS,
                                           Near Roswell Factory, Ga.,
        No. 53.   ⎠   *July 15, 1864.*

*   *   *   *   *   *   *

II. Brig. Gen. Charles R. Woods will assume command of the First Division during the temporary absence of Brig. Gen. P. J. Osterhaus.
By order of Maj. Gen. John A. Logan:

R. R. TOWNES,
Assistant Adjutant-General.

CITY POINT, *July 16, 1864—10 a. m.*

Major-General SHERMAN:

The attempted invasion of Maryland having failed to give the enemy a firm foothold North, they are now returning, with possibly 25,000 troops. All the men they have here, beyond a sufficiency to hold their strong fortifications, will be an element of weakness to eat up their supplies. It is not improbable, therefore, that you will find in the next fortnight re-enforcements in your front to the number indicated above. I advise, therefore, that if you get to Atlanta you set about destroying the railroads as far to the east and south of you as possible; collect all the stores of the country for your own use, and select a point that you can hold until help can be had. I shall make a desperate effort to get a position here which will hold the enemy without the necessity of so many men. If successful, I can detach from here for other enterprises, looking as much to your assistance as anything else.

U. S. GRANT,
Lieutenant-General.

WASHINGTON, *July 16, 1864—4.30 p. m.*

Major-General SHERMAN,
        Georgia:

General Grant wishes me to call your attention to the possibility of Johnston's being re-enforced from Richmond, and the importance of your having prepared a good line of defense against such increase of rebel force; also, the importance of getting as large an amount of supplies as possible collected at Chattanooga.

H. W. HALLECK,
Major-General and Chief of Staff.

HEADQUARTERS,
Powers' Ferry, on the Chattahoochee, Ga., July 16, 1864—11 p. m.
(Received 10.45 a. m. 17th.)

Maj. Gen. H. W. HALLECK,
        Washington, D. C.:

I have yours and General Grant's dispatches. I had anticipated all possible chances and am accumulating all the stores possible at Chattanooga and Allatoona, but I do not fear Johnston with re-enforcements of 20,000 if he will take the offensive; but I recognize the danger arising from my long line and the superiority of the enemy's cavalry in numbers and audacity. I move to-morrow from the Chattahoochee toward Decatur and Stone Mountain, east of Atlanta. All well. Copy of this to General Grant.

W. T. SHERMAN,
Major-General, Commanding.

HEADQUARTERS OF THE ARMY,
Washington, July 16, 1864.

General SHERMAN,
        Georgia, via Chattanooga:

MY DEAR GENERAL: Yours of the 9th is just received. If I have written you no "encouragement or advice" it has been mainly because you have not wanted either. Your operations thus far have been the admiration of all military men; and they prove what energy and skill combined can accomplish, while either without the other may utterly fail. In the second place, I must be exceedingly cautious about making military suggestions not through General Grant. While the general himself is free from petty jealousies, he has men about him who would gladly make difficulties between us. I know that they have tried it several times, but I do not think they will succeed. Nevertheless, I think it well to act with caution. I therefore make all suggestions to him and receive his orders. In my present position I cannot assume responsibility except in matters of mere administration or in way of advice. The position is not an agreeable one, but I am willing to serve wherever the Government thinks I can be most useful.

As you will learn from the newspapers, we have just escaped another formidable raid on Baltimore and Washington. As soon as Hunter retreated southwest from Lynchburg the road to Washington was open to the rebels, and I predicted to General Grant that a raid would be made. But he would not believe that Ewell's corps had left his front

till it had been gone more than two weeks and had already reached
Maryland.   He was deceived by the fact that prisoners captured about
Petersburg represented themselves as belonging to Ewell's old corps,
being so ordered no doubt by their officers.   We had nothing left for
the defense of Washington and Baltimore but militia, invalids, and
convalescents, re-enforced by armed clerks and quartermaster's employés.   As the lines about Washington alone are thirty-seven and a
half miles in length, laid out by McClellan for an army of 150,000, you
may judge that with 15,000 such defenders we were in no little danger
of losing the capital or Baltimore, attacked by a veteran force of
30,000.   Fortunately the Sixth Corps, under Wright, arrived just in the
nick of time, and the enemy did not attempt an assault.

Entre nous. I fear Grant has made a fatal mistake in putting himself south of James River.   He cannot now reach Richmond without
taking Petersburg, which is strongly fortified, crossing the Appomat-
tox and recrossing the James.   Moreover, by placing his army south
of Richmond he opens the capital and the whole North to rebel raids.
Lee can at any time detach 30,000 or 40,000 men without our knowing
it till we are actually threatened.   I hope we may yet have full success,
but I find that many of Grant's general officers think the campaign
already a failure.   Perseverance, however, may compensate for all
errors and overcome all obstacles.   So mote it be.

Be assured, general, that all your friends here feel greatly gratified
with your operations, and I have not heard the usual growling and
fault-finding by outsiders.   I have twice presented in writing your
name for major-general regular army, but for some reason the matter
still hangs fire.

Best regards to Thomas and McPherson.

Yours, truly,

H. W. HALLECK.

HDQRS. MILITARY DIVISION OF THE MISSISSIPPI,
In the Field, on Chattahoochee, July 16, 1864.

Generals THOMAS and MCPHERSON:

Dispatches from Generals Grant and Halleck of to-day speak of the
enemy having failed in his designs in Maryland, and cautioning me
that Lee may in the next fortnight re-enforce Johnston by 20,000.   It
behooves us, therefore, to hurry, so all will move to-morrow as far as
Nancy's Creek.

W. T. SHERMAN,
Major-General, Commanding.

HDQRS. MILITARY DIVISION OF THE MISSISSIPPI,
In the Field, on Chattahoochee River, July 16, 1864.

General THOMAS:

All are ready and will move in the morning according to Orders,
No. 35.

W. T. SHERMAN,
Major-General, Commanding.

HDQRS. MILITARY DIVISION OF THE MISSISSIPPI,
In the Field, near Chattahoochee River, July 16, 1864.

General THOMAS:

I am about moving camp to vicinity of Powers', and will visit Generals Howard and Schofield, where I can be found in case of necessity. I can't imagine what cavalry it is that General Granger reports at Claysville. What is the gun-boat about? It should be at Guntersville at once. If Johnston has ordered this movement he will not care about Huntsville or Decatur, but Stevenson and Bridgeport. The latter is of vital importance and he knows it.

W. T. SHERMAN,
Major-General, Commanding.

HEADQUARTERS DEPARTMENT OF THE CUMBERLAND,
July 16, 1864.

Major-General SHERMAN:

I cannot conceive what cavalry Granger refers to. The gun-boat has been out of my charge for more than two weeks. Granger ought to have cavalry enough left from Rousseau's expedition to whip all the cavalry the enemy can send across the Tennessee.

GEO. H. THOMAS,
Major-General, U. S. Volunteers.

HDQRS. MILITARY DIVISION OF THE MISSISSIPPI,
In the Field, at Chattahoochee River, July 16, 1864.

General THOMAS:

Have you anything further of that cavalry force at Claysville?

W. T. SHERMAN,
Major-General, Commanding.

JULY 16, 1864.

General SHERMAN:

Have heard nothing further from rebel cavalry. Am all ready and will move in the morning across Pace's Ferry.

GEO. H. THOMAS,
Major-General.

HEADQUARTERS DEPARTMENT OF THE CUMBERLAND,
In the Field, July 16, 1864.

Maj. Gen. O. O. HOWARD,
Commanding Fourth Army Corps:

GENERAL: The major-general commanding directs that at daylight to-morrow morning you move one division down the river opposite Pace's Ferry, and cover the laying of the bridges and the crossing of one division of the Fourteenth Corps, after which your division will return to its camp.

Very respectfully, your obedient servant,

WM. D. WHIPPLE,
Chief of Staff.

HEADQUARTERS FOURTH ARMY CORPS,
Powers' Ferry, Chattahoochee River, Ga., July 16, 1864.

Major-General STANLEY:

GENERAL: General Wood will move the élite of his division down the south side of the Chattahoochee River at 4.30 a. m. to-morrow for the purpose of covering the laying of a pontoon bridge at Pace's Ferry. As soon as said bridge has been laid and one division of the Fourteenth Corps crosses over the same he will return to his present camp.

By order of Major-General Howard:

J. S. FULLERTON,
Assistant Adjutant-General.

HEADQUARTERS FOURTH ARMY CORPS,
In the Field, Powers' Ferry, Chattahoochee River, Ga.,
July 16, 1864—3 p. m.

Brigadier-General WOOD,
Commanding Third Division :

You will move the élite of your division, starting at 4.30 a. m. to-morrow, down the south side of the Chattahoochee to Pace's Ferry, where you will cover the laying of a pontoon bridge over the river. As soon as the bridge has been laid, and one division of the Fourteenth Army Corps has crossed over the same, you will return with your troops to their present camp. Do not remove your pickets, but let them remain where they are. Take with you one battery and one-half of your ambulances and leave behind all of the rest of your material, camp and garrison equipage, &c.

By order of Major-General Howard:

J. S. FULLERTON,
Assistant Adjutant-General.

(Copy to General Newton.)

HEADQUARTERS DEPARTMENT OF THE CUMBERLAND,
In the Field, July 16, 1864.

Maj. Gen. J. M. PALMER,
Commanding Fourteenth Army Corps:

GENERAL: The major-general commanding directs that as soon as the bridges are laid at Pace's Ferry to-morrow morning, which will probably be about 7 o'clock, that you commence moving your corps across, posting the first division over in column on the road leading to the bridge near the mouth of Peach Tree Creek and so near the bridge as to command it. The next division will be posted with its head of column at Kyle's Bridge across Nancy's Creek on the road to Buck Head. The last division over will be posted in reserve at the fork in the road.

Very respectfully, your obedient servant,

WM. D. WHIPPLE,
Chief of Staff.

Hdqrs. Chief of Cavalry, Dept. of the Cumberland,
Near Vining's Station, Ga., July 16, 1864.
Brig. Gen. E. M. McCook,
Commanding First Cavalry Division:

The general commanding directs me to inform you that the Fourteenth Army Corps is moving and will probably cross the river to-day. You will move with your command to the position pointed out to you and patrol the river as designated.

I am, general, very respectfully, your obedient servant,
DAVID F. HOW,
Lieutenant and Acting Assistant Adjutant-General.

Decatur, *July 16, 1864.*
Brigadier-General Whipple:

The force reported at Guntersville proved to be a detachment of Rousseau's command as telegraphed this morning by Colonel Lyon, from Claysville.

R. S. GRANGER,
Brigadier-General.

Hdqrs. Military Division of the Mississippi,
In the Field, on the Chattahoochee, July 16, 1864.
Major-General Schofield,
Commanding Army of the Ohio:

General: I have just heard from General McPherson. He moves in the morning for his position on a Decatur road till abreast of you, his cavalry at or near Buchanan's. You will therefore move to-morrow to the position described in Special Field Orders, No. 35, which will be at the camp-ground you described to me to-day, with an advance down to Nancy's Creek. This will divert, too, much attention on the part of the enemy to General Thomas, who will be engaged in crossing at Pace's. General Garrard has been to Cross Keys and finds nothing on the road but bands of cavalry.

W. T. SHERMAN,
Major-General, Commanding.

Hdqrs. Military Division of the Mississippi,
In the Field, near Chattahoochee River, July 16, 1864.
General McPherson, *Roswell:*

General R. S. Granger, from Decatur, reports that a force of the enemy's cavalry, 2,800 strong, has crossed the Tennessee north of Claysville. I cannot imagine what force that can be, unless sent from Johnston's left flank, say some of W. H. Jackson's cavalry. As General Stoneman found heavy cavalry all along the Chattahoochee as far as he went, say twenty-five miles below Campbellton, it is quite probable some of Wheeler's force has been shifted to Johnston's left, in which case the cavalry force will be light in your front. I hope to start General Blair so as to reach you early to-morrow, and that he will be near enough for you to-morrow to get out as far as Buchanan's. I am about moving camp.

W. T. SHERMAN,
Major-General, Commanding.

HDQRS. MILITARY DIVISION OF THE MISSISSIPPI,
In the Field, near Chattahoochee River, July 16, 1864.

General McPHERSON,
           Roswell:

Move in the morning according to Orders 35, but don't strike for the railroad till further orders. General Corse is here. General Blair started early to-day, and will be with you to-morrow. All well here.

W. T. SHERMAN,
Major-General, Commanding.

ROSWELL BRIDGE, *July 16, 1864.*

Major-General SHERMAN:

I shall have to leave with my trains near this place at least three good regiments of infantry and one regiment of cavalry. I am waiting for Garrard to come to obtain some definite information about the road. As far as I can learn yet the Hightower trail is not practicable for troops.

JAS. B. McPHERSON,
Major-General.

HEADQUARTERS SEVENTEENTH ARMY CORPS,
Near Marietta, July 16, 1864—11 p. m.

[Lieut. Col. WILLIAM T. CLARK:]

COLONEL: I have the honor to report for the information of the major-general commanding that I arrived with my entire command within one mile of Marietta to-night. I have already issued orders for the command to move at 4 a. m. to-morrow. I will march to within four or five miles of Roswell Ferry to-morrow morning, when I will halt during the heat of the day to rest the men. I would request that I may receive some more definite instructions as to the number of days' rations I will be expected to take across the river with the command; how many ordnance wagons shall accompany the command; how much baggage officers will be allowed to take, and whether the regimental teams shall accompany the regiments. Should the general desire me to join him at once, I will move forward rapidly without halting, although I think the men will be much benefited by the midday halt.

Very respectfully, your obedient servant,
FRANK P. BLAIR, JR.,
Major-General, Commanding.

CIRCULAR.]   HEADQUARTERS FOURTEENTH ARMY CORPS,
Chattahoochee River, Ga., July 16, 1864.

To-morrow morning General Davis will move his division to Pace's Ferry at such an hour as to be prepared to cross the bridge which is expected to be prepared at that point by 7 a. m. He will immediately cross and post his division in column on the road leading to the bridge near the mouth of Peach Tree Creek, and so near to the bridge as to command it. General Johnson will cross his division at the same point as soon as General Davis' column has passed and will post his division with the head of his column at Kyle's Bridge, across Nancy's Creek, on the road to Buck Bead.   General Baird will cross as soon as the rear of General Johnson's column has passed and will post his division in reserve at the forks of the road.

By order of Maj. Gen. J. M. Palmer:

A. C. McCLURG,
Captain and Assistant Adjutant-General.

SPECIAL FIELD ORDERS, }   HDQRS. ARMY OF THE OHIO,
No. 55.   }   *Isham's Ferry, Ga., July 16, 1864.*

*   *   *   *   *   *   *

III. To-morrow morning, July 17, the corps will move to position between Island Creek and Nancy's Creek, covering the roads from Johnson's Ferry toward Cross Keys and Buck Head.   General Cox will move in advance and will march at 7 a. m.   General Cox will first move to Sandy Spring Camp-Ground, take position at that place, and send forward a brigade toward Cross Keys, with orders to reconnoiter as far as Nancy's Creek, and will await further orders before moving his division beyond the camp-ground.

General Hascall will move along the road from his present position toward the camp-ground until he reaches the Atlanta or Buck Head road, take position at that point, and send a brigade to reconnoiter toward Buck Head, as far as the main ridge between Island Creek and Nancy's Creek.   This brigade will endeavor to communicate with General Thomas' left, along the ridge, also with the brigade of General Cox, sent to reconnoiter toward Cross Keys.

General Cox will also send a regiment from the camp-ground to reconnoiter toward Pinckneyville and open communication with the right of General McPherson, who is expected to move from Roswell toward Decatur, until he comes into position on our left.   General Cox will leave his dismounted cavalry brigade and a battery to guard the bridge at Isham's Ford and such trains as may be left at this point.   The brigade will be strongly intrenched on the commanding points near the bridge, and will hold their position at all hazards.   The ordinary baggage trains and division ordnance trains will move with the troops. Other trains, when not moving to or from the depot, will be parked on the east bank of the Chattahoochee, immediately under the guns of the bridge guard.   Hereafter in sending trains to the depot for supplies special care must be taken to prevent their capture or destruction. The trains of the two divisions will habitually move together, under a common guard, the strength of which will be determined at these headquarters, according to information which may be had at the time.   No trains will be sent to the rear without orders from the commanding general.

By command of Major-General Schofield:

J. A. CAMPBELL,
Major and Assistant Adjutant-General.

SPECIAL FIELD ORDERS, }   ROSWELL BRIDGE, GA.,
No. 69.   }   *July 16, 1864.*

*   *   *   *   *   *   *

VII. In order to carry out the spirit and intention of Special Field Orders, No. 35, headquarters Military Division of the Mississippi, the following movements will take place:

1. The Fifteenth Army Corps, Maj. Gen. John A. Logan commanding, will move out from its present position at 5.30 a. m. to-morrow on the road leading to Cross Keys, following this road to a point near Providence Church, where he will take a left-hand road (sometimes called the upper Decatur road) and proceed on this until he reaches Nancy's Creek, where he will take up a good position on each side of the road and go into bivouac.

2. The Left Wing, Sixteenth Army Corps, Maj. Gen. G. M. Dodge commanding, will follow immediately after the Fifteenth Corps on the Cross Keys road to Nancy's Creek, where he will take up a good position on each side of the road and go into bivouac. He will direct the Ninth Illinois Mounted Infantry to feel out from his right for Major-General Schofield's command, and will endeavor to keep open a line of communication by means of vedettes. The pickets of the Fifteenth and Sixteenth Corps should connect.

3. Maj. Gen. F. P. Blair, on his arrival at the bridge with his command, will follow the rest of the army, and report to the major-general commanding for special instructions.

4. Brigadier-General Garrard, commanding cavalry division, will move his command at 5.30 a. m. to-morrow, crossing McAfee's Bridge, and will push out to the vicinity of Buchanan's, near the headwaters of Nancy's Creek, and take up a position covering the roads to his left and front. He will also feel to the right and open communication with the Fifteenth Army Corps. He will also leave a sufficient guard for McAfee's Bridge, and one regiment to be stationed near Roswell to form part of the guard for trains and to patrol the country in the vicinity. The trains will be compactly parked, in the most secure position which can be found, as near the bridge as practicable.

5. Each corps commander will leave one good regiment of infantry to form the guard for the train. The regiment from the Sixteenth Corps will take post at the bridge on the west side, and the other two regiments, one from the Fifteenth and one from the Seventeenth, will remain immediately with the trains.

6. Great vigilance must be exercised by the guard to prevent the train from being surprised by the enemy's cavalry.

7. All wagons and incumbrances not needed for battle must be left behind.

8. The supply train of the cavalry division will be parked with the infantry trains.

    *   *   *   *   *   *   *

By order of Maj. Gen. James B. McPherson:

WM. T. CLARK,
Assistant Adjutant-General.

SPECIAL FIELD ORDERS, }   HDQRS. 15TH ARMY CORPS,
    No. 54.   } *Near Roswell Factory, Ga., July 16, 1864.*

    *   *   *   *   *   *   *

IV. Division commanders will have their commands in readiness to move to-morrow morning, provided with three days' rations and forage and 100 rounds per man of ammunition, in addition to that already in cartridge-boxes.

    *   *   *   *   *   *   *

VI. This command will move out to-morrow morning at 5.30 o'clock on the road leading to Cross Keys, following that road to a point near

Providence Church, where it will take a left-hand road, sometimes called the upper Decatur road, and proceed on this until Nancy's Creek is reached, when a good position on each side of the road will be chosen and the troops ordered into bivouac.

VII. Brig. Gen. William Harrow, commanding Fourth Division, will have the advance, and will be followed by the divisions of Brigadier-Generals Woods and M. L. Smith, respectively.

VIII. The ammunition wagons which are intended to transport the additional 100 rounds referred to in paragraph IV of the order will follow each division, and the ambulance train of each division will likewise follow. Fifteenth Army Corps headquarters train will follow in rear of the First Division. All other wagons of the command will follow in rear of the entire command in the order of march. Two regiments of infantry will follow in the rear of the entire train as rear guard.

IX. The general supply train will be left and parked as near the river bridge as practicable, on the west side, under the direction of the chief quartermaster of the corps.

    *   *   *   *   *   *   *

By order of Maj. Gen. John A. Logan:

R. R. TOWNES,
Assistant Adjutant-General.

SPECIAL ORDERS, }   HDQRS. SEVENTEENTH ARMY CORPS,
     No. 175.   }   *In the Field, July 16, 1864.*

I. Brig. Gen. M. D. Leggett will have the advance to-morrow, and will move his command promptly at 4 a. m. on the road to Roswell Ferry.

II. Brig. Gen. W. Q. Gresham, commanding Fourth Division, will hold his command in readiness to move at 4.30 a. m., and will follow immediately in rear of the Third Division.

The trains of this command have been ordered to move at 2 a. m. on the road before indicated in advance of the troops.

By command of Maj. Gen. Frank P. Blair:

A. J. ALEXANDER,
Assistant Adjutant-General.

EAST OF CHATTAHOOCHEE RIVER, GA.,
July 17, 1864—10 p. m.   (Received 11.20 a. m. 18th.)

Maj. Gen. H. W. HALLECK,
       Washington, D. C.:

To-day we have moved out from the Chattahoochee to Nancy's Creek, General Thomas on the right from Pace's Ferry, toward Atlanta; General Schofield in the center, near Cross Keys, and General McPherson on the left near General Schofield. To-morrow I propose to advance General Thomas to Peach Tree Creek, about Buck Head; General Schofield on the Decatur road, and General McPherson to the vicinity of the railroad east of Decatur, and his cavalry division, under Garrard, will break the railroad. If we can break the railroad I propose to place the left wing across it, near Decatur, and break up the railroad eastward as far as cavalry can operate with prudence. To-day we encounter nothing but cavalry.

W. T. SHERMAN,
Major-General.

HDQRS. MILITARY DIVISION OF THE MISSISSIPPI,
In the Field, Chattahoochee River, July 17, 1864.

Major-General THOMAS:

GENERAL: If you find it difficult to pass Pace's Ferry, move one of your corps now on this side up to General Howard's, and, with the two corps, move out to the bridge at Kyle's over Nancy's Creek, leaving the other corps to cross at Pace's, or to follow the first if unable to effect a crossing at Pace's. All your army should be on Nancy's Creek to-night. General Schofield and General McPherson moved at daylight.

I am, &c.,

W. T. SHERMAN,
Major-General, Commanding.

HDQRS. MILITARY DIVISION OF THE MISSISSIPPI,
In the Field, Lot No. 165, our map, east of Chattahoochee River,
July 17, 1864.

Major-General THOMAS,
    Commanding Army of the Cumberland:

GENERAL: General Schofield has just been here and describes his position as on Nancy's Creek, his pickets on south side, near Cross Keys, about the lots 304, 315, and 316.

General McPherson is on the road from Roswell to Decatur, his advance about lot 326, about a mile above General Schofield. General Schofield says that the road represented on our maps as from Roswell to Buck Head is a broad, well traveled road and has a branch about lot No. 94, leading to Pace's Ferry. This corresponds with what General Corse tells me, that you found a large road branching to the left soon after leaving Pace's Ferry. It is well to mark this road, as it may be useful to us. General Howard can take a good road from here to Buck Head, starting at his present front and moving southeast to the main road from Roswell to Buck Head, just before it crosses Nancy's Creek. Approaching Buck Head from this quarter about the same time that Generals Schofield and McPherson get to the Peach Tree from the east, will of course relieve any pressure you may encounter on the main road.

General Schofield will move early for the Peach Tree road in front of Cross Keys, and take post about lots 239, 247, and 272, with pickets forward as far as 196, and General McPherson will seek for position in the valley of North Fork of Peach Tree, about 267, 266, 284, 285, and send General Garrard to break the road and telegraph.

You should leave a corps in front of Donaldson's, and have the other two as early as possible at and in front of Buck Head. Then feel down strong to Peach Tree and see what is there. A vigorous demonstration should be made, and caution your commanders not to exhibit any of the signs of a halt or pause, as in that event too much resistance would be made on the other flank. You know the reasons for the utmost activity and I need not repeat them. Let all your commanders have full orders to-night, and before joining General Schofield in the morning I will point out to General Howard the road by which he can reach Buck Head in five miles from here. Give orders as soon as any head of column reaches Buck Head to feel up the Peach Tree road for General Schofield, who will surely be in position before your troops can be.

I am, yours, truly,

W. T. SHERMAN,
Major-General, Commanding.

HEADQUARTERS DEPARTMENT OF THE CUMBERLAND,
July 17, 1864—8 p. m.

Major-General SHERMAN:

General Hooker has his troops posted on the intermediate road between Pace's and Powers' Ferry roads. General Palmer has Johnson on the Pace's Ferry road, and Davis on a road between that and the railroad bridge. All the troops occupy the ridge overlooking Nancy's Creek, with their skirmishers bordering the creek. Baird is in reserve behind Davis. A rebel battery with its infantry support, which has been firing on McCook's battery, posted in the redoubt to the left of the railroad, cleared out from its position on Peach Tree Creek this p. m. and retired across the creek in direction of Atlanta. Sutermeister has made excellent practice to-day, and will continue to fire at intervals through the night. I shall move my headquarters to-morrow to near Hooker, who will be in the center of my army.

GEO. H. THOMAS,
Major-General.

HOWARD'S HEADQUARTERS,
July 17, 1864—9 p. m.

General THOMAS:

Signal dispatch received. Schofield is on the road from Johnson's by Cross Keys. Palmer had better move straight for Kyle's Bridge, and Hooker from Powers' to the crossing above near Schofield; Howard in reserve.

SHERMAN,
Major-General.

HEADQUARTERS FOURTH ARMY CORPS,
Powers' Ferry, Ga., July 17, 1864.

Major-General STANLEY,
First Division, Fourth Army Corps:

GENERAL: The general commanding directs that you have everything in readiness to move at 5 a. m. to-morrow, but not to move until further orders are issued for this purpose.

Very respectfully, your obedient servant,

J. S. FULLERTON,
Assistant Adjutant-General.

(Same to Newton and Wood.)

HEADQUARTERS DEPARTMENT OF THE CUMBERLAND,
Near Vining's Station, Ga., July 17, 1864.

Maj. Gen. J. M. PALMER,
Commanding Fourteenth Army Corps:

GENERAL: The commanding general directs that you commence the execution of the orders of General Sherman (copies of which were sent you this evening) at daylight to-morrow a. m.

I am, general, very respectfully, your obedient servant,

SOUTHARD HOFFMAN,
Assistant Adjutant-General.

(Same to General Howard.)

HEADQUARTERS FOURTEENTH ARMY CORPS,
In the Field, July 17, 1864—10.45 p. m.

Brig. Gen. W. D. WHIPPLE,
Chief of Staff:

I have just received Special Field Orders, No. 36, Military Division of the Mississippi, with accompanying memorandum, and department order to commence the execution of that order at daybreak. If I were able to superintend the movements of my troops to-morrow in person I would probably need no explanation; but as I fear I will not be, I beg such directions in regard to the movements of my divisions, and such information as to what is expected of Hooker and Howard, as will enable me to accomplish what is expected of me by orders from him, supervised by General Johnson. I may add that if it is intended to maintain the right of our line on the Chattahoochee River, Davis now substantially holds up to Peach Tree Creek, and it will but remain for me to push Johnson in connection with Davis over Nancy's Creek to the ridge beyond.

Very respectfully,

JOHN M. PALMER,
Major-General, Commanding.

HEADQUARTERS DEPARTMENT OF THE CUMBERLAND,
Near Vining's Station, Ga., July 17, 1864.
(Received 9.30 a. m.)

Major-General HOOKER,
Commanding Twentieth Corps:

GENERAL: The major-general commanding directs that you this day cross the Chattahoochee River with the Twentieth Corps at Pace's Ferry after the Fourteenth Corps has crossed.

The Fourteenth Corps will, after crossing, be posted as follows: one division in column on the road leading from Pace's Ferry to the bridge over Peach Tree Creek, the head of the column at the bridge; another division in column on the road from Pace's Ferry to Buck Head, with the head of column at Kyle's Bridge over Nancy's Creek; the third division in reserve at the fork of the above-named roads. The Fourth Corps is in line in front of Powers' Ferry, connecting on the left with the Twenty-third Corps. After crossing your corps the major-general commanding directs that you post your corps somewhere between the road from Pace's Ferry to Kyle's Bridge and the Fourth Corps.

Very respectfully, your obedient servant,

WM. D. WHIPPLE,
Chief of Staff.

HEADQUARTERS CHIEF OF CAVALRY,
Near Vining's Station, Ga., July 17, 1864.

Brig. Gen. E. M. McCOOK,
Commanding First Cavalry Division:

The general commanding directs me to inform you that the brigade of Jeff. C. Davis' division will be removed to-night or to-morrow morning at daylight, and you will have your command in readiness to take up their position with a view of supporting Captain Lilly's and also Captain Sutermeister's battery.

*   *   *   *   *   *   *

I am, general, very respectfully, your obedient servant,

DAVID F. HOW,
Lieutenant and Acting Assistant Adjutant-General.

HDQRS. MILITARY DIVISION OF THE MISSISSIPPI,
Howard's Headquarters, July 17, 1864—12 m.

General SCHOFIELD:

DEAR GENERAL: Captain Bartlett is here. I have just sent back to my headquarters the draft of an order for to-morrow. Thomas will move to and beyond Buck Head. You to the Peach Tree Creek road where intersected by the road leading to Decatur. The position is on the ridge between Nancy's and Little Peach Tree. McPherson to-morrow will move to a point about four miles to your left front, and send his cavalry to the railroad. Thomas is sending a corps this way, using Howard's bridge, and I will direct them to Nancy's Creek on the direct road to Cross Keys, viz, lot 93. I suppose you to be on lot 36, with advance guard well down to the creek Nancy. I want McPherson to-night between you and Buchanan's.

Yours,

W. T. SHERMAN,
Major-General, Commanding.

JULY 17, 1864.

General SHERMAN:

I send an orderly to show you the way to my headquarters. My troops are on the ridge between Island and Nancy's Creeks, with advance at Nancy's. I hear McPherson's guns not far to my left.

Respectfully,

J. M. SCHOFIELD,
Major-General.

JULY 17, 1864—4.45 p. m.

General SHERMAN:

I have just heard directly from McPherson. He is at the crossing of Nancy's Creek on the Decatur road, one mile from Cross Keys and only a mile from my left. I expect you here about supper time. If you do not come I will call at your headquarters this evening.

Respectfully,

J. M. SCHOFIELD,
Major-General.

HDQRS. MILITARY DIVISION OF THE MISSISSIPPI,
In the Field, near Chattahoochee River, July 17, 1864.

Major-General SCHOFIELD,
Commanding Army of the Ohio:

GENERAL: Your note to the general-in-chief of 4.45 p. m. is just to hand. He had dropped a note by an orderly from you that he had already gone into camp, or else he would have bivouacked near you; he is waiting, momentarily expecting to hear from General Thomas' operations at Pace's, and will be happy to see you here.

I am, general, with much regard, yours, respectfully,

L. M. DAYTON,
Aide-de-Camp.

HEADQUARTERS ARMY OF THE OHIO,
July 17, 1864—4.30 p. m.

Brig. Gen. M. S. HASCALL,
Commanding Second Division, Twenty-third Army Corps:

GENERAL: I find General Cox and you are so far apart that it is not worth while for you to try to connect your pickets. The distance is from three to four miles. I presume the same is true with reference to General Thomas. Make your position strong, and rely on yourself. To-morrow we move through Cross Keys toward Decatur. The road Cox is on leads directly to Cross Keys; yours to Atlanta. There may be an old road leading from your position to or near Cross Keys or Decatur, leaving Buck Head to your right. Find such a road, if possible, and let me know all about it. We march at 6 a. m.

Very respectfully, your obedient servant,

J. M. SCHOFIELD,
Major-General, Commanding.

HDQRS. THIRD DIVISION, TWENTY-THIRD ARMY CORPS,
Isham's, Ga., July 17, 1864—6.30 a. m.

Colonel CRITTENDEN,
Commanding Brigade:

SIR: You will move your brigade at 9 o'clock this morning to the position indicated to you a few days ago, on the hill covering the bridge on this side. You will strongly intrench a position for the brigade, so that it may be prepared for any raid of the enemy's cavalry whether on this or the other side of the river. Rifle-pits will be dug in the bottom lands on both sides of the river, so as to protect the immediate heads of the bridge by detachments, and the most thorough means will be taken by you to guard the bridge itself, and the trains which may be parked near it. A battery of artillery will be put in position with you by Major Wells, chief of artillery, and will then be under your orders till further directions. If it is found necessary to occupy more than one of the hills, each position will be carefully intrenched, and the general position will be held at all hazards.

J. D. COX,
Brigadier-General, Commanding.

HDQRS. THIRD DIVISION, TWENTY-THIRD ARMY CORPS,
Thomason's, July 17, 1864—11.20 a. m.

Col. J. W. REILLY,
Commanding First Brigade:

SIR: Your dispatch received. Keep the bulk of your brigade on commanding ground, covering the forks where you now are, and make reconnaissance with smaller force upon each fork. It cannot be more than half a mile in your front where the Roswell Factory road comes in on the left, by which road General McPherson's force, or part of it, may be expected. A road runs off to the right a mile from here, near Wade's house, following the ridge down between Island and Nancy's Creeks. Some rebel cavalry are on this road, which is a mere cross-road. Report any information you may get, either as to roads or the enemy. I have not yet received definite orders as to the position the division shall assume. Do not display more force than is necessary.

J. D. COX,
Brigadier-General, Commanding.

HDQRS. THIRD DIVISION, TWENTY-THIRD ARMY CORPS,
Thomason's, July 17, 1864—11.30 a. m.

Major-General SCHOFIELD,
Commanding, &c.:

GENERAL: Colonel Reilly is about one mile and a half in front at the forks of the Atlanta and Cross Keys roads. The former leads along the ridge between Island and Nancy's Creeks, and unites with the one you are moving Hascall on at Burdett's, about three miles from Sandy Creek Camp-Ground, and a little more from Reilly. The road Cameron moved out on is only a plantation road. Some cavalry of the enemy are in Reilly's front on both roads, and some are seen in front of Cameron also. I have halted Reilly, ordering him to send smaller reconnaissances on both roads before him. The Roswell road comes in about a mile in front of him, but the best Roswell road is said to be that which comes in here. The triangle of roads from Burdett's is about two miles base on this road, three miles on your road, and three and a half or four from Reilly. This information is from a citizen here, who seems honest. No news of McPherson.

Very respectfully, &c.,

J. D. COX,
Brigadier-General.

HDQRS. THIRD DIVISION, TWENTY-THIRD ARMY CORPS,
Junction of Atlanta and Cross Keys Roads, July 17, 1864—6 p. m.

Major-General SCHOFIELD,
Commanding, &c.:

GENERAL: Our skirmishers have occupied the ridge on the other side of Nancy's Creek, as have General Dodge's also, connecting with ours. I have ordered Reilly to support the skirmishers with a regiment and hold the rest of his brigade in reserve on this side, near the creek. The other two brigades I have stationed as I mentioned to you. An officer of General Hascall's staff came over from him and informed me that his position is where you left it, near the Pace's Ferry road, which he says runs into this Atlanta road, making the whole distance two miles and a half. I have ordered a regiment of Byrd's command to go out a mile and have a scouting party connect with General Hascall. My headquarters are a little beyond the forks on the left of the road.

Very respectfully, &c.,

J. D. COX,
Brigadier-General, Commanding.

JULY 17, 1864.

Major-General SCHOFIELD:

GENERAL: General McPherson with one corps is at the crossing of Nancy's Creek on the Decatur road, one mile from Cross Keys. His right is not more than a mile from Reilly's left.

I am, very respectfully,

WM. J. TWINING,
Lieutenant of Engineers.

HDQRS. DEPARTMENT AND ARMY OF THE TENNESSEE,
In the Field, July 17, 1864—7.30 p. m.

Major-General SHERMAN,
Commanding, &c.:

GENERAL: I have the honor to inclose herewith a sketch* of my position, together with a report from Brig. Gen. K. Garrard, giving the position of his troops and his operations for to-day. We have met nothing but cavalry, and few of them, except in front of Dodge on the Atlanta and Roswell road, where Dibrell's brigade, with one or two pieces of artillery, was posted to check an advance across Nancy's Creek. They gave way, however, very easily when Dodge's infantry and artillery came up to the support of the Ninth Illinois, mounted, Lieutenant-Colonel Phillips commanding, and we had no difficulty in pushing our skirmishers across the creek and onto the opposite ridge. They had all the main roads, by-roads, lanes, and paths picketed, and in many cases it looks as though it was more to prevent their own men from escaping than to give notice of our advance.

Very respectfully, your obedient servant,

JAS. B. McPHERSON,
Major-General.

[Inclosure.]

HEADQUARTERS CAVALRY DIVISION,
July 17, 1864.

Maj. Gen. JOHN A. LOGAN,
Commanding Fifteenth Corps:

GENERAL: I am in camp about a mile on the left of your line. I left Colonel Long with two regiments of his brigade at the bridge to picket the Stone Mountain and the Pinckney road, and to guard the bridge. Colonel Minty's left rests near Buchanan's, and the Peach Tree road, and all roads leading from the Peach Tree road toward the river on the left are picketed. Patrols have been out well to the front, and find but few rebels, and most of their tracks lead toward Atlanta or Buck Head. I learn since being here that there are two Cross Keys. The one on the maps is the old one, where there was a post-office some years since, but the name and the post-office were transferred to the present position, some four miles to the east. This will account for the fact that both you and I are so near Cross Keys. We are some four or five miles east of the point laid down on the map as Cross Keys, and about where we were ordered. Buchanan's is only one house. Please send this to General McPherson. My headquarters are on a road leading out from your left, or about half a mile in front of a road leading just behind your line, near the house of a Mr. Chester.

Very respectfully, your obedient servant,

K. GARRARD,
Brigadier-General, Commanding Division.

* Not found.

HEADQUARTERS FIFTEENTH ARMY CORPS,
Near Cross Keys, Ga., July 17, 1864.

Lieut. Col. WILLIAM T. CLARK,
Assistant Adjutant-General:

COLONEL: A prisoner who voluntarily delivered himself up reports that Kelly's division of cavalry, about 4,000 strong, three brigades, is in the front on the road which is covered by my command, and on this side of Peach Tree Creek, and that Bate's division of infantry is on the other side of Peach Tree Creek, on same road. Also that Martin's division of cavalry is on the road in front of Dodge; also that A. J. Smith had a fight with Forrest at Tupelo; no result given. Received telegram yesterday.

Respectfully, your obedient servant,

JOHN A. LOGAN,
Major-General, Commanding.

POWERS' FERRY, GA., *July 17, 1864—9 p. m.*
(Received 11.45 p. m.)

Maj. T. T. ECKERT:

General Sherman's headquarters is now two miles from here, on Nancy's Creek. The whole of the three armies will have crossed Chattahoochee before morning. The Twentieth Corps and the Seventeenth Corps are now crossing, the Seventeenth at Roswell and the Twentieth at Pace's Ferry. Some skirmishing, but no serious resistance. McPherson is ten miles from Roswell, in direction of Stone Mountain.

J. C. VAN DUZER.

SPECIAL FIELD ORDERS,　}　HDQRS. MIL. DIV. OF THE MISS.,
No. 36.　　　　　　　}　*In the Field, Chattahoochee, July 17, 1864.*

The operations of the army for to-morrow, the 18th July, will be as follows:

I. Major-General Thomas will move forward, occupy Buck Head and the ridge between Nancy's Creek and Peach Tree, also all the roads toward Atlanta, as far as Peach Tree Creek.

II. Major-General Schofield will pass through Cross Keys and occupy the Peach Tree road where intersected by the road from Cross Keys to Decatur.

III. Major-General McPherson will move toward Stone Mountain to secure strong ground within four miles of General Schofield's position, and push Brigadier-General Garrard's cavalry to the railroad, and destroy some section of the road, and then resume position to the front and left of General McPherson.

IV. All armies will communicate with their neighbors. The general-in-chief will be near General Thomas' left, or near General Schofield.

By order of Maj. Gen. W. T. Sherman:

L. M. DAYTON,
Aide-de-Camp.

JULY 17, 1864.

Memoranda to Special Field Orders, No. 36: The map composed of two parts of the official compilation made at Marietta July 5 and 11, 1864, is the best and will be the standard for orders issued from these headquarters. As a general rule, old roads will be found to lead to Decatur, but new roads to Atlanta. The general country is very hilly and stony, but improves south and east as we approach the head of the Ocmulgee. Peach Tree Creek is considerable of a stream, but fordable at all points east of the main road from Buck Head to Atlanta. The first real lines to be found will be on the Old Peach Tree road, which starts at Turner's Ferry, keeps near the Chattahoochee, crosses Peach Tree at Moore's Mill and on a main ridge by Buck Head, Buchanan's, and Pinckneyville. Our first line must be in front of this road, leaving it clear for communication; General Thomas the right, General Schofield the center, and General McPherson the left. General Thomas will move substantially on Atlanta, General Schofield on Decatur, and General McPherson, with General Garrard's cavalry, is charged with the destruction of the railroad between Decatur and Stone Mountain. As soon as the road is broken all the armies will close on General Thomas, occupying the main roads east of Atlanta, or, in other words, the line swung across the railroad near Decatur. General Thomas will press close on Atlanta, but not assault real works, but not be deterred by cavalry or light defenses. General Schofield will threaten the neighborhood of Decatur, but Generals McPherson and Garrard will risk much and break the railroad during the 18th or 19th.

W. T. SHERMAN,
Major-General, Commanding.

HEADQUARTERS DEPARTMENT OF THE CUMBERLAND,
Near Vining's Station, Ga., July 17, 1864.

Order of the day for July 18, 1864.

In executing Special Field Orders, No. 36, from headquarters Military Division of the Mississippi, the following will be the operations of the Army of the Cumberland to-morrow:

The movements will be commenced by the Fourth Corps, Major-General Howard, and Twentieth, Major-General Hooker's corps, who will each seek a road leading from his present position to Buck Head and march upon it to that point, the former forming to the left and the latter to the right of it along the Turner's Ferry and Buck Head road. Brigadier-General Johnson's division, Fourteenth Corps, will follow the movements of Major-General Hooker, keeping his skirmishers connected with those of Major-General Hooker and forming on his right. The divisions of Brigadier-Generals Davis and Baird will maintain substantially their present positions, the former keeping his skirmishers connected with those of General Johnson.

The Fourth and Twentieth Corps will move at daylight, and the object is to gain possession of the ridge along which the Turner's Ferry and Buck Head road runs, form in front of it, and threaten Atlanta by the roads leading from it to that place; Major-General Palmer's corps on the right, Major-General Hooker's in the center, and Major-General Howard's on the left.

By command of Major-General Thomas:

WM. D. WHIPPLE,
Assistant Adjutant-General.

Special Field Orders, ⟩ Hdqrs. Dept. of the Tennessee,
      No. 70.   ⟨   Near Nancy's Creek, Ga., July 17, 1864.

  *   *   *   *   *   *   *

 VI. To carry out Special Field Orders, No. 36, headquarters Military Division of the Mississippi, a copy of which is inclosed herewith,* the following movements will take place to-morrow:

 1. The Fifteenth Army Corps, Major-General Logan commanding, will march at 5 a. m., on the Decatur road to Widow Rainey's, thence on the Stone Mountain road, by Blake's Mill, to Browning's Court-House, at the intersection of the Stone Mountain and Lawrenceville and Decatur roads, where he will hold his command in readiness to assist Brigadier-General Garrard, if he requires it, in his effort to make a break in the railroad.

 2. Major-General Dodge will move his command at 6 a. m., taking the road to his left in rear of his advance division, by Adams' across Nancy's Creek to the Peach Tree road, thence eastward on the Peach Tree road to the Decatur road from Roswell; thence Decatur road toward Peach Tree Creek, engaging the attention of the enemy, and keeping his command well in hand for any emergency.

 3. Maj. Gen. F. P. Blair will move his command at 6 a. m. on the Decatur road to Widow Rainey's, thence on the Stone Mountain road to Peach Tree Creek at Blake's Mill, following the Fifteenth Army Corps.

 4. Brig. Gen. K. Garrard will move his command at 5 a. m. by the most practicable road or roads in his front to the railroad, and do what damage he can to it by burning bridges and culverts, piling rails on the track and setting them on fire so as to heat and warp the iron, tearing up the ties, piling them up, putting the iron rails on top, and setting the ties on fire.

 5. The importance of making a break in the railroad cannot be overestimated, and the general commanding trusts that all will act with that spirit and determination which is the best guarantee of success.

  *   *   *   *   *   *   *

 By order of Maj. Gen. James B. McPherson:

         WM. T. CLARK,
        Assistant Adjutant-General.

Special Field Orders, ⟩ Hdqrs. Fifteenth Army Corps,
      No. 55.   ⟨   Near Cross Keys, Ga., July 17, 1864.

 I. The Fifteenth Army Corps will move forward at 5 a. m. to-morrow on the Decatur road to Widow Rainey's; thence on the Stone Mountain road by Blake's Mill to Bowman's [Browning's] Court-House, at the intersection of the Stone Mountain and Lawrenceville and Decatur roads, where it will be held in readiness to assist General Garrard, if he requires it, in his effort to make a break on the railroad.

 II. Brigadier-General Woods' division will have the advance and be followed by the divisions of Brig. Gens. M. L. Smith and William Harrow, respectively.

 III. The ordnance and ambulance train of each division will follow in the rear of their respective divisions, and the Fifteenth Army Corps headquarters train will follow in the rear of the Second Division ordnance and ambulance train. All other wagons will follow in the rear of the troops in the order of march.

* See p. 166.

IV. Brigadier-General Harrow will cause one brigade to march in rear of the entire train as rear guard.

V. Division commanders will not permit straggling from the ranks on any account.

By order of Maj. Gen. John A. Logan:

> R. R. TOWNES,
> *Assistant Adjutant-General.*

SPECIAL ORDERS, }   HDQRS. SEVENTEENTH ARMY CORPS,
No. 176.   }   *In the Field, July 17, 1864.*

*   *   *   *   *   *   *

III. Brig. Gen. W. Q. Gresham, commanding Fourth Division, will have the advance to-morrow, and will move his command promptly at 6 a. m. on the Decatur road to Widow Rainey's; thence on the Stone Mountain road to Peach Tree Creek at Blake's Mill, following the Fifteenth Army Corps.

By command of Maj. Gen. Frank P. Blair:

> A. J. ALEXANDER,
> *Assistant Adjutant-General.*

> EXECUTIVE MANSION,
> *Washington, July 18, 1864—11.25 a. m.*

Major-General SHERMAN,
> *Chattahoochee River, Ga.:*

I have seen your dispatches objecting to agents of Northern States opening recruiting stations near your camps. An act of Congress authorizes this, giving the appointment of agents to the States, and not to the Executive Government. It is not for the War Department, or myself, to restrain or modify the law, in its execution, further than actual necessity may require. To be candid, I was for the passage of the law, not apprehending at the time that it would produce such inconvenience to the armies in the field as you now cause me to fear. Many of the States were very anxious for it, and I hoped that, with their State bounties, and active exertions, they would get out substantial additions to our colored forces, which, unlike white recruits, help us where they come from, as well as where they go to. I still hope advantage from the law; and being a law, it must be treated as such by all of us. We here will do what we consistently can to save you from difficulties arising out of it. May I ask, therefore, that you will give your hearty co-operation.

> A. LINCOLN.

> NEAR CROSS KEYS, GA.,
> *July 18, 1864—7 p. m.* (Received 10.45 a. m. 19th.)

Maj. Gen. H. W. HALLECK,
> *Washington, D. C.:*

We moved to-day rapidly and General McPherson reached the Atlanta and Augusta road at a point seven miles east of Decatur and four miles from Stone Mountain. General Garrard's cavalry at once set to work to break up road and was re-enforced by Brig. Gen. Morgan L.

Smith's division of infantry, and they expect by night to have five miles of road effectually destroyed. Thus far we have encountered only cavalry with light resistance, and to-morrow will move on Decatur and Atlanta. I am fully aware of the necessity of making the most of time and shall keep things moving.

W. T. SHERMAN,
Major-General.

Hdqrs. Military Division of the Mississippi,
In the Field, east of Chattahoochee River, July 18, 1864—6 a. m.

General Thomas:

General: I have this moment your letter of 8 p. m. last night. I would like you to get to Buck Head early to-day and then to feel down strong on Atlanta. General Howard has already started and Generals Schofield and McPherson; I am on the point of starting and will be near General Schofield about the Cross Keys. Establish communication by courier along up to me as soon as you know any troops are in that vicinity. I may order General McPherson off on a tangent if I have anything that justifies it. I want that railroad as quick as possible and the weather seems to me too good to be wasted.

Yours, &c.,

W. T. SHERMAN,
Major-General, Commanding.

Hdqrs. Military Division of the Mississippi,
In the Field at Sam. House's, Peach Tree Road,
Five miles northeast of Buck Head, Ga., July 18, 1864.

Major-General Thomas,
Buck Head, Ga.:

General: I have reports from General McPherson to 2 p. m. He had reached the railroad at a point two miles from Stone Mountain and seven miles from Decatur; had broken the telegraphs and road, and by 5 p. m. will have four or five miles broken. To-morrow I want a bold push for Atlanta and have made my orders, which, I think, will put us in Atlanta or very close to it. Hold about Howell's Mill and the main road and let your left swing across Peach Tree about the South Fork and connect with Schofield, who will approach Decatur from the north, whilst McPherson moves down from the east. It is hard to realize that Johnston will give up Atlanta without a fight, but it may be so. Let us develop the truth.

Yours, &c.,

W. T. SHERMAN,
Major-General, Commanding.

Headquarters Department of the Cumberland,
July 18, 1864—2.15 p. m.

Maj. Gen. W. T. Sherman,
Commanding Military Division of the Mississippi:

General: General Palmer's corps occupies the Turner's Ferry and Decatur road, and he is pushing his skirmishers down to Peach Tree Creek. General Hooker's corps is on General Palmer's left, also in front of the Turner's Ferry and Decatur road. General Howard occupies

Buck Head. Both Generals Hooker and Howard will push their skir-mishers down toward Peach Tree Creek in the direction of Atlanta. General Palmer was somewhat delayed because the enemy destroyed all the bridges across Nancy's Creek, but he has been threatening and advancing continually, so that your orders have been carried out. Prisoners taken this morning report that the main body of the enemy retired last night in some hurry, as they understood, because it was reported we were crossing the river below.

Very respectfully, yours, &c.,

GEO. H. THOMAS,
Major-General, U. S. Volunteers, Commanding.

HEADQUARTERS DEPARTMENT OF THE CUMBERLAND,
July 18, 1864—7.50 p. m.

GENERAL: This dispatch was forwarded to you this p. m. at 2.15 o'clock, but the orderly has just returned after going as far as General Schofield's left without being able to hear anything as to your where-abouts. I start it out again in hopes it will reach you.

Respectfully, your obedient servant,

ROBT. H. RAMSEY,
Assistant Adjutant-General.

VINING'S SIGNAL STATION, *July 18, 1864.*

Major-General HOWARD:

Prepare to move at daylight. Will send orders by courier.

WM. D. WHIPPLE,
Assistant Adjutant-General.

HEADQUARTERS FOURTH ARMY CORPS,
Buck Head, Ga., July 18, 1864—7 p. m.

Brigadier-General WHIPPLE,
Assistant Adjutant-General and Chief of Staff:

GENERAL : Newton left camp 4.30 o'clock this morning, followed by the other divisions. Just as skirmishers emerged from the pine woods, before reaching Nancy's Creek, the rebels opened with artillery, which seemed to be a section supported by cavalry. They occupied a good elevated position across the creek, having burned the bridge. On this account they were able to hold us in check some little time. They gave way as soon as we got our artillery into a good position. We extin-guished the fire, saved a portion of the bridge, and reconstructed it. During the rest of the march to this place the rebel cavalry made quite stubborn resistance. It was a Kentucky brigade under Williams. At one place regular barricades were constructed of logs and covered with boughs. When our men approached to within 150 yards they received a volley, but in this case as in several others the skirmishers cheered and charged them out. We have had 5 men wounded; none reported killed. Two officers fell into our hands, 1 a lieutenant-colonel, killed, and a captain, severely wounded. I posted my command as directed, in advance of the Turner's Ferry road along the main ridge, all but one brigade, which was posted on the left of the Roswell Factory and Atlanta road.

Very respectfully, your obedient servant,

O. O. HOWARD,
Major-General, Commanding.

HEADQUARTERS DEPARTMENT OF THE CUMBERLAND,
In the Field, near Pace's Ferry, Ga., July 18, 1864.

Maj. Gen. J. M. PALMER,
    Commanding Fourteenth Army Corps:

GENERAL: The major-general commanding directs that at daylight to-morrow morning you send a division upon the main road leading from your front to Atlanta. Keep the head of the column covered by a strong line of skirmishers, press the enemy strongly, and be prepared to re-enforce the division should it become necessary. Major-Generals Hooker and Howard will also be instructed to send each a division in the same direction at the same time from their fronts respectively.

I am, general, very respectfully, your obedient servant,

WM. D. WHIPPLE,
Chief of Staff.

(Similar to Generals Howard and Hooker.)

P. S.—Brigadier-General Johnson's communication forwarded by you just received. The major-general commanding directs that you cross Peach Tree Creek if you can do it with one division, and push the enemy along as far as you can.

W. D. W.

HDQRS. FIRST DIVISION, FOURTEENTH CORPS,
July 18, 1864.

Capt. A. C. MCCLURG,
    Assistant Adjutant-General, Fourteenth Corps:

CAPTAIN: I have the honor to report, for the information of the major-general commanding, that my skirmishers are more than one-half of the line on Peach Tree Creek. From near the right of Colonel McCook's line (which is the left brigade) the line is slightly refused, but within a few yards of the creek and commanding it at all points. At Howell's Mill there seems to be a small force of skirmishers; they fire pretty sharply at McCook's men. The bridge is destroyed; creek deep with very abrupt and high banks; cannot be crossed so far as is reported, except by bridging. No infantry has been developed as yet, though the miller at Howell's Mill says they have infantry on the opposite bank of the creek. The ridge on the other side is not very high, nor apparently very difficult of ascent, in front of Moore's line; in some places open field; in front of McCook's heavy woods. Some of Moore's skirmishers report works. Slight skirmishing is going on all along the line. My men are intrenching on the skirmish line and my main line is being made very strong. There is an interval between my line and that of General Hooker. I have a regiment on the Buck Head road, between the two as an outpost.

Very respectfully, your obedient servant,

R. W. JOHNSON,
Brigadier-General of Volunteers.

[Indorsement.]

HEADQUARTERS FOURTEENTH ARMY CORPS,
In the Field, July 18, 1864—8.30 p. m.

This paper received this moment, and respectfully forwarded as having probably an important influence upon the plans of the general commanding for to-morrow.

I think it may be safely assumed that the enemy has crossed Peach Tree Creek, though occasional shots are heard on my extreme left, or on General Hooker's line.

JOHN M. PALMER,
Major-General, Commanding.

—

HEADQUARTERS FOURTEENTH ARMY CORPS,
Near Buck Head, July 18, 1864—8 p. m.
Brig. Gen. A. BAIRD,
Commanding Third Division, Fourteenth Army Corps:

GENERAL: General Thomas desires that you make a reconnaissance to-morrow morning toward Atlanta with your whole division. The major-general commanding the corps directs that unless you should receive the orders before that time, you move at an early hour during the cool of the morning, taking with you one battery, and upon the direct Atlanta road, through the camps of General Johnson.

I have the honor to be, general, very respectfully, your obedient servant,

A. C. McCLURG,
Captain and Assistant Adjutant-General.

———

HEADQUARTERS DEPARTMENT OF THE CUMBERLAND,
Near Pace's Ferry, July 18, 1864—10 p. m.
Brigadier-General ELLIOTT,
Chief of Cavalry, &c.:

GENERAL: The following dispatch has just been received from Major-General Stoneman, which the general commanding directs me to communicate to you, with instructions that General McCook's cavalry be on the alert:

JULY 18, 1864.
Major-General THOMAS,
Commanding, &c.:

Two parties of rebels, one of ten, the other of about twenty-five, are known to have crossed the river between Turner's Ferry and the railroad bridge. How many more parties have crossed is not known. Prisoners have been taken by my men from one of the parties, and the other was seen. The rebels have two flat-boats at the point of crossing. The district through which the parties passed back into the country is supposed to be under the control of General Elliott's cavalry.

Respectfully, &c.,

GEORGE STONEMAN,
Major-General.

I am, general, yours, very respectfully,

HENRY STONE,
Assistant Adjutant-General.

———

HEADQUARTERS CAVALRY COMMAND,
July 18, 1864—10 p. m.
Maj. Gen. GEORGE H. THOMAS:

GENERAL: Colonel Adams, commanding brigade guarding the river near the mouth of Sweet Water, has just reported to me that the enemy are crossing the river in force above the mouth of the creek, with what object or intent has not yet transpired.

Very respectfully, your obedient servant,

GEORGE STONEMAN,
Major-General.

[Indorsement.]

HEADQUARTERS ARMY OF THE CUMBERLAND,
July 19, 1864—10 a. m.

Respectfully forwarded to Major-General Sherman for his information.
This was received about ten minutes since.

GEO. H. THOMAS,
Major-General, Commanding.

HDQRS. FIRST CAV. DIV., DEPT. OF THE CUMBERLAND,
Near Railroad Bridge, July 18, 1864.

Lieut. D. F. HOW,
Acting Assistant Adjutant-General:

I have the honor to report that it was impossible for me to encamp
one brigade at the place selected at Pace's Ferry, because the roads
were crowded with and all places where there was water occupied by
wagon trains. I have encamped both brigades in the vicinity of the
fort, and am [on] the Pace's Ferry road and picketing the river. Our
infantry skirmishers are near the creek on the other bank, but the rebel
sharpshooters are still on the abutments and on the bank below. I
will put in rifle-pits to-night and try to move them out to-morrow.

Very respectfully, your obedient servant,
E. M. McCOOK,
Brigadier-General.

I discovered the rebels working on a new work this afternoon. It is
below Sutermeister's, and will enfilade him. I told him to cut the trees
away and open on it in the morning.

E. M. McCOOK,
Brigadier-General.

HDQRS. FIRST BRIGADE, FIRST CAVALRY DIVISION,
DEPARTMENT OF THE CUMBERLAND,
In the Field, July 18, 1864.

Captain LE ROY,
Assistant Adjutant-General, First Division:

The scouting party ordered to Turner's Ferry has just returned. I
found a strong picket-line on opposite side of the Chattahoochee, evidently cavalry, which seem to have recently taken their present position. The earth-work about one mile and a half from Fort McCook is
constructed for six guns. No guns visible. No boat of any description
found upon the river. No party of the enemy has crossed the river
except six or eight footmen belonging to Cheatham's division, of whom
2 were captured by Major Carter, in command of dismounted cavalry,
at Turner's Ferry, and from which probably originated the report that
the enemy had crossed between the mouth of Peach Tree Creek and
Turner's Ferry. Major Carter has 500 dismounted cavalry at Turner's
Ferry, and pickets the river from that point to the mouth of Nickajack.

I am, respectfully, your obedient servant,
J. B. DORR,
Colonel, Commanding.

HEADQUARTERS ARMY OF THE OHIO,
In the Field, Ga., July 18, 1864.

Brig. Gen. J. D. COX,
Comdg. Third Division, Twenty-third Army Corps:

GENERAL: I have the honor to inclose herewith Special Field Orders, No. 37, current series, Military Division of the Mississippi.* The commanding general directs that the Twenty-third Corps move at 5 a. m. to-morrow, in accordance with the within order, General Hascall in advance.

Very respectfully, your obedient servant,

J. A. CAMPBELL,
Major and Assistant Adjutant-General.

HDQRS. DEPARTMENT AND ARMY OF THE TENNESSEE,
Near Nancy's Creek, July 18, 1864—4.30 a. m.

Major-General SCHOFIELD,
Commanding Army of the Ohio:

GENERAL: In order to carry out the instructions of Major-General Sherman for to-day, I shall have to move General Dodge, who is nearest you, and in fact my whole command, to the east and south, which will widen the space between us. General Dodge commences his movement at 6 a. m., and will move to the left on this side of Nancy's Creek about one mile and a quarter from his present position, cross the creek and strike into the Peach Tree road about two and a half or three miles from where you strike it, passing through Cross Keys.

Yours, truly,

JAS. B. McPHERSON,
Major-General, Commanding.

HDQRS. MILITARY DIVISION OF THE MISSISSIPPI,
In the Field, on Peach Tree Road, July 18, 1864—12 m.

General McPHERSON:

I am at Sam. House's, a brick house well known, and near Old Cross Keys. A sick negro, the only human being left on the premises, says we are eleven miles from Atlanta, five from Buck Head, and a sign board says ten miles to McAfee's Bridge and eleven to Roswell Factory. At this place the main Buck Head and Atlanta road is strongly marked and forks, the right-hand looking north going to McAfee's, and the left to Roswell Factory. This left-hand road forks one mile from here, at Old Cross Keys, the main road going to Roswell and left-hand to Johnson's Ferry. The latter is the road traveled by us. I suppose all of Thomas' troops are at Buck Head, with advance guard down to Peach Tree Creek. I think I will move Schofield one mile and a half toward Buck Head, where the negro represents a road to Decatur and forward on that road a mile or so. I think Sam. House's is not far from the northwest corner of lot 273, and if I move him as contemplated he will be to-night about 202, 203. On our map a road comes from the direction of McAfee's toward Decatur, and if you can find position about 192, 191 it would best fulfill my purpose, but be careful to order Garrard to break the road to-day or to-night and report result.

* See p. 179.

I will stay here or down at the forks of the road to-night. Schofield encountered nothing but cavalry, about 500, according to the negro's report, and all retreated toward Atlanta. Tell Garrard that it will be much easier to break the telegraph and road to-day and night than if he waits longer. This negro says there is a road leading to Stone Mountain from a Mr. Lively's, on the Decatur road, on which I suppose you to be. At any rate I will be here till evening and would like to hear from you.

Yours,

W. T. SHERMAN,
Major-General.

HDQRS. DEPARTMENT AND ARMY OF THE TENNESSEE,
Blake's Mill, Ga., July 18, 1864—9.30 p. m.

Maj. Gen. W. T. SHERMAN,
Commanding Military Division of the Mississippi:

GENERAL: Inclosed please find sketch* of my position to-night and copy of Special Field Orders, No. 70, paragraph VI, from these head-quarters.†

In pursuance of this order, the different commands were in motion promptly at the hour designated, the Seventeenth Corps closing up on the Fifteenth, and the Fifteenth and Sixteenth coming together by heads of column at the Widow Rainey's, and the infantry (Fifteenth Corps) reaching a point about one mile from Braman's [Browning's] Court-House just as the last brigade of the cavalry was passing. The cavalry under Brigadier-General Garrard pushed on and struck the railroad, and five regiments were set to work to destroy it. A brigade of infantry (Lightburn's), of Morgan L. Smith's division, was also sent down, and the two forces together thoroughly destroyed over three miles of track, upsetting the ties, breaking the iron loose, piling up the ties, putting the iron on top, and setting fire to the pile. The whole of the Fifteenth Corps was marched to the immediate vicinity of Bra-man's [Browning's] Court-House, the Sixteenth to the point indicated on the map, and the Seventeenth to Blake's Mill, to be used as a reserve to re-enforce either flank in case the enemy advanced or was found in strong force. There being no water in the vicinity of Bra-man's [Browning's] Court-House just before dark, after the brigade re-turned from the railroad, the Fifteenth Corps marched to Henderson's Mill and went into camp.

There is no telegraph line along the railroad. During our operations we saw no indications of any heavy force of the enemy; nothing but cavalry, which fell back and disappeared readily on our approach.

Inclosed please find copy of report just received from General Garrard.‡

Very respectfully, your obedient servant,

JAS. B. McPHERSON,
Major-General.

HEADQUARTERS FIFTEENTH ARMY CORPS,
Henderson's Mill, Ga., July 18, 1864.

Col. W. T. CLARK,
Asst. Adjt. Gen., Army and Department of the Tennessee:

SIR: In obedience to Special Field Orders, No. 70, I moved with my command this morning at 5 o'clock from Nancy's Creek, near Cross

---

*Not found.   † See p. 168.   ‡ See Part II, p. 808.

Keys, to the intersection of the Stone Mountain and Lawrenceville roads for the purpose of assisting Brigadier-General Garrard to break the railroad, if he should need assistance. When the head of my column reached the road leading from McAfee's Bridge to Browning's Court-House, General Garrard had just arrived, moving in the direction of the railroad, some four miles distant. After his column passed, at the suggestion of the general commanding, I moved down within two miles of the railroad; then, as directed, sent one brigade of infantry, commanded by Brigadier-General Lightburn, to the railroad. He reports to me that he effectually destroyed some two miles of rail and ties of the road to within a short distance of Stone Mountain, burning water-tank, wood, &c. During the time that General Garrard and General Lightburn were destroying the road in an easterly direction, Major Hotaling, of my staff, in charge of fifty mounted men, made up of the Eighth Indiana and my escort company, moved on the main Decatur road to within three miles of Decatur, destroying two culverts and some small portion of the railroad track. In the march to and from the railroad to my present position no resistance was met anywhere that I could hear of. One prisoner was captured. He was quite unwell. I think quite a number would have been captured if we had found them, and all been in the same condition as this one. The loss in the whole command, so far as I can learn, is 1 horse with pains in his belly from eating green corn.

Respectfully,

JOHN A. LOGAN,
Major-General.

HEADQUARTERS LEFT WING, SIXTEENTH ARMY CORPS,
In the Field, near Peach Tree Creek, Ga., July 18, 1864.

Maj. Gen. J. B. MCPHERSON,
Comdg. Department and Army of the Tennessee, in Field, Ga.:

GENERAL: Scout in from Atlanta. He left there this morning. Says the enemy were moving troops all night last night there; all the wagon trains were started off on the Augusta road; that Bate's division moved up on Peach Tree road and is intrenched on south side of that creek near Howell's Bridge; that the bridge is ready to be burned. He also reports one brigade of dismounted cavalry at Buck Head, prepared to contest our advance. This morning Bate's division was the extreme right of Johnston's infantry, and Kelly's division of cavalry on north side of Little Peach Tree between me and Buck Head. This agrees with report of rebel lieutenant captured by me this morning. This scout says it is the general talk that if Atlanta falls Polk's corps will go west toward West Point, while the remainder of Johnston's army will go toward Augusta or Macon. On yesterday Hood had the left, Polk [Stewart] the center, and Hardee the right, the militia on the left. Johnston has received no re-enforcements up to to-day. The enemy are at work on their forts and intrenchments around Atlanta.

Dispatches from Richmond report their forces shelling Washington. Atlanta papers up to the 17th instant have nothing of interest in them. One editorial speculation on Sherman's probable movement thinks he may possibly move on Stone Mountain to force the evacuation of Atlanta.

I am, general, very respectfully, your obedient servant,

G. M. DODGE,
Major-General.

JULY 18, 1864—10.30 a. m.

Captain CASE:

See heavy column of dust on the roads converging beyond Kyle's Bridge; also at or near Howell's Bridge. Troops (if dust is caused by them) are moving in a large body toward Kyle's Bridge and Stone Mountain, apparently five miles from this point.

Yours, respectfully,

SAM. F. REBER,
Captain and Acting Signal Officer.

Estimated strength of Hood's army. *

HARDEE'S CORPS.

First Division, Cheatham's:
Maney's brigade	1,200	
Strahl's brigade	1,000	
Wright's brigade	1,400	
Vaughan's brigade	1,200	
		4,800

Second Division, Cleburne's:
Polk's brigade	1,000	
Govan's brigade	1,200	
Lowrey's brigade	1,500	
Granbury's brigade	1,200	
		4,900

Third Division, Walker's:
Mercer's brigade	2,000	
Stevens' brigade	1,500	
Jackson's brigade	1,000	
Gist's brigade	1,200	
		5,700

Fourth Division, Bate's:
Lewis' brigade	700	
Finley's brigade	1,000	
Tyler's brigade	1,300	
		3,000
		18,400

HOOD'S CORPS.

First Division, Hindman's:
Deas' brigade	1,200	
Manigault's brigade	1,200	
Tucker's brigade	1,000	
Walthall's brigade	1,200	
		4,600

Second Division, Stevenson's:
Cumming's brigade	1,500	
Brown's brigade	800	
Baker's brigade	1,000	
Reynolds' brigade	1,200	
		4,500

Third Division, Stewart's:
Gibson's brigade	800	
Stovall's brigade	1,200	
Clayton's brigade	1,500	
Moore's brigade	1,000	
		4,500
		13,600

---

* Memorandum found by Union forces in an old camp July 18, 1864, and filed with records of the Army of the Cumberland.

STEWART'S CORPS.

First Division, Loring's:		
Featherston's brigade	1,500	
Adams' brigade	1,500	
Scott's brigade	1,200	
		4,200
Second Division, French's:		
Cockrell's brigade	2,000	
McNair's brigade	1,000	
Sears' brigade	1,200	
		4,200
Third Division, Walthall's:		
Cantey's brigade	2,000	
Ector's brigade	1,000	
Quarles' brigade	1,000	
		4,000
		12,400
Hardee		18,400
Hood		13,600
Stewart		12,400
		44,400

CAMP, *Near Pace's Ferry, July 18, 1864—8.30 p. m.*
(Received 11 p. m.)

Maj. T. T. ECKERT:

Army pressed forward to-day from two to five miles, and now the line rests its right on Chattahoochee, between Pace's Ferry and Turner's Ferry, extends to Peach Tree Creek, and along it half a mile, and thence is deflected toward the northeast through Buck Head; General Thomas on right, Schofield in center, and McPherson on left. No enemy encountered except cavalry and artillery. Slight resistance.

J. C. VAN DUZER.

SPECIAL FIELD ORDERS, } HDQRS. MIL. DIV. OF THE MISS.,
                     In the Field, near Cross Keys, Ga.,
No. 37. }   *July 18, 1864.*

The movements of the army to-morrow, July 19, will be as follows:

I. Major-General Thomas will press down from the north on Atlanta, holding in strength the line of Peach Tree, but crossing and threatening the enemy at all accessible points to hold him there, and also taking advantage of any ground gained, especially on the extreme right.

II. Major-General Schofield will move direct on Decatur and gain a footing on the railroad, holding it, and breaking the railroad and telegraph wire.

III. Major-General McPherson will move along the railroad toward Decatur and break the telegraph wires and the railroad. In case of the sounds of serious battle he will close in on General Schofield, but otherwise will keep every man of his command at work in destroying the railroad by tearing up track, burning the ties and iron, and twisting the bars when hot. Officers should be instructed that bars simply bent may be used again, but if when red hot they are twisted out of line they cannot be used again. Pile the ties into shape for a bonfire, put the rails across, and when red hot in the middle, let a man at each end twist the bar so that its surface become spiral. General McPherson will dispatch General Garrard's cavalry eastward along the line of the railroad to continue the destruction as far as deemed prudent.

IV. All the troops should be in motion at 5 a. m., and should not lose a moment's time until night, when the lines should be closed on General Schofield about Pea Vine and Decatur.

By order of Maj. Gen. W. T. Sherman:

L. M. DAYTON,
Aide-de-Camp.

GENERAL ORDERS, }   HDQRS. DEPT. OF THE CUMBERLAND,
No. 99.   }   *Near Pace's Ferry, Ga., July 18, 1864.*

I. The batteries in each army corps of the Army of the Cumberland will in future constitute a separate command under the corps chief of artillery, subject to the direction of the corps commander and the department chief of artillery. In action or when preparing for action they will be placed in such positions as the corps chief of artillery, with the approval of the corps commander and department chief of artillery, shall select.

II. Officers now acting as chiefs of artillery of divisions, whose batteries are not serving with the army in the field, will report to their corps chiefs of artillery as their assistants. Those whose batteries are so serving will rejoin them.

III. The issuing quartermaster and commissary of subsistence at army corps headquarters shall supply the batteries of the corps artillery with quartermaster and subsistence stores.

IV. When troops are temporarily detached from any army corps they shall be accompanied by an amount of artillery proportionate to their number; and it shall be the duty of the issuing quartermaster and commissary of subsistence of the command detached to keep this artillery supplied with quartermaster and subsistence stores until it rejoins its own corps.

V. The chief of ordnance of the department will recommend an officer to act as ordnance officer for the artillery of each corps.

VI. Corps commanders will detail a sufficient infantry force as guards to the artillery trains.

VII. The medical director of the corps will assign a sufficient number of medical officers with the corps artillery, whose duties will be exclusively with that command.

VIII. All wagons belonging to the batteries, excepting three to each, and the wagons of the division ordnance trains, now used to carry artillery ammunition, will be turned over to the issuing quartermaster at corps headquarters.

By command of Major-General Thomas:

WM. D. WHIPPLE,
Assistant Adjutant-General.

HEADQUARTERS FOURTH ARMY CORPS,
Powers' Ferry, Chattahoochee River, Ga., July 18, 1864—1 a. m.

Orders of the day for the Fourth Army Corps:

The corps will move forward to-day, starting at 5 a. m. General Newton's division will lead, followed by Major-General Stanley's division, and then General Wood's. General Newton will direct his march on Buck Head, avoiding, if possible, the road leading from Pace's Ferry to the same point.

By order of Major-General Howard:

J. S. FULLERTON,
Assistant Adjutant-General.

HEADQUARTERS FOURTH ARMY CORPS,
Buck Head, Ga., July 18, 1864—9 p. m.

Orders of the day for the Fourth Army Corps for July 19, 1864, unless changed in orders to-night:

The following-mentioned reconnaissances will be made by division commanders of this corps to-morrow, each to start from camp at 6 a. m.:

I. Major-General Stanley, with one of his brigades, will move on the Decatur road as far as the north fork of Peach Tree Creek.

II. General Newton, with his reserve regiments, will move on the road next to and on the left of the Atlanta road as far as the north fork of Peach Tree Creek.

III. General Wood, with one of his reserve brigades, will move on the Atlanta road as far as Peach Tree Creek.

It is desired that the skirmish lines be strong, and that the lines of the divisions be started simultaneously, but subsequently the connection need not be kept up.

The major-general commanding will accompany the reconnaissance on the Atlanta road, and the reconnaissances on the other roads will regulate on this one.

By order of Major-General Howard:

J. S. FULLERTON,
Assistant Adjutant-General.

SPECIAL FIELD ORDERS, }　　　ON PEACH TREE, GA.,
　　No. 71.　　　　　}　　　　　　　　*July 18, 1864.*

*　　　*　　　*　　　*　　　*　　　*　　　*

III. In accordance with instructions from Military Division of the Mississippi, the following movements will be made to-morrow:

1. Major-General Logan, commanding Fifteenth Army Corps, will, at 5 o'clock, move his command toward Decatur, striking the railroad at the nearest point on his route, tearing up track, burning the ties, making the destruction complete and effectual.

2. Major-General Blair, commanding Seventeenth Army Corps, will, at 5 o'clock, move toward Decatur, following the command of General Logan, via Henderson's Mill, or by an intermediate route between the positions of General Logan and General Dodge, if a practicable road can be found. Should General Blair discover a road intermediate, leading to the railroad, his men will also be employed in tearing up tracks, burning ties, twisting rails, &c.

3. Major-General Dodge, commanding Left Wing, Sixteenth Army Corps, will, at 5 o'clock, move forward across the creek toward Decatur, striking the railroad east of that place, and employing his troops in the effectual destruction of the road.

4. Brigadier-General Garrard, commanding cavalry division, will, at 5 o'clock, move eastward along the line of the railroad, in the vicinity of Stone Mountain, continuing its destruction as far as possible.

5. The several corps of this command will pursue the line of march toward Decatur, keeping up communication with each other as far as practicable, converging at that point and continuing their work until night, when the lines will be closed on General Schofield about Pea Vine and Decatur.

6. Should indications of a heavy battle be heard, each corps will move to the right and close in on General Schofield, but not otherwise.

7. Corps commanders will see that sufficient wagons are brought forward from their trains to supply their troops with three days' rations. Empty wagons will be sent back for supplies and all trains will move under proper guards.

By order of Maj. Gen. James B. McPherson:

WM. T. CLARK,
Assistant Adjutant-General.

HEADQUARTERS DEPARTMENT OF THE CUMBERLAND,
In the Field, July 19, 1864.

Maj. Gen. W. T. SHERMAN,
Commanding Military Division of the Mississippi:

GENERAL: If you think it advisable that Major-General Stoneman should be speedily provided with the means of crossing the river, I would respectfully suggest that inasmuch as General Howard has now a trestle bridge, there is no necessity for General McPherson's bridge to remain longer at Powers' Ferry, and it could be spared to General Stoneman. This would be better than dividing my bridge.

I am, general, very respectfully, your obedient servant,

GEO. H. THOMAS,
Major-General, U. S. Volunteers, Commanding.

HDQRS. MILITARY DIVISION OF THE MISSISSIPPI,
In the Field, July 19, 1864.

General THOMAS:

I have your note of to-day about the pontoon bridge. You will remember you promised to save one bridge of pontoons of the enemy, and I thought that would be laid at Pace's, the post most easily drawn from for the use of Stoneman, but I will let Stoneman go without, for I doubt whether we can get cavalry to cross the river as long as the enemy chooses to picket it. I am intensely anxious to hear your position and whether, if we engage the enemy to-morrow, you can lend us a hand. I am satisfied both forks of Peach Tree above the forks can be forded, and I cannot hear that Howard is across even the Middle Fork. McPherson has broken the railroad to Decatur and occupies Decatur. Schofield is on a road from Doctor Powell's to Atlanta, his advance a mile and a half down the road at the Pea Vine. I beg you to send me a sketch of the position of your troops, that I may know whether to move to-morrow directly on Atlanta. If not already done, Howard should prepare bridges across both branches of Peach Tree to-night, that in case we become heavily engaged to-morrow you can re-enforce us. What about the report of Stoneman about the enemy crossing the Chattahoochee westward at Sweet Water? I think it was a party sent to prevent Stoneman's return from West Point, whither they supposed he had gone. General Corse is not yet back, but I look for him all the time.

I am, yours, truly,

W. T. SHERMAN,
Major-General.

HDQRS. MILITARY DIVISION OF THE MISSISSIPPI,
In the Field, near Decatur, Ga., July 19, 1864.

General THOMAS:

I sent General Corse to you this morning to explain the various positions of the troops and to explain my wishes. I think you have too much of your force the other side of Nancy's Creek. One division would be ample there, and all the rest in a general line, with Buck Head as a center. Howard's corps should then feel to the left and cross the forks of the Peach Tree, toward Pea Vine Creek. I take it for granted all the main crossings of Peach Tree in that quarter are well covered, but can be turned by the left. We are across all the forks of the Peach Tree, and the head of Schofield's column is beyond the forks of the road leading to Decatur and Atlanta, where Powers' is on our map. The Atlanta road is a big one and about half a mile west of Powell's forks, the left to Atlanta six miles, and the right to Pace's Ferry. After crossing the Middle Fork, a main fork of the Peach Tree, General Schofield sent Colonel Hartsuff, of his staff, to feel down. He went to the crossing places of Peach Tree, approaching from the south, and was fired on from the bank supposed to be occupied by Howard, and had an orderly wounded. I have no doubt Howard can cross anywhere above the forks.

I have seen an Atlanta paper of the 18th, containing Johnston's farewell order to his troops. From its tone and substance I infer he has been relieved by Jeff. Davis, who sent Bragg to Atlanta to bear the order. I also infer it is not for the purpose of getting another command. Hood succeeds.

You must get across Peach Tree either by moving direct on Atlanta, or, if necessary, leave a force to watch the bridge in possession of the enemy and move by the left. This is very important, and at once, as we may have to fight all of Hood's from east of Atlanta. I prefer you should let Howard open the way at once along the Pace's Ferry and Decatur road, or any other in that direction. I will push for the occupation of Decatur. and then west for Atlanta, till we know exactly what the artificial defenses are. I have already advised you that McPherson has taken the railroad between Decatur and Stone Mountain, and I expect him and Schofield to make a junction in Decatur to-day, in which case I will move Schofield on the road from Powell's to Atlanta. Schofield reports that his skirmishers are just in the edge of Decatur—1.05 p. m. A paragraph in the Atlanta paper of yesterday says the people in Montgomery were in great apprehensions about a Yankee raid, and were rushing to arms for the defense of the city. That means Rousseau.

Yours,

SHERMAN,
Major-General.

HEADQUARTERS DEPARTMENT OF THE CUMBERLAND,
July 19, 1864—3.30 p. m.

Major-General SHERMAN,
Commanding Military Division of the Mississippi:

GENERAL: I have seen your note to General Howard. I am at the crossing of Peach Tree Creek with General Wood's division, who has crossed one brigade and is crossing another on the main road to Atlanta. General Davis is across Peach Tree at two places. General Geary will cross immediately on Wood's right. The troops are all pressing forward. All my troops were between Nancy's and Peach Tree Creek last night, and your orders of yesterday were thoroughly executed.

Very respectfully,

GEO. H. THOMAS,
Major-General, U. S. Volunteers.

HDQRS. MILITARY DIVISION OF THE MISSISSIPPI,
Near Decatur, Ga., July 19, 1864.

General THOMAS,
Army of the Cumberland:

GENERAL: I have just received General Stoneman's note with your indorsement. I cannot reconcile his information with what I see and hear; yet it is possible that the enemy is crossing in force at the mouth of Sweet Water. I think it is the cavalry by way of diversion. Please send to General Stoneman again and see if he has ascertained the truth; and if you deem it necessary you can send your right corps across at Powers' Ferry and interpose between the enemy and our bridges, as also Marietta. Stoneman and McCook have force enough to check any movement of cavalry, and there is a good force of infantry at Marietta and Kenesaw, to which place information should be promptly sent.

Yours,

W. T. SHERMAN,
Major-General.

HEADQUARTERS DEPARTMENT OF THE CUMBERLAND,
July 19, 1864—4.45 p. m.

General SHERMAN:

GENERAL: Your note dated near Decatur is received. General Wood is across Peach Tree Creek on the main road to Atlanta and pushing forward. General Geary is crossing now immediately on Wood's right. General Davis has crossed at two points, near Moore's Mill and Howell's Mill. All are ordered to push for Atlanta. It appears to me this movement will relieve General Schofield in his move on Decatur. Your order, however, to General Howard has been received and he has been ordered to execute it. All my troops have been between Nancy's Creek and Peach Tree Creek, the place where you ordered them, ever since 12 o'clock yesterday, and by sundown yesterday Palmer's skirmishers were on the bank of Peach Tree Creek covering all the crossings toward Atlanta, and the enemy continually pressed at all points.

I have given orders that the troops move forward at daybreak tomorrow morning for Atlanta.

Very respectfully,

GEO. H. THOMAS,
Major-General, U. S. Volunteers, Commanding.

P. S.—An Atlanta paper of to-day has been captured by Wood's force which reports Opelika was captured yesterday and corroborates the report that Johnston has been relieved by Hood.

G. H. THOMAS.

HDQRS. MILITARY DIVISION OF THE MISSISSIPPI,
In the Field, July 19, 1864—7 p. m.

General THOMAS:

GENERAL: I have this moment received yours of 3.30, and am very glad to hear that Howard has the means to cross over to Schofield in case of need. We have had some skirmishing and abundant evidence that the whole of the rebel army is about Atlanta. The fortifications lie mostly behind the Chattahoochee and Peach Tree, and my belief is we can approach from the east with certainty of getting within cannon reach of the town, in which case it cannot be held; but to push Schofield and McPherson on the place without a certainty of your being able to effect a junction would be extra hazardous. Schofield is on a road leading from Doctor Powell's directly to Atlanta. McPherson has a corps in Decatur and the balance just northeast. Some of the enemy's cavalry retreated east. Garrard has gone east to break railroad. I am near Doctor Powell's. Before I issue my orders I want to hear that your command is where it can take part in the battle if offered outside of Atlanta. If Hood fights behind forts close to the town, I will swing in between Atlanta and the river; but if he fight outside, we must accept battle. Please to-night give me the fullest description according to the official map.

Yours, truly,

W. T. SHERMAN,
Major-General.

HEADQUARTERS DEPARTMENT OF THE CUMBERLAND,
Near Howell's Mill, Peach Tree Creek, Ga., July 19, 1864.

Maj. Gen. W. T. SHERMAN,
Commanding Military Division of the Mississippi:

GENERAL: I have the honor to report that the following movements of the troops of the Army of the Cumberland have been made this day: The divisions of Brigadier-Generals Davis and Baird, of the Fourteenth Army Corps; Brigadier-General Geary, of the Twentieth Corps, and Brigadier-General Wood, of the Fourth Corps, have crossed the Peach Tree Creek and established themselves on the south side. The division of Major-General Stanley, of the Fourth Corps, will probably get across to-night, and I have given orders for all the columns to press forward toward Atlanta at daylight in the morning. The crossing was effected by Brigadier-Generals Davis' and Wood's divisions in the face of considerable opposition by the rebels. Not so much resistance was offered to Brigadier-Generals Geary and Baird, and Brigadier-General Johnson was prevented from crossing by a mill pond in his front.

Inclosed herewith I send a Memphis Appeal of this date.

I am, general, very respectfully, your obedient servant,

GEO. H. THOMAS,
Major-General, U. S. Volunteers, Commanding.

HDQRS. MILITARY DIVISION OF THE MISSISSIPPI,
In the Field, July 19, 1864—8.10 p. m.

General THOMAS:

Good for Rousseau! Move for Atlanta at daylight, trying to connect with Schofield two miles east of Atlanta. He will move on the road from Howell's to Atlanta; McPherson by the main road, following sub-

stantially the railroad. The confusion resulting from my misunderstanding your position resulted from want of information. I supposed
your central corps to be on the main road from Buck Head to Atlanta,
the right corps extending to the mouth of Nancy's Creek, and the left,
Howard, up along the Peach Tree road. The road laid down on the map
from Buck Head, crossing Peach Tree in lot 155, where Stanley now is,
intersects another to Atlanta, crossing the South Fork, which is much
the smaller of the two, and easily fordable at lot 57. That road would
connect your left with Schofield at the very point needed. On that
road I know Howard could meet no forts or barricades, but on the direct
road I have no doubt forts will be met. With McPherson, Howard,
and Schofield, I would have ample to fight the whole of Hood's army,
leaving you to walk into Atlanta, capturing guns and everything. But
with Schofield and McPherson alone, the game will not be so certain.
I would like to have Stanley's and Newton's divisions follow that route,
and let Wood go ahead, as he is across, and effect the junction at some
point near Pea Vine, say two or three miles northeast of Atlanta. At
all events, now that I feel satisfied you can get across Peach Tree, and
as I think the opportunity the best, I will order the universal movement
on Atlanta at daylight. Communicate with me as often as possible. I
will be with Schofield, the center.

  Yours, truly,

            W. T. SHERMAN,
                Major-General.

          AT SUTERMEISTER'S BATTERY,
            July 19, 1864—11.15 a. m.
Major-General THOMAS,
  Commanding Army of the Cumberland:
  The battery being erected by the rebels is down the river, with two
embrasures bearing in that direction. It is two miles from Sutermeister and not intended to fire on his work. The bridge we saw across
a creek above the railroad is still there, and therefore I don't think it
can be Peach Tree Creek, as Davis' skirmishers were ordered to the
mouth of that creek. A deserter from the rebels at General McCook's
reports belonging to Cheatham's division, which left the large fort and
other works at about 6 p. m. yesterday.

            J. M. BRANNAN,
        Brigadier-General and Chief of Artillery.

  I will ascertain something positive as to the creek. Rebel skirmishers are pretty strong and quite active this morning.

                  J. M. B.

  If the creek we see from here is Peach Tree Creek, then our right
(Davis') is not on it.

                  J. M. B.

        HEADQUARTERS FOURTH ARMY CORPS,
            July 19, 1864—7.40 a. m.
General THOMAS,
  Commanding Department of the Cumberland:
  GENERAL: General Wood made a reconnaissance as directed, reach-
ing the vicinity of Peach Tree Creek at 6.30 a. m. I am with the recon-

naissance. Bridge is burned. A pretty fair infantry work constructed as a bridge-head beyond and manned with infantry. No artillery opened by enemy yet. He made a demonstration as if to turn our right, pushing out a line of skirmishers in a corn-field. They ran back as our artillery opened. There is considerable smoke on the main ridge half a mile toward Atlanta, but no main work, except near the bridge and river.

Respectfully,

O. O. HOWARD,
Major-General.

HEADQUARTERS FOURTH ARMY CORPS,
Near Peach Tree Creek, July 19, 1864—8 a. m.

Major-General THOMAS,
Commanding Department:

General Wood reached Peach Tree Creek at 6.30 a. m. He found the bridge burned and a pretty fair bridge-head on the other side constructed for infantry. There is considerable smoke on the ridge half a mile toward Atlanta, but no other earth-works appear except those mentioned. No artillery has yet opened.

Respectfully,

O. O. HOWARD,
Major-General.

HEADQUARTERS FOURTH ARMY CORPS,
Buck Head, Ga., July 19, 1864—9.30 a. m.

Brigadier-General WHIPPLE,
Chief of Staff:

After my previous note the enemy opened on General Wood with artillery. General Stanley made a reconnaissance on the Decatur road. He finds the bridge across the North Fork burning and very little force to oppose him. General Newton sent a regiment on the intermediate road to a point near the mouth of North Fork and finds infantry with works about to the extent of a brigade. I have directed General Stanley to put a force across North Fork if possible, and to secure and repair the bridge. The crossing at General Wood's position is the most difficult of any, and I think impracticable with any considerable force on the other side.

Very respectfully, your obedient servant,

O. O. HOWARD,
Major-General.

HEADQUARTERS DEPARTMENT OF THE CUMBERLAND,
July 19, 1864—9.15 a. m.

Major-General HOWARD,
Commanding Fourth Army Corps:

GENERAL: Your dispatch of 7.40 received. The general commanding directs that you push forward as fast as possible in the direction of Atlanta.

By command of Major-General Thomas:

J. P. WILLARD,
Captain and Aide-de-Camp.

HEADQUARTERS FOURTH CORPS,
Buck Head, July 19, 1864.

Major-General SHERMAN,
Commanding Military Division of the Mississippi:

GENERAL: General Corse just left me for General Thomas. On the main road to Atlanta I find the bridge burnt, stream about fifty paces wide, a bridge-head pretty well constructed for infantry and well manned with troops armed with rifles. No further works can be seen on the main ridge beyond the creek. I do not deem a crossing at this point practicable. On the Decatur road General Stanley finds the bridge burning, which he will try to secure and repair. Very little force in his front. This bridge was across the north fork of Peach Tree Creek. General Newton, upon an intermediate road between Stanley and Wood, finds infantry works defended by troops. On Wood the enemy opened with two pieces of artillery and made a demonstration as if to turn his right flank, but it resulted in nothing further. The rumor is (from prisoners and scouts) that Hood is in command, and that Johnston has gone east. A scout who was there reports that the rebel right flank (infantry) was last night at dark near this bridge on the Atlanta road, where Wood now is.

Respectfully, your obedient servant,

O. O. HOWARD,
Major-General.

HDQRS. MILITARY DIVISION OF THE MISSISSIPPI,
In the Field, one [mile] and a half from Decatur,
July 19, 1864—12 m.

General HOWARD:

I have received your note. It is true Johnston is relieved and gone east. I have seen a copy of his order of farewell to his troops. Hood is in command and at Atlanta.

I want Thomas to have more of his command at Buck Head. A division will be ample west of Nancy's. All the rest should be from Buck Head east. I wish him to press hard at all the crossings of the main Peach Tree Creek, but your corps should be across in the direction of Decatur or Pea Vine Creek.

General Schofield sent to communicate with you, and the bearer approached by one of the crossings, the second one from the mouth of the South Fork, but was fired on, he thinks, by your pickets, wounding an orderly, and he returned. You will have no trouble in crossing the two forks of Peach Tree any where above the forks. General Schofield now holds the forks of the Atlanta and Decatur roads, and is skirmishing on both, but thinks he will soon have the head of his column at Decatur. McPherson is approaching the same objective point from the east, having broken up the railroad good. I will write to General Thomas by a courier, and give him such orders as will enable you to put your corps across both forks of Peach Tree between Schofield and your present position.

Yours,

W. T. SHERMAN,
Major-General.

HEADQUARTERS FOURTH ARMY CORPS,
Buck Head, Ga., July 19, 1864—8 p. m.

Brigadier-General WHIPPLE, *Chief of Staff:*

GENERAL: In accordance with instructions, General Wood made a demonstration this a. m. along the Atlanta road to Peach Tree Creek. Generals Newton and Stanley at the same time making a reconnaissance with a small force on the roads to the left. The enemy was found in considerable force and well posted. His works covering the bridge were carefully constructed intrenchments. As soon as I received the order from your headquarters dated 9.15 a. m. of to-day, I ordered General Wood to force a crossing. This he did very handsomely, driving out a brigade of the enemy's infantry and taking possession of his rifle-pits. He took about 30 prisoners. General Stanley effected a crossing of the North Fork of Peach Tree Creek, extinguished the burning and repaired the bridge. Casualties of the corps about 20 killed and wounded.

Very respectfully, &c.,

O. O. HOWARD,
Major-General.

HEADQUARTERS FOURTH ARMY CORPS,
Buck Head, Ga., July 19, 1864.

Major-General STANLEY, *Commanding First Division:*

The general commanding directs that you secure the bridge, if possible, by throwing a force over the creek. Strengthen your force there, if you think it necessary, to the extent of a brigade.

Very respectfully, your obedient servant,

O. O. HOWARD,
Major-General.

HEADQUARTERS DEPARTMENT OF THE CUMBERLAND,
In the Field, near Howell's Mill, Peach Tree Creek, Ga.,
July 19, 1864.

Maj. Gen. J. M. PALMER,
Commanding Fourteenth Army Corps:

GENERAL: The major-general commanding directs that as soon as Brigadier-General Johnson can get his bridge finished that you cause his and Brigadier-General Baird's divisions to push toward Atlanta, Johnson feeling for General Hooker's right. Brigadier-General Davis' division had better remain where it is to prevent and meet any movement the enemy may make to turn our right, unless he ascertains that he (the enemy) has ceased to occupy the heights in his (Davis') front and right.

I am, general, very respectfully, your obedient servant,

WM. D. WHIPPLE,
Assistant Adjutant-General.

HEADQUARTERS TWENTIETH ARMY CORPS,
Peach Tree Creek, Ga., July 19, 1864—5 p. m.

Brigadier-General WHIPPLE, *Chief of Staff:*

GENERAL: General Geary has one brigade established on the south side of Peach Tree Creek. I have directed him to skirmish along the ridge, which is a continuation of the ridge which leads to the creek from my headquarters. Lieutenant Ludlow is now engaged in constructing a bridge for the passage of artillery and trains. We encountered but little resistance after I had gotten one regiment over the creek. My headquarters to-night same as last night.

Very respectfully, your obedient servant,

JOSEPH HOOKER,
Major-General, Commanding.

The enemy opposed to me, prisoners state, is Gates' [Gist's] brigade, Walker's division, Hardee's corps. As near as I can learn Walker's division is now drawn up in line of battle on the Atlanta road, via Howell's Mill. Prisoners state that the whole of Hardee's corps is in this neighborhood.

Respectfully,

JOSEPH HOOKER,
Major-General, Commanding.

HEADQUARTERS TWENTIETH ARMY CORPS,
Peach Tree Creek, Ga., July 19, 1864—6 p. m.

Brigadier-General WHIPPLE,
Chief of Staff:

GENERAL: I have the honor to report that I have given directions for the whole of Geary's division to cross Peach Tree Creek and establish themselves on the south side of it, and shall bring up Williams' division to support him. Prisoners state that the order was published last night relieving Johnston and putting Hood in command of their army. They do not know that any portion of their forces have been sent to our left. They say that Stewart's (Polk's) corps is on the left of Hardee's, which latter is in our front. They state further that their main line of defense is three miles from Atlanta in front of me, and about two and a half miles in the direction of the Chattahoochee. They state that the assignment of Hood gives great dissatisfaction in Hardee's corps.

Very respectfully, your obedient servant,

JOSEPH HOOKER,
Major-General, Commanding.

HEADQUARTERS DEPARTMENT OF THE CUMBERLAND,
In the Field, near Howell's Mill, Peach Tree Creek, Ga.,
July 19, 1864.

Major-General HOOKER,
Commanding Twentieth Corps:

GENERAL: The major-general commanding directs that to-morrow morning, commencing at daylight, you move your entire corps to the south side of the Peach Tree Creek, at the point where General Geary crossed his division this evening, and push out toward Atlanta. Major-Generals Palmer and Howard have been ordered to do the same, and you will, if practicable, connect with them on your right and left.

I am, very respectfully, your obedient servant,

WM. D. WHIPPLE,
Assistant Adjutant-General.

HEADQUARTERS ARMY OF THE OHIO,
In the Field, Ga., July 19, 1864.

Col. E. W. CRITTENDEN,
Commanding Cavalry Brigade, Isham's Ferry, Ga.:

COLONEL: General Stoneman reports that the enemy is crossing the river at the mouth of Sweet Water. They will doubtless attempt to destroy our trains and depot at Marietta, and may attempt to capture our bridges at the different river crossings. Keep all the trains on this side the river and under your guns. Look out for the rebels and give them a warm reception. Keep me informed of all that you learn. The supply train is ordered forward to-night.

Very respectfully, your obedient servant,
J. M. SCHOFIELD,
Major-General, Commanding.

HEADQUARTERS ARMY OF THE OHIO,
Near Decatur, Ga., July 19, 1864.

Brig. Gen. M. S. HASCALL,
Commanding Second Division, Twenty-third Army Corps:

GENERAL: General Cox is ordered to move forward on the Atlanta road at once. The commanding general desires you to move your command directly in rear of General Cox's column, keeping in close support of him, in advance of his wagons.

Very respectfully, your obedient servant,
J. A. CAMPBELL,
Major and Assistant Adjutant-General.

HEADQUARTERS ARMY OF THE OHIO,
Near Decatur, Ga., July 19, 1864—11.40 p. m.

Brig. Gen. J. D. COX,
Commanding Third Division, Twenty-third Army Corps:

GENERAL: A general movement of the army on Atlanta is ordered at 5 a. m. to-morrow. The commanding general desires you to have your command in readiness to move at that hour, and await further orders from these headquarters.

Very respectfully, your obedient servant,
J. A. CAMPBELL,
Major and Assistant Adjutant-General.

HEADQUARTERS CAVALRY COMMAND,
July 19, 1864.

Maj. Gen. GEORGE H. THOMAS:

GENERAL: The force that crossed the river last night is supposed to be a strong scouting party.

Respectfully,
GEO. STONEMAN,
Major-General.

HDQRS. CAVALRY COMMAND, DEPT. OF THE OHIO,
July 19, 1864—11 a. m.

Major-General THOMAS,
  Commanding, &c.:

I have ascertained that the rebel party that crossed the river last night near the mouth of Sweet Water Creek, probably recrossed this morning, as I cannot hear of their having gone northward, nor that they brought over any horses. The enemy's pickets near Turner's Ferry and the mouth of Nickajack were very active and unusually spiteful all night and this morning, and I have strengthened the line, keeping a limited reserve at the most central position. He appears strongest near the mouth of Sweet Water, a large cavalry camp being there.

I learn that several parties of several hundred in each party made their appearance in the country we passed over, crossing at Campbellton after we left there, three days ago. The enemy have facilities for crossing, as he has all the boats on their side, which are sunk when not required. I have one brigade near the mouth of Sweet Water watching the force opposite, another near the mouth of Nickajack, the dismounted men at Turner's Ferry, all connecting. My remaining force, acting as a reserve, and to guard our communications, is at and near the Widow Mitchell's, and from this I also send out scouts beyond the Sweet Water Town bridge. I will keep you, and through you, the commanding general, informed of everything of importance as it transpires.

Very respectfully, &c.,

GEORGE STONEMAN,
Major-General, Commanding.

(Forwarded to General Sherman by General Thomas.)

HDQRS. MILITARY DIVISION OF THE MISSISSIPPI,
In the Field, at Sam. House's, July 19, 1864—1 a. m.

General MCPHERSON:

DEAR GENERAL: I have just received your report and papers, and have read them all. The breaking the road is all right. Now we must look after Joe Johnston. Move to-day toward Decatur and co-operate with Schofield and Thomas. Schofield's advance is across Peach Tree, on the direct road to Decatur, and met little opposition. We will develop their plans to-morrow. Schofield will move early, and Thomas will press for the front. I will be near Peach Tree Creek, where the Cross (Old) Keys road crosses by a ford and bridge, which is being repaired. You had better approach Decatur from the northeast; the Lawrenceville road seems to fulfill the conditions. I will see you about Decatur to-day.

Yours, truly,

SHERMAN,
Major-General.

HDQRS. MILITARY DIVISION OF THE MISSISSIPPI,
Decatur, July 19, 1864.

Major-General MCPHERSON,
  Commanding Army of the Tennessee:

GENERAL: I am directed by the general commanding to say that General Stoneman reports the enemy as crossing in force about the mouth of Sweet Water Creek from east to west.   He advises you to get your trains on this side of the river and give such directions as to be prepared for any cavalry dash at Roswell to-night.

I am, general, yours, respectfully,

L. M. DAYTON,
Aide-de-Camp.

[July 19, 1864.—For Garrard to McPherson, reporting operations, &c., see Part II, p. 808.]

Camp on Peach Tree Creek,
July 19, 1864—11.30 p. m.

Maj. T. T. Eckert,
Washington, D. C.:

Right of line in nearly same position as at date my last.   Center advanced to Peach Tree Creek; left swung round, destroying railroad from point near Stone Mountain to Decatur, where it now rests.   I think I said our line rested on Chattahoochee, at Turner's, which was manifest blunder.   Should have said Howell's.   Rebel left is at Turner's, and right at point between Atlanta and Decatur, on Augusta railroad. Johnston is relieved by Hood.   Jeff. Davis, Bragg, and Johnston went east together four days since.   Resistance more determined to-day, and we find infantry line and intrenchments threatened.

J. C. VAN DUZER.

Special Field Orders,   Hdqrs. Mil. Div. of the Miss.,
                         In the Field, near Decatur, Ga.,
No. 39.   *July 19, 1864.*

The whole army will move on Atlanta by the most direct roads to-morrow, July 20, beginning at 5 a. m., as follows:

I. Major-General Thomas from the direction of Buck Head, his left to connect with General Schofield's right about two miles northeast of Atlanta, about lot 15, near the houses marked as "Hu." and "Col. Hoo."

II. Major-General Schofield by the road leading from Doctor Powell's to Atlanta.

III. Major-General McPherson will follow one or more roads direct from Decatur to Atlanta, following substantially the railroad.

Each army commander will accept battle on anything like fair terms, but if the army reach within cannon-range of the city without receiving artillery or musketry fire he will halt, form a strong line, with batteries in position, and await orders.   If fired on from the forts or buildings of Atlanta no consideration must be paid to the fact that they are occupied by families, but the place must be cannonaded without the formality of a demand.

The general-in-chief will be with the center of the army, viz, with or near General Schofield.

By order of Maj. Gen. W. T. Sherman:

L. M. DAYTON,
Aide-de-Camp.

HEADQUARTERS FOURTH ARMY CORPS,
Buck Head, Ga., July 19, 1864—6 p. m.

Orders of the day for the Fourth Army Corps, for July 20, 1864.

This corps will march on Atlanta, starting promptly at 5 a. m. to-morrow. The troops will move in two columns on different roads, but these columns will unite soon after leaving the other side of Peach Tree Creek. Major-General Stanley's division will constitute one column, and the other will be composed of Generals Newton's and Wood's divisions, General Newton's division to take the lead. After these two columns form a junction, Major-General Stanley's division will take the lead, followed by General Newton's and then General Wood's division. The route of march will be pointed out to division commanders before 5 a. m. to-morrow.

By order of Major-General Howard :

J. S. FULLERTON,
Assistant Adjutant-General.

———

SPECIAL FIELD ORDERS, }   NEAR DECATUR, GA.,
No. 72.   }   *July 19, 1864.*

In order to carry out Special Field Orders, No. 39, headquarters Military Division of the Mississippi, a copy of which is inclosed herewith,* the following movements will take place to-morrow:

1. Maj. Gen. John A. Logan will move his command through Decatur, on the direct road to Atlanta, starting at 5 a. m.

2. Major-General Blair will move his command, starting at 6 o'clock, into Decatur, thence south, or nearly so, a mile and a half to Schofield's house, where he will take a road leading to Atlanta and which intersects the main road from Decatur at a distance of three miles from Atlanta, coming in on the left of Major-General Logan.

3. Major-General Dodge will hold his command in his present position and be ready to follow immediately after the Fifteenth Army Corps on direct road.

4. Brigadier-General Garrard will operate upon our left flank and rear as we move toward Atlanta, and will so dispose his forces as to cover the trains in and about Decatur from any cavalry dash.

5. All wagons, except ammunition wagons and ambulances, will be left behind in the vicinity and to the north of Decatur, until the result of our advance is determined.

6. The command will move forward prepared for battle, divested of all useless incumbrances, and the major-general commanding trusts that every man will be found in ranks and in his proper place.

By order of Maj. Gen. James B. McPherson:

WM. T. CLARK,
Assistant Adjutant-General.

———

NEAR ATLANTA, GA., *July 20, 1864—9 p. m.*
(Received 12.45 p. m. 21st.)

Maj. Gen. H. W. HALLECK,
Washington, D. C.:

GENERAL: I have a dispatch from General Grant. Answer him in my name that Maj. Gen. A. J. Smith has the very orders he suggests,

———
* See p. 193.

viz, to hang on to Forrest and prevent his coming to Tennessee. I will, however, renew the orders. I advanced from the Chattahoochee in force on the 17th. On the 18th General McPherson and Garrard's cavalry reached the Augusta road and destroyed about five miles of it east of Decatur. On the 19th the whole line crossed Peach Tree Creek, General McPherson occupying Decatur. To-day we moved on Atlanta and have been fighting all day. Our line now extends from a point on the railroad two miles and a half east of Atlanta, and extends around by the north to the mouth of Peach Tree Creek. We find the enemy in force, but will close in to-morrow. By the Atlanta papers we learn that Johnston is relieved and Hood commands; that Rousseau is on the railroad at Opelika, and that most of the newspapers and people have left Atlanta. General Thomas is on my right, General Schofield the center, and General McPherson on the left, General Garrard's cavalry on the left rear of General McPherson, and Generals Stoneman and McCook on the west bank, guarding our right flank. The enemy still clings to his intrenchments. If General Grant can keep Lee from re-enforcing this army for a week, I think I can dispose of it. We have taken several hundred prisoners, and had some short severe encounters, but they were partial; but we have pressed the enemy back at all points until our rifle-shot can reach the town. If he strengthens his works I will gradually swing around between him and his only source of supplies, Macon.

> W. T. SHERMAN,
> *Major-General.*

HDQRS. MILITARY DIVISION OF THE MISSISSIPPI,
In the Field, near Decatur, Ga., July 20, 1864—1.55 a. m.

General THOMAS:

I am now in possession of your sketch, which is perfectly clear and plain. In advancing this morning, of course we will bring on a heavy battle, and should be as fully prepared as possible. I think as your troops are now disposed your right will be too strong as compared with your left. I have, therefore, to request that Stanley and Newton, of Howard's corps, move by the road Stanley is now on, making a right wheel gradually until they can meet with Schofield and Wood. In other words, I wish you to strengthen your left and risk more to your right, for the reason that as Atlanta is threatened the enemy will look to it rather than the river. Now, I have read the papers, and Rousseau has surely broken up the road about Opelika very opportunely. We have done complete work east of Decatur, and luckily it appears that a locomotive has blown up and encumbered the track on the Macon road, so now is the time for us to strike in force. Do keep me fully advised, as I am pressed from right, left, and center with questions as to the dispositions of the different commands. But all now are in good position, and it only remains to find out where is the artificial defenses of the enemy.

I am, &c.,

> W. T. SHERMAN,
> *Major-General.*

HEADQUARTERS ARMY OF THE CUMBERLAND,
July 20, 1864—12 m.

Maj. Gen. W. T. SHERMAN,
    Commanding Military Division of the Mississippi:

GENERAL: I have just completed an inspection of the lines from right to left. The enemy seems to be resisting General Palmer's extreme right very obstinately. I have therefore directed him to hold General Davis in force to observe and oppose any attempts on our right flank. The other two divisions of General Palmer's corps, General Hooker's corps, and General Newton's division, of General Howard's corps, are a mile in advance of Peach Tree Creek, their skirmishers connecting, and the troops advancing gradually. Prisoners report that the enemy's line of battle confronts my troops, with his left near Turner's Ferry, and his right resting on what I take to be Pea Vine Creek. He has a heavy line of skirmishers in my front. If the prisoners' report be true his attention is fully occupied by us, and I am in hopes Generals McPherson, Schofield, and Howard will be able to fall upon his rear without any very great difficulty. Captain Sutermeister, who commands the artillery stationed in the redoubt on the north side of the Chattahoochee, at the railroad bridge, reports considerable force of the enemy in his front in their rifle-pits. That report, taken in connection with the fact of a considerable force threatening General Davis' right, induces me to place some confidence in the reports of the deserters, which I hope may be true, as it will enable you to capture a great many prisoners. General Davis lost quite heavily yesterday, probably 200, including wounded and missing. The loss in the other commands is slight. We have taken about 50 of the enemy prisoners and buried 25 or 30 of their killed.

    Very respectfully, yours, &c.,

GEO. H. THOMAS,
Major-General, U. S. Volunteers, Commanding.

P. S.—The Stoneman raid turns out to be a humbug. I sent you his last report yesterday afternoon and hope it was received. It seems that when twenty-five of the enemy are seen anywhere, they are considered in force.

G. H. T.

WITH GENERAL HOWARD,
Four miles north of Atlanta, [July 20, 1864]—3.25 [p. m.].

General THOMAS:

From McPherson's fire, I think he is within one and a half or two miles of Atlanta. Schofield ought to be within two miles. All your troops should push hard for Atlanta, sweeping everything before them.

W. T. SHERMAN,
Major-General.

HDQRS. MILITARY DIVISION OF THE MISSISSIPPI,
In the Field, near Atlanta, Ga., July 20, 1864—6.10 [p. m.].

General THOMAS:

DEAR GENERAL: I have yours of 12 m. I have been with Howard and Schofield to-day, and one of my staff is just back from General McPherson. All report the enemy in their front so strong that I was in hopes none were left for you, but I see it is the same old game; but we must not allow the enemy to build a new system of fortifications. We cannot pass Atlanta without reducing it, and the more time we give them the harder it will be to carry. General Schofield is near the distillery, where the enemy is fortifying. General Howard is just where he first encountered the enemy, four miles back from Atlanta, and McPherson is on the railroad, about two miles and a half out, but reports a line of breast-works, but does not seem certain. I wish you to press forward all the time, and thereby contract the lines. If we can shorten our line either to the left or right, we should attempt to break up West Point. I rather incline to think it best to swing to the right, but hope to-morrow's work may develop some weak part. The enemy attempted to sally against Cox, but were quickly repulsed. I saw the skirmishers of the other division of Schofield make a dash at a line of rifle-pits, carrying it and capturing about 100 prisoners. I was anxious to-day to prevent the enemy from making a new and larger line of breast-works than had been at first prepared, which is so near Atlanta that artillery could overreach and enter the town. All the prisoners captured by Schofield are of Hood's corps, though each division commander insists he has to fight two corps. All the ground I have seen is densely wooded, but the roads are good. We will to-morrow press at all points and contract our lines, so as to spare a column for detached service. It seems to me Palmer can force the enemy to evacuate the works on this bank of the Chattahoochee or be captured. I will push Schofield and McPherson all I know how.

     Yours, truly,

W. T. SHERMAN,
Major-General, Commanding.

HEADQUARTERS ARMY OF THE CUMBERLAND,
July 20, 1864—6.15 p. m.

Maj. Gen. W. T. SHERMAN,
     Commanding Military Division of the Mississippi:

     GENERAL: The enemy attacked me in full force at about 4 p. m., and has persisted until now, attacking very fiercely, but he was repulsed handsomely by the troops all along my line. Our loss has been heavy, but the loss inflicted upon the enemy has been very severe. We have taken many prisoners, and General Ward reports having taken 2 stand of colors. I cannot make at present more than this general report, but will send you details as soon as I can get them from my corps commanders.

     Very respectfully, yours, &c.,

GEO. H. THOMAS,
Major-General, U. S. Volunteers, Commanding.

HDQRS. MILITARY DIVISION OF THE MISSISSIPPI,
In the Field, July 20, 1864—8 p. m.

General THOMAS:

     DEAR GENERAL: I have just read General Stoneman's letter, with your indorsment. We have seen enough to-day to convince us that all of Stoneman's information is incorrect. Something more than militia remain at Atlanta, and they are not demoralized. They have fought hard and persistently all day, and the heavy musketry fire still continues with Howard and Schofield. I do not hear McPherson's guns now. I will send him your letter, but fear his answer will be that he has all the rebels on his flank. I think he is already impressed with the importance of pressing hard on that flank. If we cannot break in, we must move by the right flank and interpose between the river and Atlanta, and operate against the road south. If you can advance your whole line, say to within three miles of Atlanta, I can throw a force around your rear to East Point. If you see a good chance to strike in that quarter you may call for Stoneman's and McCook's men, and let them come across by Pace's and march down this bank. My own opinion is that in the morning you will find the forts on the Chattahoochee abandoned, and think you will have no difficulty in pushing your line up close to Atlanta. At all events, try it. I will send your and Stoneman's letters to McPherson, but think the opportunity of operating on that flank, if it did exist, is now past.

Yours, truly,

W. T. SHERMAN,
Major-General.

HDQRS. FOURTH ARMY CORPS, INSPECTOR'S OFFICE,
Near Durand's Mill, on Peach Tree Creek
(South Fork), Ga., July 20, 1864.

Colonel MENDENHALL,
Assistant Inspector-General, Dept. of the Cumberland:

COLONEL: I have the honor to report that the divisions of Stanley and Wood crossed the South Fork of Peach Tree Creek to-day near Durand's Mill, and are now in position, with the left upon the Atlanta road and the right near the mouth of South Fork Peach Tree Creek. General Newton occupies the position taken by General Wood yesterday, south of the creek on the main Buck Head and Atlanta road, having gained some ground. All have had some hard fighting with the enemy's infantry and artillery. Stanley connects with General Schofield on his left, and Wood connects with King on the right. Just after dark Grose's brigade captured 42 prisoners, among them a captain belonging to Stevenson's division, Cheatham's corps (Hood's). Gibson's brigade crossed the south fork of the creek after sunset, and forms Wood's extreme right, near the junction of the two forks. Please mention this latter to General Thomas, as it was not so reported in General Howard's communication.

Respectfully,

C. H. HOWARD,
Lieutenant-Colonel and Assistant Inspector-General.

JULY 20, 1864—8.15 a. m.

General WHIPPLE:

I sent a staff officer to General Hooker, who reports Geary's division only over, distant three-quarters to one mile from my right. General Hooker is to send another division to the left of Geary. As soon as this is done I will advance a strong skirmish line to feel the enemy. It seems to me useless to attempt anything until I have a connection with Hooker, who is now too far. I respectfully await your instructions.

Respectfully, &c.,

J. NEWTON,
Brigadier-General.

P. S.—The enemy opened artillery on Hooker.

J. N.

JULY 20, 1864.

General WHIPPLE:

I am ordered to report directly to General Thomas by General Howard. I was ready to attack, when orders were received taking Wood away. I am relieving Hazen's brigade, and have sent to find the whereabouts of General Hooker, on my right. As soon as these are done I will advance a strong skirmish line of three regiments, in order to feel and ascertain what I have in front. My force is 3,200 bayonets.

Respectfully, &c.,

JOHN NEWTON,
Brigadier-General, Commanding Division.

HEADQUARTERS ARMY OF THE CUMBERLAND,
July 20, 1864—10.30 a. m.

Brig. Gen. J. NEWTON:

GENERAL: Your dispatch of 8.30 o'clock is received. I am with Major-General Hooker, who informs me that General Ward's division has gone into position between your right and General Geary's left, and closes up that interval. Prepare your command for an advance, and move forward in conjunction with General Hooker's troops. I will be over to see you in a few minutes on the Buck Head and Atlanta road.

Very respectfully, your obedient servant.

GEO. H. THOMAS,
Major-General, U. S. Volunteers, Commanding.

HEADQUARTERS ARMY OF THE CUMBERLAND,
July 20, 1864—3.45 p. m.

Brig. Gen. JOHN NEWTON:

GENERAL: The major-general commanding directs that you hold the ground you occupy at present and strengthen your position until General Hooker comes up with you.

I am, general, very respectfully, your obedient servant,

ROBT. H. RAMSEY,
Captain and Assistant Adjutant-General.

NEAR HOWELL'S BRIDGE, GA.,
July 20, 1864—1.30 p. m.

[General THOMAS:]

GENERAL: I sent you a note about half an hour since, but fixed the hour wrong, my watch having stopped. Matters remain here about as you left them this morning. General Palmer is waiting for General Hooker to advance his lines before he advances Johnson and Baird. He will then keep pace with them. The bridge will be finished in half an hour. The battery on the hill is completed, and has been firing at rebel lines. No change in enemy's position. They are strengthening their works in front of Davis. Slight skirmish fire kept up along the line.

Very respectfully, your obedient servant,
WM. D. WHIPPLE,
Assistant Adjutant-General.

NEAR BRIDGE ON MAIN ROAD TO ATLANTA
THROUGH GENERAL PALMER'S LINES,
July 20, 1864—3 p. m.

[General THOMAS:]

GENERAL: Things remain here as you left them this morning. General Palmer is waiting for General Hooker to advance before pushing forward Johnson and Baird, who will keep pace with General Geary when he starts. The battery on the hill is finished, and has been firing into what was supposed to be the rebel skirmish line. There is no perceptible change in the enemy's position. They have developed a piece or two of artillery, firing apparently by guess at the bridge they are building near here. The battery cannot be seen from any position on this side of the creek, and it is fair to presume that those at the battery cannot see the bridge. It will be done in an hour.

Very respectfully,
WM. D. WHIPPLE,
Assistant Adjutant-General.

NEAR HOWELL'S MILL, GA.,
July 20, 1864—4.45 p. m.

[General THOMAS:]

Rebs attacked us about 4 o'clock at the junction between Twentieth and Fourteenth Corps, McCook's and Knipe's brigades, and were repulsed. Attack repeated and repulsed again. The enemy is still moving troops to our left, as they have been all day.

Very respectfully, your obedient servant,
WM. D. WHIPPLE,
Assistant Adjutant-General.

The attack was very fierce and determined. Colonel McCook's adjutant was killed.

W. D. W.

HEADQUARTERS FOURTH ARMY CORPS,
Durand's Farm, Ga., July 20, 1864—7 p. m.

General WHIPPLE,
Assistant Adjutant-General and Chief of Staff:

GENERAL: I moved the two divisions, as directed, across both branches of Peach Tree Creek, formed a junction with General Schofield between four and five miles from Atlanta. We have found the enemy in strong force in our front. General Stanley drove the rebel skirmishers first from rail barricades, afterward from well-constructed rifle-pits. The enemy opened on him with musketry and artillery. General Stanley has deployed two brigades and General Wood two. General Wood's right brigade occupies General Stanley's position of last night on the other side of North Fork. General Newton's operations for the day have not been reported officially. Prisoners taken from Cheatham's and Stevenson's divisions.

Respectfully,

O. O. HOWARD,
Major-General.

Written after dusk; can't see.

HEADQUARTERS FOURTH CORPS,
Near Atlanta, Ga., July 20, 1864—8 p. m.

Major-General STANLEY,
Commanding First Division:

GENERAL: Please instruct your brigade commanders to be on the lookout for movements of the enemy to-night. If he withdraws follow him up, if possible, and annoy him as much as you can. This in accordance with instructions received from Major-General Sherman.

By order of Major-General Howard:

J. S. FULLERTON,
Assistant Adjutant-General.

(Similar verbal instructions given to General Wood.)

HEADQUARTERS DEPARTMENT OF THE CUMBERLAND,
Near Howell's Mill, near Peach Tree Creek, July 20, 1864.

Maj. Gen. O. O. HOWARD,
Commanding Fourth Army Corps:

GENERAL: The following extract from a letter from Major-General Sherman* is sent you for your information and guidance. You will follow this order should it be at variance with that given you yesterday by the major-general commanding.

I am, general, very respectfully, your obedient servant,

WM. D. WHIPPLE,
Assistant Adjutant-General.

HEADQUARTERS FOURTH ARMY CORPS,
Buck Head, Ga., July 20, 1864—6 a. m.

Brigadier-General NEWTON,
Commanding Second Division:

In accordance with instructions just received, you will move toward Atlanta along the main road, as previously directed. You will keep up communication with General Hooker's command. General Wood is

----

* See Sherman to Thomas, July 19, beginning with "The road laid down on the map" and ending "say two or three miles northeast of Atlanta," p. 186.

directed to follow General Stanley. You will rather consider yourself detached, reporting when possible directly to department headquarters. As soon as it can be done the other two divisions will be pushed back to a connection with you. From present appearances the battle will be fought by the forces to your left.

By order of Major-General Howard:

J. S. FULLERTON,
Assistant Adjutant-General.

HEADQUARTERS DEPARTMENT OF THE CUMBERLAND,
In the Field, July 20, 1864.

Maj. Gen. J. M. PALMER,
Commanding Fourteenth Army Corps:

GENERAL: The major-general commanding does not desire that you should build a wagon bridge in front of Johnson. If he has the means of crossing his infantry at the bridge you speak of in your communication, that is all he desires. The artillery and wagons can be crossed at General Geary's bridge, or at one of the others you have built, or both. Inclosed I send copy of Special Field Orders, No. 39, from headquarters Military Division of the Mississippi, and return your letter, that you may have it copied at your leisure.

I am, general, very respectfully, your obedient servant,

WM. D. WHIPPLE,
Assistant Adjutant-General.

HEADQUARTERS FOURTEENTH ARMY CORPS,
In the Field, July 20, 1864—7.30 a. m.

Brigadier-General WHIPPLE,
Assistant Adjutant-General, &c.:

GENERAL: The enemy cling with great obstinacy to our right. The colonel Thirty-fourth Illinois reports on Davis' front two lines of skirmishers and heavy columns of infantry moving to the right of Davis. Davis has just gone to see to it. Baird and Johnson are across the creek. Davis has one brigade on this side. There is skirmishing all along my front; heaviest on my right.

Respectfully,

JOHN M. PALMER,
Major-General.

HEADQUARTERS ARMY OF THE CUMBERLAND,
July 20, 1864—5 p. m.

Major-General PALMER,
Commanding Fourteenth Army Corps:

The major-general commanding directs that you send a brigade at least to support General Newton on the left at once. If it is possible for you to send a division or even two brigades, he desires you to do so. You will make your present position secure and send what force you can. The brigade must be sent at once, and be in position as soon as possible.

Very respectfully, your obedient servant,

ROBT. H. RAMSEY,
Assistant Adjutant-General.

HEADQUARTERS ARMY OF THE CUMBERLAND,
July 20, 1864—10.50 a. m.

Brig. Gen. R. W. JOHNSON,
Commanding First Division, Fourteenth Army Corps:

GENERAL: The major-general commanding directs that you push forward your command in conjunction with the movement of Major-General Hooker's troops when he moves forward. Please inform Major-General Palmer of your receipt of this order.

Very respectfully, your obedient servant,
ROBT. H. RAMSEY,
Captain and Assistant Adjutant-General.

JULY 20, 1864—11 a. m.

Capt. A. C. McCLURG,
Assistant Adjutant-General, Fourteenth Corps:

CAPTAIN: I have the honor to report, for the information of the major-general commanding corps, that I have just received orders from Major-General Thomas to push forward my command in conjunction with the movement of Major-General Hooker's troops, when he moves forward. This report is made in conformity with the request of Major-General Thomas.

Very respectfully, your obedient servant,
R. W. JOHNSON,
Brigadier-General of Volunteers.

HEADQUARTERS FOURTEENTH ARMY CORPS,
July 20, 1864.

Brigadier-General JOHNSON,
Commanding, &c.:

GENERAL: Keep all your reserves well in hand and ready to be moved in any direction. Look at once to your lines. Reports from Davis state strong force in his front and heavy columns moving to his right.

Very respectfully,

JOHN M. PALMER,
Major-General, Commanding.

HEADQUARTERS FOURTEENTH ARMY CORPS,
July 20, 1864.

General JOHNSON:

Captain Watson has been gone some time on the hunt for information as to General Hooker's purposes and movements, but has not returned. Do you know when General H[ooker] will be ready to advance? You will of course obey General Thomas' order and I will advise you at the earliest moment of any information I may get which will assist you.

Respectfully,

J. M. PALMER,
Major-General.

HEADQUARTERS FOURTEENTH ARMY CORPS,
In the Field, July 20, 1864.

Brig. Gen. R. W. JOHNSON,
Commanding First Division, Fourteenth Army Corps:

The major-general commanding directs that if General Geary throws his right forward and enables you to do so, you will relieve a portion of General Baird's left, so as to enable him to strengthen his right brigade, which is much in need of it. He desires that you have two brigades in line and one in reserve, at the same time affording General Baird all the assistance possible in the manner indicated.

[A. C. McCLURG.]

HEADQUARTERS FOURTEENTH ARMY CORPS,
July 20, 1864.

Brig. Gen. A. BAIRD:

The major-general commanding has directed General Johnson to afford you all the assistance possible. He deems the interval between Colonels Walker and Este of no importance whatever.

Very respectfully, &c.,

A. C. McCLURG.

HEADQUARTERS ARMY OF THE CUMBERLAND,
July 20, 1864—3 p. m.

Maj. Gen. JOSEPH HOOKER,
Commanding Twentieth Army Corps:

Major-General Palmer reports that he is waiting for your troops to advance before he can move. If this report is correct I wish you to push forward your command at once. General Newton has advanced his division and now occupies the ridge taken by his skirmishers an hour since, and is now about to advance his skirmish line again.

Very respectfully, yours, &c.,

GEO. H. THOMAS,
Major-General, U. S. Volunteers, Commanding.

HEADQUARTERS TWENTIETH ARMY CORPS,
July 20, 1864—3.30 p. m.

Major-General THOMAS,
Commanding Army of the Cumberland:

GENERAL: Your note of 3 p. m. just received. My lines are on the road due east and west, which I pointed out to you this morning. General Palmer's extreme left connects with it, but his right falls away to the rear and affords me little or no protection. Major-General Palmer can scarcely understand where my line is—or his own, if he makes that statement.

Very respectfully, your obedient servant,

JOSEPH HOOKER,
Major-General, Commanding.

HEADQUARTERS DEPARTMENT OF THE CUMBERLAND,
In the Field, July 20, 1864.

Maj. Gen. J. HOOKER,
Commanding Twentieth Army Corps:

GENERAL: As you will probably have breast-works constructed to-night, and as the enemy has been repulsed along the whole line in his attack of to-day, the major-general commanding directs that you press him strongly with skirmishers in the morning, for the purpose of ascertaining what has become of him, and of ascertaining his intentions. The same has been ordered for other corps of the army.

I am, general, very respectfully, your obedient servant,
WM. D. WHIPPLE,
Assistant Adjutant-General.

HEADQUARTERS ARMY OF THE OHIO,
Near Decatur, Ga., July 20, 1864.

Brig. Gen. M. S. HASCALL,
Commanding Second Division, Twenty-third Army Corps:

GENERAL: General Cox is ordered to move forward on the Atlanta road at once. The commanding general desires you to move your command directly in rear of General Cox's column, keeping within close supporting distance of him, in advance of all the wagons.

Very respectfully, your obedient servant,
J. A. CAMPBELL,
Major and Assistant Adjutant-General.

[JULY 20, 1864.]

Major CAMPBELL:

SIR: I have come across from General Logan to find out where and on what road you are moving. The Fifteenth Army Corps is moving on the main road, parallel with the railroad. I will wait here at the headquarters of Colonel Swaine's brigade until the orderly comes back.

Very respectfully,

HUGH NEILL,
Captain Company K, Eighth Missouri Mounted Infantry.

[First indorsement.]

HEADQUARTERS SWAINE'S BRIGADE,
July 20, 1864—9.30 a. m.

Respectfully forwarded, through General Hascall's headquarters, to the headquarters of the department, with request to send answer to these headquarters.

P. T. SWAINE,
Colonel, Commanding Brigade.

[Second indorsement.]

JULY 20, 1864—10.15 a. m.

CAPTAIN: The Twenty-third Corps is moving on the Atlanta road, about one mile and a half to the right of the road the Fifteenth Corps is now on. Our advance is not quite four miles from Atlanta, and has developed the enemy's works in our front.

J. A. C[AMPBELL].

HDQRS. THIRD DIVISION, TWENTY-THIRD ARMY CORPS,
July 20, 1864.

Maj. J. A. CAMPBELL,
    Assistant Adjutant-General:

MAJOR: Colonel Byrd's brigade has reported since I wrote my last note, and is now closed up on the column.

Very respectfully, &c.,

J. D. COX,
Brigadier-General.

JULY 20, 1864—10 a. m.

Major-General THOMAS,
    Commanding, &c.:

I have the honor through yourself to state for the information of the commanding general that nothing of importance transpired in this vicinity during the night, except it be that a column of cavalry of the enemy passed down on the other side of the river, reported by the officer on duty at Howell's Ferry as three miles long. I have sent a scout down to Campbellton to try to ascertain who they are, and where they have gone to. Please let one of your staff give me the state of things with you and on the left of the army. It may give me a clue to some of the various reports and rumors I hear, one of which is that a portion of Johnston's army is south of Atlanta, which of course is hardly possible. The force that passed down last night may be on the way to West Point, drawn there by Rousseau.

Very respectfully, &c.,

GEORGE STONEMAN,
Major-General.

[Indorsement.]

HEADQUARTERS ARMY OF THE CUMBERLAND,
July 21, 1864.

Respectfully forwarded to Major-General Sherman, commanding Military Division of the Mississippi, for his information.

GEO. H. THOMAS,
Major-General, U. S. Volunteers, Commanding.

HEADQUARTERS DEPARTMENT OF THE CUMBERLAND,
Near Peach Tree Creek, Ga., July 20, 1864.

Maj. Gen. GEORGE STONEMAN,
    Commanding Cavalry Force:

GENERAL: The major-general commanding directs me to acknowledge the receipt of your note of 10 a. m. this day, and to give you a summary of events occurring in this army. Our lines were yesterday pushed across Peach Tree Creek in several places, and to-day when an advance was being made by all the corps, the enemy made a furious attack on our men, commencing at about 4 p. m. on the extreme left, General Newton's lines, and extending to the extreme right. This attack was continued until night set in, and was most handsomely repulsed at all points. Our loss on some parts of the line is reported severe, but no official report has yet been made. The impression of the major-general commanding is from what he has seen and knows personally, that our loss is very light, while the rebels have lost many in killed and wounded, and those taken prisoners. General Ward, Twentieth Army Corps, reports having captured 2 stand of colors and many prisoners, and hopes to capture a whole regiment which has got into rather a tight place to get out safely.

Major-General Sherman has written a note to the major-general commanding stating that Generals McPherson, Schofield, and Howard, with two divisions of his corps, are pressing on to Atlanta, and at that time (3 p. m.) could not be more than from one mile and a half to two miles and a half distant from the city. If this report of the positions of the troops named be as stated, it is expected that we can secure many prisoners on our left, as it will be impossible for them to get away with our force in their rear.

Everything has progressed satisfactorily, and the enemy has been gloriously thrashed.

I have the honor to be, general, very respectfully, your obedient servant,

> ROBT. H. RAMSEY,
> *Captain and Assistant Adjutant-General.*

JULY 20, 1864—11 a. m.

Major-General SHERMAN,
        Commanding, &c.:

A negro, who was taken prisoner with Colonel Streight, has just come in, and, I think, brings reliable information, and, if reliable, is very important, to wit, that Johnston is retreating in haste along the Macon road. A captain who deserted and comes to us, says that Johnston cannot go by the way of West Point, as the gauge is different the other side of the river from this side. The negro says that our operations in the direction of Campbellton and Moore's Bridge caused the greatest stampede; that Jackson's division has gone to the Blue Mountain in Alabama; that he saw Wheeler near Campbellton, and that he has his whole force near there and below; that there is no force in Atlanta but the "new issue" (militia); that the army is utterly demoralized and easily frightened. The negro says he is in the Eighth Texas Regiment, Colonel Harrison's brigade, Humes' division. He has seen General Johnston often, and a short time since had his headquarters at white house, four miles from Atlanta, on or near the railroad; he wears a broad brim hat, has a gray beard and a dutch looking face; and Hood's headquarters were and are always near by. I send him to you and give you these items in order that by cross-questioning he may be detected if he is unreliable; further, that there is no sick or wounded now in Atlanta. He confirms the reports of the rebels stripping our men as soon as taken prisoners. Ask him to describe to you Streight's surrender to Forrest. I should like to have him sent back as a guide when we cross the river. We are ready to cross whenever the bridge is finished, or to cross where the bridge now is, and push down the river from Thomas' right, which I think we can easily do.

Very respectfully, &c.,

> GEORGE STONEMAN,
> *Major-General.*

HDQRS. MILITARY DIVISION OF THE MISSISSIPPI,
In the Field, July 20, 1864—8 p. m.

Major-General MCPHERSON:

DEAR GENERAL: I inclose for your perusal letters from Generals Thomas and Stoneman.* You will see that they are in error. I think our only chance of entering Atlanta by a quick move if possible is lost. Still more good results will flow from your pressing hard and close on your flank than the other, because if you can reach Atlanta with your guns or turn that flank we will capture more prisoners and property than by the other, for it will leave the enemy in a pocket whence they should not escape. We have carried several light lines of rail-pits to-day all along our lines, but have not followed up quick enough, so that I suppose in the morning we will find the remainder made into good parapets. Still do not fail to try them strong and find that flank if you can reach it. I have ordered Thomas to press close into Atlanta, and will see that Schofield and Howard do the same. I have no news later than you have from abroad.

Yours, truly,

W. T. SHERMAN,
Major-General, Commanding.

Open up a straight road to Schofield.

———

HDQRS. DEPARTMENT AND ARMY OF THE TENNESSEE,
In Field, July 20, 1864—8.45 p. m.

Major-General SHERMAN, *Comdg. Military Div. of the Mississippi:*

GENERAL: Inclosed I send you sketch of our position to-night.†

We have had some pretty lively skirmishing and have driven the enemy from several pretty strong positions, though I do not think there has been much of anything but cavalry in front of us on the left. But they have had four pieces of artillery and are armed with short Enfield rifles, making it difficult at times to dislodge them. Brigadier-General Gresham, commanding Fourth Division, Seventeenth Army Corps, was wounded in the leg below the knee by a minie-ball, which shattered the bone, and I am afraid he will lose his leg. I have assigned Brig. Gen. Giles A. Smith to the command of the division. You will see from the sketch that my left (Blair's command) is in lot 207, and the line runs nearly north, the right breaking to the rear slightly to connect with General Schofield. General Garrard's headquarters are in Decatur and his command is so disposed as to cover our rear and line of communications back to Roswell. Our losses have been comparatively light.

Very respectfully, your obedient servant,

JAS. B. MCPHERSON,
Major-General.

———

HEADQUARTERS SEVENTEENTH ARMY CORPS,
Near Atlanta, Ga., July 20, 1864.

Lieut. Col. WILLIAM T. CLARK,
Asst. Adjt. Gen., Department and Army of the Tennessee:

COLONEL: I have the honor to state, for the information of the major-general commanding, that from the best information I have been

———

* Not found as inclosures, but reference is probably to Thomas' letter of 12 m., p. 196, and Stoneman's of 11 a. m., p. 207.
† To appear in the Atlas.

able to obtain Wheeler's cavalry is on my left and rear and has patrols on the Fayetteville road and the other adjacent roads. If this is so, trains moving out of Decatur to either corps of this army are exposed to attack, as my force is not large enough to protect the flank.

Very respectfully, your obedient servant,

FRANK P. BLAIR, JR.,
Major-General.

HDQRS. MILITARY DIVISION OF THE MISSISSIPPI,
In the Field, near Atlanta, July 20, 1864—midnight.

General GARRARD,
Commanding Cavalry Division:

GENERAL: After destroying the bridge at McAfee's, which I suppose is already done, you will send to General McPherson's guard at the bridge at Roswell your wagons, led horses, and baggage, and proceed rapidly to Covington, on the main wagon and rail road east, distance about thirty miles from Decatur. Take the road by Latimar's, touching the railroad at or beyond Lithonia, and thence substantially along the railroad, destroying it effectually all the way, especially the Yellow River bridge this side of Covington, as well as the road bridge over Yellow River, after you have passed. From Covington send detachments to destroy the rail and road bridges east of Covington over the Ulcofauhachee. Try and capture and destroy some locomotives and cars, and the depots and stores at Covington, but of private property only take what is necessary for your own use, except horses and mules, of which you will take all that are fit for service, exercising, of course, some judgment as to the animals belonging to the poor and needy. On your return select your own route, but I would suggest that by way of Sheffield, Rock Bridge, and Stone Mountain, or even farther north if you prefer. I want you to put your whole strength at this, and to do it quick and well. I know it can be done. By passing Yellow River by the road bridge, and then pushing for the railroad bridges right and left, the guard will run or even burn their own bridges. You ought to catch some trains about Covington, as there is no telegraph to give them timely warning. I believe that the cavalry is mostly withdrawn from that flank of the enemy, and that you can ride roughshod over any force there; at all events, it is a matter of vital importance and must be attempted with great vigor. The importance of it will justify the loss of quarter of your command. Be prepared with axes, hatchets, and bars to tear up sections of track and make bonfires. When the rails are red hot they must be twisted. Burning will do for bridges and culverts, but not for ordinary track. Let the work be well done. The whole thing should be done in two days, including to-morrow. I will notify General McPherson that he may look out for his rear and trains.

I am, with respect, yours, truly,

W. T. SHERMAN,
Major-General, Commanding.

If the McAfee Bridge is not already burned you can send a messenger to the guard already there to do it and move to Roswell. This need not delay your departure for Covington at once.

S.

CAMP ON PEACH TREE CREEK, GA.,
July 20, 1864—10 p. m.
(Via Vining's Station. Received 11 a. m. 21st.)

Maj. THOMAS T. ECKERT, *Washington:*

Our left has pushed forward to-day to within two miles of Atlanta. Reports that the right has remained nearly in position of last night, thus developing the enemy's line and proving that our information was very nearly correct as regarded it. Enemy has assaulted several times to-day, and has been severely repulsed each time. Our casualties light, and everything favorable.

J. C. VAN DUZER.

———

SPECIAL FIELD ORDERS, No. 73.

HDQRS. DEPT. AND ARMY OF THE TENN.,
In Field, three and a half miles from Atlanta,
July 20, 1864.

I. In accordance with directions of Major-General Sherman, Brigadier-General Garrard, commanding cavalry division, will destroy McAfee's Bridge across the Chattahoochee River. General Garrard will cover the Roswell depot and protect the trains of this army.

II. Corps commanders will cause their several positions to be intrenched to-night, and will have their commands in line of battle at 3.30 to-morrow morning, ready to repel any attacks of the enemy.

*   *   *   *   *   *   *

IV. Brig. Gen. G. A. Smith, U. S. Volunteers, is hereby relieved from the command of the First Brigade, Second Division, Fifteenth Army Corps, and will forthwith report to Maj. Gen. F. P. Blair for assignment to command of the Fourth Division, Seventeenth Army Corps.

*   *   *   *   *   *

By order of Maj. Gen. James. B. McPherson:

WM. T. CLARK,
Assistant Adjutant-General.

———

NEAR ATLANTA, *July 21, 1864.*
(Received 1 p. m. 22d.)

His Excellency President LINCOLN:

Your dispatch is received. I have the highest veneration for the law, and will respect it always, however it conflicts with my opinion of its propriety. I only telegraphed to General Halleck because I had seen no copy of the law, and supposed the War Department might have some control over its operations. When I have taken Atlanta and can sit down in some peace I will convey by letter a fuller expression of my views in relation to the subject.

With great respect,

W. T. SHERMAN,
Major-General.

———

CITY POINT, VA., *July 21, 1864—10 a. m.*
(Received 6 p. m.)

Maj. Gen. W. T. SHERMAN:

The Richmond Whig of the 20th learns from the Macon Confederate that but little quartermaster or commissary stores remain in Atanta, all having been removed to safer and more secure points. It also says that it has every reason to hope that Sherman's rear will be cut in the next ten days. General Johnston has been relieved of command and General Hood takes his place, much to the surprise of the army and public; also that this change indicates that there will be no more retreating, but that Atlanta will be defended at all hazards and to the last extremity.

U. S. GRANT,
Lieutenant-General.

NEAR ATLANTA, GA., *July 21, 1864—8.30 p. m.*
(Received 11 a. m. 22d.)

Maj. Gen. H. W. HALLECK,
   Washington, D. C.:

GENERAL: Yesterday at 4 p. m. the enemy sallied from his intrenchments and fell suddenly and heavily on our line in the direction of Buck Head. The blow fell upon General Newton's division, of General Howard's corps, and on Generals Ward's, Geary's, and Williams' divisions, of General Hooker's corps, and General Johnson's, of General Palmer's. For two hours the fighting was close and severe, resulting in the complete repulse of the enemy with heavy loss in dead and wounded. He left his dead and many wounded in our possesion, we retaining undisputed possession of all the ground fought over. General Newton reports he has buried 200 of the enemy's dead, and is satisfied he wounded at least 1,200. His entire loss is only 100, as his men were partially covered by a rail barricade. At the time of the attack General Hooker was in the act of advancing his lines, so that he fought his corps uncovered, in comparatively open ground and on fair terms with the enemy. The contest was very severe. He has buried about 400 of the rebel dead, took 7 colors, and has collected many of the wounded and other prisoners. Hooker thinks the rebel wounded in his front fully equal to 4,000; but I don't like to make guesses in such matters. His own loss will be covered by 1,500. On the whole the result is most favorable to us. To-day we have gained important positions, so that Generals McPherson and Schofield, on the east, have batteries in position that will easily reach the heart of the city, and General Howard, on the north, also has advanced his lines about two miles, being within easy cannon-range of the buildings in Atlanta. He compelled the enemy to give up a long line of parapets, which constituted an advance line of intrenchments. The city seems to have a line all round it, at an average distance from the center of the town of one mile and a half, but our shot passing over this line will destroy the town, and I doubt if General Hood will stand a bombardment; still he has fought hard at all points all day. I will open on the town from the east and northeast to-morrow, and General Thomas will advance his right from the mouth of Peach Tree Creek so as to cross the railroad to the northwest of the town. I have sent General Garrard's cavalry eastward to Covington to break railroad and destroy the bridges on Yellow River and the Ulcofauhachee Creek. In the action yesterday the rebel generals O'Branan [?] and Stevens were killed, and among the dead were 3 colonels and many officers. Brigadier-General Gresham was severely wounded yesterday, but is in no danger of life or limb.

W. T. SHERMAN,
Major-General.

HEADQUARTERS DEPARTMENT OF THE CUMBERLAND,
Near Peach Tree Creek, Ga., July 21, 1864.

Maj. Gen. W. T. SHERMAN,
Commanding Military Division of the Mississippi:

GENERAL: Since my report yesterday evening at 6 p. m. I have ascertained that, with the exception of General Geary's division, my loss ha
been very slight, although exposed to as hot a fire as I have almos
ever experienced. The enemy was handsomely repulsed at all point
in every attack he made. On General Palmer he assaulted some six o
seven times. The same on General Newton. The attack on Genera
Hooker seemed to have been continuous from the time the attack firs
began until the final repulse about sundown. I passed by Genera
Geary's hospital last evening, and think he must have some 500 to 60
wounded. We took quite a number of prisoners (the exact number ha
not yet been reported), and General Ward reports that he has capture
2 stand of colors. Orders were given yesterday evening before I le
the field to press the enemy again this morning, but I doubt if we ca
accomplish very much, as he undoubtedly had yesterday strong intrenc]
ments in our front.

I am, general, very respectfully, yours, &c.,
GEO. H. THOMAS,
Major-General, U. S. Volunteers, Commanding.

HDQRS. MILITARY DIVISION OF THE MISSISSIPPI,
In the Field, near Atlanta, Ga., July 21, 1864.

Major-General THOMAS,
Army of the Cumberland:

GENERAL: After leaving you to-day I visited General Palmer an
saw his skirmishers advance well to his right flank. I am satisfied tl
enemy will not attempt to hold Atlanta and the fort at the railroa
crossing of the Chattahoochee. There is a weak place in that line, ar
it can best be reached by advancing General Johnson on the dire
road as far as possible and bringing Generals Baird and Davis well u
on his right. I do not think the enemy will assume the offensive fro
the fort on the Chattahoochee, but it may be prudent to let Gener
McCook watch him on both sides of the river. The front of Gener
Hooker is very narrow, but I admit it is the point where your line shou
be the strongest. General Howard's two divisions in this direction hav
advanced a good distance over a complete line of the enemy's defense
and I think both Generals Wood and Stanley are up to the main line
intrenchments, and that from General Wood's right rifled guns ca
reach the town. The enemy still holds the hill near where Gener
Stanley's left and General Schofield's right are, and they keep up a
infernal clatter, but it sounds to me like a waste of ammunition. Ge
eral McPherson to-day charged and carried a hill, losing 250 men, b
killing some and taking prisoners. From this hill he has an easy ran;
of the town. We will try the effect of shelling to-morrow, and duri
it you had better make all the ground you can. I do not believe tl
enemy will repeat his assaults, as he had in that of yesterday his be
troops and failed signally. Therefore I don't fear for your right flan
Still, it is well to be prudent.

Ours maps are all wrong and the quicker we can get our surveys up and publish the better. I will look to Schofield and McPherson to-morrow.

Yours, truly,

W. T. SHERMAN,
Major-General, Commanding.

HEADQUARTERS DEPARTMENT OF THE CUMBERLAND,
In the Field, July 21, 1864.

Maj. Gen. W. T. SHERMAN,
Commanding Military Division of the Mississippi:

GENERAL: Major-General Palmer reports this evening that Brigadier-General Johnson's reconnaissance, pushing near Johns', resulted in the capture of 29 prisoners from Stewart's corps, French's division, and was checked by artillery from what a very candid seeming prisoner reports was a fortified line. He says Stewart's corps is on that line. Johnson has a strong line half a mile from the artillery. Baird is on his right. General Palmer is satisfied that there is a fortified line from the river along the railroad some distance, thence east along his front and up to that point is held by Stewart's corps. The skirmishing was sharp. Our loss probably will not exceed 50. I have ordered Palmer to fortify Johnson's and Baird's present positions and have them push out again to-morrow as far as they can without bringing on a battle. I have also ordered Brigadier-General McCook to send a brigade across the river to-morrow morning to relieve General Davis' pickets along Peach Tree Creek, and when that is done for Davis to mass his division on Baird's right.

Yours, very respectfully,

GEO. H. THOMAS,
Major-General, Commanding.

P. S.—Report from General Palmer at 7.30 states that he had a conversation with "Tippen" which confirms his previous impression that the rebel works extend to the river and are held in force. The rebel guns were fired yesterday from the high hill that overlooks Atlanta. Prisoners say that our shells yesterday fell into Atlanta, producing great consternation. They also say that General Stevens, commanding a brigade, was killed, and not Stevenson.

Davis' skirmishers advanced to-day as far as the Marietta and Atlanta road. The enemy's skirmish line was formed along the railroad.

G. H. T.

HEADQUARTERS FOURTH ARMY CORPS,
Near Atlanta, Ga., July 21, 1864—7 p. m.

Brigadier-General WHIPPLE,
Chief of Staff:

GENERAL: That portion of the enemy's works between the South Fork and the main Peach Tree Creek was evacuated last night. Generals Stanley and Wood moved forward, wheeling to the left until within musketry range of the enemy's works. The left brigade of Stanley's division, having been close up to that line, did not move. From General Wood's right the enemy's line is visible to the extent of one mile.

The works seem to have been constructed some time, probably five o
six weeks. From Wood's right to Newton's left, in a straight line, i
about half a mile.   King's brigade is opposite that interval, on th
other side of the creek.   The casualties in Newton's division were abou
100. He has buried in his front about 200 of the rebel dead. Thos
between the picket-lines were buried by the enemy yesterday evening
The division made a gallant fight and deserves unqualified praise
After my report of yesterday evening Colonel Grose took 27 men an
1 captain prisoners from the skirmish rifle-pits of the enemy.

Very respectfully, your obedient servant,

O. O. HOWARD,
Major-General, Commanding.

HEADQUARTERS FOURTH ARMY CORPS,
Near Atlanta, Ga., July 21, 1864—2 p. m.

Major-General STANLEY,
Commanding First Division, Fourth Army Corps:

GENERAL: The general commanding directs that you relieve Genera
Wood's two left regiments by one regiment of your division, placing
such regiment behind the works on the other side of the ravine that lies
between you and General Wood; also to block up the ravine by felling
timber and cutting down underbrush as much as you can.

Very respectfully, your obedient servant,

J. S. FULLERTON,
Assistant Adjutant-General.

HEADQUARTERS FOURTH ARMY CORPS,
Near Atlanta, Ga., July 21, 1864—2 p. m.

Brigadier-General WOOD,
Commanding Third Division:

Major-General Stanley has been directed to relieve your two left regi
ments by a regiment from his division. The object of this is to give
you two regiments with which to strengthen your right.

By order of Major-General Howard:

J. S. FULLERTON,
Assistant Adjutant-General.

HDQRS. SECOND DIVISION, FOURTH ARMY CORPS,
Near Peach Tree Creek, Ga., July 21, 1864.

Brig. Gen. W. D. WHIPPLE,
Assistant Adjutant-General, Department of the Cumberland:

GENERAL: I have the honor to inform you that the enemy have a
continuous line of strong works at the base of the next ridge, about 500
yards in advance of my line. I sent out two regiments to develop the
enemy and found that the works were full. They are very strongly constructed with head-logs, and if not their main line of works are near it,

I think, as the line was constantly re-enforced. I am unable to find the end of the works on the right or left, and I do not think that an isolated attack with my division would be productive of beneficial results.

I am, general, very respectfully,

JOHN NEWTON,
Brigadier-General, Commanding.

(Forwarded by General Thomas to General Sherman, July 21, 1864.)

HEADQUARTERS DEPARTMENT OF THE CUMBERLAND,
Near Peach Tree Creek, Ga., July 21, 1864.

Brig. Gen. JOHN NEWTON,
Commanding Second Division, Fourth Army Corps:

GENERAL: The major-general commanding directs me to acknowledge the receipt of your note this morning, and also to say to you that he approves of your action in pushing forward in search of the enemy. The major-general commanding desires you to push up close to him and ascertain, if possible, his whereabouts definitely, but not to run any risk of bringing on a general engagement until your connection with Generals Hooker and Howard is completed. Any advantage that you may gain in pushing forward, the major-general commanding desires you to hold on to by intrenching your troops.

I have the honor to be, general, very respectfully, your obedient servant,

ROBT. H. RAMSEY,
Captain and Assistant Adjutant-General.

HDQRS. SECOND DIVISION, FOURTH ARMY CORPS,
In the Field, July 21, 1864.

Brigadier-General WHIPPLE,
Asst. Adjt. Gen. and Chief of Staff, Hdqrs. Dept. of the Cumberland:

GENERAL: I have the honor to report that my skirmishers have found the enemy 400 or 500 yards in front of my line in considerable force and occupying a strong position. They are intrenched in substantial works with a top-log, and have a skirmish line in their front. Their force I have not developed in accordance with my instructions not to bring on an engagement under present conditions, but it appears to be considerable, and has been sufficient to check my skirmishers.

I am, very respectfully, &c.,

JOHN NEWTON,
Brigadier-General.

HEADQUARTERS DEPARTMENT OF THE CUMBERLAND,
In the Field, July 21, 1864.

Brig. Gen. J. NEWTON,
Commanding Second Division, Fourth Army Corps:

GENERAL: Yours of this date received. The major-general commanding says get up as close as you can to the enemy's works and intrench your position.

Yours, very respectfully,

WM. D. WHIPPLE,
Assistant Adjutant-General.

HEADQUARTERS FOURTEENTH ARMY CORPS,
In the Field, July 21, 1864—9 a. m.

Brigadier-General WHIPPLE:

GENERAL: Please inform the general commanding that parties have been out on Johnson's front as far as Emory's house—the ground occupied by the enemy's artillery on yesterday. Mr. Shaw, of my staff, is now out with a regiment, and will learn where they are. Can I make use of General Davis, or does the order fixing him in his present position still operate?

Respectfully,

J. M. PALMER,
Major-General.

P. S.—Light skirmishing half a mile to the front.

HEADQUARTERS DEPARTMENT OF THE CUMBERLAND,
In the Field, July 21, 1864.

Maj. Gen. J. M. PALMER,
Commanding Fourteenth Army Corps:

GENERAL: Yours of 9 a. m. received. The major-general commanding thinks that General Davis' division should still hold on where he is unless he ascertains that the enemy has left his front. He can then advance with the rest of the Fourteenth Corps, refusing his right flank. In the mean time you can make use of any troops of his division that may be out of line.

I am, general, very respectfully, your obedient servant,

WM. D. WHIPPLE,
Assistant Adjutant-General.

HDQRS. SECOND DIVISION, FOURTEENTH ARMY CORPS,
July 21, 1864.

Captain McCLURG,
Assistant Adjutant-General:

CAPTAIN: Colonel Lum took possession of and held the enemy's work opposite Moore's Mill last evening. All three brigade commanders have each had a regiment out making reconnaissance since daylight. I have exhausted my patience waiting for reports. We have taken a few prisoners, another major, all belonging to French's division. They report a general movement of the enemy to his right yesterday and last night. I will report as soon as I can hear from the parties on reconnaissance.

Very respectfully,

JEF. C. DAVIS,
Brigadier-General, Commanding Division.

[Indorsement.]

HEADQUARTERS DEPARTMENT OF THE CUMBERLAND,
Near Peach Tree Creek, Ga., July 21, 1864.

Respectfully forwarded to Maj. Gen. W. T. Sherman, commanding Military Division of the Mississippi, for his information.

Just received, and despatched at once.

GEO. H. THOMAS,
Major-General, U. S. Volunteers, Commanding.

HDQRS. SECOND DIVISION, FOURTEENTH ARMY CORPS,
July 21, 1864—7 p. m.

Captain McCLURG:

CAPTAIN: For the information of the general commanding, I have the honor to state that the reconnaissance made by my troops to-day advanced as far as the Marietta and Atlanta road and threw skirmishers beyond it. The enemy's skirmish line was found running along the toll road. After remaining on the road some two hours, General Morgan's skirmishers were driven in and to the Peach Tree Creek by a force estimated at three regiments. These troops came from the enemy's works over the railroad near the river.

I am, very respectfully,

JEF. C. DAVIS,
Brigadier-General, Commanding.

[Indorsement.]

HEADQUARTERS FOURTEENTH ARMY CORPS,
July 21, 1864—7.30 p. m.

Received since my return to quarters and forwarded.

This report confirms the impression I entertain that the rebel works extend to the river and are held in force. I think my line is safe to the road to Atlanta. I have just had a conversation with "Tippen," who says the rebel guns were fired from the high hill which overlooks Atlanta. The prisoners say that shells fell into Atlanta on yesterday, producing great consternation. They also say that General Stevens, commanding a brigade, was killed yesterday, and not Stevenson.

J. M. PALMER,
Major-General.

———

HEADQUARTERS DEPARTMENT OF THE CUMBERLAND,
In the Field, July 21, 1864.

Maj. Gen. J. M. PALMER,
Commanding Fourteenth Army Corps:

GENERAL: Yours received (of 6.30). The major-general commanding directs that you cause Generals Johnson and Baird to fortify well, and push out again to-morrow as far as they can without bringing on a general engagement. Orders will to-night be sent to Brigadier-General McCook to send over a brigade of cavalry to relieve Brigadier-General Davis' pickets along Peach Tree Creek to-morrow morning. When that brigade arrives, Brigadier-General Davis' division should be massed upon Brigadier-General Baird's right and move forward with the line of the other two divisions, should they not have moved already.

Yours, very respectfully,

WM. D. WHIPPLE,
Assistant Adjutant-General.

———

HDQRS. CHIEF OF CAVALRY, DEPT. OF THE CUMBERLAND,
Near Buck Head, Ga., July 21, 1864.

Brig. Gen. E. M. McCOOK,
Commanding First Cavalry Division:

The general commanding directs that you move one brigade of your command across the river early to-morrow morning and relieve General

Davis' pickets along Peach Tree Creek, to enable General Davis to move his division on General Baird's left. The brigade will have to start very early in order to arrive at the creek in proper time. They will cross Pace's Ferry and take the right-hand road about three-quarters of a mile after crossing. Lieutenant Shaw, aide-de-camp, will show them the position they are to occupy after arriving at the creek.

I am, general, very respectfully, your obedient servant,

DAVID F. HOW,
Lieutenant and Acting Assistant Adjutant-General.

HEADQUARTERS FOURTH ARMY CORPS,
Near Durand's Mill, South Fork Peach Tree Creek,
July 21, 1864—2.45 p. m.

Major-General SCHOFIELD,
Commanding Army of the Ohio:

GENERAL: I have one small brigade in reserve, and there is quite a space between my right and Peach Tree Creek. Hood is great for attacking, and I feel that it is necessary for safety to retain this brigade in a movable condition. The enemy is in strong force throughout my entire front, also opposite the gap between Wood and Newton (the latter on the Buck Head and Atlanta main road). The works plainly visible from my right seem to have been constructed for some time. For the above reasons, if you can excuse me, I would prefer not to extend farther to the left.

Respectfully,

O. O. HOWARD,
Major-General.

HDQRS. MILITARY DIVISION OF THE MISSISSIPPI,
In the Field, near Atlanta, July 21, 1864—1 a. m.

General McPHERSON,
Army of the Tennessee:

GENERAL: I have yours of 8.45 last evening, and regret much the wound which will deprive us of the services of General Gresham. I was in hopes you could have made a closer approach to Atlanta yesterday, as I was satisfied you had a less force and more inferior works than will be revealed by daylight, if, as I suppose, Hood proposes to hold Atlanta to the death. All afternoon heavy and desperate sallies were made against Thomas, all along his lines from left to right, particularly heavy against Newton and Geary, but in every instance he was roughly handled; considerable firing has been going on all night along Howard's lines, and still continues. To-morrow I propose to press along the whole line, and try to advance Thomas, so that we will command the Chattahoochee's east bank, and contract our lines by diminishing the circle. I think to-morrow Hood will draw from his left and re-enforce his right. Nevertheless, I deem it necessary that you should gain ground so that your artillery can reach the town easily; say within 1,000 yards of the inner or main lines. I have ordered Garrard to send to Roswell his wagons and impediments and push rapidly and boldly on the bridges across the Yellow River and Ulcofauhachee, near Covington, to be gone two days. Give orders that in the mean time no trains come up to you from Roswell. He will substantially cover the road back because all the cavalry in that direction will be driven away, still some squads might be left about Stone Mountain, as he will take the direct road from Decatur to Covington, passing considerably south of Stone Mountain. Order your ordnance wagons and those that you may have left about Decatur up to your immediate rear. I will ride over to Thomas to-morrow morning and would like to hear from you before starting. If at any time you see signs of retreat on the part of the enemy follow up with all possible vigor, keeping to the left or south of Atlanta and following roads that will keep you on that flank. If Hood was as roughly handled by Thomas this afternoon as reported, and in addition the little artillery he has displayed to-day, I would not be astonished to find him off in the morning, but I see no signs looking that way yet. In case he retreats it will be toward Macon, whither all the advance stores have been sent, and most of the provisions. I want him pursued vigorously for a couple of days.

Yours, truly,

W. T. SHERMAN,
Major-General, Commanding.

IN THE FIELD, *July 21, 1864—3 p. m.*

Major-General SHERMAN,
Commanding:

GENERAL: Brigadier-General Leggett, commanding Third Division, Seventeenth Army Corps, advanced his lines and captured a hill, quite a commanding position, this forenoon; also, some 60 prisoners, principally from Cleburne's division. General Leggett is on my extreme left. The Fourth Division (late Gresham's) made a demonstration at the same time in favor of Leggett, and the loss in the two divisions is between 260 and 300 killed and wounded. The hill is two and a quarter miles from Atlanta, and a portion of the enemy's works around the town are in view. The enemy made one vigorous assault and two feeble attempts to recapture the hill, but were signally repulsed. Since that time he has been moving troops in the direction of our left. General Leggett reports having seen at least ten regiments of infantry passing in that direction. I have strengthened that portion of the line with all the available troops I have got, and I will simply remark in closing, that I have no cavalry as a body of observation on my flank, and that the whole rebel army, except Georgia militia, is not in front of the Army of the Cumberland.

Very respectfully, your obedient servant,

JAS. B. McPHERSON,
Major-General.

HEADQUARTERS SEVENTEENTH ARMY CORPS,
July 21 [22], 1864—4.30 p. m.

General SHERMAN,
Commanding:

GENERAL: The enemy attacked this morning on our left and rear, and Generals Smith and Leggett have been fighting from both sides of the works thrown up last night, repulsing Hardee's corps with heavy loss. The enemy have become quiet, and if I had a fresh brigade I could recover all that I have lost and drive the enemy easily.

FRANK P. BLAIR,
Major-General, Commanding.

HEADQUARTERS DEPARTMENT OF THE TENNESSEE,
                    In the Field, July 21, 1864—5.30 p. m.
Maj. Gen. FRANK P. BLAIR,
        Commanding Seventeenth Army Corps:

GENERAL: Have your command work industriously strengthening
their position to-night, so as to make it impregnable against any rebel
assault. Call on Brigadier-General Fuller's command (Dodge's corps)
for assistance, if you require it. Have the brush and small trees in
front of your intrenchments cut down for a distance of 80 or 100 yards,
making a sort of abatis. Impress upon the command the importance
of being on the alert at all times to repel an attack, especially about
daybreak.

        Very respectfully, your obedient servant,
                                JAS. B. McPHERSON,
                                        Major-General.

[Indorsement.]

HEADQUARTERS SEVENTEENTH ARMY CORPS,
                    Near Atlanta, July 21, 1864.

Respectfully referred to Brig. Gen. M. D. Leggett, commanding
Third Division, Seventeenth Army Corps, for his information and guidance.

General Leggett will please see that these instructions are fully and
promptly carried out, and that every effort is made to render his position as strong as possible.

        By command of Maj. Gen. F. P. Blair:

                                A. J. ALEXANDER,
                                Assistant Adjutant-General.

THREE MILES AND A HALF EAST OF ATLANTA, GA.,
                                July 21, 1864.
Maj. Gen. G. M. DODGE,
        Commanding Left Wing, Sixteenth Army Corps:

Brigadier-General Garrard's cavalry is ordered on an expedition by
Major-General Sherman which will occupy them at least two days.
This will leave Decatur defenseless, and the way open for a small body
of the enemy's cavalry to dash into our rear. You will therefore send
one brigade of Fuller's division to occupy the place, and to picket
strongly the roads to the south and east until the return of the cavalry.
You will also have your pioneer companies open a road through to
General Schofield's position in rear of our present line so that we can
communicate quickly if necessary.

        Very respectfully, your obedient servant,
                                JAS. B. McPHERSON,
                                        Major-General.

HEADQUARTERS LEFT WING, SIXTEENTH ARMY CORPS,
                    Near Atlanta, Ga., July 21, 1864.
Brig. Gen. J. W. FULLER,
        Commanding Fourth Division:

Brigadier-General Garrard's cavalry is ordered on an expedition
which will occupy them at least two days. This will leave Decatur

defenseless and the way open for a small body of the enemy's cavalry to dash into our rear. Send one brigade of your division back to occupy the place and to picket strongly the roads to the south and east until the return of the cavalry. Also have your pioneer corps open a road through to General Schofield's position, in rear of our present line, so that we can communicate quickly, if necessary. Have the commanding officer of the corps report to Lieutenant-Colonel Tiedemann for directions.

By order of Maj. Gen. G. M. Dodge:

J. W. BARNES,
Assistant Adjutant-General.

HEADQUARTERS CAVALRY DIVISION,
Decatur, July 21, 1864.

Major-General SHERMAN,
Commanding Army:

GENERAL: I have the honor to acknowledge the receipt of your orders last night at 1.30 a. m. At that time one brigade (three regiments) was at Cross Keys, ten miles from here, with pickets in every direction from three to four miles; one regiment was at McAfee's Bridge and one at Roswell, leaving me only five regiments, which were all on duty here guarding the roads. I at once took the necessary steps to carry out your instructions, and will leave here during the day, and by traveling to-night make up for the time lost in concentration. My pickets on the roads to the south and east are constantly exchanging shots with rebel cavalry pickets, and this morning one of my patrols down the Covington road captured 2 prisoners belonging to a brigade camped, when they left it, at Latimar's. As your object is to destroy the bridges and six or eight miles of road east of Stone Mountain, and as my chance of success is better by varying some from the route indicated, I deem it best to do so. I desire to succeed, as you place so much importance in having it done, and I will endeavor to do it. I would have started with my five regiments here, but my force would have been too weak to tear up railroad. If no misfortune happens I will burn the bridge east of Covington by 12 m. to-morrow, and by doing this first I catch all west of that point. I then propose breaking up everything between the two rivers. Trusting my views may meet your approval,

I remain, very respectfully, your obedient servant,

K. GARRARD,
Brigadier-General, Commanding Division.

KINGSTON, *July 21, 1864.*

Capt. C. L. WHITE,
Assistant Adjutant-General:

I have just received word that they have thrown the train off the track and torn down the telegraph line on Rome road, five miles from here. Have sent out assistance. Think there is no danger of train being burned.

Respectfully,

J. BANBURY,
Colonel, Commanding.

GENERAL THOMAS' HEADQUARTERS,
Four miles from Atlanta, July 21, 1864—7.30 p. m.

(Received 11 p. m.)

Maj. THOMAS T. ECKERT,
   Assistant Superintendent U. S. Military Telegraph:

Very little progress to-day, McPherson having gained no ground. General Palmer, on extreme right, has pushed enemy from south bank of Peach Tree Creek, and reached railroad. Skirmishing sharp and lively all day, but no general engagement. We shall bounce them to-morrow. Rousseau has been successful, and has struck railroad between Montgomery and Opelika severely—so say rebel papers.

J. C. VAN DUZER.

SPECIAL FIELD ORDERS, ⎱   HDQRS. MIL. DIV. OF THE MISS.,
               ⎰   *In the Field, near Atlanta, Ga.,*
   No. 40.   *July 21, 1864.*

The operations of the army to-morrow, July 22, will be as follows:

I. Major-Generals McPherson, Schofield, and Howard will open a careful artillery fire on the town of Atlanta, directing their shots so as to produce the best effect, and each commander will endeavor to advance his line if it can be done without a direct assault on the enemy's parapets if held in force. They will keep their men well in hand to repel assault, or to follow to the enemy's main line of intrenchments.

II. Major-General Thomas will put the whole or a part of General McCook's cavalry to watch the peninsula between Peach Tree Creek and the Chattahoochee, and will press his lines forward close upon the enemy, endeavoring to advance his right so as to extend across the railroad and main road from Marietta.

By order of Maj. Gen. W. T. Sherman:

L. M. DAYTON,
Aide-de-Camp.

SPECIAL ORDERS, ⎱   HDQRS. SEVENTEENTH ARMY CORPS,
   No. 179.   ⎰   *In the Field, July 21, 1864.*

In compliance with orders from headquarters Department and Army of the Tennessee, Brig. Gen. Giles A. Smith is hereby assigned to the command of the Fourth Division of this corps.

By command of Maj. Gen. F. P. Blair:

A. J. ALEXANDER,
Assistant Adjutant-General.

HEADQUARTERS ARMY OF THE CUMBERLAND,
Near Atlanta, Ga., July 22, 1864.

Maj. Gen. W. T. SHERMAN,
   Commanding Military Division of the Mississippi:

GENERAL: In obedience to my orders Howard's, Hooker's, and Palmer's skirmishers felt up to the enemy's position and entered his first line of works at 2 a. m., and are now pressing on. Your orders by Colonel Ewing were received by sunrise, and my previous orders modified accordingly. I will now join Palmer and put his head of column on the first road to the north of Atlanta that leads down the river. I have also ordered McCook over to operate on our flank, and have sent word to Wright to hurry up his railroad and bridge.

Very truly and respectfully,

GEO. H. THOMAS,
Major-General, U. S. Volunteers, Commanding.

HDQRS. MILITARY DIVISION OF THE MISSISSIPPI,
In the Field, two miles from Atlanta, Ga.,
July 22, 1864—11 a. m.

Major-General THOMAS:

GENERAL: We find the enemy in force inside of Atlanta, doubtless in the intrenchments as represented in the blue map as a circle of one mile and a quarter radius. We can see the buildings of town plain. The enemy fires a good deal of artillery, which passes over the house where I am. Schofield and McPherson are deploying and getting guns up, and will soon open a converging fire. I have sent word to Howard that we were mistaken in supposing the enemy gone, and have directed to continue his operations against Atlanta on that road. I sent General Corse to you to say, also, that my orders sent by Colonel Ewing were predicated on the supposition that Atlanta was given up. I want to hear from your right and front. I suppose Hood has let go the river and will make Atlanta his right and East Point his left, and endeavor to operate on our road with cavalry. I have ordered McPherson to set one corps (Dodge's) at work destroying the railroad completely back to and beyond Decatur. I suppose Garrard to be at this time near Yellow River, and during the day will break the bridges there and beyond. He will be back the day after to-morrow. If the enemy holds on to Atlanta I wish you to press down close from the north and use artillery freely, converging in the town. I will then throw McPherson again on your right to break the Macon road. I would let Stoneman try it, but I hate to base any calculations on the cavalry. McCook might attempt it, but he is not strong enough, for I take it the main cavalry force of the enemy is now on that flank.

Please give me at once the fullest information of the state of matters from the ridge as far toward Atlanta or East Point as you have ascertained.

I am, &c.,

W. T. SHERMAN,
Major-General, Commanding.

Our battery on this flank will open about 1 p. m.

HEADQUARTERS DEPARTMENT OF THE CUMBERLAND,
In the Field, two miles and a half from Atlanta, Ga.,
July 22, 1864—5 p. m.

Maj. Gen. W. T. SHERMAN,
Commanding Military Division of the Mississippi:

GENERAL: In answer to your note of 11 a. m. to-day, I have the honor to state that my right is on the Turner's Ferry and Atlanta road. We have good ground and our batteries are playing upon the fortifications upon the northwest side of the town. We can discover the enemy in his fortifications, and also in masses in front of us, his position covered by two intrenched lines of skirmishers. I think my batteries in Hooker's line, and perhaps Johnson's, can reach the town; but the right being slightly refused to cover the flank the batteries posted there cannot. McCook will be on Davis' right and rear by sunset, if he has executed the orders given him, and we will push on, closing on the enemy, if he remains in his intrenchments, early to-morrow morning. We have taken some prisoners, but have had no serious fighting to-day. The enemy is replying to our artillery fire with much spirit.

Yours, very respectfully,

GEO. H. THOMAS,
Major-General, U. S. Volunteers, Commanding.

HEADQUARTERS DEPARTMENT OF THE CUMBERLAND,
July 22, 1864.

Col. G. P. BUELL,
Commanding Pontoon Train:

COLONEL: The general commanding directs that you take up the pontoon bridge at Pace's Ferry and move down to General Stoneman, to put the bridge across at the point selected by him. After having completed this duty you will please report at these headquarters.

I am, colonel, very respectfully, your obedient servant,

HENRY STONE,
Assistant Adjutant-General.

HEADQUARTERS DEPARTMENT OF THE CUMBERLAND,
In the Field, July 22, 1864—5.30 p. m.

Col. G. P. BUELL,
Commanding Fifty-eighth Indiana Volunteers (Pontoniers):

The major-general commanding countermands the orders given you this morning to move your two bridges to Turner's Ferry and report to Major-General Stoneman, and directs that you lay them at Howell's Ferry near the railroad bridge.

Yours, very respectfully,

WM. D. WHIPPLE,
Assistant Adjutant-General.

HEADQUARTERS FOURTH ARMY CORPS,
Near Atlanta, Ga., July 22, 1864—3.15 a. m.

Brigadier-General WHIPPLE,
Chief of Staff:

GENERAL: The enemy has evacuated his works in front of General Stanley, and he has occupied them. I have no report from General Wood yet.

Very respectfully, your obedient servant,

O. O. HOWARD,
Major-General, Commanding.

HDQRS. MILITARY DIVISION OF THE MISSISSIPPI,
In the Field, near Atlanta, July 22, 1864—4.40 a. m.

General HOWARD,
Fourth Corps:

GENERAL: Schofield has reported the enemy's main line in his possession. Satisfy yourself on this point, and don't enter Atlanta, but join your army in the pursuit south.

Yours,

W. T. SHERMAN,
Major-General, Commanding.

HDQRS. SECOND DIVISION, FOURTH ARMY CORPS,
July 22, 1864.

Brig. Gen. W. D. WHIPPLE,
Assistant Adjutant-General, Dept. of the Cumberland:

GENERAL: I would respectfully inform you that the enemy have left my front, but that I am unable to advance, as General Hooker has cut in ahead of me, and his columns fill the road. Please give me instructions what to do.

I am, general, very respectfully,

JOHN NEWTON,
Brigadier-General, Commanding.

P. S.—Deserters who came in state that Loring's division was in my front yesterday, occupying the works on the left of the road from the Atlanta road toward the creek.

JOHN NEWTON.

HEADQUARTERS DEPARTMENT OF THE CUMBERLAND,
On railroad two miles from Atlanta, Ga., July 22, 1864—10 a. m.

Brig. Gen. JOHN NEWTON,
Commanding Second Division, Fourth Army Corps:

GENERAL: Yours of this date received. The major-general commanding directs that you report to Major-General Howard and notify him, unless he has already received the order, that he desires all the Army of the Cumberland to move in this direction. If he cannot move his corps at once, on account of the road being filled by General Hooker's column, he will follow that column as soon as possible.

Very respectfully, yours,

WM. D. WHIPPLE,
Assistant Adjutant-General.

HEADQUARTERS FOURTH ARMY CORPS,
Near Atlanta, Ga., July 22, 1864—12.30 p. m.

Major-General STANLEY:

GENERAL: The general commanding directs that you place all of your guns in position on your line for the purpose of firing into Atlanta and the forts around the same. Open fire at 3 p. m. All of the batteries on your left will open at the same time. Fire southwest, or on the prolongation of the roads upon which you marched toward the town. General Sherman wishes you to pass word along the lines to your right, to Wood, Newton, Hooker, Thomas, &c., that you and the forces to your left will fire, and explain to them the cause of it.

By order of Major-General Howard:

J. S. FULLERTON,
Assistant Adjutant-General.

HEADQUARTERS FOURTH ARMY CORPS,
Near Atlanta, Ga., July 22, 1864—5.40 p. m.

Major-General STANLEY,
    Commanding First Division:

The enemy's cavalry has passed around McPherson's left, and in accordance with instructions received from department headquarters the general commanding directs that you send two regiments from your division to guard the bridge you built over Peach Tree Creek.

Very respectfully, your obedient servant,

J. S. FULLERTON,
Assistant Adjutant-General.

HEADQUARTERS FOURTH ARMY CORPS,
Near Atlanta, Ga., July 22, 1864—8 p. m.

General WHIPPLE,
    Chief of Staff:

GENERAL: Lieutenant-Colonel Fullerton during my absence had directed General Stanley to send two regiments to the crossing of Peach Tree Creek by the Decatur road; but General Stanley having deployed his entire force, taking a portion of General Schofield's line, I countermanded the order. I have sent a picket force from each division to the rear, one to Newton's bridge across Peach Tree Creek, one to the Decatur road, and one to an intermediate point. Since our forces have reoccupied Decatur I presume the necessity for sending the regiments to intercept the rebel cavalry is obviated, and will not send them unless the general commanding thinks best.

Respectfully,

O. O. HOWARD,
Major-General.

HEADQUARTERS FOURTH ARMY CORPS,
Near Atlanta, Ga., July 22, 1864—8 p. m.

Brigadier-General WHIPPLE,
    Chief of Staff:

GENERAL: I have the honor to report that the enemy evacuated his works in my front between 3 and 4 o'clock this morning. Generals Stanley and Wood followed him as soon as it was light, and General Newton soon afterward. They advanced near the enemy's new line of works around Atlanta, and after some skirmishing went into line of battle about two miles from the city. The main line has not been much advanced yet. My right connects with General Hooker just on the right of the road running from Buck Head to Atlanta, and my left connects with General Schofield on the road that leads to Atlanta, near Hurt's house, as marked on the map. We have taken 90 prisoners to-day. Since I last reported to you to-day I have been obliged to string out my lines and put some of my reserves in front. Stanley's reserves relieved one of Schofield's brigades this evening, so that he (Stanley) has now no troops except those which are in line of battle.

Respectfully,

O. O. HOWARD,
Major-General.

HEADQUARTERS FOURTEENTH ARMY CORPS,
July 22, 1864—4.30 a. m.

Brig. Gen. W. D. WHIPPLE,
Assistant Adjutant-General:

GENERAL: Johnson's pickets at about 2 o'clock entered the enemy's works on his front. They are described as very solid and reported to be continuous. Parties are being pushed forward to develop the enemy's position, and Johnson's division is probably by this time in the rebel works. May I ask that King be ordered to join his division at once.

Respectfully,

JOHN M. PALMER,
Major-General.

HEADQUARTERS DEPARTMENT OF THE CUMBERLAND,
July 22, 1864.

Maj. Gen. J. M. PALMER,
Commanding Fourteenth Army Corps:

GENERAL: The enemy has evacuated Atlanta and his works around that place. The major-general commanding directs that you push on in pursuit in a southwesterly direction by the first road leading from your right, endeavoring to keep about three miles north of the Montgomery railroad. General Hooker will be on your left, if a road can be found upon which he can march running north of Atlanta.

Yours, very respectfully,

WM. D. WHIPPLE,
Assistant Adjutant-General.

HEADQUARTERS TWENTIETH ARMY CORPS,
July 22, 1864—5 a. m.

Brigadier-General WHIPPLE,
Chief of Staff:

GENERAL: My troops occupy the main line of the enemy's works in my front.

I am, general, very respectfully, your obedient servant,

JOSEPH HOOKER,
Major-General, Commanding.

HEADQUARTERS DEPARTMENT OF THE CUMBERLAND,
In the Field, July 22, 1864.

Maj. Gen. J. HOOKER,
Commanding Twentieth Army Corps:

GENERAL: The enemy has evacuated his works around Atlanta. The major-general commanding directs that you push on in pursuit by a road, if one can be found, running between the columns of Generals Palmer and Howard. General Palmer has been ordered to move in a southwesterly direction by road running from about his right, and General Howard by road running near Atlanta, but north of it and in the same direction as General Palmer. All our troops and General Schofield's move north by Atlanta.

Yours, very respectfully,

WM. D. WHIPPLE,
Assistant Adjutant-General.

HEADQUARTERS DEPARTMENT OF THE CUMBERLAND,
Near Atlanta, Ga., July 22, 1864.

Brig. Gen. W. L. ELLIOTT,
Chief of Cavalry:

GENERAL: The enemy has evacuated Atlanta. The major-general commanding directs me to say that you will order General McCook to take his command across the Chattahoochee at Pace's Landing, and then take the road down the river, crossing Peach Tree Creek at Moore's Mill, and follow the river road, covering the right flank of our army as it moves in pursuit. After he gets his troops in motion additional orders will be sent him at Moore's Mill.

I am, very respectfully, your obedient servant,

ROBT. H. RAMSEY,
Assistant Adjutant-General.

HEADQUARTERS FIRST CAVALRY DIVISION,
July 22, 1864.

General W. L. ELLIOTT,
Chief of Cavalry:

GENERAL: I have the honor to report that I found the enemy in sufficient force at the junction of this road and the Mason and Turner's Ferry road to check me. They had both infantry and artillery and I was unable to get my artillery in position to reply. It was too late for me to make a good fight. I will try it in the morning. I am, I think, about four or five miles to the right of the infantry, and will get communication some time during the night.

E. M. McCOOK,
Brigadier-General, Commanding.

IN THE FIELD, *July 22, 1864—11 o'clock.*

Brig. Gen. WILLIAM D. WHIPPLE,
Chief of Staff, Department of the Cumberland:

I cannot tell whether I will need re-enforcements until I try the enemy in the morning. The reason I suppose the force opposed to me is infantry, is based upon information received from citizens and the fact that nothing but dismounted men and artillery opposed my advance, and there were no horse tracks to indicate cavalry. I omitted to say in the dispatch I sent this evening the reason why I was too late for a decided attack this afternoon was that the enemy had torn up the bridge across the creek. My men had to get on their flank and drive them from the other side before the bridge could be repaired sufficiently for me to cross. I have a patrol from the right of my line to the river every hour. It has just been reported to me from the skirmish line that the enemy are chopping and building works very industriously. If I find their works formidable, I of course will make no assault unless ordered to do so by the general commanding. I will not, however, be kept back by any slight obstacles. They do not form a continuous line. With the infantry right I have been unable to make any connection. The country is too broken and the woods too dense for mounted men to pass through, except on roads.

I am, very respectfully, your obedient servant,

E. M. McCOOK,
Brigadier-General, Commanding.

HDQRS. CHIEF OF CAVALRY, DEPT. OF THE CUMBERLAND,
Near Atlanta, Ga., July 22, 1864.

COMMANDING OFFICER BRIGADE, FIRST CAVALRY DIVISION:

As the enemy have evacuated Atlanta, the general commanding directs that you follow up the movement of the right flank of the army until General McCook comes up.

I am, general, very respectfully, your obedient servant,

DAVID F. HOW,
Lieutenant and Acting Assistant Adjutant-General.

HEADQUARTERS ARMY OF THE OHIO,
July 22, 1864—3 a. m.

Major-General SHERMAN,
Commanding Military Division of the Mississippi:

GENERAL: The enemy has abandoned his works in front of General Hascall, and our skirmishers now occupy them. I will send forward a reconnaissance at daylight.

Respectfully,

J. M. SCHOFIELD,
Major-General.

HEADQUARTERS ARMY OF THE OHIO,
July 22, 1864—3.30 a. m.

Brig. Gen. M. S. HASCALL,
Commanding Second Division, Twenty-third Army Corps:

GENERAL: The commanding general directs that you make a reconnaissance on the road until you find the whereabouts of the enemy. As soon as the general is informed of the condition of affairs on the right he will send you the information.

Very respectfully, your obedient servant,

J. A. CAMPBELL,
Major and Assistant Adjutant-General.

HDQRS. THIRD DIVISION, TWENTY-THIRD ARMY CORPS,
July 22, 1864—5 a. m.

Maj. J. A. CAMPBELL,
    Assistant Adjutant-General:

MAJOR: The lines in our front are also found to be evacuated, our skirmishers going into them without hinderance. Three deserters have come in, reporting that they left early in the night. They know nothing of the force to the right or left of Hood's corps, to which they belonged, nor whether the intention was to go beyond Atlanta.

    Very respectfully, &c.,

                                        J. D. COX,
                                Brigadier-General, Commanding.

HEADQUARTERS ARMY OF THE OHIO,
July 22, 1864—5.30 a. m.

Brig. Gen. J. D. COX,
    Commanding Third Division, Twenty-third Army Corps:

GENERAL: Your dispatch of 5 a. m. received. Hascall has been ordered to move forward on the road until he finds the enemy or reaches Atlanta, and the commanding general desires you to follow and support him.

    Very respectfully, your obedient servant,

                                        J. A. CAMPBELL,
                            Major and Assistant Adjutant-General.

[JULY 22, 1864]—5.30 p. m.

Major-General SCHOFIELD:

General Dodge has called on me for assistance, and I am obliged to send Barter to him, leaving but one brigade here, General Logan having directed me to do this, if called on. I am three-fourths of a mile in front and left of Dodge, and they ask for Barter's brigade, because they say his left is threatened. This will indicate that my position with the remaining brigade is not very secure.

No change in front since Colonel Hartsuff left.

    Yours, &c.,

                                        J. D. COX,
                                    Brigadier-General.

My present position was shown me by General Logan, and is in itself good enough, if connected with any one.

HEADQUARTERS ARMY OF THE OHIO,
Before Atlanta, Ga., July 22, 1864—8.45 p. m.

Maj. Gen. W. T. SHERMAN,
    Commanding Military Division of the Mississippi:

GENERAL: Colonel Reilly reports that he has made a personal reconnaissance of Decatur; that the trains have all passed inside of our lines; that there is no rebel force at Decatur, and has been none but a small body of cavalry. I hope General Cox will be permitted to return to-night, even if he has to relieve Woods' division.

Very respectfully, your obedient servant,

J. M. SCHOFIELD,
Major-General, Commanding.

HDQRS. MILITARY DIVISION OF THE MISSISSIPPI,
In the Field, near Atlanta, Ga., July 22, 1864.

Major-General SCHOFIELD,
Commanding Army of the Ohio:

GENERAL: The general commanding directs me to say the relief of Cox's division by Woods', as suggested by your letter, meets his approval, and may be made to-night. General Logan, who is here, will call on you and arrange the move. I am also directed to order Captain Poe to take your engineer battalion and construct a bridge over the creek at Durand's (Williams') Mill, which will be on the most direct road to Powers' Crossing.

I am, general, yours, respectfully,

L. M. DAYTON,
Aide-de-Camp.

HEADQUARTERS ARMY OF THE OHIO,
Before Atlanta, Ga., July 22, 1864.

Brig. Gen. J. D. COX,
Commanding Third Division, Twenty-third Army Corps:

GENERAL: The commanding general directs me to inform you that it has been decided, after consultation with Generals Sherman and Logan, to relieve your two brigades by General Woods' division, and put you in General Woods' present position on General Hascall's left. General Logan will arrange the details of the movement, which will be carried out to-night. Colonel Reilly will remain in his present position, at least until morning.

Very respectfully, your obedient servant,

J. A. CAMPBELL,
Major and Assistant Adjutant-General.

HDQRS. DEPARTMENT AND ARMY OF THE TENNESSEE,
In the Field, July 22, 1864—6 a. m.

Maj. Gen. JOHN A. LOGAN,
Commanding Fifteenth Army Corps:

GENERAL: The enemy having evacuated their works in front of our lines, the supposition of Major-General Sherman is that they have given up Atlanta and are retreating in the direction of East Point. You will immediately put your command in pursuit, passing to the south and east of Atlanta, without entering the town. You will keep a route to the left of that taken by the enemy, and try to cut off a portion of them while they are pressed in rear and on our right by Generals Schofield and Thomas. Major-General Sherman desires and expects a vigorous pursuit.

Very respectfully, your obedient servant,

JAS. B. McPHERSON,
Major-General.

HDQRS. DEPARTMENT AND ARMY OF THE TENNESSEE,
July 22, 1864.

Maj. Gen. W. T. SHERMAN, *Commanding, &c.:*

DEAR SIR: I have seen all the corps commanders since I left your headquarters and made the best dispositions I could of the troops of the Army of the Tennessee. I find one division of the Seventeenth Corps somewhat despondent, but think they will hold their position; have sent them three fresh regiments to support them in holding the hill that I think is the key-point to my whole position. Some prisoners, who have just come inside of our picket-lines in General Dodge's front, report themselves from Hood's corps (now Cheatham's), which they report moving to our left, in order to attack in the morning; they say Atlanta is held by militia, and that Polk's old corps is on our extreme right, west of Atlanta. This statement may not be true, but I am inclined to think it is true from all that I have learned from other prisoners. The note to you from General Schofield giving you the information that there was nothing but a small force of cavalry in Decatur to-day, would somewhat do away with my impression about the force were it not for Colonel Sprague's report to General Dodge. He reports that he was attacked by a large force, and had lost nearly 400 men killed, wounded, and captured, as General Dodge informs me. I give you this information all as I get it, that you may judge from all information that you may get as to where troops of the enemy are and what their intentions are.

Very respectfully,

JOHN A. LOGAN,
Major-General.

CAMP ON RAILROAD,
Four miles from Atlanta, July 22, 1864—9 p. m.

Maj. THOMAS T. ECKERT,
Superintendent U. S. Military Telegraph:

At daylight to-day it was found that the rebels had gone from entire front, and General Sherman announced the occupation of Atlanta by Schofield, and ordered pursuit by Thomas and McPherson. Vigorous pursuit was made, and the enemy was found in the fortifications of Atlanta, and not Schofield. We hold road to within two miles and a half of center of place, and that is about the average distance of whole line, though Schofield and Dodge are nearer. Fighting has been severe, and we have lost General McPherson, killed by shot through lungs while on a reconnaissance. It is thought that enemy will be gone in the morning, as they have attacked and been repulsed since dark. Hood fights his graybacks desperately.

J. C. VAN DUZER,
Cipher Operator, U. S. Military Telegraph.

SPECIAL FIELD ORDERS, ⎫   HDQRS. MIL. DIV. OF THE MISS.,
⎬   *In the Field, near Atlanta, Ga.,*
No. 41.   ⎭   *July 22, 1864.*

The enemy having to-day withdrawn into his intrenchments at Atlanta, and having assaulted our left, the following general plan will be observed for to-morrow, July 23, 1864:

I. All the armies will intrench a strong front on their present lines and will hold in reserve as much infantry as possible for offensive operations. Good batteries will be constructed for the artillery and a steady fire kept up on the city of Atlanta.

II. The trains will be kept behind the main center (Major-General Howard's corps) or close up to their own reserves, and in the event of the enemy assaulting at any point all others should assault the enemy to their immediate front. By carrying any one point of the enemy's present line his whole position becomes untenable.

By order of Maj. Gen. W. T. Sherman:

L. M. DAYTON,
Aide-de-Camp.

———

CIRCULAR.]   HEADQUARTERS TWENTIETH CORPS,
ARMY OF THE CUMBERLAND,
Near Atlanta, Ga., July 22, 1864.

Appearances indicate that the enemy have only a strong rear-guard between us and Atlanta, but this we do not know positively, hence all the divisions should be held in condition for an obstinate defense in case of an assault.

The First Division will have one brigade in reserve, and that should be posted as near the right of the line as practicable, as that rests on one of the main roads leading into Atlanta. The major-general commanding suggests that a battery or two be placed in position for defending the approach by the Howell's Mill road. He also requests that the communication by the road along the ridge be kept open in order that we may have easy and quick communication between the right and left of our line. In his opinion Atlanta will be abandoned to-night, and he desires that the pickets may be directed to keep on the alert that they may be informed of the earliest movements of the enemy in their retreat, and to follow them as far as Atlanta in case they should withdraw from before our front.

It will be a great compliment to the Twentieth Corps to have it said that it was the first to enter Atlanta.

Very respectfully, yours,

H. W. PERKINS,
Assistant Adjutant-General.

———

GENERAL FIELD ORDERS, ⎫   HEADQUARTERS DEPARTMENT
               ⎬   AND ARMY OF THE TENNESSEE,
No. 3.   ⎭   *Before Atlanta, Ga., July 22, 1864.*

In pursuance of instructions from Maj. Gen. W. T. Sherman, commanding Military Division of the Mississippi, I hereby assume command of the Army of the Tennessee in the field. The department staff will remain unchanged, and reports and returns will be made as heretofore.

JOHN A. LOGAN,
Major-General.

———

SPECIAL FIELD ORDERS, ⎫   HEADQUARTERS DEPARTMENT
               ⎬   AND ARMY OF THE TENNESSEE,
No. 75.   ⎭   *Near Atlanta, Ga., July 22, 1864.*

    *   *   *   *   *   *   *

II. Brigadier-General Woods, commanding First Division, Fifteenth Army Corps, will relieve Brigadier-General Cox, commanding a division of the Twenty-third Army Corps, immediately, one brigade being relieved at a time; the brigades of General Cox marching from his present position to take up a position on the left of General Schofield's command to connect with General M. L. Smith, commanding Second Division, Fifteenth Army Corps. The movement will be made by brigade until the whole division of General Cox is relieved.

2. The entire command will be intrenched in its present position, which will be held at all hazards, especially the hill occupied by Major-General Blair.

3. The trains of this command will be kept behind the main center (Major-General Howard's command) or close up on their own reserves, and in case the enemy assault at any one point all other corps will at once assault the enemy in their immediate front.

4. This entire command will be under arms at 3.30 o'clock to-morrow morning, prepared for any emergency.

5. Corps commanders will be held responsible that their commands are amply supplied with ammunition, and caissons and cartridge-boxes will be replenished to-night.

By order of Maj. Gen. John A. Logan:

WM. T. CLARK,
Assistant Adjutant-General.

NEAR ATLANTA, GA., *July 23, 1864—10.30 a. m.*
(Received 6 p. m.)

Maj. Gen. H. W. HALLECK,
Washington, D. C.:

Yesterday morning the enemy fell back to the intrenchments proper of the city of Atlanta, which are in a general circle of a radius of one mile and a half, and we closed in. While we were forming our lines and selecting positions for batteries, the enemy appeared suddenly out of the dense woods in heavy masses on our extreme left, and struck the Seventeenth Corps (General Blair's) in flank, and was forcing it back, when the Sixteenth Corps (General Dodge's) came up and checked the movement, but the enemy's cavalry got well to our rear and into Decatur, and for some hours our left flank was completely enveloped. The fighting that resulted was continuous until night, with heavy loss on both sides. The enemy took one of our batteries (Murray's, of the Regular Army) that was marching in its place in column on the road unconscious of danger. About 4 p. m. the enemy sallied against the division of General Morgan L. Smith, which occupied an abandoned line of rifle-trenches near the railroad, east of the city, and forced it back some 400 yards, leaving in his hands for the time two batteries, but the ground and batteries were immediately after recovered by the same troops, re-enforced. I cannot well approximate our loss, which fell heaviest on the Fifteenth and Seventeenth Corps, but count it 3,000; but I know that, being on the defensive, we have inflicted equally heavy loss on the enemy. General McPherson, when arranging his troops, about 11 a. m., and passing from one column to another, unconsciously rode upon an ambuscade without apprehension and at some distance ahead of his staff and orderlies and was shot dead. His body was sent in charge of his personal staff back to Marietta and Chattanooga. His loss at that moment was most serious, but General Logan at once arranged the troops, and had immediate direction of them during the rest of the day. Our left, though refused somewhat, is still within easy cannon-range of Atlanta. The enemy seems to man his extensive parapets and, at the same time, has to spare heavy assaulting columns; but to-day we will intrench our front lines, which will give me troops to spare to meet these assaults. I cannot hear of the loss of more than a few wagons, taken by the enemy's cavalry during his temporary pause in Decatur, whence all the trains had been securely removed to the rear of the main army, under cover of a brigade of infantry, commanded by Colonel Sprague. During the heavy attack on the left, the remainder of the line was not engaged.

W. T. SHERMAN,
Major-General.

NEAR ATLANTA, GA., *July 23, 1864.*
(Received 4 p. m.)

Maj. Gen. H. W. HALLECK,
    Washington, D. C.:

General Rousseau reports from Marietta yesterday his safe return from Opelika, having destroyed that depot, 30 miles of railroad toward Montgomery, 3 miles toward Columbus, and 2 toward West Point. His entire loss 12 killed and 30 wounded. He brings in 400 mules and 300 horses.

W. T. SHERMAN,
Major-General.

HDQRS. MILITARY DIVISION OF THE MISSISSIPPI,
In the Field, near Atlanta, Ga., July 23, 1864—2 a. m.

Major-General THOMAS,
    Army of the Cumberland:

GENERAL: I have heard of General Rousseau's return to Marietta. Please order him at once to relieve General Stoneman on the other side of the river, and let General Stoneman come to me with his whole force. Please send the inclosed order for me at once. The attack on our left to-day has been desperate and persistent, and the losses on both sides quite heavy. I want you to relieve it to-morrow by an actual attack or strong demonstration on the right. I will send you word early in the day, if it is renewed. I suppose it will be kept up as long as General Garrard is out. I want General Stoneman to move out to General Garrard's relief. You can use Generals McCook and Rousseau on your right.

I am, &c.,

W. T. SHERMAN,
Major-General, Commanding.

[Inclosure.]

HDQRS. MILITARY DIVISION OF THE MISSISSIPPI,
In the Field, near Atlanta, Ga., July 23, 1864—2 a. m.

General ROUSSEAU,
    Marietta:

Your dispatch is received, and you have done well. I hate to call on you so soon for more service, but time is pressing. I want you to move down right away to the railroad bridge and relieve General Stoneman, who is watching the Chattahoochee below Turner's Ferry. He will describe to you the country and what is needed. I want him relieved as soon as possible, that he may come over here. I hope to see you in a few days.

I am, &c.,

W. T. SHERMAN,
Major-General, Commanding.

HEADQUARTERS ARMY OF THE CUMBERLAND,
July 23, 1864.

Major-General SHERMAN,
Commanding Military Division of the Mississippi:

GENERAL: Your order of last night is being carried out by my troops to-day. The enemy appears to be feeling my right and rear, but in what force I cannot ascertain, as General McCook cannot ascertain on account of the difficulties of the ground. General Rousseau has received the order to move his force to Turner's Ferry, though the movement will be somewhat delayed by his having left Marietta to visit you before the order reached him. It was sent by telegraph also, but as he had left Marietta at daylight this morning he did not receive the order before reaching my headquarters.

Very respectfully,

GEO. H. THOMAS,
Major-General, U. S. Volunteers, Commanding.

HEADQUARTERS DEPARTMENT OF THE CUMBERLAND,
Near Atlanta, July 23, 1864.

Maj. Gen. O. O. HOWARD,
Commanding Fourth Army Corps:

GENERAL: Your note of 8 p. m. was received last night. The major-general commanding says that it will not be necessary for you to send two regiments to intercept the rebel cavalry.

Yours, very respectfully,

WM. D. WHIPPLE,
Assistant Adjutant-General.

HDRS. MILITARY DIVISION OF THE MISSISSIPPI,
In the Field, near Atlanta, Ga., July 23, 1864.

General STONEMAN,
Turner's Ferry:

I sent an order for you to send a brigade of cavalry at once. I have just learned that General Rousseau has arrived at Marietta from Opelika and have ordered him to relieve you. Have all your men ready to start the moment General Rousseau comes. Turn over to him your instructions and the use of your pontoon train that he may cross over at Turner's the moment his horses are rested and General Thomas orders him.

I am, &c.,

W. T. SHERMAN,
Major-General, Commanding.

HEADQUARTERS FIRST CAVALRY DIVISION,
Turner and Mason's Ferry Road, July 23, 1864—8.30 a. m.
Lieut. D. F. HOW:

My command drove the rebels away from here this morning. The force in my front was Jackson's division. I got the report of effective force of one brigade, Harrison's, and it numbered 1,618 men. So I judge the division is strong, which is confirmed by prisoners taken. I will open communication with General Davis as soon as possible. It is about a mile from here to the river. I sent the dispatch to General Stoneman across.

Very respectfully,

E. M. McCOOK,
Brigadier-General, Commanding.

HDQRS. MILITARY DIVISION OF THE MISSISSIPPI,
In the Field, near Atlanta, Ga., July 23, 1864—8 p. m.
Major-General SCHOFIELD, *Commanding Army of the Ohio:*

GENERAL: I have examined our line of circumvallation, and have no fear of the enemy even attempting to test its strength. But until we get our cavalry in hand and position, I will not attempt anything serious. You may therefore keep things *statu quo*, and look only to your supplies of food and ammunition. I have seen General Rousseau, and am satisfied he has made a break that cuts off Alabama for a month, and he has brought us in pretty fair condition some 2,500 additional cavalry.

I am, yours, truly,

W. T. SHERMAN,
Major-General, Commanding.

HDQRS. THIRD DIVISION, TWENTY-THIRD ARMY CORPS,
Before Atlanta, July 23, 1864.
Colonel CAMERON, *Commanding Second Brigade:*

SIR: You will occupy the lines on the left of Colonel Barter's brigade, which General Woods will leave, putting in your whole command in one line, if necessary, to fill them. Then let working parties strengthen and thicken the parapet from the outside, and put in chevaux-de-frise and such abatis, &c., as you can, putting the works in the best condition and holding them at all hazards. I expect to have at least one brigade in reserve ready to support either you or Barter, though I have not yet got it relieved. I will see you in an hour, or two at furthest, after seeing General Schofield, getting some breakfast, and changing my horse.

Very respectfully, &c.,

J. D. COX,
Brigadier-General, Commanding.

HDQRS. MILITARY DIVISION OF THE MISSISSIPPI,
In the Field, near Atlanta, Ga., July 23, 1864—8 p. m.
Maj. Gen. JOHN A. LOGAN,
Commanding Army of the Tennessee:

GENERAL: I have this moment returned from an examination of our entire line. You know your own. The balance extends in a circle at about 1,000 yards distant from the enemy's lines, as far as Proctor's Creek, the whole of Palmer's corps being east and south of the railroad. All have covered their fronts with parapets so that the enemy will not attempt a sally. The question now is, What next? I will in person explain all that is necessary to produce the result aimed at as soon as General Garrard returns. You need not apprehend a renewal of the attack on the part of the enemy, but should, on the contrary, begin to feel out with skirmishers and supports into the woods east of Giles Smith's division and Dodge's corps. In the morning early let Woods' division move into Decatur, stay awhile, and return. Let details of men and pioneers begin at your very front and break up and destroy the railroad absolutely back to and including Decatur. Until we conclude upon the best manner of reducing Atlanta we cannot be better employed than in rendering the Atlanta and Augusta road useless; especially have the iron rails heated and twisted. I want your skirmishers to feel out early to-morrow in front of Dodge for a double purpose—to hold on that flank the cavalry of Wheeler, while we operate on Thomas' flank and create a diversion for Garrard, now on his return from his expedition.

I am, with respect, your obedient servant,

W. T. SHERMAN,
Major-General, Commanding.

HDQRS. MILITARY DIVISION OF THE MISSISSIPPI,
In the Field, near Atlanta, July 23, 1864—11.45 p. m.

Major-General LOGAN,
Commanding Army of the Tennessee:

GENERAL: I am directed by the general commanding to say that he prefers not to give orders as regards Roswell until he hears further from the cavalry; in the mean time let your wagons go to the railroad via Pace's Ferry and load at Vining's Station or Marietta such forage as you may need. The general understood yesterday that you had four days' supply.

I am, with much respect,

L. M. DAYTON,
Aide-de-Camp.

HEADQUARTERS LEFT WING, SIXTEENTH ARMY CORPS,
In the Field, Ga., July 23, 1864.

Major-General LOGAN,
Commanding Army of the Tennessee:

Colonel Sprague has taken up position on the left of Colonel Smith's brigade, of General Woods' division. He does not consider the position in Decatur a safe one, as the force in front and on his flank is evidently two divisions of cavalry; captured dispatches show this. He now covers road leading from main Atlanta road to Schofield's rear, and says Colonel Reilly's brigade, of Twenty-third Army Corps, is on the road leading out of Roswell road to Schofield's rear.

G. M. DODGE,
Major-General.

HEADQUARTERS LEFT WING, SIXTEENTH ARMY CORPS,
Near Atlanta, Ga., July 23, 1864.

Lieut. Col. WILLIAM T. CLARK,
Assistant Adjutant-General:

Sergeant Childs, Fourteenth Ohio Battery, came through to-day from Marietta, passing through Roswell at 2 p. m. All our trains were there with light guard. On the direct road to Decatur he passed one wagon belonging to the Seventeenth Corps, loaded with grain, burning. He came through Decatur; saw no rebels, but heard of them off the road. It appears to me that our trains are in great danger. They had not received any orders and did not know what to do.

Very respectfully, your obedient servant,

G. M. DODGE,
Major-General, Commanding.

JULY 23, 1864.

Colonel CAPRON, *Commanding Cavalry Brigade:*

Bring your command to the cross-roads, leaving a pretty strong picket guard (say 150 or 200 men) at the bridge, and send a staff officer to report to me the arrival of your command. The enemy is very active at Turner's Ferry.

Very respectfully, &c.,

STONEMAN,
General, Commanding.

CAMP THREE MILES NORTH OF ATLANTA,
July 23, 1864.—11 p. m.

Maj. T. T. ECKERT:

Enemy has been less active to-day, attacking only in front of Army of the Cumberland, and being engaged in burying dead on ground of yesterday's fight under flags of truce. General Logan commands Army of the Tennessee, and Morgan L. Smith takes the Fifteenth Corps. Our loss in yesterday's battle—of artillery, 8 guns; about 30 wagons, and 200 prisoners. As I write our heavy artillery is at work, and large fires are burning in Atlanta, supposed to be the enemy destroying stores preparatory to evacuating.

J. C. VAN DUZER,
Cipher Operator, U. S. Military Telegraph.

SPECIAL FIELD ORDERS }
        No. 76.   }

BEFORE ATLANTA, GA.,
July 23, 1864.

*   *   *   *   *   *   *

VII. Brig. Gen. M. L. Smith, commanding Fifteenth Army Corps, will direct General Woods, commanding First Division of his corps, to move into Decatur at 5 o'clock to-morrow morning, leaving along his works a heavy line of skirmishers. After remaining a while in Decatur he will return and occupy his position. General Smith will also direct details of men from General Woods' division and the pioneers from his command to commence at the extreme front of the line and destroy effectually the railroad to and including Decatur, the ties to be taken up, the rails placed upon them and bent and twisted while burning, so as to prevent any further use of the road. All details of soldiers will be sent armed, prepared for any attack of the enemy. General Woods will protect as far as possible all details employed in the destruction of the railroad. Should General Dodge be attacked, General Woods will fall upon the flank of the enemy and punish him.

2. Major-General Dodge will direct the skirmishers of his command to feel out at daylight to-morrow morning, thus keeping the enemy's cavalry on our left flank and at the same time securing a diversion while an attack is being made on the flank of General Thomas and protecting the return of General Garrard from his cavalry expedition. The skirmish line will be careful to keep its right flank connected with General Blair's pickets and will be cautioned against any attempt of the enemy to break through, to cut them off from the main line.

      *   *   *   *   *   *   *

By order of Maj. Gen. John A. Logan:

WM. T. CLARK,
Assistant Adjutant-General.

GENERAL ORDERS, ⎫   HDQRS. FIFTEENTH ARMY CORPS,
    No. 1. ⎬   *Near Atlanta, Ga., July 23, 1864.*

In pursuance of instructions from Major-General Logan, commanding Department and Army of the Tennessee, the undersigned hereby assumes command of the Fifteenth Corps.

MORGAN L. SMITH,
Brigadier-General, U. S. Volunteers.

NEAR ATLANTA, GA., *July 24, 1864—3 p. m.*
(Received 9.50 p. m.)

Maj. Gen. H. W. HALLECK, *Washington, D. C.:*

On making up reports and examining the field, I find the result of Hood's attack on our left more disastrous to the enemy than I reported. Our loss will not foot up 2,000 killed and wounded, whereas we have found over 1,000 rebels dead, which will make, with the usual proportion of wounded, a loss to the enemy of full 7,000. General Garrard has also returned, perfectly successful, having completely destroyed the two large bridges near Covington, forty miles toward Augusta, brought in 200 prisoners and some good horses, and destroyed the public stores at Covington and Conyers, including 2,000 bales of cotton, a locomotive, and a train of cars. Our communications are yet all safe, and the army in good condition in all respects. As soon as my cavalry rests I propose to swing the Army of the Tennessee round by the right rapidly and interpose between Atlanta and Macon, the only line open to the enemy.

W. T. SHERMAN,
Major-General.

NEAR ATLANTA, GA., *July 24, 1864—3 p. m.*
(Received 10 p. m.)

Maj. Gen. H. W. HALLECK, *Washington, D. C.:*

The sudden loss of McPherson was a heavy blow to me. I can hardly replace him, but must have a successor. After thinking over the whole matter, I prefer that Maj. Gen. O. O. Howard be ordered to command the Army and Department of the Tennessee. If this meets the President's approval, notify me by telegraph, when I will put him in command, and name others to fill the vacancies created.   Logan, as senior, commands the Army of the Tennessee for the present.   After we have taken Atlanta I will name officers who merit promotion.   In the mean time, I request that the President will not give increased rank to any officer who has gone on leave from sickness, or cause other than wounds in battle.

> W. T. SHERMAN,
> *Major-General.*

NEAR ATLANTA, GA., *July 24, 1864.*

General L. THOMAS, *Adjutant-General U. S. Army:*

GENERAL: It is my painful duty to report that Brig. Gen. James B. McPherson, U. S. Army, major-general of volunteers and commander of the Army of the Tennessee in the field, was killed by a shot from ambuscade about noon of yesterday.* At the time of this fatal shot he was on horseback, placing his troops in position near the city of Atlanta, and was passing by a cross-road from a moving column toward the flank of troops that had already been established on the line.   He had quitted me but a few moments before and was on his way to see in person to the execution of my orders.   About the time of this sad event the enemy had sallied from his intrenchments around Atlanta and had, by a circuit, got to the left and rear of this very line and had begun an attack which resulted in serious battle, so that General McPherson fell in battle, booted and spurred, as the gallant knight and gentleman should wish.   Not his the loss, but the country's, and the army will mourn his death and cherish his memory as that of one who, though comparatively young, had risen by his merit and ability to the command of one of the best armies which the nation had called into existence to vindicate its honor and integrity.   History tells us of but few who so blended the grace and gentleness of the friend with the dignity, courage, faith, and manliness of the soldier.   His public enemies, even the men who directed the fatal shot, ne'er spoke or wrote of him without expressions of marked respect; those whom he commanded loved him even to idolatry, and I, his associate and commander, fail in words adequate to express my opinion of his great worth.   I feel assured that every patriot in America on hearing this sad news will feel a sense of personal loss and the country generally will realize that we have lost not only an able military leader but a man who, had he survived, was qualified to heal the national strife which has been raised by ambitious and designing men.   His body has been sent North in charge of Major Willard, Captains Steele and Gile, his personal staff.

I am, with great respect,

> W. T. SHERMAN,
> *Major-General, Commanding.*

THOMAS' HEADQUARTERS, *July 24, 1864.*

Major-General SCHOFIELD:

I had Stanley prepare for any movement of the enemy which might result from your reconnaissance.   Have not heard from him yet; will send you his report.

> GEO. H. THOMAS,
> *Major-General.*

---

* He was killed July 22,

CHATTAHOOCHEE BRIDGE, GA., *July 24, 1864.*
General WHIPPLE,
    Chief of Staff:

Both my bridges are completed. The other train is here, and have one bridge almost completed. All the bridges are just below the mouth of Peach Tree Creek. Good roads on both sides of the river.
    Respectfully,
                                        GEO. P. BUELL,
                                            Commanding.

HDQRS. FIRST DIV. CAV., DEPT. OF THE CUMBERLAND,
                                        July 24, 1864.
Lieut. D. F. HOW,
    Acting Assistant Adjutant-General:

I have the honor to report that the enemy's cavalry made a demonstration against my line yesterday evening. They were repulsed; our loss 6.
    Very respectfully, your obedient servant,
                                        E. M. McCOOK,
                                Brigadier-General, Commanding.

BEFORE ATLANTA, GA., *July 24, 1864.*
Maj. Gen. W. T. SHERMAN,
    Commanding Military Division of the Mississippi:

I have the honor to state the brigade of cavalry from General Stoneman's command, which, by information from you of last evening, was to report to me this morning, has not yet reported. It is necessary that trains with forage and rations should be brought forward from Roswell. You are aware that I have no cavalry at my disposal, nor is it practicable to take a sufficient force of infantry from the lines as a guard to bring up the trains. Shall the Roswell depot be abandoned and all the trains brought forward under guard there stationed, and shall the bridge be destroyed?
    Very respectfully, your obedient servant,
                                        JNO. A. LOGAN,
                                            Major-General.

HDQRS. MILITARY DIVISION OF THE MISSISSIPPI,
    In the Field, near Atlanta, Ga., July 24, 1864.
Maj. Gen. JOHN A. LOGAN,
    Commanding Army of the Tennessee:

GENERAL: I have pretty well surveyed the whole position, and by the aid of maps and my own observations think I understand the case pretty well. Our lines are now strong in front, and we compass Atlanta from the railroad on the east to the railroad west. The enemy, having failed in his assault on your flank before it was covered by any defensible works, and having sustained most serious loss, will not again attempt it, but will await our action. I now inclose you a map* made

---
* Not found.

by General Schofield's engineers, which shows the roads to your present right rear. I sent Captain Poe to see you this morning, but from what Captain Hickenlooper says I think I may have failed to convey to you my right meaning, which is this: The only object in placing the Army of the Tennessee on that flank was to reach and destroy the railroad from Atlanta toward Augusta. That is partially done, and the work of destruction should be continued as far as possible. I wish you to keep one division or more employed day and night in breaking and burning the road until General Garrard returns. I feel no doubt but that he has succeeded in breaking the bridges across the Yellow River and the Ulcofauhachee, but he may have to fight his way back, and to relieve him I wish you to push your skirmishers out from General Dodge's front of General Blair's left, as though you were going to push your way to the east of Atlanta toward the Augusta road. To keep up this delusion, you should send a column cautiously down one of those roads or valleys southeast, and engage the enemy outside his works, but not behind his trenches. As soon as General Garrard is back you can discontinue all such demonstrations and prepare for your next move. I propose to give you timely notice to send your wagons behind General Thomas and then to move your army behind the present line to the extreme right, to reach, if possible, the Macon road, which you know to be the only road by which Atlanta can be supplied. This will leave General Schofield the left flank, which will be covered by the works he has constructed on his front, and he can use the abandoned trenches of the enemy to cover his left rear. You will no longer send your wagons by Roswell, but by Buck Head and Pace's Ferry, and when you change you will draw from the railroad bridge, to which our cars now run, and at which point we are making a pier bridge, as also two of pontoons. General Stoneman will surely be at Decatur to-day, and we will have two divisions of cavalry on our right, viz, General McCook's and [Colonel] Harrison's (General Rousseau's). Act with confidence. Know that the enemy cannot budge you from your present ground, and act offensively to show him that you dare him to the encounter. You can understand that being on the defensive he cannot afford to sally unless at great peril. General Schofield has so strengthened his front that I feel no uneasiness about that flank, and only study now to make the next move so quickly that we may reach East Point or vicinity with as little loss as possible. My headquarters are now behind General Howard's corps, General Newton's division, on the main Marietta and Atlanta road, which crosses the Chattahoochee at Pace's Ferry and passes through Buck Head. I am at a large white house near the enemy's old line of intrenchments, a prolongation of the same which passes from where I saw you yesterday by General Schofield's position. I have just heard that General Garrard is back. Go on breaking that road good.

W. T. SHERMAN,
Major-General, Commanding.

HEADQUARTERS LEFT WING, SIXTEENTH ARMY CORPS,
Near Atlanta, Ga., July 24, 1864.

Capt. L. M. DAYTON,
      Aide-de-Camp:

I respectfully request that the Third Brigade, Fourth Division, Sixteenth Army Corps, now at Decatur, Ala., be ordered to join this command. The two divisions, comprising four brigades present (two to each division), have lost in killed and wounded alone some 2,000 men, and the detaching two brigades, together with the loss from sickness, has reduced the command from 12,500 effective, which it started with, to some 6,000. One brigade, 1,800 strong, is at Rome, Ga., and one at Decatur, Ala. If either brigade or both could join me it would give us a valuable addition to the army. There are also detached the First Alabama Cavalry at Rome and the Ninth Ohio Cavalry at Decatur, besides some three regiments of colored troops belonging to this command, which makes those absent and without the command fully equal to the present. If it is possible, under the exigencies of the service, I trust the general commanding the Military Division of the Mississippi will order up a portion of my command.

I am, very respectfully, your obedient servant,

G. M. DODGE,
Major-General.

HEADQUARTERS SEVENTEENTH ARMY CORPS,
Before Atlanta, Ga., July 24, 1864.

Capt. L. M. DAYTON,
A. D. C. and A. A. A. G., Mil. Div. of the Mississippi:

CAPTAIN: I have the honor to represent for the information of the major-general commanding the Division of the Mississippi that this corps was reduced when I assumed command of it to about 10,000 effective men by leaving the strongest division at Vicksburg. Upon my arrival at Allatoona I left one brigade and two batteries, numbering about 1,200 men, to guard the depots at that place. Since that time, in the various actions in which the corps has been engaged, it has lost about 3,000 men, leaving me an effective force of only some 6,000. Under these circumstances I would most respectfully request that that portion of this corps which was left at Allatoona, and which is now stationed at Kenesaw Mountain, may be relieved by some other command and ordered to report to me for duty as soon as practicable.

I am, captain, very respectfully, your obedient servant,

FRANK P. BLAIR, JR.,
Major-General.

HDQRS. 116TH ILLINOIS INFANTRY VOLUNTEERS,
Before Atlanta, Ga., July 24, 1864.

Colonel CLARK,
Assistant Adjutant-General, Department of the Tennessee:

SIR: I have the honor of forwarding to you a stand of rebel colors captured by Lieut. Samuel R. Riggs, commanding Company E of this regiment, on the 22d of July, 1864. The circumstances are as follows: The regiment I have the honor to command was ordered to the left of the Sixteenth Army Corps. Immediately on its arrival there I was ordered back by Colonel Martin, commanding First Brigade, Second Division, Fifteenth Army Corps. I was informed that the enemy had taken our works and that they must be retaken. I was ordered to form my regiment on the right of the Sixth Missouri Infantry, to charge the enemy, and drive them from our works. When within fifty yards of the works, a rebel officer with the colors of his regiment and five of his men crossed the works, forming them on this side, and trying to get the balance of his command over. I then asked Lieutenant Riggs if he could take that stand of colors with his company. He answered, "I can." So with five of his men he charged them, killing the officer (a captain), capturing the colors and color bearer, and wounding 2 of the color guard. I will also forward you the names of the men who are entitled to the honors of helping to capture the flag: Jacob Cross, Eliphalet Greely, Joseph Goodwin, Corpl. N. Sprague, and Corpl. I. W. Rittenhouse. If consistent, I would most earnestly request that the colors be returned to Lieutenant Riggs as a reward of his bravery.

I am, sir, your obedient servant,

J. S. WINDSOR,
Commanding 116th Illinois Infantry.

[July 24, 1864.—For Garrard to Sherman, reporting results of raid to Covington, see Part II, p. 809.]

HDQRS. MILITARY DIVISION OF THE MISSISSIPPI,
In the Field, near Atlanta, Ga., July 24, 1864—2 p. m.

General GARRARD,
Decatur:

GENERAL: I am rejoiced to hear that you are back safe and successful. General Rousseau has brought me 2,500 good cavalry, having been to Opelika and destroyed thirty miles of road between West Point and Montgomery. I will give you time to rest and then we must make quick work with Atlanta. I await your report with impatience, and in the mean time tender you the assurance of my great consideration.

Your friend,

W. T. SHERMAN,
Major-General, Commanding.

HDQRS. THIRD DIVISION, FIFTEENTH ARMY CORPS,
Cartersville, Ga., July 24, 1864.

Col. BENJAMIN D. DEAN,
Twenty-sixth Missouri Infantry:

SIR: You will move with your command to Kingston, Ga., and relieve the Fifth Iowa Infantry, stationed on the Etowah River, and will assume command of the post of Kingston and Third Brigade, Third Division, Fifteenth Army Corps, relieving Col. J. Banbury, who will report to his regiment for duty.

By order of Brig. Gen. John E. Smith:

C. L. WHITE,
Captain and Assistant Adjutant-General.

HDQRS. MILITARY DIVISION OF THE MISSISSIPPI,
In the Field, near Atlanta, Ga., July 24, 1864.

Major-General SLOCUM,
Commanding Vicksburg, &c.:

GENERAL: I have received yours of July 2.* I fear you were more affected by the words of my telegram than I designed. By the lan-

---

* See Vol. XXXIX.

guage used I aimed to express emphatically how important General Grant and I deemed the intersection of the Mississippi Central and the Vicksburg and Selma roads. We had worked for it so hard that I felt sensitive when I heard the enemy were gradually closing the gap. Be assured of my sincere respect, and if you will be most active, whether successful or not, you may count on my personal and official support. This may not be a motive, but for the time being I represent the Great Valley, and I do think I appreciate the relative value of its parts.

Though far away here in Georgia thundering away at Atlanta my thoughts revert to Mississippi and that great valley, which appears to me the spinal column of America, that you will pardon me if at times I am sensitive as to the safety of its vital parts.

There is a seeming conflict of authority between General Canby's command and mine. Were I near I feel we would perfectly accord, but being so far away I will concede to him superior knowledge of the pressing necessities at local points. Therefore when he orders troops, comply with his orders, and report the troops not as transferred but as detached, and keep him advised of the tenor and purpose of any general instructions or orders from the commander of the Department of the Tennessee or from me. Our command is on the east bank and General Canby's on the west bank, but as we are off in Georgia and General Canby is near at hand, the War Department has wisely ordered that for the protection of the great interests, as it were, afloat on that river, General Canby's orders to local garrisons are good. If, as I hope will not be the case, an absolute conflict should arise, I think our commands to you would be superior, but if good sense and feeling prevail, I do not apprehend any real conflict, for the protection of the river and its commerce, which is common to our commands, must always take precedence over any mere inland expedition.

You will have heard with pain and sorrow that General McPherson was killed day before yesterday, at the beginning of a battle brought on by Hood, who attacked our left as we were closing our lines on Atlanta. General McPherson had the Fifteenth and Seventeenth Corps in line, conforming to the enemy's works, and was moving Dodge's troops obliquely by the flank to the left to form, as it were, a shoulder. General McPherson was crossing one of those valleys by a road or wood path by, as it were, a diagonal, to reach the left flank of General Blair, doubtless to prepare a place for General Dodge, and he must have encountered the advanced line of the enemy's skirmishers, who preceded the column which had reached the rear of the line of General Blair. He was shot through the breast, high up from the right side. He fell dead from his horse but a few yards from the road or path. We soon got his body and sent it to the rear and to the North. He was a noble, gallant gentleman, and the best hope for a great soldier that I had in my mind's eye. You will find many a moist eye in Vicksburg when the news of his death reaches Vicksburg. General Logan is in command of the army in the field, but the President must name his successor. In the mean time execute his general orders, and in all matters of detail your own good sense must direct.

Butterfield is home sick. Ward, Geary, and Williams command Hooker's divisions. All have done good fighting.

Your friend and servant,

W. T. SHERMAN,
Major-General, Commanding.

Special Field Orders, }   Hdqrs. Left Wing, 16th A. C.,
     No. 45.   }   *Near Atlanta, Ga., July 24, 1864.*

I. General Woods' division, of the Fifteenth Corps, has been ordered to move into Decatur at 5 o'clock this morning, and to directly return, destroying the line of the railroad for the purpose of keeping the enemy's cavalry on our left flank, and at the same time securing a diversion while an attack is being made on the flank of General Thomas and protecting the return of General Garrard from his cavalry expedition. The skirmishers of this command will feel well out at daylight this morning. The skirmish line will be careful to keep its right flank connected with General Blair's pickets, and will be cautioned against any attempt of the enemy to break through to cut them off from the main line. In case the enemy should attack, General Woods is instructed to fall upon his flank and punish him. Brig. Gen. J. W. Fuller, commanding Fourth Division, will move two regiments from his right to the left of General Sweeny's line, to occupy the position of Colonel Williamson's brigade during its absence from the line.

*   *   *   *   *   *   *

By order of Maj. Gen. G. M. Dodge:

                              J. W. BARNES,
                              Assistant Adjutant-General.

                    Near Atlanta, Ga., *July 25, 1864—8.30 p. m.*
Lieutenant-General Grant,
          Petersburg, Va.:

Your dispatch of the 21st did not come till to-day. Johnston is relieved and Hood commands. Hood has made two attempts to strike hard since we crossed the Chattahoochee, and both times got more than he bargained for. No doubt he expects to cut to my rear, but I have already cut to his rear, having broken his Augusta road out for fifty miles, and his Southern road at Opelika. None remains to him but the Macon road, and I think I will have that soon. I would rather that Hood should fight it out at Atlanta than to retreat farther toward Macon. If you can keep away re-enforcements all well. My army is all in hand, and rear well guarded.

                              W. T. SHERMAN,
                              Major-General.

                    Near Atlanta, Ga., *July 25, 1864.*
                         (Received 1 a. m. 26th.)
Col. James A. Hardie,
          Inspector-General:

I have your dispatch of yesterday, announcing the appointment of General Osterhaus as major-general. I do not object to his appointment, but I wish to put on record this my emphatic opinion, that it is an act of injustice to officers who stand by their posts in the day of danger to neglect them and advance such as Hovey and Osterhaus, who left us in the midst of bullets to go to the rear in search of personal advancement. If the rear be the post of honor, then we had better all change front on Washington.

                              W. T. SHERMAN,
                              Major-General.

NEAR ATLANTA, GA., *July 25, 1864—8 a. m.*

Maj. Gen. H. W. HALLECK, *Washington, D. C.:*

GENERAL: I find it difficult to make prompt report of results coupled with some data or information without occasionally making some mistakes. General McPherson's sudden death, and General Logan succeeding to the command, as it were, in the midst of battle, made some confusion on our extreme left, but it soon recovered and made sad havoc with the enemy, who had practiced one of his favorite games of attacking our left when in motion and before it had time to cover its weak end. After riding over the ground and hearing the varying statements of the actors on that flank, I directed General Logan to make me an official report of the actual results, and I herewith inclose it.* Though the number of dead rebels seems excessive, I am disposed to give full credit to the report that our loss, though only 3,521 killed, wounded, and missing, the enemy's dead alone on the field nearly equal that number, viz, 3,240. Happening at that point of the line when a flag of truce was sent in to ask permission for each party to bury its dead, I gave General Logan authority to permit a temporary truce on that flank alone, while our labors and fighting proceeded at all others. I also send you a copy of General Garrard's report of the breaking of railroad toward Augusta.† Now I am grouping my command to attack the Macon road, and with that view will intrench a strong line of circumvallation and flanks, so as to have as large an infantry column to co-operate as possible with all the cavalry to swing round to the south and east to control that road at or below East Point.

I have the honor to be, your obedient servant,

W. T. SHERMAN,
Major-General, Commanding.

HDQRS. MILITARY DIVISION OF THE MISSISSIPPI,
In the Field, near Atlanta, Ga., July 25, 1864.

General THOMAS:

General Garrard is back all safe, having lost but 2 men. He destroyed the bridges across the branches of the Ocmulgee, and the depots at Conyers, Covington, and Social Circle, and brought in 200 prisoners and a fine lot of fresh horses and negroes. He is now at Decatur resting, but we must all get in motion by the day after to-morrow. I thought Captain Dayton had sent you word about General Garrard's return. General Logan now foots up the killed of the enemy at 3,200, and 2,100 prisoners. Our loss in killed, wounded, and missing, 3,500 and 10 guns.

W. T. SHERMAN,
Major-General, Commanding.

HDQRS. MILITARY DIVISION OF THE MISSISSIPPI,
In the Field, near Atlanta, Ga., July 25, 1864.

General THOMAS:

Send word to General McCook and notify him to have his and Colonel Harrison's command all ready for the big raid by daylight of day after to-morrow, and that if convenient after giving his orders, I would like to see him in person to-morrow.

W. T. SHERMAN,
Major-General, Commanding.

---

*See Part III, p. 21.   † See Part II, p. 809.

HDQRS. MILITARY DIVISION OF THE MISSISSIPPI,
In the Field, near Atlanta, Ga., July 25, 1864.
General THOMAS:

I understood that General McCook's cavalry was across Proctor's Creek and held the east bank at Turner's Ferry, and ordered a pontoon bridge to be made to connect his and Colonel Harrison's cavalry, but on reaching Proctor's Creek it was found that our pickets were across the creek, but not out as far as the Turner's Ferry road. Order General McCook out early to-morrow to cover that ferry, that the bridge may be put down and Colonel Harrison and he put in communication.

W. T. SHERMAN,
Major-General, Commanding.

HDQRS. MILITARY DIVISION OF THE MISSISSIPPI,
In the Field, near Atlanta, Ga., July 25, 1864.
Major-General THOMAS, *Commanding, &c.*:

GENERAL: In the attack on the 22d our total loss 3,521 and 10 guns. Captures were 1,000 sent North, 1,017 wounded in our hands, 18 stand of colors, 5,000 stand of arms. Known dead of the enemy, 2,142, in front of the Fifteenth and Sixteenth Corps and one division of the Seventeenth Corps, and it is estimated the other division Seventeenth Corps, which repulsed six assaults of the enemy before it fell back, must have killed enough more to make his, the enemy's, loss in killed fully 3,000.

I am, general, yours, truly,

L. M. DAYTON,
Aide-de-Camp.

The known dead were those buried by us and sent over to the enemy during the truce of the following day on that front, and was on a space of ground from our main line there and the line midway between the two lines of pickets or skirmishers.

Yours, truly,

L. M. DAYTON,
Aide-de-Camp.

HEADQUARTERS FOURTEENTH ARMY CORPS,
In the Field, July 25, 1864.
Brigadier-General BAIRD:

Report from Davis' front states heavy columns of troops moving to his right. Make your line as compact as your numbers will allow, holding your reserves ready to support Walker.

Respectfully,

J. M. PALMER,
Major-General.

HEADQUARTERS TWENTIETH CORPS,
Near Atlanta, Ga., July 25, 1864—midnight.
(Received 1.30 a. m. 26th.)
Brigadier-General WILLIAMS,
Commanding First Division:

GENERAL: The major-general commanding directs me to inform you that it has been reported to him from our picket-line that the enemy have been moving all night to their left (our right), in such manner as induces him to believe that they are moving away. He wishes your pickets to be vigilant, and in case the enemy leave your front to follow as closely and as far as you can with comparative safety.

I am, general, very respectfully, your obedient servant,

H. W. PERKINS,
Assistant Adjutant-General.

HEADQUARTERS DEPARTMENT OF THE CUMBERLAND,
In the Field, July 25, 1864.

Brig. Gen. W. L. ELLIOTT,
Chief of Cavalry, Department of the Cumberland:

GENERAL: The major-general commanding directs that McCook's cavalry be ordered out as far as the Turner's Ferry road, and to cover that ferry, that a pontoon bridge may be laid at that place, and McCook and Harrison put in communication. Let this be done early to-morrow morning.

Yours, very respectfully,

WM. D. WHIPPLE,
Assistant Adjutant-General.

HDQRS. MILITARY DIVISION OF THE MISSISSIPPI,
In the Field, near Atlanta, Ga., July 25, 1864.

General McCOOK,
Commanding Cavalry Division:

GENERAL: I understood General Thomas to say yesterday that you had possession of Turner's Ferry road out for three miles from the river, and had ordered a pontoon bridge down that you would be in connection with Colonel Harrison's command on the other side of the river. I wish that bridge laid down, and you to establish communication with Colonel Harrison to-morrow. Captain Poe will see that the bridge is put down, and one of my inspectors will inspect Colonel Harrison's command to-morrow. Cover the bridge with all your cavalry.

I am, &c.,

W. T. SHERMAN,
Major-General, Commanding.

HEADQUARTERS CAVALRY DIVISION,
July 25, 1864.

Major-General SHERMAN,
Commanding Army:

GENERAL: Last night the rest of my command arrived, bringing about 30 prisoners and some hundred negroes. The depot at Social Circle and a large amount of supplies, including a lot of new Government wagons were burned. It will take three or four days to put my command in order. My wagons are not up, and I do not know where they are. I have also over 1,000 horses unshod. I can do all duty required of me on this flank, but, if possible, would like it to be so arranged as not to send me off again for some days. General Stoneman spoke to me last night, before I had time to know fully my condition, about some expedition. I could only reply that I would try to carry out all orders, but could not at that time pass my judgment in regard to its probable success or the strength I could bring to bear. If the route is taken proposed by him I think it will amount to a fight with rebel cavalry and very doubtful if much damage can be done. A raid to be a success must be made by light bodies and done quickly and the whole should be a surprise. In connection with a general advance, of course, the cavalry expect to do its share of fighting and drive off that of the enemy. But I regard the two very different affairs. I inclose you the letter of instructions asked for, and in conclusion would mention to your favorable notice my three brigade commanders, Colonel Miller, Colonel Minty, and Colonel Long. They are all good officers and manage their brigades well.

Very respectfully, your obedient servant,

K. GARRARD,
Brigadier-General, Commanding Division.

HDQRS. MILITARY DIVISION OF THE MISSISSIPPI,
In the Field, near Marietta, July 25, 1864.

General GARRARD,
Commanding Division of Cavalry :

GENERAL: Yours of to-day is received. I beg you will convey to Colonels Minty, Long, and Miller the assurances that I fully appreciate the services recently rendered. I would like to give all the time you ask for rest, reshoeing, &c., but am advised by General Grant that I must be prepared for a re-enforcement to the rebel army from Virginia, and want to prevent it. I am afraid I will have to call on you and also on General Rousseau's cavalry to start again the day after to-morrow, but I propose that yours and Rousseau's should be in the nature of support to General Stoneman and General McCook, who will be charged to make the circuit and break the Macon road well to the rear, say below McDonough.

I wanted General Stoneman to consult and advise with you and bring me your opinion, but my plan is that all my army shall swing round by the right against East Point, whilst the cavalry right and left move by a circuit, and by detachments reach the railroad so as to cut off the last link of the enemy's communications. That done, I think we can pause for rest and all sorts of repairs. Every minute we delay will add to the magnitude of the undertaking, which I take it for granted the enemy must apprehend, and will be calling in his scattered cavalry to thwart and prevent it.

I am, yours, truly,

W. T. SHERMAN,
Major-General, Commanding.

GENERAL SHERMAN'S HEADQUARTERS,
July 25, 1864.

General K. GARRARD,
Commanding Cavalry Division :

GENERAL: General Sherman says that day after to-morrow will be soon enough, provided the enemy does not leave Atlanta before that time. In the mean time he wishes us to get our commands well in hand and to be ready to act vigorously in case we are called upon suddenly to push a retreating army. The general says that you can call in the regiment you now have at the Factory bridge, and that you can replace it with such portion of your command (under an officer), as you cannot make available in the contemplated operations. This party need not, nor will it be expected to keep up communications with the left of the army, but will be considered and will act as a sort of flank guard to Marietta, and to hold the bridge for ulterior purposes, in case it may be wanted. An infantry force will also be sent there from Marietta, if necessary. The success of your recent expedition warrants the general in expecting important results from the efforts of our forces combined.

I am, very respectfully, &c.,

GEORGE STONEMAN,
Major-General.

[First indorsement.]

Respectfully referred to General Sherman, through General Logan, to know under whose orders I am serving.

I have been all day occupied in carrying out General Logan's orders and now this letter orders an entirely different disposition of my troops. Of course I do not recognize General Stoneman, but wish this matter settled in some way. I should not move for two or three days.

Very respectfully, your obedient servant,

K. GARRARD,
Brigadier-General, Commanding.

[Second indorsement.]

HDQRS. DEPARTMENT AND ARMY OF THE TENNESSEE,
Near Atlanta, Ga., July 25, 1864.

General Garrard reported to me on his return yesterday, took up a position north and east of Decatur, connecting with Colonel Sprague's brigade on my left. I learned this morning the enemy's pickets occupied the main Decatur road between that place and my front, and I accordingly requested him to throw forward his line, connect with General Dodge so that I could withdraw Sprague's brigade, and place him in reserve, the only reserve on my entire line. I also requested General Garrard to leave that portion of a regiment of his command, part of the guard at Roswell, at that place until the empty teams of his train returned to Marietta for supplies could arrive at Roswell and convey the sick to the hospitals at Marietta. All the ambulances of this army are employed in moving our hospitals to the rear, Hence the necessity of availing myself of General Garrard's empty trains. The position of General Garrard as indicated by me will give him a good camp and protect my left flank.

JOHN A. LOGAN,
Major-General.

HDQRS. MILITARY DIVISION OF THE MISSISSIPPI,
In the Field, near Atlanta, Ga., July 25, 1864.

Maj. Gen. JOHN A. LOGAN,
Commanding Army of the Tennessee:

GENERAL: I have your application for the services of General Corse, which I grant, because I want you to have good division commanders. But I beg you to see that no injustice is done to General Sweeny. I have noticed for some time a growing dissatisfaction on the part of General Dodge with General Sweeny. It may be personal. See that General Dodge prefers specific charges and specifications, and you, as the army commander, must be the judge of the sufficiency of the charges. No one but the commander of an army can arrest and send away a general; it is a high power, but I construe the power to reside with the commanders of my three armies, because each has a command other than the troops here on the spot. You, as commander of the Army of the Tennessee, should judge as to the cause of arrest and see that no injustice is done a general officer. You can see how cruel it would be to a brave and sensitive gentleman and officer to be arrested, deprived of his command, and sent to the rear at this time. I do not believe General Dodge would willingly do an act of injustice, but still you are the one to judge. I fear that General Sweeny will feel that even I am influenced against him to befriend General Corse, but it is not so. I give up General Corse because the good of the service demands that at this crisis you should have good division commanders.

I am, with respect, your obedient servant,

W. T. SHERMAN,
Major-General, Commanding.

HDQRS. THIRD BRIGADE, FIRST CAVALRY DIVISION,
La Fayette, July 25, 1864—9.30 p. m.

Major-General STEEDMAN,
Commanding District of the Etowah, Chattanooga, Tenn.:

GENERAL: My scouts have just come in, reporting a force of 2,000 rebels at Winn's Gap, within twenty miles of this place. I believe General Wheeler to be in command. With two sections of artillery I can hold the place; without it I will be compelled to fall back in case of an attack, and will require forty additional wagons to haul off ordnance stores and other property. My courier line was attacked last night by a party of rebel scouts. My scouts were also attacked yesterday evening in Broomtown Valley, by a party of Texas Rangers, which goes to show there is a new force in the neighborhood. The country is alive with rebels in scattering squads. Please send me artillery or wagons, or instructions how to act in case of an attack.

I am, general, very respectfully, your obedient servant,

J. K. FAULKNER,
Colonel, Commanding Brigade.

P. S.—The command is two-thirds dismounted, having no transportation for their saddles. My wagon train at present is loaded with stores at Rossville, Ga., on its way here.

J. K. FAULKNER.

[JULY 25, 1864.—For Giles A. Smith's congratulatory circular, embodying complimentary letter from headquarters Seventeenth Army Corps, see Part III, p. 586.]

HEADQUARTERS,
Near Atlanta, Ga., July 25, 1864.

TO THE OFFICERS AND SOLDIERS OF THE
SECOND DIVISION, SIXTEENTH ARMY CORPS:

Your general has been deprived of his command and ordered to Nashville in arrest. Before leaving he is constrained to express to you his admiration at the heroic manner in which you repulsed the terrific assault of the enemy upon your lines on the 22d instant. Feeling every confidence in you, he had looked for the displaying by you of the ordinary fortitude of soldiers in the hour of conflict, but you did more than this; with empty cartridge-boxes, and lines unbroken, you stood, trusting to your bayonets, like a wall between your country and ruin. At the order to "charge," you rushed upon the advancing columns of the enemy, and snatched victory, colors, and hundreds of prisoners from them. As if not content with the glories already won, the Second Brigade moved with alacrity to a distant part of the field, and charged like an avalanche upon a victorious column of the enemy, assisting in re-establishing our line in its former position, and again prisoners and recaptured cannon were the rewards of their efforts. Your general confesses to you freely that the evening of the 22d instant was the proudest of his life, made so by your daring, your fortitude, your heroism, and it was his desire to lead your victorious banner into the doomed city in our front; but this is not to be. It is only left with him to request of you to extend to your future commanders the confidence and cheerful obedience that you have always shown to him.

T. W. SWEENY,
Brigadier-General.

HDQRS. THIRD DIVISION, FIFTEENTH ARMY CORPS,
Cartersville, Ga., July 25, 1864.

Col. THOMAS T. HEATH,
    Commanding Fifth Ohio Cavalry:

COLONEL: You will take 200 men of your command, well mounted and supplied with ammunition and rations, if possible for four or five days, and proceed to Allatoona, getting such information of the commander of the post at that place as he may have of the road and people west of the Pumpkin Vine Creek. From thence he will proceed to Dallas, thence to Burnt Hickory (or Huntsville), thence to Van Wert, thence to Stilesborough and Euharlee, scouting them thoroughly and obtaining such information from the natives and their status as he can get through the country south of the river, between Euharlee and a point about one-half way between Rome and Kingston, returning by the way of Kingston, with all the guerrillas and scouts on the south side of the river between the points named, dead or alive. A party of fifty or sixty men (infantry) will be sent south of the river from Kingston.

By order of Brig. Gen. John E. Smith:

CARL. L. WHITE,
Captain and Assistant Adjutant-General.

NEAR ATLANTA, GA., *July 25, 1864—8 p. m.*
(Received 10.50 p. m.)

Maj. THOMAS T. ECKERT,
    Washington, D. C.:

Nothing except skirmishing and artillery practice to-day. To-morrow hope to have news for you, as movement to destroy railroad south of Atlanta starts at daylight—very strong.

J. C. VAN DUZER.

SPECIAL FIELD ORDERS, ⎱   HDQRS. MIL. DIV. OF THE MISS.,
                                      In the Field, near Atlanta, Ga.,
No. 42.   ⎰   *July 25, 1864.*

I. The several armies and bodies of cavalry will watch the enemy closely to their respective fronts, and in case the enemy retreats toward the southeast General Schofield will follow directly through Atlanta, General Thomas by roads on his right, and General Logan on his left. Generals Stoneman's and Garrard's cavalry will move by a circle to the left toward McDonough, break the railroad, and strike the enemy in front or flank, and General McCook's and Colonel Harrison's cavalry will move rapidly on Fayetteville and the railroad beyond, breaking it if possible, in advance of the enemy, and striking the enemy in flank.

II. Should the enemy remain as now, on the defensive, inside of the fortifications of Atlanta, the Macon road must be attacked by cavalry beyond Fayetteville and McDonough, and the infantry must cover the line from the Howard house, General Schofield's present center, to General Davis' position on the right, and the line extended east and south so as to reach or threaten the railroad toward East Point. To this end Generals Stoneman and Garrard will call in all detachments and send to-morrow to Roswell or in rear of the infantry all crippled stock and incumbrances, prepared to move at daylight the next morning by a circuit to the left, so as to reach the railroad below McDonough. General Stoneman will command this cavalry force, but will spare General Garrard's fatigued horses as much as possible, using that command as a reserve, and his own as the force with which to reach and break the railroad. In like manner General McCook will command the joint cavalry command, his own, and of Colonel Harrison's, but will use Colonel Harrison's fatigued command as a reserve, and his own to reach the road and break it. The railroad when reached must be substantially destroyed for a space of from two to five miles, telegraph wires pulled down as far as possible and hid in water or carried away.

III. Major-General Schofield will prepare to draw back his left division to the old rebel line, extending back from the Howard house toward the road by which General Stanley advanced, and be prepared on the withdrawal of the Army of the Tennessee to hold that line as the left flank of the grand army.

IV. Major-General Logan will to-morrow send all his trains, and sick, and impediments to the rear of General Thomas to any point near the mouth of Peach Tree Creek, and during the early morning by moonlight of the next day, viz, Wednesday, July 27, withdraw his army, corps by corps, and move it to the right, forming on General Palmer, and advancing the right as much as possible.

V. Major-General Thomas having strongly fortified his front will hold it by an adequate force, and hold the reserves at points most convenient to move to the right, from which point he will strike and destroy the railroad, or so occupy the attention of the enemy that the cavalry may do its work completely and effectually.

VI. The cavalry will, unless otherwise ordered, move out at daylight of Wednesday, 27th instant, and aim to reach and break the railroad during the day or night of the 28th, and having accomplished this work will return to their proper flanks of the army, unless the enemy should be discovered in retreat, when each force described will hang on the flanks of the retreating enemy and obstruct his retreat by all the energy in their power.

VII. All commanders will arrange that their trains be moved behind the Chattahoochee, or behind the center of the army during the time the cavalry is absent in the execution of this duty.

By order of Maj. Gen. W. T. Sherman:

L. M. DAYTON,
Aide-de-Camp.

GENERAL ORDERS, } HDQRS. MIL. DIV. OF THE MISSISSIPPI,
No. 21. } *Nashville, Tenn., July 25, 1864.*

I. General Orders, No. 20, current series, from these headquarters, is extended to include the prohibition of the exportation from this State of any agricultural produce of the kinds required for the army.

II. The use of grain for distillation within this State is prohibited.

By order of Maj. Gen. W. T. Sherman:

R. M. SAWYER,
Assistant Adjutant-General.

[JULY 25, 1864.—For congratulatory circular from headquarters Department of the Cumberland, see Part I, p. 174.]

Weekly report of effective force of the Department of the Cumberland, Maj. Gen. George H. Thomas, U. S. Army, commanding, July 25, 1864.

Command.	Headquarters.			Infantry.			Cavalry.		
	Officers.	Men.	Total.	Officers.	Men.	Total.	Officers.	Men.	Total.
Reserve Brigade, Col. H. Le Favour...	......	......	......	31	646	677	......	......	......
Post Chattanooga, Col. T. R. Stanley..	......	......	......	71	1,471	1,542	......	......	......
14th U. S. Colored Troops, Col. T. J. Morgan.	......	......	......	23	540	563	......	......	......
16th U. S. Colored Troops, Col. William B. Gaw.	......	......	......	28	579	607	......	......	......
Total............	......	......	......	153	3,236	3,389	......	......	......
Fourth Army Corps:									
Headquarters, Maj. Gen. O. O. Howard.	20	165	185	......	......	......	......	......	......
First Division, Maj. Gen. D. S. Stanley.	44	182	226	296	5,236	5,532	......	......	......
Second Division, Brig. Gen. John Newton.	32	133	165	259	3,204	3,463	......	......	......
Third Division, Brig. Gen. T. J. Wood.	42	304	346	330	4,787	5,117	......	......	......
Total............	138	784	922	885	13,227	14,112	......	......	......
Fourteenth Army Corps:									
Headquarters, Maj. Gen. J. M. Palmer.	23	445	468	......	......	......	......	......	......
First Division, Brig. Gen. R. W. Johnson.	29	137	166	262	5,144	5,406	......	......	......
Second Division, Brig. Gen. J. C. Davis.	35	87	122	257	5,233	5,490	......	......	......
Third Division, Brig. Gen. A. Baird.	35	226	261	332	5,887	6,219	......	......	......
Artillery corps	......	......	......	......	......	......	......	......	......
Detached infantry, railroad train-guards, &c.	......	......	......	73	1,155	1,228	......	......	......
Total............	122	895	1,017	924	17,419	18,343	......	......	......

Weekly report of effective force of the Department of the Cumberland, &c.—Continued.

Command.	Headquarters.			Infantry.			Cavalry.		
	Officers.	Men.	Total.	Officers.	Men.	Total.	Officers.	Men.	Total.
Twentieth Army Corps:									
Headquarters, Maj. Gen. Joseph Hooker.	17	136	153	2	61	63	3	58	61
First Division, Brig. Gen. A. S. Williams.	32	141	173	264	4,215	4,479	......	......	......
Second Division, Brig. Gen. J. W. Geary.	14	90	104	157	2,861	3,018	......	......	......
Third Division, Brig. Gen. W. T. Ward.	43	343	386	219	4,233	4,452	......	......	......
Total.........................	106	710	816	642	11,370	12,012	3	58	61
Cavalry Corps:									
Headquarters, Brig. Gen. W. L. Elliott.	10	32	42	......	......	......	......	......	......
First Division, Brig. Gen. E. M. McCook.	......	......	......	......	......	......	98	1,357	1,455
Second Division, Brig. Gen. K. Garrard.	......	......	......	......	......	......	189	4,250	4,439
Third Division, Col. W. W. Lowe..	......	......	......	......	......	......	114	1,992	2,106
Fourth Division (detached), Brig. Gen. A. C. Gillem.	11	51	62	......	......	......	87	1,841	1,928
Total.........................	21	83	104	......	......	......	488	9,440	9,928
Engineer Troops:									
Michigan Engineers and Mechanics, Col. William P. Innes.	......	......	......	53	1,199	1,252	......	......	......
Pioneer Brigade, Capt. P. O'Connell	......	......	......	18	396	414	......	......	......
Engineer Brigade, Col. J. B. Culver.	......	......	......	70	1,295	1,365	......	......	......
Total.........................	......	......	......	141	2,890	3,031	......	......	......
District of Tennessee:									
Headquarters, Maj. Gen. R. H. Milroy.	12	45	57	......	......	......	......	......	......
Fourth Division, Twentieth Army Corps, Maj. Gen. R. H. Milroy.	6	2	8	152	3,951	4,103	......	......	......
Post Nashville, Brig. Gen. J. F. Miller.	5	2	7	86	1,904	1,990	19	307	326
Fort Donelson, Lieut. Col. E. C. Brott.	2	2	4	......	......	......	......	......	......
Clarksville, Col. A. A. Smith......	4	3	7	......	......	......	......	......	......
Gallatin, Col. J. K. Miller.	......	......	......	......	......	......	......	......	......
Nashville and Northwestern Railroad, Brig. Gen. A. C. Gillem.	4	3	7	76	1,647	1,723	7	161	168
Nashville and Chattanooga Railroad, Brig. Gen. H. P. Van Cleve.	8	9	17	17	502	519	......	......	......
Convalescents, Brig. Gen. H. P. Van Cleve.	......	......	......	12	1,017	1,029	......	......	......
Nashville and Chattanooga Railroad, Col. H. K. McConnell.	......	......	......	62	1,421	1,483	......	......	......
Bridgeport, Col. W. Krzyzanowski.	7	37	44	62	1,334	1,396	......	......	......
Northern Alabama, Brig. Gen. R. S. Granger.	14	32	46	......	......	......	......	......	......
Tennessee and Alabama Railroad, Brig. Gen. J. C. Starkweather.	9	18	27	11	1,217	1,228	94	2,653	2,747
Huntsville, Ala., Col. G. M. L. Johnson.	6	......	6	7	160	167	26	640	666
11th and 12th Indiana and 2d Michigan Volunteer Cavalry.	......	......	......	......	......	......	77	1,635	1,712
Total.........................	77	153	230	485	13,153	13,638	223	5,396	5,619
Unassigned Artillery:									
Reserve Artillery, Nashville, Tenn.	7	7	14	......	......	......	......	......	......
11th Indiana Battery (in the field).	......	......	......	......	......	......	......	......	......
Total.........................	7	7	14	......	......	......	......	......	......
Grand total....................	471	2,632	3,103	3,230	61,295	64,525	714	14,894	15,608

Weekly report of effective force of the Department of the Cumberland, &c.—Continued.

Command.	Artillery.			Total.				
	Officers.	Men.	Total.	Officers.	Men.	Aggregate.	Horses.	Guns.
Reserve Brigade, Col. H. Le Favour....				31	646	677		
Post Chattanooga, Col. T. R. Stanley...	22	575	597	93	2,046	2,139	30	79
14th U. S. Colored Troops, Col. T. J. Morgan.				23	540	563		
36th U. S. Colored Troops, Col. William B. Gaw.				28	579	607		
Total	22	575	597	175	3,811	3,986	30	79
Fourth Army Corps:								
Headquarters, Maj. Gen. O. O. Howard.				20	165	185		
First Division, Maj. Gen. D. S. Stanley.	6	259	265	346	5,677	6,023	174	10
Second Division, Brig. Gen. John Newton.	5	247	252	296	3,584	3,880	225	10
Third Division, Brig. Gen. T. J. Wood.	4	264	268	376	5,355	5,731	207	9
Total	15	770	785	1,038	14,781	15,819	606	29
Fourteenth Army Corps: .								
Headquarters, Maj. Gen. J. M. Palmer.				23	445	468		
First Division, Brig. Gen. R. W. Johnson.				291	5,281	5,572		
Second Division, Brig. Gen. J. C. Davis.				292	5,320	5,612		
Third Division, Brig. Gen. A. Baird.				367	6,113	6,480		
Artillery corps........................	17	726	743	17	726	743	468	30
Detached infantry, railroad train-guards, &c.				73	1,155	1,228		
Total	17	726	743	1,063	19,040	20,103	468	30
Twentieth Army Corps:								
Headquarters, Maj. Gen. Joseph Hooker.				22	255	277	58	
First Division, Brig. Gen. A. S. Williams.	6	276	282	302	4,632	4,934	177	12
Second Division, Brig. Gen. J. W. Geary.	7	269	276	178	3,220	3,398	191	12
Third Division, Brig. Gen. W. T. Ward.	8	245	253	270	4,821	5,091	205	12
Total	21	790	811	772	12,928	13,700	631	36
Cavalry Corps:								
Headquarters, Brig. Gen. W. L. Elliott.				10	32	42	45	
First Division, Brig. Gen. E. M. McCook.				98	1,357	1,455	1,394	6
Second Division, Brig. Gen. K. Garrard.				189	4,250	4,439	4,574	6
Third Division, Col. W. W. Lowe ..				114	1,992	2,106	1,419	4
Fourth Division (detached), Brig. Gen. A. C. Gillem.	4	127	131	102	2,019	2,121	1,520	6
Total	4	127	131	513	9,650	10,163	8,952	22
Engineer Troops:								
Michigan Engineers and Mechanics, Col. William P. Innes.				53	1,199	1,252		
Pioneer Brigade, Capt. P. O'Connell				18	396	414		
Engineer Brigade, Col. J. B. Culver				70	1,295	1,365		
Total				141	2,890	3,031		
Disrtict of Tennessee:								
Headquarters, Maj. Gen. R. H. Milroy.				12	45	57		
Fourth Division, Twentieth Army Corps, Maj. Gen. R. H. Milroy.	5	220	225	163	4,173	4,336	195	12
Post Nashville, Brig. Gen. J. F. Miller.	18	493	511	128	2,706	2,834	97	31

Weekly report of effective force of the Department of the Cumberland, &c.—Continued.

Command.	Artillery.			Total.				
	Officers.	Men.	Total.	Officers.	Men.	Aggregate.	Horses.	Guns.
District of Tennessee—Continued.								
Fort Donelson, Lieut. Col. E. C. Brott.	3	162	165	5	164	169	88	11
Clarksville, Col. A. A. Smith.......	3	121	124	7	124	131	148	9
Gallatin, Col. J. K. Miller	3	119	122	3	119	122	....	6
Nashville and Northwestern Railroad, Brig. Gen. A. C. Gillem.	4	103	107	91	1,914	2,005	78	6
Nashville and Chattanooga Railroad, Brig. Gen. H. P. Van Cleve.	8	405	413	33	916	949	....	57
Convalescents, Brig. Gen. H.P.Van Cleve.	......	....	....	12	1,017	1,029	....	
Nashville and Chattanooga Railroad, Col. H. K. McConnell.	1	78	79	63	1,499	1,562	42	4
Bridgeport, Col. W. Krzyzanowski.	8	278	286	77	1,649	1,726	78	13
Northern Alabama, Brig. Gen. R. S. Granger.	5	158	163	19	190	209	100	8
Tennessee and Alabama Railroad, Brig. Gen. J. C. Starkweather.	4	128	132	118	4,016	4,134	1,773	11
Huntsville, Ala., Col. G. M. L. Johnson.	......	....	....	39	800	839	....	
11th and 12th Indiana and 2d Michigan Volunteer Cavalry.	......	....	....	77	1,635	1,712	....	
Total	62	2,265	2,327	847	20,967	21,814	2,599	165
Unassigned Artillery:								
Reserve Artillery, Nashville, Tenn.	24	712	736	31	719	750	625	24
11th Indiana Battery (in the field)..	4	127	131	4	127	131	....	6
Total	28	839	867	35	846	881	625	30
Grand total	169	6,092	6,261	4,584	84,913	89,497	13,911	391

No reports from First Ohio Volunteer Sharpshooters, One hundred and eighth Ohio Volunteer Infantry, and Fifty-eighth Indiana Volunteer Infantry, Batteries M and K, First Ohio Volunteer Artillery (unassigned artillery), and Signal Corps.

Respectfully submitted.

WM. L. PORTER,
Lieutenant and Acting Assistant Adjutant-General.

WASHINGTON, *July 26, 1864—2.30 p. m.*

Major-General SHERMAN,
Near Atlanta:

I have just seen yours complaining of the appointment of Hovey and Osterhaus. The point you make is unquestionably a good one, and yet please hear a word from us. My recollection is that both General Grant and yourself recommended both H[ovey] and O[sterhaus] for promotion, and these, with other strong recommendations, drew committals from us which we could neither honorably or safely disregard. We blamed H[ovey] for coming away in the manner in which he did, but we knew he had apparent reason to feel disappointed and mortified, and we felt it was not best to crush one who certainly had been a good soldier. As to O[sterhaus], we did not know of his leaving at the time we made the appointment, and do not now know the terms on which he left. Not to have appointed him, as the case appeared to us at the time, would have been almost, if not quite, a violation of our word. The word was given on what we thought was high merit and somewhat on his nationality. I beg you to believe we do not act in a spirit of disregarding merit. We expect to await your programme for further changes and promotions in your army. My profoundest thanks to you and your whole army for the present campaign so far.

A. LINCOLN.

CITY POINT, VA., July 26, 1864—2 p. m.
(Received 8.10 p. m.)

Hon. EDWIN M. STANTON,
        Secretary of War:

Your dispatch of 9 p. m. 24th just received.* The vacancies yet remaining for brigadier-generals I would like to have given to such men as Sherman may recommend. He has conducted his campaign with great skill and success. I would, therefore, confirm all his recommendations for department and corps commanders. No one can tell so well as one immediately in command the disposition that should be made of the material on hand. Osterhaus has proved himself a good soldier, but if he is not in the field I regret his promotion.

U. S. GRANT,
Lieutenant-General.

WASHINGTON, July 26, 1864—4 p. m.

Major-General SHERMAN,
        Georgia:

General Howard is assigned, as requested, to command the Army and Department of the Tennessee.

H. W. HALLECK,
Major-General and Chief of Staff.

NEAR ATLANTA, GA., July 26, 1864—9 p. m.
(Received 1 p. m. 27th.)

Maj. Gen. H. W. HALLECK,
        Washington, D. C.:

To-morrow we begin the move against Atlanta, having strongly intrenched our front from the railroad east of Atlanta to a hill on the south of Proctor's Creek. I move the whole Army of the Tennessee to the right, extending the line south, threatening East Point, and forcing, as I think, Hood to abandon Atlanta or allow us, at small cost, to occupy the railroad south of the town, that to the east being well destroyed. At the same time I send by the right a force of about 3,500 cavalry, under General McCook, and round by the left about 5,000 cavalry, under Stoneman, with orders to reach the railroad about Griffin. I also have consented that Stoneman (after he has executed this part of his plan), if he finds it feasible, may, with his division proper (about 2,000), go to Macon and attempt the release of our officers, prisoners there, and then to Anderson[ville] to release the 20,000 of our men,

---

* Announcing the appointment of certain brigadier-generals in the Army of the Potomac, and the appointment of Osterhaus as major-general. Also informing him (Grant) that three or four other vacancies of brigadier-general await his recommendation to be filled.

prisoners there. This is probably more than he can accomplish, but it is worthy of a determined effort. While these are in progress I will, with the main army, give employment to all of the rebel army still in Atlanta.

W. T. SHERMAN,
Major-General.

HDQRS. MILITARY DIVISION OF THE MISSISSIPPI,
In the Field, near Atlanta, Ga., July 26, 1864.
General THOMAS:

General McCook represents the enemy's cavalry to his front intrenched behind good works, extending from about White Hall down to the Chattahoochee, and he apprehended difficulty in breaking through. I have consented to his dropping down the west bank of the Chattahoochee to a point about Campbellton, crossing there and striking out for the railroad. This will turn the position of the cavalry, and force them back to meet General McCook on more open ground.

W. T. SHERMAN,
Major-General, Commanding.

HDQRS. MILITARY DIVISION OF THE MISSISSIPPI,
In the Field, near Atlanta, Ga., July 26, 1864.
General THOMAS:

Major-General Howard is ordered to the command of the Army and Department of the Tennessee. I want him in his new command at once.

W. T. SHERMAN,
Major-General, Commanding.

HDQRS. MILITARY DIVISION OF THE MISSISSIPPI,
In the Field, near Atlanta, July 26, 1864.
(Received 10 p. m.)
Major-General HOWARD:

I have this moment received a dispatch from Halleck. You are assigned to command the Army and Department of the Tennessee. I want you to-morrow to assume command and give directions to the army as it goes into position to-morrow. If you will come to my headquarters I will ride with you and explain my wishes.

I am, truly, your friend,

W. T. SHERMAN,
Major-General, Commanding.

HDQRS. MILITARY DIVISION OF THE MISSISSIPPI,
In the Field, before Atlanta, Ga., July 26, 1864.
Major-Generals THOMAS and SCHOFIELD:

GENTLEMEN: As a part of the movement to-morrow I wish, while the cavalry is moving out, say at 6 a. m., and General Logan's troops shifting from left to right, that you send from some point of the front of each division in our line of circumvallation a bold party of about a regiment strong to push back the enemy's outlying pickets and feel their position. This will have the effect of holding them and drawing there as large a body of the enemy as possible, as he will on such a display. Inasmuch as Jeff. C. Davis' division is placed as a strong right flank, and therefore will be almost entirely in reserve when the Army of the Tennessee gets to the right, I wish the demonstration to his front be still more decided, viz, a whole brigade should move on the ridge due south from the hill intrenched beyond Proctor's Creek, and should push back the enemy beyond any little rifle-pits to his main line, which will be found up on the main ridge which extends from Atlanta to East Point. This brigade should move toward the old village of White Hall, about two miles and a half from Altanta. These demonstrations should proceed slowly and deliberately, and last all day, and should be as bold and provoking to the enemy as possible, tempting him to sally out and test our present lines.

I am, &c.,

W. T. SHERMAN,
Major-General, Commanding.

HEADQUARTERS ARMY OF THE CUMBERLAND,
Near Atlanta, Ga., July 26, 1864. (Received 11.25 p. m.)

Major-General HOOKER,
Commanding Twentieth Army Corps:

GENERAL: In execution of inclosed order* from the major-general commanding the Military Division of the Mississippi, the major-general commanding the department directs that you send out from the front of each division of your corps in line one regiment to push back the enemy, as directed in the order.

I am, general, very respectfully, your obedient servant,

WM. D. WHIPPLE,
Chief of Staff.

(Same to Howard.)

HEADQUARTERS DEPARTMENT OF THE CUMBERLAND,
Near Atlanta, Ga., July 26, 1864.

Maj. Gen. J. M. PALMER,
Commanding Fourteenth Army Corps:

GENERAL: In execution of the inclosed order† the major-general commanding directs that to-morrow morning you send out a regiment from each division of your corps in line, except General Davis', to push back the enemy as directed. You will instruct General Davis to send a brigade to act as directed in the order.

I am, general, very respectfully, your obedient servant,

WM. D. WHIPPLE,
Chief of Staff.

---

* See next preceding.
† See bottom of p. 261.

HEADQUARTERS FOURTH ARMY CORPS,
Near Atlanta, Ga., July 26, 1864—7.30 p. m.

Brigadier-General WHIPPLE,
    Chief of Staff:

GENERAL: I have the honor to report that General Stanley is at present moving two of his brigades to a position on the left of Major-General Schofield's command, and that General Newton moved one of his brigades this afternoon to a position in reserve, in the rear of his present headquarters.

Very respectfully, your obedient servant,

O. O. HOWARD,
Major-General, Commanding.

HEADQUARTERS FOURTH ARMY CORPS,
Near Atlanta, Ga., July 26, 1864—5.40 p. m.

Major-General STANLEY,
    Commanding First Division, Fourth Army Corps:

GENERAL: You will immediately move two brigades of your division to the abandoned rebel works on the left of Major-General Schofield's command. Your left must rest at the point where you crossed said works in marching to your present position. Please consult with General Schofield as to picketing. This movement must be made before General Logan leaves his present position.

By order of Major-General Howard:

J. S. FULLERTON,
Assistant Adjutant-General.

HDQRS. THIRD DIVISION, TWENTY-THIRD ARMY CORPS,
Before Atlanta, Ga., July 26, 1864.

Colonel CAMERON,
    Commanding Second Brigade:

SIR: I have just seen General Logan. His troops will commence moving about midnight, beginning on the extreme left. The extreme right, which is next you, must be some hours later, but you will have to keep watch of it, and move by your left back into the new works made by the Fifteenth Corps, when they move out. Colonel Byrd is ordered to have a regiment in the same works to hold that line as skirmishers and you will support the whole skirmish line until the remainder of the division is moved into the position assigned. The skirmish line will then take position according to the orders given you this p. m., and your brigade will move inside of our works. Major Wells will be at Cockerill's battery, and you will give him immediate notice when the division on your left is in motion.

Very respectfully, &c.,

J. D. COX,
Brigadier-General, Commanding.

HEADQUARTERS ARMY OF THE OHIO,
Before Atlanta, July 26, 1864.

Brig. Gen. J. D. Cox,
Commanding Third Division, Twenty-third Army Corps:

GENERAL: The commanding general directs you to make a demonstration in your front to-morrow, as directed in inclosed extract of orders* of this date from the major-general commanding Military Division of the Mississippi.

Very respectfully, your obedient servant,
J. A. CAMPBELL,
Major and Assistant Adjutant-General.

(Same to General Hascall.)

———

HEADQUARTERS ARMY OF THE OHIO,
Before Atlanta, July 26, 1864.

Brig. Gen. M. S. HASCALL,
Commanding Second Division, Twenty-third Army Corps:

GENERAL: I have the honor to inclose herewith Special Field Orders, No. 42, current series, headquarters Military Division of the Mississippi.† The commanding general directs that you instruct your pickets to watch the enemy closely and to move forward and occupy the works on the first indication that he has evacuated. The general also directs that you put your men to work, with as little delay as possible, on the line which will be laid out by Capt. W. J. Twining, aide-de-camp.

Very respectfully, your obedient servant,
J. A. CAMPBELL,
Major and Assistant Adjutant-General.

(Same to General Cox.)

———

JULY 26, 1864.

Major-General SHERMAN,
Commanding, &c.:

In case we succeed in carrying out your wishes will it meet your approbation, should I see a good opening, if I should with a portion of the command make dash on Macon and by a vigorous stroke release the prisoners (officers) now at that point, and afterward go on to Americus and release those (privates) there. I would like to try it, and am willing to run any risks, and I can vouch for my little command. Now is the time to do it before the rebel army falls back and covers that country, and I have every inducement to try it. If we accomplish the desired object it will compensate for the loss as prisoners of us all, and I should feel compensated for almost any sacrifice.

Very respectfully, &c.,
GEORGE STONEMAN,
Major-General.

———

* See p. 261.   † See p. 255.

HDQRS. MILITARY DIVISION OF THE MISSISSIPPI,
In the Field, near Atlanta, Ga., July 26, 1864.

Maj. Gen. GEORGE STONEMAN,
Commanding Division of Cavalry:

GENERAL: I have received your letter of July 26, asking permission after breaking good the railroad below McDonough to push on [to Macon], release the officers there, and afterward to go to Anderson-[ville] and release the men confined there. I see many difficulties, but, as you say, even a chance of success will warrant the effort, and I consent to it. You may, after having fulfilled my present orders, send General Garrard back to the left flank of the army, and proceed with your command proper to accomplish both or either of the objects named. I will keep the army busy, so that you shall have nothing to contend with but the cavalry, and if you can bring back to the army any or all those prisoners of war it will be an achievement that will entitle you and the men of your command to the love and admiration of the whole country. Be careful to break telegraph wire and railroad when and where you go, especially the telegraph, as it will prevent the enemy following your movement.

W. T. SHERMAN,
Major-General, Commanding.

HDQRS. THIRD BRIGADE, FIRST CAVALRY DIVISION,
La Fayette, July 26, 1864.

Capt. S. B. MOE,
Asst. Adjt. Gen., Dist. of the Etowah, Chattanooga, Tenn.:

CAPTAIN: In reply to your communication I would respectfully state that the only re-enforcements the rebel scouts have received in addition to their numbers is the Eleventh Texas Cavalry. I am amply able to hold this place against 3,000 men. From information received this morning I am satisfied that General Wheeler is not in this section. I would much prefer remaining here with the command all together. Will start the 100 men to Nickajack Gap this evening if I receive no further orders, and will have the wagons halt until I hear from you. I will send my surplus ordnance stores, &c., back to Chattanooga for storage. Please answer immediately.

I am, captain, very respectfully, your obedient servant,

J. K. FAULKNER,
Colonel, Commanding Brigade.

HDQRS. THIRD DIVISION, FIFTEENTH ARMY CORPS,
Cartersville, Ga., July 26, 1864.

Col. BENJAMIN D. DEAN,
Commanding at Kingston:

COLONEL: You will send out Thursday next (28th instant) fifty or sixty picked men, with three days' rations and forty rounds of ammunition, under direction of Lieutenant-Colonel Buswell, to scout the country south and west of the Etowah River, and co-operate with a party of 200 cavalry under command of Colonel Heath, coming up from Dallas to Euharlee. All suspicious persons will be arrested by Colonel Buswell and brought in for such disposal as their conduct merits.

By order of Brig. Gen. John E. Smith:

CARL. L. WHITE,
Assistant Adjutant-General.

SPECIAL FIELD ORDERS, }　HDQRS. MIL. DIV. OF THE MISS.,
　　　　　　　　　　　　In the Field, near Atlanta, Ga.,
No. 43.　　　　　　　 }　　　　　　　　　*July 26, 1864.*

I. Upon the application of Maj. Gen. John A. Logan, commanding the Army of the Tennessee in the field, Brig. Gen. J. M. Corse, acting inspector-general of this army, is hereby relieved and assigned to duty with the Department and Army of the Tennessee, and will report in person to General Logan, that he may be assigned to duty according to his rank with troops.

II. The general commanding in thus relieving General Corse from a purely staff position, to enable him to accept the higher and more appropriate one in connection with troops in actual service, thanks him for his personal and official services rendered during the present campaign near his person.

III. Capt. E. C. Denig, assistant adjutant-general of volunteers, is hereby transferred from the Department and Army of the Ohio to the Department and Army of the Cumberland, and will report immediately to Maj. Gen. George H. Thomas in the field.

By order of Maj. Gen. W. T. Sherman:

L. M. DAYTON,
Aide-de-Camp.

SPECIAL FIELD ORDERS, }　HDQRS. MIL. DIV. OF THE MISS.,
　　　　　　　　　　　　In the Field, near Atlanta, Ga.,
No. 44.　　　　　　　 }　　　　　　　　　*July 26, 1864.*

I. By direction of the President of the United States, Maj. Gen. O. O. Howard, U. S. Volunteers, is assigned to command the Department and Army of the Tennessee. He will at once assume command of the Army of the Tennessee in the field.

II. Maj. Gen. George H. Thomas, commanding the Department and Army of the Cumberland, will relieve General Howard of the command of the Fourth Army Corps, that he may enter upon his new command, and will assign a general to command the Fourth Corps until the orders of the President are received.

By order of Maj. Gen. W. T. Sherman:

L. M. DAYTON,
Aide-de-Camp.

SPECIAL FIELD ORDERS, }　HDQRS. DEPT. OF THE CUMBERLAND,
No. 204.　　　　　　　 }　　　*Near Atlanta, Ga., July 26, 1864.*

*　　　*　　　*　　　*　　　*　　　*　　　*

IX. Maj. Gen. O. O. Howard, having been assigned to the command of the Army and Department of the Tennessee, is hereby relieved from the command of the Fourth Army Corps, Army of the Cumberland, and will report in person to Maj. Gen. W. T. Sherman, commanding Military Division of the Mississippi.

By command of Major-General Thomas:

WM. D. WHIPPLE,
Assistant Adjutant-General.

HEADQUARTERS FOURTH ARMY CORPS,
Near Atlanta, Ga., July 26, 1864.

To the Fourth Army Corps:

Having been assigned to another command, the duty, by no means a pleasant one, devolves upon me to take leave of a corps that I have learned to love and trust. The time of our service together has been short, but crowded with remarkable events. The words "Dalton," "Resaca," "Adairsville," "Kingston," "Cassville," "Dallas," "Kenesaw," "Smyrna Camp-Ground," and "Peach Tree Creek," suggest to us fields of conflict, more or less severe, where we have buried many an endeared comrade, where you have won honor for your country and yourselves, and where the enemy has learned anew to fear and respect the power of the Government for which we fight. It is with pain that I realize my inability to reward your cheerful devotion to duty, your arduous and prolonged labor, and your uncomplaining sacrifices. I heartily appreciate the constant co-operation of the division commanders, and the cheerful manner in which they have sustained me, and in which they have been sustained by their own officers. To them, and, through them to their commands, I tender my warmest thanks and unqualified commendation. No officer could have received more ready and untiring assistance from his staff than I have from mine. To them also I am more than grateful. Believing from my heart that our cause is right and just before God, as I take leave of you I commend you to His blessing, and trust He will assist our armies to complete the work which He has enabled them so gloriously to bring to the present stage of success.

O. O. HOWARD,
Major-General.

SPECIAL FIELD ORDERS, }   HDQRS. ARMY OF THE OHIO,
No. 62.   }   *Before Atlanta, Ga., July 26, 1864.*

*   *   *   *   *   *   *

III. To carry out the requirements of Special Field Orders, No. 42, headquarters Military Division of the Mississippi, July 25, 1864, a line of defense will be constructed to-day connecting the left of General Hascall's center brigade with the line of works abandoned by the enemy in rear of the Howard house, and the latter line will be remodeled and strengthened so as to adapt it to our use as a line of defense for the left and left rear of the army. All hospitals and trains will be moved within this new line during the day, except the trains en route to Marietta, which will remain at the latter place, or at the crossing of the Chattahoochee, until further orders. Trains will cross at Pace's or Powers' Ferry. The bridge at Isham's Ford will be destroyed, and the troops guarding it will join their division to-night. Detachments guarding trains within the line of defense will be relieved and will join their proper commands. Simultaneously with the withdrawal of the right of the Army of the Tennessee, which is expected to take place to-morrow morning, General

Cox will move back into the new line of defense, his right resting near the junction of the old rebel line and that to be constructed to-day. General Hascall will, at the same time, draw back his left to the new line prepared for it. Each division will have three brigades in line and one in reserve. The skirmish line will, unless forced back, maintain substantially its present position until the troops are established in the new line, when it will be retired so as to conform to the new position. The present line and that recently constructed by the Army of the Tennessee, as far as they are available, will be occupied by the reserve of the skirmish line, and must be held against anything less than an attack in force, and in case of an attack in force the resistance of the skirmish line in the old works must be sufficient to develop the strength and character of the attack, whether in column or line, and the real point of attack. The skirmish line will be connected with that of the troops of the Fourth Corps, General Stanley's division, which are to occupy the rear line on the left of General Cox. The skirmish line will be strong, placed well out, and must oppose an obstinate resistance to any advance of the enemy, endeavoring to ascertain and inform the commanding general as soon as possible the strength of the attacking force, and the point of the line at which the attack is really aimed. Should the enemy attack any position of the Army of the Tennessee, or of this army, during the movement, and before it shall have progressed so far as to leave the flank of this army exposed, the troops will maintain their present position, repel the attack, and await further orders. The present movements are expected to be decisive. The enemy is desperate and consequently bold. The utmost vigilance is enjoined upon all officers and men while on duty.

*   *   *   *   *   *   *

By command of Major-General Schofield:

J. A. CAMPBELL,
Major and Assistant Adjutant-General.

SPECIAL FIELD ORDERS, ⎰ HEADQUARTERS DEPARTMENT
              ⎱   AND ARMY OF THE TENNESSEE,
No. 79.   ⎰   *Before Atlanta, Ga., July 26, 1864.*

*   *   *   *   *   *

IV. In order to carry out the instructions contained in Special Field Orders, No. 42, Military Division of the Mississippi, the following movements of this army will be made:

1. Brigadier-General Woods, commanding First Division, Fifteenth Army Corps, will at 4 o'clock this p. m. march with his command and take up his position in the new line of intrenchments, his right resting on the railroad.

2. Major-General Dodge, commanding Left Wing, Sixteenth Army Corps, will at 12 o'clock to-night draw out his command and move by the nearest route to the main road running in rear of General Schofield's line, entering this road immediately to the west of the point where the new line of intrenchments crosses the railroad. General Dodge will move to the right of General Thomas' command and take up his position on the right of the corps of General Palmer.

3. As soon as the troops of Major-General Dodge have filed out, Major-General Blair will draw out his command and march by the most practicable route to the main road indicated above, following the Sixteenth Corps on that road, and taking up a position on its right.

4. When the troops of the Seventeenth Corps have filed past, Brig. Gen. M. L. Smith, commanding Fifteenth Army Corps, will draw out his command, following the Seventeenth Army Corps, and moving last the division of Brigadier-General Woods. The Fifteenth Army Corps will take up a position on the right of the Seventeenth Army Corps, one division being held in reserve. The new line to be occupied on the right will be thrown forward as far as practicable.

5. That portion of the artillery which can be drawn out during the day will be designated by Captain Hickenlooper, chief of artillery, and a position assigned it in the new line. The remaining artillery will be drawn out immediately after dark, the wheels muffled with grain sacks, and every precaution used to make the movement as silently as possible.

6. All the trains, except one wagon with ammunition for each regiment and battery, will be sent to-day to a point in rear of the center of the army and there parked.

7. Corps commanders will, under the direction of Captain Reese, chief engineer, cause good roads to be constructed during the day for their commands to move out upon, and staff officers will make themselves thoroughly acquainted with the route to be taken by each division.

8. All arrangements to accomplish these movements will be made during the day, so that the troops can be drawn out with celerity and without confusion.

V. Brig. Gen. J. M. Corse, having reported to these headquarters, in accordance with Special Field Orders, No. 43, Military Division of the Mississippi, will forthwith report to Major-General Dodge, commanding Left Wing, Sixteenth Army Corps, for assignment to the command of the Second Division, Sixteenth Army Corps.

      *   *   *   *   *   *   *

By order of Maj. Gen. John A. Logan:

WM. T. CLARK,
Assistant Adjutant-General.

SPECIAL FIELD ORDERS, } HDQRS. FIFTEENTH ARMY CORPS,
     No. 62.   }   *Before Atlanta, Ga., July 26, 1864.*

      *   *   *   *   *   *   *

III. The division of General Harrow will move at 12 o'clock, following the Seventeenth Corps. General Lightburn will put his division in motion so as to close upon General Harrow at the crossing of the railroad on the road to the Howard house. General Woods will move so as to close up on General Lightburn. Commands will not be given except in a very low tone of voice. Headquarters wagons of divisions, brigades, and of these headquarters, except one to carry rations, will pass the Howard house and follow the wagons of General Logan's headquarters immediately after dark to-night.

IV. Pickets will be relieved when the rear of the division passes the new works. Ammunition wagons and ambulances will precede the division to which they pertain. Picket officers from each division of the Army of the Tennessee will get notice to withdraw their pickets from the white house on the railroad as soon as the rear of the Second Division, Fifteenth Corps, passes through the new line of works.

By order of Brig. Gen. M. L. Smith:

R. R. TOWNES,
Assistant Adjutant-General.

SPECIAL FIELD ORDERS, } HDQRS. LEFT WING, 16TH ARMY CORPS,
No. 47. } *Near Atlanta, Ga., July 26, 1864.*

I. Brig. Gen. J. M. Corse, having reported to these headquarters for duty, is, in accordance with Special Field Orders, No. 79, headquarters Department and Army of the Tennessee, hereby assigned to the command of the Second Division, Sixteenth Army Corps. All books, maps, and papers appertaining to headquarters of the division will be turned over to Brigadier-General Corse, and the division staff will report to him for duty. Col. E. W. Rice, Seventh Iowa Infantry Volunteers, will again assume command of the First Brigade.

II. In making the movement to-night as specified in extract IV, Special Field Orders, No. 79, headquarters Department and Army of the Tennessee (a copy of which is inclosed), the Second Division will have the advance, moving promptly at 12 o'clock to-night. The Fourth Division will remain in its present position till the Second has withdrawn from its works, when it will closely follow. All wagons, with the exception of one wagon loaded with ammunition to each regiment and battery, will move this p. m. to a position near where the advanced supply train is now stationed, in the rear of the center of the army.

* * * * * * *

V. The following additional instructions in relation to the movement to-night will be observed: At 8 p. m. Col. J. W. Sprague, commanding Second Brigade, Fourth Division, will move out and go into position on the left of Brigadier-General Woods' division, Fifteenth Army Corps, in the new intrenchments north of the railroad, and will join his division as it passes through these intrenchments during the night. The Second Brigade, Second Division, will draw out with the Seventeenth Army Corps, and join its division to-morrow morning at the creek near General Sherman's headquarters, where the command will bivouac. The troops must be moved quietly, without sound of bugle or drum, and all teams, except one wagon of ammunition to a regiment and battery, must move off early to-night and go into park with the trains in rear of the center of the army before 11 p. m., so that the entire road is clear for troops. The ammunition wagons will move in advance of the divisions. Division picket officers will report to Capt. H. L. Burnham at these headquarters, at 10 p. m., for instructions in relation to withdrawing the picket-lines, which is not to be done until the entire army has moved out.

By order of Maj. Gen. G. M. Dodge:

J. W. BARNES,
Assistant Adjutant-General.

SPECIAL ORDERS, } HDQRS. SEVENTEENTH ARMY CORPS,
No. 184. } *Before Atlanta, Ga., July 26, 1864.*

* * * * * * *

XXX. In compliance with orders from headquarters Department and Army of the Tennessee, this command will be prepared to move at 12.30 to-morrow morning. As soon as the Sixteenth Army Corps has filed out, Brig. Gen. Giles A. Smith, commanding Fourth Division, will move his command by the left flank on the road running near his left to the railroad by these headquarters, where he will halt. Brigadier-General Leggett, commanding Third Division, Seventeenth Army Corps, will move his command simultaneously with the Fourth Division on a road leading from his left rear along the rear of the Fifteenth Army Corps, striking the railroad at the same point as the Fourth Division, where he will await further orders. Upon moving beyond the railroad the Third Division will take the advance.

By command of Maj. Gen. Frank P. Blair:

ROWLAND COX,
Assistant Adjutant-General.

[JULY 26, 1864.—For General Orders, No. 8, headquarters Seventeenth Army Corps, conferring a medal of honor upon Private George J. Reynolds, Company D, Fifteenth Iowa Infantry, for recovering the body of General McPherson, &c., see Part III, p. 556.]

NEAR ATLANTA, GA., *July 27, 1864.*
(Received 12.05 a. m. 29th.)

His Excellency President LINCOLN,
Washington:

SIR: Your dispatch of yesterday is received. I beg you will not regard me as fault finding, for I assert that I have been well sustained in every respect during my entire service. I did not suppose my dispatches would go outside the offices at the War Department. I did not suppose you were troubled with such things. Hovey and Osterhaus are both worthy men, and had they been promoted on the eve of the Vicksburg campaign, it would have been natural and well accepted; but I do think you will admit that their promotion, coming to us when they had gone to the rear, the one offended because I could not unite in the same division five infantry and five cavalry regiments, and the other for temporary sickness. You can see how ambitious aspirants for military fame regard these things. They come to me and point them out as evidences that I am wrong in encouraging them to a silent, patient discharge of duty. I assure you that every general of my army has spoken of it and referred to it as evidence that promotion results from importunity and not from actual service. I have refrained from recommending any thus far in the campaign, as I think we should reach some stage in the game before stopping to balance accounts or writing history. I assure you that I do think you have conscientiously acted throughout the war with marked skill in the matter of military appointments, and that as few mistakes have been made as could be expected. I will furnish all my army and division commanders with a copy of your dispatch, that they may feel reassured.

With great respect,

W. T. SHERMAN,
Major-General.

NEAR ATLANTA, GA., *July 27, 1864—8.30 p. m.*
(Received 8 p. m. 28th.)

Maj. Gen. H. W. HALLECK,
Washington, D. C.:

My two cavalry expeditions are off to make a wide circuit and reach the Macon road well to the southeast of Atlanta, and the Army of the Tennessee is shifted to the extreme right, reaching well toward the railroad, so that I think to-morrow must develop something. The cavalry will have to fight the enemy's cavalry, and we can hold the infantry and artillery to Atlanta and force them to extend and choose between Atlanta and East Point. I don't think the enemy can hold both. All are well pleased with General Howard's appointment but Generals Logan and Hooker. The former thought he ought to have been allowed the command of the army in the field until the end of the campaign; but I explained to him that a permanent department commander had to be appointed at once, as discharges, furloughs, and much detailed business could alone be done by a department commander. General Hooker is offended because he thinks he is entitled to the command. I must be honest and say he is not qualified or suited to it. He talks of quitting. If General Thomas recommends, I shall not object. He is not indispensable to our success. He is welcome to my place if the President awards it, but I cannot name him to so important a command as the Army of the Tennessee. All is well. The enemy to-day offered no serious opposition to the changes of to-day, and our skirmishing and artillery were just enough to make things interesting.

W. T. SHERMAN,
Major-General, Commanding.

NEAR ATLANTA, GA., July 27, 1864—11 p. m.
(Received 7.30 p. m. 28th.)

Maj. Gen. H. W. HALLECK,
Washington, D. C.:

General Hooker has applied to be relieved of the command of the Twentieth Army Corps, assigning as a reason the appointment of General Howard, his junior, to command the Army of the Tennessee. General Thomas asks the following appointments: General D. S. Stanley to command the Fourth Corps, vice Howard, transferred; General H. W. Slocum to command the Twentieth Corps, vice Hooker, relieved at his own request. I approve these nominations, and ask orders by telegraph that General Slocum may be summoned from Vicksburg, where he now is.

W. T. SHERMAN,
Major-General, Commanding.

HEADQUARTERS DEPARTMENT OF THE CUMBERLAND,
Before Atlanta, July 27, 1864.

ADJUTANT-GENERAL U. S. ARMY,
Washington:

Major-General Hooker desires to be relieved from the command of the Twentieth Army Corps. Am I authorized to order him to report to you at Washington?

GEO. H. THOMAS,
Major-General, Commanding.

WASHINGTON, D. C.,
[July 27, 1864]—4.15 p. m.

Maj. Gen. GEORGE H. THOMAS:

The Secretary of War authorizes you to order General Hooker to report to the Adjutant-General of the Army. Acknowledge receipt.

E. D. TOWNSEND,
Assistant Adjutant-General.

JULY 27, 1864.

General THOMAS:

Send me the papers about Hooker to-night, and make specific recommendations to fill the vacancies. Make Hooker resign his post as commander of the Twentieth Corps, that he cannot claim it and occasion delay in filling the vacancy.

> W. T. SHERMAN,
> *Major-General.*

HEADQUARTERS DEPARTMENT OF THE CUMBERLAND,
In the Field, July 27, 1864.

Maj. Gen. W. T. SHERMAN,
Commanding Military Division of the Mississippi:

GENERAL: Inclosed herewith I have the honor to transmit a copy of a communication this day received from Major-General Hooker, with my order in the case. Major-General Howard having been placed in command of the Department and Army of the Tennessee, I would recommend that Maj. Gen. D. S. Stanley, commanding First Division of the Fourth Army Corps, be placed in command of the corps. Major-General Hooker having, at his own request, been relieved from the command of the Twentieth Army Corps, I would recommend that Maj. Gen. H. W. Slocum be placed in command of that corps.

I am, general, very respectfully, your obedient servant,

> GEO. H. THOMAS,
> *Major-General, Commanding.*

[Inclosure No. 1.]

HDQRS. 20TH ARMY CORPS, ARMY OF THE CUMBERLAND,
Near Atlanta, Ga., July 27, 1864.

Brigadier-General WHIPPLE:

SIR: I have just learned that Major-General Howard, my junior, has been assigned to the command of the Army of the Tennessee. If this is the case I request that I may be relieved from duty with this army. Justice and self-respect alike require my removal from an army in which rank and service are ignored. I should like to have my personal staff relieved with me.

> JOSEPH HOOKER,
> *Major-General.*

[Inclosure No. 2.]

SPECIAL FIELD ORDERS, } HDQRS. DEPT. OF THE CUMBERLAND,
No. 205.   }   *Near Atlanta, Ga., July 27, 1864.*

*   *   *   *   *   *   *

VII. At his own request, Maj. Gen. J. Hooker, commanding the Twentieth Army Corps, is relieved from duty with the Army and Department of the Cumberland. He will repair to Washington, D. C., and report to the Adjutant-General for orders. Major-General Hooker's personal staff is also relieved from duty with this army that they may accompany the general. The quartermaster's department will furnish the necessary transportation. Brig. Gen. A. S. Williams, commanding First Division, Twentieth Army Corps, will succeed Major-General Hooker in command of the corps until an assignment to that command is made by the President of the United States.

By command of Major-General Thomas:

WM. D. WHIPPLE,
Assistant Adjutant-General.

HDQRS. FIRST CAV. DIV., DEPT. OF THE CUMBERLAND,
Opposite Campbellton, July 27, 1864—9 p. m.

Capt. L. M. DAYTON,
Aide-de-Camp:

I arrived opposite Campbellton at 4 p. m. The rebels have the whole river picketed in this vicinity, though not in sufficient force to have prevented my crossing. The pontoon train, however, at the hour I write, is not yet within six miles of me. Captain Kossak has found it impossible to pull it up with his mules. I will take some of my cavalry horses and pull it up. This delay will involve the probable necessity of crossing below here, as the attention of the enemy has, I think, been attracted to this point for some reason, as there have been none of them here recently until last night, when a brigade came down to picket their different ferries. I have endeavored to conceal my force, and think the rebels are not yet seriously alarmed. I expected to have reached Fayetteville to-night, and but for the disability on the part of the pontoon train would have done so. I now think I will be able to cross by daybreak at some point. Nothing has been found on this side of the river except small scouting parties of Texas cavalry. It is twenty-six miles from here to the point from which we moved our camp this morning.

I am, captain, very respectfully, your obedient servant,

E. M. McCOOK,
Brigadier-General, Commanding Division.

CARTERSVILLE, *July 27, 1864.*

Lieut. D. F. HOW,
Acting Assistant Adjutant-General:

Colonel Murray telegraphs that Captain Cummings, Third Kentucky Cavalry, routed Jordan's guerrillas yesterday, killing Captain McElroy, wounding Jordan and quite a number of his party. He is still in pursuit. A scouting party has just returned from Stilesborough, having met a party of twenty or twenty-five rebels. They captured horses and equipments, but failed to take any of the party.

J. KILPATRICK,
Brigadier-General.

HDQRS. MILITARY DIVISION OF THE MISSISSIPPI,
In the Field, near Atlanta, Ga., July 27, 1864.

General SCHOFIELD:

I am at General Davis' headquarters. The Army of the Tennessee is approaching the right flank, which is on the Turner's Ferry road four miles from the Chattahoochee and about the same distance from Atlanta. I propose to extend on a ridge due south, so that by facing left the right of our line will be a strong threat to East Point. I took it for granted the enemy would shift to this flank, but gradually we can make him extend till he is out of Atlanta. Listen well for sounds of action on the part of the cavalry. It would be well to burn that big brick house unless you picket it. A regiment should also patrol back toward Decatur occasionally.

W. T. SHERMAN,
Major-General, Commanding.

HDQRS. MILITARY DIVISION OF THE MISSISSIPPI,
In the Field, near Atlanta, July 27, 1864.

General SCHOFIELD:

I am just back from the extreme right. General Howard will have two corps in on the right intrenched, the other in reserve. Our cavalry is now out a day and to-morrow the effect of these two moves will be felt. I wish you to-morrow to let your skirmishers be bold, even to rashness, and show a good many men at open spaces. If you don't occupy that brick house as an outpost burn it.

W. T. SHERMAN,
Major-General, Commanding.

HEADQUARTERS ARMY OF THE OHIO,
Before Atlanta, Ga., July 27, 1864.

Major-General SHERMAN:

My demonstration to-day showed the enemy still in force in front of my center, near the railroad. About 500 cavalry made their appearance near the same point this p. m. and moved toward Decatur. I have a regiment of cavalry, Seventh Ohio, Colonel Garrard commanding, which arrived from the North to-day too late to join General Stoneman. I have ordered it to operate on my left as far out as Decatur.

J. M. SCHOFIELD,
Major-General.

HEADQUARTERS ARMY OF THE OHIO,
Before Atlanta, Ga., July 27, 1864—9 p. m.

Major-General SHERMAN:

I have your dispatch of 8.45. The brick house you refer to was burned this evening. I will press the enemy to-morrow as you desire.

J. M. SCHOFIELD,
Major-General.

HEADQUARTERS SEVENTEENTH ARMY CORPS,
Before Atlanta, Ga., July 27, 1864.

Lieut. Col. WILLIAM T. CLARK,
Assistant Adjutant-General, Dept. and Army of the Tennessee:

COLONEL: I have the honor to report, for the information of the major-general commanding, that in obedience to instructions from him I advanced the Third Division of this corps, immediately on its arrival, with instructions to proceed and take up a position on General Dodge's right, and on the extension of the line occupied by his command. After a sharp skirmish, which made it necessary to advance slowly, it was found inadvisable to advance farther in consequence of the darkness and difficult nature of the ground. In consequence of the road being blocked up by wagons and artillery, the Fourth Division did not reach the vicinity of the position assigned it until almost dark. It was, however, moved rapidly forward with the view to connect with the right of the Third Division; before reaching the Third Division, however, it became dark, and it was considered by the officer commanding the troops, as well as myself, to be entirely impracticable to advance farther. I therefore formed it in a strong position, the left resting on the rear of the right of the Third Division, and the right thrown back so as to form almost a right angle with the line occupied by that division, thereby securing my right flank and rear.

Very respectfully, your obedient servant,

FRANK P. BLAIR, JR.,
Major-General.

SPECIAL FIELD ORDERS, ⎰ HDQRS. DEPT. OF THE CUMBERLAND,
No. 205.   ⎱   *Near Atlanta, Ga., July 27, 1864.*

*   *   *   *   *   *   *

X. The First Division of Cavalry (McCook's) will be relieved by the Third Division of Cavalry (Kilpatrick's) in the following manner: Tenth Ohio and detachment of Second Kentucky Cavalry, with one section of Beebe's (Tenth Wisconsin) battery, will proceed without delay and report to Colonel Harrison, commanding Second Brigade, Third Division of Cavalry, with the army at the front. On the arrival of this command, Brigadier-General McCook will proceed with his division to the District of the Etowah, headquarters Cartersville, and relieve Brigadier-General Kilpatrick, commanding Third Division of Cavalry, carrying out the instructions heretofore given to the commander of the Third Division. Upon being relieved, Brigadier-General Kilpatrick will proceed with the remainder of his command, after it is concentrated at Cartersville, Ga., and join the army at the front.

By command of Major-General Thomas:

WM. D. WHIPPLE,
Assistant Adjutant-General.

ORDERS.]   HEADQUARTERS FOURTH ARMY CORPS,
Near Atlanta, Ga., July 27, 1864.

Maj. Gen. O. O. Howard having been ordered to the command of the Army of the Tennessee, the undersigned hereby assumes command of this corps.

D. S. STANLEY,
Major-General.

SPECIAL FIELD ORDERS, ⎰ HDQRS. ARMY OF THE OHIO,
                    ⎱   *In the Field, near Atlanta, Ga.,*
No. 63.   ⎱   *July 27, 1864.*

I. Capt. Theodore Cox, assistant adjutant-general of volunteers, having reported at these headquarters, in compliance with Special Orders, No. 239, current series, War Department, Adjutant-General's Office, is hereby assigned to duty as assistant adjutant-general of the Third Division, Twenty-third Army Corps, and will report in person, without delay, to Brig. Gen. J. D. Cox, commanding.

II. To-morrow, commencing at 7 a. m., a strong demonstration will be made by the Twenty-third Corps upon the enemy in its front for the purpose of diverting attention as much as possible from movements on our right. The skirmish line will be re-enforced and pushed out boldly, even at the risk of a sharp engagement. General Cox will send a strong regiment, with one or more at proper distances to support it, to feel for and make a strong demonstration upon the enemy's right. Colonel Garrard will move with his regiment of cavalry in conjunction with this infantry force and cover its left, pressing the enemy vigorously, and endeavoring to drive back whatever cavalry he may have upon his flank. The troops engaged in this demonstration should make considerable display, but carefully conceal their real strength. The troops must be ready to move at a moment's notice if the enemy be found in retreat, or to have withdrawn from his works in our immediate front.

By command of Major-General Schofield:

J. A. CAMPBELL,
Major and Assistant Adjutant-General.

GENERAL FIELD ORDERS, } HEADQUARTERS DEPARTMENT
No. 5.   } AND ARMY OF THE TENNESSEE,
Before Atlanta, Ga., July 27, 1864.

In pursuance of orders from the President, the undersigned hereby assumes command of the Department and Army of the Tennessee. I assure the gallant soldiers of this renowned army that I fully realize the delicate nature of my responsibility. Your late beloved commander was my personal friend, and while I unite with you in profound sympathy and regret for our irreparable loss, it shall be my constant aim to emulate his noble example.

O. O. HOWARD,
Major-General.

SPECIAL ORDERS, } HDQRS. FIRST DIVISION, 14TH CORPS,
No. 122.   } *Before Atlanta, Ga., July 27, 1864.*

*   *   *   *   *   *   *

II. In obedience to department orders the Second Regiment Ohio Volunteers is relieved from duty with this division, and will at once comply with the said order. The loss of the Second Ohio will be seriously felt, as a better or more gallant regiment cannot be found in service. The good conduct of the officers and men, both in camp and in battle, has challenged the admiration of the division commander, and when they leave for their homes they will carry with them his best wishes for their future happiness and prosperity. While your division commander rejoices at your prospect of soon being with your families, and congratulates them on your safe return, he deeply sympathizes with the families and friends of those who will be missing at your last reveille. The brilliant record of your regiment will be a source of pride to you in all time to come, and though your hardships have been great these will be forgotten and you will refer to your services in the army as constituting the most pleasant and agreeable part of your lives. My thanks are especially due to Col. A. G. McCook, who has commanded the regiment with so much skill and ability. As a regimental and brigade commander I have found him prompt, brave, skillful, and efficient.

  *   *   *   *   *   *   *

By command of Brigadier-General Johnson:

G. W. SMITH,
Captain and Acting Assistant Adjutant-General.

GENERAL FIELD ORDERS,)   HDQRS. FIFTEENTH ARMY CORPS,
   No. 2.   )   *Before Atlanta, Ga., July 27, 1864.*

I. The undersigned hereby reassumes command of the Fifteenth Army Corps.

II. Brig. Gen. M. L. Smith will reassume command of the Second Division, relieving Brigadier-General Lightburn.

JOHN A. LOGAN,
Major-General.

SPECIAL FIELD ORDERS,)   HDQRS. FIFTEENTH ARMY CORPS,
   No. 63.   )   *Before Atlanta, Ga., July 27, 1864.*

Brig. Gen. C. R. Woods, commanding First Division, will, as soon as the moon rises to-night, move into position on the right of the Seventeenth Army Corps, and form in two lines.

Brig. Gen. William Harrow, commanding Fourth Division, will form with a brigade front on the right of Brigadier-General Woods, refusing his entire line about right angles with General Woods. As soon as he shall have gone into position the rest of his troops will be formed in line in reserve.

Brig. Gen. M. L. Smith, commanding Second Division, will, as soon as General Harrow shall have gone into position, form one brigade on his right, and refuse the line thus formed, and place one brigade in reserve to the right and rear of his front line.

It is important that these movements be made before daylight, and division commanders should communicate with each other at once, through staff officers, the better to facilitate the movement. All wagons that are necessary to be had by the command will be brought forward and parked at convenient distances in the rear, the rest will be left in charge of Captain Emery, acting chief quartermaster, until needed. Ammunition sufficient to make 100 rounds per man will be brought forward to-night and placed near enough to the several commands to be accessible, should it be needed. Each division commander should know just where to get it.

By order of Maj. Gen. John A. Logan:

R. R. TOWNES,
Assistant Adjutant-General.

WAR DEPARTMENT,
July 28, 1864—8.30 p. m.

Maj. Gen. W. T. SHERMAN,
  Comdg. Army of the Mississippi, before Atlanta, Ga.:

The Secretary of War directs that you forward to the Department, as soon as practicable, a list of colonels whom you desire promoted to the rank of brigadier-general of volunteers. There will probably be eight appointments made for your army. Please indicate your preference for those you desire to receive the first appointments.

JAMES A. HARDIE,
Colonel and Inspector-General.

NEAR ATLANTA, GA., July 28, 1864—9 p. m.
(Received 29th.)

Major-General HALLECK, Washington, D. C.:

The enemy again assaulted to-day; this time on our extreme right, to which flank I had shifted the Army of the Tennessee, to gain ground toward the railroad. The blow fell upon the Fifteenth Corps, which handsomely repulsed it, capturing 4 regimental flags. The attack was kept up for five hours. Our men were partially covered, while the enemy were exposed. Our loss is comparatively small, while that of the enemy is represented as heavy. I will give approximate figures to-morrow. The cavalry has now been out two days, and to-morrow should show the effect. I feel confident they will reach the Macon road. Our right is about a mile distant from the railroad, but the ground is very difficult. I may be forced to extend still farther to command it. We have had heavy cannonading all day, the enemy using ordnance as heavy as 6-inch rifled guns. Bragg has been to Atlanta on a second visit.

W. T. SHERMAN.

SHERMAN'S HEADQUARTERS, July 28, 1864.

Maj. Gen. GEORGE H. THOMAS:

Order Davis' division to leave his camp and move to Turner's Ferry, and then, by a road leading toward East Point, to feel forward for Howard's right, back into some known point of Turner's Ferry. I will be over on that flank all day and await to reach out as far as possible.*

W. T. SHERMAN.

Brig. Gen. J. C. DAVIS, Commanding, &c.:

Herewith find copy of telegram from the general commanding the Military Division of the Mississippi, forwarded for your information and guidance. March at once in conformity to its directions.

Respectfully,

JOHN M. PALMER.

HDQRS. MILITARY DIVISION OF THE MISSISSIPPI,
In the Field, near Atlanta, Ga., July 28, 1864.

General THOMAS:

Before coming in to-night I ordered back the division of General Williams' corps, which I called on to be near at hand; also the brigade

---

* As recorded in Sherman's letter-book, this dispatch reads: "Order Davis' division to leave his camps and move to Turner's Ferry, and then, by road leading to East Point, to feel forward for Howard's right. I want to connect Howard's right, back with some known point of Turner's Ferry. I will be over on that flank all day, and want to reach out as far as possible." See, also, Morgan's quotation, Part I, p. 650.

of General Palmer which went over to General Howard. General Jeff. Davis was approaching at dark, and it was supposed would be in position to-night. It took wrong road. General Howard repulsed all attacks and inflicted heavy loss, his own being light. By daylight he will be well intrenched.

> W. T. SHERMAN,
> *Major-General, Commanding.*

> SHERMAN'S HEADQUARTERS,
> *July 28, 1864.* (Received 9.15 p. m.)

General THOMAS:

Try and thin your strong lines as much as possible to-morrow, so as to make good reserves for action. Let these reserves be ready to move at any moment. Our cavalry surely will reach the Macon road to-night, and to-morrow the enemy will do something desperate.

> W. T. SHERMAN,
> *Major-General.*

> HDQRS. MILITARY DIVISION OF THE MISSISSIPPI,
> *In the Field, near Atlanta, Ga., July 28, 1864.*

General THOMAS:

Let two of your Napoleons or 20-pounder Parrott batteries keep up fire on Atlanta all night, each battery throwing a shot every fifteen minutes, partly for effect and partly as signal to our cavalry.

> W. T. SHERMAN,
> *Major-General, Commanding.*

> HEADQUARTERS FOURTH ARMY CORPS,
> *Near Atlanta, Ga., July 28, 1864—8.50 p. m.*

Brig. Gen. W. D. WHIPPLE,
  Chief of Staff, Army of the Cumberland:

GENERAL: In obedience to General Thomas' order I pushed the rebel lines on my front at 4 p. m. We carried three rifle-pits in front of General Wood's and Colonel Grose's divisions, capturing 20 prisoners. These men belonged to Cheatham's division, late Walker's division. Cheatham's division had gone off to oppose our right, leaving his pickets. The enemy showed at least a continuous line of troops in their works on my front, and moved men rapidly from General Geary's or General Newton's front to the works opposite General Wood's right, where they were most seriously threatened. The rebels still hold a line of light works, a continuous rifle-pit, about 200 yards in advance of their main intrenchments. The prisoners represent that no re-enforcements have joined them, and that Steve Lee now commands Hood's corps, Cheatham having returned to his division, and that they will try to hold Atlanta. The prisoners were taken principally by Gibson's brigade. We had 1 man killed and a few wounded. The rebels can very easily reach our skirmish line with canister. I think any attack upon their main line, excepting by a regular well managed assaulting column, must have failed. I am sorry General Newton did not take the enemy's picket-line on his front; he could easily have done so.

Very respectfully, your obedient servant,

D. S. STANLEY,
Major-General.

P. S.—Since writing the foregoing, my provost-marshal reports that he has now 40 enlisted men and 3 commissioned [officers] prisoners in his hands, who were captured this afternoon.

D. S. STANLEY,
Major-General.

HEADQUARTERS FOURTEENTH ARMY CORPS,
July 28, 1864—1.45 p. m.

Brig. Gen. W. D. WHIPPLE, *Assistant Adjutant-General:*

GENERAL: Howard has sent word that the rebels are passing to his right on the Sandtown road, and asks assistance. Morgan, with Davis' division, started very promptly, and I have no more troops to spare from my own lines. He had not, when his messenger started, heard from Morgan.

Respectfully,

JOHN M. PALMER,
Major-General.

HDQRS. SECOND DIVISION, FOURTEENTH ARMY CORPS,
July 28, 1864.

Major-General PALMER, *Commanding Corps:*

GENERAL: The order to move with my division has been received. I am too sick to go, and have turned over the command to General Morgan. I regret being sick; am too weak to sit on my horse. Perhaps I will be better by this afternoon; hope so.

Very respectfully,

JEF. C. DAVIS,
Brigadier-General, Commanding Division.

HDQRS. THIRD DIVISION, FOURTH ARMY CORPS,
Near Atlanta, Ga., July 29, 1864.

Lieut. Col. J. S. FULLERTON:

COLONEL: Moore, a scout, whom I sent out on the 26th in the forenoon, returned this p. m. and makes the following statement: General S. D. Lee arrived about the 25th instant from Mississippi and brought 3,500 troops with him. These were dismounted cavalry, are now used as infantry, and are in the intrenchments. Moore says he went to the depot every time the cars came into Atlanta, and that the trains were loaded with re-enforcements of the Georgia militia. He says many arriving in this way. Moore says he heard Judge Wright and Ridley, citizens, say that there would be enough of the re-enforcements to make a small corps for General Cheatham. Moore says the rebels acknowledge they were defeated yesterday, and he heard officers talking who said they had lost between 8,000 and 9,000. Moore says he heard in Atlanta

yesterday afternoon that there had been an engagement yesterday at
11 a. m., between our cavalry, under General Garrard, and the rebel
cavalry, under Wheeler, in the direction of Yellow River, but he was
not able to learn any of the details.   Moore says that the understanding
prevails in the rebel army that Atlanta is to be defended to the last
extremity, but that much dissatisfaction prevails among the common
soldiery about the removal of General Johnston and the manner in
which General Hood has handled the army since taking command of it.
The soldiers were dissatisfied with the attacks that Hood has made.
Moore says the supply of forage and subsistence is very short indeed,
produced by there being now but one line of railroad.   When he was
in Atlanta he could get no corn for his horse; hitherto he had got
plenty.   He says he heard it said that if the rebels were driven out of
Atlanta they would try to make their first stand at East Point.   Moore
says Stewart's and Lee's corps made the attack yesterday morning, but
were subsequently re-enforced by a part of Hardee's corps, which had
been left in the works.   After the fighting ceased a part of the troops
were brought back to occupy the intrenchments around the town.   Moore
says they kept a strong line in their works.   Moore says our shells fall
into the town and annoy them very much, though they have inflicted
no great loss.   General Bragg is still in Atlanta.   General Johnston is in
Macon.   General Loring was wounded in the fight yesterday severely.
Moore says he heard officers saying that they would get re-enforcements of militia and conscripts to make up for their late losses.   Moore
brings a paper of this date.

Respectfully submitted, with the newspaper, for the information of
the corps and department commanders.

TH. J. WOOD,
Brigadier-General of Volunteers, Commanding.

HEADQUARTERS TWENTIETH CORPS,
Near Atlanta, Ga., July 28, 1864.

Brig. Gen. W. T. WARD, *Commanding Third Division:*

GENERAL: The brigadier-general commanding the corps directs that,
pursuant to orders of the major-general commanding Department of
the Cumberland, you hold your division in readiness to move at daybreak to-morrow morning in such direction as may hereafter be indicated.   It is expected that the operations of the cavalry may provoke
some desperate operations upon the part of the enemy.

I have the honor to be, general, very respectfully, your obedient
servant,

S. E. PITTMAN,
Captain and Acting Aide-de-Camp.

HDQRS. DEPARTMENT AND ARMY OF THE TENNESSEE,
Before Atlanta, Ga., July 28, 1864.

Maj. Gen. W. T. SHERMAN,
Commanding Military Division of the Mississippi:

GENERAL: The corps of Hood attacked us to-day at 11.30 a. m. on
the right of my line, mainly opposite the Fifteenth Corps, with lines
extending beyond my right flank.   The assaults were pertinaciously
kept up for four hours with scarcely any intermission, and were invariably repulsed.   The enemy's dead lie thickly on our front.   We
took several stand of colors and quite a number of prisoners.   Gen-

eral Logan bore the brunt of the battle, and his command acquitted itself nobly. Generals Blair and Dodge weakened their lines to the lowest limits in order to extend his flank and re-enforce him at any point. Our casualties are small, owing to the fact that we had just covered ourselves with rough barricades. Some of Polk's command was engaged in the last assaults. I will make a more specific report as soon as I can get the requisite returns from the different commands.

Very respectfully, your obedient servant,

O. O. HOWARD,
Major-General.

THOMAS' HEADQUARTERS,
July 28, 1864.

Major-General SCHOFIELD:

General Howard is being hard pressed on our right and I desire that you press the enemy with vigor in your front, and, if practicable, break their lines, which must be light held. Howard has been attacked, first in flank, then on his whole front, but at last report had repulsed the enemy.

W. T. SHERMAN,
Major-General.

HEADQUARTERS ARMY OF THE OHIO,
Before Atlanta, Ga., July 28, 1864.

Major-General SHERMAN:

Your dispatch is received. I have a brigade on the railroad pressed close to the enemy's works, which appear to be held in sufficient force to resist an assault. They have a heavy cross-fire of artillery. It seems to me impossible to carry any point of the enemy's line without going beyond the defenses of the town, which would take me far from the rest of the army. I will reconnoiter carefully and will endeavor to gain a point of the enemy's line, if I can see any chance of success.

J. M. SCHOFIELD,
Major-General.

HEADQUARTERS ARMY OF THE OHIO,
Before Atlanta, Ga., July 28, 1864.

Colonel WARNER,
Acting Inspector-General, Thomas' Headquarters:

My demonstration in front of my left shows the enemy apparently in force in his works. No change appears along my front.

J. M. SCHOFIELD,
Major-General.

HDQRS. MILITARY DIVISION OF THE MISSISSIPPI,
In the Field, near Atlanta, Ga., July 28, 1864.

General SCHOFIELD:

I am starting off to the right again. I want to watch the effect on that flank. Keep things lively in your front, and let that cavalry regiment feel out eastward and south, as far as they can venture.

W. T. SHERMAN,
Major-General, Commanding.

HEADQUARTERS ARMY OF THE OHIO,
July 28, 1864—3.30 p. m.

Major-General THOMAS:

I have very little hope of being able to carry any point of the enemy's works, since I can't go beyond the strong defenses of Atlanta. I will, however, move a considerable force well to my left, make some display and press strongly so as to draw off as much force from your front as possible.

J. M. SCHOFIELD,
Major-General.

[Indorsement.]

JULY 28—4 p. m.

Major-General STANLEY:

Should you discover that the enemy attempts to withdraw any of his forces from your front, I wish you to take advantage of it to drive him as far as possible. See General Schofield's dispatch within.

GEO. H. THOMAS,
Major-General.

Please return.

G. H. T.

———

HEADQUARTERS ARMY OF THE OHIO,
Before Atlanta, Ga., July 28, 1864—8.15 p. m.

Major-General SHERMAN:

I have kept up my demonstration during the day, and extended it about a mile beyond the railroad. The enemy has continually moved troops to his right, and met me in strong works with a good deal of artillery, and men enough to resist an assault.

J. M. SCHOFIELD,
Major-General.

———

HDQRS. MILITARY DIVISION OF THE MISSISSIPPI,
In the Field, near Atlanta, Ga., July 28, 1864.

General SCHOFIELD:

One of my aides is just in from General Howard. He repulsed all attacks handsomely, the enemy leaving his dead in our possession. The number, though heavy, not yet ascertained. Our loss light, the men having temporary barricades.

W. T. SHERMAN,
Major-General, Commanding.

———

HDQRS. MILITARY DIVISION OF THE MISSISSIPPI,
In the Field, near Atlanta, Ga., July 28, 1864.

General SCHOFIELD:

I have your two dispatches. I hardly expected you could carry the enemy's works, but the attack on General Howard was so persistent that I did not know but that Hood had actually stripped his line of all but the militia. Up to the time of my leaving the field no figures were given, but it was reported that the attack came from Hood's corps and fell on the Fifteenth Corps. The repulse was complete, and we hold the ground.

W. T. SHERMAN,
Major-General, Commanding.

HDQRS. MILITARY DIVISION OF THE MISSISSIPPI,
In the Field, near Atlanta, Ga., July 28, 1864.
General SCHOFIELD:

General Howard's conduct to-day had an excellent effect on his command. After the firing had ceased he walked the line, and the men gathered about him in the most affectionate manner, and he at once gained their hearts and confidence. I deem this a perfect restoration to confidence in themselves and leader of that army.

W. T. SHERMAN,
Major-General, Commanding.

HDQRS. MILITARY DIVISION OF THE MISSISSIPPI,
In the Field, near Atlanta, Ga., July 28, 1864.
General SCHOFIELD:

If you have not already a command by one of your batteries of the Decatur road and railway, clear out the trees, so that your shot and shell can reach them easily about the brick house you burned.

W. T. SHERMAN,
Major-General, Commanding.

HDQRS. MILITARY DIVISION OF THE MISSISSIPPI,
In the Field, near Atlanta, Ga., July 28, 1864.
General SCHOFIELD:

Let one of your batteries, 20-pounder Parrott or Napoleon, throw a shot into Atlanta every fifteen minutes during the night, partly for effect and partly for signals to our cavalry.

W. T. SHERMAN,
Major-General, Commanding.

HEADQUARTERS ARMY OF THE OHIO,
July 28, 1864—9 p. m.
Major-General SHERMAN:

I have your dispatch. Howard's success is splendid and must go far toward determining a speedy evacuation of Atlanta. I will carry out your directions about the night firing and command of the Decatur road.

J. M. SCHOFIELD,
Major-General.

HEADQUARTERS ARMY OF THE OHIO,
Near Atlanta, Ga., July 28, 1864.
Brig. Gen. J. D. COX,
Commanding Third Division, Twenty-third Army Corps:

GENERAL: General Sherman informs r > that Howard repulsed the enemy handsomely in every attack, his dead being left in our hands; our men fought behind breast-works and suffered but slight loss.

Figures are not given, but the loss of the enemy is said to be heavy. The general desires that the woods be cleared away so that one of your batteries shall have full command of the Decatur road about the brick house.

Very respectfully, your obedient servant,

J. M. SCHOFIELD,
Major-General, Commanding.

HDQRS. THIRD DIVISION, TWENTY-THIRD ARMY CORPS,
Before Atlanta, July 28, 1864.

Colonel CAMERON,
Commanding Second Brigade:

SIR: The reconnaissance ordered from corps headquarters had better go out near the site of the brick house, pushing to the front of your old position. The regiment in support can occupy either your old line of works or that last built by the Fifteenth Corps. Let the movement be pushed so as to develop the enemy's force in your front and fully detect any movement or withdrawal on their part. For the rest see the order sent last night, which the commandant of the detachment should carefully study.

Yours, respectfully,

J. D. COX,
Brigadier-General, Commanding.

HDQRS. THIRD DIVISION, TWENTY-THIRD ARMY CORPS,
Before Atlanta, July 28, 1864—11.30 a. m.

Col. D. CAMERON,
Commanding Second Brigade:

SIR: The order I sent by Lieutenant Coughlan was that you should push pretty well to the right, inasmuch as you did not seem to find much resistance in your immediate front, and the distance you had advanced made it proper to take your supports nearer to the advanced line than the line of works would be. The object was, as stated in the first order, to use the full strength of one regiment in developing the enemy's position and force in front, and hold the other well in hand to support the first, or to cover a retreat, if you should be attacked by heavy force. The feeling to the right is necessary, because that is the point of danger, and where you must be most guarded. This was simply in extension of the written orders sent, and by no means inconsistent with the spirit and general purpose, but rather in furtherance of both. I greatly regret you did not see it so. The reconnaissance will be continued as far as it can be done consistently with keeping open your communication with the division, and the direction is toward the principal line of works the enemy occupy commanding the railroad, &c. Please report progress, &c.

J. D. COX,
Brigadier-General, Commanding.

HDQRS. THIRD DIVISION, TWENTY-THIRD ARMY CORPS,
Before Atlanta, July 28, 1864.

Maj. J. A. CAMPBELL,
Assistant Adjutant-General, Army of the Ohio:

MAJOR: I have the honor to inclose, for the information of the commanding general, a report just received from Colonel Cameron of his reconnaissance to the front. His orders (sent since this report of his was written, though before I received it) are to continue pushing as long as he can do so without serious loss and without compromising his power to return to the position of the division.

Very respectfully, your obedient servant,

J. D. COX,
Brigadier-General, Commanding.

[Inclosure.]

AT THE BRICK HOUSE,
Near Atlanta, July 28, 1864—10.30 a. m.

Brigadier-General Cox,
Commanding Third Division, Twenty-third Corps:

GENERAL: I moved out with the Sixty-third Indiana and Sixty-fifth Illinois at 7 this morning, carrying out your instructions. We have pushed in the enemy's skirmishers to their former position and now occupy with our reserves the advanced pits of the former skirmish line of the Fifteenth Corps. Our line of vedettes are about 100 yards ahead of this. The enemy has a strong skirmish line and is skirmishing with our men. The enemy's position is in full view. They show a force, I should judge from the reports of Major Wilcox (in charge of the line), quite sufficient to hold it. Four companies of the Sixty-third Indiana are in position to the left of the brick house, and where, in my judgment, they should at present remain. The rest of the regiment is forward. I have sent four companies of the Sixty-fifth Illinois Volunteers forward on the right, extending to the creek. Their reserves occupy the advanced skirmish line formerly held by us. Our skirmishers have advanced here and drawn the fire of the enemy, who has a strong skirmish line also in this direction and a battery in position, from which they have thrown several shells. The enemy has a battery in position near the railroad, in plain view of our skirmishers. This is the battery to which their prisoners belong. Major Wilcox reports the enemy moving artillery toward our left, and that working parties are actually employed along the line strengthening the main line of works. We can keep up a brisk skirmish with the enemy, but, in my judgment, a farther advance is not practicable. I have one-half of my force on the skirmish line and the other half on the works of the Fifteenth Corps and the works formerly held by ourselves. I will not change this arrangement unless otherwise directed. Skirmishing has become very active on the left.

Very respectfully, your obedient servant,

DANIEL CAMERON,
Colonel, Commanding Brigade.

HEADQUARTERS THIRD DIVISION,
July 28, 1864.

Major CAMPBELL,
Assistant Adjutant-General, Department of the Ohio:

MAJOR: The general directs me to inclose to you the accompanying report made by Colonel Cameron of his operations to-day.

Most respectfully, your obedient servant,

H. W. WELLS,
Major and Chief of Artillery.

[Inclosure.]

HDQRS. SECOND BRIG., THIRD DIV., TWENTY-THIRD CORPS,
Near Atlanta, Ga., July 28, 1864.

Major WELLS,
Actg. Asst. Adjt. Gen., Third Division, Twenty-third Corps:

MAJOR: I have the honor to report the result of the reconnaissance made this afternoon by the Second Brigade, Third Division. Like that made this morning by two regiments of the brigade, it resulted in our driving the enemy to their works, developing their line, and showing the position of their artillery. The works in our front are strong and held by a considerable force. In the front of the brigade artillery opened from three different positions; I should say from eight pieces. The enemy's force this morning was but slight; about 2 p. m. they commenced moving heavy forces to the left (cavalry and infantry); from the skirmish line they could be distinctly seen and heard fortifying. As their troops passed our skirmish line near the railroad they were in full sight and were fired at by our men. Our advance was a surprise. Four large dwellings have been burned by them to-day as they fell back. Three of our regiments advanced to the left of the railroad and one to the right. The enemy's line extended far to the left of ours. Our losses 14 wounded and killed. We advanced within 250 yards of their works.

I have the honor to be, &c., yours,

DANIEL CAMERON,
Colonel, Commanding, &c.

NEAR ATLANTA, GA., *July 28, 1864—8 p. m.*

Maj. T. T. ECKERT:

Howard's command got into position on right this day, and were attacked at once, the weight falling on Fifteenth Corps. Enemy charged four times in very dense timber, and were repulsed as often—with what loss I cannot say; our loss not a hundred. At this hour rebels are massing against right, while Schofield and Stanley are ready to attack on our left as soon as our right is pressed heavily. Assignment of Howard to the Army of the Tennessee causes some discontent, but not as much as I feared. No news from cavalry raid on Macon railroad.

J. C. VAN DUZER.

CLYDE, OHIO, *July 29, 1864.*
(Received 10 a. m.)

His Excellency President LINCOLN:

We have the honor to report that the remains of the distinguished Major-General McPherson are now here, at the home of his childhood and residence of his widowed mother. Some of his personal staff, a guard of honor, and a proper military escort, with many distinguished strangers and a large concourse of citizens are here, prepared to deposit in his last resting place, at 10 o'clock to-day, what now remains of the illustrious dead.

C. W. PAGE,
Chairman Committee.
R. A. FOSTER,
Secretary.

CITY POINT, VA., *July 29, 1864—12 m.*

Maj. Gen. H. W. HALLECK,
    Chief of Staff:

I would approve of making the appointments of corps commanders recommended by General Thomas. In relieving General Slocum from command at Vicksburg, I would direct General Canby to send a suitable major-general from his military division. General Dana would prob-ably be the best man, but I would leave this to Canby, knowing that he would make a proper selection.

U. S. GRANT,
    Lieutenant-General.

NEAR ATLANTA, GA., *July 29, 1864—8.30 p. m.*
(Received 10.45 p. m.)

Maj. Gen. H. W. HALLECK,
    Washington, D. C.:

The result of the enemy's attack yesterday, chiefly on the Fifteenth Corps, is thus reported by General Howard :

We have counted 642 rebel dead, and there are still others in front of our lines. It is fair to presume that their wounded are five or six times that of their dead. Over 100 prisoners are in hand, and others being gathered up in the woods.

Howard estimates the enemy's loss at 5,000, and our loss at less than 600. General W. H. T. Walker was killed on the 22d, and it is now reported by prisoners that Wheeler was killed yesterday. Stephen D. Lee, Loring, and Stewart severely wounded yesterday. We are so near the enemy's line that their artillery prevents our advancing the lines so as to take full advantage of battle, they gathering into the city the wounded and more remote dead. The parapets of Atlanta present a well-filled line wherever we approach them. General Thomas is to-day making a strong reconnaissance in force toward East Point, and General Schofield on the left. Our cavalry has now been out three days, and must have done its work about Griffin.

W. T. SHERMAN,
    Major-General.

HDQRS. MILITARY DIVISION OF THE MISSISSIPPI,
    In the Field, near Atlanta, Ga., July 29, 1864.
(Received 2.50 a. m. 30th.)

Col. JAMES A. HARDIE,
    Inspector-General, Washington, D. C.:

In compliance with your dispatch of the 28th instant, I now send you the names of eight colonels who are recommended by their immediate and superior commanders for promotion, and I earnestly recommend that they be appointed brigadier-generals: Col. William Grose, Thirty-sixth Indiana; Col. Charles C. Walcutt, Forty-sixth Ohio; Col. James W. Reilly, One hundred and fourth Ohio; Col. L. P. Bradley, Fifty-first Illinois; Col. J. W. Sprague, Sixty-third Ohio; Col. Joseph A. Cooper, Sixth East Tennessee; Col. John T. Croxton, Fourth Kentucky; Col. William W. Belknap, Fifteenth Iowa. Three of them are from each of the armies of the Cumberland and Tennessee, and two of the Army of the Ohio, and are all at their posts doing good service.

W. T. SHERMAN,
    Major-General.

HDQRS. MILITARY DIVISION OF THE MISSISSIPPI,
In the Field, near Atlanta, Ga., July 29, 1864.

General THOMAS:

Until the result of our cavalry is known, I want the utmost activity on our flanks. General Howard by this time must have his line strong. I wish you to take General Davis' division and one of General Williams' and operate from General Howard's right flank toward East Point. Don't form a line, but move so as to occupy or threaten the railroad. General Schofield will do the same on the left. I will stay at home to-day to be convenient to the telegraph. Keep me well advised. Don't extend the line permanently, but operate in the nature of a strong reconnaissance toward East Point, having General Howard's lines as a point of departure and safety.

W. T. SHERMAN,
Major-General, Commanding.

HDQRS. MILITARY DIVISION OF THE MISSISSIPPI,
In the Field, near Atlanta, Ga., July 29, 1864.

General THOMAS:

Have those two divisions moved to our right, and when? General Howard reports that appearances are that Hardee's corps is between his right and Turner's Ferry. If so, we ought to strike it, or between it and Atlanta, at once.

W. T. SHERMAN,
Major-General, Commanding.

DAVIS' HEADQUARTERS, ARMY OF THE CUMBERLAND,
July 29, 1864—1 p. m.

Major-General SHERMAN,
Commanding Military Division of the Mississippi :

The two divisions were ordered out as soon as your dispatch was received at 7 a. m. Davis' division is moving now by Howard's right, and Ward's division is moving in support of Davis. I do not know what is on General Howard's right, as I have not heard from him to-day. General Morgan was ordered to move toward the railroad by Howard's right, in compliance with your orders.

GEO. H. THOMAS,
Major-General, U. S. Volunteers, Commanding.

HEADQUARTERS DEPARTMENT OF THE CUMBERLAND,
July 29, 1864.

Major-General SHERMAN:

I have just returned from the right. I have intrenched Morgan on the Howell's (or Green's) Ferry road, to the right and southwest of Logan. He has complete control of that road, and has his skirmishers out half a mile to his front. They have driven the rebels into intrenched rifle-pits, and report intrenched lines heavily manned a short distance in rear of their skirmish rifle-pits. I also directed Ward to take position on Morgan's right and refuse his right, so as to make a strong right flank.

Ward fronts the Howell's Ferry road, and runs along it toward the Chattahoochee for half a mile and then falls back this way. Howard had good ground to fight over yesterday. I saw several dead rebels that Ward's men were burying. If, after intrenching, Howard will thin out and extend to his right, Morgan and Ward can move still farther to the right, and might perhaps overlap the enemy. Whilst Morgan and Ward made their advances, I had Williams, Johnson, and Baird make strong reconnaissances to their fronts. They all report their belief that the enemy has either retired altogether, or has withdrawn the greater part of his forces, and only now has a weak skirmish line covering his fortifications around the city. I have directed them to feel strongly to-night, and determine whether the enemy has retired or not.

GEO. H. THOMAS,
Major-General.

(Copy to Generals Howard and Schofield.)

HEADQUARTERS DEPARTMENT OF THE CUMBERLAND,
July 29, 1864.

Major-General SHERMAN:

I will send to General Morgan immediately for the strength of the Tenth Illinois. I take great pleasure in announcing the capture, this morning, of an entire rebel regiment—115 officers and men—by the First Division, Twentieth Corps, whilst advancing its lines in obedience to my orders of last night. The position gained is very advantageous to us also, as it will enable me to shorten my lines considerably and have a better view of the ground in front.

GEO. H. THOMAS,
Major-General.

HDQRS. MILITARY DIVISION OF THE MISSISSIPPI,
In the Field, near Atlanta, Ga., July 29, 1864.

General THOMAS:

Send me the names of three colonels in your command you want made brigadiers. Col. James A. Hardie, Inspector-General, notifies me that there are eight to be made out of my division. I give three to you, three to the Tennessee, and two to Ohio Department.

W. T. SHERMAN,
Major-General, Commanding.

SHERMAN'S HEADQUARTERS,
July 29, 1864.

General THOMAS:

I have ordered Howard to extend his lines to-morrow as much as possible toward East Point, and wish you to continue the movement still farther, to draw the enemy out of Atlanta by threatening the railroad below. I send you a copy of Schofield's dispatch.* I will order him to keep up the attraction on the left and feel Atlanta pretty strong.

W. T. SHERMAN,
Major-General.

---

*See p. 293, beginning, "Colonel Reilly has just returned," &c.

Official copy respectfully furnished Maj. Gen. J. M. Palmer, who will give the necessary orders to General Davis to carry out General Sherman's instructions. When General Howard extends, you can move out and show this order to General Ward, who will move within supporting distance of him.

By command of Major-General Thomas:

WM. D. WHIPPLE,
Assistant Adjutant-General.

Official copies of the foregoing referred to Brig. Gen. J. C. Davis, with instructions to carry out their provisions.

A. C. McCLURG,
Captain and Assistant Adjutant-General.

HEADQUARTERS DEPARTMENT OF THE CUMBERLAND,
Before Atlanta, Ga., July 29, 1864.

Brig. Gen. A. S. WILLIAMS,
Commanding Twentieth Army Corps:

GENERAL: In accordance with orders from headquarters Military Division of the Mississippi, the major-general commanding directs that you send one division of your corps to operate in conjunction with Brig. Gen. Jeff. C. Davis from Major-General Howard's right flank toward East Point. The division which you send will be held in reserve, to act as a support to General Davis' division, the latter conducting the reconnaissance. Major-General Howard's lines will be used as a point of departure and safety for the reconnaissance.

I am, general, very respectfully, your obedient servant,

WM. D. WHIPPLE,
Assistant Adjutant-General.

HEADQUARTERS TWENTIETH CORPS,
Near Atlanta, Ga., July 29, 1864.

Brigadier-General GEARY,
Commanding Second Division:

GENERAL: The brigadier-general commanding the corps directs that you feel with your pickets during the night well out. The indications during the day have been that the enemy have been evacuating the town or intend to do so. A picket-line may be left in our front to deceive us; if so the general commanding desires that in the morning at daylight parties may be sent out from each division to test it, and if possible to break it and occupy the town.

I am, general, very respectfully, your obedient servant,

H. W. PERKINS,
Assistant Adjutant-General.

HEADQUARTERS TWENTIETH CORPS,
Near Atlanta, Ga., July 29, 1864—10.15 a. m.

Brig. Gen. W. T. WARD,
Commanding Third Division:

GENERAL: I am directed by the brigadier-general commanding the corps to inclose herewith a copy of an order from the major-general commanding the department to send the reserve division to support General Jeff. Davis' division upon a reconnaissance.*   General Williams desires that you execute the order without delay.

I have the honor to be, general, yours, respectfully,

S. E. PITTMAN,
Captain and Acting Aide-de-Camp.

HEADQUARTERS ARMY OF THE OHIO,
Before Atlanta, Ga., July 29, 1864.

Major-General SHERMAN:

I have sent a brigade of infantry with Colonel Garrard's cavalry to make a detour to the left and threaten the enemy's extreme right, reconnoitering all the roads to the east and south. I will also keep up activity along my front.

J. M. SCHOFIELD,
Major-General.

HEADQUARTERS ARMY OF THE OHIO,
Before Atlanta, Ga., July 29, 1864.

Major-General SHERMAN:

Colonel Reilly has just returned from his reconnaissance to the left. He passed the left of the line occupied by the Army of the Tennessee during the battle of the 22d, and struck the rebel intrenchments about six miles from Atlanta, and three miles from the Decatur road. He drove before him a considerable force of cavalry, mostly militia, and found a brigade or more of regular infantry in the intrenchments. He kept up his demonstrations during the day and retired at night with slight loss.

J. M. SCHOFIELD,
Major-General.

HDQRS. MILITARY DIVISION OF THE MISSISSIPPI,
In the Field, near Atlanta, Ga., July 29, 1864.

General SCHOFIELD:

General Thomas has got two divisions to the right of General Howard, and to-morrow will push forward close to the railroad. General Thomas thinks the enemy must be very weak in Atlanta. Feel your front strong in the morning, and repeat the movement on the left. It is time we heard something of our cavalry.

W. T. SHERMAN,
Major-General, Commanding.

HEADQUARTERS ARMY OF THE OHIO,
Before Atlanta, Ga., July 29, 1864.

Major-General SHERMAN,
Commanding Military Division of the Mississippi:

There is a large quantity of bridge timber on the railroad near the brick house; shall I destroy it?

J. M. SCHOFIELD,
Major-General.

---

* See Whipple to Williams, p. 292.

HDQRS. MILITARY DIVISION OF THE MISSISSIPPI,
In the Field, near Atlanta, Ga., July 29, 1864.

Major-General SCHOFIELD:

No, do not destroy the bridge.

W. T. SHERMAN,
Major-General, Commanding.

HEADQUARTERS ARMY OF THE OHIO,
Before Atlanta, Ga., July 29, 1864.

Brig. Gen. M. S. HASCALL,
Commanding Second Division, Twenty-third Army Corps:

GENERAL: The commanding general desires to know whether your demonstrations to-day drew any artillery fire from the enemy or developed any force in your front more than a skirmish line. General Thomas reports that it is the impression of his division commanders in front of the city on the right that the enemy has withdrawn everything but his skirmish line. If you have any reason to believe such is the condition of affairs in your front the commanding general desires you to push forward either to-night, or at daylight in the morning, and ascertain the true condition of affairs.

Very respectfully, your obedient servant,

J. A. CAMPBELL,
Major and Assistant Adjutant-General.

HEADQUARTERS ARMY OF THE OHIO,
Before Atlanta, Ga., July 29, 1864.

Brig. Gen. J. D. COX,
Commanding Third Division, Twenty-third Army Corps:

GENERAL: Please send a brigade to make a vigorous demonstration upon the enemy's extreme right. The brigade might go as far east as Decatur, thence south and west, but must of course be handled with discretion as well as vigor. Colonel Garrard with his regiment of cavalry will be ordered to report to the brigade commander and act with the infantry. The main object is a diversion in favor of our cavalry, also to prevent any movement of the enemy's cavalry upon our flank or rear.

Very respectfully, your obedient servant,

J. M. SCHOFIELD,
Major-General, Commanding.

HDQRS. THIRD DIVISION, TWENTY-THIRD ARMY CORPS,
Before Atlanta, July 29, 1864—9.15 a. m.

Maj. J. A. CAMPBELL,
Assistant Adjutant-General, &c.:

SIR: The dispatch of the commanding general is received. I have ordered Colonel Reilly to move out his brigade at once, for the proposed demonstration, taking the road near General Hascall's old front (on 20th instant) leading into the Decatur and Atlanta road, near where the left of the Army of the Tennessee formerly was, thence to the position occupied by me during the night of the 22d, and which is about one mile and a half from Decatur. Here a road runs to the south, and I have directed that after sending a portion of his force into Decatur and clearing it, his principal reconnaissance be pushed by this south road till he finds the enemy's extreme right and fully carries out the instructions of the general's dispatch, keeping communication by flankers (as he may) with our picket-line in the new works made by the Army of the Tennessee. If the commanding general desires to modify these instructions I would like to be informed early. Also where Colonel Garrard will report to Colonel Reilly.

Very respectfully, your obedient servant,

J. D. COX,
Brigadier-General, Commanding.

HEADQUARTERS ARMY OF THE OHIO,
Before Atlanta, Ga., July 29, 1864.

Brig. Gen. J. D. COX,
Commanding Third Division, Twenty-third Army Corps:

GENERAL: The commanding general directs me to acknowledge the receipt of your dispatch of 9.15 a. m., and to inform you that Colonel Garrard has been ordered to report to Colonel Reilly on the Atlanta and Decatur road. Your instructions to Colonel Reilly will not be modified at present.

Very respectfully, your obedient servant,

J. A. CAMPBELL,
Major and Assistant Adjutant-General.

HDQRS. THIRD DIVISION, TWENTY-THIRD ARMY CORPS,
Before Atlanta, July 29, 1864.

Maj. J. A. CAMPBELL,
Assistant Adjutant-General, Army of the Ohio:

MAJOR: I have the honor to hand you copies of dispatches* sent Colonel Cameron yesterday. Immediately after receiving the order from corps headquarters in the night of the 27th I sent Colonel Cameron a copy, simply directing him to make the reconnaissance in accordance with it. I then sent dispatch No. 1 to him at 5 o'clock in the morning. Between 7 and 8 I was myself near the batteries occupied by our troops in the old line, and hearing only a little skirmishing toward the right of his line of skirmishers, I sent my aide, Lieutenant Coughlan, with verbal directions to Colonel Cameron to push his advanced regiment more vigorously, and if the resistance was, as it seemed, chiefly on his right, to make the movement take that direction, moving up his supports from the works, and holding them well in hand to press the enemy, or to cover a retreat if his advance should meet a force greater than the whole of his. He appeared unwilling, as Mr. Coughlan reports, to receive any verbal instructions, saying he already had his orders in writing. After waiting more than an hour after Lieutenant Coughlan's return, and hearing no lively skirmishing, I sent dispatch No. 2, and a little later urged the same in person on Colonel Cameron's coming himself to report progress.

Very respectfully, your obedient servant,

J. D. COX,
Brigadier-General, Commanding Division.

* See p. 286.

HEADQUARTERS ARMY OF THE OHIO,
Before Atlanta, Ga., July 29, 1864.

Col. ISRAEL GARRARD, *Commanding Seventh Ohio Cavalry:*

COLONEL: Colonel Reilly, commanding brigade, Third Division, Twenty-third Army Corps, has been ordered to make a vigorous demonstration upon the enemy's extreme right. The object is a diversion in favor of our cavalry and also to prevent any movement of the enemy's cavalry upon our flank or rear. The commanding general directs that you report with your regiment to Colonel Reilly and act with the infantry. Colonel Reilly's brigade is now moving toward Decatur on the Atlanta and Decatur road, and you will report to him on the road.

Very respectfully, your obedient servant,

J. A. CAMPBELL,
Major and Assistant Adjutant-General.

HDQRS. FIRST BRIGADE, CAVALRY CORPS,
Near General Stanley's Line, outside the Skirmish Line,
July 29, 1864.

Major CAMPBELL,
Assistant Adjutant-General, Army of the Ohio:

MAJOR: I have the honor to report that the scouting party under Captain Rankin, Seventh Ohio Volunteer Cavalry, which has just returned from Decatur, reports no enemy in that direction, and none have passed through since the cavalry force that followed General Stoneman. The report of citizens, negroes, and the condition of the roads since the rain of day before yesterday, all sustain the correctness of this report.

Very respectfully, your obedient servant,

ISRAEL GARRARD,
Colonel, Commanding.

SHERMAN'S HEADQUARTERS,
July 29, 1864.

General SCHOFIELD:

Send me the names of two colonels—names you want made brigadier-generals. Keep things active on your front and flank. The utmost activity should be kept up till our cavalry is heard from. Thomas will make a strong demonstration toward East Point with two divisions of his reserve.

W. T. SHERMAN,
Major-General.

HEADQUARTERS DEPARTMENT OF THE TENNESSEE,
July 29, 1864.

Major-General SHERMAN:

I have reliable information that Hardee is making a movement of some kind and some indications that he is trying to place his force between me and Turner's Ferry. What is the extent of General Thomas' demonstration on my right, and when will it take place?

O. O. HOWARD,
Major-General.

HDQRS. MILITARY DIVISION OF THE MISSISSIPPI,
In the Field, near Atlanta, Ga., July 29, 1864.

General HOWARD:

General Thomas' demonstration will be with two divisions, and should be progressing now. I will inquire of him when it started. If we discern such a move you can let go your lines and throw your force with Thomas' reserves between Hardee and Atlanta. I think you will find it an infantry force to interpose between our cavalry, which is out, and its return. But it will not return that way.

W. T. SHERMAN,
Major-General, Commanding.

HDQRS. MILITARY DIVISION OF THE MISSISSIPPI,
In the Field, near Atlanta, Ga., July 29, 1864.

General HOWARD:

Avail yourself of the good opportunity of General Thomas' reconnaissance in force to push your vedettes well out toward White Hall. Secure the enemy's dead, count them, and have them buried. Our cavalry operations must now be presumed to be felt.

W. T. SHERMAN,
Major-General, Commanding.

HEADQUARTERS DEPARTMENT OF THE TENNESSEE,
July 29, 1864.

Major-General SHERMAN:

General Thomas occupies a good position across the Sandtown road, masking the Fifteenth Army Corps. If desirable, I can move forward in the morning, relieving General Thomas so that he can extend his lines still farther.

O. O. HOWARD,
Major-General.

HDQRS. MILITARY DIVISION OF THE MISSISSIPPI,
In the Field, near Atlanta, Ga., July 29, 1864.

General HOWARD:

You may extend to the front and right toward East Point as much as possible, and General Thomas will also continue in the same direction. I think we can draw the enemy out of Atlanta or force him to the attack, which is to be desired. I will be over to-morrow.

W. T. SHERMAN,
Major-General, Commanding.

HOWARD'S HEADQUARTERS,
July 29, 1864.

General SHERMAN:

My officers and scouts report no enemy toward the west, nor between me and Turner's Ferry.

O. O. HOWARD,
Major-General.

HDQRS. MILITARY DIVISION OF THE MISSISSIPPI,
In the Field, near Atlanta, Ga., July 29, 1864.

General HOWARD:

Telegraph me the names of three colonels that you want made briga-dier-generals. Go on and strengthen your position. Study its roads and front. General Thomas will make a strong demonstration on your right.

W. T. SHERMAN,
Major-General, Commanding.

HDQRS. SECOND DIVISION, FIFTEENTH ARMY CORPS,
Near Atlanta, Ga., July 29, 1864.

Brig. Gen. GILES A. SMITH,
Comdg. Fourth Division, Seventeenth Army Corps:

The general commanding thanks you for the assistance rendered him yesterday by sending to his support the Fifteenth Iowa and Thirty-second Ohio Regiments, under command of Col. William W. Belknap.

The general also thanks Colonel Belknap and his brave men for the efficient manner in which they performed their duty.

By order of Brig. Gen. M. L. Smith:

G. LOFLAND,
Assistant Adjutant-General.

HEADQUARTERS LEFT WING, SIXTEENTH ARMY CORPS,
Before Atlanta, Ga., July 29, 1864.

Brig. Gen. J. M. CORSE,
Comdg. Second Division, Sixteenth Army Corps:

GENERAL: You will immediately relieve a regiment of General Ful-ler's command immediately on your right with a regiment of General Rice's brigade now in reserve. You will hold Lieutenant-Colonel Phil-lips' command in reserve ready to move at a moment's warning, should occasion require.

By order of Maj. Gen. G. M. Dodge:

GEO. C. TICHENOR,
Lieutenant and Aide-de-Camp.

HDQRS. SECOND DIVISION, SIXTEENTH ARMY CORPS,
In the Field, near Atlanta, Ga., July 29, 1864.

Brig. Gen. E. W. RICE,
Commanding First Brigade:

The general commanding desires you to push forward your skirmish line for the purpose of ascertaining what is in your front, observing due caution.

Very respectfully, your obedient servant,

L. H. EVERTS,
Assistant Adjutant-General.

Hdqrs. Second Brig., Third Div., 15th Army Corps,
Resaca, Ga., July 29, 1864.

Maj. S. B. Moe,
   Assistant Adjutant-General:

Major : A detachment of the Third Kentucky Cavalry, under the command of Captain Cummings, numbering 250 men, returned from Pickens County to-day, having been out seven days. They engaged Jordan's band of guerrillas, killing 9 and wounding 4; the latter made good their escape. Pickens County is thoroughly loyal. Nearly 1,000 persons met at Jasper to congratulate our troops upon their success. A company of home guards, numbering 128, was raised on the spot. A delegation of five waited on me to-day and applied for arms. I believe I can arm 400 loyal men in Gordon, Pickens, Gilmer, and Murray Counties. I respectfully request that arms be obtained for this purpose at the earliest practicable moment.

Very respectfully, your obedient servant,

GREEN B. RAUM,
Colonel, Commanding Brigade.

Before Atlanta, Ga., *July 29, 1864—10.30 p. m.*

Maj. T. T. Eckert :

Two divisions of the Army of the Cumberland went to right to-day, and Thomas has put them in position. Says united testimony of all his generals is that enemy holds Atlanta with mere shell of an army. Stoneman heard from at Fayetteville. Successful so far. Six hundred and forty-two dead rebels counted and buried by Logan to-day. They must have lost 3,000 at least, while Logan's entire casualties are less than 500. We look for decisive action to-morrow. No fears of result.

J. C. VAN DUZER.

Special Field Orders, }   Hdqrs. Army of the Ohio,
   No. 65.   }   *Before Atlanta, Ga., July 29, 1864.*

*   *   *   *   *   *   *

II. The commanding general takes pleasure in announcing to the troops of this command the result of the engagement of yesterday. The enemy repeatedly attacked, with great vigor and in heavy force, the Army of the Tennessee, commanded, since the death of the lamented General McPherson, by General Howard. At every point the enemy was repulsed with tremendous slaughter, our forces capturing several stand of colors and a number of prisoners. The rebels did not lose less than 10,000 in killed, wounded, and prisoners, while our loss did not exceed 2,000. Our victory was complete.

By command of Major-General Schofield:

J. A. CAMPBELL,
Major and Assistant Adjutant-General.

Special Field Orders, }   Headquarters Department
                       }   and Army of the Tennessee,
   No. 82.   }   *Before Atlanta, Ga., July 29, 1864.*

*   *   *   *   *   *   *

IV. Maj. Gen. G. M. Dodge, commanding Left Wing, Sixteenth Army Corps, will reduce his command to one good line, keeping not more than one brigade as a reserve, relieving a portion of General Blair's left.

Maj. Gen. F. P. Blair, commanding Seventeenth Army Corps, will diminish his command to one line also, not holding more than one brigade as a reserve, relieving a portion of General Logan's left.

Maj. Gen. John A. Logan, commanding Fifteenth Army Corps, will then complete his line of works to his right. The object being to extend the line as far as possible to the right, the intrenchments will be made strong and ground cleared well to the front. Corps commanders will report the execution of this order of the completion of their line.

*   *   *   *   *   *   *

XI. Corps commanders will be prepared at 8 a. m. to-morrow to move their commands forward, in order to extend our lines as far to the right as possible and relieve the troops of Major-General Thomas' command, now occupying a position on our right flank.

By order of Maj. Gen. O. O. Howard:

WM. T. CLARK,
Assistant Adjutant-General.

WAR DEPARTMENT,
July 30, 1864.

Maj. Gen. W. T. SHERMAN,
Commanding, &c., before Atlanta, Ga.:

Cols. William Grose, Thirty-sixth Indiana; Charles C. Walcutt, Forty-Sixth Ohio; James W. Reilly, One hundred and fourth Ohio; Luther P. Bradley, Fifty-first Illinois; John W. Sprague, Sixty-third Ohio; Joseph A. Cooper, Sixth Tennessee; John T. Croxton, Fourth Kentucky, and William W. Belknap, Fifteenth Iowa Volunteers, were this day appointed brigadier-generals of volunteers. The appointments will be forwarded without delay

JAS. A. HARDIE,
Colonel and Inspector-General.

HDQRS. MILITARY DIVISION OF THE MISSISSIPPI,
In the Field, near Atlanta, Ga., July 30, 1864.
(Received 9.45 p. m.)

Col. JAMES A. HARDIE,
Inspector-General, Washington, D. C.:

Be pleased to convey my thanks to the President for his prompt bestowal of the appointments as brigadier-generals on the eight most worthy colonels named in your dispatch to-day.

W. T. SHERMAN,
Major-General, Commanding.

HDQRS. MILITARY DIVISION OF THE MISSISSIPPI,
In the Field, near Atlanta, Ga., July 30, 1864.

General THOMAS:

Send two or three of your best scouts across to the west bank of the Chattahoochee, and down till they come to where General McCook crossed with his pontoons. Ascertain if the bridge is still down and guarded, and how guarded, and with orders to send us back word and news from our cavalry.

W. T. SHERMAN,
Major-General, Commanding.

HDQRS. MILITARY DIVISION OF THE MISSISSIPPI,
In the Field, near Atlanta, Ga., July 30, 1864.

General THOMAS:

I am starting for General Howard's headquarters. Any message for me will reach me there. I have ordered Captain Poe to examine and select a line as a left flank in case I have to throw General Schofield on the right.

W. T. SHERMAN,
Major-General, Commanding.

SHERMAN'S HEADQUARTERS,
July 30, 1864.

General THOMAS:

Our right is too much refused to be a threat. I will go to Schofield's to-morrow and examine a point near Stanley's left to see what chance to break in there. As soon as the cavalry returns I will probably throw Schofield over, and in the mean time want that flank well studied. I would like to have you go to Davis' division and cause a bold reconnaissance over toward East Point.

W. T. SHERMAN,
Major-General.

CONFIDENTIAL.]   HEADQUARTERS FOURTH ARMY CORPS,
Near Atlanta, Ga., July 30, 1864—2 p. m.

Colonel GROSE,
Commanding First Division, Fourth Army Corps:

COLONEL: The requirements of the service may render it necessary for the divisions of this corps to extend and still further thin out their lines. To prepare for this, which may occur to-morrow, all of the men with tools will be put to work at once to strengthen our present defenses. The parapets are deemed sufficiently strong already, and additional strength can be best given by increasing our abatis and fastening it to the ground by strong cross stakes; the cutting and tangling of brushwood, to give a better range and increased obstacle, will be particularly attended to. The passages to the front through the abatis must only be, in number, one to each battalion, and only wide enough for a single file.

By order of Major-General Stanley:

J. S. FULLERTON,
Assistant Adjutant-General.

(Same to Generals Newton and Wood.)

HEADQUARTERS DEPARTMENT OF THE CUMBERLAND,
In the Field, July 30, 1864.

Maj. Gen. J. M. PALMER, *Commanding Fourteenth Army Corps:*

GENERAL: The following copy of a telegram* just received from Major-General Sherman is sent you for your information. You will please give General Davis the necessary orders to carry the order contained therein into execution.

Yours, very respectfully,

WM. D. WHIPPLE,
Assistant Adjutant-General.

----

* See above, beginning, "Our right is too much refused," &c.

HDQRS. FIRST DIVISION, FOURTEENTH ARMY CORPS,
Near Atlanta, Ga., July 30, 1864.

Capt. A. C. MCCLURG,
Assistant Adjutant-General, Fourteenth Corps:

CAPTAIN: Please say to General Palmer that Colonel Taylor, in charge of the picket-line, has just come in, and reports the line strongly intrenched. He says there is an elegant place for a section of artillery at the point on the railroad at which my left rests. The embrasures of the rebel work are in full view. Guns placed there would have to be sunk or otherwise strongly protected. The men at work on the skirmish line were subjected to a pretty heavy fire from the rebel fort, though not one single man was killed or wounded.

Respectfully, your obedient servant,

R. W. JOHNSON,
Brigadier-General.

HEADQUARTERS,
Myers' House, July 30, 1864.

Captain MCCLURG,
Assistant Adjutant-General, Fourteenth Army Corps:

CAPTAIN: I have the honor to report everything quiet on General Morgan's front last night; little firing on the skirmish line. Morgan is intrenched on the road in advance of Howard's right. Ward is on his right. Generals Thomas and Howard put them in position last evening. Howard is to conform his lines to theirs to-day.

Very respectfully,

JEF. C. DAVIS,
Brigadier-General.

HEADQUARTERS TWENTIETH ARMY CORPS,
Near Atlanta, Ga., July 30, 1864.

Brigadier-General WHIPPLE,
Chief of Staff:

GENERAL: I have the honor to report that I advanced this morning the picket-lines of the corps to the high ground in front of the former line. In front of the First Division nearly the whole of the enemy's pickets were captured by us (about 100 prisoners). Our loss is slight, 4 men wounded. I shall establish the picket-line of the corps on the advanced position gained by us.

I am, general, very respectfully, your obedient servant,

A. S. WILLIAMS,
Brigadier-General, Commanding.

HEADQUARTERS TWENTIETH CORPS,
Near Atlanta, Ga., July 30, 1864.

Brigadier-General GEARY,
Commanding Second Division:

GENERAL: The brigadier-general commanding the corps directs me to inform you that the picket-line of the First Division has been considerably advanced this morning, and that he wishes you to advance the right of your picket-line, if you have not already done so, to connect with it in the advance position. He captured 100 prisoners, with very slight loss to us.

I am, general, very respectfully, your obedient servant,

H. W. PERKINS,
Assistant Adjutant-General.

HEADQUARTERS ARMY OF THE OHIO,
Before Atlanta, Ga., July 30, 1864—6 p. m.

Major-General SHERMAN:

A rebel scouting party which came into Decatur this morning informed the citizens that the railroad had been cut by our cavalry at a place called Jonesborough, as it was understood by Colonel Garrard, who brought the report.

J. M. SCHOFIELD,
Major-General.

(Copy to Thomas and Howard.)

HDQRS. MILITARY DIVISION OF THE MISSISSIPPI,
In the Field, near Atlanta, Ga., July 30, 1864.

General SCHOFIELD:

I am starting for the right. It may become necessary to shift you to the extreme right, in which case our left will be back of Pea Vine Creek, from General Wood's right back to the rebel lines, with a detachment at Buck Head, but this I do not propose till General Garrard is back.

W. T. SHERMAN,
Major-General, Commanding.

HDQRS. MILITARY DIVISION OF THE MISSISSIPPI,
In the Field, near Atlanta, Ga., July 30, 1864.

General SCHOFIELD:

I have been over to the right to-day. Our troops are on the Sandtown road. The enemy must follow that movement, and if they hold a force on your left front, it is only for effect. They will weaken about General Stanley. I will come over to-morrow. I hope to hear of our cavalry to-morrow. When it is back, I will probably shift you over to the right.

W. T. SHERMAN,
Major-General, Commanding.

HEADQUARTERS ARMY OF THE OHIO,
July 30, 1864—8 p. m.

Major-General SHERMAN:

The enemy has shown more force than usual in his main works in my front to-day, and has been erecting a battery a short distance in front of his old works on the railroad bridge, where I pressed him closely on the 28th. Colonel Garrard reports no movement on our left, except a small body of cavalry, which he drove from Decatur this morning.

J. M. SCHOFIELD,
Major-General.

HEADQUARTERS ARMY OF THE OHIO,
July 30, 1864.

Major-General SHERMAN:

I have your dispatch expressing your desire that I advance my picket-line in front of the distillery near the road leading to Atlanta. I tried that on the 28th and found it impracticable, for this reason, viz, the point referred to is in a large re-entering angle of the enemy's works, and the enemy's picket-line in that vicinity is enfiladed by the artillery of both the adjacent salients. Neither the enemy's picket-line, nor even the main curtain in rear, should be held by our troops until those salients are carried. One of them is three-quarters of a mile to my left, and hence beyond my reach. The other is somewhat to my right. I will see General Stanley and ascertain what can be done about this latter salient. Perhaps we can drive in the skirmishers around it and keep down its fire with our sharpshooters.

Respectfully,

J. M. SCHOFIELD,
Major-General.

HDQRS. MILITARY DIVISION OF THE MISSISSIPPI,
In the Field, near Atlanta, Ga., July 30, 1864.

General SCHOFIELD:

Order Colonel Garrard to feel into Decatur again in the morning, and, without seeming anxious, to pick up any further news of our cavalry. Where did General Garrard leave his wagons and lame horses?

W. T. SHERMAN,
Major-General, Commanding.

HEADQUARTERS ARMY OF THE OHIO,
Before Atlanta, Ga., July 30, 1864.

Maj. Gen. W. T. SHERMAN:

I do not know where General Garrard left his wagons and horses. They were not reported to my quartermaster.

J. M. SCHOFIELD,
Major-General.

HEADQUARTERS ARMY OF THE OHIO,
Before Atlanta, Ga., July 30, 1864.

Col. ISRAEL GARRARD,
Commanding Seventh Ohio Cavalry:

COLONEL: The commanding general desires you to feel into Decatur with your regiment to-morrow morning, and, if possible, pick up some information about the movements of our cavalry. Do not appear to be anxious to obtain the information or intimate that we are not already informed of all the movements of Generals Stoneman and Garrard, but find out from the citizens or others where the cavalry is and what it has accomplished. Please report the result of your inquiries as soon as you have procured any reliable information.

Very respectfully, your obedient servant,

J. A. CAMPBELL,
Major and Assistant Adjutant-General.

HEADQUARTERS SEVENTEENTH ARMY CORPS,
In the Field, July 30, 1864.

Lieut. Col. W. T. CLARK,
Assistant Adjutant-General, Dept. and Army of the Tennessee:

COLONEL: I have the honor to report that I have occupied the line designated for this corps, extending from the point previously occupied by the left of my right (Fourth) division to the point on the ridge to the extreme right indicated by Lieutenant-Colonel Strong. Several hours since the men commenced building works, and they are now sufficiently advanced to insure the safety of the men.

Very respectfully, your obedient servant,

FRANK P. BLAIR, JR.,
Major-General, Commanding.

HEADQUARTERS SEVENTEENTH ARMY CORPS,
Before Atlanta, Ga., July 30, 1864.

Capt. L. M. DAYTON,
Aide-de-Camp and Actg. Asst. Adjt. Gen., Mil. Div. of the Miss.:

CAPTAIN: I have the honor to represent that in the recent operations this command has become reduced to about 6,400 effective men. A large number of the officers and men of this corps have been left behind sick and slightly wounded in hospitals at Cairo, Nashville, Louisville, Huntsville, and Rome, and I am satisfied there are many of them ready for the field who have been improperly detailed at these points and at Saint Louis, Mo. I have, therefore, the honor to request that Maj. G. W. Kennard, Twentieth Illinois Infantry Volunteers, may be sent to these points for the purpose of collecting and returning all men fit for duty to this command, with full authority to send to the front all officers and men who, in his opinion, have been improperly detailed or are absent without proper authority from this command. In the recent battles Major Kennard's regiment has been reduced to about twenty-five men, with whom there are two line and one field officer, so that he can easily be spared, and as he is an active and efficient officer, I am satisfied he will be able to collect a large number of men who will otherwise remain as extra nurses and servants to officers.

I am, very respectfully, your obedient servant,

FRANK P. BLAIR, JR.,
Major-General.

HDQRS. MILITARY DIVISION OF THE MISSISSIPPI,
In the Field, near Atlanta, July 30, 1864.

JOHN A. SPOONER, Esq.,
Agent for the Commonwealth of Massachusetts, Nashville:

SIR: Yours from Chattanooga of July 28 is received, notifying me of your appointment by your State as lieutenant-colonel and provost-marshal for Georgia, Alabama, and Mississippi, under the act of Congress approved July 4, 1864, to recruit volunteers to be credited the quotas of the States, respectively. On applying to General Webster at Nashville, he will grant you a pass through our lines to these States, and as I have had considerable experience in those States would suggest recruiting depots to be established at Macon and Columbus, Miss.; Selma, Montgomery, and Mobile, Ala., and Columbus, Milledgeville, and Savannah, Ga.

I do not see that the law restricts you to black recruits, but you are at liberty, I suppose, to collect white recruits also. It is waste of time and money to open rendezvous in Northwest Georgia, for I assure you I have not seen an able-bodied man, black or white, fit for a soldier, who was not in this army or the one opposed to it. You speak of the impression going about that I am opposed to the organization of colored regiments. My opinions are usually very positive, and there is no reason why you should not know them. Though entertaining profound reverence for our Congress, I do doubt their wisdom in the passage of this law, first, because civilian agents about an army are a nuisance; second, the duty of citizens to fight for their country is too sacred a one to be peddled off by buying up the refuse of other States; third, it is unjust to the soldiers and volunteers who are fighting, as those who compose this army are doing, to place them on a par with the class of recruits you are after; fourth, the negro is in a transition state, and is not the equal of the white man; fifth, he is liberated from his bondage by act of war, and the armies in the field are entitled to all his assistance in labor and fighting in addition to the proper quota of the States; sixth, this bidding and bartering for recruits, white and black, has delayed the re-enforcement of our armies at the time when such re-enforcements would have enabled us to make our successes permanent; seventh, the law is an experiment which, pending war, is unwise and unsafe, and has delayed the universal draft which I firmly believe will become necessary to overcome the widespread resistance offered us, and I also believe the universal draft will be wise and beneficent, for, under the providence of God, it will separate the sheep from the goats, and demonstrate what citizens will fight for their country and what will only talk. No one shall infer from this that I am not the friend of the negro as well as the white race. I contend that the treason and rebellion of the master freed the slave, and I and the armies I have commanded have conducted to safe points more negroes than those of any other general officer in the army, but I prefer some negroes as pioneers, teamsters, cooks, and servants; others gradually to experiment in the art of the soldier, beginning with the duties of local garrison, such as we had at Memphis, Vicksburg, Natchez, Nashville, and Chattanooga. But I would not draw on the poor race for too large a proportion of its active, athletic young men, for some must remain to seek new homes and provide for the old and young, the feeble and helpless.

These are some of my peculiar notions, but I assure you they are shared by a large proportion of our fighting men.

You may show this to the agents of the other States in the same business with yourself.

I am, &c.,

W. T. SHERMAN,
Major-General.

(Copy to Generals Thomas, Schofield, Howard, and Webster.)

BEFORE ATLANTA, GA., *July 30, 1864—9 p. m.*

Maj. T. T. ECKERT:

Our line was extended nearly two miles down the Sandtown road to-day without meeting any resistance, and is now intrenched in the new position. The failure of enemy to attack while movement was in progress, and reports of scouts and rebel prisoners that Stoneman had destroyed the railroad at Jonesborough, give rise to rumor of evacuation of Atlanta, which I am inclined to credit the more because of great activity of their artillery until just now.

J. C. VAN DUZER.

Consolidated semi-monthly field return of artillery in the Army of the Ohio for July 30, 1864.

Battery.	Division.	Effective force.				Rounds of ammunition on hand.	Horses.	Casualties.		Loss of horses.
								Men.		
		Officers.	Men.	Guns.	Caissons.			Killed.	Wounded.	
19th Ohio	Second	4	88	4	4	464	60			10
22d Indiana	do	3	111	4	4	204	86		2	5
1st Michigan Artillery, (F).	do	4	96	4	4	734	81	1	2	4
15th Indiana	Third	3	108	4	4	640	74			3
23d Indiana	do	4	117	4	4	445	68			3
1st Ohio Volunteer Light Artillery (D).	do	4	106	4	5	640	72	*a*1	1	
24th Indiana *b*	Cavalry Corps									
Total		22	626	24	25	3,127	441	2	5	25

a Died.
b No report; Cavalry Corps is on an expedition.

I certify that the above report is correct.

G. W. SCHOFIELD,
Lieut. Col. and Chief of Arty. and Ord., Dept. of the Ohio.

GENERAL ORDERS, } WAR DEPT., ADJT. GENERAL'S OFFICE,
No. 238.   }   *Washington, July 30, 1864.*

The following assignments are hereby made:

1. Maj. Gen. O. O. Howard to the command of the Army and Department of the Tennessee.

2. Maj. Gen. H. W. Slocum to the command of the Twentieth Army Corps, vice Major-General Hooker, who is relieved at his own request.

3. Maj. Gen. D. S. Stanley to the command of the Fourth Army Corps, vice Major-General Howard, transferred to the Army and Department of the Tennessee.

By order of the President of the United States:

E. D. TOWNSEND,
Assistant Adjutant-General.

SPECIAL FIELD ORDERS, }   HEADQUARTERS LEFT WING,
                       }   SIXTEENTH ARMY CORPS,
No. 50.   }   *Near Atlanta, Ga., July 30, 1864.*

*   *   *   *   *   *   *

II. The Seventeenth Army Corps are moving to the right, and the Fourth Division will stretch out their line as far as possible and cover the ground left vacant, drawing out troops from the left if necessary.

Second. Brig. Gen. J. M. Corse will stretch out the Second Division and occupy the ground vacated by General Fuller. The movement will be made immediately.

*   *   *   *   *   *   *

By order of Maj. Gen. G. M. Dodge:

J. W. BARNES,
Assistant Adjutant-General.

NEAR ATLANTA, GA., *July 31, 1864—8 p. m.*
(Received 12.15 p. m. August 1.)

Maj. Gen. H. W. HALLECK, *Washington, D. C.:*

No change since my last. Weather has been intensely hot, and to-day it is raining hard. General Garrard's cavalry is back. General Stoneman placed it at Flat Rock to cover his movement south. General Garrard reports the enemy's cavalry all round him for two days, when he charged out and went to Latimar's, where he heard that General Stoneman had passed Covington, so he got two full days' start for Macon. I will not hear of him for some days. From rumors among the people, I think he struck the road, for it is reported broken at Jonesborough. To-morrow night I will move General Schofield to the extreme right and draw the enemy out to East Point. His works are too strong for an assault, and we cannot spare the ammunition for a bombardment.

W. T. SHERMAN,
Major-General.

HDQRS. MILITARY DIVISION OF THE MISSISSIPPI,
In the Field, near Atlanta, Ga., July 31, 1864.

General WEBSTER, *Nashville:*

Many prisoners escaped from the enemy are coming in the lines, whom I pass to you by the general's direction, and you will forward to their regiments, allowing, say, a week's leave at home.

L. M. DAYTON,
Aide-de-Camp.

HEADQUARTERS DEPARTMENT OF THE CUMBERLAND,
Extreme Right, July 31, 1864—9.30 a. m.

Major-General SHERMAN:

GENERAL: I find that General Howard has simply taken up the line occupied by General Morgan on the afternoon of the 29th. If he would straighten his line and intrench it, his right would be much nearer the railroad. Generals Morgan and Ward could have supported his right whilst he was intrenching. Taking up the line he did rendered it necessary for General Morgan to extend his line along the road to Green's Ferry or isolate his command. The reconnaissance has been ordered as you directed, but General Morgan will have to return in consequence of General Howard having taken up his old line instead of extending his, Howard's, line toward the railroad, as I should have thought he would have done.

Respectfully,

GEO. H. THOMAS,
Major-General.

HDQRS. MILITARY DIVISION OF THE MISSISSIPPI,
In the Field, near Atlanta, Ga., July 31, 1864.

General THOMAS:

I have further news of General McCook. The officer who commands the pontoon train is back with his boats at Vining's. At 2 p. m. on Friday General McCook was across at Rivertown with 3,000 men and started out. That night the officer saw large fires in the direction of the railroad. He was ordered to come back to Vining's, with his boat train by General McCook, who expected to come back by a circuit north.

W. T. SHERMAN,
Major-General, Commanding.

(Same to Generals Schofield and Howard.)

———

HEADQUARTERS DEPARTMENT OF THE CUMBERLAND,
July 31, 1864—8 p. m.

Major-General SHERMAN:

I have just returned from the right. General Howard's troops only occupy the intrenchments made by Morgan and Ward, whereas he should have extended his line toward the railroad, throwing out as his intrenchments were completed. Morgan and Ward could then have supported his right as he extended his lines. I think Howard's army will reach very nearly to the railroad when intrenched and thrown out as my troops are. Should Schofield move to the right he will surely reach the road; thus Morgan and Ward can be held in reserve and in support of the right flank as it progresses toward the railroad. The reconnaissance you ordered was made to-day by Morgan. He found the enemy covered by a strong infantry skirmish line with artillery on a road leading direct to East Point from a house on the Green's Ferry road, about a mile from the rear of our right. The troops moved about a mile and a half on that road before encountering the enemy. Morgan returned to his camp toward night, as I did not deem it prudent to have him so far to Howard's right. I think I understand the directions of all the roads leading toward East Point from all points directly in our rear.

GEO. H. THOMAS,
Major-General.

———

HDQRS. MILITARY DIVISION OF THE MISSISSIPPI,
In the Field, near Atlanta, Ga., July 31, 1864.

General THOMAS:

I have your dispatch, which is most satisfactory. I think General Schofield, supported by Generals Davis and Ward, will reach the railroad. At all events, it is our true move. General Garrard's cavalry can occupy General Schofield's lines, and General Stanley's left, refused along Pea Vine, will make good flank, covering Buck Head and the Pace's Ferry road. This will enable you with your main army to press on Atlanta, whilst General Howard advances his right and General Schofield extends, supported by Generals Davis and Ward, will make an army equal to Hood's movable column. I think I appreciate General Garrard's good qualities, but he is so cautious that if forced to make a bold move to the relief of General McCook I doubt if he would attempt it. General Stoneman went with a full knowledge of his risk; but General McCook will have reason to expect co-operation from about McDonough, and may be disappointed when he finds his bridge gone and a new road ahead closed by Wheeler. He has, however, a bold and well-appointed force and can fight his way back; still, for his sake, we must occupy the attention of the enemy as much as possible.

W. T. SHERMAN,
Major-General, Commanding.

HDQRS. MILITARY DIVISION OF THE MISSISSIPPI,
In the Field, near Atlanta, Ga., July 31, 1864.

Generals THOMAS and HOWARD:

A cavalryman, just in, says General Garrard is coming in by the Peach Tree road; had a small fight first day, none since. Says General Stoneman has gone on, so that branch of the raid seems to be doing well. I now want news of General McCook. As soon as General Garrard comes I will order some cavalry down the west bank of the Chattahoochee to see to General McCook's bridge. Though the heat is intense, the time is for a bold reconnaissance and threat about East Point.

W. T. SHERMAN,
Major-General, Commanding.

HDQRS. MILITARY DIVISION OF THE MISSISSIPPI,
In the Field, near Atlanta, Ga., July 31, 1864.

Generals THOMAS and HOWARD:

I am just back from an interview with General Schofield. General Garrard is back. He was sent by General Stoneman to Flat Rock, where he was surrounded by Wheeler's cavalry, but he remained two days, expecting General Stoneman to send him orders, when he broke out to Latimar's, where he heard General Stoneman had gone to Covington and beyond. Not having further orders he came home via the Peach Tree road. His fight was a small affair, losing only 1 officer and 6 men wounded, and riding down one brigade of the enemy. He thinks Wheeler still remains on the right of Atlanta, extending the infantry line. I think General Stoneman has gone to Macon, east of Yellow River, and that it is well. I have ordered General Garrard in on our left, and to-morrow night will let him fill with a skirmish line General Schofield's position, and move all of General Schofield to the right of General Howard, and wish the divisions of Generals Davis and Ward in reserve on the right to strike a blow beyond our new right flank when intrenched. Our right flank must be advanced in close and absolute contact with the enemy, and with General Schofield on that flank I think we can make him quit Atlanta, or so weaken his lines that we can break through somewhere, the same as our Kenesaw move. Study the road so that Generals Schofield and Howard may have a line close up to the enemy, as close as possible. I will send a regiment of cavalry down the west bank of the Chattahoochee to feel for General McCook. I must have a bolder commander for General Garrard's cavalry and want General Thomas to name to me General Kilpatrick or some good brigadier for the command.

W. T. SHERMAN,
Major-General, Commanding.

HEADQUARTERS DEPARTMENT OF THE CUMBERLAND,
July 31, 1864—8.30 p. m.

Major-General SHERMAN:

I do not know of a better cavalry commander in my army than Garrard. He is an excellent administrative officer, and I have no doubt you will find on inquiry that his orders from Stoneman were indefinite. Garrard is much more judicious than Kilpatrick, who can knock up his horses as rapidly as any man I know. I think if you will bear with Garrard you will find in a short time he will be the best cavalry commander you have.

GEO. H. THOMAS,
Major-General.

———

HDQRS. 14TH ARMY CORPS, DEPT. OF THE CUMBERLAND,
July 31, 1864—6 a. m.

Brig. Gen. W. D. WHIPPLE,
Assistant Adjutant-General:

GENERAL: Brigadier-General Davis expressed to Mr. Shaw upon the delivery of the order of the major-general commanding the military division his inability to understand the method of the proposed reconnaissance. He says his division is in line, the enemy being in position about 1,200 yards to his front, and the division of Brigadier-General Ward in position on his right. If he advances it amounts to an assault upon the enemy's position. If he withdraws with a view to passing to General Ward's rear he leaves a gap. As this is the fourth order from the headquarters of the military division imposing special duties upon Davis' division away from his corps, I do not feel at liberty to interfere even by advice; but as he still nominally belongs to the Fourteenth Corps, hope I will be pardoned for acting in the matter so far as to communicate his difficulties and in asking from the proper authority such further and more precise instructions as it may be thought proper to give him.

Very respectfully,

JOHN M. PALMER,
Major-General.

———

HDQRS. MILITARY DIVISION OF THE MISSISSIPPI,
In the Field, near Atlanta, Ga., July 31, 1864.

General SCHOFIELD:

It is going to be terrifically hot, but I must ask you to meet me at 10 a. m. at General Wood's, with your maps and any notes of observations of the enemy's works between your left and General Stanley's center.

W. T. SHERMAN,
Major-General, Commanding.

———

HDQRS. MILITARY DIVISION OF THE MISSISSIPPI,
In the Field, near Atlanta, Ga., July 31, 1864.

General SCHOFIELD:

I have news from General Garrard. He camped eighteen miles from here last night, on the Peach Tree road, and is coming toward Buck

Head now; had a small fight first day; since, nothing. I think I under-stood the man, and that General Stoneman has gone on to Macon and Anderson[ville]; a desperate move, but may succeed for its desperation.

W. T. SHERMAN,
Major-General, Commanding.

HEADQUARTERS ARMY OF THE OHIO,
July 31, 1864.

Major-General SHERMAN:

I had started Colonel Garrard to aid General McCook in recrossing the river. I will order him back now that I know McCook is going the other way.

J. M. SCHOFIELD,
Major-General.

HEADQUARTERS ARMY OF THE OHIO,
In the Field, Ga., July 31, 1864.

Col. ISRAEL GARRARD,
Commanding Seventh Ohio Cavalry:

COLONEL: In compliance with orders from Major-General Sherman, you will move with your regiment across the Chattahoochee at or near the railroad bridge; thence down the west bank of the river to a point (understood to be near Campbellton) where General McCook left his pontoon bridge after crossing the river on his present raid. The object of your expedition is to aid General McCook in recrossing the river on his return. It is understood that General McCook left a regiment of cavalry with his bridge for the above purpose. If you find this to be the case, you will join that regiment and act in concert with it in carrying out General McCook's instructions. In any event, you will watch carefully for General McCook's troops for some distance up and down the river, endeavor to give early information of their return, and learn at what point they propose to cross, so as, if practicable, to have the bridge laid by the time his troops reach the river. You will use your utmost endeavors to assist General McCook's troops in a safe passage of the river. Having completed this duty, you will report for further in-structions at these headquarters.

Very respectfully, your obedient servant,

J. M. SCHOFIELD,
Major-General, Commanding.

HDQRS. FIRST BRIG., CAV. COMMAND, DEPT. OF THE OHIO,
Sunday, July 31, 1864.

Maj. J. A. CAMPBELL,
Assistant Adjutant-General, Army of the Ohio:

I have the honor to report that the most thorough and careful inves-tigation of all the news and reports among the citizens of Decatur has satisfied me that there was a fight of no great importance with the rear of Stoneman's column near Flat Rock, but further than that I do not consider the reports to be entirely reliable. They are all founded on the report brought to a Mrs. Smith by a rebel patrol, Tom Jones, who told her that things were going badly; that Stoneman had left a small force to hold them in check at Flat Rock and had gone across to Jonesborough and destroyed the road for ten miles, and was going on down toward Macon, destroying the road; that on Wednesday the troops in Atlanta had been allowed to plunder the stores and take all the liquors and goods.

Very respectfully, your obedient servant,

ISRAEL GARRARD,
Colonel Seventh Ohio Vol. Cavalry, Commanding Brigade.

There was a vedette (rebel) near the town as we entered it, and while there, some three hours, some ten or twelve showed themselves on the far side of some old fields half a mile beyond our picket. They left when fired on.

I. G.

HEADQUARTERS DEPARTMENT OF THE TENNESSEE,
July 31, 1864.

Major-General SHERMAN:

My skirmishers were pushed forward early this morning and a strong line in front of General Logan in nature of a reconnaissance. General Logan's skirmishers came up on the enemy's line of skirmishers occupying rifle-pits from three-quarters of a mile to a mile from their main works, which can be plainly seen. They appear to be strongly intrenched all the way to my extreme right. Artillery was heard moving out from Atlanta, which stopped in front of General Logan's line. Our vedettes are now close upon the enemy.

O. O. HOWARD,
Major-General.

BEFORE ATLANTA, GA., *July 31, 1864.*

Maj. Gen. W. T. SHERMAN,
Commanding Military Division of the Mississippi:

My scouts find only cavalry pickets of this army beyond our infantry flank. I did not know General Thomas would make a reconnaissance to-day on my right until I heard the firing. Should I take steps to advance prior to General Schofield's arrival, *i. e.*, to close in on the enemy, it can easily be done. Captain Poe took a map with the information as to White Hall, &c., that you required.

O. O. HOWARD,
Major-General.

HDQRS. MILITARY DIVISION OF THE MISSISSIPPI,
In the Field, near Atlanta, Ga., July 31, 1864.

General HOWARD:

I would like to have a line of ground examined in front of what on your topographical maps is called the Asylum, east and south. On studying my maps I think the road by which the enemy came the other day to attack you is the old Sandtown road, and that it passes by White

Hall. White Hall is well fortified, but a point of the railroad between there and East Point is not. I have ordered General Thomas to repeat the reconnaissance toward East Point. I will be with General Schofield to-day.

> W. T. SHERMAN,
> *Major-General.*

HDQRS. MILITARY DIVISION OF THE MISSISSIPPI,
In the Field, near Atlanta, Ga., July 31, 1864.

General HOWARD:

I would like you to advance your right to-morrow from about the meeting-house toward East Point, ready for General Schofield to prolong your line. Generals Davis' and Ward's divisions are at hand to back you. General Thomas has made reconnaissances half a mile toward East Point. I expect both White Hall and East Point are fortified, but there must be a weak point in the long curtain between.

> W. T. SHERMAN,
> *Major-General, Commanding.*

HDQRS. MILITARY DIVISION OF THE MISSISSIPPI,
In the Field, near Atlanta, Ga., July 31, 1864.

General HOWARD:

General Garrard did not destroy any of the railroad. He was posted at Flat Rock by General Stoneman to occupy the attention of the enemy's cavalry, which he (Stoneman) pressed to his rear and south. All we know of the Macon road is from a Colonel Garrard, with General Schofield, who visited Decatur and learned from a woman that the enemy's cavalry had been to Decatur, and reported that our cavalry had got on the road at Jonesborough and burned ten miles of the road and was going on down burning as he went. General Garrard staid two days at Flat Rock; says he was completely surrounded, but cut his way out, though his loss was trifling. The locomotives that are whistling near you may be bagged.

> W. T. SHERMAN,
> *Major-General, Commanding.*

HEADQUARTERS SEVENTEENTH ARMY CORPS,
DEPARTMENT AND ARMY OF THE TENNESSEE,
Before Atlanta, Ga., July 31, 1864.

Capt. L. M. DAYTON,
A. D. C. and A. A. G., Military Division of the Mississippi:

CAPTAIN: The following regiments and detachments were detailed from this corps to take part in the Red River expedition, under General A. J. Smith, viz, Third Iowa Infantry Volunteers, Forty-first Illinois Infantry Volunteers, Eighty-first Illinois Infantry Volunteers, Ninety-fifth Illinois Infantry Volunteers, Fourteenth Wisconsin Infantry Volunteers, Thirty-third Wisconsin Infantry Volunteers, Fifty-eighth Ohio Infantry Volunteers. I heard unofficially that upon their return to the Mississippi River they were ordered to rejoin this corps, but were detained at Memphis to take part in the recent operations of General A. J. Smith in Mississippi. Learning that this expedition has accomplished its purpose and has returned to Memphis, I have the honor to request that if consistent with the interests of the public service, these regiments and detachments may be ordered to rejoin this command without delay.

Very respectfully, your obedient servant,

FRANK P. BLAIR, JR.,
Major-General.

CARTERSVILLE, GA., *July 31, 1864.*

Lieut. D. F. How,
Acting Assistant Adjutant-General:

Captain Estes has just returned from a scout in the direction of Frogtown. He captured 60 mules, 15 horses, brought in 40 sides of harness leather, and killed 5 of Jordan's guerrillas. All quiet throughout the entire country.

J. KILPATRICK,
Brigadier-General.

SPECIAL FIELD ORDERS, } HDQRS. ARMY OF THE OHIO,
No. 67. } *Before Atlanta, Ga., July 31, 1864.*

* * * * * * *

V. To-morrow, the 1st of August, all empty supply trains will be sent to the depot, and all other trains in rear of the Army of the Cumberland near the railroad, and be parked at a point to be selected by the chief quartermaster. The field hospitals will also be moved to-morrow to some point in rear of the center of the Army of the Cumberland. All practicable preparations will be made to withdraw the troops from their present position on the left at dark to-morrow evening, but special care must be observed to avoid doing anything within view of the enemy which might indicate that such movement is contemplated. Further orders relative to the movement will be issued to-morrow.

* * * * * * *

By command of Major-General Schofield:

J. A. CAMPBELL,
Major and Assistant Adjutant-General.

SPECIAL FIELD ORDERS, } HDQRS. FIFTEENTH ARMY CORPS,
No. 65. } *Before Atlanta, Ga., July 31, 1864.*

I. In pursuance of Special Field Orders, No. 46, dated headquarters Military Division of the Mississippi, July 30, 1864, Brig. Gen. Charles C. Walcutt, U. S. Volunteers, is hereby assigned to the command of the Second Brigade, Fourth Division, and will report accordingly to Brig. Gen. William Harrow, commanding Fourth Division.

* * * * * * *

By order of Maj. Gen. John A. Logan:

R. R. TOWNES,
Assistant Adjutant-General.

Abstract from returns of the Department of the Cumberland, Maj. Gen. George H. Thomas, U. S. Army, commanding, for the month of July, 1864.

[Compiled mainly from subordinate returns.]

Command.	Present for duty.		Aggregate present.	Aggregate present and absent.	Pieces of artillery.		Headquarters.
	Officers.	Men.			Heavy.	Field.	
General headquarters	50	384	465	550			In the Field, Ga.
Fourth Army Corps (Stanley):							
Headquarters	7		7	8			Near Atlanta, Ga.
First Division (Grose)	313	5,368	6,782	11,502			Do.
Second Division (Newton)	248	3,085	4,086	10,579			Do.
Third Division (Wood)	266	3,847	4,945	10,955			Do.
Artillery (Bridges)	21	826	897	1,124		35	Do.
Total Fourth Army Corps.	855	13,126	16,717	34,168		35	
Fourteenth Army Corps (Palmer):							
Headquarters	6		6	6			Near Atlanta, Ga.
First Division (Johnson)	295	6,050	7,269	12,814			Do.
Second Division (Davis)	253	5,227	6,129	10,354			Do.
Third Division (Baird)	303	5,604	6,674	11,561			Do.
Artillery (Houghtaling)	18	675	738	916		34	Do.
Total Fourteenth Army Corps.	875	17,556	20,816	35,651		34	
Twentieth Army Corps (Williams):							
Headquarters	16	70	86	97			Near Atlanta, Ga.
First Division (Knipe)	270	4,299	5,344	9,604			Do.
Second Division (Geary)	168	3,070	3,989	8,712			Do.
Third Division (Ward)	228	4,145	5,386	10,005			Do.
Artillery (Reynolds)	23	734	826	1,014		36	Do.
Total Twentieth Army Corps.*	705	12,318	15,631	29,432		36	
Cavalry Corps (Elliott):							
Headquarters	7		7	8			
First Division (McCook)	161	2,975	3,916	7,985		4	
Second Division (Garrard)	177	4,087	5,044	9,852		6	
Third Division (Kilpatrick)	181	3,699	4,509	7,361		4	
Fourth Division (Thornburgh).	129	2,953	3,537	5,140		8	
Detached (Palmer)	20	337	428	681			
Total Cavalry Corps	675	14,051	17,441	31,027		22	
Reserve Brigade (Le Favour)	29	795	1,003	1,532			Near Atlanta, Ga.
Post of Chattanooga (Stanley)	92	2,075	2,589	3,761	16	66	
Veteran Reserve Corps (Gazzam)	17	446	923	1,011			Nashville, Tenn.
Engineer Troops:							
Engineer Brigade (Culver)	69	1,342	1,794	2,219			Lookout Mountain.
Pioneer Brigade (O'Connell)							
1st Michigan Engineers (Innes).	43	1,006	1,653	1,789			Cartersville, Ga.
Total engineer troops	112	2,348	3,447	4,008			
Unassigned Troops:							
Infantry	98	2,258	2,905	3,277			Cartersville and Rome, Ga., and Chattanooga, Tenn.
Artillery†	20	640	695	873		35	
Total unassigned	118	2,898	3,600	4,150		35	

* The Fourth Division reported at Nashville, Tenn.

† At Bridgeport, Stevenson, Tullahoma, and near Atlanta.

Abstract from returns of the Department of the Cumberland, &c.—Continued.

Command.	Present for duty.		Aggregate present.	Aggregate present and absent.	Pieces of artillery.		Headquarters.
	Officers.	Men.			Heavy.	Field.	
District of Tennessee (Rousseau):							
Headquarters..................	3	....	3	3	....	....	Nashville, Tenn.
First Brigade, Fourth Division, Twentieth Army Corps (Doolittle).	75	2,054	2,612	3,072	....	....	Do.
Unassigned regiments, Fourth Division, Twentieth Army Corps.	131	3,140	4,066	4,912	....	....	Do.
9th Ohio and 20th Indiana Batteries.	7	245	272	313	....	12	Do.
Nashville (Miller)	89	1,940	2,381	3,101	14	48	
Fort Donelson (Brott)........	1	127	140	163	......	6	
Gallatin (J. K. Miller).......	3	120	134	150	......	6	
Clarksville (Smith)	1	98	139	161	......	6	
Nashville and North Western Railroad (Gillem).	87	2,018	2,869	3,117	......	6	Nashville.
Nashville and Chattanooga Railroad (Milroy).	162	3,933	4,668	4,959	29	28	Tullahoma.
District of Northern Alabama (Granger).	174	4,220	5,168	5,856	......	12	Decatur, Ala.
Total District of Tennessee.	733	17,895	22,452	25,807	43	124	
Grand total	4,261	83,892	105,084	171,097	59	352	
Grand total according to monthly return of the department.	4,275	83,957	105,140	171,036	32	318	

Abstract from returns of the Department of the Tennessee, Maj. Gen. Oliver O. Howard, U. S. Army, commanding, for the month of July, 1864

[Compiled mainly from subordinate returns.]

Command.	Present for duty.		Aggregate present.	Aggregate present and absent.	Pieces of artillery.		Headquarters.
	Officers.	Men.			Heavy.	Field.	
General headquarters*	24	20	83	114	....	....	Near Atlanta, Ga.
Fifteenth Army Corps (Logan):							
Headquarters.................	11	34	47	48	....	....	Near Atlanta, Ga.
First Division (Woods)......	220	3,044	4,101	6,643	......	10	Do.
Second Division (M. L. Smith)	167	2,454	3,413	6,411	......	7	Do.
Third Division (J. E. Smith).	255	4,757	6,017	7,610	......	10	Cartersville, Ga.
Fourth Division (Harrow)...	144	3,198	4,078	7,310	......	10	Near Atlanta, Ga.
Total Fifteenth Army Corps.	797	13,487	17,656	28,022	......	37	
Sixteenth Army Corps:							
Headquarters.................	4	....	4	4	....	....	Memphis, Tenn.
Left Wing (Dodge):							
Headquarters............	10	27	39	40	....	....	In the Field, Ga.
Second Division (Corse)..	205	4,770	6,171	8,954	......	10	Near Atlanta, Ga.
Fourth Division (Fuller).	192	4,620	5,534	8,698	5	16	Do.
U. S. Colored Infantry (Campbell).	42	916	1,260	1,930	......	....	Athens, Ala.
Cavalry (Spencer)	25	427	533	756	....	....	In the Field.
Total Left Wing.......	474	10,760	13,537	20,378	5	26	

* Includes detachment Signal Corps and Fourth Independent Company Ohio Cavalry.

Abstract from returns of the Department of the Tennessee, &c.—Continued.

Command.	Present for duty.		Aggregate present.	Aggregate present and absent.	Pieces of artillery.		Headquarters.
	Officers.	Men.			Heavy.	Field.	
Sixteenth Army Corps—Cont'd.							
Right Wing (A. J. Smith):							
Headquarters............	2	....	2	2	......	......	Memphis, Tenn.
First Division (Mower)..	183	3,950	5,076	9,672	......	14	Do.
Third Division (Shaw) ..	220	4,603	5,765	9,376	......	20	Do.
Brigade U. S. Colored Troops (Bouton).	91	2,525	3,447	3,719	......	6	Do.
Brigade Seventeenth Army Corps* (Ward).	......	....	......	......	......	......	
Total Right Wing.....	496	11,078	14,290	22,769	......	40	
Total Sixteenth Army Corps.	974	21,838	27,831	43,151	5	66	
District of West Tennessee (Washburn):							
Headquarters...............	4	....	4	4	......	......	Memphis, Tenn.
District of Memphis (Buckland).	458	8,952	12,326	14,172	102	4	Do.
Division Seventeenth Army Corps (J. B. Moore).	57	1,288	1,658	2,784	......	......	Do.
Cavalry Division (Grierson).	287	8,367	11,004	14,527	......	6	Do.
District of Western Kentucky (Paine).	225	4,909	6,441	7,231	28	7	Paducah, Ky.
Total District of West Tennessee.	1,031	23,516	31,433	38,718	130	17	
Seventeenth Army Corps (Blair):							
Headquarters..............	21	18	42	51	......	......	Before Atlanta, Ga.
First Division (Dennis)......	79	2,152	2,672	4,440	......	......	Morganza, La.
Third Division (Leggett)....	141	3,085	3,894	7,063	......	14	Before Atlanta, Ga.
Fourth Division (G. A. Smith)	147	3,480	4,248	6,759	......	23	Do.
Total Seventeenth Army Corps.	388	8,735	10,856	18,313	......	37	
District of Vicksburg (Slocum):							
Headquarters............	11	....	11	12	......	......	Vicksburg, Miss.
First Division (Dennis)†.....	......	....	......	......	......	......	
Maltby's brigade	47	1,420	1,938	3,059	......	12	Do.
Colored troops (Hawkins) ...	208	3,901	5,335	6,043	......	8	Do.
Cavalry (Kerr)...............	82	2,034	2,953	3,314	......	......	Do.
Detachments U. S. Colored Infantry (Thomas).	8	239	373	423	......	......	Davis' Bend, Miss.
Defenses of Natchez, Miss. (Brayman).	120	3,600	4,782	5,766	......	......	
Mississippi Marine Brigade (Ellet).	29	679	895	1,289	......	......	
Total District of Vicksburg.	505	11,873	16,287	19,906	......	20	
Grand total Department of the Tennessee.	3,719	79,469	104,146	148,224	135	177	
Grand total according to monthly return of the department.	3,618	75,683	97,545	141,306	68	150	

* Reported in District of West Tennessee with division Seventeenth Army Corps, under Colonel Moore.

† Reported in Seventeenth Army Corps.

Abstract from returns of the Department of the Ohio, Maj. Gen. John M. Schofield, U. S. Army, commanding, for the month of July, 1864.

[Compiled mainly from subordinate returns.]

Command.	Present for duty.		Aggregate present.	Aggregate present and absent.	Pieces of artillery.		Headquarters.
	Officers.	Men.			Heavy.	Field.	
General headquarters.............	46	....	46	46	......	......	In the Field, Ga.
Twenty-third Army Corps (Schofield):							
Headquarters.................	14	62	76	77	......	......	In the Field, Ga.
First Division*............							
Second Division (Hascall)...	291	5,141	6,523	11,902	......	......	Near Atlanta, Ga.
Third Division (Cox)........	314	6,943	8,195	13,688	......	......	In the Field, Ga.
Fourth Division (Ammen)...	161	3,689	5,071	7,331	......	89	Knoxville, Tenn.
Fifth Division† (Burbridge)..	428	8,414	10,512	15,116	16	70	Lexington, Ky.
Cavalry Corps‡ (Stoneman)..	214	4,490	5,425	7,619	......	......	In the Field, Ga.
Heavy artillery (Gibson).....	44	1,314	1,587	1,818	......	......	Cleveland, Tenn.
Engineer troops§ (McClure)							
Total Twenty-third Army Corps.	1,466	30,053	37,387	57,551	16	159	
Grand total Department of the Ohio.	1,512	30,053	37,433	57,597	16	159	
Grand total according to monthly return of the department.	1,430	29,755	36,969	56,220	(‖)	(‖)	

Abstract from returns of the District of Kentucky (or Fifth Division, Twenty-third Army Corps), Maj. Gen. Stephen G. Burbridge, U. S. Army, commanding, for the month of July, 1864.

Command.	Present for duty.		Aggregate present.	Aggregate present and absent.	Pieces of artillery.		Headquarters.
	Officers.	Men.			Heavy.	Field.	
General headquarters.............	......	......	......	......	......	......	Lexington, Ky.
First Division (McLean):							
Headquarters.................	3	....	3	4	......	......	Lexington, Ky.
First Brigade (Hobson).......	100	1,930	2,200	2,727	......	2	Lebanon, Ky.
Second Brigade (J. M. Brown)	52	972	1,139	1,492	......	......	Lexington, Ky.
Third Brigade (Hanson)	54	1,459	1,982	2,673	......	8	Mount Sterling, Ky.
Fourth Brigade (Ratliff)......	60	1,236	1,600	2,417	8	7	Lexington, Ky.
Camp Nelson, Ky. (Fry)	76	1,035	1,316	1,501	......	......	
Pieces of artillery¶.........	......	......	......	......	71	32	
Total First Division........	345	6,632	8,240	10,814	79	49	
Second Division (Ewing):							
Headquarters.................	2	....	2	2	......	......	Louisville, Ky.
First Brigade (Fairleigh)	52	1,199	1,475	2,761	4	27	Louisville, &c., Ky.
Second Brigade (Grider)......	29	583	795	1,539	4	26	Bowling Green, Ky.
Total Second Division......	83	1,782	2,272	4,302	8	53	
Total District of Kentucky.	428	8,414	10,512	15,116	87	102	

* Troops temporarily assigned to Second and Third Divisions, Twenty-third Army Corps.

† District of Kentucky. No return of district found. Only returns of First and Second divisions.

‡ Compiled from tri-monthly report of July 20.

§ Composed of infantry details, and accounted for with their regiments.

‖ Pieces of artillery not accounted for.

¶ In fortifications at Covington, Camp Nelson, Frankfort, Paris, and Louisa, Ky.

NEAR ATLANTA, GA., *August 1, 1864—8 p. m.*
(Received 1.30 p. m. 2d.)
Maj. Gen. H. W. HALLECK,
Washington, D. C.:

Colonel Brownlow reports from Marietta that he has just reached there, having escaped from a disaster that overtook General McCook's cavalry expedition at Newnan. He reports the expedition reached the railroad and destroyed more road than the rebels can repair in fifteen days, and burned 500 baggage wagons, including the headquarters trains of the rebel army, but was overtaken at Newnan by rebel cavalry and infantry, and after a hard fight had to surrender. Colonel Harrison was killed.* I can hardly believe it, as he had 3,000 picked cavalry. Colonel Brownlow commanded one of the regiments, and brought in with him but few men. I have sent for him from Marietta, to inquire more closely into the matter. I have reported General Garrard's safe return. General Stoneman used him as a cover to get a good start, so that he will probably reach Macon, and it may be Andersonville, but will have to run the gauntlet to get back safe. The loss of this cavalry is a serious one to me, but we are pushing the enemy close. Considerable re-enforcements of militia and dismounted cavalry have reached Atlanta, under Stephen D. Lee.

W. T. SHERMAN,
Major-General.

NEAR ATLANTA, GA., *August 1, 1864—10 p. m.*
(Received 1 p. m. 2d.)
Maj. Gen. H. W. HALLECK,
Washington, D. C.:

Colonel Brownlow is here and reports that General McCook proceeded according to his orders, and reached the Macon railroad and destroyed twelve miles and a bridge over a branch of White Water, which, he says, is as long as that over Chattahoochee. He also destroyed 500 wagons, among them the headquarters wagons of Hood and Hardee. Unfortunately, instead of completing the circuit by the east and north, he then turned back and commenced breaking up the West Point road, about Newnan, when he was attacked by infantry and cavalry in overwhelming force, and Brownlow says all were killed or captured, except such as cut their way out. Nearly 500 are now back in Marietta, and he thinks more will get in. Colonel Brownlow's account is not yet satisfactory to me, but is the best I can get.

W. T. SHERMAN,
Major-General.

HDQRS. MILITARY DIVISION OF THE MISSISSIPPI,
In the Field, near Atlanta, Ga., August 1, 1864.
General WEBSTER,
Nashville:

I am afraid that General McCook's command of cavalry, 3,000 strong, has been caught and captured at Newnan, after having broken the railroad and burned 300 wagons of the enemy; so Colonel Brownlow reports by telegraph from Marietta, he having escaped. Order General

---
*A mistake; he was captured.

Burbridge, in Kentucky, and General Rousseau, to send me all the cavalry that can possibly be spared, as the enemy will surely be on our railroad very soon.

> W. T. SHERMAN,
> *Major-General, Commanding.*

HEADQUARTERS DEPARTMENT OF THE CUMBERLAND,
August 1, 1864.

Major-Generals SHERMAN and HOWARD:

The firing you have heard was from the skirmishers in Palmer's and Williams' lines, driving in the rebel pickets. They have been driven into their intrenchments and are now held there by our sharpshooters.

> GEO. H. THOMAS,
> *Major-General.*

HDQRS. MILITARY DIVISION OF THE MISSISSIPPI,
In the Field, near Atlanta, Ga., August 1, 1864.

General THOMAS:

General Howard reports an unusual movement of troops out of Atlanta to his right. I am very anxious to hear the substance of Colonel Brownlow's story. I am told by General Barry's aide that he saw Colonel Brownlow at your camp. I cannot understand Brownlow's return if McCook had surrendered.

> W. T. SHERMAN,
> *Major-General, Commanding.*

HEADQUARTERS DEPARTMENT OF THE CUMBERLAND,
August 1, 1864—9 p. m.

Major-General SHERMAN:

Colonel Brownlow reports that McCook destroyed twelve miles of the Macon railroad, and a bridge over the White Water, longer than the Chattahoochee bridge. He also destroyed over 500 wagons, Hood's, Hardee's, and other headquarters wagons among them. Unfortunately he then turned back on his old route and commenced to destroy the West Point road, when he was attacked on the 29th [30th], near Newnan, by infantry and cavalry in overwhelming numbers, surrounded, and all who did not cut their way through were either killed or captured. There are nearly 500 now in Marietta, and Brownlow thinks many more will find their way in. The First Wisconsin was cut off near Campbellton, and returned two days ago. I will send you his report in the morning.

> GEO. H. THOMAS,
> *Major-General.*

SHERMAN'S HEADQUARTERS,
August 1, 1864.

Major-General THOMAS:

I wish you to see that some one officer, say the colonel of a small infantry regiment, be at the railroad bridge and occupy the rebel intrenchments toward Vining's and about Turner's Ferry, and collect in them all the scattered detachments about there, and see that wagons are not grouped outside. Easton should use the bridge as his depot, instead of Vining's, but a picket should be on the hill overlooking Vining's. The guards at Marietta are enough. Kilpatrick's cavalry should be between Marietta and the railroad bridge, with patrols down about Sweet Water. A regiment of men in the old rebel intrenchments will be a perfect protection to the bridges and our depot on the other side.

W. T. SHERMAN,
Major-General.

HDQRS. MILITARY DIVISION OF THE MISSISSIPPI,
In the Field, near Atlanta, Ga., August 1, 1864.

General THOMAS:

You had better order General Kilpatrick to march at once down by Marietta to our right flank, and to gather up the fragments of General McCook's cavalry and put it in shape, for the enemy will surely cross over to that flank. Also, if you have any regiment of cavalry up at Chattanooga, it could patrol about Resaca till we get more cavalry down. It may be that more of General McCook's men may escape.

W. T. SHERMAN,
Major-General, Commanding.

HEADQUARTERS FOURTH ARMY CORPS,
August 1, 1864.

Brig. Gen. WILLIAM GROSE,
Commanding First Division:

GENERAL: By direction of the department commander, the Fourth Corps, aided by Garrard's cavalry, will maintain a force in General Schofield's works to-morrow. General Wood will maintain his present line, holding as many troops as possible ready to move to threatened points. General Grose will extend his left by placing Taylor's and Kirby's brigades in the present position of the two right brigades of Hascall's division. General Kimball's brigade will take post in the works on General Grose's left. These three brigades should relieve all of Hascall's division. General Garrard will relieve General Cox. The present picket-line of General Schofield will be maintained. The troops will move into position at night-fall to-night. All wagons of General Grose's division, excepting necessary ammunition wagons, will be sent within the new line made to-day. General Grose will retain four pieces of artillery in good position.

D. S. STANLEY,
Major-General.

(Same to Generals Newton and Wood.)

HEADQUARTERS FOURTH ARMY CORPS,
August 1, 1864—5 p. m.

Brig. Gen. WILLIAM GROSE,
Commanding First Division:

GENERAL: In relieving General Hascall to-night caution your men to observe silence as much as possible. Our duty to-morrow is risky, but it is directed by General Thomas, and we must depend upon vigilance, bravery of our men, and our strong works. I will be on the ground very early in the morning. I think we can make the thing safe, and it may be of vast importance to the movement on the right of the army.

Your obedient servant,

D. S. STANLEY,
Major-General.

HDQRS. CHIEF OF CAVALRY, DEPT. OF THE CUMBERLAND,
August 1, 1864.

General J. KILPATRICK, *Cartersville, Ga.:*

Proceed with your division to Chattahoochee River, taking the Sand-town road. Should you find any stragglers from First Division, bring them up with you. We hear the division inflicted considerable damage on the enemy, but was afterward overpowered by cavalry and infantry. Please answer.

W. L. ELLIOTT,
Brigadier-General and Chief of Cavalry.

MARIETTA, GA., *August 1, 1864.*

General W. D. WHIPPLE, *Assistant Adjutant-General:*

Col. James P. Brownlow has just come in here with a very few straggling cavalry, entirely demoralized. Brownlow is barefooted. He reports that our cavalry destroyed the West Point and Macon Railroad to such an extent that it will require fifteen days to repair it; that they burnt 500 wagons, including Hood's and Hardee's, and nearly all other headquarters trains; that after doing this damage they went to Newnan, Ga., where General McCook's division was attacked by Kelly's and Humes' divisions of cavalry and a division of infantry, and that McCook and his command were nearly all captured. Harrison killed. I start immediately for camp, and will bring Brownlow with me.

J. G. PARKHURST,
Colonel and Provost-Marshal-General.

HEADQUARTERS ARMY OF THE OHIO,
Before Atlanta, Ga., August 1, 1864.

Major-General SHERMAN:

Everything is so wet that I do not think anything can be done toward destroying the Decatur road to-day. However, I will try it if you desire.

J. M. SCHOFIELD,
Major-General.

SHERMAN'S HEADQUARTERS,
August 1, 1864. (Received 10.50 a. m.)

General SCHOFIELD:

I guess we will trust to the railroad being enough broken, but I want some noise on that flank, as I fear that the enemy's cavalry may all turn on McCook. We hear from down the river that he broke twelve miles of the Macon road, and burned 300 wagon loads of clothing.

W. T. SHERMAN,
Major-General.

SHERMAN'S HEADQUARTERS,
August 1, 1864. (Received 1.30 p. m.)

General SCHOFIELD:

You may fire from ten to fifteen shots from every gun you have in position into Atlanta that will reach any of its houses. Fire slowly and with deliberation between 4 p. m. and dark. I have inquired into our reserve supply and the occasion will warrant the expenditure. Thomas and Howard will do the same.

W. T. SHERMAN,
Major-General.

VINING'S, *August 1, 1864—9 a. m.*

Maj. J. A. CAMPBELL,
Assistant Adjutant-General Department of the Ohio:

I have the honor to report that the Ninth Ohio Cavalry, the regiment left by General McCook in charge of the pontoon train, returned here with it the day after he crossed, as ordered to do by General McCook. The regiment has no orders with regard to watching the river for his return. The First Wisconsin Cavalry, part of General McCook's command, came back the next morning after he crossed the river, and is now in camp somewhere in this vicinity. The Ninth Ohio Volunteer Cavalry and First Wisconsin Cavalry are under the command of Colonel Hamilton, Ninth Ohio Volunteer Cavalry. The ranking officer, Colonel Hamilton, is not here at present; he left here an hour ago for headquarters of General Sherman. Under these circumstances I have deemed it proper to report the facts and await your orders to move the pontoon train down the river to the vicinity of Campbellton, and watch the river for the return of General McCook. General McCook crossed below Campbellton, about thirty miles from here. At the rate the train moves it will take two days to move to that point.

ISRAEL GARRARD,
Colonel Seventh Ohio Volunteer Cavalry.

HOWARD'S HEADQUARTERS,
August 1, 1864—12.30 p. m.

Major-General SHERMAN:

Old Mr. Bowen, living just beyond the right of our line, says we have not yet reached the Sandtown road proper. The Green's Ferry road leads to White Hall, the Sandtown road and that being the same road from Atlanta to a point this side of White Hall.

O. O. HOWARD,
Major-General.

HDQRS. MILITARY DIVISION OF THE MISSISSIPPI,
In the Field, near Atlanta, Ga., August 1, 1864.

General HOWARD:

General Schofield has just been here. His troops are drawing out of their old lines, and will move for the right early in the morning. When he reaches you give him the right direction, so that when in position he will be within cannon-range of the railroad.

W. T. SHERMAN,
Major-General, Commanding.

HDQRS. MILITARY DIVISION OF THE MISSISSIPPI,
In the Field, near Atlanta, Ga., August 1, 1864.

General HOWARD:

You may, between 4 p. m. and dark, fire from ten to fifteen shots from each gun in position that will reach any part of Atlanta. I have inquired into our reserve supply, and it will warrant the expenditure. I will order the shipment by cars of your horses. Who has them in charge at Chattanooga?

W. T. SHERMAN,
Major-General, Commanding.

———

HEADQUARTERS DEPARTMENT OF THE TENNESSEE,
August 1, 1864.

Major-General SHERMAN:

General Corse reports an unusual movement of troops and trains to my right since 5 o'clock this evening. My scouts report cavalry pickets opposite my right flank. I have not noticed any attempt as yet to turn it.

O. O HOWARD,
Major-General.

———

HDQRS. DEPARTMENT AND ARMY OF THE TENNESSEE,
Before Atlanta, Ga., August 1, 1864.

Maj. Gen. JOHN A. LOGAN, *Comdg. Fifteenth Army Corps:*

I have requested General Blair to extend his line so as to fill one-half of the interval between the present right of his new line and the left of yours. My impression is that you will find your new line shorter than you anticipate, and hope when you get your batteries in position you will have as much reserve as you had before.

Very respectfully, your obedient servant,

O. O. HOWARD,
Major-General.

———

HDQRS. DEPARTMENT AND ARMY OF THE TENNESSEE,
Before Atlanta, Ga., August 1, 1864.

Maj. Gen. F. P. BLAIR,
Commanding Seventeenth Army Corps:

I think when you get your battery into position you can take one-half of the space between the right of your new line and the left of General Logan's, as you described it to-day. Please extend your line, thinning out on your left where your works are so complete, with a view to this. General Logan will be requested to take the remainder of the interval.

Very respectfully, your obedient servant,

O. O. HOWARD,
Major-General.

———

HEADQUARTERS SEVENTEENTH ARMY CORPS,
Before Atlanta, Ga., August 1, 1864.

Brig. Gen. M. D. LEGGETT, *Commanding Third Division:*

GENERAL: General Smith, commanding Fourth Division, has been directed to extend his line more to the right, taking a portion of the interval between him and Logan. The major-general commanding desires you to communicate with him, and when he makes this disposition extend toward him as much as possible, thinning out along your left for that purpose.

I am, very respectfully, your obedient servant,

ROWLAND COX,
Assistant Adjutant-General.

HDQRS. SECOND DIVISION, SIXTEENTH ARMY CORPS,
Before Atlanta, Ga., August 1, 1864.

Captain BARNES,
Assistant Adjutant-General, Sixteenth Army Corps, &c.:

CAPTAIN: I have the honor to report, for the information of the general commanding the corps, that the artillery fire from this division front resulted in developing a 20-pounder battery immediately adjoining the siege piece that had opened so frequently on our lines during the past three days. Also assured the chief of artillery of the fact that with the 3-inch ordnance he can shell the center of the city of Atlanta with tolerable accuracy. The rifled 32-pounder did not open. I further report that the officers and men of the battery in my front have noticed an unusual movement of troops and trains toward our right during the greater portion of the afternoon. The skirmish line, with the exception of the advance of one or two posts, is substantially the same. No casualties have been ascertained as resulting from the enemy's shells thus far.

I am, very respectfully, your obedient servant,

JNO. M. CORSE,
Brigadier-General, Commanding.

HDQRS. MILITARY DIVISION OF THE MISSISSIPPI,
In the Field, near Atlanta, Ga., August 1, 1864.

General JOHN E. SMITH,
Cartersville:

I fear the enemy has caught one of my raiding parties, under General McCook, at Newnan. You must be on the lookout, as the enemy will surely be on our railroad, but I shall expect them about Marietta or Vining's.

W. T. SHERMAN,
Major-General, Commanding.

HDQRS. THIRD DIVISION, FIFTEENTH ARMY CORPS,
Cartersville, Ga., August 1, 1864.

Lieut. Col. PREN METHAM,
Commanding Eightieth Ohio Infantry
(Through Headquarters Post Allatoona):

SIR: On the reception of this order, you will move by dirt road with your command to Resaca, Ga., and on your arrival there report to Col. Green B. Raum, commanding Second Brigade, Third Division, for assignment to duty.

By order of Brig. Gen. John E. Smith:

CARL. L. WHITE,
Captain and Assistant Adjutant-General.

NEAR ATLANTA, GA., *August 1, 1864—9 p. m.*

Major ECKERT:

Our cavalry, under General McCook, reached the Macon road, burned a bridge, and destroyed railroad for twelve miles as thoroughly as possible. Burned several trains of wagons—500 in all—including 300 loads of clothing, and Hood's headquarters train, but failed to get away; was attacked, cut off, defeated, and the greater part captured, including the general. Colonel Brownlow, who escaped, says the railroad cannot be repaired under fifteen days. Stoneman not heard from. Schofield's command swings from left to right to-day, and tomorrow he and Howard, with divisions of Davis and Ward, will go for East Point.

VAN DUZER.

SPECIAL FIELD ORDERS, }   HDQRS. MIL. DIV. OF THE MISS.,
                                   In the Field, near Atlanta, Ga.,
No. 48.   }   *August 1, 1864.*

I. During the next series of operations General Thomas will be the left, General Howard center, and General Schofield the right army. The two divisions of Generals Davis and Ward will continue to be held in reserve toward the right, and in case the enemy attack that flank, these divisions will report to and during the action obey General Schofield's orders. When not engaged General Thomas will post them so as to cover his communications from danger coming from the southeast.

II. Brigadier-General Garrard's cavalry will relieve General Schofield on the left and occupy in part his trenches, patrol the roads about Decatur, and picket toward Roswell. He will report to General Thomas, and be prepared to sally out as cavalry from his trenches, in case of necessity.

III. All trains of wagons going to and from the depots of Vining's and Marietta will follow roads converging at the railroad bridge, and never go north of Buck Head or south of Turner's.

IV. General Thomas will cause a new infantry flank to be prepared on his left, north of the Buck Head road, connecting General Stanley's front lines with the old rebel parapet near Peach Tree Creek.

By order of Maj. Gen. W. T. Sherman:

L. M. DAYTON,
Aide-de-Camp.

SPECIAL FIELD ORDERS, }   HDQRS. ARMY OF THE OHIO,
No. 68.   }   *Before Atlanta, Ga., August 1, 1864.*

*   *   *   *   *   *   *

VI. The troops will withdraw from their present position and move toward the right this evening. The movement will commence at dark and will be made by brigades from the left. Each brigade will remain in position until the preceding one has got into the road and is well under way, so that the troops may not be detained in positions exposed to the enemy's artillery fire. The movement should be made quietly and in good order, with as little noise or display as possible. The picket-line will remain in its present position until it shall be relieved by other troops, or until notified that our troops are withdrawn and that a new picket-line has been established by General Stanley's corps and General Garrard's cavalry, when our picket-line will quietly retire and join the corps. The divisions will march to points selected by Captain Twining, chief engineer, behind the new flank line of the Army of the Cumberland, and there bivouac for the night. The march will be resumed at 6 a. m. to-morrow. A detachment from the Second Division will be posted by Captain Twining at short intervals along the route of to-night's march to keep fires burning to light the road and guide the column. Army headquarters will be to-night near headquarters of the military division.

*   *   *   *   *   *   *

By command of Major-General Schofield:

J. A. CAMPBELL,
Major and Assistant Adjutant-General.

GENERAL FIELD ORDERS, } HEADQUARTERS DEPARTMENT
                                               AND ARMY OF THE TENNESSEE,
       No. 6.   } *Before Atlanta, Ga., August 1, 1864.*

The following officers are announced as members of the staff and staff corps of this department and army. They will be obeyed and respected accordingly: Lieut. Col. C. H. Howard, senior aide-de-camp; Maj. T.W. Osborn, First New York Artillery, chief of artillery; Capt. H. M. Stinson, aide-de-camp; Capt. F. W. Gilbreth, aide-de-camp; Capt. W. M. Beebe, Forty-first Regiment Ohio Infantry, acting aide-de-camp; Capt. E. H. Kirlin, volunteer aide-de-camp.

By order of Maj. Gen. O. O. Howard:

WM. T. CLARK,
Assistant Adjutant-General.

GENERAL FIELD ORDERS, } HEADQUARTERS DEPARTMENT
                                               AND ARMY OF THE TENNESSEE,
       No. 7.   } *Before Atlanta, Ga., August 1, 1864.*

Capt. A. Hickenlooper, Fifth Ohio Battery, in addition to his duties as judge-advocate of the department, will act as assistant chief of artillery of the army in the field, and will be obeyed and respected accordingly.

By order of Maj. Gen. O. O. Howard:

WM. T. CLARK,
Assistant Adjutant-General.

NEAR ATLANTA, GA., *August 2, 1864.*

General L. THOMAS,
       Adjutant-General U. S. Army:

If you have any negro regiments fit for duty I would like to have them in front of Nashville; that would enable me to bring to the front brigades that properly belong to the corps at the front. Could not some general order be made for white recruits to be sent from the States as fast as they are made, to be put in with our old men? Losses in battle and sickness from work and weather is beginning to tell on the strength of my army. If this matter pertains to the Provost-Marshal-General, I would request you to notify him that I would prefer to have recruits come to me daily by tens and hundreds than to await them in larger bodies more difficult to transport. Our cars could bring me 400 daily without overloading.

W. T. SHERMAN,
Major-General.

HDQRS. MILITARY DIVISION OF THE MISSISSIPPI,
In the Field, near Atlanta, Ga., August 2, 1864.

General WEBSTER,
Nashville:

Too many citizens manage to come to the front. Be even more stringent than heretofore. Grant no passes beyond Chattanooga, and only the smallest possible number that far. Surgeons can fill the offices of the Sanitary Commission, and chaplains minister to the wants of the soldiers. If any recruits are coming from the North, I want them forwarded with dispatch by the cars.

W. T. SHERMAN,
Major-General, Commanding.

NASHVILLE, *August 2, 1864.*

Major-General SHERMAN:

The cavalry horses in this district are less than 3,000 all told. Had I not better order cavalry from Memphis to this line by such route as will avoid the necessity of fighting any force of the enemy before reaching us; and also demonstrate from Memphis by such other troops as may be available.

J. D. WEBSTER,
Brigadier-General.

HDQRS. MILITARY DIVISION OF THE MISSISSIPPI,
In the Field, near Atlanta, Ga., August 2, 1864.

General WEBSTER,
Nashville:

Don't call for any cavalry from Memphis. General A. J. Smith has his orders to watch Forrest, and if he comes to Tennessee to follow him to Decatur. He will want all his cavalry. Only collect the scattered detachments of cavalry and order more horses to be purchased to remount the dismounted cavalry in General Thomas' department at Columbia and elsewhere. A good many of General McCook's cavalry are coming in by squads to Marietta.

W. T. SHERMAN,
Major-General, Commanding.

NASHVILLE, *August 2, 1864.*

Major-General SHERMAN:

Can pick up from the corrals and teams here about 1,200 horses, besides the 3,000 now in use, mentioned in telegraph this forenoon. Will send 600 to Decatur at once to remount a regiment there. Will use the others to mount cavalry here. Will push them forward as fast as possible.

J. D. WEBSTER,
Brigadier-General.

HDQRS. MILITARY DIVISION OF THE MISSISSIPPI,
In the Field, near Atlanta, Ga., August 2, 1864.

General THOMAS:

I am quite unwell to-day. General Schofield is marching for and will take up position on the right. I think well of General Stanley's keeping a mere line of display where General Schofield was for a few days, and if you can occupy General Palmer's place in the main line by withdrawing General Ward's division, it would give us General Palmer's corps as a working force in reserve on the right. As soon as General Schofield selects his right flank we must assume the offensive against the railroad between White Hall and East Point. I have no doubt that General McCook damaged the Southern road and that provisions and ammunition will be short in the rebel camp. But we must look to our own depots. Please do all that is possible to organize a force of cavalry about Marietta, composed of General Kilpatrick's division and such of General McCook's as have returned. Also have the old rebel lines west of Chattahoochee lightly guarded to cover our bridges. Order all bridges above Pace's, except that at Roswell, to be destroyed.

W. T. SHERMAN,
Major-General, Commanding.

HEADQUARTERS DEPARTMENT OF THE CUMBERLAND,
August 2, 1864.

Major-General SHERMAN:

Yours received. Orders have been given to Kilpatrick to move down to Marietta and guard the road from the river to that place. A regiment has been sent to occupy the old rebel works across the river toward Vining's and at Turner's Ferry. The First Wisconsin Cavalry has been ordered down the river to pick up the scattered men of McCook's command. The remaining four guns of the battery McCook had with him have been put in the works near the railroad bridge, and Major Purdy with the 280 men with which he returned, and all others he can collect, ordered to the same place.

GEO. H. THOMAS.

HDQRS. MILITARY DIVISION OF THE MISSISSIPPI,
In the Field, near Atlanta, Ga., August 2, 1864.

General THOMAS:

General Schofield is in position on General Howard's right and extends one mile and a half in a south course, his right being one and one-half southeast of lot 213. He faces a branch of Utoy Creek, and General Howard thinks the East Point and Atlanta road lies on the ridge opposite, which the enemy holds in force. General Schofield represents Utoy Creek opposite his right as about the size of Olley's Creek, and thinks its passage will be seriously resisted. Better get General Palmer's corps ready and we must break through somewhere. The rest of our line should make dashes and secure lodgments close up under the main works.

W. T. SHERMAN,
Major-General, Commanding.

SHERMAN'S HEADQUARTERS,
August 2, 1864.

General STANLEY:

Order just received from Washington assigns you to command of the Fourth Corps.

W. T. SHERMAN,
Major-General, Commanding.

STANLEY'S HEADQUARTERS,
August 2, 1864.

Major-General SHERMAN:

Telegram received. Much obliged to you. Will do my best to merit the confidence. Deserter just in says order read last night to rebel army says they captured 500 of McCook's command and dispersed the rest. Hardee has resigned. Cleburne commands his corps.

D. S. STANLEY,
Major-General.

HEADQUARTERS FOURTH ARMY CORPS,
Near Atlanta, Ga., August 2, 1864.

Brigadier-General GROSE,
First Division, Fourth Army Corps:

GENERAL: You will hold the line you now occupy until otherwise ordered. The contemplated movement of the troops of this corps to our new and interior line will not be made perhaps for some days. Move all of your wagons within said interior line of works, except headquarters trains, if it be necessary that they should be kept outside. Do not leave your commissary train outside of the same longer than may be necessary to issue to the troops.

By order of Major-General Stanley:

J. S. FULLERTON,
Assistant Adjutant-General.

(Same to Generals Newton and Wood.)

HDQRS. DEPARTMENT OF THE CUMBERLAND,
Near Atlanta, Ga., August 2, 1864.

Maj. Gen. J. M. PALMER,
Commanding Fourteenth Army Corps:

GENERAL: General Ward's division, of the Twentieth Corps, has been ordered to return from its present position, and occupy that portion of our lines now held by the Fourteenth Army Corps, with the exception of one brigade, which you will be requested to leave in position on your present right. When your two divisions, less the one brigade, are drawn out of the line, you will order them, also General Davis' division, massed in rear of General Schofield's right flank.

I am, general, very respectfully, your obedient servant,

WM. D. WHIPPLE,
Assistant Adjutant-General.

HEADQUARTERS TWENTIETH CORPS,
Near Atlanta, Ga., August 2, 1864.

Brig. Gen. W. T. WARD,
    Commanding Third Division:

GENERAL: In compliance with inclosed order the general command-ing the corps directs that you move your division this afternoon, camp-ing it for the night in rear of the position now occupied by the Fourteenth Corps, and be in readiness to relieve by daylight to-morrow morning all of the Fourteenth Corps now in the front line, except one brigade (the extreme right of the Fourteenth Corps).

I am, general, very respectfully, your obedient servant,

H. W. PERKINS,
Lieutenant-Colonel and Assistant Adjutant-General.

[Inclosure.]

HEADQUARTERS DEPARTMENT OF THE CUMBERLAND,
Near Atlanta, Ga., August 2, 1864.

Brig. Gen. A. S. WILLIAMS,
    Commanding Twentieth Army Corps:

GENERAL: The major-general commanding directs that General Ward's division of your corps be ordered to return from its present po-sition near our right and be placed in the line as arranged between you and the major-general commanding, relieving all but one brigade of the Fourteenth Corps.

Yours, very respectfully,

WM. D. WHIPPLE,
Assistant Adjutant-General.

HDQRS. MILITARY DIVISION OF THE MISSISSIPPI,
In the Field, near Atlanta, Ga., August 2, 1864.

General SLOCUM,
    Vicksburg:

You are assigned to command the Twentieth Corps. Turn over your command to the officer next in rank, and come and command your corps in the field. I will extend General Washburn's district over Vicksburg and Natchez, so that the river can be controlled by one mind. Come via Cairo and Nashville.

W. T. SHERMAN,
Major-General, Commanding.

HDQRS. MILITARY DIVISION OF THE MISSISSIPPI,
In the Field, near Atlanta, Ga., August 2, 1864.

General ROBERT S. GRANGER,
    Decatur, Ala.:

If that brigade of the Sixteenth Corps commanded by Colonel Howe can possibly be spared, I want it sent to the front by the cars. Our losses have been heavy and we want that brigade more than you can possibly do. I have asked General Lorenzo Thomas to send you some negro regiments, which will do to hold block-houses and intrenched places. General A. J. Smith will watch Forrest, and if he moves toward

Tennessee General Smith will come to Decatur. Stephen D. Lee re-enforced General Hood in Atlanta with troops brought from Mississippi. As long as General Smith hovers between Memphis and Forrest, the latter will hardly venture across the Tennessee River. Answer by telegraph.

W. T. SHERMAN,
Major-General, Commanding.

NASHVILLE, TENN., *August 2, 1864.*

Major-General SHERMAN:

After relieving brigade of Sixteenth Army Corps there will be but one regiment of infantry, 600 strong, to garrison Decatur. The works are very extensive and can only be held effectually by present garrison. If, however, we have nothing to apprehend from Forrest we can with one regiment of infantry and our cavalry hold it against all the force Roddey can bring. I must say I feel a little apprehension. A good portion of Forrest's force may slip by Smith, and that with Roddey's command make a dash on our road and Decatur. This you will see, by communications captured from Patterson and forwarded to General Thomas, they had in contemplation before Smith's advance called them into Mississippi. I will order the brigade to be prepared to leave as soon as transportation can be furnished. I have just finished inspection of the troops and defenses the entire length of the road and find them in pretty good condition.

R. S. GRANGER,
Brigadier-General.

SHERMAN'S HEADQUARTERS,
August 2, 1864. (Received 1.10 p. m.)

General SCHOFIELD:

Describe to me your new position. I have just sent a telegraph operator on to your old headquarters, so that we will have telegraphic communication from right to left.

W. T. SHERMAN,
Major-General.

HEADQUARTERS ARMY OF THE OHIO,
August 2, 1864—1.45 p. m.

Major-General SHERMAN:

I have reconnoitered to the point reached by Morgan's division on his reconnaissance the other day, which is on the prolongation of Howard's new line and less than a mile from his right. I will put my troops in there and connect with Howard. The position faces a branch of Utoy Creek and is a mile south of Wilson's house, now occupied by Bowen. My infantry is not up. When I get it in position I will reconnoiter farther and give you a more accurate description. The enemy's intrenchments are visible in front of Howard's right, across the creek. I have not yet been able to determine how far they extend, but will try to do so when my troops get up.

J. M. SCHOFIELD,
Major-General.

HEADQUARTERS ARMY OF THE OHIO,
Before Atlanta, Ga., August 2, 1864.

Major-General SHERMAN:

From all that I can see, I judge that the enemy's infantry line bends back opposite my left center and runs from that point nearly south behind a small branch of the creek in front of Howard and myself. The force in front of my right appears to be cavalry. To seriously threaten the enemy's flank and railroad communication it will be necessary to cross the creek in front of my right and reach the Sandtown road, which is about a mile beyond the creek. If this move can be made with a sufficiently large force the result must be very decisive. Please inform me if you desire me to push forward to-morrow, and also whether Morgan's and Ward's divisions will be absolutely under my command, or only to be called upon when the necessity arises. At present they are in easy supporting distance, but if I move they should move with me.

Respectfully,

J. M. SCHOFIELD,
Major-General.

HDQRS. MILITARY DIVISION OF THE MISSISSIPPI,
In the Field, near Atlanta, Ga., August 2, 1864.

General SCHOFIELD:

I would like to have you to prepare a crossing-place over the Utoy. General Davis' division will remain to-morrow, and during the day, if all is quiet, Ward's will return to occupy the line now held by Palmer's corps, and all of Palmer's corps will come to Davis' and advance with yours, or even beyond you, as an attacking column. I will be over to-morrow.

W. T. SHERMAN,
Major-General, Commanding.

HDQRS. MILITARY DIVISION OF THE MISSISSIPPI,
In the Field, near Atlanta, Ga., August 2, 1864.

General SCHOFIELD:

Will you have your command in position and intrenched by morning? How far do you reckon you are off from the railroad?

W. T. SHERMAN,
Major-General, Commanding.

HEADQUARTERS ARMY OF THE OHIO,
Before Atlanta, Ga., August 2, 1864.

Major-General SHERMAN:

My troops are in position, and will be well intrenched to-night. I have prolonged Howard's new line along the branch of Utoy Creek about a mile and a half, and have a good flank. I think no point of my line is nearer the railroad than Howard's right, which I estimate to be between one mile and a quarter and one mile and three-quarters. My right is not as far forward as I hoped it would be, but I have gone as far as it was possible to-day. To cross the creek will be a day's work, and I reckon must be done in force. The situation seems very similar to that at Olley's Creek, but I presume a single division will not be permitted to do what one did there. What means the unusual silence along the lines to-day?

Respectfully,

J. M. SCHOFIELD,
Major-General.

HDQRS. MILITARY DIVISION OF THE MISSISSIPPI,
In the Field, near Atlanta, Ga., August 2, 1864.
(Received 8.45 p. m.)

General SCHOFIELD:

Your dispatch is received. I cannot account for the silence to-day, unless the enemy awaits our initiative.

W. T. SHERMAN,
Major-General.

HEADQUARTERS DEPARTMENT OF THE TENNESSEE,
August 2, 1864.

Major-General SHERMAN:

Our lines face a branch of Utoy. This branch seems to be nearly parallel with the East Point and Atlanta wagon road. Schofield's right is about one mile and a half to the southeast of lot 213. I believe he has one division in position, probably well intrenched, before this time. The branch of the Utoy is said to be fordable. The general will certainly cross the creek if it is possible to do so, and if the rebel works change direction where I think they do, he can cross without difficulty. His right is on a high ridge, that should be intrenched to debouch from.

O. O. HOWARD,
Major-General.

HDQRS. MILITARY DIVISION OF THE MISSISSIPPI,
In the Field, near Atlanta, Ga., August 2, 1864.

General HOWARD:

General Ransom is assigned to you. He is an excellent division commander.

W. T. SHERMAN,
Major-General, Commanding.

HEADQUARTERS DEPARTMENT OF THE TENNESSEE,
August 2, 1864.

Major-General SHERMAN:

I assisted General Schofield in reconnoitering the ground on my right flank this a. m., and at 3 p. m. moved forward my command to occupy my new line. General Schofield extends that line over a mile to the southwest. We both face the western branch of Utoy Creek. The rebel works are parallel with mine on the other side of that creek and in plain view and apparently extend about half a mile beyond my right flank, where they seem to refuse. I could see no works in front of General Schofield's right. The rebel skirmishers and mine are now close together, and we have a battery constructed from which I think we may reach the railroad, though it is not in sight.

O. O. HOWARD,
Major-General.

HDQRS. MILITARY DIVISION OF THE MISSISSIPPI,
In the Field, near Atlanta, Ga., August 2, 1864.

General HOWARD:

If yours and General Schofield's lines run southwest and face Utoy Creek, I fear we are rather leaving than nearing the railroad. Is Utoy Creek easily passed? Will General Schofield have his men in position and covered by morning?

W. T. SHERMAN,
Major-General, Commanding.

HDQRS. MILITARY DIVISION OF THE MISSISSIPPI,
In the Field, near Atlanta, Ga., August 2, 1864.

General HOWARD:

General Schofield has started his troops and himself. You will probably understand the object of extending the right as much as any one, and I beg you will aid General Schofield in getting a good position. General Thomas will see about putting General Ward's division back, and having all of General Palmer's corps as a right reserve. We should have the Sandtown road, and our right should, if possible, be within cannon-range of the railroad. I am quite unwell to-day.

W. T. SHERMAN,
Major-General, Commanding.

HEADQUARTERS DEPARTMENT OF THE TENNESSEE,
August 2, 1864.

General SHERMAN:

GENERAL: I am very sorry to hear that you are ill. I will meet General Schofield and do everything in my power to facilitate operations. Hood may possibly attempt a blow on him, but with Palmer's and this army close at hand he will be likely to get badly whipped.

O. O. HOWARD,
Major-General.

HEADQUARTERS DEPARTMENT OF THE TENNESSEE,
August 2, 1864.

General SHERMAN:

My signal officer reports as follows:

I see something more than 100 men with bundles, without arms, moving into Atlanta under guard.

O. O. HOWARD,
Major-General.

HdQRS. MILITARY DIVISION OF THE MISSISSIPPI,
In the Field, near Atlanta, Ga., August 2, 1864.

COMMANDING OFFICER AT MARIETTA:

Report to me direct any men of General McCook's got in, and also if General Kilpatrick has come down with his cavalry from Cartersville.

W. T. SHERMAN,
Major-General, Commanding.

MARIETTA, *August 2, 1864.*

Major-General SHERMAN:

Nothing here in regard to Kilpatrick's command. From McCook's command the First Wisconsin Cavalry came here and have gone to near Campbellton under orders of General Elliott; strength not reported. There are here 230 men of McCook's command, with four pieces of artillery, about to move, under General Elliott's orders, to railroad bridge at Chattahoochee River. Captain McCormick, of General Elliott's staff, is here looking after and reorganizing them.

SAML. ROSS,
Colonel Twentieth Connecticut, Commanding Post.

MARIETTA, *August 2, 1864.*

Maj. Gen. W. T. SHERMAN:

Respectfully report my arrival here with 95 men of my command, having been in Brigadier-General McCook's expedition with 170. In the engagement near Newnan was cut off from the main body, losing the difference in men. The command, horses and men, is in exhausted condition.

OWEN STAR,
Major Second Kentucky Cavalry, Commanding Regiment.

BEFORE ATLANTA, GA., *August 2, 1864—9.30 p. m.*

Maj. T. T. ECKERT:

To-day has been used in getting troops into position to attack. Corps are now in line from left to right in this order: Twentieth, Fourth, Sixteenth, Seventeenth, Fifteenth, and Twenty-third, with Fourteenth in reserve in rear of Twenty-third. Can't say when the word will be given to attack, but expect it to-morrow. No further news from cavalry expedition.

J. C. VAN DUZER.

SPECIAL FIELD ORDERS, ⎞ HdQRS. MIL. DIV. OF THE MISS.,
                      ⎟   *In the Field, near Atlanta, Ga.,*
No. 49.   ⎠   *August 2, 1864.*

I. Brig. Gen. T. E. G. Ransom, U. S. Volunteers, having in pursuance of Special Orders, No. 34, paragraph IV, dated headquarters Armies of the United States, June 12, 1864, reported for duty, is hereby assigned to duty with the Department and Army of the Tennessee, and will report in person to Maj. Gen. O. O. Howard, commanding.

*   *   *   *   *   *   *

By order of Maj. Gen. W. T. Sherman:

L. M. DAYTON,
Aide-de-Camp.

SPECIAL FIELD ORDERS, ⎱   HEADQUARTERS LEFT WING,
                         ⎰   SIXTEENTH ARMY CORPS,
        No 53.   *Near Atlanta, Ga., August 2, 1864.*

  *   *   *   *   *   ***

III. Brig. Gen. T. E. G. Ransom, U. S. Volunteers, having reported to these headquarters for duty in compliance with extract V, Special Field Orders, No. 86, Department and Army of the Tennessee, is hereby assigned to the command of the Fourth Division, Sixteenth Army Corps.

Brig. Gen. J. W. Fuller will assume command of the First Brigade, Fourth Division, Sixteenth Army Corps.

  *   *   *   *   *   *   ***

By order of Maj. Gen. G. M. Dodge:

           J. W. BARNES,
          Assistant Adjutant-General.

GENERAL ORDERS, ⎱   HDQRS. SEVENTEENTH ARMY CORPS,
    No. 9.   ⎰   *Before Atlanta, Ga., August 2, 1864.*

I. Capt. E. M. Joel, assistant quartermaster, having reported to these headquarters for duty, is announced as acting chief quartermaster of the corps. He will be obeyed and respected accordingly.

II. Capt. J. W. Barlow, U. S. Army, is announced as chief engineer on the staff of the major-general commanding. He will be obeyed and respected accordingly.

By command of Maj. Gen. Frank P. Blair:

           A. J. ALEXANDER,
          Assistant Adjutant-General.

GENERAL ORDERS, ⎱   HDQRS. SEVENTEENTH ARMY CORPS,
    No. 10.   ⎰   *Before Atlanta, Ga., August 2, 1864.*

In order to improve the efficiency of the engineer department of this corps, the following directions will be strictly observed by all officers detailed upon engineering duty:

1. Whenever an engineer officer of a division leaves the division the commanding officer will immediately assign some one to perform his duties until an officer can be procured to take his place.

2. Division engineers will, without fail, report daily to the chief engineer of the corps any change which may take place in the position of his division, accompanying such report by a sketch as accurate as circumstances will permit. He will also endeavor to gain information of the nature of the country, roads, &c., in the vicinity of the division, particularly toward the front, and will cause a detail of the pioneer corps to invariably prepare a good road parallel to the front, and covered as much as possible from the enemy's fire. He will keep an official journal of all engineer operations performed by the division, which must be forwarded to the chief engineer at these headquarters by noon every Saturday, instead of every ten days, as was previously required. In these reports the movements of the division must be stated, also the names of all officers and enlisted men on engineer duty, and what they are doing. The division engineer should pay the greatest attention to the laying out of field-works, as the direction of a very small portion of

the line may decidedly affect the issue of an attack upon it, and in the construction of such work the pioneer corps will observe and obey the instructions given by the division engineer.

3. Division commanders will at once fill up the pioneer corps to the maximum in accordance with General Orders, No. 47, headquarters Department of the Tennessee, July 24, 1863, and have the corps constantly supplied with the number of tools provided by said order. The commanders of pioneer corps will not omit to make their weekly returns of tools, &c., to these headquarters by noon every Saturday, and their monthly returns will also be promptly forwarded.

It is hoped that the division commanders and pioneer officers will do everything in their power to further the efficiency of the engineer department of the corps, which can only be done by an earnest co-working of all who are interested in its advancement.

By order of Maj. Gen. Frank P. Blair:

> A. J. ALEXANDER,
> *Assistant Adjutant-General.*

CITY POINT, *August 3, 1864.*
(Received 6.30 a. m. 4th.)

General HALLECK,
 Chief of Staff:

Richmond Dispatch of to-day contains the following:

MACON, *August 1, 1864—6 p. m.*

Our cavalry under General Iverson attacked the enemy yesterday near Clinton. The Yankees, commanded by General Stoneman, were routed, and Stoneman, 25 officers, and about 500 prisoners, with 2 pieces of artillery, surrendered, and have just reached the city. The rest of the Yankee force is scattered and flying toward Eatonton.

> U. S. GRANT,
> *Lieutenant-General.*

NEAR ATLANTA, GA., *August 3, 1864—9 p. m.*
(Received 11 p. m. 4th.)

Maj. Gen. H. W. HALLECK,
 Washington, D. C.:

We have had pretty lively times to-day generally, closing in, taking some 200 or 300 prisoners. Under the pressure I got two divisions across the head of Utoy Creek, well toward the railroad, and to-morrow will push still more on that flank. General McCook, after all, has got in, bringing 1,200 of his men. He reports that on July 29 he broke the West Point road at Palmetto, and then crossed over to the Macon road, at Lovejoy's, where he took up 2 miles of track, burned 2 trains, 100 bales of cotton, and 5 miles of telegraph. He fell upon the rebel wagon train and burned over 500 wagons and killed 800 mules. He captured 72 officers and 350 men, but his progress eastward and north, according to the plan, was stopped by a superior force of cavalry and he turned toward Newnan, where he was completely surrounded. He ordered two of his small brigades to make their way to the Chattahoochee while he held the enemy. About 500 of them are in, but the balance, about 1,000, are doubtless captured or killed. He then with 1,200 men charged through in column, riding down Ross' (Texas) brigade and capturing Ross, the commander; but he had to drop all pris-

oners and incumbrances to save his command. He crossed the Chattahoochee below Franklin and up by Dallas to Marietta. The plan was
for him to meet General Stoneman at Lovejoy's, but he did not meet
him. Prisoners report that Yankee cavalry were shelling Macon on
the 1st instant, so I think General Stoneman has a chance of rescuing
those prisoners. It was a bold and rash adventure, but I sanctioned
it, and hoped for its success from its very rashness. I think that all
Georgia is now in my front, and he may meet but little opposition and
succeed in releasing those prisoners. The difficulty will then commence for them to reach me. My lines are very strong, and cover well
all our bridges across Chattahoochee. I will use my cavalry hereafter to cover the railroad, and use infantry and artillery against Atlanta. A large part of Hood's army is militia, that cannot be trusted
in the open field, and I think we have crippled the three fighting corps
now commanded by Stewart, Stephen D. Lee, and Hardee. It is even
whispered that Hardee has resigned; but this is as yet but the story of
deserters.

W. T. SHERMAN,
Major-General.

Near Atlanta, Ga., August 3, 1864—11.30 p. m.
(Received 11 p. m. 4th.)

Maj. Gen. H. W. Halleck,
  Washington, D. C.:

In order to make my campaign conclusive I should have a large
cavalry force. We find great difficulty in procuring horses. I understand there are 2,000 at Saint Louis. Can I not have them? Recruits
also should be sent to Nashville, and sent forward daily, and distributed
as they come.

W. T. SHERMAN,
Major-General.

Hdqrs. Military Division of the Mississippi,
In the Field, near Atlanta, Ga., August 3, 1864.

General Webster,
  Nashville:

General McCook is safe. He is in with 1,200 of his command. About
500 had got into Marietta before him. Still I will need cavalry.

W. T. SHERMAN,
Major-General, Commanding.

Nashville, August 3, 1864.

Major-General Sherman:

Lewis Merrill, chief of Cavalry Bureau at Saint Louis, telegraphs
me he has 2,000 cavalry horses on hand, and will send them to me if
they will allow it at Washington. This in reply to a telegram from
me. They might give you 1,000 of these animals if you request it, if
not all. They will deny me. I have asked too often.

J. L. DONALDSON,
Senior and Supervising Quartermaster.

HDQRS. MILITARY DIVISION OF THE MISSISSIPPI,
In the Field, near Atlanta, Ga., August 3, 1864.
General THOMAS:

I am on the point of starting to the right. Will move headquarters to the neighborhood of General Howard. Have you any reports from the front? There seems an unusual quiet prevailing.
W. T. SHERMAN,
Major-General, Commanding.

———

HEADQUARTERS DEPARTMENT OF THE CUMBERLAND,
In the Field, August 3, 1864.
Major-General SHERMAN:

I have had no report from the front this morning. I am just leaving to ride along the line, and if I hear anything will at once inform you.
GEO. H. THOMAS,
Major-General, Commanding.
Per H. S.

———

HDQRS. MILITARY DIVISION OF THE MISSISSIPPI,
In the Field, near Atlanta, Ga., August 3, 1864.
General THOMAS:

I am just in from the right. General Schofield has one division across Utoy, and General Baird was crossing at 6 p. m.; pretty severe skirmish but no battle. I came by General Logan's, who has been fighting with artillery and picket-lines all day. He carried a line and took 50 prisoners. Enemy retook the pits, but our skirmishers got in safe. General Logan again took them, with 150 prisoners, his loss very small. He was still hammering away when I left him along his line, and this relieved the pressure on Generals Schofield and Baird. I think by morning he will have a lodgment across Utoy, on or very near the big Sandtown road, that will seriously threaten the railroad. I have heard of General McCook and am well pleased. I heard very heavy firing up your way. Tell me all about it.
W. T. SHERMAN,
Major-General, Commanding.

———

HEADQUARTERS DEPARTMENT OF THE CUMBERLAND,
August 3, 1864.
Major-General SHERMAN:

The firing you heard was Stanley making a demonstration with his skirmish line. The enemy's skirmishers replied briskly, wounding perhaps 50 of our men. We captured about that number of rebels. Sutermeister is firing upon the town to-night.
GEO. H. THOMAS,
Major-General.

———

HEADQUARTERS DEPARTMENT OF THE CUMBERLAND,
August 3, 1864.
Major-General SHERMAN:

McCook is all right, near Dallas, with 1,200 men. I send his report to you.* Will have him reorganize to-morrow at the railroad bridge.

———

* See Part II, p. 761.

Have just returned from the extreme left. We keep up a pretty good display, and I think we can make the rebels believe we occupy the whole line. Have directed Stanley to advance his skirmish line. No reports from him yet. We are well up to the rebel works. Williams will improve his line to-morrow. I will visit the railroad bridge to-morrow, and then go to the right, unless you wish me to remain here.

GEO. H. THOMAS,
Major-General.

Hdqrs. Military Division of the Mississippi,
In the Field, near Atlanta, Ga., August 3, 1864.

General Thomas:

I would rather have you defer your visit to the railroad bridge another day. I think that to-morrow we can force the rebels to attack our right or be in a tight place. I will be there, and want you to take advantage of any change.

W. T. SHERMAN,
Major-General, Commanding.

Schofield's Headquarters,
August 3, 1864. (Received 12.20 p. m.)

Generals Thomas and Stanley:

I have the dispatch showing the enemy moving to meet ours on this flank. This p. m. Hascall's division, of Schofield, and one of Palmer's will cross Utoy Creek to the east, and will so threaten the railroad that I think the enemy will so far weaken the defenses of Atlanta that a bold dash might make a lodgment about Wood's front; at all events make the attempt with a strong line of skirmishers. Howard has successfully advanced his line, taking the enemy's pits and his skirmishers.

W. T. SHERMAN,
Major-General.

Thomas' Headquarters,
August 3, 1864—2 p. m.

Major-General Sherman:

I have been out to the Augusta railroad to-day. The rebels are still there, but I will have them felt this p. m. to ascertain their strength.

GEO. H. THOMAS,
Major-General.

Howard's Headquarters,
August 3, 1864. (Received 11 a. m.)

Major-General Stanley,
    Commanding Fourth Corps:

Our movements to-day on the extreme right will surely draw the enemy to East Point. He may possibly attack on our left, but I think not. We should, however, feel every approachable point of Atlanta and make him develop his force. The extreme silence and absence of artillery, when he must see troops moving at Palmer's front, are suspicious. If you want to communicate with me during the day, I will be at or near Schofield's. I would like any symptoms, however trivial, reported. I would like to have the skirmishers about Wood's and Newton's front to push a reconnaissance as far forward as is possible, and to use some considerable artillery about 4 p. m.

W. T. SHERMAN,
Major-General, Commanding.

(Same to General Thomas.)

HEADQUARTERS FOURTH ARMY CORPS,
August 3, 1864—8.30 p. m.

Major-General SHERMAN:

I have the honor to report, in answer to your inquiry, that I carried the picket-line on the whole corps front, excepting Gibson's [brigade], of Wood's division. Newton's men went within 100 yards of the star fort. The rebels opened from at least twenty pieces. The rebels rallied and drove back Hazen's skirmishers. We took about 40 prisoners. Three of Cheatham's brigades are certainly in our front. They say Cleburne is on the rebel right. We could see troops move in and deploy in the works during the fight. I send through General Thomas a Chattanooga Rebel paper of the 3d of August. Stoneman was at Clinton on the 1st. He has destroyed Oconee bridge, burned cars, &c., on Central Railroad. I had 30 or 40 killed and wounded to-day. My belief is that the rebel force is quite strong on this front yet. Gibson met a destructive fire of musketry and canister.

D. S. STANLEY,
Major-General.

HEADQUARTERS FOURTH ARMY CORPS,
August 3, 1864—8.30 a. m.

Brigadier-General WHIPPLE, *Chief of Staff:*

I think of pushing a reconnaissance out from the left of my line, and of opening artillery upon the city. I may attack the rebel picket-line. Would like the opinion of General Thomas.

D. S. STANLEY,
Major-General.

AUGUST 3, 1864.

General STANLEY, *Commanding Fourth Army Corps:*

The general commanding directs that you organize a strong skirmish line and make a bold dash against the enemy, capturing their picket-line at any rate.

By command of Major-General Thomas:

HENRY STONE,
Assistant Adjutant-General.

HEADQUARTERS FOURTH ARMY CORPS,
Near Atlanta, Ga., August 3, 1864.

Brigadier-General WHIPPLE,
Assistant Adjutant-General and Chief of Staff:

GENERAL: I have the honor to report the following as the result of our operations this afternoon:

At 4.30 p. m. I advanced the re-enforced skirmish lines of Grose's, Wood's, and Newton's divisions. I carried the rebel picket-lines on the whole corps front excepting in front of Gibson's brigade, of Wood's division. Gibson met a destructive fire of musketry and canister. Newton's men went within 100 yards of the star fort. The rebels opened upon us at least twenty pieces of artillery. After Hazen had taken the enemy's skirmish rifle-pits, about three-quarters of a mile from our works and about 100 yards from the enemy's works, the rebels sallied out and drove his skirmishers back. We have taken about 40 prisoners. Three of Cheatham's brigades are in our front. The prisoners report that Cleburne's division is on the rebel right. We could see troops move in and occupy the works during the fight. We lost about 30 killed and wounded. My belief is that the rebel force is quite strong in my front yet. The rebels' right, as pointed out by the deserter you sent to me, rests on the Augusta railroad, with their right thrown back.

D. S. STANLEY,
Major-General, Commanding.

(Forwarded to General Sherman by General Thomas.)

HEADQUARTERS FOURTH ARMY CORPS,
Near Atlanta, Ga., August 3, 1864—2.30 p. m.

Brigadier-General GROSE,
     Commanding First Division, Fourth Army Corps:

GENERAL: The general commanding directs me to say that in accordance with instructions received from department headquarters, General Wood's troops will make a dash at about 4.30 this p. m., for the purpose of trying to capture or drive in the enemy's skirmish line. If a favorable point is discovered or opportunity is offered in your front, your troops will make a like attempt.

Very respectfully, your obedient servant,
J. S. FULLERTON,
Assistant Adjutant-General.

(Verbal orders similar to the above given to Generals Newton and Wood.)

HDQRS. SECOND DIVISION, FOURTH ARMY CORPS,
August 3, 1864.

General WAGNER,
     Commanding Second Brigade:

GENERAL: You will immediately re-enforce your skirmish line with one regiment as support. You will advance your skirmish line at 4.30 p. m. precisely, taking the enemy's skirmish pits; when this is done part of your supports will continue to occupy the present skirmish pits. Put a good officer in command. Draw in all your working parties and have your line fully manned. Get your time at these headquarters. You have no time to lose.

By order of Brigadier-General Newton:

J. S. RANSOM,
Captain and Acting Assistant Adjutant-General.

HEADQUARTERS FOURTH ARMY CORPS,
August 3, 1864.　(Received 10.20 a. m.)

Major-General SHERMAN:

One of our signal officers reports that the rebels are leaving the front of our left and are moving off to their left; are passing through Atlanta. He says no artillery with them. General Stanley is in front; will send your dispatch to him at once. He has gone to push a reconnaissance from Grose's front.

J. S. FULLERTON,
Assistant Adjutant-General

———

STANLEY'S HEADQUARTERS,
August 3, 1864—1.20 p. m.

Capt. L. M. DAYTON,
Actg. Asst. Adjt. Gen., Hdqrs. Mil. Div. of the Mississippi:

The troops reported as leaving my front by the signal officers were replaced by other rebel troops. About one small brigade moved west through Atlanta. We can yet see their artillery in position.

D. S. STANLEY,
Major-General.

———

HEADQUARTERS FOURTH ARMY CORPS,
August 3, 1864.

Major-General HOWARD:

We carried the rebel skirmish rifle-pits along our entire front. Newton reports that he carried three lines, and Gibson's brigade the same. Skirmishers of Hazen's and Knefler's brigades driven back. The enemy showed quite strong force. Opened at least twenty pieces artillery. We have lost 30 men. Have taken about 40 prisoners. Cheatham's division in front of Wood and Newton. Prisoners report Cleburne's division on right.

J. S. FULLERTON,
Assistant Adjutant-General.

———

HDQRS. MILITARY DIVISION OF THE MISSISSIPPI,
In the Field, near Atlanta, Ga., August 3, 1864.

General STANLEY:

General Hascall is across Utoy Creek and General Baird is passing. Watch well the effect on the extreme left, and at whatever points signal officers can see in Atlanta.

W. T. SHERMAN,
Major-General, Commanding.

———

HEADQUARTERS DEPARTMENT OF THE CUMBERLAND,
Near Atlanta, Ga., August 3, 1864.　(Received 10.15 a. m.)

Maj. Gen. D. S. STANLEY,
Commanding Fourth Army Corps:

GENERAL: The major-general commanding directs that you strip the south end of the bridge at Powers' Ferry, and move the guard down to Pace's Ferry and guard the bridge at that point.

Very respectfully, your obedient servant,
HENRY STONE,
Assistant Adjutant-General.

HEADQUARTERS DEPARTMENT OF THE CUMBERLAND,
Near Atlanta, August 3, 1864.

Brigadier-General WILLIAMS, *Commanding Twentieth Corps:*

I send you below a copy of telegram* just received at these head-quarters. General Thomas has gone to some point on the lines. I shall forward this to him at once, and you will please act on it so far as relates to your corps, unless otherwise ordered by him.

Very respectfully,

HENRY STONE,
Assistant Adjutant-General.

A copy has been sent to General Stanley.

H. S.

HEADQUARTERS TWENTIETH CORPS,
Near Atlanta, Ga., August 3, 1864.

Brig. Gen. W. T. WARD, *Commanding Third Division:*

GENERAL: The general commanding directs that you commence the construction of breast-works on the new line now being located by Lieutenant Ludlow, engineer of the corps, at once, if it is possible to work there in the daylight without drawing a fire from the enemy. If you find it impracticable to work at them during the daytime he desires that you will put a strong force at work to-night, as he desires that they may be finished and occupied by morning. Lieutenant Ludlow is now on the line and will give you such information as you may need. Major Reynolds, chief of artillery, will select the position for the artillery, and the general wishes that the earth-works at the points he selects may be constructed with special reference to the protection of the artillery.

Very respectfully, your obedient servant,

H. W. PERKINS,
Lieutenant-Colonel and Assistant Adjutant-General.

HDQRS. CHIEF OF CAVALRY, DEPT. OF THE CUMBERLAND,
Near Atlanta, Ga., August 3, 1864.

Brig. Gen. E. M. McCOOK,
Commanding First Cavalry Division, Marietta, Ga.:

The general commanding directs that you move with your command to the railroad bridge north of the Chattahoochee. He congratulates you and your command on your success during the late raid.

DAVID F. HOW,
Lieutenant and Acting Assistant Adjutant-General.

HDQRS. CHIEF OF CAVALRY, DEPT. OF THE CUMBERLAND,
August 3, 1864.

General J. KILPATRICK,
Cartersville, or en route to Marietta, Ga.:

I have reports that 500 to 1,000 rebels crossed Chattahoochee at Campbellton last night and moved in direction of Burnt Hickory. Look out for them on railroad.

W. L. ELLIOTT,
Brigadier-General and Chief of Cavalry.

---

*See Sherman to Thomas and Stanley, p. 342.

HDQRS. MILITARY DIVISION OF THE MISSISSIPPI,
In the Field, near Atlanta, Ga., August 3, 1864.

General GRANGER,
　　Decatur:

I want that brigade. Stephen D. Lee is here from Mississippi with 3,500 cavalry, dismounted. Deserters say also that Forrest is here, but, if so, only for consultation. Get General Lorenzo Thomas to give you some negro regiments to hold the railroad stations and bring forward any troops you can get. Consult General Rousseau.

W. T. SHERMAN,
Major-General, Commanding.

HDQRS. DEPARTMENT OF THE CUMBERLAND,
OFFICE PROVOST-MARSHAL-GENERAL,
Near Atlanta, Ga., August 3, 1864.

Brig. Gen. W. D. WHIPPLE,
　　Chief of Staff:

GENERAL: I have the honor to submit the following for your information: J. M. Glass, scout, left the town of Atlanta this morning about 9 o'clock; says that Roddey and Humes (or Holmes) have arrived with re-enforcements, said to number 10,000 men, principally dismounted cavalry. Three thousand militia arrived last night from below; saw this force marching through town this morning. One battalion, commanded by Youngblood, from Columbus, arrived about one week ago. Trains appear to be running regularly to and from Macon. Trains came in on that road last night and this morning. About 600 prisoners were sent off yesterday by railroad to Macon. Generals Bragg and Johnston are in the city; did not hear anything said about Johnston resuming the command; understood they had nine or ten 64-pounders in position; think the principal strength of the enemy is on their left and left center. Colonel Hill, provost-marshal-general, being intoxicated, could not get a pass to enable him (Glass) to visit the lines. The enemy seems to be putting every man into the ranks they can get hold of. Colonel Hill told me they were mounting some new 32-pounder Parrotts in front; did not learn at what part of the line, but understood they were placed in the forts. The enemy say they have captured General Stoneman and 500 of his command, a large portion of the number officers. Stoneman is said to have arrived in front of Macon and commenced shelling the town. The convalescents and militia opposed him, and kept him at bay until General Wheeler's cavalry got in his rear. Stoneman fought his way back fifteen miles before he was taken. That part of his command not killed or captured is reported scattered, with cavalry after them. This information is from a telegram received by General Hood from Macon. McCook destroyed about one mile and a half of the railroad between Jonesborough and Griffin. The road is repaired, however, and trains are running as before. Glass says he came out on south side of Augusta railroad and passed through the works on our left thrown up by General McPherson. Says Martin's division of cavalry is about half way between Atlanta and Decatur, and that there is only a small force opposite our left, composed of militia and a few cavalry. Saw one fort in front of McPherson's old works; saw four guns in it—12 or 20 pounders. There is no forage in the city whatever. Stock is being fed on small patches of green corn in and around the town. They appear to have plenty of subsistence on hand for present use; could not learn whether they had any supply on hand. Since Walker's death, his old division has been cut up and put into Cleburne's and Cheatham's divisions. General Hood's headquarters is in White Hall street, near Rodgers' tannery.

I am, general, very respectfully, your obedient servant,

ED. C. DENIG,
Assistant Adjutant-General.

SHERMAN'S HEADQUARTERS,
August 3, 1864.

General SCHOFIELD:

We are moving to-day, and the general had just ridden off for your flank as yours came. Last from McCook is from deserter, who says order was read stating capture of 500 of his men, and rest killed and dispersed by Wheeler. Some are still reaching our lines. Hardee has resigned, by disagreement with Hood.

L. M. DAYTON,
Aide-de-Camp.

HEADQUARTERS ARMY OF THE OHIO,
Near Atlanta, Ga.; August 3, 1864.

Major-General SHERMAN:

Hascall and Baird are in position, and intrenched. The enemy's artillery fire was quite heavy just before dark, and caused some loss. We will have batteries in position to respond fully in the morning. Hascall captured 49 prisoners from the enemy's skirmish line during his advance. His loss is only about 20 killed and wounded.

J. M. SCHOFIELD,
Major-General.

HDQRS. THIRD DIVISION, TWENTY-THIRD ARMY CORPS,
Before Atlanta, August 3, 1864—7 a. m.

Colonel BARTER,
Commanding Fourth Brigade:

You will move your remaining two regiments immediately to Colonel Casement's left, and put them in line between him and Colonel Crittenden. I have just learned that there is a gap there unfilled. Please use haste in moving, as the gap must not be left unfilled a moment longer than absolutely necessary. When your troops are ready to start report in person to me in advance and I will give more particular instructions.

J. D. COX,
Brigadier-General, Commanding.

CAMP OF SEVENTH OHIO VOLUNTEER CAVALRY,
August 3 [4], 1864.*

Maj. J. A. CAMPBELL,
Assistant Adjutant-General, Army of the Ohio:

MAJOR: I have the honor to report that I made a scout on the road to Sandtown as far as the bridge over Utoy Creek, seven miles from

---

* See Wherry to Garrard, August 4, p. 362.

this point, and made a scout on the road that crosses Utoy Creek at Dollars' Mill. This last road leaves the main road about five miles from here. There has not been for some days any rebel force across Utoy Creek (on this side). The scouts made to-day have crossed Utoy Creek at three places and nothing has been met with but six or seven rebel cavalrymen that were part of a scout of about twenty-five, probably, that went back over the creek at Dollars' Mill.

Very respectfully, your obedient servant,

ISRAEL GARRARD,
Colonel Seventh Ohio Volunteer Cavalry.

NEAR ATLANTA, GA., *August 3, 1864—8.30 p. m.*

Major ECKERT:

No fight yet. Right pushed across Utoy Creek toward railroad near East Point, without finding anything but skirmish line, which retired upon being pressed. McCook has turned up near Dallas, having cut his way through the enemy with 1,200 men. Only 1,000 men of his command now missing, under General Croxton, and they may be safe. No news from Stoneman except from rebels, who say Wheeler caught and thrashed him fifteen miles from Macon after he had shelled that town.

J. C. VAN DUZER.

SPECIAL FIELD ORDERS, } HEADQUARTERS DEPARTMENT
                                   OF THE CUMBERLAND,
No. 212.   } *Near Atlanta, Ga., August 3, 1864.*

*   *   *   *   *   *   *

VII. Maj. Gen. D. S. Stanley, U. S. Volunteers, having been assigned by the President of the United States to the command of the Fourth Army Corps, Brig. Gen. Nathan Kimball, U. S. Volunteers, is assigned to the command of the First Division of that corps.

*   *   *   *   *   *   *

By command of Major-General Thomas:

WM. D. WHIPPLE,
Assistant Adjutant-General.

CITY POINT, VA., *August 4, 1864.*

Major-General SHERMAN:

Richmond Dispatch to-day [yesterday] contains following:

MACON, *August 1.*

Our cavalry under General Iverson attacked the enemy yesterday near Clinton. The Yankees, commanded by General Stoneman, were routed, and about 500 prisoners, with 2 pieces of artillery, surrendered, and have just reached the city. The rest of the Yankee force is scattered and flying toward Eatonton.

U. S. GRANT,
Lieutenant-General.

CITY POINT, VA., *August 4, 1864—10 a. m.*

Major-General SHERMAN:

Richmond papers of yesterday announce the capture of General Stoneman and 500 of his party near Macon, Ga. The capture took place the 31st of July. Have you heard anything of this?

U. S. GRANT,
Lieutenant-General.

NEAR ATLANTA, GA., *August 4, 1864.*
(Received 10.20 p. m.)

Lieut. Gen. U. S. GRANT, *City Point:*

General Stoneman had only 2,300 men; 900 have got in. I fear the balance are captured as related in your dispatch. General Stoneman was sent to break railroad, after which I consented he should attempt the rescue of our prisoners at Andersonville.

W. T. SHERMAN,
Major-General.

NEAR ATLANTA, GA., *August 4, 1864—1.30 p. m.*
(Received 9 p. m. 5th.)

Lieut. Gen. U. S. GRANT, *City Point:*

I have your second dispatch about General Stoneman. I have newspapers with dates from Macon of the 1st, speaking of Stoneman's capture as a rumor, but not as a fact. He started from here in connection with two other parties that have got back. He had 2,300 men, and after breaking the Macon road, he was to make an effort to rescue our prisoners. Colonel Adams, with 900 of his men, got back to Marietta to-day and telegraphs me he was attacked at Clinton, Ga., by overwhelming numbers, and they fear he is captured. It may be so, but I hope he may, like McCook, dodge and get in. Washburn is moving from Holly Springs on Columbus, Miss. He thinks that Forrest is dead of the wound received in his battle with General Smith. The country in which I am operating is very difficult for a large army, and the defensive positions very strong and hard to circumvent, but perseverance will move mountains. I ought to be better advised of your plans and movements. I hear you have blown up the outer bastion of Petersburg, but don't know how near you are to getting full possession of the place, or its bearing on Richmond. Hood uses his militia to fill his lines, and shows a bold front wherever I get at him.

W. T. SHERMAN,
Major-General.

NEAR ATLANTA, GA., *August 4, 1864.*
(Received 10.40 p. m.)

COMMISSARY-GENERAL OF SUBSISTENCE U. S. ARMY:

Cannot something be done at Washington to stimulate the Quartermaster's Department to greater exertions in the way of transportation of our subsistence stores from the Ohio River to Nashville? Our supplies will soon be exhausted, and no visible and adequate means have been instituted to bring additional stores forward.

A. BECKWITH,
Colonel and Chief Commissary.

HDQRS. MILITARY DIVISION OF THE MISSISSIPPI,
In the Field, near Atlanta, Ga., August 4, 1864.

General WEBSTER,
    Nashville:

As some confusion and misunderstanding has occurred relative to my orders as to newspapers and newspaper carriers, I will repeat that it is a small business for me to attend to it in the midst of an active campaign, and one that ought never to reach my notice. The military railroad is to carry supplies for the army. It cannot carry all the supplies allowed by law and usage, and therefore preference must be given to some things over others: First, ammunition; second, clothing; third, provisions for men; fourth, forage for horses; and as I cannot in person supervise the bills of lading or loading of trains, I leave this to the quartermaster at Nashville, who has the best knowledge of the state of supplies forward and at the depot, as well as the capacity of the cars. Newspapers are a kind of freight, and as such I do not object to the quartermaster at Nashville shipping any number of bundles consigned to any of the posts forward, because they occupy little space, and the bulk of such newspapers cannot materially affect the quantity of provisions shipped; but newsvenders, like any other merchants, must not travel in the cars to sell their goods any more than grocers or hucksters. They may send bundles of their papers in the cars by consent of the quartermaster who loads the cars. Every army commander can send his mail messengers daily each way, and these may carry papers as a part of the army mails, and the orders of Generals Thomas, Howard, and Schofield for officers and men are military orders of transportation that quartermasters will respect the same as mine. Passes to citizens as far as Chattanooga, in very limited numbers, may be granted by the authority of either of these army commanders, and they may send to the rear car-loads of prisoners, refugees and citizens, without limit, but I have ordered that on no pretense must citizens come this side of Chattanooga, for I find them useless mouths that we cannot afford to feed. My orders also are that officers must live on the soldier's ration; yet if the quartermaster at Nashville can keep our supplies up, and also send supplies to officers above the rations without interfering with the regular freight, he may do so. In other words, I hold the officers of the quartermaster's department responsible that the army stores take precedence of all other stores, and if he sends anything else he cannot allege it as a reason for a failure to keep up the regular supplies. The railroad has supplied us well, better than I expected, and I am willing to continue to trust the regular quartermasters who thus far have managed the business well. There is and can be no conflict of orders. No one can question my orders when they are positive, but I do not choose to make orders touching freight absolutely positive, save in large articles, such as cotton and produce, that would, if attempted, soon absorb our cars, and thereby diminish the ability of our railroad to handle the vast amount of supplies on which we depend. All I order as to newspapers is that no monopoly should be allowed, and officers can be supplied as in other mail matters, and venders may get the quartermaster at Nashville to carry their bundles, but not their carriers. These are superfluous.

W. T. SHERMAN,
Major-General, Commanding.

NASHVILLE, TENN., *August 4, 1864.*

General SHERMAN:

Orders were given to the military conductors to carry out your instructions to Colonel Donaldson to exclude newspapers from the trains. The provost-marshal, Department of the Cumberland, has detailed military messengers, authorizing them to carry newspapers for traders. There will be a conflict of authorities unless it can be more clearly understood who commands.

> J. D. WEBSTER,
> *Brigadier-General.*

HDQRS. MILITARY DIVISION OF THE MISSISSIPPI,
In the Field, near Atlanta, Ga., August 4, 1864.

General THOMAS:

Will you let General Elliott get a return of all the cavalry not of General Garrard's proper command, including Generals McCook's, Kilpatrick's, and Stoneman's, and Colonel Hamilton's commands, and propose an organization that will make all efficient? Colonel Adams has got to Marietta with 900 of General Stoneman's command. The rest are, I fear, lost to us.

> W. T. SHERMAN,
> *Major-General, Commanding.*

HEADQUARTERS ARMY OF THE CUMBERLAND,
August 4, 1864—6 p. m.

Major-General SHERMAN:

Elliott will get a return of the cavalry as you directed as soon as possible. I heard heavy cannonading for a few moments about 3 p. m. Was there any serious fighting on the right?

> GEO. H. THOMAS,
> *Major-General, U. S. Volunteers, Commanding.*

HDQRS. MILITARY DIVISION OF THE MISSISSIPPI,
In the Field, near Atlanta, Ga., August 4, 1864.

General THOMAS:

Nothing was done on the right. General Palmer's troops seem immovable, but I have ordered operations to be resumed in the morning, and to be continued till we get possession of the Sandtown road.

> W. T. SHERMAN,
> *Major-General, Commanding.*

HDQRS. MILITARY DIVISION OF THE MISSISSIPPI,
In the Field, near Atlanta, Ga., August 4, 1864.

Major-General THOMAS:

General Morgan L. Smith is reported as suffering so much from his old wound that he must go away. I can give Hazen a division in the Army of the Tennessee if you will consent to his transfer. It will make a good opening for his promotion, and the advancement of some good colonel.

> W. T. SHERMAN,
> *Major-General.*

HEADQUARTERS DEPARTMENT OF THE CUMBERLAND,
August 4, 1864.

Major-General SHERMAN:

If I could have known this yesterday I would have consented to General Kimball's going to General Howard. General Hazen is so identified with the Fourth Corps that I would like very much to keep him with it. I will consent to the transfer of General Kimball to the Army of the Tennessee, and then place Hazen in command of the First Division, Fourth Corps, or consent to the transfer of Major-General Milroy to the Army of the Tennessee.

GEO. H. THOMAS,
Major-General, U. S. Volunteers, Commanding.

HEADQUARTERS ARMY OF THE CUMBERLAND,
August 4, 1864.

Major-General STANLEY,
Commanding Fourth Corps:

I wish you to have persons on your lookout stations all along the line to observe closely the movements of the enemy, and hold your troops ready to take advantage of any opportunity to move on their intrenchments. General Sherman thinks his movements this morning will either force them to attack him or place their communications in a critical condition. One of my scouts came in last night. He reports their force opposed to you as weak, its right flank supported by a brigade of cavalry. Martin's division of cavalry is posted on the south of the railroad, and about half way between Atlanta and Decatur. Garrard had better send out a small scouting party of active and intelligent men to find Martin's division and reconnoiter this position, with a view of attacking him if the ground be favorable. McCook has got back with about 1,200 men.

GEO. H. THOMAS,
Major-General, U. S. Volunteers, Commanding.

P. S.—You had better make your headquarters at the house recently occupied by General Sherman, leaving the telegraph office at Wood's headquarters.

G. H. T.

HEADQUARTERS FOURTH ARMY CORPS,
August 4, 1864.

Brigadier-General WHIPPLE,
Chief of Staff:

Colonel Kirby, of Grose's division, just reports as follows: "Our lookout reports that they discover the enemy moving columns of troops to our left." They could discover one entire regiment, and then portions of columns marching by the flank as they moved past an open space. I am just starting over to the left to investigate this matter.

D. S. STANLEY,
Major-General.

HEADQUARTERS FOURTH ARMY CORPS,
Near Atlanta, Ga., August 4, 1864—7.40 p. m.

Brigadier-General WHIPPLE, *Chief of Staff:*

The following just received:

Colonel POST:

My lookout reports that rebel troops appear to be moving in two columns, but cannot tell in what direction on account of the dust.

BENNETT,
Colonel Seventy-fifth Illinois.

Colonel Post's lookout reports the rebels moving from our left toward town. I spent the afternoon at the angle; nothing observed but the movements of two small rebel regiments, one to the right and one to the left.

D. S. STANLEY,
Major-General.

———

SCHOFIELD'S HEADQUARTERS,
August 4, 1864.

Major-General THOMAS:

I have no orders to-day from any quarter. The orders of the day imply co-operation with General Schofield. General S[chofield] has shown me copy.

J. M. PALMER,
Major-General.

[Indorsement.]

Major-General PALMER:

Carry out the instructions contained in the order.

GEO. H. THOMAS,
Major-General.

———

SCHOFIELD'S HEADQUARTERS,
August 4, 1864.

Maj. Gen. G. H. THOMAS,
Commanding Department of the Cumberland:

The orders seem to be intended to give General Schofield control over my troops. Shall I turn them over to him?

J. M. PALMER,
Major-General.

[Indorsement.]

Major-General PALMER:

No. Inform General Schofield that you are ready to co-operate with him. General Sherman does not intend to place you under General Schofield's orders.

GEO. H. THOMAS,
Major-General.

———

HDQRS. MILITARY DIVISION OF THE MISSISSIPPI,
In the Field, near Atlanta, Ga., August 4, 1864.

General PALMER:

You will during the movement against the railroad report to and receive orders from General Schofield. General Thomas will person-

ally look to the front of Atlanta.   General Howard will co-operate with
General Schofield, and General Schofield, re-enforced by your corps, is
charged to reach the railroad.   Obey his orders and instructions.
Acknowledge receipt.

W. T. SHERMAN,
Major-General, Commanding.

HEADQUARTERS FOURTEENTH ARMY CORPS,
In the Field, August 4, 1864.

Major-General SHERMAN,
     Commanding:

  I am General Schofield's senior.   We may co-operate but I respectfully decline to report to or take orders from him.

  Respectfully,

JNO. M. PALMER,
Major-General.

HDQRS. MILITARY DIVISION OF THE MISSISSIPPI,
In the Field, near Atlanta, Ga., August 4, 1864.

General PALMER:

  I was under the impression that General Schofield ranked you.   I
had not thought of the relative rank.   Co-operate heartily and the same
result will be obtained.   I will see you this afternoon.   I assure you
that I have no disposition to qualify your true rank.

W. T. SHERMAN,
Major-General, Commanding.

HEADQUARTERS FOURTEENTH ARMY CORPS,
August 4, 1864—1 p. m.

Maj. Gen. JOHN M. SCHOFIELD:

  I have this moment received a telegraphic order from Major-General
Sherman directing me to report to you and obey your orders, and your
Special Field Orders, No. 71, prescribing the movement of troops to-day.
I respectfully decline obedience to either.   You are my junior.   While it
was a question of co-operation, I raised no question about our respective
rights and rank, and I have no doubt, influenced as we both are by
friendly feelings and a desire to attain the best results, we should have
operated to-day harmoniously.   I did not claim to command your troops
from motives of delicacy.   I will not obey either General Sherman's
order or yours, as they violate my self-respect.   I will nothing of this
sort under orders, whatever I may yield to courtesy.

  Respectfully,

JOHN M. PALMER,
Major-General.

HEADQUARTERS ARMY OF THE OHIO,
Before Atlanta, Ga., August 4, 1864—3 p. m.

Maj. Gen. JOHN M. PALMER,
  Commanding Fourteenth Army Corps:

  GENERAL: I have just received your communication of 11 a. m. [1
p. m.?] to-day, and beg leave to correct your impression that you are my

senior, which you give as your reason for refusing to obey my orders, and that of General Sherman directing you to report to me. You are my junior for two reasons, first, because I have the senior commission, and second, because I am by the President's order commander of a separate army. I regret extremely that any misunderstanding exists on this subject.

Very respectfully, your obedient servant,

J. M. SCHOFIELD,
Major-General, Commanding.

HDQRS. MILITARY DIVISION OF THE MISSISSIPPI,
In the Field, near Atlanta, Ga., August 4, 1864—10.45 p. m.

General PALMER:

From the statements made by yourself and General Schofield to-day, my decision is that he ranks you as major-general, being of same date of commission by previous rank as brigadier-general. The movements for to-morrow are so important that the orders of the superior on that flank should be minutely followed. General Schofield's orders for movement to-morrow must be regarded as military orders and not in the nature of co-operation. I did hope that there was no necessity of making this decision, but it is better for all parties interested that no question of rank should occur during active battle. The Sandtown road and the railroad, if possible, must be gained to-morrow if it costs half your command. I regard the loss of time this afternoon as equal to the loss of 2,000 men.

W. T. SHERMAN,
Major-General, Commanding.

HEADQUARTERS FOURTEENTH ARMY CORPS,
In the Field, August 4, 1864—11.55 p. m.

Maj. Gen. W. T. SHERMAN:

Dispatch of 10.45 of this p. m. this moment received. I am unable to acquiesce in the correctness of the decision that Major-General Schofield legally ranks me. I do not argue the question, but repeat the facts. General Schofield was appointed brigadier-general on the 21st of November, 1861, and I was appointed to the same on the 20th of December of the same year. At the session of Congress 1862-'63 General Schofield and myself were promoted to the rank of major general of volunteers. My appointment was confirmed by the Senate and his expired by constitutional limitation. Not having been confirmed by the Senate his name, therefore, does not appear in the list of major-generals in the Army Register of April 1, 1863. He was reappointed by the President and confirmed since the commencement of the present campaign. His commission must be a year in date junior to my own, though he is said to take rank from the 29th of November, 1862.

The question of rank has arisen by accident and I agree with you that it is better for the interest of all parties that it should be decided but I cannot acquiesce in the correctness of the decision made. I respectfully ask, therefore, that some officer be designated to whom may turn over the command of the Fourteenth Army Corps.

I think I need not assure you or General Schofield that I am not influenced by any desire to command him, nor that, if I deemed it consist ent with my self-respect to waive the question or my views of our relative rank, I would obey his orders as cheerfully as I would those of any gentleman connected with the army.

I am, very respectfully,

JOHN M. PALMER,
Major-General.

HEADQUARTERS TWENTIETH CORPS,
Near Atlanta, Ga., August 4, 1864—9 a. m.

Brig. Gen. J. F. KNIPE, *Commanding First Division:*

GENERAL: The general commanding the corps directs me to send you the inclosed order of Major-General Sherman* and to say that the withdrawal of troops from this part of the line for important operations on the right possibly may induce the enemy to make a demonstration and perhaps an attack on our lines. He directs that all the troops be kept well in hand at the breast-works; that all the reserves be stationed at the weakest points in the lines, and everything be in readiness for immediate use. The reserves of the First Division will be held near the railroad. The general desires that all commanding officers will be with their commands during the day and see personally to the dispositions.

I am, general, very respectfully, your obedient servant,

H. W. PERKINS,
Lieutenant-Colonel and Assistant Adjutant-General.

(Same to Generals Geary and Ward.)

HEADQUARTERS TWENTIETH CORPS,
Near Atlanta, Ga., August 4, 1864.

Brig. Gen. W. T. WARD, *Commanding Third Division:*

GENERAL: The general commanding the corps directs that you push the work on the new breast-works to the utmost, and occupy them with your troops at the earliest possible moment. General Thomas has so ordered.

I am, general, very respectfully, your obedient servant,

H. W. PERKINS,
Lieutenant-Colonel and Assistant Adjutant-General.

SIGNAL DEPT., ARMY OF THE CUMBERLAND,
August 4, 1864.

Brigadier-General WILLIAMS,
Commanding Twentieth Army Corps:

GENERAL: I have the honor to report the following just received from station of observation at General Geary's headquarters:

Can see no movement whatever in Atlanta nor along the works. Some of the works in front of Twentieth Army Corps very strong, having in some cases two rows sharpened sticks and one and two rows abatis. Can see considerable artillery firing at a point due southwest from here.

I am, very respectfully, your obedient servant,

W. W. HOPKINS,
First Lieutenant and Acting Signal Officer.

---

* See p. 364.

DECATUR, *August 4, 1864.*

Major-General SHERMAN:

Two regiments of brigade, now loading on cars, will be off soon. Others will follow soon as transportation is furnished to four guns belonging to brigade artillery, without horses and short of men. Shall they go forward? Rousseau is looking up all the troops he can find. Don't know how he has succeeded. Will apply for negro regiments. If I can get them I can forward Tenth Indiana Cavalry, 900 strong. Six companies of Ninth, also dismounted, could be replaced by colored troops.

R. S. GRANGER,
Brigadier-General.

HEADQUARTERS ARMY OF THE OHIO,
Near Atlanta, Ga., August 4, 1864.

Major-General SHERMAN:

Colonel Garrard drove the rebel pickets across Utoy Creek, at Dollars' Mill, and at the bridge near its mouth, so that there is now no rebel cavalry this side of the creek. I propose in the morning to work forward from Hascall's left toward the high wooded hill occupied by the rebel artillery, thus shortening the line across to Howard, and if possible gain the hill. I can do nothing on my right until Palmer works up onto the Sandtown road. I will hold Cox ready to strike there as soon as the movement on the right will justify it.

Respectfully,

J. M. SCHOFIELD,
Major-General.

HDQRS. MILITARY DIVISION OF THE MISSISSIPPI,
In the Field, near Atlanta, Ga., August 4, 1864.

General SCHOFIELD:

I am willing you should attempt to carry that wooded hill to the left front of General Hascall, but its value is not great as compared to advancing our extreme right to and beyond the Sandtown road. So we conform our general line close to theirs, it makes little difference to us where their line is.

W. T. SHERMAN,
Major-General, Commanding.

HDQRS. MILITARY DIVISION OF THE MISSISSIPPI,
In the Field, near Atlanta, Ga., August 4, 1864.
(Received 9.50 a. m.)

General SCHOFIELD:

As a preliminary move to that prescribed in orders, I suggest you dispatch at once a brigade of General Palmer's reserve down the peninsula between Utoy and Chattahoochee toward Utoy Post-Office, to have the effect of making the enemy believe we propose to extend our lines down the big Sandtown road; the cavalry to move on their right, and none to go beyond Utoy Creek. The cavalry to remain and demonstrate as though we intended to cross there, and the infantry to rejoin its division.

W. T. SHERMAN,
Major-General, Commanding.

HDQRS. MILITARY DIVISION OF THE MISSISSIPPI,
In the Field, near Atlanta, Ga., August 4, 1864.

General SCHOFIELD:

As soon as you have made enough roads and bridges to have easy communication across Utoy, I will come down to General Howard's right and your left. I think that dam might be cut away and a couple crossing-places made near General Cox's left and center. I want the heavy columns to move as early as 3 p. m., and there should be at least one road per division across Utoy and up the hill.

W. T. SHERMAN,
Major-General, Commanding.

HEADQUARTERS ARMY OF THE OHIO,
August 4, 1864—11.30 a. m.

Major-General SHERMAN:

We have good facilities for crossing the creek. I have ordered all preparations for the attack to be made by 2 o'clock, though we may not be ready before 3. Do you desire it made at any particular hour? General Palmer is sending a brigade to the right, as you suggested. Will you be here in person? General Palmer is making preparations to execute your orders, but expects orders through General Thomas.

J. M. SCHOFIELD,
Major-General.

HDQRS. MILITARY DIVISION OF THE MISSISSIPPI,
In the Field, near Atlanta, Ga., August 4, 1864.

General SCHOFIELD:

I have notified other commanders that the attack will commence at 3 p. m. That will be early enough. In the mean time make all preparations, especially to look to your connection with General Howard. I will be over. General Palmer will be ordered to report to you with his command.

W. T. SHERMAN,
Major-General, Commanding.

AUGUST 4, 1864.

General SCHOFIELD:

I am just starting for your flank. Go on and I will overtake you.

W. T. SHERMAN,
Major-General.

HDQRS. MILITARY DIVISION OF THE MISSISSIPPI,
In the Field, near Atlanta, Ga., August 4, 1864.
(Received 9.20 p. m.)

General SCHOFIELD:

That is very well as to your left, but I want to assume the offensive on the right, and wish you to order General Palmer to advance his left division till he reaches the Sandtown road, and its right supported by General Davis' division. General Johnson's division should reach the

Sandtown road more to the right, and close to the left on General Davis. The connection between you and General Howard is not important. Slash down the timber in the valley of Utoy, and a single battery with a regiment of skirmishers will hold a mile against the whole of Hood's army. I want all of your army and General Palmer's corps to turn the enemy's left, and the sooner it is done the better. I wish you to make written orders, so that Generals Palmer and Baird cannot mistake them. Their delay this afternoon was unpardonable. If the enemy ever gets a column through our lines, we will let go our breast-works and turn on his flanks, and, therefore, I do not care about our line being continuous and uniform. If they sally it will be quick and by some well-defined road.

W. T. SHERMAN,
Major-General, Commanding.

HEADQUARTERS ARMY OF THE OHIO,
August 4, 1864—9.20 p. m.

Major-General SHERMAN:

I have your dispatch directing me to order certain movements by General Palmer's corps. I did not understand that the question of rank raised by General Palmer was settled. In his reply to my orders for to-day's movements and your order to report to me he said: "I will not obey either General Sherman's order or yours," the reason being his assumed seniority. In subsequent conversations he still maintained the same ground and I did not understand him to yield or you to decide the question after you arrived but to waive it, with the remark that no such question could arise between such men, and that we could co-operate harmoniously. I feel confident that General Palmer understands the question as having been so waived. Please inform me if you gave General Palmer distinctly to understand that he is to obey my orders. Please have it understood before I send him orders for to-morrow. It is a very delicate and unpleasant matter for me to correspond with him about.

Respectfully,

J. M. SCHOFIELD,
Major-General.

HEADQUARTERS ARMY OF THE OHIO,
Before Atlanta, Ga., August 4, 1864—12.15 p. m.

Maj. Gen. J. M. PALMER,
Commanding Fourteenth Army Corps:

GENERAL: Major-General Schofield directs me to inform you that the attack to-day will be made at 3 p. m. instead of at 2 p. m., as previously ordered. The general desires you, however, to continue your preparations in order to be sure to be ready at that hour.

Very respectfully, your obedient servant,

J. A. CAMPBELL,
Major and Assistant Adjutant-General.

(Same to Generals Cox and Hascall.)

HEADQUARTERS ARMY OF THE OHIO,
Near Utoy Creek, Ga., August 4, 1864.

General THOMAS:

General Sherman directed me to telegraph you and say the troops of Generals Schofield and Palmer were advancing across Utoy Creek and toward the Sandtown road. General Sherman is on the hill this side of the creek and just above Herring's Mill.

W. C. BARTLETT,
Captain and Aide-de-Camp.

(Same to General Stanley.)

HEADQUARTERS ARMY OF THE OHIO,
Before Atlanta, Ga., August 4, 1864.

Brig. Gen. R. W. JOHNSON,
Commanding Fourteenth Army Corps:

GENERAL: Major-General Schofield directs me to forward you the inclosed Special Field Orders, No. 71, current series, from these headquarters, for to-morrow's movements of the Fourteenth and Twenty-third Army Corps.* The order is sent to you as the senior and commanding general of the Fourteenth Army Corps, as Major-General Palmer still adheres to the views he expressed on yesterday. In order to prevent any delay, Generals Baird and Morgan have been furnished with copies of the inclosed orders direct from these headquarters.

Very respectfully, your obedient servant,

J. A. CAMPBELL,
Major and Assistant Adjutant-General.

HDQRS. THIRD DIVISION, TWENTY-THIRD ARMY CORPS,
Utoy Creek, August 4, 1864—3.30 p. m.

Major-General SCHOFIELD,
Commanding Army of the Ohio:

SIR: I have made a personal reconnaissance of General Hascall's right and Baird's left. General Baird has not yet moved and told me five minutes ago he had as yet no orders. Reilly's brigade is in the creek bottom ready to cross. I have halted the others in the road out of sight. Any advance from Hascall's right will be taken in rear by the enemy's fire until General Baird's right is swung forward so as to continue the direction of the line in its prolongation as it leaves Hascall. A little farther to the left the ground is open and an advance would have no cover whatever. There is a ridge running straight forward from Hascall's right on which a movement can be made whenever it is covered from the rear fire of which I have spoken. An officer whom I take to be one of General Palmer's staff has just passed seeking General Baird.

Very respectfully, &c.,

J. D. COX,
Brigadier-General, Commanding.

---

* See p. 364.

HEADQUARTERS ARMY OF THE OHIO,
Before Atlanta, Ga., August 4, 1864—9 p. m.

Brig. Gen. M. S. HASCALL,
Commanding Second Division, Twenty-third Army Corps:

GENERAL: General Palmer is ordered to press forward onto the Sandtown road in the morning; and the programme of to-day in substance is still to be pursued during the morning. Until Palmer's movements enable Cox to work from your right we will direct our attention to your left. It occurs to me that your reserve brigade can work forward and get to the low ridge in front of your left and near the hill occupied by the rebel artillery, and I think it not improbable that we may be able to gain that hill. At all events, we will shorten the line across to Howard, and make a strong diversion in favor of operations to the right. Study the matter and see what can be done. We ought to begin pretty early in the morning.

Very respectfully, your obedient servant,
J. M. SCHOFIELD,
Major-General, Commanding.

HEADQUARTERS ARMY OF THE OHIO,
Near Atlanta, Ga., August 4, 1864.

Col. ISRAEL GARRARD,
Commanding Seventh Ohio Cavalry:

COLONEL: Your dispatch of to-day (dated yesterday, the 3d instant) has been received and read by the major-general commanding, who directs me to inform you that to-morrow (the 5th instant) General Howard will send over a regiment of mounted infantry to co-operate with you on your right. The commanding general desires you, with this regiment, to guard all the fords and bridges of Utoy Creek below the point where General King's brigade crossed, and prevent enemy's crossing.

Very respectfully, your obedient servant,
WM. M. WHERRY,
Major and Aide-de-Camp.

HDQRS. MILITARY DIVISION OF THE MISSISSIPPI,
In the Field, near Atlanta, Ga., August 4, 1864.

General HOWARD:

General Thomas is willing to give General Kimball, but says General Hazen is so identified with the Fourth Corps that he cannot spare him.

W. T. SHERMAN,
Major-General, Commanding.

HDQRS. MILITARY DIVISION OF THE MISSISSIPPI,
In the Field, near Atlanta, Ga., August 4, 1864.

General HOWARD:

Order more and better bridges over Proctor's Creek. There should be two good ones where there is now one, and another opposite Davis' hill, where the old mill was.

W. T. SHERMAN,
Major-General, Commanding.

HEADQUARTERS LEFT WING, SIXTEENTH ARMY CORPS,
Near Atlanta, Ga., August 4, 1864.

Lieut. Col. WILLIAM T. CLARK,
Assistant Adjutant-General:

I have the honor to report that in accordance with orders I advanced my skirmish line to-day, taking the rebel rifle-pits just before dark. The enemy attacked my line heavily along its entire front and drove me back. I re-enforced the line until I had five regiments engaged, and retook the pits and now hold them. The ground, however, is untenable, from the fact that at dark the advance of the troops on my left had not connected, my line being in advance of their skirmishers, and General Leggett reported that he could not hold his line, and fell back to the old line. I therefore ordered that my line should be held and intrenched as far in advance of the old line as the connection on the right and left would admit. Prisoners captured say that our extreme advance was within 600 yards of their main works.

I am, very respectfully, your obedient servant,
G. M. DODGE,
Major-General, Commanding.

[AUGUST 4, 1864.—For Logan to Clark, reporting skirmish on August 3, with table of casualties, see Part III, p. 87.]

MARIETTA, *August 4, 1864.*

Major-General SHERMAN:

Colonel Adams, commanding brigade of Stoneman's cavalry, is here with the First and Eleventh Kentucky, about 900 strong. He thinks that the balance of the command are prisoners, including General Stoneman. He cut the railroad south of Macon. The command was overwhelmed by the rebels between Monticello and Clinton.

SAML. ROSS,
Colonel Twentieth Connecticut Volunteers, Commanding.

HDQRS. MILITARY DIVISION OF THE MISSISSIPPI,
In the Field, near Atlanta, Ga., August 4, 1864.

Colonel ROSS,
Marietta:

Let Colonel Adams collect all of General Stoneman's cavalry, make his depot at Marietta, and picket Roswell in connection with the regiment of infantry there. I will trust that General Stoneman will fight his way out like General McCook. Tell Colonel Adams to make a minute report of the facts and let me draw conclusions.

W. T. SHERMAN,
Major-General, Commanding.

ROME, *August 4, 1864.*

Major-General STEEDMAN:

A considerable body of the enemy are reported to have crossed the Coosa below here for the purpose of making a raid upon the railroad.

WM. VANDEVER,
Brigadier-General, Commanding.

NEAR ATLANTA, GA., *August 4, 1864—11 p. m.*

Maj. THOMAS T. ECKERT:

Nothing accomplished to-day, movements having been brought to deadlock by squabble about rank between Schofield and Palmer, which at this hour is unsettled. Hope to do something to-morrow but cannot say exactly what. No further news from Stoneman's force.

J. C. VAN DUZER.

SPECIAL FIELD ORDERS, } HDQRS. MIL. DIV. OF THE MISS.,
                      In the Field, near Atlanta, Ga.,
No. 51.   }   *August 4, 1864.*

The order of movement of the army to-day will be as follows:

I. Major-General Schofield with his own command and General Palmer's corps will move directly on the railroad which leads south out of Atlanta, at any point between White Hall and East Point, and will not stop until he has absolute control of that railroad, but must not extend more to the right than is absolutely necessary to that end.

II. Major-Generals Thomas and Howard will press close on the enemy at all points, and re-enforce well the points of the line where the enemy is most likely to sally, viz, on the Decatur, Buck Head, and Turner's Ferry roads, but more especially watch the outlet along the railroad, viz, General Williams' front.

III. On the right we must assume the offensive and every man be prepared to fight, leaving knapsacks, &c., in the present trenches. Wagons will not be taken east of Utoy Creek until General Schofield has secured position on the railroad or so near it that it can be reached by musket-balls and canister. If necessary to secure this end ordinary parapets must be charged and carried, and every hour's delay enables the enemy to strengthen. Therefore let it be done to-day.

By order of Maj. Gen. W. T. Sherman:

L. M. DAYTON,
Aide-de-Camp.

SPECIAL FIELD ORDERS, }   HDQRS. ARMY OF THE OHIO,
No. 71.   }   *Near Atlanta, Ga., August 4, 1864.*

I. To carry out the orders for the day from headquarters Military Division of the Mississippi the following movements will be made: Generals Baird's and Hascall's divisions will press forward close to the enemy's works from left to right, make a strong and continuous demonstration, and even attack in case the character of the enemy's works or the strength of his forces indicate that they can be carried. General Palmer will support General Baird's right, with one division in reserve. General Cox's division (three brigades), of the Twenty-third Army Corps, and one division of General Palmer's corps will be formed into strong columns of attack to the right and rear of General Baird's, prepared to attack the enemy's position in their front at 2 p. m. The advance of the attacking force will be immediately preceded by a very strong line of skirmishers, to drive the enemy into his intrenchments, and press close enough to be able to reconnoiter well the position. The commanders of the attacking force will quickly reconnoiter the enemy's lines and select their points of attack. If it be found that the enemy's works are only ordinary parapets and without impassable abatis or other serious obstructions in front, the assault will be made at once, so as not to leave time for the enemy to re-enforce the points threatened. If the commanders judge that the enemy's line cannot be carried, the assault will be delayed and the reconnaissance continued to the right. If a point of the enemy's line be carried, the advantage will be pressed as vigorously as practicable until a point be gained commanding at short musket-range the railroad. The point of the railroad to be gained is about east or southeast from the point of attack. General Cox will swing forward Barter's and Crittenden's brigades, so as to substantially connect General Howard's right and General Hascall's left, and strongly intrench the new position. General Cox's attacking column will form on the left, immediately to Baird's right, and that of General Palmer's corps on the right. General Palmer's reserve division will support the right.

*   *   *   *   *   *   *

IV. The movements of the Fourteenth and Twenty-third Corps to-morrow will be as follows, viz: At 5 a. m. General Johnson will move for the Sandtown road and push forward vigorously along that road until he connects with, or comes in close supporting distance to, General Davis. At 6 a. m. General Baird will push forward his whole line, conforming it substantially to the direction of the enemy's works, until he drives in the enemy's skirmishers and draws the fire of their line. General Davis' division will advance in support of General Baird's right, and, if it can be done without seriously exposing his own flank, will prolong General Baird's line until he crosses the Sandtown road; in which case General Johnson, on coming up, will be in reserve. If General Davis finds it impracticable to cross the road before General Johnson comes up, he will refuse his right until General Johnson arrives within supporting distance, when General Davis will swing forward, leaving General Johnson in reserve. General Baird will move without reference to his connection with General Hascall. General Cox will promptly fill any gap which may be [made] by his movement and will support him in case of an attack by the enemy. In addition to the above, General Cox will hold his division in readiness to be used as an assaulting force at any point which may be selected after the movements above ordered have been executed. If in the above movement either division reach a point of the enemy's line which, in the opinion of the division commander, can be carried, he will assault at once, notifying his superior officer and the commanders of the adjacent divisions of his intentions, so that they may promptly take advantage of any success he may gain. If the troops find themselves confronting positions too strong to be carried, they will intrench at once, and prepare to hold their lines with as small force as practicable, when the movement will be continued to the right, with a view to turn the enemy's left or reach a point of his lines which can be assaulted with success. Promptness and vigor are essential to the success of this movement. If General Palmer finds that he can reach the enemy's flank by detaching a division a short distance to the right, he will send the division with orders to strike the flank vigorously and, by forcing the enemy back, secure its connection with the corps. In case of such a movment, General Cox will move to the right as a reserve. General Johnson will watch well his right and rear during his advance on the Sandtown road, and keep a strong skirmish line well out in those directions. General Hascall will thin out his line as much as he can with safety, so as to obtain a strong reserve for use at other points of the field. He will use his artillery freely, and press his skirmishers during the movements on his right.

By command of Major-General Schofield:

J. A. CAMPBELL,
Major and Assistant Adjutant-General.

Special Field Orders, ⎰ Headquarters Department
                                               ⎱ and Army of the Tennessee,
    No. 88.   ⎱ *Before Atlanta, Ga., August 4, 1864.*

   *   *   *   *   *   *   *

IV. Major-General Schofield having been ordered to move his command, with the corps of Major-General Palmer, in order to throw himself across the railroad, commencing the movement at 3 o'clock this p. m., the following are the orders for this army:

1. At 2.30 p. m. to-day the line of skirmishers will be doubled, and the enemy pressed hard along the whole line.

2. All the men in the trenches will stand under arms during the demonstration, without their knapsacks.

3. Major-General Logan's division will be held where it now is, in readiness to move to any point at a moment's warning.

4. It is desirable that corps commanders personally superintend the movement of the skirmishers, using their artillery when and where they deem necessary with a view to keeping the enemy in his works and to deceive him as to the real movement.

5. The general or some of his staff will be at De Gress' battery near the right of line.

   *   *   *   *   *   *   *

VIII. Brig. Gen. Morgan L. Smith, U. S. Volunteers, will as soon as able for duty proceed to Memphis, Tenn., and report to Maj. Gen. C. C. Washburn for assignment to the command of the District of Vicksburg. The major-general commanding takes this occasion to express his sincere regret that the failing health of General Smith has compelled him to leave the front, where during this campaign he has so gallantly distinguished himself, and added to his already brilliant reputation as a skillful and an accomplished officer, winning the confidence and esteem of his superiors and endearing himself to this whole command.

IX. Major-General Dodge, commanding Left Wing, Sixteenth Army Corps, will direct the Ninth Illinois Cavalry* to establish their headquarters on the Green's Ferry road, and form a line of pickets from the right of the infantry or cavalry (if there be any cavalry on the right of the line) to the main Utoy Creek, keeping up their patrol, and reporting the result frequently to these headquarters. Major-General Dodge will cause his front to be reconnoitered by his engineer officer with a view to the establishment of a new advanced line to connect with the new line to be established in front of the Seventeenth Army Corps.

2. Major-General Blair, commanding Seventeenth Corps, will cause his front to be reconnoitered with a view to the establishment of a new line. He will direct his engineer officer to act in concert with the engineer officers of the Fifteenth and Sixteenth Corps, under the supervision of Capt. C. B. Reese, chief engineer.

3. Major-General Logan, commanding Fifteenth Army Corps, will cause his front to be reconnoitered, and will connect his advanced line

---

* Mounted infantry.

with the Seventeenth Corps, directing his engineers to co-operate with the engineers of the Seventeenth Army Corps, under the direction of Capt. C. B. Reese, chief engineer.

4. The object being to advance as rapidly and as far as possible toward the enemy's position, corps commanders will act in concert, secure all vantage ground and every commanding position.

By order of Maj. Gen. O. O. Howard:

WM. T. CLARK,
Assistant Adjutant-General.

SPECIAL FIELD ORDERS, } HDQRS. LEFT WING, 16TH ARMY CORPS,
No. 54.   }   *Near Atlanta, Ga., August 4, 1864.*

I. In order to successfully carry out Special Field Orders, No. 88, Department and Army of the Tennessee, the following instructions will be complied with as near as possible by division commanders:

First. The skirmish line will be doubled, ready to advance before the appointed time. As good a knowledge of the ground will be obtained as possible, and when the advance is made, the batteries will open upon the skirmish line of the enemy and his rifle-pits carried; the move to be made in conjunction on the right with the Seventeenth Corps and on the left, if practicable, with the Twentieth Corps.

Second. After the enemy's line is carried and during the time batteries will continue to play upon the enemy's main works or any of his troops that may be discerned. Commanders of divisions will have an understanding with the division commanders on their right and left, so that the advance can be made in unison.

Headquarters of the general commanding will be on the hill near the signal station.

By order of Maj. Gen. G. M. Dodge:

J. W. BARNES,
Assistant Adjutant-General.

HDQRS. MILITARY DIVISION OF THE MISSISSIPPI,
In the Field, near Atlanta, Ga., August 5, 1864.
(Received 11 a. m. 6th.)

Hon. E. M. STANTON,
Secretary of War:

The time has now come that we must have the exclusive use of the Northwestern road from Nashville to Reynoldsburg. It has been substantially done for some time, but Governor Johnson retains the management of it for some reason, under your former orders; but to be of service to us in the present emergency it must be in the control of Mr. Anderson, superintendent of military roads, that trains may run continuously from the Tennessee River, at Reynoldsburg, to our camp. This main road has been admirably managed, and has supplied this vast army, so that not a man, horse, or mule has been for a day without food and abundant supplies of clothing and ammunition. Our progress may be slow to you all at a distance, but if you ever cross this ground you will not accuse us of being idlers.

W. T. SHERMAN,
Major-General, Commanding.

WASHINGTON, *August 5, 1864—10.15 a. m.*

Major-General SHERMAN,
    Near Atlanta, Ga.:

Your request about horses from Saint Louis has been anticipated. Instead of 2,000 on hand, they will not be able to send you 1,000 in less than a week. The country is nearly exhausted of cavalry horses, and unless there is a greater economy in their use the men must very soon go afoot.

H. W. HALLECK,
    Major-General and Chief of Staff.

HDQRS. MILITARY DIVISION OF THE MISSISSIPPI,
    In the Field, near Atlanta, Ga., August 5, 1864.

Governor ANDREW JOHNSON,
    Nashville, Tenn.:

We will now need the exclusive use of the railroad from the Tennessee to Nashville, to be operated by the same parties who now operate the Chattanooga. Cars will load at Reynoldsburg and come to our camp. I will instruct General Webster to make all the orders necessary to make the transfer. If the road and fixtures are incomplete, we will take it as it is and make the best use we can of it.

W. T. SHERMAN,
    Major-General, Commanding.

HDQRS. MILITARY DIVISION OF THE MISSISSIPPI,
    In the Field, near Atlanta, Ga., August 5, 1864.

General WEBSTER,
    Nashville:

See Governor Johnson and arrange for transferring the railroad to the Tennessee, from Reynoldsburg to Nashville, to Mr. Anderson, superintendent of road, that he may use his trains from Reynoldsburg to our camp at Atlanta. Notify Colonel Donaldson to use that road hereafter, and to make temporary sheds at the river. Telegraph to Admiral Porter as to patrolling the river up as far as Reynoldsburg, and see General Rousseau as to guarding it to Nashville. Make all arrangements that the route may be entire and complete under one single management. When the Cumberland River rises so as to be available it may again, so far as I am concerned, go back to the management of Governor Johnson. I will telegraph the Secretary of War as to the necessity of this change.

W. T. SHERMAN,
    Major-General, Commanding.

SCHOFIELD'S HEADQUARTERS,
    August 5, 1864.

Major-General SHERMAN:

Nothing done, nor will anything be done to-day.

WILLARD WARNER,
    Lieutenant-Colonel, &c.

HDQRS. MILITARY DIVISION OF THE MISSISSIPPI,
In the Field, near Atlanta, Ga., August 5, 1864.

General THOMAS,
Army of the Cumberland:

Yesterday General Palmer raised the question of rank with General Schofield. I went in person and found that General Schofield ranked General Palmer as a brigadier; but General Palmer was appointed and confirmed major-general to date November 29, 1862. General Schofield was also nominated from same date, but the Senate would not confirm. But since that session the Senate has confirmed, and General Schofield has his commission of same date as General Palmer, and ranks him by virtue of prior commission. I have so decided, and General Palmer asks to be relieved of his command and to be ordered North. I declined and ordered him emphatically to go on to-day and execute the plan prescribed for yesterday, in connection with and under command of General Schofield. I have another letter from him, asking to be relieved after to-day's operations. Now, what say you? General Davis is unwell and General Johnson ranks him. That is the largest corps we have, and thus far has not sustained heavy loss in this campaign. It moves slowly and reluctantly and there is something wrong. What are your plans and wishes? General Schofield reports that General Johnson's division has reached the Sandtown road well to the right by a road I put it on last night. General Morgan's division also has reached it, and General Baird is swinging by a left wheel, so his right flank will reach it. Generals Schofield and Palmer have both gone out to complete the movement, which involves a push toward the railroad till our right flank is near enough the railroad to control it by short-range artillery. There was sharp firing for a few moments this morning, but it has ceased now, so that I begin to think we will succeed on that flank without the serious battle I apprehended. Still, keep your ears open, and if you hear heavy musketry over near White Hall, either make a break into Atlanta or so occupy the lines that the enemy may not detach too heavily against Generals Schofield and Palmer. Generals Howard and Schofield will connect by a shorter line across the head of Utoy Creek. Our cavalry has scouted down to the mouth of Utoy Creek.

W. T. SHERMAN,
Major-General, Commanding.

HEADQUARTERS DEPARTMENT OF THE CUMBERLAND,
August 5, 1864—9.30 a. m.

Major-General SHERMAN:

Your dispatch received. I regret to hear that Palmer has taken the course he has, and as I know he intends to offer his resignation as soon as he feels he can do so without injury to himself I recommend that his application to be relieved from the command of the Fourteenth Army Corps be granted. I earnestly recommend Brig. Gen. J. C. Davis for major-general U. S. Volunteers for past services and uniform gallantry in battle, and apply to have him assigned to the command of the Fourteenth Army Corps. I have everybody on the lookout for any movement of the enemy.

GEO. H. THOMAS,
Major-General, U. S. Volunteers.

HDQRS. MILITARY DIVISION OF THE MISSISSIPPI,
In the Field, near Atlanta, Ga., August 5, 1864.

General THOMAS:

Your dispatch is received. I will send a copy of it to General Palmer and give him a couple of hours to think of it, and if he reiterates his application I will leave you to accept and let him go. I will then indorse your recommendation of General Jeff. C. Davis as major-general and commander of the Fourteenth Corps. I don't want General Palmer to make so fatal a mistake as he seems bent on committing.

W. T. SHERMAN,
Major-General, Commanding.

SHERMAN'S HEADQUARTERS,
August 5, 1864.

Generals THOMAS and SCHOFIELD:

The following dispatch has just come through General Howard:

The pickets report heavy movements of trains toward our right. The rebel skirmishers are very active along the whole line. It may be an evacuation, or they may be massing their forces on Schofield.

GILES A. SMITH,
Brigadier-General.

General Giles A. Smith is about Howard's center, in front of where the battle of the 28th was fought, therefore opposite to and nearest White Hall. Let Stanley pitch in again and generally let all our lines be active. If our movements had been more positive to-day I should infer that the enemy was quitting Atlanta to make sure of East Point.

W. T. SHERMAN,
Major-General.

HDQRS. MILITARY DIVISION OF THE MISSISSIPPI,
In the Field, near Atlanta, Ga., August 5, 1864.

General THOMAS:

General Schofield telegraphs:

I am compelled to acknowledge that I have totally failed to make any aggressive movement with the Fourteenth Corps. The efforts yesterday and to-day on this flank have been more than mere failures. I have ordered General Johnson to relieve General Hascall this evening, and propose to take my own troops to the right and try to recover what has been lost by two days' delay. The force may very likely be too small.

From what I saw myself there was a manifest determination not to move toward the enemy. General Davis' division is a mile farther west than when it started. I see no help for it but to lose the services of the corps and let General Schofield feel for the enemy eastward, while the Fourteenth intrenches against a squad of cavalry that may be on the flank. Colonel Warner, of my staff, rode out half a mile in front of the extreme front and saw no sign of an enemy. I will have General Palmer report in the morning, and if he wishes to go it is best he should.

W. T. SHERMAN,
Major-General, Commanding.

HDQRS. DEPT. OF THE CUMBERLAND, *August 5, 1864.*

Major-General SHERMAN:

I am surprised to receive such a report of the Fourteenth Corps, for it has always been prompt in executing any work given to it heretofore. If General Palmer is an obstacle to its efficiency, I would let him go. I had the Fourth and Twentieth Corps demonstrate strongly on the enemy's line from 12 m. until night. They found the intrenchments heavily manned. I will have the skirmishers feel forward again to-night to see if the enemy have left. The Fourth and Twentieth Corps now occupy the whole line held by the Twenty-third, Twentieth, and Fourth Corps before the movement on the right commenced, consequently they are in single line, and it will be impossible to form an assaulting column. I sent Whipple to the right to-day. He has just returned and informed me that all that was done to-day on the right was done by Baird's division, which advanced in obedience to Schofield's orders, but not being supported either on its right or left, General Baird fell back to his former position after having driven the enemy from two lines of rifle-pits, and capturing 160 prisoners, losing about 100 men himself.

GEO. H. THOMAS,
Major-General.

HDQRS. MILITARY DIVISION OF THE MISSISSIPPI,
In the Field, near Atlanta, Ga., August 5, 1864.

General THOMAS:

Colonel Warner, one of my inspectors-general, who was on the right all day, reports nothing done or would be done. Will General Johnson be any better than General Palmer? I would prefer to move a rock than to move that corps. On the defensive it would be splendid, but for offensive it is of no use. It must have a head that will give it life and impulse. I was ashamed yesterday and kept away on purpose to-day to see if orders would not move it, but if an enemy can be seen by a spy-glass the whole corps is halted and intrenched for a siege. Unless it will attack I must relieve it in orders and state the reason. I will call for official reports and act to-night. Is General Johnson capable of handling the corps till we can have General Davis commissioned and ordered to the command?

W. T. SHERMAN,
Major-General, Commanding.

HEADQUARTERS DEPARTMENT OF THE CUMBERLAND,
August 5, 1864.

Major-General SHERMAN:

Johnson ought to be able to maneuver the corps. He has commanded a division for more than two years.

GEO. H. THOMAS,
Major-General.

HDQRS. MILITARY DIVISION OF THE MISSISSIPPI,
In the Field, near Atlanta, Ga., August 5, 1864.

Generals THOMAS and HOWARD:

I hear General Schofield engaged well off to the right. Always push up against Atlanta at the weakest points in your front assaulting

parties, who may during an attack at the right gain one of their redoubts or salients, which will settle the question quick; at all events
will keep employed a large force to hold their lines.

W. T. SHERMAN,
Major-General, Commanding.

SHERMAN'S HEADQUARTERS,
August 5, 1864.

General THOMAS:

Generals Schofield and Palmer must be engaged. We can hear the
musketry.

W. T. SHERMAN,
Major-General.

HDQRS. MILITARY DIVISION OF THE MISSISSIPPI,
In the Field, near Atlanta, Ga., August 5, 1864.

General THOMAS:

I telegraphed to General R. S. Granger this morning that he need
not send the battery along with the infantry brigade. If not needed at
Decatur order General Granger to send it to Nashville in reserve. I
know that the slowness of the troops on the right was not the fault of
the men, but the want of proper direction on the part of the commanders. First, was the question of rank; and next, the course taken was
too far west, away from the railroad rather than toward it. To-night
General Schofield will put General Johnson in the trenches, take his
out, and move perpendicular to the road, and not extend to the right
more than is necessary, and will have Generals Baird and Morgan in
support. If we can keep the forts of Atlanta full, with four divisions in
hand, we can whip any force outside of rebel intrenchments, and will
have General Johnson near enough for support. All our line is well
developed, but is generally strengthened by good abatis and parapet,
and conforms pretty close to the enemy, so that if we force the enemy to
stick in his trenches General Schofield should surely reach the railroad
and overcome any force the enemy has outside. I have no doubt by
our delay the enemy is better prepared than he would have been could
we have moved quick, as I ordered yesterday. Last night I could see
the cars, say a mile and a quarter due southeast, whereas Generals
Baird and Johnson to-day moved southwest, or nearly due west, away
from the enemy. But we will try again to-morrow, and persevere to
the end. I have written to General Palmer at length, and asked him
to come and see me very early in the morning, and if he wants to go I
will assent, and in that event will make the recommendations you suggested this morning. I have personally examined our line from right
to left, and feel no uneasiness as to the enemy making a sally. I know
it will be hard to make an assaulting column, but all I want is to force
the enemy to hold troops at all points, so as not to mass too heavy on
our right.

W. T. SHERMAN,
Major-General, Commanding.

SIGNAL DEPARTMENT, ARMY OF THE CUMBERLAND,
Howard's House, August 5, 1864—9 a. m.

Captain CASE:

I see no indications of troops moving from my front. Everything is quiet as can be. I can hear no artillery and see no smoke of battle in direction of Palmer and Schofield. Will keep a good lookout and re-port often. The telegraph has not yet reached here.

Very respectfully,

FORAKER,
Acting Signal Officer.

_____

HOWARD'S HOUSE, *August 5, 1864—12.30 p. m.*

Captain CASE:

Nothing new on our front. I hear heavy artillery firing in direction of our extreme right. Some of our shells burst over city.

B. FORAKER,
Acting Signal Officer.

_____

HEADQUARTERS DEPARTMENT OF THE CUMBERLAND,
In the Field, August 5, 1864.   (Received 7.30 a. m.)

Maj. Gen. D. S. STANLEY,
Commanding Fourth Army Corps:

GENERAL: The indications are that Major-Generals Schofield and Palmer are engaged with the enemy, as the musketry can be heard. The major-general commanding directs that you observe closely the indications of the battle, and should our troops advance upon the town that you be prepared to take advantage of such movement.

Yours, very respectfully,

WM. D. WHIPPLE,
Assistant Adjutant-General.

_____

AUGUST 5, 1864.

Major-General STANLEY,
Commanding Fourth Corps:

How are things going on your front? Do you observe any movements of the enemy?

GEO. H. THOMAS,
Major-General, U. S. Volunteers, Commanding.

_____

HEADQUARTERS FOURTH ARMY CORPS,
Near Atlanta, Ga., August 5, 1864—8.40 a. m.

Brigadier-General WHIPPLE,
Chief of Staff:

The enemy has been skirmishing in front of my left since sunrise; the skirmishing is on the left and rear of the line toward Decatur. I have just ordered General Wood to send two regiments to re-enforce the left, and am now starting for that point.

D. S. STANLEY,
Major-General.

HEADQUARTERS ARMY OF THE CUMBERLAND,
August 5, 1864—12.40 p. m. (Received 12.50 p. m.)

General STANLEY:

Schofield is heavily engaged with the enemy. Watch them closely in your front and take advantage of any attempt they may make to withdraw from your front. Threaten them all along your line. Tell Garrard to keep a good lookout on his front and take advantage immediately of any favorable opportunity to move against the enemy.

GEO. H. THOMAS,
Major-General, Commanding.

HEADQUARTERS FOURTH ARMY CORPS,
Near Atlanta, Ga., August 5, 1864—4.45 p. m.

Brigadier-General WHIPPLE,
Chief of Staff:

I attacked the rebels with a heavy skirmish line along my whole front; drove them from their rifle-pits in front of Grose's position from Wood's front. We received a heavy fire from their main works, musketry and artillery. From Grose's we received a heavy fire from their main works and a heavy out-work 100 yards in front of the main work. I see no chance to carry their main work without severe loss. I have not heard from Newton yet. I am now moving regiments to the front and will make a reconnaissance, feeling for their right. No movements of the enemy except manning the works have been observed. They have been discovered at work all day.

D. S. STANLEY,
Major-General.

HEADQUARTERS FOURTH ARMY CORPS,
Howard's House, August 5, 1864—12.50.

Captain BRIDGES,
Chief of Artillery:

Open with rifled guns and solid shot from 12-pounders on rebel front and city.

D. S. STANLEY,
Major-General.

HEADQUARTERS,
August 5, 1864.

Generals NEWTON and WOOD:

Schofield is heavily engaged with the enemy. Re-enforce your skirmish line; open fire and advance your skirmishers where you can threaten the enemy, and if he leaves his works to re-enforce his left take advantage to push into his works. Make his skirmish line hot for him; open deliberately with solid shot on his batteries.

D. S. STANLEY,
Major-General.

HDQRS. MILITARY DIVISION OF THE MISSISSIPPI,
In the Field, near Atlanta, August 5, 1864.

General STANLEY:

A heavy movement of troops is reported out of Atlanta, south through White Hall. Let your extreme left feel forward strong and fire half dozen shots with artillery in quick succession or by volleys, something different from the usual way.

W. T. SHERMAN,
Major-General, Commanding.

HEADQUARTERS FOURTH ARMY CORPS,
August 5, 1864—10 p. m.

Brigadier-General KIMBALL,
Commanding First Division, Fourth Army Corps:

Direct the artillery on your front to fire six volleys at intervals of ten minutes into Atlanta. Let your skirmishers keep up fire and notice if the rebels return fire. Do you see any sign of their quitting? If so, push skirmishers up. General Sherman thinks they may quit. Our forces did nothing on the right to-day. Baird captured 150 on skirmish line, but not being supported fell back to his intrenchments. Please answer.

D. S. STANLEY,
Major-General.

HEADQUARTERS DEPARTMENT OF THE CUMBERLAND,
In the Field, August 5, 1864.

Brigadier-General WILLIAMS,
Commanding Twentieth Army Corps:

Major-General Sherman reports that he can hear musketry on the front of Generals Palmer and Schofield and concludes that they must be engaged. The major-general commanding directs that you observe well the indications of the battle, and if there is any move of our troops toward the town that you be prepared to take advantage of it.

Very respectfully,

WM. D. WHIPPLE,
Assistant Adjutant-General.

STATION OBSERVATION, *August 5, 1864.*

Capt. A. K. TAYLOR,
Acting Signal Officer, Commanding:

CAPTAIN: No change since morning. Very few rebels seen during the skirmishing this afternoon along the front of the Fourth and Twentieth Army Corps. Saw rebel skirmishers firing from pits close to line of works near white frame house in front of First Division.

Very respectfully, your obedient servant,

W. W. HOPKINS,
First Lieutenant and Acting Signal Officer.

STATION OBSERVATION, *August 5, 1864.*

Capt. A. K. TAYLOR,
Acting Signal Officer, Twentieth Army Corps :

CAPTAIN: Directly south from here can see men at work on a fort. Twenty degrees east of south is a fort with embrasures fallen in on sides. This is in front of Twentieth Army Corps, and from this point to southeast along same front very few men can be seen in the enemy's works. Can see no movements of troops.

Very respectfully, your obedient servant,

W. W. HOPKINS,
First Lieutenant and Acting Signal Officer.

HDQRS. MILITARY DIVISION OF THE MISSISSIPPI,
In the Field, near Atlanta, Ga., August 5, 1864.

General THOMAS,
Commanding Department of the Cumberland:

GENERAL: General Milroy's letter of July 26, with your indorsement, is now before me. He asks to suppress the sale and circulation in his district of certain mischievous and treasonable newspapers, and transmits certain slips as proof of the mischievous tendency of their contents. I have no objection whatever, but in human nature there is so much of the mule left that prohibition of a newspaper increases its circulation. So long as the freedom of the press is one of the foundation stones of our Government, I think we must allow it to work out its solution, the *reductio ad absurdum* of the mathematician. It has been the chief cause of this horrid war. It has undermined all that was good and generous and magnanimous in the character of the American people. It has made false issues, it has kindled the wildest passions and kept them alive, till reason no longer even pretends to enter into our national affairs. It has cost us two thousand millions of dollars, has destroyed half a million of the finest young men of our country, and filled the land from Maine to Louisiana with widows and cripples, yet it is insatiate. It claims to be a power above Government, feeds upon slander and falsehood, and perfectly revels in murder and bloodshed. Yet you and I, with our large and well appointed armies, can neither check nor control it. The suppression of the few mentioned by General Milroy would be like damming a few of the tributaries of the Kanawha to stop the flood of the Mississippi. If General Milroy finds anybody selling mischievous matter within the sphere of his authority he might give him a good sound thrashing or put him in the stocks, but he cannot reach the editors who make money in New York or Chicago or Louisville by pandering to the tastes of certain cliques. My own opinion is that the freedom of the press to publish mischievous political matter, personal slander, and libel, and garbled statements of facts, like freedom of speech, can only be regulated by wise statute laws or by the laws of nature. As the press has now more power than the Congress, that makes our laws, we are now going through the expensive natural progress which will result in no law at all, but every man will defend his own property and reputation by the knife and pistol, and it is probable it will produce the result which history demonstrates in other similar cases, that the people will discover that it is better to curtail the liberty of the press as well as the liberty of speech, and devise some proper punishment for falsehood and slander in newspapers as is partially the case with individuals.

Each military commander subject to me may suppress all disorders and immoralities in the sphere of his command as he best may, but my belief is that the proper remedy is in punishing the men who publish malicious and false articles, if residing in his jurisdiction, or in punish-ing ignominiously the circulators of the books and papers containing the nuisance. A mere order of suppression simply excites the curi-osity of the thoughtless, who, through the mails, can easily defeat any effort at suppression. Thus, let the commanding officer at Nashville put in a public stocks any venders of obscene or libelous sheets, and give a good horsewhipping to any editor who would dare advise our soldiers to avoid their honorable contracts of enlistment, confiscate his press, and use his types for printing quartermasters' blanks. This is all the notice I would take of such things at this epoch of the storm the unlicensed press has brought upon our country.

I am, with respect, your obedient servant,

W. T. SHERMAN,
Major-General, Commanding.

HDQRS. MILITARY DIVISION OF THE MISSISSIPPI,
In the Field, Near Atlanta, Ga., August 5, 1864.

General R. S. GRANGER,
　　Decatur:

Keep the battery and send only the infantry of Colonel Howe's bri-gade. They need not bring wagons; we have enough here. Send the balance of men and horses of the Ninth Ohio Cavalry, Colonel Ham-ilton, to Marietta, where he is with his regiment. Rousseau's com-mand lost but little in the McCook expedition, except in the person of Colonel Harrison, who is, I think, a prisoner and not killed as first re-ported. I have seen an intercepted rebel letter speaking of him as a prisoner. Nine hundred of General Stoneman's men are in; balance, about 1,200, are still out, and I have a hope they will fetch up at Pensa-cola or somewhere, like General McCook. General Washburn dispatches from Memphis, August 2, that he is marching with a strong army on Columbus, Miss. He thinks Forrest died of his wound received in his fight with General A. J. Smith. Get your cavalry well together in as good order as possible, under some young active commander, but I have no idea now that any attempt will be made on Tennessee as long as General Washburn keeps things moving there, and I hammer away at Atlanta. All well.

W. T. SHERMAN,
Major-General, Commanding.

DECATUR, *August 5, 1864.*

Maj. Gen. W. T. SHERMAN:

The last train loaded with the Third Brigade has pulled out for Chat-tanooga.

R. S. GRANGER,
Brigadier-General.

HDQRS. MILITARY DIVISION OF THE MISSISSIPPI,
In the Field, near Atlanta, Ga., August 5, 1864.
(Received 7.20 a. m.)

General SCHOFIELD:

I want to hear more noise on your flank. If General Palmer will not go into action, and General Jeff. Davis be present, turn over the orders to him, but time is precious, and that attack must be pushed to-day all the time.

W. T. SHERMAN,
Major-General, Commanding.

HEADQUARTERS ARMY OF THE OHIO,
August 5, 1864—7.25 a. m.

Major-General SHERMAN:

General Palmer has this moment informed me of your refusal to relieve him, and his final decision to go on the field and carry out my orders. He is now starting. I have been trying nearly all night to get things in working shape, but with very little progress. I hope now to get started. Johnson reached the Sandtown road last night, and Morgan's skirmishers are on it this morning. He reports strong resistance. I will do all in my power to press the attack. Davis is not here, and if he were, Johnson is his senior.

J. M. SCHOFIELD,
Major-General.

HDQRS. MILITARY DIVISION OF THE MISSISSIPPI,
In the Field, near Atlanta, Ga., August 5, 1864.

General SCHOFIELD:

Dispatch received. All right. Press that attack on the right. I will judge by the sound, and if I judge you are too hard pressed will order Generals Thomas and Howard to assault somewhere. Get some part of your command where you can reach easily the railroad with short-range guns, and then intrench a strong flank. It is worth a battle, and the closer the first advantages are followed up the better. The weakest point of the enemy must be mathematically at some point between Atlanta and East Point. Keep me often advised of progress, and I will come over any minute you say, but can better handle the whole army from here by the telegraph.

W. T. SHERMAN,
Major-General, Commanding.

HDQRS. MILITARY DIVISION OF THE MISSISSIPPI,
In the Field, near Atlanta, Ga., August 5, 1864.

General SCHOFIELD:

Now is the time for you to push. General Thomas is hard at work well on the other flank.

W. T. SHERMAN,
Major-General, Commanding.

HEADQUARTERS ARMY OF THE OHIO,
Near Atlanta, Ga., August 5, 1864.

Major-General SHERMAN:

Palmer is developing his troops along the enemy's line, which is found to run nearly south from Hascall's right, and to be very strong. As soon as Palmer gets two divisions in position Johnson will make a rapid detour to the right, and try to strike the enemy in flank or in point of his line which is not held in force. Cox will take Johnson's place as reserve on the right, and if Johnson fail Cox will assault immediately. This movement is to be made at 2 o'clock. I think we are progressing pretty well, though slowly. Have captured about 200 prisoners. General Howard asks me to inform you that his signal officer reports that a large column of cavalry is passing into Atlanta from the enemy's left, probably one brigade.

J. M. SCHOFIELD,
Major-General.

HEADQUARTERS ARMY OF THE OHIO,
Near Atlanta, Ga., August 5, 1864.

Major-General SHERMAN:

Your dispatch is received. The enemy appears to have a continuous line to our right, behind the Sandtown road, but I presume held only by cavalry. I will get that, and then try to break toward the railroad.

J. M. SCHOFIELD,
Major-General.

HDQRS. MILITARY DIVISION OF THE MISSISSIPPI,
In the Field, near Atlanta, Ga., August 5, 1864.

General SCHOFIELD:

Your dispatch is received. I have sent copies to each of the other army commanders, and ordered them to press forward and threaten all points.

W. T. SHERMAN,
Major-General, Commanding.

HDQRS. MILITARY DIVISION OF THE MISSISSIPPI,
In the Field, near Atlanta, Ga., August 5, 1864.

General SCHOFIELD:

I have been listening since 2 p. m. for the sounds of battle on your flank. How are you progressing?

W. T. SHERMAN,
Major-General, Commanding.

HDQRS. MILITARY DIVISION OF THE MISSISSIPPI,
In the Field, near Atlanta, Ga., August 5, 1864.

General SCHOFIELD:

One of my staff reports nothing done on that flank. Is it possible you cannot move those troops? Let me know the truth, and, if necessary, I will withdraw them and substitute others.

W. T. SHERMAN,
Major-General, Commanding.

HEADQUARTERS ARMY OF THE OHIO,
August 5, 1864—4 p. m.

Major-General SHERMAN:

Johnson is moving. Did not get started until after 3. I hear nothing from him but light skirmishing.

J. M. SCHOFIELD,
Major-General.

HEADQUARTERS ARMY OF THE OHIO,
Before Atlanta, Ga., August 5, 1864—7.15 p. m.

Maj. Gen. W. T. SHERMAN,
Commanding Military Division of the Mississippi:

GENERAL: Your dispatch is received. I am compelled to acknowledge that I have totally failed to make any aggressive movement with the Fourteenth Corps, and have very little hope of being able to do better. The efforts of yesterday and to-day on this flank have been much worse than mere failures. I have ordered Johnson to relieve Hascall this evening, and propose to-morrow to take my own corps onto the right and try to recover what has been lost by two days' delay. The force may very likely be too small.

Very respectfully, your obedient servant,

J. M. SCHOFIELD,
Major-General, Commanding.

HDQRS. MILITARY DIVISION OF THE MISSISSIPPI,
In the Field, near Atlanta, Ga., August 5, 1864.

General SCHOFIELD:

Very well; take your divisions and order in writing both Generals Baird and Morgan to follow your movement, either in support or in echelon, with General Johnson to hold the tête-de-pont, push out for the Sandtown road, and, if possible, a position where you can control the railroad. I will have General Palmer come up, and, if he wants to resign, will consent; in which case General Johnson will remain as corps commander until other promotions can be made. Try and make an early start; the delay may have deceived the enemy, unless he can see your force. Those divisions of the Fourteenth Corps are the strongest and best in the army, and all they want is a good leader. Give direction to your movement, and they will support your flank perfectly. I will see that Generals Thomas and Howard occupy the attention of the whole line.

W. T. SHERMAN,
Major-General, Commanding.

HDQRS. 14TH ARMY CORPS, DEPT. OF THE CUMBERLAND,
August 5, 1864—12.45 a. m.

Maj. Gen. J. M. SCHOFIELD,
Commanding, &c.:

GENERAL: I have to acknowledge by your courier the receipt of telegraphic note from Major-General Sherman, in which he intimates his decision of the question discussed by us on yesterday adverse to my views. I forward you an open note to Major-General Sherman, which you will read and will then oblige me by forwarding to him, as I am unable to direct my orderly to his headquarters.* I have the honor to inform you at the same time that, in my opinion, Brig. Gen. R. W. Johnson is the senior brigadier-general in this corps, and suggest that, until General Sherman shall otherwise direct, all orders for its commanding officer be addressed to him.

    Respectfully,

JOHN M. PALMER,
Major-General.

HEADQUARTERS ARMY OF THE OHIO,
Near Atlanta, Ga., August 5, 1864—8.30 a. m.

Maj. Gen. J. M. PALMER,
    Commanding Fourteenth Army Corps:

    GENERAL: Will you please inform your division commanders that you are acting under my orders to-day? In an emergency it may be necessary to give them orders directly. I have just heard from General Sherman. He desires us to press vigorously and endeavor to gain a point commanding the railroad to-day, and intrench it.

    Very respectfully, your obedient servant,

J. M. SCHOFIELD,
Major-General, Commanding.

HEADQUARTERS FOURTEENTH ARMY CORPS,
August 5, 1864.

Major-General SCHOFIELD,
    Commanding:

    GENERAL: I have informed my division commanders that your orders given them through General Johnson are to be obeyed, and that you command them. I add that I am in good faith conforming for the day to General Sherman's order, and regret that you should have apprehensions that I would do otherwise.

    Respectfully,

J. M. PALMER.

HEADQUARTERS ARMY OF THE OHIO,
In the Field, Ga., August 5, 1864.

Maj. Gen. J. M. PALMER,
    Commanding Fourteenth Army Corps:

    GENERAL: Permit me to assure you that I have not had the slightest apprehension as to your sincere intention to carry out General Sherman's orders. My request was based upon the information that General Baird had not been notified of the arrangement for the day, and my apprehension that you might not think to notify him. I simply desire to avoid misapprehension and consequent mistakes.

    Very respectfully, your obedient servant,

J. M. SCHOFIELD,
Major-General, Commanding.

---

*See August 4, 11.55 p. m., p. 356.

HEADQUARTERS ARMY OF THE OHIO,
Before Atlanta, Ga., August 5, 1864.

Brig. Gen. R. W. JOHNSON,
Commanding Fourteenth Army Corps:

GENERAL: The major-general commanding directs me to forward you the following statement for your information and guidance: Major-General Howard reports a heavy movement of the enemy's trains toward our right, and great activity on part of rebel skirmishers on his (General Howard's) front. This may indicate an evacuation by the rebels of Atlanta, or a preparation on their part to mass troops to attack our right, or more probably both; in which case the attack will be very heavy. The general directs that this information be given you that you may make such preparations as, in your judgment, appear necessary.

Very respectfully, your obedient servant,

W. C. BARTLETT,
Captain and Aide-de-Camp.

(Same to Generals Hascall and Cox.)

HEADQUARTERS FOURTEENTH ARMY CORPS,
August 5, 1864—5 a. m.

Maj. Gen. W. T. SHERMAN,
Commanding:

GENERAL: I would be obliged to you that in addition to, and as part of the order relieving me, you would order me to report to the Adjutant-General, from Illinois, by letter.

Respectfully,

JOHN M. PALMER.

HEADQUARTERS FOURTEENTH ARMY CORPS,
In the Field, August 5, 1864.

Maj. Gen. W. T. SHERMAN,
Commanding, &c.:

GENERAL: I am very greatly obliged to you for your expressions of kindness, but regret exceedingly that you decline to accede to my request to be relieved. I have joined General Schofield with a larger force than his own. I have seen much more service in the face of the enemy. I have a commission much older in fact, whatever may be the form; and this question of rank-raising with me is so decided that I lose all practical control over my corps, that, too, at a time of great probable difficulty. As you have declined to relieve me, I go, of course, to the field, and will do what I can to give success to the operations of the day, but I urge that you will reconsider your refusal to relieve me and permit me at the close of the day to turn the command over to Brigadier-General Johnson, who is the senior brigadier-general in the corps.

I am, very respectfully,

JOHN M. PALMER,
Major-General, Commanding.

Hdqrs. Military Division of the Mississippi,
In the Field, near Atlanta, Ga., August 5, 1864.

General Palmer,
At the Front:

I have communicated to General Thomas the substance of our former notes and messages, and have received the following reply by telegraph:

I regret to hear that Palmer has taken the course he has, and as I know he intends to offer his resignation as soon as he can properly do so I recommend that his application be granted.

Now, if General Schofield has a major-general's commission going back to equal date with yours, though confirmed subsequent, with retroactive effect, he ranks you by reason of former superior commission, and if you resign because you measure your number of men as greater than his, and your services in battle as giving you greater right to command, you commit the mistake of substituting your own individual opinion over the established law and military usage. The special assignment of General Schofield to the command of a separate army and department shows that he enjoys the confidence of the President, even above his mere lineal rank. If you want to resign, wait a few days and allege some other reason—one that will stand the test of time. Your future is too valuable to be staked on a mistake. Your case clearly falls under an old Article of War: "When two or more commands happen together, the officer highest in rank commands the whole." General Schofield ranks you by his commission, and it would not do for military men to discuss the nice question of how far back the President and Senate may give effect to a commission. I again ask you not to disregard the friendly advice of such men as General Thomas and myself, for you cannot misconstrue our friendly feelings toward you.

I am, &c.,

W. T. SHERMAN,
Major-General, Commanding.

Headquarters Fourteenth Army Corps,
August 5, 1864—12.30 p. m.

Maj. Gen. W. T. Sherman,
Commanding, &c.:

General: Your note by courier and duplicate by telegraph have just reached me. I assure you I am unaffectedly grateful to you for the personal direction this correspondence is assuming and for your friendly expressions toward me. I beg to assure you that I am of opinion that the ultimate decision of the question under discussion is not as free from doubt as you seem to suppose, but there are arguments more potent than even would be the certainty that I was right in my construction of the law. These are, that possibly my withdrawal from command might occasion inconvenience, and that the friendly advice of yourself and General Thomas is against me. For these reasons I request that pending active operations my application to be relieved be regarded as withdrawn.

Respectfully,

JOHN M. PALMER,
Major-General.

Hdqrs. Military Division of the Mississippi,
In the Field, near Atlanta, Ga., August 5, 1864.

General Palmer:

I would like to have you to come and see me as early in the morning as convenient. If you think of resigning it is probably better it should be now, as I fear the intention lessens your interests in our operations. Should you agree with me in this, turn over the command to General Johnson, and then you can assign as a reason anything you prefer. I would suggest that you put it on the ground of a prior resolve as soon as the campaign was over, and it having settled down into a quasi siege, you request now to be relieved and to be permitted to go to Illinois; or, if you prefer it, the reason that you considered your rank superior to General Schofield's. To be honest, I must say the operations on that flank yesterday and to-day have not been satisfactory. Yet I will not say that there has been want of energy or skill, but events have not kept pace with my desires.

W. T. SHERMAN,
Major-General, Commanding.

Headquarters Fourteenth Army Corps,
Before Atlanta, Ga., August 5, 1864—10.05 p. m.

[General Sherman:]

General: I confess my surprise at the contents of your telegraphic note, this moment received.

Waiving any statement of what were my purposes and intentions in respect to quitting the service, I will frankly say that if I were in your place, at the head of an army, I would require of my subordinates the faithful and energetic performance of their respective duties, and if my plans failed of execution, I would ascertain the cause and punish the delinquent vigorously, as no man is to be regarded when contrasted with [the] great cause of the country.

I am not surprised that you are dissatisfied with the operations of the army on this flank on yesterday and to-day, for I am also dissatisfied, and think much more ought to have been done, and readily confess myself in some measure responsible. Still I do earnestly protest against your inference of a want of interest in our operations. On yesterday you were present, and I will not speak of what I said or did. To-day I exerted myself more, I think, than any officer on the field to carry out General Schofield's orders, until the afternoon, near night, I found that aside from Baird's handsome operation in the forenoon nothing would be accomplished. I am to blame, however, in this, that I have not done as you obviously intend doing in my case—hold some one responsible for the failures. I think I could select the proper objects of responsibility more accurately than you have done in selecting me. I am so well convinced that this campaign has been lengthened out by the negligence and inattention of officers, and will be hereafter lengthened and drawn out from the same cause, that I accept your intimation to me not as offensive (though I think unjust), but as a sign of a purpose on your part, in future, to inquire into the causes of our almost daily failures to meet your avowed expectations, and when the cause is discovered to apply the correction. If you will do this justly, without favor or affection, I will venture my life that you will be astonished at the result. I will accept your offer to relieve me, not upon the ground that your suspicion of a want of interest is well founded, nor that I am in any other than the manner already admitted responsible for the unsatisfactory results on this flank, but upon the principle that as you are responsible to the country for this campaign every subordinate officer employed ought upon the first intimation from you of a want of confidence step out of the way promptly and feel that he is serving the country in doing so. Pardon this long letter. I will call upon you to-morrow morning and present a formal application to be relieved.

Respectfully,

JOHN M. PALMER,
Major-General.

HDQRS. THIRD DIVISION, TWENTY-THIRD ARMY CORPS,
Utoy Creek, August 5, 1864—7.20 a. m.

Major-General SCHOFIELD,
Commanding Army of the Ohio:

SIR: Colonel Walker, commanding brigade in General Baird's division, gives me the following, as obtained from rebel deserters and prisoners, who appeared candid: "The rebel line has a large re-entrant angle along Generals Hascall's and Baird's fronts; it then refuses, but follows near the creek and the Sandtown road all the way to the river. For about a mile to Hascall's right the trenches are held by infantry, beyond that by cavalry. Immediately in this front they report the lines very strong, having, as they say, three lines of intrenchments and with at least twenty pieces of artillery within half a mile. They seemed positive that the trenches were continued to the river or near it, though inferior in strength, as soon as they pass the infantry line." The enemy made a little brush at Baird's skirmish line this morning, but it amounted to nothing. General Hascall says he saw General Baird a few minutes ago, and that General Baird says he is without orders this morning.

Very respectfully, &c.,

J. D. COX,
Brigadier-General, Commanding.

HEADQUARTERS ARMY OF THE OHIO,
In the Field, Ga., August 5, 1864—10.45 a. m.

Brig. Gen. J. D. COX,
Comdg. Third Division, Twenty-third Army Corps:

GENERAL: Baird and Morgan are developing their lines along those of the enemy and expect to be in position and intrenched by 1 o'clock. Johnson is then to make a rapid detour to the right and endeavor to strike the enemy's flank or a point where his line is weak. You will move toward the right so as to take Johnson's place as reserve and at the same time make an assault if you find any point near the right where success seems probable. If Johnson succeeds your assault will probably not be necessary. If he fail, his effort will probably draw off some troops and thus increase your chances. I am willing you should be rather rash than prudent in this case. Johnson is to start promptly at 2 o'clock. Look out for an attack from the enemy on your right.

Very respectfully, your obedient servant,

J. M. SCHOFIELD,
Major-General, Commanding.

HDQRS. THIRD DIVISION, TWENTY-THIRD ARMY CORPS,
Near Utoy Creek, August 5, 1864—11.30 a. m.

Major-General SCHOFIELD,
 Commanding Army of the Ohio:

 Your dispatch ordering me to the right is received, and I will put the division in motion at once.

J. D. COX,
Brigadier-General, Commanding.

HEADQUARTERS ARMY OF THE OHIO,
Before Atlanta, Ga., August 5, 1864.

Col. ISRAEL GARRARD,
 Commanding Seventh Ohio Cavalry:

 COLONEL: The commanding general directs that you relieve the pickets of General Palmer's escort now on the road that General Johnson moved out on, and picket that road, as well as the road to the right. Please relieve the pickets of General Palmer's escort as soon as possible to-night.

 Very respectfully, your obedient servant,

J. A. CAMPBELL,
Major and Assistant Adjutant-General.

HDQRS. ARMY AND DEPARTMENT OF THE TENNESSEE,
August 5, 1864—10.30 a. m.

[General SCHOFIELD:]

 GENERAL: I find the line occupied by your brigade much more extended than I thought yesterday evening. It will take nearly, if not quite, all of my reserve to fill it. Please not remove the brigade until you absolutely need it. When you do so need it I will take care of myself.

O. O. HOWARD,
Major-General.

 P. S.—Signal officer reports large columns of cavalry passing into town from enemy's left flank; probably one brigade. Please notify General Sherman.

O. O. H.,
Major-General.

HEADQUARTERS ARMY OF THE OHIO,
In the Field, Ga., August 5, 1864—11.15 a. m.

Maj. Gen. O. O. HOWARD,
 Commanding Army of the Tennessee:

 GENERAL: Your dispatch is received. I will not take the brigade away until absolutely necessary. I do not expect to need it to-day unless to protect my right rear along the Howell's Ferry road.

 Very respectfully, your obedient servant,

J. M. SCHOFIELD,
Major-General, Commanding.

HEADQUARTERS LEFT WING, SIXTEENTH ARMY CORPS,
                    Near Atlanta, Ga., August 5, 1864.

Brig. Gen. J. M. CORSE,
        Commanding Second Division:

General Howard desires a demonstration made during the afternoon, while the fighting is going on at the right.   He thinks, however, the putting in of the new line may attract the attention of the enemy. Get your working parties out, support them well, and occasionally use artillery against the enemy. If you discover the enemy leaving or materially weakening their front, take advantage of it immediately and gain any advantage you can.
        Respectfully, your obedient servant,
                                G. M. DODGE,
                                Major-General, Commanding.

                    BEFORE ATLANTA, GA., *August 5, 1864.*

Maj. Gen. G. M. DODGE,
        Commanding Left Wing, Sixteenth Army Corps:

The following dispatch has just been received from General Giles A. Smith through headquarters Seventeenth Army Corps:

> The pickets report heavy movements of trains on our right.   The rebel skirmishers are very active along the whole line.   It may be an evacuation, or they may be massing their forces on Schofield.

The major-general commanding requests that you direct your skirmishers to be on the *qui vive* and unusually vigilant in the morning, and should the rebel skirmishers show any disposition to retire to follow them up vigorously.   General Logan has been directed to fire from one of his batteries upon the enemy's position one gun every ten minutes during the night.
        Very respectfully, your obedient servant,
                                WM. T. CLARK,
                                Assistant Adjutant-General.

HDQRS. DEPARTMENT AND ARMY OF THE TENNESSEE,
                    Before Atlanta, Ga., August 5, 1864.

Maj. Gen. F. P. BLAIR,
        Commanding Seventeenth Army Corps:

The report of General Giles A. Smith has been received. The general requests that you direct your skirmishers to be on the *qui vive* and unusually vigilant in the morning, and should the rebel skirmishers show any disposition to retire to follow them up vigorously. General Logan has been directed to fire from one of his batteries upon the enemy's position one gun every ten minutes during the night.
        Very respectfully, your obedient servant,
                                WM. T. CLARK,
                                Assistant Adjutant-General.

HDQRS. DEPARTMENT AND ARMY OF THE TENNESSEE,
August 5, 1864.

Maj. Gen. JOHN A. LOGAN,
Commanding Fifteenth Army Corps:

The following telegram is just received, and corps commanders are requested to act in accordance with suggestions therein contained:

Generals THOMAS and HOWARD:

I hear Schofield engaged well off to the right. Always push up against Atlanta at the weakest points in your front assaulting parties, who may during an attack at the right gain one of their redoubts or salients, which will settle the question quick; at all events will keep employed a large force to hold their lines.

W. T. SHERMAN,
Major-General.

By order of Maj. Gen. O. O. Howard:

WM. T. CLARK,
Assistant Adjutant-General.

MARIETTA, *August 5, 1864.*

Capt. L. M. DAYTON:

I sent all the men of my command that were fit for duty to Roswell Factory, as directed by General Sherman. I have no further news from the remainder of General Stoneman's command. My horses I sent to Roswell are much broken down, and feet worn out for want of shoes. I have more transportation than is necessary, and can have 200 or 300 more men for duty by turning over pack-saddles and mounting on the pack animals. Lieutenant-Colonel Smith, of General Stoneman's command, will report in person this morning to General Sherman.

S. ADAMS,
Colonel First Kentucky Cavalry.

NEAR ATLANTA, GA., *August 5, 1864—9.30 p. m.*

Major ECKERT:

Operations to-day complete failure, or worse. Schofield and Palmer were ordered to carry a point which would command railroad south of Atlanta, while the other corps made active diversions in favor of the movement. The attacking force moved early, and the whole line was engaged, but when Schofield and Palmer found the enemy they stopped and intrenched. There they stay yet, while they make no progress, and the rebels have time to mass men and throw up earth-works, or to evacuate as they choose. They are very actively doing one or the other now; which it is, daylight will tell. Had we done anything to-day I should think they were on the wing.

J. C. VAN DUZER.

SPECIAL FIELD ORDERS,   }   HDQRS. MIL. DIV. OF THE MISS.,
                     }   *In the Field, near Atlanta,*
     No. 52.   }   *August 5, 1864.*

I. Brig. Gen. John McArthur is hereby assigned to the command of the district of country embracing Kenesaw, Marietta, Roswell, and the west bank of the Chattahoochee River and the Sweet Water.

First. He is charged with guarding the railroad from Big Shanty to the Chattahoochee and protecting our stores at Marietta and Vining's.

Second. He will personally visit the points of interest and distribute the troops embraced in his command according to his judgment, and cause redoubts and block-houses to be at once made to give additional security to the railroad and places of deposit.

Third. He will cause camps to be prepared, one for each of the armies in the field, where he will assemble the detachments of recruits and convalescents arriving, and sick and discharged men going to the rear, and give dispatch to their movements.

Fourth. He will report to and receive instructions directly from these headquarters.

II. In pursuance of orders from Lieutenant-General Grant, commanding the Armies of the United States, the Tenth Regiment Illinois Infantry Volunteers is hereby transferred from the Department and Army of the Cumberland to the Department of the Tennessee, and the commanding officer will report to Maj. Gen. O. O. Howard, commanding.

III. In order that the relative strength of the armies may remain unchanged, the Seventeenth Regiment New York Volunteer Infantry is hereby transferred from the Department of the Tennessee to the Department of the Cumberland, and the commanding officer will report to Maj. Gen. George H. Thomas, commanding.

By order of Maj. Gen. W. T. Sherman:

L. M. DAYTON,
Aide-de-Camp.

SPECIAL FIELD ORDERS, }   HEADQUARTERS DEPARTMENT
                                                OF THE CUMBERLAND,
No. 214.   }   *Near Atlanta, Ga., August 5, 1864.*

*   *   *   *   *   *   *

VI. Brig. Gen. William Grose is assigned to the command of the Third Brigade, First Division, Fourth Army Corps, and will report accordingly.

*   *   *   *   *   *   *

By command of Major-General Thomas:

WM. D. WHIPPLE,
Assistant Adjutant-General.

CIRCULAR.]   HEADQUARTERS FOURTEENTH ARMY CORPS,
                              Near Atlanta, Ga., August 5, 1864.

Brigadier-General Johnson will advance, relieve Brigadier-General Hascall's troops near the mill, and at once strengthen the works so that he can hold them with a light line. Brigadier-General Baird will strengthen his works and obstruct the front so that he can hold with a light line and withdraw troops for his reserve. Brigadier-General Morgan will also strengthen his line as ordered above and be ready to hold with a small force and assist in the offensive operations of to-morrow.

By command of Maj. Gen. J. M. Palmer:

A. C. McCLURG,
Captain and Assistant Adjutant-General.

SPECIAL FIELD ORDERS, } HDQRS. ARMY OF THE OHIO,
  No. 72.   *Near Atlanta, Ga., August 5, 1864.*

* * * * * * *

III. General Palmer will push forward and firmly establish the right of his line this evening. General Cox will cover General Palmer's right and be ready for aggressive operations early in the morning. As soon as General Johnson returns from his demonstration this evening, he will relieve General Hascall and occupy the trenches. General Hascall on being relieved will move under cover to the rear and bivouac for the night. At 5 a. m. he will move to the right and take position in reserve to General Cox, prepared to support him in his movement. General Palmer will thin his line as much as practicable, so as to obtain a strong reserve for aggressive operations on his right.

IV. To-morrow, the 6th instant, a vigorous effort will be made to turn the enemy's left or break his line near the Sandtown road. The troops will be prepared to move at 6 a. m., but will wait orders to commence the movement. General Cox in advance will press forward in a southerly direction until he reaches the Sandtown road, and then along that road, or on more favorable ground not far to the right or left, until he strikes the enemy's line or flank, the latter to be preferred if it does not require too great separation from the rest of the army. If General Cox deems it practicable to carry the enemy's position, he will attack without unnecessary delay; otherwise he will report the facts and await further orders. General Hascall will follow in close supporting distance from General Cox, and will cover his right during the movement. General Morgan will connect the skirmishers of the troops now in position with those of General Cox in motion, and move forward with the latter, supporting his skirmishers as far as may be necessary. He will also hold his division in readiness to move promptly, as may be ordered during the day. Generals Baird and Johnson will hold the present lines of the Fourteenth and Twenty-third Corps, and keep up a steady pressure with artillery and skirmishers during the early part of the day. General Baird will also be prepared to move out promptly in support of the contemplated attack, as may be ordered at any time during the day. In case of General Baird's movement, General Johnson will, unless otherwise ordered, throw back his right into the tête-de-pont constructed by General Hascall and hold that position. All trains will be kept in rear of Utoy Creek. Colonel Garrard's cavalry will scout on all roads leading to the right and right rear of the infantry during the day. The troops will be kept well massed and in hand, ready to meet an attack from any direction.

By command of Major-General Schofield:

       J. A. CAMPBELL,
    Major and Assistant Adjutant-General.

   WASHINGTON, D. C., *August 6, 1864—1.45 p. m.*

Major-General SHERMAN:

An order by the President, under the act of Congress for the military possession of the Northwestern Railroad, has been issued, and will be forwarded you by the Adjutant-General. Do not imagine that we are impatient of your progress; instead of considering it slow, we regard it rapid, brilliant, and successful beyond our expectations. Take your time, and do your work in your own way. This Department is only anxious to afford you every assistance within its power.

       E. M. STANTON,
       Secretary of War.

WAR DEPARTMENT, ADJUTANT-GENERAL'S OFFICE,
Washington, August 6, 1864.

Special orders relating to the Northwestern Railroad, from Nashville to Reynoldsburg:

Whereas the exclusive use of the Northwestern Railroad, from Nashville to Reynoldsburg, is necessary for the military operations under command of Major-General Sherman, the President does therefore order and direct that Major-General Sherman take military possession of the said Northwestern Railroad, its stock, equipments, appendages, and appurtenances for the exclusive use of the United States, and hold, use, manage, and employ the same by his officers, agents, superintendents, and employés exclusively for the use aforesaid so long, and to such extent, as in his judgment such exclusive use is required for military operations, or until further orders, and that all conflicting orders and authority be, and they are hereby, revoked and annulled.

By order of the President:

E. D. TOWNSEND,
Assistant Adjutant-General.

WAR DEPARTMENT,
August 6, 1864.

Brigadier-General JOHNSON,
Military Governor, &c., Nashville, Tenn.:

On the direct application of General Sherman and his representation that the exclusive use of the Northwestern Railroad, from Nashville to Reynoldsburg, is necessary for the success of his military operations, the President, under the provisions of the act of Congress, has, by order of this date, authorized and directed him to take military possession of said railroad, its rolling-stock, equipment, appendages, and appurtenances for exclusive military use, and revoked all prior and conflicting orders and authority.

EDWIN M. STANTON,
Secretary of War.

NEAR ATLANTA, GA., *August 6, 1864—3 p. m.*
(Received 11.50 a. m. 7th.)

Maj. Gen. H. W. HALLECK, *Washington, D. C.:*

General Palmer has resigned his command of the Fourteenth Army Corps, and General Thomas has relieved him of the command. General Thomas recommends the promotion of General Jeff. C. Davis as a major-general and assignment to the command of the corps. In the event the President will not consent to this, General Thomas asks the promotion and assignment of General J. M. Brannan. I approve his recommendations, and ask a speedy return.

W. T. SHERMAN,
Major-General.

NEAR ATLANTA, GA., *August 6, 1864—9 p. m.*
(Received 5.30 p. m. 7th.)

Maj. Gen. H. W. HALLECK, *Washington, D. C.:*

We have now developed our line along with the enemy from the Augusta railroad, on our left, to Utoy Post-Office, on our right, and the enemy faces us in force at all points with equal force and superior works. General Schofield tried to break through at a point near our right with a brigade (General Reilly's), but his men were caught in the entanglement and lost probably 500. We have skirmished heavily along the whole line, using artillery freely, but have made no impression. I will continue to work to the right to find the extreme flank and threaten the railroad, if possible, to draw him out of Atlanta or force him to attack us; but our line is already too extended and weak. By means of his militia (of which he has the whole population of Georgia) he is enabled to use his three regular corps as reserves. Our loss to-day will foot up 1,000. I will soon need re-enforcements, and if you can replace General A. J. Smith at Memphis with negro or fresh troops I would order him here via Decatur. He must now be en route for Columbus, Miss. I have called forward a brigade from Decatur. I am now convinced that General Stoneman surrendered near Macon with 700 of his men, ordering two small brigades to break out and get in. One (Colonel Adams'), with 900 men, is in, but their time is out and they will be discharged. The other brigade (Capron's) I fear was scattered and picked up in detail. His entire loss will be about 1,300. General McCook's loss is 500. Damage done road, cars, and bridges was very large, but the enemy run cars into Atlanta from Macon.

> W. T. SHERMAN,
> *Major-General.*

HDQRS. MILITARY DIVISION OF THE MISSISSIPPI,
In the Field, near Atlanta, Ga., August 6, 1864.

General THOMAS:

General Palmer is just started for your headquarters. When you have taken official action on his application, let me know it, that I may urge the speedy appointment of General Jeff. Davis to the command. General Johnson has not the ability or vigor necessary to so large a command.

> W. T. SHERMAN,
> *Major-General, Commanding.*

HEADQUARTERS DEPARTMENT OF THE CUMBERLAND,
August 6, 1864—12 m.

Major General SHERMAN:

The enemy have been feeling our lines from Williams' right toward the left, apparently to see whether we have weakened our lines or not. The skirmishing on the left is probably for the same purpose, but it will be well to ascertain whether he intends more serious work, which Stanley can do by sending Garrard to feel his flanks. Howard thinks he is trying to get out of Atlanta clear. That may be, but Stanley must be watchful and not give ground until he can see he intends to attack him, then have him withdraw gradually to new line and let him come on until he becomes well entangled in the abatis before opening fire on him, but not leave present position until he thinks it absolutely necessary.

> GEO. H. THOMAS,
> *Major-General.*

(Copy to General Stanley.)

HDQRS. MILITARY DIVISION OF THE MISSISSIPPI,
In the Field, near Atlanta, August 6, 1864.

General THOMAS:

Your dispatch is received. Your instructions to General Stanley are exactly right. Only hold fast that left flank as long as possible, because I think the enemy may be repairing the Augusta road and it is important we control it from our left flank. General Stanley should fight for it hard, and I don't believe the enemy will venture an attack as long as they know we are working on the other flank. General Schofield is making slow but sure progress.

W. T. SHERMAN,
Major-General, Commanding.

———

HDQRS. MILITARY DIVISION OF THE MISSISSIPPI,
Near Atlanta, Ga., August 6, 1864.

Major-General THOMAS:

General Schofield reports at 12.30 that he had crossed the main road, the Sandtown, and found the enemy's line. He had attacked but did not succeed, but will repeat it again farther to the right. Order your batteries to be demonstrative and engage the enemy's at all points along your line during the day. We cannot hear the sound of his musketry.

W. T. SHERMAN,
Major-General.

(Same to General Howard.)

———

HEADQUARTERS DEPARTMENT OF THE CUMBERLAND,
August 6, 1864—2 p. m.

Major-General SHERMAN:

General Palmer has decided to go, and I have relieved him from the command of the Fourteenth Army Corps. I respectfully recommend Brig. Gen. J. C. Davis as major-general U. S. Volunteers, and request that he be assigned to the command of the Fourteenth Corps. Should there be any objection to General Davis I respectfully recommend the promotion of Brig. Gen. J. M. Brannan, with the request that he be assigned to the command of the Fourteenth Corps.

GEO. H. THOMAS,
Major-General, U. S. Volunteers, Commanding.

———

HDQRS. MILITARY DIVISION OF THE MISSISSIPPI,
In the Field, near Atlanta, August 6, 1864.

General THOMAS:

General Schofield has been at work to-day with his two divisions, and holds General Johnson in support. He has just finished working up his measurements and locates himself at the forks of the Utoy Creek, two miles west of East Point. Though our line is extended, we cannot do better than to control and strengthen by defenses our present front, and let General Schofield work so as to threaten East Point. I do not believe the enemy can defend so long a line, and he may be forced to choose between the two, Atlanta and East Point. Unless he has repaired the Augusta road, of which there are no signs, or unless he can drive back General Johnson's flank, which controls that road, he will be compelled to give up Atlanta to secure East Point. General Schofield asks for a couple of topographical engineers. He lost his only one yesterday. Can you spare him one or two. If so, order them to report to him. He tried to break through the enemy's lines by a brigade to-day, but failed, losing 500 men. Instead of going round East Point I would prefer the enemy to weaken so we may break through at some point, and wish you to continue to make such an effort. I will instruct General Howard to do the same about the head of Utoy Creek, his right.

W. T. SHERMAN,
Major-General, Commanding.

HOWARD'S HOUSE, *August 6, 1864.*
Capt. C. R. CASE:
All quiet on this flank. Can see but few of the enemy in their works. Cannot see as many pieces of artillery as I did yesterday. Shells from the Twentieth Corps burst near the center of the city.
A. F. BERRY,
Signal Officer.

HOWARD'S HOUSE, *August 6, 1864—9 a. m.*
Capt. C. R. CASE,
Chief Signal Officer, Department of the Cumberland:
Can hear heavy musketry and artillery on our right. Can see no movement of troops on this flank. Rebels just threw a shell at my station; but it fell a little short.
A. F. BERRY.

HEADQUARTERS FIRST DIVISION, FOURTH ARMY CORPS,
August 6, 1864—7.30 a. m. (Received 8.30 a. m.)
Major-General STANLEY,
Commanding Fourth Army Corps:
The rebels are evidently hunting for our left in considerable force; they made an attack on the left of my picket-line, but were held in check; they are moving still to our left, and heavy skirmishing going on on my left. I hope that the cavalry will stand. Would suggest that they be re-enforced from some other quarter.
Respectfully,

NATHAN KIMBALL,
Brigadier-General, Commanding.

HOWARD'S HOUSE, *August 6, 1864—12.30 p. m.*
Brig. Gen. W. D. WHIPPLE:
No attack excepting coming suddenly from the direction of the match factory on the Roswell road could affect my position. I have two regiments guarding the breast-works on the Roswell road.
D. S. STANLEY,
Major-General.

HEADQUARTERS FOURTH ARMY CORPS,
Near Atlanta, Ga., August 6, 1864—3.45 p. m.

General NEWTON,
Commanding Second Division:

GENERAL: In accordance with the dispatches (official copies of which are herewith inclosed), you will strengthen your skirmish line, and threaten the enemy. Also make a show of your infantry in the main lines, and such movements as may lead the enemy to suppose that you are about to make a general advance and attack.

By order of Major-General Stanley:

J. S. FULLERTON,
Assistant Adjutant-General.

(Same to Generals Wood and Kimball.)

STANLEY'S HEADQUARTERS,
August 6, 1864.

General WHIPPLE,
Chief of Staff:

Is the demonstration upon the enemy's line to be one of artillery alone?

D. S. STANLEY,
Major-General.

HDQRS. DEPARTMENT AND ARMY OF THE CUMBERLAND,
August 6, 1864.

Maj. Gen. D. S. STANLEY,
Commanding Fourth Army Corps:

The general commanding directs that you threaten the enemy with infantry without moving on his lines.

By command of Major-General Thomas:

HENRY STONE,
Assistant Adjutant-General.

(Copies to Generals Wood and Newton.)

HOWARD'S HOUSE, *August 6, 1864.*

Brig. Gen. W. D. WHIPPLE:

The demonstration on our left was made by Maney's brigade, of Cheatham's division. We learn from a deserter that this brigade is posted south of the railroad, and that they are very anxious to learn what we have here. We had 1 man killed and our picket-line slightly forced back. It is now re-established.

D. S. STANLEY,
Major-General.

(Copy to General Sherman.)

STATION OBSERVATION, *August 6, 1864—8.45 a. m.*

Capt. A. K. TAYLOR,
    Acting Signal Officer, Commanding:

CAPTAIN: There seems to be more men about the enemy's works than yesterday. No other change that I can see. Occasional artillery shot on the left from our guns. It is too smoky to see very well.

Very respectfully, your obedient servant,

W. W. HOPKINS,
    First Lieutenant and Acting Signal Officer.

HDQRS. CHIEF OF CAVALRY, DEPT. OF THE CUMBERLAND,
    August 6, 1864.

Brig. Gen. E. M. McCOOK,
    Commanding First Cavalry Division, Marietta, Ga.:

The general commanding directs that you move with your command to vicinity of railroad bridge. The commanding officer at Marietta will send all men belonging to your division, if they arrive there, to the bridge. The Fourth Tennessee Cavalry gone to Decatur, Ala.; the Ninth Ohio can get its own supplies, as it does not belong to your division.

By order, &c.:

DAVID F. HOW,
    Lieutenant and Acting Assistant Adjutant-General.

OFFICERS' PRISON,
    Macon, Ga., August 6, 1864.

Major-General SHERMAN,
    Commanding Division of the Mississippi:

I have the honor of making the following report: On the 30th of July, near Newnan, Ga., General McCook ordered me to dismount two of my regiments to fight the enemy on foot. The Fourth Tennessee and Fifth Iowa were dismounted, when I dismounted, directing my orderly to follow me with my horse. We drove the enemy for one mile through the woods. I there found the enemy in overwhelming numbers in front, and that they were passing in my rear between my line and the main line of our force. We here commenced retreating and fighting the enemy in our rear. My horse had failed to come up with me. After three personal encounters with the enemy I was separated from my force, and, suffering with cramp in my right leg, I was forced to surrender to a party of the enemy then confronting me. Six of my line officers, 4 of my surgeons, and about 50 of my men were taken with me. They are all retained as prisoners. I am in fine health, not wounded, as reported.

T. J. HARRISON,
    Colonel, Commanding Cavalry.

DECATUR, ALA., *August 6, 1864.*

Major-General SHERMAN:

Infantry brigade Sixteenth Army Corps all gone. Received a dispatch last night that sixty horses were coming for battery. Under these circumstances shall I forward the battery? I have no particular use for it here, but it is in poor condition. All right about Parson Johnson, and Mead reported with 250 men north of the river, between Flint and Paint Rock. Anderson after them with about 400 of his regiment. I don't believe Forrest dead, nor expect him here, though some of his men have very recently been killed by my scouting parties in Middle Tennessee. Hammer at Atlanta; we rejoice at every blow.

R. S. GRANGER,
Brigadier-General.

DECATUR, ALA., August 6, 1864.

Brigadier-General WHIPPLE,
    Assistant Adjutant-General:

Major-General Sherman having asked what troops can be spared from this district, I have notified him and Major-General Rousseau that the Tenth Indiana Cavalry could be replaced by a regiment of colored troops if there was one disposable to relieve it. Colored troops will do for the block-houses. As there is no probability of the Ninth Ohio or the Fourth Tennessee returning to this district, I do not think it advisable to part with more cavalry. I have the honor to report the Third Brigade, Sixteenth Corps, as being relieved from duty here and now en route for the front; same reported to Major-General Rousseau.

R. S. GRANGER,
Brigadier-General.

SCHOFIELD'S HEADQUARTERS,
August 6, 1864—5.45 a. m.

General SHERMAN:

Please inform me if there are any changes along the line this morning before I start out.

J. M. SCHOFIELD,
Major-General.

HDQRS. MILITARY DIVISION OF THE MISSISSIPPI,
In the Field, near Atlanta, August 6, 1864.

General SCHOFIELD:

No changes are reported along the line. Use all the force you can, and don't make too wide a circuit. I will reiterate to Generals Thomas and Howard to occupy the attention of the enemy along every yard of our lines.

W. T. SHERMAN,
Major-General, Commanding.

HEADQUARTERS ARMY OF THE OHIO,
In the Field, August 6, 1864—8.20 a. m.

General SHERMAN:

We are about starting. I will keep you advised of progress. Our skirmishers have been pushed well forward, and find lines apparently strong in front of our right.

J. M. SCHOFIELD,
Major-General.

Hdqrs. Military Division of the Mississippi,
In the Field, near Atlanta, Ga., August 6, 1864.

General Schofield:

Keep me well advised to-day, that I may co-operate from all points. I want to know when you are in secure possession of the big Sandtown road, and then of the railroad.

W. T. SHERMAN,
Major-General, Commanding.

Headquarters Army of the Ohio,
Near Atlanta, Ga., August 6, 1864.

Major-General Sherman:

Your dispatch is received. I have a division covering the Sandtown road, where it debouches from the enemy's line, and hard at work intrenching. All my troops are well in hand to meet an attack. Hood can't hit me without crossing the main Utoy south of the road and passing around some distance through a forest. I think very likely he will try it, and rather hope he will. If he does not, I propose to try to break the salient of his lines between the forks of Utoy, and then work toward East Point, with my right resting on the main creek.

J. M. SCHOFIELD,
Major-General.

Headquarters Army of the Ohio,
Near Atlanta, Ga., August 6, 1864.

Major-General Sherman:

I have got a force across the main road, and have made a vigorous assault upon what appears to be the enemy's main line, but without success. Our loss is quite severe. I am about to try it again farther to the right.

J. M. SCHOFIELD,
Major-General.

Hdqrs. Military Division of the Mississippi,
In the Field, near Atlanta, August 6, 1864.

General Schofield:

Your dispatch is received. Go on and do the best the case admits of. I am sure both Generals Thomas and Howard will give full employment to all the forces on their front. If we can reach a point on the right, where our shot will command the railroad, then we can afford to rest.

W. T. SHERMAN,
Major-General, Commanding.

Headquarters Army of the Ohio,
Near Atlanta, Ga., August 6, 1864.

Major-General Sherman:

In my movement this morning I made a circuit to the right far enough to strike beyond what appeared to be, and probably was, yesterday the enemy's flank, but found intrenchments of ordinary strength with extensive entanglements in front. Reilly assaulted gallantly and energetically, and I believe with more than ordinary confidence of success on the part of himself and men. But the obstructions were so great that it was found impossible to reach the parapet. Reilly's loss is about 500 men, including many valuable officers. After this failure, I made a much larger circuit to the right for the purpose of reaching the enemy's flank or a point of his line not protected by abatis. I struck the point where the Sandtown road crosses the main Utoy Creek. Here the enemy's line makes a sharp salient, bending back along the north bank of the creek. The main line was prolonged by cavalry, with artillery, toward the Chattahoochee. General Hascall sent two brigades, under General Cooper, to clear this flank, which he did by crossing the creek, but too late for any further operations. We are intrenching the ground we have gained, and will be ready for work again in the morning. The losses in Cox's and Hascall's divisions are probably not more than 1,000 men. I have not thought it advisable to put in more men than the Twenty-third Corps to-day, except in making demonstrations to draw the enemy from the points of attack. General Johnson has been with me during the day and has promptly executed all my orders. Colonel Warner, who left me late this evening, can explain to you more fully our situation. If you take the blue colored map of Atlanta and vicinity, the forks of the Utoy Creek southeast of the town of Utoy is, I believe, Hascall's position. I will determine more accurately to-night.

J. M. SCHOFIELD,
Major-General.

HDQRS. MILITARY DIVISION OF THE MISSISSIPPI,
In the Field, near Atlanta, August 6, 1864.

General SCHOFIELD:

I have your dispatch. There is no alternative but for you to continue to work on that flank with as much caution as possible, and it is possible the enemy may attack us, or draw out. He must defend that road.

W. T. SHERMAN,
Major-General, Commanding.

HEADQUARTERS ARMY OF THE OHIO,
Near Atlanta, Ga., August 6, 1864.

Major-General SHERMAN:

We are working hard for the big road. The ground is very rough. I am confident of getting the road, but doubt my ability to either reach the enemy's left or break his lines, but will give it a fair trial.

J. M. SCHOFIELD,
Major-General.

HEADQUARTERS ARMY OF THE OHIO,
August 6, 1864.

Major-General SHERMAN:

The rough measurements we have been able to make to-day place me much farther south and east than I had supposed. Contracting them as much as possible, my right is about due west from East Point, and not more than two miles from it. If this be true, I have struck the flank of the defenses of East Point. You will readily recognize the position on the blue map. If possible, I wish you would send me one or two good topographical engineers for a few days. The only one I had was killed day before yesterday. It is very important now for me to have accurate surveys.

J. M. SCHOFIELD,
Major-General.

HDQRS. MILITARY DIVISION OF THE MISSISSIPPI,
In the Field, near Atlanta, Ga., August 6, 1864.

General SCHOFIELD:

I will try to send you some engineers to-morrow. I will have to borrow of other armies. Continue to work to-morrow in such a manner as to best threaten the railroad at or below East Point, and keep your own and the Fourteenth Corps united, so as to defend yourselves against the enemy should he let go Atlanta and shift to his communications. If you can threaten that road he is bound to choose, and you know what choice he will make. I advise you to see to-night that the right, by which the big Sandtown road comes out from the enemy to your line, is well covered, for he will, if at all, sally by well-known roads. The valleys of the two forks of Utoy can easily be held by a thin line and an entanglement of timber. General Thomas will continue to press Atlanta up the valley of Proctor's Creek, and General Howard by Utoy. The militia, by which Hood holds his long lines of intrenchments, are worthless, save for that purpose, but they enable him to use his good troops, distributed, doubtless, by brigades, to rush to threatened points. I don't think he will mass them all, unless he gives up Atlanta and throws his force at one move to East Point. If you be at the forks of the main Utoy, two miles west of East Point, your cavalry should cross the upper fork, and picket the crossing at Utoy Post-Office. You should also open a more direct road to where your headquarters are, which serves as a key point.

W. T. SHERMAN,
Major-General, Commanding.

HEADQUARTERS FOURTEENTH ARMY CORPS,
August 6, 1864—1.15 a. m.

Major-General SCHOFIELD,
 Commanding, &c.:

GENERAL: From the contents of a telegraphic note received a few hours ago, through your office from General Sherman, I infer he has made up his mind to relieve me from the command of this corps, upon grounds, however, totally different from those involved in the discussions of yesterday. He intimates such a purpose, and directs me to turn over the command to Brigadier-General Johnson. I send your order to General J[ohnson] with the information above. If anything shall occur to leave me in command, I will see that all that's possible is done to effect the objects of to-morrow's movements.

Respectfully,

JOHN M. PALMER,
Major-General.

HEADQUARTERS FOURTEENTH ARMY CORPS,
Near Atlanta, August 6, 1864.

[General SCHOFIELD:]

GENERAL: When I left you this evening I told you that I could replace General Morgan's division, but I find after filling the gap between Howard and myself that I have only five small regiments left; with these I could replace one brigade. This, with his reserve brigade, will give you two brigades upon which you can rely to assist in any movement contemplated on the right. In this calculation I assume that the present line is to be held. The gap proves to be much greater than I first supposed. If you can, please telegraph Howard that I connect closely with him.

Respectfully, your obedient servant,

R. W. JOHNSON,
Brigadier-General.

AUGUST 6, 1864—10 a. m.

Brigadier-General REILLY,
Commanding, &c.:

After reflecting on the statement of the guide, I incline to the opinion that the movement through the strip of wood, and so up on the ridge, may be made with very strong prospect of success. If it looks so to you also, you may support Colonel Mottley very closely with the regiment, and bring down the whole brigade earlier than we contemplated when I left you. Once on the ridge, we may push rapidly and strongly to the left along it, and since I left you I have learned that General Morgan will probably be able to swing forward and connect by a cross-ridge as soon as you get fairly astride of the one you are going for. It seems to be a spur of a main ridge running along from General Morgan's front.

J. D. COX,
Brigadier-General, Commanding.

HDQRS. THIRD DIVISION, TWENTY-THIRD ARMY CORPS,
Utoy Creek, August 6, 1864—2.30 p. m.

Col. J. S. CASEMENT,
Commanding Second Brigade:

General Hascall is trying to find the flank of the enemy farther to the right. General Schofield directs that you make a demonstration in his favor. Do this by advancing a line of skirmishers up toward the works so as to keep the enemy in the belief that we shall again assault them there. Take advantage of the same opportunity to have all our wounded and dead brought off that can possibly be reached. Make it a point of honor to leave as few of ours to fall into the rebel hands as possible.

Very respectfully, &c.,

J. D. COX,
Brigadier-General, Commanding.

HEADQUARTERS ARMY OF THE OHIO,
In the Field, Ga., August 6, 1864.

Lieut. Col. G. W. SCHOFIELD,
Chief of Artillery and Ordnance:

COLONEL: The commanding general directs that you send Colonel Barter's brigade out the road taken by General Johnson, and let him occupy the right of the works this side of Utoy Creek. Inform General Howard.

Very respectfully, your obedient servant,
WM. M. WHERRY,
Major and Aide-de-Camp.

HEADQUARTERS ARMY OF THE OHIO,
In the Field, Ga., August 6, 1864.

Maj. W. W. WHEELER,
Provost-Marshal-General, Army of the Ohio:

MAJOR: Colonel Barter's brigade is in reserve in the works occupied by General Johnson yesterday—the extreme right of the line occupied last night, right resting on the south bank of Utoy Creek, connecting with the troops now in line by his left.

Very respectfully, your obedient servant,
WM. M. WHERRY,
Major and Aide-de-Camp.

HEADQUARTERS DEPARTMENT OF THE TENNESSEE,
August 6, 1864.

Major-General SHERMAN:

Signal officer reports he has seen over 100 wagons moving out of Atlanta in a southwest direction, while there were not more than ten going in. As far as he can see, enemy's troops do not appear at all harassed or excited.

O. O. HOWARD,
Major-General.

HDQRS. MILITARY DIVISION OF THE MISSISSIPPI,
In the Field, near Atlanta, August 6, 1864.

General HOWARD:

I have no idea that the enemy will leave Atlanta until compelled to do so. General Schofield is making slow but sure progress on our right, but I expect each minute to hear him heavily engaged. Study your front so that you can keep employed on it as much of the enemy as possible, that General Schofield will have the less to deal with.

W. T. SHERMAN,
Major-General, Commanding.

HEADQUARTERS DEPARTMENT OF THE TENNESSEE,
August 6, 1864.

Major-General SHERMAN:

I have directed General Dodge to move forward his line to connect with line of Seventeenth Corps, which has just been constructed. General Logan has relieved the brigade of Schofield's on the right, and thus thoroughly obstructing the space through which the enemy could come from that quarter. I have requested Johnson to swing his left up on to a pine ridge just in front of it. All these movements will occupy the enemy, it being uncertain what we are really doing.

O. O. HOWARD,
Major-General.

HDQRS. MILITARY DIVISION OF THE MISSISSIPPI,
In the Field, near Atlanta, August 6, 1864.

General HOWARD:

General Schofield tried to break through the enemy's lines about Cherburg, but failed, losing about 500 men. He is now down on main Utoy at a point about two miles from East Point. This extension weakens our lines, but we must do this or assault. I will order him with due caution to continue to threaten East Point and his lines of communication. We know he will let go the former. General Thomas will continue to strengthen his line by works, and shorten it when possible, and I want you to do the same. Gain ground to the front whenever you can, thereby diminishing the length of your line, and being that much nearer the enemy is a more dangerous threat to him, preventing him detaching as against General Schofield, unless he lets go Atlanta. I have an idea you could work up some on your right along Utoy. I will ride your lines to-morrow and see you. General Dodge will have another brigade to-morrow from Decatur. It left in cars yesterday and day before.

W. T. SHERMAN,
Major-General, Commanding.

HEADQUARTERS ARMY OF THE OHIO,
Near Atlanta, Ga., August 6, 1864.

Major-General HOWARD:

General Johnson informs me that he now connects closely with you, whether by swinging forward or extending he does not say. I understand there was very little firing in that gap to-day. I have had a pretty hard day's work, and believe I have reached about the end of Hood's rope.

J. M. SCHOFIELD,
Major-General.

HEADQUARTERS ARMY OF THE OHIO,
Near Atlanta, Ga., August 6, 1864.

Maj. Gen. O. O. HOWARD,
Commanding Army of the Tennessee:

GENERAL: It is quite important that I have to-day the use of that portion of Cox's division now on this side of the creek. I do not like to withdraw them and leave a gap, for all my trains must be left here, and a breach would result in their loss, though I should not fear any thing more serious. If you can hold that space I shall be very glad to withdraw my troops. Please inform me.

Very respectfully, your obedient servant,

J. M. SCHOFIELD,
Major-General, Commanding.

HEADQUARTERS ARMY OF THE TENNESSEE,
August 6, 1864—6 a. m.

Major-General SCHOFIELD,
  Commanding Army of the Ohio:

DEAR GENERAL: I can hold the present lines, but cannot prevent the enemy from entering between us after putting every man into position, so that I have no second line or reserves. However, I will do my best if you deem it necessary to take the brigade.

Respectfully,

O. O. HOWARD,
Major-General.

HDQRS. DEPARTMENT AND ARMY OF THE TENNESSEE,
  Near Atlanta, Ga., August 6, 1864—8 a. m.

General SCHOFIELD,
  Commanding, &c.:

I have directed General Logan to relieve your brigade, and have ordered the Ninth Illinois Mounted Infantry to watch the space between us.

O. O. HOWARD,
Major-General.

Would be sent by telegraph, but it is not in working order.

HOWARD'S HEADQUARTERS,
August 6, 1864. (Received 10 a. m.)

General SCHOFIELD:

GENERAL: I have ordered your brigade relieved. Quite a serious demonstration is taking place on my left; may result in an attack; so please let your brigade remain near by as long as you can; but take it when you absolutely require it.

O. O. HOWARD,
Major-General.

HEADQUARTERS ARMY OF THE OHIO,
  Near Atlanta, Ga., August 6, 1864.

Major-General HOWARD:

I will let the troops remain till I absolutely need them. I have some apprehension for the safety of my right rear, and would like to have a reserve near my present headquarters. But I will risk it for a time.

Respectfully,

J. M. SCHOFIELD,
Major-General.

HOWARD'S HEADQUARTERS,
August 6, 1864.

General SCHOFIELD:

The rebels made a demonstration with strong skirmish line along front of Sixteenth and Seventeenth Corps this morning and extended to Twentieth Corps this afternoon. I ordered a demonstration for your relief, opening with artillery and musketry. Rebels replied with some musketry and several batteries of artillery, making a good deal of noise. I am yet in doubt whether any musketry firing occurred between Johnson and myself. I hope Johnson's left has swung up onto that ridge, as it will secure the safety of the trains and will relieve your reserve brigade entirely; he may already have done so. My staff officers have explained to me your present position.

O. O. HOWARD,
Major-General.

HEADQUARTERS ARMY OF THE OHIO,
Near Atlanta, Ga., August 6, 1864.

Major-General HOWARD:

Your telegram is received. I have ordered the brigade to be kept within supporting distance of your right until I absolutely require it.

J. M. SCHOFIELD,
Major-General.

HEADQUARTERS DEPARTMENT OF THE TENNESSEE,
August 6, 1864—11.45 a. m.

Colonel EWING,
    Acting Inspector-General:

There is nothing particular requiring the presence of the general commanding at these headquarters. I have just returned from the right, where I have been advancing my line. Blair and Morgan are in position and now intrenching.

O. O. HOWARD,
Major-General.

BEFORE ATLANTA, GA., *August 6, 1864.*

Maj. Gen. JOHN A. LOGAN,
    Commanding Fifteenth Army Corps:

The major-general commanding directs that the following telegram to him from General Sherman be sent to you, and that you cause your batteries to open on the enemy's works, keeping up a regular cannonade, and to advance your skirmish line as if for an attack:

General Schofield reports at 12.30 that he had crossed the main road, the Sandtown, and found the enemy's line. He had attacked but did not succeed, but will repeat it again farther to the right. Order your batteries to be demonstrative and engage the enemy's at all points along your line during the day. We cannot hear the sound of his musketry.

W. T. SHERMAN,
Major-General.

Very respectfully, your obedient servant,

SAML. L. TAGGART,
Assistant Adjutant-General.

(Same to General Blair.)

HEADQUARTERS LEFT WING, SIXTEENTH ARMY CORPS,
Near Atlanta, Ga., August 6, 1864.
Brig. Gen. J. M. CORSE,
Commanding Second Division:

General Ransom and the Seventeenth Army Corps are moving into the new line by direction of the department commander. Have your line finished up as soon as possible. I think Welker's battery better remain in its present position. I have ordered Ransom to throw a regiment on his left, facing north, connecting his left with the main line occupied by you. I will be out this p. m. and see if we cannot in some manner shorten the line. Strengthen the new line as much as possible.

I am, very respectfully, your obedient servant,
G. M. DODGE,
Major-General, Commanding.

HDQRS. MILITARY DIVISION OF THE MISSISSIPPI,
In the Field, near Atlanta, Ga., August 6, 1864.
Major-General DODGE:

DEAR SIR: Yours of this date is received. I know nothing of General A. J. Smith's assignment to the command of the Sixteenth Corps. Among a batch of special orders received from Washington was one assigning Maj. John Hough to duty, with General A. J. Smith as commanding the Sixteenth Corps. It may be as commanding that part of the corps on the Mississippi, where the records still are. This is all any one knows about it. General Grant supposed you would succeed General Hurlbut, but I know nothing further than the above. I take pleasure in saying you have ever done your whole duty with zeal and fervor.

With respect, &c.,
W. T. SHERMAN,
Major-General, Commanding.

HDQRS. MILITARY DIVISION OF THE MISSISSIPPI,
In the Field, near Atlanta, August 6, 1864.
General McARTHUR,
Marietta:

You may order the bridge at Roswell to be burned, and draw in the regiment of infantry and cavalry now there; the river being fordable, there is no use in having detachments out exposed.
W. T. SHERMAN,
Major-General, Commanding.

KINGSTON, *August 6, 1864.*
Capt. L. M. DAYTON,
Aide-de-Camp:

There are several small bodies of enemy's cavalry hovering on our line watching an opportunity to burn bridges and trains, but I think I can take care of them. Everything right, and going on well. Will go as far as the Chattahoochee with permission.
JAMES B. STEEDMAN,
Major-General.

BEFORE ATLANTA, GA., *August 6, 1864—9 p. m.*
(Received 12 m. 7th.)

Maj. THOMAS T. ECKERT:

Palmer was relieved this morning of the command of the Fourteenth Corps, which has been handled to-day by Brigadier-General Johnson, under direction of General Schofield. Some ground has been gained on right, but not enough to enable us to command railroad yet. An attack by Schofield's corps on enemy's earth-works was repulsed with loss of 1,000 men in all. Farther extension to railroad found rebel flank; too late for further operations, but there is promise of success at daylight. Something done; prospects brighten a little. Our line of battle thirteen miles long. Generals report operations and receive orders by telegraph.

J. C. VAN DUZER.

SPECIAL FIELD ORDERS, ⎱   HEADQUARTERS DEPARTMENT
                                          OF THE CUMBERLAND,
No. 215. ⎰   *Near Atlanta, Ga., August 6, 1864.*

*   *   *   *   *   *   *

III. At his own request Maj. Gen. J. M. Palmer is relieved from the command of the Fourteenth Army Corps, on duty in the Department of the Cumberland, and will proceed to Carlinville, Ill., whence he will report by letter to the Adjutant-General U. S. Army, at Washington, D. C. The officers composing the general's personal staff are also relieved from duty, that they may accompany him. The quartermaster's department will furnish the necessary transportation for the general, his staff, and the authorized number of servants and horses.

*   *   *   *   *   *   *

By command of Major-General Thomas:

WM. D. WHIPPLE,
Assistant Adjutant-General.

SPECIAL FIELD ORDERS, ⎱   HEADQUARTERS DEPARTMENT,
                                          AND ARMY OF THE TENNESSEE,
No. 90. ⎰   *Before Atlanta, Ga., August 6, 1864.*

*   *   *   *   *   *   *

X. Corps commanders will at 6 o'clock to-morrow morning, the 7th instant, move forward a sufficient number of their troops to occupy and hold the new line of works.

By order of Maj. Gen. O. O. Howard:

WM. T. CLARK,
Assistant Adjutant-General.

WASHINGTON, D. C., *August 7, 1864.*

Major-General SHERMAN,
Commanding, &c.:

Your progress, instead of appearing slow, has received the universal commendation of all loyal citizens, as well as of the President, War Department, and all persons whose commendation you would care for.

The enemy detaching a portion of his force to secure the crops of the Shenandoah Valley, and raid into Maryland and Pennsylvania to call attention from them, has called me here to organize our forces to drive the enemy south. I came from the Monocacy yesterday afternoon, after having put all our forces in motion after the enemy, and after having put Sheridan in command, who I know will push the enemy to the very death. I will telegraph you in future more frequently than heretofore.

U. S. GRANT,
Lieutenant-General.

HDQRS. MILITARY DIVISION OF THE MISSISSIPPI,
In the Field, near Atlanta, August 7, 1864—8 p. m.
(Received 3.30 a. m. 8th.)

Lieutenant-General GRANT,
Washington:

I was gratified to learn you were satisfied with my progress. Get the War Department to send us recruits daily as they are made, for we can teach them more war in our camps in one day than they can get at a rendezvous in a month. Also tell Mr. Lincoln that he must not make the least concession in the matter of the September draft. It is right, and popular with the army, and the army is worth considering. I am glad you have given General Sheridan the command of the forces to defend Washington. He will worry Early to death. Let us give those southern fellows all the fighting they want, and when they are tired we can tell them we are just warming to the work. Any signs of let up on our part is sure to be falsely construed, and for this reason I always remind them that the siege of Troy lasted six years, and Atlanta is a more valuable town than Troy. We must manifest the character of dogged courage and perseverance of our race. Don't stay in Washington longer than is necessary to give impulse to events, and get out of it. It is the center of intrigue. I would like to have General Mower made a major-general. He is a real fighter.

W. T. SHERMAN,
Major-General, Commanding.

NEAR ATLANTA, GA., *August 7, 1864—8 p. m.*
(Received 2.30 a. m. 8th.)

Maj. Gen. H. W. HALLECK,
Washington, D. C.:

Have received to-day the dispatches of the Secretary of War and Lieutenant-General Grant, which are very satisfactory. We keep hammering away here all the time, and there is no peace inside or outside of Atlanta. To-day General Schofield got round the flank of the line assaulted yesterday by General Reilly's brigade, turned it, and gained the ground where the assault was, with all our dead and wounded. We continued to press on that flank, and brought on a noisy but not a bloody battle. We drove the enemy behind his main breast-works, which cover the railroad from Atlanta to East Point. We captured a good many of the skirmishers, which are of their best troops, for the militia hug the breast-works close. I do not deem it prudent to extend more to the right, but will push forward daily by parallels, and make the inside of Atlanta too hot to be endured. I have sent to Chattanooga for two 30-pounder Parrotts, with which we can pick out almost any house in the town. I am too impatient for a siege, but I do not know but here is as good a place to fight it out as farther inland. One thing is certain, whether we get inside of Atlanta or not, it will be a used-up community by the time we are done with it.

W. T. SHERMAN,
Major-General.

WASHINGTON, *August 7, 1864—10.30 p. m.*

Major-General SHERMAN:

General Washburn has been directed to send you all the troops he can spare from his command.

H. W. HALLECK,
Major-General.

HDQRS. MILITARY DIVISION OF THE MISSISSIPPI,
In the Field, near Atlanta, Ga., August 7, 1864.

Maj. Gen. H. W. HALLECK,
    Chief of Staff, Washington, D. C.:

GENERAL: In order that you may have a proper understanding of the recent cavalry operations from this army that terminated somewhat unsuccessfully, I will explain. On the 25th of July I had driven the enemy to his inner intrenchments of Atlanta, and had by Garrard's division of cavalry broken the road leading to Augusta about the branches of the Ocmulgee, forty miles east, and had by McPherson's army taken up two sections of rails of about five miles each, near Stone Mountain and Decatur. I then proposed to throw the Army of the Tennessee rapidly round by the right, so as to approach the only remaining railroad left to the enemy, leading due south for six miles, and then branching to Macon on the one hand and West Point, on the Chattahoochee, on the other. To accomplish this I placed General Stoneman with his own division of cavalry, 2,300 strong, and Garrard's division, about 3,500, on my left near Decatur, and on the right General McCook with a small division of about 1,300, and a part of Harrison's, just arrived under Rousseau, from the raid to Opelika. This force was about 1,700. Both expeditions started punctually on the 27th, and acted under my written orders, No. 42, a copy of which is inclosed.* The day before starting General Stoneman addressed me a note,† a copy of which is inclosed, asking leave, after fulfilling his orders, to push on and release our prisoners known to be confined at Macon and Andersonville. I gave my consent in a letter,† a copy of which is also inclosed. Nothing but the natural and intense desire to accomplish an end so inviting to one's feelings would have drawn me to commit a military mistake, at such a crisis, as that of dividing and risking my cavalry, so necessary to the success of my campaign. Stoneman ordered Garrard to move to Flat Rock, doubtless to attract the attention of the enemy, while he passed behind him and on to McDonough and the railroad about Lovejoy's, where he would have met McCook, but for some reason he did not go to McDonough, but to Covington, and down on the east side of Ocmulgee to Clinton, when he sent detachments that burned the Oconee bridge, seventeen locomotives, over 100 cars, tore down telegraph wire, and damaged the railroad east of Macon considerably. He

---

* See p. 255.
† See pp. 264, 265.

attempted to get into Macon; shelled the town, but fell back to Clinton. Finding the enemy gathering in too large a force, he seems to have turned back, but the roads were obstructed, and he fought till his ammunition was exhausted, and he seems to have given up. He told his brigade commanders, Adams and Capron, he would with 700 men engage the attention of the enemy, while they might escape. Adams has come in with his brigade, 900 strong; Capron is not in, and I think the bulk of his command were captured. About forty stragglers of it have got in. I have no doubt Stoneman surrendered in the manner and at the time described by the Macon paper I sent you yesterday. Garrard remained at Flat Rock until the 29th, and hearing nothing of Stoneman he came in without loss or serious opposition. McCook crossed the Chattahoochee at Rivertown, below Campbellton, by a pontoon bridge, which he sent back, intending to come in by a circuit east and north. At 2 p. m. of the 28th he left the banks of the Chattahoochee and struck the West Point branch at Magnolia Station, which he burned and tore up track. He then by a rapid night march pushed for Fayetteville, where he found the roads and by-ways full of army wagons belonging to the army in Atlanta, embracing the headquarters teams of all the generals. All were burned good, and about 800 mules sabered. He then pushed on for the railroad at Lovejoy's, where he destroyed full two miles of track, the depot, a lot of cotton and stores, and carried off five miles of telegraph wire. Up to that time he had not encountered any opposition, for Stoneman's and Garrard's movements out from Decatur had attracted the enemy's cavalry. Having, as he supposed, broken the road enough, and supposing his best way back was by Newnan, he turned in that direction. He had 73 officers and 350 men prisoners, mounted on all sorts of horses and mules; still he reached Newnan, where the enemy began to gather about him and oppose him. He thinks two brigades of dismounted cavalry, acting as infantry, had been stopped en route from Mississippi for Atlanta by the break he had made in the railroad and happened there. These, in addition to two divisions of cavalry, headed him off whichever way he turned. He fought hard for five hours, until he exhausted his artillery ammunition, when he chopped up the wheels, spiked and plugged the guns. He then kept Harrison's brigade, and directed the smaller ones, commanded by General Croxton and Colonel Torrey, to cut out. He continued to fight until near night, when he dashed through an infantry line, reached the Chattahoochee, crossed his men, and got in. Harrison is a prisoner, I think; of Croxton I can hear nothing. But nearly all the men not killed and wounded are in. McCook left his prisoners free, and his wounded in charge of his surgeons. His management was all that could be expected throughout.

With great respect,

W. T. SHERMAN,
Major-General.

NASHVILLE, *August 7, 1864.*

Major-General SHERMAN:

The Northwestern Railroad is now run by Mr. Anderson, though not formally turned over by Governor Johnson. A depot is established at Johnsonville, and supplies are arriving by that line. The navy has been notified to patrol the Tennessee River to Johnsonville and Reynoldsburg. General Gillem has been guarding the road, and I have had several conferences with him as to increasing the force there, as the increasing importance of the line seemed to require more. Will confer with

General Rousseau and see that all is done which can insure safety and full working of the road. Colonel Donaldson fully appreciates its importance.

J. D. WEBSTER,
Brigadier-General.

———

NASHVILLE, *August 7, 1864.*

Major-General SHERMAN:

The Northwestern Railroad has been under the exclusive control of the military authorities so far as transportation and supplies for the Government are concerned since 9th of June, and the transfer now proposed had already taken place. Even transportation of citizens was only on military authority. It has been understood and was intended that so soon as the military authorities placed the rolling-stock on at their discretion time-tables for running continuously through to the farthest point would be established. The road is still unfinished; the work is progressing as rapidly as possible. This State is largely interested in this road, innocent persons beyond its limits holding the bonds issued for its construction. An effort was made by certain parties some time since to take charge of road before it was even in running order. It is hardly necessary for me to state that there might be parties interested in various ways in having the immediate and direct supervision of the road a little farther removed for other than military purposes. I repeat that for all military and Government purposes the road has been under military control since the cars have been running over it. It seems to me the same and stronger reasons for taking the Nashville and Louisville have existed since the Federal troops first entered Nashville. The Government has paid hundreds of thousands for the use of that road, which found its way into the pockets of traitors, and are for the support of treason.

A. JOHNSON,
Military Governor.

———

HDQRS. MILITARY DIVISION OF THE MISSISSIPPI,
In the Field, near Atlanta, August 7, 1864.

Colonel DONALDSON,
Quartermaster, Nashville:

Take military possession of the Northwestern Railroad, under the laws of Congress, by order of the President of the United States, a copy of which orders will reach you by mail.* Place the road and its equipments in the charge of the general superintendent, with orders to use it exclusively for military uses and transportation. Make such temporary store-houses as will accommodate the business of the season of low water, and call on General Rousseau to guard it according to his judgment of the danger to its safety. As this transfer is made by virtue of an act of Congress, I think an accurate inventory of the road, its stock and material on hand, should be made, and a regular set of books opened of its business, that a future settlement may be made with the owners of the road if entitled to compensation. I do not see why the cars might not be loaded at Reynoldsburg and unloaded here in our camp.

W. T. SHERMAN,
Major-General, Commanding.

———

* See p. 391.

HDQRS. MILITARY DIVISION OF THE MISSISSIPPI,
In the Field, near Atlanta, August 7, 1864.

Major-General THOMAS:

The line assaulted yesterday was an incomplete one. By feeling its left, Bate's division evacuated and fell back to the real line, which is nearer the railroad. I ordered the skirmishers to be pushed in and the strength demonstrated, and developed heavy musketry fire and artillery. We have gained valuable ground and full possession of the real Sandtown road. Our lines are close up and by morning will be intrenched, so we will keep on working by that flank, but I want the whole line advanced whenever it be possible, and that General Thomas bring from Chattanooga two 30-pounder Parrotts on siege carriages and batter the town. The closer we press our lines we contract and strengthen. General Schofield's right does not yet really threaten the railroad, though a full mile nearer East Point than last night.

W. T. SHERMAN,
Major-General, Commanding

(Same to General Howard.)

HEADQUARTERS OF MAJOR-GENERAL SCHOFIELD,
August 7, 1864.

General THOMAS:

Telegraph to Chattanooga and have two 30-pounder Parrotts sent down on the cars, with 1,000 shells and ammunition. Put them into your best position, and knock down the buildings of the town. Slow progress here.

W. T. SHERMAN,
Major-General.

HEADQUARTERS DEPARTMENT OF THE CUMBERLAND,
August 7, 1864—8.30 p. m.

Major-General SHERMAN:

The guns have been ordered by express train with ammunition, and I will look up the best position for them to-morrow. Have directed Elliott to make arrangements for the distribution of the horses. He thinks he can bring up McCook's division to about 3,000. McCook's men are constantly coming in and Kilpatrick reports that he has taken some prisoners, rebel cavalry, near Campbellton. The enemy still occupies his intrenchments in my front in considerable force.

GEO. H. THOMAS,
Major-General, U. S. Volunteers, Commanding.

HOWARD'S HOUSE, *August 7, 1864—7.30 a. m.*

Captain CASE,
    Chief Signal Officer:

Cannot see any change in enemy's lines since yesterday. Guns in same position. Can see a few men loitering behind their works. Cannot see any troops moving. It is very quiet.

BURTON,
Signal Officer.

HOWARD'S HOUSE, *August 7, 1864—1 p. m.*

Captain CASE,
    Chief Signal Officer, Department of the Cumberland:

See column of dust south of here, distant about eight miles. Cannot tell which way it is moving.

H. H. BURTON,
    Lieutenant and Acting Signal Officer.

STATION OBSERVATION, *August 7, 1864—9.25 a. m.*

Capt. A. K. TAYLOR,
    Acting Signal Officer, Commanding:

CAPTAIN: No change since yesterday except greater activity along the enemy's lines. They are issuing clothing at four-gun fort.

Very respectfully, your obedient servant,

W. W. HOPKINS,
    First Lieutenant and Acting Signal Officer.

STATION OBSERVATION, *August 7, 1864.*

Capt. A. K. TAYLOR,
    Acting Signal Officer, Commanding:

CAPTAIN: No change along line since morning. Heavy cannonading on our right this afternoon. Dense volume of smoke arose out of the city this evening for a few minutes near tall brick smoke-stack.

Very respectfully, your obedient servant,

W. W. HOPKINS,
    First Lieutenant and Acting Signal Officer.

Statement of J. M. Glass (scout).

OFFICE PROVOST-MARSHAL-GENERAL,
    Near Atlanta, Ga., August 7, 1864.

Says he left Atlanta, Ga., yesterday morning about 10 o'clock; says the right of the enemy's line is held by militia supported by one brigade of Hardee's corps; with this exception all the old troops are on the center and on the left. Hardee's corps is on the left flank of the army. From the best information he could get thinks there are at least 15,000 militia. One brigade of militia came in from some point below on the 4th instant. Learned that 1,700 of General Stoneman's command were captured; heard a rumor to the effect that General Wheeler will be relieved of his command because he did not capture the whole of Generals Stoneman's and McCook's commands. Two brigades of Wheeler's corps were sent to Flat Shoals on the 5th instant. An orderly on duty at General Hood's headquarters told him, Glass, that General Lee was expected from Virginia, also that General Ewell was looked for at Atlanta with his corps, said to be 32,000 strong. Same orderly said that he believed from the manner in which things were going on about headquarters that preparations were being made for a sudden flank movement of some kind. The large guns have all been removed from the fort east of the cemetery. Do not think Hood is accumulating supplies in Atlanta; think they only arrive as they are needed by the troops. Trains are running regularly on the Macon and Atlanta road. Two hundred prisoners were sent below on the 5th instant. Our wounded prisoners are kept in the southeast portion of the town. Says he came out of Atlanta past the cemetery, thence on the Decatur road south of the Augusta railroad to Decatur. Says there are no troops in Decatur or to the right. Says there are no rebel works nor troops between our works and the railroad. South of the railroad the enemy has two lines of works held by militia. The right of the enemy's line of infantry is within one mile of Decatur. The two brigades of cavalry sent to Flat Shoals are from Martin's division, which was camped in the rear of the infantry between Atlanta and Decatur; only one brigade there now. Glass thinks that from the hint he received from General Hood's inspector-general, viz, to come over last night, that they did not want him there to-day.

Respectfully forwarded for the information of the general commanding.

ED. C. DENIG,
Captain and Assistant Adjutant-General.

HDQRS. MILITARY DIVISION OF THE MISSISSIPPI,
In the Field, near Atlanta, August 7, 1864.

Brig. Gen. R. S. GRANGER,
Decatur, Ala.:

I don't want the artillery; we have enough. If not needed at Decatur, put the men and guns on the cars and send them to Nashville in reserve. Turn over the horses to the cavalry. Do all that is possible to put your cavalry in the best order, and feel down into Alabama as far and as often as is prudent. General A. J. Smith will make a clean sweep this time.

W. T. SHERMAN,
Major-General, Commanding.

HDQRS. MILITARY DIVISION OF THE MISSISSIPPI,
In the Field, near Atlanta, August 7, 1864.

Major-General SCHOFIELD:

I don't apprehend the enemy's cavalry will get in behind you north of Utoy Creek, but it is well to be prudent. You can use all the cavalry belonging to your army, and may send to Marietta and secure the horses of Colonel Adams' brigade and mount other men. I think some of Colonel Capron's men are in too. If Colonel Garrard watches the passes of Utoy and blocks all roads not guarded that flank is a strong one. A very few infantry well posted would make it more secure. Continue to work on the enemy's left night and day and give him no rest. I will see to all other points.

W. T. SHERMAN,
Major-General, Commanding.

HEADQUARTERS ARMY OF THE OHIO,
Near Atlanta, Ga., August 7, 1864—8.30 p. m.

Major-General SHERMAN:

Our line is swung forward until it faces nearly due east from Morgan's center to Cox's center, from which last point it is somewhat refused. This must, I think, bring Cox's center within a mile of the railroad. We cross both the Sandtown and Campbellton roads near their intersection, which seems to be between our line and that of the enemy. I have not yet learned the final result of the operations of Johnson's left. Will inform you when I hear from him. We have got good positions for artillery, and are putting in batteries all along the line to-night. I have seen Colonel Garrard and given him orders about picketing our right, but apprehend that his force (400 men) is entirely inadequate.

J. M. SCHOFIELD,
Major-General.

HDQRS. MILITARY DIVISION OF THE MISSISSIPPI,
In the Field, near Atlanta, August 7, 1864.

General SCHOFIELD:

That's right. Go on in your own way to accomplish the end and keep your five divisions so as to hold the enemy till a battle is fought. I will look a little closer at General Howard's front to see if there is not a weak place there in the enemy's line; there should be about the head of Utoy, north fork. I will then work my way down to you on the extreme right.

W. T. SHERMAN,
Major-General, Commanding.

HEADQUARTERS SECOND DIVISION,
August 7, 1864—12 m.

Major-General SCHOFIELD,
    Commanding Army of the Ohio:

GENERAL: I have Hobson's brigade on the Bald Hill, which has been the bone of contention, and two prisoners taken say that their division (Bate's, of Hardee's corps) fell back last night to their main work about a mile east or back, in consequence of my attack on their left last night. I am moving forward with my whole division, and will push out a reconnaissance at once.

MILO S. HASCALL,
Brigadier-General of Volunteers.

These prisoners say their works do not extend within two miles of East Point. The enemy thought I had turned his extreme left and was making direct for East Point.

M. S. H.

HEADQUARTERS DEPARTMENT OF THE TENNESSEE,
August 7, 1864.

Major-General SHERMAN:

LOOKOUT STATION—10.20 a. m.

A column of the enemy just moved toward their left. On account of the conformation of the ground and the dust I cannot tell how large a force. In the column I discovered two flags, white ones like signal flags. A train of twelve wagons and two ambulances followed the column. One train, freight, arrived this a. m. in Atlanta.

FISH,
Signal Officer.

O. O. HOWARD,
Major-General.

(Same to General Schofield.)

HOWARD'S HEADQUARTERS,
August 7, 1864. (Received 8.30 p. m.)
Major-General SCHOFIELD:

General Dodge advanced his skirmishers, taking 27 prisoners. Sixteenth and Seventeenth Corps main lines advanced about 300 paces and intrenched. Fifteenth Corps advancing and intrenching to-night near our present skirmish line. It is reported that one of Baird's wagons and some men were captured between here and Chattahoochee. Is not Utoy Creek picketed by your cavalry?

O. O. HOWARD,
Major-General.

[AUGUST 7, 1864.—For R. W. Johnson to Schofield, reporting operations of the Fourteenth Corps, see Part I, p. 510.]

HEADQUARTERS ARMY OF THE OHIO,
Near Atlanta, Ga., August 7, 1864.
Major-General HOWARD:

My cavalry is picketing Utoy Creek, and Colonel Garrard thinks no rebel cavalry has passed this way; but he has only 400 men, which, I apprehend, is entirely too small to guard so long a line.

J. M. SCHOFIELD,
Major-General.

BEFORE ATLANTA, GA., *August 7, 1864.*
Brigadier-General WILLIAMS,
Commanding Twentieth Army Corps:

GENERAL: Brigadier-General Corse informs me that you promised to move up the right of your line to the hill immediately on his left as soon as he had gained possession of the ridge in his front. General Corse has already moved his line forward and is intrenched, but it will be impossible for him to extend his line, not even the length of a regiment. Will you be kind enough to connect the right of your line if you can with the left of General Corse's division, and oblige,

Very respectfully, your obedient servant,
O. O. HOWARD,
Major-General.

HDQRS. SIGNAL DETACHMENT, FIFTEENTH ARMY CORPS,
August 7, 1864.
Maj. Gen. JOHN A. LOGAN,
Commanding Fifteenth Army Corps:

SIR: I have the honor to state that I took my position in lookout station at 7 a. m., but on account of fog it was sometime before I could see with any correctness. At 10.30 a. m. I sent a message to Maj. Gen. O. O. Howard stating that a column of the enemy just moved toward their left. I was unable to count the files, but saw two regimental flags, twelve wagons, and two ambulances move by with column. One train of freight cars loaded with white sacks, apparently corn or meal, passed into Atlanta at 11 a. m. At 1.30 p. m. a train consisting of eight freight and three passenger cars left the town empty. At 2 p. m. a freight train of fifteen cars, empty, left town. At 4.30 a passenger train with eight freight cars attached came in sight; the engine backed into town without the passenger cars. At 5 p. m. a freight train of thirteen cars loaded with white sacks, as before, passed into town. During the day several trains from twelve to thirty wagons each passed into town from the southwest loaded with fodder, partly dry and partly green; some loads looked like wheat or oats. The enemy's lines as far as I can see appear to be unchanged. My observations lead me to believe that the enemy are repairing the Augusta railroad.

I am, sir, most respectfully, your most obedient servant,

SAMUEL EDGE,
First Lieutenant, Acting Signal Officer, Comdg. Detachment.

HDQRS. DEPARTMENT AND ARMY OF THE TENNESSEE,
Before Atlanta, Ga., August 7, 1864.

Maj. Gen. JOHN A. LOGAN,
Commanding Fifteenth Army Corps:

GENERAL: The general commanding requests me to say that your proposition to advance your lines meets his hearty approval. You will accordingly move forward your right to the hill which your skirmishers now occupy, establishing your line so as to connect in a direct line as near as may be with your present left. You will also please direct General Woods to throw forward his right so as to form the shortest practicable line to the creek. Please have the new position intrenched to-night and your troops moved into the works.

Very respectfully, your obedient servant,

WM. T. CLARK,
Assistant Adjutant-General.

MARIETTA, GA., *August 7, 1864.*

Major-General SHERMAN,
Commanding:

The bridge at Roswell has been destroyed and the regiment reported here. The commanding officer informs me that yesterday afternoon he saw clouds of dust some distance to the left, on the opposite side of the river, as of troops moving in that direction. Have you sent any cavalry around your left?

J. MCARTHUR,
Brigadier-General.

HDQRS. MILITARY DIVISION OF THE MISSISSIPPI,
In the Field, near Atlanta, August 7, 1864.

General MCARTHUR:

Your dispatch received. General Garrard's cavalry on our left flank frequently patrols up as far as McAfee's Bridge above Roswell. The dust may have been his cavalry. Still I know the enemy will attempt by his cavalry to strike our road, and I want you to keep all on the look-out, and to fight like the devil. If any party allows itself to be surprised or defeated, he [the commander] had better drown himself.

W. T. SHERMAN,
Major-General, Commanding.

SPECIAL FIELD ORDERS, ⎞ HDQRS. MIL. DIV. OF THE MISS.,
                      ⎟   *In the Field, near Atlanta,*
    No. 53.   ⎠   *August 7, 1864.*

1. The following officers being the seniors of their departments with the army in the field, are hereby relieved from duty with the Department of the Cumberland, and will in person report at these headquarters for duty, viz: Lieut. Col. L. C. Easton, chief quartermaster; Capt. T. G. Baylor, chief ordnance officer.

By order of Maj. Gen. W. T. Sherman:

                                    L. M. DAYTON,
                                    Aide-de-Camp.

SPECIAL FIELD ORDERS, ⎞   HDQRS. ARMY OF THE OHIO,
    No. 74.   ⎠   *Near Atlanta, Ga., August 7, 1864.*

*   *   *   *   *   *   *

II. The Fourteenth and Twenty-third Corps, as far as General Cox's right, will press the enemy closely during the day to-morrow, and gain and intrench as much ground as practicable. Each division will endeavor, if the commanders deem it practicable, to carry a point of the enemy's works. General Hascall will make a reconnaissance to the right, and endeavor to reach and turn the enemy's flank. Intrenchments must be made very strong and held with small force, so as to leave large reserves for operations, either offensive or defensive, upon the right.

By command of Major-General Schofield:

                                    J. A. CAMPBELL,
                          Major and Assistant Adjutant-General.

            HDQRS. MILITARY DIVISION OF THE MISSISSIPPI,
                In the Field, near Atlanta, August 8, 1864.

General THOMAS:

The enemy's cavalry manifests activity on our right, threatening to cross Utoy Creek to General Schofield's rear. He has little or no cavalry. I want him to-morrow to develop well the enemy's flank, which I believe is along the south fork of Utoy Creek, covering East Point. To enable him to do this I want a general cannonading to-morrow, the 4½-inch guns included, if they come in time; and I want you to order General Garrard to send a brigade out to and beyond Decatur on your left, and let General Kilpatrick move down to Sandtown and feign as though intending to cross over. Send orders for him to-night, that the effect may be felt as early in the day as possible. I cannot move General Schofield with any activity as long as that cavalry hovers on his right and rear. We are now as much extended as possible, and must test the strength of our flanks and line.

                                    W. T. SHERMAN,
                                    Major-General, Commanding.

            THOMAS' HEADQUARTERS, *August 8, 1864.*

Major-General SHERMAN:

Your dispatch about the cavalry received. Will be attended to immediately.

                                    GEO. H. THOMAS,
                                    Major-General.

HDQRS. MILITARY DIVISION OF THE MISSISSIPPI,
In the Field, near Atlanta, August 8, 1864.

General THOMAS:

Where is General Kilpatrick's cavalry at this time?

W. T. SHERMAN,
Major-General, Commanding.

THOMAS' HEADQUARTERS,
August 8, 1864.

General SHERMAN:

General Kilpatrick's headquarters are at the junction of Powder Springs and Sandtown roads. He covers Sweet Water and patrols to Dallas.

S. HOFFMAN,
Assistant Adjutant-General.

HDQRS. MILITARY DIVISION OF THE MISSISSIPPI,
In the Field, near Atlanta, August 8, 1864.

General THOMAS:

Order Captain Merrill to meet General Cullum at Nashville about the end of this week to consult about the defenses of Nashville. This by General Halleck's order. General Schofield has made some progress on the right, but not enough. General Howard has also advanced his line somewhat. Let me know if the 4½-inch guns have come and where you will place them. A very good place will be on General Ward's right, on account of the opening made by the valley of Proctor's Creek, giving a plain view of the very heart of the town. I would like to have them at work to-morrow.

W. T. SHERMAN,
Major-General, Commanding.

HEADQUARTERS DEPARTMENT OF THE CUMBERLAND,
August 8, 1864.

Major-General SHERMAN:

The 4½-inch guns have not yet arrived. They are not due until to-morrow. I have selected a very good point for them on Geary's left, where you can get a fair view of the town, and half a mile nearer than any other position. It was reported that they were to leave Chatta-nooga at 8 a. m. to-day. The position selected enfilades White Hall street, upon which is General Hood's headquarters, and the battery is being built to-night.

GEO. H. THOMAS,
Major-General.

HEADQUARTERS ARMY OF THE CUMBERLAND,
August 8, 1864.

Major-General SHERMAN:

Lieutenant Wharton, Engineers, informs me that there are not enough topographical engineers in this army to supply its necessary wants; consequently I shall not be able to spare any to General Schofield.

GEO. H. THOMAS,
Major-General, U. S. Volunteers, Commanding.

AUGUST 8, 1864.

Captain CASE, *Chief Signal Officer:*

Can see no change in enemy's lines. Can see them bringing water from their works. Hear brisk cannonading on right.

BURTON.

HEADQUARTERS FOURTH ARMY CORPS,
August 8, 1864.

Brig. Gen. W. D. WHIPPLE,
Chief of Staff:

GENERAL: The appearance of the enemy's line in front of this corps remains unchanged so far as can be ascertained by observation. Since the capture of their pickets in the demonstrations made last week the enemy have strengthened their line, and in our last attempt promptly re-enforced their pickets and showed a disposition to maintain the line. A lieutenant and private from Vaughan's brigade, Cheatham's division, deserted and came into our lines this morning. They came directly through their own pickets. The lieutenant's account of their line is essentially the same as given by previous prisoners and deserters, *i. e.*, the main works are filled by militia, and that Cheatham's and Cleburne's divisions are camped behind the main line, confronting the Fourth Corps, and doing the picketing for the militia. He does not know of the position of the remaining division of Hardee's corps, Bate's, but thinks it is similarly employed. I have no reason to doubt the statement of this man, and he says he was along the line and saw the troops he mentions yesterday. Two brigades of dismounted cavalry extend the rebel right beyond the right of the infantry south of the railroad. It appears somewhat strange the rebels can oppose these old troops to us here and yet meet the movements upon our right. The lieutenant represents the defenses north and east of Atlanta as very perfect and that there is nothing south in the way of fortifications.

Very respectfully, your obedient servant,

D. S. STANLEY,
Major-General.

HDQRS. SECOND BRIGADE, SECOND CAVALRY DIVISION,
Buck Head, Ga., August 8, 1864.

Capt. ROBERT P. KENNEDY,
Assistant Adjutant-General, Second Cavalry Division:

CAPTAIN: I have the honor to report, for the information of the brigadier-general commanding, that I sent a scouting party of one battalion to McAfee's Bridge at an early hour this morning. Lieutenant-Colonel Patten, First Ohio Cavalry, was in charge of this party, and has returned with his command. He reports having found no force of rebel cavalry in that neighborhood, nor could he hear of anything more than small squads. He saw but one or two stragglers of General Stoneman's command. He lost one horse killed, by being fired upon by a squad of men who escaped in the woods. From the best information he could gather he deemed it useless to remain longer, and returned to camp this evening.

I am, very respectfully, your obedient servant,

ELI LONG,
Colonel, Commanding Brigade.

HDQRS. CHIEF OF CAVALRY, DEPT. OF THE CUMBERLAND,
        Near Atlanta, Ga., August 8, 1864—11.30 p. m.
Brig. Gen. J. KILPATRICK, *Comdg. Third Cavalry Division:*

The enemy's cavalry on the south side of the Chattahoochee threatens General Schofield's right flank on or near the Sandtown and Atlanta road. The general commanding directs that you make a demonstration opposite to and below Sandtown as if you intended to cross the river. Make the greatest show of force by countermarching command. Let this be done at an early hour but without harassing your animals more than is necessary.

I am, general, very respectfully, your obedient servant,

DAVID F. HOW,
        Lieutenant and Acting Assistant Adjutant-General.

HDQRS. MILITARY DIVISION OF THE MISSISSIPPI,
        In the Field, near Atlanta, August 8, 1864.
                        (Received 9.05 a. m.)
Major-General SCHOFIELD:

I wish you to develop the enemy's position and strength on the right as soon as you can, that I may adopt some well-defined plan for further operations.

W. T. SHERMAN,
        Major-General, Commanding.

HEADQUARTERS ARMY OF THE OHIO,
        Near Atlanta, Ga., August 8, 1864—10.30 a. m.
Major-General SHERMAN:

I will push forward and develop the enemy's position as rapidly as practicable. I have just returned from the extreme right, which is near Utoy Creek. The enemy is behind intrenchments south of the creek and facing toward my flank. I have sent Hascall to cross the creek and try to clear that flank, while the rest of the corps is pushing forward. I think the force south of the creek is only cavalry with artillery.

J. M. SCHOFIELD,
        Major-General.

HEADQUARTERS ARMY OF THE OHIO,
        In the Field, August 8, 1864—11.15 a. m.
Major-General SHERMAN:

General Hascall reports the enemy advancing in force on or near his right. He has consequently suspended his movement and is preparing to receive an attack.

J. M. SCHOFIELD,
        Major-General.

HDQRS. MILITARY DIVISION OF THE MISSISSIPPI,
        Proctor's Creek, August 8, 1864—1 p. m.
General SCHOFIELD:

Your dispatches of 10.30 and 11.15 a. m. are received. I have been along General Corse's line, also General Williams', and we are preparing for a dash at another hill looking into the very streets of Atlanta. I expect the 30-pounder Parrotts up this p. m. and will use them freely. I have renewed my orders to attack at all points on hearing the sounds of battle over at your flank. I think you have force enough to fight all of Hood's movable army if he comes outside his trenches. Go on, press him close, and trust to the chances of battle on anything like fair terms.

W. T. SHERMAN,
Major-General, Commanding.

HEADQUARTERS ARMY OF THE OHIO,
Near Atlanta, Ga., August 8, 1864—1.50 p. m.

Major-General SHERMAN:

A column of cavalry and infantry is reported moving around my right. This is doubtless the same force before reported advancing toward my right. I presume the design is to cross Utoy Creek and strike our trains. I will try to prevent it, but may not be able.

J. M. SCHOFIELD,
Major-General.

(Same to General Thomas.)

HDQRS. MILITARY DIVISION OF THE MISSISSIPPI,
In the Field, near Atlanta, August 8, 1864.
(Received 2.50 p. m.)

General SCHOFIELD:

If infantry has passed round your right flank they could be caught by detaching a division from your line to move down the Sandtown road to the forks; but the report is so indefinite that I cannot understand the movement. If you can catch any enemy outside of breast-works attack him vigorously. One of Johnson's divisions could hold the tête-de-pont, and you have four divisions for battle.

W. T. SHERMAN,
Major-General, Commanding.

HEADQUARTERS ARMY OF THE OHIO,
Near Atlanta, Ga., August 8, 1864—3.50 p. m.

Major-General SHERMAN:

The force moving to my right is not an army, but a raiding force. The only question was whether I could afford to spare from other operations force enough to meet it at the numerous points where it might come. I wished to put you on your guard about trains. I do not hear of any attempt of the enemy to cross Utoy and presume Hascall's movements have caused them to fall back. This rain makes it very difficult to move, but I hope to accomplish our object before dark.

J. M. SCHOFIELD,
Major-General.

HEADQUARTERS ARMY OF THE OHIO,
Near Atlanta, Ga., August 8, 1864—6 p. m.

Major-General SHERMAN:

We have developed the enemy's line to Utoy Creek. It runs nearly south from the salient in front of Morgan's left center. We are about as close to it as we can get. Cox's right rests substantially on the creek. Hascall had to bridge the creek to make his movement to the right. He has a brigade across and on the ridge beyond. It has met a pretty stubborn resistance, but not such as to indicate a large infantry force. The enemy's cavalry is all along Utoy Creek beyond our right, but has made no attempt to cross. The ground is open from Cox's right toward the railroad. The enemy's line does not appear to cross the open ground. What appears to be the railroad crosses this open ground about a mile from Cox's right. I will try to learn all about it before dark. Hascall can't do much more to-day.

J. M. SCHOFIELD,
Major-General.

HEADQUARTERS ARMY OF THE OHIO,
Near Atlanta, August 8, 1864—8.30 p. m.

Major-General SHERMAN:

Hascall only succeeded in getting one brigade across the creek and intrenched. The enemy is pretty strong in front of that brigade, and has used artillery freely. Hascall is making good roads and bridges across the creek. It seems clear that we are as near to the railroad as we can get on this side of the creek without breaking the rebel lines. To cross the creek takes us around below East Point. Whether one division is sufficient force to make that move with, seems extremely doubtful. Possibly the demonstration may be sufficient to make Hood let go of Atlanta. I am satisfied Cox's right is not more than a mile from East Point.

J. M. SCHOFIELD,
Major-General.

HDQRS. MILITARY DIVISION OF THE MISSISSIPPI,
In the Field, near Atlanta, August 8, 1864.
(Received 9 40 p. m.)

General SCHOFIELD:

I have your dispatch. Continue to press by the right. It is impossible for the enemy to extend much farther. Thomas and Howard will continue to press forward. If Garrard watches well the passes of Utoy Creek, I have no fears of that flank. If Cox has a view of the railroad over clear ground to his right, distant only a mile, our rifle guns will reach it. Still, Hascall should move straight toward it, and intrench as close as he can get. I think that open ground is below East Point, and the railroad you see is the West Point road, which the enemy does not use. East Point is at the head of the south fork of Utoy. I have your dispatch of 8.30. See in person to the point occupied by Hascall. Let good bridges and roads be prepared, and intrench the point as a flank to threaten below East Point. Strengthen the main line as much as possible, so that, if the enemy will fight on that flank, you will have as much force as possible to support, but explain to Hascall if they allow him to intrench they will not attack him, but feign, for the purpose of breaking out somewhere else.

W. T. SHERMAN,
Major-General, Commanding.

HEADQUARTERS ARMY OF THE OHIO,
Near Atlanta, Ga., August 8, 1864—10 p. m.

Major-General SHERMAN:

Your dispatches of 9.20 and 9.50 are received. When Hascall crosses the creek and begins to operate toward East Point there will be several miles of rebel cavalry line facing our rear, which I must detach infantry to operate against. The creek can be crossed anywhere at low water except near the mouth. The rebel cavalry attempted to cross at two points this evening. First at the bridge, which fortunately had been destroyed, and subsequently at a ford where I had some troops stationed, where skirmishing was going on at dark. From the forks of the creek up they can cross anywhere as soon as my infantry is withdrawn. The force sent across the creek will, from the nature of the ground, have to act entirely independently, and having no cavalry on its flanks will have to rest both flanks on the creek. The commanding ground on the opposite side of the creek is at least a mile from Cox's right. I do not think a single division can accomplish anything, but I will try what can be done.

J. M. SCHOFIELD,
Major-General.

HDQRS. MILITARY DIVISION OF THE MISSISSIPPI,
In the Field, near Atlanta, Ga., August 8, 1864.

General SCHOFIELD:

I will order Kilpatrick's cavalry down on the other bank of the Chattahoochee to feign a crossing at Sandtown. As soon as I learn where Kilpatrick is I will tell you where its effect may be felt. It seems to me a part of the Fourteenth Corps could be spared from the lines to watch the flank between Cox's right and Utoy Post-Office. Certainly it don't need all of the Fourteenth Corps and Cox's division to watch the line between the two forks of Utoy. It looked to me as though two divisions could hold that ridge against a sally, giving you three divisions to operate with.

W. T. SHERMAN,
Major-General, Commanding.

HDQRS. MILITARY DIVISION OF THE MISSISSIPPI,
In the Field, near Atlanta, Ga., August 8, 1864.

General SCHOFIELD:

General Thomas says that Kilpatrick is at the junction of the Sandtown and Powder Springs roads. I have ordered him to send instructions for him to move down to Sandtown and feign as though crossing. This will engage their attention, and I don't believe the enemy will put any considerable cavalry force above Utoy Creek. I think Garrard below the forks and a brigade of infantry down the Sandtown road, near Utoy Post-Office, will make that flank perfect.

W. T. SHERMAN,
Major-General, Commanding.

AUGUST 8, 1864.

Major-General SCHOFIELD:

Colonel Casement covers the reported gap between Generals Cox and Hascall. Casement is on the right of Barter, who occupies a ridge that partially runs out at his line. There is a creek between Barter and Casement. General Hascall has just thrown his left forward and will connect with Casement's right. The reported movement of the rebels in three lines I do not credit. All I can definitely learn is that the rebels were moving toward our right, and apparently for the purpose of strengthening their line in front of General Hascall. I have not seen the general himself; he may have other information. I will follow up General Hascall's movement and report if anything occurs.

Very respectfully, your obedient servant,

WM. J. TWINING,
Lieutenant of Engineers.

HDQRS. SECOND DIVISION, TWENTY-THIRD ARMY CORPS,
August 8, 1864—12.30 p. m.

Major-General SCHOFIELD,
Commanding Army of the Ohio:

GENERAL: Colonel Swaine just sends word that a column of infantry and cavalry are now passing around to his right, about 1,000 yards off. I have just sent him word to open on them with three Parrott guns, which I have up there, and to press out his skirmishers and ascertain the true state of the case. I had given Colonels Strickland and Hobson half an hour to complete their new line preparatory to my advance, and by that time will ascertain the true state of the case.

MILO S. HASCALL,
Brigadier-General.

HDQRS. SECOND DIVISION, TWENTY-THIRD ARMY CORPS,
August 8, 1864—3.30 p. m.

Major-General SCHOFIELD,
Commanding Twenty-third Corps:

GENERAL: Yours of 1.30 just received. About 12.30 I took Colonel Strickland, Colonel Hobson, and General Cooper to the point where I now am (in front of Colonel Casement's line on the open field), showed them the ground I wanted them to advance over, and instructed Colonel Strickland to advance his brigade at once, and sent two staff officers with him to help him along and report progress. I cannot imagine what detains them, unless the heavy rain has swollen the stream in our front so as to render its passage very difficult. I expect to hear them open every minute now. There is a tremendous large open field in front of where I am, on the right of which I am having my force advanced. Plenty of rebels, rifle-pits, artillery, and trains are visible. It will not be possible for me to advance as far as the farther end of the field, as it is from one mile and a half to two miles. I will report progress directly, as I have sent another staff officer to hurry the troops along. I can see everything from where I am.

Truly, yours,

MILO S. HASCALL,
Brigadier-General.

HEADQUARTERS SECOND DIVISION,
August 8, 1864—6 p. m.

Major-General SCHOFIELD,
Commanding Twenty-third Corps:

GENERAL: I have brought General Cooper's brigade down to where Major Campbell saw me, and fortifying it, Colonel Hobson on his right to connect with Colonel Swaine, and Colonel Strickland to hold a position on the far side of the creek to secure a foothold on that side. I have ordered two good roads and bridges made, connecting Colonel Strickland with this side, which will enable him to reach this side, if he should be pressed there. He has met a tolerably heavy force over there, and the enemy are now using artillery freely on him. I can easily fall back into my old position with the whole division, if it is necessary. My present position overlooks a vast extent of country and is good on that account. Please answer by bearer.

MILO S. HASCALL,
Brigadier-General.

P. S.—General Cox, I think, should bring forward Casement and connect with my left.

HEADQUARTERS ARMY OF THE OHIO,
In the Field, Ga., August 8, 1864.

Lieut. Col. G. W. SCHOFIELD,
Chief of Artillery and Ordnance, Army of the Ohio:

COLONEL: The commanding general directs that you have Colonel Crittenden's men under arms and on the alert, watching well to the west. The enemy is reported moving round to the right of our lines, and may intend to cross Utoy Creek and strike our rear. Inform Colonel Garrard and let him scout out toward General Hascall's right, and you to inform General Howard that the troops are there, and can be called upon in case of necessity on his right.

Very respectfully, your obedient servant,

WM. M. WHERRY,
Major and Aide-de-Camp.

HDQRS. THIRD DIVISION, TWENTY-THIRD ARMY CORPS,
Before Atlanta, August 8, 1864.

Brigadier-General REILLY,
Commanding First Brigade:

General Schofield directs that we advance our lines if possible, swinging in the right to get new tenable ground nearer the enemy until the position, &c., of their works is definitely ascertained. Colonel Byrd reports their principal line visible on the next ridge along his front, about 250 yards distant. Can you report anything from your front on this subject? If you can swing out your skirmish line Byrd and all left of you will keep pace with it. General S[chofield] is urgent that the effort should be very strong till we can report definitely our distance from the rebel fortifications. Show this to Barter and he will act in concert with you. I will be over as soon as this storm passes, and meanwhile the order is to push.

J. D. COX,
Brigadier-General, Commanding.

HDQRS. THIRD DIVISION, TWENTY-THIRD ARMY CORPS,
South Bank Utoy Creek, August 8, 1864.

Colonel BARTER,
Commanding Brigade:

SIR: General Hascall is about to make a reconnaissance in the direction of the flank of the rebel works seen from Cockerill's battery, and you will please keep watch of any movement in that direction, and if you hear or see him at work, make a strong demonstration with your skirmish line and endeavor to capture the skirmishers in your front. The rebel skirmish line must be pushed back, as it is entirely too near both you and Reilly, and the works of the rebels must be developed so that we shall know definitely their position and distance, and the nature of the intervening ground. Show this to General Reilly, who will please regard it as an order for him to co-operate and perform the same work along his line in conjunction with you. General Schofield intimated that he should reluctantly yield to your request to be permitted to resign.

Very respectfully, &c.,

J. D. COX,
Brigadier-General, Commanding.

HDQRS. THIRD DIVISION, TWENTY-THIRD ARMY CORPS,
Before Atlanta, August 8, 1864—3.30 p. m.

Maj. J. A. CAMPBELL,
Assistant Adjutant-General, &c.:

SIR: In obedience to the orders of the commanding general, my kirmish line, strongly re-enforced, has been pushed along Colonel Byrd's front, on my left. He reports the main continuous line of the enemy's works about 250 yards distant from his breast-works, and visible at intervals through the woods, running parallel to ours. He reports no good position in his front between his own and the enemy's, whose skirmishers, he says, are close to their works. General Reilly and Colonel Barter have not yet reported fully, but I have little doubt the line is continuous along our entire front, at a distance not varying much from that reported by Colonel Byrd.

Very respectfully, your obedient servant,

J. D. COX,
Brigadier-General, Commanding.

HOWARD'S HEADQUARTERS,
August 8, 1864.

Major-General SHERMAN:

Signal officer's report, viz:

9.15 A. M.

A very heavy detail of fatigue men, negroes, just passed toward the enemy's left. They took the right-hand road at the forks. They will number about 300, perhaps more. Their line in front appears unchanged.

O. O. HOWARD,
Major-General.

HOWARD'S HEADQUARTERS,
August 8, 1864. (Received 2.50 p. m.)

Major-General SCHOFIELD:

I have sent the Ninth Illinois Cavalry* down on our right flank to watch the movements of the enemy and guard against any attempt to get in our rear.

O. O. HOWARD,
Major-General.

Tell me of what service I can be to you.

O. O. HOWARD.

———

HOWARD'S HEADQUARTERS,
August 8, 1864.

General SHERMAN:

I have ordered what little reserve I have to be held in hand on the Green's Ferry road. I will go to General Schofield's headquarters. Please communicate with me there, if there are any orders.

O. O. HOWARD,
Major-General.

———

HDQRS. MILITARY DIVISION OF THE MISSISSIPPI,
In the Field, near Atlanta, August 8, 1864.

Major-General HOWARD:

There is a wooded hill to General Corse's left and front, on which I was told General Williams' skirmishers were yesterday. It seemed to be on the south of Proctor's Creek. That hill would be a strong left flank to you. In front of General Corse's left center seemed an orchard near to a rebel work, and it may be within the re-entrant of their salients, but if we could get a battery near there it would make sad havoc in Atlanta.

W. T. SHERMAN,
Major-General, Commanding.

———

HEADQUARTERS DEPARTMENT OF THE TENNESSEE,
August 8, 1864.

Major-General SHERMAN:

I am just starting to reconnoiter that position.

O. O. HOWARD,
Major-General.

———

HDQRS. MILITARY DIVISION OF THE MISSISSIPPI,
In the Field, near Atlanta, August 8, 1864.

General HOWARD:

General Schofield reports his line close up to the rebel lines from your right to the crossing of the south fork of Utoy, which he thinks is one mile from East Point; he thinks he sees the railroad, but if so, it is the West Point railroad, which is not the one we want. His line gives General Hascall's division in excess, one brigade of which is across Utoy and on the ridge which he is fortifying. He says the enemy manifests considerable resistance, but if he is allowed to fortify south of that fork of Utoy, they will not attack that flank, and will

———

* Mounted infantry.

either await our further development or try to break through somewhere else. I think they will await our initiative, trusting to catch us
in an assault. I did not learn if General Corse got that hill on his left
front. I would like to get a good battery as near it as possible that
will reach the heart of Atlanta and reduce it to ruins, and to keep up
a fire that will prevent wagon supply trains from coming into town.
There is little use of your firing from the right of your line, as that end
of town is of little depth or importance. General Blair's front is the
only part of your line where a sally need be expected.

W. T. SHERMAN,
Major-General, Commanding.

HEADQUARTERS DEPARTMENT OF THE TENNESSEE,
August 8, 1864.

Major-General SHERMAN:

Dispatches received. General Corse reports that he advanced
within forty yards of the top of the ridge which he was to take; this
at 7 p. m. The enemy resisted pretty stubbornly, but he holds his
ground and is intrenched; says no one advanced on his left until 8.45,
the last report from him, there being some misunderstanding, and the
failure in concert of action on the part of General Williams. His communication has been referred to General Williams. General Dodge
thinks they will take the ridge to-night; if not, in the morning.

O. O. HOWARD,
Major-General.

HDQRS. MILITARY DIVISION OF THE MISSISSIPPI,
In the Field, near Atlanta, Ga., August 8, 1864.

Major-General HOWARD:

Has the brigade from Decatur arrived? I would like you, if possible, to hold the line from Proctor's Creek to the north branch of Utoy.
This would clearly define your line from General Thomas to General
Schofield, and every yard of advance would contract your line and
strengthen your reserve.

W. T. SHERMAN,
Major-General, Commanding.

HEADQUARTERS DEPARTMENT OF THE TENNESSEE,
August 8, 1864.

Major-General SHERMAN:

A part at least of the brigade has arrived. I will ask Dodge as
to the remainder. My right now rests on the north branch of Utoy.
I will reconnoiter at once with regard to the left. General Williams
and myself already connect on our new line.

O. O. HOWARD,
Major-General.

HEADQUARTERS DEPARTMENT OF THE TENNESSEE,
August 8, 1864.

Major-General SHERMAN:

Colonel Garrard, commanding cavalry regiment, reports that several
hundred enemy's cavalry have halted and gone into camp beyond Utoy

Creek, about two miles from its mouth, in plain view of Colonel Garrard's pickets. I have sent a squadron—perhaps 200—mounted infantry in that direction. At last accounts General Schofield was going on with his movements.

O. O. HOWARD,
Major-General.

Hdqrs. Department and Army of the Tennessee,
Before Atlanta, Ga., August 8, 1864.

Maj. Gen. JOHN A. LOGAN,
Commanding Fifteenth Army Corps:

General Schofield reports his right being turned. The major-general commanding directs that you order your reserve immediately into our old line of works on the Green's Ferry road, holding them there prepared to support the right.

Very respectfully, your obedient servant,

WM. T. CLARK,
Assistant Adjutant-General.

(Same to General Blair, Seventeenth Army Corps.)

Headquarters Fifteenth Army Corps,
Before Atlanta, Ga., August 8, 1864.

Brigadier-General LIGHTBURN,
Commanding Second Division:

GENERAL: General Schofield reports his right being turned, and Major-General Logan in pursuance of instructions from Major-General Howard directs that you order your reserves into our old line of works on the Green's Ferry road, holding them in readiness to support the right.

By order of Major-General Logan:

R. R. TOWNES,
Assistant Adjutant-General.

Headquarters Left Wing, Sixteenth Army Corps,
Near Atlanta, Ga., August 8, 1864.

Lieut. Col. WILLIAM T. CLARK,
Assistant Adjutant-General, Dept. and Army of the Tennessee:

COLONEL: General Corse reports that he is now (8.45 p. m.) within forty yards of the top of the ridge on which the dead trees are. He says no one advanced on his left until just now, there being some misunderstanding in the matter. He is about advancing to the top, but I judge the enemy is holding the ridge pretty stubbornly. General Corse is intrenching the ridge this side, and if he gets the other to-night will intrench that. In accordance with your orders I have directed my front line to move into the new works at 6 a. m. to-morrow. If I understand the ground the Twentieth Corps should move up also, or it will expose General Corse's left, especially if he should gain the farther ridge. General Ransom is intrenching his line where Major-General Howard directed. The enemy has attacked General Corse twice, but so far he has held all the ground taken to-day.

Very respectfully, your obedient servant,

G. M. DODGE,
Major-General.

BEFORE ATLANTA, GA., *August 8, 1864.*

Maj. T. T. ECKERT,
    Superintendent U. S. Military Telegraph:

No fighting since last communication. Armies both stretching toward right, striving to turn a flank, and so far rebels have the best of it. Attempted to-day to get in our rear by crossing Utoy Creek, but were stopped by destroying the bridge. Line of battle now sixteen miles long.

J. C. VAN DUZER,
    Cipher Operator, U. S. Military Telegraph.

SHERMAN'S HEADQUARTERS,
    August 8, 1864.

General THOMAS:

Orders for to-morrow, August 9: All the batteries that can reach the buildings of Atlanta will fire steadily on the town to-morrow, using during the day about fifty rounds per gun, shell and solid shot. General Schofield will, during the cannonading, completely develop the enemy's strength and position on his left flank.

W. T. SHERMAN,
    Major-General.

(Same to Generals Schofield and Howard.)

SPECIAL FIELD ORDERS,) HEADQUARTERS DEPARTMENT
                       }   AND ARMY OF THE TENNESSEE,
    No. 92.   )   *Before Atlanta, Ga., August 8, 1864.*

*   *   *   *   *   *   *

IX. Corps commanders will cause their present skirmish lines to be intrenched completely to-night, and will move into them a sufficient number of troops to hold and occupy them to-morrow morning at 6 o'clock. Care will be taken to complete the connection between the several corps.

By order of Maj. Gen. O. O. Howard:

WM. T. CLARK,
    Assistant Adjutant-General.

SPECIAL FIELD ORDERS,) HDQRS. LEFT WING, 16TH A. C.,
    No. 57.   )   *Before Atlanta, Ga., August 8, 1864.*

*   *   *   *   *   *   *

IV. In order to properly carry out Special Field Orders, No. 92, headquarters Department and Army of the Tennessee (a copy of which is herewith inclosed),* the skirmish line will be strengthened to-night, and sufficient working details will be made to throw up works during the night sufficiently strong to protect the troops, connections being made on right and left with the Twentieth and Seventeenth Corps. At 6 a. m. to-morrow troops sufficient to fill the works will be moved in and they will strengthen the position in every possible way. Batteries will be erected on prominent points. The reserves will be held under arms in the line of works, ready for any emergency. A portion

*See next preceding.

of the position to be taken is so near the enemy that the works must be strengthened as much as possible during the night, and great vigilance observed that the working parties are not driven off.

By order of Maj. Gen. G. M. Dodge:

J. W. BARNES,
Assistant Adjutant-General.

Abstract from report of the effective force of the cavalry of the Military Division of the Mississippi, August 8, 1864.

Command.	Present for duty.			Total present.			Mounted and equipped for line of battle.		
	Officers.	Men.	Total.	Officers.	Men.	Total.	Officers.	Men.	Total.
Cavalry, Department of the Cumberland, Brig. Gen. W. L. Elliott.	10	31	41	10	61	71	.....	.....	.....
First Cavalry Division, Brig. Gen. E. M. McCook.	9	78	87	9	78	87	.....	.....	.....
First Brigade, Maj. R. Root..	11	217	228	11	217	228	11	66	77
Second Brigade, Lieut. Col. H. P. Lamson.	43	469	512	47	588	635	33	301	334
18th Indiana Battery:									
Lieutenant Rippetoe....	3	122	125	3	122	125	3	122	125
Lieutenant Thomas	1	63	64	1	63	64	.....	.....	.....
Total First Cavalry Division.*a*	67	949	1,016	71	1,068	1,139	47	489	536
Second Cavalry Division, Brig. Gen. K. Garrard.	199	4,177	4,376	236	4,878	5,114	210	4,132	4,342
Third Cavalry Division, Brig. Gen. J. Kilpatrick.	13	30	43	13	30	43	13	30	43
First Brigade, Lieutenant-Colonel Klein.	19	458	477	26	558	584	19	330	349
Second Brigade, Lieut. Col. F. A. Jones.	57	1,012	1,069	65	1,123	1,188	59	633	692
Third Brigade, Col. E. H. Murray.	69	1,221	1,290	78	1,510	1,588	72	905	977
10th Wisconsin Battery, Capt. Y. V. Beebe.	4	105	109	5	120	125	4	105	109
Total Third Cavalry Division.	162	2,826	2,988	187	3,341	3,528	167	2,003	2,170
Total cavalry, Department of the Cumberland.	438	7,983	8,421	504	9,348	9,852	424	6,624	7,048
Major-General Stoneman's command:									
Cavalry, Department of the Ohio, Col. Silas Adams.	8	.....	8	8	.....	8	8	.....	8
First Brigade, Maj. W. Carter.	22	528	550	22	528	550	22	528	550
Second Brigade, Major Rowland.	30	778	808	30	778	808	30	677	707
Third Brigade, Major Coates	11	371	382	11	371	382	11	154	165
24th Indiana Battery, Lieutenant Allen.	1	67	68	1	67	68	.....	.....	.....
Total......................	72	1,664	1,736	72	1,664	1,736	71	854	926
9th Ohio Cavalry,*b* Col. W. D. Hamilton.	22	418	440	26	474	500	22	237	259
4th Tennessee Cavalry,*c* Maj. M. Stephens.	9	229	238	9	229	238	9	20	29
Grand total	541	10,294	10,835	611	11,715	12,326	526	7,735	8,261

a The Third Brigade of this division is guarding the line of Atlantic and Western Railroad.
b Unassigned regiment; encamped Vining's Station.
c This regiment belongs to Fourth Cavalry Division, Department of the Cumberland, and has been ordered to Decatur, Ala.

Abstract from report of the effective force of the cavalry, &c.—Continued.

Command.	Dismounted.			Horses.		Mules.		Guns.
	Officers.	Men.	Total.	Serviceable.	Unserviceable.	Serviceable.	Unserviceable.	
Cavalry, Department of the Cumberland, Brig. Gen. W. L. Elliott.	.....	.....	.....	54	.....	.....	.....	.....
First Cavalry Division, Brig. Gen. E. M. McCook.	.....	2	2	93	5	.....	.....	.....
First Brigade, Maj. R. Root ..	.....	9	9	66	144	.....	.....	.....
Second Brigade, Lieut. Col. H. P. Lamson.	.....	43	43	335	158	.....	.....	.....
18th Indiana Battery: Lieutenant Rippetoe.....	.....	.....	.....	90	24	.....	.....	4
Lieutenant Thomas......	1	63	64	.....	.....	.....	.....	.....
Total First Cavalry Division.	1	117	118	574	331	.....	.....	4
Second Cavalry Division, Brig. Gen. K. Garrard.	.....	67	67	4,763	611	.....	.....	.....
Third Cavalry Division, Brig. Gen. J. Kilpatrick.	.....	.....	.....	56	.....	.....	.....	.....
First Brigade, Lieutenant-Colonel Klein.	.....	175	175	341	190	.....	.....	432
Second Brigade, Lieut. Col. F. A. Jones.	1	271	272	544	337	110	35	1,090
Third Brigade, Col. E. H. Murray.	1	141	142	980	518	.....	.....	1,513
10th Wisconsin Battery, Capt. Y. V. Beebe.	.....	.....	.....	105	3	.....	.....	4
Total Third Cavalry Division.	2	587	589	2,026	1,048	110	35	3,039
Total cavalry, Department of the Cumberland.	3	771	774	7,417	1,990	110	35	3,043
Major-General Stoneman's command: Cavalry, Department of the Ohio, Col. Silas Adams.	.....							
First Brigade, Maj. W. Carter.	.....			23	26			
Second Brigade, Major Rowland.	.....			220	477			
Third Brigade, Major Coates.	.....			181	124			
24th Indiana Battery, Lieutenant Allen.	.....				12			
Total				424	639			
9th Ohio Cavalry, Col. W. D. Hamilton.	.....	32	32	83	246	58	40	460
4th Tennessee Cavalry, Maj. M. Stephens.	.....			29	181			194
Grand total	3	803	806	7,953	3,056	168	75	3,717

W. L. ELLIOTT,
Brigadier-General and Chief of Cav., Dept. of the Cumberland.

CITY POINT, VA., *August 9, 1864—11.30 a. m.*

Major-General SHERMAN,
Commanding, &c., near Atlanta, Ga.:

The enemy having drawn to your front most of his forces west of Alabama, can you not re-enforce from Mississippi garrisons? I will ask to have all Western recruits sent immediately to you. Your views about showing no despondency, but keeping the enemy, with his last man now in the field, constantly employed, are the same I have often expressed.

We must win, if not defeated at home.   Every day exhausts the enemy at least a regiment, without any further population to draw from to replace it, exclusive of losses in battle.   I would suggest the employment of as many negroes as you can get for teamsters, company cooks, pioneers, &c., and keep the enlisted men in the ranks, and the shipment to Nashville of every unemployed negro, big and little.   By sending some of your disabled officers you might collect a considerable force from Northern hospitals.   Deserters coming in daily keep us well posted as to the position of Lee's forces.   Stories of deserters are not to be relied on, but they give their regiment, brigade, and division correctly, and many of them coming locate the whole.   I think no troops have gone from here to Hood.

U. S. GRANT,
Lieutenant-General.

Washington, August 9, 1864.

Major-General Sherman:

Dispatch of August 2 received.   There are no negro regiments avail able at present.   Recruits from Western States will be sent you in the mode you desire.

E. D. TOWNSEND,
Assistant Adjutant-General.

Near Atlanta, Ga., August 9, 1864—8.30 p. m.
(Received 2.20 p. m. 10th.)

Maj. Gen. H. W. Halleck,
Washington, D. C.:

Schofield developed the enemy's position to below East Point.   His line is well fortified, embracing Atlanta and East Point, and his redoubts and lines seem well filled.   Cavalry is on his flanks.   Our forces, too, are spread for ten miles.   So Hood intends to stand his ground. I threw into Atlanta about 3,000 solid shot and shell to-day, and have got from Chattanooga four 4½-inch rifled guns, and will try their effect. Our right is below Utoy Creek.   I will intrench it and the flanks and study the ground a little more before adopting a new plan.   We have had considerable rain, but on the whole the weather is healthy.   Colonel Capron, of Stoneman's command, with several squads of men are in at Marietta, and will reduce his loss below 1,000.

W. T. SHERMAN,
Major-General.

Nashville, August 9, 1864.

Major-General Sherman:

We have military possession of the Northwestern Railroad, and are working it to Colonel McCallum's satisfaction, connecting through to Johnsonville, the terminus on the Tennessee River.   It is not, however, formally transferred by Governor Johnson, and I have made the communication to him.   The road has been built for the most part by the United States, and no private parties have anything to do with it. Will send you by mail the orders under which I have proceeded to construct the road.

J. L. DONALDSON.

SHERMAN'S HEADQUARTERS,
August 9, 1864.

Generals THOMAS and HOWARD:

Schofield has his right division up to the enemy below Utoy Creek and south of East Point, and yet the enemy overlap him with redoubts and men. They must have more men than we estimate, or are thinly strung out; their line must be full fifteen miles long. Of course the bulk must be militia. I want our lines and flanks strengthened as much as possible with parapets and abatis, Thomas to get his 4½-inch guns to work, and study the ground a little more before adopting new plans. We are as much extended now as is prudent.

W. T. SHERMAN,
Major-General.

HDQRS. MILITARY DIVISION OF THE MISSISSIPPI,
In the Field, near Atlanta, August 9, 1864.

Major-General THOMAS:

I have examined the cavalry reports. You will please organize all on your returns according to the best interests of the service, and I will instruct General Schofield to do the same. As soon as he gets a return I will order Colonel Hamilton to you or General Schofield. I think the latter, as General Schofield should have something in lieu of what General Stoneman lost. Colonel Capron, long missing, is at Marietta, and reports a good many scattered detachments coming in. You can increase your divisions of Generals Kilpatrick and McCook by calling forward some of the cavalry in Tennessee, which cannot be needed there, save to allay the fears of the old women. Forrest is in no condition to enter Tennessee, and General A. J. Smith is after him.

W. T. SHERMAN,
Major-General, Commanding.

HDQRS. MILITARY DIVISION OF THE MISSISSIPPI,
In the Field, near Atlanta, August 9, 1864.

General THOMAS:

I will have to give General Schofield the Ninth Ohio Cavalry, Colonel Hamilton. With this regiment, and the wreck of General Stoneman's command, he can make a small brigade, enough to picket his flank on the Utoy Creek. If General Elliott has put the regiment on any kind of duty, please order him to have Colonel Hamilton to report to General Schofield.

W. T. SHERMAN,
Major-General, Commanding.

HDQRS. MILITARY DIVISION OF THE MISSISSIPPI,
In the Field, near Atlanta, August 9, 1864.

General THOMAS:

Send me word when the 4½-inch guns come, as I want to come over and watch the effect of a few of the first shots.

W. T. SHERMAN,
Major-General, Commanding.

THOMAS' HEADQUARTERS,
August 9, 1864.

Major-General SHERMAN:

I expect the 4½-inch guns to-day. Will send you word as soon as they arrive.

GEO. H. THOMAS,
Major-General.

HEADQUARTERS DEPARTMENT OF THE CUMBERLAND,
Before Atlanta, August 9, 1864—8.30 p. m.

Major-General SHERMAN:

The ammunition will be here to-morrow morning for the 4½-inch guns. The battery is formed and three of the guns here now. I have already made my intrenchments almost impregnable, but will have them re-examined for additional improvements if necessary. Deserters and refugees report to-night that Farragut has passed into Mobile Bay with his gun-boats and transports, and it is believed in Atlanta that he has possession of Mobile.

GEO. H. THOMAS,
Major-General, U. S. Volunteers.

HDQRS. MILITARY DIVISION OF THE MISSISSIPPI,
In the Field, near Atlanta, August 9, 1864.

General THOMAS:

I have a dispatch from General Meigs that Colonel Mackay is appointed as your assistant quartermaster, Colonel Easton as chief, and Colonel Bingham as inspector for me. I believe the report of the Mobile matter. It was, as you remember, a part of the original design. Now if General Canby can follow it up it will be of vast assistance to us. Get your guns well into position, and the moment the ammunition comes, let them open slowly, and with great precision, making all parts of the town unsafe. Guns of that caliber with good shells have a better effect than any I ever used.

W. T. SHERMAN,
Major-General, Commanding.

HOWARD'S HOUSE, *August 9, 1864—8.30 a. m.*

Captain CASE:

There is more stir than usual among the citizens and soldiers. Can see them moving in all directions. The battle-flags still remain in position.

BERRY,
Signal Officer.

HOWARD'S HOUSE, *August 9, 1864—10 a. m.*

Captain CASE:

The rebels are busily engaged in strengthening their abatis along the line as far as can see.

BERRY.

HOWARD'S HOUSE, *August 9, 1864.*
Captain CASE,
    Chief Signal Officer:

All quiet on this front. The enemy did not reply to our shelling.
They fired but two or three shots.
                                        A. F. BERRY,
                                            Signal Officer.

STANLEY'S HEADQUARTERS,
                        August 9, 1864.
Captain CASE,
    Signal Officer:

The shots were fired from a fort directly east of Atlanta.
                                        A. F. BERRY.

STATION OBSERVATION, *August 9, 1864—9.25 a. m.*
Capt. A. K. TAYLOR,
    Acting Signal Officer:

CAPTAIN: No change along line since yesterday. Working party on
fort to right, south from here.
    Yours, &c.,
                                        W. W. HOPKINS,
                            First Lieutenant and Acting Signal Officer.

SIGNAL DEPARTMENT, ARMY OF THE CUMBERLAND,
                    Station Observation, August 9, 1864.
Capt. A. K. TAYLOR,
    Acting Signal Officer, Commanding:

CAPTAIN: I have to make following report of the artillery firing along
front to-day as seen from tree at General Geary's headquarters. The
explosion of shells could be seen from a point southeast around to south.
Shells burst in front, above, and in rear of the large redoubt southeast,
and between it and four-gun fort. I saw none strike either, although they
burst very low. The most noticeable effect of the shelling was in front
of General Geary's division at a fort and house. This fort was struck;
also the works near it, and the house had quite a large hole knocked
in it besides being riddled. Shells burst over the works here and in the
woods to rear of them. The shells, which were few, I saw burst along
to south, were in rear of enemy's works. Shells exploded over the city
and in it, judging from the sound. A small piece was knocked off top
of brick smoke-stack in town. The rebels who have usually been loung-
ing around their works went into the ditches, seldom showing themselves, and this evening could be seen coming out for their rations, but
a shell bursting near soon dispersed them. Horses which have been
daily grazing around large redoubt were led off. The enemy fired from
fort in front of First Division for a short time this evening. Their shots
seemed to be directed at battery of 20-pounder Parrotts and one on line
in front of it. This was the only place I saw them fire from during the
day.
    Very respectfully, your obedient servant,
                                        W. W. HOPKINS,
                                Lieutenant and Acting Signal Officer.

STANLEY'S HEADQUARTERS, *August 9, 1864.*
Brig. Gen. W. D. WHIPPLE:

Three rebel colors were seen moving along the works south of the Augusta railroad, from the rebel right to left, and toward the railroad just at dusk. It may be relieving regiments. No other change.

D. S. STANLEY.

HEADQUARTERS FOURTEENTH ARMY CORPS,
Near Atlanta, Ga., August 9, 1864.
Brig. Gen. W. D. WHIPPLE,
  Chief of Staff, Department of the Cumberland:

On the evening of the 5th I was ordered by Major-General Palmer to move out my division on the road leading by Mr. Bankston's house, cross the Utoy, and encamp for the night. On the 6th I was ordered to move up to the Sandtown road, and march by that road toward Atlanta until I came up to General Davis' division, when I would find myself in reserve. This movement was performed, though slowly, on account of the stubborn resistance offered by the enemy. Arriving in rear of Davis, and finding our right and rear exposed, I formed my division in the rear of the right, and had a strong line of works constructed. About 3.30 p. m. General Cox arrived with his division, and said he had been ordered to relieve me.' I immediately called upon General Schofield, who informed me that he had ordered me to make a reconnaissance to the right to develop the enemy's position, and that I had been ordered to move at 2 p. m. My skirmishers and command had to be relieved, which consumed near an hour, and about 4 p. m., with my small division (3,000), I cut loose from the entire army. The dense undergrowth prevented very rapid movement, and I was unable to proceed more than a mile, where the rebel works appeared to be as strong as at any point I had come in contact with them. Later I received an order to relieve General Hascall, which I did after dark and before daylight on the morning of the 7th. On the 7th I was placed in command of the corps and ordered to advance upon the works to cover the movements on the right. The advance was announced, and the men moved forward rapidly, capturing the enemy's first line of rifle-pits with 172 prisoners. In this attempt the entire line was advanced, the rebels were driven into their main works, and the entire line of the corps advanced and fortified. Our loss during the operations of the 6th and 7th was 2 officers and 68 enlisted men killed; 15 officers and 398 enlisted men wounded, and 16 enlisted men missing. Total loss, 17 officers and 482 enlisted men; aggregate, 499. The rebels in my front have no skirmishers out except at a few points. On the 8th little could be done, though batteries were placed in position. On the 9th we kept up a vigorous firing with artillery and small-arms with no visible result.

Very respectfully, your obedient servant,

R. W. JOHNSON,
Brigadier-General.

The prisoners captured by Generals Baird and Morgan on the 5th—151 in number—were delivered to and receipted for by Lieutenant Duffield, assistant provost-marshal-general, Department of the Cumberland. One hundred and seventy-three prisoners, captured since then, and principally by General King, have been turned over to the provost-marshal of the Army of the Ohio, copies of the lists and receipts for whom are herewith transmitted.

R. W. J.

HEADQUARTERS DEPARTMENT OF THE CUMBERLAND,
Near Atlanta, August 9, 1864. (Received 12 m.)

Brig. Gen. A. S. WILLIAMS,
Commanding Twentieth Army Corps:

GENERAL: The major-general commanding desires that you will move up the right of your line so as to connect with the left of the Army of the Tennessee.

Very respectfully, yours,

WM. D. WHIPPLE,
Assistant Adjutant-General.

HEADQUARTERS DEPARTMENT OF THE CUMBERLAND,
Near Atlanta, Ga., August 9, 1864.

Brig. Gen. K. GARRARD,
Commanding Second Cavalry Division:

GENERAL: The major-general commanding directs that at as early an hour as possible this morning you send a brigade out to and beyond Decatur on our left to make a demonstration against the enemy. General Kilpatrick's division is ordered to threaten a crossing of the Chattahooche near Campbellton. The enemy's cavalry manifested unusual activity on our right yesterday, threatening to cross Utoy Creek. This movement of the cavalry is ordered to occupy the attention of the enemy's and prevent him in any way embarrassing the movements of General Schofield to-day while he endeavors to find the rebel left flank.

Yours, very respectfully,

WM. D. WHIPPLE,
Assistant Adjutant-General.

MARIETTA, *August 9, 1864.*

Major-General SHERMAN:

I arrived here yesterday. Am not in condition to report in person to-day. Small detachments of my brigade are hourly arriving. Will muster them to-day, and will report in person to-morrow unless otherwise ordered.

HORACE CAPRON,
Colonel, Commanding Brigade.

Statement of W. H. Gates (citizen).

OFFICE PROVOST-MARSHAL-GENERAL,
Near Atlanta, Ga., August 9, 1864.

Left Atlanta on the evening of the 8th instant and came with his wife to Decatur. Saw no pickets on the way who halted him until within three miles of Decatur; saw but few troops on the road, and those he saw were cavalry. Thinks there are no troops east of the cemetery except cavalry pickets. There is a camp of cavalry three miles south of Decatur. The State troops occupy the trenches on the north and northeast side of town, and their front is picketed by Cheatham's troops. The State troops number about 20,000. The whole rebel force is estimated at 60,000. There is one heavy gun located north of the female college. All business in Atlanta is suspended; the goods have been removed to other points in the State. There is but one grocery running in Atlanta and no stores or other business places. Hotels are closed.

Most of the shells from Federal guns strike in the vicinity of the depot, the larger part of them south of the depot. Seven shells have been sent through the Western and Atlantic Depot. In order for the gun firing from Marietta street to strike the commissary depot it should be depressed a little and the aim taken about 100 yards to the left of its usual range; the shells go about sixty feet over the commissary stores. No buildings have been burned by the shells. The subsistence on hand amounts to about six days. There have been several rumors of a new commander for the rebel army. One report was that Lee was coming to Atlanta and Jeff. Davis was going to command the Eastern army. The last report was that Beauregard was going to relieve Hood. A report came into Atlanta on or about the 5th instant from Brigadier-General Page, commanding Fort Morgan, in Mobile Bay, to General Higgins, that three gun-boats and fourteen ships had passed Fort Morgan into the bay. The rebel gun-boat Tennessee surrendered after a terrific fight, the Gaines was beached, the Selma was captured. The Tecumseh sunk under the guns of the water battery. Federal troops were landed on Dauphin Island; city in great excitement. General Maury called all citizens to arms.

[Indorsement.]

NEAR ATLANTA, GA., *August 9, 1864.*

Respectfully forwarded for the information of the general commanding.

J. G. PARKHURST,
Colonel and Provost-Marshal-General, Dept. of the Cumberland.

HEADQUARTERS DEPARTMENT OF THE CUMBERLAND,
August 9, 1864. (Received 8.50 a. m.)

Major-General SCHOFIELD

General Elliott reports to me that he yesterday saw a large herd of cattle and mules on this side of the Chattahoochee, below Proctor's Creek, as he was on his way to visit General Kilpatrick at Sweet Water Town; he also informs me that the enemy's cavalry is on this side of Chattahoochee, a short distance below Turner's Ferry, and could very easily capture the herd where it is at this time. He suggests that it be moved to this side of Proctor's Creek, unless you have a guard sufficiently large to insure its safety against capture.

GEO. H. THOMAS,
Major-General, Commanding.

(Same to General Howard.)

HDQRS. MILITARY DIVISION OF THE MISSISSIPPI,
In the Field, near Atlanta, August 9, 1864.
(Received 8.15 a. m.)

General SCHOFIELD:

Don't delay your movements to-day or make them dependent on the sounds of artillery, for you cannot hear the guns of General Thomas that bear on the city, while only four of General Howard's can reach the town. You may persevere in a general activity along the whole line. Orders were sent to General Kilpatrick during the night.

W. T. SHERMAN,
Major-General, Commanding.

HEADQUARTERS ARMY OF THE OHIO,
Near Atlanta, Ga., August 9, 1864.

Major-General SHERMAN:

Hascall has advanced onto the prolongation of Cox's line. In his front is a broad open valley running south and containing a small branch of Utoy Creek. Across this valley about southeast from his position is a large redoubt resembling those of Atlanta. About 100 yards of curtain can be seen on each side of it facing northwest. In front of Cox's right the enemy's line bends back so as to face southwest. Utoy Creek runs between this last line and the one of which the large redoubt forms part. It is probably a mile or more from Cox's right to the redoubt and nearly due south or a little east of south.

J. M. SCHOFIELD,
Major-General.

HEADQUARTERS ARMY OF THE OHIO,
Near Atlanta, August 9, 1864—1.25 p. m.

Major-General SHERMAN:

I have been across the creek and examined the ground in front of Hascall. He can gain some ground toward East Point and come nearly on the prolongation of our line this side of the creek. We are now pushing forward our right and will do so as far as practicable. You are mistaken about the extent of our lines. The Fourteenth Corps and Cox's division are in a single line with very small reserves.

J. M. SCHOFIELD,
Major-General.

HDQRS. MILITARY DIVISION OF THE MISSISSIPPI,
In the Field, near Atlanta, August 9, 1864.

General SCHOFIELD:

Your dispatch is received. All we can now do is to shorten our lines when practicable, strengthen the front and flanks as much as possible with parapets and abatis, and study the ground. We are extended enough. There must be some weak points in the enemy's line which we must study and develop. If we can't do that we must cut loose from our base and go south, a measure almost too rash to undertake, but inevitable unless we can draw Hood out otherwise.

W. T. SHERMAN,
Major-General, Commanding.

HDQRS. MILITARY DIVISION OF THE MISSISSIPPI,
In the Field, near Atlanta, Ga., August 9, 1864.

General SCHOFIELD:

Col. Horace Capron reports his arrival at Marietta. Says small detachments of his men are coming in; that he will muster them and report in person to-morrow. I have ordered him not to hurry, but to collect all men he can and report to you by telegraph and letter.

W. T. SHERMAN,
Major-General, Commanding.

HDQRS. MILITARY DIVISION OF THE MISSISSIPPI,
In the Field, near Atlanta, August 9, 1864.

General SCHOFIELD:

If you have a good cavalry brigadier I will give you Colonel Hamilton's regiment, Ninth Ohio, with a full regiment and nearly 500 horses, to make a brigade of cavalry, but I must have a real head, one that will give it personal attention.

W. T. SHERMAN,
Major-General, Commanding.

SCHOFIELD'S HEADQUARTERS,
August 9, 1864.

Major-General SHERMAN:

I have no good cavalry commander. Colonel Adams is probably the best I have. Can you not assign one from some other department? It is very important now for me to have a good man to collect my scattered fragments and bring them into serviceable shape.

Respectfully,

J. M. SCHOFIELD,
Major-General.

HDQRS. MILITARY DIVISION OF THE MISSISSIPPI,
In the Field, near Atlanta, August 9, 1864.

General SCHOFIELD:

I have no cavalry commander at all. All the cavalry of the old Army of the Tennessee is back in Mississippi, and General Thomas' cavalry is not well commanded. Colonel Adams told me his time was out, and he was going back to Kentucky to reorganize. You must secure his horses and appraise them, as they belong to the men. Colonel Capron is back; how is he?

W. T. SHERMAN,
Major-General, Commanding.

HEADQUARTERS ARMY OF THE OHIO,
Near Atlanta, Ga., August 9, 1864.

Major-General SHERMAN:

I don't know Colonel Capron personally, but understand he is not of much account. Colonel Garrard is the best man I have, but he is wanting in dash. I have ordered the appraisal of Colonel Adams' horses, and will try to get my cavalry in shape as soon as possible. I cannot do better for the present than to put Colonel Garrard in command, unless Colonel Hamilton is better. I know nothing of him.

J. M. SCHOFIELD,
Major-General.

HDQRS. MILITARY DIVISION OF THE MISSISSIPPI,
In the Field, near Atlanta, August 9, 1864.

General SCHOFIELD:

I have not the least objection in the world to paymasters coming to the front, only it is risky to bring too many greenbacks. I advise all that it is safe to pay the bulk in checks, and only enough greenbacks for, say, one-fourth. General Thomas says deserters report Admiral

Farragut inside of Mobile Bay. I hope it is true. I will assign Colonel Hamilton to you, and leave you to pick out a commander of brigade.

W. T. SHERMAN,
Major-General, Commanding.

HDQRS. THIRD DIVISION, TWENTY-THIRD ARMY CORPS,
Before Atlanta, August 9, 1864—1 p. m.
Col. J. S. CASEMENT, *Commanding Second Brigade:*

SIR: I am ordered to put Byrd, Reilly, and Barter in one line substantially. This will probably crowd out all of your brigade from the new line, but one regiment. If that is so, I desire the Sixty-third Indiana to be the regiment left there, for reasons which I mentioned last evening, and the rest of your brigade would be held substantially in reserve in the position it occupied this morning.

Very respectfully, &c.,

J. D. COX,
Brigadier-General, Commanding.

HEADQUARTERS LEFT WING, SIXTEENTH ARMY CORPS,
Near Atlanta, Ga., August 9, 1864.
Lieut. Col. WILLIAM T. CLARK, *Assistant Adjutant-General:*

In accordance with orders from department headquarters I occupied my advance works this morning at 6 o'clock, but up to this time, 10 a. m., no movement on the right or left of me has been made, a skirmish line only connecting with my front line.

I am, very respectfully, your obedient servant,

G. M. DODGE,
Major-General, Commanding.

BEFORE ATLANTA, GA., *August 9, 1864.*
Maj. Gen. F. P. BLAIR,
Commanding Seventeenth Army Corps:

The general commanding directs me to say that the new line in process of completion was occupied this a. m. as directed along the entire front, with the exception of a space between the Fifteenth and Seventeenth Corps, concerning which some misunderstanding exists. This new line is occupied as strongly as is now necessary for a fighting line, and more troops will probably be in the way of the working parties. In order to settle the division between your corps and the Fifteenth Corps, the general requests that you will direct the engineer officer of your corps to meet the engineer officer of the Fifteenth Corps, with Capt. C. B. Reese, chief engineer, at these headquarters at 2 o'clock this p. m. These three officers will determine the division to prevent any further misunderstanding.

Very respectfully, your obedient servant,

SAML. L. TAGGART,
Assistant Adjutant-General.

P. S.—It is proper to add that the conformation of the ground lengthens the line to be occupied by the Fifteenth Corps, throwing more than one brigade to the right.

(Same to General Logan, commanding Fifteenth Army Corps.)

Hdqrs. Second Division, Fifteenth Army Corps,
Before Atlanta, Ga., August 9, 1864.

Lieut. Col. R. R. Townes,
    Assistant Adjutant-General, Fifteenth Army Corps:

Colonel: I have the honor to report that my command was to-day employed in finishing a new line of works in advance of the one now occupied, which was completed this evening, except head-logs and abatis. The abatis could not be made in daylight and will, therefore, be finished to-night. I would also report that the new line was occupied to-day, by direction of the major-general commanding the department, by troops sufficient to make one rank. Nothing special occurred in front. Picket-firing was quite brisk, and a few shells thrown from the enemy's batteries.

Respectfully submitted.

J. A. J. LIGHTBURN,
Brigadier-General of Volunteers.

Hdqrs. Fourth Division, Fifteenth Army Corps,
August 9, 1864.

Lieutenant-Colonel Townes,
    Assistant Adjutant-General:

In accordance with instructions from corps headquarters, I caused my line in front to be strengthened as far as I could, and have moved a portion of my command forward, but the work on my left, and which Captain Klostermann said could be completed by the Seventeenth Corps, is untouched, and to move my line forward would leave it without connection on the left. What shall I do? By advancing my line, unless the Seventeenth Corps moves up and shares this ground, I will not have troops enough to more than put a single line by using them all. The weak part of the line is on the left, between the Fifteenth and Seventeenth Corps, owing to the exposed position and the complete curve, which would hide an approaching enemy until within a few yards. I am having the brush chopped and the work extended toward the Seventeenth Corps, but cannot surely believe that we are expected to keep feeling for the right of the Seventeenth Corps. By so doing I will so weaken the point indicated as to render it very insecure.

Respectfully, your obedient servant,

WILLIAM HARROW,
Brigadier-General.

Headquarters Left Wing, Sixteenth Army Corps,
Near Atlanta, Ga., August 9, 1864.

Brig. Gen. J. M. Corse,
    Commanding Second Division:

General: Your note is received. If the Twentieth Corps comes up you will be all right. I am anxious to have a good, large, strong battery put in on your front where you deem best. I leave it to you. If you can get to work on it to-night so much the better, as we may want to use it. The Seventeenth Army Corps is moving up this p. m., so that both of our flanks will be secure. Make your front as strong as possible. So long as we are so near the enemy we are likely to suffer from his sharpshooters, but we can force them back as soon as connections are perfected. Have your picket-line watch closely for any movement of the enemy to-night.

I am, very respectfully, your obedient servant,

G. M. DODGE,
Major-General, Commanding.

HDQRS. DEPARTMENT AND ARMY OF THE TENNESSEE,
Before Atlanta, Ga., August 9, 1864.

Maj. Gen. G. M. DODGE,
Commanding Left Wing, Sixteenth Army Corps:

GENERAL: The following dispatch is received, and the major-general commanding directs me to send you copy for your information:

Major-General HOWARD:

I saw General Thomas at 1 o'clock, and explained to him the position of General Ward's line with [regard] to General Corse, and he ordered the former to connect his line of battle with the latter's. This will include the hill we were on this morning.

WILLIAM F. BARRY,
Brigadier-General.

Respectfully, yours,

SAML. L. TAGGART,
Assistant Adjutant-General.

[Indorsement.]

AUGUST 9, 1864.

Referred to General Corse for his information.

DODGE,
General.

HDQRS. MILITARY DIVISION OF THE MISSISSIPPI,
In the Field, near Atlanta, August 9, 1864.

WILLIAM HARKER, Esq.,
McDonough, Ill.:

DEAR SIR: Yours of July 5 came to hand duly, and I asked General Newton, commanding the division to which General Harker belonged, to give me a more full account than the mere official statement ordinarily given. I have this moment received General Newton's paper, which comes, you will observe, from L. P. Bradley, now a brigadier-general, but then a colonel. The position we attacked was a difficult one, but very important, and had General Harker lived I believe we would have carried the parapet, broken the enemy's center, and driven him pell-mell into the Chattahoochee. General Harker, though quite young for his rank, was regarded as one of our best young generals, of rising fame, and his loss was deeply felt by me. He was universally esteemed, none more so; but death, you know, chooses a shining mark; and this has been very strongly exemplified in this campaign, for I have lost some of my best brigadiers and commanders. The nature of the country, its forests, its narrow defiles and mountain passes, all expose the leaders to the danger of ambush and unexpected shots; but General Harker fell in an assault, always one of the most dangerous moves of our dangerous life. I beg to record the high opinion I had of

General Harker, and the hopes I had of a long and bright future to him, but it is ordered otherwise and we must submit. Be pleased to accept the assurances of my sincere condolence and respect.

W. T. SHERMAN,
Major-General, Commanding.

BEFORE ATLANTA, GA., *August 9, 1864—9 p. m.*
Major ECKERT:

No movement to-day, severe rain-storm preventing. Prisoners and deserters all bring rumors of capture of Mobile by General Granger's forces. Have you any news from that point?

J. C. VAN DUZER.

GENERAL ORDERS, ⎱ WAR DEPT., ADJT. GENERAL'S OFFICE,
No. 241. ⎰ *Washington, August 9, 1864.*

Bvt. Maj. Gen. J. C. Davis is assigned to the command of the Fourteenth Army Corps, according to his brevet rank, vice Major-General Palmer, relieved at his own request.

By order of the President of the United States:

E. D. TOWNSEND,
Assistant Adjutant-General.

SPECIAL FIELD ORDERS, ⎱ HDQRS. DEPT. OF THE CUMBERLAND,
No. 218. ⎰ *Near Atlanta, Ga., August 9, 1864.*

* * * * * * *

II. Special Field Orders, No. 205, paragraph X, July 27, 1864, from these headquarters, is revoked. The First Division Cavalry (McCook's) will proceed to the District of the Etowah, headquarters Cartersville, Ga. The horses and equipments of the First Brigade, First Division Cavalry, will be turned over to the Second Brigade, First Division. The several brigades of the First Division Cavalry will take post as follows: First Brigade (dismounted) at or near Kingston, Ga.; the Second Brigade at or near Cartersville, Ga., and the Third Brigade at or near Calhoun, Tenn. The dismounted men of the First Division will be mounted and equipped at Nashville, Tenn., and sent to the division as soon as possible. The transportation of the First Division Cavalry will be recruited and organized under existing orders. Brigadier-General McCook, commanding First Division, will exercise a supervision over the several brigades of his division with a view to its instruction, discipline, and preparing it for active service as soon as possible, and will visit the several brigades for that purpose whenever necessary. The several brigades of this division will be concentrated as much as is possible to afford protection to the railroad, the mounted force patrolling the railroad and scouting the country between the Etowah River and Ellijay, and Spring Place.

* * * * * * *

By command of Major-General Thomas:

WM. D. WHIPPLE,
Assistant Adjutant-General.

SPECIAL FIELD ORDERS, } HDQRS. FIFTEENTH ARMY CORPS,
No. 73.   }   *Before Atlanta, Ga., August 9, 1864.*

*   *   *   *   *   *   *

III. Division commanders will complete the new line of works and occupy them to-night, if possible, with artillery and infantry, or have it ready to occupy in the morning. In case of an attack the new line is the one to be defended; should not be crowded with troops, but sufficient room for them to work freely must be given, and the reserves thus obtained will be placed in position in the old works.

By order of Maj. Gen. John A. Logan:

R. R. TOWNES,
Assistant Adjutant-General.

HDQRS. MILITARY DIVISION OF THE MISSISSIPPI,
In the Field, near Atlanta, August 10, 1864—8 p. m.

Lieut. Gen. U. S. GRANT,
Washington, D. C.:

Your dispatch of the 9th is received. It is to replace our daily losses that I propose that all recruits made daily in the Western States instead of accumulating at depots, should at once come to Nashville and be sent here on the cars, which can bring 400 a day without interfering with freights. I have ordered General Washburn, at Memphis, to have General A. J. Smith, who is now marching on Columbus, Miss., come to Decatur, Ala., whence I can bring to this army certain regiments and fragments that properly belong here, and a division that I originally designed to form a part of this army. The balance of infantry and cavalry I would send back via Savannah and Jackson, Tenn. My lines are now ten miles long, extending from the Augusta road on the left, round to East Point on the south. I cannot extend more without making my lines too weak. We are in close contact and skirmishing all the time. I have just got up four 4½-inch rifled guns with ammunition, and propose to expend about 4,000 rifled shot in the heart of Atlanta. We have already commanded it with our lighter ordnance. Since July 28 General Hood has not attempted to meet us outside of his parapets. In order to possess and destroy effectually his communications I may have to leave a corps at the railroad bridge, well intrenched, and cut loose with the balance and make a desolating circle around Atlanta. I do not propose to assault the works, which are too strong, or to proceed by regular approaches. I have lost a good many regiments and will lose more by the expiration of service, and this is the only reason why I want re-enforcements. I have killed, crippled, and captured more of the enemy than we have lost by his acts.

W. T. SHERMAN,
Major-General, Commanding.

HDQRS. MILITARY DIVISION OF THE MISSISSIPPI,
In the Field, near Atlanta, August 10, 1864.

General THOMAS:

General Schofield has examined closely his whole line, which lies south, a little east, parallel with the enemy, one brigade being on the Campbellton road south of Utoy. He is not absolutely certain that his right is near the West Point railroad, and yet urges that another corps can reach the Macon road, and wants to make Proctor's Creek our left flank, draw our supplies from Turner's Ferry, and keep on extending. My own experience is the enemy can build parapets faster than we march, and it would be the same thing by extending right or left. In a single night we would find ourselves confronted with parapets which we would fear to attack in the morning. He describes the country south of Utoy as more open and better cultivated. I want the 4½-inch and 20-pounder guns to hammer away, and I will think of the next move.

W. T. SHERMAN,
Major-General, Commanding.

(Same to General Howard.)

HDQRS. MILITARY DIVISION OF THE MISSISSIPPI,
In the Field, near Atlanta, August 10, 1864.

General THOMAS:

I don't hear the 4½-inch guns. Tell General Brannan to keep them going. Time is too valuable to be wasted. I have a report of the lay of ground south of Utoy from General Schofield, about which I have asked him some questions, when I will telegraph you substance. I have a dispatch from General Grant, in Washington, of the 9th, but nothing of interest. Louisville papers contain news of Admiral Farragut's passage of the Mobile forts.

W. T. SHERMAN,
Major-General, Commanding.

THOMAS' HEADQUARTERS,
August 10, 1864.

General SHERMAN:

The 4½-inch guns have been firing every five minutes since 5 p. m. I will order them to increase. The battery on Williams' front has been ordered ready as soon as possible and will fire when completed. The shells from the 4½-inch guns burst beautifully.

GEO. H. THOMAS,
Major-General.

SHERMAN'S HEADQUARTERS,
August 10, 1864.

Major-General THOMAS:

I have your last dispatch. I hear the guns and the shells also. The enemy's battery of 32-pounders rifled are firing on us here from the White Hall fort to draw off or divert our fire. Keep up a steady, persistent fire on Atlanta with the 4½-inch guns and 20-pounder Parrotts, and order them to pay no attention to the side firing by which the enemy may attempt to divert their attention. I think those guns will make Atlanta of less value to them as a large machine-shop and depot of supplies. The inhabitants have, of course, got out.

W. T. SHERMAN,
Major-General.

HEADQUARTERS DEPARTMENT OF THE CUMBERLAND,
August 10, 1864—10.30 p. m.

Major-General SHERMAN:

A staff officer has been sent to place the 4½-inch guns in position on General Williams' right, with orders to commence firing as soon as in position. Orders have gone out to fire continually all night without regard to time or side issues.

GEO. H. THOMAS,
Major-General.

SHERMAN'S HEADQUARTERS,
August 10, 1864.

Major-General THOMAS:

I hear Brannan's guns at Geary's battery, and hear the shells burst in Atlanta. Send word to the battery to work all night and not limit themselves to 5-minute guns, but to fire slowly and steadily each gun as it is ready; also order the gun on Williams' front to be got ready and put to work with similar orders to-night. Howard will get his 20s near the same point, which he pronounces much better than that at Geary's, which he visited with me to-day. Williams' right and Howard's left are on Proctor's Creek, from which you look up the valley to what seems the heart of Atlanta, the ridge on which are the railroad and White Hall being plainly visible, as also that by which the Marietta road enters the town, the intervening angle being cleared ground giving a fine field of fire. I think the 4½-inch gun on Williams' right can demolish the big engine-house.

W. T. SHERMAN,
Major-General.

STANLEY'S HEADQUARTERS,
August 10, 1864—6.30 p. m.

Brigadier-General WHIPPLE:

General Wood's lookout in front of Knefler's brigade reports the passage of some of the enemy's troops with wagons toward our left. He could form no definite idea of the number. I do not consider the report of much importance. Have instructed Kimball to keep strict watch. The lookout at Howard's house reports all quiet in Atlanta and no movements observed.

D. S. STANLEY,
Major-General.

HEADQUARTERS FOURTEENTH ARMY CORPS,
Near Atlanta, Ga., August 10, 1864.

Brig. Gen. W. D. WHIPPLE,
Assistant Adjutant-General, Chief of Staff:

The corps remained to-day in its old position. A constant firing of skirmishers kept up, with occasional artillery firing. Losses, 3 enlisted men killed, 12 enlisted men wounded. Several deserters came into our lines and will be forwarded to department headquarters.

Respectfully, your obedient servant,

R. W. JOHNSON,
Brigadier-General.

SHERMAN'S HEADQUARTERS,
August 10, 1864.   (Received 7.50 a. m.)

General SCHOFIELD:

I will go to Thomas' front to-day to watch the effect of the new battery of 30-pounder Parrotts. I want you to go on perfecting your line and flank, and study as far as possible the roads and lay of the country. Be sure that your advanced line of pickets is close up to the enemy, to be sure they occupy their main line with something more than a mere thin line of vedettes.

W. T. SHERMAN,
Major-General.

SCHOFIELD'S HEADQUARTERS,
August 10, 1864.

Major-General SHERMAN:

I have been all along Hascall's skirmish line and carefully reconnoitered the enemy's position. My report of last evening was based upon the observations of others, and was essentially accurate. The enemy's line from a point in front of Cox's right runs substantially as I described it, viz, southeast or south-southeast. This line is an ordinary infantry parapet, recently constructed, and contains one battery about half a mile from Cox's right. The line is visible for a mile or more. There are no works visible southwest of the creek in front of Hascall, and there appears to be no force there but cavalry. It is evident the enemy is simply prolonging his line in advance of our movement and essentially parallel to the Macon railroad.

J. M. SCHOFIELD,
Major-General.

HDQRS. MILITARY DIVISION OF THE MISSISSIPPI,
In the Field, near Atlanta, August 10, 1864.

General SCHOFIELD:

Your report is received. Do you think General Hascall can reach the West Point railroad from his position without assaulting parapets? Do you think a further prolongation would enable us to reach the Macon road without cutting loose from our base? How are the roads south of Utoy? Do you observe any change in the character of the country? We are now cannonading with $4\frac{1}{2}$-inch rifle bolts, and have 4,000 of them on hand.

W. T. SHERMAN,
Major-General, Commanding.

HEADQUARTERS ARMY OF THE OHIO,
August 10, 1864.

Major-General SHERMAN:

Either our maps or surveys or both are so evidently erroneous that I am very uncertain about the distance from Hascall's present position to the West Point railroad, but I have no doubt he can reach it without assaulting parapets, and by moving nearly in a southeasterly direction from his present position the distance may be a little more than a mile and it may be three miles. I think it probable that another corps on this flank would be able to prolong the line to the Macon railroad, or better, that one corps, in addition to mine, could swing loose from the flank of the Fourteenth, strike in rear of East Point, and get a position crossing the railroad, from which we could not be driven. The country south of Utoy appears less broken and much more cultivated than north of it. Hascall is on the main Campbellton road. There is said to be a big road a short distance in his front leading to East Point. I have not been able to learn of any others in that vicinity. Can you not take Proctor's Creek for your left flank, bring supplies by Turner's Ferry, and thus throw even two corps yet to the right? It appears to me that such a move if made rapidly ought to bring success.

J. M. SCHOFIELD,
Major-General.

HDQRS. MILITARY DIVISION OF THE MISSISSIPPI,
In the Field, near Atlanta, August 10, 1864.

General SCHOFIELD:

I have your dispatch. I am deliberating what to do next, but despair of making a quick move. It takes two days to do what ought to be done in one. We are now bombarding the town of Atlanta, and I will await its effect, but rather prefer to cast loose from our base altogether to extending any more.

W. T. SHERMAN,
Major-General, Commanding.

HEADQUARTERS ARMY OF THE OHIO,
August 10, 1864.

Major-General SHERMAN:

The question is a difficult one. I will get all the additional information I can about the country, roads, distances, &c., to aid you in determining what to do.

J. M. SCHOFIELD,
Major-General.

SHERMAN'S HEADQUARTERS,
August 10, 1864.   (Received 10.55 p. m.)

General SCHOFIELD:

I will come down to-morrow and go with you to Hascall's position. I suppose Hamilton's regiment of cavalry has reported to you. Kilpatrick is on the opposite bank at Sandtown. Order Colonel Garrard to-morrow to replace his bridge over Utoy and feel across to the south bank of the creek.

W. T. SHERMAN,
Major-General.

SCHOFIELD'S HEADQUARTERS,
August 10, 1864.

Major-General SHERMAN:

I will make a thorough examination of my lines and reconnaissance of the enemy's with a view to carrying out your plans. Along a large portion of our line we have driven the enemy into his works, and do not allow him to put out pickets at all. I will try to accomplish the same all along. I can also do something in the way of reconnaissance in force toward the enemy's rear when it is desired to draw him off temporarily in that direction. I will also try to find a point of the enemy's line which can be broken.

J. M. SCHOFIELD,
Major-General.

HEADQUARTERS ARMY OF THE OHIO,
Before Atlanta, Ga., August 10, 1864.

Col. ISRAEL GARRARD,
    Commanding Cavalry Division:

COLONEL: The major-general commanding directs me to inform you that General Kilpatrick with his force is on the opposite bank of the Chattahoochee, making a demonstration as if to cross at Sandtown, which he thinks will make the enemy's cavalry timid, and he desires you to feel across the Utoy Creek with as large a portion of your force as you can use for the purpose, and drive the enemy back, feeling as far in the direction of the right of General Hascall as you can get, and report as early as possible the result of your observations.

Very respectfully, your obedient servant,
WM. M. WHERRY,
Major and Aide-de-Camp.

The major-general directs me to add that if you find on crossing the creek that it will be practicable for you to hold an advanced line from the right of the infantry to the Chattahoochee, he desires you will do so.

Very respectfully, your obedient servant,
WM. M. WHERRY,
Major and Aide-de-Camp.

HDQRS. MILITARY DIVISION OF THE MISSISSIPPI,
In the Field, near Atlanta, August 10, 1864.

General HOWARD:

I am going this morning to General Thomas' front to watch the effect of the new battery of 4½-inch guns. All you can do is to keep your line of skirmishers up, so as to compel the enemy to keep his forts and main line full of men.

W. T. SHERMAN,
Major-General, Commanding.

HDQRS. MILITARY DIVISION OF THE MISSISSIPPI,
In the Field, near Atlanta, August 10, 1864.

General HOWARD:

I hear General Brannan's guns and hear the shells burst in Atlanta. The shells that burst near you are from the enemy's big guns, which have been put in the fort at White Hall. Hood is anxious to draw our fire from the town to their fort at White Hall, which is of no value to us. Let us destroy Atlanta and make it a desolation.

W. T. SHERMAN,
Major-General, Commanding.

HEADQUARTERS DEPARTMENT OF THE TENNESSEE,
August 10, 1864.

Maj. Gen. W. T. SHERMAN,
  Commanding Military Division of the Mississippi:

Instead of a greater detour, could not the present left of Fourteenth Corps (with cavalry to Proctor's Creek) form a good flank, throwing the rest of the army to right of Schofield's rapidly? Green's Ferry and Sandtown, and perhaps Turner's Ferry, roads could be kept open. Such an extension must bring the enemy out of Atlanta. I mean the above with other dispositions as you proposed to-day. It is possible, the works being so strong, that the cavalry could hold the present lines of the Fourth Corps, so as to move that over without difficulty.

O. O. HOWARD,
Major-General.

HDQRS. MILITARY DIVISION OF THE MISSISSIPPI,
  In the Field, near Atlanta, August 10, 1864.

General HOWARD:

I thank you for the suggestion. I am studying all the combinations possible and beg you to think also, and communicate to me, but be careful to keep your own confidence. I spoke of the same thing to-day to General Thomas, and he goes to look at the railroad bridge to see to a proper cover there for the wagons and a corps. I want to expend 4,000 heavy rifle-shots on the town before doing anything new, and then will be prepared to act quick. General Schofield has been reconnoitering the right all day, and after he has answered a few more of my questions I will give you the substance of his report.

W. T. SHERMAN,
Major-General, Commanding.

HDQRS. MILITARY DIVISION OF THE MISSISSIPPI,
  In the Field, near Atlanta, August 10, 1864.

General HOWARD:

Can't you get in your 20-pounders to-night in General Corse's battery and put them to work? The moon gives light enough, and night is better than day for artillery. General Brannan has three 4½-inch guns in General Geary's battery, and one on General Williams' right.

W. T. SHERMAN,
Major-General, Commanding.

HEADQUARTERS DEPARTMENT OF THE TENNESSEE,
August 10, 1864.

Major-General SHERMAN:

My battery on Corse's left is completed and I will put in the guns in the morning. This position and the one on Williams' right are the best for damaging the town I have seen.

O. O. HOWARD,
Major-General.

HDQRS. MILITARY DIVISION OF THE MISSISSIPPI,
In the Field, near Atlanta, August 10, 1864.

General HOWARD:

The 4½-inch guns are in position on the front of General Geary's division, Twentieth Corps, and will begin firing this evening, and continue until the ammunition is used up.

W. T. SHERMAN,
Major-General, Commanding.

(Same to General Schofield.)

HEADQUARTERS DEPARTMENT OF THE TENNESSEE,
August 10, 1864.

Major-General SHERMAN:

I can get the guns at work. The pioneers are trimming down the bushes. Shells are exploding constantly near my headquarters. I hope it is not Brannan's aiming down this way. Don't hear any other firing.

O. O. HOWARD,
Major-General.

HEADQUARTERS FIFTEENTH ARMY CORPS,
Before Atlanta, Ga., August 10, 1864.

Lieut. Col. W. T. CLARK,
Assistant Adjutant-General:

COLONEL: I have the honor to report after a careful examination by my engineer officers that no continuous defensive line can be formed in my present front, and that detached works can only be established a short distance in front of the left of General Harrow's line, which, when erected, would not, in my judgment, be tenable.

Very respectfully, your obedient servant,

JOHN A. LOGAN,
Major-General, Commanding.

HDQRS. FIRST DIVISION, FIFTEENTH ARMY CORPS,
Near Atlanta, Ga., August 10, 1864.

Lieut. Col. R. R. TOWNES,
Assistant Adjutant-General, Fifteenth Army Corps:

COLONEL: The works occupied yesterday were strengthened to-day. No occurrence of interest to report, except lively skirmishing and some artillery practice.

I have the honor to be, colonel, your obedient servant,

C. R. WOODS,
Brigadier-General.

HDQRS. SECOND DIVISION, FIFTEENTH ARMY CORPS,
Near Atlanta, Ga., August 10, 1864.

Lieut. Col. R. R. TOWNES,
Assistant Adjutant-General, Fifteenth Army Corps:

I have the honor to report that nothing of interest occurred in my front to-day. The enemy was quite busy with his artillery to-day, doing us but little damage, considering the amount of firing done. My command occupied the new line this morning one hour before daylight, keeping one regiment in reserve, which occupies that portion of the old line on the right of De Gress' battery. A portion of the troops in the line were occupied in trimming up and strengthening the work, and to-night will complete it, extending and throwing forward my right to connect more perfectly with General Woods' division and cover a ravine.

All of which is respectfully submitted.

J. A. J. LIGHTBURN,
Brigadier-General of Volunteers.

BEFORE ATLANTA, GA., *August 10, 1864—10 p. m.*

Maj. T. T. ECKERT,
 Assistant Superintendent U. S. Military Telegraph:

Still extending our line to the right, and find enemy on our front everywhere. Have got four 4½-inch Rodman guns into position to-day, which burst their shells in Atlanta, and will keep that city awake. No other news.

J. C. VAN DUZER,
Cipher Operator, U. S. Military Telegraph.

SPECIAL FIELD ORDERS, ⎰ HDQRS. ARMY OF THE OHIO,
  No. 77. ⎱ *Near Atlanta, Ga., August 10, 1864.*

I. The term of service of the First Regiment East Tennessee Infantry having nearly expired, the regiment will be relieved from duty with the army in the field, on the 11th instant; will move, by rail if practicable, to Knoxville, Tenn., and will there be mustered out of the service. This gallant regiment, first among the patriotic men of East Tennessee to take up arms in defense of the Union, has gained an enviable reputation by its three years of faithful and efficient service, and, especially during the present campaign, has won, together with its comrades of the Twenty-third Corps, enduring fame. To Col. R. K. Byrd and the officers and men of his regiment I tender a soldier's appreciation and regard for soldierly fidelity and gallantry, and bid them farewell, with the hope that they may soon find in their homes in Tennessee the peace and prosperity for which they have fought so long and well.

J. M. SCHOFIELD,
Major-General, Commanding.

SPECIAL FIELD ORDERS, ⎰ HDQRS. DEPT. OF THE TENNESSEE,
  No. 94. ⎱ *Before Atlanta, Ga., August 10, 1864.*

Corps commanders will thoroughly reconnoiter the front, with a view to the practicability of a nearer approach to the rebel works, and so locating detached works or batteries as to hold the lines with a smaller number of men. The enemy will be annoyed by the skirmishers and our artillery as much as possible, so as to force him to remain inside his works.

* * * * * * *

By order of Maj. Gen. O. O. Howard:

WM. T. CLARK,
Assistant Adjutant-General.

NEAR ATLANTA, GA., *August 11, 1864—8 a. m.*
(Received 1 p. m.)

Hon. E. M. STANTON,
 Secretary of War :

Glorious news of Mobile just received. I have the same news, embracing the capture of Mobile City, through deserters. Now, if General Canby can follow it up by the capture of the Alabama River, my position would be much improved. All well here. I am knocking Atlanta with 4½-inch rifle-shells.

W. T. SHERMAN,
Major-General.

NEAR ATLANTA, GA., *August 11, 1864—9 a. m.*
(Received 3.20 p. m.)

Maj. Gen. H. W. HALLECK,
 Washington, D. C.:

If it be as reported, that Admiral Farragut has taken Mobile City, or even Blakely, it would help me if he were to send a few of his vessels to demolish old Fort Saint Mark's, and then go up the Appalachicola as far as the depth of water will permit. The old arsenal at the mouth of Flint River is an important point to be destroyed or even threatened.

W. T. SHERMAN,
Major-General.

HDQRS. MILITARY DIVISION OF THE MISSISSIPPI,
In the Field, near Atlanta, August 11, 1864.

General THOMAS:

General Howard reports that General Corse advanced his skirmish line this morning, taking a certain hill which I have wanted for a week. He took some prisoners, dismounted cavalry, of Ferguson's brigade. Prisoners say our folks have the city of Mobile.

W. T. SHERMAN,
Major-General, Commanding.

(Same to General Schofield.)

HDQRS. MILITARY DIVISION OF THE MISSISSIPPI,
In the Field, near Atlanta, August 11, 1864.

General THOMAS:

General Corse this morning fought for a hill which to my eye is 300 yards nearer the heart of Atlanta than General Geary's battery. The hill is next to General Williams' right, where I ordered one of the 4½-inch guns yesterday. General Barry tells me that General Brannan instead of sending that gun to General Williams' right sent it to the same point the other three were. You will please have General Brannan report what this means; why my orders were not obeyed; why when ordered to place that gun on General Williams' right he sent it in an opposite direction.

W. T. SHERMAN,
Major-General, Commanding.

HDQRS. MILITARY DIVISION OF THE MISSISSIPPI,
In the Field, near Atlanta, August 11, 1864.

General THOMAS, or if absent,
General STANLEY:

Some prisoners report the enemy engaged in repairing the Augusta road. Send word to General Garrard that I would like to know at once what truth there is in this.

W. T. SHERMAN,
Major-General, Commanding.

STANLEY'S HEADQUARTERS,
August 11, 1864—1.25 p. m.

Major-General SHERMAN:

General Garrard just reports as follows:

Please tell General Sherman that men from Stoneman's command are daily coming in; that they come along the railroad and that on Sunday nothing had been done toward repairing the road. A large part of their cavalry is now in the neighborhood of Covington, and it is generally believed that they will soon make a grand raid to Tennessee or Kentucky. An officer who has just got in staid in that neighborhood three days, as he could not get out of the way of their cavalry. He says he has never seen so much cavalry in one body. Persons from near Atlanta also report the rebel cavalry moving over toward Covington.

D. S. STANLEY,
Major-General.

HDQRS. MILITARY DIVISION OF THE MISSISSIPPI,
In the Field, near Atlanta, August 11, 1864.

General STANLEY:

General Schofield will to-morrow move out from our extreme right to reconnoiter in force, and to break the West Point railroad. It is important that the enemy should be well held to his parapet all day. Let your pickets make a dash at theirs about daylight near the old distillery in front of the Howard house, and report to me very early the appearance of things there.

W. T. SHERMAN,
Major-General, Commanding.

HEADQUARTERS DEPARTMENT OF THE CUMBERLAND,
August 11, 1864—9.30 p. m.

Major-General SHERMAN:

Your dispatch to General Thomas received. The 4½-inch gun you ordered to be placed in position on Williams' right was sent there to-day about 3 p. m. General Barry is mistaken as to the gun being sent to the same position the other three are. It never was moved from the camp near the railroad till to-day, when it was sent to Williams' right. General Barry sent for the gun to be placed in position on General Corse's line. I telegraphed him twice relative to it, and informed him the gun was waiting in rear of General Williams' right, where it was originally intended to be placed. He replied that he would send Lieutenant Smith, Fifth United States, for it. Your orders have not been disobeyed, but on the contrary carried into execution as soon as the battery was completed to receive the gun.

J. M. BRANNAN,
Brigadier-General and Chief of Artillery.

HDQRS. CHIEF OF ARTY., DEPT. OF THE CUMBERLAND,
August 11, 1864.
Brigadier-General BARRY,
     Chief of Arty., Mil. Div., General Sherman's Hdqrs.:

General Thomas says you can have the 4½-inch gun, as we don't intend to use it. Please order some officer of General Howard's army to receipt for it.

J. M. BRANNAN,
Brigadier-General and Chief of Artillery.

HDQRS. CHIEF OF ARTY., DEPT. OF THE CUMBERLAND,
Near Atlanta, Ga., August 11, 1864.
Brigadier-General BARRY,
     Chief of Artillery, General Sherman's Headquarters:

The 4½-inch gun to be turned over to the Army of the Tennessee is waiting in rear of the position on the right of the Twentieth Corps, in which it was previously intended to place it. Please send for it as soon as convenient.

J. M. BRANNAN,
Brigadier-General and Chief of Artillery.

HOWARD'S HOUSE, *August 11, 1864—12.30 p. m.*
Captain CASE:

Skirmishing quite brisk this a. m. Rebels threw a few shells at us this a. m. Quiet now. Cannonading still going on briskly on our right. Shells from our big guns explode on the outskirts of city. I saw an engine and six empty cars in city this a. m.

BURTON.

STATION OBSERVATION, *August 11, 1864—10.10 a. m.*
Capt. A. K. TAYLOR,
     Acting Signal Officer:

CAPTAIN: Working party at four-gun fort on left, just where line of works joins it on west side.
     Very respectfully, yours,

W. W. HOPKINS,
First Lieutenant and Acting Signal Officer.

STATION OBSERVATION, *August 11, 1864—2.20 p. m.*
Capt. A. K. TAYLOR,
     Acting Signal Officer:

CAPTAIN: Men still at work on four-gun fort and on large fort south, three miles distant.
     Very respectfully, yours,

W. W. HOPKINS,
First Lieutenant and Acting Signal Officer.

HEADQUARTERS FOURTEENTH ARMY CORPS,
Near Atlanta, Ga., August 11, 1864.

Brig. Gen. W. D. WHIPPLE,
A. A. G. and Chief of Staff, Dept. of the Cumberland:

The lines of the Fourteenth Corps remain unchanged to-day. Constant picket-firing, with occasional artillery, was kept up during the day. One or more cannon belonging to the enemy were destroyed or disabled. This is confirmed by deserters. Deserters represent the rebel army as much dissatisfied with Hood. Their losses are heavy from our artillery. I have directed the batteries on my front to keep up a steady fire upon their lines to-morrow. Few shots were fired by the rebels to-day from their artillery. My lines are so extended that the men are constantly on duty in the trenches and are, of course, somewhat worn and fatigued. This is not mentioned by way of complaint, but simply to let the department commander know that we (the Fourteenth Corps) are not idle.

Respectfully, your obedient servant,

R. W. JOHNSON,
Brigadier-General.

HEADQUARTERS SECOND CAVALRY DIVISION,
August 11, 1864.

Brig. Gen. W. L. ELLIOTT,
Chief of Cavalry, Hdqrs. Dept. of the Cumberland:

GENERAL: I have the honor to report, for the information of the major-general commanding department, that through officers and men of Stoneman's command I learn that the rebel cavalry is concentrating in large force at Monticello, some fifteen or twenty miles south of Covington and on the east of the Ocmulgee. An officer of the Fourteenth Illinois, wounded in the shoulder, is now in my camp; he has been two years in service, and has seen large bodies of cavalry together. Saw Stoneman's and my division together; he was three days in the vicinity of this cavalry, and saw it passing on the road, says he never saw so much cavalry before. Says Breckinridge is there, and that soldiers, officers, and negroes all say that there is to be a big raid to Tennessee. Negroes told him and as he laid by the roadside he overheard the rebels talk. He left Monticello four days ago. A private of same regiment also reports that he had to conceal himself three days near Covington as the roads were full of rebel cavalry going south. Deserters from Atlanta also report that Wheeler's command or portions of it have gone toward Covington. One man of the Fifth Indiana who left Covington on Monday reports four brigades to have passed there on that day en route to Madison. He says the bridge (railroad) over the Yellow River is not repaired, and he could see no attempts to repair the railroad.

Very respectfully, your obedient servant,

K. GARRARD,
Brigadier-General, Commanding Division.

HDQRS. MILITARY DIVISION OF THE MISSISSIPPI,
In the Field, near Atlanta, August 11, 1864.

General SCHOFIELD:

I do want to know where our right flank is, how far from one of the two roads south of Atlanta; and as we cannot reach the Macon road I would like to say at least we had found out where the West Point road is. When reached, it should be torn up for a couple of miles, and then the force employed should return to the right flank of the army. I don't limit you to one division, but you can take the whole five, or only such part as you may deem sufficient to accomplish the end. It appears that Colonel Hamilton, Ninth Ohio, reported with his regiment to General Howard with 200 men. He reported to me in person he had a full regiment, of which 500 were here mounted, balance at Decatur, Ala. I have ordered General Howard to cause Colonel Hamilton to report to you at once. We believe the enemy has his three corps distributed— Hardee, right; Lee, left; and Stewart, center; old troops on picket and in rear; militia in trenches. The right is three miles east of Atlanta, center about railroad, and left about East Point. I believe a skirmish line can hold any part of our front, but in making a detachment due caution should be exercised. It appeared to me far more prudent to vacate or thin out your line; in other words, to extend the Fourteenth Corps and send out two divisions, say Generals Hascall's and Baird's, with your cavalry as vedettes, and a good engineer officer to sketch the country. But as you already have a better knowledge of the country than I, I leave it to you. It does seem to me with an enemy besieged we should be a little more enterprising.

W. T. SHERMAN,
Major-General, Commanding.

HEADQUARTERS ARMY OF THE OHIO,
August 11, 1864.

Maj. Gen. W. T. SHERMAN:

From all the information I can get the distance from Hascall's position to the railroad is probably about two miles. He will have to travel somewhat farther to avoid moving in view of and parallel to the enemy's works. I think there cannot be much difficulty in reaching the road and getting back. Whether he can stay there long enough to do much damage is more doubtful.

J. M. SCHOFIELD,
Major-General.

HEADQUARTERS ARMY OF THE OHIO,
August 11, 1864.

Major-General SHERMAN:

I do not see how I can support Hascall in his proposed movement or be prepared to cut in between East Point and any infantry sent to molest him, unless the enemy abandon his lines in front to attack him, which does not seem probable. My troops will be stretched out in line three miles long, and in no condition to move. While the enemy's lines in front are held I must either let Hascall take care of himself or abandon my lines and concentrate my troops to support him. If the division go on such an expedition I see no way but to risk its loss or its safety in retreat. I think the risk would not be very great, but of this you can judge quite as well as I. If you think the object to be gained worth the risk I will start Hascall early in the morning.

J. M. SCHOFIELD,
Major-General.

HDQRS. MILITARY DIVISION OF THE MISSISSIPPI,
In the Field, near Atlanta, August 11, 1864.
General SCHOFIELD:

Can't you make up a detachment strong enough to feel by the nearest line, and ascertain exactly the distance to the West Point railroad, and to break it? It is reported the enemy is repairing the Augusta road. This, if true, will have an effect on our next move.

W. T. SHERMAN,
Major-General, Commanding.

———

HEADQUARTERS ARMY OF THE OHIO, *August 11, 1864.*
Major-General SHERMAN:

Your dispatch is received. I could spare a division for the expedition you refer to. Hascall's present position is of no value to our line, considered defensively. I think he might push out to the West Point railroad, break it, and return without running very great risk. Less than a division would hardly suffice, for it would have to fight cavalry on nearly all sides.

J. M. SCHOFIELD,
Major-General.

———

HDQRS. MILITARY DIVISION OF THE MISSISSIPPI,
In the Field, near Atlanta, August 11, 1864.
General SCHOFIELD:

There must be some confusion in your or my dispatches of yesterday and to-day. I understood you last night that General Hascall had one brigade on the right, south and east of Utoy Creek, that the ground was open, and that the pickets and flankers could see the West. Point railroad, and that the enemy's line was parallel with the Macon road. This corresponds with all probabilities. You also report that there was no redoubt, as first supposed, in the direction of the West Point road, which also corresponds with all our information. You also suggested that instead of making a continuous line to reach the road that it be done by a detachment, stating that you believed one division enough. You say, I think General Hascall might push out to the West Point railroad, break it, and return without running very great risk, there being nothing but cavalry in that direction, and now you speak of it as of extraordinary hazard. It was I that suggested that it would be prudent to be prepared to support General Hascall, and as our line is already drawn out, thought the support necessary could better come from your five divisions than to draw from any more distant point. Now, let me understand what has made you change your mind on this subject. The dispatch from which I quote is dated to-day, and if not properly sent by the wires please correct it. The dispatch was in answer to mine asking if this very thing were not feasible, and I certainly construed your answer as affirmative. If it involves extra hazard I don't want it done, because I have not yet made up my mind whether to swing round Atlanta by the east or south, but I want to fight Hood the earliest possible moment he will come out of his trenches, and would risk a good deal to draw him out. There is no doubt of it, our movements all are too slow to be productive of good results. I feel mortified that he holds us in check by the aid of his militia.

W. T. SHERMAN,
Major-General, Commanding.

HEADQUARTERS ARMY OF THE OHIO,
August 11, 1864—9.30 p. m.

Major-General SHERMAN:

I will try to explain fully the situation and why I regard the move as suggested by you extra hazardous. You have correctly understood my dispatches about the enemy's works. There are none visible covering the West Point road, and those visible run substantially parallel to the Macon road. Relative to the distance from Hascall to the West Point you have misunderstood me. My picket officers reported they saw what appeared to be a railroad, as I telegraphed you, but I subsequently stated that I knew very little about the distance; that it might be a little more than a mile and it might be three miles, but that I thought Hascall might strike the road and return without any great risk. I still think the same, viz, that a light force, just large enough to sweep away the cavalry, can make a rapid march to some point of the road, break it, and return without much risk. Such a force can make a circuit through the woods, keep out of the enemy's view, do its work, and return before a large force can concentrate against it. I would expect this force, if threatened by superior numbers, not to fight but to fall back behind the flank of our intrenched position, which it could do with safety so long as this position is held. On the other hand, to make the move with a large force, I must virtually abandon my lines, send my transportation and hospitals to the rear, and separate my command from three to five miles from the right of the Army of the Tennessee, a movement which has, as I understand, invariably been regarded too hazardous. I take it for granted that any attack upon Hascall in his movement would not come from the enemy's line in my front but from his reserves, which might be nearly the whole of his veteran troops. I would not hesitate to fight all of those with my two corps, but I would want all my troops concentrated and prepared in advance. I have not the slightest hesitation in making the effort to strike and break the railroad, though I may fail in the attempt, but I did think you expected me to do more than I could safely attempt in the event of my meeting unexpected resistance, and I am free to say I felt not a little chagrined at your imputation of want of enterprise. There is also some confusion about my estimate of force necessary to cut the road. I suggested that instead of a continuous line my corps and one other be detached from the flank of the Fourteenth and strike in rear of East Point, cutting the Macon road, meaning to seize and hold a position there. To detach the Fourteenth with mine would separate us three miles farther from the army than what I suggested. I have not in the least changed my opinion as to the practicability of making a mere raid or reconnaissance to the West Point road with a single division, or of gaining and holding a point of the Macon road with two corps, starting from the right of the Fourteenth. I regret that I have failed to make myself understood.

J. M. SCHOFIELD,
Major-General.

HDQRS. MILITARY DIVISION OF THE MISSISSIPPI,
In the Field, near Atlanta, August 11, 1864.

General SCHOFIELD:

I have read and considered your dispatch. It is a physical impossibility for the enemy to ascertain the force which moves against the railroad and to act against it with any more than one-third of his reserves.

The other two-thirds will be from four to eight miles off. Colonel Garrard's cavalry passed along the flank to-day unopposed, and I do not think the West Point road more than two miles from General Hascall's present flank. You will, therefore, make the expedition with one division, the other either placed intermediate or ready to act. Of course without abandoning our present base or dividing our forces into two equal parts I have no other corps to give you. You may consider it a reconnaissance in force not to go over three miles from General Cox's present right. I know a full proportion of the enemy is on our left and center, and if any change occurs in the night I will be sure to advise you. Our heavy ordnance, playing for the past thirty hours from the Buck Head road into Atlanta, has kept to the parapets a full proportion of the enemy all the way round to your old position and beyond, and if I am to give weight to the testimony from official sources the enemy at this moment exhibits most force on his present right. I have no idea that he can throw on you even a third of his reserve force, because he will look upon the movement as a decoy to weaken his line somewhat that we may break in. Besides, we know his line as well as ours is so stretched out that his reserves are not over 1,000 men per mile, for his infantry line three miles east of the Howard house round to the Macon road below East Point is full fifteen miles long, requiring at his parapets 40,000 men, leaving him no reserve on that flank that can disturb two divisions. We must act. We cannot sit down and do nothing because it involves risk. Being on the offensive we must risk, and that is the flank on which we calculated to make the risk, indeed have been maneuvering to that end ever since the Army of the Tennessee shifted from left to right.

W. T. SHERMAN,
Major-General, Commanding.

HEADQUARTERS ARMY OF THE OHIO,
August 11, 1864.

Major-General SHERMAN:

I will thin out the Fourteenth Corps so as to relieve Cox, and will send Hascall, supported by Cox, to destroy the road. I may overestimate the difficulties and dangers of this movement. I have made several like it, which were regarded somewhat hazardous, but they were trifling compared to this. I will do the best I can, and hope at least to remove your impression that I have shown a want of enterprise.

J. M. SCHOFIELD,
Major-General.

HDQRS. MILITARY DIVISION OF THE MISSISSIPPI,
In the Field, near Atlanta, August 11, 1864.

General SCHOFIELD:

To make sure I am right in my conclusion that the enemy is as strong on his right as left, I will now order General Stanley at daylight to make a pretty sharp dash opposite the Howard house, at that hill to the left of the distillery, and to report to me the result as early as possible.

W. T. SHERMAN,
Major-General, Commanding.

HDQRS. MILITARY DIVISION OF THE MISSISSIPPI,
In the Field, near Atlanta, August 11, 1864.
(Received 3.30 p. m.)

General SCHOFIELD:

General Stanley informs me that officers and men of General Stoneman's command, just in, report at Covington all the enemy's cavalry assembling for a grand raid to Tennessee and Kentucky. If this be so the cavalry cannot be on your flank, nor is it possible for the enemy to follow General Hascall with infantry unless they let go their parapets, in which event you should be prepared to let go too. This is all I mean, to have one or two divisions on that flank ready, in case General Hascall becomes heavily engaged, to march in such a direction, not to his rear, but to his front, to relieve him of pressure. We all know that the enemy holds us by inferior force, and I may have to let go our parapets altogether, for it seems we are more besieged than they. Send General Hascall to feel for that road in the morning, and have all your command, if necessary, ready to let go their parapets and engage the enemy, and if that be not sufficient I will order General Howard to do the same.

W. T. SHERMAN,
Major-General, Commanding.

HEADQUARTERS ARMY OF THE OHIO,
Near Atlanta, Ga., August 11, 1864—3.45 p. m.

Major-General SHERMAN:

I have the evidence of two days' fighting that the force of the enemy's cavalry on my flank is considerable, certainly enough to surround an infantry division, but this is by no means a serious matter. It occurs to me that if the enemy send infantry to meet Hascall he will not take them from my front, leaving me free to follow them up, but will bring them from other parts of his line little more distant, measured on his interior lines, but much more so on ours. I wish, however, simply to understand fully what you wish me to do, and I will do it as well as I know how. Do you desire Hascall to remain in any advanced position or simply to break the road and return? How much work ought he to do, or how long should he continue his work, or must this be determined hereafter? Is the object simply a reconnaissance, or an extensive destruction of the road, or to draw the enemy out of his works, or all of them? I want to give Hascall full instructions as possible before he starts.

J. M. SCHOFIELD,
Major-General.

HEADQUARTERS ARMY OF THE OHIO,
Near Atlanta, Ga., August 11, 1864.

Major-General SHERMAN:

The news from Mobile is very encouraging. Will you be able to break the enemy's line from the hill which Corse has taken? At what time to-day may I look for you here?

J. M. SCHOFIELD,
Major-General.

HDQRS. MILITARY DIVISION OF THE MISSISSIPPI,
In the Field, near Atlanta, August 11, 1864.

General SCHOFIELD:

I will not be able to come down to-day. I want to watch the effect of the heavy bombardment. I would like to have the division of General Hascall feel out this morning or early to-morrow for that railroad, and be prepared to support him or cut in between East Point and any infantry sent to molest him.

W. T. SHERMAN,
Major-General, Commanding.

HDQRS. MILITARY DIVISION OF THE MISSISSIPPI,
In the Field, near Atlanta, August 11, 1864—10 a. m.

General SCHOFIELD:

The hill that General Corse has taken will in nowise help us to break the enemy's line. On the contrary, it is opposite the big fort at White Hall that seems the strongest of the whole defenses of Atlanta, and from which they fire the heaviest guns. It is merely a means to contract his line and give him a reserve. I am hard at work writing. Don't wait for me. I will overtake you wherever you may be.

W. T. SHERMAN,
Major-General, Commanding.

HEADQUARTERS ARMY OF THE OHIO,
August 11, 1864—8.30 p. m.

Major-General SHERMAN:

Colonel Garrard has returned from his scout. He crossed the Utoy Creek at the bridge, and went as far as Sandtown; thence toward Atlanta two miles and a half, and to the Owl Rock Church and across the right of General Hascall's position. He found only cavalry pickets on any of the roads. The large cavalry camps appeared to be a day or two old. Citizens informed him that Armstrong's division—three brigades—had camped near the church night before last and started for Campbellton yesterday morning, saying they were going on a raid. General Kilpatrick had shelled Sandtown day before yesterday, but none of his troops were in sight to-day.

J. M. SCHOFIELD,
Major-General.

HDQRS. MILITARY DIVISION OF THE MISSISSIPPI,
In the Field, near Atlanta, August 11, 1864.

General SCHOFIELD:

Dispatch received. Am glad to hear that Colonel Garrard has connected Sandtown with General Hascall's position. Armstrong will not make a raid on us from the direction of Campbellton. General Kilpatrick can whip his division if he crosses the Chattahoochee.

W. T. SHERMAN,
Major-General, Commanding.

SCHOFIELD'S HEADQUARTERS,
August 11, 1864.

General SHERMAN:

Colonel Hamilton has not yet reported with his regiment.

J. M. SCHOFIELD,
Major-General.

———

HEADQUARTERS ARMY OF THE OHIO,
August 11, 1864.

Brig. Gen. R. W. JOHNSON,
Commanding Fourteenth Army Corps:

GENERAL: To enable me to execute General Sherman's orders for to-morrow it will be necessary for me to have Cox out of line, and you will have to relieve him. Please thin out to-night and get in reserve enough to hold Cox's present line. You can relieve him early in the morning, letting his pickets remain. I will send full instructions to-night.

Very respectfully,

J. M. SCHOFIELD,
Major-General.

———

HEADQUARTERS ARMY OF THE OHIO,
In the Field, before Atlanta, Ga., August 11, 1864.

Brig. Gen. J. D. COX,
Commanding Third Division:

GENERAL: The commanding general directs me to inform you that he has ordered General Johnson to relieve all of your division, except your pickets, early to-morrow morning. This will be necessary in order to enable him to carry out General Sherman's instructions. Full instructions will be given to-night or in the morning.

Very respectfully, your obedient servant,

J. A. CAMPBELL,
Major and Assistant Adjutant-General.

———

HEADQUARTERS ARMY OF THE OHIO,
Near Atlanta, Ga., August 11, 1864.

Brig. Gen. J. D. COX,
Commanding Third Division, Twenty-third Army Corps:

GENERAL: The commanding general directs me to inform you that General Johnson will extend his line toward your left so as to relieve one of your brigades which he desires you to place in position near General Hascall's right as a reserve. In case of an attack on that flank during the absence of the commanding general he desires you to take command of the two divisions. The general will be over in the course of the morning with General Sherman.

Very respectfully, your obedient servant,

WM. M. WHERRY,
Major and Aide-de-Camp.

HEADQUARTERS ARMY OF THE OHIO,
In the Field, Ga., August 11, 1864.

Brig. Gen. M. S. HASCALL,
Commanding Second Division, Twenty-third Army Corps:

GENERAL: The major-general commanding directs me to inform you that General Cox is ordered to place a brigade in reserve near your right, and in case of an attack during the absence of the commanding general, General Cox will assume command of both divisions.

Very respectfully, your obedient servant,
WM. M. WHERRY,
Major and Aide-de-Camp.

HEADQUARTERS ARMY OF THE OHIO,
Near Atlanta, Ga., August 11, 1864.

Brig. Gen. M. S. HASCALL,
Commanding Second Division, Twenty-third Army Corps:

GENERAL: Early to-morrow you will have to start on a sort of raid to find and break the West Point railroad. I will send you full instructions to-night, and see you in the morning before you start; meanwhile make your preparations. Send all your wagons and artillery which you do not want with you this side of the creek to-night and be ready to march light and without incumbrance. A good place for your wagons will be in rear of Cox's headquarters. I think one battery without caissons will be sufficient to take with you.

Very respectfully, your obedient servant,
J. M. SCHOFIELD,
Major-General, Commanding.

P. S.—Don't make any change until dark, lest the enemy may observe it.

Very respectfully, &c.,
J. M. SCHOFIELD,
Major-General, Commanding.

HEADQUARTERS ARMY OF THE OHIO,
Before Atlanta, Ga., August 11, 1864—9 p. m.

Brig. Gen. M. S. HASCALL,
Commanding Second Division, Twenty-third Army Corps:

GENERAL: The commanding general directs me to say you need not remove any of your artillery to the rear, as General Cox will move into your works and protect what you leave there.

Very respectfully, your obedient servant,
WM. M. WHERRY,
Major and Aide-de-Camp.

HDQRS. CAVALRY COMMAND, DEPT. OF THE OHIO,
Before Atlanta, Ga., August 11, 1864.

Maj. J. A. CAMPBELL,
Assistant Adjutant-General:

MAJOR: I have the honor to report that, under the orders of last night to scout the country south of Utoy Creek, I took about 450 men of the Ninth Michigan Cavalry, Seventh Ohio Cavalry, and Ninth Illinois

Mounted Infantry, and crossed Utoy Creek at the bridge. Rebel vedettes were found not far from the bridge and again at Sandtown.
There was a picket-post near Sandtown, on the Fayetteville road;
when driven from it they retreated southward. He showed but a
small force, and there appeared to be no re-enforcement of the rebel
picket. I concluded that it was a post of observation only. General
Kilpatrick had shelled Sandtown day before yesterday, but there were
none of his troops in sight from Sandtown. I then took the road from
Sandtown to Atlanta and returned on it two miles and a half to the
road that leads to Owl Rock Church. I made a scout out on this to the
camp-ground. Many fires of a large camp were still smoking. A respectable citizen, an old man, Mr. McWilliams, who lives near the
church, stated that Armstrong's division of three brigades had camped
there night before last, and had left there yesterday morning on the
road toward Campbellton, saying that they were going on a raid. A
small force of about 200 came back over the road this morning, and
turned down the road that takes them either to East Point or Atlanta.
A number of picket-posts at cross-roads on the Sandtown road were
found, but the corn blades were two days or more old. It was evident
that the cavalry had been moved out of that part of the country. On
reaching the post of the cavalry on the Sandtown road in rear of the
infantry position, I sent that which I had with me to their old positions on Utoy Creek and in camp near my quarters, and took the other
portion and made a scout through to the vicinity of the right of General Hascall's position, but found no rebels in the rear of it. I do not
think it practicable to picket the line of road traveled to-day, and think
that the line of Utoy Creek is the best one for the protection of the
flank from the right of our line to the river. There are no natural advantages on the line of the Sandtown road.

Very respectfully, your obedient servant,

ISRAEL GARRARD,
Colonel, Commanding.

HDQRS. MILITARY DIVISION OF THE MISSISSIPPI,
In the Field, near Atlanta, August 11, 1864.

General HOWARD:

Colonel Hamilton was ordered to report with his regiment to General
Schofield and not to you. Please have him do so at once. In a close
campaign like this, when horses are so scarce, generals must do without cavalry escorts. I have none.

W. T. SHERMAN,
Major-General, Commanding.

HOWARD'S HEADQUARTERS,
August 11, 1864.

General SHERMAN:

Colonel Hamilton, Ninth Ohio Cavalry, has with him but 200 men. I
had him relieve the men of the Ninth Illinois Mounted Infantry at
different headquarters. Is your order to him intended as a transfer
to the Department of the Ohio, or only a temporary assignment for
duty? For temporary duty on the right the Ninth Illinois Mounted
Infantry is better prepared just now.

O. O. HOWARD,
Major-General.

HDQRS. MILITARY DIVISION OF THE MISSISSIPPI,
In the Field, near Atlanta, August 11, 1864.

General HOWARD:

The transfer of the Ninth Ohio was made permanent, at Colonel Hamilton's representation that he belonged to no brigade and had 400 men. General Schofield having lost General Stoneman needs cavalry on his flank. We must put our joint shoulders to the wheel and scrape up all the horses we can, else the enemy will ride all around and over us.

W. T. SHERMAN,
Major-General, Commanding.

HOWARD'S HEADQUARTERS,
August 11, 1864.

General SHERMAN:

I have not the slightest objection to the transfer of the Ninth Ohio Cavalry. I found it in this command, and was using a portion of it. Every effort to secure cavalry will meet with my hearty co-operation.

O. O. HOWARD,
Major-General.

HOWARD'S HEADQUARTERS,
August 11, 1864.

General THOMAS,
Commanding Department of the Cumberland:

Have you any infantry near Vining's Station or railroad bridge, and what cavalry have you on river below? I ask with a view to proper protection for my trains.

O. O. HOWARD,
Major-General.

[AUGUST 11, 1864.]

Maj. Gen. O. O. HOWARD,
Commanding Army of the Tennessee:

Stanley has a guard at Pace's Ferry. There are parts of two regiments at the railroad bridge, and Kilpatrick's cavalry is posted along the river from railroad bridge to Sandtown.

GEO. H. THOMAS,
Major-General, U. S. Volunteers, Commanding.

HEADQUARTERS LEFT WING, SIXTEENTH ARMY CORPS,
Near Atlanta, Ga., August 11, 1864.

Lieut. Col. WILLIAM T. CLARK,
Asst. Adjt. Gen., Department and Army of the Tennessee:

COLONEL: Brigadier-General Corse reports to me to-night that he has but nine companies in reserve. General Corse says he has been obliged to put one regiment more on his left to connect with the Twentieth Army Corps. He has one regiment and two companies on the skirmish line, which takes all of his command except nine companies, as stated. His men have been in the trench now two days and nights without relief. I do not think I can relieve him, for General Ransom has one regiment on his left as a reserve to cover the gap between him and General Corse, should it become necessary. This will leave him two regiments in reserve. It seems to me that the Twentieth Corps should relieve one regiment on the left of General Corse's line. Please call General Howard's attention to this, as I informed him differently to-night, not knowing of General Corse's new disposition of troops.

I am, very respectfully, your obedient servant,

G. M. DODGE,
Major-General, Commanding.

HEADQUARTERS SEVENTEENTH ARMY CORPS,
Before Atlanta, Ga., August 11, 1864.

Lieut. Col. WILLIAM T. CLARK,
Assistant Adjutant-General, Army of the Tennessee:

COLONEL: I desire to call the attention of the major-general commanding to the fact that the line occupied by the Fourth Division of this corps has become extended to such an extent by the recent movements that neither the division commander (General Giles A. Smith) nor myself consider it safe without some reserve. It is in a very exposed position, and there is not in the division enough men to give a man for every two feet of front. I have been informed that the Sixteenth Corps has been re-enforced by a brigade.

I am, colonel, very respectfully, your obedient servant,

FRANK P. BLAIR, JR.,
Major-General.

SPECIAL FIELD ORDERS, ⎱   HDQRS. ARMY OF THE OHIO,
    No. 79.   ⎰   *Near Atlanta, Ga., August 11, 1864.*

I. Col. Israel Garrard, Seventh Ohio Cavalry, is hereby assigned to the command of all the cavalry of the Army of the Ohio serving with the troops in the field. Colonel Garrard will at once proceed to organize the cavalry and prepare it for active field service as soon as possible. Regimental and other commanders will make their reports to Colonel Garrard, as required by existing orders and regulations. All the members of the corps staff of the Cavalry Corps of the Army of the Ohio will report for duty to Colonel Garrard.

*   *   *   *   *   *   *

XIII. Early to-morrow General Hascall will move forward and endeavor to reach the West Point railroad, as near as practicable to East Point, thoroughly destroy the road for a distance of two or three miles, and return to the rear of his present line. General Johnson will thin out his line to-night and relieve General Cox's division at daylight in the morning. General Cox will occupy General Hascall's works as soon as vacated, and will support General Hascall in his operations, if necessary; especially in case of an attack or threatened attack upon his left. Colonel Garrard will operate upon General Hascall's right, and endeavor to clear the enemy's cavalry from his flank. He will scout and picket all roads leading from General Hascall's right to the Chattahoochee. The pickets should be very vigilant during the day, so as to detect at once any movement of troops about the enemy's lines. In case of the withdrawal of troops from any portion of the lines in his front General Johnson will endeavor to secure possession of them.

By command of Major-General Schofield:

J. A. CAMPBELL,
Major and Assistant Adjutant-General.

SPECIAL FIELD ORDERS, }   HDQRS. LEFT WING, 16TH A. C.,
            No. 59.   }   *Near Atlanta, Ga., August 11, 1864.*

*   *   *   *   *   *   *

II. First. Every battery in the command will be placed in position in the front line. Strong works will be built to hold them, and, when necessary, they will be casemated. This should be done by daylight to-morrow, the 12th instant.

Second. As soon as all batteries are in position, whenever the enemy open a gun upon any part of the line every gun that can be brought to bear upon it will be immediately brought into action and continue to fire until the enemy's guns are silenced.

Third. The skirmish line will be instructed to keep a hot fire upon the enemy's skirmish line, or main line, and especially upon the embrasures of his batteries during the day, and every opportunity will be taken to force the enemy's skirmishers into their main works. During the night the skirmish line will not fire unless the enemy advance.

Fourth. Division commanders will select some point on the line to approach the enemy's works, and commence to work up to them by parallels and saps.

*   *   *   *   *   *   *

By order of Maj. Gen. G. M. Dodge:

J. W. BARNES,
Assistant Adjutant-General.

WASHINGTON, *August 12, 1864—11 a. m.*

Major-General SHERMAN:

I have the pleasure of informing you that your appointment as major-general in the regular army has been ordered to-day, and will be immediately forwarded by mail. General Mower is appointed major-general of volunteers. His appointment will also be transmitted to you.

EDWIN M. STANTON,
Secretary of War.

NEAR ATLANTA, GA., *August 12, 1864—7.30 p. m.*
(Received 1.30 a. m. 13th.)

Hon. E. M. STANTON,
          Secretary of War:

Please convey to the President my thanks for the honor conferred on me. I would have preferred a delay until the close of the campaign. Also for the commission for General Mower, whose task was to kill Forrest. He only crippled him, but he is a young and game officer. All well.

W. T. SHERMAN,
Major-General.

HEADQUARTERS DEPARTMENT OF THE CUMBERLAND,
          Before Atlanta, August 12, 1864.

DEAR SHERMAN: I am sure you will feel convinced on receiving copies of Brannan's two telegrams* of yesterday to Barry that he did not for one moment think of embarrassing operations by any act of

* See p. 458.

jealousy toward the Army of the Tennessee. Indeed I do not understand why Barry should have reported to you that Brannan was making obstacles about placing the gun on Howard's left after receiving the telegrams referred to. I visited the bridge yesterday, and have sent Wharton down this morning to make a thorough reconnaissance and sketch of the ground so that Williams may be able to understand the orders which it will be necessary to give him relative to preparing for the defensive. I have already taken measures to mobilize my army when it becomes necessary to make the move you spoke to me about day before yesterday. I have also taken measures to find out more about the concentration of the enemy's cavalry at Monticello. I do not understand why they assemble there if a raid into Tennessee and Kentucky is intended, as reported. I hope to know something about their intentions in a day or two. Nearly all the ammunition for the $4\frac{1}{2}$-inch guns, which Baylor has been able to get down, has been expended now. The whole will be used up by to-morrow night. I sincerely hope the reports we hear of the movements about Mobile may prove true.

Yours, truly,

GEO. H. THOMAS,
Major-General, U. S. Volunteers.

SHERMAN'S HEADQUARTERS,
August 12, 1864.

Major-General THOMAS:

I have your note. Assure General Brannan of my entire satisfaction. General Barry, in referring to his dispatches, found he had read it wrong. The dispatch was clear. I am perfectly satisfied that General Brannan did right and Barry led me into the error. Meet Generals Schofield and Howard at my headquarters at 10 a. m. to-morrow. I have just returned from the extreme right. I think the position of Schofield's corps, at least two miles below Utoy, is a threat to that flank that cannot be disregarded by Hood. Watch the motions in Atlanta as close as possible. I have no doubt of the news from Mobile. I know officially per Canby that the attempt was to be made, and it is more successful than I hoped for from the destruction of the rebel gunboats, without which they cannot defend the city.

W. T. SHERMAN,
Major-General.

HDQRS. MILITARY DIVISION OF THE MISSISSIPPI,
In the Field, near Atlanta, August 12, 1864.

General BRANNAN:

I will show your dispatch to General Barry. The facts seem different than as represented to me. Yet too much time has been consumed, and I want more rapidity of firing, both for effect and that time may be allowed to remove the guns back to a safe place in case the whole army is required to move quick. I was offended about the gun, because it looked as though you begrudged the Army of the Tennessee the use of a single gun, a spirit of jealousy when there should be a generous rivalry and desire to oblige, but I trust I am mistaken in this also.

W. T. SHERMAN,
Major-General, Commanding.

HDQRS. CHIEF OF ARTY., DEPT. OF THE CUMBERLAND,
August 12, 1864.

Major-General SHERMAN,
    Commanding Military Division:

Your dispatch of this date received. You are mistaken as to any spirit of jealousy on the part of the Army of the Cumberland toward the Army of the Tennessee, so far as I am concerned. As soon as General Barry informed me (3 p. m. yesterday) that he desired a 4½-inch gun to place on General Corse's front it was instantly ordered with a supply of ammunition. If I am to be censured for disobedience of orders on the report of General Barry it would be well for him to obtain facts. I inclose copies of telegrams to him.* The firing shall continue with the rapidity you desire.

I am, general, very respectfully, your obedient servant,
                                        J. M. BRANNAN,
        Brig. Gen. and Chief of Artillery, Dept. of the Cumberland.

HDQRS. MILITARY DIVISION OF THE MISSISSIPPI,
    In the Field, near Atlanta (at General Schofield's),
                                August 12, 1864—11 a. m.

General THOMAS:

I am at General Schofield's headquarters, which is now on the Sandtown road, and I should think nearly abreast of East Point. The general is out on a reconnaissance in force, and I wish you to keep things lively, that no concentrating or massing may be made as against General Schofield.

                                        W. T. SHERMAN,
                                        Major-General, Commanding.

HEADQUARTERS DEPARTMENT OF THE CUMBERLAND,
                                        August 12, 1864.

Major-General SHERMAN:

I have kept up a continuous demonstration on the enemy all day, both skirmishing and artillery firing. No movements of his troops have been reported to me by any of my officers on lookout.

                                        GEO. H. THOMAS,
                                        Major-General.

THOMAS' HEADQUARTERS,
                    August 12, 1864—10.30 p. m.

Major-General SHERMAN:

Two 20-pounder Parrott guns have burst; have caused the firing to cease with the two others till morning. The ammunition for 4½-inch guns (1,100 rounds) will be here by 8 a. m. to-morrow, when the firing will be immediately resumed. Your dispatch of this evening received; will be over in the morning and bring a rebel paper giving account of the Mobile affair.

                                        GEO. H. THOMAS,
                                        Major-General, U. S. Volunteers.

* See p. 458.

STANLEY'S HEADQUARTERS,
August 12, 1864—7.20 a. m.

Major-General SHERMAN:

I regret to say that your dispatch was received at these headquarters just five minutes ago. I will at once send telegraphic instructions to Kimball, in accordance therewith. Am now starting for the left.

D. S. STANLEY,
Major-General.

———

HEADQUARTERS FOURTH ARMY CORPS,
August 12, 1864—9.30 a. m.

Major-General SHERMAN:

No change discovered within the enemy's works this morning. The same force and disposition of force observed to-day as yesterday. I am just about to try to capture his picket-line near the railroad.

D. S. STANLEY,
Major-General.

———

HOWARD'S HOUSE, *August 12, 1864—2.30 p. m.*

Capt. L. M. DAYTON:

We can see no change in the rebel lines during our demonstration. We can see them stand to arms in their works, but cannot determine their strength. The line appears as well manned as heretofore. The rebels re-enforced their skirmish line when we advanced.

D. S. STANLEY,
Major-General.

———

KIMBALL'S HEADQUARTERS,
August 12, 1864.

Captain DAYTON:

I received General Sherman's dispatch too late to make any surprise of the rebel pickets. I will try this to-morrow at daylight. I will engage and drive in their pickets now. No change in this line. By deserters I learn that Cheatham's division, with some cavalry, guard their right.

D. S. STANLEY,
Major-General.

———

HEADQUARTERS FOURTH ARMY CORPS,
August 12, 1864—7 p. m.

Brigadier-General KIMBALL,
Commanding First Division, Fourth Army Corps:

I do not deem it advisable, under the circumstances, to attack the rebel pickets in the morning.

D. S. STANLEY,
Major-General.

HEADQUARTERS FOURTEENTH ARMY CORPS,
Near Atlanta, Ga., August 12, 1864.

Brig. Gen. W. D. WHIPPLE,
Assistant Adjutant-General and Chief of Staff:

Last night I received an order from General Schofield to extend my line to the right in order to relieve the Twenty-third Corps, as it was intended to be moved to the right to destroy the railroad. My part was performed, but if the Twenty-third Corps did anything I have failed to hear of it. Thirty-eight prisoners of war and deserters have been forwarded since my report of the 9th. A deserter who came in late this evening reports that the rebels have a line of works about one mile and a quarter in the rear of those now occupied, to which they design falling back to-night. I inclose casualty report for yesterday.*

Respectfully, your obedient servant,

R. W. JOHNSON,
Brigadier-General.

STATION OBSERVATION, *August 12, 1864—9.25 a. m.*

Capt. A. K. TAYLOR,
Acting Signal Officer:

CAPTAIN: Men at work on four-gun fort, same place as yesterday.

Very respectfully, yours,

W. W. HOPKINS,
First Lieutenant and Acting Signal Officer.

HEADQUARTERS DEPARTMENT OF THE CUMBERLAND,
Chattanooga, August 12, 1864.

Lieut. Col. R. M. SAWYER,
Asst. Adjt. Gen., Military Division of the Mississippi:

COLONEL: In compliance with your telegram of 10th instant inclosed please find list of Western veteran troops serving in this department. The report is not very complete, owing to the fact that reports have not been received from many of the commands since their return from furlough, in consequence of the movements of the army and the troops being on the march or in line of battle. If the inclosed be not satisfactory it will be necessary to send to each command for the data from which to compile the required list, the reports being received at these headquarters in a consolidated form by divisions. The estimate of the strength of each regiment is in all probability not too great, no allowance being made for the casualties of the present campaign. Many non-veterans still serving with their regiments are not included.

Very respectfully, your obedient servant,

HENRY M. CIST,
Captain and Assistant Adjutant-General.

---

* See Part I, p. 510.

[Inclosure.]

List of Western veteran regiments, &c., in the Department of the Cumberland.

Command.	Date of report.	Veterans.	Recruits gained.	Aggregate.
5th Ohio Volunteer Infantry	Mar. 1, 1864	128	155	283
13th Ohio Volunteer Infantry		181		
14th Ohio Volunteer Infantry	Mar. 1, 1864	421	215	636
15th Ohio Volunteer Infantry	Apr. 1, 1864	301	313	614
17th Ohio Volunteer Infantry		326		
19th Ohio Volunteer Infantry		310		
21st Ohio Volunteer Infantry	Mar. 1, 1864	252	196	448
26th Ohio Volunteer Infantry	....do	185	89	274
29th Ohio Volunteer Infantry	....do	304	110	414
31st Ohio Volunteer Infantry	....do	259	375	634
33d Ohio Volunteer Infantry	....do	219	166	385
36th Ohio Volunteer Infantry		343		
38th Ohio Volunteer Infantry	Mar. 1, 1864	462	219	681
40th Ohio Volunteer Infantry		172		
41st Ohio Volunteer Infantry	Mar. 1, 1864	196	80	276
49th Ohio Volunteer Infantry		261		
51st Ohio Volunteer Infantry	Mar. 1, 1864	237	248	485
55th Ohio Volunteer Infantry	....do	314	94	408
61st Ohio Volunteer Infantry		118		
64th Ohio Volunteer Infantry	Mar. 1, 1864	226	70	296
65th Ohio Volunteer Infantry	Apr. 1, 1864	170	17	187
66th Ohio Volunteer Infantry	Mar. 1, 1864	255	52	307
69th Ohio Volunteer Infantry		302		
71st Ohio Volunteer Infantry	Apr. 1, 1864	302	117	419
73d Ohio Volunteer Infantry	Mar. 1, 1864	....	111	
74th Ohio Volunteer Infantry	....do	159	131	290
82d Ohio Volunteer Infantry	....do	265	142	407
9th Indiana Volunteer Infantry	....do	280	135	415
17th Indiana Volunteer Infantry (mounted)	....do	278		
22d Indiana Volunteer Infantry		312		
27th Indiana Volunteer Infantry		152		
29th Indiana Volunteer Infantry	Mar. 1, 1864	32	87	119
30th Indiana Volunteer Infantry		120		
31st Indiana Volunteer Infantry		285		
33d Indiana Volunteer Infantry		448		
35th Indiana Volunteer Infantry	Mar. 1, 1864	182	68	250
37th Indiana Volunteer Infantry		193		
38th Indiana Volunteer Infantry	Mar. 1, 1864	218	78	296
40th Indiana Volunteer Infantry		246		
42d Indiana Volunteer Infantry	Mar. 1, 1864	215	99	314
44th Indiana Volunteer Infantry		264		
51st Indiana Volunteer Infantry	Apr. 1, 1864	291	24	315
57th Indiana Volunteer Infantry		215		
58th Indiana Volunteer Infantry		202		
10th Illinois Volunteer Infantry	Mar. 1, 1864	378	184	562
16th Illinois Volunteer Infantry	....do	378	308	686
34th Illinois Volunteer Infantry	....do	296	188	484
36th Illinois Volunteer Infantry	....do	211	52	263
38th Illinois Volunteer Infantry		171		
42d Illinois Volunteer Infantry		226		
44th Illinois Volunteer Infantry		224		
51st Illinois Volunteer Infantry		146		
59th Illinois Volunteer Infantry	Mar. 1, 1864	248	89	371
60th Illinois Volunteer Infantry		333		
4th Kentucky Volunteer Infantry		215		
18th Kentucky Volunteer Infantry	Mar. 1, 1864	175	45	220
21st Kentucky Volunteer Infantry	....do	296	14	310
23d Kentucky Volunteer Infantry		192		
28th Kentucky Volunteer Infantry		243		
9th Michigan Volunteer Infantry	Mar. 1, 1864	289	210	499
10th Michigan Volunteer Infantry		391		
13th Michigan Volunteer Infantry	Apr. 1, 1864	190	383	573
14th Michigan Volunteer Infantry		350		
3d Wisconsin Volunteer Infantry	Mar. 1, 1864	238	300	538
13th Wisconsin Volunteer Infantry	Apr. 1, 1864	392	59	451
15th Missouri Volunteer Infantry		168		
2d Minnesota Volunteer Infantry	Mar. 1, 1864	244	143	387
8th Kansas Volunteer Infantry		205		
1st Ohio Volunteer Cavalry	Mar. 1, 1864	331	335	666
* 3d Ohio Volunteer Cavalry	....do	296		
4th Ohio Volunteer Cavalry	....do	194	160	354
8th Indiana Volunteer Cavalry		296		
2d Kentucky Volunteer Cavalry		184		
3d Kentucky Volunteer Cavalry		237		
4th Kentucky Volunteer Cavalry	Mar. 1, 1864	110	26	136
6th Kentucky Volunteer Cavalry		76		
2d Michigan Volunteer Cavalry		320		
5th Iowa Volunteer Cavalry	Mar. 1, 1864	416	197	613

List of Western veteran regiments, &c., in the Department of the Cumberland—Cont'd.

Command.	Date of report.	Veterans.	Recruits gained.	Aggregate.
1st Ohio Volunteer Artillery:				
Battery B	Apr. 1, 1864	67	13	80
Battery C	Mar. 1, 1864	63	30	93
Battery F	Apr. 1, 1864	73	66	139
Battery G	....do	15	24	39
Battery K		50		
6th Ohio Independent Battery		66		
12th Ohio Independent Battery	Mar. 1, 1864	33	30	63
13th Indiana Independent Battery		76		
Battery C, 1st Illinois Volunteer Artillery	Mar. 1, 1864	41	24	65
2d Illinois Volunteer Artillery:				
Battery H	Apr. 1, 1864	64	17	81
Battery I	Mar. 1, 1864	65	70	135
Battery E, 1st Michigan Volunteer Artillery	Apr. 1, 1864	58		
5th Wisconsin Independent Battery	Mar. 1, 1864	86	57	143
8th Wisconsin Independent Battery	....do	77	62	139
Battery G, 1st Missouri Volunteer Artillery		30		
2d Minnesota Independent Battery		46		
1st Kansas Independent Battery		43		

> HENRY M. CIST,
> *Captain and Assistant Adjutant-General.*

HDQRS. DEPARTMENT OF THE CUMBERLAND,
　　　Chattanooga, August 12, 1864.

HDQRS. FIRST DIVISION, FIFTEENTH ARMY CORPS,
　　　Near Atlanta, Ga., August 12, 1864.

Lieut. Col. R. R. TOWNES,
　Assistant Adjutant-General, Fifteenth Army Corps:

COLONEL: I have the honor to report that this forenoon a work for two pieces was built near center of my First Brigade, and occupied by two 12-pounder Napoleons. They commenced shelling the rebel rifle-pits at 3 p. m. with effect, driving the rebels temporarily from a portion of their pits. During the night I propose to construct another work in a more advanced position. Nothing further of interest to report.

I am, respectfully,

> W. A. GORDON,
> *Assistant Adjutant-General.*

(For Brig. Gen. C. R. Woods, momentarily absent.)

Statement of J. Milton Glass (scout).

OFFICE PROVOST-MARSHAL-GENERAL,
　　　DEPARTMENT OF THE CUMBERLAND,
　　　　Near Atlanta, August 12, 1864.

Reports that he left Atlanta about 9 o'clock this morning; was not allowed to visit the lines while there. Saw four large pieces of artillery moving down the Macon railroad toward East Point. Day before yesterday shells passed over General Hood's headquarters and struck 300 or 400 yards beyond; Hood's headquarters are near where White Hall street intersects Faith's alley. These shells appeared to come from the Fifteenth Corps. This morning shells from the Twentieth and Fourth Corps struck at the corner of McDonough street and Faith's alley. The supply trains belonging to Hardee's corps are camped to the right of the cemetery between First street and the Augusta railroad, near Elmore street; can be easily reached by batteries in Fourth Corps. Says no change has taken place in the position of the enemy's corps except that they are strengthening their left by artillery. The buildings in the fair-grounds are used as hospitals for their wounded. Says when he went into town yesterday he was not halted nor asked for a pass till he got into town; went into town from Paul Jones', southeast from Decatur two miles, and returned same way. Says the works along the Augusta railroad are held by militia and dismounted cavalry in small force and without artillery.

[Indorsement.]

Respectfully forwarded for the information of the major-general commanding.

ED. C. DENIG,
Captain and Assistant Adjutant-General.

HDQRS. MILITARY DIVISION OF THE MISSISSIPPI,
In the Field, near Atlanta, August 12, 1864.

General SCHOFIELD:

We could not get General Stanley's operator last night, but he got the orders this morning and says he will attend to them at once. I will come over in about an hour and follow to your right. All our big guns are now in position, three firing along the Buck Head road and one at the depot up the valley of Proctor's Creek.

W. T. SHERMAN,
Major-General, Commanding.

SHERMAN'S HEADQUARTERS,
August 12, 1864.

General SCHOFIELD:

Meet Generals Thomas and Howard at my headquarters at 10 a. m. [to-morrow]. Collect to-night the names of as many resident farmers as you can, as I have copy of a rebel map with names on it and ruled to lots. I will have copies made enough for us all. The name of the man who lived at the house we were in this evening will enable us to locate our line exactly.

W. T. SHERMAN,
Major-General.

HEADQUARTERS ARMY OF THE OHIO,
In the Field, before Atlanta, Ga., August 12, 1864—2 a. m.

Brig. Gen. J. D. COX,
Commanding Third Division:

GENERAL: The commanding general directs that your division will pass by General Hascall's command and take the advance in the movement to-morrow morning, and he desires you to make all necessary arrangements. The general will see you at an early hour in the morning and give full instructions.

Very respectfully, your obedient servant,

J. A. CAMPBELL,
Major and Assistant Adjutant-General.

HEADQUARTERS ARMY OF THE OHIO,
Near Atlanta, Ga., August 12, 1864—2 a. m.

Brig. Gen. M. S. HASCALL,
Commanding Second Division, Twenty-third Army Corps:

GENERAL: The commanding general directs me to acknowledge receipt of your letter* of 11.30 p. m. [August 11], and to say, in reply, that General Cox's division will be substituted for your command, in the advance to-morrow.

Very respectfully, &c

WM. M. WHERRY,
Major and Aide-de-Camp.

HDQRS. THIRD DIVISION, TWENTY-THIRD ARMY CORPS,
August 12, 1864—11.15 a. m.

Major-General SCHOFIELD, *Commanding Army of the Ohio:*

Colonel Garrard reports to me that a dismounted force has been placed by the enemy in position across the Campbellton road, about half a mile west of here. Casement is feeling forward and to the right, and as soon as Reilly is in position I will have him support Garrard in a reconnaissance to the right to develop fully what there is on that flank. This has to be done, of course, before Casement can make much progress to the front, especially as he finds the detour to the right to avoid open country more considerable than we expected.

Very respectfully, &c.,

J. D. COX,
Brigadier-General, Commanding.

HDQRS. THIRD DIVISION, TWENTY-THIRD ARMY CORPS,
August 12, 1864—11.40 a. m.

Major-General SCHOFIELD, *Commanding Army of the Ohio:*

Lieutenant Reynolds, signal officer, reports rebels in line in upper part of open country in front of us, making earth-works, and others moving still farther toward our right, apparently extending the line. From the direction I should expect this to be seen from the point I left you in. Supposing you would wish to know this immediately I send the report, although so soon after my last dispatch. Nothing further from the right as yet.

Very respectfully, &c.,

J. D. COX,
Brigadier-General, Commanding.

HDQRS. THIRD DIVISION, TWENTY-THIRD ARMY CORPS,
August 12, 1864—12.40 [p.] m.

Major-General SCHOFIELD, *Commanding, &c.:*

Casement is a mile west of where I left you, and has been obliged to keep on the north side of the Campbellton road all the way to avoid going into open ground. He then has to go around a large open field on the north side, which he is now doing, with some chance of finding cover to cross the road there. There is, however, so much open land

---

* Not found.

that it is nearly hopeless to avoid the force being fully seen, as rebel vedettes are along our front the whole distance. I have no hesitation in saying that any road to the railroad which is not exceedingly long and circuitous must lead through the open valleys around us. The force reported by Garrard proves to be only vedettes.

Very respectfully, your obedient servant,

J. D. COX,
Brigadier-General.

HDQRS. THIRD DIVISION, TWENTY-THIRD ARMY CORPS,
August 12. 1864—2.30 p. m.

Major-General SCHOFIELD,
Commanding, &c.:

SIR: I have passed beyond the cross-road between the Sandtown and Campbellton road, about a quarter of a mile to the forks of the C[ampbellton] and East Point roads. The E[ast] P[oint] road comes back sharply. Casement is out on it, pushing toward the wooded hill seen from General Hascall's front. The vedettes on the extreme right (Campbellton road) keep up a lively skirmish. The line of the C[ampbellton] road from Hascall's right to this point is a very pretty one for a defensive line if the flank is not too exposed. Captain Twining will wait till Casement gets farther on so as to be able to report definitely whether the wooded hill referred to is held in any considerable force. The line of rebel works is distinctly seen at intervals all the way down to the point stated by Mr. Willis to be near East Point.

Very respectfully, your obedient servant,

J. D. COX,
Brigadier-General, Commanding.

HDQRS. CAVALRY COMMAND, DEPT. OF THE OHIO,
Before Atlanta, Ga., August 12, 1864.

Maj. J. A. CAMPBELL,
Assistant Adjutant-General:

MAJOR: I have the honor to report that the scouts ordered this morning to scout from the bridge over Utoy to Sandtown, and from Donahue's Mill to the cross-roads near the Owl Rock Church, met heavy pickets of the enemy, indicating that the country over which I scouted yesterday had been reoccupied. The enemy's pickets made a stubborn resistance, but were driven in, and scouts made as far as Sandtown and to the cross-roads near the Owl Rock Church.

Very respectfully, your obedient servant,

ISRAEL GARRARD,
Colonel, Commanding.

HOWARD'S HEADQUARTERS,
August 12, 1864.

Major-General SHERMAN:

Signal officer reports 5.10 p. m. three trains of cars loaded with troops just arrived at Atlanta. No. 1, four passenger and seven freight cars; No. 2, thirteen freight cars; No. 3, seventeen freight cars, full outside and inside.

O. O. HOWARD,
Major-General.

HDQRS. MILITARY DIVISION OF THE MISSISSIPPI,
In the Field, near Atlanta, August 12, 1864.

General HOWARD:

Meet Generals Thomas and Schofield at my headquarters at 10 a. m. to-morrow. I am just from General Schofield's right. General Cox was out about two miles, and we could see the enemy trying to throw up fresh rifle-pits farther south. I will describe more fully to-morrow.

W. T. SHERMAN,
Major-General, Commanding.

HDQRS. SECOND DIVISION, FIFTEENTH ARMY CORPS,
Near Atlanta, Ga., August 12, 1864.

Lieut. Col. R. R. TOWNES,
Assistant Adjutant-General, Fifteenth Army Corps:

I have the honor to report that nothing of importance has occurred in my front during the day. Quite an artillery duel has been kept up, but I have sustained no damage by it. There was quite a heavy infantry fire in my front about 10 o'clock last evening, but I think the cause was more imaginary than real by both parties.

Very respectfully, your obedient servant,

J. A. J. LIGHTBURN,
Brigadier-General of Volunteers.

NEAR ATLANTA, GA., *August 12, 1864—8 p. m.*

Maj. T. T. ECKERT,
Assistant Superintendent U. S. Military Telegraph:

General Schofield felt forward again to-day for West Point railroad, south of East Point, but without success, finding enemy in earthworks on his front. It is evident that there are more rebels before us than we had supposed. Our artillery annoys them severely, causing their troops to remain in the trenches, as our shells reach over their camp near Atlanta. I have neglected to mention that the bridge over Chattahoochee is done, and trains run to our position. Nothing further from Mobile.

J. C. VAN DUZER,
Cipher Operator, U. S. Military Telegraph.

GENERAL ORDERS, } HDQRS. MIL. DIV. OF THE MISSISSIPPI,
No. 22. } *Nashville, Tenn., August 12, 1864.*

I. Deserters from the rebel army required by standing orders to be sent north of the Ohio River and discharged, as well as refugees, male and female, escaping from the dangers of civil war at the South, will, on arrival at Cairo or Louisville, be forwarded at the expense of the United States, if unable to pay their own way, to Cincinnati or Saint Louis by water, or to any point not over 100 miles by railroad.

II. Commanding officers at Cairo and Louisville will, through the agents of the Christian Commission or labor agencies, endeavor to put this class of people in the way of honest employment as much as possible.

By order of Maj. Gen. W. T. Sherman:

R. M. SAWYER,
Assistant Adjutant-General.

Near Atlanta, Ga., *August 13, 1864—8 a. m.*
(Received 11 p. m.)

Maj. Gen. H. W. Halleck,
       Washington, D. C.:

We have now pressed the enemy's lines from east around to East Point on the south. The nature of ground, with its artificial defenses, makes it too difficult to assault, and to reach the Macon road by a farther extension will be extra hazardous. I have ordered army commanders to prepare for the following plan: Leave one corps strongly intrenched at the Chattahoochee bridge in charge of our surplus wagon trains and artillery; with 60,000 men, reduced to fighting trim, to make a circuit of devastation around the town, with a radius of fifteen or twenty miles. To do this I go on the faith that the militia in Atlanta are only good for the defense of its parapets and will not come out. I want a good corps commander for the Fourteenth Corps, in place of General Palmer, and Jeff. Davis is the best officer in that corps. I prefer him much to General Brannan. I would like the utmost activity to be kept up in Mobile Bay, and, if possible, about the mouth of Appalachicola. Also, to be assured that no material re-enforcements have come here from Virginia. If I should ever be cut off from my base, look out for me about Saint Mark's, Fla., or Savannah, Ga.

                                   W. T. SHERMAN,
                                        Major-General.

Near Atlanta, Ga., *August 13, 1864—11.30 p. m.*
(Received 11 a. m. 14th.)

Maj. Gen. H. W. Halleck,
       Washington, D. C.:

In making the circuit of Atlanta, as proposed in my dispatch of to-day, I necessarily run some risk. If there be any possibility of Admiral Farragut and the land forces of Granger taking Mobile (which rebel prisoners now report, but the report is not confirmed by Macon papers of the 11th, which I have seen), and, further, of pushing up to Montgomery, my best plan would be to wait awhile as now, and at the proper time move down to West Point and operate into the heart of Georgia from there. Before cutting loose, as proposed, I would like to know the chances of our getting the use of the Alabama River this campaign. I could easily break up the railroad back to Chattanooga and shift my whole army down to West Point and Columbus, a country rich in corn, and make my fall campaign from there. I know Fort Morgan must succumb in time.

                                   W. T. SHERMAN,
                                        Major-General.

Headquarters Army of the Cumberland,
                                   August 13, 1864.

Major-General Sherman:

Garrard has already received orders to scout as far as Roswell. He sent a scouting party some distance beyond Decatur, both south and in the direction of Covington, yesterday, but discovered nothing. Have sent orders for Kilpatrick to put down the bridge at Sandtown.

                                   GEO. H. THOMAS,
                              Major-General, U. S. Volunteers, Commanding.

HOWARD'S HOUSE, *August 13, 1864—9 a. m.*

Captain CASE:

Can see three regiments in rear of rebel main line. One about south 30 degrees west, near the fort on their right, one in front of the medical college, and one west near the fort where the large guns are. They are pitching tents and putting up shelters as though they had just moved in. In other parts of the line everything seems to be same as usual. Can see seven battle-flags. Some firing on the skirmish line.

FORAKER.

HOWARD'S HOUSE, *August 13, 1864.*

Captain CASE,
Chief Signal Officer:

No change in the rebel lines in the front since morning. Hear heavy artillery firing beyond the city about south 4 degrees west.

FORAKER.

HEADQUARTERS FOURTH ARMY CORPS,
Near Atlanta, Ga., August 13, 1864—1.30 a. m.

Brigadier-General WHIPPLE,
Chief of Staff:

General Kimball just reports that the pickets in his front near the brown house report that a rebel column has been passing their front toward our left for the last hour and a half, and that the enemy has kept up a constant skirmish fire all night. I have just directed General Wood to send two regiments at once to the Roswell road as a support for General Kimball's left.

D. S. STANLEY,
Major-General.

HEADQUARTERS DEPARTMENT OF THE CUMBERLAND,
Camp near Atlanta, August 13, 1864.
(Received 9.50 a. m.)

Maj. Gen. D. S. STANLEY,
Commanding Fourth Army Corps:

GENERAL: General Garrard has been ordered to send a scouting party in the direction of Decatur, for the purpose of ascertaining the amount of those movements the enemy made last night and his apparent intentions, and the major-general commanding directs that you be on the watch for the earliest information or signs of movement of the enemy.

Yours, respectfully,

WM. D. WHIPPLE,
Assistant Adjutant-General.

KIMBALL'S HEADQUARTERS,
August 13, 1864—8.30 a. m.

Colonel FULLERTON:

COLONEL: I have delayed answering yours until I could ascertain more certainly the facts as to the movement last night. It is certain that there was a movement of troops in front of Taylor, but where to I cannot find out; deserters say that they know of no movement on their right. I find all about as usual. The rebels did make a reconnaissance with scouts along our picket-line in front of Opdycke. Two regiments from General Wood reported at early dawn; they are in line on the left of the cavalry. I will retain them there until evening unless otherwise ordered.

NATHAN KIMBALL,
Brigadier-General, Commanding.

HDQRS. FIRST DIVISION, FOURTH ARMY CORPS,
August 13, 1864—9.30 a. m.

Colonel FULLERTON,
Assistant Adjutant-General:

COLONEL: Since my dispatch at 8.30 a. m. the signal officer reports that the rebel line in front of Kirby's pickets has been strengthened by at least three regiments. This begins more fully to develop the movements of last night. The guns remain as before.

NATHAN KIMBALL,
Brigadier-General.

HDQRS. FIRST BRIG., FIRST DIV., FOURTH ARMY CORPS,
August 13, 1864—12 midnight.

Maj. W. H. SINCLAIR,
Assistant Adjutant-General:

My brigade officer of the day reports that by the aid of a fire in front of the enemy's works he saw five regiments passing to our left, and then the fire was put out. He also says that he could distinctly hear loud cries from women and children, as if praying, &c. There is now quite a fire burning in the town. The shelling from the enemy has done me no injury, though uncomfortably close.

Very respectfully, your obedient servant,

I. M. KIRBY,
Colonel, Commanding.

P. S.—I will be on the alert before daylight.

I. M. KIRBY.

HEADQUARTERS DEPARTMENT OF THE CUMBERLAND,
Camp near Atlanta, Ga., August 13, 1864.

Brig. Gen. K. GARRARD,
Commanding Second Cavalry Division:

GENERAL: Major-General Stanley reports that the enemy were marching last night toward our left. The major-general commanding directs that you send a scouting party in the direction of Decatur for the purpose of ascertaining if possible whether the enemy has moved, where he is, and what are his apparent intentions.

Yours, respectfully,

WM. D. WHIPPLE,
Assistant Adjutant-General.

HDQRS. SECOND BRIGADE, SECOND DIVISION CAVALRY,
                    Buck Head, Ga., August 13, 1864.
Capt. R. P. KENNEDY,
    Assistant Adjutant-General, Second Cavalry Division:

CAPTAIN: I have the honor to report that the battalion of my command sent out this morning has returned. They proceeded beyond Decatur on the McDonough road some two or three miles, and also some five or six miles north and east of the town, without encountering any of the enemy or learning anything of any movements on their part.

I am, very respectfully, your obedient servant,
                                    ELI LONG,
                            Colonel, Commanding Brigade.

HDQRS. THIRD DIVISION, TWENTY-THIRD ARMY CORPS,
                            August 13, 1864.
Maj. J. A. CAMPBELL,
    Assistant Adjutant-General, Army of the Ohio:

MAJOR: Colonel Garrard reported last evening an appearance of increased cavalry force in his front pressing him closely. I therefore marched General Reilly's brigade across from the Campbellton road to the Sandtown road, and put them in camp on that road beyond the hospitals, &c., and just in rear of the cavalry camp. I put Colonel Stiles' brigade between the Sandtown road and General Hascall's headquarters, where I had one regiment the night before, and placed Colonel Casement's brigade in his old works just in rear of the line where he relieved part of General Hascall's command two days ago.

Very respectfully, your obedient servant,
                                    J. D. COX,
                            Brigadier-General, Commanding.

HEADQUARTERS DEPARTMENT OF THE TENNESSEE,
                            August 13, 1864.
Major-General SHERMAN:

General Logan reports that General Woods advanced and took the enemy's rifle-pits, capturing 65 prisoners—4 commissioned officers and 61 enlisted men. This in front of the extreme right of my line.
                                    O. O. HOWARD,
                                        Major-General.

HDQRS. FIRST DIVISION, FIFTEENTH ARMY CORPS,
                    Near Atlanta, Ga., August 13, 1864.
[Lieut. Col. R. R. TOWNES,
    Assistant Adjutant-General, Fifteenth Army Corps:]

COLONEL: I have the honor to report that I advanced my skirmishers this afternoon and took the intrenched skirmish line of the enemy in my front, with a loss of 1 man killed and 1 accidentally wounded. I have directed Colonel Smith to hold the line at all hazards if it takes his whole brigade to do so. The line is by this time well secured by reversing the enemy's pits. I have 61 privates and 4 officers as prisoners, who will be forwarded within half an hour. The Fourteenth Corps got 27 prisoners that were sent back by my men or driven into their lines. They neither fired a shot nor advanced a man, but still claim the prisoners as captured by them.

I am, colonel, very respectfully, your obedient servant,

C. R. WOODS,
Brigadier-General, Commanding.

HDQRS. SECOND DIVISION, FIFTEENTH ARMY CORPS,
Near Atlanta, Ga., August 13, 1864.

Lieut. Col. R. R. TOWNES,
Assistant Adjutant-General, Fifteenth Army Corps:

I have the honor to report nothing special in my front to-day, except that I advanced the right of my skirmish line to connect with General Woods' left, taking three skirmish pits occupied by the rebels in my front, which drew a considerable fire from the enemy's batteries, doing me but little damage.

Very respectfully, your obedient servant,

J. A. J. LIGHTBURN,
Brigadier-General of Volunteers.

HDQRS. MILITARY DIVISION OF THE MISSISSIPPI,
In the Field, near Atlanta, August 13, 1864.

General McARTHUR,
Marietta:

See at once as to who and what force broke the road at or near Acworth. It is, in my judgment, a mere cut, having a bearing on something beyond.

W. T. SHERMAN,
Major-General, Commanding.

BIG SHANTY, GA., *August 13, 1864—12.50 p. m.*

Major-General SHERMAN:

Damage to railroad repaired. Enemy's force, about seventy-five, came on the Alabama road, about one mile south of Acworth, and returned same way. Nobody hurt and no serious damage to engine. I have taken measures to prevent a recurrence.

J. McARTHUR,
Brigadier-General.

HDQRS. MILITARY DIVISION OF THE MISSISSIPPI,
In the Field, near Atlanta, August 13, 1864.

General McARTHUR,
Marietta:

Make somebody suffer for the break of the railroad at Acworth; somebody over in the direction of Roswell or McAfee's Bridge. It would be well to keep a good picket out in that direction. The Macon papers announce the capture of Marietta by their cavalry. That indicates a purpose. I think you had better bring the Kenesaw force close in, with a regiment to picket the mountain, with a signal station.

W. T. SHERMAN,
Major-General, Commanding.

MARIETTA, *August 13, 1864.*

General SHERMAN:

Following telegram just received:

BIG SHANTY.

VAN DYNE:

Train No. 2, first section, engine 25, was fired upon one mile south of Acworth; the road entirely torn up for 8 rods; engine 25 badly off; ties all burnt and iron bent. I have brought my train back to Big Shanty, and will wait orders from you.

SULLIVAN,
Conductor.

I will send a construction train at once to repair track.

J. B. VAN DYNE,
Master of Transportation.

CALHOUN, GA., *August 13, 1864.*

Maj. Gen. J. B. STEEDMAN,
Commanding District of the Etowah:

Citizens from Pickens County report that Colonel Hart's Sixth Georgia (rebel) Cavalry Regiment, with one other battalion, are at Jasper. They state their number at 1,500, but I think greatly overestimate their strength. It is probable they may be a part of the same gang that tore up the road last night. I start a scout of 100 men on Jasper road at 3 o'clock to-morrow morning.

J. K. FAULKNER,
Colonel, Commanding.

PROPOSITION.]   HDQRS. DEPT. AND ARMY OF THE TENN.,
Before Atlanta, Ga., August 13, 1864.

Accumulate all impedimenta not going at proposed depot prior to movement, and move trains of Armies of the Ohio and the Cumberland, under cover as much as possible, to vicinity of Utoy Creek, there to be parked and guarded by infantry; this the day before the troops draw out. Then:

First. Move Fourth Corps in the night to position in rear of Fourteenth Corps, so that the Twentieth Corps can withdraw at daylight and march to proposed depot, cavalry following closely Twentieth Corps, and taking up position on the south side of Proctor's Creek. Next night let trains of Army of the Tennessee move down Green's Ferry road, under guard, toward Sandtown, and park near Utoy Creek.

Second. At daylight Armies of the Ohio and the Cumberland move out simultaneously, by two routes if possible, in direction of Fairburn, Army of the Ohio to halt in position, Army of the Cumberland to form on its left, and the Army of the Tennessee, marching at same hour, to pass via Utoy or Sandtown to the rear and right of the other two armies. The three armies will march by three roads if possible, not more than two miles apart. The cavalry (Kilpatrick's) intended to cover the right flank to precede the Army of the Ohio, and that intended for the left flank to follow the Army of the Tennessee as far as Utoy Creek.

Respectfully submitted.

O. O. HOWARD,
Major-General.

CITY POINT, VA., *August 14, 1864—8.30 p. m.*
Major-General SHERMAN:

No division or brigade has gone from here west, and I shall endeavor to keep the enemy busy that none will go. The great danger has been of troops going from Lee to join Early in the Shenandoah Valley. I attempted a surprise on the north side of the river last night with the hope of getting near to Richmond and getting cavalry on their railroads on that side of the river. The enemy were found fortified, and their works manned by a division of Longstreet's corps, which I supposed had gone to join Early. The great danger you have to apprehend is from Kirby Smith getting his men across the Mississippi. The move you propose is a little hazardous, but I believe it will succeed. If you do not force the enemy out to fight, you will easily get back to your base. Our move to-day has resulted in the capture of 6 pieces of artillery and some prisoners, and probably the killing and wounding of 500 or 600 of the enemy. In killed and wounded our loss will probably reach 400.

U. S. GRANT,
Lieutenant-General.

WASHINGTON, *August 14, 1864—2 p. m.*
Major-General SHERMAN,
  Near Atlanta, Ga.:

Our official information extends only to the passage of the forts by the fleet and Granger's landing on Dauphin Island. Through the rebel papers we learn that Forts Gaines and Powell were captured and destroyed. I have seen nothing to indicate that either Fort Morgan or Mobile had been taken, and I have no reason to hope that the fleet or Granger's command will be able to open the Alabama River. Your dispatch will be sent to General Grant for his reply.

H. W. HALLECK,
Major-General and Chief of Staff.

HDQRS. MILITARY DIVISION OF THE MISSISSIPPI,
  In the Field, near Atlanta, August 14, 1864.
General THOMAS:

General McArthur, at Marietta, reports small bodies of cavalry approach Marietta from the northeast. General Garrard should send frequently up to Roswell and McAfee's. You may order General Kilpatrick to lay down a bridge at Sandtown, and be prepared to scour the country down as far as Camp Creek.

W. T. SHERMAN,
Major-General, Commanding.

HEADQUARTERS DEPARTMENT OF THE CUMBERLAND,
August 14, 1864.

Major-General SHERMAN:

Garrard has already received orders to scout as far as Roswell. He sent a scouting party some distance beyond Decatur, both south and in the direction of Covington, yesterday, but discovered nothing. Have sent orders for Kilpatrick to put down the bridge at Sandtown.

GEO. H. THOMAS,
Major-General.

HDQRS. MILITARY DIVISION OF THE MISSISSIPPI,
In the Field, near Atlanta, August 14, 1864.

General THOMAS:

Colonel Raum, commanding at Resaca, reports Wheeler passed Old-town going north at daylight this morning with 3,000 cavalry and wagon train. He should never be allowed to return. What think you of taking advantage of the occasion to put all our cavalry in motion?

W. T. SHERMAN,
Major-General, Commanding.

HDQRS. MILITARY DIVISION OF THE MISSISSIPPI,
In the Field, near Atlanta, August 14, 1864.

General THOMAS:

My telegraph operator says he heard the operator at Resaca say that he heard a fragment of a message coming from Chickamauga Station to the effect that Wheeler was at Dalton and had demanded the surrender of the place. The wires are again broken beyond Resaca.

W. T. SHERMAN,
Major-General, Commanding.

HDQRS. MILITARY DIVISION OF THE MISSISSIPPI,
In the Field, near Atlanta, August 14, 1864.

General THOMAS:

I would not be surprised if Wheeler is up at Dalton. If so, now is the time for General Elliott to collect all his cavalry and make a break round the enemy by either flank. I send you a copy of dispatch* just received from General J. E. Smith.

W. T. SHERMAN,
Major-General, Commanding.

HEADQUARTERS DEPARTMENT OF THE CUMBERLAND,
August 14, 1864.

Major-General SHERMAN:

I think it better to pursue Wheeler with our cavalry than to attempt another raid with it on the enemy's communications during Wheeler's absence; but Elliott will be over to see you.

GEO. H. THOMAS,
Major-General.

---

* See p. 501.

HDQRS. MILITARY DIVISION OF THE MISSISSIPPI,
In the Field, near Atlanta, August 14, 1864.

General THOMAS:

The telegraph has just announced the capture, by the rebel cavalry, of a drove of 1,000 cattle about Adairsville. Let General McCook have a determined pursuit and General Garrard a brigade ready to push across to and beyond Canton, to prevent the driving away of these cattle.

W. T. SHERMAN,
Major-General, Commanding.

HDQRS. MILITARY DIVISION OF THE MISSISSIPPI,
In the Field, near Atlanta, August 14, 1864.

General THOMAS:

We should either act offensively with our cavalry or so place it that it catch Wheeler on his return. Let General Elliott give orders that those cattle must be recovered at all hazards, and we will await further news as to the force Wheeler carried off with him; but Generals Garrard's and Kilpatrick's cavalry could operate in the absence of Wheeler from Decatur without risk.

W. T. SHERMAN,
Major-General, Commanding.

HEADQUARTERS DEPARTMENT OF THE CUMBERLAND,
August 14, 1864.

Major-General SHERMAN:

Your dispatch received and shown to Elliott. He will be over to see you. But do you think it prudent to risk any more cavalry on their communications until our force is materially increased?

GEO. H. THOMAS,
Major-General.

HDQRS. MILITARY DIVISION OF THE MISSISSIPPI,
In the Field, near Atlanta, August 14, 1864.

General THOMAS:

General Elliott is here. Inasmuch as we propose to throw the bulk of our army on the enemy's communications I will not risk our cavalry, but will get General Elliott to have General Kilpatrick make a bold reconnaissance toward Fairburn and engage any cavalry he meets to test its strength; General Schofield's cavalry to go with him.

W. T. SHERMAN,
Major-General, Commanding.

SHERMAN'S HEADQUARTERS,
August 14, 1864.

General STANLEY or General GARRARD:

GENERAL: What part of the parapets does Garrard's cavalry occupy?

W. T. SHERMAN,
Major-General.

STANLEY'S HEADQUARTERS, *August 14, 1864.*

General SHERMAN:

Garrard's cavalry occupies the reverse side of the old rebel works; they extend about half a mile from the Howard house.

D. S. STANLEY,
Major-General.

HEADQUARTERS FOURTH ARMY CORPS,
Near Atlanta, Ga., August 14, 1864—2.35 a. m.

Brigadier-General WHIPPLE, *Chief of Staff:*

General Kimball has just sent a dispatch to these headquarters stating that Colonel Kirby, in a note dated midnight, reports as follows:

My brigade officer of the day reports that by the aid of a fire in front of the enemy's works he saw five regiments passing to our left, and then the fire was put out. He also says he could hear loud cries from women and children, as if praying, &c. There is now quite a fire in the town.*

I will make preparations to meet every attack that may be made upon our left at daylight.

Very respectfully,

D. S. STANLEY,
Major-General.

STANLEY'S HEADQUARTERS, *August 14, 1864.*

Brig. Gen. W. D. WHIPPLE, *Assistant Adjutant-General:*

The moving of Garrard will render it impossible for me to hold the same picket-line on the left. I can, however, modify it, so as not to make much change.

D. S. STANLEY,
Major-General.

HEADQUARTERS FOURTH ARMY CORPS,
August 14, 1864—11 p. m.

Brigadier-General KIMBALL,
Commanding First Division, Fourth Army Corps:

All of Garrard's cavalry are to be drawn off. Relieve his pickets at daylight in the morning. You will have to reduce your pickets to the number necessary to keep up appearances.

D. S. STANLEY,
Major-General, Commanding.

HEADQUARTERS FOURTH ARMY CORPS,
August 14, 1864.

Brigadier-General KIMBALL:

Colonel Miller's brigade is ordered to be withdrawn to go in pursuit of rebel raiders who have captured a drove of 1,000 beef-cattle near Adairsville. You will be obliged to relieve his pickets as soon as it can be done, and in the morning Minty's pickets will take place upon your left.

D. S. STANLEY,
Major-General.

---

* For full text of this dispatch, see Kirby to Sinclair, p. 484.

STATION OBSERVATION,
At General Geary's Headquarters, August 14, 1864.

Capt. A. K. TAYLOR,
     Acting Signal Officer :

CAPTAIN: I have to report that the shells fired from the heavy guns, with but few exceptions, exploded in the city. The shells fired from a battery, I think on General Ward's line, exploded in front, above, and to rear of the enemy's works south and distant from station two miles and a half. The men in these works confined themselves closely all day to their bomb-proofs. In a direction 10 degrees west of south, and distant three miles and a half, the enemy were working on a fort all day. This evening heard rumbling in direction of the city as if the cars were running in. Considerable firing, both artillery and musketry, on right this evening.

     Very respectfully, your obedient servant,
         W. W. HOPKINS,
         Captain and Acting Signal Officer.

SHERMAN'S HEADQUARTERS,
August 14, 1864.

General McCOOK:

Cannot John E. Smith's infantry drive that brigade at Fairmount? I think that Steedman at Chattanooga will come out and meet Wheeler at or near Dalton. I have just ordered Garrard and Kilpatrick to take advantage of the absence of Wheeler to strike the enemy's flanks. Collect your men and be ready to catch detachments of Wheeler on their return.

         W. T. SHERMAN,
         Major-General.

CARTERSVILLE, GA., *August 14, 1864.*

Maj. Gen. W. T. SHERMAN:

I think there will be no difficulty in driving the brigade at Fairmount away, and that it was only left to cover the retreat of the party with cattle. They retreated toward Jasper, and the force I sent out this morning may intercept them there. I sent all I had, but still fear they are too weak. Colonel Faulkner had sent 250 men when he attacked them at Fairmount. I think Wheeler is after the tunnel.

         E. M. McCOOK,
         Brigadier-General.

CARTERSVILLE, *August 14, 1864.*

Major-General SHERMAN:

Colonel Faulkner has just returned from pursuit of the party that captured cattle. It was Hannon's brigade, four regiments, and two pieces artillery. Major Fidler drove in enemy's pickets at Fairmount. Colonel Faulkner telegraphs that his horses are exhausted, and that Wheeler with 6,000 men is on Oldtown road from Tilton to Dalton, and had demanded surrender of Dalton. Forces ought to be concentrated up there. The Second Brigade detachments still out. I have nothing to take the offensive with.

         E. M. McCOOK,
         Brigadier-General.

Hdqrs. Chief of Cavalry, Dept. of the Cumberland,
August 14, 1864.

Brig. Gen. E. M. McCook,
    Comdg. First Cavalry Division, Cartersville, Ga.:

Ascertain if possible the route which the rebels have taken. A brigade of cavalry is ready to move in any direction and cut off their retreat.

By order, &c.:

DAVID F. HOW,
Lieutenant and Acting Assistant Adjutant-General.

Hdqrs. Chief of Cavalry, Dept. of the Cumberland,
August 14, 1864.

Brig. Gen. E. M. McCook,
    Comdg. First Cavalry Division, Cartersville, Ga.:

You will make a determined pursuit after the rebel cavalry who captured the cattle above Adairsville. Take your whole force.

By order, &c.:

DAVID F. HOW,
Lieutenant and Acting Assistant Adjutant-General.

[August 14, 1864.—For McCook to How, reporting Wheeler's raid, &c., see Part II, p. 765.]

Hdqrs. Chief of Cavalry, Dept. of the Cumberland,
August 14, 1864.

Brig. Gen. J. Kilpatrick,
    Commanding Third Cavalry Division:

The general commanding directs that you cross the Chattahoochee, fortify the position at the bridge, and scout and clear the country of rebels to Camp Creek. Your train will be kept near the railroad bridge until your position on the south side is securely established.

I am, general, very respectfully, your obedient servant,

DAVID F. HOW,
Lieutenant and Acting Assistant Adjutant-General.

Hdqrs. Chief of Cavalry, Dept. of the Cumberland,
August 14, 1864.

General Kilpatrick:

You will make a bold reconnaissance in the direction of Fairburn to railroad if you can reach it. It is reported that Wheeler with 6,000 cavalry and artillery has gone north. If true, you will have only Jackson's cavalry to contend with. If the opportunity offers try to break him up. General Schofield's small force of cavalry will be ordered to co-operate with you. It is on the south side of Utoy Creek, and will report to you at Sandtown to-morrow.

W. L. ELLIOTT,
Brigadier-General and Chief of Cavalry.

HDQRS. CHIEF OF CAVALRY, DEPT. OF THE CUMBERLAND,
                                        August 14, 1864.

General GARRARD, *General Stanley's Headquarters:*

You will with your entire cavalry force to-morrow early, and by easy marches, test the strength of the enemy's cavalry on our left flank without risking too much. Give him a hard fight if the opportunity offers. There is no doubt that Wheeler is about Dalton with a large force, variously reported at from 3,000 to 6,000. If the opportunity offers to reach the Macon road without too much risk, don't fail to avail yourself of it.

                                        W. L. ELLIOTT,
                            Brigadier-General and Chief of Cavalry.

Statement of J. B. Jordan, Captain Company G, Thirty-sixth Alabama Infantry, C. S. Army.

HEADQUARTERS DEPARTMENT OF THE CUMBERLAND,
                    OFFICE PROVOST-MARSHAL-GENERAL,
                        Near Atlanta, Ga., August 14, 1864.

Captain Jordan says he came into our lines of his own accord yesterday evening. His regiment belongs to Holtzclaw's brigade, Clayton's division, of Lee's corps, numbers about 250 men, and is the strongest regiment in the brigade. Says their division is about 2,500 strong, is in front of the Fourteenth Corps, the left resting on the Sandtown road and the right a little to the left, in front of General R. W. Johnson's headquarters. Brigadier-Generals Stovall, Baker, Holtzclaw, and Gibson are the brigade commanders and are in position from right to left in the order named. Holtzclaw and Baker have Alabama troops; Gibson has Louisiana troops, and his is counted the best fighting brigade in the corps; Stovall has Georgia troops, and his men are very much demoralized, won't fight, and are constantly deserting. Clayton's division is on the left of the corps (Lee's). Hindman's division, now commanded by General Brown, of Tennessee, is in the center, and Stevenson's is on the right. Thinks their division, Clayton's, is fully as strong as either of the others. All the regiments of their corps are very much extended, in many places the line being one rank and the men three feet apart. Gibson's brigade, the left flank of their division, is one rank, with no reserves, and covers at least half a mile. Has not been to the left of their army and can give no particulars about position of troops there, except that Hardee's corps (except Cheatham's division) is on the left of Lee's, and holds the left flank of the army; thinks the extreme left is near the river. Stewart's corps is on Lee's right; says Stewart's divisions are much stronger than theirs; when he first came to them at Resaca some of his regiments numbered 1,500 men; thinks the right of Stewart's corps is about half a mile from the Augusta railroad. The militia are on Stewart's right, and are about 5,000 or 6,000 strong. Cheatham's division, of Hardee's corps, holds the right flank of the army and pickets the front of the militia; thinks Cheatham's division is about 3,000 strong. Does not know of any reserves in rear of the line at any point, and is pretty confident that there are none. No re-enforcements have been received except militia and men from convalescent camps and hospitals; says a large number of men have been added to the army from these sources; thinks the aggregate number since Hood has been in command, including cooks, teamsters, and other detailed men, will reach 15,000 men. His own company, Jordan's, numbered 14 men at Kenesaw, and yesterday mustered 34 guns; has received 12 men since the fight on the 22d. All he can say about the cavalry is that it is on the flanks; says Wheeler's command numbers 25,000 men; has not heard of any raid contemplated by him. The whole army is said to be 75,000 men. With regard to its morale Captain Jordan says it is greatly demoralized, both officers and men feel that they are whipped. The officers will not acknowledge it, but the men feel that there is no longer any chance of success, and, although they will fight desperately if attacked in their works, they would refuse to make a general charge; says he is confident that if the men could be made to know how they would be treated after coming over the majority of Hood's soldiers would desert him, and that if the practice of the picket-lines agreeing to a truce for a few hours at a time was encouraged a great many men would desert them every day. Their men have great confidence in the honor of our soldiers, and a proposition to cease firing is at once accepted. It was during one of these armistices along the picket-lines that he questioned our pickets as to the kind of treatment he would receive in case he deserted, and was told he would be sent North. Their men are taught to believe that the Government would force them into the army as soon as they came over; says he has been looking for an opportunity to desert during the whole campaign and improved the first opportunity after being assured that he would be sent North and allowed to stay there. Since the 20th of July only about one-quarter rations have been issued. There are no supplies of any kind in Atlanta. They are shipped from below as they are needed by the troops, two or three days' supply being issued at a time. The ration consists of bacon and corn bread and occasionally beef; has often seen his men eat a day's supply at a meal and then not be satisfied. Officers draw rations with their men. The supply of ammunition is very small; men are ordered not to fire when upon picket duty or when acting as sharp-shooters unless sure of their mark, and whenever an assault is ordered or an attack expected an order is issued cautioning the men to be saving of the cartridges. Our artillery is often not replied to because of the scarcity of ammunition. One-third of the men in the trenches are kept up all night, and at 3 o'clock the whole force is ordered under arms until daylight.

Captain Jordan describes the breast-works as being very strong, and protected by abatis constructed with great care and extending along the whole line; thinks the weakest part of the line is that portion held by the militia. The works there are the same, and were constructed by old troops, but the militia will not stand; does not know what damage was done to the railroad by Stoneman, but learned that all bridges south of Macon for a distance of thirty miles were burned, together with some engines and cars at or near Griswold Station; states that one of his men who was sick at Montgomery came over the Atlanta and West Point Railroad, and that about three miles at each end of the break was repaired. Parties were employed repairing the road at each end of the break. Has not heard anything in regard to the Augusta railroad, whether it is being repaired or not. States that supplies are scattered from Atlanta to Macon, no great quantity at any one point.

[Indorsement.]

HDQRS. DEPARTMENT OF THE CUMBERLAND,
OFFICE PROVOST-MARSHAL-GENERAL,
Near Atlanta, Ga., August 14, 1864.

Respectfully submitted for the information of the general commanding.

ED. C. DENIG,
Assistant Adjutant-General.

Statement of William McNabb (citizen).

OFFICE PROVOST-MARSHAL-GENERAL,
DEPARTMENT OF THE CUMBERLAND,
Near Atlanta, Ga., August 14, 1864.

Says he is a citizen of Dalton, Ga.; has been in the employ of the Confederate Government on the Western and Atlantic Railroad for three years; has been at Griswold Station with rolling-stock of the road. Came through Atlanta and Decatur day before yesterday. States that on the Central road General Stoneman burned all the bridges, trestles, depot buildings and Government store-houses between Macon and McIntire Station, a distance of sixty miles; did not disturb the track. A large lot of quartermaster's stores, which had been sent from Griswold to Gordon Station, were burned at that station, together with 4 trains, 4 engines, and about 50 cars, which were standing on the side track at Gordon and Griswold. The first trestle south of Macon has been rebuilt and others are being framed at Millen Station, ten miles from Macon. Does not know whether the Atlanta and West Point Road is being repaired or not. Says he was in Augusta last Sunday, August 7. A bridge is being framed at Augusta to replace the one destroyed over the Alcova River. Saw workmen clearing off the timber and apparently getting ready to rebuild the bridge destroyed across the Yellow River. Learned from railroad men and workmen at Alcova Station that the road would be repaired as far as Covington. Did not see or hear of any bridge being built over Yellow River. Says they were looking for another raid. Understood that about 2,000 of Wheeler's command started from Covington last week on a raid in our rear; was told this by citizens near Jonesborough.

[L. dorsement.]

OFFICE PROVOST-MARSHAL-GENERAL,
DEPARTMENT OF THE CUMBERLAND,
Near Atlanta, Ga., August 14, 1864.

Respectfully forwarded for the information of the general commanding.

ED. C. DENIG,
Captain and Assistant Adjutant-General.

HDQRS. MILITARY DIVISION OF THE MISSISSIPPI,
In the Field, near Atlanta, Ga., August 14, 1864.
(Received 2.45 p. m.)

General SCHOFIELD:

Send an aide to the Campbellton road where we were the other evening, and report to me to-night if the enemy have erected a battery at the point where we saw them at work. Also any other appearances on that flank indicative of an accumulation of troops there. I would also like to have a rough sketch of the lay of the ground and roads from your old headquarters, to what we term Utoy Post-Office, and the point to which General Cox extended his reconnaissance.

W. T. SHERMAN,
Major-General, Commanding.

SCHOFIELD'S HEADQUARTERS,
August 14, 1864.

Major-General SHERMAN:

I will send an officer at once to ascertain about the battery and troops on the enemy's left. I will also have the sketch you desire made as soon as possible.

J. M. SCHOFIELD,
Major-General.

HEADQUARTERS ARMY OF THE OHIO,
Near Atlanta, Ga., August 14, 1864.

Major-General SHERMAN:

The officer I sent to the right reports three strong batteries along the edge of the woods near East Point, all looking down the valley toward Hascall's position. The one most to our right is where you saw the enemy working day before yesterday. The others are visible from a point on the Campbellton road, a few hundred yards west of where you were. The batteries are connected by infantry parapets, which, however, are not visible south or west of the left battery. Probably the line there bends southeast through the woods. A large force is working on each battery; but very few men are seen elsewhere. There has been no indication of movement of troops there to-day.

J. M. SCHOFIELD,
Major-General.

SCHOFIELD'S HEADQUARTERS,
August 14, 1864.

Major-General SHERMAN:

Captain Twining has sent Captain Poe a map of all the surveys we have been able to make up to-day. To-morrow I will have it improved and extended as far as possible, and also get what information I can from citizens.

J. M. SCHOFIELD,
Major-General.

HDQRS. MILITARY DIVISION OF THE MISSISSIPPI,
In the Field, near Atlanta, August 14, 1864.
(Received 8.45 p. m.)

General SCHOFIELD:

There is no doubt Wheeler is up about Dalton with a large cavalry force. I want our cavalry now to feel the enemy's flanks strong, and will order General Kilpatrick to cross at Sandtown and make a bold push for Fairburn, and General Garrard in like manner to feel well round the enemy's right flank. Let your cavalry go down in the morning to Sandtown and report for the expedition to General Kilpatrick.

W. T. SHERMAN,
Major-General, Commanding.

SCHOFIELD'S HEADQUARTERS,
August 14, 1864.

Major-General SHERMAN:

Your dispatch is received, and I will order Colonel Garrard to move accordingly early in the morning and report to General Kilpatrick at Sandtown.

J. M. SCHOFIELD,
Major-General.

HEADQUARTERS ARMY OF THE OHIO,
In the Field, August 14, 1864.

Maj. Gen. W. T. SHERMAN,
Commanding Military Division of the Mississippi:

GENERAL: In accordance with the desire expressed by you yesterday to General Thomas, General Howard, and myself, I have the honor to submit the following plan of operations, having for its object to compel the enemy to abandon his works about Atlanta and give battle on equal terms or retreat below East Point. The plan which suggests itself to me is but a modification and extension of the one followed up to this time. The proposed modification to consist of a more rapid, continuous, and systematic transfer of corps from left to right, and a temporary abandonment of our base. The transfer may be made by one corps, or, probably better, two corps at a time; the movement to be repeated daily until the object shall be gained. One corps should at all times be kept in reserve upon the right to meet an attack, this corps going into position the moment the next one arrives to take its place as reserve. Or, if the movement be made two corps at a time, the reserve corps of the preceding day and one of the newly arrived corps can go into position each day. It is my opinion that this movement can be made so rapidly as to reach and control the Macon railroad in from three to five days, after which the road can be so thoroughly destroyed as to be no longer available to the enemy. The same would, of course, be true of the West Point road. If, contrary to my belief, the enemy should prolong his lines so rapidly as to prevent our reaching the Macon road by simple extension of our line, he will at least be drawn far away from Atlanta, and his lines so rapidly constructed will often run through open fields where abatis cannot be constructed in so short a time. There will then be two alternatives left us: one to break the imperfect lines near the enemy's left flank, and the other to draw one or two corps from our left, as if to continue the movement to the right and send them rapidly by a short circuit to the left and seize Atlanta, or some more convenient point of the enemy's abandoned lines. The enemy must keep all of his small veteran force concentrated upon his left to prevent our success in the first movement, in which case the latter will be entirely practicable. My conviction of the feasibility of this plan is the result of continued observation and experience during almost the entire campaign. There has, I believe, been no time when if our movements from one flank to the other had been followed up as rapidly as the troops could have been transferred and got into position success would not have been speedy and certain.

To carry out this plan the troops along the road below Etowah should be concentrated at Marietta or other point to guard such stores as are not carried with the troops, and other points of the railroad abandoned. The movement can be commenced with supplies enough for twenty

days. If the enemy detach force enough to capture Marietta we cannot fail to turn his flank and destroy his army and still have on hand
ten days' supplies. The crossing at Sandtown can be controlled with
the left of the army resting on lower Utoy (our present right), and I
think the plan cannot require any farther movement to the right. The
enemy will hardly venture to send infantry across the Chattahoochee
while we have possession of Sandtown. Our trains between Utoy and
Camp Creek will be quite secure, and need be no incumbrance in this
movement. In a rapid prolongation of our lines we have great advantage over the enemy in this: All our troops are veterans, while, probably, more than half of his are militia. He must concentrate his veterans to meet each movement, and then after he has intrenched his
extended line his veterans must be relieved by militia and prepared to
meet the next movement. On this account it would probably be best
to move two corps at a time, as it would require all of the enemy's available veterans to meet this force. It is hardly possible that the enemy
can endure three such battles, as he can thus be compelled to fight
in as many consecutive days.

In case this plan should be adopted, even in its main features, I
would suggest that in the first movement General Thomas put his two
corps in on the right of the Fourteenth, leaving mine in reserve, as it
virtually is now, and let me make the next move on his right, or even
on the right of General Howard, if that be preferred. This will bring
General Thomas' three corps together and allow mine to take a more
hazardous part (if not more important one) in a movement which I
recommend.

I would also suggest as a matter of detail what I consider an improve-
ment upon the prevalent mode of making such movements, viz, that instead of gradually unfolding from the flank of the corps already in position,
the corps moving in detach itself a mile or so from the flank and march
in strong order of battle directly upon the point to be gained. In the
comparatively open country to our present right this method will be
entirely practicable and much more rapid and decisive than the prevalent method. I feel confident that this plan ought to succeed, and its
hazards appear less to me than any other that promises success. Yet
I suggest it with diffidence, and do not feel at all sure that it is as good
a plan as that suggested by you yesterday, though the latter seems
very difficult of execution. I am carefully considering the details of
movement involved in your plan, and will give you my views as soon
as possible. Meanwhile I am preparing the position I now occupy as
a pivot on which the first portion of that movement can be made.

I have the honor to be, very respectfully, your obedient servant,
                                        J. M. SCHOFIELD,
                                                  Major-General.

                    ————

HEADQUARTERS ARMY OF THE OHIO,
                    Near Atlanta, Ga., August 14, 1864.
Col. ISRAEL GARRARD,
        Commanding Cavalry Division, Army of the Ohio:
COLONEL: General Sherman is informed that a large body of the
enemy's cavalry is now north of the Chattahoochee, making a raid
upon our rear, and he desires to take advantage of their absence to
operate on the enemy's flanks. General Kilpatrick will cross the river
at Sandtown to-morrow, and operate on the enemy's left, while Gen-

eral Garrard will operate upon the enemy's right. You will please move close to Sandtown early to-morrow with your command, aid General Kilpatrick in crossing the river, and report to him for duty during the expedition. Until General Kilpatrick gets across the river, try to scout all the roads from the river to the right of our infantry. General Kilpatrick will have instructions from General Sherman for further operations.

Very respectfully, your obedient servant,

J. M. SCHOFIELD,
Major-General, Commanding.

HEADQUARTERS ARMY OF THE OHIO,
Near Atlanta, Ga., August 14, 1864—11 a. m.

Brig. Gen. M. S. HASCALL,
Commanding Second Division, Twenty-third Army Corps :

GENERAL: The commanding general desires you to push out your skirmish line so far as to cover the Campbellton road for half a mile to the right of your present position.

Very respectfully, your obedient servant,

J. A. CAMPBELL,
Major and Assistant Adjutant-General.

HDQRS. MILITARY DIVISION OF THE MISSISSIPPI,
In the Field, near Atlanta, August 14, 1864.

General McARTHUR:

General Garrard will scout with his cavalry up Chattahoochee as far as Roswell and McAfee's. If small parties of cavalry approach Marietta, you should ambuscade them with infantry. It has a better effect than to run them down by cavalry.

W. T. SHERMAN,
Major-General, Commanding.

HDQRS. SECOND DIVISION, FIFTEENTH ARMY CORPS,
Near Atlanta, Ga., August 14, 1864.

Lieut. Col. R. R. TOWNES,
Assistant Adjutant-General, Fifteenth Army Corps :

I have the honor to report nothing unusual in my front to-day. The usual amount of picket-firing was kept up, with some artillery, doing but little damage, as shown by the list of casualties. On last night I straightened and intrenched the skirmish line on my right, upon the ground gained by the advance of yesterday, which, to a certain extent, relieved that portion of my line from exposure to the enemy's sharpshooters.

Very respectfully, your obedient servant,

J. A. J. LIGHTBURN,
Brigadier-General of Volunteers.

HEADQUARTERS SIGNAL DETACHMENT,
Before Atlanta, Ga., August 14, 1864.

Maj. Gen. JOHN A. LOGAN,
Commanding Fifteenth Army Corps:

SIR: I have the honor to submit the following as my report for to-day: Lieutenant Fish, one of my officers, went to observation station early in the morning and reports as follows: I found everything as before, with one exception, viz, a casemated fort for two guns is being erected at the right (enemy's right) and in rear of six-gun fort. Three trains of cars arrived at Atlanta during the day: No. 1, of four platform and two box-cars, used as a construction train; No. 2, of four passenger and five freight cars; No. 3, of fifteen freight cars, doors closed; could not see with what loaded, or whether loaded or not. Train ran slow; engine appeared to be working hard.

I have the honor to be, sir, your most obedient servant,

SAMUEL EDGE,
First Lieutenant and Chief Acting Signal Officer.

HDQRS. THIRD DIVISION, FIFTEENTH ARMY CORPS,
Cartersville, August 14, 1864.

Major-General SHERMAN:

A drove of cattle was this a. m. captured together with escort. Have sent out all available cavalry and 300 infantry. Commanding officer at Adairsville telegraphs 6 p. m.—

That a captured prisoner reports the force to consist of 6,000 men under General Wheeler, with ten pieces of artillery, and that the party capturing the cattle were 2,000 strong, with two pieces artillery, and that their main force is pushing still farther north.

I cannot get any reliable information, but do not think there is more than 1,000 or 1,500. I understand further that the telegraph operators at Resaca and Calhoun heard a message from a colonel at Dalton to General Steedman, stating that the rebels had demanded the surrender of that place.

JNO. E. SMITH,
Brigadier-General.

(Copy forwarded by General Sherman to Generals Thomas, Howard, and Schofield.)

HDQRS. MILITARY DIVISION OF THE MISSISSIPPI,
In the Field, near Atlanta, August 14, 1864.

General J. E. SMITH:

If Wheeler has passed north, look well to the security of the Etowah bridge and Allatoona. Have as strong a force collected as possible, and watch to catch parties on their return. General Steedman has force enough. In an emergency like this, you can call on the force at Rome, which is not on the main line, and therefore not essential.

W. T. SHERMAN,
Major-General, Commanding.

HdQRS. MILITARY DIVISION OF THE MISSISSIPPI,
            In the Field, near Atlanta, August 14, 1864.

General J. E. SMITH,
        Cartersville:

I have sent a brigade of General Garrard's cavalry over toward Canton to intercept those cattle. Tell General McCook it is important that party represented as 200 strong that has been on the road should be hunted down, else you will have no peace on the road.

                                W. T. SHERMAN,
                                Major-General, Commanding.

HdQRS. MILITARY DIVISION OF THE MISSISSIPPI,
            In the Field, near Atlanta, August 14, 1864.

General J. E. SMITH.
        Allatoona:

Use all the infantry you can spare in connection with cavalry, and interpose so as to prevent the escape up the valley of the Etowah of the party who captured the drove of cattle at Adairsville.

                                W. T. SHERMAN,
                                Major-General, Commanding.

                                CARTERSVILLE, *August 14, 1864.*

Major-General SHERMAN:

Two hundred and fifty cavalry left at daylight this a. m. for Jasper, by way of Pine Log; 100 more follow at 1 p. m. and 200 by way of Canton to Long Swamp Valley. Will send infantry to Hightower.

                                JNO. E. SMITH,
                                Brigadier-General.

HdQRS. MILITARY DIVISION OF THE MISSISSIPPI,
            In the Field, near Atlanta, August 14, 1864—10.30 p. m.

General JOHN E. SMITH:

The general commanding directs that you collect as strong an infantry force as possible from Rome and other points at the most favorable place to strike Wheeler on his return; and also to obstruct the passes and crossings of the river, and arrange for giving him ambush reception. Obstruct the roads in order to catch his artillery if possible.

                                L. M. DAYTON,
                                Aide-de-Camp.

HdQRS. MILITARY DIVISION OF THE MISSISSIPPI,
            In the Field, near Atlanta, August 14, 1864.

General VANDEVER,
        Rome:

You know our navy is in Mobile Bay, and have captured the rebel gun-boats, and I think they can take Mobile. Also General A. J. Smith is moving on Columbus, Miss., and farther this way. Now is the time for your Alabama cavalry to move straight down along the Coosa to gather horses and recruits. They should be very kind to the poor farmers and people, but give the guerrillas and Clanton's men all the fighting they want. I don't care about their running too much risk; but by moving by moonlight and laying by of days, they can create a good diversion. Infantry should also move occasionally down the valley.

> W. T. SHERMAN,
> *Major-General, Commanding.*

HDQRS. MILITARY DIVISION OF THE MISSISSIPPI,
In the Field, near Atlanta, Ga., August 14, 1864.

General VANDEVER,
> *Rome:*

Don't send off that cavalry or recall it till we know more about the force which is on our road above Resaca.

> W. T. SHERMAN,
> *Major-General, Commanding.*

MARIETTA, *August 14, 1864.*

Major-General SHERMAN:

All quiet here to-day. Cannot hear of the enemy being near. The troops are well in hand and prepared to strike.

> J. McARTHUR,
> *Brigadier-General.*

RESACA, *August 14, 1864—7.30 p. m.*

Major-General SHERMAN:

The enemy, reported to be under Wheeler, commenced passing Old-town, eighteen miles east, going north, at daylight. They passed during the day until 1 p. m. with wagon train. My scouts think they numbered at least 3,000. A force of 700 is now at Fairmount, being part of the force which captured Captain Thornton and drove. Colonel Faulkner with 250 cavalry skirmished with them, and returned to Calhoun this evening. The enemy is moving upon Tilton. I will have over 300 men there and a block-house. Dalton is threatened. I have 700 men there and four guns. There is a brigade of cavalry at Calhoun under Colonel Faulkner, besides half a regiment of infantry. I have half a regiment of infantry at Adairsville and two regiments at Kingston.

> G. B. RAUM,
> *Colonel, Commanding Brigade.*

RESACA, *August 14, 1864—11 p. m.*

General SHERMAN:

An orderly just arrived from Tilton. All safe there. Dalton has been attacked and reported captured. No trains burnt. My patrols from Tilton north found all right. The commanding officer at Tilton is sanguine of saving the bridge.

> G. B. RAUM,
> *Colonel, Commanding Brigade.*

MARIETTA, *August 14, 1864.*

General SHERMAN:

We have four trains at Kingston and two at Marietta. They will be ready to move north at 2.30 a. m. Will it be safe, and shall I send them on to Chattanooga?

Very respectfully,

J. B. VAN DYNE,
Master Railroad Transportation.

AUGUST 14, 1864.

General SMITH,
  Cartersville, Ga.:

Colonel Faulkner reports enemy with artillery four miles south Calhoun; he does not report his strength. Have you not mounted force enough to get in their rear with safety to your command?

JAS. B. STEEDMAN,
Major-General.

HEADQUARTERS,
Cleveland, August 14, 1864.

General STEEDMAN:

Captain Crowell, commanding company at Varnell's Station, sends a dispatch that 2,000 rebels are attacking Dalton. The artillery is distinctly heard by him. He wishes artillery sent to him. If no artillery can be sent, he wants a company of infantry. What shall I do?

H. G. GIBSON,
Second Ohio Heavy Artillery.

[AUGUST 14, 1864.—For correspondence between Wheeler and Laiboldt, relating to the surrender of Union forces at Dalton, see Part I, p. 324.]

DALTON, *August 14, 1864.*

Major-General STEEDMAN:

Wheeler has demanded surrender of this post. Send re-enforcements.

B. LAIBOLDT,
Colonel, Commanding.

CALHOUN, *August 14, 1864.*

Maj. Gen. JAMES B. STEEDMAN,
  Commanding, Chattanooga:

There are of General McCook's division at this place 300 mounted and 234 dismounted men available. The enemy has attacked a guard with large lot of cattle, four miles below here. He is using two pieces of artillery. I have sent all my effective mounted force to the relief of the guard, and to ascertain the force of the enemy.

J. K. FAULKNER,
Colonel, Commanding.

SPECIAL FIELD ORDERS, }   HDQRS. MIL. DIV. OF THE MISS.,
     No. 55.   }   *In Field, near Atlanta, August 14, 1864.*

   I. Brig. Gen. W. B. Hazen, U. S. Volunteers, with the consent of his present commanding officers, is hereby transferred from the Department of the Cumberland to the Department of the Tennessee, and will report in person to Maj. Gen. O. O. Howard, commanding, that he may be assigned to the command of a division according to his rank.

        *   *   *   *   *   *   *

   By order of Maj. Gen. W. T. Sherman:
                                L. M. DAYTON,
                                       Aide-de-Camp.

                                EXECUTIVE MANSION,
                Washington, D. C., August 15, 1864—11 a. m.
Major-General SHERMAN,
     Near Atlanta, Ga.:

   If the Government should purchase on its own account cotton northward of you, and on the line of your communications, would it be an inconvenience to you or detriment to the military service for it to come to the North on the railroad?

                                      A. LINCOLN.

     HDQRS. MILITARY DIVISION OF THE MISSISSIPPI,
        In the Field, near Atlanta, August 15, 1864.
                        (Received 8.45 a. m.)
General THOMAS:

   Colonel Raum, at Resaca, reports the enemy's cavalry on the railroad near Tilton tearing up track. Give orders that will insure great economy in provisions and forage until we can estimate the time required to repair damages. I have nothing from beyond Resaca. General John E. Smith, at Cartersville, will collect all the infantry that can be spared from the defense of material points about Allatoona and go up the road.
                          W. T. SHERMAN,
                        Major-General, Commanding.

(Same to Generals Schofield and Howard.)

                     SHERMAN'S HEADQUARTERS,
            August 15, 1864.   (Received 9.45 a. m.)
General THOMAS:

   The following dispatch just received:

                     RESACA, *August 15, 1864—9 a. m.*
General SHERMAN:

   Dalton is invested, the enemy using artillery. A bridge near that place is burnt; one mile of track south of Tilton burnt at 3 a. m. Bridge all right. The enemy retreated before the arrival of my troops.
                           G. B. RAUM,
                     Colonel, Commanding Brigade.
                         W. T. SHERMAN,
                            Major-General.

(Same to Generals Schofield and Howard.)

HDQRS. MILITARY DIVISION OF THE MISSISSIPPI,
In the Field, near Atlanta, August 15, 1864.

General THOMAS:

What is the substance of the report that the rebel cavalry were near Vining's Station? I have nothing further from Dalton or thereabouts.

W. T. SHERMAN,
Major-General, Commanding.

THOMAS' HEADQUARTERS,
August 15, 1864.

Major-General SHERMAN:

When at your headquarters I ordered out a force to ascertain the truth of the report about the rebel cavalry. Have not yet heard from them, but will report as soon as I receive any reliable information.

GEO. H. THOMAS,
Major-General.

THOMAS' HEADQUARTERS,
August 15, 1864.

Major-General SHERMAN:

I sent to Vining's to see what preparations had been made to receive the 500 cavalry reported approaching that place. I have just learned that everything was in readiness, but that nobody but the courier who came to the telegraph office had seen or heard anything of the rebels Two trains came down from Marietta whilst Whipple was at Vining's.

GEO. H. THOMAS,
Major-General.

SHERMAN'S HEADQUARTERS,
August 15, 1864. (Received 5.05 p. m.)

General THOMAS:

The following just received and given for information:

RESACA, *August 15, 1864—p. m.*

All quiet at Tilton. Citizens coming into that place report that re-enforcements reached Dalton during the night, and that the firing this morning was northeast of that place and was gradually decreased in sound. About half a mile of railroad and a bridge were destroyed near Dalton. I will receive more definite information soon.

G. B. RAUM,
Colonel, Commanding Brigade.

L. M. DAYTON,
Aide-de-Camp.

(Same to Generals Howard and Schofield.)

HDQRS. MILITARY DIVISION OF THE MISSISSIPPI,
In the Field, near Atlanta, Ga., August 15, 1864.
(Received 7.55 p. m.)

General THOMAS:

General John E. Smith has gone up the road with 2,000 men in cars. Wheeler failed to take Dalton, and has gone northeast, where he cannot do us much harm. I will order that he be kept in that direction. He may disturb some of General Schofield's garrisons; but if he could not take Tilton or Dalton, he will not venture much, and all above will be on their guard and prepared. As soon as this news is confirmed and ratified, I will put in execution our plans. So get ready. I want to hear of Generals Kilpatrick's and Garrard's expeditions before making orders.

W. T. SHERMAN,
Major-General, Commanding.

(Same to Generals Schofield and Howard.)

SHERMAN'S HEADQUARTERS,
August 15, 1864.

General THOMAS:

Following received from Colonel Raum, at Resaca:

I can now give you particulars of the Dalton affair. The town was sieged about 6 p. m. yesterday. Colonel Laiboldt occupied the fort and declined to surrender. Early this morning General Steedman arrived there with one New York and one Ohio regiment and six companies of negro troops, and immediately attacked the enemy, and after four hours' fighting drove them toward Spring Place. The enemy's loss heavy. We are collecting the dead and wounded. Colonel Laiboldt expects another attack. The enemy supposed to be 6,000 strong, with two batteries. I had two companies at the water-tank, one mile and three-quarters south of Dalton. They were attacked at daylight this morning, and after four hours' fighting surrendered. The railroad is destroyed from the tank north to Dalton. The enemy still in the neighborhood of Tilton. General Smith, with 2,000 men, is due here at 11 o'clock. The cavalry at Calhoun, I think, should be ordered to this place to-night.

G. B. RAUM,
Colonel, Commanding Brigade.

W. T. SHERMAN,
Major-General.

HEADQUARTERS DEPARTMENT OF THE CUMBERLAND,
Before Atlanta, Ga., August 15, 1864.

Maj. Gen. W. T. SHERMAN,
Commanding Military Division of the Mississippi:

GENERAL: I have the honor to submit the following plan for the withdrawal of my troops from the left, and concentrating them on the right, and at the same time place the Twentieth Corps in the fortifications at the railroad bridge.

First. Have all the wagons that are to be taken with the troops moved over to the right, and parked in some secure position. Then, early in the evening, about 8 o'clock, move General Stanley's entire force from the intrenchments, and mass them on advantageous ground somewhere about the Meyer house. This will enable General Stanley to cover the retirement of the Twentieth Corps, which should be able to commence its movement by 12 o'clock at night. About 2 a. m. both General Stanley's and General Williams' pickets might be withdrawn, General Stanley's pickets taking post in front of his line, near the Meyer house, and General Williams' pickets covering his march to the river. General Garrard's cavalry should preserve its position on the extreme left, and look out for the flank during the movement of the two corps, commencing to fall back when General Stanley's pickets move, and so conduct his movement as to place his troops between General Williams' skirmishers and the enemy if General Williams is pursued. General Garrard should maintain his position until General Williams has reached his position at the bridge and adjusted his troops.

Second. General Williams having adjusted his troops to cover the railroad bridge, General Garrard should move by the right and place himself on the right and rear of General Howard to protect his flank. After General Williams has passed toward the river General Stanley could continue his march and go into camp behind and near the extreme right. If possible General Stanley should reach the position on the extreme right the first day, as it would enable his troops to have the whole of the second day to rest.

Third. In continuance of the movements for the concentration of the army, the second day General Howard could move from his position on the left of the Fourteenth Corps, and place his troops on the extreme right as you design, and the Fourteenth Corps shift its position from the left to the right of General Schofield's corps, and in front of the Fourth Corps or on its right flank. This will place the troops in position in the order in which you designed moving them, with General Garrard's cavalry on the left flank.

I am, general, very respectfully, your obedient servant,
GEO. H. THOMAS,
Major-General, U. S. Volunteers, Commanding.

HDQRS. MILITARY DIVISION OF THE MISSISSIPPI,
In the Field, near Atlanta, August 15, 1864.
General THOMAS:

Your written communication is received and read. As soon as we know the extent of Wheeler's operations I will make my specific orders. I have Generals Howard's and Schofield's papers also. Go on and make all possible preparations preliminary to the move.
W. T. SHERMAN,
Major-General, Commanding.

CALHOUN, *August 15, 1864—10.40 p. m.*
General W. T. SHERMAN:

Colonel Faulkner's scouts report the enemy have crossed to north side of Coosawattee. They have gone from Dalton northeast.
E. M. McCOOK,
Brigadier-General.

SHERMAN'S HEADQUARTERS,
August 15, 1864.
General McCOOK:

In the absence of General Smith, take command of all forces in Allatoona, and be sure to protect the rations deposited there. Can't you hear of those cattle? Until Wheeler is disposed of, everything of value should be collected in Allatoona.
W. T. SHERMAN,
Major-General.

HDQRS. CHIEF OF CAVALRY, DEPT. OF THE CUMBERLAND,
August 15, 1864.

General W. D. WHIPPLE:

GENERAL: General Garrard was with me until 12 or 1 a. m., after receipt of the orders from General Sherman. He got provisions yesterday, but will not have forage until 12 m. to-day. He says he knows the strength of the enemy's cavalry on our left—a brigade or division behind breast-works, and with their horses in rear. That he sends scouts, a company or more, to Decatur, and even below it. The pickets of the enemy and reserves fall back to main line. That Colonel Long, with brigade and two pieces of artillery, went beyond Decatur, and could not draw rebel cavalry from support of their infantry. He thinks that one brigade will obtain as much information as a division. That if the object is to attack the remaining cavalry he should go toward Covington, where it is said they have their broken-down horses. If the object is to break the Macon road, with his knowledge of the country and roads, he would avoid the flank of the enemy near Atlanta and strike the road quickly. He represents the country as affording nothing for man or horse. Would not our trains be in danger if Garrard's entire division should go, with brigade or division of rebel cavalry in front of our left? I told General G[arrard] I would represent the case to General Thomas at an early hour and let him know.

Respectfully, your obedient servant,

W. L. ELLIOTT,
Brigadier-General, &c.

HDQRS. CHIEF OF CAVALRY, DEPT. OF THE CUMBERLAND,
August 15, 1864.

General GARRARD:

Have presented your statement to General Thomas; he says he cannot give you more definite orders—to use your discretion. I say, if the enemy won't come out and fight you you can't make him, but can drive him to his works. If, in connection with your reconnaissance, you think you cannot strike the railroad, I would not attempt it. Such is my understanding of General Sherman's orders.

W. L. ELLIOTT,
Brigadier-General, Chief of Cavalry.

HDQRS. CHIEF OF CAVALRY, DEPT. OF THE CUMBERLAND,
August 15, 1864.

General GARRARD, or
COMMANDING OFFICER SECOND CAVALRY DIVISION,
General Stanley's Headquarters:

Five hundred rebel cavalry are reported moving on Vining's Station. Send a cavalry force there immediately, without regard to other orders.

W. L. ELLIOTT,
Brig. Gen., U. S. Vols., Chief of Cav., Dept. of the Cumberland.

HDQRS. CHIEF OF CAVALRY, DEPT. OF THE CUMBERLAND,
                    Near Atlanta, Ga., August 15, 1864.
Capt. R. P. KENNEDY,
      Assistant Adjutant-General, General Garrard's Headquarters:

If the force ordered to Vining's Station, via Pace's Ferry, in pursuit of 500 rebel cavalry reported to be marching on Vining's, has not started or is not available, send courier to General Garrard with this communication. The pursuit of rebels above referred to is to take precedence of all other orders.

                              W. L. ELLIOTT,
      Brig. Gen., U. S. Vols., Chief of Cav., Dept. of the Cumberland.

HDQRS. CHIEF OF CAVALRY, DEPT. OF THE CUMBERLAND,
                    Near Atlanta, August 15, 1864.
Lieut. WILLIAM B. RIPPETOE,
      Eighteenth Indiana Battery:

The general commanding directs me to inform you that there is a report of 500 cavalry moving toward Vining's Station. Have your men well in hand to guard against any surprise.

I am, very respectfully, your obedient servant,
                              DAVID F. HOW,
      Lieutenant and Acting Assistant Adjutant-General.

STATION OBSERVATION,
      Near General Geary's Headquarters, August 15, 1864.
Capt. A. K. TAYLOR,
      Acting Signal Officer:

CAPTAIN: I have to report that the enemy were at work to-day at same place reported yesterday, and this evening at fort south and distant from station two miles and a half. The greater number of shells from siege guns exploded in that part of the city between my station and church spires. Three exploded over the city and one in front and close up to six-gun fort in front of the right of General Geary's division, and one over the works a short distance farther to the enemy's left. I noticed several times this afternoon considerable smoke rising in rear of large brick and square stone buildings just to my left of brick smoke-stack.

I am, very respectfully, your obedient servant,
                              W. W. HOPKINS,
      Captain and Acting Signal Officer.

SHERMAN'S HEADQUARTERS,
      August 15, 1864. (Received 12.30 p. m.)
General SCHOFIELD:

General Howard's signal officer reports a column of infantry, followed by wagons, passing to our right. Do you know whether Kilpatrick is on this side or not? Keep a good lookout in the direction of that road, where we saw the wagons, and report any movements of interest. I think Kilpatrick will make the road at Fairburn.

                              W. T. SHERMAN,
                                    Major-General.

SCHOFIELD'S HEADQUARTERS,
August 15, 1864—12.30 p. m.

Major-General SHERMAN:

Colonel Garrard moved down early this morning to join Kilpatrick, but I have heard nothing from them. I will send an officer at once to watch the road along the enemy's left and report.

J. M. SCHOFIELD,
Major-General.

HEADQUARTERS ARMY OF THE OHIO,
August 15, 1864—1 p. m.

Major-General SHERMAN:

I have just returned from extreme right. The enemy seems to have completed his works as far as the point where you saw them working the other day. Beyond that nothing can be seen. The enemy shows no force in or about his works on his left. I have laid out my lines preparatory to the proposed movement, and will have them constructed to-night. I have not yet been able to learn enough of the roads to be clear as to the details of the movement.

J. M. SCHOFIELD,
Major-General.

HEADQUARTERS ARMY OF THE OHIO,
Near Atlanta, Ga., August 15, 1864.

Major-General SHERMAN:

I am preparing to carry on the next move about twelve days' supplies, which I can make last twenty days if necessary. Shall we leave all baggage wagons in rear? Will there be time to send wagons to the rear after your orders are issued, or shall it be done at once?

J. M. SCHOFIELD,
Major-General.

HDQRS. MILITARY DIVISION OF THE MISSISSIPPI,
In the Field, near Atlanta, August 15, 1864.
(Received 9 p. m.)

General SCHOFIELD:

There will be plenty of time to dispose of wagons after my orders are issued. I want to hear of Generals Kilpatrick and Garrard before making my orders, but I am more and more satisfied the movement we contemplate is the true one to be made. I think Generals Steedman and John E. Smith will drive Wheeler far away and repair our road in two days. Give me the earliest news of the cavalry on your flank.

W. T. SHERMAN,
Major-General, Commanding.

HEADQUARTERS ARMY OF THE OHIO,
Near Atlanta, Ga., August 15, 1864.

Major-General SHERMAN:

I do not believe Wheeler can hurt us at all seriously; he cannot do more than break the road in a few places and possibly pick up one or two of my small garrisons and thus relieve Steedman of the dispute about internal discipline. I will give you my earliest news about the cavalry; a few artillery shots were heard in that direction this evening. I apprehend we will be troubled to find roads enough to move as rapidly as you desire, and with sufficient concentration near the left. That is the only difficulty I apprehend. Perhaps the cavalry will be able to give us better information.

> J. M. SCHOFIELD,
> *Major-General.*

> HEADQUARTERS ARMY OF THE OHIO,
> *Near Atlanta, Ga., August 15, 1864.*

Major-General SHERMAN:

My signal officer reports no movement of troops can be seen about the enemy's left. He can see distinctly the road beyond the big field, but cannot see beyond the woods. One of my signal officers who went out with Colonel Garrard left him at 1 o'clock near Sandtown. Kilpatrick had not yet joined him. He had not met even a picket of the enemy.

> J. M. SCHOFIELD,
> *Major-General.*

> HOWARD'S HEADQUARTERS,
> *August 15, 1864.*

Major-General SHERMAN:

Following just received from signal officer:

I have just seen a large body of infantry passing to the enemy's left. Did not see the head of column, but counted four regiments followed by several wagons.

> O. O. HOWARD,
> *Major-General.*

> HDQRS. MILITARY DIVISION OF THE MISSISSIPPI,
> *In the Field, near Atlanta, August 15, 1864.*

General HOWARD:

The infantry is doubtless the result of General Kilpatrick's movement on that flank, but let the signal officers watch and report everything of interest.

> W. T. SHERMAN,
> *Major-General, Commanding.*

> HDQRS. SIGNAL DETACH., FIFTEENTH ARMY CORPS,
> *Before Atlanta, Ga., August 15, 1864.*

Maj. Gen. JOHN A. LOGAN,
> *Commanding Fifteenth Army Corps:*

SIR: I have the honor to submit the following as my report for to-day. The officer on the observation station reports the following:

At 10.40 a. m. one passenger and one freight train left Atlanta apparently empty. At 5.10 p. m. one train of cars, three passenger, one baggage, and five freight cars, apparently the same train that left town at 10.40 a. m., arrived; also a train of eighteen cars, five of them loaded with white sacks. The rest of the train appeared to be empty. Green corn was hauled in and issued to the rebel troops in their works this p. m.

I am, sir, very respectfully, your obedient servant,

SAMUEL EDGE,
First Lieutenant and Chief Acting Signal Officer.

HDQRS. DEPARTMENT AND ARMY OF THE TENNESSEE,
Before Atlanta, Ga., August 15, 1864.

Maj. Gen. JOHN A. LOGAN,
Commanding Fifteenth Army Corps:

The inclosed telegram is just received. The major-general commanding requests that you take such measures as will insure the economy recommended.

Colonel Raum, at Resaca, reports the enemy's cavalry on the railroad near Tilton tearing up track. Give orders that will insure great economy in provisions and forage till we can estimate the time required to repair damages. I have nothing from beyond Resaca. General John E. Smith, at Cartersville, will collect all the infantry that can be spared from defense of material points about Allatoona and go up the road.

W. T. SHERMAN,
Major-General.

Very respectfully, your obedient servant,

WM. T. CLARK,
Assistant Adjutant-General.

(Same to Generals Blair and Dodge.)

HDQRS. MILITARY DIVISION OF THE MISSISSIPPI,
In the Field, near Atlanta, August 15, 1864.

General JOHN E. SMITH,
Resaca or beyond:

If Wheeler has gone above Dalton consult with General Steedman and telegraph me, and I will instruct as soon as I can learn the destination. Try, if possible, to force him to get back to Georgia through the passes of North Carolina, which will ruin his horses.

W. T. SHERMAN,
Major-General, Commanding.

HDQRS. MILITARY DIVISION OF THE MISSISSIPPI,
In the Field, near Atlanta, August 15, 1864.

General JOHN E. SMITH,
Cartersville:

There are four trains of cars at Kingston, which I have ordered to drop back to Cartersville. I will order General McArthur to load with troops two trains now at Marietta, and hold subject to your orders. Whilst cut off from Steedman take control of all matters below the break, and use superhuman efforts to prevent Wheeler getting out with prisoners or plunder. By getting infantry to central points, and timely obstructing roads, &c., cavalry can be circumvented. General McCook will give directions to use bodies of cavalry. The posts and block-houses, if defended obstinately, will not be attacked by Wheeler.

> W. T. SHERMAN,
> *Major-General, Commanding.*

HDQRS. MILITARY DIVISION OF THE MISSISSIPPI,
In the Field, near Atlanta, August 15, 1864.

General JOHN E. SMITH,
Cartersville:

You had better fill all the cars you can get with infantry at Rome, Marietta, and Allatoona, and proceed up the road as far as possible to act against Wheeler in concert with what General Steedman will do from the other end of the line. The bridges should be strongly defended, but other points might be stripped of their garrisons to increase the force to the capacity of available cars. All should move in one group of trains.

> W. T. SHERMAN,
> *Major-General, Commanding.*

CARTERSVILLE, *August 15, 1864.*

Major-General SHERMAN:

I have not been able to communicate with Rome. Have ordered train of cars sent out for two regiments. Do not hear from Marietta. Soon as possible will take two regiments from this place, one from Kingston, and what I get from Rome and Marietta, and go up the road as directed. The cavalry sent out yesterday have not been heard from. Three hundred and fifty were ordered to go out by way of Pine Log to Jasper, and 200 up the river road via Ball Ground to Hannagen in Long Swamp Valley, to intercept the cattle at Hightower. This force was sent out under the information that there was but 300 or 400 of the enemy. The infantry ordered to Canton have been ordered back.

> JNO. E. SMITH,
> *Brigadier-General.*

CARTERSVILLE, *August 15, 1864—6.30 p. m.*

Major-General SHERMAN:

I am just starting up the road with about 2,000 men. Dispatch received from Resaca says the rebel force is moving northeast from Dalton; burned a bridge below Dalton, and tore up the track. My cavalry not heard from.

> JNO. E. SMITH,
> *Brigadier-General.*

HDQRS. MILITARY DIVISION OF THE MISSISSIPPI,
In the Field, near Atlanta, August 15, 1864.

Colonel RAUM:

General Smith is ordered to send up all trains at Marietta and Allatoona as far as possible loaded with infantry. I have no doubt General Steedman will go to the relief of Dalton. No matter what happens hold on to Resaca to the death. I want to catch Wheeler if possible. If possible send word to General Steedman by Snake Creek Gap and Johnson's Crook.

> W. T. SHERMAN,
> *Major-General, Commanding.*

RESACA, *August 15, 1864—7 p. m.*

General SHERMAN:

The force which crossed last evening below Field's Mill was 2,000 strong, under General Martin, composed of the First, Third, Fourth, and Sixth Georgia Cavalry, a Mississippi regiment, and some Alabama cavalry. This force destroyed the railroad near Tilton. The force which crossed at the same time at Field's Mill is estimated at 1,000. They had four pieces of artillery. Wheeler was with the column which passed up yesterday morning by Oldtown. Their horses considerably jaded. I think all are north of the river. Some soldiers told their friends Wheeler would go to East Tennessee.

> G. B. RAUM,
> *Colonel, Commanding Brigade.*

HDQRS. MILITARY DIVISION OF THE MISSISSIPPI,
In the Field, near Atlanta, August 15, 1864.

Colonel RAUM,
　Resaca:

General Smith on arrival can command all forces in and about Resaca, including the cavalry at Calhoun. Wheeler won't attack infantry in position. The prisoners taken by him should be rescued, and he should not be allowed to return down the valley, but be forced up toward Tennessee.

> W. T. SHERMAN,
> *Major-General, Commanding.*

RESACA, *August 15, 1864—9 a. m.*

General SMITH,
　Cartersville:

Dalton is invested and the enemy using artillery. Between 2 and 4 this morning the enemy destroyed about one mile of road south of Tilton and have moved toward Spring Place. I have sent the Eightieth Ohio to Tilton. Is it possible to send troops from Rome, Kingston, and Calhoun to the relief of Dalton? There are two trains here could be used. The cavalry at Calhoun are not acting under my orders.

> G. B. RAUM,
> *Colonel, Commanding Brigade.*

RESACA, *August 15, 1864—1 p. m.*

General JOHN E. SMITH:

Last night a strong force of the enemy passed north, crossing the Coosawattee below Field's Mill. I think it is the force reported at Fairmount. Cannonading continued north of Tilton two hours ago. We sent courier to Chattanooga.

> G. B. RAUM,
> *Colonel, Commanding.*

HDQRS. THIRD DIVISION, FIFTEENTH ARMY CORPS,
Cartersville, August 15, 1864.

Colonel DEAN:

SIR: If there is a train of empty cars at Kingston, send it to Rome at once. Write to commanding officer to send, by direction of General Sherman, two of his best infantry regiments with 100 rounds ammunition per man. A train guard of fifty men should be sent with it. Hold your command in readiness to move on receipt of orders.

JNO. E. SMITH,
Brigadier-General.

HDQRS. THIRD DIVISION, FIFTEENTH ARMY CORPS,
Cartersville, Ga., August 15, 1864.

Brigadier-General VANDEVER,
Commanding at Rome, Ga.:

SIR: By direction of Major-General Sherman you will send at once to Kingston, Ga., two of the best and largest regiments of infantry of your command. They will be supplied before starting with 100 rounds ammunition per man and three days' rations.

I am, general, very respectfully, your obedient servant,

JNO. E. SMITH,
Brigadier-General.

HDQRS. THIRD DIVISION, FIFTEENTH ARMY CORPS,
Cartersville, Ga., August 15, 1864.

Brigadier-General VANDEVER,
Commanding at Rome, Ga.:

GENERAL: You will have in readiness two of your strongest regiments with 100 rounds ammunition and three days' rations to embark on the cars upon their arrival, by direction of Major-General Sherman.

Very respectfully, your obedient servant,

JNO. E. SMITH,
Brigadier-General.

HDQRS. MILITARY DIVISION OF THE MISSISSIPPI,
In the Field, near Atlanta, August 15, 1864.

General MCARTHUR, *Marietta:*

Wheeler has gone north as far as Dalton, and nothing will threaten you. There are two trains of cars at Marietta. Load them with troops and hold subject to the order of General John E. Smith at Cartersville, who will try to prevent Wheeler getting back with prisoners or plunder.

W. T. SHERMAN,
Major-General, Commanding.

HDQRS. MILITARY DIVISION OF THE MISSISSIPPI,
In the Field, near Atlanta, August 15, 1864.

General MCARTHUR:

Make up two trains of cars loaded with infantry, and send up to General John E. Smith, at Cartersville.

W. T. SHERMAN,
Major-General, Commanding.

MARIETTA, *August 15, 1864.*

Major-General SHERMAN:

I am loading three regiments, numbering 1,000 men. I have about 750 left for duty here.

J. McARTHUR,
Brigadier-General.

———

ROME, *August 15, 1864.*

Major-General SHERMAN:

Colonel Dean sends to me for re-enforcements.

WM. VANDEVER,
Brigadier-General.

———

HDQRS. MILITARY DIVISION OF THE MISSISSIPPI,
In the Field, near Atlanta, August 15, 1864.

General VANDEVER, *Rome:*

Have two good regiments ready to embark in cars that General John E. Smith will send for you, to join an expedition to go up to Resaca to attack Wheeler, who is damaging our road. Let the balance of the garrison be confined to one or two redoubts, and on the exhibition on the part of the people of any hostility, burn the town down.

W. T. SHERMAN,
Major-General, Commanding.

———

ROME, *August 15, 1864.*

Maj. Gen. W. T. SHERMAN:

Have sent two regiments to report to General Smith. Cavalry returned from toward Blue Mountain. Enemy 1,500 strong there. Took some prisoners and captured 75 mules and horses; destroyed a cotton factory. Obtained a Mobile paper of 9th with an account of the success of gun-boats in the bay.

WM. VANDEVER,
Brigadier-General.

———

HDQRS. MILITARY DIVISION OF THE MISSISSIPPI,
In the Field, near Atlanta, August 15, 1864.

General VANDEVER, *Rome:*

Have your dispatch. I suppose Clanton is still at Blue Mountain. I am willing he should stay there. I hear that Wheeler failed to surprise Dalton, and has gone up into East Tennessee. He cannot do much harm there. Let your cavalry pick up as many horses and mules as possible, also recruits, and be most active. I expect soon to make a move that will bring things to a crisis.

W. T. SHERMAN,
Major-General, Commanding.

———

ROME, *August 15, 1864.*

Major-General SHERMAN:

Dispatches received. Three days ago I sent cavalry expedition toward Jacksonville. Expect to return to-day. Yesterday sent party to Adairsville. Will return to-day.

WM. VANDEVER,
Brigadier-General.

HDQRS. MILITARY DIVISION OF THE MISSISSIPPI,
In the Field, near Atlanta, Ga., August 15, 1864.

J. B. VAN DYNE, *Master of Transportation, Marietta:*

Let the trains at Kingston drop back to Cartersville, and hold the trains at Marietta ready to carry troops to any point needed.

W. T. SHERMAN,
Major-General, Commanding.

MARIETTA, *August 15, 1864.*

General SHERMAN:

I have ordered all trains at Kingston back to Cartersville, and have trains at Marietta ready to move when called for. I am also holding two trains at Resaca. If you desire them elsewhere they will be ready to move at any time.

J. B. VAN DYNE,
Master of Railroad Transportation.

MARIETTA, *August 15, 1864.*

Major-General SHERMAN:

Telegram just received. Shall I send an engine with Captain Van Duzer's telegraphic material from Kingston to Resaca? I have a small locomotive at Rome which would be able to do the work he requires.

J. B. VAN DYNE,
Master of Transportation.

HDQRS. MILITARY DIVISION OF THE MISSISSIPPI,
In the Field, near Atlanta, August 15, 1864.

J. B. VAN DYNE, *Marietta:*

General McArthur will send up to Allatoona and beyond two trains of cars loaded with soldiers to join four more trains at Cartersville, loaded also with troops from Rome and Kingston. Let Captain Van Duzer send with one of these his telegraph wire and repair party. Risk your locomotives and cars as little as possible till the end of this raid.

W. T. SHERMAN,
Major-General, Commanding.

HDQRS. THIRD BRIG., SECOND DIV., 16TH ARMY CORPS,
Rome, Ga., August 15, 1864.

Lieut. Col. F. J. HURLBUT, *Fifty-seventh Illinois Infantry:*

COLONEL: You will take command of the two regiments (Thirty-ninth Iowa and Fifty-seventh Illinois Infantry) and move to Kingston, Ga., by rail at once, reporting to General John E. Smith at Kingston.

By order of Col. R. Rowett:

J. S. ROBINSON,
Lieutenant and Acting Assistant Adjutant-General.

CLEVELAND, *August 15, 1864.*

Brigadier-General AMMEN:

The enemy has attacked Dalton in force, General Steedman says a large force, and has sent re-enforcements there. Captain Crowell reports the number at 2,000, and heavy artillery heard at Varnell's Station all day. I am in a poor position for defense here owing to General Steedman's order, and do not expect to save the depot or public stores in case of attack. I would like to have you come here and see for yourself.

H. G. GIBSON,
Colonel Second Ohio Heavy Artillery.

CLEVELAND, *August 15, 1864.*

General AMMEN:

Captain Crowell, at Varnell's, reports Dalton in possession of the rebels; General Steedman thinks it is not the case. I have sent a train to Varnell's to bring away the garrison if the commander thinks he cannot hold his position.

H. G. GIBSON,
Colonel Second Ohio Heavy Artillery.

CIRCULAR.]   ARTILLERY HDQRS., MIL. DIV. OF THE MISS.,
Before Atlanta, August 15, 1864.

The entire supply of field artillery ammunition with the army to-day and at all accessible depots (exclusive of the contents of the ammunition chests) being 212 rounds per gun of 3-inch, 246 rounds of 12-pounder, and 235 rounds of 20-pounder, and existing circumstances rendering communication with Chattanooga uncertain for some days to come, it is important that all unnecessary or doubtful expenditure of field artillery ammunition be prohibited, and the strictest economy in its use be for the present enjoined upon battery commanders.

WILLIAM F. BARRY,
Brigadier-General, Chief of Artillery.

Semi-monthly field report of the artillery of the Army of the Tennessee.

Batteries	Effective force.		Guns.	Caissons.	Rounds ammunition on hand.	Horses.	Casualties—men.	
	Officers.	Men.					Killed.	Wounded.
Fifteenth Army Corps, Maj. T. D. Maurice, chief of artillery:								
4th Ohio Independent...................	4	95	6	6	698	119	......	......
2d Missouri Artillery (F)...............	1	93	4	4	517	65	......	1
1st Illinois (A and B).................	1	103	4	4	389	70	......	......
1st Illinois (H)......................	2	84	3	4	333	72	......	......
1st Illinois (F)......................	2	123	6	......	192	51	......	......
1st Iowa.............................	1	80	4	4	643	65	......	2
Sixteenth Army Corps, Maj. William H. Ross, chief of artillery:								
1st Michigan (C)......................	4	116	4	4	800	61	......	......
14th Ohio	4	160	6	6	1,170	87	......	1
1st Missouri (H)	2	81	6	6	768	106	......	2
1st Michigan (B)	3	87	6	6	1,070	83	......	......
2d United States (F).................	1	52	......	......	......	......	......	......

Semi-monthly field report of the artillery of the Army of the Tennessee—Continued.

Batteries.	Effective force.		Guns.	Caissons.	Rounds ammunition on hand.	Horses.	Casualties— men.	
	Officers.	Men.					Killed.	Wounded.
Seventeenth Army Corps, Maj. John T. Cheney, chief of artillery:								
3d Ohio	2	116	4	4	254	66	......	......
1st Illinois (D)	4	134	4	4	257	76	......	......
1st Michigan (H)	3	100	6	6	913	80	......	......
15th Ohio Independent	3	114	6	6	701	88	......	......
2d Illinois (F)	3	118	4	4	482	63	1	......
1st Minnesota	5	138	6	6	1,124	89	......	......
10th Ohio a	2	123	3	4	811	53	......	......
1st Missouri (C) a	2	103	4	4	608	45	......	......
Total	50	2,020	86	82	11,730	1,339	1	10

a At Marietta.

T. W. OSBORN,
Major and Chief of Artillery, Dept. and Army of the Tenn.

BEFORE ATLANTA, GA., *August 15, 1864.*

Consolidated semi-monthly field return of the artillery of the Army of the Cumberland, August 15, 1864.

Batteries.	Effective force.		Guns.	Caissons.	Rounds of ammunition on hand.	Horses.	Casualties.		
							Men.		Loss of horses.
	Officers.	Men.					Killed.	Wounded.	
Fourth Army Corps:									
Artillery Brigade Headquarters	6	88	......	......		23	......	......	......
5th Indiana Battery	4	120	6	6	830	93	......	......	......
Independent Pennsylvania (B)	2	110	4	5	548	80	......	......	......
1st Ohio Artillery (A)	4	134	6	6	641	97	......	......	......
1st Illinois Artillery (M)	2	101	4	6	419	102	......	......	2
Bridges' Battery (Illinois)	1	109	5	6	610	110	......	......	......
6th Ohio Battery	5	153	4	6	638	97	......	......	2
1st Ohio Artillery (M)	4	118	6	6	842	104	......	......	......
Fourteenth Army Corps:									
1st Illinois Artillery (C)	4	113	6	6	800	74	......	......	......
2d Illinois Artillery (I)	3	138	6	6	980	91	......	......	......
7th Indiana Battery	4	111	4	6	670	57	......	......	......
5th Wisconsin Battery	4	140	6	6	644	96	......	......	......
19th Indiana Battery	3	115	4	6	675	96	......	......	......
20th Indiana Battery	3	140	6	6	705	112	......	......	......
Twentieth Army Corps:									
Artillery Brigade Headquarters	8	17	......	......			......	......	......
1st New York Artillery (M)	2	123	6	6	768	88	......	......	......
1st Ohio Artillery (C)	5	128	6	6	768	92	......	......	......
13th New York Battery	5	109	6	6	759	95	......	......	......
1st Michigan Artillery (I)	3	107	6	6	1,200	89	1	2	......
1st New York Artillery (I)	3	142	6	6	944	81	......	2	......
Independent Pennsylvania (E)	3	142	6	6	1,200	94	......	......	......
11th Indiana Battery a (detached)	5	127	9	6	1,816	106	......	......	......
Total	83	2,585	112	119	16,457	1,877	1	4	4

a Two 20-pounder Parrott guns disabled August 12, 1864, the muzzles being torn off in firing.

J. M. BRANNAN,
Brigadier-General, Chief of Artillery.

Consolidated semi-monthly field return of artillery serving in the Army of the Ohio for August 15, 1864.

Designation of batteries.	Division.	Effective force.				Rounds of ammunition on hand.	Horses.	Casualties.					
		Officers.	Men.	Guns.	Caissons.			Officers prisoners.	Men.				Loss of horses.
									Killed.	Wounded.	Prisoners.		
19th Ohio	Second	4	83	4	4	485	74			1			
1st Michigan Light Artillery (F).*a*	....do	3	88	3	4	725	67		1				3
22d Indiana	....do	3	115	4	4	486	84						8
1st Ohio Light Artillery (D)	Third	4	105	4	4	718	70						2
23d Indiana	....do	3	114	4	4	374	80						
15th Indiana	....do	3	107	4	4	530	77						1
24th Indiana	Cavalry Corps	1	67	2	4	259	4	3				47	52
Total		21	679	25	28	3,577	456	3	1	1	47		66

a Fourteen unserviceable horses.

I certify the above report is correct.

G. W. SCHOFIELD,
Lieut. Col. and Chief of Arty. and Ord., Dept. of the Ohio.

HEADQUARTERS ARMY OF THE OHIO,
Before Atlanta, Ga., August 16, 1864.

HDQRS. MILITARY DIVISION OF THE MISSISSIPPI,
In the Field, near Atlanta, Ga., August 16, 1864.

Hon. E. M. STANTON,
Secretary of War, Washington, D. C.:

I need a good cavalry brigadier very much, and recommend Col. Eli Long, Fourth Ohio Cavalry, now here, and who merited promotion for good service the time I went to Knoxville. He is a junior colonel now, and the cavalry is not commanded to my satisfaction.

W. T. SHERMAN,
Major-General, Commanding.

CITY POINT, *August 16, 1864—10 a. m.*

General SHERMAN:

Saturday night last I threw the Second and Tenth Corps, with a division of cavalry, to the north of the James River, for the purpose of employing the enemy and keeping him from sending off any of his forces, and to make him recall some from the Shenandoah Valley, if I could. We have kept him constantly occupied since, and prisoners report with very heavy loss. Two general officers have been killed and their bodies left in our hands. I shall keep the enemy so employed that he will not send troops to Atlanta.

Yours,

U. S. GRANT,
Lieutenant-General.

Hdqrs. Military Division of the Mississippi,
        In the Field, near Atlanta, August 16, 1864.

Major-General HALLECK,
        Chief of Staff, Washington, D. C.:

GENERAL: It occurs to me that preliminary to a future report of the history of this campaign, I should record certain facts of great personal interest to officers of this command.

General McPherson was killed by the musketry fire at the beginning of the battle of July 22. He had in person selected the ground for his troops, constituting the left wing of the army, I being in person with the center, General Schofield. The moment the information reached me I sent one of my staff to announce the fact to General John A. Logan, the senior officer present with the Army of the Tennessee, with general instructions to maintain the ground chosen by General McPherson if possible, but if pressed too hard to refuse his left flank, but at all events to hold the railroad and main Decatur road; that I did not propose to move or gain ground by that flank, but rather by the right, and that I wanted the Army of the Tennessee to fight it out unaided. General Logan admirably conceived my orders and executed them, and if he gave ground on the left of the Seventeenth Corps, it was properly done by my orders, but he held a certain hill by the right division of the Seventeenth Corps, the only ground on that line the possession of which by an enemy would have damaged us by giving a reverse fire on the remainder of the troops. General Logan fought that battle out as required unaided, save by a small brigade sent by my orders from General Schofield to the Decatur road well to the rear, where it was reported the enemy's cavalry had got into the town of Decatur and was operating directly on the rear of Logan, but that brigade was not disturbed, and was replaced that night by a part of the Fifteenth Corps, next to General Schofield, and General Schofield's brigade brought back, so as to be kept together on its own line.

General Logan managed the Army of the Tennessee well during his command, and it may be that an unfair inference might be drawn to his prejudice, because he did not succeed to the permanent command. I was forced to choose a commander, not only for the army in the field, but of the Department of the Tennessee, covering a vast extent of country with troops much dispersed. It was a delicate and difficult task, and I gave preference to Maj. Gen. O. O. Howard, then in command of the Fourth Army Corps in the Department of the Cumberland. Instead of giving my reasons I prefer that the wisdom of the choice be left to the test of time. The President kindly ratified my choice, and I am willing to assume the responsibility. I meant no disrespect to any officer, and hereby declare that General Logan submitted with the grace and dignity of a soldier, gentleman, and patriot, resumed the command of his corps proper (Fifteenth), and enjoys the love and respect of his army and his commanders.

It so happened that on the 28th of July I had again thrown the same army to the extreme right, the exposed flank, where the enemy repeated the same maneuver, striking in mass the extreme corps deployed in line and refused as a flank (the Fifteenth, Major-General Logan), and he commanded in person, General Howard and myself being near, and that corps, as heretofore reported, repulsed the rebel army completely, and next day advanced and occupied the ground fought over and the road the enemy sought to cover. General Howard, who had that very day assumed his new command, unequivocally gave General Logan all the credit possible, and I also beg to add my unqualified admiration of the bravery, skill, and, more yet, good sense that influenced him to bear a natural disappointment and do his whole duty like a man. If I could bestow on him substantial reward it would afford me unalloyed satisfaction, but I do believe, in the consciousness of acts done from noble impulses and gracefully admitted by his superiors in authority, he will be contented. He already holds the highest known commission in the army, and it is hard to say how we can better manifest our applause.

At the time of General Howard's selection, Major-General Hooker commanded the Twentieth Army Corps in the Army of the Cumberland, made up for his special accommodation out of the old Eleventh and Twelfth Corps, whereby General Slocum was deprived of his corps command. Both the law and practice are and have been to fill vacancies in the higher army commands by selection. Rank or dates of commission have not controlled, nor am I aware that any reflection can be inferred unless the junior be placed immediately over the senior, but in this case General Hooker's command was in no manner disturbed. General Howard was not put over him, but in charge of a distinct and separate army. No indignity was offered nor intended, and I must say that General Hooker was not justified in retiring. At all events had he spoken or written to me I would have made every explanation and concession he could have expected, but could not have changed my course, because then, as now, I believe I did right and for the good of our country and cause. As a matter of justice General Slocum, having been displaced by the consolidation, was deemed by General Thomas as entitled to the vacancy created by General Hooker's voluntary withdrawal and has received it.

With great respect,

W. T. SHERMAN,
Major-General, Commanding.

SHERMAN'S HEADQUARTERS, *August 16, 1864.*

General THOMAS:

The operator at Cartersville began a message, saying six regiments were approaching Cartersville. I think all the enemy's cavalry must be up there, and it may be necessary to send ours after it. They may do so much damage to the railroad that it will take a long time to repair it.

W. T. SHERMAN,
Major-General.

THOMAS' HEADQUARTERS, *August 16, 1864.*

Major-General SHERMAN:

Are there not some troops at Cartersville? Do you wish the cavalry sent up to Cartersville?

GEO. H. THOMAS,
Major-General.

SHERMAN'S HEADQUARTERS, *August 16, 1864.*

General THOMAS:

There are troops at Allatoona and the bridge. I have called for a report since John E. Smith went up the road with 2,000 men, made up at Marietta, Rome, and Allatoona, but I have no report of what force remains. The telegraph wire does not work beyond Allatoona. Don't send the cavalry, but let Garrard be notified that he may have to go. We must clear our lines.

> W. T. SHERMAN,
> *Major-General.*

HEADQUARTERS DEPARTMENT OF THE CUMBERLAND,
August 16, 1864.

Major-General SHERMAN:

If you think a cavalry raid can destroy the Macon road sufficiently to force Hood to retreat, I think now would be a good time to send against it.

> GEO. H. THOMAS,
> *Major-General, U. S. Volunteers, Commanding.*

HEADQUARTERS DEPARTMENT OF THE CUMBERLAND,
August 16, 1864.

Major-General SHERMAN:

General Kilpatrick reports that he forced the enemy back into his camp near the railroad, five miles above Fairburn Station; destroyed the station and public buildings, telegraph and railroad for about three miles. Jackson's division has thus far refused to give him battle. He anticipates an attempt will be made to prevent his return this morning, and feels confident he can destroy Jackson, provided cavalry alone meets him.

> GEO. H. THOMAS,
> *Major-General.*

HDQRS. MILITARY DIVISION OF THE MISSISSIPPI,
In the Field, near Atlanta, August 16, 1864.

General THOMAS:

The news from General Kilpatrick is first rate. He has acted so as to show the enemy that he will fight. I do believe he, with his own and General Garrard's cavalry, could ride right round Atlanta and mash the Macon road all to pieces, but I don't want to risk our cavalry. I don't fear the enemy trying to cut off his return. General Schofield's position is such that infantry will not leave their lines to go down to Camp Creek.

> W. T. SHERMAN,
> *Major-General, Commanding.*

HDQRS. MILITARY DIVISION OF THE MISSISSIPPI,
In the Field, near Atlanta, August 16, 1864.

General THOMAS:

I have sent a courier to General Kilpatrick to make inquiries about the country about Mount Gilead and Fairburn Station, and will hear by daylight. I do believe Hood has but little provisions, and the facilities for repairs do not compare with ours. Cavalry could make in a

single night breaks of ten or fifteen miles which I think would lessen
his hold of Atlanta.   Also, the position of our infantry would make a
cavalry raid from our right flank little hazardous.

W. T. SHERMAN,
Major-General, Commanding.

HDQRS. MILITARY DIVISION OF THE MISSISSIPPI,
In the Field, near Atlanta, August 16, 1864.
General THOMAS:

General Schofield reports that General Kilpatrick did not find the
enemy's cavalry at his old camp at Mount Gilead Church; but I don't
know where that church is.   It is manifest that all the efficient cavalry
of the enemy is to our rear.   They will tear up all the road beyond
Cartersville; but I think Wheeler has been driven off toward East
Tennessee, and trust that General John E. Smith will return to Cartersville; he has cars enough.   There are three regiments and eight
guns at Allatoona and Etowah bridge, and I have ordered General
McArthur to send any re-enforcements he can spare, and call on us to
replace them at Marietta.   I do think our cavalry should now break
the Macon road good.   If we can save our rations at Marietta and Allatoona, and break the Macon road for many miles, we can wait as long
as Hood.   What say you to letting General Kilpatrick have two of
General Garrard's brigades, and then to strike across to the Macon
road and tear it up good?   He has scouted the country now and knows
it, and can act with confidence and due caution.   General Schofield is
well on that flank and makes a good cover.   I like the plan better than
to send General Garrard up to Cartersville, for the enemy will simply
run off, but General Kilpatrick, with two good brigades, can reach
across to the Macon road about Rough and Ready, and tear up about
six or eight miles by to-morrow night or next day.

W. T. SHERMAN,
Major-General, Commanding.

HDQRS. MILITARY DIVISION OF THE MISSISSIPPI,
In the Field, near Atlanta, August 16, 1864.
General THOMAS:

Until General Garrard is in, General Kilpatrick should remain near
Sandtown or General Schofield's flank, in a threatening attitude, to
prevent Jackson's cavalry going over to join whatever Wheeler left to
watch that flank.   If Wheeler took out 6,000 with him I don't believe
4,000 good cavalry remains to the enemy in our front.

W. T. SHERMAN,
Major-General, Commanding.

HDQRS. MILITARY DIVISION OF THE MISSISSIPPI,
In the Field, near Atlanta, August 16, 1864.
General THOMAS:

General Stanley reports General Garrard as back.   Has he reported?
General Stanley says some cavalry passed to our rear at Cross Keys
and killed a picket.   Does General Garrard manifest enough activity?
Get his report and let me have the substance.

W. T. SHERMAN,
Major-General, Commanding.

HEADQUARTERS DEPARTMENT OF THE CUMBERLAND,
August 16, 1864—10 a. m.

Major-General SHERMAN:

Garrard returned last night about 12 o'clock. His report is being copied to be sent to you. I think you will find it satisfactory. Several of the colonels of Garrard's division rank Long. The only way that I can see how he can be placed in command of the division will be by getting him promoted. I think Garrard's services on the Augusta road show how thoroughly he performs his work when he undertakes what he has to do. By not rashly pushing on to the main road, regardless of the forces opposed to him, he has preserved to us his fine division, with which I believe he will yet do good service.

GEO. H. THOMAS,
Major-General.

HDQRS. MILITARY DIVISION OF THE MISSISSIPPI,
In the Field, near Atlanta, August 16, 1864.

General THOMAS:

I am willing to admit that General Garrard's excessive prudence saves his cavalry to us, but though saved, it is as useless as so many sticks. Saving himself, he sacrifices others operating in conjoint expeditions. I am so thoroughly convinced that if he can see a horseman in the distance with a spy-glass he will turn back, that I cannot again depend on his making an effort, though he knows a commander depends on him. If we cannot use that cavalry now, at this moment, when can we? Wheeler is out of the way, and when shall we use cavalry, if not now? If we wait till Wheeler returns, of course an opportunity is lost, which never is repeated in war.

W. T. SHERMAN,
Major-General, Commanding.

HDQRS. MILITARY DIVISION OF THE MISSISSIPPI,
In the Field, near Atlanta, August 16, 1864.

General THOMAS:

General Garrard will not attempt anything if there be a show of resistance. If you consent, and can give the command of that cavalry to Colonel Long, I will put General Garrard on my staff and send him to Nashville to supervise the equipment and armament of our cavalry, the same office held by General W. S. Smith, resigned.

W. T. SHERMAN,
Major-General, Commanding.

HEADQUARTERS ARMY OF THE CUMBERLAND,
August 16, 1864.

Major-General SHERMAN:

I would be perfectly willing to see Long placed in command of a division of cavalry, and should have given him a division last winter if his rank had been high enough. Have you seen Colonel Warner since he was here this morning?

GEO. H. THOMAS,
Major-General, U. S. Volunteers, Commanding.

HDQRS. MILITARY DIVISION OF THE MISSISSIPPI,
In the Field, near Atlanta, August 16, 1864.

General THOMAS:

I have seen Colonel Warner and am willing to leave that cavalry for the present as it is, but if we ever have to use it offensively it will need a more active leader. I have made a special recommendation in Colonel Long's case, and hope he will be promoted; you may tell him so. General Schofield has word from General Kilpatrick at noon, when he was moving toward the flank and trying to get a fight out of some cavalry, but I think the enemy's cavalry has orders to avoid fight now that Wheeler is absent.

W. T. SHERMAN,
Major-General, Commanding.

HEADQUARTERS DEPARTMENT OF THE CUMBERLAND,
August 16, 1864—11.30 a. m.

Major-General SHERMAN,
Commanding Military Division of the Mississippi:

GENERAL: I do not know how to overcome the difficulty of finding a commander for the division now commanded by Garrard, unless you could have Long promoted. I regard Long as a very efficient officer, who, by his services during this war, has dearly earned his promotion, not only for gallantry, but on account of his administrative ability and experience. He enjoyed the high opinion of the late Major-General Sedgwick, who, as major of the First Cavalry, predicted for him much distinction, should he ever have the opportunity.

Very respectfully, your obedient servant,

GEO. H. THOMAS,
Major-General, U. S. Volunteers, Commanding.

SHERMAN'S HEADQUARTERS,
August 16, 1864.

General THOMAS:

I agree with you as to Long. I owe him a promotion from a promise made at Knoxville and will recommend him at once, but our telegraph is down. Do I understand if Long can be promoted you will approve him as the division commander? I don't want to act in this matter without your full and cordial consent, as this cavalry is properly in your command, and it is for you to regulate it. I want that road broken bad, and I believe now is the time.

W. T. SHERMAN,
Major-General.

SHERMAN'S HEADQUARTERS,
August 16, 1864.

General THOMAS:

Cannot you give General Johnson command of Nashville, and put Miller, say, at Murfreesborough or Columbia? Davis has received a brevet commission, which will give him the command.

W. T. SHERMAN,
Major-General.

HEADQUARTERS DEPARTMENT OF THE CUMBERLAND,
August 16, 1864.

Major-General SHERMAN:

Have you any objections to putting Johnson in command of Louisville? I do not think he would like to serve in the Army of the Cumberland any longer, as he regards the placing of Davis in command of the corps as a personal insult.

GEO. H. THOMAS,
Major-General, U. S. Volunteers, Commanding.

HDQRS. MILITARY DIVISION OF THE MISSISSIPPI,
In the Field, near Atlanta, Ga., August 16, 1864.

General THOMAS:

General Davis is here and is the bearer of a request from General Johnson to have command at Louisville or Nashville. I have telegraphed to General Schofield as to the former. He, General Johnson, came to see me yesterday on the same subject, but so many people were present that he did not have a chance to speak to me privately, and asked General Davis to see me, and General Davis is now here for that purpose. He says he thinks General Johnson would rather have a local command than one in the field.

W. T. SHERMAN,
Major-General, Commanding.

HDQRS. MILITARY DIVISION OF THE MISSISSIPPI,
In the Field, near Atlanta, August 16, 1864.

General THOMAS:

We will commence the movement against the railroad about Jonesborough Thursday night unless something occurs in the mean time to mar the plan. I will make my orders, and the preliminary preparations may be begun. If Wheeler interrupts our supplies, we can surely cut off those of Hood, and see who can stand it best.

W. T. SHERMAN,
Major-General, Commanding.

(Same to Generals Schofield and Howard.)

HDQRS. MILITARY DIVISION OF THE MISSISSIPPI,
In the Field, near Atlanta, August 16, 1864.

General STANLEY:

Have you heard anything from General Garrard since he started out?

W. T. SHERMAN,
Major-General, Commanding.

STANLEY'S HEADQUARTERS,
August 16, 1864.

General SHERMAN:

Have not heard anything. Will send down to his headquarters and see if they have any information from him.

D. S. STANLEY,
Major-General.

STANLEY'S HEADQUARTERS,
August 16, 1864.

Major-General SHERMAN

General Garrard came back last night. He had some fighting with the rebels. He found them in force, about seven regiments. They fell back behind breast-works. Some rebel cavalry passed our flank about Cross Keys yesterday. They killed one man on picket. I presume General Garrard has already reported.

D. S. STANLEY,
Major-General.

STANLEY'S HEADQUARTERS,
August 16, 1864—10.30 p. m.

Major-General SHERMAN:

The following just received from my staff officer, Captain Steele, now at Howard's house:

General STANLEY:

Have seen troops passing a fire due west from this point going southward. A building now burning in same direction. First Brigade pickets report unusual activity among the rebels at sundown; say they heard commands given and wagons moving. Enemy sounded tattoo as usual at 9 p. m. on their right.

STEELE.

He will remain at Howard's house until 12 o'clock to report movements of enemy.

D. S. STANLEY,
Major-General.

STANLEY'S HEADQUARTERS,
August 16, 1864—11 p. m.

General W. D. WHIPPLE:

Report from Newton's front: Some movement of the enemy going on; words of command can be heard, and artillery or wagons can be heard moving. More than the usual force could be seen in their works on Newton's front this p. m.

D. S. STANLEY,
Major-General.

HEADQUARTERS FOURTH ARMY CORPS,
Near Atlanta, Ga., August 16, 1864—8.45 p. m.

General NEWTON,
Commanding Second Division, Fourth Army Corps:

GENERAL: Certain movements of the enemy that have been discovered since dark indicate that he is at present preparing for an attack, or to withdraw from Atlanta. Please have your pickets instructed without delay to be on the alert, and to watch closely for any movement that may be made in their front.

By order of Major-General Stanley:

J. S. FULLERTON,
Assistant Adjutant-General.

(Same to General Wood.)

HDQRS. MILITARY DIVISION OF THE MISSISSIPPI,
In the Field, near Atlanta, August 16, 1864.

General ELLIOTT or THOMAS:

Have you anything from Generals Garrard and Kilpatrick?

W. T. SHERMAN,
Major-General, Commanding.

HEADQUARTERS DEPARTMENT OF THE CUMBERLAND,
August 16, 1864.

Major-General SHERMAN:

The following received from Kilpatrick, dated August 15, 9 p. m., near Camp Creek, en route from Fairburn:

Thus far my reconnaissance has been a success. I crossed the river at 11 a. m., and passed out at once for Fairburn. I forced the enemy back into his camp near railroad, five miles above the station. Destroyed the station, public buildings, telegraph and railroad for about three miles. Jackson's division of cavalry has thus far refused to give me battle. I rather expect an attempt will be made in the morning to prevent my return. This will give me the opportunity I seek to destroy Jackson and his command, provided his cavalry alone meets me.

The regiment from Garrard's division sent after a party of rebel cavalry reported as being near Vining's Station, have returned to camp this morning. They report all quiet. No sign of any rebels. Nothing from General Garrard's command.

W. L. ELLIOTT,
Brigadier-General and Chief of Cavalry.

HDQRS. MILITARY DIVISION OF THE MISSISSIPPI,
In the Field, near Atlanta, August 16, 1864.

General ELLIOTT:

The news from General Kilpatrick is first rate. He acts in earnest. I believe General Kilpatrick, with his own and General Garrard's cavalry, could go straight for Rough and Ready, and break the Macon road all to pieces.

W. T. SHERMAN,
Major-General, Commanding.

[AUGUST 16, 1864.—For Kenner Garrard to Elliott, reporting operations, &c., see Part II, p. 809.]

HDQRS. CHIEF OF CAVALRY, DEPT. OF THE CUMBERLAND,
Near Atlanta, Ga., August 16, 1864.

Brig. Gen. K. GARRARD,
Commanding Second Division Cavalry:

The general commanding directs that you have your command in readiness for a move of the army of from ten to fifteen days.

I am, general, very respectfully, your obedient servant,

DAVID F. HOW,
Lieutenant and Acting Assistant Adjutant-General.

HDQRS. CHIEF OF CAVALRY, DEPT. OF THE CUMBERLAND,
Near Atlanta, Ga., August 16, 1864.
Brig. Gen. J. KILPATRICK,
Commanding Third Cavalry Division:

The general commanding directs that you occupy Sandtown with your command, and scout as far as Camp Creek.

I am, general, very respectfully, your obedient servant,
DAVID F. HOW,
Lieutenant and Acting Assistant Adjutant-General.

HEADQUARTERS THIRD CAVALRY DIVISION,
Sandtown, Ga., August 16, 1864.
Brigadier-General ELLIOTT,
Chief of Cavalry, Department of the Cumberland:

GENERAL: I have the honor to report that I have returned to this point and my command has gone into camp. I succeeded in reaching and destroying the depot and public buildings at Fairburn, telegraph wire and railroad track for about three miles. Drove Ross' brigade, of Jackson's division, out of his camp, situated on Camp Creek, about three miles from the railroad, and went into camp late last evening near that point. I marched at an early hour this morning, crossing Camp Creek, and moved to attack Jackson's division, said to be situated on Camp Creek road, near East Point, but I was unable to find any force of the enemy. I scouted the entire country between Camp Creek and the railroad to within one mile and a half of East Point. I was informed that the enemy had here a considerable force of infantry, and a part of Jackson's division of cavalry, dismounted and in the trenches. The enemy seemed to make but little or no effort to prevent me from reaching the railroad at any point below East Point Station. I infer from this that the road is to be abandoned. The enemy's cavalry has certainly all been withdrawn from this portion of his line save two brigades, of Jackson's division, which force is not at all formidable. You will see by the accompanying sketch* that if I am able to maintain the line of pickets indicated, the enemy's lines will be very much contracted and both railroads exposed to raids from this point.

I am, general, very respectfully, your obedient servant,
J. KILPATRICK,
Brigadier-General of Volunteers.

HDQRS. MILITARY DIVISION OF THE MISSISSIPPI,
In the Field, near Atlanta, August 16, 1864.
General SCHOFIELD:

General Kilpatrick reports he reached Fairburn, burned the depot, public buildings and stores, tore up three miles of track, and Jackson refused to fight him. At 9 p. m. last night he was this side of Camp Creek, hoping that Jackson would come out. Let your right division know this, and should they observe infantry move out, we must go also.
W. T. SHERMAN,
Major-General, Commanding.

---

* To appear in the Atlas.

Hdqrs. Military Division of the Mississippi,
In the Field, near Atlanta, August 16, 1864.
(Received 10 a. m.)

Generals Schofield and Howard:

General Garrard is back; went seven miles; saw some horsemen and came back. General John E. Smith is at Resaca, and the enemy is at Spring Place. I think Generals Smith and Steedman can so manage that Wheeler will be driven north. Has General Schofield heard from his cavalry this morning?

W. T. SHERMAN,
Major-General, Commanding.

Headquarters Army of the Ohio,
Near Atlanta, Ga., August 16, 1864.

Major-General Sherman:

I have heard nothing from my cavalry this morning. I am now with General Howard on our extreme right and will watch the enemy. There is no sign of movement yet.

J. M. SCHOFIELD,
Major-General.

Headquarters Army of the Ohio,
August 16, 1864—1.45 p. m.

Major-General Sherman:

I have just heard from Kilpatrick through Colonel Garrard. His dispatch is dated 12 m. Kilpatrick had moved up the Campbellton road toward the right of our infantry to a cross-road leading to Mount Gilead Church, where the rebel cavalry is encamped, with the intention of moving out and attacking them. My troops are ready to move at once if the enemy send infantry against our cavalry.

J. M. SCHOFIELD,
Major-General.

Schofield's Headquarters,
August 16, 1864.

Major-General Sherman:

Colonel Garrard informs me that General Kilpatrick did not find the enemy's cavalry at their old camp near Mount Gilead Church.

J. M. SCHOFIELD,
Major-General.

Hdqrs. Military Division of the Mississippi,
In the Field, near Atlanta, August 16, 1864.
(Received 10.20 p. m.)

General Schofield:

Have you an idea where Mount Gilead Church is? Ascertain if possible from General Kilpatrick if he does not think with two of General Garrard's brigades in addition to his own he could break the Macon road effectually. I do not think General Garrard will try.

W. T. SHERMAN,
Major-General, Commanding.

HEADQUARTERS ARMY OF THE OHIO,
Near Atlanta, Ga., August 16, 1864.

Major-General SHERMAN:

I understand Mount Gilead Church to be near Camp Creek, and about due south from Utoy Post-Office. I will ascertain more accurately from Colonel Garrard. My messenger has already started for Kilpatrick to get his report. I will send another with the question you ask about breaking the Macon road.

J. M. SCHOFIELD,
Major-General.

HDQRS. MILITARY DIVISION OF THE MISSISSIPPI,
In the Field, near Atlanta, August 16, 1864.
(Received 10 p. m.)

General SCHOFIELD:

The enemy's cavalry is now threatening Cartersville and Allatoona. I am satisfied that all the effective cavalry of the enemy is to our rear and would like to have ours dash at the Macon road. If you can communicate with General Kilpatrick to-night, I would like a definite report of his operations.

W. T. SHERMAN,
Major-General, Commanding.

HEADQUARTERS ARMY OF THE OHIO,
Near Atlanta, Ga., August 16, 1864.

Major-General SHERMAN:

I doubt whether I can communicate with Kilpatrick to-night, but will try.

J. M. SCHOFIELD,
Major-General.

HDQRS. MILITARY DIVISION OF THE MISSISSIPPI,
In the Field, near Atlanta, August 16, 1864.

Major-General SCHOFIELD:

Who have you in command of Louisville and that district, and would you be willing for the general to assign to you General Johnson, of the Fourteenth Corps, to command there? He would like the place

L. M. DAYTON,
Aide-de-Camp.

SCHOFIELD'S HEADQUARTERS,
August 16, 1864.

Capt. L. M. DAYTON:

I believe Louisville is in the district commanded by General Hugh Ewing, but the city is commanded by a colonel. I would not like to displace General Ewing, but General Johnson might be given command of Louisville and vicinity as a separate district. I am entirely willing to have General Johnson assigned to me, and will ask General Burbridge to arrange the commands so as to be satisfactory to both General Johnson and General Ewing.

J. M. SCHOFIELD,
Major-General.

HEADQUARTERS ARMY OF THE OHIO,
August 16, 1864.

Major-General SHERMAN,
   Commanding Military Division of the Mississippi:

GENERAL: I respectfully suggest the following details in the execution of the plan proposed by you on the 13th instant:

First day. Twentieth Corps to take its position on the Chattahoochee and the Fourth Corps in rear of the Fourteenth, the trains which are to move with the army being previously parked along the Utoy, and those to be left in rear sent to the bridge-head.

Second day. General Howard to move via Utoy Post-Office to the south bank of Utoy Creek. General Thomas to pass around General Schofield, beyond the Campbellton road. General Howard's trains to move to where the road from Utoy Post-Office to Campbellton crosses a branch of Utoy Creek, those of Generals Thomas and Schofield, near the Campbellton road, in rear of General Thomas.

Third day. General Howard to move via Elton to Fairburn, General Thomas via Mount Gilead Church to Red Oak, General Schofield to follow General Thomas. Trains to follow General Howard on the road his troops take and ones intermediate between Generals Thomas and Howard. Generals Thomas and Schofield to march by the right flank in strong order of battle (three parallel columns), using the wagon road for artillery and ammunition wagons alone, and cutting roads where necessary for the infantry to the left of the wagon road. I deem this order of march necessary for the reason that the enemy will most probably attack our left during the third day's march. General Kilpatrick to cover the interval between the heads of column and General Howard's right. General Garrard to cover the rear from General Schofield's left to the Chattahoochee. Upon reaching the West Point road General Schofield to take position facing East Point, Generals Thomas, Howard, and Kilpatrick to deploy along the road and destroy it.

   I am, general, very respectfully, your obedient servant,
                                   J. M. SCHOFIELD,
                                        Major-General.

HEADQUARTERS ARMY OF THE OHIO,
   Near Atlanta, Ga., August 16, 1864—9 a. m.

Brig. Gen. M. S. HASCALL,
   Commanding Second Division, Twenty-third Army Corps:

GENERAL: I am directed by the major-general commanding to inform you that Kilpatrick has reached Fairburn, burned the depot, torn up track, &c. At 9 p. m. last night he was this side of Camp Creek, hoping that Jackson would come out and fight him. He also directs me to request you to have your troops in readiness to move at a moment's notice, and if the enemy's infantry is seen moving out, inform him of it at once, as in such a case we must also move out and meet them. The general will be at the front and see you there in the course of the morning.

   Very respectfully, your obedient servant,
                                   GEO. W. SCHOFIELD,
                        Lieut. Col. and Chief of Artillery and Ordnance.

(Same to General Cox.)

HEADQUARTERS ARMY OF THE OHIO,
August 16, 1864—2 p. m.

Brigadier-General COX,
Commanding Third Division, Twenty-third Army Corps:

GENERAL: I am informed that General Kilpatrick is about moving out to attack the rebel cavalry near Mount Gilead Church. At 12 m. he was on the Campbellton road at the cross-road leading to the church, and I believe about a mile and a half from your right. If he meet rebel infantry he will call upon you for aid, in which case please move to his support at once; and in case of need call out two of Hascall's brigades to support you.

Respectfully,

J. M. SCHOFIELD,
Major-General.

HDQRS. CAVALRY DIVISION, DEPARTMENT OF THE OHIO,
Cross-Roads, nine miles from Atlanta, August 16, 1864—12 m.

Maj. J. A. CAMPBELL,
Assistant Adjutant-General, Army of the Ohio:

MAJOR: I am requested by General Kilpatrick to present his compliments to Major General Schofield, and inform him that the railroad was cut at Fairburn, and the depot burned there last evening, and the enemy's cavalry found to be in force equal to two brigades, with four guns, near Camp Creek; that he has moved up on this road (the same that General Cox crossed in his reconnaissance a few days ago) to a cross-road that leads to Mount Gilead Church, near which the rebel cavalry is encamped, with the intention of moving on them. I have the honor to report that if a new line of picket-posts is established from the right of our lines to the river, my picket-lines on Utoy Creek will not be needed, and I can bring these companies on picket up to the new line. This line will probably be the road we are now on, from the river to these cross-roads. From here to the right of our lines it will probably be back from it.

Very respectfully, your obedient servant,

ISRAEL GARRARD.

HEADQUARTERS ARMY OF THE OHIO,
Near Atlanta, Ga., August 16, 1864—2 p. m.

Col. ISRAEL GARRARD,
Commanding Cavalry Division:

COLONEL: I have your dispatch of 12 m. Present my compliments to General Kilpatrick, and tell him I have ordered General Cox's division of infantry to support him in his operations in case the enemy send infantry to oppose him. If he will call on General Cox, in case of need, the latter will move to his aid at once. If General Kilpatrick establishes his line from the river to the cross-roads, or in any other position in advance of the one you have heretofore occupied, move yours forward so as to connect between him and the infantry, holding your picket-line as far forward as practicable. It is very desirable to have the main road on which you now are entirely crossed by our pickets.

Very respectfully, your obedient servant,

J. M. SCHOFIELD,
Major-General, Commanding.

HDQRS. CAVALRY DIVISION, ARMY OF THE OHIO,
Utoy, August 16, 1864—7 p. m.

Maj. J. A. CAMPBELL,
Assistant Adjutant-General, Army of the Ohio:

MAJOR: I have the honor to acknowledge the receipt of the letter of Major-General Schofield, and to inform him that I communicated to Brigadier-General Kilpatrick his message to him by letter this evening. There was no enemy found at the camp where they were found last night. To-day my division was posted across the road leading to Atlanta, my outposts occupying the same ground they did the day I was protecting the right flank of General Cox's division. I will not be able to picket on the line of the road until I have ascertained by reconnaissance of the country and roads this side of that road where I can post reserves so as to make the pickets safe. My pickets at the cross-roads were attacked as soon as I left this evening and driven back. I have sent seventy-five men out to a point near there with orders to advance to the cross-roads at daylight. There is another cross-roads half a mile east that will have to be picketed simultaneously in order to give security to either post. Rebel infantry were out at the cross-roads last evening. I have withdrawn my pickets from the line of Utoy Creek in the rear of General Kilpatrick's line.

Very respectfully, your obedient servant,

ISRAEL GARRARD,
Colonel, Commanding Division.

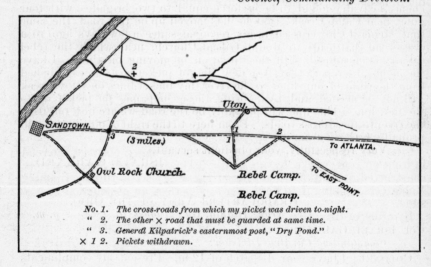

No. 1.   The cross-roads from which my picket was driven to-night.
"   2.   The other × road that must be guarded at same time.
"   3.   General Kilpatrick's easternmost post, "Dry Pond."
× 1 2.   Pickets withdrawn.

[AUGUST 16, 1864.—For Israel Garrard to Schofield, 11 p. m., reporting operations, &c., see Part II, p. 922.]

HOWARD'S HEADQUARTERS,
August 16, 1864.

General SHERMAN:

According to your suggestion, I am going down on the right to-day.

O. O. HOWARD,
Major-General.

HDQRS. SECOND DIVISION, FIFTEENTH ARMY CORPS,
Before Atlanta, Ga., August 16, 1864.

Lieut. Col. R. R. TOWNES,
Assistant Adjutant-General, Fifteenth Army Corps:

COLONEL: I have the honor to report that nothing unusual occurred in my front to-day. The enemy seems to have had a new set of men on his skirmish line to-day, who were inclined to fire more than yesterday, and were less careful about exposing themselves.

Very respectfully, your obedient servant,

J. A. J. LIGHTBURN,
Brigadier-General of Volunteers.

HEADQUARTERS LEFT WING, SIXTEENTH ARMY CORPS,
Near Atlanta, Ga., August 16, 1864.

Lieut. Col. WILLIAM T. CLARK,
Asst. Adjt. Gen., Department and Army of the Tennessee:

COLONEL: General Corse reports the enemy unusually quiet in his front. The 4½-inch Rodman will be finished and in position by 9 p. m., when it will open. The picket officer reports that troops have been seen moving toward the enemy's right (our left). This movement was visible from his front for about forty-five minutes.

I am, very respectfully, your obedient servant,

G. M. DODGE,
Major-General, Commanding.

HDQRS. SECOND DIVISION, SIXTEENTH ARMY CORPS,
Before Atlanta, Ga., August 16, 1864.

Col. R. N. ADAMS,
Commanding Second Brigade:

COLONEL: You will immediately and thoroughly obstruct the road in front of your works by an abatis. The same will also be at once constructed in front of the works of the Sixty-sixth Illinois Infantry Volunteers, making it in both cases as perfect an obstruction as possible.

By order of Brig. Gen. J. M. Corse:

LOUIS H. EVERTS,
Assistant Adjutant-General.

RESACA, *August 16, 1864—6 a. m.*

General W. T. SHERMAN:

I am here with Colonel Watkins and 210 cavalry, all his available force. Can I go on with them and General Smith, or do you desire me to return to Cartersville personally? Your dispatch was received at Calhoun last night. Please answer immediately.

E. M. McCOOK,
Brigadier-General.

SHERMAN'S HEADQUARTERS,
August 16, 1864.

General MCCOOK:

Remain with General Smith and help him all you can. If you can keep Wheeler up about Spring Place and Cleveland, do so. Telegraph to Colonel Donaldson, Nashville, to send down cavalry by cars, and also call for all cavalry you can hear of that is within reach. I want Wheeler dogged, the prisoners and plunder rescued, and his force damaged all that is possible. Kilpatrick has already driven Jackson off the West Point road, and mashed that again, and Garrard is out on the other flank. I will avail myself all I can of Wheeler's absence to destroy the railroads south and the cavalry he has left behind. Did you hear anything of the cavalry you sent out from Cartersville?

W. T. SHERMAN,
Major-General.

RESACA, *August 16, 1864—10.30 a. m.*

Maj. Gen. W. T. SHERMAN:

I have heard nothing of the cavalry I sent from Cartersville. You will be telegraphed from there as soon as anything comes. Will send courier through to Dalton with dispatch to General Steedman containing what you direct about cavalry from Nashville.

E. M. McCOOK,
Brigadier-General.

RESACA, *August 16, 1864.*

Maj. Gen. W. T. SHERMAN:

Cavalry just come in from near Spring Place. Struck the enemy's pickets two miles from the town. Martin is at Spring Place with force; scouts report them about 2,000 strong. Wheeler encamped there last night, and citizens report that he was going to Cleveland with the rest of his command, while Martin remained at Spring Place. General Smith is sending this information to General Steedman by courier. I think Martin holds this point in order to control the only roads over which Wheeler could retreat eastward. I telegraphed to Rome to-day to send any cavalry they had over here.

E. M. McCOOK,
Brigadier-General.

HDQRS. FIRST CAV. DIV., DEPT. OF THE CUMBERLAND,
Cartersville, Ga., August 16, 1864.

Brig. Gen. E. M. McCOOK, *Kingston, Ga.:*

All the information we can get seems to indicate that the enemy are concentrating for an attack on this place from the south side of the Etowah. Scouts have been sent out to ascertain their force and movements. Colonel Alexander, commanding fortifications at the bridge, advises the removal of all trains under the guns of the fort at the bridge. Unless otherwise directed by you, all the wagons and supply trains will be moved under the guns of the fort and the troops bivouacked in their present position on the Stilesborough road, prepared for an attack from that direction.

J. A. S. MITCHELL,
Captain and Inspector.

CARTERSVILLE, GA., *August 16, 1864.*

Brigadier-General SMITH,
        Resaca, Ga.:

GENERAL: I report the enemy (General Wheeler) having crossed at Frog Town and above, from 10,000 to 15,000 strong, between Friday noon and Sunday night. They moved in three columns, Wheeler passing through Jasper with a very large force on Saturday night and Sunday. General Wheeler said he intended striking Dalton, Kingston, Resaca, Tilton, and Tunnel Hill, then move into Tennessee. They reported 30,000 General Lee's infantry following the force of General Wheeler. They have made no attempt to carry off the cattle south, but keep them with their column. The country about Jasper is full of rebels hunting down Union men, shooting some, and burning houses. I marched six miles beyond Jasper on the east, and have been ten hours out of the saddle since I left camp. Paine and Edwards, the two guides, were captured. Country eaten out of subsistence. The enemy had fourteen pieces of artillery.

I am, general, very respectfully, your obedient servant,
                        THOMAS T. HEATH,
                Colonel Fifth Ohio Volunteer Cavalry.

RESACA, *August 16, 1864.*

Major-General SHERMAN:

I move out this a. m. for Spring Place. Shall be governed by circumstances, as I cannot communicate with General Steedman in less than twenty-four hours from time of my arrival last night, 11.30 o'clock, at which time I sent couriers. Wheeler has concentrated his forces. I think if he is north I can accomplish what you desire by moving to Spring Place. I have 2,200 men, five days' supplies, and one section artillery. Colonel Raum will forward any communication you may have to make.

                        JNO. E. SMITH,
                        Brigadier-General.

RESACA, *August 16, 1864—12 m.*

Major-General SHERMAN:

The operators at Cleveland report the enemy moving toward Charleston, having passed within one mile of that place last night. I have sent out cavalry in direction of Spring Place; have not heard from them.

                        JNO. E. SMITH,
                        Brigadier-General.

RESACA, *August 16, 1864—2.30 p. m.*

General SHERMAN:

Six rebel regiments reported within ten miles of Cartersville. Waiting to hear from General Steedman.

                        JNO. E. SMITH,
                        Brigadier-General.

HDQRS. MILITARY DIVISION OF THE MISSISSIPPI,
In the Field, near Atlanta, Ga., August 16, 1864.

General JOHN E. SMITH,
Resaca:

I have your dispatch of 12 m. and Colonel Raum's of 10.30 a. m. You should make a junction with the Dalton force as soon as possible, restore the telegraph and railroad, and feel out to Spring Place. If Wheeler goes up into East Tennessee, well; only get word to Chattanooga and Nashville as soon as possible; I would rather he was there than here. Do all you can to rescue his prisoners, and don't let him return. Get on the road by which he went and obstruct it by all the means in your power. It may be he has gone up into East Tennessee with a part, and a part remains; in that event fall upon the latter and drive it as far as your men have endurance. Clean out Spring Place, move its inhabitants north and burn the town, if you think they have connived or played spies on our road. Communicate these views to General Steedman and I will approve whatever you or he may do.

W. T. SHERMAN,
Major-General, Commanding.

HDQRS. MILITARY DIVISION OF THE MISSISSIPPI,
In the Field, near Atlanta, August 16, 1864.

General JOHN E. SMITH,
Resaca:

I hear nothing of the six regiments near Cartersville. The wire was interrupted for some hours, but now is working well. If Martin's division be at Spring Place and Wheeler above Dalton, Martin should be attacked by infantry, and the road occupied and obstructed by all possible ways, so that he cannot move artillery or wagons. As soon as you communicate with General Steedman, and he is satisfied he can handle Wheeler, return to your post with the command. The stores in Allatoona are so valuable that I don't want to risk them too much. Wheeler's move north was forced upon him, and if he could be hemmed in he won't fight hard. He depends on sudden dashes and surprise. I have broken the West Point road good, and will try the Macon road, without which Hood cannot feed his army. Wheeler will find it hard to feed his men and horses up there. General Steedman can call from above a good many troops, and horses will be along soon.

W. T. SHERMAN,
Major-General, Commanding.

HDQRS. MILITARY DIVISION OF THE MISSISSIPPI,
In the Field, near Atlanta, Ga., August 16, 1864.

General JOHN E. SMITH,
Resaca:

I do not think you should attack Wheeler in position with your force. Better wait till you act in concert with General Steedman, who can bring to Dalton from the rear a good force that can do the thing sure

W. T. SHERMAN,
Major-General, Commanding.

RESACA, *August 16, 1864—10.20 a. m.*

General SHERMAN:

An officer just from Dalton left there at 7 a. m.   Martin's division was moving from the east upon Dalton.   Colonel Laiboldt had moved out to feel of them.   Skirmishing had commenced.   The colonel feels secure. He has two pieces of artillery.   General Smith still here.

G. B. RAUM,
Colonel, Commanding Brigade.

HDQRS. MILITARY DIVISION OF THE MISSISSIPPI,
In the Field, near Atlanta, August 16, 1864.

Colonel RAUM,
Resaca:

Keep me well advised, especially as to how soon the railroad will be repaired, as I want to make another move of great importance as soon as I can calculate the great question of supplies.   All well here.

W. T. SHERMAN,
Major-General, Commanding.

HDQRS. MILITARY DIVISION OF THE MISSISSIPPI,
In the Field, near Atlanta, August 16, 1864.

Colonel RAUM,
Resaca:

It is very important to resume telegraphic communication with Chattanooga.   We have stores enough for two weeks.   I want Wheeler opposed at all points and when possible dogged; he can do us no danger up toward Cleveland.   If Martin's division be at Spring Place it should be attacked and driven north.

W. T. SHERMAN,
Major-General, Commanding.

RESACA, *August 16, 1864—7 p. m.*

Major-General SHERMAN:

I am just from Tilton.   The track south of there will be repaired by 11 o'clock to-night.   As soon as repaired I will go by railroad to the break south of Dalton, take with me the section men, and assist in the repairs there.   The telegraph, I think, can be repaired to Dalton to-morrow.   I will take any dispatch that you wish to send.

G. B. RAUM,
Colonel, Commanding Brigade.

CARTERSVILLE, GA., *August 16, 1864.*

Brigadier-General MCARTHUR,
Commanding at Marietta:

GENERAL: Can you send me 300 muskets, caliber .58? I am threatened with an attack by six regiments rebel cavalry, and require the above-mentioned arms to arm dismounted cavalry and convalescents. I will send train for the same.

I am, general, very respectfully, your obedient servant,

J. I. ALEXANDER,
Colonel, Commanding Post.

HDQRS. MILITARY DIVISION OF THE MISSISSIPPI,
In the Field, near Atlanta, Ga., August 16, 1864.

COMMANDING OFFICER,
Cartersville:

Has nothing been heard of the cavalry sent out by General McCook? What was the occasion of the wire being interrupted? I have ordered a sufficient force to Allatoona in case of need, but the Etowah bridge is more important than Cartersville, and should you be threatened by superior force, move to the bridge, and all trains into Allatoona.

W. T. SHERMAN,
Major-General, Commanding.

CARTERSVILLE, GA., *August 16, 1864.*

Brigadier-General SMITH,
Via Resaca:

One of our scouting parties has just returned. I am satisfied that there is no considerable force below us, on the opposite side of the river. Everything is in good order here, and I feel sure that we are equal to any emergency that is likely to arise.

I am, general, very respectfully, your obedient servant,

J. I. ALEXANDER,
Colonel, Commanding Post.

ALLATOONA, *August 16, 1864.*

Major-General SHERMAN:

No news of the cavalry or of the cattle has been received at this post.

J. E. TOURTELLOTTE,
Lieutenant-Colonel Fourth Minnesota Volunteers, Commanding.

HDQRS. MILITARY DIVISION OF THE MISSISSIPPI,
In the Field, near Atlanta, Ga., August 16, 1864.

COMMANDING OFFICER AT ALLATOONA:

What force have you at Allatoona, and what at the bridge?

W. T. SHERMAN,
Major-General, Commanding.

ALLATOONA, *August 16, 1864.*

Major-General SHERMAN:

I have at this place 500 guns and 4 pieces of artillery. At the bridge across Allatoona Creek there are 70 guns.

J. E. TOURTELLOTTE,
Lieutenant-Colonel, Commanding.

HDQRS. MILITARY DIVISION OF THE MISSISSIPPI,
In the Field, near Atlanta, Ga., August 16, 1864.

COMMANDING OFFICER AT ALLATOONA:

Defend that place and those stores at all costs. Send me word if anything occurs, that I may, if necessary, send you re-enforcements.

W. T. SHERMAN,
Major-General, Commanding.

HDQRS. MILITARY DIVISION OF THE MISSISSIPPI,
In the Field, near Atlanta, Ga., August 16, 1864.

General MCARTHUR,
  Marietta:

Communicate with Colonel Tourtellotte, commanding at Allatoona, and if you have reason to believe our stores there in danger, send by cars all the men you can spare, and send cars to me for re-enforcements for Marietta.

W. T. SHERMAN,
Major-General, Commanding.

HDQRS. MILITARY DIVISION OF THE MISSISSIPPI,
In the Field, near Atlanta, Ga., August 16, 1864.

Colonel TOURTELLOTTE,
  Allatoona:

I have instructed General McArthur, in case the stores in Allatoona Pass are endangered, to send you re-enforcements by cars from Marietta, and I will replace them from here. Send word to the bridge and Cartersville that if attacked they must fight to the last. Cavalry will not attack troops in position, because half the men must watch the horses. The bridge, the stores, and the Allatoona depot must be held, cost what it may.

W. T. SHERMAN,
Major-General, Commanding.

HDQRS. MILITARY DIVISION OF THE MISSISSIPPI,
In the Field, near Atlanta, Ga., August 16, 1864.

Colonel TOURTELLOTTE,
  Allatoona:

What force is at the Etowah bridge and Cartersville?

W. T. SHERMAN,
Major-General, Commanding.

ALLATOONA, *August 16, 1864.*

Major-General SHERMAN:

One regiment and four pieces of artillery at Etowah bridge.

J. E. TOURTELLOTTE,
Lieutenant-Colonel, Commanding.

ALLATOONA, *August 16, 1864.*

Major-General SHERMAN:

There were two regiments and four-gun battery at Etowah bridge and one regiment at Cartersville, but think one regiment at least was sent away yesterday.

J. E. TOURTELLOTTE,
Lieutenant-Colonel, Commanding.

MARIETTA, *August 16, 1864.*

General SHERMAN:

The train I sent to Cartersville this p. m. has just returned. The arms were distributed at Etowah bridge. The conductor reports that they were expecting an attack, both at the bridge and at Cartersville.

                                        J. B. VAN DYNE.

MARIETTA, *August 16, 1864.*

Major-General SHERMAN.

At 4 p. m. to-day we had four trains at Resaca, one at Kingston, and two at Cartersville. At 5.10 p. m. I sent a train of four cars from Marietta to Cartersville with 300 muskets and a guard of 75 men. I have four engines and forty cars at Marietta, and the regular hospital train is at the front.

                              J. B. VAN DYNE,
                                   Master of Transportation.

DALTON, *August 16, 1864.*

Major-General STEEDMAN:

I just received following note from J. E. Smith, brigadier-general:

RESACA, *August 15—11.30 p. m.*

I have just arrived with 2,000 men. General Sherman directs me to communicate with General Steedman; if he is not there you will communicate such information as you may have of the movements of enemy. General Sherman desires that Wheeler be driven toward Tennessee and not be allowed to return down the valley. I shall move out toward Spring Place in the morning. You will telegraph General Steedman and send me reply as soon as possible.

Yours, respectfully,

                                        J. E. SMITH,
                                         Brigadier-General.

I shall endeavor to find out Wheeler's whereabouts, and do all in my power with the troops at my disposal to accomplish the desired object. Please answer immediately.

                                   B. LAIBOLDT,
                              Colonel, Commanding Post.

DALTON, *August 16, 1864—6 a. m.*

Major-General STEEDMAN,
          Chattanooga:

I just received information that Martin's (rebel) division is in camp four miles from here on this side of the river.

                                   B. LAIBOLDT,
                                   Colonel, Commanding.

DALTON, *August 16, 1864—7 p. m.*

Major-General STEEDMAN:

The enemy is collecting forces on the Spring Place road, near Thompson's Mill, and the Connesauga River. Citizens report that their intention is to blow up the tunnel.

                                   B. LAIBOLDT,
                                   Colonel, Commanding.

GRAYSVILLE, *August 16, 1864.*

Major MOE,
      Assistant Adjutant-General:

Rebels in force in Parker's Gap. They have run our scouts into this post. They are from 600 to 700 strong. I have sent scouts out to feel the enemy.

S. CRANE,
Captain, Commanding.

———

BLOCK-HOUSE, GRAYSVILLE, *August 16, 1864—7 p. m.*

Major MOE,
      Assistant Adjutant-General:

We are attacked here, but still hold the bridge. Scouts report heavy force of the enemy. Answer.

S. CRANE,
Captain, Commanding.

———

CLEVELAND, *August 16, 1864.*

Brigadier-General AMMEN:

The enemy which were within a mile of this place last night have turned toward Charleston. They are 2,500 strong, with cavalry and artillery.

H. G. GIBSON,
Colonel Second Ohio Heavy Artillery.

———

LOUDON, *August 16, 1864.*

Capt. W. P. AMMEN,
      Assistant Adjutant-General:

The following just received from Cleveland:

Lieut. Col. M. L. PATTERSON:

Twenty-five hundred rebels, said to be under Kirby Smith, encamped near here last night, and went toward Charleston this morning; did not attack; are now at least 400 at Benton, driving up stock.

H. G. GIBSON,
Colonel.

I have sent out scouts in direction of Sweet Water, also ordered scouts to be sent out from Kingston in the direction of Charleston.

M. L. PATTERSON,
Lieutenant-Colonel, Commanding.

———

LOUDON, *August 16, 1864.*

Capt. W. P. AMMEN,
      Assistant Adjutant-General:

Dispatch received from department provost-marshal at Athens states the rebels are crossing the river at Columbus coming from Benton. Colonel Ewing, commanding at Charleston, sends for me to send men to Athens. He fears that place will be attacked before morning. I dispatched him that I had not the men to spare.

M. L. PATTERSON,
Lieutenant-Colonel, Commanding.

35 R R—VOL XXXVIII, PT V

SPECIAL FIELD ORDERS,   HDQRS. MIL. DIV. OF THE MISS.,
     No. 57.   *In the Field, near Atlanta, August 16, 1864.*

The movement of the army against the Macon railroad will begin Thursday night, August 18, and will be continued on the following general plan:

I. All army commanders will send across the Chattahoochee River and within the old rebel works at the bridge and down as far as Turner's Ferry all surplus wagons, horses, men, and materials not absolutely necessary to the success of the expedition, and will collect in their wagons with best teams bread, meat, sugar, coffee, &c., for fifteen days after the 19th instant, and ammunition, and park them near Utoy Creek.

First move: General Kilpatrick's cavalry will move to Camp Creek; General Schofield will cover the Campbellton road, and General Thomas will move one corps (General Williams') to the Chattahoochee bridge, with orders to hold it, Pace's Ferry bridge, and a pontoon bridge (Captain Kossak's), at Turner's Ferry, ready to be laid down if necessary. The other corps, General Stanley's, will move south of Proctor's Creek, to near the Utoy, behind the right center of the Army of the Tennessee, prepared to cover the Bell's Ferry road. General Garrard's cavalry will fall behind Peach Tree Creek, and act against the enemy should he sally against General Williams' or General Stanley's corps during the movement.

Second move: The Army of the Tennessee will withdraw, cross Utoy Creek, and move by the most direct road toward Fairburn, going as far as Camp Creek. General Thomas will mass his two corps, Generals Stanley's and Johnson's, below Utoy Creek, and General Garrard's cavalry will join General Thomas by the most direct road or by way of Sandtown bridge, and act with him during the rest of the move. General Schofield will advance abreast of and in communication with the Army of the Tennessee as far as Camp Creek.

Third move: The Armies of the Ohio and Tennessee will move direct for the West Point road, aiming to strike it between Red Oak and Fairburn. General Thomas will follow well closed up in two columns, the trains between. General Kilpatrick will act as the advance, and General Garrard will cover the rear, under direction of General Thomas. The bridges at Sandtown will be kept and protected by a detachment of cavalry detailed by General Elliott, with a section of guns or four-gun battery.

II. During the movement, and until the army returns to the river, the utmost care will be taken to expose as little as possible the trains of cars and wagons. The depots at the bridge, at Allatoona, and Marietta will be held against any attack, and communication kept up with the army as far as possible by way of Sandtown. On reaching any railroad, the troops will at once be disposed for defense, and at least one-third put to work to tear up track and destroy iron, ties, and all railroad materials.

By order of Major-General Sherman:

                             L. M. DAYTON,
                                Aide-de-Camp.

———

SPECIAL FIELD ORDERS,   HEADQUARTERS DEPARTMENT
                           AND ARMY OF THE TENNESSEE,
     No. 100.   *Before Atlanta, Ga., August 16, 1864.*
       *   *   *   *   *   *   *

XIII. The Fourth Division, Sixteenth Army Corps, Brigadier-General Ransom commanding, will form the left flank of this army, taking up a good position on Proctor's Creek. To this end, Major-General Blair, commanding Seventeenth Army Corps, will cause General Ransom's division to be relieved, and will then in conjunction with Major-General Logan, commanding Fifteenth Corps, occupy the entire line to the new right of the Sixteenth Corps. Capt. C. B. Reese, chief engineer, will indicate to General Ransom the position to be occupied by him. These dispositions will be made after dark to-morrow, the 17th instant, and corps commanders will make all necessary arrangements during the day, in order that the movement may be effected with celerity and without noise.

By order of Maj. Gen. O. O. Howard:

WM. T. CLARK,
Assistant Adjutant-General.

HDQRS. MILITARY DIVISION OF THE MISSISSIPPI,
In the Field, near Atlanta, Ga., August 17, 1864.
(Received 6 p. m. 18th.)

Maj. Gen. H. W. HALLECK,
Washington, D. C.:

Your dispatch of yesterday is received.* We must have the Alabama River, and, if I remember the bay, the best river channel is on the Tensas side; but, of course, I must trust to Admiral Farragut and General Canby. I have a tight grip on Atlanta, and was on the point of swinging round to the southeast when Wheeler went to my rear with 6,000 cavalry; he has passed into East Tennessee, having damaged us but little. I will avail myself of his absence to reciprocate the compliment, and to-morrow night the Macon road must be broken good. General Kilpatrick will undertake it. Wheeler cannot disturb Knoxville or Loudon. He may hurt some of the minor points, but, on the whole, East Tennessee is a good place for him to break down his horses, and a poor place to steal new ones. All well.

W. T. SHERMAN,
Major-General.

NEAR ATLANTA, *August 17, 1864—11.30 a. m.*
(Received 7 p. m. 18th.)

Maj. Gen. H. W. HALLECK,
Washington, D. C.:

The trouble about cotton is the time consumed in loading and unloading. It is all we can do to get supplies up, for I have to make allowance for our road being broken one-third the time. There is very little cotton in North Georgia, but I will order quartermasters to collect all and send it to Colonel Donaldson at Nashville, where the Treasury Department may have it or buy it of nominal owners.†

W. T. SHERMAN,
Major-General.

---

* Probably of August 14, 2 p. m., p. 488.
† Sent in reply to the President's inquiry of August 15 (see p. 505), which, as received by General Sherman, was signed H. W. Halleck.

HDQRS. MILITARY DIVISION OF THE MISSISSIPPI,
In the Field, near Atlanta, August 17, 1864.

General THOMAS :

I have a message from General Kilpatrick, inclosing a copy of his report to General Elliott.* He thinks it not only possible but comparatively easy to break the railroad to Macon effectually. I do not want to move this vast army and its paraphernalia round Atlanta unless forced to do so, and it does seem the enemy has offered us the very opportunity we seek. We know positively that Wheeler is above Dalton, and that he must have taken the very flower of his cavalry. He has, and may do us harm, but that we cannot help. I do not think he can carry any point of our road that he can maintain, and his own necessities will force him back soon with jaded and worn-out horses. Now, ours can be quickly moved to Sandtown at a walk, and according to General Kilpatrick can reach Red Oak or any point below the enemy's infantry, and by a single dash can beat the remaining cavalry of the enemy and break up many miles of that railroad. General Garrard with one brigade could amuse those on the east, and General Kilpatrick with his own and the two brigades of General Garrard, under Colonel Long, could make in a single move a break that would disturb Hood seriously. The risk will be comparatively small, as General Schofield can act in support with his whole command. I am perfectly alive to the fact that the loss of our cavalry would be most serious, but I do think such an opportunity if neglected will never again appear. In this combination I would merely suspend the final execution of the movement of the whole army till the result of this move is reached. I think we could give General Kilpatrick such orders that he would not be rash, and General Schofield could move to his right a couple of miles, and make it certain that Hood would not attempt to use infantry to interpose to the return of our cavalry. Don't make any orders till you and I have perfectly agreed on this plan. In the mean time anything done toward the movement of the whole army will not be lost, as it simply amounts to sending to the bridge all the loose ends. I have sent for General Kilpatrick to come up.

W. T. SHERMAN,
Major-General, Commanding.

HDQRS. MILITARY DIVISION OF THE MISSISSIPPI,
August 17, 1864.

General THOMAS:

I wish you to notify General Garrard to have one of his brigades ready to make a demonstration, without risking battle, on our left, and have the effective part of two brigades, under Long if possible, ready to move this night by moonlight by Pace's Ferry and Sandtown bridges, to operate under Kilpatrick, on our right. They will not move till I see Kilpatrick in person and have a clear understanding. Stanley's line should be most persistent in annoying the enemy, and making feints as though looking for a place to assault. Though you may continue to make preparations to move the infantry as heretofore ordered, do not actually move till further orders.

W. T. SHERMAN,
Major-General.

---

* See p. 531.

[Indorsement.]

HEADQUARTERS DEPARTMENT OF THE CUMBERLAND,
Near Atlanta, August 17, 1864.

Respectfully referred to Major-General Stanley, with instructions to carry out so much of this order as relates to his corps.

By command of Major-General Thomas:

HENRY STONE,
Assistant Adjutant-General.

HEADQUARTERS DEPARTMENT OF THE CUMBERLAND,
August 17, 1864.

Major-General SHERMAN:

Your dispatch directing the movement of the cavalry has been received, and the necessary orders given Garrard; also orders to keep the enemy fully occupied to-morrow and next day.

GEO. H. THOMAS,
Major-General.

HEADQUARTERS DEPARTMENT OF THE CUMBERLAND,
August 17, 1864.

Major-General SHERMAN:

General Kimball reports that the enemy appears to be massing in front of his Second Brigade. I have directed him to be on the alert and endeavor to detect what movement is attempted as soon as possible. Should he mass on my left it will offer a favorable opportunity to Kilpatrick.

GEO. H. THOMAS,
Major-General.

HDQRS. MILITARY DIVISION OF THE MISSISSIPPI,
In the Field, near Atlanta, August 17, 1864.

General THOMAS:

I would be glad to know the enemy is massing against General Kimball, but your signal officer at the Howard house reports 10 a. m. that but few troops appear on the line there; that the front line seems almost abandoned, and but few people can be seen in the city; but let us watch them close until all is ready. I expect General Kilpatrick here this p. m., when I will make distinct and final orders. If General Kilpatrick starts from General Schofield's right, General Garrard's two brigades could move by the road this way, saving six or eight miles by moving by moonlight.

W. T. SHERMAN,
Major-General, Commanding.

HDQRS. MILITARY DIVISION OF THE MISSISSIPPI,
Near Atlanta, August 17, 1864.

General THOMAS:

General Kilpatrick is here and gives me a description of his position at Sandtown that convinces me he can, in connection with Schofield, so effectually destroy the Macon railroad that it cannot be used in two weeks, and that too without risking his cavalry. You will, therefore, order General Garrard to send to Sandtown, via Pace's Ferry and the west bank, the two brigades of cavalry, heretofore notified, with a battery of artillery, to move to-night and report on arrival to General Kilpatrick at Sandtown. The horses should be well fed, and could take some wagons of shelled corn as far as Sandtown, when the wagons may return. Men provided with full ammunition and five days' bread, sugar, coffee, and plenty of salt. General Kilpatrick will keep his command concealed all day to-morrow and move to-morrow night, cross the West Point road above Fairburn, reach the Macon road near Jonesborough, face toward East Point, and break road to the south. The dispatch from Cartersville I sent you an hour since is conclusive that Wheeler is away, and but little cavalry is left here. Kilpatrick will want a diversion day after to-morrow, and I will see that Schofield makes a considerable one, and I wish you to have Garrard's remaining brigade and Stanley's division give full occupation to that flank; I will risk the other. Instruct Garrard to be sure to send the pioneers along with the cavalry, provided with the tools to break up railroad. Kilpatrick represents forage abundant down there. Kilpatrick ranks Garrard, and the latter may go along if you prefer.

W. T. SHERMAN,
Major-General.

NOTE.—Instead of moving via Pace's Ferry the two brigades will move to-night on this (east) side of the river to Sandtown.
By order of Brigadier-General Elliott:

DAVID F. HOW,
Lieutenant and Acting Assistant Adjutant-General.

HEADQUARTERS DEPARTMENT OF THE CUMBERLAND,
August 17, 1864.

Major-General SHERMAN:

The report of General Kimball that the enemy seemed to be massing on his left, as if with the intention of attacking him, does not seem to be well founded. General Stanley reports that he cannot perceive any evidence of the enemy, though he observes more than the usual activity along their lines.

GEO. H. THOMAS,
Major-General, U. S. Volunteers, Commanding.

HDQRS. MILITARY DIVISION OF THE MISSISSIPPI,
In the Field, near Atlanta, August 17, 1864.

General THOMAS:

I now have positive and official information that General Wheeler has gone up into East Tennessee beyond Spring Place. We will repair all damages to railroad and telegraph to-night. I will not move our infantry, but break the Macon road all to pieces with our cavalry to-morrow night. Therefore be active and demonstrate against Atlanta to occupy the front and make believe we will attack them in their trenches during to-morrow and next day.

W. T. SHERMAN,
Major-General, Commanding.

(Same to Generals Schofield and Howard.)

HEADQUARTERS DEPARTMENT OF THE CUMBERLAND,
August 17, 1864.

Major-General SHERMAN:

Information from all sources seems to confirm the report that Wheeler has taken off the greater part of his cavalry. I therefore think this will be as good a time as could be taken to make another raid on the Macon railroad, but if you send Kilpatrick I would insist on his taking the most practicable route and avoid the enemy's infantry as much as possible.

GEO. H. THOMAS,
Major-General.

HDQRS. MILITARY DIVISION OF THE MISSISSIPPI,
In the Field, near Atlanta, August 17, 1864.

Major-General THOMAS,
Commanding Army of the Cumberland:

GENERAL: I beg you will convey the following orders to govern General Kilpatrick in his movement on the Macon road. It is not a raid, but a deliberate attack for the purpose of so disabling that road that the enemy will be unable to supply his army in Atlanta. He will have his own division of cavalry and two good brigades from General Garrard's division. With these he will move to-morrow night, aiming to cross the West Point road between Red Oak and Fairburn. If he has time he should remove a small section of the road without using fire, simply to lessen the chances of an infantry force being sent to intercept his return. He should then move in force to the nearest point of the Macon road, about Jonesborough, and should destroy as much of that road as he possibly can do, working steadily until forced to take to his arms and horses for battle. He should avoid battle with infantry or artillery, but may safely fight any cavalry he encounters, because we know that the enemy has sent Wheeler with full 6,000 cavalry up into East Tennessee. I leave the extent of the break to General Kilpatrick, but will only say that he cannot destroy too much. Having fulfilled his task he will return and resume his post on the right flank of the army and send General Garrard's brigades back to their division on the left. General Schofield will be instructed to move to his right as far as prudent the day after to-morrow and all the army should so engage the attention of the enemy that he cannot detach infantry as against General Kilpatrick. Instruct the general to advise us at the earliest possible moment of his success.

I am, with respect, yours, truly,

W. T. SHERMAN,
Major-General, Commanding.

THOMAS' HEADQUARTERS,
August 17, 1864.

Major-General SHERMAN:

Your dispatch ordering the preparation of two brigades of General Garrard's cavalry to report to General Kilpatrick has been received, and the necessary orders have been given, not only to Garrard, but to Stanley, regarding the demonstration on the enemy.

GEO. H. THOMAS,
Major-General.

HOWARD'S HOUSE, *August 17, 1864—8 a. m.*
Captain CASE :

I cannot discover anything new in enemy's lines. I can see but the upper part of the large fort southwest of here on the south side of the city. Cannot see any embrasures. Think it is a barbette fort. Saw but one man in it yet. Can see no guns in it. Think the fort faces southeast. Very few people to be seen in the city, and very little firing on skirmish line. Cannot see any more marks with the big glass than I could with my own.

BURTON.

HOWARD'S HOUSE, *August 17, 1864—10 a. m.*
Captain CASE:

There does not seem to be as many troops behind the works to the left of enemy's fort on our extreme left. Cannot see as many shelters there as usual. It is remarkably quiet, and scarcely any one to be seen in the city; only an occasional artillery shot heard on our right. The battle-flag that has been flying from their first line is gone.

BURTON.

VINING'S, *August 17, 1864.*
Captain CASE:

Heavy column of dust one-half mile length, south 20 degrees, five miles from here, moving to the west.

BRENT,
Lieutenant and Signal Officer.

HEADQUARTERS FOURTH ARMY CORPS,
Near Atlanta, Ga., August 17, 1864—1.45 p. m.
General WHIPPLE, *Chief of Staff:*

GENERAL: The communication of Colonel Bennett, Seventy-fifth Illinois, and indorsed by General Kimball, seems to have created a wrong impression. While the enemy have displayed much activity along his line to-day, and his troops have been seen getting into line apparently to change position, there are no more, if as many, troops visible to-day as yesterday. I have four good lookouts along the line of my front, and every movement of the enemy is closely watched and reported to me. I am carrying out the order of General Sherman transmitted through your headquarters, and have ordered Captain Bridges, chief of artillery, to open along the line during the p. m.

I am, your obedient servant,

D. S. STANLEY,
Major-General.

HEADQUARTERS FOURTH ARMY CORPS,
August 17, 1864—2 p. m.
Brigadier-General WHIPPLE, *Chief of Staff:*

General Wood is very anxious that the order transferring Post's regiment to the Third Division and the Twenty-third Kentucky to the First Division should be issued at once, as he wants Post installed before the contemplated movement. Could you send the order this afternoon?

Your obedient servant,

D. S. STANLEY,
Major-General.

HEADQUARTERS DEPARTMENT OF THE CUMBERLAND,
Before Atlanta, Ga., August 17, 1864.

Maj. Gen. D. S. STANLEY, *Commanding Fourth Army Corps:*

The major-general commanding directs me to acknowledge the receipt of your report of this morning, announcing the massing of the enemy on your left. In reply the major-general commanding would caution you to be watchful at every point, and endeavor to discover if possible what the movement may really be; whether it be with the intention of an attack on your lines, or if it be only a massing of his forces preparatory to his withdrawal. That some movement is being made by him in the disposition of his forces is evident, and we should be on the *qui vive* to improve any advantages which present themselves, as well as to secure ourselves from any damage by his attack on us. The major-general commanding desires that you take the precaution to prevent any stampeding of your troops and be ready to repel any ordinary attack that may be made upon you, and in case an overwhelming force should be thrown against you, one over which you could not hope to be successful, that you withdraw your troops in good order and without confusion. The major-general commanding desires also that you inform General Garrard of your impressions as to the designs of the enemy, but not to say that they are massing on him or yourself unless it is positively known to be so. Great caution will need to be exercised, and it is hoped all will be well. Please report any further indications that may be seen in your front of movement on the part of the enemy.

I have the honor to be, general, very respectfully, your obedient servant,

ROBT. H. RAMSEY,
Assistant Adjutant-General.

HEADQUARTERS FOURTH ARMY CORPS,
Near Atlanta, Ga., August 17, 1864—12.25 p. m.

General KIMBALL:

GENERAL: The following is just received from General Sherman, through department headquarters:

Stanley's line should be most persistent in annoying the enemy and making feints, as though looking for a place to assault.

W. T. SHERMAN,
Major-General.

Division commanders will, with their pickets, keep up a persistent fire to annoy the enemy. General Kimball will repeat the maneuvers that he executed a few days ago, viz, send a regiment at a time out to the vicinity of the railroad and try and create an impression upon the enemy that he is massing troops to assault their lines. Generals Newton and Wood will cause their men to display unusual activity in their camps, and if possible march troops in the enemy's view, letting them file past in sight of the enemy, then disappear, and again, after marching behind a hill or through thick timber, reappear and try and create the impression that a heavy column is massing on our left (the enemy's right). One good place for this is in rear of where the divisions of Generals Wood and Kimball join. Whenever this is practicable, have it done.

By command of Major-General Stanley:

WM. H. SINCLAIR,
Major and Assistant Adjutant-General.

(Same to Generals Newton and Wood.)

HEADQUARTERS FOURTH ARMY CORPS,
Near Atlanta, Ga., August 17, 1864—7.45 p. m.

General KIMBALL:

GENERAL: By instructions received from the headquarters of the department, the movements of this corps, indicated by instructions this morning for to-morrow evening at dark, are postponed until further and definite orders. It is desirable, however, that everything should be kept in as much readiness for movement as possible. To this end the supply and ordnance trains provided for in this morning's note will be kept loaded ready to move, and all surplus baggage will be sent to the corps train at Vining's Station. By General Sherman's order all the demonstrations of force and disposition to attack possible must be kept up to-morrow and next day. To this end regiments must be paraded frequently and marched near the line of works from one part of the line to another. Reveille, without drums or bugles, will be at 3.30 to-morrow morning, and the regiments will all be paraded and some portions of them marched along the line as indicated. Fires for the purpose of raising smoke must be kept up in the woods to the rear of our lines, giving the impression of increased force.

By order of Major-General Stanley:

J. S. FULLERTON,
Assistant Adjutant-General.

(Same to Generals Newton and Wood.)

HEADQUARTERS FOURTEENTH ARMY CORPS,
Near Atlanta, Ga., August 17, 1864.

[Brig. Gen. WILLIAM D. WHIPPLE:]

GENERAL: Nothing new occurred on the front of the Fourteenth Corps to-day. One prisoner and one deserter received to-day. The troops in our front have been changed to prevent desertions. If I was supplied with the President's proclamation and General Orders, No. 64, War Department, 1863, I think I could induce the greater portion of the Georgia and Alabama troops to join us.

Respectfully, your obedient servant,

R. W. JOHNSON,
Brigadier-General of Volunteers, Commanding.

HDQRS. CHIEF OF CAVALRY, DEPT. OF THE CUMBERLAND,
Near Atlanta, Ga., August 17, 1864.

Brig. Gen. K. GARRARD,
Commanding Second Division Cavalry:

I am directed by the general commanding to say that you will have one of your brigades ready to make a demonstration, without risking battle, on our left. You will also have the effective force of two brigades, under command of Colonel Long, ready to move to-night by moonlight, via Pace's Ferry and Sandtown bridge, to Sandtown.

I have the honor to be, very respectfully, &c.,

DAVID F. HOW,
Lieutenant and Acting Assistant Adjutant-General.

HEADQUARTERS DEPARTMENT OF THE CUMBERLAND,
Before Atlanta, Ga., August 17, 1864.
Brig. Gen. K. GARRARD,
Commanding Second Cavalry Division:

The major-general commanding directs me to inform you that he is in receipt of a report from Major-General Stanley of a movement on the part of the enemy on our left. He desires you to keep a strict lookout, and watch any movement that may be made by him, exercising great caution to prevent a stampede on the part of your command and prepared to resist any ordinary attack made on your lines. Should, however, the force sent against you be more than you could successfully cope with, you will be expected to withdraw your troops in good order. Please report any indications of a movement on the part of the enemy.

I have the honor to be, general, very respectfully, your obedient servant,

ROBT. H. RAMSEY,
Assistant Adjutant-General.

HDQRS. MILITARY DIVISION OF THE MISSISSIPPI,
In the Field, near Atlanta, August 17, 1864—10.40 a. m.
General SCHOFIELD:

I think I will defer the grand movement for a day or so, and precede it by a cavalry movement on the Macon road between Rough and Ready and Jonesborough. I propose to give General Kilpatrick his whole division and two of General Garrard's brigades to move quietly down to Camp Creek, and then by a rapid movement strike and break thoroughly the Macon road, your infantry to co-operate and divert attention. We know that Wheeler is well to the north with a large part of the cavalry, and now is the time. I expect General Kilpatrick up. Any preparations for the infantry move will be all right, and we need only postpone the time of execution.

W. T. SHERMAN,
Major-General, Commanding.

HEADQUARTERS ARMY OF THE OHIO,
August 17, 1864.
Major-General SHERMAN:

At what time will Kilpatrick start? I propose to push out in the direction that Cox took the other day and threaten East Point. If Kilpatrick is to start to-morrow night, probably I had better push out some distance to-morrow, fortify and stay there, and then press East Point closely the next day. If he is to start in the morning I ought to press closely to-morrow. Please inform me whether this accords with your views.

J. M. SCHOFIELD,
Major-General.

HDQRS. MILITARY DIVISION OF THE MISSISSIPPI,
In the Field, near Atlanta, August 17, 1864—6.45 p. m.
General SCHOFIELD:

To-night two brigades of cavalry will march down to Sandtown, and to-morrow night General Kilpatrick will start out with his own command and the two brigades for Fairburn, and then for Jonesborough, where I want him to make a most thorough break in the road. He will therefore not manifest himself to the enemy till the next morning. I want you to-morrow to act so as to give the impression that we propose to extend our lines. Your dispatch is just received. I see you anticipate my wishes, only, in addition, I want, in case the enemy do sally, to fight him on that flank, even if I have to bring General Thomas from the left. But if General Kilpatrick can, as I believe, in the absence of Wheeler, whip the cavalry that remains, all we have to do is to see that he is not interfered with by infantry. Therefore, to-morrow a mere development will do, but next day we must be ready to let go, and make toward Red Oak, if necessary, to help General Kilpatrick.

W. T. SHERMAN,
Major-General, Commanding.

HDQRS. THIRD CAV. DIV., DEPT. OF THE CUMBERLAND,
August 17, 1864.

Major-General SCHOFIELD:

GENERAL: I send you the report of my operations of yesterday by one of my aides to make certain that you get it.* I am satisfied that with two of General Garrard's brigades and my own division I can break the Macon road effectually at any point the major-general commanding may be pleased to indicate. Such an opportunity to strike the enemy a terrible blow has never offered. If it is decided to make the attempt, I should wish to see you and will visit your headquarters for that purpose.

Very respectfully, your obedient servant,

J. KILPATRICK,
Brigadier-General of Volunteers.

HEADQUARTERS DEPARTMENT OF THE TENNESSEE,
August 17, 1864.

Major-General SHERMAN:

Prisoners captured by General Logan this morning report that the enemy sent all their reserves and all the men they could spare yesterday over to their extreme left.

O. O. HOWARD,
Major-General.

HDQRS. MILITARY DIVISION OF THE MISSISSIPPI,
In the Field, near Atlanta, August 17, 1864.

General HOWARD:

I have telegraphed to Generals Thomas and Schofield the substance of your dispatch to the effect that prisoners report that the enemy's reserves were all moved to the left. I will probably postpone our grand movement for a day or so and send General Kilpatrick with all our cavalry on the Macon road, supported by General Schofield.

W. T. SHERMAN,
Major-General, Commanding.

---

*See p. 531. Report forwarded by Schofield to Sherman.

HOWARD'S HEADQUARTERS,
August 17, 1864.

General SHERMAN:

I have just returned from reconnoitering with General Logan on extreme right. Shall I countermand orders preparatory to a movement,
or merely postpone?

O. O. HOWARD,
Major-General.

HDQRS. MILITARY DIVISION OF THE MISSISSIPPI,
In the Field, near Atlanta, August 17, 1864.

General HOWARD:

Make preparations, but merely postpone. If the cavalry can do what
we want, there is no need of moving the whole army.

W. T. SHERMAN,
Major-General, Commanding.

HDQRS. MILITARY DIVISION OF THE MISSISSIPPI,
In the Field, near Atlanta, Ga., August 17, 1864.

General HOWARD:

I now have positive intelligence that Wheeler is gone into East Tennessee with a large force of cavalry, and now is the time to strike the
Macon road with cavalry. I will concentrate five brigades at Sandtown
to-night under General Kilpatrick. To-morrow night he will move out to
Fairburn, and then to Jonesborough, smashing the road badly. Therefore to-morrow keep up a steady pressure, and make demonstrations, as
though looking for a place to assault, and next day keep up a lively
activity along the whole line, so that infantry cannot be spared to go
out to protect the railroad. I think Hood has made a mistake in sending his cavalry now, and propose to take advantage of it. If the cavalry cannot do the job, of necessity we must then go out in force.

W. T. SHERMAN,
Major-General, Commanding.

HDQRS. DEPARTMENT AND ARMY OF THE TENNESSEE,
Before Atlanta, Ga., August 17, 1864.

Maj. Gen. JOHN A. LOGAN,
Commanding Fifteenth Army Corps:

GENERAL: General Howard directs that every embrasure in your
redoubts be screened so that the enemy can by no possibility see your
guns; then, in case of removal, the enemy will not discover the withdrawing of the guns.

Very respectfully, your obedient servant,

T. W. OSBORN,
Maj. and Chief of Arty., Dept. and Army of the Tennessee.

(Same to Generals Blair and Dodge.)

HDQRS. SECOND DIVISION, FIFTEENTH ARMY CORPS,
Before Atlanta, Ga., August 17, 1864.

Lieut. Col. R. R. TOWNES,
Assistant Adjutant-General, Fifteenth Army Corps:

COLONEL: I have the honor to report nothing of interest to-day. I inclose herewith a report from Colonel Jones, commanding First Brigade. It seems that these truces have been practiced by other corps, which have given them some precedence; whether sanctioned by their commanding officer or not I am unable to say, and I have never had the general's views on the subject, but I think it unmilitary and have given orders positively forbidding it, and unless otherwise directed will severely punish any violation of the order.

Very respectfully, your obedient servant,

J. A. J. LIGHTBURN,
Brigadier-General of Volunteers.

[Inclosure.]

HDQRS. FIRST BRIG., SECOND DIV., 15TH ARMY CORPS,
Before Atlanta, Ga., August 17, 1864.

Capt. G. LOFLAND,
Asst. Adjt. Gen., Second Div., Fifteenth Army Corps:

SIR: I have the honor to report that last evening intercourse was carried on between a portion of the pickets of my command and the enemy's opposite to them; papers, &c., were exchanged. Rufus Ready, Company F, Sixth Missouri Veteran Volunteers, went over to the enemy's rifle-pits for the purpose of making an exchange of some kind and was retained by them. I had no knowledge of the affair until this morning, when immediate measures were taken to keep the men in their proper places. It seems that the picket officer of this brigade permitted two men to meet a similar number midway between the enemy's line and our own for the purpose of exchanging papers. Afterwards advantage was taken of this precedent and meetings were had which ended in the retention of Ready by the enemy. Owing to the previous good service rendered by Captain Kendrick as brigade picket officer, I had deferred taking any active steps in the case, but think that I can assure you that nothing of the kind will occur again while I have the honor to command this brigade. Nothing further of note occurred on the line.

I am, sir, very respectfully, your obedient servant,

THEO. JONES,
Colonel, Commanding.

ALLATOONA, *August 17, 1864.*

Major-General SHERMAN:

Seven hundred recaptured cattle are at Allatoona on the way to the front.

J. E. TOURTELLOTTE,
Lieutenant-Colonel, Commanding.

RESACA, *August 17, 1864—7 a. m.*

General SHERMAN:

I left Dalton at 4 o'clock this morning. Went by railroad within two miles and a half of that place; found nearly two miles of road badly torn up and very small force at work. I will send 250 men with material, which is being loaded, and will hasten repairs. I think the road will be all right by 10 o'clock this p. m. The telegraph should be repaired by noon. General Steedman moves at 6 a. m., with 1,800 men and three pieces of artillery. General Smith has already gone. They aim to strike the enemy at Spring Place. Our loss at Dalton was 10 killed and 55 wounded. The enemy lost 200 killed and wounded. We captured 2 surgeons and 40 wounded. So says General Steedman.

G. B. RAUM,
Colonel, Commanding Brigade.

HDQRS. MILITARY DIVISION OF THE MISSISSIPPI,
In the Field, near Atlanta, August 17, 1864.

Colonel RAUM,
Resaca:

Your report of this morning is received, and is very satisfactory. I have no doubt about the result of the move against Spring Place. Martin will quit. I want you to caution all posts below you toward Kingston to be wide awake. All well here.

W. T. SHERMAN,
Major-General, Commanding.

RESACA, *August 17, 1864—11 a. m.*

Major-General SHERMAN:

As small items are sometimes important, I give you the following: A squad of Seventh Kentucky Cavalry arrived at Calhoun this morning, and report having gone within four miles of Fairmount. They heard that rebels, with captured cattle, were in town. They also heard of four rebel couriers, who crossed at Field's Mill this morning, inquiring the way to Spring Place.

GREEN B. RAUM,
Colonel, Commanding Brigade.

HDQRS. MILITARY DIVISION OF THE MISSISSIPPI,
In the Field, near Atlanta, August 17, 1864.

Colonel RAUM,
Resaca:

I am making certain preparations, and want you to give me the most minute facts, that I may draw conclusions. I got your dispatch about the cattle being reported still at Fairmount and the scouts crossing at Field's Mill. I want to hear the earliest possible news from Generals Steedman and John E. Smith.

W. T. SHERMAN,
Major-General, Commanding.

RESACA, *August 17, 1864—2.30 p. m.*

General SHERMAN:

I am just from Tilton. Your dispatch of 1.45 p. m. received. A dispatch written at Tilton is my answer, as follows:

The Seventeenth Iowa prisoners, of whose capture I advised you, were paroled by Wheeler eight miles beyond and northeast of Spring

Place last evening about sundown. They were escorted to that place. I reached here at noon. They report that Wheeler had a very heavy force—from 10,000 to 12,000. Before the prisoners were paroled the entire force moved off north on the Federal road. General Steedman obtained information that Wheeler had divided his force, sending one column against Cartersville, one against Cleveland, and one toward Chattanooga. General Steedman, with his force, has returned to Chattanooga. These facts I learn from an officer from Dalton. I have sent a courier to General Smith. Telegraphed General Steedman via Dalton. Train now on the way with message. I have advised post commanders. You shall be in telegraphic communication with Chattanooga to-night, if not now. I have put 300 men on the repairs of railroad, and will work every hour until they are completed. Trains are at Resaca to convey General Smith in any direction. I think he will return to Resaca to-night. I will send you copy of Wheeler's letter to General Steedman in reference to paroling the prisoners. I ask that you order them on duty.

2.45 P. M.

Since reaching the telegraph office I have received the following letter from General Steedman, which shows that Captain Cilley, captain and assistant adjutant-general, who gave me the information alluded to, was mistaken:

DALTON, August 17, 1864.

COLONEL: Please inform General Smith that the enemy has gone to East Tennessee. They report having captured Cleveland, but I do not credit the report. Push the work on the railroad with all possible dispatch. Use the siding at Calhoun, and, if necessary, send to Adairsville and get all the iron you can. Colonel Laiboldt has sent a small regiment to the bridge two miles south of this point to protect the working party. I have sent for ties and iron, with which any sidings you may take up can be replaced. Dispatch General Sherman that the enemy has gone to East Tennessee, and I have returned to Chattanooga to protect the Chickamauga bridges. The force of the enemy consists of at least 5,000, nine small brigades, and may reach 7,000. My belief is they intend to capture Knoxville.

JAMES B. STEEDMAN,
Major-General.

I have sent a courier to General Smith from here. I give you the conflicting accounts as to Wheeler's strength for what they are worth. My own opinion is that he has between 6,000 and 7,000 men.

G. B. RAUM,
Colonel, Commanding.

RESACA, August 17, 1864.

General SHERMAN:

I neglected to state in my dispatch of 2.30 p. m. that the enemy seemed greatly elated at their success in destroying the railroad. Officers expressed the opinion that it would require several weeks to make repairs. There was no effort made to conceal the direction in which they were going, but rather a desire to indicate it. The prisoners were sent by the most direct route to Tilton. It will not be necessary to take up side tracks to repair the railroad.

G. B. RAUM,
Colonel, Commanding.

RESACA, *August 17, 1864—4 p. m.*

General SHERMAN:

I give below a copy of Wheeler's letter to General Steedman:

HEADQUARTERS CAVALRY CORPS, ARMY OF TENNESSEE,
August 16, 1864.

Maj. Gen. GEORGE [JAMES] B. STEEDMAN,
Commanding Communications, Army of the Cumberland:

GENERAL: Colonel Hawkins, commanding my scouts, having some months since entered into an agreement with General Granger, commanding the line of communications of the Army of the Cumberland, for the exchange of such prisoners as might be captured in the rear of the army, and as their compact was approved by the commanding officer of the Army of the Cumberland, and also by myself, I feel it my duty to return to you the prisoners which were captured in and around Dalton. I have heard such statements as to lead me to believe that you will approve of the course pursued by me, if you desire to lessen the horrors attending upon war, and that you will aid me in lessening the afflictions of those captured. I rely upon you to release such prisoners of my command as you may capture, or have heretofore captured, and direct them to rejoin me until the number equals that which I have returned of yours. I will keep an accurate account of the number returned to you, and also of those of my command which you may release. I have paroled these prisoners, and shall consider them exchanged as soon as you may commence sending my prisoners to me, or to our lines.

Respectfully, general, your obedient servant,

JOS. WHEELER,
Major-General, C. S. Army.

G. B. RAUM,
Colonel, Commanding.

RESACA, *August 17, 1864—4.30 a. m.*

General SHERMAN:

I move out to Spring Place. General Steedman moves from Dalton at 6 a. m. with 1,800 men and one section artillery.

JNO. E. SMITH,
Brigadier-General.

HDQRS. MILITARY DIVISION OF THE MISSISSIPPI,
In the Field, near Atlanta, August 17, 1864.

General JOHN E. SMITH:

I have your dispatch of this morning. With yours and General Steedman's forces acting conjointly you can whip all of Wheeler's cavalry. Don't depend on artillery, but get to close quarters with the small-arms, and shoot rebel cavalry horses whenever you get a chance.

W. T. SHERMAN,
Major-General, Commanding.

RESACA, *August 17, 1864—10.30 p. m.*

Major-General SHERMAN:

I have just returned from Spring Place, where I arrived at 1.30 p. m. Wheeler's command had left yesterday p. m. in direction of Cleveland. Sent scouts out to see if any portion had gone south or east. They report that none have taken those directions. They reported that they had 10,000 men. Citizens say the horses were generally in good condition, and that men said they were going to Tennessee. Cannonading was heard in direction of Cleveland at 2.30 p. m. Commanding officers: Wheeler, Martin, Kelly, Robertson, Allen, Williams, Dibrell, and Colonel Hannon.

JNO. E. SMITH,
Brigadier-General.

RESACA, *August 17, 1864.*

General W. L. ELLIOTT,
Chief of Cavalry:

Have just returned from Spring Place with Watkins. Wheeler left there yesterday evening after the cavalry scout attacked their pickets, and has moved toward Cleveland. Heard cannonading in that direction this p. m. Will send Watkins to Fairmount to-morrow, as citizens report some of their cattle were there yesterday. General Croxton is at Kingston.

E. M. McCOOK,
Brigadier-General.

CARTERSVILLE, *August 17, 1864.*

Maj. Gen. W. T. SHERMAN:

Major Briggs, in command of 250 men of the Second Brigade, First Cavalry Division, has returned, having gone five miles and a half beyond Jasper. He reports that Wheeler in person, with from 5,000 to 7,000 cavalry, and eight pieces of artillery, passed through Jasper twenty-four hours in advance of him, leaving a strong rear guard of 800 to 1,200 in that place, so that he was compelled to go around it. He, Wheeler, went toward Dalton, saying that he intended holding the railroad fifteen days. From Jasper he moved his force in three columns toward Dalton, Tilton, and Calhoun. Major Briggs thinks no attempt was made to drive the cattle captured back across the Etowah, but that they went along with the main force of the enemy. The rebels gave out reports of rebel infantry following them. They also said they were going to East Tennessee to form a junction with forces from Lee. General McCook is out with Colonel Watkins' brigade.

J. A. S. MITCHELL,
Captain and Acting Assistant Inspector-General.
(In absence of General McCook.)

CARTERSVILLE, *August 17, 1864.*

General W. L. ELLIOTT:

The following is just received by telegram from Resaca, 17th:

Capt. J. A. S. MITCHELL:

General McCook left here this morning for Spring Place. General Steedman thinks that enemy has gone to East Tennessee. The railroad is not threatened. Yesterday evening Wheeler was on the Federal road, going north in great numbers. There were no enemy at Spring Place.

G. B. RAUM,
Colonel, Commanding Brigade.

Scouts are kept out in the direction of Fairmount, Jasper, and Canton from the portion of the Second Brigade here that had horses able for duty.

J. A. S. MITCHELL,
Captain and Inspector.

CARTERSVILLE, *August 17, 1864.*

Maj. Gen. W. T. SHERMAN:

McCook's cavalry has returned, and a report of their operations has been sent to the front. The wire was not cut, but worked very hard during early part of the night. I don't think the enemy will attack this place just now. The six rebel regiments reported six miles below here yesterday were not there. Eighty or 100 guerrillas gave rise to the report. I have cavalry patrols well out.

JESSE I. ALEXANDER,
Colonel, Commanding.

CHATTANOOGA, *August 17, 1864.*
(Received 19th.)

Major-General THOMAS:

I have driven Wheeler's forces all off our main line, except a few small squads he has left to annoy us, and will have trains running to the front to-night. He has gone in the direction of Knoxville with his whole force, except one regiment, which camped near Red Clay last night. He destroyed in all about two miles of track, burned two water-tanks and two small bridges near Dalton, and captured about 150 of our men. My loss, killed and wounded, including 17 Laiboldt lost, is about 50. We killed and wounded fully 200 of the enemy. Will report by courier. He skirmished a little at Cleveland, but did no damage.

Very respectfully, &c.,

JAMES B. STEEDMAN,
Major-General.

GRAYSVILLE, *August 17, 1864.*

Maj. S. B. MOE,
Assistant Adjutant-General:

I just arrived at this point and find a quarter of a mile of track torn; will reach Chattanooga to-night, if possible; have been repairing road all day. Wheeler has gone to East Tennessee with his whole force, except one regiment left to cut the road.

JAMES B. STEEDMAN,
Major-General.

CLEVELAND, *August 17, 1864.*

Major-General STEEDMAN:

The advance of 5,000 rebels is reported within six miles of this place, on the Dalton road; 200 encamped at Ooltewah last night. Please send me re-enforcements.

H. G. GIBSON,
Colonel Second Ohio Heavy Artillery.

HDQRS. SECOND BRIG., FOURTH DIV., 23D ARMY CORPS,
Knoxville, Tenn., August 17, 1864.

COMMANDING OFFICERS AT MARYVILLE AND SEVIERVILLE:

SIRS: It is reported that a large force of the enemy crossed the Hiwassee at Columbus yesterday evening and are now moving up the

McGhee road, which runs through Maryville and Sevierville. You will at once send out scouts and take such other means of ascertaining the movements of the enemy as may be in your power. Should the report prove true you will on the approach of the enemy fall back on this place, not precipitately but in good order, and learn if possible the number of the force, by whom commanded, and the point to which they are moving.

By command of Brigadier-General Tillson:

W. W. DEANE,
Captain and Assistant Adjutant-General.

LOUDON, *August 17, 1864.*

Capt. W. P. AMMEN,
Assistant Adjutant-General:

All telegraphic communication is cut off west of this place. I shall rely on my scouts for information, as I have them out on all roads.

M. L. PATTERSON,
Lieutenant-Colonel, Commanding.

LOUDON, *August 17, 1864.*

Capt. W. P. AMMEN,
Assistant Adjutant-General:

Lieutenant Marshman, who has been commanding at Athens, says, from Charleston, that Wheeler is at Athens with 5,000 men, six pieces artillery. Colonel Ewing, at Charleston, says his scouts report rebels crossing Hiwassee at Columbus yesterday from noon till midnight in direction of Athens.

M. L. PATTERSON,
Lieutenant-Colonel.

LOUDON, TENN., *August 17, 1864.*

Brigadier-General AMMEN:

The following just received:

Wheeler reported near Athens. Can you fully protect the bridge against 2,000 or 3,000 men with light artillery?

J. B. STEEDMAN,
Major-General.

A 20-pounder Parrott gun would be of great advantage in case I am attacked by 2,000 or 3,000 men.

M. L. PATTERSON,
Lieutenant-Colonel, Commanding.

LOUDON, *August 17, 1864.*

Capt. W. P. AMMEN,
Assistant Adjutant-General:

Just arrived here. Colonel Byrd and his regiment, with the regular train that left this morning, met the rebels about a mile this side of Athens. Colonel Byrd deployed two companies of skirmishers, and drove them into and out of town; they were about sixty in number, and

were tearing up track and tearing down the wires. Under the superintendence of Mr. Hoxie they commenced repairing the track, but seeing the enemy on two different roads, appearing that they were to cut
off their retreat, Colonel Byrd deemed it prudent to fall back on Loudon. He says there is nothing certain about their numbers, but the
rumors among the citizens are that there are over 3,000. Scouts of Colonel Patterson, on Madisonville and Tellico roads, report no enemy, and
all think it improbable that the enemy have moved toward Maryville.
Colonel Byrd wants to move down toward Athens to-morrow morning,
but he wants 100 or 200 additional men from this place. Hoxie, railroad superintendent, wishes to run down a construction train early to
repair the road so that the train can go through on time. Please see
General Tillson and send instructions immediately. The rebels completely gutted Athens. No news of train from Chattanooga. Rumors
at Athens of fighting at Charleston. Shall I come back with the men
I brought down, or send them and remain myself? All think if they
intend attacking Loudon it will be to-morrow at daylight.

N. A. REED,
Aide-de-Camp.

LOUDON, *August 17, 1864—8.55 p. m.*

Captain AMMEN:

The following from Colonel Byrd, Charleston:

From all the information there is about 3,000 or 4,000, with eight pieces of artillery,
and they say they are coming to Loudon. Train left Charleston at 6 o'clock. Shall
I come up on it or not?

N. A. REED,
Aide-de-Camp.

CHARLESTON, *August 17, 1864.*

Capt. W. P. AMMEN:

They left Benton last night and crossed the river, going in the direction of Athens, is the latest that is reliable.

M. B. EWING.

CHARLESTON, *August 17, 1864.*

Capt. W. P. AMMEN:
      Assistant Adjutant-General:

The latest is that a large force, reported at from 4,000 to 5,000, going
in the direction of Athens.

M. B. EWING.

CLEVELAND, *August 17, 1864.*

Capt. W. P. AMMEN,
      Assistant Adjutant-General:

The last report comes from Lieutenant-Colonel Ewing, at Charleston,
who telegraphs that Lieutenant Marshman, Second Ohio Heavy Artillery, had just arrived from Athens and reported Wheeler there with
5,000 men and six pieces of artillery. They seem to be on a foraging
expedition, and avoid all places where troops are.

H. G. GIBSON,
Colonel Second Ohio Heavy Artillery.

KINGSTON, GA., *August 17, 1864—3 p. m.*

Maj. T. T. ECKERT:

For the first time since Sunday morning we have telegraphic communication with Chattanooga. Wheeler has been on the line and has kept it down since that time between here and Dalton, and has destroyed the railroad—to what extent I am as yet not informed. He attacked Dalton, but was repulsed, and retreated toward Spring Place, pursued by Generals Steedman and John E. Smith, who will give him no rest. Matters at Atlanta as at last advices, except that the left is retired to prepare for flank movement in earnest in a few days.

J. C. VAN DUZER,
Captain, &c.

SPECIAL FIELD ORDERS, ⎱ HDQRS. DEPT. OF THE CUMBERLAND,
     No. 226.   ⎰   *Near Atlanta, Ga., August 17, 1864.*

*   *   *   *   *   *   *

II. Pursuant to Special Field Orders, No. 57, from headquarters Military Division of the Mississippi, Major-General Stanley, commanding Fourth Army Corps, will, early during the day to-morrow, dispose of his wagons as directed in paragraph I of the order referred to, sending those which he is to take on the march to the rear of the position he is directed to occupy, south of Proctor's Creek. At 8 p. m. he will withdraw his entire corps from the breast-works, except a picket-line, and mass it on advantageous ground, somewhere about the Meyer house, and cover the withdrawal of General Williams' corps.

The pickets of the Fourth Corps will withdraw at 12 midnight, retiring by the left flank, and march to join their corps. After General Williams' corps has withdrawn, General Stanley will continue his march to the position indicated, south of Proctor's Creek, to near the Utoy. Brigadier-General Williams, commanding Twentieth Army Corps, will send his wagons to the rear early in the day to-morrow, and at 12 midnight will withdraw from the breast-works, the pickets following immediately after the passage of those of the Fourth Corps.

He will move to the Chattahoochee River and take up the position indicated in the order from the headquarters Military Division of the Mississippi. The movements directed for the cavalry are so clearly defined in General Sherman's order, that no further instructions are considered necessary in this order.

*   *   *   *   *   *   *

By command of Major-General Thomas:

WM. D. WHIPPLE,
Assistant Adjutant-General.

HEADQUARTERS FOURTH ARMY CORPS,
Near Atlanta, Ga., August 17, 1864—10 a. m.

GENERAL: To carry out Special Field Orders, No. 57, Division of the Mississippi, division commanders will at once select a sufficient number of their best wagons to carry 100 rounds musket-cartridges per man; fifteen days' forage of six pounds per animal per day must also be carried in each of said wagons. In like manner they will select the best teams from the supply train, and load them with sufficient rations to give, with the three days' carried by the men, fifteen days' rations, commencing on the 20th. The ammunition wagons will move at noon to-morrow to a position west of Proctor's Creek, and park in rear of General Sherman's headquarters. The supply train will move by the Marietta and Atlanta road from the railroad bridge, and park at the same place to-morrow (near General Sherman's headquarters).

All surplus wagons will be sent back to Vining's Station to be parked by Colonel Hayes, chief quartermaster. These can be moved back this p. m. and to-morrow a. m.

Headquarters wagons, ambulances, and all extra caissons and artillery wagons will be sent out of the way before sundown to-morrow. Men going on picket to-morrow will be prepared for the march. In executing the movement at dark to-morrow every precaution of secrecy will be observed.

Second. To enable the First Division to carry its subsistence General Newton's chief quartermaster will turn over to the quartermaster of the First Division ten wagons and teams of the average quality.

Third. All men, animals, and material not fit for active service will be left with the surplus wagons at Vining's Station. Details from the ordnance guard will be left with surplus ordnance train.

By command of Major-General Stanley:

J. S. FULLERTON,
Assistant Adjutant-General.

(To division commanders.)

SPECIAL FIELD ORDERS, ⎱   HDQRS. ARMY OF THE OHIO,
⎰   *In the Field, near Atlanta, Ga.,*
No. 85.   ⎰   *August 17, 1864.*

*   *   *   *   *   *   *

IX. To-morrow General Cox will move forward toward the enemy's left, to the position reached by him in his reconnaissance on the 12th instant, and fortify so as substantially to extend our line parallel to that of the enemy's. General Hascall will throw forward his right into the works vacated by General Cox, and hold his two right brigades in readiness to support General Cox if necessary.

General Hascall and General Morgan will push forward their skirmishers, using artillery freely, and endeavor to gain possession of the valley in front of General Morgan's right and General Hascall's left. General activity will be kept up along the lines during the day.

By command of Major-General Schofield:

J. A. CAMPBELL,
Major and Assistant Adjutant-General.

SPECIAL FIELD ORDERS, ⎱   HEADQUARTERS DEPARTMENT
⎰   AND ARMY OF THE TENNESSEE,
No. 101.   ⎰   *Before Atlanta, Ga., August 17, 1864.*

In order to carry out the instructions contained in Special Field Orders, No. 57, Military Division of the Mississippi, the following movements and dispositions will be made:

1. Corps commanders will select from their trains their best wagons and teams, and cause them at once to be loaded with fifteen days' rations of bread, meat, sugar, coffee, and salt, 100 rounds of ammunition to the man, and forage equal, if it can be obtained, to half rations to the animals for fifteen days. Forage must be taken from the country to make up the deficiency. These trains will, except the ammunition, one wagon to each regiment and battery, cooking utensils. &c., for the men, the

medical wagons and ambulances be parked to-morrow evening, the 18th instant, under the supervision of Col. J. D. Bingham, chief quartermaster, at the point where the Turner's Ferry road crosses Proctor's Creek, and be prepared to move at a moment's notice on Friday morning, the 19th instant, in the direction indicated in Special Field Orders, No. 57, Military Division of the Mississippi. All the remaining trains and material and all the artillery, except two batteries to a division, will be sent across the Chattahoochee River, and within the old rebel works at the bridge, and as far down as Turner's Ferry if necessary. The batteries to be sent to the rear will be indicated by Major Osborn, chief of artillery, and will be subject to the orders during the absence of this army of the commanding officer of the troops guarding the depot of supplies, &c.

2. Major-General Logan, commanding Fifteenth Army Corps, will, unless otherwise ordered, at 8 o'clock on Friday evening, the 19th instant, withdraw his command, moving out on the Green's Ferry road, crossing Utoy Creek at Judge Wilson's, then proceeding by the most direct road toward Fairburn, marching the first day as far as Camp Creek.

3. Major-General Blair, commanding Seventeenth Army Corps, will, at the same hour, unless otherwise directed, draw out his command by the road past Ezra Church, inside our old line of works, striking the Green's Ferry road near Wilson's, and following up the Fifteenth Army Corps.

4. Major-General Dodge, commanding Left Wing, Sixteenth Army Corps, will, as soon as the troops of Major-General Blair commence to draw out, fall back with his command to the position occupied by the Fifteenth Army Corps in the battle of July 28. When the rear of General Blair's column has passed, General Dodge will take up his line of march on a road to the north of the Green's Ferry road, striking that road near Wilson's, and following up the Seventeenth Army Corps. General Dodge's command will form the rear guard of the army.

5. Corps commanders will cause their engineer and staff officers to make themselves thoroughly acquainted with all the roads on which their commands are to march, and, wherever practicable, new roads will be made to facilitate the movement.

6. The necessary disposition of troops will be made during the day on Friday, the 19th instant, in order that the movement may be executed with dispatch and silently.

*   *   *   *   *   *   *

VIII. Corps commanders will cause their commands to be active during to-morrow and next day, occupying the enemy's attention, and, if possible, inducing the belief that we are to attack them in their trenches. Rebel skirmishers should be taken whenever practicable.

*   *   *   *   *   *   *

By order of Maj. Gen. O. O. Howard:

WM. T. CLARK,
Assistant Adjutant-General.

SPECIAL FIELD ORDERS, }   HDQRS. FIFTEENTH ARMY CORPS,
     No. 79.   }   *Before Atlanta, Ga., August 17, 1864.*

*   *   *   *   *   *

V. Brig. Gen. W. B. Hazen, U. S. Volunteers, having reported to these headquarters, in compliance with Special Field Orders, No. 101, extract

V, dated headquarters Department and Army of the Tennessee, August 17, 1864, is hereby assigned to command the Second Division, and will relieve Brig. Gen. J. A. J. Lightburn, who will, upon being relieved, assume command of the Second Brigade, Second Division.

*   *   *   *   *   *   *

By order of Maj. Gen. John A. Logan:

R. R. TOWNES,
Assistant Adjutant-General.

WASHINGTON, *August 18, 1864—5.35 p. m.*

Major-General SHERMAN:

The appointment of Colonel Long as brigadier has been made and will be forwarded to you by mail immediately. We have recent news from Mobile. Nothing new from General Grant. The enemy is concentrating on Sheridan in large force in the Shenandoah Valley.

E. M. STANTON,
Secretary of War.

CITY POINT, VA., *August 18, 1864.*

Major-General SHERMAN:

Richmond papers of the 17th give it as the opinion of military men that Atlanta can hold out one month yet. In the mean time, like Micawber, they expect something to turn up. If you can hold fast as you are now and prevent raids upon your rear you will destroy most of that army. I never would advise going backward even if your roads are cut so as to preclude the possibility of receiving supplies from the North, but would recommend the accumulation of ordnance stores and supplies while you can, and if it comes to the worst move south as you suggested. I have forced the enemy to move a large force north of the James River, and am now moving one corps by our left around Petersburg. I expect no great results, but will probably cut the Weldon road again, and will also demonstrate to the enemy that he has now the minimum garrison possible to hold his present lines with, and that to hold his roads he must re-enforce.

U. S. GRANT,
Lieutenant-General.

NEAR ATLANTA, GA., *August 18, 1864—6 p. m.*
(Received 12.30 p. m. 19th.)

Maj. Gen. H. W. HALLECK,
Washington, D. C.:

We have been hammering away at Atlanta, and I was going to put a corps (intrenched) at the railroad bridge, and with the balance swing round by the south and east; but Hood has sent off his cavalry, which touched our road at two or three points, which are already repaired, and that cavalry has gone up into East Tennessee, leaving me now superior in cavalry, and I hope the opportunity thus given me will save me the risk and excessive labor of making a wide circuit in this hot weather. To-night General Kilpatrick will start for the Macon road with five brigades of cavalry, which can whip all the enemy's cavalry present, and to-morrow I will demonstrate along my whole line to give

General Kilpatrick time to make a good break in that road, so vital to Hood. We all feel confident we can succeed, and for that reason I do not regret that Wheeler has gone up to East Tennessee. I think we have force enough at Knoxville, the Gap, and Kingston to hold vital points until necessity will force Wheeler to come back; but I will leave him to be attended to by those in my rear.

W. T. SHERMAN,
Major-General, Commanding.

AUGUST 18, 1864—4 a. m.

General THOMAS:

The shelling of our lines is to withdraw our attention from some other point. Send word to Stanley and Garrard, to the bridge and Marietta, to be on their guard.

W. T. SHERMAN,
Major-General.

THOMAS' HEADQUARTERS,
August 18, 1864.

Major-General SHERMAN:

Your dispatch of this morning relative to the defenses of Vining's and bridge-head has been received, and will be attended to immediately.

GEO. H. THOMAS,
Major-General.

SHERMAN'S HEADQUARTERS,
August 18, 1864.

General THOMAS:

Also have Stanley watch well the left, and see if he can report anything.

W. T. SHERMAN,
Major-General.

THOMAS' HEADQUARTERS,
August 18, 1864.

Major-General SHERMAN:

Your dispatches of this morning have been received, and the orders given.

GEO. H. THOMAS,
Major-General.

THOMAS' HEADQUARTERS,
August 18, 1864.

Major-General SHERMAN:

Major Edie, commanding Second Brigade, First Division, Fourteenth Army Corps, reports 10 o'clock last night enemy been moving to our left three hours. The instructions for General Kilpatrick sent me in note have been forwarded to him.

GEO. H. THOMAS,
Major-General.

HDQRS. MILITARY DIVISION OF THE MISSISSIPPI,
In the Field, near Atlanta, Ga., August 18, 1864.

General THOMAS:

There are always at the bridge enough troops in the shape of train guards and wagon escorts, but it is proper some one colonel should be known as the commanding officer. You may name one and instruct him to picket well up the river, and on any alarm to hold the signal hill over Vining's, and the redoubts at the bridge, and make it his duty to notify you of anything worthy of your attention.

W. T. SHERMAN,
Major-General, Commanding.

———

THOMAS' HEADQUARTERS,
August 18, 1864.

Major-General SHERMAN:

No change in the appearance of things upon the rebel side in front of the Fourth Corps.

GEO. H. THOMAS,
Major-General.

———

HDQRS. MILITARY DIVISION OF THE MISSISSIPPI,
In the Field, near Atlanta, Ga., August 18, 1864.

General THOMAS:

Both Generals Howard and Schofield report the enemy to their front unchanged. I don't understand why the wires are down between Vining's and Marietta. Can you signal to Kenesaw and ask if all is right? As auxiliary we had better keep up signals from your headquarters to signal hill, or Vining's, Kenesaw, and Allatoona.

W. T. SHERMAN,
Major-General, Commanding.

———

THOMAS' HEADQUARTERS,
August 18, 1864.

Major-General SHERMAN:

I have officers enough to establish stations here at Vining's and Marietta or Kenesaw. If General Howard can send a couple to Allatoona we can have a complete line as far as that point. I ordered up ammunition early this morning, and the big guns will continue firing as soon as it arrives.

GEO. H. THOMAS,
Major-General, U. S. Volunteers.

———

HDQRS. MILITARY DIVISION OF THE MISSISSIPPI,
In the Field, near Atlanta, August 18, 1864—12 m.

General THOMAS:

I will order General Howard to establish a signal station on the hill at Allatoona in correspondence with one at Kenesaw.

W. T. SHERMAN,
Major-General, Commanding.

HEADQUARTERS DEPARTMENT OF THE CUMBERLAND,
Before Atlanta, Ga., August 18, 1864—10 a. m.

Maj. Gen. W. T. SHERMAN,
Commanding Military Division of the Mississippi:

GENERAL: I have the honor to inclose copies of reports just received from points on my line relative to movements on the part of the enemy. I have ordered every movement carefully and closely watched, and all are on the alert. I am satisfied no movement can be made by him without its being at once detected, and myself made cognizant of the fact.

I am, general, very respectfully, your obedient servant,

GEO. H. THOMAS,
Major-General, U. S. Volunteers, Commanding.

[Inclosure No. 1.]

HEADQUARTERS,
August 18, 1864—6 a. m.

[Col. J. S. FULLERTON:]

COLONEL: I have been around my lines this morning, and have demonstrated, kindled fires, and got up a muss generally. The rebs in my front keep very close, few to be seen; their picket-line is strong. Last night the enemy was very quiet; but few lights were seen in their camp. Colonel Kirby lost 5 men from his picket-line, belonging to Twenty-first Illinois Veteran Infantry; they are reported captured. It is said that an officer came to the vedette, and after being challenged answered that he was officer of the day, and desired the sentinel to go farther out. Soon four other sentinels, hearing a scuffling, advanced, and they have not been heard of since. This is all that I can gather. The query with me is, have these men been captured or have they deserted. Their captain, with whom I conversed this morning, says that they are good men and very sharp, and that if captured they will give no information. These men know nothing of the indicated movement.

I am, colonel, very respectfully, your obedient servant,

NATHAN KIMBALL,
Brigadier-General, Commanding Division.

[Inclosure No. 2.]

STATION OBSERVATION, *August 18, 1864.*

[Capt. A. K. TAYLOR:]

CAPTAIN: Squad of eighteen men with knapsacks, &c., on marched from four-gun fort toward town. Regiment moving out works on right of fort; they move toward rear of fort. Both battle-flags gone from here.

Very respectfully, your obedient servant,

W. W. HOPKINS,
Captain and Acting Signal Officer.

Part of men now standing in line in works.

HDQRS. MILITARY DIVISION OF THE MISSISSIPPI,
In the Field, near Atlanta, August 18, 1864—10.15 a. m.

General THOMAS:

General Barry says your big guns were ordered to stop firing as soon as the ammunition then on hand was exhausted. You understand of course that I have suspended the movement contemplated for to-night until General Kilpatrick tries his hand. Keep the big guns going, and damage Atlanta all that is possible.

W. T. SHERMAN,
Major-General, Commanding.

HEADQUARTERS DEPARTMENT OF THE CUMBERLAND,
August 18, 1864—11.55 a. m.

Major-General SHERMAN:

Signal officer at Howard's house reports at 10 a. m. a heavy cannonading for about half an hour previous in direction south 20 degrees east from his position. Some of the shells burst over the northern part of Atlanta. I send this that you may know what batteries were firing and where the shells reached. But little picket-firing in my front now, though it was quite sharp for three or four hours from daylight.

GEO. H. THOMAS,
Major-General, U. S. Volunteers.

(Same to Generals Schofield and Howard.)

HDQRS. MILITARY DIVISION OF THE MISSISSIPPI,
In the Field, near Atlanta, August 18, 1864—12 m.

General THOMAS:

General Kimball's report is received and is perfectly satisfactory. The movement from the enemy's left to right last night was the division sent to East Point when General Schofield was feeling that flank a little too close for Hood's comfort. It was recalled last night on the supposition that Wheeler was on our road and we would be sending back. Time and circumstances all favor the Kilpatrick move, and I hope he will make a good job.

W. T. SHERMAN,
Major-General, Commanding.

HDQRS. MILITARY DIVISION OF THE MISSISSIPPI,
In the Field, near Atlanta, August 18, 1864—1.15 p. m.

General THOMAS:

The shots that go so deep into the city are from 10-pounder Parrotts in General Ransom's front, which is the second division to the right of General Williams; he is well in the re-entrant between Atlanta and White Hall, looking up Proctor's Creek. The 4½-inch gun of General Corse has an equally good position. We are in close musket-range of the enemy's main line. That General Kilpatrick may succeed perfectly and do plenty of damage, it is, of course, important to draw off from him all the cavalry we can. I wish you to instruct General Garrard minutely; he will obey orders, but if left to himself does not persevere long enough. I think by daylight he ought to be in Decatur, then move some four or five miles in the direction of Flat Rock and skirmish with the enemy, then toward Stone Mountain, and then swinging round toward the Peach Tree road come home, as it were trolling off any party of cavalry that may be kept by Hood to watch his right flank. General Kilpatrick will be near Fairburn at daylight, with his horses cool and fresh. He will then push rapidly for Jonesborough, and ought to be there by 1 or 2 p. m. to-morrow. If he can then have twelve hours of uninterrupted work he can do much damage. General Garrard should therefore maneuver and threaten all day and night to-morrow and into next day. He should keep a respectable force of the enemy's cavalry in sight all the time, for, if after him, they cannot be bothering General Kilpatrick, whose real task is not to fight but to work.

> W. T. SHERMAN,
> *Major-General, Commanding.*

> HDQRS. MILITARY DIVISION OF THE MISSISSIPPI,
> *In the Field, near Atlanta, August 18, 1864.*

General THOMAS:

Hood may attempt to pass round our left flank to our rear, following the cavalry movement, in which event I will move General Schofield, and if need be General Howard, in that direction. Therefore ascertain as soon as possible if any infantry has passed out of Atlanta to the east.

> W. T. SHERMAN,
> *Major-General, Commanding.*

> SHERMAN'S HEADQUARTERS,
> *August 18, 1864.*

General THOMAS:

Let General Garrard look well around Decatur to see if enemy's infantry is moving outside fortifications of Atlanta in direction of Roswell.

> W. T. SHERMAN,
> *Major-General.*

> HEADQUARTERS DEPARTMENT OF THE CUMBERLAND,
> *Before Atlanta, Ga., August 18, 1864.*
> (Received 2 p. m.)

Maj. Gen. D. S. STANLEY,
Commanding Fourth Army Corps:

GENERAL: For the purpose of aiding General Kilpatrick in his operations on the Macon railroad as much as possible, I desire you to concentrate on your left flank as large a force as you can, without weakening your lines too much (by daylight to-morrow morning, 19th), and make a strong demonstration, and attract the enemy toward you as much as possible, and endeavor to hold him opposite you during the day. It is hoped that General Kilpatrick will be able to reach the Macon road at Jonesborough between 12 m. and 2 p. m. to-morrow, 19th, and if he can have from that time until 10 p. m. to work uninterruptedly, he ought to be able to destroy so much of the road as to make it impossible to operate it for at least ten days, by which time it is supposed Hood will be starved out. Similar instructions have been given to General Garrard, who will operate on the enemy's flank still farther to your left. It is also desirable for you to make a similar demonstration on the morning of the 20th, to enable General Kilpatrick to withdraw.

Very respectfully, yours, &c.,
GEO. H. THOMAS,
Major-General, U. S. Volunteers, Commanding.

HEADQUARTERS DEPARTMENT OF THE CUMBERLAND,
Before Atlanta, Ga., August 18, 1864—2 p. m.

Brig. Gen. K. GARRARD,
Commanding Second Cavalry Division:

GENERAL : To facilitate the success of General Kilpatrick as much as possible, I wish you to be in Decatur by daylight to-morrow morning (19th) with the effective force you have with you. Then move in the direction of Flat Rock and Atlanta, and so attract the enemy's attention by skirmishing and threatening as to induce him to believe that you are about to attack his flank, then by moving off toward Stone Mountain, draw him after you as far as possible, and swing round toward your present position in the direction of the Peach Tree road. This movement should be continued throughout the day, and the enemy should be threatened again early on the morning of the 20th instant by a similar movement as the one above directed. By this means it is hoped you will be able to hold all the cavalry the enemy now has on his right flank, and thereby give General Kilpatrick at least twelve hours on the Macon road. He expects to reach Fairburn by daylight to-morrow (19th) with his horses fresh and cool. He will then push rapidly for Jonesborough, which place he should reach by 2 p. m., and if uninterrupted he will have from that time until dark, and for some hours during the night, to break up and destroy the railroad, and whatever stores, material, and rolling-stock he may meet with. You will therefore perceive the necessity for occupying the attention of the enemy as much as possible to draw from General Kilpatrick all the cavalry you can for at least to-morrow and next day (19th and 20th).

Very respectfully, yours, &c.,
GEO. H. THOMAS,
Major-General, U. S. Volunteers, Commanding.

HEADQUARTERS FOURTH ARMY CORPS,
August 18, 1864—8 p. m.

Brig. Gen. NATHAN KIMBALL,
Commanding First Division:

GENERAL: In order to favor the movement of General Kilpatrick I am ordered to make the strongest demonstration possible upon the left at daylight in the morning. I have directed General Wood to send two regiments (three if they can be spared) to Colonel Opdycke's position. These regiments, with Opdycke's brigade, will occupy Colonel Kirby's position, giving Kirby's brigade to operate with. The brigade will march just at dawn over to the railroad, where the main body will be held in reserve, regiments being sent to the left and front to reconnoiter. The brigade will remain near the railroad all forenoon; the men will get their breakfast in the new position at the time Kirby's brigade marches to the railroad. One of Taylor's regiments will move to the left and occupy a position midway, covering the deep ravine on your left. I will try to be on the ground myself. It may be advisable to move artillery over. We must do all we can to deceive the enemy and make him expect assault.

Very respectfully, your obedient servant,

D. S. STANLEY,
Major-General.

HDQRS. FIRST BRIG., FIRST DIV., 4TH ARMY CORPS,
August 18, 1864—2.20 a. m.

Captain MASON,
Assistant Adjutant-General:

I have just had report from my officer of the day that a picket-post of ours had been captured. The location and circumstance create quite a surprise in my mind. The post was about the left of my picket-line and nearly in front of the left of my line of battle. The country immediately in front of the captured post is densely wooded, to the front and right is the deep cut and heavy embankment on the railroad, admirably adapted for the concealment of any movements of the troops. The circumstances attending the capture are these: A vedette (stationed a short distance in front of the post) was heard to challenge some person and get the reply "relief guard." Immediately thereafter a slight scuffle ensued, without any outcry. After waiting a moment or two, four men, composing the post, started out to reconnoiter. Nothing had been heard from these men, not even the slightest noise, for two hours, when the officer in command of the station sent the sergeant of the guard in to make this report. No enemy has ever been discovered in that vicinity before by my men. The enemy's railroad trains are very busy to-night.

I am, very respectfully, your obedient servant,

I. M. KIRBY,
Colonel, Commanding Brigade.

HDQRS. SECOND DIVISION, FOURTH ARMY CORPS,
August 18, 1864.

Lieut. Col. J. S. FULLERTON,
Assistant Adjutant-General, Fourth Army Corps:

COLONEL: Permit me to offer a few suggestions for the consideration of the general commanding, which I consider applicable to our present position and equally so whether we are to retain our present line or to abandon it:

First. To suspend all fire along the lines from midnight till reveille, and after that, unless for some reason the pickets are ordered to fire, and in case of the pickets being compelled to fire, that they report to brigade commander what the object is.

Second. To restrain artillery fire at daybreak, if practicable, because that might indicate that we retained our line or the contrary.

Third. That the smokes in our rear be increased and extended, and that reveille be without drums or bugles, and no drums or bugles be sounded before 12 m. I offer these suggestions respectfully in view of the indications on my own line, without asserting them as applicable to the line of the whole corps.

Very respectfully, your obedient servant,

JOHN NEWTON,
Brigadier-General, Commanding.

HEADQUARTERS FOURTH ARMY CORPS,
Near Atlanta, Ga., August 18, 1864—8.30 p. m.

General NEWTON,
Second Division, Fourth Army Corps:

GENERAL: The general commanding directs me to say, in reply to your report just received, that he approves of your suggestions in endeavoring to draw out the enemy's pickets in the morning, and he wishes you to adopt the plan you have mentioned. At daylight to-morrow a demonstration will be made with a brigade in front of General Kimball's left to draw off attention from General Kilpatrick's movements. The brigade will be pushed out toward the railroad, and will be kept well out all day. Two or three of General Wood's regiments will be also withdrawn to be moved over to the left; this will weaken our lines very much; therefore, the general commanding directs that you keep a close watch for any movement the enemy may make during the day to take advantage of such movements on the part of Generals Wood's and Kimball's troops.

Very respectfully, your obedient servant,

J. S. FULLERTON,
Assistant Adjutant-General.

HEADQUARTERS FOURTH ARMY CORPS,
August 18, 1864—7.30 p. m.

Brigadier-General WOOD,
Commanding Third Division:

In order to favor General Kilpatrick I am ordered to make as strong a demonstration as possible on the left at daylight to-morrow morning. I must draw on General Kimball for all the troops to do this, and I do not think I can safely carry out my plan with less than a brigade. In order to aid in guarding General Kimball's line, I wish you to send two regiments, or three if you think safe, to start at 3 o'clock in the morning, carrying three days' rations with them, to march by way of General Kimball's headquarters to the position of Opdycke's brigade, upon Kimball's left. At daylight make a demonstration by firing, similar to the orders practiced to-day.

Very respectfully, your obedient servant,

D. S. STANLEY,
Major-General.

HEADQUARTERS FOURTH ARMY CORPS,
Near Atlanta, Ga., August 18, 1864—8.45 p. m.

Brigadier-General WOOD,
Commanding Third Division:

It is supposed that the enemy opened his artillery upon us this morning to ascertain whether we had fallen back from our lines during last night. He may do likewise in the morning. Therefore you had better have your pickets instructed to cease firing altogether toward morning, and do not reply to any fire from the enemy's artillery. Such action may cause the enemy to advance his skirmishers and give us an opportunity to capture some of them These same directions have been sent to General Newton.

By order of Major-General Stanley:

J. S. FULLERTON,
Assistant Adjutant-General.

HEADQUARTERS FOURTEENTH ARMY CORPS,
Before Atlanta, Ga., August 18, 1864.

Brig. Gen. W. D. WHIPPLE,
Chief of Staff, Department of the Cumberland:

GENERAL: Reports during last night from the picket-lines indicate a movement of the enemy toward our left. This morning, under orders from General Schofield, I pressed forward my skirmishers and found the enemy still in force in my front. A deserter reports the rebels preparing to evacuate Atlanta and take position near East Point. I inclose yesterday's report of casualties, &c.* Eight deserters forwarded to-day.

Very respectfully, your obedient servant,

R. W. JOHNSON,
Brigadier-General, Commanding.

HDQRS. CHIEF OF CAVALRY, DEPT. OF THE CUMBERLAND,
Near Atlanta, Ga., August 18, 1864.

Brig. Gen. K. GARRARD,
Commanding Second Cavalry Division:

General Kilpatrick reports that his command will make to-night for the direction of Jonesborough, on the Macon railroad. The general commanding directs that you endeavor to attract the attention of the enemy this evening and early to-morrow morning, with a view if possible to draw his cavalry toward our left and from the route to be taken by General Kilpatrick.

I am, general, very respectfully, your obedient servant,

DAVID F. HOW,
Lieutenant and Acting Assistant Adjutant-General.

HDQRS. THIRD BRIGADE, SECOND CAVALRY DIVISION,
Near Atlanta, August 18, 1864.

Captain KENNEDY,
Assistant Adjutant-General:

CAPTAIN: The patrol from Decatur has returned. They went into town, found no rebels there. None have been there since our reconnaissance on Monday except small scouting parties of eight or ten. Eleven or twelve were in town this morning. They captured two of our stragglers yesterday. Reported that they frequently capture men at Mrs. Seely's, on Peach Tree Creek, said woman being in concert with the rebels. No infantry been near there. Ferguson's command camped one mile and a half from Decatur, with pickets on Atlanta road, one mile

---

* Not found.

west of town. All the scouts in town have been of Ferguson's command. The Cross Keys patrol reports scouting parties through that country yesterday. Twenty-five at Cross Keys last night.

I am, captain, very respectfully, your obedient servant,

A. O. MILLER,
Colonel, Commanding Brigade.

HDQRS. CHIEF OF CAVALRY, DEPT. OF THE CUMBERLAND,
Near Atlanta, Ga., August 18, 1864.

Brig. Gen. J. KILPATRICK,
Commanding Third Division Cavalry:

I am directed by the general commanding to acknowledge the receipt of your communication* of 10 a. m., and to say that our cavalry on our left is on Augusta railroad, near and east of Atlanta. Decatur is occupied alternately by scouts from both armies. Should you find it necessary to return by our left, the route by Flat Rock, Latimar's, and Decatur would probably be the best. You will have many officers of Garrard's division, who can give you more information about South River and its branches than I am able to get for you. The entire cavalry force on the left cannot be detached, but orders will be given to make a demonstration this evening and early to-morrow morning to engage the attention of the enemy's cavalry on our left and draw him in that direction.

I am, general, very respectfully, your obedient servant,

DAVID F. HOW,
Lieutenant and Acting Assistant Adjutant-General.

Statement of J. Milton Glass (scout).

OFFICE PROVOST-MARSHAL-GENERAL,
Near Atlanta, Ga., August 18, 1864.

Went into Atlanta past our left flank on 13th instant; saw one brigade of Martin's division of cavalry between the cemetery and Decatur. Strahl's brigade, of Cheatham's division, holds the extreme right of the enemy's infantry line and is in position about one mile from the cemetery toward Decatur on the south side of the railroad. Says the militia commences on the left of Strahl's brigade. Lee's corps is on the left of the militia and Stewart on his left. Hardee is on the extreme left; Cleburne's division holds the left flank and is in position, the left resting opposite Mims', five or six miles southwest of East Point. Says he rode along the lines from Atlanta to East Point on Monday; left East Point yesterday morning and went to Fairburn. Did not see or hear of any reserves along their lines; says their lines are very thin. The country between the enemy and Fairburn is open; nothing there but a few cavalry pickets and scouts. Saw large squads of negroes along the railroad from East Point to Fairburn, felling timber and throwing up breast-works. General Toombs arrived there about one week ago with some militia; was told at the Camp of Direction that Toombs was second in command of the militia, and that there were 30,000 of them, including the troops brought up some time ago by Generals Roddey and Lee. Was told also that these troops, the 30,000, were to be organized into two corps. Says this Camp of Direction is a

---

* Not found.

sort of headquarters for guards and couriers. Says that Wheeler started from Covington with about 6,000 men, and that Lewis with about 800 Kentuckians crossed the Chattahoochee below Campbellton and passed our right flank. Thinks it was Lewis' brigade that cut the railroad at Acworth. Says the enemy was very anxious to learn from him what force was after Wheeler. Heard that Morgan was to form a junction with Wheeler some place near Cleveland in East Tennessee. Reports the Atlanta and West-Point Railroad in running order. Trains passed through Fairburn yesterday morning for Atlanta. Reports the depot buildings and car sheds destroyed by Kilpatrick. Says that a large block of buildings near the corner of Marietta and Woodley streets was fired by our shells on Saturday night and destroyed. The buildings contained cotton and a large drug store; another building in same part of town was destroyed Sunday evening. Visited several camps; the men appear to have plenty of rations and forage from day to day, but there is no supply on hand; supplies are all brought from Macon. Says there are six strong forts at East Point all ready for artillery; none in them yet. On the evening of the 15th instant a train of fifteen cars loaded with infantry went down the Macon road; did not learn to what point; and on the 16th another train full of troops, about 1,000 men, went down same road. Says no train came up from Macon on 16th and that the cause of detention was not known at headquarters. Thinks Wheeler has all their mounted force off with him, except the brigade on their right near Decatur, and about two small brigades picketing and scouting between East Point and Fairburn.

[Indorsement.]

Respectfully forwarded for the information of the major-general commanding.

ED. C. DENIG,
Captain and Assistant Adjutant-General.

HEADQUARTERS ARMY OF THE OHIO,
In the Field, August 18, 1864—2.40 a. m.

Maj. Gen. W. T. SHERMAN,
Commanding Military Division of the Mississippi:

GENERAL: Major Edie, commanding Second Brigade, First Division, Fourteenth Army Corps, informs me through General Johnson that his pickets report the enemy passing for three hours (his dispatch dated at 10 p. m.) to our left. General Johnson in his indorsement says a copy has been sent to General Thomas. My telegraph operator failed to connect with yours, and I send this by courier for your information.

Very respectfully, your obedient servant,

J. M. SCHOFIELD,
Major-General.

SHERMAN'S HEADQUARTERS,
August 18, 1864. (Received 4.35 a. m.)

General SCHOFIELD:

Your dispatch received. Have you observed anything further during the night?

W. T. SHERMAN,
Major-General.

HEADQUARTERS ARMY OF THE OHIO,
Near Atlanta, Ga., August 18, 1864.

Major-General SHERMAN:

General Johnson's pickets report the enemy moving to our left for three hours previous to 10 p. m. No further information has been received.

J. M. SCHOFIELD,
Major-General.

HDQRS. MILITARY DIVISION OF THE MISSISSIPPI,
In the Field, near Atlanta, August 18, 1864.

General SCHOFIELD:

The enemy may attempt to occupy us with his militia and move to our left and rear. General Thomas is advised, and in that event I will want your whole army to move in the same direction. Be prepared and keep ready. I have notified General Thomas.

W. T. SHERMAN,
Major-General, Commanding.

HDQRS. MILITARY DIVISION OF THE MISSISSIPPI,
In the Field, near Atlanta, August 18, 1864—7 a. m.

General SCHOFIELD:

I wanted to come down to the extreme right to-day, and may still, but I must watch matters to our rear. Hood no doubt supposes he has put Wheeler on our line, and is demonstrating accordingly; he has small parties to cut our wires nightly. We cannot now get Marietta. Nevertheless, unless something very extraordinary takes place to-day, I want General Kilpatrick to start and break up that Macon road all to pieces. Keep your own cavalry as vedettes on your right flank, and to-morrow they might venture as close East Point as possible and break up some more of that railroad, while General Kilpatrick draws their cavalry toward Jonesborough, as they will be sure to watch if they don't fight him. Use your troops to-day as though investing and feeling their left flank, but to-morrow venture out a little. Keep me well advised of all facts that will enable me to divine Hood's scheme.

W. T. SHERMAN,
Major-General, Commanding.

SCHOFIELD'S HEADQUARTERS,
August 18, 1864.

General SHERMAN:

Cox is working forward to extend our lines toward East Point. Hascall and Morgan are fighting to get their skirmishers in possession of the valley in their front. I will watch the enemy closely and keep you advised of everything.

J. M. SCHOFIELD,
Major-General.

HEADQUARTERS ARMY OF THE OHIO,
Near Atlanta, Ga., August 18, 1864.

Major-General SHERMAN:

I have extended my line for more than a mile substantially parallel to that of the enemy and have a pretty good flank. The enemy's works appear to be occupied only in moderate force. They have shown no movement during the day. I propose to-night to draw out two brigades of each division of the Fourteenth Corps, leaving one brigade of each division, including Hascall's, to hold the present lines. This will give me a movable force of about 18,000 men with which to make my movement against the enemy's left. This will of course leave our lines very weak, but I reckon strong enough against any probable attack.

J. M. SCHOFIELD,
Major-General.

———

SCHOFIELD'S HEADQUARTERS,
August 18, 1864.

General SHERMAN:

Our demonstrations show no apparent diminution of the enemy's force in front of the Fourteenth Corps.

J. M. SCHOFIELD,
Major-General.

———

HDQRS. MILITARY DIVISION OF THE MISSISSIPPI,
In the Field, near Atlanta, August 18, 1864—11.30 a. m.

General SCHOFIELD:

Our telegraph now works to Chattanooga. The conclusion my mind has arrived at is that Hood sent Wheeler's cavalry to occupy our road at Dalton; that he had re-enforced East Point with a division of his old corps, which last night was brought back on the supposition that Wheeler had succeeded, and we would begin to detach to our rear. Now, of all times, is the time for our cavalry to do its work well, and if you hear nothing from me before 3 o'clock, send a messenger to General Kilpatrick with a note stating that all things are most favorable for his work; to break as much of the Macon road as he possibly can, and, as he swings back, to rest on the West Point road at some point below Fairburn, and make another big tear up. If he feels master of the situation on the road he cannot tear up too much track nor twist too much iron. It may save this army the necessity of making a long, hazardous flank march. Tell him what you will do to-morrow to occupy the enemy's infantry on that flank, and assure him I will cause the same along our whole line, especially on our extreme left. I will see that General Garrard risks all he can to amuse what cavalry the enemy has about Decatur and Stone Mountain.

W. T. SHERMAN,
Major-General, Commanding.

———

SCHOFIELD'S HEADQUARTERS,
August 18, 1864.

General SHERMAN:

Your dispatch is received. At 3 o'clock I will send an officer to General Kilpatrick with a letter explaining your wishes, and also what will be done by the infantry to aid him.

J. M. SCHOFIELD,
Major-General.

HDQRS. MILITARY DIVISION OF THE MISSISSIPPI,
In the Field, near Atlanta, August 18, 1864—7.45 p. m.

General SCHOFIELD:

Your dispatch is received. All right. The enemy's cavalry has made its appearance near Acworth, so I believe General Kilpatrick will find his road clear. I would not move far to-morrow, unless you detect the enemy moving also.

W. T. SHERMAN,
Major-General, Commanding.

HEADQUARTERS ARMY OF THE OHIO,
Near Atlanta, Ga., August 18, 1864.

Major-General HOWARD:

We have had considerable skirmishing and some artillery firing during the day. Nothing more serious. I have extended my line more than a mile toward the West Point railroad and fortified.

J. M. SCHOFIELD,
Major-General.

HEADQUARTERS ARMY OF THE OHIO,
In the Field, before Atlanta, Ga., August 18, 1864.

Brigadier-General JOHNSON,
Commanding Fourteenth Army Corps:

GENERAL: The major-general commanding has information that the enemy were moving toward our left during last night. He desires you to push out a line of skirmishers in your front immediately and ascertain, if possible, whether they occupy their position in force or not.

Very respectfully, your obedient servant,

WM. M. WHERRY,
Major and Aide-de-Camp.

HEADQUARTERS ARMY OF THE OHIO,
August 18, 1864.

Brigadier-General JOHNSON,
Commanding Fourteenth Army Corps:

GENERAL: The enemy appears to be contemplating some kind of a move to-day; General Sherman thinks probably to our rear, and directs that we be prepared to make a corresponding move at any moment. Our trains should be kept hitched and everything ready to move.

Very respectfully,

J. M. SCHOFIELD,
Major-General.

HEADQUARTERS ARMY OF THE OHIO,
Near Atlanta, Ga., August 18, 1864.

Brigadier-General KILPATRICK,
Commanding Cavalry Division, Army of the Cumberland:

GENERAL: General Sherman directs me by telegraph to inform you that everything is most favorable for your work, and he wishes you to do it well; to break as much of the Macon road as you possibly can, and, as you swing back, to rest on the West Point road somewhere below Fairburn, and make another big break there. If you find you are master of the situation on that road, take time enough and destroy as long a line of track as possible. Do the work thoroughly by heating and twisting the rails, and burning ties, &c. In places where you have not time to work, you can still do great damage by prying up the track (rails and ties together), propping it up above the surface of the ground, piling in large quantities of dry fence rails and burning them. There is good reason to hope that you may be able to accomplish what the whole army would otherwise have to do, at great risk, by a long and difficult flank movement. Early to-morrow I will move with a corps of infantry toward the railroad near East Point, and engage the enemy so as to prevent his sending infantry to oppose you. General Sherman directs me to assure you that he will have the same done all along the line, especially on our extreme left, and he will see that Garrard occupies the attention of the enemy's cavalry about Decatur and Stone Mountain. The most abundant success attend you.

Very respectfully, your obedient servant,

J. M. SCHOFIELD,
Major-General, Commanding.

Hdqrs. Military Division of the Mississippi,
In the Field, near Atlanta, August 18, 1864.

General Howard:

Feel the enemy to your front, and ascertain if they occupy their positions in force or only as a blind. They contemplate something to-day.

W. T. SHERMAN,
Major-General, Commanding.

(Same to General Schofield.)

Howard's Headquarters,
August 18, 1864.

General Sherman:

I ordered a demonstration last night, directing corps commanders to feel for the enemy. I have sent for them since receiving your dispatch, so as to secure concert of action.

O. O. HOWARD,
Major-General.

Hdqrs. Military Division of the Mississippi,
In the Field, near Atlanta, August 18, 1864—8.30 a. m.

General Howard:

The reason for feeling the lines this morning and to-day is that a Colonel Edie, commanding brigade of Fourteenth Corps, reports the enemy moving for three hours past his position toward our left.

W. T. SHERMAN,
Major-General, Commanding.

HDQRS. MILITARY DIVISION OF THE MISSISSIPPI,
In the Field, near Atlanta, August 18, 1864—11 a. m.

General HOWARD:

Our telegraph wires are cut so often that it is prudent to have signal telegraph back as far as Allatoona. General Thomas can make stations back to Kenesaw. I wish you to have a station on the hill at Allatoona in connection with General Thomas' station on Kenesaw.

W. T. SHERMAN,
Major-General, Commanding.

HOWARD'S HEADQUARTERS,
August 18, 1864.

General SHERMAN:

My chief signal officer will have an office opened at Allatoona at once.

O. O. HOWARD,
Major-General.

HOWARD'S HEADQUARTERS,
August 18, 1864 -

Major-General SHERMAN:

Signal officers report a column of infantry, nearly a division strong, moving from the works in front of the Twentieth Corps, moving north of the Turner's Ferry road, and to their left, accompanied by some artillery.

O. O. HOWARD,
Major-General.

HOWARD'S HEADQUARTERS,
August 18, 1864.

General SHERMAN:

Following messages just received from signal officer:

1 P. M.

A column of troops, at least a brigade strong, just passed south along the enemy's line. The head of column had passed before I discovered it. They passed a point between me and the churches.

1.05 P. M.

A brigade of infantry has just passed in front of the fort, moving toward our right.

O. O. HOWARD,
Major-General.

HOWARD'S HEADQUARTERS,
August 18, 1864.

Major-General SHERMAN:

I have been along my entire line this a. m. Considerable artillery was developed by the demonstration, and a strong skirmish line throughout. Not many men can be seen in the main works in front of General Logan, but I do not think they have been removed. The division previously reported consisted of seven regiments of infantry. When last seen they were moving opposite the left of the Fifteenth Corps, going toward our left. There were a great many stragglers.

O. O. HOWARD,
Major-General.

HEADQUARTERS FIFTEENTH ARMY CORPS,
Before Atlanta, Ga., August 18, 1864.

Maj. Gen. P. J. OSTERHAUS,
Commanding First Division, Fifteenth Army Corps:

GENERAL: At 4 p. m. this afternoon a strong demonstration will be made by your command, using artillery freely, for the purpose of developing the strength of the enemy in your front. Display freely the colors and make every threatening movement that you think proper to discover the strength of the enemy, and, if possible, draw him from his fortifications. Keep your command well in hand for any emergency.

By order of Maj. Gen. John A. Logan:

R. R. TOWNES,
Assistant Adjutant-General.

(Same to Generals Hazen and Harrow.)

HDQRS. FIRST DIVISION, FIFTEENTH ARMY CORPS,
Before Atlanta, Ga., August 18, 1864.

Lieut. Col. R. R. TOWNES,
Assistant Adjutant-General, Fifteenth Army Corps:

COLONEL: In pursuance of instructions from headquarters Fifteenth Army Corps, I made a demonstration with a view to develop the enemy's force at 4 p. m., while the artillery opened a lively fire on the rebel lines. At the appointed hour I pushed strong re-enforcements forward to the lines held by the reserve of our pickets. The pickets themselves advanced in converging lines toward and in neck of timber in my front held by the enemy's sharpshooters. My pickets advanced from 200 to 300 yards and dislodged the rebels from their first line of rifle-pits. The ground gained is now occupied by my troops, and will be intrenched in compliance with your orders received since.

I am, respectfully, your obedient servant,

P. JOS. OSTERHAUS,
Major-General of Volunteers.

HDQRS. SECOND DIVISION, FIFTEENTH ARMY CORPS,
Before Atlanta, Ga., August 18, 1864.

Lieut. Col. R. R. TOWNES,
Assistant Adjutant-General, Fifteenth Army Corps:

I have the honor to report that I assumed command of this division at about 1 p. m. to-day. At 4 p. m., in obedience to orders, a strong demonstration was made along the line of the division, eliciting a weak fire of artillery from positions to the right and left of my division, but none in its immediate front. None of the enemy were seen during the demonstration, but their shelters were seen in a few places and afterward a few men walking about on all points of the line. But a few muskets were fired in reply to ours. I have no reason for believing that any change has taken place in the positions of any of the enemy's troops in my front during the day.

I am, very respectfully, your obedient servant,

W. B. HAZEN,
Brigadier-General of Volunteers.

HEADQUARTERS LEFT WING, SIXTEENTH ARMY CORPS,
August 18, 1864—9 a. m.

Brig. Gen. J. M. CORSE,
Commanding Second Division:

At 10 a. m. to-day open every gun on your line and continue to fire upon the enemy's line, also have the entire skirmish line open a heavy fire on the enemy. Should an opportunity offer, and the enemy leave their skirmish line, take advantage of it to occupy it.

Respectfully,

G. M. DODGE,
Major-General.

HEADQUARTERS LEFT WING, SIXTEENTH ARMY CORPS,
Near Atlanta, Ga., August 18, 1864.

Lieut. Col. WILLIAM T. CLARK,
Asst. Adjt. Gen., Department and Army of the Tennessee:

COLONEL: In accordance with instructions received this morning, my command opened with all batteries and the skirmish line opened a heavy fire on the enemy. We received only an occasional response, but the enemy could be seen in his main works in considerable force, especially when we first opened. Afterward they kept very low. The signal officer reports that the firing of batteries was excellent, doing considerable damage. More teams than usual have been noticed going in and out of town.

I am, very respectfully, your obedient servant,

G. M. DODGE,
Major-General, Commanding.

RESACA, *August 18, 1864—9.35 a. m.*

Major-General SHERMAN:

I go back to Cartersville this morning; came from Spring Place yesterday. The enemy left there the evening before, just after their pickets were driven in by my scouts, and have gone toward Cleveland. Citizens state they learned from deserters Wheeler designed passing from Cleveland, between Chattanooga and Bridgeport, into Alabama, and join Forrest there. Watkins' horses nearly used up. All able to march started for Fairmount. The Rome cavalry did not come over, and I have none except the small force at Cartersville, who came in from Jasper yesterday. Do you desire them to remain there or be sent to East Tennessee, to follow the enemy? Answer at Cartersville.

E. M. McCOOK,
Brigadier-General.

CARTERSVILLE, *August 18, 1864.*

Major-General SHERMAN:

I just received this dispatch from Colonel Watkins:

CALHOUN, *August 18.*

Have just received positive information that there were three regiments of rebels at Jasper yesterday, and that they moved toward Fairmount yesterday evening or last night.

I have ordered all my cavalry here (480) to be in readiness to move to-night, and unless you give other instructions will march to Fairmount and try to drive these fellows out of the country. Please answer.

E. M. McCOOK,
Brigadier-General.

SHERMAN'S HEADQUARTERS,
August 18, 1864—5.30 p. m.

Brig. Gen. E. M. McCOOK:

I would like to have a good force scour the country from Fairmount to Canton. I will give occupation to all the rebel army here, and I suppose that Wheeler is off on a wild-goose chase. Your force is not enough, but General Smith can make up a command of infantry, which, with your cavalry, could get on the road below Fairmount and give the rebel cavalry great trouble. They are doubtless left behind to watch for Wheeler's return. All roads should be obstructed about Talking Rock, or any by which Wheeler will attempt to return. I would like, if possible, those cattle to be recovered or prevented reaching Atlanta or Covington. General Smith can give you several infantry regiments, and they can march by moonlight and lay by in the heat of the day. These, with your small force of cavalry as scouts, can whip any cavalry left by Wheeler on the road.

W. T. SHERMAN,
Major-General.

RESACA, *August 18, 1864—12 m.*

Major-General SHERMAN:

I left the break at 9.20; delayed an hour and a half by engine getting off track. Trains can now run through to Chattanooga. An unnecessary delay of twelve hours has resulted from the withdrawal of the working party and guard sent from Dalton. The arrangements there have not been equal to the occasion. Thanks are due Captain Nevins, First Michigan Engineers, A. W. Mears, division master of repairs, and G. J. Spears, superintendent of bridge carpenters, and their men, for the energy they have displayed. I have no further news of the enemy.

G. B. RAUM,
Colonel, Commanding Brigade.

HDQRS. MILITARY DIVISION OF THE MISSISSIPPI,
In the Field, near Atlanta, August 18, 1864—3 p. m.

Colonel RAUM,
Resaca:

Your dispatch received. Wheeler can do comparatively little harm in East Tennessee. Put the paroled men to duty. It is a well estab-

lished rule that the enemy must hold and keep prisoners, for we always
have the chances of rescue. I want those cattle recovered if possible,
and any detachments of the enemy left behind Wheeler.

W. T. SHERMAN,
Major-General, Commanding.

RESACA, *August 18, 1864—4 p. m.*

General SHERMAN:

General J. E. Smith has just telegraphed me from Kingston; part of
his command has gone south and part still here. Colonel Watkins says
he has reliable information that three regiments of the enemy left
Pine Log yesterday for Fairmount. The presence of the enemy at that
place is reported by a citizen who passed there last evening.

G. B. RAUM,
Colonel, Commanding.

RESACA, *August 18, 1864.*

General SHERMAN:

The balance of General J. E. Smith's moving command has just gone
south.

G. B. RAUM,
Colonel, Commanding.

CARTERSVILLE, *August 18, 1864—4.30 p. m.*

Major-General SHERMAN:

I left Resaca at 11 a. m. this day, having telegraphed to General
Steedman upon my arrival from Spring Place at 10.30 p. m. 17th instant,
asking what disposition he wished made of the troops under my command. Not receiving any answer, I relieved the troops and sent
them to their respective commands. I feel confident that I can hold
Etowah and Allatoona, but the road is not sufficiently guarded above
Kingston to Dalton. Since my arrival here Colonel Watkins telegraphed
General McCook he had reliable information that three regiments had
left Pine Log and were marching to Fairmount. It is reported that there
is a force in the vicinity of Canton. Scouting party sent out yesterday
afternoon to Canton have not reported.

JNO. E. SMITH,
Brigadier-General.

HDQRS. MILITARY DIVISION OF THE MISSISSIPPI,
In the Field, near Atlanta, August 18, 1864—5.30 p. m.

General JOHN E. SMITH:

Now that Wheeler has gone into East Tennessee and we are all right
here, I think you had better make up an infantry force out of the Rome
and Allatoona garrisons to go to Pine Log and Fairmount, and attack
any force remaining in that neighborhood. To-night I will give employment to all the Confederate cavalry here, and General McCook has not
enough to venture out alone; you could use troops that are fresh, and
the moonlight nights are the very thing for marching.

W. T. SHERMAN,
Major-General, Commanding.

Hdqrs. Military Division of the Mississippi,
In the Field, near Atlanta, August 18, 1864—3.30 p. m.

General STEEDMAN, *Chattanooga:*

I want a full report of matters and things up your way. Let Wheeler go as far into Tennessee and Kentucky as he pleases, but keep him off our main road.

W. T. SHERMAN,
Major-General, Commanding.

Hdqrs. Third Division, Fifteenth Army Corps,
Cartersville, Ga., August 18, 1864—10 p. m.

Lieut. Col. JOHN E. TOURTELLOTTE,
Commandiug at Allatoona:

Recall your forces at once, and barricade all the roads you can to-night. The force estimated at 2,000 camped nine miles from you, near the intersection of the old Marietta and Acworth roads. Close your lines against all citizens for the present.

Very respectfully, your obedient servant,

JNO. E. SMITH,
Brigadier-General.

CARTERSVILLE, *August 18, 1864.*

Major-General STEEDMAN:

Telegraphic communication cut off below Allatoona since 7 p. m. Have ordered the two regiments from Rome here by direction of General Sherman. I expect an attack in this direction. What do you hear of Wheeler?

JNO. E. SMITH,
Brigadier-General.

Hdqrs. Military Division of the Mississippi,
In the Field, near Atlanta, August 18, 1864—10 a. m.

General McARTHUR, *Marietta:*

You know that Wheeler has gone into East Tennessee. General John E. Smith will doubtless return and send you the two regiments with him. The enemy cannot attack Marietta now, for we have the superiority of cavalry. Do the best you can and make one redoubt impregnable, and the enemy will not attack.

W. T. SHERMAN,
Major-General, Commanding.

Hdqrs. Military Division of the Mississippi,
In the Field, near Atlanta, August 18, 1864—7.15 p. m.

General McARTHUR, *Marietta:*

Inquire closely into the firing on the train near Acworth. I think that Wheeler left a small force near Canton, which may be down about Acworth. Send a force there to-night and ambush them. I start all my cavalry to-night to the rear of Atlanta.

W. T. SHERMAN,
Major-General, Commanding.

MARIETTA, *August 18, 1864.*

General SHERMAN:

The train, engine 142, from Allatoona, just arrived. The conductor reports as follows: As the train was nearing the road crossing, half a mile north of Acworth, they saw a small force of cavalry riding rapidly from the east toward the track. They succeeded in crossing track about thirty yards ahead of the engine. They quickly dismounted and fired upon the engine and train. The train kept on and reported to our forces at Acworth and Big Shanty. The fireman and one brakeman missing. No other force of the enemy was seen.

J. B. VAN DYNE.

LOUDON, *August 18, 1864—2.20 p. m.*

Capt. W. P. AMMEN,
    Assistant Adjutant-General:

Courier from Colonel Byrd, at Sweet Water; he says all right this far. I hear of nothing that ought to alarm us. The repairers are evidently working on line, so judge that Colonel Byrd has arrived at Athens without trouble.

N. A. REED,
Aide-de-Camp.

LOUDON, TENN., *August 18, 1864—8.40 p. m.*

Captain AMMEN:

Following just received from Charleston:

They seem to be principally on the north side of the Hiwassee, fording the river near Benton. The citizens report that they intend attacking this place to-night or in the morning. It is reported that they have a force of 2,000 or 5,000, with artillery.

M. B. EWING,
Lieutenant-Colonel.

From all the information we can get they are six miles above this place on the river, not very far from Benton, though most of the force is at Spring Creek, but some say the most of them have crossed the river and are marching toward Athens and Loudon.

R. K. BYRD,
Colonel, Commanding.

I have given you all that I have. The road is cut about two miles this side of Cleveland. The rebels burned and tore up the road for one mile.

R. K. BYRD,
Colonel, Commanding.

This is all we have at present. Everything is in the very best condition, in my opinion. I have visited the pickets this p. m. and found them all right; have thrown out additional advance pickets since dark; all watchful and ready. Construction train just in from Charleston. A captain of First Tennessee reports the same as telegraphs above. He says at Athens the citizens report that a brigade of cavalry passed that place on a back road three miles from town about an hour and a half before sundown, moving this way.

N. A. REED,
Aide-de-Camp.

LOUDON, *August 18, 1864—9.05 p. m.*

Capt. W. P. AMMEN, *Assistant Adjutant-General:*

Having only supplied Colonel Byrd with 6,000 rounds, we have plenty of ammunition. Colonel Patterson wishes me to say to you there are only four pieces of artillery here, and thinks if they are crossing with eight he should have more.

N. A. REED,
Aide-de-Camp.

LOUDON, TENN., *August 18, 1864—9.25 p. m.*

Capt. W. P. AMMEN:

Passenger train just arrived; report nearly the same as previous dispatches, and about as uncertain. Colonel Patterson wishes me to state that from conductors and passengers he learns that Humes' division crossed the railroad at Riceville, between Charleston and Athens, and feeling some alarm for Kingston, has dispatched courier. The conductor states the remaining divisions are said to be following Humes', which has the advance, but no account of their having crossed the road has been received. The rebels burned the depot at Athens last night and inflicted much damage on town. Train has just left for Knoxville.

N. A. REED,
Aide-de-Camp.

LOUDON, TENN., *August 18, 1864.*

Capt. W. P. AMMEN, *Assistant Adjutant-General:*

Courier from Colonel Byrd states that he had arrived all right at Philadelphia. Citizen from that place writes by same courier that he had heard this morning from ten miles below Philadelphia and there was no trouble. Two men fleeing with their goods from Athens report a force from Chattanooga as having engaged the rebels near Athens last night. They know nothing for certain, but only heard it.

N. A. REED,
Aide-de-Camp.

LOUDON, TENN., *August 18, 1864.*

Capt. W. P. AMMEN:

As all the scouts sent out have now returned and have failed to report any enemy, and sufficient time has elapsed for Colonel Byrd to have reported any disaster, I think all chances for attack at this point to be past, and so, unless advised to the contrary, I shall return on first train that appears.

N. A. REED,
Aide-de-Camp.

LOUDON, TENN., *August 18, 1864—11 p. m.*

Captain AMMEN, *Assistant Adjutant-General:*

Courier just in from Kingston. Major Reeves reports two regiments of rebels in Meigs County at 12 m., twenty-three miles from Kingston, moving in that direction.

M. L. PATTERSON,
Lieutenant-Colonel, Commanding.

Weekly report of effective force of the Third and Fourth Divisions, Seventeenth Army Corps, Maj. Gen. Frank P. Blair commanding, August 18, 1864.

Command	Headquarters			Infantry			Artillery			Total				
	Officers.	Men.	Total.	Officers.	Men.	Total.	Officers.	Men.	Total.	Officers.	Men.	Aggregate.	Horses.	Guns.
Seventeenth Army Corps, general and staff	20	200	220							20	200	220		
Third Division, general a and staff	14	40	54							14	40	54		
20th Illinois Infantry Volunteers, Capt. J. H. Austin				3	35	38				3	35	38		
First Brigade, Col. G. E. Bryant	6	38	44	42	1,208	1.250				48	1,246	1,294		
Second Brigade, Lieut. Col. G. F. Wiles	6	28	34	38	797	835				44	825	869		
Third Brigade, Maj. Asa Worden	4	22	26	26	584	610				30	606	636		
Artillery, Capt. W. S. Williams	1	2	3				7	315	322	8	317	325	166	14
Total	31	130	161	109	2,624	2,733	7	315	322	147	3,069	3,216	166	14
Fourth Division, general b and staff	11	53	64							11	53	64		
First Brigade, Col. B. F. Potts	6	29	35	56	1,128	1,184				62	1,157	1,219		
Second Brigade, Col. John Logan c														
Third Brigade, Brig. Gen. W. W. Belknap	7	10	17	41	944	985				48	954	1,002		
Artillery, Capt. W. Z. Clayton							9	364	373	9	364	373	205	14
Pioneer corps, Capt. J. H. Davis				3	88	91				3	88	91		
Detachment Thirty-third Wisconsin Infantry, Lieutenant Stark				1	61	62				1	61	62		
Total	24	92	116	101	2,221	2,322	9	364	373	134	2,677	2,811	205	14
Grand total	75	422	497	210	4,845	5,055	16	679	695	301	5,946	6,247	371	28

a Brig. Gen. Charles R. Woods.
b Brig. Gen. G. A. Smith.
c At Marietta, Ga.

FRANK P. BLAIR, Jr.,
Major-General, Commanding.

ARTILLERY HDQRS., MIL. DIV. OF THE MISSISSIPPI,
Before Atlanta, August 18, 1864.

Brigadier-General BRANNAN,
    Chief of Artillery, Department of the Cumberland:

GENERAL: The movement of the army which involves the sending to the rear the 4½-inch siege guns having been temporarily suspended (of which fact Major-General Thomas has been advised), Major-General Sherman directs me to say that the fire of the three 4½-inch guns on Geary's front will be resumed and will be continued at the same rate as heretofore as long as possible. Captain Baylor informs me that there are upward of 1,500 rounds of ammunition for these guns at Chattahoochee railroad bridge depot.

    I am, general, &c.,

                            WM. F. BARRY.

SPECIAL FIELD ORDERS, }   HDQRS. ARMY OF THE OHIO,
     No. 86.   }   *Near Atlanta, Ga., August 18, 1864.*

    *   *   *   *   *   *   *

    V. To-night General Johnson will withdraw from the trenches two brigades of each division of his corps, distributing the third brigade of each so as to occupy the division front. The troops withdrawn will remain out of the enemy's view until morning, when they will march to the right of the Twenty-third Corps, the head of column to reach Utoy Creek, near the Sandtown road, by 6 a. m. The tents should be left standing and every means adopted to keep the enemy in ignorance of the diminution of force. The troops will probably return to their present position to-morrow night or the next day. General Hascall will in like manner distribute one brigade so as to hold his present line and report to General Cox with his other two brigades, and act under his command during the day. All trains will be kept hitched up during the day and ready to move to the rear in case of danger. No wagons will accompany the troops beyond General Hascall's present works. Colonel Garrard, commanding cavalry division, will continue to operate on the right of the infantry. Further orders will be given in the morning.

    *   *   *   *   *   *   *

    By command of Major-General Schofield:

                        J. A. CAMPBELL,
              Major and Assistant Adjutant-General

HDQRS. MILITARY DIVISION OF THE MISSISSIPPI,
In the Field, near Atlanta, August 19, 1864—10.45 a. m.

General GRANT,
    City Point:

    I have your two dispatches of 14th and 16th, also that of 18th. I will never take a step backward, and have no fears of Hood. I can whip him outside of his trenches, and think in time I can compel him to come out. I think at this moment I have a fine cavalry force on the only road which can feed him, and if necessary will swing my whole army across it also.

                      W. T. SHERMAN,
              Major-General, Commanding.

NEAR ATLANTA, *August 19, 1864—7 p. m.*
(Received 2.20 p. m. 20th.)
General H. W. HALLECK,
Washington:

I have Secretary Stanton's dispatch announcing the promotion of Colonel Long, a hard-working and worthy cavalry officer. We have had heavy demonstrations all day, especially on our flanks, to hold the enemy while our cavalry is out after the Macon road. I hope this time the work will be better done than before. We control all other railroads. General Dodge received a ball wound in his forehead, but it is pronounced not serious. All well.

W. T. SHERMAN,
Major-General, Commanding.

———

THOMAS' HEADQUARTERS,
August 19, 1864.
Major-General SHERMAN:

I send following message, Vining's, &c. Can't that have been Kilpatrick?

VINING'S, *August 19, 1864—1.30 a. m.*
Captain CASE,
Chief Signal Officer:

Immense fire south by 15 degrees west, thirteen miles from here.

BRENT,
Signal Officer.

GEO. H. THOMAS,
Major-General.

———

HDQRS. MILITARY DIVISION OF THE MISSISSIPPI,
In the Field, near Atlanta, August 19, 1864—8.45 a. m.
General THOMAS:

Fairburn is south 15 degrees west of Vining's. I have no doubt the fire referred to by the signal officer was caused by General Kilpatrick; he probably reached the railroad about that hour; but the distance from Vining's is greater than thirteen miles, near twenty.

W. T. SHERMAN,
Major-General, Commanding.

———

HDQRS. MILITARY DIVISION OF THE MISSISSIPPI,
In the Field, near Atlanta, August 19, 1864—9.30 p. m.
Generals THOMAS and HOWARD:

General Schofield has been to the Newnan road at the point marked "Bacon" on the map. Enemy has a strong fort in the northeast corner of 190, whence his works run southeast to the West Point railroad. No opposition to General Schofield, who found the lines guarded, but none outside; he observed no movement down the road. What news have you?

W. T. SHERMAN,
Major-General, Commanding.

HEADQUARTERS ARMY OF THE CUMBERLAND,
August 19, 1864—10 p. m.

Major-General SHERMAN:

Signal officer at Howard's house reports saw column smoke south of Atlanta, distant about eight or ten miles. General Stanley reports having advanced a strong line of skirmishers in his front, and drove the enemy's skirmishers into their main works, but found them too strong to attempt assault. He has kept them fully occupied. He will to-morrow morning move the rifle-pits as far as the railroad, and then throw out a strong brigade beyond the railroad to see if he can find their flank, and drive it in. Our cavalry has kept that of the enemy fully occupied from daylight this morning, taking a few prisoners between Decatur and Atlanta.

GEO. H. THOMAS,
Major-General, U. S. Volunteers, Commanding.

HOWARD'S HOUSE, *August 19, 1864—2 p. m.*

Captain CASE:

I feel satisfied there are but few rebels in the works in this front. Have not seen fifty all day. Can see four or five guns (6-inch). See no movements of any description. The enemy have not fired a shot in reply to our artillery. Can see no smoke or dust in the direction of Macon yet.

Very respectfully,

A. F. BERRY,
Signal Officer.

HOWARD'S HOUSE, *August 19, 1864—6 p. m.*

Captain CASE:

Saw a large column of smoke south of Atlanta about eight or ten miles distant. Our troops advanced this p. m. at 5 o'clock, and after a brisk skirmish retired. We lost only few men. Don't know the number. Could see but very few in enemy's lines.

BERRY.

HEADQUARTERS FOURTH ARMY CORPS,
Near Atlanta, Ga., August 19, 1864.

Brig. Gen. WILLIAM D. WHIPPLE,
Chief of Staff, Department of the Cumberland:

GENERAL: I moved Kirby's brigade to the railroad at daybreak and sent strong reconnoitering parties toward Atlanta and south toward the battle-ground of the Seventeenth Corps. About one division of the enemy was seen going into the rebel works opposite our lines and the flank works running south of Atlanta. We drove the enemy out of his works, which he appears to man quite as strongly as heretofore. The regiments are now intrenching or improving the intrenchments at the angle near the railroad to give the idea of a permanent extension of our line. General Grose on his front also made a vigorous advance and his skirmishers engaged the rebel main line. No rebels will leave that part of the works. I will make additional movements this evening. We were so unfortunate as to lose one of the best officers in the corps, killed, Captain Rains, Ninetieth Ohio Infantry Volunteers. But few other casualties.

Your obedient servant,

D. S. STANLEY,
Major-General, Commanding.

STANLEY'S HEADQUARTERS,
August 19, 1864—1 p. m.

Brig. Gen. W. D. WHIPPLE,
Chief of Staff:

I have tested every part of the enemy's line this morning, and do not think I can take it with the troops at my disposal. I will engage the enemy to the best of my ability this evening.

D. S. STANLEY,
Major-General.

STANLEY'S HEADQUARTERS,
August 19, 1864.

General SHERMAN:

I saw no indications of a fire at 3 p. m., but about 5 o'clock saw a considerable column of smoke in south part of city. Signal officers report seeing column of smoke about ten miles south of Atlanta during the afternoon.

D. S. STANLEY,
Major-General.

HEADQUARTERS FOURTH ARMY CORPS,
Near Atlanta, Ga., August 19, 1864—1.25 p. m.

General KIMBALL:

GENERAL: A telegram, of which the following is a copy, has just been received by the major-general commanding:

SHERMAN'S HEADQUARTERS,
August 19, 1864.

General THOMAS:

General Howard's signal officer reports cars loaded with soldiers sent down the railroad. Of course Hood will try to defend that road at all cost, and we should take advantage of detachments made for that purpose. Better let all your line feel forward as far as prudent, and if a safe place be found make a lodgment.

W. T. SHERMAN,
Major-General.

In accordance with the above you will re-enforce your picket-line and make such other disposition of your troops as may be necessary, "and feel forward as far as prudent" at 5 o'clock this p. m., "and if a safe place be found make a lodgment."

By order of Major-General Stanley:

J. S. FULLERTON,
Assistant Adjutant-General and Chief of Staff.

(Same to Generals Newton and Wood.)

HEADQUARTERS FOURTH ARMY CORPS,
Near Atlanta, Ga., August 19, 1864—9.10 p. m.

Brigadier-General KIMBALL,
Commanding First Division, Fourth Army Corps:

GENERAL: Our demonstrations in favor of Kilpatrick will continue to-morrow. This is in accordance with instructions received from department headquarters. At daybreak to-morrow you will station two regiments of Opdycke's brigade and one regiment of Taylor's brigade in the works about the "burnt brick house," and also so as to cover the ravine between your present left and said house. You will also at the same time move a brigade toward the enemy's right flank and execute the movement in such a manner as to lead him to think you are hunting for it (the flank). Move toward the position where the right flank of the enemy appeared to be to-day, not down the railroad, though you will have to send pickets in that direction and make as large a show of force as possible. General Wood has been directed to send two regiments to report to you at daylight to-morrow. They will report at the same place that the two regiments reported this morning.

By command of Major-General Stanley:

J. S. FULLERTON,
Assistant Adjutant-General and Chief of Staff.

HEADQUARTERS FOURTH ARMY CORPS,
Near Atlanta, Ga., August 19, 1864—8.45 p. m.

Brigadier-General NEWTON,
Commanding Second Division, Fourth Army Corps:

GENERAL: You will keep up the demonstration that you have been making to-day in favor of General Kilpatrick during to-morrow. Do this by engaging the enemy's skirmishers. Do not advance your troops unless the situation of the enemy in your front will allow you to do so with comparative safety.

By order of Major-General Stanley:

J. S. FULLERTON,
Lieutenant-Colonel and Chief of Staff.

HEADQUARTERS FOURTH ARMY CORPS,
Near Atlanta, Ga., August 19, 1864—8.45 p. m.

Brigadier-General WOOD,
Commanding Third Division:

Our demonstrations in favor of Kilpatrick will continue during to-morrow. You will therefore send two regiments to the same point that you sent the two this morning on General Kimball's left. Start them from their camp at 3 o'clock in the morning. Engage the enemy's skirmishers through the day, and keep up the same show and activity that you have exhibited to-day; also, watch closely for any movements that the enemy may make.

By order of Major-General Stanley:

J. S. FULLERTON,
Assistant Adjutant-General.

HEADQUARTERS FOURTEENTH ARMY CORPS,
Near Atlanta, Ga., August 19, 1864.

[General W. D. WHIPPLE:]

GENERAL: Last night I received orders to withdraw from the Fourteenth Corps all excepting three brigades, and move to the right of the Twenty-third Corps. This was accomplished by 5 o'clock this morning. This force was to support a movement to be made by a part of the Twenty-third Corps. Nothing was accomplished during the day, and the troops returned to their positions after dark this evening. Nothing of interest occurred on the line during the day. I inclose casualty report of yesterday.*

Respectfully, your obedient servant,

R. W. JOHNSON,
Brigadier-General of Volunteers, Commanding.

STATION OBSERVATION,
At General Geary's Headquarters, August 19, 1864—6.35 p. m.

Brigadier-General WILLIAMS,
Commanding Twentieth Army Corps:

GENERAL: I have the honor to report that the enemy's troops in works on right of four-gun fort moved up as reported yesterday and occupied trenches. A squad of twelve marched to rear into ravine; all had knapsacks and arms. The six-gun fort in front General Geary was struck frequently during day by shells from heavy gun on left, one causing something like an explosion of a caisson. This same report, general, has been sent by the chief signal officer to General Thomas.

Very respectfully, your obedient servant,

W. W. HOPKINS,
Captain and Acting Signal Officer.

HDQRS. MILITARY DIVISION OF THE MISSISSIPPI,
In the Field, near Atlanta, August 19, 1864—8.30 a. m.

General ROUSSEAU,
Nashville:

Wheeler has passed to my rear with 6,000 men, and was yesterday in East Tennessee. You must attend to him if he approaches your district.

W. T. SHERMAN,
Major-General, Commanding.

HEADQUARTERS DEFENSES
NASHVILLE AND CHATTANOOGA RAILROAD,
Tullahoma, Tenn., August 19, 1864.

Captain CAIN,
Fifth Tennessee Volunteer Cavalry:

CAPTAIN: From information received from General Sherman I learn that the rebel General Wheeler is getting into East Tennessee with 6,000 men, and may strike at this railroad. If he should attempt to do so you

---

* Not found.

are in a position where you will most likely receive the first news of his approach. You will therefore keep a sharp lookout; keep scouting parties well out on all the roads east and southeast, and guard well against a surprise, and be sure you have timely notice of his approach, and upon the first certain notice of his approach send couriers both to me at this place and to General Van Cleve at Murfreesborough. Put your command in the best order for active operations. Collect in all stragglers and keep your men well in hand. Get everything ready for falling back on short notice, and be prepared to move what Government stores you can, and what you cannot move be prepared to destroy. When you are certain that Wheeler is approaching you will fall back to this place. If you should find that impossible you will fall back on Murfreesborough. In either case keep your force, with the exception of a small advance guard, between the enemy and your transportation. Inform the Union citizens that there is danger, that they may be prepared to act as they think best for their safety. Be sure you are not alarmed by guerrillas alone to evacuate the place without cause. Be vigilant, brave, and calm, and there will be no danger of being gobbled. Wheeler may turn his attention toward Knoxville and not come this way. It would be well to give out to the inhabitants that you are to make a stand and hold the place till relieved.

I am, captain, very respectfully,

R. H. MILROY,
Major-General, Commanding.

P. S.—I have concluded to send Major Waters, of the Fifth Tennessee Cavalry, to take command at McMinnville, and the above instructions to Captain Cain will be carried out by Major Waters.

R. H. MILROY,
Major-General, Commanding.

HEADQUARTERS ARMY OF THE OHIO,
Near Atlanta, Ga., August 19, 1864.

Brig. Gen. R. W. JOHNSON,
Commanding Fourteenth Army Corps:

GENERAL: General Schofield desires you to withdraw four brigades from your line to-morrow morning (as you did this morning) for to-morrow's operations.

Very respectfully, your obedient servant,

J. A. CAMPBELL,
Major and Assistant Adjutant-General.

HEADQUARTERS ARMY OF THE OHIO,
Near Atlanta, Ga., August 19, 1864.

Major-General SHERMAN:

Considerable artillery firing was heard from our right this morning, commencing at daylight and lasting about two hours. It first appeared to be near Fairburn, and moved continually toward Jonesborough. The enemy is very quiet in our front this morning and shows no change. Our skirmishers have advanced some distance, and Cox is about to move forward with four brigades.

J. M. SCHOFIELD,
Major-General.

HDQRS. MILITARY DIVISION OF THE MISSISSIPPI,
In the Field, near Atlanta, August 19, 1864—7.30 a. m.

General SCHOFIELD:

Your dispatch is received. General Stanley, on the other flank, is operating in like manner. General Garrard, with his remaining brigade, was to be in Decatur at daylight to move toward Flat Rock and engage a brigade of cavalry on that flank, and move off toward Stone Mountain and swing round toward camp, to repeat the same to-morrow morning. If my presence is wanted over there let me know, and I come at once. All is not yet satisfactory to our rear.

W. T. SHERMAN,
Major-General, Commanding.

HEADQUARTERS ARMY OF THE OHIO,
Near Atlanta, Ga., August 19, 1864.

Major-General SHERMAN:

I will reconnoiter forward to a point where I can better watch the enemy and be ready to attack him if he shows any sign of movement.

J. M. SCHOFIELD,
Major-General.

HDQRS. MILITARY DIVISION OF THE MISSISSIPPI,
In the Field, near Atlanta, August 19, 1864—10.15 a. m.

General SCHOFIELD:

I have your dispatch. I have heard from General Kilpatrick at 11 o'clock last night, five miles south of Camp Creek. Ross' brigade in his front and retreating. He reported he would be on the Macon road at 12.30 to-day. Keep your cavalry well out as vedettes, and demonstrate as strong as you can. General Stanley is at work to the other flank.

W. T. SHERMAN,
Major-General, Commanding.

SCHOFIELD'S HEADQUARTERS,
August 19, 1864—2 p. m.

General SHERMAN:

We have extended our demonstration along the enemy's line as far as the large battery on the Newnan road. My skirmishers are now within 300 yards of that battery. The enemy has been compelled to bring up reserves and occupy his works in force. I am now sending another force still farther to the right to threaten the enemy's left.

J. M. SCHOFIELD,
Major-General.

HDQRS. MILITARY DIVISION OF THE MISSISSIPPI,
In the Field, near Atlanta, August 19, 1864—3.10 p. m.

General SCHOFIELD:

Should your demonstration carry you to the West Point railroad break it, and let that seem to be partially the object of the movement, and also it will prevent an infantry force from being thrown down to-night to interfere with General Kilpatrick's return.

W. T. SHERMAN,
Major-General, Commanding.

SCHOFIELD'S HEADQUARTERS,
August 19, 1864—7 p. m.

General SHERMAN:

The large battery which we struck in the first move is, I believe, about the northeast corner of lot 190, where two roads come into the Newnan road. From that point the enemy's lines seem to run southeast to the West Point railroad, striking it near Bacon. In the second move we crossed the Newnan road at Diggs'. Did not get across Camp Creek, but moved up the Newnan road until we developed the enemy in force in their works. Citizens and prisoners say the enemy's lines extend to the railroad, but do not know whether beyond or not.

                                        J. M. SCHOFIELD,
                                                Major-General.

HDQRS. MILITARY DIVISION OF THE MISSISSIPPI,
In the Field, near Atlanta, August 19, 1864—8.15 p. m.

General SCHOFIELD:

I can trace your movement by the map perfectly well. I think it well still to display a force about Diggs' until we know that General Kilpatrick is back behind Camp Creek. Have you seen your cavalry during the day? General Stanley moved in force across the railroad about the brick house, and set his men to work enlarging and strengthening his lines in that quarter. To produce the proper effect he sent a brigade across to General McPherson's battle-ground, and found the enemy intrenched on that hill, about half a mile out. I have not heard of General Garrard's cavalry, but am satisfied the enemy has been held to his lines to-day, and General Kilpatrick has had a good chance to work. Generals Stanley and Garrard will renew their operations in the morning and all the line will be active until General Kilpatrick is back, of which, I think, you will have the first notice. We have fired the town twice to-day, a heavy fire burning at daylight and about 3 p. m. General Dodge got a bad wipe across the forehead, but the wound is not dangerous. Nothing positive done along our lines, as nothing was attempted, but, although we displayed large force on our flanks, wide apart, I thought the enemy would make some demonstration against our center, but nothing of the kind. Telegraph and railroad at work again. Wheeler is above Cleveland, but I hear nothing of him, save that he did no damage at Cleveland.

                                        W. T. SHERMAN,
                                            Major-General, Commanding.

HEADQUARTERS ARMY OF THE OHIO,
Near Atlanta, Ga., August 19, 1864.

Major-General SHERMAN:

My cavalry has been well forward on my right and in communication with the infantry during the day; also picketing all roads to the right. A rebel cavalryman, captured this morning, says one of Armstrong's brigades was in front of Kilpatrick last night, and another started after him this morning; that there is very little cavalry left on the flank. My cavalry has met nothing but light pickets. I will keep up a show of force about Diggs' to-morrow, and I think threaten the railroad with a light force a little more toward Red Oak, which will deter the enemy from sending infantry to trouble Kilpatrick on his return.

                                        J. M. SCHOFIELD,
                                                Major-General.

SHERMAN'S HEADQUARTERS,
August 19, 1864. (Received 8.45 p. m.)

General SCHOFIELD:

According to the doctrine of chances, on the supposition that Kilpatrick breaks the road, of which, I think, there is no doubt, the enemy should try to break our center. Therefore, let orders be made that in case of any indications of such an event the wings will close on the center. The center is defined to be from the Buck Head road, Newton's, to the poor-house, or the Fifteenth Corps.

W. T. SHERMAN,
Major-General.

(Same to Generals Thomas and Howard.)

HEADQUARTERS ARMY OF THE OHIO,
Near Atlanta, Ga., August 19, 1864.

Major-General SHERMAN:

In my present position I hold my lines with very light force, keeping reserves where they can be quickly concentrated at any point. I do not quite understand whether you mean that the wings shall close upon the center upon indication of an attempt to break our center, or not until an indication that it is broken.

J. M. SCHOFIELD,
Major-General.

HDQRS. MILITARY DIVISION OF THE MISSISSIPPI,
In the Field, near Atlanta, August 19, 1864—12 midnight.

General SCHOFIELD:

The notice to close on the center was given in case of the center being broken and communication between the parts cut off. Otherwise the operations begun to-day to continue till General Kilpatrick is back.

W. T. SHERMAN,
Major-General, Commanding.

HEADQUARTERS DEPARTMENT OF THE TENNESSEE,
August 19, 1864.

Major-General SHERMAN:

I have ordered an immediate demonstration along my entire front. I fear Hood has ample time to move his troops by cars to the point threatened, but I hope not.

O. O. HOWARD,
Major-General.

HDQRS. MILITARY DIVISION OF THE MISSISSIPPI,
In the Field, near Atlanta, August 19, 1864—11.15 a. m.

General HOWARD:

General Kilpatrick reported last night at 11 o'clock he would be on the road at 12.30 to-day. He will cut the road and force the infantry to disembark. No train can carry more than 800 men, and General Kilpatrick can work on both sides of that train. Being mounted he can circumvent any infantry except at a single point, and he is not limited to any point. He can be at Jonesborough at noon, tear up a few rails, and ten miles below in a couple of hours. I think General Kilpatrick equal to anything Hood can now do. Still we should take advantage of the detachment of his best troops for that duty.

W. T. SHERMAN,
Major-General, Commanding.

HOWARD'S HEADQUARTERS,
August 19, 1864.

General SHERMAN:

Train which left Atlanta at 9.35 returned at 11.35 empty. Know it is same train by peculiarity of one of the cars. Another train which left at 11.10 returned at 11.40 empty.

O. O. HOWARD,
Major-General.

HEADQUARTERS DEPARTMENT OF THE TENNESSEE,
August 19, 1864.

Major-General SHERMAN:

Demonstration in front of the Fifteenth Corps developed more force of the enemy than yesterday. In front of the other corps about the same. No news.

O. O. HOWARD,
Major-General.

HEADQUARTERS DEPARTMENT OF THE TENNESSEE,
August 19, 1864.

Major-General SHERMAN:

General Dodge is wounded in the side of the head by a musket-ball; not seriously.

O. O. HOWARD,
Major-General.

HEADQUARTERS DEPARTMENT OF THE TENNESSEE,
August 19, 1864.

Major-General SHERMAN:

The skirmishing you hear is apparently between me and the Fourteenth Corps. Have not heard from my right yet.

O. O. HOWARD,
Major-General.

HEADQUARTERS DEPARTMENT OF THE TENNESSEE,
August 19, 1864.

Major-General SHERMAN:

The firing to-night occurred in the front of the right of the Fifteenth Corps. The enemy attempted to capture our working parties. They failed. General Lightburn was wounded at De Gress' battery in a similar manner to General Dodge. The officers and men on the right of the Fifteenth Corps have observed fires in the direction of Macon since 6 o'clock. One of my staff just returned reports he saw the fires still burning.

O. O. HOWARD,
Major-General.

HOWARD'S HEADQUARTERS,
August 19, 1864. (Received 11.15 a. m.)

General SCHOFIELD:

Following just received from signal officer:

A long train of cars, loaded on top with troops, just moved down to the barracks, where it took on more troops and then moved south.

O. O. HOWARD,
Major-General.

HDQRS. DEPARTMENT AND ARMY OF THE TENNESSEE,
Before Atlanta, Ga., August 19, 1864.

Maj. Gen. JOHN A. LOGAN,
Commanding Fifteenth Army Corps:

GENERAL: Major-General Howard desires you to throw forward two regiments in some secure place near the skirmish line, say on General Hazen's front, and direct them to open fire by file, keeping it up for about half an hour. The same plan will be pursued in front of the Sixteenth and Seventeenth Corps, all with a view to give the appearance of a general assault. There is plenty of ammunition at Marietta.

Very respectfully, your obedient servant,

WM. T. CLARK,
Assistant Adjutant-General.

[Indorsement.]

HEADQUARTERS FIFTEENTH ARMY CORPS,
Before Atlanta, August 19, 1864.

Respectfully referred to General Hazen, who is hereby instructed to act in accordance with suggestions in inclosed communication.

By order of Major-General Logan:

R. R. TOWNES,
Assistant Adjutant-General.

HEADQUARTERS FIFTEENTH ARMY CORPS,
Before Atlanta, Ga., August 19, 1864.

Lieut. Col. WILLIAM T. CLARK,
Assistant Adjutant-General:

COLONEL: I have the honor to report that the demonstration was made to-day at 12 m. in compliance with instructions, and that it did not result in developing any greater force of the enemy than on yesterday. They replied briskly with musketry and artillery. The firing to-night commenced on General Osterhaus' working party and afterward extended generally along the whole line. Brigadier-General Lightburn was wounded severely in the head while at De Gress' battery.

Very respectfully, your obedient servant,

JOHN A. LOGAN,
Major-General.

HdQrs. Second Division, Fifteenth Army Corps,
Before Atlanta, Ga., August 19, 1864.
Lieut. Col. R. R. Townes,
Assistant Adjutant-General, Fifteenth Army Corps:

I have the honor to report that at 12 m. to-day orders were received to make a demonstration along the line of the division, which was at once obeyed by sending forward two regiments, displaying troops, firing with artillery and infantry. The enemy at once replied all along the line with some infantry, and from three positions in my immediate front with the artillery, probably not more than a section, at each place. This was in addition to firing with artillery from the two positions fired from last evening. Excepting a brisk and ineffective fire for about ten minutes along the picket-line last night nothing else of importance has transpired in the front of this line for the last twenty-four hours.

I am, respectfully, your obedient servant,

W. B. HAZEN,
Brigadier-General of Volunteers.

Headquarters Department of the Tennessee,
Before Atlanta, Ga., August 19, 1864.
Maj. Gen. F. P. Blair,
Commanding Seventeenth Army Corps:

In visiting the lines yesterday I observed that opposite the left of General Leggett the rebels, as skirmishers, occupy a continuous line of rifle-pits. If your engineer can put up a work for a couple of guns, temporarily, I think you can drive them out. Please investigate the matter and report to me the result.

Very respectfully,

O. O. HOWARD,
Major-General.

HdQrs. Military Division of the Mississippi,
In the Field, near Atlanta, August 19, 1864—2 p. m.
General Steedman,
Chattanooga:

Where did Wheeler cross the Hiwassee? Did the commanding officers at Loudon and Knoxville have notice of his coming? Keep me well advised of his movements; also Generals Rousseau and Burbridge. Lookout for his return. I want him headed off if he attempts to come back.

W. T. SHERMAN,
Major-General, Commanding.

Chattanooga, *August 19, 1864.*
Capt. L. M. Dayton,
Aide-de-Camp:

Wheeler is reported to have crossed the Hiwassee at Columbus. Loudon had notice of his coming. I keep men scouting south and east of Cleveland.

JAMES B. STEEDMAN,
Major-General.

HDQRS. MILITARY DIVISION OF THE MISSISSIPPI,
In the Field, near Atlanta, August 19, 1864—9 a. m.

General JOHN E. SMITH,
Cartersville:

If you send to Canton notify the people that if our road is let alone we will feed ourselves, but if it be interrupted we will of necessity strip the country and destroy all things within reach.

W. T. SHERMAN,
Major-General, Commanding.

HEADQUARTERS FOURTH TENNESSEE INFANTRY,
Kingston, Tenn., August 19, 1864—8 p. m.

Capt. H. C. CONNELLY,
Acting Assistant Inspector-General:

CAPTAIN: Yours per courier received. Reports just in from scout below Post Oak say the rebels are crossing Tennessee River at Brady's Ferry, about twenty-five miles below this place, variously estimated from 2,000 to 5,000. Reports from south side of Tennessee say two regiments were crossing at the same place, this about 11 a. m. Cannot find out which direction they are moving. My scouts nearly form a connected line from Cumberland Mountain to Sweet Water Valley. I am confident that they cannot surprise us. The three pieces of artillery here have each 100 rounds of grape-shot and shell. The steamers on which they belong speak of running up to Loudon if the rebels attack us here, and will take off the pieces with them, for the captains say that they have orders from General Thomas to not run without them aboard. The ammunition sent from Loudon is received. Will fix up receipts, &c., as soon as possible.

The men are all anxious to have the rebels try us, and I have the utmost confidence in them. I am inclined to think that the intention of the rebels is to make a raid through Middle Tennessee and cut communication off from Nashville, though I may be wrong, but will try to be ready for them when they come. If we are attacked you shall know it at once.

Very respectfully, your obedient servant,

T. H. REEVES,
Major, Commanding Regiment.

CARTERSVILLE, *August 19, 1864.*

Major-General SHERMAN:

Colonel Cooper started to Fairmount at 4 o'clock yesterday; reports rebel force gone. A few scattering ones at Jasper.

E. M. McCOOK,
Brigadier-General.

CHATTANOOGA, TENN., *August 19, 1864—9 p. m.*
(Received 2.40 a. m. 20th.)

Maj. THOMAS T. ECKERT:

Situation at front not materially changed since my last. Kilpatrick is to-day raiding the Macon railroad with an infantry support, and has besides his own division two brigades of Garrard's, under Long. General Sherman expects much from the movement. Railroad hence to Atlanta all right again, and Wheeler is now in East Tennessee above the Hiwassee, no doubt on the same route he went over last year, and will be next heard from on the Nashville railroad in vicinity of Wartrace or Duck River bridge. He has not less than 5,000 men and ten guns. Two wires to Kingston, and business will be more promptly forwarded if rebels don't keep both cut, as has been the case for the last three or four days. Awful hot.

J. C. VAN DUZER.

SPECIAL FIELD ORDERS, }   HDQRS. MIL. DIV. OF THE MISS.,
                              In the Field, near Atlanta,
No. 58.   }   *August 19, 1864.*

I. Brig. Gen. R. W. Johnson, U. S. Volunteers, is hereby announced as chief of cavalry of the Military Division of the Mississippi. He will take post at headquarters, Nashville, Tenn.

II. General Johnson, as chief of cavalry, will have charge of all remounts, care of horses that are issued to the cavalry by the quartermaster's department or by the purchasing officers of the Cavalry Bureau, will direct their issue and determine the order in which horses shall be issued, giving preference always to the best cavalry troops dismounted, or to such as take best care of their horses.

III. He will from time to time make inspection of the different cavalry commands; will make his reports to the head of the Cavalry Bureau, Washington, D. C., and to these headquarters, and may call for reports of all men, horses, equipments, arms, &c., pertaining to that branch of service in this command.

* * . * * * * *

By order of Maj. Gen. W. T. Sherman:

L. M. DAYTON,
Aide-de-Camp.

GENERAL ORDERS, }   HDQRS. CAV. DIV., ARMY OF THE OHIO,
No. 3.   }   *Before Atlanta, Ga., August 19, 1864.*

Col. Horace Capron, Fourteenth Illinois Cavalry Volunteers, is hereby assigned to the command of the First Brigade, Cavalry Division, Army of the Ohio. The brigade will be composed of the following regiments: Fourteenth Illinois Cavalry Volunteers, Eighth Michigan Cavalry Volunteers, Fifth Indiana Cavalry Volunteers, Sixth Indiana Cavalry Volunteers. Colonel Capron will at once proceed to organize the brigade to make it as effective as possible. Regimental commanders will make their reports to Colonel Capron, as required by existing orders and regulations.

By command of Israel Garrard, colonel, commanding division:

T. F. ALLEN,
Captain and Acting Assistant Adjutant-General.

SPECIAL FIELD ORDERS, }   HDQRS. FIFTEENTH ARMY CORPS,
No. 81.   }   *Before Atlanta, Ga., August 19, 1864.*

I. Division commanders will, at 12 m. to-day, make such a demonstration as to induce the enemy to believe we are going to assault their works.

By order of Maj. Gen. John A. Logan:

R. R. TOWNES,
Assistant Adjutant-General.

GENERAL ORDERS, ⎰ HDQRS. LEFT WING, 16TH ARMY CORPS,
No. 47.   ⎱   *Near Atlanta, Ga., August 19, 1864.*

In compliance with instructions received, I hereby assume temporary command of the Left Wing, Sixteenth Army Corps.

T. E. G. RANSOM,
Brigadier-General.

HDQRS. MILITARY DIVISION OF THE MISSISSIPPI,
In the Field, near Atlanta, August 20, 1864.

Maj. Gen. H. W. HALLECK,
      Washington:

GENERAL: I received last night your dispatch of 19th concerning jurisdiction on the Mississippi.* As long as we can all pull together it makes little difference who commands, and I perfectly accord to General Canby the control of matters on the great river. I have sent by telegraph to General Washburn a copy of your dispatch, with an order to be governed by it, but it will need some further orders to make things straight. I will see General Howard to-day, and we will submit some proposition that will give General Canby all the troops of the Department of the Tennessee resting on the Mississippi, but for the sake of accountability we should have sent to this army certain detachments that resulted from the General Banks expedition. You will remember that I made up my Meridian force out of the Sixteenth and Seventeenth Corps, and when General Banks asked for 10,000 men for one month on Red River we made up the force by using troops, non-veterans, and availed ourselves of the lull to furlough the veterans. In this operation some considerable confusion was made in old divisions, brigades, and even regiments, so that still fractions of these are here and the other fractions down the Mississippi, making it very difficult to preserve the standard organizations. My orders to General Washburn were to let General A. J. Smith sweep across North Mississippi and reach either Eastport or Decatur, whence I would draw these fragments and the division of General A. J. Smith, which was designed to form a part of General McPherson's column, and send the balance, including the cavalry, back. I only gave this order after I knew that Stephen D. Lee had joined General Johnston at Atlanta with a large part of the Mississippi army. I think it would be well, if possible still, to send here by river and rail, if necessary, the fragments to which I refer, which cannot amount to more than 2,000 or 3,000 men, and leave General Canby the balance.

Our casualties here from death, wounds, and sickness have been and must continue large, but we lose more by the expiration of service of regiments and individuals. I think more than half this army is entitled to discharge between this and October, so that if Hood can simply hold on here he will be enabled to defeat us by the superior method they have of recruitment. In the South all men are soldiers, and they are not held for limited terms, but for life if the war lasts that long. In the end we must adopt the same plan, but in the mean time may lose the result of all former labors and have to commence *de novo.*

If General Canby can hold the river and prevent Kirby Smith passing over (which he cannot, for the men pass by individuals and meet at some rendezvous in Mississippi, whence they come in organized masses to Hood), he will accomplish the same result as here. Also the

---

* See Vol. XXXIX, Part II.

operations up the Alabama are of equal assistance to me. I would not take Mobile City, for that would simply tie up a garrison, whereas now General Dabney Maury holds it with a Confederate garrison which is lost to our opponents. A single gun-boat can watch Fort Morgan, two more the river at and near Mobile, and, if I am not in error, General Gordon Granger's troops could go up the old Spanish channel by Blakely and reach Selma, and it may be Montgomery, which would compel Hood to detach as against him, for a large portion of the Confederate supplies come through the reach of the Alabama River between Selma and Montgomery.

I beg you will submit these views to the lieutenant-general commanding, and I will be perfectly satisfied if the troops hitherto subject to my orders can be directed to the accomplishment of these ends.

I am, with great respect, your obedient servant,

W. T. SHERMAN,
Major-General, Commanding.

NEAR ATLANTA, GA., *August 20, 1864—7 p. m.*
(Received 11 p. m.)

Maj. Gen. H. W. HALLECK,
Washington, D. C.:

General Kilpatrick is out yet, and I infer has broken the Macon road, because three trains of cars left Atlanta and returned, backing the trains. Our infantry to-day was on the West Point road at Red Oak, five miles below East Point. General Lightburn was struck in the head last evening by a sharpshooter, very much as General Dodge, but will get well. We have kept up brisk skirmishing all day. Our road is now repaired and in good order. Wheeler is above the Hiwassee.

W. T. SHERMAN,
Major-General.

NASHVILLE, *August 20, 1864—5 p. m.*

Major-General SHERMAN:

Sixteen hundred and seventy-five men, recruits returning from furlough, convalescents, have been sent to the front within the last ten days. Surgeons are busy at the different hospitals here, at Louisville, Jeffersonville, and other places, weeding out those fit for duty. Every exertion is being made to forward all who arrive here. No new troops have reported.

R. M. SAWYER,
Assistant Adjutant-General.

HDQRS. MILITARY DIVISION OF THE MISSISSIPPI,
In the Field, near Atlanta, August 20, 1864—9.15 a. m.

General THOMAS:

I leave in a short time for General Howard's headquarters, and then over to General Schofield's right. I would like to have before starting or by the time I reach General Schofield's any news of General Stanley's operations or of General Garrard's if heard from.   Large fires were reported last night below Atlanta, but almost too near for General Kilpatrick.

W. T. SHERMAN,
Major-General, Commanding.

HEADQUARTERS ARMY OF THE CUMBERLAND,
August 20, 1864.

Major-General SHERMAN,
    At Schofield's:

General Stanley reports that the brigade started out on his left, drove back the enemy's skirmishers one mile, and found the right of his infantry line, took 8 prisoners from Strahl's brigade, who report that Ferguson's brigade of cavalry left their right at daylight yesterday morning, and that they have now only two new regiments of Georgia cavalry on their right.   From Garrard's report of last evening I think Ferguson's brigade must be after or watching his brigade in the vicinity of Decatur.   The signal officer at the Howard house reported at 7 a. m. to-day that he saw a larger force of the enemy in the works opposite General Stanley's left this morning than he had observed there yesterday or the day before.   I hope Stanley's demonstration may have the effect of causing the enemy to concentrate on the Decatur road and thereby relieve pressure on our right and draw off any troops that he may think of sending against Kilpatrick.

GEO. H. THOMAS,
Major-General, U. S. Volunteers.

HDQRS. MILITARY DIVISION OF THE MISSISSIPPI,
In the Field, near Atlanta, August 20, 1864—7 p. m.

General THOMAS:

I have been to General Schofield's.   General Jeff. Davis reached the West Point road and tore up a section to prevent infantry going out to bother General Kilpatrick on his return.   The signal officer at General Howard's reports three trains of cars that went out of Atlanta returned, backing into the station, so I infer they could not go ahead.   Nothing from General Kilpatrick.   An officer was up from Sandtown bridge saying he had 600 men there, and all was quiet.   I hope General Kilpatrick has reached the road and has made a good job.

W. T. SHERMAN,
Major-General, Commanding.

HEADQUARTERS DEPARTMENT OF THE CUMBERLAND,
August 20, 1864—7.30 p. m.

Major-General SHERMAN:

I forwarded Stanley's report of operations since 3 a. m. about 1 o'clock to-day.   He has kept the enemy fully occupied ever since yesterday noon; so has Garrard's brigade.   We have made three captures of rebel scouts, and from papers found on one of them I infer Hood is exceedingly anxious to know where our left flank is and its strength.

Geary's signal officer reports having observed the light of a large fire last night in the direction of Rough and Ready Station just before the storm came on.

GEO. H. THOMAS,
Major-General.

————

STANLEY'S HEADQUARTERS,
August 20, 1864.

General THOMAS:

I have been out on the left since 3 a. m., and have just returned. We drove the enemy's skirmishers back one mile and found the right of his infantry line. Took 8 prisoners from Strahl's brigade, and they report that Ferguson's brigade of cavalry left their right at daylight yesterday a. m., and only the two regiments of new Georgia cavalry are now on the right of their infantry. I was just writing a full report when your dispatch was received. Will start it off in a few minutes.

D. S. STANLEY,
Major-General.

————

HEADQUARTERS FOURTH ARMY CORPS,
Near Atlanta, Ga., August 20, 1864—10.30 a. m.

Brigadier-General WHIPPLE, *Chief of Staff:*

GENERAL: I have the honor to report that the reconnaissance I proposed making last evening was accomplished this morning by Brigadier-General Grose, with six regiments of his brigade, Colonel Opdycke's brigade supporting his left flank. The course of march was nearly due south from the burnt house on the railroad. The rebel skirmishers were driven back about a mile, when they made a stand in the works at the angle occupied by the Seventeenth Corps some weeks ago. As the brigade was advanced a good distance beyond support it was not deemed prudent to advance farther. Our losses were: Major Carter, Ninth Indiana, badly contused by a spent ball; 1 man mortally and 2 severely wounded. We captured 8 men of the Forty-first Tennessee Infantry, Strahl's brigade, Cheatham's division. From these we learned that we struck the extreme right of the brigade and the right of the rebel army, excepting the two new regiments of Georgia cavalry, who scampered off as soon as our skirmishers met them. The prisoners state that Ferguson's brigade of cavalry left their (Strahl's) right at daylight yesterday morning. The prisoners confirm the report of the putting up of the big guns on the new fort southeast of the city. They say the fort is for sixteen guns. They gave the information which our observation leads to, that the rebels have a line of works covering the south of the city. I do not think an attack upon the enemy's right could be made decisive with less than a corps, and then not certainly, as an attacking force would meet several successive works. Strahl's brigade, however, could be sent flying with a good division. The rebels have re-enforced their lines in front of us with additional militia. I do not know the country, but I believe Miller's brigade of cavalry could go around and smash up the Georgia cavalry. They won't fight much. My men charged the enemy behind works and behaved well. The Ninth Indiana took the prisoners.

Your obedient servant,

D. S. STANLEY,
Major-General.

HEADQUARTERS FOURTH ARMY CORPS,
August 20, 1864.
Brig. Gen. W. D. WHIPPLE,
　　　Chief of Staff:

GENERAL: The inclosed papers,* taken from a rebel scout killed near Decatur by Colonel Miller's command this morning, show Hood is anxious to know the exact location of our left. Whether for curiosity, or because he thinks of an enterprise, it is hard to tell.

　　Your obedient servant,
D. S. STANLEY,
Major-General.

HEADQUARTERS FOURTH ARMY CORPS,
Near Atlanta, Ga., August 20, 1864—10.30 a. m.
Brigadier-General GARRARD,
　　Commanding Second Cavalry Division:

The general commanding desires me to inform you that he made a demonstration upon the enemy's right at daylight this morning. He struck the rebel cavalry and the right of the rebel infantry line and took 8 infantrymen prisoners. They belonged to Strahl's brigade. From them it was learned that Ferguson's cavalry brigade left the right of the rebel line at daylight yesterday morning to move after Kilpatrick, and that the only cavalry now left there are the new Georgia troops. This cavalry run at almost the first shot that we fired this morning. It would be probably an easy matter for Miller's brigade to strike and disperse this force.

　　Very respectfully, your obedient servant,
J. S. FULLERTON,
Assistant Adjutant-General.

HEADQUARTERS SECOND CAVALRY DIVISION,
August 20, 1864. (Received 1 p. m.)
Major-General STANLEY:

GENERAL: My brigade has just returned from Decatur. They drove in the pickets, &c., yesterday and also this morning, and were skirmishing at the same time with your troops. They could not draw the enemy far from their works. A few men of the enemy were killed and a few captured. On one were found the inclosed papers,* which may interest you.

　　Very respectfully,

K. GARRARD,
Brigadier-General.

HEADQUARTERS FOURTEENTH ARMY CORPS,
Near East Point, August 20, 1864.
[General W. D. WHIPPLE:]

GENERAL: Four brigades of my command were withdrawn from my line to-day and sent to the right to act with the Twenty-third Corps. Two of these brigades, under Morgan, were sent down in the direction of Red Oak, striking the West Point railroad about half a mile

---

* Not found.

north of Red Oak, destroying about 200 yards of it, and returned. General Morgan captured about 20 prisoners. More of the railroad would have been destroyed, but the command was ordered in by General Schofield. Morgan marched about twenty miles to-day.

Respectfully, your obedient servant,

R. W. JOHNSON,
Brigadier-General.

HDQRS. FIRST BRIG., SECOND DIV., 14TH ARMY CORPS,
In the Field, August 20, 1864.

Capt. T. W. MORRISON,
Asst. Adjt. Gen., Second Div., Fourteenth Army Corps:

CAPTAIN: I have the honor to report that in compliance with orders from division headquarters, my command moved early this morning to the right and in rear of trenches lately occupied by Second Division, Twenty-third Army Corps. About 8.30 a. m. I received orders to make a reconnaissance with my own and the Third Brigade toward Red Oak Station, on Atlanta and West Point Railroad. When within two miles and a half of the station, on the Newnan road, the First Brigade was left to cover certain roads leading in the direction of East Point, while the Third Brigade moved toward Red Oak, striking the Atlanta and West Point Railroad half a mile east of that station, cutting the telegraph wire and tearing up portion of the railroad track. From here the troops moved by the most direct route back to camp. The heavy rains made the creeks almost impassable, and some delay occurred in crossing Camp Creek on my return. The troops met with no resistance until reaching the railroad, where I found a small force of the enemy's cavalry. Distance marched during the day, fully twenty miles. Prisoners captured by both brigades, some 12 or 14. Full reports have not been received. Casualties, none.

Very respectfully, your obedient servant,

JAMES D. MORGAN,
Brigadier-General.

NEW YORK, *August 20, 1864.*

Maj. Gen. W. T. SHERMAN:

Are the assignments made for the Fourth, Fourteenth, and Twentieth Corps? Do I get either?

DANL. BUTTERFIELD,
Major-General.

HEADQUARTERS SECOND CAVALRY DIVISION,
August 20, 1864.

Brig. Gen. W. D. WHIPPLE,
Chief of Staff, Department of the Cumberland:

GENERAL: I have the honor to report the return of the brigade sent to Decatur. Little information was gained. The pickets, &c., were driven in yesterday and this morning, but the rebels could not be persuaded to follow us back and fight. The roads were patrolled beyond Decatur several miles. The impression is that Wheeler has left considerable of his force in and about Lawrenceville, and that the railroad at Covington is about being repaired. An Irishman just from there says the timbers for the bridge over the Ulcofauhachee are on the ground and the bridge about being rebuilt. The brigade camped near Decatur last night and returned this afternoon.

Very respectfully, your obedient servant,

K. GARRARD,
Brigadier-General, Commanding Division.

HDQRS. DETACHMENT THIRD CAVALRY DIVISION,
Sandtown, Ga., August 20, 1864.

Brigadier-General ELLIOTT,
Chief of Cavalry, Department of the Cumberland:

GENERAL: I have the honor to report that Lieutenant-Colonel Klein, commanding First Brigade, Third Cavalry Division, has just returned to this place with his command. Lieutenant-Colonel Klein was detached from Brigadier-General Kilpatrick's command on the night of the 18th instant with about 300 men, and proceeding toward the Atlanta and Macon Railroad he struck that road at Fayette at noon of the 19th instant. At this place he destroyed one-quarter of a mile of track and captured a train of 8 cars, which he destroyed, together with the locomotive. Another train arriving from the north with an infantry force, and being also attacked by cavalry, he was compelled to leave the railroad. Being unable to rejoin General Kilpatrick, in the direction of Atlanta, he returned to this place with the loss of 2 men.

I have the honor to be, general, very respectfully, your obedient servant,

M. T. PATRICK,
Lieut. Col. Fifth Iowa Cav., Comdg. Detachment Third Cav. Div.

HEADQUARTERS DISTRICT OF NORTHERN ALABAMA,
Decatur, August 20, 1864.

Major-General ROUSSEAU, *Nashville:*

The cavalry is all in at this point. Colonel Prosser returned to-day from his expedition to Moulton. He was attacked last night by the enemy under Patterson, 500 or 600 strong. He killed 15 of them; number of wounded unknown. Our loss is 1 man slightly wounded; we had several horses killed and wounded. Colonel Prosser brought in a number of prisoners. Please let me know where Wheeler's force was when last heard from.

R. S. GRANGER,
Brigadier-General.

SCHOFIELD'S HEADQUARTERS,
August 20, 1864.

General SHERMAN:

I have started Cox and Davis to continue operations on the extreme right, and will probably remain in camp until you arrive unless something serious occurs on the field. I am trying to get my cavalry in shape, which I find difficult enough. I will have six regiments dismounted. Is there any chance of getting horses at Nashville?

J. M. SCHOFIELD,
Major-General.

SHERMAN'S HEADQUARTERS,
August 20, 1864.

General SCHOFIELD:

I will be over to-day, but must spend some time with General Howard to arrange as to certain troops still in Mississippi. If you go to the extreme right of your lines I will join you there.

W. T. SHERMAN,
Major-General.

———

HDQRS. THIRD DIVISION, TWENTY-THIRD ARMY CORPS,
Camp Creek Church, August 20, 1864—1.30 p. m.

Major-General SCHOFIELD,
Commanding, &c.:

The command reached here a little after noon with very slight opposition, the rebel vedettes falling back with but few shots. Colonel Stiles' brigade is on the left, General Cooper's on the right, Colonel Bond's in reserve. The right crosses the road at Diggs', the left is refused with an interval between the brigades of about one-quarter of a mile, the whole covered by a connected line of skirmishers, which is continuous all the way to my camp. A regiment is at Widow Lee's, and covering the road to Bacon's Post-Office. It is raining hard and steadily. If it clears in time I purpose sending a regiment to push as far up toward East Point as possible. At present the woods are so wet as to make it very difficult to do so with any effect.

Very respectfully, &c.,

J. D. COX,
Brigadier-General, Commanding.

———

HDQRS. SECOND DIVISION, FOURTEENTH ARMY CORPS,
August 20, 1864—3.30 p. m.

Major-General SCHOFIELD,
Commanding:

GENERAL: A part of my troops have reached Red Oak and are tearing up the track at this time. I have ordered Morgan to return. They met but little resistance. All the rebel cavalry have gone to the rear in pursuit of Kilpatrick.

Very respectfully,

JEF. C. DAVIS,
Brigadier-General, Commanding Division.

———

HOWARD'S HEADQUARTERS,
August 20, 1864.

Major-General SHERMAN:

Following from signal officer:

3.35 P. M.

Three trains of cars have just arrived; first, eight cars; second, six cars; third, train same that left at 3.45 p. m. yesterday. They carried a few men on them, and all backed in.

O. O. HOWARD,
Major-General.

HEADQUARTERS SECOND DIVISION, FIFTEENTH CORPS,
Near Atlanta, Ga., August 20, 1864.
Lieut. Col. R. R. TOWNES,
 Assistant Adjutant-General:

I have the honor to report that the lines of this division have been very quiet for the past twenty-four hours, that excepting the firing about 10 p. m. last night and the wounding of General Lightburn, nothing has occurred in the division requiring notice.

I am, respectfully, your obedient servant,
       W. B. HAZEN,
        Brigadier-General.

———

HOWARD'S HEADQUARTERS,
August 20, 1864.
General SCHOFIELD:

Twenty-five rebel cavalry were seen by my scouts near Judge Wilson's, prowling in your rear. If not closely watched they will pick up many of our men.

       O. O. HOWARD,
        Major-General.

———

HOWARD'S HEADQUARTERS,
August 20, 1864—5 p. m.
General SCHOFIELD:

The following just received from signal officer:

A train of fifteen freight cars just left Atlanta, loaded with troops inside and outside; tops of cars were crowded.

       O. O. HOWARD,
        Major-General.

———

CARTERSVILLE, *August 20, 1864.*
Major-General SHERMAN:

Having ascertained that there is a force of about 1,200 rebels five miles southwest of Stilesborough I placed 1,000 infantry and 400 cavalry under General McCook's orders. He moved out at 3 this a. m.

       JNO. E. SMITH,
        Brigadier-General.

———

HDQRS. MILITARY DIVISION OF THE MISSISSIPPI,
In the Field, near Atlanta, August 20, 1864—9.15 p. m.
General JOHN E. SMITH,
 Cartersville:

The force you describe as about Stilesborough is Clanton's, from the neighborhood of Talladega. General Vandever's cavalry is after it. Head it off and if possible capture it. It is a very indifferent force, that General Rousseau drove with great ease. It was doubtless ordered to co-operate with Wheeler and is behind time.

       W. T. SHERMAN,
        Major-General, Commanding.

CARTERSVILLE, *August 20, 1864.*

Major-General SHERMAN:

General McCook has returned with the infantry, not finding the enemy. The cavalry has been sent to Dallas. No force at Fairmount or Jasper; only small parties of ten to twenty scattered about in the mountains.

JNO. E. SMITH,
Brigadier-General.

CARTERSVILLE, *August 20, 1864—11.40 p. m.*

Major-General SHERMAN:

General McCook returned with the infantry at 12 m. to-day. Colonel Heath returned at 10 p. m., having captured 2 prisoners. No force of the enemy found. Reported the return of General McCook at 1 p. m. to-day.

JNO. E. SMITH,
Brigadier-General.

HDQRS. MILITARY DIVISION OF THE MISSISSIPPI,
In the Field, near Atlanta, August 20, 1864—8.15 p. m.

COMMANDING OFFICERS,
Marietta, Allatoona, Kingston, Cartersville, and Resaca:

Try to ambush the scamps that cut our telegraph wire. Signal stations will be kept up at Vining's, Kenesaw, and Allatoona; and operators should send by signal notice of the time and place of break in the wires, that steps may be taken which will lead to the capture of the men who are employed for the purpose.

W. T. SHERMAN,
Major-General, Commanding.

HDQRS. MILITARY DIVISION OF THE MISSISSIPPI,
In the Field, near Atlanta, August 20, 1864—9.15 p. m.

General VANDEVER,
Rome:

General John E. Smith reports from Cartersville a force of 1,200 below Stilesborough, and has sent out 1,400 men to head it off. Between you at Rome and General John E. Smith at Cartersville that force should be caught. Send out every man you can spare, and do all that is possible.

W. T. SHERMAN,
Major-General, Commanding.

ROME, *August 20, 1864.*

Major-General SHERMAN:

Clanton has crossed the Coosa at Gadsden with 1,200 men and gone north. My cavalry is following him.

WM. VANDEVER,
Brigadier-General.

Hdqrs. Military Division of the Mississippi,
In the Field, near Atlanta, August 20, 1864—10 p. m.

General Steedman,
    Chattanooga:

General Vandever reports Clanton has passed the Coosa on his way north. He will come up doubtless by way of La Fayette in concert with Wheeler. Be on your guard and prevent a junction if possible. Call for cavalry and infantry from above.

W. T. SHERMAN,
Major-General, Commanding.

Rome, *August 20, 1864.*

Major-General Steedman:

The rebel General Clanton crossed the Coosa at Gadsden on Tuesday last with 1,200 cavalry, and proceeded north to strike the railroad, either between Bridgeport and Chattanooga or between Stevenson and Huntsville. My cavalry is after him. I had a courier killed last night bringing this intelligence.

WM. VANDEVER,
Brigadier-General.

Chattanooga, *August 20, 1864.*

Maj. Gen. L. H. Rousseau,
    Nashville:

General Vandever telegraphs from Rome that General Clanton crossed the Coosa at Gadsden Tuesday with 1,200 men (cavalry), and proceeded north to strike the railroad between this point and Huntsville. Reports from Charleston, Tenn., say that a portion of Wheeler's raiders have gone to Cotton Port, on Tennessee River, but from most reliable information I get I think most of his forces have taken the direction of Knoxville.

JAMES B. STEEDMAN,
Major-General, U. S. Volunteers.

Chattanooga, *August 20, 1864.*

Capt. L. M. Dayton,
    Aide-de-Camp:

A party of Wheeler's raiders were seven miles southeast of Charleston last night. They are moving east toward Maryville, Tenn.

J. B. STEEDMAN,
Major-General.

Dalton, *August 20, 1864.*
(Received 22d.)

General William D. Whipple,
    Assistant Adjutant-General:

We have been scouting in this district under orders of General Steedman. If we are to proceed to Atlanta without delay please telegraph him.

WM. J. PALMER,
Colonel, Commanding Fifteenth Pennsylvania Cavalry.

DALTON, *August 20, 1864.*

Major-General STEEDMAN:

We arrived here this evening, having thoroughly scouted the country from Graysville, through Parker's Gap eastward on the old Alabama road, to within twelve miles of Cleveland, thence across to Red Clay and to Varnell's Station, thence via Tunnel Hill to Dalton. There are no rebels, even in small parties, within that range, and none to be heard of nearer than East Tennessee. The rebel cavalry that cut the road at Graysville was a Kentucky brigade, under General Williams, numbering about 900 men, which came through Parker's Gap and McDaniel's Gap, and went back the same way. The last of these left the old Alabama road at Blackburn's, eight miles from Parker's Gap, near which they fed on Wednesday at 3 p. m., and took the road to Red Clay, but turned off toward Cleveland. Some of the soldiers told the people they were going to Kentucky. The rebels fed their horses on green corn, with what hay and sheaf oats they could pick up. They also said they were to meet General Vaughn at Charleston, on the Hiwassee River.

WM. J. PALMER,
Colonel, Commanding.

CHATTANOOGA, TENN., *August 20, 1864—9 p. m.*
(Received 11.10 p. m.)

Maj. THOMAS T. ECKERT:

No movement of the army to-day. No news of cavalry expedition south of Atlanta, but the fact that railroad trains that took out troops to meet it backed up to Atlanta again indicates success. Large fires seen last night south of Atlanta. Wheeler not heard from since last advice. Railroad and telegraph from here to Knoxville still broken, and scouts bring rumors that Wheeler will attack Loudon before crossing mountains.

J. C. VAN DUZER.

SPECIAL FIELD ORDERS,)   HDQRS. ARMY OF THE OHIO,
No. 88.   }   *Near Atlanta, Ga., August 20, 1864.*

I. To-day General Cox will continue his demonstration upon the enemy's left, using his own division and two brigades of General Hascall's. He will occupy the Newnan road to Diggs' during the day. General Johnson will send two brigades to reconnoiter and threaten the railroad about Red Oak. Colonel Garrard's cavalry will operate in conjunction with this force.

*   *   *   *   *   *   *

III. The major-general commanding is pained to find it necessary again to call the attention of the officers and men of this command to the disgraceful practice of marauding and plundering which, in spite of past orders, is still prevalent in the command. All officers and soldiers are strictly forbidden to pass beyond the skirmish line, except by order of a division commander. When foraging parties are sent out they must be sufficiently strong to protect themselves and always in charge of a trustworthy commissioned officer who will be held to a rigid responsibility for the good conduct of the party. Any soldier found entering the house of a citizen without permission, or taking the property of citizens, or committing any outrage whatever, will be punished with the severest penalty of the law. The attention of all commanding officers of cavalry, as well as infantry, is called to this order. It must be enforced and obeyed.

By command of Major-General Schofield:

> J. A. CAMPBELL,
> *Major and Assistant Adjutant-General.*

GENERAL ORDERS,)   HDQRS. SEVENTEENTH ARMY CORPS,
    No. 11.   }   *Before Atlanta, Ga., August 20, 1864.*

The following officers are announced as members of the staff and staff corps on duty at these headquarters. They will be respected and obeyed accordingly: Capt. A. Hickenlooper, Fifth Ohio Battery, acting assistant inspector-general; First Lieut. William Henley, Twenty-ninth Missouri Infantry Volunteers, acting aide-de-camp.

By command of Maj. Gen. F. P. Blair:

> [ROWLAND COX,]
> *Assistant Adjutant-General.*

HDQRS. MILITARY DIVISION OF THE MISSISSIPPI,
In the Field, near Atlanta, Ga., August 21, 1864—10 a. m.

(Received 8 p. m.)

Maj. Gen. H. W. HALLECK,
     Washington, D. C.:

General Howard and I have talked over the affairs of the Department of the Tennessee, and admit the wisdom of General Canby exercising command of all the troops on the Mississippi. To preserve organizations already existing without materially diminishing the military force on the Mississippi, we ask that certain fragments of regiments and brigades, not exceeding in the aggregate 2,500 men, be allowed to come to their organization here. Also, if possible, that a division of the Seventeenth Corps, originally designated as part of General McPherson's column, but detained up Red River, be also allowed to come by any route deemed advisable by General Washburn. To accomplish these results General Howard sends to-day a staff officer to Louisville to confer with you by telegraph, and then to go to Memphis and accomplish whatever you may conclude. Be assured that General Howard and I both cheerfully concede anything that will produce good results. I think it would be well not to change the limits of departments, but to have all troops now belonging to the Department of the Tennessee still make returns to General Howard, but be subject to the military orders of General Canby, to whom they could make reports of effective force that would satisfy his purposes. All well. Expect to hear of General Kilpatrick every hour. Nothing further of Wheeler.

> W. T. SHERMAN,
> *Major-General, Commanding.*

SHERMAN'S HEADQUARTERS,
August 21, 1864.

General THOMAS:

General Steedman reports some of Wheeler's men last night near Charleston, but says they have moved toward Maryville. I think you had better hurry forward all the cavalry you can from Nashville and group it under McCook about Dalton until Wheeler either goes into Kentucky or comes back to Georgia. Our roads are more threatened from the direction of East Tennessee than from here.

W. T. SHERMAN,
Major-General.

HEADQUARTERS DEPARTMENT OF THE CUMBERLAND,
August 21, 1864.

Major-General SHERMAN:

Did you receive Colonel Klein's report* forwarded this morning? He broke the road near Fayette and destroyed a train of cars with locomotive, but being attacked by cavalry, supported by infantry, and cut off, as he says, from Kilpatrick, returned to Sandtown with but very little loss. If he broke the road between Atlanta and Kilpatrick, and then succeeded in effecting his escape, there can be but little doubt of Kilpatrick's success, if he worked away from Atlanta, as there is but little probability of his meeting serious opposition from the direction of Macon. Orders about concentrating all cavalry coming to the front at Dalton have been given.

GEO. H. THOMAS,
Major-General.

HDQRS. MILITARY DIVISION OF THE MISSISSIPPI,
In the Field, near Atlanta, August 21, 1864—12 m.

General THOMAS:

I received Colonel Klein's report. I feel certain that General Kilpatrick is doing good work; still it is time for us to hear from him direct.

W. T. SHERMAN,
Major-General, Commanding.

STANLEY'S HEADQUARTERS,
August 21, 1864—2.45 p. m.

General WHIPPLE:

Five deserters from Maney's and Vaughan's brigades, Cheatham's division, just in. Yesterday at noon these two brigades moved to the right of the railroad, re-enforcing Strahl, on rebel right. They heard the railroad was cut night before last. A colonel said the cutting the road would not interfere with supplies for the army.

D. S. STANLEY,
Major-General.

HDQRS. CHIEF OF CAVALRY, DEPT. OF THE CUMBERLAND,
Near Atlanta, Ga., August 21, 1864.

Brig. Gen. K. GARRARD, *Comdg. Second Division Cavalry:*

After crossing at Sandtown you will extend from General Stanley's left to the Chattahoochee, and on the south side of Utoy Creek. General Stanley it is expected will be in position to-day.

I am, general, very respectfully, your obedient servant,

W. L. ELLIOTT,
Brigadier-General and Chief of Cavalry.

---

* See Part II, p. 868.

HEADQUARTERS ARMY OF THE OHIO,
Near Atlanta, Ga., August 21, 1864.

Major-General SHERMAN:

Prisoners captured by General Cox last evening report that Kilpatrick struck the railroad at Jonesborough the morning after he started. Very distant artillery firing was heard in the direction of Macon from our extreme right last evening. I have learned nothing further indicative of Kilpatrick's movements. Cox is making a demonstration on the right to aid him in his return. The enemy is using his artillery quite freely in front of the Fourteenth Corps this morning.

J. M. SCHOFIELD,
Major-General.

SHERMAN'S HEADQUARTERS,
August 21, 1864.

General SCHOFIELD:

How far out did Cox go to-day? Did he observe anything different from usual. Have you heard anything from Kilpatrick?

W. T. SHERMAN,
Major-General.

SCHOFIELD'S HEADQUARTERS,
August 21, 1864.

General SHERMAN:

I have no report yet from Cox, and have heard nothing of Kilpatrick. I doubt if he can get across Camp Creek since the rain.

J. M. SCHOFIELD,
Major-General.

HDQRS. THIRD DIVISION, TWENTY-THIRD ARMY CORPS,
Camp, August 21, 1864.

Major-General SCHOFIELD,
Commanding Army of the Ohio:

SIR: In addition to the dispatch sent you yesterday I have the honor to report that during the movement on my right General Reilly pushed forward his brigade to the advanced point occupied by him the day before, and Colonel Casement connected by swinging forward his line of skirmishers. The enemy made a dash with some force, about 2 p. m., to get in between Reilly and Stiles, but were unsuccessful, and retired after a brisk skirmish. The line of vedettes became broken necessarily by the movement, and I have reason to believe that my aide, Mr. Coughlan, was captured. He had been to General Reilly with orders and started to return to me, passing in rear of the skirmish line, and has not since been heard of. The probability is that, not being aware that any portion of the chain of vedettes had left their position, he passed through the gap about the time of the demonstration by the enemy at that point and was surrounded before he was aware of it. If there is any proper means of doing so I should like very much to make inquiry of the enemy whether he was wounded. The gap in the skirmish line was closed as soon as Colonel Stiles became aware of it, and it could not have existed long. Citizens on the Newnan road report that the rebels do not expect to keep open the West Point road, and, making a merit of necessity, profess to have made arrangements to abandon it. They report General Kilpatrick's cavalry in the vicinity of Jonesborough night before last. Very distant cannonade was heard yesterday afternoon in a southerly direction. Your orders as to the demonstration to-day will be carried out by Reilly's brigade and part of Stiles'. The order in regard to foraging is substantially the same as one I had issued for my own command. I regret General Morgan did not arrest the plunderers he saw, as I should like to know whether they belonged to this division and to what regiments.

Very respectfully, &c.,
                              J. D. COX,
                    Brigadier-General, Commanding.

                    HEADQUARTERS ARMY OF THE OHIO,
                    In the Field, August 21, 1864—5 a. m.

Brig. Gen. J. D. COX,
        Commanding, &c.:

GENERAL: The commanding general directs me to say that he desires you to continue to make a show of a demonstration to-day until we hear from General Kilpatrick. He does not wish you to use much force nor to go very far, merely enough to compel the enemy to occupy his works in force.

I have the honor to be, very respectfully, your obedient servant,
                              WM. M. WHERRY,
                        Major and Aide-de-Camp.

                              HOWARD'S HEADQUARTERS,
                                   August 21, 1864.

Major-General SHERMAN:

A train of eleven freight-cars, one baggage, and one passenger-car, all empty except the passenger-car, which had a few persons in it, has just left Atlanta.

                              O. O. HOWARD,
                                   Major-General.

        HDQRS. SIGNAL DETACH., FIFTEENTH ARMY CORPS,
                    Before Atlanta, Ga., August 21, 1864.

Maj. Gen. JOHN A. LOGAN,
        Commanding Fifteenth Army Corps:

SIR: I have the honor to state that there has been very little of interest transpired to-day. The rebel lines appear to be unchanged. At 5 p. m. a train of cars, four freight and one passenger, with a few passengers, arrived in Atlanta—freight-cars empty. At 6 p. m. a train of freight-cars, empty, left Atlanta. I shall comply hereafter with your order.

I am, sir, very respectfully, your obedient servant,
                              SAMUEL EDGE,
                First Lieutenant and Chief Acting Signal Officer.

CARTERSVILLE, *August 21, 1864.*

Maj. Gen. W. T. SHERMAN:

The force that has been threatening the road south of the Etowah was part of Clanton's. We captured 2 of their scouts. I had cavalry as far as Dallas yesterday. Clanton's men have gone back toward Alabama.

E. M. McCOOK,
Brigadier-General.

CHATTANOOGA, *August 21, 1864.*

Capt. L. M. DAYTON, *Aide-de-Camp:*

I have ordered the Fifteenth Pennsylvania Cavalry to remain at Dalton a few days, scouting the country in that vicinity.

J. B. STEEDMAN,
Major-General.

HDQRS. MILITARY DIVISION OF THE MISSISSIPPI,
In the Field, near Atlanta, August 21, 1864—3 p. m.

General STEEDMAN, *Chattanooga:*

You may detain the Fifteenth Pennsylvania Cavalry at Dalton till I make further inquiry. Look out for Clanton from the south. I think you may gobble him up, as he doubtless calculates to meet Wheeler at Dalton or Graysville. Get down all the cavalry you can from above.

W. T. SHERMAN,
Major-General, Commanding.

HDQRS. MILITARY DIVISION OF THE MISSISSIPPI,
In the Field, near Atlanta, August 21, 1864—3 p. m.

General STEEDMAN, *Chattanooga:*

I have instructed General Thomas to assemble as much cavalry as he can about Dalton, from which it seems to me the road can be better watched than from any other point. Should Wheeler get the road about Athens could we communicate with Knoxville by the river and Kingston?

W. T. SHERMAN,
Major-General, Commanding.

CHATTANOOGA, *August 21, 1864.*

Major-General SHERMAN:

I sent scouting party this morning from Dalton to Alpine, by way of Villanow, and another to La Fayette, through Ship's Gap. We can communicate with Kingston or Loudon by river. The enemy are destroying the track of the Knoxville road. The Loudon bridge is safe.

J. B. STEEDMAN,
Major-General.

CHATTANOOGA, *August 21, 1864.*

Capt. L. M. DAYTON, *Aide-de-Camp:*

I have ordered a detachment of the Fifteenth Pennsylvania Cavalry to scout in the direction of La Fayette and Alpine. Telegraph work-

ing east only to Cleveland. Have ordered Brown's home guards to
scout about Ellijay and in the direction taken by Wheeler. The Ninth
Pennsylvania Cavalry is expected here to-day. Will detain a few days
until I can learn something definite of Wheeler's whereabouts.

J. B. STEEDMAN,
Major-General.

HDQRS. MILITARY DIVISION OF THE MISSISSIPPI,
In the Field, near Atlanta, Ga., August 21, 1864—8 p. m.

General STEEDMAN, *Chattanooga:*

I have your dispatch of to-day, and if a gun-boat can get up to
Kingston it would be well to send it. Wheeler cannot do us serious
harm up there, and cavalry has not the industry to damage railroads
seriously. General Schofield thinks Knoxville has provisions for three
months, and is very strongly fortified, so you need not bother Wheeler
there further than to keep him watched by scouts and citizens, and let
me know his future course. I don't want him to come back by way of
the Oostenaula. Now is the time to get all your forces in good position to move rapidly against his flank if he comes back anywhere between Spring Place and Talking Rock. Dalton is the best point from
which to watch him, and I think it would be well to make a bridge
across the Connesauga, near the mouth of Cooyehuttee, on the road
from Dalton to Spring Place, and build a small, but strong, redoubt
between the forks at the bridge, as a threat to that flank. I don't
know the ground at Dalton or Spring Place, but by the maps I know
if you have a respectable force at Dalton, and the Spring Place road
fortified as I describe, Wheeler will not dare pass down this way. If
he go into Kentucky by Cumberland Gap or Somerset there are forces
enough to attend to him there. I feel confident General Grant will
give Lee enough to do, so he cannot detach any considerable force
toward Knoxville.

W. T. SHERMAN,
Major-General, Commanding.

ROME, *August 21, 1864.*

Maj. Gen. W. T. SHERMAN:

My scouts, just returned from Randolph County, Ala., report the
rebels abandoning the railroad between Atlanta and Montgomery, and
moving everything around to the Charleston road. Rebels report that
our forces occupy Mobile. A small party passed near Stilesborough
last evening, and heard of no rebels. There is a force at Cedartown
and Cave Spring.

WM. VANDEVER,
Brigadier-General, Commanding.

ROME, *August 21, 1864.*

Major-General SHERMAN:

Dispatch received at 11 a. m. Will turn out all the force that can
possibly be spared. Two of my regiments are already with General
Smith, and the cavalry after Clanton.

WM. VANDEVER,
Brigadier-General.

Hdqrs. Military Division of the Mississippi,
In the Field, near Atlanta, August 21, 1864—6 p. m.

General VANDEVER, *Rome:*

I had understood that all the troops taken by General John E. Smith to Resaca had returned to their several posts. General Steedman reports that Clanton's force has returned toward Alabama. Do the best you can.

W. T. SHERMAN,
Major-General, Commanding.

CHATTANOOGA, TENN., *August 21, 1864.*

SHOLES:

Say to General Sherman that operator arrived here from Charleston this evening and reports Wheeler's headquarters at Athens and his troops occupying the country from Charleston to near Loudon, and making quite thorough job of destruction of railroad and telegraph line. One mile of road and two of telegraph yet to be repaired this side of Charleston. Wheeler tells inhabitants he is to remain there, and that the State is to be reoccupied from east.

J. C. VAN DUZER.

CHATTANOOGA, TENN., *August 21, 1864.*
(Received 22d.)

Maj. T. T. ECKERT:

Position before Atlanta very little changed. Part of cavalry force returned, having struck Macon road at Fayette and been attacked by superior force. Main force under Kilpatrick not heard from, and fears begin to be felt that it has come to grief. Wheeler's headquarters at Athens, Tenn., and his troops hold country from near Loudon to Hiwassee, having made clean sweep of railroad and telegraph. No attempt is made to drive him out, he being as little bother there as anywhere. Scouts, deserters, and spies report the occupation of Mobile by General Granger.

J. C. VAN DUZER.

Hdqrs. Military Division of the Mississippi,
In the Field, near Atlanta, August 21, 1864—3 p. m.

Maj. Gen. DANIEL BUTTERFIELD, *New York City:*

General Stanley has the Fourth Corps, General Slocum the Twentieth, and General Jeff. C. Davis the Fourteenth, all on the nomination of General Thomas. We must have corps commanders present.

W. T. SHERMAN,
Major-General, Commanding.

SPECIAL FIELD ORDERS, }   Hdqrs. Army of the Ohio,
        No. 89.   }   *Near Atlanta, Ga., August 21, 1864.*

*   *   *   *   *   *   *

II. The Sixteenth Illinois Cavalry and Twelfth Kentucky Cavalry are hereby detached from the Third Division, Twenty-third Army Corps, and will report to Col. Israel Garrard, commanding cavalry division, to be assigned to the dismounted cavalry brigade.

*   *   *   *   *   *   *

VI. The following regiments, viz, the Fourteenth Illinois Cavalry, the Eighth Michigan Cavalry, the Fifth and Sixth Indiana Cavalry, having lost on the late raid under Major-General Stoneman a large portion of their arms and horses, and it being impossible to rearm and equip them as cavalry for several weeks, it is hereby ordered that they be temporarily armed and equipped as infantry. The commanding officers of the above-named regiments will without delay turn over to the proper ordnance officer such cavalry arms, accouterments, equipments, and ammunition as there may be left in their respective commands, and will draw from the same officer and arm their men with Springfield rifled muskets and accouterments. The turning over of the above-named ordnance and ordnance stores will be preceded by an inspection for the purpose of determining their actual condition. The necessary receipts and invoices will be given.

By command of Major-General Schofield:

> J. A. CAMPBELL,
> *Major and Assistant Adjutant-General.*

GENERAL ORDERS, }   HDQRS. FOURTEENTH ARMY CORPS,
No. 11.   }   *Near East Point, Ga., August 21, 1864.*

Having been appointed chief of cavalry for the Military Division of the Mississippi, I relinquish the command of the Fourteenth Corps to Bvt. Maj. Gen. J. C. Davis, a true and tried soldier. Let your past conduct be a guide for your future, and history will be bright with the record of your brilliant and honorable services. To every officer and enlisted man in this command my thanks are due for their zeal and devotion to duty manifested by them under all circumstances.

By command of Brig. Gen. R. W. Johnson:

> A. C. McCLURG,
> *Captain and Assistant Adjutant-General.*

NEAR ATLANTA, GA., *August 22, 1864—10 p. m.*
(Received 11 p. m. 23d.)

Maj. Gen. H. W. HALLECK,
Washington, D. C.:

General Kilpatrick is back. He had pretty hard fighting with a division of infantry and three brigades of cavalry. He broke the cavalry into disorder and captured a battery, which he destroyed, except one gun, which he brought in in addition to all his own. He also brought in 3 captured flags and 70 prisoners. He had possession of a large part of Ross' brigade, but could not encumber himself with them. He destroyed 3 miles of the road about Jonesborough, and broke pieces for about 10 miles more, enough to disable the road for ten days. I expect I will have to swing across to that road in force to make the matter certain. General Kilpatrick destroyed 2 locomotives and trains. It has been very quiet with us here. Wheeler is about Athens, Tenn., and General Steedman will move out against him from Chattanooga.

> W. T. SHERMAN,
> *Major-General.*

HEADQUARTERS DEPARTMENT OF THE CUMBERLAND,
August 22, 1864.
Maj. Gen. W. T. SHERMAN:
General Garrard reports Kilpatrick at Decatur on his return.
GEO. H. THOMAS,
Major-General, Commanding.

HDQRS. MILITARY DIVISION OF THE MISSISSIPPI,
In the Field, near Atlanta, Ga., August 22, 1864.
Maj. Gen. GEORGE H. THOMAS, U. S. Volunteers,
Commanding:
I wish to see General Kilpatrick soon as possible.
W. T. SHERMAN,
Major-General.

HDQRS. MILITARY DIVISION OF THE MISSISSIPPI,
In the Field, near Atlanta, Ga., August 22, 1864—6.30 p. m.
General THOMAS:
Telegraph me in general terms the result of General Kilpatrick's trip. General Schofield inquires for Captain Bartlett. If General Kilpatrick be tired, let him rest with you and let Captain Bartlett stop with me on his way home.
W. T. SHERMAN,
Major-General, Commanding.

HEADQUARTERS DEPARTMENT OF THE CUMBERLAND,
August 22, 1864—7.30 p. m.
Major-General SHERMAN:
General Kilpatrick is about to start for your headquarters. He reports having torn up four miles connectedly of railroad between Rough and Ready and Jonesborough, and ten miles at intervals, and destroyed two trains, including the one destroyed by Klein. He virtually captured Ross and brigade, but could not bring the men away. He was attacked by Jackson's cavalry and a division of infantry but effected his escape before the enemy could surround him, and brought off his own artillery and one piece of the 4 captured. Two pieces and 9 caissons were destroyed by him. He brought in about 70 prisoners and 3 battle-flags; all his own wounded. Has 97 killed and missing, among the missing 4 officers. Brigadier-General Long was wounded slightly in two places. He speaks in high terms of the behavior of his whole command. Captain Bartlett is well and on the road with him to your headquarters.
GEO. H. THOMAS,
Major-General.

HDQRS. SIGNAL PARTY, TWENTIETH ARMY CORPS,
August 22, 1864.
Brigadier-General WILLIAMS,
Commanding Twentieth Army Corps:
GENERAL: I have the honor to report the following observations made to-day: The enemy have had working parties engaged at different places along their line of works—on the traverses along works to right

of four-gun fort, on the side of six-gun fort struck by the shells from heavy gun on our left, and along works south to 15 degrees west of south, distance three miles. They have also put up a number of board shelters along the works on both sides four-gun fort and to right of six-gun fort. There are two battle-flags flying from the line of works to left of four-gun fort not seen there yesterday.

Very respectfully, your obedient servant,

W. W. HOPKINS,
Lieutenant and Acting Signal Officer.

SHERMAN'S HEADQUARTERS,
August 22, 1864.
(Received 8 a. m.)

General SCHOFIELD:

I will go over to General Thomas and on the railroad on our flank. Has anything occurred that I should know ?

W. T. SHERMAN,
Major-General.

(Similar to General Howard.)

SCHOFIELD'S HEADQUARTERS,
August 22, 1864.

General SHERMAN:

Nothing of importance has occurred on this flank. A negro who came in last night reports that Ross' brigade and battery were captured by Kilpatrick on the 20th; says he saw the captain of the battery yesterday and heard him make the statement.

J. M. SCHOFIELD,
Major-General.

SCHOFIELD'S HEADQUARTERS,
August 22, 1864.

Major-General SHERMAN:

Rebel deserters repeat the report that Ross' brigade of rebel cavalry was captured by Kilpatrick.

J. M. SCHOFIELD,
Major-General.

SHERMAN'S HEADQUARTERS,
August 22, 1864. (Received 6 p. m.)

General SCHOFIELD:

General Thomas reports from General Garrard that Kilpatrick is at Decatur.

L. M. DAYTON,
Aide-de-Camp.

(Same to General Howard.)

HEADQUARTERS SIGNAL DETACHMENT,
Before Atlanta, Ga., August 22, 1864.

Maj. Gen. JOHN A. LOGAN,
Commanding Fifteenth Army Corps:

SIR: I have the honor to transmit the observations of my officers and myself of to-day.

Observations of Lieut. C. H. Fish from the lookout station:

Everything very quiet along the lines; a train of five freight, two platform, three passenger, and one baggage cars arrived at Atlanta at 5.30 p. m. There were a few persons on it; probably fifty. I have observed for several days a body of men at work on what appeared to be a new line of works on east side of Marietta railroad. To-day I have been able to better determine the nature of the work. A line of works runs parallel to the railroad directly opposite of railroad buildings, terminating in a strong fort. In front of this line rifle-pits for skirmishers are already made.

CH. H. FISH,
Lieutenant.

Observations of Lieut. J. H. Weirick along the line:

I was at battery De Gress to-day making observations of rebel lines and movements. Their lines unchanged except on one point in front of Second Division, Fifteenth Army Corps, where no rebels could be seen for three or four days until this morning, when they appeared in considerable number and were busy all day building shelter, completing earth-works, &c.

J. H. WEIRICK,
Lieutenant.

Observations of myself from station in tree: The enemy are busy strengthening their works and building new ones in front of the Twentieth Corps. The new casemate battery and six-gun fort south of big gun and in front of the left of the Sixteenth Corps appear to be temporarily abandoned, casemates and embrasures being thickly covered with brush. At 4 p. m. three ladies, two girls, and a citizen, with a black servant girl, all of them well dressed, took quite a promenade on the large work in front of the main part of town. The enemy issued green corn again to their men in the rifle-pits this p. m. The box-cars reported by Lieutenant Fish appeared to be loaded.

Men seem to be very scarce in front of the Sixteenth Corps. The big gun stands in the same position.

I have the honor to be, sir, very respectfully, your obedient servant,

SAMUEL EDGE,
First Lieutenant and Chief Acting Signal Officer.

CARTERSVILLE, GA., *August 22, 1864.*

Brig. Gen. W. L. ELLIOTT,
Chief of Cavalry, Department of the Cumberland:

I received your telegram to-day concerning Colonel Palmer's force. If any mounted force should be placed at my command sufficiently large to be effective, I desire to ask you as to the disposition of them. If the object is simply to scout along the road the force is at present probably as well disposed for that purpose as it could be; if, on the contrary, you design to intercept Wheeler should he endeavor to return south by his old route, all the cavalry should be concentrated at Dalton, Resaca, or Spring Place. Dalton is probably the best point from which to defend the road. I deem it impossible, however, for any cavalry force you could concentrate at present to intercept Wheeler if he desires to avoid you, as he can back through Ellijay and Jasper or through Ducktown and Amicalola Falls or through Cooper's Gap to Dahlonega and cross the

Chattahoochee any place above there. It might be hard for his force to procure subsistence over these routes, but no more difficult than over the route he has already marched, where everything has already been consumed. Talking Rock is another important point, and scouting parties sent there and to Pine Log Post-Office continually will give notice of any attempt on the road south of the Coosawattee. I am satisfied that the recent attacks on the road south of the Etowah have been encouraged and assisted by citizens. If some terrible lesson is not taught them now our line of communications will suffer through the whole campaign. If they learn that when they destroy our railroad we will destroy their houses I think they will be willing to quit. The experiment is worth trying at any rate.

I am, general, very respectfully, your obedient servant,
E. M. McCOOK,
Brigadier-General, Commanding Division.

RESACA, GA., *August 22, 1864.*
Capt. L. M. DAYTON, *Aide-de-Camp:*

The enemy is reported in heavy force at Holly Creek Mill, ten miles east of Tilton. They arrived there after 4 this p. m. I suppose it is part of Wheeler's force returning. I am yet unable to estimate the number.

G. B. RAUM,
Colonel, Commanding Brigade.

RESACA, GA., *August 22, 1864.*
Maj. S. B. MOE,
Assistant Adjutant-General:

The enemy was in heavy force at 4 this p. m. at Holly Creek Mill, ten miles east of Tilton. It may be that Wheeler is returning and that a large part of his force is at Spring Place. I have notified Tilton, Dalton, and Tunnel Hill.

GREEN B. RAUM,
Colonel, Commanding Brigade.

HDQRS. MILITARY DIVISION OF THE MISSISSIPPI,
In the Field, near Atlanta, August 22, 1864—10.15 p. m.
General G. B. RAUM, *Resaca:*

General Steedman reported this forenoon that Wheeler was north of Hiwassee River and could not ford it. Please telegraph to General Steedman such information as you are able to get, and also keep us advised promptly as possible.

W. T. SHERMAN,
Major-General, Commanding.

RESACA, *August 22, 1864—11.20 p. m.*
Capt. L. M. DAYTON, *Aide-de-Camp:*

I have just received your dispatch, also one from Colonel Laiboldt, Dalton, stating that scouts coming in to-night report bodies of rebel cavalry moving down the Westfield pike toward Ellijay. It may be that the force reported at Holly Creek are there for the purpose of covering the return of Wheeler's whole force. General J. E. Smith sent a brigade of infantry to Dalton to-night. I have advised General Steedman, and the commanders at Tunnel Hill, Dalton, Calhoun, Adairsville, Kingston, and General Smith at Cartersville.

> G. B. RAUM,
> *Colonel, Commanding Brigade.*

CHATTANOOGA, *August 22, 1864.*
(Received 5.40 p. m.)

Brig. Gen. JOHN E. SMITH:

Send me five regiments to Chattanooga instead of Dalton as soon as you can procure transportation. Exercise your own judgment where to take them from.

> JAMES B. STEEDMAN,
> *Major-General.*

CARTERSVILLE, *August 22, 1864.*

Major-General STEEDMAN:

I have two of Vandever's regiments here, which, with the Fifth and Tenth Iowa Infantry at Kingston, I have in readiness to send to Dalton as soon as transportation arrives. Do you wish me to uncover Etowah and Allatoona by sending up a brigade in addition? General Sherman instructs me not to uncover these points.

> JNO. E. SMITH,
> *Brigadier-General.*

CHATTANOOGA, *August 22, 1864.*

Major-General SHERMAN:

Wheeler is now between the Hiwassee and Little Tennessee Rivers, both too high to ford. I think I can force him back through the mountains toward North Carolina by concentrating force at Charleston, and moving on him from that place. I have force enough and can concentrate them in time. I await your orders; concentrating at Dalton as you directed.

Respectfully,

> JAMES B. STEEDMAN,
> *Major-General.*

HDQRS. MILITARY DIVISION OF THE MISSISSIPPI,
In the Field, near Atlanta, August 22, 1864—12 m.

General STEEDMAN:

I have your dispatch to-day relative to attacking Wheeler. I am at General Thomas' now, and he will see and approve this dispatch. If you have force sufficient send word to Loudon and Knoxville, by the west bank and most rapid way, stating the time and manner of your movement; then concentrate your command at Charleston; send a detachment rapidly up to Columbus to intrench there and picket the river fords. With the balance of your command move rapidly toward Tellico, and there turn on Wheeler, trying to break up his command into fragments, and capture his wagons, artillery, plunder, and all you can. If another plan suggests itself to you I don't hold you to mine, but give it, as I have been up to that country. General Kilpatrick is out, and we have no news of him except a negro reports that on the 20th he captured Ross' brigade and battery. Keep me advised, and also General John E. Smith at Cartersville, in your absence from the district.

W. T. SHERMAN,
Major-General, Commanding.

HDQRS. MILITARY DIVISION OF THE MISSISSIPPI,
In the Field, near Atlanta, August 22, 1864—10.30 p. m.
General STEEDMAN, *Chattanooga:*

General Kilpatrick is back all right; had pretty hard fighting with cavalry and infantry, but brought in 3 captured flags and 1 extra gun. Captured a whole battery, which he broke up. He destroyed enough road to last ten days, by which time I will reach it again.

W. T. SHERMAN,
Major-General, Commanding.

ROME, GA., *August 22, 1864.*
Major-General STEEDMAN:

Clanton was at Guntersville yesterday morning, waiting for Wheeler, who was expected to make a circuit across the railroad north of Chattanooga.

WM. VANDEVER,
Brigadier-General.

ROME, *August 22, 1864.*
Major-General STEEDMAN:

No further news from Clanton. First Alabama Cavalry following them.

WM. VANDEVER,
Brigadier-General.

HEADQUARTERS DISTRICT OF THE ETOWAH,
Chattanooga, Tenn., August 22, 1864.
Major BARNES, *Cleveland, Tenn.:*

You will move with your entire effective force to or near Columbus, occupying all fordable places in that vicinity on the Hiwassee. You will start at 7 a. m. to-morrow, August 23, provided with three days' rations. You will report frequently all that you may learn regarding Wheeler. Send reports to Charleston after 11 a. m.

By command of Major-General Steedman:

S. B. MOE,
Assistant Adjutant-General.

SPECIAL FIELD ORDERS, } HEADQUARTERS DEPARTMENT
                        AND ARMY OF THE TENNESSEE,
No. 106.   }   *Before Atlanta, Ga., August 22, 1864.*

*   *   *   *   *   *   *

XIII. Brig. Gen. M. D. Leggett, having been granted a leave of absence on surgeon's certificate of disability, Brig. Gen. Charles R. Woods, U. S. Volunteers, is relieved from command of the First Brigade, First

Division, Fifteenth Army Corps, and assigned to the temporary command of Third Division, Seventeenth Army Corps, and will forthwith report accordingly.

By order of Maj. Gen. O. O. Howard:

WM. T. CLARK,
Assistant Adjutant-General.

Weekly report of effective force of the Department of the Cumberland, Maj. Gen. George H. Thomas, U. S. Army, commanding, August 22, 1864.

Command.	Headquarters.			Infantry.			Cavalry.		
	Officers.	Men.	Total.	Officers.	Men.	Total.	Officers.	Men.	Total.
Reserve Brigade, Col. H. Le Favour. *a*	2	9	11	22	688	710	......	......	......
11th Indiana Battery, Capt. A. Sutermeister. *b*	......	......	......						
Post Chattanooga, Col. T. R. Stanley.	14	11	25	66	1,731	1,797	......	......	......
14th U. S. Colored Troops, Col. Thomas J. Morgan.	......	......	......	29	622	651			
16th U. S. Colored Troops, Col. William B. Gaw.	......	......	......	26	656	682			
Total..................	16	20	36	143	3,697	3,840	......	......	......
Fourth Army Corps:									
Headquarters, Maj. Gen. D. S. Stanley.	22	167	189	......	......	......			
First Division, Brig. Gen. N. Kimball.	40	196	236	283	5,018	5,301	......	......	......
Second Division, Brig. Gen. John Newton.	36	126	162	271	3,529	3,800			
Third Division, Brig. Gen. Thomas J. Wood.	42	306	348	262	4,127	4,389	......	......	......
Artillery, Capt. L. Bridges.	7	91	98	......	......	......			
Total..................	147	886	1,033	*816	12,674	13,490	......	......	......
Fourteenth Army Corps:									
Headquarters, Bvt. Maj. Gen. J. C. Davis.	23	445	468	......	......	......			
First Division, Brig. Gen. W. P. Carlin.	29	151	180	247	4,894	5,141	......	......	......
Second Division, Bvt. Maj. Gen. J. C. Davis.	32	92	124	243	4,727	4,970			
Third Division, Brig. Gen. A. Baird.	33	207	240	247	4,478	4,725	......	......	......
Artillery..................									
Detached regiments, train-guards.	......	......	......	54	793	847	......	......	......
Total..................	117	895	1,012	791	14,892	15,683	......	......	......
Twentieth Army Corps:									
Headquarters, Brig. Gen. A. S. Williams.	17	126	143	1	63	64	3	50	53
First Division, Brig. Gen. Joseph F. Knipe.	38	198	236	250	3,980	4,230	......	......	......
Second Division, Brig. Gen. J. W. Geary.	15	90	105	149	3,091	3,240			
Third Division, Brig. Gen. W. T. Ward.	41	375	416	210	4,031	4,241	......	......	......
Artillery, Major Reynolds.	8	17	25	......	......	......			
Total..................	119	806	925	610	11,165	11,775	3	50	53
Cavalry Command:									
Headquarters, Brig. Gen. W. L. Elliott.	10	31	41	......	......	......			
First Division, Brig. Gen. E. M. McCook. *c*	......	......	......	......	......	......	47	489	536
Second Division, Brig. Gen. K. Garrard. *b*	......	......	......	......	......	......	220	4,111	4,331
Third Division, Brig. Gen. J. Kilpatrick. *b*	......	......	......	......	......	......	159	2,119	2,278
Total..................	10	31	41	......	......	......	426	6,719	7,145

a August 8, 1864.   *b* August 15, 1864.   *c* August 6, 1864.

Weekly report of effective force of the Department of the Cumberland, &c.—Continued.

Command.	Headquarters.			Infantry.			Cavalry.		
	Officers.	Men.	Total.	Officers.	Men.	Total.	Officers.	Men.	Total.
Engineer Troops:									
Michigan Engineers and Mechanics, Col. William P. Innes.				53	1,380	1,433			
Pioneer Brigade, Capt. N. Thatcher.				9	193	202			
Engineer Brigade, Col. William B. McCreery.				76	1,254	1,330			
58th Indiana Volunteer Infantry, Col. George P. Buell.a				22	258	280			
Total................				160	3,085	3,245			
District of Tennessee:									
Headquarters, Maj. Gen. L. H. Rousseau.	16	45	61						
Fourth Division, Twentieth Army Corps, Maj. Gen. L. H. Rousseau.	6	2	8	172	4,601	4,773			
Post Nashville. Tenn., Brig. Gen. J. F. Miller.	5	4	9	100	2,072	2,172	6	150	156
Artillery Reserve, Col. James Barnett.	8	7	15						
Fort Donelson, Tenn., Lieut. Col. E. C. Brott.	2	2	4						
Clarksville, Tenn., Col. A. A. Smith.	4	3	7						
Gallatin, Tenn., Col. S. K. N. Patton.									
Nashville and Northwestern Railroad, Tennessee, Brig. Gen. A. C. Gillem.	3	3	6	48	1,266	1,314			
Nashville and Chattanooga Railroad, Tennessee, Brig. Gen. H. P. Van Cleve.	8	9	17	27	802	829			
Nashville and Chattanooga Railroad, Tennessee, Maj. Gen. R. H. Milroy.	7	5	12	54	1,209	1,263			
Post Stevenson, Ala., Col. W. C. Wilson.				26	570	596			
Post Bridgeport, Col. W. Krzyzanowski.	7	33	40	33	665	698			
District of Northern Alabama, Brig. Gen. R. S. Granger.	6	27	33						
Post Decatur, Ala., Col. C. C. Doolittle.	1	3	4						
Post Huntsville, Ala., Col. G. M. L. Johnson.							32	734	766
Pulaski, Tenn., Brig. Gen. J. C. Starkweather.	9	18	27				55	1,616	1,671
Columbia, Tenn., Col. William B. Sipes.							18	984	1,002
Fourth Division Cavalry, Lieut. Col. J. M. Thornburgh.	6	30	36				80	1,450	1,530
2d Michigan, 10th, 11th, and 12th Regiments Indiana Cavalry.							77	2,775	2,352
Total................	88	191	279	460	11,185	11,645	268	7,209	7,477
Grand total	497	2,829	3,326	2,980	56,698	59,678	697	13,978	14,675

a August 1, 1864.

Weekly report of effective force of the Department of the Cumberland, &c.—Continued.

Command.	Artillery.			Total.		Aggregate.	Horses.	Guns.
	Officers.	Men.	Total.	Officers.	Men.			
Reserve Brigade, Col. H. Le Favour.	....	....	....	24	697	721	....	....
11th Indiana Battery, Capt. A. Sutermeister.	5	127	132	5	127	132	....	9
Post Chattanooga, Col. T. R. Stanley.	18	598	616	98	2,340	2,438	31	67
14th U. S. Colored Troops, Col. Thomas J. Morgan.	....	....	....	29	622	651	....	....
16th U. S. Colored Troops, Col. William B. Gaw.	....	....	....	26	656	682	....	....
Total....................	23	725	748	182	4,442	4,624	31	76
Fourth Army Corps:								
Headquarters, Maj. Gen. D. S. Stanley.	....	....	....	22	167	189	....	....
First Division, Brig. Gen. N. Kimball.	....	....	....	323	5,214	5,537	....	....
Second Division, Brig. Gen. John Newton.	....	....	....	307	3,655	3,962	....	....
Third Division, Brig. Gen. Thomas J. Wood.	....	....	....	304	4,433	4,737	....	....
Artillery, Capt. L. Bridges.	26	837	863	33	928	961	655	35
Total....................	26	837	863	989	14,397	15,386	655	35
Fourteenth Army Corps:								
Headquarters, Bvt. Maj. Gen. J. C. Davis.	....	....	....	23	445	468	....	....
First Division, Brig. Gen. W. P. Carlin.	....	....	....	276	5,045	5,321	....	....
Second Division, Bvt. Maj. Gen. J. C. Davis.	....	....	....	275	4,819	5,094	....	....
Third Division, Brig. Gen. A. Baird.	....	....	....	280	4,685	4,965	....	....
Artillery.....................	22	766	788	22	766	788	477	32
Detached regiments, train-guards.	....	....	....	54	793	847	....	....
Total....................	22	766	788	930	16,553	17,483	477	32
Twentieth Army Corps:								
Headquarters, Brig. Gen. A. S. Williams.	....	....	....	21	239	260	50	....
First Division, Brig. Gen. Joseph F. Knipe.	....	....	....	288	4,178	4,466	....	....
Second Division, Brig.Gen. J. W. Geary.	....	....	....	164	3,181	3,345	....	....
Third Division, Brig. Gen. W. T. Ward.	....	....	....	251	4,406	4,657	....	....
Artillery, Major Reynolds.	21	750	771	29	767	796	534	36
Total....................	21	750	771	753	12,771	13,524	584	36
Cavalry Command:								
Headquarters, Brig. Gen. W. L. Elliott.	....	....	....	10	31	41	54	....
First Division, Brig. Gen. E. M. McCook.	....	....	....	47	489	536	574	4
Second Division, Brig.Gen. K. Garrard.	....	....	....	220	4,111	4,331	4,533	6
Third Division, Brig. Gen. J. Kilpatrick.	....	....	....	159	2,119	2,278	2,138	4
Total....................	....	....	....	436	6,750	7,186	7,299	14
Engineer Troops:								
Michigan Engineers and Mechanics, Col. William P. Innes.	....	....	....	53	1,380	1,433	....	....
Pioneer Brigade, Capt. N. Thatcher.	....	....	....	9	193	202	....	....
Engineer Brigade, Col. William B. McCreery.	....	....	....	76	1,254	1,330	....	....
58th Indiana Volunteer Infantry, Col. George P. Buell.	....	....	....	22	258	280	....	....
Total....................	....	....	....	160	3,085	3,245	....	....

Weekly report of effective force of the Department of the Cumberland, &c.—Continued.

Command.	Artillery.			Total.		Aggregate.	Horses.	Guns.
	Officers.	Men.	Total.	Officers.	Men.			
District of Tennessee:								
Headquarters, Maj. Gen. L. H. Rousseau.	......	......	......	16	45	61	......	......
Fourth Division, Twentieth Army Corps, Maj. Gen. L. H. Rousseau.	3	133	136	181	4,736	4,917	97	6
Post Nashville, Tenn., Brig. Gen. J. F. Miller.	12	329	341	123	2,555	2,678	86	24
Artillery Reserve, Col. James Barnett.	20	637	657	28	644	672	533	30
Fort Donelson, Tenn., Lieut. Col. E. C. Brott.	5	153	158	7	155	162	88	13
Clarksville, Tenn., Col. A. A. Smith.	3	104	107	7	107	114	186	6
Gallatin, Tenn., Col. S. K. N. Patton.	3	131	134	3	131	134	......	6
Nashville and Northwestern Railroad, Tennessee, Brig. Gen. A. C. Gillem.	4	103	107	55	1,372	1,427	78	6
Nashville and Chattanooga Railroad, Tennessee, Brig. Gen. H. P. Van Cleve.	12	380	392	47	1,191	1,238	......	57
Nashville and Chattanooga Railroad, Tennessee, Maj. Gen. R. H. Milroy.	3	89	92	64	1,303	1,367	3	9
Post Stevenson, Ala., Col. W. C. Wilson.	4	133	137	30	703	733	9	6
Post Bridgeport, Col. W. Krzyzanowski.	6	256	262	46	954	1,000	27	5
District of Northern Alabama, Brig. Gen. R. S. Granger.	......	......	......	6	27	33	......	......
Post Decatur, Ala., Col. C. C. Doolittle.	6	195	201	7	198	205	164	11
Post Huntsville, Ala., Col. G. M. L. Johnson.	......	......	......	32	734	766	......	......
Pulaski, Tenn., Brig. Gen. J. C. Starkweather.	......	......	......	64	1,634	1,698	442	......
Columbia, Tenn., Col. William B. Sipes.	3	118	121	21	1,102	1,123	203	6
Fourth Division Cavalry, Lieut. Col. J. M. Thornburgh.	5	120	125	91	1,600	1,691	968	6
2d Michigan, 10th, 11th, and 12th Regiments Indiana Cavalry.	......	......	......	77	2,275	2,352	338	......
Total......	89	2,881	2,970	905	21,466	22,371	3,222	191
Grand total	181	5,959	6,140	4,355	79,464	83,819	12,268	384

No report from First Ohio Volunteer Sharpshooters, Battery I, First Ohio Volunteer Artillery, Thirty-seventh Indiana, Seventy-eighth Pennsylvania, and One hundred and eighth Ohio Volunteer Infantry.

Respectfully submitted.

WM. L. PORTER,
Lieutenant and Acting Assistant Adjutant-General.

Near Atlanta, Ga., *August 23, 1864—11.30 p. m.*
(Received 24th.)

Maj. Gen. H. W. Halleck, *Washington, D. C.:*

All well. Give currency to the idea that I am to remain quiet till events transpire in other quarters, and let the idea be printed, so as to reach Richmond in three days. You understand the effect.

W. T. SHERMAN,
Major-General.

HDQRS. MILITARY DIVISION OF THE MISSISSIPPI,
In the Field, near Atlanta, August 23, 1864—9.15 a. m.

General THOMAS:

As near as I can make out the rebels have repaired the Macon road, and we must swing across it. Let me know when you will be ready to execute the former plan.

W. T. SHERMAN,
Major-General, Commanding.

HEADQUARTERS DEPARTMENT OF THE CUMBERLAND,
August 23, 1864.

Major-General SHERMAN:

The teams of my command have only five days' forage on hand; otherwise my command will be ready to commence the movement to-morrow. Colonel Mackay tells me that in three days the whole army could be supplied with ten days' forage.

GEO. H. THOMAS,
Major-General.

SHERMAN'S HEADQUARTERS,
August 23, 1864.

Major-General THOMAS:

General Kilpatrick represents the corn-fields very extensive down on Flint River and the country about Jonesborough, so I think we can safely depend on forage. Still I think it well to have corn in bags, and this could follow us, via Sandtown, on the third day. I would like to begin the movement to-morrow night.

W. T. SHERMAN,
Major-General.

THOMAS' HEADQUARTERS,
August 23, 1864.

General SHERMAN:

I would like to commence the movement without being hurried, and can do so by Thursday night. I think the cavalry ought to have a little rest and time to shoe up. I will be perfectly prepared by Thursday with provisions, and can arrange to get forage by Sandtown the day after, if forage comes down.

GEO. H. THOMAS,
Major-General.

HDQRS. MILITARY DIVISION OF THE MISSISSIPPI,
In the Field, near Atlanta, August 23, 1864—1.30 p. m.

General THOMAS:

Yours received. The general wants all fully prepared without undue haste, and will therefore postpone until Thursday night.

L. M. DAYTON,
Aide-de-Camp.

HDQRS. MILITARY DIVISION OF THE MISSISSIPPI,
In the Field, near Atlanta, August 23, 1864—6 p. m.

General THOMAS:

Inasmuch as we have postponed our movement till Thursday night I think it would be well for General Garrard to send out the brigade that did not go with General Kilpatrick out to Stone Mountain to-morrow, and let it break up another five miles of road to make a sure thing of that road.

W. T. SHERMAN,
Major-General, Commanding.

HDQRS. MILITARY DIVISION OF THE MISSISSIPPI,
In the Field, near Atlanta, August 23, 1864—7.30 p. m.

General THOMAS:

Have your signal corps provided with rockets, and agree upon signals by rockets or signal smoke for a few simple messages such as "All well," "Send boats to Campbellton," "Send a brigade, division, or regiment to Campbellton," also "Look out for us at Roswell." These signals may be of use to us when we get beyond safe distance for couriers via Sandtown.

W. T. SHERMAN,
Major-General, Commanding.

THOMAS' HEADQUARTERS,
August 23, 1864.

General SHERMAN:

My signal officers have rockets, and will arrange a code.

GEO. H. THOMAS,
Major-General.

HOWARD'S HOUSE, *August 23, 1864—7.40 a. m.*

Captain CASE:

But very few men to be seen in enemy's works this morning. White house, in front of here and just in front of enemy's works, destroyed by fire last night. Very little firing this a. m.

H. H. BURTON,
Lieutenant and Acting Signal Officer.

HDQRS. CHIEF OF CAVALRY, DEPT. OF THE CUMBERLAND,
Near Atlanta, Ga., August 23, 1864.

Brig. Gen. K. GARRARD, *Comdg. Second Division Cavalry:*

The general commanding directs that you send out Colonel Miller's brigade very early to-morrow morning, to destroy as much of the Atlanta and Augusta Railroad as possible, and return to-morrow.

I am, general, respectfully, your obedient servant,

DAVID F. HOW,
Lieutenant and Acting Assistant Adjutant-General.

[AUGUST 23, 1864.—For Kilpatrick to Elliott, relative to damage done to railroad, &c., see Part II, p. 855.]

SHERMAN'S HEADQUARTERS,
August 23, 1864.

General SCHOFIELD:

I think the rebels have already repaired the Macon road. How soon can you be ready to execute our former plan?

W. T. SHERMAN,
Major-General.

———

SCHOFIELD'S HEADQUARTERS,
August 23, 1864.

Major-General SHERMAN:

I think I can be ready to-morrow. Will know definitely as soon as I can hear from my commissary at Marietta.

J. M. SCHOFIELD,
Major-General.

———

HDQRS. MILITARY DIVISION OF THE MISSISSIPPI,
In the Field, near Atlanta, August 23, 1864—10.30 a. m.

General SCHOFIELD:

Get General Morgan to give you the best idea he can of the roads from your flank to Red Oak, with as many names as possible; also get a diagram of the roads from your old headquarters (Wilson's) to Utoy Post-Office and Red Oak and Fairburn. Captain Bartlett can fill in for you some.

W. T. SHERMAN,
Major-General, Commanding.

———

HEADQUARTERS ARMY OF THE OHIO,
Near Atlanta, Ga., August 23, 1864.

Major-General SHERMAN:

I have on hand supplies for the grand movement, and only need long enough notice to send my baggage wagons to the rear. I will have maps about Utoy, Red Oak, &c., completed this evening.

J. M. SCHOFIELD,
Major-General.

———

HDQRS. MILITARY DIVISION OF THE MISSISSIPPI,
In the Field, near Atlanta, August 23, 1864—3 p. m.

General SCHOFIELD:

General Thomas reports he will be ready for Thursday night. Therefore make all possible preparations in the mean time.

W. T. SHERMAN,
Major-General, Commanding.

(Same to General Howard.)

HDQRS. THIRD DIVISION, TWENTY-THIRD ARMY CORPS,
                    Near East Point, August 23, 1864.

Maj. J. A. CAMPBELL,
        Assistant Adjutant-General, &c.:

SIR: Lieutenant-Colonel Miner, commanding Seventh Ohio Volunteer Cavalry, reports some force of rebel infantry moving off to his right about a mile from here. I have ordered a reconnaissance from Third Brigade to determine what the movement may be.

Very respectfully, &c.,

J. D. COX,
                            Brigadier-General, Commanding.

HDQRS. MILITARY DIVISION OF THE MISSISSIPPI,
        In the Field, near Atlanta, August 23, 1864—9.15 a. m.

General HOWARD:

I think the rebels have repaired the Macon road. How soon can you be ready to execute the former plan of swinging our whole army by the right across by Fayetteville or Jonesborough?*

W. T. SHERMAN,
                        Major-General, Commanding.

HDQRS. SIGNAL DETACH., FIFTEENTH ARMY CORPS,
            Before Atlanta, Ga., August 23, 1864.

Maj. Gen. JOHN A. LOGAN,
        Commanding Fifteenth Army Corps:

SIR: I have the honor to submit the following as my report of to-day: First Lieut. C. H. Fish, of this detachment, took his position on lookout station at 7 a. m. At 7.30 a. m. two engines, with some cars, passed into Atlanta. The fog prevented the counting of the cars or seeing what was on them. At 9.15 a. m. an engine with one box-car left town. At 2 p. m. an engine with two box-cars left town; no men to be seen on them. At 3 p. m. the engine and car that left at 9.15 a. m. returned, closely followed by the other engine. No men to be seen on them. At 6 p. m. a train of seventeen freight and one passenger cars left Atlanta. Nothing aboard but a few men. The enemy are tearing down old barracks and using the lumber for shelters along their line of works. First Lieut. J. H. Weirick, of this detachment, reports the rebels busy extending and completing their skirmish pits. Enemy's main lines unchanged as far as I can see them from my position at De Gress' battery and other points along the line. The enemy are still working slowly on their new forts and rifle-pits in front of the Twentieth Corps.

I am, sir, very respectfully, your obedient servant,

SAMUEL EDGE,
            First Lieutenant and Chief Acting Signal Officer.

RESACA, *August 23, 1864—8 a. m.*

Maj. S. B. MOE,
        Assistant Adjutant-General:

Cannot send an infantry force toward Holly Creek without uncovering the bridge. What a squadron of cavalry can do to ascertain the

----
*Answer not found.

strength, &c., of the enemy will be done.   Last night I advised Colonel
Watkins, at Calhoun, to send a cavalry force to Jasper to ascertain
whether the enemy was moving down in that direction.   He might send
a part of his force via this place to Holly Creek.

GREEN B. RAUM,
Colonel, Commanding Brigade.

RESACA, *August 23, 1864.*

Capt. L. M. DAYTON,
Aide-de-Camp:

I have no further information this morning.   I sent a squadron of
cavalry toward Holly Creek Mill at daylight.

G. B. RAUM,
Colonel, Commanding Brigade.

RESACA, *August 23, 1864—1 p. m.*
(Received 3 p. m.)

Capt. L. M. DAYTON,
Aide-de-Camp:

Lieutenant Hunter, who had command of the advance guard of the
squadron sent toward Holly Creek Mill, is just in.   He reports that one
mile and a half this side of the mill Captain Robinson, commanding the
column, was attacked in the rear by a force estimated at 500.   Lieutenant
Hunter went to the mill, crossed the creek, turned west and reached
Tilton with the advance guard.   Captain Robinson and his men have
not reported.   Citizens estimate the force variously at from 500 to 2,000.

G. B. RAUM,
Colonel, Commanding Brigade.

HDQRS. MILITARY DIVISION OF THE MISSISSIPPI,
In the Field, near Atlanta, August 23, 1864—4 p. m.

Colonel RAUM:

Have you not force enough to go out to Holly Creek by night and
bounce that party?   It is there to cover a courier line back to Hood.
I suppose General Steedman to be now up about Charleston and Columbus, and that Wheeler must go north or on into North Carolina.

W. T. SHERMAN,
Major-General, Commanding.

RESACA, *August 23, 1864.*

Capt. L. M. DAYTON,
Aide-de-Camp:

Captain Robinson has just got in without loss.   He reports the enemy
about 300 strong near Holly Creek Mill, and that 400 camped last night
on Holly Creek where the Federal road crosses.   No further news of the
force reported passing down the Westfield pike.

G. B. RAUM,
Colonel, Commanding Brigade.

RESACA, *August 23, 1864.*

Major-General SHERMAN:

I have 410 muskets besides 100 cavalry. I can take the cavalry and, say, 200 infantry, and move out within an hour and see what can be done for the fellows near Holly Creek.

G. B. RAUM,
Colonel, Commanding Brigade.

RESACA, *August 23, 1864—5.45 p. m.*

Capt. L. M. DAYTON,
Aide-de-Camp:

Colonel Raum has just started for Holly Spring Creek with 50 cavalry and 200 infantry.

WM. W. McCAMMON,
Acting Assistant Adjutant-General.

HDQRS. MILITARY DIVISION OF THE MISSISSIPPI,
In the Field, near Atlanta, August 23, 1864—6.30 p. m.

Colonel RAUM,
Resaca:

Your force is too small to venture. Make sure of Resaca and wait General Steedman's action.

W. T. SHERMAN,
Major-General, Commanding.

RESACA, *August 23, 1864—9 p. m.*

Capt. L. M. DAYTON,
Aide-de-Camp:

The general's dispatch of 7.20 [6.30] p. m. overtook me on the way to Holly Creek. I think Resaca would have been safe. I have just returned. I will try to have 500 of the dismounted cavalry at Calhoun brought to this place so I can take the offensive, if necessary. The force near Holly Creek, whatever it may be, has made no offensive movements to-day.

G. B. RAUM,
Colonel, Commanding Brigade.

HDQRS. MILITARY DIVISION OF THE MISSISSIPPI,
In the Field, near Atlanta, August 23, 1864—11.30 p. m.

COMMANDING OFFICER,
Resaca:

That bridge at Resaca must not be risked, but 300 men in the two redoubts can defend themselves and the bridge against all Wheeler's cavalry.

W. T. SHERMAN,
Major-General, Commanding.

RESACA, *August 23, 1864—12 midnight.* ·

Capt. L. M. DAYTON:

The four pieces of artillery are manned, in addition to the number of men reported with my present force. I expect to whip any number brought against me. The bridge will never be destroyed until after the destruction of the garrison.

G. B. RAUM,
Colonel, Commanding Brigade.

CHATTANOOGA, *August 23, 1864.*
(Received 8.30 a. m.)

General SMITH:

Rebel forces reported last night at Holly Spring Mill. Do you hear anything of them?

JAS. B. STEEDMAN,
Major-General.

CARTERSVILLE, *August 23, 1864—8.30 a. m.*

Major-General STEEDMAN,
Chattanooga:

Troops left here at 12.30 a. m. last night, of which I advised you by telegraph. I get no news from the enemy.

JNO. E. SMITH,
Brigadier-General.

CARTERSVILLE, *August 23, 1864—8.40 p. m.*

Major-General SHERMAN:

I have sent to Chattanooga two regiments from Rome, one from Allatoona, one from Etowah, and one from Kingston, to report to General Steedman, last night. Leaves me two small regiments at Allatoona and two at Etowah and this place.

JNO. E. SMITH,
Brigadier-General.

DALTON, *August 23, 1864.*

Major-General STEEDMAN:

A company of forty soldiers sent from Resaca met the enemy near Spring Place (at the mills on Connesauga River) from 100 to 200 strong. Our men were repulsed, four of them coming in here this a. m. One of the home guards just arriving, and reports a fight with the rebels near Spring Place last night, in which Captain Woody and another man were wounded.

B. LAIBOLDT,
Colonel, Commanding.

HEADQUARTERS DISTRICT OF THE ETOWAH,
Chattanooga, August 23, 1864.

Capt. L. M. DAYTON,
Aide-de-Camp to Major-General Sherman:

A party of Wheeler's raiders were seen to the southeast of Charleston last night. They are moving toward Maryville, Tenn.

J. B. STEEDMAN,
Major-General.

———

DALTON, *August 23, 1864.*

Major-General STEEDMAN:

I sent out one company yesterday morning eastward to Holly Creek, beyond Spring Place, and another through Ship's Gap to Summerville via Broomtown Valley; the last will not return till to-night. The first company returned last evening, and report a body of 500 rebel cavalry lying on the Westfield turnpike at the foot of the Cohutta Mountain, about twenty miles from here on the road to Ellijay. They are apparently holding that gap for the protection of couriers or other communications between Wheeler and Atlanta. They came there on Sunday from the diretion of Columbus, having been sent to learn the old Federal road in the neighborhood of Cohutta Springs on Saturday evening, and to proceed in the direction of Ellijay. This body has two companies guarding the ford of Hold's Creek. I do not think they intend to harass the railroad but merely to hold that gap.

WM. J. PALMER,
Colonel, Commanding Fifteenth Pennsylvania Cavalry.

———

HEADQUARTERS DISTRICT OF THE ETOWAH,
Chattanooga, August 23, 1864.

Col. L. D. WATKINS,
Calhoun, Ga.:

Send all your mounted force effective for a march by way of Spring Place and Cohutta Springs toward Savannah, on the Hiwassee River. Colonel Palmer sends a detachment from Dalton by way of Spring Place to Columbus; try to communicate with him. He reports 500 rebel cavalry at the foot of Cohutta Mountain on Westfield road, evidently keeping open communication between Wheeler and Atlanta. Try to break up the line and move on same route to the Hiwassee and co-operate with Colonel Palmer.

J. B. STEEDMAN,
Major-General.

———

ROME, *August 23, 1864.*

Major-General SHERMAN:

My cavalry has returned. It accomplished nothing. They report Clanton at Guntersville, with means of crossing the river. Wheeler was expected back that way after cutting the railroads beyond Chattanooga. My two regiments sent to General Smith have not returned. I am informed they have gone to Chattanooga.

WM. VANDEVER,
Brigadier-General.

Hdqrs. Chief of Cavalry, Dept. of the Cumberland,
                                Chattanooga, Tenn., August 23, 1864.
Capt. A. P. Gallagher,
        Co. C, 4th Indiana Cav., Comdg. Detach. 1st Car. Div.:

The general commanding directs that you proceed to-morrow morning with your company and the detachments from other regiments of the First Cavalry Division to Dalton, Ga. 'You will on arriving there report by telegraph to Brig. Gen. E. M. McCook, commanding First Division Cavalry, at Cartersville, Ga., and await instructions from him respecting your future movements. Two days' forage will be carried upon your horses and three days' rations in haversacks by your men. Your command will be fully armed and equipped and have forty rounds of ammunition per man. Two extra horseshoes and nails will also be carried by each man. You will, on the march, keep your command well closed up, and allow no straggling or pillaging. On camping at night post pickets to guard the approaches to your camp, and while on the march and in camp be vigilant against surprise. You will avail yourself of all opportunities to graze your horses after your day's march. As you will reach Dalton at the end of the second day you can obtain forage and rations for your command from the post commander during your stay there.

I am, captain, very respectfully, your obedient servant,

                                        J. E. JACOBS,
                        Captain and Assistant Adjutant-General.

                Chattanooga, Tenn., *August 23, 1864—9 a. m.*
                                        (Received 2.10 p. m.)
Maj. T. T. Eckert:

General Kilpatrick has returned, having destroyed a few miles of the Macon road, and fought Ross' cavalry, capturing a battery and 3 stand of colors. Wheeler has thrown part of his command to north bank of the Tennessee, and yesterday captured men, mules, and wagons within ten miles of here. I think Steedman is too late with his movement, and then Wheeler will strike Nashville road. Too much rain.

                                J. C. VAN DUZER,
                        Captain, &c., U. S. Military Telegraph.

                Chattanooga, Tenn., *August 23, 1864—10 p. m.*
                                        (Received 11.40 p. m.)
Maj. Thomas T. Eckert:

Nothing from Wheeler or the front at Atlanta to-day. Flank movement to our right and the rear of Atlanta will begin day after to-morrow, if no unexpected delay.

                                J. C. VAN DUZER.

Special Field Orders, }   Hdqrs. Mil. Div. of the Miss.,
        No. 59.   }   *In the Field, near Atlanta, August 23, 1864.*

In order to carry out the provisions of the act of Congress approved July 2, 1864, and the regulations of the Secretary of the Treasury relative to trade and intercourse with States and parts of States in insurrection, and to make the operations of trade just and fair both as to the people and the merchant, the following general rules will be observed in this military division as near as the state of the country will permit:

I. All trade is prohibited near armies in the field or moving columns of troops save that necessary to supply the wants of the troops themselves. Quartermasters and commissaries will take such supplies as are needed in the countries passed through, leaving receipts and taking the articles up on their returns. When cotton is found, and transportation is easy and does not interfere with the supplies to the army dependent upon the route, the quartermaster will ship the cotton to the quartermaster at Nashville or Memphis, who will deliver it to the agent of the Treasury Department. It will be treated as captured property of an enemy and invoiced accordingly. No claim of private interest in it will be entertained by the military authorities.

II. In departments and military districts embracing a country within our military control, the commanders of such departments and districts may permit a trade in articles, not contraband of war or damaging to the operations of the army at the front, through the properly appointed agents and sub-agents of the Treasury Department, to an extent proportionate to the necessities of the peaceful and worthy inhabitants of the localities described; but as trade and the benefits of civil government are conditions not only of fidelity of the people, but also of an ability to maintain peace and order in their district, county, or locality, commanding officers will give notice that all trade will cease where guerrillas are tolerated or encouraged, and, moreover, that in such districts and localities the army or detachments sent to maintain the peace must be maintained by the district or locality that tolerates or encourages such guerrillas.

III. All military officers will assist the agents of the Treasury Department in securing possession of all abandoned property and estates subject to confiscation under the law.

IV. The use of weapons for hunting purposes is too dangerous to be allowed at this time, and therefore the introduction of all arms and powder, percussion caps, bullets, shot, lead, or anything used in connection with fire-arms, is prohibited absolutely, save by the proper agents of the United States; and when the inhabitants require and can be trusted with such things for self-defense, or for aiding in maintaining the peace and safety of their families and property, commanding officers may issue the same out of the public stores in limited quantities.

V. Medicines and clothing, as well as salt, meats and provisions, being quasi-contraband of war according to the condition of the district or locality where offered for sale, will be regulated by local commanders in connection with the agents of the Treasury Department.

VI. In articles non-contraband, such as the clothing needed for women and children, groceries and imported articles, the trade should be left to the Treasury agents as matters too unimportant to be noticed by military men.

VII. When military officers can indicate a preference to the class of men allowed to trade they will always give preference to men who have served the Government as soldiers and are wounded or incapacitated from further service by such wounds or sickness. Men who manifest loyalty by oaths and nothing more are entitled to live, but not to ask favors of a Government that demands acts and personal sacrifice.

By order of Maj. Gen. W. T. Sherman:

L. M. DAYTON,
Aide-de-Camp.

SPECIAL FIELD ORDERS, }   HDQRS. ARMY OF THE OHIO,
        No. 91.   }   *Before Atlanta, Ga., August 23, 1864.*

*   *   *   *   *   *   *

VI. The troops will be prepared to march on Friday, the 26th instant, with nine days' rations in haversacks. Until further orders three days' rations of all, except fresh beef, will be required to last five days. Full rations of beef will be issued. Regimental and headquarters transportation will be reduced to what is absolutely necessary to carry cooking utensils and provisions for officers for twenty days. All surplus transportation will be sent across the Chattahoochee at Turner's Ferry on the 25th, and will be left in charge of Colonel Capron, commanding dismounted cavalry. All sick and wounded will be sent to the rear on the same day. Every effort must be made to preserve secrecy relative to the proposed movement. Conversation between pickets is strictly prohibited.

By command of Major-General Schofield:

J. A. CAMPBELL,
Major and Assistant Adjutant-General.

SPECIAL ORDERS, }   HDQRS. SEVENTEENTH ARMY CORPS,
        No. 210.   }   *Before Atlanta, Ga., August 23, 1864.*

*   *   *   *   *   *   *

II. Brig. Gen. Charles R. Woods, U. S. Volunteers, having reported, in compliance with Special Field Orders, No. 106, Department and Army of the Tennessee, is temporarily assigned to the command of the Third Division, and will forthwith report accordingly.

*   *   *   *   *   *   *

By command of Maj. Gen. F. P. Blair:

ROWLAND COX,
Assistant Adjutant-General.

NEAR ATLANTA, GA., *August 24, 1864—7.15 p. m.*
(Received 12.15 a. m. 25th.)

Maj. Gen. H. W. HALLECK,
        Washington, D. C.:

Heavy fires in Atlanta all day, caused by our artillery. I will be all ready and will commence the movement round Atlanta by the south to-morrow night, and for some time you will hear little of me. I will keep open a courier line with Chattahoochee bridge by the way of Sandtown. The Twentieth Corps will hold the bridge, and I will move with the balance of the army, provisioned for twenty days.

W. T. SHERMAN,
Major-General.

HDQRS. MILITARY DIVISION OF THE MISSISSIPPI,
        In the Field, near Atlanta, August 24, 1864—8 a. m.

General THOMAS:

I will ride down to the bridge to-day to see the lay of the ground and the character of the redoubts there. Go on and make all the preparations possible, so that our movement when begun may proceed rapidly and safely. Our maps should be compiled, and as many roads laid down between Red Oak and Jonesborough as we can be sure of existence.

W. T. SHERMAN,
Major-General, Commanding.

(Same to Generals Schofield and Howard.)

———

HDQRS. MILITARY DIVISION OF THE MISSISSIPPI,
In the Field, near Atlanta, August 24, 1864—7 p. m.

General THOMAS:

I was at the bridge to-day and telegraphed you from· there that it would be well to send pioneers to mark and begin the line for a bridge-head; also a cavalry company could go through the woods in every direction and order all the drift to get over the river. I came round by Turner's Ferry and found men encamped everywhere; a battery belonging to General McCook. All had better move to-morrow, so that Generals Williams and Stanley will have the road clear. The telegraph superintendent may take up his wire to-morrow after 9 o'clock.

W. T. SHERMAN,
Major-General, Commanding.

———

THOMAS' HEADQUARTERS,
August 24, 1864.

Major-General SHERMAN:

Your telegram from the bridge was received.* Orders have been given for the removal of all the drift to the bridge; also pioneers and a regiment from each brigade to prepare abatis and lay out the works. The cavalry command will also be sent out.

GEO. H. THOMAS,
Major-General.

P. S.—Where will you have your headquarters to-morrow night? Mine will be behind the right of the Fourteenth Army Corps.

G. H. T.

———

SHERMAN'S HEADQUARTERS,
August 24, 1864.

General THOMAS:

I will move my headquarters to Utoy Creek, near the left division of General Schofield. No particular spot, but will leave word with Cox or Hascall—the latter, I think.

W. T. SHERMAN,
Major-General.

———

HEADQUARTERS FOURTH ARMY CORPS,
Before Atlanta, Ga., August 24, 1864.

Brigadier-General KIMBALL,
Commanding First Division, Fourth Army Corps:

GENERAL: The contemplated movements of the divisions of this corps, as indicated in letters of instructions to division commanders, dated at these headquarters August 17, 10 a. m., and which movements

———

* See in Ramsey to Williams, p. 651.

were postponed until further orders, in accordance with instructions from department headquarters, received August 17, p. m., will commence just after dark to-morrow evening. During to-day and to-morrow morning you will send all of your surplus men, horses, wagons—ammunition and baggage wagons, &c.—and material not absolutely necessary for the success of the expedition, to Vining's Station, on the other side of the Chattahoochee River, and you will send a small force to the same place to guard such. Let every preparation for this movement be completed by to-morrow noon. Place a good and reliable division officer of the day, or commander of your division pickets, on duty to-morrow. A staff officer will be sent to you to point out the route of march for your division, and further instructions will be given in reference to the time and manner of withdrawing your pickets.

By order of Major-General Stanley:

J. S. FULLERTON,
Lieutenant-Colonel and Chief of Staff.

(Same to Generals Newton and Wood.)

HEADQUARTERS DEPARTMENT OF THE CUMBERLAND,
Before Atlanta, Ga., August 24, 1864.
(Received 3.20 p. m.)

Brig. Gen. A. S. WILLIAMS, *Comdg Twentieth Army Corps:*

GENERAL: I am directed by the major-general commanding to send you the following copy of a dispatch just received from Major-General Sherman, with instructions that its requirements may be at once complied with:

CHATTAHOOCHEE BRIDGE, *August 24, 1864.*

General THOMAS:

You had better order down the pioneers and working parties with Lieutenant Ludlow, engineer department, and prepare the bridge-head before the troops come down; the two small redoubts here on this side are inefficient and of little account. It may be the troops will not have time to cover themselves and the bridge before Hood may strike them, as his first impression may and will be that our whole army is retiring.

W. T. SHERMAN,
Major-General.

I have the honor to be, general, very respectfully, your obedient servant,

ROBT. H. RAMSEY,
Assistant Adjutant-General.

HDQRS. SIGNAL DETACH., TWENTIETH ARMY CORPS,
In the Field, August 24, 1864.

Brigadier-General WILLIAMS, *Comdg. Twentieth Army Corps:*

GENERAL: I have the honor to report that at least three houses, two frame and one brick, were destroyed by the fire in Atlanta this afternoon. Our shells burst in the city to right and left of brick stack.

Very respectfully, your obedient servant,

W. W. HOPKINS,
Captain and Acting Signal Officer.

[AUGUST 24, 1864.—For Miller to Kennedy, reporting operations on railroad between Decatur and Stone Mountain, see Part II, p. 851.]

DECATUR, *August 24, 1864.*

General GEORGE H. THOMAS:

The very last from a reliable and intelligent refugee, who is vouched for by our scout as being truly loyal, is, Roddey returned to Moulton last night. His command will be there to-day. He is ordered to remain in the valley, but to strike at our railroads, and if possible to attack Decatur from the north. General Smith is between Pontotoc and Okolona, moving toward Columbus. Forrest is in the field, but is retreating south of Columbus, having told the citizens he could not hold the place without re-enforcements. Forrest only lost his little toe, but is reported twice 6,000 little toes still under his command. Clanton is reported in the eastern part of this (Morgan) county with 1,500 men.

R. S. GRANGER,
Brigadier-General.

HEADQUARTERS DEPARTMENT OF THE CUMBERLAND,
August 24, 1864.

Brig. Gen. R. S. GRANGER,
      Decatur, Ala.:

Yours received. Watch Roddey and Clanton well, and prevent them from crossing the river and attacking your post or line of communications.

WM. D. WHIPPLE,
Assistant Adjutant-General.

NASHVILLE, *August 24, 1864.*

General WHIPPLE:

General Granger telegraphs from Decatur that Roddey has returned to Moulton, and has orders to remain in the valley and strike at our communications, and if possible attack Decatur from the north side of the river. He says General Smith is between Pontotoc and Okolona, moving toward Columbus. Forrest in the field again, retreating south of Columbus, telling citizens he could not hold the place without re-enforcements. His force is reported to be 6,000.

L. H. ROUSSEAU,
Major-General.

HDQRS. MILITARY DIVISION OF THE MISSISSIPPI,
In the Field, near Atlanta, August 24, 1864—8 p. m.

General GRANGER,
      Decatur:

I am satisfied the enemy designs to make desperate attempts on our road. I have your dispatch, and think it probable Roddey is over there, also Clanton. Do the best you can and keep General Rousseau advised. Cavalry usually do so little damage to a road that it can be repaired faster than they damage it. Guard well the vital points, such as bridges and tunnels, and when the enemy scatters, as he is sure to do, pitch into his detachments.

W. T. SHERMAN,
Major-General, Commanding.

HEADQUARTERS ARMY OF THE OHIO,
Near Atlanta, Ga., August 24, 1864.

Major-General SHERMAN:

I will make all possible preparations. My staff officers are in search of information about roads beyond Red Oak.

J. M. SCHOFIELD,
Major-General.

HDQRS. MILITARY DIVISION OF THE MISSISSIPPI,
In the Field, near Atlanta, August 24, 1864—7 p. m.

General SCHOFIELD:

I have been out all day. Will move my camp to-morrow somewhere below General Hascall on Utoy Creek. The telegraph wire will be taken down at 9 a. m. to-morrow, so make all your dispatches before. Nothing from General Steedman, who is after Wheeler above the Hiwassee.

W. T. SHERMAN,
Major-General, Commanding.

HEADQUARTERS ARMY OF THE OHIO,
August 24, 1864.

Col. HORACE CAPRON,
Commanding Cavalry:

You will concentrate all your command at Turner's Ferry to guard train of the Army of the Ohio. Consult with commanding-general of the Twentieth Army Corps, who will probably be left in command of troops on the Chattahoochee, as to the movements and disposition of train.

By order of General Schofield:

J. A. CAMPBELL,
Major and Assistant Adjutant-General.

HEADQUARTERS ARMY OF THE OHIO,
August 24, 1864.

Col. HORACE CAPRON,
Commanding Cavalry:

The trains of the Army of the Ohio will be sent to Turner's Ferry to-morrow, to be placed under your charge; you will act until further orders under the direction of the officer in command of troops at the Chattahoochee.

By order of General Schofield:

J. A. CAMPBELL,
Major and Assistant Adjutant-General.

HOWARD'S HEADQUARTERS,
August 24, 1864.

General SHERMAN:

Do you wish me to delay till Friday night or follow General Thomas' movement immediately, provided it can be done?

O. O. HOWARD,
Major-General.

Hdqrs. Military Division of the Mississippi,
In the Field, near Atlanta, August 24, 1864—3 p. m.

General Howard:

I think it will be as much as we can do the first day to get General Williams down to the bridge, and General Stanley south of Proctor's Creek. Consult with General Thomas as to the first move.

W. T. SHERMAN,
Major-General, Commanding.

Hdqrs. Military Division of the Mississippi,
In the Field, near Atlanta, August 24, 1864—7 p. m.

General Howard:

I have been out all day at the river—the railroad bridge and Turner's; will move my camp to-morrow to Utoy Creek, below General Hascall. The telegraph wire will be gathered in to-morrow at 9 o'clock, so make your dispatches before. I would rather have your left near where it is, and unless you and General Thomas have made other arrangements, will instruct him to have General Stanley also stop at least a division about the Turner's Ferry road, so as to support your left to-morrow night and next day.

W. T. SHERMAN,
Major-General, Commanding.

Headquarters Department of the Tennessee,
August 24, 1864.

Major-General Sherman:

I have seen General Thomas and learn from him that he intended to cover the movement of the Twentieth Corps with Fourth Corps near Proctor's Creek, and then move the Fourth Corps at once in rear of Fourteenth; and I have already made a new flank near Ezra Church and given my orders to withdraw the Sixteenth and part of the Seventeenth into the new works in conjunction with General Thomas' first movement. I could not fight a battle on the old ground unless the enemy would come square in front. If the Fourth Corps stops on that flank all right, otherwise I should prefer to withdraw into my new lines.

O. O. HOWARD,
Major-General.

Hdqrs. Military Division of the Mississippi,
In the Field, near Atlanta, August 24, 1864—8.15 p. m.

General Howard:

Yours of August 24 is received. All right. Make the movement to-morrow night and next day according to your better knowledge of the ground. Take due precaution that all your trains are covered or moved behind the Chattahoochee, under protection of the Twentieth Corps.

W. T. SHERMAN,
Major-General, Commanding.

HEADQUARTERS DEPARTMENT OF THE TENNESSEE,
August 24, 1864.

Major-General SHERMAN:

A fire seems to be raging in Atlanta, direction 10 degrees south of east from my tree. Can see heated air rising in dense column; seems to be spreading; town is filled with smoke. I have directed my heavy guns to fire on the town.

O. O. HOWARD,
Major-General.

HOWARD'S HEADQUARTERS,
August 24, 1864.

Major-General SHERMAN:

3.30 p. m.—Fire reported spreading in Atlanta. 4 p. m.—It broke out in rear of large block. Eighteen box and one passenger cars arrived, empty.

O. O. HOWARD,
Major-General.

HOWARD'S HEADQUARTERS,
August 24, 1864.

General SHERMAN:

Signal report 6 p. m says: A train of eight freight-cars, loaded with boxes, bundles of goods, and other articles, just left Atlanta; about forty men on the train. The fire is still burning and spreading.

O. O. HOWARD,
Major-General.

HEADQUARTERS ARMY OF THE CUMBERLAND,
August 24, 1864.

Major-General HOWARD:

The road past Utoy Creek will not be used by me after Friday morning. I will park my trains as far to the right rear of the Fourteenth Army Corps as it will be safe.

GEO. H. THOMAS,
Major-General, U. S. Volunteers, Commanding.

HOWARD'S HEADQUARTERS,
August 24, 1864.

Major-General THOMAS:

I meant Utoy Place, not creek. I wish to know if I can march a column via Utoy or Kennedy's house without interfering with you or Schofield, and I wish to park my trains a little nearer the Chattahoochee than yourself.

O. O. HOWARD,
Major-General.

THOMAS' HEADQUARTERS,
August 24, 1864.

Major-General HOWARD:

The road you indicate will not be used by my troops after Friday morning.

GEO. H. THOMAS,
Major-General, U. S. Volunteers, Commanding.

HEADQUARTERS FIFTEENTH ARMY CORPS,
Before Atlanta, Ga., August 24, 1864.

Maj. Gen. P. J. OSTERHAUS,
Commanding First Division:

GENERAL: The following telegram is just received from Major-General Howard:

Major-General LOGAN:

Please satisfy yourself fully as to whether there is anything more than a skirmish line in your front or not, and report.

O. O. HOWARD,
Major-General.

You will take the necessary measures to ascertain whether or not there is more in your front than is indicated in the telegram, taking care not to expose your lines too freely, and report your operations to these headquarters.

By order of Major-General Logan:

H. N. WHEELER,
Assistant Adjutant-General.

HEADQUARTERS SIGNAL DETACHMENT,
Before Atlanta, Ga., August 24, 1864.

Maj. Gen. JOHN A. LOGAN,
Commanding Fifteenth Army Corps:

SIR: I have the honor to submit the following as my report of to-day. Lieutenant Fish, of this detachment, took position on lookout station at 8 a. m. and reports the following:

At 11.30 a. m. I discovered a column of smoke rising from Atlanta. I examined it closely, but could not determine from what it originated. The fire emitted black smoke for a space of five minutes, then white smoke, something like steam. Heated air could be seen to rise in thick white clouds. It was still burning at dark. At 11.40 a. m. a train of eighteen box-cars left town; doors closed; could not tell if loaded or not. At 4.30 p. m. a train of eighteen box-cars and one passenger-car arrived, all empty. At 4.50 p. m. a train of four passenger and five box cars arrived; they appeared to be empty. At 6 p. m. a train of eight box-cars, loaded with boxes, bundles of clothing or bedding, and other articles, left town, also about thirty-five men on board. The six-gun fort in front of the Seventeenth Corps has part of the embrasures casemated. A battery in the Seventeenth Army Corps almost destroyed one of the casemates to-day; their firing was very good.

Lieutenant Weirick, of this detachment, reports from Captain De Gress' battery:

I notice the following changes on the rebel lines in front of Fifteenth Army Corps: During the last twenty-four hours considerable timber has been cut in front of their main lines. They have extended and completed some of their advance skirmish pits and pitched some additional tents or flies in rear of main works, apparently officers' quarters; otherwise their lines appear unchanged.

At 12 m. I received information from General O. O. Howard that it was currently reported that the rebels were evacuating Atlanta. I therefore proceeded to the lookout station and examined entirely the enemy's lines, but could see nothing to justify the report. A large fire appeared in Atlanta that I could tell but very little about. The smoke appeared like that of burning grain. I then proceeded to Captain De Gress' battery; while there I discovered considerable movements along the rebel line. They appeared to be fixing up their equipments; most of them moved back to a camp or new line in rear of the one in sight. At 5 p. m. I returned to the lookout on tree and discovered a few men leaving the rifle-pits in front of Twentieth Corps with their equipments; they appeared to be militia. At 6 p. m. I saw four old citizens, well dressed, come out on the big work in front of town. They appeared to be agitated and excited. It is evident from their motion and downcast appearance that there is some move about to take place. Two more large fires occurred, one in the evening and the other at about dark; appeared to be large buildings of some kind. From my observations this afternoon I am satisfied that the enemy are about to make a grand move of some sort. The rebels fired their big gun three times, once before dark and twice after. Very few pieces of artillery in sight.

I am, very respectfully, your obedient servant,

SAMUEL EDGE,
First Lieutenant and Chief Acting Signal Officer.

RESACA, *August 24, 1864.*

Capt. L. M. DAYTON,
   Aide-de-Camp:

I have positive information that on the 17th instant the cattle captured near Calhoun were within fifteen miles of Athens, Ga., under escort of two regiments of mounted infantry. They passed up through Ellijay. I think troops left at Fairmount to cover the removal of cattle near Holly Creek have withdrawn.

GREEN B. RAUM,
Colonel, Commanding.

CLEVELAND, TENN., *August 24, 1864.*

Maj. S. B. MOE,
   Assistant Adjutant-General, Chattanooga:

The 300 rebels, telegraphed you about by Colonel Palmer yesterday, as reported by citizens in Holly Creek, are only thirty bushwhackers and citizens. Captain Woody, Murray County Home Guards, was wounded in a skirmish with them near Westfield late the night of 22d. One hundred mounted men said to be at Ellijay; none nearer. On Friday thirty-eight of Wheeler's men passed down Federal road across to Ellijay with dispatch; none have been seen since.

CHAS. B. LAMBORN,
Lieutenant-Colonel Fifteenth Pennsylvania Cavalry.

LOUDON, TENN., *August 24, 1864.*

Major-General STEEDMAN:

GENERAL: I have the honor to make you acquainted with the following account of the proceedings of the raiding party from the south, in this vicinity for your information:

On Saturday last a detachment from this place had a skirmish with the enemy near Sweet Water early in the morning, and finding their strength too great fell back. In the afternoon, near Philadelphia, had another skirmish, and 3 men captured, 1 of whom made his escape, but no one killed or wounded. The loss of the enemy in killed and wounded in these two skirmishes was 6 or more. We captured 1 from the Sixth Georgia Cavalry. That day the enemy moved to the south of this place and crossed the Little Tennessee at different fords the 20th and 21st. The 22d some crossed the Holston at Louisville and cut the telegraph at Concord, and did a little damage to railroad, and then returned to the south side of the river the next day. Railroad and telegraph to Knoxville now repaired. I inclose copies of telegrams from General Tillson, which will inform you of the subsequent movements of the enemy. The railroad and telegraph between Philadelphia and Athens are badly injured. The construction train is here, and will proceed at once to repair the road and telegraph as rapidly as possible. There is no injury to either between Loudon and Philadelphia. The country has been thoroughly scouted, and we feel assured that they have all crossed to the other side of the Little Tennessee River. I felt confident of being able to defend the place and protect the bridge, but had not force to attack the enemy in the field. Loudon and Kingston were not molested. General Tillson is at Knoxville, and as the place is very strongly fortified there is no cause of fear. I return this p. m. to Knoxville, having made arrangements here for the safety of bridge, &c. Shall spare no effort for the security of the garrisons, &c., under my command, and shall use every endeavor to harass and defeat the enemy. Capt. W. W. Cushing, military conductor, is just in from Charleston; reports no rebels, but road very much destroyed between Athens and Charleston.

I am, general, most respectfully, your obedient servant,

J. AMMEN,
Brig. Gen., U. S. Vols., Comdg. Fourth Division, 23d Army Corps.

[Inclosure No. 1.]

KNOXVILLE, *August 24, 1864.*

Lieutenant REED, *Aide-de-Camp:*

I have just received definite information of the enemy from a scout I sent out to Maryville last night. The brigade of which I telegraphed you last night as being on the Boardman Ferry road was only a part of the enemy's force. They also passed up Tar Creek road, and the main body on the Sevierville road. They are crossing French Broad in several places. See next dispatch for balance.

TILLSON.

[Inclosure No. 2.]

KNOXVILLE, *August 24, 1864.*

Lieutenant REED, *Aide-de-Camp:*

Their force is from 2,500 to 3,000, with five pieces of artillery. I have sent the information to Gillem and suggested to him the propriety of turning back, if possible, and striking the enemy before he can cross the river and concentrate. The affair at Maryville turned out of small consequence; nobody killed or wounded on our side, and only 18 or 20 captured, some of whom have since escaped; the rest, it is stated, have been paroled by enemy.

TILLSON.

[Inclosure No. 3.]

KNOXVILLE, *August 24, 1864.*

Lieutenant REED, *Loudon:*

We have captured one of General Humes' body guard. He tells a straightforward, truthful story, apparently. He says the enemy's force consists of Humes' division, Ashby's and Harrison's brigades, Kelly's division, Robertson's and Iverson's brigades, and Williams' independent brigade, in all, from twenty-five to thirty regiments and nine pieces of artillery. He says they expected to join Morgan at the Plains and make for Middle Tennessee.

DAVIS TILLSON,
Brigadier-General.

SPECIAL ORDERS,   }   WAR DEPT., ADJT. GENERAL'S OFFICE,
No. 279.   {   *Washington, August 24, 1864.*

*   *   *   *   *   *   *

19. Permission to remain at Carlinville, Ill., until further orders, is hereby granted Maj. Gen. John M. Palmer, U. S. Volunteers.

*   *   *   *   *   *   *

By order of the Secretary of War:

E. D. TOWNSEND,
Assistant Adjutant-General.

SPECIAL FIELD ORDERS,   }   HDQRS. MIL. DIV. OF THE MISS.,
{   *In the Field, near Atlanta, Ga.,*
No. 60.   {   *August 24, 1864.*

It being represented by A. W. Smith, special agent of the Post-Office Department, that the mail cars are daily encumbered with about fifty men, detailed by divisions, brigades, and regiments, who profess to be after their mails, but are in reality engaged in traffic, it is ordered:

I. The special agent of the Post-Office Department will bring the army mail to the nearest practicable point by rail to the army and there deliver the bags only to corps messengers, duly appointed by a corps order, approved by the army commander.

II. Each army corps commander will arrange to receive his mail of the agent of the Post-Office Department at the end of the railroad, and will have it brought to his headquarters and there distributed to divisions, brigades, and regiments, according to his own plan.

III. Army commanders, viz, Cumberland, Tennessee, and Ohio, may send special messengers through to Nashville, Chattanooga, and Knoxville and back, but these must confine their business to that defined in their written orders. The same privilege cannot be conceded to any others, because we have not the facilities and quantity of cars needed for more than the absolute necessities of the army.

*   *   *   *   *   *   *

By order of Maj. Gen. W. T. Sherman:

L. M. DAYTON,
Aide-de-Camp.

SPECIAL FIELD ORDERS, ⎰ HDQRS. DEPT. OF THE CUMBERLAND,
    No. 233.   ⎱   *Near Atlanta, Ga., August 24, 1864.*

      *   *   *   *   *   *   *

XV. Brevet Brigadier-General Colgrove is hereby assigned to the command of the First Brigade, Third Division, Fourth Corps, and will report accordingly.

      *   *   *   *   *   *   *

By command of Major-General Thomas:

WM. D. WHIPPLE,
Assistant Adjutant-General.

GENERAL ORDERS, ⎰   HDQRS. FOURTEENTH ARMY CORPS,
    No. 13.   ⎱   *Near East Point, Ga., August 24, 1864.*

Having been assigned to that duty by order of the President of the United States, expressed in General Orders, No. 241, War Department, current series, Adjutant-General's Office, I hereby assume command of the Fourteenth Army Corps.

The following officers are announced as a part of the corps staff: Capt. A. C. McClurg, assistant adjutant-general, chief of staff; Capt. T. W. Morrison, U. S. Volunteers, assistant adjutant-general; Capt. John F. Squier, Seventy-fourth Illinois Volunteers, aide-de-camp; Lieut. Thomas J. Carney, Thirty-fourth Illinois Volunteers, aide-de-camp; Lieut. Col. A. von Schrader, U. S. Volunteers, assistant inspector-general; Lieut. Col. J. R. Paul, U. S. Volunteers, chief commissary of subsistence; Capt. J. E. Remington, U. S. Volunteers, chief quartermaster; Maj. Charles Houghtaling, First Illinois Artillery, chief of artillery; Maj. John B. Lee, One hundred and twenty-fifth Illinois Volunteers, provost-marshal; Capt. Jesse Fulmer, Fifteenth U. S. Infantry, commissary of musters; Capt. A. S. Cole, chief signal officer; Capt. W. H. Collins, One hundred and fourth Illinois Volunteers, chief of ambulances.

By command of Bvt. Maj. Gen. J. C. Davis:

A. C. McCLURG,
Assistant Adjutant-General and Chief of Staff.

ORDERS.]   HEADQUARTERS TWENTIETH ARMY CORPS,
                      Near Atlanta, Ga., August 24, 1864.

The divisions of this corps will be held in readiness to move to-morrow night, the 25th, at such hour as may be hereafter designated.

The First Division, with Colonel Harrison's brigade, of the Third Division, to move to the Chattahoochee River at the railroad bridge; the Second Division to the river at Pace's Ferry; the Second and Third Brigades of the Third Division to the river at Turner's Ferry. Positions will be taken at each of these crossings for their protection. At daybreak to-morrow morning each division commander will send all of his pioneers, with one regiment from each of his brigades, to the position he is to occupy, for the purpose of constructing intrenchments and abatis. General Ward and General Geary will each send a competent staff officer to locate their lines. Lieutenant Ludlow, engineer, will superintend the erection of the works at the railroad crossing. Major Reynolds, chief of artillery, will assign one battery to each General Ward's and General Geary's divisions, to march with them, and dur ing the day to-morrow will select positions at the railroad crossing for the other four batteries, which will march with the First Division. The ordnance and regimental trains of the First and Third Divisions will start early to-morrow, and be parked on this side of the river at the crossings they are respectively to hold. The trains of the Second Division will march simultaneously with the division, taking an interior road. The caissons of the batteries will accompany the ordnance trains of the division to which the battery is assigned. All trains must be out of the way, so that when the troops commence the march they will have a clear road. Further instructions will be given regarding the withdrawal of the picket-line.

By command of Brigadier-General Williams:

H. W. PERKINS,
Assistant Adjutant-General.

SPECIAL FIELD ORDERS, }   HEADQUARTERS DEPARTMENT
                           AND ARMY OF THE TENNESSEE,
No. 108.   }   *Before Atlanta, Ga., August 24, 1864.*

*   *   *   *   *   *   *

II. Special Field Orders, No. 101, August 17, from these headquarters, and Special Field Orders, No. 58, Military Division of the Mississippi, will be carried into effect as follows:

1. All the trains will be loaded to-day as therein indicated, and be ready to move, under the direction of the chief quartermaster, to-morrow morning at 9 o'clock.

2. All wagons, artillery, &c., to go to the rear as specified in said order, will be sent to-day.

3. Major-General Blair and General Ransom will to-morrow evening move their commands into the new work. The hour of moving will be made known hereafter.

4. The line of march will be as indicated, Major-General Logan, moving out first with his command, and Major-General Blair on a separate road, followed by the Left Wing, Sixteenth Army Corps, under command of Brigadier-General Ransom. The time of moving will be given.

5. All other provisions of Special Field Orders, No. 101, will be observed as far as practicable.

*   *   *   *   *   *   *

By order of Maj. Gen. O. O. Howard:

WM. T. CLARK,
Assistant Adjutant-General.

GENERAL ORDERS, }   HDQRS. LEFT WING, 16TH ARMY CORPS,
No. 48.   }   *Near Atlanta, Ga., August 24, 1864.*

The following-named officers are announced as aides-de-camp on the staff of the general commanding, and will be obeyed and respected accordingly: Capt. George S. Doane, Eleventh Regiment Illinois Infantry Volunteers; Lieut. J. D. Tredway, Twenty-third Regiment Wisconsin Infantry Volunteers.

By order of Brig. Gen. T. E. G. Ransom:

J. W. BARNES,
Assistant Adjutant-General.

SPECIAL FIELD ORDERS, ⎞   HEADQUARTERS LEFT WING,
                      ⎟   SIXTEENTH ARMY CORPS,
      No. 70.   ⎠   *Near Atlanta, Ga., August 24, 1864.*

*   *   *   *   *   *   *

II. In addition to the orders from military division and department headquarters forwarded to division commanders for their information and guidance, they are instructed to be ready to withdraw their commands into the new works to-morrow morning at a moment's notice, the movement to commence from the right of each division at the same time, each division taking the most direct road in rear of the old works to its new position.

Second. The ammunition and regimental wagons and ambulances will be ready to move at 9 a. m. to a point, to be designated by each division commander, in rear of the new works.

Third. The skirmishers of the Second Division will be withdrawn to the new line heretofore designated as soon after the division moves as the division commander may deem prudent. Care will be taken to notify and connect with the skirmishers of the Fourth Division, the left of whose line will retire to conform with the new line of the Second Division.

Fourth. The Ninth Illinois Mounted Infantry will picket Proctor's Creek, connecting the left of the skirmish line of the Second Division, reporting direct to these headquarters.

Fifth. The second move will be made in the following order, viz: First. Trains of both divisions, in the same order of march as the divisions, each accompanied by a detail from the pioneer corps, following in the rear of the Seventeenth Army Corps, and, if practicable, on an interior road hereafter to be designated. Second. Fourth Division Third. Second Division. The Ninth Illinois will receive further instructions at the time this move is to be made.

Sixth. The command will be supplied with three days' rations in haversacks from the morning of the 26th instant.

By order of Brig. Gen. T. E. G. Ransom:

J. W. BARNES,
Assistant Adjutant-General.

———

HEADQUARTERS LEFT WING, SIXTEENTH ARMY CORPS,
Near Atlanta, Ga., August 24, 1864.

SOLDIERS: It becomes necessary for me to relinquish my command for a short time. No one can regret this more than I do. Upon leaving you I cannot refrain from extending to you my heartfelt thanks for the efficient and brave manner in which you have supported me throughout this campaign. Whether on the battle-field, in the trenches, or on the march, you have given that earnest, zealous, and efficient attention to your duties that always insures success.

From Chattanooga to Atlanta, through a campaign unparalleled in its severity and its successes, you have done your full share ; your comrades are buried on every field, and while we deeply mourn their loss we have the satisfaction of knowing that they fell nobly doing their duty. I leave you in the hands of able and tried commanders give them the same cheerful support you have always given me, and there will be no fears of the result. I shall watch your course with the same interest ; your victories will be mine. May God bless and protect you.

G. M. DODGE,
Major-General.

HEADQUARTERS DEPARTMENT OF THE CUMBERLAND,
In the Field, Ga., August 25, 1864.

Col. M. F. MOORE, *Commanding:*

COLONEL: The general commanding directs that you withdraw your brigade to-night at the same time that the troops of General Davis' division are withdrawn. You will accompany their movement across Proctor's Creek, and then proceed as speedily as possible to join your proper division in the Fourteenth Army Corps.

Very respectfully, your obedient servant,

HENRY STONE,
Assistant Adjutant-General.

HEADQUARTERS TWENTIETH CORPS,
Near Atlanta, Ga., August 25, 1864—6.45 p. m.

Brig. Gen. WILLIAM D. WHIPPLE, *Chief of Staff:*

GENERAL: A deserter from Stevenson's division, just brought in, says that the report has been circulated on the enemy's picket-line that the Federal army will fall back to-night, and thinks an attempt to follow will be made to-morrow. The report was spread among them this morning.

Very respectfully, your obedient servant,

A. S. WILLIAMS,
Brigadier-General, Commanding.

HEADQUARTERS TWENTIETH CORPS,
Near Atlanta, Ga., August 25, 1864.

Col. BENJAMIN HARRISON,
Comdg. First Brigade, Third Division, Twentieth Corps:

COLONEL: The general commanding the corps directs that for orders concerning the movements of your brigade to-night, you report to Brigadier-General Knipe, commanding First Division, as your brigade is to march with that division and take position with it near the railroad crossing over the Chattahoochee River.

I am, colonel, very respectfully, your obedient servant,

H. W. PERKINS,
Lieutenant-Colonel and Assistant Adjutant-General.

P. S.—Orders to the above effect have been sent to General Ward.

NASHVILLE, TENN., *August 25, 1864.*

General WHIPPLE, *Assistant Adjutant-General:*

General Carter telegraphs that Wheeler has crossed the river above Knoxville, and will likely be down upon our communications this side of Chattanooga.

L. H. ROUSSEAU,
Major-General.

HEADQUARTERS ARMY OF THE CUMBERLAND,
August 25, 1864.

Maj. Gen. L. H. ROUSSEAU, *Nashville, Tenn.:*

Yours received. General Thomas says watch Wheeler and protect the road to the best of your ability. He wishes you also to see that the rebel forces do not cross the Tennessee and attack the Tennessee and Alabama Railroad. They can only do so upon flat-boats, which can be prevented by watchfulness. Moreover the gun-boat will soon be down the river.

WM. D. WHIPPLE,
Assistant Adjutant-General.

NASHVILLE, *August 25, 1864.*

General W. T. SHERMAN:

  Arrived yesterday. Second Michigan mounted and ready for the front; Ninth Pennsylvania mounted and leaving for front by rail. Will mount 300 men per day, beginning to-morrow. Could mount two regiments by taking horses from Government wagons, ambulances, and dismounting clerks and other fancy persons. Recommend that an order be issued requiring mules only to be used in teams. The finest horses in this city are in Government wagons. Shall Second Michigan be sent by land or rail?

R. W. JOHNSON,
Brigadier-General.

HEADQUARTERS DEPARTMENT OF THE CUMBERLAND,
Near Atlanta, Ga., August 25, 1864.

Maj. Gen. O. O. HOWARD,
  Commanding Army of the Tennessee:

  GENERAL: From what I have been told by General Brannan, I fear there is some difference in the manner in which we interpret Special Field Orders, No. 57, from headquarters Military Division of the Mississippi. General Brannan informs me that in conversation with you you told him that you were going to swing back your left to-night. As General Stanley is required to move his corps to-night from our extreme left to behind the right center of the Army of the Tennessee, I would respectfully suggest that you should not withdraw your left from its present position until General Stanley has taken up his, as indicated in the first move of Orders, No. 57. General Stanley's movement will undoubtedly occupy him during the greater portion of this night, and should you swing back your left until after his corps has passed, you expose him to an attack in flank, for the consequences of which I cannot be held responsible.

  Yours, very respectfully,

GEO. H. THOMAS,
Major-General, U. S. Volunteers, Commanding.

HEADQUARTERS DEPARTMENT OF THE TENNESSEE,
Before Atlanta, Ga., August 25, 1864—8 p. m.

Maj. Gen. GEORGE H. THOMAS,
  Commanding Department and Army of the Cumberland:

  I do not intend to move till Friday night. I merely ordered a refusal of my left to Ezra Church, for as soon as Williams is withdrawn I am obliged to do it, as I cannot extend my line to hold the line of Proctor's Creek. I will, however, hold that line—Proctor's Creek—till an hour before daylight to-morrow night if possible with my picket-line. I had intended to have ordered an earlier refusal of line but have postponed on reception of your note. Surely Stanley will be past my left by that time.

Respectfully,

O. O. HOWARD,
Major-General.

How about the Fourteenth Corps? When I withdraw at dark Friday will it be withdrawn in conjunction?

HDQRS. SIGNAL DETACH., FIFTEENTH ARMY CORPS,
Before Atlanta, Ga., August 25, 1864.

Maj. Gen. JOHN A. LOGAN,
Commanding Fifteenth Army Corps:

SIR: I have the honor to submit the following as my report of the day. Lieutenant Fish, of this detachment, took his position on lookout station at 7.30 p. m. and reports the following:

At 10.05 a. m. a train of thirteen box and one passenger cars arrived in Atlanta. The doors were shut; could not tell if loaded or not; a few men in passenger-cars. At 5 p. m. a train of fifteen box-cars arrived in Atlanta with between 150 to 200 men on board. They appeared to have other freight besides the men. At 5.35 p. m. a train of three passenger, one baggage, and seven box cars arrived in town. Baggage-car well filled with what appeared to be trunks, and quite a number of passengers. At 6 p. m. a train of eighteen box-cars loaded quite heavy with men and freight left town. At 6.20 p. m. a train of four cattle-cars loaded with men and freight left town, also one box-car with two engines in front; the hind engine had no fire in.

Lieutenant Weirick, of this detachment, reports:

Everything on the rebel lines in front of the Fifteenth Corps unchanged. From my own observation the rebel forts and lines as far as I can see appear unchanged. Very little sign of an evacuation. The men on the cars appeared unarmed, probably convalescents. The train of five cars and two engines were well filled with men sitting on top of some kind of freight. One of the engines appeared to be disabled. A fatigue party of forty men and an officer on horseback came from the rebel left and moved to their right a little before dark. The men had picks, shovels, and axes.

I am, sir, very respectfully, your obedient servant,

SAMUEL EDGE,
First Lieutenant, Chief Acting Signal Officer.

CHARLESTON, *August 25, 1864.*

Capt. L. M. DAYTON,
Aide-de-Camp:

Wheeler reported over the Little Tennessee and crossing the Holston. Will know positively to-day.

J. B. STEEDMAN,
Major-General.

NASHVILLE, TENN, *August 25, 1864.*

Brig. Gen. R. S. GRANGER,
        Decatur, Ala.:

The forces at McMinnville report that a brigade of rebel cavalry staid at Polk's place last night. If that be true, they are after the Chattanooga road. Colonel Spalding has been ordered to move his two regiments to Decherd in the morning.

B. H. POLK,
Major and Assistant Adjutant-General.

NASHVILLE, TENN., *August 25, 1864.*

Brig. Gen. R. S. GRANGER,
        Commanding District of Northern Alabama, Decatur, Ala.:

General Carter telegraphs that Wheeler has crossed the river above Knoxville and will be upon us. All our cavalry should be ready to move at any moment. Clanton and Roddey, I think, will cross and act in concert with Wheeler. The menace of Decatur was no doubt a sham. A large portion of the cavalry must be moved to the Nashville and Chattanooga Railroad, to points to be indicated hereafter. If practicable, the rebel flat-boats you referred to should be destroyed, but not to interfere with the disposition above indicated.

By command of Major-General Rousseau:

B. H. POLK,
Major and Assistant Adjutant-General.

KNOXVILLE, TENN., *August 25, 1864.*

General STEEDMAN,
        Chattanooga:

The enemy crossed the Holston, two miles below Strawberry Plains, yesterday and last night. He is apparently moving toward Big Creek Gap. Our cavalry, numbering seventy, had a skirmish with the enemy and was worsted. We have no cavalry here and cannot pursue to advantage. The force of the enemy is probably 4,000, with four or nine pieces of artillery. Did not attack garrison at Plains, and did but little damage to railroad. All quiet here.

J. AMMEN,
Brigadier-General of Volunteers.

LOUDON, *August 25, 1864.*

Capt. W. P. AMMEN,
        Assistant Adjutant-General:

The gun-boat Stone River, with six guns of Tenth Indiana Battery, is now here, laying at Huff's Ferry. Will leave for Chattanooga in about an hour. If you have any news for General Steedman telegraph and I will send it down. Captain Naylor, an old friend of yours, is in command of the boat. All quiet on river below.

M. L. PATTERSON,
Lieutenant-Colonel, Commanding.

CHATTANOOGA, TENN., *August 25, 1864—9 p. m.*

Maj. T. T. ECKERT,
    Washington :

Armies finally in motion. Headquarters Army of the Cumberland struck camp at 9 a. m. this day, and my front office is now at Chattahoochee, near the railroad bridge, where Stanley, with the Fourth Corps, is intrenched. General Steedman telegraphs from Charleston, Tenn., that Wheeler has crossed the Little Tennessee, and is crossing Holston, going to Middle Tennessee or Kentucky, probably the former, to destroy railroads.

                                                  J. C. VAN DUZER.

———

SPECIAL FIELD ORDERS,)   HDQRS. DEPT. OF THE CUMBERLAND,
       No. 234.   }   *On Lick Skillet Road, Ga., August 25, 1864.*

I. Bvt. Maj. Gen. J. C. Davis, having been assigned to the command of the Fourteenth Army Corps, according to his brevet rank, vice Major-General Palmer, relieved at his own request, will be relieved in command of the Second Division, Fourteenth Corps, by Brig. Gen. James D. Morgan, U. S. Volunteers.

    *   *   *   *   *   *   *

By command of Major-General Thomas:

                                            WM. D. WHIPPLE,
                                        Assistant Adjutant-General.

———

HEADQUARTERS FOURTH ARMY CORPS,
    Before Atlanta, Ga., August 25, 1864—10 a. m.

Order of the day for Fourth Army Corps, August 25, 1864:

The movement of this command from its present lines will commence at night-fall this evening. Colonel Opdycke will withdraw his brigade first, and he will move it promptly by the best road to General Newton's headquarters, where he will rejoin his division. Next, Brigadier-General Kimball will withdraw his division, commencing on the left, and he will march to the present corps headquarters. As soon as General Kimball passes the left of Brigadier-General Wood's division he, General Wood, will withdraw his division and follow him. General Newton will in turn withdraw by his left as soon as General Wood's division has passed the same. General Newton's division and the artillery will move on the " outside" road, which passes in the rear of department headquarters. Captain Steele, aide-de-camp, will guide this column. All of the columns will march right in front. Brigade commanders will assemble their battalion commanders and enjoin secrecy upon them in this movement, and instruct them to see that all commands are given in an ordinary tone of voice. They will also instruct their captains to prevent talking in the ranks and by the pickets. The pickets of General Kimball's division and Colonel Opdycke's brigade will move back into the main works promptly at 11 o'clock this p. m. As soon as they arrive in the main works the whole line will move to the right, commencing on the left, and they will keep the road near the breast-works, and be ready to repulse any sudden attack that may be made. The picket officers of the day will meet at General Kimball's headquarters at 4 o'clock this afternoon for consultation. They must have a perfect understanding as to where to find each other to-night, and General Newton's picket officer will notify the picket officer of General Geary's division, Twentieth Corps, where to meet him and where he can be found to-night. In no case will the pickets of any division or brigade fall back until those on their left have done so. Lieutenant Taylor, aide-de-camp, will accompany the picket officer of the First Division, and will guide the whole picket-line in moving off to-night. By promptness the pickets should all be in the main works by midnight.

By order of Major-General Stanley:

J. S. FULLERTON,
Assistant Adjutant-General.

GENERAL ORDERS,) HDQRS. CAV. DIV., ARMY OF THE OHIO,
    No. 6.   )   *Before Atlanta, Ga., August 25, 1864.*

The colonel commanding has had, in common with every officer and soldier of his command, occasion to know from personal observation that horses and mules captured from the enemy, and taken from disloyal citizens, have not been treated as the property of the Government, but have been claimed as the private property of both officers and soldiers, and as such have been the subject of trade and sale between soldiers, and between soldiers and officers, and in many instances have been sold to the Government buyers, to private horse dealers, or shipped to the homes of their pretended owners. In common with all honest men, both soldiers and officers of this command, the colonel commanding desires that these dishonest practices be stopped, and that our Government be no more defrauded by any one of this command of its right to captured property. The two desirable objects to be attained are: first, that the captured horses and mules shall become the property of the United States; second, that the individual company or regiment making the capture shall have the privilege of the use of it. Both of these desirable ends can be attained by frequent inspection of companies and regiments, and the branding of all horses and mules found to be without the brand. It is well known to all cavalrymen that it is almost, if not entirely, impossible that there should be a fair, bona fide purchase of a horse from a citizen or soldier in this country. The colonel commanding, therefore, desires it to be known to his command, that it will give him pleasure to see all his officers and men well mounted on captured horses bearing the brand of the Government, and trusts that the only claim any one in this command may ever make to a captured horse may be to use it in the service of the Government. It is therefore ordered that all horses and mules captured from the enemy or taken from citizens be branded with the Government brand as soon as practicable after the capture; and that captured horses and mules in excess of the need of the company or regiments be turned over to the regimental, brigade, or division quartermaster for issue to other portions of the command. Company and regimental officers are charged with the duty of making inspections, which will be necessary to carry this order into effect, and will be held responsible for such neglect as will countenance or encourage the conversion of captured property to private use. It will be the duty of the acting assistant inspectors-general of this command to report to these headquarters the names of officers having in their commands unbranded animals.

This order to be read to each company in this command within forty-eight hours.

By command of Israel Garrard, colonel, commanding:

T. F. ALLEN,
Captain and Acting Assistant Adjutant-General.

NEAR EAST POINT, GA., *August 26, 1864—6.45 p. m.*
Maj. Gen. H. W. HALLECK,
          Washington, D. C.:

I have moved the Twentieth Corps to the Chattahoochee bridge, where it is intrenched, and with the balance of the army am moving for Jonesborough on the Macon road. Last night we made the first move without trouble; to-night I make the second, and the third will place the army massed near Fairburn. If Hood attacks he must come out, which is all we ask. All well thus far.

W. T. SHERMAN,
Major-General.

HEADQUARTERS FOURTH ARMY CORPS,
          Utoy Creek, Ga., August 26, 1864—10 p. m.
Brigadier-General WHIPPLE,
          Chief of Staff:

I have the honor to report the following operations of this corps to-day: At daylight this morning my command was in position, two divisions on the other side of Proctor's Creek (Generals Newton's and Wood's), on the ridges about one-quarter of a mile therefrom, and my other division (General Kimball's) on the hill on this side of the creek, the same hill formerly fortified by General Davis. Soon after my troops had taken these positions the enemy's skirmishers opposed and engaged them. A lively skirmish was then kept up until about 10 a. m., when our pickets at the creek were withdrawn. The enemy did not appear disposed to attack us, and, therefore, in accordance with instructions, I commenced to withdraw my troops at about 9 a. m., and marched them to Utoy Creek, where I arrived at 4 p. m. The First Division is in reserve a short distance back from the creek, and the Second and Third Divisions are in line of battle facing the creek, and are on the ridges about a quarter of a mile from it, General Newton's division on the right of the Sandtown road, and General Wood's on the left.

D. S. STANLEY,
Major-General.

HEADQUARTERS FOURTH ARMY CORPS,
          Utoy Creek, Ga., August 26, 1864—11 p. m.
Brigadier-General KIMBALL,
          First Division:

GENERAL: The following is a copy of a dispatch just received from department headquarters:

HEADQUARTERS DEPARTMENT OF THE CUMBERLAND,
          Camp on Campbellton Road, August 26, 1864.
Maj. Gen. D. S. STANLEY,
          Commanding Fourth Army Corps:

The major-general commanding directs that to-morrow morning you march your corps by the road running nearly due south from the Widow Kennedy's to Mount Gilead Church, on or near the eastern branch of Camp Creek, and take up a position at that place. Be prepared to move out at 8 o'clock, and a guide will be sent to conduct you to the place mentioned.

Yours, very respectfully,

WM. D. WHIPPLE,
Assistant Adjutant-General.

In accordance with the above you will make every preparation to move at 8 a. m. to-morrow.

By command of Major-General Stanley:

J. S. FULLERTON,
Assistant Adjutant-General.

(Same to Generals Newton and Wood.)

HDQRS. THIRD BRIG., THIRD DIV., 14TH ARMY CORPS,
August 26, 1864.

[Maj. JAMES A. LOWRIE,
Assistant Adjutant-General:]

MAJOR: My lookouts report seeing, about half an hour since, rebel troops moving. The troops seemed to be about two miles distant to the left of my brigade, toward Atlanta. The column was about twenty minutes in motion, since which all has been quiet; probably a brigade. The direction they were taking it was difficult to determine, on account of the trees and the haziness of the atmosphere. The lookout thought their direction was to our left, their right, though not certain. No apparent changes in my front.

Respectfully,

GEO. P. ESTE,
Colonel, Commanding.

HEADQUARTERS TWENTIETH CORPS,
Near Atlanta, Ga., August 26, 1864—1 p. m.

Brig. Gen. W. D. WHIPPLE,
Chief of Staff:

GENERAL: I have the honor to report that this corps is in position as ordered at Pace's, Montgomery's, and Turner's Ferries. The withdrawal was effected last night without molestation from the enemy. Scouts that I have sent out to-day report the enemy's scouting parties at Howell's Mill and in the vicinity of the old headquarters of the Department of the Cumberland, but no force. Our positions have been strengthened so as to be safe. The bridge at Turner's Ferry is complete. General Slocum has arrived and will assume command of the corps to-morrow.

I am, general, very respectfully, your obedient servant,

A. S. WILLIAMS,
Brigadier-General, Commanding.

HDQRS. SECOND DIVISION, TWENTIETH ARMY CORPS,
Pace's Ferry, Ga., August 26, 1864.

Lieut. Col. H. W. PERKINS,
Assistant Adjutant-General, Twentieth Corps:

COLONEL: Brigadier-General Geary directs me to state to you, for the information of the general commanding corps, that this division reached Pace's Ferry about daylight this morning and was placed in position on chain of hills east of the Chattahoochee River, the left resting near the river, about 500 yards above the bridge at the ferry, the right resting near the river, about two miles by course of works below the bridge. Our pickets that were left in front of Atlanta last night rejoined the division here, two hours after daylight, having come the entire route unmolested. About noon slight skirmishing commenced between our pickets and the enemy's cavalry, who are developed in rather heavy force in our present front. A portion of their cavalry (dismounted) charged on our picket-line and were instantly driven back, with a loss of 3 captured. Slight picket-firing continued during the afternoon. General Geary directs me to say that the series of hills on which our line is formed make a naturally strong line of defense, but that the number of troops in this division is not sufficient to hold the position against a very heavy attack by infantry. Defensive works are rapidly being completed throughout the entire line, which is about two miles and a half in length. Much of the timber has already been slashed, as abatis, and that work will be steadily pushed to completion. The general is busy along the lines and has no opportunity to address you over his own signature.

I have the honor to be, very respectfully, your obedient servant,

W. T. FORBES,
Captain and Acting Assistant Adjutant-General.

HEADQUARTERS TWENTIETH CORPS,
Near Atlanta, Ga., August 26, 1864.

Colonel MINTY,
Commanding Cavalry Brigade:

COLONEL: The general commanding directs me to inform you that scouts sent from these headquarters toward Roswell Factory report a force of the enemy's cavalry, 400 strong, on this side of the river at Roswell, located there (as the citizens say) for the purpose of making demonstrations on our trains. The general desires that you make such disposition of your troops (those that are to remain up the river from here) as will prevent the enemy from molesting in any way the wagon trains now posted on the north side of the river in this vicinity. He has directed his escort to picket for to-night the road along the railroad and the one which passes by signal hill. All other roads and approaches between the latter and the river he wishes you to place guards and vedettes on. Please answer.

I am, colonel, very respectfully, your obedient servant,

H. W. PERKINS,
Lieutenant-Colonel and Assistant Adjutant-General.

HDQRS. DEPARTMENT AND ARMY OF THE TENNESSEE,
Before Atlanta, Ga., August 26, 1864.

Maj. Gen. JOHN A. LOGAN,
Commanding Fifteenth Army Corps:

GENERAL: The major-general commanding directs that the time for the commencement of the movement to-night be 8 o'clock. He also directs that your pickets and skirmishers be not withdrawn until the rear of the column is well under motion. A staff officer (Lieutenant-Colonel Strong) will superintend their withdrawal.

Very respectfully, your obedient servant,

SAML. L. TAGGART,
Assistant Adjutant-General.

HDQRS. DEPARTMENT AND ARMY OF THE TENNESSEE,
Before Atlanta, Ga., August 26, 1864.

Brig. Gen. T. E. G. RANSOM,
Commanding Left Wing, Sixteenth Army Corps:

Major-Generals Logan and Blair will commence their movement to-night at 8 o'clock. Lieutenant-Colonel Strong will superintend the withdrawal of the pickets and skirmishers.

By order of Maj. Gen. O. O. Howard:

SAML. L. TAGGART,
Assistant Adjutant-General.

HDQRS. SIGNAL DETACH., FIFTEENTH ARMY CORPS,
Before Atlanta, August 26, 1864.

Maj. Gen. JOHN A. LOGAN,
Commanding Fifteenth Army Corps:

SIR: I have the honor to submit the following as my report for to-day:

Lieutenant Fish, of this detachment, was on the station at 7.30 a. m. and reports the following:

The enemy could be seen, gathered in groups, looking intently toward our late lines. At 10.15 a. m. a train of five freight-cars left Atlanta; they appeared to be loaded. At 11 a. m. a few straggling rebels could be seen rambling about the works lately held by the Twentieth Army Corps. These stragglers picked up a few of our men that straggled behind, probably from the Fourth Army Corps, as a portion of that corps were in that vicinity. At 11.30 a. m. a locomotive left Atlanta alone. At 1 p. m. I discovered a column of infantry moving toward the enemy's left. I did not see the head of column; counted five stand of colors; a portion of the column was mounted infantry, about 300. At 3.15 p. m. a train of twelve box-cars, all empty, arrived in Atlanta. At 4.15 p. m. a train of three passenger and four freight cars arrived in Atlanta with a few passengers aboard. At 5.45 p. m. a train of fifteen freight-cars, a portion of which were cattle-cars, arrived in Atlanta; there were a few men in each car. At 6 p. m. a train of seventeen freight-cars, loaded with what appeared to be army stores, left town; immediately following this freight train was a train of six passenger and two baggage cars, with two extra locomotives attached.

Lieutenant Weirick, of this detachment, reports the following:

All quiet and unchanged, with the exception of rebel skirmishers, who kept up a constant fire at our skirmishers on main lines of Fifteenth Army Corps. At 6 p. m. communicated movements to our right and front.

As for myself, I was on the lookout station most of the day, and indorse the above statement of Lieutenant Fish.

I am, sir, very respectfully, your obedient servant,

SAMUEL EDGE,
First Lieutenant and Chief Acting Signal Officer.

HDQRS. MILITARY DIVISION OF THE MISSISSIPPI,
In the Field, Mount Gilead, Ga., August 26, 1864.

General STEEDMAN,
Chattanooga:

If Wheeler goes up into East Tennessee beyond the Holston let him go. The people must rally and destroy bridges and roads, and worry him. He cannot do us any harm, but will simply consume the grain and hay needed by the people. He cannot disturb Loudon or Knoxville. Let General McCook increase his cavalry from Nashville, and after a while we will send him to attend to Wheeler, who is well out of our way.

W. T. SHERMAN,
Major-General, Commanding.

ATHENS, <i>August 26, 1864.</i>
(Via Charleston.)

Maj. S. B. MOE, <i>Assistant Adjutant-General:</i>

We are halted here by what appears to be authenticated rumors that our forces at Knoxville have forced Wheeler back in this direction. Have sent scouting parties to ascertain. I sent orders to the cavalry to retire to Dalton and Cleveland. You will control their future movements, holding them and the 1,200 at Dalton guarding the Spring Place road, to form junction with me if necessary. Let General Sherman know. I am watching Wheeler, and will attack him if he attempts to recross the Little Tennessee. Send no cars for me until further orders.

JAS. B. STEEDMAN,
Major-General.

HDQRS. FOURTH DIV. CAV., ARMY OF THE CUMBERLAND,
Pulaski, Tenn., August 26, 1864—10.20 a. m.

Maj. B. H. POLK:

The following dispatch has just been received from Lieutenant-Colonel Thornburgh, commanding First Brigade, Fourth Division Cavalry, Army of the Cumberland:

Indications are that Roddey is preparing to cross Tennessee River between Elk River and Florence with about 2,000 men.

GEO. SPALDING,
Colonel, Commanding.

HDQRS. FOURTH DIV. CAV., ARMY OF THE CUMBERLAND,
Pulaski, Tenn., August 26, 1864.

Brig. Gen. R. S. GRANGER,
Commanding District of Northern Alabama:

The following telegram has been received from Major-General Rousseau:

A brigade of rebel cavalry is reported near the Polk place.

Sent the Tenth and Twelfth to Decherd.

GEO. SPALDING,
Colonel, Commanding.

HDQRS. FOURTH DIV. CAV., ARMY OF THE CUMBERLAND,
Pulaski, Tenn., August 26, 1864.

Lieut. Col. W. J. CLIFT,
Commanding Second Brigade, Fourth Division Cavalry:

General Rousseau states rebel brigade moving toward the railroad from Polk's place. You will proceed as soon as you can travel with the entire effective force of your command to Decherd Station, Tenn., by the most direct route; the men will carry four days' rations in haversacks. You will take a sufficient number of teams to carry 100 rounds of ammunition per man. You will relieve your pickets immediately. Two efficient officers will be left in charge of camp of each regiment.

By order of Col. George Spalding:

HERVEY A. COLVIN,
Lieutenant and Acting Assistant Adjutant-General.

HDQRS. SECOND BRIG., THIRD DIV., 15TH ARMY CORPS,
Resaca, Ga., August 26, 1864.

Capt. S. M. BUDLONG,
Actg. Asst. Adjt. Gen., Third Division, Fifteenth Corps:

CAPTAIN: I have directed Colonel Hall to survey a route for a road as near as possible along the railroad between Calhoun and Adairsville, crossing the Oothkaloga Creek railroad bridges. If this route proves practicable I propose opening a wagon road, and throwing two bridges across that creek, and then obstruct all fords on the creek east of the railroad. I have also directed him to erect a stockade for the accommodation of forty men at a point half way between the two block-houses, to which point roads converge from the country.

I am, captain, very respectfully, your obedient servant,

GREEN B. RAUM,
Colonel, Commanding Brigade.

KNOXVILLE, TENN., *August 26, 1864.*

Lieut. Col. M. L. PATTERSON,
Loudon:

The enemy came down the Emory road or Beaver Creek road inquiring for Lee's and Black's fords below Clinton. A portion of them are on the road from Ball Play to Campbell's Station, encamped. Yesterday they tried to burn the bridge at Strawberry Plains but failed, as the garrison there of 150 men, with two pieces of artillery, drove them away without any loss on our side, but some to them. If they attempt the bridge at Loudon you can keep them away by sending infantry to this side into the two works by railroad, near end of bridge (one already occupied by Fourth Tennessee), and some at this end of bridge. Do not send out too far on this side, except scouts. You may expect assistance soon. You can whip them easily if they do not improve very much. If the gun-boat helps Major Reeves, Kingston will be safe with moderate fighting and tolerable management. Their whole force is evidently on this side, and they do not intend to fight much if they can avoid it. Our estimate of their numbers is right. You know what we thought. They certainly intend to cross to Middle Tennessee or Kentucky. You can whip them easily. They tried to apply torches to the bridge at Strawberry Plains, but the guns on this side were in the way. You can do as well with your guns. Shut the cut as before in railroad and man the fort opposite. The two forts on this side, with a few skirmishers in front to observe and afterward fall back into the works and to the end of the bridge on this side, will make the defense good, probably the best.

Very respectfully, your most obedient servant,

J. AMMEN,
Brigadier-General of Volunteers, Commanding Division.

KNOXVILLE, TENN., *August 26, 1864.*

Major SMITH,
  Strawberry Plains:

We have certain information that the whole force of the enemy has crossed the Clinch River at Lee's Ferry. The last brigade crossed this a. m. Send this information to Gillem with all the dispatch possible. It is supposed the enemy are making for Middle Tennessee.

                                        J. AMMEN,
                          Brigadier-General of Volunteers.

GENERAL ORDERS, } HDQRS. MIL. DIV. OF THE MISSISSIPPI,
  No. 24.   }   *Nashville, Tenn., August 26, 1864.*

Pursuant to assignment by the Secretary of War, Col. Langdon C. Easton, quartermaster, U. S. Army, is hereby announced as chief quartermaster of the Military Division of the Mississippi. He will be respected accordingly.

By order of Maj. Gen. W. T. Sherman:

                                        R. M. SAWYER,
                              Assistant Adjutant-General.

SPECIAL FIELD ORDERS, } HDQRS. FOURTEENTH ARMY CORPS,
  No. 1.   }   *Before Atlanta, August 26, 1864.*

The following will be the movement of the Fourteenth Army Corps during the night of the 26th of August:

General Carlin will withdraw his division from its present position simultaneously with the withdrawal of the Army of the Tennessee on his left, and passing in rear of the other divisions by the most practicable road, will take position with his right resting upon the Twenty-third Corps, refusing his line so as to run parallel with the south branch of the Utoy Creek, posting two brigades in front line and one in reserve. General Baird will withdraw his division in the same way, following General Carlin, and take position on Carlin's left, continuing his line down the creek, with two brigades in front line and one in reserve. Generals Carlin and Baird will each post their divisions with two brigades in the front line and one in reserve. General Morgan, following General Baird, will withdraw and take position on Baird's left, unless General Baird's line should reach that of the Fourth Corps, in which case he will place his troops in reserve in rear of General Baird's left. The picket-line of the respective divisions will remain in their present position until near daylight unless driven in by the enemy, in which case they will fall back, skirmishing, to their commands. All hospitals, and trains, and batteries not in position, will be removed this afternoon to the rear of the positions indicated, the batteries being withdrawn with and protected by the troops with which they are now posted in line, under the superintendence of the chief of artillery. During the movement now commenced the corps will be held in position and maneuvered as to moving column, and officers kept in their places and men in their ranks. Trains will be placed in secure positions and guarded carefully.

By order of Bvt. Maj. Gen. J. C. Davis:

                                        A. C. McCLURG,
                    Assistant Adjutant-General and Chief of Staff.

SPECIAL FIELD ORDERS, ⎰ HDQRS. FIFTEENTH ARMY CORPS,
     No. 87.   ⎱   *Before Atlanta, Ga., August 26, 1864.*

I. In order to carry out the instructions in Special Field Orders, No. 101, and paragraph II of Special Field Orders, No. 108, from headquarters Department and Army of the Tennessee—

First. Maj. Gen. P. Joseph Osterhaus, commanding First Division, will this evening withdraw his command, moving out on the road surveyed by Captain Klostermann, engineer officer, crossing Utoy Creek near Judge Wilson's, thence proceeding by road designated by Captain Klostermann, engineer officer, to Camp Creek.

Second. Immediately after the troops of Major-General Osterhaus' division have moved out of position, Brigadier-General Hazen, commanding Second Division, will withdraw his command and closely follow that of Major-General Osterhaus.

Third. Immediately after the troops of Brigadier-General Hazen have moved out of position, Brigadier-General Harrow, commanding Fourth Division, will withdraw his command, and closely follow that of Brigadier-General Hazen.

Fourth. Headquarters wagons and ambulances will precede their respective divisions and will be moved out this afternoon to Utoy Creek, where the supply train is parked, and await the arrival of the division to which they belong, and then move in their proper place. Care must be taken not to delay the column. All other wagons will be sent during the afternoon to the place where our line of march crosses Utoy Creek, there to await the arrival of their respective divisions.

Fifth. A strong skirmish line will be maintained until the troops of the last division have withdrawn from the main line of works. They will then be withdrawn to the main line of works by signal agreed upon by their respective division picket officers, and then held until the column is well out of the road, when they will be conducted by their respective officers by the most practicable road to their commands.

Sixth. The time for withdrawing will be announced during the day by General Howard.

   *   *   *   *   *   *   *

By order of Maj. Gen. John A. Logan:

                              R. R. TOWNES,
                            Assistant Adjutant-General.

GENERAL ORDERS, ⎰ HDQRS. LEFT WING, 16TH ARMY CORPS,
     No. 49.   ⎱   *Near Atlanta, Ga., August 26, 1864.*

Capt. Frederick Welker, First Regiment Missouri Light Artillery, is hereby assigned to duty temporarily as chief of artillery of the Left Wing, Sixteenth Army Corps. He will be respected and obeyed accordingly.

By order of Brig. Gen. T. E. G. Ransom:

                              J. W. BARNES,
                            Assistant Adjutant-General.

          HEADQUARTERS FOURTEENTH ARMY CORPS,
               Near East Point, Ga., August 27, 1864.

Brigadier-General WHIPPLE,
     Chief of Staff, Department of the Cumberland:

GENERAL: I have the honor to report that soon after my skirmish line withdrew from the opposite bank of the creek (Utoy) the enemy

established his there.   Light skirmishing has been kept up during the
day since.   I do not think there is a greater force than a skirmish line.
A brigade of infantry has been posted southeast of Patterson's, with
orders to guard the trains there as directed.

I am, very respectfully, your obedient servant,

JEF. C. DAVIS,
Brevet Major-General, Commanding.

HEADQUARTERS DEPARTMENT OF THE CUMBERLAND,
Mount Gilead Church, August 27, 1864.

Bvt. Maj. Gen. J. C. DAVIS, *Comdg. Fourteenth Army Corps:*

GENERAL: The major-general commanding directs that at daylight
to-morrow morning you commence the march for this place, moving by
Patterson's into the Campbellton road, moving along that road to the
cross-roads, about a mile from our camp of last night.   At this point
leave the Campbellton road and move upon the one inclining to the left
and passing Peyton Holbrook's and the Widow Smith's on to this point,
where you will reach the left of the Fourth Corps.   You will pass the
latter, move on to its right, by which time further orders will be given
you.   You will this afternoon seek for some road running to the right
of the one I have described and in a general parallel direction, on
which you will move your wagons and park them in an open space near
this place.   You will report to-night whether you have succeeded in
finding such a road for your wagons, and in the morning come on in
advance of your troops, as the major-general commanding desires to see
you.

Yours, very respectfully,

WM. D. WHIPPLE,
Assistant Adjutant-General.

HEADQUARTERS FOURTEENTH ARMY CORPS,
Near East Point, Ga., August 27, 1864.

Brig. Gen. WILLIAM D. WHIPPLE, *Assistant Adjutant-General:*

GENERAL: Your communication directing me to move my command
to Mount Gilead Church, commencing the movement at daylight in the
morning, came to hand at 5.30 p. m.   I was out reconnoitering the roads
in the vicinity of Patterson's at the time.   I did not receive it myself
until dark.   My troops will move as directed.   I will report in person
in advance of the column.   My general supply trains, under charge of
the corps quartermaster, will move from Patterson's on some road as
near parallel as can be found to the one on which the troops march, and to
the right of the one occupied by General Stanley's corps.   My quartermaster informs me that such a road can be found.   I had but little time
to make inquiry myself about the roads in that direction.   I have sent
an engineer to make a reconnaissance, with a view to finding a road
in that direction.   He will report by morning.

I am, general, very respectfully, your obedient servant,

JEF. C. DAVIS,
Brevet Major-General, Commanding.

P. S.—Since writing the above the engineer has reported a practicable
road in the direction desired, and my trains will move on it accordingly.

JEF. C. DAVIS,
Commanding Corps.

HEADQUARTERS TWENTIETH CORPS,
Chattahoochee Bridge, August 27, 1864.

Brigadier-General WHIPPLE,
        Chief of Staff:

GENERAL: I have the honor to report that I have to-day assumed the command of the Twentieth Corps. The corps is in position as directed at Pace's, Montgomery's, and Turner's Ferries, and intrenched. Yesterday afternoon Geary's division, at Pace's Ferry, had some sharp skirmishing with the enemy's cavalry, capturing a few prisoners. My head quarters are near the railroad bridge.

        I am, general, very respectfully, your obedient servant,
                        H. W. SLOCUM,
                        Major-General, Commanding.

[Indorsement.]

Respectfully forwarded as a partial answer to Captain Dayton's note of this evening.

No report has been received of any firing in that direction to-day.
                        WM. D. WHIPPLE,
                        Assistant Adjutant-General.

HDQRS. FIRST DIVISION, TWENTIETH ARMY CORPS,
                        August 27, 1864.

Capt. S. E. PITTMAN,
        Acting Aide-de-Camp, Twentieth Army Corps:

I am directed by General Knipe to inform you that the picket-line of this division is continuous, and extends along the whole front of the division; that the picket-line does not connect with General Geary's, though a connection can be easily made by throwing forward the right of General Geary's picket-line, connecting with the line of this division near Howell's Mill road and in front of the hill now occupied by Colonel Pardee. The citizen spoken of came through our line at Moore's Mill.

        I have the honor to be, very respectfully, your obedient servant,
                        JAMES FRANCIS,
                        Major and Acting Assistant Inspector-General.

HDQRS. CHIEF OF CAVALRY, DEPT. OF THE CUMBERLAND,
                        Near Mount Gilead Church, August 27, 1864.

Brig. Gen. K. GARRARD,
        Commanding Second Division Cavalry:

I am directed by the general commanding to say that General Stanley will march to vicinity of Mount Gilead Church to-day, and that you will then act on the left flank and rear of General Schofield's corps. His headquarters are in the vicinity of W. Holbrook's, fronting East Point and Atlanta. General Thomas desires daily reports from you while conforming to the movements of General Schofield.

        I am, general, very respectfully, your obedient servant,
                        DAVID F. HOW,
                        Lieutenant and Acting Assistant Adjutant-General.

HEADQUARTERS ARMY OF THE OHIO,
Near Atlanta, Ga., August 27, 1864.

Brig. Gen. J. D. COX,
Commanding Third Division, Twenty-third Army Corps:

GENERAL: The commanding general directs me to inform you that it is possible we may have to withdraw from our present position to-night. He desires you to have your trains in readiness to move back at 4 this p. m. Further orders will be given.

Very respectfully, your obedient servant,
WM. M. WHERRY,
Major and Aide-de-Camp.

HEADQUARTERS ARMY OF THE OHIO,
Near Atlanta, Ga., August 27, 1864.

Brig. Gen. M. S. HASCALL,
Commanding Second Division, Twenty-third Army Corps:

GENERAL: The commanding general directs me to inform you that your division will not be required to move to-night.

Very respectfully, your obedient servant,
J. A. CAMPBELL,
Major and Assistant Adjutant-General.

HDQRS. DEPARTMENT AND ARMY OF THE TENNESSEE,
Near Widow Forsyth's, Ga., August 27, 1864.

Maj. Gen. W. T. SHERMAN,
Commanding, &c.:

GENERAL: We had little difficulty in drawing out last night; some shelling. I heard of but one casualty, but we found the roads rough and the bottoms marshy, so that with great difficulty and delay we made the march. General Logan is now pretty well across Camp Creek, about due south from this place. General Blair is crossing at William Campbell's, about a mile farther to the right. Kilpatrick reports himself across Camp Creek and about a mile south of Enon Church. Logan's position is 71. Have no word from Schofield as yet. A great portion of the Sixteenth and Seventeenth Corps have been broken of their rest two nights. I would prefer not to march till to-morrow morning if this will do. My headquarters are on the Campbellton road, near Widow Forsyth's, one mile east of Dry Pond.

Respectfully, your obedient servant,
O. O. HOWARD,
Major-General.

HDQRS. DEPARTMENT AND ARMY OF THE TENNESSEE,
Near Widow Forsyth's, Ga., August 27, 1864.

Maj. Gen. W. T. SHERMAN,
Commanding Military Division of the Mississippi:

GENERAL: I have complied with your directions. General Garrard was on his way some little time ago to Utoy and probably ere this has reported to you. For the safety of our rear against small squads of the enemy and to keep us informed about larger bodies I hope you will see General Garrard, for I do not think he now has a correct notion of the position of the different corps, though he may.

Very respectfully, your obedient servant,

O. O. HOWARD,
Major-General.

P. S.—Quite heavy cannonading was heard by one of my staff officers between 12 and 1 o'clock to-day in the direction of the railroad bridge.

O. O. H.,
Major-General.

HEADQUARTERS FIFTEENTH ARMY CORPS,
In Field, on Wolf Creek, Ga., August 27, 1864.

Lieut. Col. WILLIAM T. CLARK, *Assistant Adjutant-General:*

COLONEL: I have the honor to report that I have placed my command in position on a line of ridges extending across Wolf Creek, about three-quarters of a mile south of Aldrich's house, fronting south-south-east. General Harrow forms the left, General Hazen the center, and General Osterhaus the right. The pickets of General Harrow extend to Camp Creek, and those of General Osterhaus connect with those of the Seventeenth Corps. The position is a good defensive one. My batteries are in position, and the men are engaged in throwing up works.

My headquarters are on the right of the road near Aldrich's house. See inclosed map.*

Very respectfully, your obedient servant,

JOHN A. LOGAN,
Major-General.

HDQRS. SECOND DIVISION, FIFTEENTH ARMY CORPS,
In the Field, Ga., August 27, 1864.

Lieut. Col. R. R. TOWNES,
Assistant Adjutant-General, Fifteenth Army Corps:

I have the honor to report that this division was withdrawn from its recent position at 8.30 last evening, with the loss of 1 enlisted man killed by a shell, and arrived at this point at about 11 a. m. to-day. The position of this division at present is shown by the accompanying sketch.* It has already a good defensive line of rifle-pits with a broad belt abatis and entanglement in its front. The hill marked A in the sketch commands all the lines of this corps besides seeing them all in reverse. Were this position to be maintained it is my opinion the hill should be fortified.

I am, very respectfully, your obedient servant,

W. B. HAZEN,
Brigadier-General.

KNOXVILLE, *August 27, 1864.*

Colonel PATTERSON, *Loudon:*

The enemy crossed at Lee's Ferry, and will go toward Sparta, probably. They inquired for road to Crossville, &c. Please send word to General Steedman. All quiet here.

J. AMMEN,
Brigadier-General.

---

* Not found.

HEADQUARTERS U. S. FORCES,
Loudon, Tenn., August 27, 1864—10.30 a. m.

Brigadier-General AMMEN,
Knoxville, Tenn.:

GENERAL: I have the honor to acknowledge your dispatch by courier. My scouts report General Steedman at Athens, on his return to Chattanooga. He advanced some distance this side of Athens. I have sent him a dispatch by courier, telling him where the enemy is.

A dispatch from Major Reeves, which left Kingston at 4 o'clock last evening, reports that his outposts were attacked and driven in. He also reports the capture by the enemy of a lieutenant and 9 men out of a scout of twelve men who had been sent out to feel the enemy. A large fire in that vicinity last night indicates that the enemy occupy Kingston, although I hope for the best. I am expecting a courier every minute from the major.

I have the honor to remain, your obedient servant,

M. L. PATTERSON,
Lieutenant-Colonel, Commanding.

LOUDON, *August 27, 1864.*

Brigadier-General AMMEN:

Dispatch just received from Kingston says reliable information states Wheeler was crossing Emory River at Park's Ferry last night and this morning, said to be 2,500 strong. Major Reeves thinks they will attack him to-night or in the morning. I don't think Wheeler will attack at Kingston. Major Reeves asks re-enforcements. Shall I send them down; [how] many?

M. L. PATTERSON,
Lieutenant-Colonel, Commanding.

KNOXVILLE, *August 27, 1864.*

Colonel PATTERSON,
Loudon:

Send courier to General Steedman and inform him of movements of the enemy. If necessary send to Charleston, so as to telegraph to him at Chattanooga. He will want to protect railroad toward Nashville.

J. AMMEN,
Brigadier-General of Volunteers.

LOUDON, *August 27, 1864—5.45 p. m.*

Capt. W. P. AMMEN:

Dispatch just received from Kingston states Wheeler estimated to have 3,000 or 4,000, passing down on northwest side Clinch River. Will camp at Post Oak Springs to-night, seven miles below Kingston.

M. L. PATTERSON,
Lieutenant-Colonel.

LOUDON, *August 27, 1864—6.40 p. m.*

Capt. W. P. AMMEN:

We have sent courier to General Steedman, giving him all the info
mation we have up to this p. m. Shall I send another? Some comps
nies of First Ohio leave here at 8 o'clock to re-enforce Major Reeve
Shall send courier ahead, with instructions that if the re-enforcement
are not needed to have them turned back.

                    M. L. PATTERSON,
                        Lieutenant-Colonel, Commanding.

LOUDON, *August 27, 1864.*

Capt. W. P. AMMEN,
    Assistant Adjutant-General:

I sent out, found General Steedman near Athens with strong forc
Sent courier to him this a. m., telling where the enemy was reported
be. Advised Major Reeves to communicate with General Steedma
General Ammen's communication of yesterday received 10 o'clock th
morning.

                    M. L. PATTERSON,
                        Lieutenant-Colonel, Commanding.

LOUDON, *August 27, 1864.*

Capt. W. P. AMMEN,
    Assistant Adjutant-General:

All quiet here. Courier just in from Kingston. Major Reeves w
attacked last evening 4 o'clock. Skirmished with the enemy until dar
drove them off. Twelve of his scouts were attacked; four have got i
Report the others either killed or captured.

                    M. L. PATTERSON,
                        Lieutenant-Colonel, Commanding.

MARIETTA, *August 27, 1864.*

SHOLES:

Wheeler passed west between Knoxville and Clinton, saying that
should strike Nashville and Chattanooga Railroad near Murfreesb
ough. General Rousseau is notified. I am informed by Major Ecke
that rebels in Shenandoah Valley say that Hood is dead and Lon
street in command at Atlanta. Report not credited entirely, but whe
abouts of latter not known for two weeks past.

                    J. C. VAN DUZER.

HEADQUARTERS FOURTH ARMY CORPS,
    Utoy Creek, August 27, 1864—6 a. m.

Order of march for Fourth Army Corps for to-day, August 27:

General Wood's division will lead, followed by General Kimbal
division. Then will follow the artillery, then the ordnance trains (in t
same order in which the divisions march), then the hospital train a

extra ambulances, then all other wagons, and following these General Newton's division will march. General Wood will take with his division the two batteries formerly attached thereto. Five ammunition wagons and fifteen ambulances will accompany each division. To-day head-quarters trains will follow the division to which they belong.

By order of Major-General Stanley:

J. S. FULLERTON,
Assistant Adjutant-General.

SPECIAL FIELD ORDERS, }
  No. 2.   }

HDQRS. 14TH ARMY CORPS,
Before Atlanta, Ga., August 27, 1864.

Each division commander will at once establish a line of pickets in his own front upon the line of the Utoy Creek, General Carlin's connecting on the right with those of the Twenty-third Corps, and the line connecting on the left with the pickets of the Fourth Corps. All regimental and other wagons, except hospital wagons, and ambulances and ammunition trains, and one wagon each to division and brigade headquarters, and (when they have the tools) one wagon to each brigade for intrenching tools, will be collected under the division quartermaster and reported to-day to Captain Remington, chief quartermaster of the corps, on the farm of Mrs. Patterson, on the Campbellton road. During the projected movements the trains will be moved and parked under Captain Remington's directions. The troops will be in readiness to move at 3 o'clock this afternoon.

By order of Bvt. Maj. Gen. J. C. Davis:

A. C. McCLURG,
Assistant Adjutant-General and Chief of Staff.

SPECIAL FIELD ORDERS, }
  No. 3.   }

HDQRS. 14TH ARMY CORPS,
Near East Point, Ga., August 27, 1864.

The movement which was contemplated for this afternoon will begin at daylight to-morrow.

General Morgan will move his division from its present position at 4 a. m., striking the main Campbellton road with the head of his column at or near the Widow Holbrook's, at which point he will receive further instructions. General Baird will move his division at 5 a. m., following General Morgan. General Carlin will move his division at 6 a. m., following General Baird. The ammunition trains will move upon the main Campbellton road in the order in which their divisions march, following in the rear of the troops of the corps and pursuing the route they have taken.

By order of Bvt. Maj. Gen. J. C. Davis:

A. C. McCLURG,
Assistant Adjutant-General and Chief of Staff.

GENERAL ORDERS, }
  No. 10.   }

HEADQUARTERS TWENTIETH CORPS,
Chattahoochee River, August 27, 1864.

In compliance with General Orders, No. 238, of July 30, 1864, Adjutant-General's Office, the undersigned hereby assumes command of the Twentieth Army Corps.

The following-named staff officers are hereby announced: Maj. E. W. Guindon, aide-de-camp; Capt. W. W. Moseley, aide-de-camp; Capt. W. G. Tracy, aide-de-camp.

H. W. SLOCUM,
Major-General.

SPECIAL ORDERS,   HEADQUARTERS TWENTIETH CORPS,
  No. 69.   *Chattahoochee River, Ga., August 27, 1864.*

I. The First Brigade, Third Division, is hereby relieved from further duty with the First Division, and until it rejoins its division will report to corps headquarters for orders. Colonel Harrison will at once post his brigade in accordance with the verbal instructions given him by the corps commander.

 *   *   *   *   *   *   *

IV. Brig. Gen. A. S. Williams, U. S. Volunteers, having been relieved from the command of the Twentieth Corps, will resume the command of the First Division, and Brigadier-General Knipe will resume command of the First Brigade, First Division.

By command of Major-General Slocum:

H. W. PERKINS,
Assistant Adjutant-General.

SPECIAL FIELD ORDERS,   HDQRS. ARMY OF THE OHIO,
  No. 95.   *Before Atlanta, Ga., August 27, 1864.*

 *   *   *   *   *   *   *

VIII. The following movement will be made to-morrow, viz: Promptly at daylight the division trains will move out on the Sandtown road toward Patterson's and join the corps train, leaving a few ambulances with the troops. The entire train will then move in rear of the troops and train of the Fourteenth Corps (not interfering with the latter) via Patterson's and Mount Gilead to the valley of Camp Creek, in rear of General Stanley's present position, where it will park until further orders. As soon as the trains are out of the way and the Fourteenth Corps has withdrawn from its present position (soon after daylight), General Hascall will draw back to his new line, covering the Campbellton road, and General Cox will simultaneously draw back to the Mount Gilead road and take position, covering that road, with his left near Mrs. Holbrook's. When the trains reach their park at Camp Creek General Hascall will move down to Mount Gilead, passing General Cox, and will occupy the position now held by the Fourth Corps as soon as the latter has moved out. General Cox will prepare to throw back his left, so as to cover the road, as soon as General Hascall shall have passed. General Garrard's cavalry division is to connect with the left and cover the rear of the infantry during the movement. Colonel Garrard will operate from the left of General Thomas along the front of the Twenty-third Corps, observing the enemy until the corps, by its advance from Mount Gilead, shall again encounter the enemy's pickets. Generals Cox and Hascall will keep their skirmish lines, with very strong supports, well out toward the enemy. Orders for further movements will be given during the day.

By command of Major-General Schofield:

J. A. CAMPBELL,
Major and Assistant Adjutant-General.

GENERAL ⎰ HDQRS. DEPT. AND ARMY OF THE TENN.,
FIELD ORDERS, ⎱　　　　　*Near Widow Forsyth's,*
No. 12.　　　　*On Campbellton Road, Ga., August 27, 1864.*

While the general commanding assures the officers and men of this army of his appreciation of the very satisfactory manner in which the late delicate and important movements have been made, he desires to call the attention of corps, division, brigade, and regimental commanders, in our future movements in the face of the enemy, to the necessity of keeping the columns well closed up, and preventing straggling by proper rear guards.

2. The artillery especially requires notice, and chiefs of artillery will be held responsible that their batteries are kept constantly closed up, receiving the individual attention of their commanding officers wherever bad places in the roads shall be likely to occasion delay.

3. At the hour of retreat to-day there will be a roll-call in every regiment, battery, and detachment of this command, when every absentee will be accounted for and patrols sent out to pick up stragglers and men who have fallen by the way, weary from the march.

4. The attention of corps commanders is called to the orders requiring the pioneer corps to accompany the advance of the column, in order thoroughly to repair the roads, and so complete their work that the command can move on without delay.

By order of Maj. Gen. O. O. Howard:

WM. T. CLARK,
Assistant Adjutant-General.

SPECIAL ⎰ HDQRS. DEPT. AND ARMY OF THE TENN.,
FIELD ORDERS, ⎱　　　　　*Near Widow Forsyth's,*
No. 111.　　　　*On Campbellton Road, August 27, 1864.*

Maj. Gen. John A. Logan, commanding Fifteenth Army Corps, will cause two bridges across each of the creeks, Camp and Wolf, to be immediately constructed at suitable points in his front.

II. Maj. Gen. F. P. Blair, commanding Seventeenth Army Corps, will cause two bridges across each of the creeks, Camp and Wolf, to be immediately constructed at suitable points in his front.

III. Brig. Gen. T. E. G. Ransom, commanding Left Wing, Sixteenth Army Corps, will direct the pioneer corps of his command, in charge of Lieutenant-Colonel Tiedemann, to report forthwith to Major-General Blair for temporary duty.

IV. In accordance with instructions from headquarters Military Division of the Mississippi, this army will move to-morrow at 7 a. m., in two columns, to the vicinity of New Hope Church, situated between Fairburn and Red Oak. The right column will comprise the Seventeenth Corps, Major-General Blair, followed by the Left Wing, Sixteenth Corps, Brigadier-General Ransom; the left column, the Fifteenth Corps, Major-General Logan, followed by the general train and a brigade from Left Wing, Sixteenth Army Corps, as rear guard. The routes are being reconnoitered, and will be indicated before the hour of march. Corps and division commanders will familiarize themselves as much as possible with all the roads in their front. In addition to the permanent guard the Left Wing, Sixteenth Army Corps, Brigadier-General Ransom commanding, will furnish a rear guard of one brigade for the general train.

General Kilpatrick will move in such a manner as to cover the right, and, if possible, mask the movement so that the infantry will not be noticed.

*   *   *   *   *   *   *

VII. Major-General Blair will, at the hour heretofore ordered, move forward with his command, followed by Left Wing, Sixteenth Army Corps, Brigadier-General Ransom commanding, on the direct road in his front toward Sidling, or Shadna, on the West Point railroad (the same heretofore noted as New Hope).

2. Major-General Logan will at the same hour move forward with the left column on the road in his immediate front, passing by or near Sewell's, and pursuing a route to the left of that followed by Major-General Blair. He will construct a road to move on beyond Sewell's, should no practicable route from that point be discovered. The command will go into position to the left of Fairburn, about one-third the distance between that point and Red Oak. The routes to be pursued and the positions to be occupied are indicated on the accompanying map.

By order of Maj. Gen. O. O. Howard:

WM. T. CLARK,
Assistant Adjutant-General.

SPECIAL FIELD ORDERS, {   HDQRS. 15TH ARMY CORPS,
                                 In the Field, on Wolf Creek, Ga.,
No. 88.   }   *August 27, 1864.*

I. Brig. Gen. William Harrow, commanding Fourth Division, will extend his picket-line on the left in a northeasterly direction to Camp Creek, and join on the right with the picket-line of Brig. Gen. W. B. Hazen, commanding Second Division.

II. Maj. Gen. P. Joseph Osterhaus will connect his picket line on the left with that of Brig. Gen. W. B. Hazen, and on the right with that of the Seventeenth Army Corps.

III. The picket-line must be thrown well forward, and the pickets instructed to be unusually vigilant. Division picket officers must make frequent visits to the picket-lines of their respective commands and see that the duty is performed properly.

*   *   *   *   *   *   *

VII. In accordance with instructions from headquarters Department and Army of the Tennessee, the command forming the left column will move at 7 a. m. to the vicinity of New Hope Church, situated between Fairburn and Red Oak.

First. Maj. Gen. P. Joseph Osterhaus' command will have the advance and will be followed by the commands of Brigadier-Generals Hazen and Harrow respectively.

Second. Ten wagons of ammunition, the ambulance and medicine wagons, will follow each division. All other wagons will follow the corps in the order of march superintended by the chief quartermaster of the corps.

Third. Brig. Gen. William Harrow will detail two regiments as train guard, to be disposed at proper intervals through the train. The ranking officer of the two regiments selected will have charge of the entire guard and train and will see that it is kept well closed up.

Fourth. Division commanders must cause their troops to march in good order and keep well closed up, and to this end will designate a staff officer to ride along the line of march frequently and give notice to rigade commanders of any break that may occur in their lines, with rders to at once close it up by marching in quick, and if necessary in louble quick, time.

Fifth. Straggling must under no circumstances be allowed. Division ommanders must give the most stringent instructions regarding it, for hey will themselves be held responsible here. Each regiment should letach a small rear guard, under an officer who can be relied on to revent it in his command.

Sixth. The route to be taken will be indicated before the hour of narch.

By order of Maj. Gen. John A. Logan:

R. R. TOWNES,
Assistant Adjutant-General.

SPECIAL FIELD ORDERS, } HDQRS. LEFT WING, 16TH A. C.,
                             Near Campbellton Road, Ga.,
No. 72.   }   *August 27, 1864.*

*　　　*　　　*　　　*　　　*　　　*　　　*

II. In carrying out the provisions of Special Field Orders, No. 111, extract IV, headquarters Department and Army of the Tennessee, the Second Division, Brig. Gen. J. M. Corse commanding, will take the advance, following closely in rear of the Seventeenth Corps. Brig. Gen. J. W. Fuller, commanding Fourth Division, will designate one brigade of his command to act as rear guard for the general train, which moves in the left column, in rear of the Fifteenth Corps. Brig. Gen. J. W. Fuller, with his command, will follow the Second Division, General Corse commanding, with the exception of the ordnance trains, which will move in the immediate rear of each division. All teams will move in rear of the Fourth Division in the same order of march as divisions. Brig. Gen. J. W. Fuller will designate two regiments to act as rear guard to these trains and to gather up all stragglers.

By order of Brig. Gen. T. E. G. Ransom:

J. W. BARNES,
Assistant Adjutant-General.

SPECIAL ORDERS, } HDQRS. SEVENTEENTH ARMY CORPS,
No. 214.   }   *In the Field, Ga., August 27, 1864.*

In order to carry out Special Field Orders, No. 111, extract IV, headquarters Department and Army of the Tennessee, the following dispositions will be made:

First. Brig. Gen. Charles R. Woods, commanding Third Division, will have the advance, and will move his command promptly at 7 a. m. to-morrow, on the direct road to New Hope Church.

Second. The Fourth Division, Brig. Gen. Giles A. Smith commanding, will follow immediately in the rear of the Third Division.

The route will be indicated by a member of the staff of the major-general commanding.

By command of Maj. Gen. F. P. Blair:

ROWLAND COX,
Assistant Adjutant-General.

NEAR WEST POINT RAILROAD,
August 28, 1864—4 p. m.
(Received 29th.)
Maj. Gen. H. W. HALLECK,
Washington, D. C.:

Army of the Tennessee is on the West Point railroad near Fairburn; Army of the Cumberland is on the same road at Red Oak; and that of the Ohio will be to-night at Camp Creek. Enemy has made no serious opposition to our movement.

W. T. SHERMAN,
Major-General.

HEADQUARTERS DEPARTMENT OF THE CUMBERLAND,
Near Cook's House, August 28, 1864.
Maj. Gen. W. T. SHERMAN,
Commanding Military Division of the Mississippi:

GENERAL: I have General Davis in position on commanding ground, his left resting on the railroad, his line extending south to within a mile of the Jonesborough road, from New Hope or Fairburn. I suppose it runs nearly east and west. General Morgan has a strong picket on that road, and General Davis' right flank is completely covered by the breaks of the ground and General Morgan's picket. General Stanley has been ordered to post his pickets on the north of the railroad, his left extending toward Mims' house, and covering the road by which the troops marched. The trains are getting into position on the right and rear of our position. Major-General Howard is about a mile in rear of our right. Will we march to-morrow, or will we remain here to destroy the railroad? I had almost forgotten to report that General Morgan's picket officer on the Jonesborough road reports that the woman living on that road at his picket-post says that a considerable body of rebel cavalry had passed there, and that they had informed her that the rebel army was moving toward Jonesborough.

Very respectfully, yours, &c.,

GEO. H. THOMAS,
Major-General, U. S. Volunteers, Commanding.

HDQRS. MILITARY DIVISION OF THE MISSISSIPPI,
In the Field, Red Oak, Ga., August 28, 1864—6.45 p. m.
Major-General THOMAS,
Commanding:

GENERAL: We will remain here to-morrow. I wish the railroad thoroughly destroyed as far forward as possible, and to the rear until you meet General Howard's troops. Let the destruction be so thorough that not a rail or tie can be used again. My own experience demonstrates the proper method to be: To march a regiment to the road, stack arms, loosen two rails opposite the right and two opposite the left of the regiment, then to heave the whole track, rails and ties, over, breaking it all to pieces, then pile the ties in the nature of crib work and lay the rails over them, then by means of fence rails make a bonfire, and when the rails are red-hot in the middle let men give the rail a twist, which cannot be straightened without machinery. Also fill up some of the cuts with heavy logs and trunks of trees and branches and cover up and fill with dirt. Please give minute instructions on this subject to-night, and have the work commenced as early in the morning as possible, taking proper precaution also to guard against attack on either the working parties or the general position. General Howard has received similar instructions and General Schofield will be moved to your left front.

W. T. SHERMAN,
Major-General, Commanding.

HEADQUARTERS DEPARTMENT OF THE CUMBERLAND,
Red Oak, Ga., August 28, 1864.

Maj. Gen. D. S. STANLEY,
Commanding Fourth Army Corps:

GENERAL: I have the honor, by direction of the major-general commanding, to inclose you an official copy of a letter received from Major-General Sherman for your information and direction.* In addition or explanation the major-general commanding directs that you throw forward one division of your corps on the left of the railroad as far to the front as possible, and while care should be exercised that it be not suddenly attacked, your whole line will needs be guarded against such a movement on the part of the enemy. General Davis will throw forward a division on the right of the railroad. The track will be effectually destroyed from your most advanced position as far back as the line now held by General Howard. The major-general commanding directs that when the rails are red-hot in the center of the rail one soldier can take hold of each end, and by giving it a twist it will prevent its use again without first being rerolled. The present opportunity to break the railroad effectually should not be passed by unimproved.

I am, general, very respectfully, your obedient servant,

ROBT. H. RAMSEY,
Assistant Adjutant-General.

HEADQUARTERS FOURTH ARMY CORPS,
Near Red Oak Station, Ga., August 28, 1864—11.30 p. m.

Brigadier-General KIMBALL,
First Division, Fourth Army Corps:

GENERAL: The general commanding directs that you readjust your lines to-morrow morning, and build a strong barricade along your front. We will remain in our present position to-morrow. He also directs that you instruct Colonel Taylor to report with his brigade to General Wood to-morrow, to assist him in destroying the track of the Atlanta and West Point Railroad. Have these troops make preparations to perform such duty as soon as rations are issued to them in the morning.

Very respectfully, your obedient servant,

J. S. FULLERTON,
Assistant Adjutant-General.

---

* See next, *ante.*

HEADQUARTERS FOURTH ARMY CORPS,
Near Red Oak, Ga., August 28, 1864—11.30 p. m.

General NEWTON,
   Second Division, Fourth Army Corps:

GENERAL: We will remain here to-morrow. You will readjust your lines early in the morning and construct strong barricades in your front.

By order of Major-General Stanley:

J. S. FULLERTON,
Assistant Adjutant-General.

HEADQUARTERS FOURTH ARMY CORPS,
Near Red Oak, Ga., August 28, 1864—11.45 p. m.

Brigadier-General WOOD,
   Commanding Third Division:

Herewith inclosed please find copy of instructions from Major-General Sherman in reference to destroying the track of the Atlanta and West Point Railroad.* In accordance therewith, and with instructions received from department headquarters, you will throw forward two brigades of your division and Taylor's brigade, of General Kimball's division (which will report to you for duty to-morrow), "on the left of the railroad, as far to the front as possible," and thoroughly destroy the railroad track. "Care should be exercised that you be not suddenly attacked." You will take with you one battery and leave behind all pack-mules and teams, shelter-tents, &c., so that the troops may move as light as possible. Your camp will be guarded during your absence by the brigade you leave behind. Also instruct the commanding officer of such brigade to construct strong barricades along your front after you have readjusted your lines, early to-morrow morning. General Schofield will cover your left flank.

By order of Major-General Stanley:

J. S. FULLERTON,
Assistant Adjutant-General.

HEADQUARTERS DEPARTMENT OF THE CUMBERLAND,
Red Oak, August 28, 1864.

Maj. Gen. J. C. DAVIS,
   Commanding Fourteenth Army Corps:

GENERAL: I have the honor, by direction of the major-general commanding, to inclose you an official copy of a letter received from Major-General Sherman for your information and direction.* In addition or explanation the major-general commanding directs that you throw forward one division of your corps on the right of the railroad as far to the front as possible, and while care should be exercised that it be not suddenly attacked, your whole line will needs be guarded against a similar movement on the part of the enemy. General Stanley will throw a division forward on the left of the railroad. The track will be effectually destroyed from your most advanced position as far back as the line now held by General Howard. The major-general commanding directs that when the rails are red-hot in the center of the rail one soldier can

----

* See p. 688.

take hold of each end, and by giving it a twist it will prevent its use again without first being rerolled. The present opportunity to break the railroad effectually should not be passed by unimproved.

I am, general, very respectfully, your obedient servant,

ROBT. H. RAMSEY,
Assistant Adjutant-General.

HEADQUARTERS FOURTEENTH ARMY CORPS,
Red Oak Station, Ga., August 28, 1864.

Brig. Gen. W. P. CARLIN,
Commanding First Division, Fourteenth Army Corps:

The general commanding directs that at an early hour to-morrow morning you send out your largest brigade upon the railroad with instructions to make a reconnaissance to your front and to destroy the road as effectively and as far as possible, and that you send another brigade to the rear with orders to destroy the road thoroughly in that direction. The general also wishes you as early as possible to open a wagon road from your lines to the cleared farm land in your rear upon the south side of the railroad.

Very respectfully, your obedient servant,

A. C. McCLURG,
Assistant Adjutant-General and Chief of Staff.

HDQRS. MILITARY DIVISION OF THE MISSISSIPPI,
In the Field, near West Point Railroad, August 28, 1864—4 p. m.

General SLOCUM,
Bridge:

Army of the Tennessee is on the West Point railroad near Fairburn, Cumberland at Red Oak, and Ohio will be on Camp Creek to-night. We will break it good and move on to the other at once. Keep me advised of all things of interest, if possible, via Campbellton, and when you feel strong at the bridge give a help to Marietta. Order as many stores to your position as possible.

W. T. SHERMAN,
Major-General, Commanding.

HEADQUARTERS TWENTIETH CORPS,
Chattahoochee River, August 28, 1864.

Lieut. M. J. KELLY,
Chief of Couriers:

LIEUTENANT: Your note of this morning is just received. General Slocum is absent from headquarters along the lines. The firing yesterday was at Turner's Ferry. The enemy's cavalry, with a section of artillery, appeared in front of Ward's division and fired a few rounds, which were returned. After a slight skirmish with our infantry they retired, and all has been quiet since. They have made no demonstrations on Williams' division at the railroad crossing, though their cavalry picket along the front of that division. On the 26th, Geary's division, at Pace's Ferry, had a sharp skirmish with cavalry (dismounted), but nothing since. The demonstration of yesterday amounted to nothing— merely reconnoitering to ascertain whether or not Turner's Ferry was held by us. The enemy have cavalry on all the roads leading from the river to Atlanta. Our positions at each of the three ferries have been strengthened so as to be perfectly safe, and we have one brigade on the north side of the river at this point, which occupies a portion of the old rebel works, and completely protects the depot and trains here from any attack in the rear. Colonel Minty has one regiment of cavalry up the river from here toward Roswell Factory and two regiments at Sandtown. The enemy's cavalry hold Roswell. Their force there is supposed to be about 400. They scout down the river as far as Soap Creek. A patrol this moment returned reports the enemy in front of Ward's division withdrawn. The patrolling party, starting from Turner's Ferry, went out on the road to Atlanta three miles, took a road to the left, and came in to our lines again at this point. The general will, I presume, make a reconnaissance to-morrow morning. Is it your intention to keep open the communication by courier line to this point via Sandtown?

    Yours, respectfully,

H. W. PERKINS,
Assistant Adjutant-General.

(Forwarded by General Thomas to General Sherman.)

HEADQUARTERS DEPARTMENT OF THE CUMBERLAND,
Red Oak, Ga., August 28, 1864.

Col. H. LE FAVOUR,
    Commanding Reserve Brigade:

    COLONEL: The major-general commanding directs that you place your brigade on the railroad early to-morrow morning just in front of your camp, for the purpose of tearing up the track and effectually destroying the road by burning ties and twisting the rails. Your brigade will destroy to the rear, working along until it meets with General Howard's troops, which will approach you from the rear. General Howard's troops are now about one mile and a half back. By heating the rails red-hot in the center, one soldier taking each end can give them such a twist as will effectually prevent them being used again without first being rerolled.

    I have the honor to be, colonel, very respectfully, your obedient servant,

ROBT. H. RAMSEY,
Assistant Adjutant-General.

CARTERSVILLE, GA., *August 28, 1864—3.30 p. m.*

Col. O. H. LA GRANGE,
    Commanding Second Brigade:

    General Smith says citizens report a large body of rebels two miles and a half east of this point, and desires 100 men sent to occupy the road where it intersects the railroad between here and Allatoona. Send out the men immediately and let them hold this point, and from time to time report anything they may observe. Our pickets at Allatoona were fired on this afternoon, killing 2, wounding 2.

    I am, colonel, your very obedient servant,

E. M. McCOOK,
Brigadier-General, Commanding.

AUGUST 28, 1864—12 m.

General SHERMAN:

The enemy is forming outside of his works in front of Cox as if to attack. A brigade is formed, and more can be seen coming out of the woods. I will inform you more definitely soon. I have not been able to commence my movement until now on account of the roads being blocked. I will now wait until I see the meaning of this movement of the enemy.

J. M. SCHOFIELD,
Major-General.

AUGUST 28, 1864—1.30 p. m.

General SHERMAN:

The force which appeared in Cox's front was, I think, only a brigade. It disappeared in the woods near the Newnan road. Quite a large militia force has been moving to our left during the morning and occupying our old works on the north side of Utoy. This is what I make out of all reports. I am going on with my movement.

J. M. SCHOFIELD,
Major-General.

HEADQUARTERS ARMY OF THE OHIO,
In the Field, Mount Gilead, August 28, 1864.

Major-General SHERMAN,
    Commanding Military Division of the Mississippi:

GENERAL: I occupy the works vacated by General Stanley, with my left resting at Mrs. Holbrook's. The enemy made a demonstration upon Cox's right about noon, but got back into his works as quickly as possible upon finding that we were in force. We then withdrew without annoyance. General Garrard is on my left, keeping pace with me and covering the trains. If I do not hear from you before morning, I will move out early on the road taken by Wood this evening until I connect substantially with General Thomas (preserving a front toward East Point) or until I receive your orders. My movement will have to be governed somewhat by the trains, for there is still a vast part of them in this valley.

Very respectfully,

J. M. SCHOFIELD,
Major-General.

HDQRS. MILITARY DIVISION OF THE MISSISSIPPI,
In the Field, Red Oak, Ga., August 28, 1864—6.45 p. m.

Major-General SCHOFIELD,
    Commanding, &c.:

GENERAL: You had better move your trains by the middle road of the three in front of Mount Gilead Church. It will come out at Red Oak where there are cleared fields of corn—this is the same by which General Thomas moved his trains, and they report it very good. Move your troops by Redwine's across Camp Creek to Oliver's house, and thence to General Stanley's left, about a mile from Oliver's house, leaving a strong left flank near the Oliver house. Instruct General Garrard to feel eastward from the Oliver house and to reconnoiter well to the east and north, reaching, if possible, the point marked on our map as Trimble's Mill.

W. T. SHERMAN,
Major-General, Commanding.

HEADQUARTERS ARMY OF THE OHIO,
In the Field, Ga., August 28, 1864.

Brigadier-General GARRARD,
   Commanding Cavalry Division, Army of the Cumberland:

GENERAL: I send you a map showing my present position, and from which you can see what my probable movement will be to-morrow. General Thomas is now on the railroad about Red Oak, and General Howard has crossed it, between Red Oak and Fairburn. To-morrow I shall probably move to or near the railroad via Mims' and Trimble's. With the aid of Colonel Garrard you will, I think, be able to keep up connection with my left, and cover all roads on which army trains are moving. This being the object, it does not matter about preserving your line so far advanced as it is now. As fast as you have to gain ground to the right to keep pace with my movement, and the trains get out of your way, you can draw back your line until it rests along Camp Creek instead of Utoy. I would like, however, to have the Sandtown road covered during to-morrow if practicable, on account of some forage trains which I hope will arrive by that route. Please arrange with Colonel Garrard as to the position of the line which he shall hold. The cavalry ought to be pretty strong immediately on my left. If anything occurs to modify the proposed movement for to-morrow, I will inform you in the morning.

   Very respectfully, your obedient servant,

J. M. SCHOFIELD,
Major-General, Commanding.

HDQRS. DEPARTMENT AND ARMY OF THE TENNESSEE,
On the West Point Railroad, August 28, 1864.

Maj. Gen. W. T. SHERMAN,
   Commanding Military Division of the Mississippi:

GENERAL: Arrived at 11 o'clock this a. m., and troops now going into position.

   Very respectfully, your obedient servant,

O. O. HOWARD,
Major-General.

P. S.—General Kilpatrick arrived before 8 a. m.; encountered considerable cavalry, which he drove back.

O. O. H.

HDQRS. MILITARY DIVISION OF THE MISSISSIPPI,
August 28, 1864.

General HOWARD:

   General Thomas' column is on the railroad at Red Oak also; communicate with him up the Newnan road. Do the job of tearing up, burning, and twisting in the most approved style. You can't do too much of it. I don't think the enemy yet understand our movement.

They have made no effort to stop us, only cavalry holding the road. Schofield reports a force which he thinks may threaten him. In case of heavy battle up our way come up the Newnan road.

> W. T. SHERMAN,
> *Major-General.*

HDQRS. MILITARY DIVISION OF THE MISSISSIPPI,
In the Field, Red Oak, Ga., August 28, 1864—6.45 p. m.
Major-General HOWARD, *Commanding, &c.:*

GENERAL: Colonel Wilson is here. I wrote you by Captain Knox. Our movement has been slower on the left on account of the proximity to the enemy, and a necessity for greater caution. General Thomas is in position, his two corps crossing the railroad and facing Atlanta. General Schofield still remains about Mount Gilead Church. We will remain on the road to-morrow, and break it in the most thorough manner possible. General Thomas will work forward and break to you. I want you to do the best job of railroad destruction on record, using General Kilpatrick to cover you while at work, and to explore roads to the east and make such reconnaissances toward Campbellton as would be useful to us in the future; also fill up some cuts in the railroad with logs and trees covered with dirt, so we may rest perfectly satisfied as regards the use of this railroad during the remainder of this campaign. It is more important that each bar of iron should be heated and twisted than a great amount of imperfect work done, for if the iron can be used again in this wooded country ties can be easily supplied.

Yours, &c.,

> W. T. SHERMAN,
> *Major-General, Commanding.*

HEADQUARTERS FIFTEENTH ARMY CORPS,
In the Field, near Fairburn, Ga., August 28, 1864.
Brig. Gen. WILLIAM HARROW, *Comdg. Fourth Division:*

GENERAL: The major-general commanding directs that as soon as your troops have a little rest and get some coffee, you march a brigade or more to the railroad and commence its destruction at the right of General Osterhaus' line and extend to our picket-line toward Atlanta. The work must be done complete by burning the ties and warping, twisting, and bending the iron in such a manner as to preclude its future use. The telegraph poles will be cut down and burned and the wire broken in pieces and carried off a considerable distance from the road into the woods and, if possible, concealed. The execution of this order will be reported in writing to these headquarters.

By order of Maj. Gen. John A. Logan:

> R. R. TOWNES,
> *Assistant Adjutant-General.*

HDQRS. THIRD CAV. DIV., DEPT. OF THE CUMBERLAND,
Shadna Church, August 28, 1864—6 p. m.
Lieut. Col. W. T. CLARK,
Assistant Adjutant-General, Army of the Tennessee:

COLONEL: My command is in position on the right of General Blair, with one brigade thrown forward on the Jonesborough road. My lines extend along from the front of this brigade across the road and railroad to a point about half a mile from the road. My artillery is in position, covering the country in the direction of Jonesborough and Fairburn. I have cut a road from the rear and center of my command through the country, striking the road upon which we advanced this morning in rear of your headquarters. I await further orders.

I am, colonel, very respectfully, your obedient servant,

J. KILPATRICK,
Brig. Gen. of Volunteers, Comdg. Third Cavalry Division.

LOUDON, *August 28, 1864.*

Capt. W. P. AMMEN, *Assistant Adjutant-General:*

By dispatch per courier all was quiet at Kingston up to 6 p. m. last evening. Major Reeves had sent steamer to Chattanooga with dispatches to General Steedman, informing him of strength of enemy and their probable course, which he thought would be Murfreesborough, and that they would reach there in about four days. No fears are felt for safety of Kingston. Re-enforcements sent last night. All quiet here.

M. L. PATTERSON,
Lieutenant-Colonel, Commanding.

CAMP ON CHATTAHOOCHEE, *August 28, 1864—8 p. m.*
(Received 12.10 a. m. 29th.)

Maj. THOMAS T. ECKERT:

Officers in from front report General Thomas' headquarters near Red Oak, and army in position on Macon railroad, having found but few Johnnies and met with no serious resistance. One hundred prisoners have arrived here. Slocum is in command Twentieth Corps. No news from Wheeler. Railroad is repaired nearly to Athens, Tenn. I go front to-morrow.

J. C. VAN DUZER.

HEADQUARTERS FOURTH ARMY CORPS,
Mount Gilead Church, Ga., August 28, 1864—5.45 a. m.

Orders of the day for the Fourth Army Corps for August 28, 1864: The corps will be ready to move at 7 a. m., but it will not move until further orders are given. General Newton's division will lead, General Wood's will follow, then General Kimball's. The line of march will be directly southward to the railroad. The two batteries formerly attached to the Second Division will accompany it. One battery will accompany each of the other divisions. Headquarters trains will follow the divisions to which they belong. All other trains and the surplus artillery will move on the road to the right of the road on which the troops march. On this road the artillery will move first, then the hospital trains, then the ammunition trains, then the general supply train. These trains will move in the order in which the divisions march, and they will be conducted by Captain Schoeninger, assistant chief quartermaster. Fifteen ambulances and five ammunition wagons will accompany each division on the march.

By order of Major-General Stanley:

J. S. FULLERTON,
Assistant Adjutant-General.

Supplement.

6.15 A. M.

Orders of the day are changed, in this, that General Kimball's division will lead, followed by General Newton, then General Wood. General Kimball will take the two batteries formerly attached to his division; General Newton will take but one battery with him.

By order of Major-General Stanley:

J. S. FULLERTON,
Assistant Adjutant-General.

SPECIAL ⎫ HDQRS. DEPT. AND ARMY OF THE TENN.,
FIELD ORDERS, ⎬　　　　*Near Shadna Church,*
No. 112. ⎭　　*On West Point Railroad, Ga., August 28, 1864.*

Corps commanders will direct all empty wagons and surplus animals in their commands, not necessary for immediate use, to be sent at daylight to-morrow, in charge of a competent officer, back to the old corral at Chattahoochee railroad bridge, there to remain until further orders. When forage arrives at that point these teams will be loaded and sent forward if communication is opened and intact, which fact will be learned from Major-General Slocum, commanding Twentieth Corps.

2. No more grain will at present be issued in this command except for artillery and riding horses and the animals belonging to the ordnance trains; all other animals must obtain subsistence from the country. Quartermasters will be governed accordingly.

II. This army will move forward in two columns to-morrow at 7 a. m. in the following order:

1. Maj. Gen. John A. Logan, commanding Fifteenth Corps, will pursue the direct route toward Jonesborough, crossing Pond Creek and Shoal Creek, aiming to reach the vicinity of Renfroe Place.

2. The Left Wing, Sixteenth Corps, Brigadier-General Ransom commanding, will have the advance of the right column, moving on a road to the right of that pursued by the Fifteenth Corps, and followed by the Seventeenth Corps, Major-General Blair commanding. Should the column of General Ransom at any point intercept the column of the left, he will construct a road to the right, pursuing a line of march converging toward Renfroe Place. The trains in charge of the chief quartermaster will follow the Fifteenth Army Corps, and a brigade from the Seventeenth Army Corps will form the rear guard. Major-General Blair will accordingly detail a brigade to report to Capt. J. T. Conklin, chief quartermaster at these headquarters, at 6 a. m. to-morrow, to relieve the brigade from the Left Wing, Sixteenth Army Corps, now the rear guard of the train. The accompanying map will indicate the route to be followed. Brig. Gen. J. Kilpatrick, commanding cavalry division, will make the same disposition of his command as of to-day, conforming his line of march to that pursued by this army.

III. Capt. William Kossak, aide-de-camp, is relieved from duty as engineer in charge of pontoon train. He will turn the command of the pioneers over to Lieutenant Shaffer, who will report to Captain Woodward, who will assume command of the train. Captain Kossak will then without delay report to Major-General Blair, commanding Seventeenth Army Corps, for assignment to duty as chief engineer.

IV. In accordance with instructions from Major-General Sherman, the movements indicated in Special Field Orders, No. 112, extract II, of this date, from these headquarters, are suspended, and will not be made until further orders.

V. Maj. Gen. John A. Logan, commanding Fifteenth Corps, will immediately direct the officer in charge of the guards for the trains of his corps to throw out a strong line of pickets well to the east and north of his trains in order to prevent any cavalry dash by the enemy upon them. General Logan will direct the officer in command of the guard in future to report through these headquarters to the chief quartermaster, in order that he may be advised upon what troops he may depend for the proper protection of the trains under his charge.

By order of Maj. Gen. O. O. Howard:

WM. T. CLARK,
Assistant Adjutant-General.

SPECIAL FIELD ORDERS, }   HDQRS. FIFTEENTH ARMY CORPS,
          No. 89.   }   *Near Fairburn, Ga., August 28, 1864.*

*   *   *   *   *   *   *

II. In pursuance of orders this command will move forward at 7 a. m. to-morrow on the direct route toward Jonesborough, crossing Pond Creek and Shoal Creek, aiming to reach the vicinity of Renfroe Place.

III. Brig. Gen. W. B. Hazen's command will have the advance, and will be followed by the commands of Brig. Gen. William Harrow and Maj. Gen. P. Joseph Osterhaus, respectively.

IV. The same general disposition of trains as indicated in Special Field Orders, No. 88, of yesterday, will be observed.

V. Major-General Osterhaus will dispose a sufficient number of troops, with the wagons moving immediately in rear of the column, to protect them.

VI. The rule relating to straggling must be regarded strictly.

VII. Division commanders are hereby directed to act in compliance with instructions contained in Special Field Orders, No. 112, Department and Army of the Tennessee, herewith inclosed.*

VIII. In accordance with instructions from department headquarters, the movements indicated in Special Field Orders, No. 89, extract II to VI, of this date, from these headquarters, are suspended, and will not be made until further orders.

IX. Brig. Gen. William Harrow, commanding Fourth Division, will forthwith throw out a strong line of pickets well to the east and north of the general supply train parked immediately in rear of department headquarters, in order to prevent any cavalry dash by the enemy upon them.

By order of Maj. Gen. John A. Logan:

R. R. TOWNES,
Assistant Adjutant-General.

[AUGUST 28, 1864.—For General Orders, No. 13, headquarters Seventeenth Army Corps, conferring medals of honor, see Part III, p. 556.]

---

* See p. 697.

SPECIAL ORDERS, }   HDQRS. SEVENTEENTH ARMY CORPS,
    No. 215.   }   *In the Field, Ga., August 28, 1864.*

I. This command will move forward at 7 a. m. to-morrow. The Fourth Division, Brig. Gen. Giles A. Smith commanding, will have the advance, and will move promptly at the hour indicated, following the Left Wing of the Sixteenth Army Corps. The Third Division, Brig. Gen. C. R. Woods •commanding, will follow immediately in rear of the Fourth.

II. Brig. Gen. Giles A. Smith, commanding Fourth Division, will cause one of the brigades of his command to report to Capt. J. T. Conklin, chief quartermaster, Department and Army of the Tennessee, at 6 a. m. to-morrow, for the purpose of relieving a brigade of the Left Wing, Sixteenth Army Corps, on duty as guard for train. General Smith will please report to these headquarters the brigade assigned to this duty.

By command of Maj. Gen. F. P. Blair:

ROWLAND COX,
Assistant Adjutant-General.

HDQRS. MILITARY DIVISION OF THE MISSISSIPPI,
In the Field, Red Oak, Ga., August 29, 1864—8 p. m.

Major-General THOMAS,
    Commanding Army of the Cumberland:

GENERAL: I have seen General Howard. You will move to-morrow for Shoal Creek Church and on to the road leading from Decatur to Fayetteville, half way between Morrow's Mill and the Renfroe Place (Couch's). Move the head of your column by Mrs. Long's place, taking care to leave room for General Schofield to pass the same point up toward Morrow's Mill. Please report to me if Generals Davis or Stanley moved toward East Point far enough to secure the road by which I design General Schofield to move, viz, from D. Mims' up along the railroad to the road represented as leading down to Mrs. Long's. General Howard starts at 7 a. m. I would like you to reach Shoal Creek Church as early as 10 a. m. at furthest, to cover General Howard's movement, who will, if possible, reach Jonesborough to-morrow.

Yours, &c.,

W. T. SHERMAN,
Major-General, Commanding.

HEADQUARTERS DEPARTMENT OF THE CUMBERLAND,
Red Oak, August 29, 1864.

Maj. Gen. W. T. SHERMAN,
    Commanding Military Division of the Mississippi:

GENERAL: Your note of this evening received. I presume that Davis moved sufficiently far toward East Point to secure the road you speak of. General Carlin reports having destroyed the road two miles above his camp, which must have taken him above that point. The head of my column will be at Shoal Creek Church by 8 a. m., unless strongly resisted. My columns will move by Mrs. Long's place and cover the Decatur and Fayetteville road.

Yours, respectfully,

GEO. H. THOMAS,
Major-General, Commanding.

HEADQUARTERS DEPARTMENT OF THE CUMBERLAND,
Red Oak, August 29, 1864.

Maj. Gen. D. S. STANLEY,
Commanding Fourth Army Corps:

GENERAL: The major-general commanding directs that you move your column at 6 a. m. to-morrow from its present position by the road leading past Ballard's, Godby's, and Miller's to Mrs: Long's, thence to the Decatur and Fayetteville road, and take up a position on the left of the Fourteenth Army Corps and covering the above-named road. Your wagons will move by the road which will be taken by the Fourteenth Corps, and which crosses the railroad a short distance southwest of Red Oak and which runs in nearly a direct line to Long's. Inclosed I send you a copy of the instructions given to General Davis.* After taking up your position you will connect by your pickets with General Davis on your right and feel for the Twenty-third Army Corps on your left.

Yours, very respectfully,

WM. D. WHIPPLE,
Assistant Adjutant-General.

HEADQUARTERS FOURTH ARMY CORPS,
Red Oak, August 29, 1864—9 p. m.

Brigadier-General WHIPPLE,
Chief of Staff:

The occupation of the troops of this corps to-day consisted in adjusting and barricading the lines occupied by the corps last evening, and in breaking up the railroad toward East Point. The latter was done by Brig. Gen. T. J. Wood with two brigades, Post's and Knefler's, of his division, and Taylor's brigade, of Kimball's division. In conjunction with General Carlin's division General Wood thoroughly destroyed the railroad three miles in advance of our lines. We met only a few cavalry skirmishers. As, from information received from citizens and contrabands, the point reached by the working party was two miles and a half from the rebel lines, it was not deemed advisable to push farther forward. Three men of Kimball's division, who had a pass to go out for roasting-ears, to keep behind the force on the railroad, were captured by the enemy.

Very respectfully, your obedient servant,

D. S. STANLEY,
Major-General.

HEADQUARTERS FOURTEENTH ARMY CORPS,
Red Oak Station, August 29, 1864.

[Brig. Gen. WILLIAM D. WHIPPLE:]

GENERAL: I have the honor to report that during to-day my command lay in position, its line running north and south, with the left resting near Red Oak Station. During the morning my First Division, General Carlin, destroyed the West Point railroad from two miles in his front to about one mile in his rear, where he found the road destroyed by the troops of General Howard. General Carlin's troops

---

found the enemy in an intrenched position between two and three miles in his front. Two different regiments were sent out upon reconnaissance upon the front and right of General Morgan, one of which supported the troops of General Carlin, and returned at 2 p. m., when they returned. The other, the Tenth Michigan, marched a little south of east as far as the Shoal Creek Church, and cutting out a road to that point, or near it, for the troops to march upon in the contemplated movements of to-morrow, they met the enemy's cavalry in some force and drove them back beyond the church. The Twenty-first Wisconsin, accompanied by Lieutenant Carney, of my staff, was sent out upon a road lying south of my right, and running a little south of east, keeping nearly parallel with the route of the Tenth Michigan and striking the Jonesborough or Flat Shoal road near Dodd's house. It also skirmished slightly with rebel cavalry, inflicting some damage upon them, but losing none themselves.

My loss during the day is only 1 man missing.

I am, very respectfully,

JEF. C. DAVIS,
Brevet Major-General.

HEADQUARTERS DEPARTMENT OF THE CUMBERLAND,
Red Oak, Ga., August 29, 1864.

Maj. Gen. J. C. DAVIS,
Commanding Fourteenth Army Corps:

GENERAL: The major-general commanding directs that to-morrow morning at 6 o'clock you move your corps from your present position to Shoal Creek Church and, if no serious resistance is offered you, on to Couch's, taking up a position near that place and connecting by your pickets with the Fourth Corps, which will be on your left, and the Army of the Tennessee on your right. Your wagons will be moved by the road indicated by you running to the right of and in the same direction as that taken by your troops, and at night parked in rear of the corps.

Very respectfully, your obedient servant,

WM. D. WHIPPLE,
Assistant Adjutant-General.

HDQRS. FIRST DIVISION, FOURTEENTH ARMY CORPS,
August 29, 1864.

Capt. A. C. MCCLURG,
Asst. Adjt. Gen., Hdqrs. Fourteenth Army Corps:

CAPTAIN: I have the honor to report to the general commanding the corps that his instructions concerning the destruction of the railroad have been executed. It is thoroughly destroyed for at least two miles above my camp, about half a mile having been destroyed by General Wood's division, Fourth Corps. The cavalry pickets of the enemy were driven back a mile, when a considerable force was met in fortifications. This was as far as prudence would permit me to go with one brigade. The railroad thus embraced within our lines was as much as two brigades could destroy by 2 p. m. to-day, when I withdrew the whole force; the men being much fatigued.

Very respectfully, your obedient servant,

W. P. CARLIN,
Brigadier-General, Commanding.

HEADQUARTERS TENTH MICHIGAN INFANTRY,
In Camp, near East Point, Ga., August 29, 1864.

Col. CHARLES M. LUM,
    10th Michigan, Comdg. 1st Brig., 2d Div., 14th Army Corps:

COLONEL: In accordance with orders and instructions received from General Morgan, I moved my regiment in nearly an easterly direction for about two miles through plantations and open timber. I then moved about east of southeast for near one mile, striking the Fairburn road about one-quarter of a mile below Shoal Creek Church. As we came in sight of the road at Cole's, we found a small force of the enemy (about twenty-five). Our skirmishers charged across an open field for about 300 yards. The rebels started for their horses and we fired on them. They ran, leaving a portion of their horses, saddles, and arms. I found that we had struck the rear guard of a cavalry force that commenced passing the church at 8 a.m. The last of the column passed at 11.45 a.m. I threw out skirmishers in rear and flankers and took position on the ridge at the church. The enemy moved down in line extending across the road and field into the timber on either side, covering the trail on which we advanced. I found on inquiry from my guide that we could get back by moving on the Fayette and Atlanta road. I moved out on this road about one mile and a half, turned to the left, and struck our outward path at Kimberly's plantation. I then cut the road out for about one mile and a half toward the church, leaving about three-quarters of a mile uncut, but plainly blazed. We found the enemy in squads along the road on our return march. Captured 1 prisoner, who reports that Hardee's corps moved down on the Montgomery railroad to-day.

I have to report the capture of 8 horses, 7 mules, and 9 guns. We destroyed about 20 guns. The cavalry force was represented as consisting of Armstrong's brigade and three regiments of Martin's brigade.

I am, colonel, very respectfully, your obedient servant,

                        H. S. BURNETT,
            Major, Commanding Tenth Michigan Infantry.

                    AUGUST 29, 1864—6.30 p.m.

Major-General SLOCUM, *Marietta:*

The following just received, with request that an answer be returned by bearer, after which the courier line is to be withdrawn until the movement is over:

                    RED OAK, *August 29, 1864.*

General SLOCUM:

The major-general commanding directs that you assume command of and collect together all stragglers who are to be found in your vicinity. Those that are armed, organize for the defense of the tête-de-pont; those that are unarmed put to work upon the defenses. The same will apply to detachments of convalescents, &c., en route to join their regiments. He also directs that you keep out pickets and watch well the movements of the enemy, and should he leave Atlanta, to occupy the place by, say, one division, if you can do so without endangering the safety of the tête-de-pont. It seems impossible that the rebels should be able to carry away all their artillery and ammunition, and if you cannot hold the place you may possibly destroy this artillery and ammunition.

                    WM. D. WHIPPLE,
                  Assistant Adjutant-General.

If you will telegraph an answer I will have it sent forward to-night so that it will get through.

                    H. W. PERKINS,
                  Assistant Adjutant-General.

TELEGRAPH OPERATOR,
   Bridge:

You had better ask the operator of Marietta if General Slocum is still there. He may have left there to return here; if so this dispatch need not be sent. Please send me word by the bearer if you reach the general there.

H. W. PERKINS,
Assistant Adjutant-General.

HEADQUARTERS TWENTIETH ARMY CORPS,
   Chattahoochee River, August 29, 1864—8 p. m.

Brigadier-General WHIPPLE,
   Chief of Staff:

GENERAL: I have the honor to acknowledge the receipt of your communication of to-day from Red Oak. At the time of its reception General Slocum was, and still is, absent at Marietta, where he has gone to make a personal inspection of the defenses. Your letter was telegraphed to him. A copy of his reply is herewith inclosed. In reference to the stragglers and convalescents, your order has been anticipated. The enemy have retired from our immediate front, and are now picketing in our old line of works about Atlanta. A reconnaissance will be sent out to-morrow toward Atlanta to enter the place if possible. Our position here has been so strengthened that it may be considered perfectly safe.

I am, general, very respectfully, your obedient servant,

H. W. PERKINS,
Lieutenant-Colonel and Assistant Adjutant-General.

[Inclosure.]

MARIETTA, *August 29, 1864.*

Col. H. W. PERKINS:

Write to General Thomas that I have collected and armed all convalescents and stragglers; that our position is a very strong one; that I will keep a close watch in the direction of Atlanta and try to carry out his orders. Tell him I am now at Marietta, but will return to the bridge to-night.

H. W. SLOCUM,
Major-General.

NASHVILLE, *August 29, 1864.*

Brig. Gen. W. D. WHIPPLE,
   Assistant Adjutant-General:

A courier in at Gallatin from Carthage reports Wheeler at Sparta with 12,000 men and six pieces of artillery. General Granger reports a part of Roddey's and Forrest's force across the river near Savannah, with nine regiments near Tuscumbia, preparing to cross at Bledsoe.

L. H. ROUSSEAU,
Major-General.

NASHVILLE, TENN., *August 29, 1864.*

Brigadier-General WHIPPLE:

General Steedman telegraphs that some 3,000 or 4,000 of Wheeler's force were reported north of Kingston yesterday morning, moving toward Sparta and McMinnville.   General Granger telegraphs that Roddey with 3,000 men and nine pieces of artillery is preparing to cross the Tennessee in boats, and, if possible, at the Shoals.

                                    LOVELL H. ROUSSEAU,
                                               Major-General.

                                    NASHVILLE, TENN., *August 29, 1864.*
Brig. Gen. H. P. VAN CLEVE,
          Murfreesborough:

A courier in at Gallatin from Carthage reports Wheeler at Sparta. Keep scouts out on the road to Lebanon as far up as Jefferson Crossing, ten or twelve miles.   A scout has been sent from here to Lebanon.

By command of Major-General Rousseau:
                                    B. H. POLK,
                              Major and Assistant Adjutant-General.

                                    NASHVILLE, TENN., *August 29, 1864.*
Brig. Gen. R. S. GRANGER,
          Decatur:

A courier just in at Gallatin from Carthage reports Wheeler at Sparta, with large force and six pieces of artillery.   No orders have been given to Colonel Spalding since he was ordered to send the two regiments to Decherd, of which order you were at once notified.   You will be notified when orders are given direct to your troops.

By command of Major-General Rousseau:
                                    B. H. POLK,
                              Major and Assistant Adjutant-General.

                                    NASHVILLE, TENN., *August 29, 1864.*
                              (Received at Tullahoma 8.45 p. m.)
Major-General MILROY:

A courier from Carthage to Gallatin reports Wheeler at Sparta, with a large force and six pieces of artillery.   What is the force at Duck River, Elk River, and at the Tunnel?   They should be increased.   The force at Decherd should be sent to Elk and Duck Rivers.   Send the two pieces of artillery formerly at Elk River back to that place.

By command of Major-General Rousseau:
                                    B. H. POLK,
                              Major and Assistant Adjutant-General.

                                    NASHVILLE, TENN., *August 29, 1864.*
Maj. Gen. R. H. MILROY,
          Tullahoma:

General Steedman will send 200 men to Stevenson, 200 to the Tunnel, and 300 to report to you at Tullahoma; strengthen the force at Duck River and Elk River.   General Steedman reports the enemy 2,000 strong near Pikeville, moving down the Sequatchie Valley.   Keep your cavalry well in hand.

By command of Major-General Rousseau:
                                    B. H. POLK,
                              Major and Assistant Adjutant-General.

HDQRS. DEFENSES NASHVILLE AND CHATTANOOGA R. R.,
Tullahoma, Tenn., August 29, 1864—11 p. m.

Col. W. J. CLIFT, *Commanding Second Brigade Cavalry:*

COLONEL: A telegram just received from Major-General Rousseau ordering you back to this place and Decherd. You will remain at Manchester till morning, then fall back to this place with half of your force, sending the other half to Decherd from Manchester. Send forward couriers immediately upon the receipt of this to recall Major Waters and the ammunition wagon sent from here this evening. If you leave Manchester in the morning before Major Waters reaches you leave one or two companies there to support him. Keep us advised by couriers of the movements of the enemy.

By command of Major-General Milroy:

JNO. O. CRAVENS,
Assistant Adjutant-General.

NASHVILLE, *August 29, 1864.*

Major-General STEEDMAN :

Please send 200 men to Stevenson, 200 to the Tunnel, and 300 to report to General Milroy at Tullahoma, and if you can spare it, one regiment to Bridgeport. General Milroy telegraphs that his cavalry has engaged the enemy at McMinnville.

L. H. ROUSSEAU,
Major-General.

NASHVILLE, *August 29, 1864.*

Maj. Gen. J. B. STEEDMAN:

A courier in at Gallatin from Carthage reports Wheeler at Sparta with 12,000 men and six pieces of artillery. He is evidently coming this way. General Granger reports a part of Roddey's and Forrest's force across the river, near Savannah, with nine regiments near Tuscumbia, preparing to cross at Bledsoe. Can you not loan me a small force to strengthen Stevenson and the road this side?

L. H. ROUSSEAU,
Major-General.

HDQRS. MILITARY DIVISION OF THE MISSISSIPPI,
In the Field, August 29, 1864.

Major-General SCHOFIELD:

I have been down to General Howard. The railroad is well broken down two miles and a half below Fairburn, which is six miles from here. Several cuts are also filled with trees, rocks, and earth. We will move to-morrow for our next objective. Howard will move for Jonesborough; Thomas via Shoal Creek Church, Mrs. Long's, and Couch's, on the road from Morrow's Mill, toward Fayetteville. I want you to cover the movement with your two divisions and the cavalry of Garrard. It may be best for you to occupy the parapets made by Stanley and Davis until your trains are well toward Shoal Creek Church, and then move toward any strong position south and west of Morrow's Mill, covering the Decatur road and in communication with Thomas at Couch's. I don't know how far toward East Point Davis and Stanley went to-day, but if you can I want you to gain your position via D.

Mims' and the road across by Mrs. Long's. If you find this difficult, maintain a defensive position till the trains are well out, and then follow Thomas' movement as far as Long's, and thence to the one described.

W. T. SHERMAN,
Major-General.

HEADQUARTERS CAVALRY DIVISION,
August 29, 1864.

[General SCHOFIELD:]

GENERAL: My headquarters are at Wait's house, on the south side of Camp Creek, and my two brigades lie to the left, along the creek. I cover all the roads and ground from Mims' around to the Sandtown road, a mile west of Patterson's, and also picket to my left rear. My line is along outside of your position last night, and the Sandtown road is watched at three points. Colonel Garrard's regiment, which was on my right, is camped near Mount Gilead Church, inside of my pickets, and near a regiment of mine on picket. I do not know where the colonel is, and have not communicated with him. A few rebels are now in the fort, on the old line near the Sandtown road. Small parties have run in on me on all roads during the day, but no indication of any large force. The road to Sandtown is not now safe except for armed men, and wagons should have guards. As your left is not as far beyond Mims' as I expected, I am closer in on you than I otherwise would have been.

Very respectfully, your obedient servant,

K. GARRARD,
Brigadier-General.

HEADQUARTERS ARMY OF THE OHIO,
In the Field, Ga., August 29, 1864.

Brigadier-General GARRARD,
  Comdg. Cavalry Division, Army of the Cumberland:

GENERAL: I send you the plan of operations for to-morrow, and a map which will enable you to understand it. In conforming to the infantry movement you will doubtless have to draw back your line somewhat and contract your left, or at least weaken it. All roads leading toward East Point should be held by the cavalry in strong force, as soon as abandoned by the infantry, and as far forward as practicable. I think you might during the day, as the infantry move off, draw back your main force to the railroad above Red Oak, and picket along Camp Creek with a strong head picket toward East Point. Colonel Garrard's force will, I think, be sufficient to operate between the railroad and the left of the infantry.

Very respectfully, your obedient servant,

J. M. SCHOFIELD,
Major-General, Commanding.

HDQRS. DEPARTMENT AND ARMY OF THE TENNESSEE,
Near Shadna Church, on West Point Railroad, Ga.,
August 29, 1864.

Maj. Gen. JOHN A. LOGAN, *Commanding Fifteenth Army Corps:*

GENERAL: The major-general commanding directs me to state that Brigadier-General Ransom has been ordered to proceed with his command along the railroad to Fairburn, for the purpose of destroying the road. He directs that you make the destruction of the railroad within your lines thorough and complete by bending and twisting every rail, rendering it totally unfit for further use, burning every tie, and filling up the cuts with logs, stones, and earth—in short making a complete annihilation of the road.

Very respectfully, your obedient servant,

SAML. L. TAGGART,
Assistant Adjutant-General.

(Same to General Blair, commanding Seventeenth Army Corps.)

HDQRS. THIRD DIVISION, SEVENTEENTH ARMY CORPS,
Near Shadna Church, August 29, 1864.

Col. A. J. ALEXANDER,
Assistant Adjutant-General, Seventeenth Army Corps:

I have the honor to report that my command destroyed road as follows: First Brigade, 420 yards, ties burned, rails doubled; Second Brigade, 200 yards, ties all burned, rails all broken; Third Brigade, 270 yards, ties burned, rails doubled; total, 890 yards. In addition the cuts in rear of my line are being rapidly filled with brush and earth mixed. The destruction is complete.

I am, colonel, very truly, yours,

CHAS. R. WOODS,
Brigadier-General.

HEADQUARTERS FOURTH ARMY CORPS,
Near Red Oak Station, Ga., August 29, 1864—8 p. m.

Orders of the day for the Fourth Army Corps for to-morrow, August 30, 1864:

The corps will move to-morrow morning, starting at 6 a. m. General Newton's division will lead, followed by General Wood, and then General Kimball. The line of march will be pointed out to General Newton in the morning. Ten ammunition wagons, fifteen ambulances, two wagons for division headquarters, and one wagon for each brigade headquarters will follow each division on the march. All other wagons and ambulances will move on the same road taken by the general supply train. The artillery of the corps will move with the troops on the same road. Captain Bridges, chief of artillery, will distribute it in the column, placing with each division the batteries formerly attached to the same. The trains of the corps will follow the Fourteenth Army Corps on the same road in the order in which the divisions to which they belong will march. The ammunition train will move first, followed by the ambulances, then the hospital trains, then the general supply train. Surplus limbers will move with the artillery; ordnance train and surplus headquarters trains will move with the division ambulance trains. The artillery wagons will move with the general supply train.

By order of Major-General Stanley:

J. S. FULLERTON,
Assistant Adjutant-General.

Special Field Orders,) Hdqrs. Fourteenth Army Corps,
     No. 4.   }   *Red Oak Station, Ga., August 29, 1864.*

The movements of the corps to-morrow will be as follows :

General Morgan will move his division at 6 o'clock by the most direct road to Shoal Creek Church, and take position at that place. General Baird will move his division upon the same road, following General Morgan as soon as the road is clear, and prepared to support General Morgan's left, should resistance be met sufficient to render it necessary. General Carlin will move his division at 5.30 a. m. by a road starting near these headquarters and running to the right of and parallel to the one taken by the other two divisions, and intersecting the Jonesborough or Flat Shoal road at Dodd's house near the Shoal Creek Church. He will move prepared, in case of emergency, to support General Morgan's right. The head of the two columns of troops will if possible keep up constant communication. The artillery as assigned will accompany their respective divisions. On arriving at the church the troops will be massed on the best ground which presents itself for forming lines of battle, and will be held in readiness for a farther advance as soon as practicable roads can be found.

The ordnance and hospital trains and other wagons heretofore allowed to accompany the moving column will follow General Carlin's division in the following order: General Carlin's, General Morgan's, General Baird's. These will be followed by the general supply train of the corps.

By order of Bvt. Maj. Gen. J. C. Davis:

                  A. C. McCLURG,
          Assistant Adjutant-General and Chief of Staff.

———

Special Field Orders,) Hdqrs. Army of the Ohio,
     No. 97.   }   *Near Atlanta, Ga., August 29, 1864.*

I. The plan of operations for to-morrow is as follows: The Army of the Tennessee to move from Fairburn to Renfroe Place (near Jonesborough); the Army of the Cumberland, from Red Oak, via Shoal Creek Church, to Couch's; the Army of the Ohio, via Red Oak and Mims', by Mrs. Long's, to Murry's [Morrow's] Mill.

II. General Cox will follow immediately in rear of General Stanley, from his present position to Red Oak, then take the East Point road and move to the intersection of the Jonesborough road, a short distance beyond Mims'. He will go into position so as to cover the Jonesborough road, and fortify. General Hascall will follow General Cox to the position described above, pass him on the Jonesborough road, move to the intersection of the road from Shoal Creek Church to East Point, take position facing East Point and Rough and Ready, and fortify; General Cox will then pass General Hascall and move to Mrs. Long's, where General Hascall will join him. The divisions will then move together to Murry's [Morrow's] Mill. Colonel Garrard will follow the movement of the infantry, keeping connection with the infantry left and in conjunction with General Garrard, scouting thoroughly all roads leading toward the Macon railroad. The division ammunition and baggage trains will follow the troops. Other trains will follow the trains or troops of the Army of the Cumberland to Shoal Creek Church, where they will await further orders.

III. The following must be strictly observed in the movement of trains in connection with troops, viz : Where delay occurs at the head of the

column by skirmishing or otherwise, the trains will at once move into
park in the nearest open ground to the head of the train, leaving the
road free for the passing of troops. Artillery should in general observe
the same rule. In no case must artillery or wagons be permitted to
double up in the road or occupy it unnecessarily.

By command of Major-General Schofield:

J. A. CAMPBELL,
Major and Assistant Adjutant-General.

SPECIAL | HDQRS. DEPT. AND ARMY OF THE TENN.,
FIELD ORDERS, } *Near Shadna Church,*
No. 113. | *On West Point Railroad, Ga., August 29, 1864.*

*   *   *   *   *   *   *

IV. From a most reliable source a report has reached these headquarters that there has been from this army to-day between 1,500 or
2,000 stragglers, a great many of them teamsters, and that numbers
of them have been guilty of the vilest conduct, entering houses where
there were women and little children, and utterly destroying everything,
stealing knives, forks, and spoons, opening trunks, &c. Corps commanders will take measures and prevent conduct so shameful and so
disgraceful to our army. It is not the good soldiers who do these
things, but the vilest miscreants. Corps commanders will be sustained
in the infliction of punishment immediate and adequate to stop such
offenses.

V. This army will move forward to-morrow morning at 7 o'clock in
accordance with the instructions contained in Special Field Orders, No.
112, extract II, from these headquarters, of August 28, 1864.*

By order of Maj. Gen. O. O. Howard:

WM. T. CLARK,
Assistant Adjutant-General.

SPECIAL FIELD ORDERS, } HDQRS. FIFTEENTH ARMY CORPS,
No. 90. | *Near Fairburn, Ga., August 29, 1864.*

*   *   *   *   *   *   *

III. Paragraphs I, II, III, IV, V, and VI of Special Field Orders,
No. 89, from these headquarters, will be executed to-morrow. The command will therefore move as therein indicated at 7 a. m. August 30.

IV. Brigadier-General Hazen will, on moving out to-morrow morning, throw forward two regiments as advance guard and protect his
flank by strong lines of flankers.

*   *   *   *   *   *   *

By order of Maj. Gen. John A. Logan:

R. R. TOWNES,
Assistant Adjutant-General.

SPECIAL FIELD ORDERS, } HEADQUARTERS LEFT WING,
| SIXTEENTH ARMY CORPS,
No. 73. | *Near Shadna Church, Ga., August 29, 1864.*

On the march to-morrow the Second Division, Brig. Gen. J. M. Corse
commanding, will take the advance, moving promptly at 6.45 a. m.
The Fourth Division, Brig. Gen. J. W. Fuller commanding, will follow

* See p. 697.

immediately in rear of the Second Division. All trains will follow the Fourth Division, ordnance trains moving first, followed by headquarters and regimental trains in their regular order. A staff officer from each division will be detailed daily to superintend the movement of the trains, and will be held responsible for any unnecessary delay when on the march. The rear guard will be particularly instructed to pick up all stragglers. The Ninth Illinois, mounted, and the pioneer corps of both divisions, in charge of Lieutenant Beers, will report at these headquarters at 6.15 a. m. to-morrow. A report showing number of wagons in division ordnance trains, division and brigade headquarters and regimental trains, will be forwarded by division commanders to these headquarters to-morrow morning.

By order of Brig. Gen. T. E. G. Ransom:

J. W. BARNES,
Assistant Adjutant-General.

SPECIAL ORDERS,   }   HDQRS. SEVENTEENTH ARMY CORPS,
    No. 216.   }   *Shadna Church, Ga., August 29, 1864.*

*   *   *   *   *   *   *

III. In pursuance of orders from headquarters Department and Army of the Tennessee, Special Orders, No. 215, and Special Orders, No. 215, extract II, of August 28, 1864, from these headquarters, will be carried into effect to-morrow, all movements and dispositions to be made as therein ordered.

By command of Maj. Gen. F. P. Blair:

ROWLAND COX,
Assistant Adjutant-General.

HEADQUARTERS FOURTH ARMY CORPS,
Niles' House, near Flat Shoal Creek, Ga.,
August 30, 1864—8.20 p. m.

Brig. Gen. W. D. WHIPPLE,
   Chief of Staff, Department of the Cumberland:

GENERAL: I have the honor to report that this corps left its lines near Red Oak at 6 o'clock this a. m.; marched two miles up the Newnan road, turning at Ballard's house on the road to Mrs. Long's. One mile from the Ballard house we ran into the Fourteenth Corps, and were detained for three hours. After passing it we encountered the enemy's pickets about half a mile from Mrs. Long's house. We drove them off the Flat Shoal road, and they made a stand at Mann's house, where they were covered with rail barricades. We again drove them back. General Newton then placed his division in line of battle at Mann's house, facing northeast. I made arrangements to cover what I supposed to be the Decatur and Fayetteville and the Flat Shoal roads. I then rode over to General Baird's, at Couch's house, and made a reconnaissance of a line to connect with him by pickets. When I returned to General Newton he informed me that he had reliable information that the enemy was intrenched in his front and was in force. I then determined to place Generals Kimball's and Wood's divisions on his left. While making this formation I received instructions from Major-General Thomas to place these two divisions on the Decatur road, connecting with General Baird. I at once posted them in what I supposed to be the proper position (having received no instructions as to the direction of the line), by connecting with Baird's left, and then running my line across the Decatur road so that it faced northeast. General Newton reports that he has not yet been able to find General Schofield's right. General Newton's division is but one line. A boy, the son of a rebel soldier who lives in this neighborhood, and who left his father with the rebel troops this morning, states that they are in our front and have breast-works about Morrow's Mill and between the forks of the creek, over three miles long. This is also reported by two other citizens. A woman reports that it is Cheatham's division in our front, and that it came there last night. My position, with the exception of the connection between Generals Kimball and Newton, is strong.

Very respectfully, your obedient servant,

D. S. STANLEY,
Major-General.

HDQRS. SECOND DIVISION, FOURTH ARMY CORPS,
In the Field, August 30, 1864.

Lieut. Col. J. S. FULLERTON,
Asst. Adjt. Gen. and Chief of Staff, Fourth Army Corps:

COLONEL: I have the honor to report, for the information of the general commanding, that this afternoon Colonel Opdycke, commanding my First Brigade, made a reconnaissance, under instructions, on the Rough and Ready road. He discovered the enemy in respectable force three-quarters of a mile from my present position. They were well fortified and appeared very saucy and independent. The reconnoitering party were unable to determine whether the enemy were on this side of the creek or the other, although their force and works were in plain view. The pickets this afternoon report the enemy felling timber to the north. My proper front is almost directly east. A considerable force of the enemy's cavalry were discovered this afternoon near the house where General Stanley turned off to post me in my present position.

I have the honor to be, very respectfully, your obedient servant,

JOHN NEWTON,
Brigadier-General, Commanding.

HDQRS. SECOND DIVISION, FOURTH ARMY CORPS,
In the Field, August 30, 1864—8 p. m.

Lieut. Col. J. S. FULLERTON,
Asst. Adjt. Gen. and Chief of Staff, Fourth Army Corps:

COLONEL: I have the honor to report that Lieutenant-Colonel Olson, Thirty-sixth Illinois, of my division, reports that he saw a column of troops moving into position northeast of Mann's house at about sundown this evening. Colonel Opdycke, from his position, about 600 yards in advance of the works, heard the movement of artillery. The major-general commanding can judge whether this was General Schofield's troops or not. I incline to think it was not.

I am, sir, very respectfully, your obedient servant,

JOHN NEWTON,
Brigadier-General, Commanding.

HEADQUARTERS FOURTEENTH ARMY CORPS,
Near Couch's House, Ga., August 30, 1864—9 p. m.

Brig. Gen. W. D. WHIPPLE,
  A. A. G. and Chief of Staff, Dept. of the Cumberland:

GENERAL: I have the honor to report that at 5.30 o'clock this morning the First Division of my corps moved from its position in front of Red Oak Station to a road which runs in a southeasterly direction from a point south of Red Oak Station, and strikes the Flat Shoal road near the Rev. Mr. Dodd's house. Marching to this point the division moved upon the latter road to the Shoal Creek Church, which point it reached at 8.45 a. m. The Second Division, followed by the Third, moved at 6 a. m. upon a road leading to the front from the position occupied by the extreme right of the corps, running north of, but nearly parallel to, the one upon which the First Division moved. These roads converge at the Shoal Creek Church. The head of the column of the Second Division reached the church at 8.30 a. m., just fifteen minutes before the First Division appeared in sight. To this point the ammunition, hospital, and headquarters trains of the corps had moved in the rear of the First Division, followed by the corps supply trains. Resting for an hour at the church, the corps moved eastward toward Couch's house, the Second Division, followed by the First, moving upon one road, and the Third Division marching upon a road nearly parallel, but north of this one, and converging at Couch's. The Third Division being in advance, skirmished with the rebel cavalry, and drove them back without loss. The corps went into position a little in advance or eastward of the Jonesborough and Fayetteville road, the lines running nearly north and south, and the right being refused across the road. The left of the corps rests near Couch's house, and there connects with General Stanley's right. On arriving at our present position, two regiments were sent down the road to Renfroe's and opened communication with General Howard's forces at that point. The trains have made but little progress this side of the Shoal Creek Church, having been, as reported by some of the officers in charge, cut out of the road by the general supply trains of department headquarters and the pontoon train. Several of the pontoon wagons were stuck in the mud, blockading the road.

I am, general, very respectfully, your obedient servant,
                                      JEF. C. DAVIS,
                            Brevet Major-General, Commanding.

HEADQUARTERS TWENTIETH CORPS,
Chattahoochee River, August 30, 1864.

Brigadier-General WILLIAMS,
  Commanding First Division:

GENERAL: The major-general commanding directs that you order Brigadier-General Ruger to make this morning a reconnaissance toward Atlanta to develop the whereabouts of the enemy. He will take eight companies from each regiment of his brigade, and a battery of artillery will be ordered to report to him to accompany the reconnaissance. The general desires that he will start as soon as possible this morning.

I am, general, very respectfully, your obedient servant,
                                      H. W. PERKINS,
                              Assistant Adjutant-General.

HDQRS. THIRD DIVISION, TWENTY-THIRD ARMY CORPS,
August 30, 1864.

Major-General SCHOFIELD,
         Commanding, &c.:

SIR: I am now (1.15 p. m.) at the forks of the East Point road and the road crossing the railroad and leading to Widow Long's. The Fourth Corps is just ahead of me, and going on the latter road. I am going in position. The ground is not very good, and the connections with the Newnan road make the left especially weak. I shall keep as much reserve as I can consistently with covering the railroad and the little commanding ground on the left.

Very respectfully, your obedient servant,
                              J. D. COX,
                         Brigadier-General, Commanding.

HDQRS. THIRD DIVISION, TWENTY-THIRD ARMY CORPS,
August 30, 1864.

General M. S. HASCALL,
         Commanding Second Division:

I find the Fourth Corps is not all out yet, and have overtaken them less than half a mile from my former position. I was misinformed when I sent my message by your orderly, and hasten to correct it. I will send you word when they really get off.

Yours, &c.,
                              J. D. COX,
                         Brigadier-General, Commanding.

HEADQUARTERS ARMY OF THE OHIO,
In the Field, Ga., August 30, 1864.

Col. ISRAEL GARRARD,
         Commanding Cavalry Division, Army of the Ohio:

COLONEL: The commanding general desires you, if possible, to move from your present position, via Mims' and Trimble's Mill, down to the point at the intersection of the Jonesborough and East Point road, where you will meet the infantry, instead of following in the rear of the infantry, as directed in your orders of last night. Please report to the commanding general as soon as possible whether it is possible for you to march by the road above indicated, and, if you find it cannot be done, move as directed last night, in the rear of the infantry.

Very respectfully, your obedient servant,
                              J. A. CAMPBELL,
                         Major and Assistant Adjutant-General.

HEADQUARTERS ARMY OF THE OHIO,
In the Field, Ga., August 30, 1864.

Brigadier-General GARRARD,
         Commanding Cavalry Division, Army of the Cumberland:

GENERAL: The commanding general desires you to occupy, substantially, the present position occupied by his infantry, crossing the rail-

road, and all roads to the left of it. Colonel Garrard will cover all
roads between you and the infantry. The infantry will move out at
early daylight, say 4.30 a. m. to-morrow.

Very respectfully, your obedient servant,

WM. M. WHERRY,
Major and Aide-de-Camp.

HEADQUARTERS SECOND CAVALRY DIVISION,
On Camp Creek, August 30, 1864.

Brig. Gen. W. D. WHIPPLE,
Chief of Staff, Department of the Cumberland:

GENERAL: On leaving Decatur I was directed to send daily repor
to department headquarters under the impression that this was to
notify the chief of cavalry of my station daily. The only day one of
his staff officers has not been in my camp I reported by letter. Last
evening I received a note from Captain Ramsey, assistant adjutant-
general, saying that the commanding general wanted daily reports from
me. I have been in the rear, conforming my movements to the infantry and wagon trains, getting into position after night. Day before
yesterday my pickets were on the Sandtown and Atlanta road, just
south of Utoy Creek, and picketing beyond the creek up to Judge
Wilson's, and then back toward Sandtown, and connecting with left of
the infantry. Yesterday my line run farther south, but picketed on
the Sandtown road, where the trains of the Army of the Tennessee
crossed it. Last night my division camped on Camp Creek, and my
line runs from there out to the Campbellton road, and then leaves that
road and runs to my left and rear a mile west of Patterson's. The
three roads at Mims' are strongly picketed, and patrols go out in sight
of the Newnan road. Small parties run in on my pickets, but no large
force has as yet disturbed me. Guards should now be sent with ambulances or wagons going to Sandtown. It will not always be possible
for me to report at night, for it is often very late before I can report,
when I will report early next morning.

Very respectfully, your obedient servant,

K. GARRARD,
Brigadier-General, Commanding Division.

HDQRS. SECOND CAV. DIV., DEPT. OF THE CUMBERLAND,
Red Oak, August 30, 1864.

Brig. Gen. W. D. WHIPPLE,
Chief of Staff, Department of the Cumberland:

GENERAL: I have the honor to make my daily report. My command
is near this point. My pickets reach on the south side of Camp Creek
from Trimble's Mill to where the Campbellton road crosses the creek,
and then around on the West Point road far enough west to cover all
the roads used by trains. It is a very difficult matter for me to keep
informed of the movements of the army, as so many delays have
occurred. In the morning I examine the country in my front, then
judge of the probable advance of the trains, and establish my new
pickets. Then I move my command forward, and then withdraw the
old pickets. This keeps me occupied all day, and into the night some-

times, though I move but a few miles a day. Only small parties have struck my pickets. As General Schofield moves so far to the east of the roads used by trains I may have to divide my command to cover the rear. One of my brigades (Minty's) was left to patrol and guard the river toward Roswell and down to Sweet Water.

Very respectfully, your obedient servant,

K. GARRARD,
Brigadier-General, Commanding Division.

NASHVILLE, TENN., *August 30, 1864.*

Brig. Gen. W. D. WHIPPLE, *Assistant Adjutant-General:*

The enemy drove our small cavalry force from McMinnville last evening, and this morning a portion of the rebel command attacked and captured a part of our forces at Lebanon, put out there as a party for observation. I am unable yet to tell the number of the enemy or divine their exact intentions.

L. H. ROUSSEAU,
Major-General.

CHATTANOOGA, *August 30, 1864.*

Major-General SHERMAN:

Major-General Rousseau reports large force of enemy at Sparta, Tenn. Citizens from Sequatchie Valley report a force this side of Pikeville, coming down the valley. General Granger reports portion of Roddey's and Forrest's forces north of the Tennessee, near Savannah, with nine regiments preparing to cross at Bledsoe, near Tuscumbia. By request of Major-General Rousseau I have sent four regiments to be used by him to protect the road to Nashville. I can send more troops if he requires them. The Ninth Pennsylvania Cavalry is here; I shall detain it a few days. The Seventy-first Ohio Infantry proceeded to the front on the 28th instant.

JAMES B. STEEDMAN,
Major-General.

NASHVILLE, TENN., *August 30, 1864.*

Major-General MILROY, *Tullahoma:*

What news have you from the vicinity of Murfreesborough. Have you strengthened the force at Elk River and Duck River? The enemy were undoubtedly at Lebanon this morning. Keep scouts from your cavalry well out to give timely notice of their approach.

By command of Major-General Rousseau:

B. H. POLK,
Major and Assistant Adjutant-General.

NASHVILLE, *August 30, 1864.*
(Received at Tullahoma 10.50 p. m.)

Major-General MILROY:

General Steedman telegraphs that Wheeler's force, independent of Forrest and Morgan, is at least 6,000 strong, and artillery.

B. H. POLK,
Major and Assistant Adjutant-General.

MURFREESBOROUGH, *August 30, 1864.*
(Received at Tullahoma 4.23 p. m.)

Maj. J. O. CRAVENS,
    Assistant Adjutant-General:

A scout sent out this morning was fired on near Woodbury by a party of rebels. Citizens report the rebels moving this way, their force not known.

H. P. VAN CLEVE,
Brigadier-General.

NASHVILLE, TENN., *August 30, 1864.*

General R. H. MILROY, *Tullahoma:*

A report from Colonel Patton is that a company of East Tennessee cavalry was captured by the rebels near Lebanon at 3 o'clock this morning.

B. H. POLK,
Major and Assistant Adjutant-General.

AUGUST 30, 1864—1 a. m.

General GRANGER, *Decatur, Ala.:*

My scouts just come in and report that Wheeler's command will strike Elk River bridge and Sulphur trestle simultaneously at daybreak. I go in for one place and Colonel Campbell the other.

JOHN C. STARKWEATHER,
Brigadier-General, Commanding.

CHATTANOOGA, TENN., *August 30, 1864.*

General WHIPPLE:

I have just ordered General Smith to relieve Colonel Lowe and men in accordance with Major-General Thomas' instructions.

J. B. STEEDMAN,
Major-General.

MARIETTA, GA., *August 30, 1864—8.30 p. m.*
(Received 12 p. m.)

Maj. THOMAS T. ECKERT:

No news from Sherman to-day. Slocum pushed reconnaissance within two miles of Atlanta, finding only cavalry, and not much of that. He had only a brigade and moved slowly, but will know by daylight whether enemy still occupies Atlanta or not.

J. C. VAN DUZER.

LOUISVILLE, KY., *August 30, 1864—11.30 a. m.*

Maj. THOMAS T. ECKERT:

Portion of Wheeler's force said to be across Cumberland, and coming toward Gallatin, Tenn. Wheeler sent word to commander of post he had captured two companies of his command; would soon capture remainder.

S. BRUCH.

Circular.]   Headquarters Twentieth Corps,
Chattahoochee River, Ga., August 30, 1864.

Each division commander will to-morrow send out from his front at 6 a. m. a reconnoitering party of from 200 to 300 strong to feel carefully to the front and ascertain the position of the enemy. Immediately on the return of these parties a report of all information gained by them will be forwarded to these headquarters.

By command of Maj. Gen. H. W. Slocum:

H. W. PERKINS,
Assistant Adjutant-General.

Special Field Orders, ?   Hdqrs. Army of the Ohio,
No. 98.   )   *Red Oak, Ga., August 30, 1864.*

I. The troops will move promptly at 4.30 a. m. to-morrow—early daylight—by the right flank, in their present order, on the road to Shoal Creek Church. The skirmish line will be kept out well to the left and will move parallel to the column. At Mrs. Long's the head of the column will be turned toward Morrow's Mill, and the leading division—General Hascall's—will go into position on favorable ground on the road leading to Shoal Creek Church. If at any time during the march the enemy should appear on the flank the troops will immediately move into position under the direction of the division commanders and prepare to give battle. Whenever practicable the infantry will move through fields, leaving the road to the artillery, which will move up promptly so as to shorten the column as much as possible. The trains will take the right-hand road, about half a mile from General Hascall's present right, leading toward the Rev. Dodd's, and will move on that road until they find a road leading to the left toward the position likely to be occupied by the troops at Morrow's Mill. General Cox will send one regiment as rear guard to the train. Between the present position of the troops and the forks of the road the troops must keep to the left of the road to leave it free for the train. Colonel Garrard's cavalry will push out as far as practicable on all the roads to the left of the road on which the infantry moves, and will continue to occupy all the roads from the new position as far as the West Point railroad, connecting with General Garrard's cavalry, which will occupy the position now occupied by the infantry.

By command of Major-General Schofield:

J. A. CAMPBELL,
Major and Assistant Adjutant-General.

Couch's House, *August 31, 1864—8 a. m.*
(Received 5 a. m. September 9.)

Maj. Gen. H. W. Halleck,
Washington, D. C.:

At this time I would not suggest a change in the geographical lines of the Departments of the Ohio and the Cumberland because Generals Thomas and Schofield are now in actual battle and cannot give their attention to the necessary details. I will see both of them to-day and will then communicate my opinion. We reached the West Point railroad, and broke up twelve miles of it thoroughly; then marched on a big left-wheel for the Macon road, General Schofield on the left, aiming for Rough and Ready, General Thomas center, and General Howard right, aiming for Jonesborough. The left and center as yet have met little or no opposition, but General Howard has fought two brigades of cavalry all the way from Fairburn. Last night darkness overtook him within a mile of Jonesborough, having pushed the cavalry so close that he secured the Flint River bridge. To-day I press at all points, but expect to make a lodgment on the road at or below Jonesborough, when I propose to swing the whole army upon it and break it all to pieces. I expect, and am prepared for, hard fighting, and have the army well in hand.

W. T. SHERMAN,
Major-General.

HDQRS. MILITARY DIVISION OF THE MISSISSIPPI,
In the Field, August 31, 1864.
Major-General THOMAS,
Commanding Army of the Cumberland:

I have reports from Generals Howard and Schofield, and from a signal dispatch of the former I infer Hardee will attempt to-night to move back to Atlanta to form a junction with Hood. It also appears that Stanley ranks Schofield, raising that old question of who commands. Of course my decision is that the senior commission, which is Stanley's; but as my instructions have been made to Schofield, I wish you would make them to Stanley to move very early in the morning down on Jonesborough (or the enemy wherever he may be), breaking railroad as he moves south. I don't believe anybody recognizes how important it is now to destroy this railroad. Should it appear the enemy is trying to make a junction round by the east, we must strike him in motion.

I am, &c.,

W. T. SHERMAN,
Major-General.

HEADQUARTERS DEPARTMENT OF THE CUMBERLAND,
Renfroe's, August 31, 1864—7 p. m.
Major-General SHERMAN,
Commanding Military Division of the Mississippi:

GENERAL: What do you think of this: Let Stanley and Schofield, covered by Garrard, destroy the railroad to-morrow to their rear until they come down to Baird; then for me to draw off the Army of the Cumberland and throw it on the railroad east of Fayetteville, say at Lovejoy's, or some point below, Howard confronting and holding the enemy at Jonesborough. Prisoners taken by Stanley report five trains in Atlanta which cannot get out; they also confirm the report that the militia and probably one corps have been left in Atlanta. I understand that General Howard repulsed the enemy, inflicting a heavy loss upon him; if so, I think the move on Fayetteville would be eminently beneficial. I am happy to report that General Baird is also on the railroad; he reached it at 5 p. m., and set 400 men at work immediately to destroy the road. I think Hood has gone up or ordered to Macon.

Respectfully,

GEO. H. THOMAS,
Major-General, U. S. Volunteers, Commanding.

P. S.—All the prisoners captured by Baird say there are but two corps in Jonesborough. Baird has taken between 40 and 50 prisoners.

G. H. THOMAS,
Major-General, U. S. Volunteers.

HDQRS. MILITARY DIVISION OF THE MISSISSIPPI,
In the Field, August 31, 1864—9 p. m.

Major-General THOMAS:

Inasmuch as I have already given orders to Schofield, based on the idea that he and Stanley move down the railroad, breaking it, till they come to Baird and Davis, near Jonesborough, I think we had better adhere to that plan till we develop the first step in the enemy's game, after he knows we are between him and Atlanta. I wish you to order Kilpatrick the moment he learns the enemy has gone south to hurry to Fayette Station and Griffin, hang on the flanks of the enemy while we push him to the rear. I propose to go as far as Griffin, utterly destroying the road, and then act according to circumstances. I would rather you should follow the enemy as he retreats, leaving the Army of the Tennessee to swing by the right, and that of the Ohio by the left. I am glad to hear that Baird also is on the railroad, and now the sooner we get all our army together in close order the better. You may put Davis in on the left of Howard, ready for Baird and Stanley to come up along the railroad. If Hood remains in Atlanta and Hardee commands at Jonesborough the latter may attempt to get back to Atlanta, in which event he may to-night run up against Baird, who should be put on his guard. You may give all the necessary orders that will bring your command together to attack and pursue that part of the Confederate army now at Jonesborough by whatever road it takes, and I will give directions to the other armies to operate on its flanks. As soon as it is demonstrated on what road it retreats we can arrange to head it off. My own impression is that Hardee will try to join Hood in Atlanta. May send Schofield to-night, and I am anxious that Howard should keep in close contact. Audenried, of my staff, went about dark with orders to Schofield to the above effect, and for him and Stanley to work down the railroad to-night if possible, otherwise early in the morning. I will come down early also.

Yours, truly,

W. T. SHERMAN,
Major-General.

HDQRS. MILITARY DIVISION OF THE MISSISSIPPI,
In the Field, near Jonesborough, August 31, 1864—11 p. m.

Major-General THOMAS, *Commanding Army of the Cumberland:*

GENERAL: I wish you would instruct General Slocum at the bridge to feel forward to Atlanta, as boldly as he can, by the direct road leading from the bridge, and to send any cavalry force he can raise over toward Decatur to watch the movements of the enemy in that quarter. Advise him fully of the situation of affairs here, and assure him that we will fully occupy the attention of the rebel army outside of Atlanta.

Yours, truly,

W. T. SHERMAN,
Major-General, Commanding.

HEADQUARTERS FOURTH ARMY CORPS,
Near Morrow's Mill, August 31, 1864—8 p. m.

Brigadier-General WHIPPLE, *Chief of Staff:*

My corps moved to-day from its position on the road from Long's to Couch's to Morrow's Mill. Here we met the enemy in intrenchments very well finished, but occupied only by dismounted cavalry. We drove these out, and as soon as General Schofield's forces had come up pushed out for the Macon railroad, which we reached at the big bend about the same time or a little later than General Cox. My corps is in position in strong line, the left resting upon the railroad, my right at Morrow's Mill. The working parties will go to work to burn up the track at 3 o'clock in the morning, unless I receive other instructions.

Very respectfully,

D. S. STANLEY,
Major-General.

HEADQUARTERS DEPARTMENT OF THE CUMBERLAND,
Renfroe's, August 31, 1864.

Maj. Gen. D. S. STANLEY,
Commanding Fourth Army Corps:

GENERAL: The major-general commanding directs that to-morrow morning early you commence the destruction of the Macon and Western Railroad in conjunction with General Schofield, who will receive orders from General Sherman. You will destroy as far as you can in the direction of Jonesborough, or until you meet with General Baird's division, of the Fourteenth Corps, which you will probably find engaged in the same work. Should you meet with or overtake General Baird, you will report for further orders. General Garrard has been ordered to cover the flank of your column during its march down the road.

Yours, very respectfully,

WM. D. WHIPPLE,
Assistant Adjutant-General.

P. S.—General Baird struck the railroad at 5 p. m. to-day and went to work immediately breaking the road.

HEADQUARTERS FOURTH ARMY CORPS,
Morrow's Mill, Ga., August 31, 1864.

General NEWTON:

You will send all the pioneers of your division, under charge of an energetic officer, to begin tearing up railroad track at 3 o'clock to-morrow morning, commencing on the left of the corps where we join General Schofield's corps, and working south; each division commander will send with his pioneers one regiment to protect the men while at work. The senior officer of the three regiments will command the whole. Have the details on the ground (left of General Wood's division) and at work by 3 a. m.

By command of Major-General Stanley:

WM. H. SINCLAIR,
Major and Assistant Adjutant-General.

(Same to Generals Kimball and Wood.)

HEADQUARTERS FOURTH ARMY CORPS,
Near Morrow's Mill, August 31, 1864—9.30 p. m.

Maj. Gen. J. M. SCHOFIELD:

GENERAL: I have reported my position to General Thomas, and will undoubtedly receive instructions from him. I have given orders to commence destroying the railroad at 3 a. m. As your movement up the road will separate us several miles, and as we are liable to attack in flank, I prefer to hold on to our intrenched lines until Cox returns from Rough and Ready, and is closed up in support; no time will be lost in the mean time, as I will have strong working parties.

Your obedient servant,

D. S. STANLEY,
Major-General.

HEADQUARTERS FOURTEENTH ARMY CORPS,
August 31, 1864—3 a. m.

[Brig. Gen. WILLIAM D. WHIPPLE:]

GENERAL: I will immediately order out a brigade to Renfroe's, and will report. Will order them to keep up connection with General Howard, and will order a report from those which have returned.

Very respectfully,

JEF. C. DAVIS,
Brevet Major-General, Commanding.

HEADQUARTERS ARMY OF THE CUMBERLAND,
Poplar Springs, Ga., August 31, 1864.

Maj. Gen. J. C. DAVIS,
Commanding Fourteenth Army Corps:

GENERAL: The major-general commanding directs that the following letter of instructions from Major-General Sherman be copied for your information and guidance:

HEADQUARTERS MILITARY DIVISION OF THE MISSISSIPPI,
In the Field, August 31, 1864.

General THOMAS:

I send you for perusal Howard's letter of 3 a. m.* He did not get the road, though I doubt not he is too close for the comfort of the enemy. He must not fail in this. Order one of Davis' divisions down at once to Renfroe's, and move all your trains well to your right, so that you can rapidly fling your whole command over to Jonesborough. Then let Davis send out from his front, obliquely to the right front, a strong skirmish line with supports, as though to reach the railroad three or four miles above Jonesborough. Have Stanley do the same toward, but below, Rough and Ready. Impress upon these commanders that it is not so necessary to have united lines, but rather columns of attack. We are not on the defensive, but offensive, and must risk everything rather than dilly-dally about. We must confuse the enemy. As soon as Schofield gets up I will put him against Rough and Ready till he meets formidable resistance.

W. T. SHERMAN,
Major-General, Commanding.

The messengers to Schofield are back and Stanley may look for him about Morrow's in two hours at furthest.

Yours, respectfully,

WM. D. WHIPPLE,
Assistant Adjutant-General.

(Same to General Stanley.)

---

* See p. 725.

HEADQUARTERS ARMY OF THE CUMBERLAND,
Couch's House, August 31, 1864.

Bvt. Maj. Gen. J. C. DAVIS,
Commanding Fourteenth Army Corps:

GENERAL: Direct General Morgan to move with his division at once
and take up a position on General Baird's right, on the east side of the
Rough and Ready and Jonesborough road, so as to threaten the Macon
railroad between Rough and Ready and Jonesborough. Threaten the
enemy strongly, but do not push so far as to give him an advantage.
In other words, do not go beyond supporting distance from General
Howard, in case the enemy should turn on you. Endeavor to communicate with General Howard by your right and rear, giving him your
position, and satisfying yourself with reference to his position on your
right. You need not be under much apprehension as regards your left,
as Generals Stanley and Schofield will be between you and Rough and
Ready, and covering the only practicable wagon route between Rough
and Ready and Jonesborough by which the enemy could move to attack
you. I wish General Morgan to be in position before sunset. General
Carlin will cover the trains completely at Renfroe Place.

Very respectfully, yours, &c.,

GEO. H. THOMAS,
Major-General, U. S. Volunteers, Commanding.

HEADQUARTERS ARMY OF THE CUMBERLAND,
Couch's House, August 31, 1864—5 p. m.

Brig. Gen. A. BAIRD:

GENERAL: General Schofield has possession of the railroad below
Rough and Ready, and by this time is strongly fortified, and has already commenced the destruction of the railroad. Make your position
strong, and then make a strong demonstration toward the road east of
you early to-morrow morning. You need not have much apprehension
as to your left, as Generals Schofield and Stanley will effectually cover
you in that direction. Keep a sharp lookout toward your right and
south, as the enemy still confronts General Howard. I have sent General Carlin to his relief, although I believe there is no necessity for it;
so you will have to make the most of your four brigades. Handle them
judiciously and energetically, and all will go well. If you think you
will need more ammunition send for it to Renfroe's, and get it up by
daylight to-morrow morning.

Respectfully, yours,

GEO. H. THOMAS,
Major-General, U. S. Volunteers, Commanding.

HEADQUARTERS FOURTEENTH ARMY CORPS,
At Renfroe's House, August 31, 1864.

[Brig. Gen. WILLIAM D. WHIPPLE:]

GENERAL: I have the honor to submit the following report of the
operations of the Fourteenth Corps during to-day: In obedience to instructions received from General Sherman, during the night, I sent one
of Carlin's brigades to take post at Renfroe's house to protect our trains
ordered to that point, which it did at daylight. In compliance with

orders from Major-General Thomas, commanding, I ordered General Baird to take two brigades of his own division and one of General Morgan's and make a reconnaissance and demonstration on the railroad in front of our position at Couch's house. This movement has been successful, and General Baird's division, with one brigade of Morgan's division, are now in position holding the railroad east of Couch's house. A few minutes after 3 o'clock an order was received to recall General Morgan (who had previously been directed to move to the support of General Baird, with his other two brigades), and to place him in position at Renfroe's house, in order to relieve Carlin, who was ordered to move rapidly to the support of General Howard, commanding the Army of the Tennessee, near Jonesborough. These movements were promptly executed. About dark General Carlin's division returned, and I ordered it to take position, occupying the works which they had last night built and held.

In compliance with orders my trains have been moved from their position of last night and parked in the field in the rear of Renfroe's house, where my headquarters now are. My troops have been ordered to be ready to march to-morrow morning at daylight.

I am, general, very respectfully, your obedient servant,

JEF. C. DAVIS,
Brevet Major-General, Commanding.

HEADQUARTERS FOURTEENTH ARMY CORPS,
Near Couch's House, Ga., August 31, 1864.

Brig. Gen. W. P. CARLIN,
Commanding First Division, Fourteenth Army Corps:

The general commanding directs that you move the remainder of your division to Renfroe's, with your trains, and take position east of that point, thoroughly covering and securing the cross-road which there converges. General Baird has been directed with his division to make a strong reconnaissance and demonstration toward the railroad in front of his position.

Very respectfully, your obedient servant,

A. C. McCLURG,
Assistant Adjutant-General and Chief of Staff.

HEADQUARTERS ARMY OF THE CUMBERLAND,
Couch's House, August 31, 1864.

General W. P. CARLIN,
Commanding First Division, Fourteenth Army Corps:

GENERAL: Move at once to the support of General Howard, on the Jonesborough road. Send forward a staff officer to General Howard's headquarters to receive instructions where you are to go to take your position in line.

Respectfully, yours,

GEO. H. THOMAS,
Major-General, U. S. Volunteers, Commanding.

HEADQUARTERS FOURTEENTH ARMY CORPS,
Near Couch's House, August 31, 1864.

Brig. Gen. J. D. MORGAN,
Commanding Second Division, Fourteenth Army Corps:

GENERAL: The general commanding directs that you order your reserve brigade to report at once to General Baird, to participate in a reconnaissance and demonstration which will be made this a. m. under his command to the front and right. General Carlin has been ordered to move his division to Renfroe's, and you will occupy and secure the works vacated by him.

Very respectfully, your obedient servant,
A. C. McCLURG,
Assistant Adjutant-General and Chief of Staff.

HEADQUARTERS FOURTEENTH ARMY CORPS,
Near Couch's House, Ga., August 31, 1864.

Brig. Gen. A. BAIRD,
Commanding Third Division, Fourteenth Army Corps:

The general commanding directs that with two brigades of your own division and one of General Morgan's, which will be ordered to report to you immediately, you make a reconnaissance and demonstration to the front and right of your present position toward the railroad above Jonesborough, in conformity with the following instructions from General Sherman, transmitted through General Thomas, which are copied for your information:

HEADQUARTERS MILITARY DIVISION OF THE MISSISSIPPI,
In the Field, Ga., August 31, 1864.

General THOMAS:

*   *   *   *   *   *   *

Order one of Davis' divisions down at once to Renfroe's, and move all your trains well to your right, so that you can rapidly fling your whole command over to Jonesborough. Then let Davis send out from his front, obliquely to the right front, a strong skirmish line with supports, as though to reach the railroad three or four miles above Jonesborough. Have Stanley do the same toward, but below, Rough and Ready. Impress upon these commanders that it is not so necessary to have united lines, but rather columns of attack. We are not on the defensive, but offensive, and must risk everything rather than dilly-dally about. We must confuse the enemy. As soon as Schofield gets up I will put him against Rough and Ready till he meets formidable resistance.

W. T. SHERMAN,
Major-General, Commanding.

The movement should begin immediately.
By order of Bvt. Maj. Gen. Jeff. C. Davis:
A. C. McCLURG,
Assistant Adjutant-General and Chief of Staff.

HEADQUARTERS FOURTEENTH ARMY CORPS,
Near Couch's House, Ga., August 31, 1864.

Brig. Gen. A. BAIRD,
Commanding Third Division, Fourteenth Army Corps:

I have just seen General Sherman, and he informed me that he desired you to push your reconnaissance with vigor. After crossing the creek you will deploy a heavy line of skirmishers, and push them forward to the wagon road over which the enemy's wagon train was passing this morning. Should you meet with no great resistance push on to the railroad. Support your skirmish line well with reserves and artillery. Leave a brigade in a good position to cover the bridge over which you expect to return.

I am, very respectfully,

JEF. C. DAVIS,
Brevet Major-General, Commanding.

HEADQUARTERS ARMY OF THE TENNESSEE,
August 31, 1864—3 a. m.

Major-General SHERMAN,
Commanding:

GENERAL: Kilpatrick made an attempt to get upon the railroad, but met with so strong resistance that he gave it up for daylight. He says Logan's center is about 800 yards from the depot. The town is to our right and the depot in the direct front. The Sixteenth Corps is on the west side of the river, and prolonging the line of Logan. The Seventeenth Corps did not get up; is three miles back. I intended to place it in position facing north, virtually prolonging Logan's left; it will move at daylight in the morning. My only exposure is in that direction. If you will push hard enough to prevent the enemy from striking me this side of Flint River it will be all right; my officers apprehend it more than I do. My information is that the enemy had here four brigades of infantry on our arrival, and more are coming. I understand your anxiety to get the road; no exertion will be spared as soon as we can see. The Seventeenth Corps will move up at daylight.

Respectfully,

O. O. HOWARD,
Major-General.

[Indorsements.]

Generals Thomas and Schofield, read and return.

SHERMAN.

HEADQUARTERS ARMY OF THE CUMBERLAND,
Poplar Springs, August 31, 1864.

This paper has been read, and your instructions will be carried out.

GEO. H. THOMAS,
Major-General, Commanding.

HDQRS. MILITARY DIVISION OF THE MISSISSIPPI,
In the Field, August 31, 1864—6 a. m.

General O. O. HOWARD:

I have yours of 3 a. m. I am satisfied you have as many men as can operate at that point now. Let Kilpatrick reach well to the right, break the telegraph, and take up a few rails, but I want you to get possession and fortify some one point of the road itself anywhere near Jonesborough. Davis is all ready with his whole corps to move to your assistance, and I will order him to feel forward toward a point north of Jonesborough. As soon as Schofield gets up I will put him and Stanley toward Rough and Ready, and Garrard's cavalry down toward Fayetteville. We must have that road, and it is worth to us a heavy battle, and make good all the ground you have, and if your guns command any reach of the road it will be a great gain, but we want the road itself. Keep me fully advised, and I will see that you are supported either by direct help or by auxiliary attacks above and below you, but understand that my hope of success rests mainly with you. I am in the dead certainty of having heavy masses in close support, which are soon to be intrenched. Let your trains come down well, close to your bridge, and I will move a division of Davis' to the forks—Renfroe's—to cover that point.

Yours,

W. T. SHERMAN,
Major-General.

HDQRS. DEPARTMENT AND ARMY OF THE TENNESSEE,
August 31, 1864—9.10 a. m.

Major-General SHERMAN,
Commanding Military Division of the Mississippi:

GENERAL: I have sent Kilpatrick to the right with all his cavalry; he has secured a bridge over the Flint River about a mile from rail-road. The enemy is shoving troops down here with great rapidity, and preparing, I think, to attack Logan's position. I have strengthened Logan by a division of Ransom's on the right, by a brigade of General Blair's on the left. It seems to me that it would be better to push General Davis straight to Flint River on my left. He cannot be far off from me. I have a battery being put in position, which will fire straight into the depot at a range of 600 yards, and another position where the trains can be seen passing. I propose to keep at work at them, but do not think I could carry any point of Logan's front by assault. If the enemy will attack, as I think he will, that will simplify the matter.

Respectfully,

O. O. HOWARD,
Major-General.

AUGUST 31, 1864—12.30 [p. m.].

General HOWARD:

Your dispatch is received. Of course, now an attack by you on Jonesborough is out of the question, but you can make that position impregnable, and we can operate beyond. Baird is now moving toward the road four miles north of you, and Schofield about the mills, which of course is the strongest part of the enemy's works. I expect Garrard's cavalry can be relieved of guarding Schofield's trains to-day, and I will send it to Kilpatrick. The enemy is too smart for us, and we may have to maneuver thus down to Macon. It may be that some accident will happen, of which we can take advantage. Get your guns in position and damage trains passing, but it is useless to waste ammunition on the depot already reported burned by Kilpatrick. I cannot move the troops 100 yards without their stopping to intrench, though I have not seen an enemy. I have got Baird across Flint River about due east of this point. Thomas is at Renfroe's, and will come to your aid if you need him, but I think you have as many men as can operate at that point, and as soon as I can hear from Schofield further I will commence to move toward Griffin, the next accessible point. I have no idea that Hardee will attack you, if you have any cover whatever. Get as many guns in as possible, so that by a simultaneous discharge you can knock a train to pieces at one discharge. It is only on condition that you can get on the road that I would put all of Thomas' troops on that side of the Flint.

Yours,

W. T. SHERMAN,
Major-General.

HDQRS. DEPARTMENT AND ARMY OF THE TENNESSEE,
August 31, 1864—3.45 p. m.

Maj. Gen. W. T. SHERMAN,
Commanding, &c.:

GENERAL: The enemy attacked us in three distinct points, and were each time handsomely repulsed.

Very respectfully, your obedient servant,

O. O. HOWARD,
Major-General.

Major-General Logan says the enemy made two distinct attacks on his lines and were repulsed.

O. O. H.

HDQRS. MILITARY DIVISION OF THE MISSISSIPPI,
In the Field, August 31, 1864.

Major-General HOWARD:

I have your dispatch. Hold your own. Carlin's division is near you. Schofield and Stanley are on the railroad two miles south of Rough and Ready; headed off a train of cars loaded with troops making south, so you have Hardee all right. Watch him close and be prepared with Davis to follow him. He must retreat to McDoncugh or down the road. I must interpose our whole army between Atlanta and the enemy now in Jonesborough. Let your whole command know and feel I am thinking of them, and that I have got the railroad above them.

Yours,

W. T. SHERMAN,
Major-General.

HDQRS. DEPARTMENT AND ARMY OF THE TENNESSEE,
Near Jonesborough, Ga., August 31, 1864.

Maj. Gen. W. T. SHERMAN,
Commanding Military Division of the Mississippi:

GENERAL: Your letter is received. I have the honor to report the following as the result of the day's operations: About 3 o'clock the enemy attacked the position of Major-General Logan and General Corse, who occupied the right of the line on the other side of Flint River, and was handsomely repulsed. He repeated the attack at three different points on the line with the same result. One division of the Seventeenth Corps, General Woods commanding, was moved across the river and went into position on the left. One of his brigades was attacked and the enemy repulsed promptly. Cleburne's division, failing to make any impression on the right of my line across the river, moved down to the bridge held by General Kilpatrick's cavalry, upon whom they advanced in three lines. The cavalry held their position until their ammunition was exhausted, when they retired across the bridge, but were not followed up, nor have they been by the enemy. Upon learning the situation of General Kilpatrick, General Giles A. Smith's division, of Blair's corps, was moved over to protect the train and to repulse any attack on my right. I directed General Carlin to cover the Fayetteville road so that my right flank and trains may be considered sufficiently protected. The First Regiment Missouri Engineers, which reported during the day over 1,000 strong, now occupies the works vacated by General Blair's command. I have published the contents of your very gratifying letter to this command. Inclosed I send you the latest dispatch from the signal officer. It would appear that the enemy contemplates making connection again with his forces at East Point or Atlanta.

I have the honor to be, very respectfully, your obedient servant,

O. O. HOWARD,
Major-General.

[Inclosure.]

LOOKOUT STATION, *August 31, 1864—6.10 p. m.*
Captain HOWARD:

A very strong column of the enemy is now moving to their right. Has been moving about three-quarters of an hour. They pass directly through town toward Atlanta.

FISH,
Lieutenant and Acting Signal Officer, Fifteenth Army Corps.

HDQRS. SIGNAL DETACH., FIFTEENTH ARMY CORPS,
Near Jonesborough, Ga., August 31, 1864.
Maj. Gen. JOHN A. LOGAN,
Commanding Fifteenth Army Corps:

SIR: I have the honor to submit the following as my report for the day. Lieutenant Fish, of this detachment, reports as follows:

In the morning Lieutenant Edge and self made a station of observation in a tall pine, where we had a good view of town and a portion of the enemy's lines, that fronting First and Fourth Divisions, Fifteenth Army C rps. In front of these divisions the enemy had massed a large force. In an open field fronting the First Division a line of battle was formed extending up into the timber to their left out of sight. A battery of four guns was with this line. Lieutenant Edge went down to the line to direct our battery in firing, I watching the shots and signaling to him the effect and range. While engaged in signaling to him this line of battle was formed, faced to the rear, and marched back to the edge of the timber about 100 yards, the battery put in position, and a barricade of rails made. Another column moved up and formed in their front and moved obliquely toward the right of First Division, Fifteenth Corps. A portion of their line was badly broken up by our shells and ran in wild confusion, but rallied on reaching cover, and reformed their lines. At this time two batteries opened on our line and cross-fired on my tree, a good many shells bursting in and around it. Nearly all their shells passed over our main line. I had to leave my tree, and reported what I had seen to the general commanding the corps. As soon as it was possible I went back to my station, saw the enemy busily engaged in removing their dead and wounded. A large detail was at work with stretchers, and their ambulances very active. At 5 p. m. a column of the enemy moved from the left up in front of the First and Fourth Divisions, Fifteenth Army Corps, and formed two lines of battle, placed a battery in position, and made preparation as if intending another charge.

I immediately reported this to the commanding general personally, then went back to my tree; found a very heavy column of the enemy, both infantry and artillery, moving to their right. This column was nearly an hour and a half passing a given point. There were five batteries that I saw. The infantry and two of these batteries passed on through town toward Atlanta; the other three batteries were parked in town. The skirmish line in front of the Fifteenth Army Corps was heavily re-enforced. Their line of rear skirmishers was left very weak. No artillery left on the line that I could see. I remained at my station until 7 p. m. The rear of the enemy's column had just passed through town. I reported in person to the commanding general the condition of enemy's lines in his front.

As for myself, I went to the front of our corps and built a station on a tree; saw a brigade of the enemy (and several regiments) lying in an open field in front of First Division, Fifteenth Army Corps. Proceeded to a battery in front of my station, and, with the aid of Lieutenant Fish, who was left on the tree, I directed the shooting of our guns on rebel brigade, which caused great confusion and drove them out. They then reformed in column of regiments and moved to their front, with two batteries of artillery, apparently to make a charge on the right of the Fifteenth Corps. I then proceeded in person to the general commanding the corps and reported to him, and also to Maj. Gen. O. O. Howard, all I had seen.

I have the honor to be, sir, your most obedient servant,

SAMUEL EDGE,
First Lieutenant and Chief Acting Signal Officer.

HEADQUARTERS FIFTEENTH ARMY CORPS,
In the Field, on Flint River, August 31, 1864.

Brig. Gen. W. B. HAZEN,
Commanding Second Division:

GENERAL: The major-general commanding directs that you push forward your skirmishers to-night, so as to cover as many of the enemy's dead as possible, and in the morning at daylight to advance your skirmish line for the purpose of ascertaining if the enemy are still in force in your front. The other division commanders have the same instructions.

By order of Maj. Gen. John A. Logan:

R. R. TOWNES,
Assistant Adjutant-General.

HEADQUARTERS LEFT WING, SIXTEENTH ARMY CORPS,
Near Jonesborough, Ga., August 31, 1864.

Brig. Gen. J. M. CORSE,
Commanding Second Division:

Major-General Howard, commanding department, directs that you push forward your pickets as far as possible to-night. The object is to ascertain what the enemy is doing, but not to bring on an engagement. It is officially reported that General Thomas is on the railroad, two miles this side of Rough and Ready, and the general commanding department thinks that Hardee may withdraw from our front to-night. If he does he desires to be informed of the movement as soon as possible.

By order of Brig. Gen. T. E. G. Ransom:

J. W. BARNES,
Assistant Adjutant-General.

HEADQUARTERS SEVENTEENTH ARMY CORPS,
Near Flint River, Ga., August 31, 1864.

Brig. Gen. C. R. WOODS,
    Commanding Third Division:

GENERAL: I send inclosed a letter from Maj. Gen. O. O. Howard, indorsed for your action. The major-general commanding desires you to move your command across the river at once and get them in position for the object indicated. You will then send word to General Smith (who will fire the signal guns), and move forward at once.

I have the honor to be, very respectfully, your obedient servant,

A. J. ALEXANDER,
Assistant Adjutant-General.

[Inclosure.]

HDQRS. DEPARTMENT AND ARMY OF THE TENNESSEE,
Near Jonesborough, Ga., August 31, 1864.

Maj. Gen. F. P. BLAIR,
    Commanding Seventeenth Army Corps:

GENERAL: The major-general commanding directs that you hold a division of your command in readiness to make a reconnaissance in force this afternoon at 4 o'clock. The point to debouch from is near the brigade of your command already across the river. General Logan will make a strong demonstration along his entire front at the same hour. General Ransom will make a feint of moving to the right. The object of the reconnaissance is to obtain information of the position and strength of the enemy's forces, to ascertain whether his lines are continuous beyond our left, to occupy his attention while Generals Thomas and Schofield are endeavoring to get upon the railroad, and certainly get upon the railroad ourselves if able at any point. When General Blair is ready to debouch from the lines he will give a signal of six guns in quick succession from a battery this side of the river. The major-general commanding will be present on the left at the hour named.

Very respectfully, your obedient servant,

S. L. TAGGART,
Assistant Adjutant-General.

[Indorsement.]

HEADQUARTERS SEVENTEENTH ARMY CORPS,
Flint Creek, Ga., August 31, 1864.

Respectfully referred to Brig. Gen. C. R. Woods, commanding Third Division, whose command is detailed for this duty.

This will include the brigade already across the river, with the exception of one regiment which it is understood has been detached by Major-General Logan.

By order of Major-General Blair:

A. J. ALEXANDER.

HDQRS. MILITARY DIVISION OF THE MISSISSIPPI,
In the Field, August 31, 1864.

General SCHOFIELD,
    Army of the Ohio:

I wrote you in the night and the couriers are back with a receipt, so I suppose you are moving toward Mrs. Long's or Morrow's Mill. I was at Morrow's yesterday and it seemed a good point, but examine well. I do not think the enemy will attack now, because Howard is within 800 yards of the railroad at Jonesborough, intrenched. He has three bridges and feels strong, but the darkness of night prevented him reaching the road, but he was to resume operations at daylight. I have ordered one of Davis' divisions down to Renfroe's, and expect to send the whole to Howard's flank, but will keep Stanley near him, but will soon send him to the right and let you stand the brunt if Hardee comes out of Rough and Ready. He has some works about the Mount Zion Church, and likely has his corps there. It is not as good as yours. I don't wish you to attack it in position, but to hold it, and as much more as possible, for the other, which is the real attack. After selecting your ground feel the enemy with skirmishers, and if possible you may push in a strong party by Thames' Mill, aiming to reach the railroad about two miles below Rough and Ready. This can only be done, of course, in case of what I want to prevent—Hood fronting Howard with all his combined force. Relieve Howard all you can, but prepare to take advantage of all successes. I want Garrard's cavalry the moment you can spare him, and you can spare him the moment you have a good flank. Colonel Garrard with his cavalry can serve as vedettes. The moment you can spare Garrard send him to me. I send Audenried to you, who will describe to you the roads, positions, fields of grass, corn, &c.

W. T. SHERMAN,
Major-General, Commanding.

AUGUST 31, 1864—7.30 a. m.

General SHERMAN:

My troops are now at Kinney's. I will be closed up on Stanley very soon. The enemy has made no show this morning.

Respectfully,

J. M. SCHOFIELD,
Major-General.

HEADQUARTERS ARMY OF THE OHIO,
August 31, 1864—8.15 a. m.

General SHERMAN:

Captain Audenried has just handed me your dispatch of this morning and explained your wishes. My troops are now massing near Stanley's left, and reconnoitering the ground toward the mill. I will get my troops into the desired position without delay, and then commence to demonstrate against Hardee and toward the railroad. I will do all I can to carry out your instructions. I will be able to send you Garrard's cavalry soon.

Respectfully,

J. M. SCHOFIELD,
Major-General.

AUGUST 31, 1864—12.30 p. m.

General SHERMAN:

We have crossed the creek at Morrow's Mill and are pushing toward the railroad. Stanley is striking south of Rough and Ready, and I will aim at that point, holding roads toward East Point. Prisoners say Hardee's and Stewart's corps both went toward Jonesborough last night. My cavalry has been well out on the left and found nothing. I think Stanley and I had better push for the railroad here. Had not General Garrard better do the same?

Respectfully,

J. M. SCHOFIELD,
Major-General.

Hdqrs. Military Division of the Mississippi,
In the Field, August 31, 1864—2 p. m.

General SCHOFIELD:

Your information corresponds with that of our information here. Baird is on the road leading straight down from Rough and Ready to Jonesborough, about five miles north of Jonesborough. Howard found a strong and threatening force in his front, but is strongly posted 600 to 800 yards from the depot. If you and Stanley will make a lodgment on the railroad below Rough and Ready, Howard can hold the enemy at Jonesborough till you do infinite mischief, and Davis can hold the flank. Break the telegraph at once if possible, to cut off communication. It is Hardee's and Lee's corps at Jonesborough, and Stewart's and militia remain in Atlanta and East Point. You can use Garrard if sure of getting the railroad to-day. If you reach the road don't waste a minute till you have destroyed a good section and make a good lodgment. Keep me well advised.

W. T. SHERMAN,
Major-General.

[Indorsement.]

General STANLEY:

I send you this for your information. Cox is within half a mile of the railroad, but is meeting pretty strong resistance—has got the road. I will leave Hascall to hold all roads coming to our left. Your corps and Cox will be able to hold and destroy the road.

Yours, &c.,

J. M. SCHOFIELD,
Major-General.

AUGUST 31, 1864—4 p. m.

General SHERMAN:

I struck the railroad a mile below Rough and Ready at 3 o'clock. Have Cox's division in position fortifying and breaking track. Stanley is now coming in on my right, and we will soon be abundantly strong. The enemy was running cars down with troops up to the moment we reached the road. They held a pretty good position, well fortified, but we pushed in a strong force at once, and drove them out before they had time to re-enforce very much. The enemy retreated toward Rough and Ready.

Respectfully,

J. M. SCHOFIELD,
Major-General.

HDQRS. MILITARY DIVISION OF THE MISSISSIPPI,
In the Field, August 31, 1864.

Major-General SCHOFIELD:

I have your dispatch and am rejoiced. I think we have now a good game. Break road down toward Jonesborough. The bulk of the enemy's good troops are there; they attacked Howard twice and were repulsed. Put Garrard's cavalry at your back; work down the road, burning and breaking the road good. Howard and Davis will hold on to Hardee and Lee. Baird has four brigades on the road from Rough and Ready, five miles above Jonesborough. Tell Garrard to push the enemy up to Rough and Ready, breaking road as he goes, and you with Stanley move south doing the same. I will give you timely notice if Hardee turns to you in force. Don't get off the track; hold it fast; we will get our whole army on the railroad as near Jonesborough as possible and push Hardee and Lee first, and then for Atlanta. Inspire your men with the importance of their work, and trust to me to fall on Hardee's flank or rear if he turns north, and the cavalry of Garrard can guard your rear toward Atlanta. If you get abreast of Baird, communicate with him and he will join you, but break the road good as you move south.

Yours,

W. T. SHERMAN,
Major-General, Commanding.

———

HEADQUARTERS ARMY OF THE OHIO,
August 31, 1864—8.15 p. m.

Major-General SHERMAN,
Commanding Military Division of the Mississippi:

GENERAL: I have received your dispatch of this p. m. and also your instructions sent by Captain Audenried. I have seen Garrard and given him all necessary instructions. At daylight Cox will push up toward Rough and Ready to help Garrard to sweep in there, and will also destroy the track in that direction, while Stanley is getting under way below. I have sent a copy of your instructions to Stanley and will see him at daylight. I think you may rely upon our pushing the work with vigor. Cox has driven the enemy back nearly to Rough and Ready, where they seem to be in considerable force. Two trains arrived apparently with troops after we got on the railroad. This evening there are sounds of a movement to the south on a road not far east of the railroad. I have sent a party to push out and ascertain what it is if possible. I will inform you at once if I learn anything important. My men are too much fatigued to work more to-night, but we will begin again at dawn of day.

Very respectfully, your obedient servant,

J. M. SCHOFIELD,
Major-General.

P. S.—General Cox reports as the result of his reconnaissance to his front that he pushed out about two miles, finding many small roads, but no traveled one, and encountering no enemy.

Respectfully,

J. M. SCHOFIELD,
Major-General.

HDQRS. MILITARY DIVISION OF THE MISSISSIPPI,
In the Field, Couch's House, August 31, 1864—9.15 p. m.

General SCHOFIELD:

As the question of rank will come up, I will decide it now, and beg you to acquiesce whatever your present opinion may be. Whenever two or more officers happen together on a common duty calling for a common head, even for a minute, the officer highest in rank present must give the necessary orders. Your own, Stanley's, and Davis' commands will to-morrow form a common movement requiring a common head in case of battle or extreme danger, and whoever happens to rank must command and be held responsible. The real point is your being a separate army commander, but the overruling necessity of the well established principle before recited takes precedence, or in a combined army like this, embracing three, the latter lose their separate character and become parts or components of the single army. I have and shall continue to keep each army separate, employed as far as may be on tasks proportioned to the strength of each, but when these unexpected combinations arise from the nature of things a fixed rule had better be established now. My decision, I repeat, is that when current events carry your corps and another together in a common object your rank is then determined by the well established rule, and as a separate army commander you have no legal right to exercise that authority over an officer of superior rank in another separate army, but the one having the highest commission must command the whole. Please act on this decision. I will be near Jonesborough to-morrow, prepared to act promptly, according to the signs, but again beg to impress on you and all the great importance of destroying that railroad absolutely beyond hope of repair.

I am, &c.,

W. T. SHERMAN,
Major-General, Commanding.

HEADQUARTERS ARMY OF THE OHIO,
August 31, 1864—8 p. m.

Major-General STANLEY,
Commanding Fourth Army Corps:

GENERAL: I inclose you a copy of a dispatch from General Sherman giving his plan of operations for to-morrow.* I have seen Garrard, and he will strike in toward Rough and Ready early in the morning. At the same time I will send Cox up toward Rough and Ready to break the road as far as practicable and help Garrard to get between us and Atlanta. Meanwhile Hascall will move down and join Cox. I propose that you move forward at daylight toward Jonesborough, covering the railroad and the main wagon road, breaking the track as much as you can, and I will follow as soon as Cox is done above and Hascall joins. I will complete the destruction of the road in your rear, and be ready to re-enforce you if you meet the enemy in force. During the day we can alternate according to circumstances. Please inform me if this meets your views, or suggest any change which may occur to you by which we can work together to the best advantage.

Very respectfully,

J. M. SCHOFIELD,
Major-General.

---

* See Sherman to Schofield, p. 733.

HEADQUARTERS ARMY OF THE OHIO,
In the Field, Ga., August 31, 1864—7.30 p. m.

Brig. Gen. M. S. HASCALL,
Comdg. Second Division, Twenty-third Army Corps:

GENERAL: Cox got the railroad at 3 o'clock and Stanley joined him about 4. We are well intrenched and have the road secure. To-morrow promises to be a day of hard work, and I hope profitable, perhaps decisive. I want you to move down with two brigades and join Cox in the morning, leaving one brigade at the cross-roads beyond Huis' Mill, with orders to be ready to march at a moment's notice. General Garrard, with his cavalry, will move by Huis' Mill in the morning, and strike toward and above Rough and Ready, while Cox will move on the same place from his present position. As soon as they develop what is north of us the brigade you leave behind can probably join you. Please start as soon as you can see to march in the morning; come down the road by Johnson's to Morrow's Mill, then take the Rough and Ready road. Let your trains wait near Morrow's Mill for further orders. Time is important.

Very respectfully, your obedient servant,

J. M. SCHOFIELD,
Major-General, Commanding.

HDQRS. THIRD DIVISION, TWENTY-THIRD ARMY CORPS,
August 31, 1864—1.10 p. m.

Major-General SCHOFIELD,
Commanding, &c.:

GENERAL: I am at Thames' house. A little cavalry in front, making it necessary to deploy some skirmishers. It is one mile and a half to the railroad by nearest road, which forks about half a mile beyond to the left. It is half a mile farther by the right fork of the road. I suppose you desire me to take the right fork so as to keep near Fourth Corps. Mr. Thames says Stanley cannot strike the railroad less than three miles below where I shall reach it by the right-hand road.

J. D. COX,
Brigadier-General, Commanding.

HEADQUARTERS ARMY OF THE OHIO,
August 31, 1864—9 p. m.

Brig. Gen. J. D. COX,
Commanding Third Division:

GENERAL: Please push forward a brigade or more toward Rough and Ready in the morning to find what is there and destroy the track; also to assist General Garrard, who will approach the railroad at that point and open communication with you. He is to push in across the road and hold any force coming from Atlanta, while we move south. Start at dawn of day. Let our men understand how important is to-morrow's work. General Sherman expresses the highest gratification at what they have done to-day, and asks another big day's work to-morrow.

Very respectfully,

J. M. SCHOFIELD,
Major-General.

AUGUST 31, 1864.

Maj. J. A. CAMPBELL,
      Assistant Adjutant-General, Army of the Ohio:

MAJOR: I have the honor to inform you that the breast-works of the enemy along the line of the creek near Dodson's were evacuated last night. A prisoner captured states that the rebel infantry have fallen back to their works near Rough and Ready, and that the cavalry is also near that point. A rebel picket was found on the Atlanta road, but none on the road leading east past Dodson's. My scouting parties have not yet returned. No firing has been heard in the direction of either scouting party since the picket was driven in.

Very respectfully, your obedient servant,

ISRAEL GARRARD,
Colonel, Commanding Division.

————

HDQRS. CAVALRY DIVISION, ARMY OF THE OHIO,
August 31, 1864—9 p. m.

Maj. J. A. CAMPBELL,
      Assistant Adjutant-General, Army of the Ohio:

MAJOR: I have the honor to report that I sent the Ninth Ohio Volunteer Cavalry out east from this point, on the left flank, and that I have not had any report from it. I suppose it to have communicated with that part of the Twenty-third Corps beyond Murray's [Morrow's] Mill. I sent a scout across to Dodson's, that followed the road around to the railroad, driving a picket most of the way. I also sent one up to the railroad on the Atlanta road. This last, under Major Rice, First Ohio Squadron, advanced until it reached a point about two miles or less from East Point, where it came on a force that it did not attempt to drive, as it was superior in numbers and in the vicinity of breast-works, some infantry, and some cavalry. While occupying an advanced position Major Rice captured Maj. J. Y. Rankin, commissary of subsistence, who was looking for his train, that had left East Point for Rough and Ready. He left Atlanta this afternoon between 2 and 3 o'clock. I send you the papers of to-day. He belongs to Granbury's brigade, Cleburne's division, Hardee's corps. My quarters to-night are two miles out on the road where the road leading east by Dodson's turns out, just to the rear of the left of the infantry line.

Very respectfully, your obedient servant,

ISRAEL GARRARD,
Colonel, Commanding Cavalry Division.

————

HDQRS. THIRD CAV. DIV., DEPT. OF THE CUMBERLAND,
On Flint River, August 31, 1864.

Brigadier-General ELLIOTT,
      Chief of Cavalry, Department of the Cumberland:

GENERAL: I left my camp yesterday morning at 6.30 in advance of General Ransom's column. Met the enemy two miles out, and drove him back to the cross-roads, five miles from the railroad. Here he made a determined resistance, with the assistance of 400 infantry. He was again driven back from one position to another till a favorable opportunity offered, when I rushed the Ninety-second Illinois forward, saved the bridge, and crossed in face of rifle-pits. Captain Estes and the officers and men of the Ninety-second Illinois are alone entitled to all the praise for this successful exploit. Three regiments of my division were at once crossed and pushed into the right of the infantry, and made a deliberate effort to reach the road below Jonesborough. The enemy in front of my cavalry was driven to within 300 yards of the track, but we could not reach it, owing to my small force and the fact that it was quite dark. My people fell back to a strong position, and at daylight this a. m. recrossed the river. I will send you during the day a nominal list of casualties. As soon as Major-General Howard finds that his left flank is safe, by his directions I will cross the river below Jonesborough, and reach the railroad, if possible. One hour of daylight would have given me the road last evening.

I am, general, very respectfully, your obedient servant,

J. KILPATRICK,
Brigadier-General of Volunteers.

HDQRS. THIRD CAV. DIV., DEPT. OF THE CUMBERLAND,
Near Flint River, August 31, 1864.

Lieut. DAVID F. HOW,
Acting Assistant Adjutant-General, Hdqrs. Chief of Cavalry:

I have the honor to report that I forced a passage on the river half a mile below Jonesborough, drove in the enemy's pickets directly in his rear to a point within half a mile of the town, dismounted an entire brigade, sent the horses back across the river, and held the position. Repulsed two determined attacks of rebel infantry, and only retired when nearly enveloped, as I have since been informed, by the rebel General Cleburne's entire division. The enemy forced me from the banks of the river, crossed on a bridge constructed by my people, attacked the Ninety-second Illinois in a position a few hundred yards from the river on the crest of the hill, was repulsed, and retired across the river. In the mean time Captain Qualman, Third Indiana Cavalry, with a strong force of picked men, dashed in on the railroad four miles below, effectually destroyed upward of fifty yards of track, burning the ties and bending the rails, and brought with him into camp about half a mile of telegraph wire. He lost 1 man killed. My people are now guarding all the roads leading from fords or bridges as far down as the point where the Jonesborough and Fayetteville road crossed the river. I will make every effort to learn the position, strength, and movements of the enemy, and keep you advised.

I am, sir, very respectfully, your obedient servant,

J. KILPATRICK,
Brigadier-General of Volunteers.

NEAR JONESBOROUGH, GA., *August 31, 1864.*

Brig. Gen. J. KILPATRICK,
Commanding Cavalry Division:

Major-General Howard directs me to say that a large force of the enemy is in his front, quite enveloping his position; that there are indications that the enemy is disposed to attack, and that consequently he cannot at present detach any portion of his command for the purpose of operating with you. He desires you to make a dash upon the road and destroy the telegraph wire if possible. Just as soon as it can be done the infantry will be pushed over into the road.

I have the honor to be, general, very respectfully, your obedient servant,

SAML. L. TAGGART,
Assistant Adjutant-General.

HEADQUARTERS THIRD CAVALRY DIVISION,
On Flint River, August 31, 1864.

Lieutenant-Colonel CLARK, *Assistant Adjutant-General:*

COLONEL: Your dispatch has been received. I have opened communication with your infantry on the right, which now occupies a position from a half to three-quarters of a mile from this point. The shells from one of your batteries reach the enemy's position, the left of which rests on the Fayetteville road, not quite half a mile from Jonesborough. I have a lookout upon a house overlooking the enemy's left. A small force of cavalry is now passing down the railroad, with, it is thought, one piece of artillery and two covered wagons. No infantry can be seen on or passing to the right. Fearing that this force of cavalry was moving to intercept my men already sent to destroy the wire, I have ordered Colonel Jones, with his brigade, to attack in flank and hold them in check until the object of the expedition is accomplished. A train of cars is now passing south; brakemen can be seen on the cars, but no troops. The country on both sides of the river about this point is quite open. I have 100 men at a good ford one mile and a half below this point, and a sufficient force is at the bridge burned by the rebels five miles farther down. I expect the bridges are quite all burnt for a considerable distance down, but any of them can be repaired in a very short time. Our position is now so very near the railroad that any formidable force of cavalry can strike it at pleasure.

Very respectfully,

J. KILPATRICK,
Brigadier-General.

NASHVILLE, TENN., *August 31, 1864.*

Col. D. C. McCALLUM, *Chattanooga:*

The enemy as early as this morning were at Woodbury and McMinnville, and to-night were found in camp seven miles east of Wartrace. I do not think the Nashville and Chattanooga Railroad safe for trains, but I think trains may yet safely run to Stevenson and by the way of Huntsville.

L. H. ROUSSEAU,
Major-General.

NASHVILLE, *August 31, 1864.*

Major-General STEEDMAN:

Our wires went down between La Vergne and Murfreesborough and near Decherd early this morning, so we have had no word from General Van Cleve, at Murfreesborough, or General Milroy, at Tullahoma. The enemy in small force have torn up the track this side of La Vergne, and between there and Murfreesborough, doing but small damage. Citizens report hearing firing in direction of Murfreesborough during the day. Commanding officer at Columbia says that citizens from Shelbyville report fighting in direction of Wartrace, more likely Elk River. General Rousseau has gone out with force—my excuse for telegraphing.

B. H. POLK,
Major and Assistant Adjutant-General.

TULLAHOMA, *August 31, 1864.*

Major-General STEEDMAN:

Wheeler's forces captured a company of Tennessee cavalry at Lebanon yesterday morning. They were skirmished by General Van Cleve's scouts near Woodbury. A cavalry scout sent out from Duck River bridge drove in pickets of a heavy force of the enemy six miles east of that place yesterday evening. On yesterday the enemy attacked and drove in small force stationed at Tracy City, and destroyed a railroad bridge. Colonel Krzyzanowski reports the enemy at Jasper yesterday. The telegraph all north of Duck River was cut last night. I know not what damage, if any, has been done to the railroad north of that place, but will soon know. No trains from Nashville since 6 p. m. last night.

R. H. MILROY,
Major-General.

P. S.—Later: Fighting reported at Decherd at 10.45 a. m.

R. H. M.

BRIDGEPORT, *August 31, 1864.*

Major-General STEEDMAN:

A member of the detachment of the Fifth Tennessee Cavalry has brought the following communication:

TRACY CITY, *August 31, 1864.*

We had a fight yesterday with a detachment of Wheeler's brigade, and repulsed him. They claim to have had about 300 men. The enemy is reported to be about three-quarters of a mile from here, waiting for a piece of artillery. We can hold this place until we are re-enforced, unless they get artillery. We cannot get away without being captured by their cavalry. We have about thirty-five men and want help.

General, I am unable to send any re-enforcements from here. Can I request you for help for the troops at Tracy City? I have a pilot who can conduct the troops on a road about sixteen miles from this place.

An immediate answer most respectfully requested.

W. KRZYZANOWSKI,
Colonel, Commanding.

HEADQUARTERS DISTRICT OF THE ETOWAH,
Chattanooga, August 31, 1864.

Colonel KRZYZANOWSKI, *Bridgeport:*

I sent a strong force of cavalry to the enemy's rear this morning, who will drive them from the vicinity of Tracy City to-morrow, if they do not leave sooner. I think they will hear of them, and leave to-night.

J. B. STEEDMAN,
Major-General.

BRIDGEPORT, *August 31, 1864.*

Major-General STEEDMAN:

My scouts report that Wheeler came into Jasper with 1,600 men at 1 p. m.

W. KRZYZANOWSKI,
Colonel, Commanding Post.

———

COWAN, *August 31, 1864.*

Major-General STEEDMAN:

I have sent a heavy guard three miles north. The railroad is torn up and some ties burned; not much damage done yet. They are near Decherd. My men came up to their pickets. All quiet here and at the Tunnel.

C. H. JACKSON,
Lieutenant-Colonel, Commanding.

———

COWAN, *August 31, 1864.*

General STEEDMAN:

Five hundred rebel cavalry passed here at 2 o'clock this p. m., skirmishing with my outposts. Communications north of here are cut.

C. H. JACKSON,
Lieut. Col., Eighteenth Wisconsin Volunteers, Commanding.

———

DECATUR, *August 31, 1864.*

Major-General SHERMAN:

I have reliable information that Clanton's force received orders Sunday evening to go to Atlanta, and left. I can get no information as to the whereabouts of Wheeler. I have a force—concentrated and provided with three days' rations, ready to throw them upon any point of the road, if I can get information and a train I have ordered—of One hundred and second Ohio, Thirteenth Wisconsin, and Seventy-third Indiana from river, except one company at most exposed points commanded by each regiment.

R. S. GRANGER,
Brigadier-General.

———

ROME, *August 31, 1864.*

Major-General STEEDMAN:

GENERAL: I am satisfied that the enemy contemplate an attack on this place. Can you not send back my two regiments?

WM. VANDEVER,
Brigadier-General, Commanding.

———

LOUISVILLE, *August 31, 1864—7 a. m.*

Major ECKERT:

Both lines between Nashville and Chattanooga cut south of Christiana, Tenn., and heavy firing heard south of there. Work to Chattanooga via Huntsville and Stevenson. Line from Chattanooga to front O. K.

S. BRUCH.

CAMP ON CHATTAHOOCHEE, *August 31, 1864—9.30 p. m.*
(Received 2.30 a. m. September 1.)

Maj. THOMAS T. ECKERT:

Wheeler to-day cut railroad and telegraph, first near Wartrace, and later between Elk River and Cumberland Mountains. His operations have been in a line near Cowan. No communication with Sherman since my last; but heavy artillery firing was heard southeast of Atlanta this morning, distance about fifteen miles from Vining's. Slocum's reconnaissance found too many rebels before Atlanta, and returned.

J. C. VAN DUZER.

HDQRS. MILITARY DIVISION OF THE MISSISSIPPI,
In the Field, near Renfroe's Place, August 31, 1864—5.45 p. m.

[General SHERMAN:]

GENERAL: There is no musketry to be heard at all, but occasionally the report of artillery on our left. Our trains are moving to the front. Colonel Strong, of General H[oward's] staff, just passed, on his way to the right, to verify the report of one of Kilpatrick's men, who says that General K[ilpatrick], who was holding a bridge over Flint River, two miles south of the right of the Army of the Tennessee, has been driven away from the river by rebel infantry. A rebel prisoner belonging to Cleburne's division says they were ordered to move to the south and turn our right.

Respectfully,

CHARLES EWING,
Acting Inspector-General.

[AUGUST 31, 1864.—For General Field Orders, No. 13 (congratulatory), from headquarters Department and Army of the Tennessee, see Part III, p. 49.]

Consolidated semi-monthly field return of artillery serving in the Army of the Ohio for the fifteen days ending August 31, 1864.

Battery.	Division.	Effective force.				Rounds of ammunition on hand.	Horses.	Casualties.	
		Officers.	Men.	Guns.	Caissons.			Men wounded.	Loss of horses.
19th Ohio	Second	4	79	4	4	513	69	1	5
1st Michigan (F)	do	2	89	4	4	808	68	......	9
22d Indiana	do	2	111	4	4	451	63	......	18
15th Indiana	Third	3	102	4	4	629	72	1	5
1st Ohio (D)	do	4	98	4	4	800	66	1	4
23d Indiana	do	2	116	4	4	394	67	......	13
24th Indiana	Cavalry Corps	1	61	2	2	400	36	......	2
Total		18	656	26	26	3,995	441	3	56

I certify that the above report is correct.

G. W. SCHOFIELD,
Lieutenant-Colonel and Chief of Artillery and Ordnance.

HEADQUARTERS ARMY OF THE OHIO,
Decatur, Ga., September 10, 1864.

Abstract from returns of the Department of the Cumberland, Maj. Gen. George H. Thomas, U. S. Army, commanding, for the month of August, 1864.

[Compiled mainly from subordinate returns.]

Command.	Present for duty.		Aggregate present.	Aggregate present and absent.	Pieces of artillery.	
	Officers.	Men.			Heavy.	Field.
General headquarters..	51	366	453	526	......	......
Fourth Army Corps (Stanley):						
Headquarters..	7	....	7	7	......	......
First Division (Kimball).........................	306	4,911	6,236	10,852	......	......
Second Division (Newton).....................	266	3,117	4,091	9,961	......	......
Third Division (Wood)...........................	238	3,807	4,735	9,433	......	......
Corps artillery (Bridges)	29	783	853	1,116	......	35
Total Fourth Army Corps...................	846	12,618	15,922	31,369	......	35
Fourteenth Army Corps (Davis):						
Headquarters..	7	....	7	7	......	......
First Division (Carlin)	262	5,107	6,348	11,797	......	......
Second Division (Morgan).....................	220	4,685	5,581	9,884	......	......
Third Division (Baird)	250	4,426	5,264	10,766	......	......
Corps artillery (Houghtaling)	20	668	728	905	......	34
Total Fourteenth Army Corps...........	759	14,886	17,928	33,359	......	34
Twentieth Army Corps (Slocum):						
Headquarters..	16	66	88	99	......	......
First Division (Williams)	276	4,260	5,217	9,473	......	......
Second Division (Geary)........................	176	3,130	4,028	8,644	......	......
Third Division (Ward)...........................	223	3,995	5,155	9,775	......	......
Corps artillery (Reynolds)	26	719	776	1,000	......	36
Total Twentieth Army Corps*.............	717	12,170	15,264	28,991	......	36
Cavalry Corps (Elliott):						
Headquarters..	7	....	7	8	......	......
First Division (McCook)........................	172	3,538	4,499	8,035	......	4
Second Division (Garrard).....................	171	3,501	4,401	9,708	......	4
Third Division (Kilpatrick)...................	166	3,554	4,336	7,390	......	4
Fourth Division (Spalding)...................	141	3,373	4,085	5,041	......	6
Detached (Palmer)................................	23	394	490	684	......	......
Total Cavalry Corps...........................	680	14,360	17,818	30,866	......	18
Post of Chattanooga (Stanley)...................	102	2,484	3,049	4,423	16	66
Engineer Troops:						
Engineer Brigade (McCreery)	70	1,361	1,790	2,193	......	......
Pioneer Brigade (O'Connell)	....	....	....	....	......	......
1st Michigan Engineers (Innes)	38	999	1,664	1,776	......	......
1st U. S. Veteran Volunteer Engineers (Merrill)......	18	614	842	906	......	......
Total Engineer Troops	126	2,974	4,296	4,875	......	......
Reserve Brigade (Le Favour).....................	24	778	973	1,526	......	......
Veteran Reserve Corps (Gazzam)................	3	418	849	943	......	......
Unassigned troops:						
Infantry †	92	2,094	2,886	3,388	......	......
Artillery ‡...	12	447	480	712	......	27
Total unassigned	104	2,541	3,366	4,100	......	27
District of Tennessee (Rousseau):						
Headquarters..	3	....	3	3	......	......
First Brigade, Fourth Division, Twentieth Army Corps (Doolittle).	69	1,945	2,564	3,046	......	......
Unassigned regiments, Fourth Division, Twentieth Army Corps.	138	2,932	3,716	4,559	......	......
9th Ohio and 20th Indiana Batteries	4	124	142	149	......	......

* The Fourth Division reported at Nashville, Tenn.
†At Chattahoochee River, Ga., Chattanooga, Tenn., and Rome, Ga.
‡At Bridgeport, Ala., Atlanta, Ga., Chattanooga, Tenn., Jonesborough, Ga., and steamer Stone River.

Abstract from returns of the Department of the Cumberland, &c.—Continued.

Command.	Present for duty.		Aggregate present.	Aggregate present and absent.	Pieces of artillery.	
	Officers.	Men.			Heavy.	Field.
District of Tennessee (Rousseau)—Continued.						
Nashville (Miller)	62	1,417	1,687	2,006	14	40
Springfield (Downey)	12	331	418	727		
Fort Donelson (Brott)	2	131	144	166		6
Clarksville (Smith)	3	*121	137	160		6
Gallatin (J. K. Miller)	4	120	135	150		
Nashville and Northwestern Railroad (Thompson)	50	1,471	1,706	1,803		6
Nashville and Chattanooga Railroad (Milroy)	82	1,860	2,069	2,455	31	41
District of Northern Alabama (Granger)	174	4,226	5,165	5,854	4	8
Total District of Tennessee	603	14,678	17,886	21,078	49	107
Grand Total	4,015	78,273	97,804	162,056	65	323
Grand total according to monthly return of the department.	4,023	78,561	97,914	162,087	36	321

Abstract from returns of the Department of the Tennessee, Maj. Gen. Oliver O. Howard, U. S. Army, commanding, for the month of August, 1864.

[Compiled mainly from subordinate returns.]

Command.	Present for duty.		Aggregate present.	Aggregate present and absent.	Pieces of artillery.	
	Officers.	Men.			Heavy.	Field.
General headquarters*	23	33	96	117		
Fifteenth Army Corps (Logan):						
Headquarters	13	30	45	50		
First Division (Osterhaus)	218	2,739	3,746	6,187		10
Second Division (Hazen)	142	2,083	2,947	5,688		7
Third Division (J. E. Smith)	235	4,414	5,695	7,299		10
Fourth Division (Harrow)	165	3,378	4,257	7,090		10
Total Fifteenth Army Corps	773	12,644	16,690	26,314		37
Sixteenth Army Corps:						
Headquarters	4		4	4		
Left Wing (Ransom):						
Headquarters	9	28	38	40		
Second Division (Corse)	169	4,076	5,370	8,309		12
Fourth Division (Fuller)	186	3,684	4,482	8,645		
First Brigade U. S. Colored Infantry (Campbell)	41	960	1,254	1,934		
Cavalry (Spencer)	24	487	613	773		
Total Left Wing	429	9,235	11,757	19,701		12
Right Wing (A. J. Smith):						
Headquarters	3		3	3		
First Division (Mower)	235	4,655	5,945	9,623		14
Third Division (Shaw)	241	4,866	5,873	9,278		20
Brigade U. S. Colored Troops† (Bouton)						
Total Right Wing	479	9,521	11,821	18,904		34
Total Sixteenth Army Corps	912	18,756	23,582	38,609		46

* Includes detachment Signal Corps and Fourth Independent Company Ohio Cavalry.

† Reported in the District of West Tennessee.

Abstract from returns of the Department of the Tennessee, &c.—Continued.

Command.	Present for duty.		Aggregate present.	Aggregate present and absent.	Pieces of artillery.	
	Officers.	Men.			Heavy.	Field.
Seventeenth Army Corps (Blair):						
Headquarters	21	26	104	122	......	..
First Division (Dennis)	123	3,262	3,948	4,870	......	14
Third Division (Woods)	115	2,485	3,163	6,993	......	10
Fourth Division (G. A. Smith)	134	3,245	3,864	7,206	......	23
Total Seventeenth Army Corps	393	9,018	11,079	19,191	......	47
District of West Tennessee (Washburn):						
Headquarters	4	....	4	4	......	..
District of Memphis (Buckland)	432	8,359	11,748	13,527	96	12
First Brigade U. S. Colored Troops (Bouton)	102	2,630	3,277	3,474	......	6
Cavalry Division (Grierson)	290	8,470	10,496	14,759	......	11
Division Seventeenth Army Corps *(J. B. Moore)						
District of Western Kentucky† (Paine)	154	3,186	4,550	7,355	7	..
Total District of West Tennessee	982	22,645	30,075	39,119	103	29
District of Vicksburg (Dana):						
Headquarters	12	....	12	12	......	..
First Division‡ (Dennis)						
Maltby's brigade	62	1,984	2,573	2,897	......	12
Colored Troops (Hawkins)	206	4,515	5,823	6,320	......	10
Cavalry (Osband)	66	1,736	2,767	3,144	......	..
Defenses of Natchez, Miss. (Brayman)	119	3,330	4,449	5,258	6	27
Mississippi Marine Brigade§ (Ellet)						
Total District of Vicksburg	465	11,565	15,624	17,631	6	49
Grand total Department of the Tennessee	3,548	74,661	97,146	140,981	109	208
Grand total according to monthly return of the department.	3,519	73,564	95,666	139,237	68	174

Abstract from returns of the Department of the Ohio, Maj. Gen. John M. Schofield, U. S. Army, commanding, for the month of August, 1864.

[Compiled mainly from subordinate returns.]

Command.	Present for duty.		Aggregate present.	Aggregate present and absent.	Pieces of artillery.	
	Officers.	Men.			Heavy.	Field.
General headquarters	46	....	46	46		
Twenty-third Army Corps (Schofield):						
Headquarters	14	62	76	77	......	..
Second Division (Hascall)	248	4,536	5,703	11,689	......	..
Third Division (Cox)	236	5,163	6,083	11,644	......	..
Fourth Division (Ammen)	128	3,672	4,851	7,346	......	73

* Reporting to Department of Arkansas.
† Also reported in the Department of the Ohio, to which it was transferred August 7.
‡ Reported in Seventeenth Army Corps.
§ Ordered to be disbanded.

Abstract from returns of the Department of the Ohio, &c.—Continued.

Command.	Present for duty.		Aggregate present.	Aggregate present and absent.	Pieces of artillery.	
	Officers.	Men.			Heavy.	Field.
Twenty-third Army Corps (Schofield)—Continued.						
Fifth Division* (Burbridge)	591	13,040	15,742	19,894	16	70
Cavalry Division† (Stoneman)	214	4,490	5,425	7,619		
Heavy Artillery (Gibson)	42	1,289	1,525	1,808		
Engineer Troops‡ (McClure)						
Total Twenty-third Army Corps	1,473	32,252	39,405	60,077	16	143
District of Western Kentucky§ (Paine):						
Headquarters	2		2	2		
Paducah, Ky. (Barry)	29	667	1,118	3,755		
Cairo, Ill. (S. Meredith)	33	535	780	881	7	
Columbus, Ky. (McArthur)	90	1,984	2,650	2,837		
Total District of Western Kentucky	154	3,186	4,550	7,475	7	
Grand total	1,673	35,438	44,001	67,598	23	143
Grand total according to monthly return of the department.‖	1,295	27,672	34,152	54,091	(¶)	(¶)

[AUGUST 31, 1864.—For roster of troops in the Military Division of the Mississippi, not serving in the Atlanta campaign, see Vol. XXXIX, Part II.]

————

HEADQUARTERS ARMY OF THE CUMBERLAND,
In the Field, Smith's House, near crossing of Mill Creek,
September 1, 1864—12 m.

Maj. Gen. W. T. SHERMAN,
Commanding Military Division of the Mississippi:

GENERAL: General Stanley is at Morrow's Station. He reports to me that all the road to his rear, as far as his camp of last night, has been destroyed. I have ordered him to concentrate there, and to move right down upon Jonesborough. He will connect with General Davis' left, which will make our line complete. My skirmish line has moved forward now and driven the enemy from the ridge bordering Mill Creek on the south.

Respectfully, yours,

GEO. H. THOMAS,
Major-General, U. S. Volunteers, Commanding.

———

* District of Kentucky. No return of district found—only returns of First and Second Divisions.
† Compiled from tri-monthly reports of July 20.
‡ Composed of infantry details, and accounted for with their regiments.
§ Transferred to the Department of the Ohio August 7.
‖ Exclusive of the District of Western Kentucky, not borne on the return.
¶ Pieces of artillery not accounted for.

HDQRS. MILITARY DIVISION OF THE MISSISSIPPI,
In the Field, near Jonesborough, September 1, 1864.

Major-General THOMAS,
Commanding Army of the Cumberland:

In order that no doubt may exist as to future operations, I wish your army to press directly after the enemy southward with all the speed and vigor possible till we reach Griffin, where I will make new orders. I regret to learn that General Stanley remained to-day for hours on the railroad awaiting orders, when he heard firing heavy to his front and right. I may be in error, but such is reported to me by Captain Audenried and Captain Poe. I knew you had given him orders, and think we should not overlook it. I don't know why Stanley could not have pushed along the railroad while General Davis was heavily engaged, and absolutely enveloped the enemy in Jonesborough. Now he has time to fortify, and we may be compelled to modify all our plans. If General Stanley lost a minute of time when he should have been in action, I beg you will not overlook it, as it concerns the lives of our men and the success of our arms. General Davis' attack, though some hours later than I expected, was still spirited and good, and was measurably successful. I suppose now Stewart has made his junction, which improves our chances at Atlanta, but gives us harder work out here. Please renew your orders to General Slocum to make a dash at Atlanta before the enemy has time to haul off the artillery and stores.

Yours, truly,

W. T. SHERMAN,
Major-General, Commanding.

HEADQUARTERS DEPARTMENT OF THE CUMBERLAND,
In the Field, September 1, 1864. (Received 7.30 p. m.)

Maj. Gen. D. S. STANLEY,
Commanding Fourth Army Corps:

GENERAL: The major-general commanding directs that you complete the adjustment of your lines to-night, closing well upon the left of the Fourteenth Army Corps, and move upon the enemy's works at daylight in the morning (to-morrow). Unless you receive contradictory orders, you will move in conjunction with the Fourteenth Corps.

Yours, very respectfully,

WM. D. WHIPPLE,
Assistant Adjutant-General.

HEADQUARTERS FOURTH ARMY CORPS,
Near Jonesborough, Ga., September 1, 1864—7.45 p. m.

Brigadier-General WHIPPLE, *Chief of Staff:*

I have the honor to report that I commenced to tear up the railroad this morning at 3 o'clock where I struck the road yesterday, and have destroyed it up to the point where my right now rests, save about 400 yards of track torn up by General Baird. At 3.30 p. m. I received orders from Major-General Thomas to push forward for Jonesborough. About two miles from Jonesborough I commenced to deploy part of my force to try and outflank the enemy and favor General Davis' assault. Kirby's and Grose's brigades, of the First Division, were advanced, with Taylor's brigade in reserve, and on the left Newton's division was deployed and advanced. Wood's division was massed in reserve. We drove the enemy about half a mile, but we could not get up to their works in time to storm them before dark, on account of the great difficulty the troops experienced in getting through the dense jungle in their front. Kirby found the enemy in strong works. Grose reports that they are in works in his front, and that there is an almost impassable ravine before him. Newton's skirmishers report that they saw works, but I do not believe this. Our lines face nearly southwest. I have sent to see whether Schofield has advanced on my left. I do not believe he is on a line with me, and I will look out for my own left.

D. S. STANLEY,
Major-General, Commanding.

HEADQUARTERS FOURTH ARMY CORPS,
Morrow's Mill, Ga., September 1, 1864.

General KIMBALL:

GENERAL: The corps will march immediately for Jonesborough. General Kimball's division will lead, marching on the railroad. General Newton will follow General Kimball. General Wood, with his division, will take the main Griffin road, taking with him all the artillery except two pieces, which will accompany General Kimball on the railroad. General Wood will be careful not to get in advance of the column moving down the railroad, and will keep a strong advance well out in his front.

By command of Major-General Stanley:
WM. H. SINCLAIR,
Major and Assistant Adjutant-General.

(Same to Generals Newton and Wood.)

HDQRS. SECOND DIVISION, FOURTH ARMY CORPS,
September 1, 1864—6 a. m.

Brigadier-General WAGNER:

GENERAL: The general commanding directs that you evacuate your position, and move your command to this place at once. The division is ordered to move immediately.

By order of Brigadier-General Newton:
GEORGE LEE,
Assistant Adjutant-General.

CONFIDENTIAL.] HDQRS. SECOND DIVISION, 4TH ARMY CORPS,
September 1, 1864.

General WAGNER, *Commanding Second Brigade:*

GENERAL: In accordance with instructions just received from corps headquarters, you will be prepared to move upon the enemy's works at daylight to-morrow. Make every preparation to-night to carry out this order; distribute sixty rounds of ammunition per man. The ammunition train will be found near these headquarters.

By order of Brigadier-General Newton:
J. S. RANSOM,
Captain, &c.

P. S.—You will send in a report of casualties sustained to-day sometime to-night.

HEADQUARTERS DEPARTMENT OF THE CUMBERLAND,
Near Renfroe's, Ga., September 1, 1864.

Major-General DAVIS,
     Commanding Fourteenth Army Corps:

GENERAL: The general commanding directs that you move at once, with General Morgan's division and two brigades of General Carlin's division, and join General Baird. You will then move in support of General Howard's left, supporting Baird as you approach Jonesborough, and while he is destroying the railroad. The brigade of Carlin, which is detached, will remain at this point to protect your train against any movement of the enemy from the direction of Fayetteville. If you can get into position quicker by following the Jonesborough road and taking post on Howard's left, you are at liberty to do so.

I am, general, very respectfully, your obedient servant,
                                   HENRY STONE,
                         Captain and Assistant Adjutant-General.

HEADQUARTERS FOURTEENTH ARMY CORPS,
Mrs. Smith's House, near Rough and Ready Road,
September 1, 1864.

Brig. Gen. W. P. CARLIN,
     Commanding First Division, Fourteenth Army Corps:

GENERAL: The following instructions from the major-general commanding are furnished for your guidance:

The general commanding directs that you move at once, with General Morgan's division and two brigades of General Carlin's division, and join General Baird. You will then move in support of General Howard's left, supporting Baird as you approach Jonesborough, and while he is destroying the railroad.

Your division will form the advance of the column moving down the Rough and Ready road. Jonesborough is represented as being five miles from this point. You will advance along it two or two and a half miles, select a good position, and form your lines facing Jonesborough. Throw out flankers well to your right and left, particularly the latter. General Morgan will follow you and will be prepared to support you. Move vigorously and report frequently. General Davis will be found at this point or along the Rough and Ready road. Move as soon as your troops are rested.

By order of Bvt. Maj. Gen. Jef. C. Davis:
                                   A. C. McCLURG,
                      Assistant Adjutant-General and Chief of Staff.

HEADQUARTERS FOURTEENTH ARMY CORPS,
Renfroe's House, September 1, 1864.

Brig. Gen. J. D. MORGAN,
     Commanding Second Division, Fourteenth Army Corps:

You will move your division to the position of General Baird as contemplated in your orders yesterday, following General Carlin, who is now moving to that point.

By order of Bvt. Maj. Gen. Jef. C. Davis:
                                   A. C. McCLURG,
                      Assistant Adjutant-General and Chief of Staff.

HEADQUARTERS DEPARTMENT OF THE CUMBERLAND,
Near Renfroe's House, September 1, 1864.

Maj. Gen. H. W. SLOCUM,
Commanding Twentieth Army Corps:

GENERAL : There is but little doubt that the three corps of the rebel army are now at Jonesborough. This is the concurrent testimony of the prisoners captured. If this is the case, it is undoubtedly Hood's intention to evacuate the place, and has at this time, probably, only a force of militia there for the purpose of getting away the heavy artillery and stores. If this is the case, you might possibly by a dash capture the place with artillery and stores. The major-general commanding directs that you make the effort, but without exposing the tête-de-pont to capture. The Fourteenth Corps this afternoon made a spirited assault upon the enemy's works, capturing a line of intrenchments, 2 batteries of artillery, 2 stand of colors, and about 200 prisoners.

Yours, very respectfully,

GEO. H. THOMAS,
Major-General, U. S. Volunteers, Commanding.

HEADQUARTERS TWENTIETH CORPS,
Chattahoochee River, Ga., September 1, 1864.

Brig. Gen. J. W. GEARY,
Commanding Second Division:

GENERAL: The major-general commanding directs that you send out to-morrow morning in the direction of Atlanta a reconnoitering party of about 500 men to ascertain the position and intention of the enemy. Please report all information obtained immediately on the return of the expedition. General Ward also sends out a party of 1,000 men for the same purpose.

I am, general, very respectfully, your obedient servant,

H. W. PERKINS,
Lieutenant-Colonel and Assistant Adjutant-General.

HDQRS. CHIEF OF CAVALRY, DEPT. OF THE CUMBERLAND,
Near Renfroe's, Ga., September 1, 1864.

Brig. Gen. J. KILPATRICK,
Commanding Third Division Cavalry:

I am directed by the general commanding to say that you will, with your command, closely watch the enemy, and should he retreat you will harass him as much as possible by keeping on his flank and rear; and should the retreat be in the direction of Macon the Army of the Cumberland will follow him as far as Griffin. Whenever the opportunity offers to break the railroad without much risk, do so. Give the earliest reliable information of the movements of the enemy.

I am, general, very respectfully, your obedient servant,

DAVID F. HOW,
Lieutenant and Acting Assistant Adjutant-General.

HDQRS. CHIEF OF CAVALRY, DEPT. OF THE CUMBERLAND,
Near Renfroe's, Ga., September 1, 1864.

Brig. Gen. J. KILPATRICK,
Commanding Third Division Cavalry:

I am directed by the general commanding to say that should the enemy retreat south you will hurry to Fayette Station and Griffin and hang on his flank, while the Army of the Cumberland pushes him to the rear. Send information as to the movements of the enemy as soon as you learn anything of them.

I am, general, very respectfully, your obedient servant,

DAVID F. HOW,
Lieutenant and Acting Assistant Adjutant-General.

HEADQUARTERS THIRD CAVALRY DIVISION,
On Flint River, September 1, 1864.

Lieut. DAVID F. HOW,
Acting Assistant Adjutant-General:

LIEUTENANT: A citizen came into my lines near the burnt bridge over Flint River on the Jonesborough road. He has been sent to General Howard's headquarters. He came from Macon last evening and left Jonesborough at sunrise this a. m. He reports that the rebel army is strengthening and extending their lines about Jonesborough; that no troops are moving down the railroad, but all are in position and busily at work; that the railroad as far down as Griffin is guarded by cavalry only; that last evening General Hood was in Atlanta with one corps of regular troops and the Georgia militia, and that Hardee with his own and Lee's corps was at Jonesborough, and although the repulse was quite disastrous, Hood intended to hold Jonesborough and if possible Atlanta. For the last hour the enemy has been extending his works along the line of railroad in direction of the bridge on Fayetteville road. Several regiments can be seen at work. I do not think from all I can learn that the enemy is at present retreating. Rest assured that I will not be slow to strike him when an opportunity offers.

Very respectfully, your obedient servant,

J. KILPATRICK,
Brigadier-General of Volunteers.

HDQRS. DEPARTMENT AND ARMY OF THE TENNESSEE,
Near Jonesborough, Ga., September 1, 1864.

Maj. Gen. W. T. SHERMAN,
Commanding Military Division of the Mississippi:

GENERAL: I have the honor to report the following as the result of the operations of this army to-day: The Seventeenth Corps, which was on my left, was, about 3.30 o'clock this p. m., relieved by the Fourteenth Corps, and by your instructions ordered to the right. Major-General Blair reports that he has one division across the river and has advanced a heavy skirmish line and finds the enemy in strong position. The operations of the cavalry to-day are given in the inclosed note from General Kilpatrick. During the attack of the Fourteenth Corps the Fifteenth Corps made a vigorous demonstration on the enemy, and at some points drove them from their skirmish pits into their main line, capturing some prisoners. This movement was also participated in by General Ransom, commanding Sixteenth Corps, all having been made to create a diversion in favor of the attacking column on the left. Casualties for the day not yet reported.

I am, general, very respectfully, your obedient servant,

O. O. HOWARD,
Major-General.

[Inclosure.]

HDQRS. THIRD CAV. DIV., DEPT. OF THE CUMBERLAND,
On Flint River, September 1, 1864.

Lieutenant-Colonel CLARK,
Assistant Adjutant-General, Army of the Tennessee:

COLONEL: General Blair has arrived at this point. I am moving with my entire command to the bridge below. A train of cars passed down to Lovejoy's Station two hours ago loaded with infantry. They are now intrenching above Lovejoy's Station. This is the only infantry on the railroad between Jonesborough and Griffin.

Very respectfully,

J. KILPATRICK,
Brigadier-General.

HDQRS. MILITARY DIVISION OF THE MISSISSIPPI,
In the Field, September 1, 1864—8 p. m.

Major-General HOWARD,
Commanding Army of the Tennessee:

GENERAL: In order that you may act advisedly, I will merely state that Jonesborough is of no value to us, but we are now trying to cripple and destroy the army now there. Thomas will push him in the direction of the railroad south. Schofield will operate on the east and you on the west of the railroad. If he retreats we will follow without halt or delay, if possible, to Griffin. If he remains in Jonesborough we must envelop him and destroy his communications south, as they are already destroyed north. Your troops are now well disposed, and Blair can do good service by feeling out and reaching the railroad if possible. He should not be content with a cavalry break, but one of some extent, and well done. Send word to Osterhaus to have his artillery officers listen for the cars to-night, and if heard to open artillery on them at random. If the enemy retreats I think you could make best progress by marching rapidly to Fayetteville, and then toward Griffin, falling on the flanks of the enemy. I suppose the bridge is destroyed, but General Thomas has a pontoon train that could march there in one day. This train is at Renfroe's, eight miles from Fayetteville, from which there are several roads across Flint River, the one fulfilling most conditions being the one toward Fayette Station. · Still, if you can learn of roads east of Flint River that will be available, and yet not bring you in contact with Thomas' troops, it would be the safest, as all the army will then be together, and no part separated by an impassable stream. Should the enemy remain in Jonesborough to-morrow hold your line as now, and give to Blair's movements all the force you can.

Yours, truly,

W. T. SHERMAN,
Major-General, Commanding.

HEADQUARTERS FIFTEENTH ARMY CORPS,
September 1, 1864—4.05 a. m.

Colonel CLARK, *Assistant Adjutant-General:*

Major-General Logan directs me to report that the pickets of each division report that the enemy have been moving to our right for three hours, apparently in great confusion. Wagons are easily heard moving from any point on our line.

Very respectfully, your obedient servant,

R. R. TOWNES,
Lieutenant-Colonel and Assistant Adjutant-General.

[Indorsement.]

HDQRS. DEPARTMENT AND ARMY OF THE TENNESSEE,
September 1, 1864.

Respectfully referred to Major-General Sherman for his information. Preparations are made to follow. Generals Logan, Ransom and Kilpatrick have been notified.

Respectfully,

O. O. HOWARD,
Major-General.

———

NEAR JONESBOROUGH, GA., *September 1, 1864.*

Maj. Gen. JOHN A. LOGAN, *Commanding Fifteenth Army Corps:*

The major-general commanding directs that as soon as you observe any movement upon the advancing columns of Schofield and Stanley you will open fire with musketry along your line, and make sallies, feigning an attack, and as much as possible attract the attention of the enemy.

Very respectfully, your obedient servant,

SAML. L. TAGGART,
Assistant Adjutant-General.

———

HDQRS. DEPARTMENT AND ARMY OF THE TENNESSEE,
Near Jonesborough, Ga., September 1, 1864.

Maj. Gen. JOHN A. LOGAN, *Commanding Fifteenth Army Corps:*

GENERAL: The major-general commanding directs that you cause occasional shots from your batteries to be fired upon the town during the night, care being taken not to expend too large an amount of ammunition.

Very respectfully, your obedient servant,

SAML. L. TAGGART,
Assistant Adjutant-General.

———

HEADQUARTERS SIGNAL DETACHMENT,
Near Jonesborough, Ga., September 1, 1864.

Maj. Gen. JOHN A. LOGAN, *Commanding Fifteenth Army Corps:*

SIR: I have the honor to submit the following as my report of to-day. Lieutenant Fish, of this detachment, reports as follows:

I was out on my tree at 7 a. m.; examined the enemy's lines carefully; found a strong line of battle formed in front of Fifteenth Army Corps; men busy at work on a second line of earth-works. This line is on the east and south of the field sides, where their lines were formed yesterday that charged the Fifteenth Army Corps. I immediately reported what I had seen to the major-general commanding. As the fog and smoke rose I discovered enemy's line of skirmishers had been advanced about fifty yards. At 12.30 p. m. I discovered two trains of cars moving toward Macon; appeared to be empty. A few minutes after a column of infantry passed from their left to right. There were three regiments in the column. In a short time the line in front of the Fifteenth Army Corps was weakened by removing men enough to cover the front lately occupied by the three regiments. Shortly after the Army of the Cumberland became engaged another column of five regiments moved from their left to right. This column was nicely shelled by a battery in Fourth Division, Fifteenth Army Corps. I also discovered the enemy driving their beef-cattle through town; were going in a hurry. I assisted a battery of Napoleon guns in Fourth Division, Fifteenth Army Corps, in getting the range of enemy's rifle-pits. They did some good firing, driving the enemy from their works in great confusion. During the latter part of the day I reported to Captain Hoover verbally, and also to Lieutenant Edge. My tree was in plain view of the enemy's skirmishers, and the men in two of their pits made me their target, firing a good many shots at me, two of which struck the tree but a short distance from me. I was out of the tree only time enough to take my dinner, and remained there until too dark to see anything.

As for myself, I sent, by an order of the general commanding the corps, an officer to the station early in the morning, and as soon as I could make it convenient I went to the front myself. After taking a good look at everything, I proceeded to a battery in front and directed the shelling of the rebel lines. Then I returned and reported to the general commanding the corps. At 2 p. m. I went to the front again; found the enemy again at work; proceeded to battery and directed the firing, which stopped the rebels working and drove them out of their works. I then returned to the tree station to assist Lieutenant Fish, where I remained till dark.

I have the honor to be, sir, your obedient servant,

SAMUEL EDGE,
First Lieutenant and Chief Acting Signal Officer.

HEADQUARTERS ARMY OF THE OHIO,
September 1, 1864—5 a. m.

Major-General SHERMAN,
Commanding Military Division of the Mississippi:

GENERAL: I will waive for the time being my own opinion on the question of rank, and act heartily in accordance with your decision. All is quiet here so far. Our men are at work on the railroad.

Very respectfully,

J. M. SCHOFIELD,
Major-General.

HEADQUARTERS, &C.,
Near Jonesborough, September 1, 1864—8.20 a. m.

General SCHOFIELD:

I have your note of 5 a. m., and think my decision as to rank is the law, but I am none the less obliged for your prompt and cordial assent to my conclusions. In promising to keep the three armies separate as far as possible, I do as much as you can expect. Howard assents to my proposition. I have just ordered a sketch of Howard's position, which I send with this, and shall expect you and Stanley pretty soon. Davis is moving into position now. Thomas is at Renfroe's, and I will be in this neighborhood to-day. I think you will find plenty of roads along down the railroad, also from any point of it across to us. All the people hereabouts know the main stream, which is on our map as Crooked Creek, as Flint River, but up above Jonesborough it is easily bridged. Baird has bridges, and so will Davis. Howard has four, the upper or northern one being about one mile and a half above Jonesborough road. Press steadily down with Stanley, and the moment you can reach me with your orders and form a part of the main army, that anomalous character of detachment ceases and you are then the Army of the Ohio.

I am, yours,

W. T. SHERMAN,
Major-General, Commanding.

HDQRS. MILITARY DIVISION OF THE MISSISSIPPI,
In the Field, September 1, 1864.

Major-General SCHOFIELD:

GENERAL: From reports of my staff I think enough of the railroad has been broken until we have conquered the army now lying at Jonesborough. We had pretty hard fighting with them this afternoon, and I think had all our force been engaged we would have beaten them, but now Stewart's corps will effect its junction and the enemy will fortify. Yet he may underrate our strength, and I wish you to-morrow early to get over to the northeast of Jonesborough and approach from that quarter, and should the enemy retreat follow him with energy, hanging on his left flank; follow roads east of the railroad as far as Griffin. Thomas will follow the railroad substantially and Howard will keep to the right. I don't see any reason why the enemy should elect to hold Jonesborough defensively, as we have broken his road, so if you find him intrenched don't assault, but feel below the town. Howard has Blair's corps, with Kilpatrick's cavalry, across Flint River, feeling out for the railroad below Jonesborough. If you think Stewart's corps has passed around by the east from Atlanta and joined Hood at Jonesborough you may order Garrard up to act with you around to the south of Jonesborough, but if there be anything to our rear keep him holding all roads by which Hardee or Hood—both are now represented as present—can receive re-enforcements from the rear. At all events call Garrard close up, that he may be within reach if needed, which will be the case if the enemy retreats to-morrow. His movements are so slow that you had better send to him to-night specific orders. Now that the army is united you are of course subject to no one's orders but mine. But if fighting occurs, or you have a chance to attack, the orders are always to attack. We don't care about Jonesborough, but we want to destroy our enemy.

Yours, truly,

W. T. SHERMAN,
Major-General, Commanding.

HEADQUARTERS ARMY OF THE OHIO,
September 1, 1864—7.15 p. m.

Major-General SHERMAN,
Commanding Military Division of the Mississippi:

GENERAL: My troops are massed in rear of Stanley's left. I found it impossible to deploy them before dark. I have found a country road leading around not far from Stanley's left and striking the McDonough road about two miles from Jonesborough, by which I can get in to-morrow, if that be in accordance with your plans. I have heard nothing from Garrard since he reached Rough and Ready this morning. Doubt-less you have later information. Cox spent some time in waiting for him to get on the road, but the time was not lost, for Cox overtook Stanley before he had begun to deploy. We have made the destruction of the road very thorough. My headquarters are near the railroad where the Flat Rock road strikes it.

Very respectfully,

J. M. SCHOFIELD,
Major-General.

P. S.—I received your dispatch from Howard's headquarters at 2.30 p. m.

J. M. S.

HOWARD'S HEADQUARTERS,
September 1, 1864.

General SCHOFIELD:

I have yours announcing the destruction up, including Rough and Ready. I want all your troops down on Stanley's left, and the cavalry very far to Atlanta. Slocum is ordered to watch Atlanta from the bridge. If there be anything more at Jonesborough than Hardee's and Lee's corps nobody knows it, and we have here plenty of prisoners from these two corps and no others. These corps are not intrenched farther than a straight barricade this side of and parallel to the railroad. If Stewart comes down he will come round by Decatur and McDonough. By moving quick we can prevent this, and that is one reason. Inasmuch as your troops have pushed the enemy beyond Rough and Ready, let Cox follow Hascall at once, keeping your corps in the nature of a strong left flank, prepared to swing round east of the railroad. I sent you a sketch showing Howard's position. Hardee cannot move south now without our seeing him, and if all of our army is concentrated on him we should make quick work. Hardee reports 35,000 men, but no one believes he has more than 20,000. Howard disabled 4,000, and has the dead and a great many wounded. Two hundred and fifty will cover his whole loss. The prisoners say they were assured before the attack that we had no intrenchments, whereas the trenches were good and strong.

Yours,

W. T. SHERMAN,
Major-General, Commanding.

HEADQUARTERS ARMY OF THE OHIO,
Jones' House, September 1, 1864.

General COX,
Commanding Third Division:

GENERAL: The commanding general desires you to please inform him as soon as General Garrard comes up to you. General Hascall is at this point with his division.

Very respectfully,

J. A. CAMPBELL,
Major and Assistant Adjutant-General.

The bearer will bring the answer.

J. A. CAMPBELL,
Assistant Adjutant-General.

HEADQUARTERS ARMY OF THE OHIO,
In the Field, September 1, 1864.

Brigadier-General Cox, *Commanding Third Division:*

GENERAL: The commanding general directs me to inform you that General Hascall is now moving down the railroad in rear of the Fourth Corps, and he wishes you to follow as a rear guard, moving on the main wagon road running on the right-hand side of the railroad, your trains in front. He desires the trains to move forward at once, and the troops when General Garrard shall have arrived.

Very respectfully, your obedient servant,

WM. M. WHERRY,
Major and Aide-de-Camp.

P. S.—The general directs me to add that if you find at any time that General Hascall's rear is in advance he wishes you to put a small force to move on the railroad to act as rear guard there.

Respectfully,

WM. M. WHERRY,
Major and Aide-de-Camp.

HEADQUARTERS ARMY OF THE OHIO,
Near Jonesborough, Ga., September 1, 1864.

Brig. Gen. J. D. Cox,
Commanding Third Division, Twenty-third Army Corps:

GENERAL: The commanding general desires you to have your command in readiness to move at 6 a. m. to-morrow. Detailed instructions will be given you before that hour.

Very respectfully, your obedient servant,

J. A. CAMPBELL,
Major and Assistant Adjutant-General.

(Same to General Hascall.)

Statement of George M. Rose (scout).

HDQRS. DEPARTMENT OF THE CUMBERLAND,
OFFICE PROVOST-MARSHAL-GENERAL,
September 1, 1864.

Left camp yesterday morning; went down the East Point and Fayetteville road. At Thornton's, five miles north of Fayetteville, overtook four of the enemy's scouts. About one mile and a half farther, found a cavalry picket, about forty men; flanked this party and afterward came up in their rear; learned from one of the party that twenty-five of them belonged to Armstrong's command and the balance to the Second Mississippi Cavalry. The latter had just arrived from Powder Springs, where they had been stealing horses. One lieutenant and five men remained at this place, Favor's house, all night; the balance went to Jonesborough yesterday evening. Saw no troops at Fayetteville, except a few scouts; one of these said Hardee and Lee's corps of infantry and two brigades of cavalry were at Jonesborough; could not learn who was in command. Returning, left Fayetteville about 10 o'clock last night and came back on the main F[ayette] and E[ast] P[oint] road. Found the same picket at Favor's house and none this side of there. Talked with citizens at Fayetteville and on the road and think the strength of our force here is not known.

[Indorsement.]

HDQRS. DEPARTMENT OF THE CUMBERLAND,
OFFICE PROVOST-MARSHAL-GENERAL,
September 1, 1864.

Respectfully transmitted for the information of the general commanding.

ED. C. DENIG,
Assistant Adjutant-General, in charge of Army Scouts.

NASHVILLE, *September 1, 1864.*
(Received at Tullahoma 12.20 p. m.)

Major-General MILROY:

Wheeler is on the Murfreesborough pike, ten miles out. General Rousseau is fighting him with cavalry and infantry between here and Murfreesborough, and if you have a force you can spare, he wishes [thinks] you had better send it up this way. General Rousseau is in command of the forces that are out.

B. H. POLK,
Major and Assistant Adjutant-General.

NASHVILLE, *September 1, 1864.*
(Received at Tullahoma 4.20 p. m.)

Major-General MILROY:

At 1 p. m. General Rousseau was driving the enemy slowly near La Grange. You had better perhaps move your main force of cavalry up the road.

B. H. POLK,
Major and Assistant Adjutant-General.

NASHVILLE, *September 1, 1864.*
(Received at Tullahoma 5.30 p. m.)

Major-General MILROY:

Have just had dispatch from General Rousseau; he is slowly driving the enemy. He directs that you send the brigade of cavalry with you to meet him at Murfreesborough.

B. H. POLK,
Major and Assistant Adjutant-General.

NASHVILLE, TENN., *September 1, 1864.*

Brigadier-General GRANGER, *Decatur:*

Nothing from General Rousseau later than 8 a. m., at which time he was fighting Wheeler's forces, ten miles out on the Murfreesborough pike, and slowly driving him. The road is good south of Bell Buckle, Captain Baird, aide on General Milroy's staff, having just passed over it.

B. H. POLK,
Major and Assistant Adjutant-General.

CHATTANOOGA, *September 1, 1864.*

Major-General ROUSSEAU:

I will operate against Wheeler from this way with cavalry and infantry.

J. B. STEEDMAN,
Major-General.

NASHVILLE, *September 1, 1864—12.30 a. m.*

Major-General STEEDMAN:

General Rousseau encountered the enemy to-night on the Murfreesborough pike near the insane asylum. He don't know what force. Beyond Antioch the road appeared to be burning for a distance of from two to four miles. A prisoner just captured says there are parts of the three divisions this side of Murfreesborough, and that Wheeler commands in person. It is generally believed that the larger force is south of Murfreesborough. There are very few available troops here, and the general is out with a small force. I will send your dispatch offering assistance as early as I can, but I have no doubt it would be very acceptable to the general.

B. H. POLK,
Major and Assistant Adjutant-General.

STEVENSON, *September 1, 1864.*

Major-General ROUSSEAU:

Am here with 3,000 infantry; will reach you as soon as possible. Telegraph to me at Tullahoma.

J. B. STEEDMAN,
Major-General.

NASHVILLE, *September 1, 1864—1.30 p. m.*

Major-General STEEDMAN:

Two hours after sun-up to-day General Rousseau sent in a courier with dispatch from ten miles out on Murfreesborough pike, saying he had met the enemy in force under Wheeler himself and was fighting him, and that he was satisfied Wheeler's force largely exceeded his own.

B. H. POLK,
Major and Assistant Adjutant-General.

NASHVILLE, TENN., *September 1, 1864—3.30 p. m.*

[General ROUSSEAU:]

DEAR GENERAL: Your note just received. We are getting the quartermaster's men armed, also the nurses and convalescents in hospital. These, with 500 men of the commissary department, will make us strong. We will make a good fight if the enemy leave your front and come against the town, which I do not think they will undertake. Give them enough of it in your own style.

Truly, yours,

J. D. WEBSTER.

Granger is all right, so we need fear no demonstration from that direction. I have telegraphed to Steedman to move up rapidly from his side.

HEADQUARTERS U. S. FORCES,
Pulaski, September 1, 1864.

Lieutenant KNEELAND,
Acting Assistant Adjutant-General, Decatur:

Scout from Florence has just returned. Did not meet with the 100 men from Tennessee brigade. Met the enemy near Bainbridge Ferry yesterday at about 10 a. m.; attacked them; was successful in first charge, driving them, killing 3 first fire; enemy fell back; scouts followed until they struck the main body, where the scouts where driven back with loss of 7 men—1 killed, 1 mortally wounded, balance missing. Enemy must have suffered severely in both attacks, from all accounts. Conflicting statements as to their artillery. Some told the scouts four and some six pieces, and the force ran from 500 to 2,000. I am satisfied it is the force I reported to you through my Savannah scout. I have sent to Fayetteville scouts, also to Florence, to learn all that is possible as to enemy's movements, numbers, &c. I understand that Third Tennessee has been sent to Athens, from your dispatch. Unless I hear from you to the contrary I shall make my headquarters at Elk River bridge, moving at about 6 p. m. Cannot a telegraph operator be sent to Elk River bridge?

> JOHN C. STARKWEATHER,
> *Brigadier-General, Commanding.*

COLUMBIA, *September 1, 1864.*

Maj. B. H. POLK, *Assistant Adjutant-General:*

Scouts report that rebels going toward Columbia on road from Murfreesborough. Can you give me any information?

> WM. B. SIPES,
> *Colonel, Commanding.*

DECATUR, *September 1, 1864.*

Maj. B. H. POLK:

The following dispatch just received from Stevenson, dated yesterday:

At 2 o'clock this afternoon 400 of Wheeler's forces crossed the Nashville railroad, two miles north of Cowan Station. Captured 7 men and 3 wagons.

> JOHN HUSTON,
> *Major 102d Ohio Volunteer Infantry.*

This looks like a great scattering of the flock. Roddey was at Lamb's Ferry yesterday, with about 1,600 men.

> R. S. GRANGER,
> *Brigadier-General.*

DECATUR, *September 1, 1864—2.50 p. m.*

Maj. B. H. POLK, *Assistant Adjutant-General:*

The following telegrams are just received: •

COLUMBIA, *September 1, 1864.*

General GRANGER:

No further information obtained of rebel movements. My scouts were attacked near Shelbyville last night. I fell back to within ten miles of Columbia. Advanced this morning at daybreak, but had not met the enemy at last reports.

> WM. B. SIPES,
> *Colonel, Commanding.*

PULASKI, *September 1, 1864.*

General GRANGER:

My scouts have come in, and report all quiet at Fayetteville and Winchester. I believe that Wheeler is not about there. Have left all my troops at Elk River bridge, except 100 men. Have sent troops to Sulphur trestle; will leave the troops at both points for a day or two.

> JNO. C. STARKWEATHER,
> *Brigadier-General.*

> R. S. GRANGER,
> *Brigadier-General.*

CHATTANOOGA, *September 1, 1864.*

Major-General SHERMAN:

I will assist General Rousseau to open road to Nashville with 4,000 men. I started cavalry yesterday morning by way of Sequatchie Valley, and leave this morning with infantry by rail to Decherd.

JAMES B. STEEDMAN,
Major-General.

NASHVILLE, TENN., *September 1, 1864—3 p. m.*

Major-General BURBRIDGE:

Wheeler's whole force is now this side of Murfreesborough. Major-General Rousseau is skirmishing with them ten miles out. Force of rebels reported at Lebanon. Nothing from Forrest and artillery. High water on Tennessee has probably prevented their crossing to co-operate with Wheeler. Nothing from Sherman for some days.

J. D. WEBSTER,
Brigadier-General.

DECATUR, ALA., *September 1, 1864.*
(Received 2d.)

Brig. Gen. WILLIAM D. WHIPPLE:

Wheeler's forces reported near Franklin, and on road from Murfreesborough to Columbia. Roddey has crossed at Bainbridge with 2,000 men and five or six pieces of artillery. Lines down between here and Nashville. I have been trying to get transportation for 2,000 men and two pieces of artillery to move to such points on the road as required assistance. It has not come. I have been re-enforcing General Starkweather with such forces as I can get to him on a construction train. I have sent to Sulphur trestle two pieces of artillery and four companies, and to Elk River bridge Third Tennessee, Seventy-third Indiana, and two pieces of artillery. As soon as I can get the One hundred and second Ohio I will go up the road myself, though I am looking for a tap between this and Stevenson. A number of boats are reported crossing at Bainbridge to-day. General Starkweather now reports 600 cavalry and three pieces of artillery one mile and a half from Sulphur trestle. Very latest. Fire burning on track four miles north of Franklin.

R. S. GRANGER,
Brigadier-General.

Instructions to Division Commanders.

HEADQUARTERS FOURTH ARMY CORPS,
Near Jonesborough, Ga., September 1, 1864—7.30 p. m.

GENERAL: Orders have been received from department headquarters for this corps to move upon the enemy's works at daylight in the morning, in conjunction with the Fourteenth Army Corps. Readjust your lines and make every preparation to-night to carry out this order. Distribute plenty of ammunition to your men to-night.

By order of Major-General Stanley:

J. S. FULLERTON,
Assistant Adjutant-General.

(To Generals Kimball, Newton, and Wood.)

SPECIAL FIELD ORDERS, }   HDQRS. 15TH ARMY CORPS,
                      In the Field, on Flint River, Ga.,
     No. 91.   }   *September 1, 1864.*

I. Division commanders will expend as little ammunition as possible and fire only when absolutely necessary while situated so far from depot of supplies.

*   *   *   *   *   *   *

III. Division commanders are reminded of the fact that the supply of ammunition for artillery is rapidly decreasing, and that it should be carefully expended. They will only use it in case of absolute necessity, or when ordered by superior commanders. These instructions will be communicated to chiefs of artillery of divisions by division commanders.

By order of Maj. Gen. John A. Logan:

                                R. R. TOWNES,
                            Assistant Adjutant-General.

Consolidated semi-monthly field return of the artillery of the Army of the Cumberland, September 1, 1864.

Battery	Effective force.		Guns.	Caissons.	Rounds of ammunition on hand.	Horses.	Casualties.	
	Officers.	Men.					Men killed.	Loss of horses.
Fourth Army Corps:								
Artillery brigade headquarters	7	91	......	......	......	24	......	......
5th Indiana Battery	4	119	6	6	814	80	......	8
Independent Pennsylvania Artillery (B)	5	108	4	5	555	70	2	......
1st Ohio Artillery (A)	4	130	6	6	724	88	1	......
1st Illinois Artillery (M)	4	97	4	6	1,054	108	......	......
Bridges' Illinois Battery	1	104	4	6	1,110	101	......	......
6th Ohio Battery	5	133	4	6	680	101	......	......
1st Ohio Artillery (M)	4	117	6	6	832	100	......	......
Fourteenth Army Corps:								
1st Illinois Artillery (C)*a*	6	156	6	6	1,190	74	......	......
19th Indiana Battery*b*	3	108	4	6	612	56	......	......
2d Illinois Artillery (I)*c*	3	137	6	6	701	85	......	......
5th Wisconsin Battery	4	139	6	6	693	90	......	......
20th Indiana Battery	2	122	6	6	920	100	......	......
7th Indiana Battery	4	103	4	6	1,436	50	......	......
11th Indiana Battery (detached)	5	127	5	2	220	94	......	......

a Detail of 2 commissioned officers and 43 men.   *b* Detail of 28 men.   *c* Detail of 33 men.

On account of the separation from the main command of the Twentieth Army Corps and the cavalry divisions, reports from the artillery serving in them have not been received. They will be consolidated and forwarded on a special report.

                           J. M. BRANNAN,
                Brigadier-General and Chief of Artillery.

Brig. Gen. WILLIAM F. BARRY,
     Chief of Artillery, Military Division of the Mississippi.

Additional semi-monthly field return of the artillery of the Army of the Cumberland, September 1, 1864.

Battery.	Effective force.		Guns.	Caissons.	Rounds of ammunition on hand.	Horses.	Casualties—men.	
	Officers.	Men.					Killed.	Wounded.
Twentieth Army Corps:								
Artillery brigade headquarters	9	17	....	....	....	....	....	....
1st New York Artillery (M)............	2	120	6	6	768	85	....	....
1st Ohio Artillery (C)	5	120	6	6	768	90	1	....
13th New York Independent..............	5	108	6	6	752	94	....	....
1st New York Artillery (I)	4	142	6	6	1,200	80	....	1
1st Michigan Artillery (I)..............	3	103	6	6	1,178	77	....	1
Independent Pennsylvania (E)	3	134	6	6	1,200	89	....	1
5th Artillery (K) (detached)	2	69	4	4	....	109	....	....
Total	33	813	40	40	5,866	624	1	3

J. M. BRANNAN,
Brigadier-General and Chief of Artillery.

HDQRS. CHIEF OF ARTY., DEPT. OF THE CUMBERLAND,
Atlanta, Ga., September 9, 1864.

Brig. Gen. W. F. BARRY,
Chief of Artillery, Military Division of the Mississippi.

Semi-monthly field report of the artillery of the Army of the Tennessee and including the 3d of September, 1864.

Batteries.	Effective force.		Guns.	Caissons.	Rounds of ammunition on hand.	Horses.	Casualties.			
							Killed.		Wounded.	
	Officers.	Men.					Officers.	Men.	Officers.	Men.
FIFTEENTH ARMY CORPS.										
First Division.										
Fourth Ohio, Independent.......	2	127	6	6	569	116	1	......	....	3
Second Missouri Artillery (F)....	1	93	4	4	578	64	....	......	....	....
First Illinois, { (A)	1	99	4	4	467	74	....	......	....	....
{ (H)	2	86	3	4	373	78	....	1	....	1
{ (F)	1	117	6	6	598	85	....	1	....	3
First Iowa...................	1	77	4	4	510	60	....	......	....	3
Total	8	599	27	28	3,095	477	1	2	....	10
SIXTEENTH ARMY CORPS.										
Second Division.										
First Missouri Artillery (H)*a*....	3	80	6	6	768	108	....	......	....	1
First Michigan (C)............	4	99	4	4	812	71	....	......	....	2
Fourteenth Ohio Independent ..	3	129	6	6	1,273	99	....	......	....	2
First Michigan (B)*b*............	2	118	6	6	1,070	72	....	....	....	....
Total	12	426	22	22	,923	350	....	......	....	5

a 1 officer and 37 men attached.   *b* 10 men attached.

Semi-monthly field report of the artillery of the Army of the Tennessee, &c.—Continued.

Batteries.	Effective force.				Rounds of ammunition on hand.	Horses.	Casualties.			
							Killed.		Wounded.	
	Officers.	Men.	Guns.	Caissons.			Officers.	Men.	Officers.	Men.
SEVENTEENTH ARMY CORPS.										
Third Division.										
Third Ohio Independent *a*										1
First Illinois (D)................	2	98	4	4	331	69				1
First Michigan (H)...............	3	96	6	6	550	94				
Fifteenth Ohio Independent	3	92	4	4	481	67				
First Missouri (C) *b*	2	100	4	4	608	44				
Second Illinois (F)...............	3	97	4	4	433	67				
Tenth Ohio Independent *b*	2	119	3	4	811	47				
First Minnesota Independent ...	3	120	6	6	1,051	86				
Total	18	722	31	32	4,265	474				2
Grand total	38	1,747	80	82	11,283	1,301	1	2		17

a On duty temporarily in Twentieth Army Corps.   *b* At Marietta, Ga.

T. W. OSBORN,
Major and Chief of Artillery, Dept. and Army of the Tennessee.

NEAR ATLANTA, GA., *September 3, 1864.*

ATLANTA, GA., *September 2, 1864.*
(Received 10.05 p. m.)

Hon. E. M. STANTON,
Secretary of War:

General Sherman has taken Atlanta. The Twentieth Corps occupies the city. The main army is on the Macon road, near East Point. A battle was fought near that point, in which General Sherman was successful. Particulars not known.

H. W. SLOCUM,
Major-General.

CITY POINT, VA., *September 2, 1864—9.30 p. m.*
(Received 3d.)

Major-General SLOCUM,
Near Atlanta, Ga.:

While you are cut off from communication with General Sherman, telegraph your situation daily to General Halleck.

U. S. GRANT,
Lieutenant-General.

NASHVILLE, TENN., *September 2, 1864.*

Major-General SHERMAN, *Near Atlanta:*

Wheeler's main force was yesterday morning ten miles from here on the Murfreesborough road. General Rousseau, with 3,000 men, skirmished with him all day. In the afternoon Wheeler left that road and went across to the Alabama road, Rousseau following. The enemy is now on the Alabama and the Northwestern roads. Fear he will do serious mischief at the latter. Think he has not destroyed important bridges on the other two. We can take care of Nashville, but may not be able to capture the enemy's force. All well here.

J. D. WEBSTER,
Brigadier-General.

Hdqrs. Military Division of the Mississippi,
In the Field, September 2, 1864—4 a. m.

Major-General THOMAS:

At 2 a. m. I heard heavy firing and saw a large fire in the direction of Atlanta. I have just heard more firing seemingly nearer. Garrard is to our rear, with orders to cover us from all approach from that quarter. I have not yet clearly ascertained if Stewart is with the army in Jonesborough, but think he may have swung around Stanley and come in from the east. If so, any force approaching our rear would not be very formidable, though we must be prepared. I think you had better move your headquarters and trains in near your rear, where the trains will be less exposed, and if Schofield's trains be near Renfroe's, as I suppose them to be, you had better order them down to Flint River nearer Howard's left, on Davis' right. Schofield is across the railroad, massed on Stanley's left, but I have ordered him if any danger approach our rear he must go and meet it. In the mean time you had better send a strong picket up the road to Couch's, to guard that point till your trains are close into your troops. I think Garrard can cover the roads, yet he may not know them.

W. T. SHERMAN,
Major-General.

Hdqrs. Military Division of the Mississippi,
September 2, 1864—9.15 a. m.

Major-General THOMAS,
Commanding Department of the Cumberland:

GENERAL: General Sherman desires that you will leave General Davis' corps at the north of Jonesborough for the present.

Very respectfully, your obedient servant,
J. P. WILLARD,
Captain and Aide-de-Camp.

Hdqrs. Military Division of the Mississippi,
In the Field, near Lovejoy's, Ga., September 2, 1864—8 p. m.

Major-General THOMAS:

Until we hear from Atlanta the exact truth, I do not care about your pushing your men against breast-works. Destroy the railroad well up to your lines; keep skirmishers well up, and hold your troops in hand for anything that may turn up. As soon as I know positively that our troops are in Atlanta I will determine what to do. I have ordered General Schofield to feel for the McDonough road, to prevent re-enforcements coming to the enemy from that direction.

Yours, &c.,
W. T. SHERMAN,
Major-General, Commanding.

HEADQUARTERS FOURTH ARMY CORPS,
Two miles from Lovejoy's Station, Ga.,
September 2, 1864—12.15 p. m.

Major-General THOMAS,
    Commanding Department of the Cumberland:

We are about two miles from Lovejoy's Station. The enemy is about one mile this side of the same and about half a mile this side of the McDonough and Fayette road. We can see them busily fortifying. They have a good line already. I think their object is to hold this road to make a junction with troops at McDonough. I also think Lee's corps is expected from that direction. I am now deploying skirmishers and will push forward with my whole force.

D. S. STANLEY,
Major-General.

HEADQUARTERS FOURTH ARMY CORPS,
Near Lovejoy's Station, Ga., September 2, 1864—7.30 p. m.

Brigadier-General WHIPPLE,
    Chief of Staff:

GENERAL: I have the honor to report that at 5 a. m. I started after the enemy, who retreated from my front last night, arriving at Jonesborough at 5.30 a. m. I awaited orders to proceed, and received them at 7.30 a. m., when I started down the railroad. At 12 m. I arrived within about two miles of Lovejoy's, where we met the enemy. Seeing that he had a strong position, and was behind earth-works, I commenced to deploy my troops and make preparations to advance on the left of the railroad, while the Army of the Tennessee advanced on the right. All of my command was deployed, and part of it in single line. At 3.20 p. m. General Howard sent me word that he had just given the orders to advance, and I at once ordered my division commanders to press forward and take the enemy's works if possible. The Second Division passed through a dense jungle, while the First and Third Divisions passed through an almost impassable swamp, through deep ravines, and over steep ridges. I have never seen the enemy take a stronger position, or one of more difficult approach. On the left we reached the enemy's works, and the Third Division assaulted them at 5.30 p. m. It was impossible to reach them at an earlier hour. In this assault Knefler's brigade, Third Division, got into the works, but could not hold them. Kimball, who was on the extreme left, was unable to take the works, being exposed to a heavy cross-fire of artillery. Newton's division did [not] progress much, as the Army of the Tennessee did not move up. General Schofield was one mile in the rear when we assaulted the works, but he now connects with my left. I think the enemy's right this evening is about the center of my left division. Knefler's loss was very severe. Captain Miller, his assistant adjutant-general, and an aide-de-camp, were killed. General Wood was wounded, and Colonel Post took command of the division. Colonel Manderson, Nineteenth Ohio, was severely wounded.

D. S. STANLEY,
Major-General.

HEADQUARTERS DEPARTMENT OF THE CUMBERLAND,
Near Lovejoy's, September 2, 1864. (Received 8.30 p. m.)

Maj. Gen. D. S. STANLEY,
 Commanding Fourth Army Corps:

 GENERAL: The major-general commanding directs that to-night you break the railroad thoroughly for a distance of one mile to your rear. To-morrow morning at daylight press with your entire line upon the enemy's position, and if you think it practicable assault them.
 Yours, very respectfully,

WM. D. WHIPPLE,
Assistant Adjutant-General.

HEADQUARTERS FOURTH ARMY CORPS,
Near Lovejoy's Station, Ga., September 2, 1864—8.40 p. m.

Brigadier-General WHIPPLE,
 Chief of Staff:

 Your note dated September 2 instructing me to thoroughly destroy a mile of railroad track to-night, and then at daylight to-morrow morning to press the enemy with my entire line for the purpose of making an assault if practicable, was received at 8.30 this p. m. My troops are all deployed close up to the enemy in dense woods, and it will be impossible to withdraw them to break the road to-night. I examined the enemy's works closely this evening, and I do not think they can be successfully assaulted. I tried it this afternoon. After the hard climbing and working through the entanglements this afternoon, my troops are nearly exhausted.

D. S. STANLEY,
Major-General.

 P. S.—They are also constructing breast-works to-night.

HEADQUARTERS DEPARTMENT OF THE CUMBERLAND,
Jonesborough, September 2, 1864.

Maj. Gen. J. C. DAVIS,
 Commanding Fourteenth Army Corps:

 GENERAL: Your corps is to form the rear guard to the entire army during its farther march south until further orders. The major-general commanding directs that you form your line facing north and across the roads leading through here from Atlanta, with your picket-line along the line of the rebel breast-works from which you drove them last night. Brigadier-General Garrard's division of cavalry will cover your front and give you timely information of any movements of the enemy from the direction of Atlanta and on your flanks. Your train can be parked in Jonesborough. You will probably march on to-day or to-morrow. From information received Hardee's corps, with some militia, has gone to Lovejoy's Station, and the other portion of the army which was here, back to Atlanta. Two negroes just from Atlanta report that General Slocum was last night shelling the town, and the militia was in great consternation at the time they left.
 Yours, respectfully,

WM. D. WHIPPLE,
Assistant Adjutant-General.

HEADQUARTERS ARMY OF THE CUMBERLAND,
Jonesborough, Ga., September 2, 1864.

Maj. Gen. J. C. DAVIS,
    Commanding Fourteenth Army Corps:

GENERAL: I am directed by the major-general commanding to inform
you that he desires you to at once order your corps of pioneers to report
to Colonel Flad, Army of the Tennessee, by him to be set to work destroying the railroad. You will also issue orders for the arrest of all
straggling soldiers without arms, citizens following the army, and those
on no apparent duty, who will be disposed of by Colonel Flad in destroying the railroad; also your troops will, after they have rested this
afternoon, destroy the road back from your present position to where
General Baird left it broken yesterday.

I am, general, very respectfully, your obedient servant,
                                    R. H. RAMSEY,
                                Assistant Adjutant-General.

HEADQUARTERS FOURTEENTH ARMY CORPS,
Jonesborough, Ga., September 2, 1864.

Brig. Gen. W. D. WHIPPLE,
    Asst. Adjt. Gen. and Chief of Staff, Dept. of the Cumberland:

GENERAL: At an early hour this morning my pickets were pushed
to the front from my position on the battle-field of yesterday. They
found no enemy. After issuing three days' rations to the men my
corps was moved into position near Jonesborough as follows: Morgan
in advance, taking position near the depot, followed by Carlin's and
Baird's divisions. Here I received orders from the general commanding to halt and form my lines facing northward and crossing the railroad, and in the future movements of the army southward my corps
was to act as rear guard. The trains of the corps were moved from
their former position and all were parked near this place by 4 p. m.
Colonel Taylor's brigade, forming the guard to the trains, reported
here at sunset. In compliance with orders a regiment for pioneer
duty reported to Colonel Flad, of the Army of the Tennessee, to
assist in the destruction of the railroad. A part of General Baird's
command was engaged all day tearing up the road in accordance
with orders received from General Thomas in person. A part of General Morgan's division will be detailed for the same duty to-morrow.
No casualties are reported. This report has been delayed by the non-
reception of any report of operations from General Baird.

I am, general, very respectfully, your obedient servant,
                                    JEF. C. DAVIS,
                            Brevet Major-General, Commanding.

HEADQUARTERS DEPARTMENT OF THE CUMBERLAND,
Two miles south of Jonesborough, Ga., September 2, 1864.

Major-General SLOCUM,
    Commanding Twentieth Army Corps:

GENERAL: Major-General Sherman requests me to state that he is
very anxious to know the particulars of the capture of Atlanta. As we
have rumors to the effect that you now occupy that city, he wishes you

to send your dispatch to him in cipher. He also requests that you telegraph to Major-General Halleck at the War Department, Washington, that he, General Sherman, is strongly posted on the Macon railroad.

Very respectfully, your obedient servant,

M. J. KELLY,
First Lieut. Fourth Cavalry, U. S. Army, and Chief of Couriers.

HEADQUARTERS TWENTIETH CORPS,
Chattahoochee Bridge, Ga., September 2, 1864—2.30 a. m.
Brig. Gen. A. S. WILLIAMS,
Commanding First Division:

GENERAL: The major-general commanding desires that you send out as soon as possible this morning a reconnoitering party toward Atlanta, to ascertain where and what the firing is. Parties have been ordered out from Second and Third Divisions, but they will not get started as soon as you. The general desires to get as early information as possible, and has ordered twenty men of his escort to report to you for messengers.

I am, general, very respectfully, your obedient servant,

H. W. PERKINS,
Lieutenant-Colonel and Assistant Adjutant-General.

[SEPTEMBER 2, 1864.]
Colonel PERKINS:

COLONEL: Direct General Geary to move all his command, except one brigade, to Atlanta. He must hold the right of his line, leaving the artillery on the hill. Direct Williams to move all, except one brigade, distributing the remaining brigade along his line. Send forward what artillery can be spared.

Yours, respectfully,

H. W. SLOCUM.

Send an engine over the railroad at once.

HDQRS. THIRD DIVISION, TWENTIETH ARMY CORPS,
September 2, 1864. (Received 1 p. m.)
Lieut. Col. H. W. PERKINS,
Assistant Adjutant-General:

COLONEL: The city authorities have surrendered to my reconnoitering party, and my troops now occupy the same (Atlanta).

I am, colonel, very respectfully, your obedient servant,

W. T. WARD,
Brigadier-General.

SEPTEMBER 2, 1864.
Lieut. Col. H. W. PERKINS,
Assistant Adjutant-General, Twentieth Army Corps:

As my troops took Atlanta, courtesy, if not justice to me, demands that I may be permitted to occupy the same. If not inconsistent with the public interest, I desire to be permitted to move my division to

Atlanta and to leave the dismounted cavalry to guard this ford.   If I am not permitted to move to said place, I sincerely hope and earnestly request some of my command may be sent there to take charge of said town.

Yours, with sincere esteem,

W. T. WARD,
Brigadier-General.

HEADQUARTERS TWENTIETH CORPS,
Chattahoochee Bridge, September 2, 1864.

Colonel MINTY,
Commanding Cavalry at Sandtown:

COLONEL: The major-general commanding directs me to inform you that our large reconnoitering parties sent out this morning report that Atlanta is evacuated, and that our people are now in there.   He directs that you send one regiment of cavalry from Sandtown to Atlanta at once.   The general is just leaving for that point.

I am, colonel, very respectfully, your obedient servant,

H. W. PERKINS,
Lieutenant-Colonel and Assistant Adjutant-General.

HDQRS. CHIEF OF CAVALRY, DEPT. OF THE CUMBERLAND,
Near Jonesborough, Ga., September 2, 1864.

Brig. Gen. K. GARRARD,
Commanding Second Division Cavalry:

The Army of the Cumberland marches in the direction of Griffin, with the Army of the Tennessee on the right and that of the Ohio on the left.   General Thomas directs that you cover the trains of the Army of the Cumberland, giving information of any attempt on the part of the enemy to attack them or our rear.   General Schofield's cavalry will probably cover the rear of his army.   If so, keep up communication with it.   No reports received from you for August 31 and September 1.   Please acknowledge receipt of this order.

I am, general, very respectfully, your obedient servant,

W. L. ELLIOTT,
Brigadier-General and Chief of Cavalry.

HEADQUARTERS SECOND CAVALRY DIVISION,
September 2, 1864.

Brig. Gen. W. D. WHIPPLE,
Chief of Staff, Department of the Cumberland:

GENERAL: I have the honor to report my camp on the Jonesborough road, about four miles from Rough and Ready, acting with the Twenty-third Corps and covering the rear.   Yesterday from Rough and Ready I sent parties out to the north and east, but gained no reliable information.

Very respectfully, your obedient servant,

K. GARRARD,
Brigadier-General, Commanding Division.

HDQRS. CHIEF OF CAVALRY, DEPT. OF THE CUMBERLAND,
Jonesborough, Ga., September 2, 1864.

Brig. Gen. K. GARRARD, *Comdg. Second Division Cavalry:*

You will, with your division, feel up in the direction of Atlanta. Rebels report the city in our possession. Let us know the exact state of affairs. Send scouts in the direction of Flat Rock and roads leading toward Decatur. General Davis' corps is left here to cover the trains. You have authority from Generals Sherman and Thomas to open any dispatches for them from the direction of Atlanta. Send them forward via this place to Lovejoy's. Lee's corps is reported to have gone from here to Atlanta, and to be returning to join Hardee at Lovejoy's.

I am, general, very respectfully, your obedient servant,

W. L. ELLIOTT,
Brigadier-General and Chief of Cavalry.

HDQRS. THIRD CAV. DIV., DEPT. OF THE CUMBERLAND,
Glass' Bridge, on Flint River, September 2, 1864—4.30 p. m.

Major-General HOWARD, or
Brigadier-General ELLIOTT:

GENERAL: The enemy are still passing to the right and on a road this side of the railroad, artillery, infantry, wagons, and cavalry, but my force is too weak to break through the infantry and cavalry line, which is now protecting the flanks of this moving column. Heavy columns of dust can be seen along the line of the railroad and in the direction of McDonough. I feel quite confident that the enemy are retreating. I have sent over several messengers asking for information as to the intended movements of our army, in order that I might know how to maneuver my cavalry, and also for instructions. The required information has not been sent me. My instructions from General Elliott are that, if I find the enemy to be retreating down the railroad, I must move my command quickly to the vicinity of Fayette Station and Griffin, and annoy his flank until our army moves upon his rear. There are no bridges below this point; all are burned, and the river is too wide for me to rebuild them. I am now but fifteen miles from Griffin, and will make every effort to carry out the general's instructions. I suppose our army to be moving down the railroad. I have a good bridge built at this point, and have had some very sharp fighting, the enemy using artillery, with cavalry, supported by infantry. Two of our prisoners have just come into my lines, having escaped from Andersonville.

Very respectfully, your obedient servant,

J. KILPATRICK,
Brigadier-General, Commanding.

[Indorsement.]

HDQRS. CHIEF OF CAVALRY, DEPT. OF THE CUMBERLAND,
September 2, 1864—10.30 p. m.

Respectfully forwarded.

In the absence of instructions as to the movements of the army for to-morrow, and on account of General Kilpatrick's inability to cross Flint River, instructions have been sent him to communicate with the right of the army and let his movements conform thereto.

W. L. ELLIOTT,
Brigadier-General and Chief of Cavalry.

(Forwarded to General Sherman by General Thomas.)

CALHOUN, *September 2, 1864.*

Brig. Gen. WILLIAM D. WHIPPLE :

My regiment is here—440 officers and men, all well armed, equipped, and mounted. Can I not bring them at once to the front? Please answer.

WM. J. PALMER,
Colonel, Commanding Fifteenth Pennsylvania Cavalry.

[Indorsement.]

HDQRS. CHIEF OF CAVALRY, DEPT. OF THE CUMBERLAND,
September 4, 1864.

Colonel Palmer has been ordered to report for orders to General Mc-Cook, and the order has been reiterated to him; but no reply received to the dispatches. I send the order again to him.

W. L. ELLIOTT,
Brigadier-General and Chief of Cavalry.

DECATUR, ALA., *September 2, 1864.*

Major-General THOMAS, and
Major-General SHERMAN :

The following telegram was sent to Major-General Rousseau, which is nearly a repetition of two sent some days since. No transportation has arrived. It is now too late to come through, as the road is cut in several places. I have heard of no bridge being burned.

HEADQUARTERS DISTRICT OF NORTHERN ALABAMA,
Decatur, Ala., September 1, 1864.

Major-General ROUSSEAU,
Nashville, Tenn. :

I deem it indispensable to the safety of the road—indeed the only plan that suggests itself to me for its protection against so large a force as Wheeler's on the road—that a train or trains [be prepared] capable [of] carrying 1,500 infantry and two pieces of artillery—mounted artillery. The horses must go with the guns. This force to go up the road as far as Columbia, and fight the head of Wheeler's columns. With this force I would be nearly 2,000 strong at Columbia, and with the cavalry at Pulaski, 3,000. If this suggestion is accepted, will you please send the transportation at once. I have the Thirteenth Wisconsin, One hundred and second Ohio, and Seventy-third Indiana Infantry.

R. S. GRANGER,
Brigadier-General.

HDQRS. MILITARY DIVISION OF THE MISSISSIPPI,
In the Field, September 2, 1864—8 p. m.

General HOWARD :

You know that General Garrard reports General Slocum in possession of Atlanta. I have sent couriers to learn the exact truth. If it be so, we don't care about pushing the enemy any farther at this time. Had we prevented his making intrenchments it would have been well, but, as he has a strong line, I do not wish to waste lives by an assault. You may therefore order the skirmishers close up, but hold your lines so as not to suffer much. If the enemy be gone in the morning occupy his lines to your front and await orders.

Yours,

W. T. SHERMAN,
Major-General.

HEADQUARTERS FIFTEENTH ARMY CORPS,
Near Lovejoy's, September 2, 1864.

Major-General OSTERHAUS:

GENERAL: The major-general commanding directs that you construct a strong line of works in your front to-night, and make good roads and bridges in rear of every second regiment in line, that ammunition may be easily transported to the front.

By order of Maj. Gen. John A. Logan:

R. R. TOWNES,
Assistant Adjutant-General.

HEADQUARTERS LEFT WING, SIXTEENTH ARMY CORPS,
Jonesborough, Ga., September 2, 1864.

Lieut. Col. WILLIAM T. CLARK,
Assistant Adjutant-General:

My pickets advanced to the town and found no enemy. I have ordered two regiments into the town. My pickets are now south of it and still advancing.

Very respectfully, your obedient servant,

T. E. G. RANSOM,
Brigadier-General, Commanding.

HDQRS. MILITARY DIVISION OF THE MISSISSIPPI,
In the Field, September 2, 1864—4 a. m.

General SCHOFIELD:

I have your dispatch of 7.15 last evening, since which time you have a letter from me. I heard explosions and firing about Atlanta at 2 o'clock, and at this moment I hear more seemingly nearer us, but due north; it must be Garrard, but what force he engages I don't know. Please ascertain whether Stewart's corps came into Jonesborough from the direction of Flat Rock, and let me know. If the firing at the north be not explained, prepare to meet any interruption of our operations from that quarter, and act without further orders if the occasion calls for it, otherwise I want you to attack Jonesborough from the east. Try and communicate with Garrard, and ascertain what the force to our rear is, and move to meet it. Our trains are at the Renfroe Place, out about four miles northwest of Jonesborough. I am near General Howard, at the Flint River, two miles northwest of Jonesborough. A road leads from here due east a little north, which I think passes by where you are.

Yours,

W. T. SHERMAN,
Major-General, Commanding.

HEADQUARTERS ARMY OF THE OHIO,
September 2, 1864—8 a. m.

Major-General SHERMAN,
Commanding Military Division of the Mississippi:

GENERAL: I have your dispatches of 8 last evening and 4 this morning. I have heard from Garrard this morning. The noise last night sounded to him as to us, to be at Atlanta. The last, about 4 o'clock, probably at East Point. We watched it closely. Very large fires were visible in the direction of Atlanta. Brilliant flashes followed at regular intervals by loud explosions, far too loud for any artillery, and then by very rapid explosions of shells. The interval between the flash and explosion gave the distance to Atlanta. All the circumstances indicate the burning of magazines at Atlanta. At the time of the later and near explosions the fires and flashes were not visible. I have no doubt these last were at East Point. I cannot explain the phenomena of last night in any other way. No battle I have ever witnessed would begin to account for it. Citizens here report that a large column of rebel troops passed down the Flat Rock road, just in front of Stanley, yesterday morning. What troops they were I have not yet learned, but am searching for information. Garrard's cavalry went yesterday to about two miles this side of East Point, met some cavalry, and returned. Prisoners and citizens there all said that Stewart's corps and the militia were still about Atlanta. I have sent an infantry reconnaissance up the Flat Rock road to see what can be learned in that direction. Garrard will be here soon, when I will get him started off toward the east. As soon as I can learn that there is no force in our rear I will move in and attack the enemy's right.

Very respectfully,

J. M. SCHOFIELD,
Major-General.

SEPTEMBER 2, 1864—10.25 a. m.

General SHERMAN:

A negro who has just come in from Atlanta says our troops attacked the place about dark last night. The enemy immediately retreated on the McDonough road in great confusion and disorder, all the citizens joining in the flight. Houses were burned, magazines blown up, and a wagon train of ammunition burned. I have my head of column on the McDonough road (one division), the other is moving more to the left, but has a road by which it can join the first if necessary. I have sent to find a road leading substantially parallel to the railroad, if you desire me to pursue toward Griffin.

I hope to hear from you soon, as Colonel Warner must have reached you before now.

Very respectfully,

J. M. SCHOFIELD,
Major-General.

SEPTEMBER 2, 1864—12.45.

General SHERMAN:

I have your orders sent by Colonel Ewing and Colonel Schofield, and am pushing on rapidly. I understand the game, and it is one worth any amount of effort. I sent the colonel simply to give you the information about Lee's movement.

Respectfully,

J. M. SCHOFIELD,
Major-General.

HDQRS. MILITARY DIVISION OF THE MISSISSIPPI,
In the Field, September 2, 1864—8 p. m.

Major-General SCHOFIELD:

I have strong evidence that the enemy blew up his magazines and abandoned Atlanta to General Slocum. If this be so, it is unnecessary for us to go farther at this stage. I have parties breaking up the railroad from Jonesborough to our lines, and to-morrow wish you to feel for the McDonough road, so as to command it if possible, but keep up strong connection with General Stanley and do not assault works of the enemy. If he gives you a fair chance punish him. I have couriers back to ascertain the exact state of affairs in Atlanta, and will be governed by what I hear.

Yours,

W. T. SHERMAN,
Major-General, Commanding.

HEADQUARTERS ARMY OF THE OHIO,
September 2, 1864—9.30 p. m.

Major-General SHERMAN,
Commanding Military Division of the Mississippi:

GENERAL: After a long and most tedious march over all sorts of roads, I was barely able to get one division in position on Stanley's left some time after dark. My artillery and trains are not even yet off the road. I found the country roads, by which I was compelled to march, very crooked and difficult. No enemy except cavalry pickets appeared on my flank during the day. I gained no positive information of the enemy's movements, but all reports corroborate the one I sent you this morning about the retreat from Atlanta, destruction of property, &c. General Garrard informs me he sent a regiment to the McDonough road and struck a rear guard retreating southward, but it was too strong for him to attack, I have just received your dispatch of 8 p. m., and will feel out for the McDonough road in the morning. I understand you to mean the road from Fosterville to McDonough. Please inform me if I am not right. I think I can reach that road if Lee does not come in on Hardee's right to-night. But the country is very open in that direction, and hence it will be difficult to make any move not in plain view of the enemy without detaching my corps some distance from Stanley. But I will examine the ground carefully and proceed with due caution.

Very respectfully,

J. M. SCHOFIELD,
Major-General.

HDQRS. MILITARY DIVISION OF THE MISSISSIPPI,
In the Field, September 2, 1864—11.20 p. m.

General SCHOFIELD:

Yours of 9.30 is received. The road I want to watch is the one indicated as from McDonough to Fosterville, but there will be one to Lovejoy's also, from the nature of things. What I want to know is, is the stand made at Lovejoy's a prearranged thing or mere accident? If the latter, a junction should be prevented; if the former, it demonstrates a more formidable position than its mere appearance would indicate. Keep up your connection with Stanley, but try to prevent or delay a concentration of the rebel army in our front. Nothing positive from Atlanta, and that bothers me.

W. T. SHERMAN,
Major-General.

HEADQUARTERS ARMY OF THE OHIO,
Near Jonesborough, Ga., September 2, 1864—4.15 a. m.

Brig. Gen. J. D. COX,
    Commanding Third Division, Twenty-third Army Corps:

GENERAL: The major-general commanding directs me to say to you that he had the following instructions from General Sherman, viz: "If Stewart's corps has passed down from Atlanta and joined Hood at Jonesborough, you may order Garrard up to act with you around the south of Jonesborough, but if there be anything to our rear, keep him, holding all roads by which Hardee or Hood can receive re-enforcements from the rear. At all events call Garrard down close up, that he may be in reach if needed." He therefore desires you to inform him exactly where your troops are; give him all information you have in regard to Stewart's movements, and take steps to ascertain the facts in regard to it. It is his impression that Stewart has joined Hood. Your forces are probably much farther away now than is desirable should they be needed east and south of Jonesborough. He desires me also to inform you that our troops are mostly in line of battle confronting the enemy in Jonesborough. These headquarters are near the track, four miles by rail from that place.

Very respectfully, your obedient servant,
GEORGE W. SCHOFIELD,
Lieutenant-Colonel and Chief of Artillery and Ordnance.

P. S.—The general wishes to know where you locate the firing or explosions heard since 1 o'clock this morning, and what it appears to have been.

Please keep in hourly communication with these headquarters during the day.

Very respectfully, your obedient servant,
GEORGE W. SCHOFIELD,
Lieutenant-Colonel and Chief of Artillery and Ordnance.

SEPTEMBER 2, 1864.

General COX:

We are to pursue parallel to the railroad. Hascall is on the Jonesborough and McDonough road, about two miles from Jonesborough, and is about starting south. You may join him by taking the first road to the right; it is only about one mile and a half. Probably Reilly had better follow Hascall.

Respectfully,

J. M. SCHOFIELD,
Major-General.

HEADQUARTERS SECOND CAVALRY DIVISION,
September 2, 1864.

Lieut. Col. G. W. SCHOFIELD, *Headquarters Army of the Ohio:*

COLONEL: Yesterday every one said (prisoners and citizens) that Stewart's corps and militia were in Atlanta and East Point; also that Armstrong's brigade cavalry [was] near East Point; also that a large train of wagons passed down toward Jonesborough under guard of cavalry night before last. The regiment which went toward East Point met considerable opposition about two miles this side of East Point, and failed to get there. My troops are near the point where your headquarters train crossed the Jonesborough road, and covering roads to rear and toward East Point. No roads to my knowledge leave the railroad to the east this side of Rough and Ready, and I cannot tell what may be the movements of the enemy until I find some road leading east near this point. It would be impossible to prevent re-enforcements reaching Hood from Atlanta, as there are plenty of roads bearing east from that place, and then cross-roads in the neighborhood of McDonough to Jonesborough. The firing seemed in the direction of Atlanta, but whether it was from guns or some explosions could not be ascertained, though several of us listened to determine. I will order my command under saddle and report in person to the general.

Very respectfully, your obedient servant,

K. GARRARD,
Brigadier-General, Commanding Cavalry.

NASHVILLE, TENN., *September 2, 1864—3 p. m.*
(Received 5.40 p. m.)

Maj. Gen. M. C. MEIGS, *Quartermaster-General:*

I have a brigade of 4,000 quartermasters' men organized under arms, and the spirit of officers and men is admirable. I reviewed them last evening with General Miller, commanding post, and he was exceedingly pleased with their appearance. In a pinch they can defend Nashville alone. Last evening Rousseau engaged Wheeler about four miles this side of La Vergne and drove him. It is said he is making for the Tennessee and Alabama road at Franklin to destroy it, and perhaps threaten our communication by the Cumberland River. Steedman is said to be at Murfreesborough with 3,000 infantry and cavalry.

J. L. DONALDSON,
Colonel, Chief Quartermaster.

CHATTAHOOCHEE RIVER, *September 2, 1864.*
(Received 10 p. m.)

Major-General MEIGS, *Quartermaster-General:*

Atlanta taken; abandoned by Stewart last night, after destroying his stores and ammunition, five engines and train of cars. Stewart was in command of Hood's old corps, and held the city, while General Sherman is said by the citizens to have fought and whipped Hood near East Point, on the line of the Macon road, cutting the rebel army in two. Stewart will have trouble to rejoin Hood. Hardee killed. Enemy's loss estimated by the citizens very heavy. Our losses not known. Not yet in communication with Sherman.

W. G. LE DUC.

HEADQUARTERS FOURTH ARMY CORPS,
Near Jonesborough, September 2, 1864—7.30 a. m.

Order of the day for the Fourth Army Corps for to-day:

The troops of this corps will march at once, moving southward after the enemy. The column will move on the railroad, and the artillery, ambulances, and headquarters trains will move on the dirt road on this side of the railroad. General Newton's division will lead, followed by General Wood's, then General Kimball's.

By order of Major-General Stanley:

WM. H. SINCLAIR,
Assistant Adjutant-General.

NEAR LOVEJOY'S STATION,
Twenty-six miles south of Atlanta, Ga.,
September 3, 1864—6 a. m.
(Received 5.30 p. m. 4th.)

Maj. Gen. H. W. HALLECK, *Washington, D. C.:*

As already reported, the army drew from about Atlanta, and on the 30th had made a good break of the West Point road and reached a good position from which to strike the Macon railroad, the right (General Howard's) near Jonesborough, the left (General Schofield's) near Rough and Ready, and the center (General Thomas') at Couch's. General Howard found the enemy in force at Jonesborough, and intrenched his troops, the salient within half a mile of the railroad. The enemy attacked him at 3 p. m., and was easily repulsed, leaving his dead and wounded. Finding strong opposition on the right, I advanced the left and center rapidly to the railroad, made a good lodgment, and broke it all the way from Rough and Ready down to Howard's left, near Jonesborough, and by the same movement I interposed my whole army between Atlanta and the part of the enemy intrenched in and around Jonesborough. We made a general attack on the enemy at Jonesborough on September 1, the Fourteenth Corps, General Jeff. C. Davis, carrying the works handsomely, with 10 guns and about 1,000 prisoners. In the night the enemy retreated south, and we have followed him to another of his well-chosen and hastily constructed lines, near Lovejoy's. Hood, at Atlanta, finding me on his road, the only one that could supply him, and between him and a considerable part of his army, blew up his magazines in Atlanta and left in the night-time, when the Twentieth Corps, General Slocum, took possession of the place. So Atlanta is ours, and fairly won. I shall not push much farther on this raid, but in a day or so will move to Atlanta and give my men some rest. Since May 5 we have been in one constant battle or skirmish, and need rest. Our losses will not exceed 1,200, and we have possession of over 300 rebel dead, 250 wounded, and over 1,500 well prisoners.

W. T. SHERMAN,
Major-General.

WAR DEPARTMENT,
September 3, 1864.

Major-General SLOCUM, *Atlanta:*

Accept my thanks for your telegram communicating the welcome news from Atlanta. Please keep me advised of events.

EDWIN M. STANTON,
Secretary of War.

ATLANTA, GA., *September 3, 1864—9.30 p. m.*
(Received 4.30 p. m. 4th.)

Major-General HALLECK,
Chief of Staff:

Sherman, with his entire army, except this corps, is near Jonesborough, on the Macon road. Hood's army is south of him, except the troops left in Atlanta, consisting of militia and about one division of old troops. These troops, when they evacuated this place, took the McDonough road, and will probably effect a junction with their main army. Sherman has captured 2 batteries and 2,000 prisoners. The enemy, on evacuating, destroyed 7 locomotives and 81 cars, loaded with ammunition, small-arms, and stores, and left here 14 pieces of artillery, most of them uninjured, and a large number of small-arms. We have taken 200 prisoners, and deserters are constantly coming into our lines. We have on hand a good supply of ammunition, subsistence stores, and clothing. I earnestly hope that paymasters may be sent here as soon as possible, as some of my command have not been paid for eight months.

H. W. SLOCUM,
Major-General.

HDQRS. MILITARY DIVISION OF THE MISSISSIPPI,
In the Field, near Lovejoy's Station, September 3, 1864.

Major-General SLOCUM,
Atlanta, Ga.:

Move all the stores forward from Allatoona and Marietta to Atlanta. Take possession of all good buildings for Government purposes, and see they are not used as quarters. Advise the people to quit now. There can be no trade or commerce now until the war is over. Let Union families go to the North with their effects, and secesh families move on. All cotton is tainted with treason, and no title in it will be respected. It must all go to Nashville as United States property, and pretended claimants may collect testimony for the pursuit of the proceeds of sale after they reach the U. S. Treasury in money.

W. T. SHERMAN,
Major-General, Commanding.

NASHVILLE, TENN., *September 3, 1864—2.30 p. m.*
(Received 6 p. m.)

Major-General HALLECK,
Chief of Staff:

Telegram for General A. J. Smith received.* Do not know where he is. General Rousseau has fought Wheeler two days, driving him. Wheeler came within fifteen miles of this city, on the Chattanooga road, of which he destroyed some miles, but no important bridges. It can soon be repaired. Night before last he crossed over to the Alabama road, where General Rousseau had heavy skirmishing with him. Yesterday Wheeler retreated toward Columbia; is now across the West Harpeth, below Franklin, Rousseau pursuing. Rebel General Kelly is mortally wounded, and in our hands. Our loss is not heavy. If General Steedman can get up in time on the other side Wheeler can be cap-

---
* See p. 789.

tured or his whole force dispersed. He will probably give us but little more trouble. We are reliably informed that Forrest intended co-operating with Wheeler, but we do not know that he has succeeded in crossing the Tennessee.

J. D. WEBSTER,
Brigadier-General.

[SEPTEMBER 3, 1864.—For Whipple to Stanley, inclosing copy of Special Field Orders, No. 63, from headquarters Military Division of the Mississippi (see p. 790), and conveying instructions in accordance therewith, see Part I, p. 934.]

HEADQUARTERS FOURTH ARMY CORPS,
Near Lovejoy's, September 3, 1864.

General KIMBALL:

GENERAL: Official information has just been received from Major-General Sherman that we have Atlanta. On the night of September 1 Hood abandoned the city, and retreated with the force he had there. He destroyed 80 railroad cars of ammunition, blew up the magazines at Atlanta, and destroyed his siege guns. General Slocum occupies the city. A large amount of rebel public property was destroyed. Please have this information published to your regiments.

By order of Major-General Stanley:

WM. H. SINCLAIR,
Assistant Adjutant-General.

Send copy to Newton and Wood.

HEADQUARTERS FOURTH ARMY CORPS,
Near Lovejoy's Station, Ga., September 3, 1864.

The following-mentioned regiments will accompany the train of this corps that moves to the rear from Jonesborough early to-morrow morning. They will be under the temporary command of Colonel Dunlap, Third Kentucky Infantry, who will report to these headquarters for instructions without delay. The regiments will march to Jonesborough this afternoon: The Third Kentucky Infantry Volunteers and the Thirty-sixth Indiana Infantry Volunteers, the non-veterans of the Thirty-first Indiana Infantry Volunteers.

By order of Major-General Stanley:

J. S. FULLERTON,
Assistant Adjutant-General.

HEADQUARTERS DEPARTMENT OF THE CUMBERLAND,
Near Lovejoy's Station, September 3, 1864.

Maj. Gen. J. C. DAVIS,
Commanding Fourteenth Army Corps:

GENERAL: The major-general commanding directs that to-morrow you send back to Atlanta all wagons of your corps not absolutely required to transport the stores now on hand. These wagons will be loaded with the captured arms in your possession and the cotton captured in Jonesborough. Your sick and wounded who are able to travel will be sent back at the same time, and the whole guarded by a brigade to be detailed by yourself. The prisoners now in your hands you will send to Atlanta in charge of this brigade. You will direct the trains and commanding officer of the brigade to report to Major-General Slocum, commanding at Atlanta, and remain there until further orders. Direct your ordnance officer to retain charge of the captured arms until he can turn them over properly to the chief of ordnance of the department. All the prisoners now at these headquarters will this a. m. be sent to be forwarded with the others.

Very respectfully,

WM. D. WHIPPLE,
Assistant Adjutant-General.

HEADQUARTERS FOURTEENTH ARMY CORPS,
Jonesborough, Ga., September 3, 1864.

Lieut. Col. J. W. LANGLEY,
Comdg. Third Brig., Second Div., Fourteenth Army Corps:

COLONEL: Your brigade having been detailed as an escort for prisoners of war, and the trains containing sick and wounded which are to be sent back to Atlanta, you will immediately start with the prisoners, march a little beyond the hospitals of the corps, take position covering them and encamp for the night. To-morrow morning at daylight you will take charge of the whole and march to Atlanta, reporting to Major-General Slocum, commanding at that place. You will exercise great caution and care, and move as rapidly as the condition of the sick and wounded men will admit. The general commanding thinks you can reach Atlanta to-morrow night.

By order of Bvt. Maj. Gen. J. C. Davis:

A. C. McCLURG,
Assistant Adjutant-General and Chief of Staff.

HEADQUARTERS FOURTEENTH ARMY CORPS,
Jonesborough, Ga., September 3, 1864.

[Brig. Gen. WILLIAM D. WHIPPLE:]

GENERAL: I have the honor to report that no change has taken place in the general position of my lines to-day. During the early part of the morning two regiments from the First Division were engaged tearing up the railroad until the order was countermanded by General Sherman's order. A reconnoitering force of two regiments from the same division, under command of Col. William B. Anderson, Sixtieth Illinois, moved out six miles in the direction of McDonough to Lee's Mill. They communicated with General Garrard's cavalry, but obtained little intelligence of the enemy, and did not communicate with the Twenty-third Corps. In compliance with instructions, I have ordered my sick and wounded to be prepared to move at daylight to-morrow to Atlanta, together with all the prisoners of war captured by my command and those turned over to me by Colonel Parkhurst, under guard of the Third Brigade, Second Division, which has been detailed to accompany them to Atlanta. I will have the wounded rebel prisoners, in hospitals in the vicinity of Jonesborough, removed to this place to-morrow morning.

I am, general, very respectfully, your obedient servant,

JEF. C. DAVIS,
Brevet Major-General, Commanding.

[SEPTEMBER 3, 1864.—For Slocum to Whipple (two dispatches), reporting occupation of Atlanta, &c., see Part II, p. 20.]

HEADQUARTERS DEPARTMENT OF THE CUMBERLAND,
Near Lovejoy's Station, September 3, 1864.

Maj. Gen. H. W. SLOCUM,
Commanding Twentieth Army Corps:

GENERAL: The major-general commanding directs that you assume command at Atlanta and the fortifications around the place, and move up from the Chattahoochee your entire corps, with the exception of one brigade, which you will leave at the railroad bridge. The guard at Pace's Ferry will be withdrawn. You will direct the proper officers to take charge of and account for such property as may be found there, have the town thoroughly policed, and permit no one to take quarters there, except upon the orders of General Sherman, General Thomas, or yourself. You will direct Colonel Wright to repair the railroad into the town. The troops will be disposed in the fortifications for defense.

Yours, very respectfully,

WM. D. WHIPPLE,
Assistant Adjutant-General.

HEADQUARTERS TWENTIETH CORPS,
Atlanta, Ga., September 3, 1864.

Brig. Gen. A. S. WILLIAMS,
Commanding First Division:

GENERAL: The major-general commanding directs that you bring the whole of your division to this point. Colonel Harrison has been ordered to occupy and hold the bridge-heads on the south side of the Chattahoochee, where your brigade is now posted.

I am, general, very respectfully, your obedient servant,

H. W. PERKINS,
Assistant Adjutant-General.

HEADQUARTERS FIRST DIVISION, TWENTIETH CORPS,
Atlanta, Ga., September 3, 1864.

Col. H. BOUGHTON,
Commanding Third Brigade:

COLONEL: I am directed by the brigadier-general commanding the division to instruct you to move your brigade forward to this place, starting to-morrow morning at an early hour. Your command will be relieved by Colonel Harrison; still your movements need not be delayed by him. You may send him word, however, upon receipt of this at what hour you expect to move. Upon arriving at the eastern end of the town, say the termination of Decatur street, you will report in person at these headquarters for instructions.

I have the honor to be, colonel, your obedient servant,

S. E. PITTMAN,
Captain and Assistant Adjutant-General.

HEADQUARTERS FIRST DIVISION, TWENTIETH CORPS,
Atlanta, Ga., September 3, 1864.

Lieutenant-Colonel THOMSON,
Commanding Detachment Third Brigade:

The brigadier-general commanding desires that you place the two regiments of Third Brigade under your command in the trenches on the left of General Ruger's brigade. If possible extend your line so as to cover the Peach Tree Creek road. If you cannot make a continuous line so far, put three or four companies on that road where it cuts the breast-works, and obstruct the road if not already obstructed. You can get into this position at any hour before dark.

I have the honor to be, colonel, your obedient servant,

S. E. PITTMAN,
Captain and Assistant Adjutant-General.

HEADQUARTERS TWENTIETH CORPS,
Atlanta, Ga., September 3, 1864.

Col. BENJAMIN HARRISON,
Commanding at Chattahoochee River:

COLONEL: The major-general commanding directs me to inform you that he has ordered General Williams' troops all forward to this point, and also General Geary's. He directs that you send one regiment to hold the bridge-heads on the south side of the Chattahoochee at the railroad ferry and a company to hold Pace's Ferry. At the latter bridge you can take up about fifty feet of the flooring from the south end of the bridge, which a guard of a company at the north end will make safe. The bridge at Turner's Ferry is to be taken up, and the dismounted cavalry, under Colonel Capron, are to hold the ford, being posted on the north side of the river. He further directs that you order forward to this point all the stragglers and convalescents you have now in charge, with such guard as may be necessary, with instructions to report to Colonel Cogswell, commandant of the post. You will afford the different departments every facility for loading stores that are to be transferred from your post to this point.

I am, colonel, very respectfully, your obedient servant,

H. W. PERKINS,
Lieutenant-Colonel and Assistant Adjutant-General.

HDQRS. CHIEF OF CAVALRY, DEPT. OF THE CUMBERLAND,
Camp two miles and a half from Lovejoy's, September 3, 1864.

Brig. Gen. K. GARRARD,
Commanding Second Cavalry Division:

GENERAL: The general commanding directs that you take up your position south of the road from Jonesborough to Flat Rock and covering it. You will observe well the roads leading toward McDonough, and have your scouting parties advance as far as that place; ascertain, if possible, the movements and intentions of the enemy, reporting the same promptly to these headquarters. A wagon train will leave Jonesborough to-morrow morning for Atlanta. Prevent any of the enemy's cavalry from getting onto that road.

I am, general, very respectfully, your obedient servant,

DAVID F. HOW,
Lieutenant and Acting Assistant Adjutant-General.

HEADQUARTERS SECOND CAVALRY DIVISION,
September 3, 1864.

Brig. Gen. W. L. ELLIOTT,
Chief of Cavalry, Department of the Cumberland:

GENERAL: I have the honor to report that my division is to the rear and east (left) of Jonesborough, covering the roads leading to that place. The party I sent to Atlanta has not returned to my headquarters, and I cannot report state of affairs there. The parties sent out to the east gained no new information, but confirm what I reported through one of my staff officers.

Very respectfully, your obedient servant,

K. GARRARD,
Brigadier-General.

I would report the position of my headquarters, but cannot fix it nearer than a mile from the Jonesborough and Stockbridge road, and between that and the Jonesborough and McDonough road.

HEADQUARTERS SECOND CAVALRY DIVISION,
September 3, 1864.

Brigadier-General ELLIOTT,
Chief of Cavalry, Department of the Cumberland:

GENERAL: I have the following information to report which I am confident is accurate. On the 1st of September Lee's corps left Jonesborough at daylight and moved toward Atlanta, and camped for the night near the Atlanta and McDonough road where the road from Jonesborough, on which they marched, struck it. On the morning of the 2d they turned toward McDonough. On the 2d [1st], in the morning, Stewart's corps moved out of Atlanta to within sight of the Chattahoochee River and halted. In the mean time the militia were hurried out of Atlanta toward McDonough, but a few miles out took an easterly road. In the afternoon Stewart's corps returned to Atlanta and at night moved down the McDonough road, leaving Loring's division as rear guard and to destroy property. Quarles' brigade, Loring's division, the rear guard, did not leave until daylight.

Very respectfully, your obedient servant.

K. GARRARD,
Brigadier-General, Commanding Division.

My party from Atlanta has returned.

HEADQUARTERS SECOND CAVALRY DIVISION,
September 3, 1864.

Brig. Gen. W. D. WHIPPLE,
  Chief of Staff, Department of the Cumberland:

GENERAL: My daily reports have not been very regularly made during the past few days, but I have been doing all that I could to meet the requirements of the occasion. On yesterday morning, by heavy patrols to the north and east, I learned that Atlanta was evacuated, and that Lee's and Stewart's corps had gone toward McDonough; that I at once reported to General Sherman, as he was in doubt of the position of the enemy. Considering information the most valuable at the time, I have for two days employed what force I could spare from my division to obtain it. To-day I reported to General [Elliott] full information of the time and route of Lee's and Stewart's corps and the militia. I think I made Stewart's corps leave Atlanta and go to the Chattahoochee and return to Atlanta, on the 2d instant, instead of the 1st, as was the case; it was an oversight on my [part] not intended. Hood remained in Atlanta till daylight on the 2d, and passed eight miles east of here on the Atlanta and Griffin road at 11 a. m. yesterday. It was impossible to make many captures, as all the roads to the east were strongly guarded. I have only few prisoners, but Hardee's, Stewart's, and Lee's corps, and the militia are represented. Yesterday I sent one company to Atlanta; it returned to-day.

Very respectfully, your obedient servant,

K. GARRARD,
Brigadier-General, Commanding.

HEADQUARTERS THIRD CAVALRY DIVISION,
Glass' Bridge, Flint River, September 3, 1864.

Brigadier-General WHIPPLE,
  Chief of Staff, Department of the Cumberland:

GENERAL: Captain Brink has returned, bringing me information desired in reference to our army. I had a scout last night inside the enemy's lines. Portions of Armstrong's and Ross' commands, mounted and dismounted, watch the enemy's left flank directly opposite me. The enemy, so far as I can learn, unless he has moved during the night, is intrenched about Lovejoy's Station, his lines crossing the Jonesborough road and extending to this point. Several car-loads of wounded passed down the road yesterday. Did not stop at but passed through Griffin. Scouts report the enemy's wagon trains to be moving toward Griffin, many of them loaded with green corn. At 2 p. m. yesterday large trains were passing through Fayette Station. As soon as the enemy is forced back beyond Lovejoy's Station I will cross and press in toward Griffin, communicating with our army to the left.

Very respectfully, your obedient servant,

J. KILPATRICK,
Brigadier-General of Volunteers.

HDQRS. CHIEF OF CAVALRY, DEPT. OF THE CUMBERLAND,
Camp near Lovejoy's, Ga., September 3, 1864.

Brig. Gen. J. KILPATRICK,
  Commanding Third Division Cavalry:

The general commanding directs me to inform you that the army will move back to-morrow in the direction of Atlanta. One day's rations have been issued from supply train at these headquarters to some sixty sick and wounded of your division in hospital near Jonesborough. Send ambulances to get them to-day, with a supply of rations.

I am, general, very respectfully, your obedient servant,

DAVID F. HOW,
Lieutenant and Acting Assistant Adjutant-General.

HDQRS. DEPARTMENT AND ARMY OF THE TENNESSEE,
Near Lovejoy's Station, Ga., September 3, 1864.

Capt. L. M. DAYTON,
Aide-de-Camp, Military Division of the Mississippi:

CAPTAIN: The general commanding requests me to state that the column of the enemy which appeared in front of the Fifteenth and Seventeenth Corps is reported by General Blair as moving off toward Griffin.

Very respectfully, your obedient servant,

SAML. L. TAGGART,
Assistant Adjutant-General.

HDQRS. SECOND DIVISION, FIFTEENTH ARMY CORPS,
In the Field, Ga., September 3, 1864.

Lieut. Col. R. R. TOWNES,
Assistant Adjutant-General, Fifteenth Army Corps:

I am now prepared to report the result of the enemy's assault upon this division on the 31st ultimo, as follows: Killed of the enemy and buried, 186; captured unhurt, 99; captured and wounded, 79; total, 364. There were also taken 2 stand of colors and over 1,000 stand small-arms. The usual proportion wounded give about 1,000 wounded, and among them was known to be Maj. Gen. Patton Anderson.

I am, very respectfully,

W. B. HAZEN,
Brigadier-General.

HEADQUARTERS FIFTEENTH ARMY CORPS,
In the Field, near Lovejoy's, Ga., September 3, 1864.

Brig. Gen. WILLIAM HARROW,
Commanding Fourth Division:

GENERAL: You will be prepared in the morning to construct a barricade on the most defensible ground in rear of the cotton gin, with the left resting on the railroad and running out to a point to be designated by Captain Reese, engineer officer of department staff.

By order of Maj. Gen. John A. Logan:

R. R. TOWNES,
Assistant Adjutant-General.

HEADQUARTERS ARMY OF THE OHIO,
Near Lovejoy's Station, Ga., September 3, 1864—9 a. m.

Major-General SHERMAN,
Commanding Military Division of the Mississippi:

GENERAL: Prisoners report that Lee's corps joined Hardee yesterday afternoon, and that Stewart was at McDonough at 4 o'clock.

If this is true both are probably here now. The enemy's line has been considerably extended eastward since last evening, and is probably beyond my reach. It appears to run along a high ridge immediately in front of the McDonough road and behind Walnut Creek. I am feeling well to the left with skirmishers to see if I can reach the enemy's left on the McDonough road.

Very respectfully,

J. M. SCHOFIELD,
Major-General.

HEADQUARTERS ARMY OF THE OHIO,
Near Lovejoy's Station, Ga., September 3, 1864—6.15 p. m.
Major-General SHERMAN,
Commanding Military Division of the Mississippi:

GENERAL: Colonel Garrard reports that he reached the McDonough and Fosterville road three or four miles from Lovejoy's Station. Citizens on the road say that troops, said to be Lee's corps, were passing this morning toward Lovejoy's, and that stragglers were still passing when he reached the road. The people spoke of it as a very large force with a great amount of artillery. As near as Colonel Garrard could ascertain the column was three or four hours in passing. A negro also reports a large number of troops joining the force in our front to-day.

Very respectfully,

J. M. SCHOFIELD,
Major-General.

SEPTEMBER 3, 1864—5 p. m.
Maj. J. A. CAMPBELL,
Assistant Adjutant-General, Army of the Ohio:

MAJOR: I have the honor to report that I went across on to the McDonough and Fayetteville road, striking it between three and four miles from Lovejoy's Station. Citizens report that infantry from Atlanta, said to be Lee's corps, was moving all the morning, and that the stragglers were still passing when we reached the road. A large wagon train was moving on Thursday night and yesterday to Lovejoy's Station. Last night Ross' brigade of cavalry camped just this side of the road, and moved on this morning to Bear Creek Station, below Lovejoy's. The force that moved on the road this morning had artillery. The people speak of there being a great deal of artillery, and of the infantry being very great in quantity, but as near as I could ascertain it took the regular column some three or four hours to pass.

Very respectfully, your obedient servant,

ISRAEL GARRARD,
Colonel, Commanding.

HEADQUARTERS ARMY OF THE OHIO,
In the Field, September 3, 1864.
Col. ISRAEL GARRARD,
Commanding Cavalry Division, Army of the Ohio:

COLONEL: The commanding general directs me to inform you that the enemy's cavalry is reported formed on his right, threatening our trains, and he desires you to extend your right so as to connect with our infantry's left and protect our trains. Watch the country well on what will be your front and report any movement you may observe.

Very respectfully, your obedient servant,

J. A. CAMPBELL,
Major and Assistant Adjutant-General.

HEADQUARTERS ARMY OF THE OHIO,
In the Field, Ga., September 3, 1864.

Col. ISRAEL GARRARD,
Commanding Cavalry Division, Army of the Ohio:

COLONEL: The commanding general directs that you arrest all stragglers and foragers your men may find, except such as are foraging under written orders from the commanding officer of their division, as directed in paragraph III, Special Field Orders, No. 88, current series, from these headquarters.* All men you may arrest will be sent to the provost-marshal at these headquarters.

Very respectfully, your obedient servant,

J. A. CAMPBELL,
Major and Assistant Adjutant-General.

HEADQUARTERS,
Columbia, Tenn., September 3, 1864.

Major-General ROUSSEAU,
Commanding U. S. Forces:

GENERAL: Hearing nothing of either Colonels Spalding or Grummond, and my command being entirely worn down, I have gone into camp on the road leading south from this place. I have directed that Colonels Spalding and Grummond and the battery encamp north of the river. I have sent reconnoitering parties on the Mount Pleasant and Pulaski roads, and also on the Morefield road, which leads down the railroad. The road between this point and Pulaski was intact up to this afternoon. There is no telegraphic communication. The railroad is not damaged but for a mile or two this side of Spring Hill, and I think you had better have the train from here bring down the infantry, and they may be able to ride thus even to Pulaski. Any way, it will save ten or fifteen miles and place them where they can support me to-morrow. I shall try and determine to-night whither they have gone, whether down the railroad toward Pulaski or toward Florence or directly west toward the Tennessee River.

Very respectfully, your obedient servant,

JNO. T. CROXTON,
Brigadier-General of Volunteers.

IN THE FIELD, *Franklin, September 3, 1864.*

Maj. B. H. POLK:

Say to General Granger that General Steedman has been requested to come around by Huntsville with 3,400 infantry and help us. Direct General Granger to send up his cavalry along the line of the railroad to resist the destruction of the road by Wheeler, who is now going down

---

* See p. 620.

it toward Columbia. The cavalry can rely for support on the block-houses, if hard pressed. Wheeler seems to be on the river, and doing little or no damage to the road; we are pursuing.

L. H. ROUSSEAU,
Major-General.

NASHVILLE, TENN., *September 3, 1864.*

General BURBRIDGE:

Wheeler is making from East Tennessee toward the Nashville and Chattanooga Railroad, and his force has been encountered at three or four places east of the road, at one or two points as near as seven miles distant. He will likely strike the road between Murfreesborough and Cowan.

B. H. POLK,
Major and Assistant Adjutant-General.

HEADQUARTERS U. S. FORCES,
Carthage, Tenn., September 3, 1864.

Lieut. E. S. RICHARDS,
Acting Assistant Adjutant-General, Nashville:

SIR: I have the honor to report that all is quiet at this post. The troops from Granville, consisting of Companies B, C, D, E, and F, First Tennessee Mounted Infantry, have fallen back to this place, but a portion of the command are on the opposite bank of the river from Granville, watching that point. As yet no attempt has been made to capture the forces here. No rebels have been on this side of the Cumberland as known of. I have had the surrounding country full of spies since Monday last, and have been kept fully posted. The rebels left Alexandria last night, moving in the direction of Lebanon. A great many stragglers have been left in the country. In order to clear the country of these men effectually, and to prevent them from bushwhacking, it will require a heavy force to commence work at once, and that energetically. If allowed time to rest and concentrate these stragglers will commit innumerable outrages. In order to effectually and speedily clear the country of all stragglers I respectfully but earnestly request that the Fifth Tennessee Cavalry be ordered to report to me for duty. They can and will do the work. They have been tried, and I have only to point to their achievements for proof of their success in guerrilla warfare. I wish this communication to be laid before His Excellency Governor Johnson, and shall expect his aid in this matter. It is due to the families of my men that their fathers, brothers, and husbands should be here to protect them. If attacked at this post I shall fight as long as ammunition will last and the troops hold out. We are well prepared to act on the defensive, but can do nothing on the offensive.

Very respectfully, your obedient servant,

W. B. STOKES,
Colonel Fifth Tennessee Cavalry, Commanding.

[Indorsement.]

HDQRS. DEFENSES NASHVILLE AND CHATTANOOGA R. R.,
Tullahoma, September 19, 1864.

Respectfully returned.

As there is now no enemy to endanger the Nashville and Chattanooga Railroad, except guerrillas, who are disheartened by the total failure of the recent big raid, and as I have here three companies of the Twelfth Indiana Cavalry, mounted, with whom I can keep the country in the vicinity of the railroad pretty well scouted, and as the Fifth Tennessee, by going to its gallant colonel for the service he requires, will use up a large portion of the guerrillas who endanger the railroad, I can, with the assistance of the Twelfth Indiana Cavalry and other regiments ordered to report to me, protect the railroad. I recommend that the regiment be ordered to him for such length of time as may be thought best.

R. H. MILROY,
Major-General, Commanding.

WASHINGTON, *September 3, 1864—10.30 a. m.*

Maj. Gen. A. J. SMITH:

It is General Grant's wish that you act with your command against Wheeler's cavalry raiders.

H. W. HALLECK,
Major-General and Chief of Staff.

NASHVILLE, *September 3, 1864—12 m.*
(Received 2 p. m.)

Maj. T. T. ECKERT,
Superintendent U. S. Military Telegraph :

Wheeler came within seven miles of Nashville; crossed Nashville and Chattanooga Railroad, cutting it and telegraph pretty badly; thence went and cut railroad and telegraph between here and Franklin. He is now ten miles south of Franklin, going toward Columbia, with General Rousseau close after, skirmishing. Telegraph to Chattanooga be up to-day. Railroad will be repaired in few days; think damage is slight. Telegraph works to front via Chattanooga and Knoxville.

SAM. BRUCH,
Captain, &c.

SPECIAL
FIELD ORDERS,
No. 62.
HDQRS. MIL. DIV. OF THE MISSISSIPPI,
In the Field, near Lovejoy's,
September 3, 1864.

The general commanding announces with great pleasure that he has official information that our troops under Major-General Slocum occupied Atlanta yesterday at 11 a. m., the enemy having evacuated the night before, destroyed vast magazines of stores, and blowing up, among other things, eighty car-loads of ammunition, which accounts for the sounds heard by us on the night of the 1st instant. Our present task is, therefore, well done, and all work of destruction on the railroad will cease.

By order of Maj. Gen. W. T. Sherman:

L. M. DAYTON,
Aide-de-Camp.

Special } Hdqrs. Mil. Div. of the Mississippi,
Field Orders, } *In the Field, near Lovejoy's Station, Ga.,*
No. 63. } *September 3, 1864.*

I. Army commanders will, during to-day, send to Jonesborough all sick and wounded men, all empty wagons and prisoners of war, also all surplus wheels not needed for a five days' stay in front, ready to start to-morrow morning at 6 o'clock from Jonesborough for Atlanta. Each army will send a regiment to escort these wagons, and General Thomas will send an experienced colonel to conduct the train into Atlanta, there to await further orders.

II. The army will be prepared to move back to-morrow or next day, the Army of the Cumberland to Atlanta and Chattahoochee bridge, the Army of the Tennessee to East Point, and the Army of the Ohio to Decatur. Major-General Thomas will have General Garrard's cavalry ready to act as the rear guard.

By order of Maj. Gen. W. T. Sherman:

L. M. DAYTON,
Aide-de-Camp.

———

Special } Headquarters Department
Field Orders, } and Army of the Tennessee,
No. 116. } *Near Lovejoy's Station, Ga., September 3, 1864.*

The major-general commanding Military Division of the Mississippi, not desiring to prevent the enemy from pushing toward or around our right, the following will be the dispositions for the day:

1. Major-General Blair will inspect the extreme right, and secure it against any reverse fire, shortening his lines if necessary so as to have some reserve.

2. Major-General Logan will hold his front line with as few troops as he deems safe, and put the rest comfortably in camp.

3. General Ransom will encamp his troops, with a view to resting them, pushing skirmishers far out toward our right flank.

4. Brigadier-General Kilpatrick, while he will conform the operations of his command to the foregoing, will at the same time keep a sharp lookout on our right flank, advising the general commanding of any movement of the enemy.

*   *   *   *   *   *   *

VI. The following are the orders and dispositions of this army in the preparations to move back, in pursuance of Special Field Orders, No. 63, Military Division of the Mississippi:

1. Major-General Logan will, with his reserves, at once form a barricade on the most practicable defensive ground in the rear of the cotton-gin; this reserve position will be occupied by the division of Brigadier-General Hazen, who will form the rear guard of the right column; General Logan will then reduce his front line as much as possible, holding, however, to the last, the hill now occupied by General Harrow.

2. Brigadier-General Ransom, commanding Left Wing, Sixteenth Army Corps, will, with his reserves, construct a barricade on the right of that to be made by the Fifteenth Corps, retaining General Fuller's division as rear guard of the left column. General Ransom will also, in conjunction with the commands on his left, reduce his front to a thin line, moving all troops not necessary to hold it to the rear of his barricade.

3. Major-General Blair will, at the hour of withdrawal, carefully move back his corps through to the rear of his barricades, take the advance on the road pursued by the Sixteenth Corps, forming the left column.

4. The right column, under Major-General Logan, will pursue the road on which he advanced, drawing out at the same hour with the Sixteenth and Seventeenth Corps.

5. All trains, ammunition wagons, ambulances, &c., will be sent in advance. The hour of moving the trains and troops will be designated hereafter.

*   *   *   *   *   *   *

By order of Maj. Gen. O. O. Howard:

WM. T. CLARK,
Assistant Adjutant-General.

[SEPTEMBER 4, 1864.—For Grant to Sherman, acknowledging receipt of dispatch announcing capture of Atlanta, &c., see Part I, p. 87.]

HDQRS. MILITARY DIVISION OF THE MISSISSIPPI,
In the Field, near Lovejoy's, twenty-six miles south of Atlanta,
September 4, 1864.

General HALLECK:

MY DEAR FRIEND: I owe you a private letter, and believe one at this time will be acceptable to you. I appreciate your position and the delicate responsibilities that devolve on you, but believe you will master and surmount them all. I confess I owe you all I now enjoy of fame, for I had allowed myself in 1861 to sink into a perfect "slough of despond," and do believe if I could I would have run away and hid from the dangers and complications that surrounded us. You alone seemed to be confident, and opened to us the first avenue of success and hope, and you gradually put me in the way of recovering from what might have proved an ignoble end. When Grant spoke of my promotion as a major-general of the regular army, I asked him to decline in my name till this campaign tested us. Even when my commission came, which you were kind enough to send, I doubted its wisdom, but now that I have taken Atlanta as much by strategy as by force, I suppose the military world will approve it.

Through the official bulletins you are better acquainted with all the steps of our progress than any other man in the country, but I will try and point out to you more clearly the recent achievement. By the rapid falling off of my command, by expiration of service, I found myself reduced in number, close up against Atlanta, which was so protected by earth-works that I dared not assault. Fortunately Hood detached 6,000 of his best cavalry to our rear, and I quickly sent my cavalry to break the Macon road, over which his provisions and supplies came. I knew my cavalry was the superior to his, but he managed skillfully to send a brigade of infantry, which, in connection with his cavalry, about 4,000, managed so to occupy mine that though Kilpatrick reached the road he could work but little. The damage was soon repaired, and nothing was left me but to raise the siege, and move with my army. I moved one corps by night back to the bridge, which had been intrenched, using mostly old rebel works, then withdrawing from the left I got my whole army over on the West Point road, from Red Oak to

Fairburn, with the loss of but one man. There I spent one day and broke twelve miles of that road good. I then moved rapidly so that my right flank was within half a mile of the Macon road at Jonesborough, and the left two miles and a half from Rough and Ready. Hood had first sent Lee's corps to Jonesborough and Hardee's to Rough and Ready, but the Army of the Tennessee (my right) approached Jonesborough so rapidly that Hardee's corps was shifted at night also to that flank. Seeing his mistake I ordered Howard rapidly to intrench and hold his position, "threatening," and threw the balance of my army on the road from Rough and Ready to within four miles of Jonesborough. The moment that was done, I ordered Thomas and Schofield to rapidly break up that road, and without rest to turn on Jonesborough and crush that part. My plan was partially, but not thoroughly, executed. Hardee assaulted Howard, but made no progress; left his dead, about 400, and wounded in our hands, and fell behind his own works. I expected Thomas to be ready by 11 a. m., but it was near 4 when he got in; but one corps, Davis', charged down and captured the flank with 10 guns and many prisoners, but for some reason Stanley and Schofield were slow, and night came to Hardee's relief, and he escaped to the south. Hood finding me twenty miles below him on his only railroad, and Hardee defeated, was forced to abandon Atlanta, and retreated eastward, and by a circuit has got his men below me on the line to Macon. I ought to have reaped larger fruits of victory. A part of my army is too slow, but I feel my part was skillful and well executed. Though I ought to have taken 10,000 of Hardee's men, and all his artillery, I must content myself with 500 dead, 2,000 wounded, 2,000 prisoners, 10 guns on the field and 14 in Atlanta, 7 trains of cars captured and burned, many stragglers fleeing in disorder, and the town of Atlanta, which, after all, was the prize I fought for.

The army is in magnificent heart, and I could go on, but it would not be prudent. Wheeler is still somewhere to my rear, and every mile costs me detachments which I can illy spare. This country is so easily fortified that an enemy can stop an army every few miles. All the roads run on ridges, so that a hundred yards of parapet, with abatis, closes it, and gives the wings time to extend as fast as we can reconnoiter and cut roads. Our men will charge the parapet without fear, but they cannot the abatis and entanglements, which catch them at close range. I stay here a few days for effect, and then will fall back and occupy Atlanta, giving my command some rest. They need it. The untold labor they have done is herculean, and if ever you pass our route you will say honestly that we have achieved success by industry and courage. I hope the administration will be satisfied, for I have studied hard to serve it faithfully.

I hope anything I may have said or done will not be construed unfriendly to Mr. Lincoln or Stanton. That negro letter of mine I never designed for publication, but I am honest in my belief that it is not fair to our men to count negroes as equals. Cannot we at this day drop theories, and be reasonable men? Let us capture negroes, of course, and use them to the best advantage. My quartermaster now could give employment to 3,200, and relieve that number of soldiers who are now used to unload and dispatch trains, whereas those recruiting agents take them back to Nashville, where, so far as my experience goes, they disappear. When I call for expeditions at distant points, the answer invariably comes that they have not sufficient troops. All count the negroes out. On the Mississippi, where Thomas talked about 100,000 negro troops, I find I cannot draw away a white soldier, because they are indispensable to the safety of the river. I am willing to use them as far as possible, but object to fighting with "paper" men. Occasionally an exception occurs, which simply deceives. We want the best young white men of the land, and they should be inspired with the pride of freemen to fight for their country. If Mr. Lincoln or Stanton could walk through the camps of this army and hear the soldiers talk they would hear new ideas. I have had the question put to me often: "Is not a negro as good as a white man to stop a bullet?" Yes, and a sand-bag is better; but can a negro do our skirmishing and picket duty? Can they improvise roads, bridges, sorties, flank movements, &c., like the white man? I say no. Soldiers must and do many things without orders from their own sense, as in sentinels. Negroes are not equal to this. I have gone steadily, firmly, and confidently along, and I could not have done it with black troops, but with my old troops I have never felt a waver of doubt, and that very confidence begets success. I hope to God the draft will be made to-morrow; that you will keep up my army to its standard, 100,000 men; that you will give Canby an equal number; give Grant 200,000, and the balance keep on our communications, and I pledge you to take Macon and Savannah before spring, or leave my bones. My army is now in the very condition to be supplied with recruits. We have good corporals and sergeants, and some good lieutenants and captains, and those are far more important than good generals. They all seem to have implicit confidence in me. They observe success at points remote, as in this case of Atlanta, and they naturally say that the old man knows what he is about. They think I know where every road and by-path is in Georgia, and one soldier swore that I was born on Kenesaw Mountain. George Thomas, you know, is slow, but as true as steel; Schofield is also slow and leaves too much to others; Howard is a Christian, elegant gentleman, and conscientious soldier. In him I made no mistake. Hooker was a fool. Had he staid a couple of weeks he could have marched into Atlanta and claimed all the honors. I therefore think I have the army on which you may safely build. Grant has the perseverance of a Scotch terrier. Let him alone, and he will overcome Lee by untiring and unceasing efforts. The Mobile column is the one that needs a head, and no time should be wasted on the city. The river, Montgomery, and Columbus, Ga., are the strategic points. The latter has a double line by Montgomery and the Appalachicola River. It will not be safe to push this line farther until that is done, but stores and supplies may be accumulated here, and the country behind Chattahoochee purged a little more.

To-morrow is the day for the draft, and I feel far more interested in it than any event that ever transpired. I do think it has been wrong to keep our old troops so constantly under fire. Some of those old regiments that we had at Shiloh and Corinth have been with me ever since, and some of them have lost 70 per cent. in battle. It looks hard to put those brigades, now numbering less than 800 men, into battle. They feel discouraged, whereas if we could have a steady influx of recruits the living would soon forget the dead. The wounded and sick are lost to us, for once at a hospital they become worthless. It has been very bad economy to kill off our best men and pay full wages and bounties to the drift and substitutes. While all at the rear are paid regularly, I have here regiments that have not been paid for eight months, because the paymaster could not come to them. The draft judiciously used will be popular, and will take as many opponents of the war as advocates, whereas now our political equilibrium at the North seems disturbed by the absence of the fighting element, whereas the voting population is made up of sneaks, exempts, and cowards. Any nation would perish under such a system if protracted.

I have not heard yet of the Chicago nominations, but appearances are that McClellan will be nominated. The phases of "Democracy" are strange indeed. Some fool seems to have used my name. If forced to choose between the penitentiary and White House for four years, like old Professor Molinard, I would say the penitentiary, thank you, sir. If any committee would approach me for political preferment, I doubt if I could have patience or prudence enough to preserve a decent restraint on myself, but would insult the nation in my reply.

If we can only carry our people past this fall, we may escape the greatest danger that ever threatened a civilized people. We as soldiers best fulfill our parts by minding our own business, and I will try to do that.

I wish you would thank the President and Secretary for the constant support they have given me, and accept from me my personal assurance that I have always felt buoyed up by the knowledge that you were there.

Your sincere friend,

W. T. SHERMAN.

———

NEAR LOVEJOY'S, GA., *September 4, 1864—9 a. m.*
Maj. Gen. H. W. HALLECK, *Washington, D. C.:*

The Twentieth Corps now occupies Atlanta and the Chattahoochee bridges. The main army is now here, grouped below Jonesborough. The enemy holds a line facing us, with front well covered by parapets, and flanks by Walnut Creek on the right and a confluent of Flint River on his left. His position is too strong to attack in front, and to turn it would carry me too far from our base at this time. Besides, there is no commensurate object, as there is no valuable point to his rear till we reach Macon, 103 miles from Atlanta. We are not prepared for that, and I will gradually fall back and occupy Atlanta, which was and is our grand objective point, already secured. For the future I propose that of the drafted men I receive my due share, say 50,000; that an equal or greater number go to General Canby, who should now proceed with all energy to get Montgomery and the reach of the Alabama River above Selma; that when I know he can move on Columbus, Ga., I move on La Grange and West Point, keeping to the east of the Chattahoochee; that we form a junction, repair roads to Montgomery, and open up the Appalachicola and Chattahoochee Rivers to Columbus, and move from it as a base straight on Macon. This campaign can be made in the winter, and we can safely rely on the corn of the Flint and Chattahoochee to supply forage. If the Tensas Channel of the Alabama can be used, General Gardner, with the rebel garrison, could continue to hold Mobile for our use when we want it. I propose to remove all the inhabitants of Atlanta, sending those committed to our cause to the rear, and the rebel families to the front. I will allow no trade, manufactories, nor any citizens there at all, so that we will have the entire use of railroad back, as also such corn and forage as may be reached by our troops. If the people raise a howl against my barbarity and cruelty I will answer that war is war, and not popularity-seeking. If they want peace they and their relatives must stop war.

W. T. SHERMAN,
Major-General.

HEADQUARTERS DEPARTMENT OF THE CUMBERLAND,
September 4, 1864—12 m.

Major-General SHERMAN,
Commanding Military Division of the Mississippi:

GENERAL: Lieutenant Wharton, my engineer, has just returned from an examination of the enemy's lines in front of Stanley. He reports them very strong and still being strengthened by the enemy amid a constant and hot skirmish. He believes the enemy intends to hold his present line.

Respectfully, &c.,

GEO. H. THOMAS,
Major-General, U. S. Volunteers, Commanding.

HEADQUARTERS FOURTEENTH ARMY CORPS,
Jonesborough, Ga., September 4, 1864.

Brigadier-General WHIPPLE,
Chief of Staff, Department of the Cumberland:

GENERAL: I have the honor to report that my sick, wounded, captured ordnance, and prisoners of war left for Atlanta this morning, escorted by a brigade of Morgan's division. They moved at daylight. I am now engaged in removing the rebel wounded scattered about in the neighborhood to this place. I have but forty-five empty wagons left with which to remove them and the cotton alluded to in the general's order. They will not be sufficient to more than transport the wounded, if that. There are many empty wagons belonging to other commands moving to the rear. Why can they not be required to do some of this work?

I am, respectfully,

JEF. C. DAVIS,
Brevet Major-General, Commanding.

HEADQUARTERS FOURTEENTH ARMY CORPS,
Jonesborough, Ga., September 4, 1864.

[Brig. Gen. WILLIAM D. WHIPPLE:]

GENERAL: I have the honor to report that all has been quiet upon my front to-day, and no change has taken place in the position of my lines. As more fully reported in my letter of this morning, the empty wagons of my command were loaded with the sick and wounded and ordnance stores captured from the enemy, and, together with all prisoners of war in my possession, were forwarded to Atlanta under escort of a brigade from Second Division. Two hundred and thirty-four rebel wounded, surgeons, chaplains, and attendants have been collected in this neighborhood during the day, and all but about eighty, who are too badly wounded, will be sent to Atlanta in the morning. Twenty-one rebel deserters have been received during the day.

I am, very respectfully, your obedient servant,

JEF. C. DAVIS,
Brevet Major-General, Commanding.

HEADQUARTERS SECOND CAVALRY DIVISION,
September 4, 1864.

Brigadier-General ELLIOTT,
  Chief of Cavalry, Department of the Cumberland:

GENERAL: The rebel pickets were withdrawn from all roads to the east of this, except on the McDonough road, by 4 p. m. yesterday, and their army may now be regarded as south of us. On the McDonough road the cavalry of the Army of the Ohio was skirmishing yesterday and drove in their pickets to within a few miles of McDonough. I do not know if they reached that point, but think not. My command will be on the Jonesborough and Flat Rock road to-day.

Very respectfully, your obedient servant,
K. GARRARD,
Brigadier-General, Commanding Division.

HDQRS. CHIEF OF CAVALRY, DEPT. OF THE CUMBERLAND,
Camp near Lovejoy's, September 4, 1864.

Brig. Gen. K. GARRARD,
  Commanding Second Division Cavalry:

The general commanding directs that you have your command in readiness to march to-morrow, although the precise hour cannot be stated, and that you cover the rear and right flank of General Schofield's corps in its march to Decatur, Ga. You will ascertain from General Schofield when his command will move, allowing it to pass to the north of you. On the arrival of General Schofield's corps at Decatur you will, with your command, take post, headquarters at Cross Keys, picketing from Stone Mountain to the crossing of the Chattahoochee on the road from Pinckneyville to Warsaw. It is designed to establish a signal station on Stone Mountain, if, in connection with General Schofield's cavalry, it can be made secure. You will keep yourself informed of any movements of the enemy toward Lawrenceville. On your arrival at Cross Keys establish a courier line, in charge of a non-commissioned officer, to these headquarters at or near Atlanta.

I am, general, very respectfully, your obedient servant,
DAVID F. HOW,
Lieutenant and Acting Assistant Adjutant-General.

HEADQUARTERS SECOND CAVALRY DIVISION,
September 4, 1864.

Brig. Gen. W. D. WHIPPLE,
  Chief of Staff, Department of the Cumberland:

GENERAL: I have nothing of interest to report to-day. My headquarters are at Mount Zion Church, about four miles northeast of Jonesborough, and my pickets cover all roads as far north as Rough and Ready.

Very respectfully, your obedient servant,
K. GARRARD,
Brigadier-General, Commanding Division.

HDQRS. SECOND BRIGADE, THIRD CAVALRY DIVISION,
Camp in the Field, September 4, 1864.
Captain ESTES,
 Assistant Adjutant-General:

I have the honor to report that scouting parties sent out from my command report my front strongly picketed by the enemy, apparently cavalry, on the right, and infantry or dismounted cavalry on the left. Several of their posts were driven in, developing quite a strong force in position behind a swampy ravine running nearly parallel to the Glass road. The scouts also report a plantation road, extending from near James Bull's house, on the Glass road, through the plantations of Mr. Dorsey and Mr. Crawford. I also learn from citizens that the same road extends to Lovejoy's Station. The Glass road appears to be open from my position to Flint River, except perhaps small patrols of the enemy.
 Very respectfully,

             F. A. JONES,
          Lieutenant-Colonel, Commanding.

            NEAR LOVEJOY'S STATION,
                September 4, 1864.
Maj. Gen. JOHN A. LOGAN,
 Commanding Fifteenth Army Corps:

The heavy rains having rendered the route to be taken by the left column, as indicated in Special Field Orders, No. 116, extract VI, impracticable, General Blair will withdraw on the road by which he approached, taking the advance, followed by the Left Wing, Sixteenth Army Corps.
 By order of Maj. Gen. O. O. Howard:

            WM. T. CLARK,
          Assistant Adjutant-General.

        HEADQUARTERS ARMY OF THE OHIO,
    Near Lovejoy's Station, Ga., September 4, 1864.
Maj. Gen. W. T. SHERMAN,
 Commanding Military Division of the Mississippi:

GENERAL: In compliance with your request, I have the honor to submit my views upon the questions of rank arising under the act of Congress approved April 4, 1862. These questions may be thus stated:

First. When a corps is temporarily detached from the army to which it belongs to operate with another army, whose commander is assigned by the President, under the act of April 4, 1862, but who is junior by commission to the corps commander, is this corps commander entitled by law to command the combined force?

Second. Is there any provision of law for such command?

The first question can probably best be answered, and the difficulty of the second illustrated by considering a case which has occurred and which is likely to be a very common one. General A commands an army consisting of two corps, whose commanders, Generals B and C, are senior by commission to General A. General D commands a corps of another army and is senior to General A but junior to Generals B and C. General D's corps is detached and ordered to operate with

General A's army. The sixty-second Article of War directs that in such case the officer highest in rank by commission there on duty shall command the combined force, "unless otherwise specially directed by the President of the United States." But the officer highest in rank is General B or C, who must therefore command (according to the sixty-second Article of War), unless otherwise specially directed by the President. But neither General B nor C can take the command, for the President has otherwise directed by making them subordinate to General A, under the act of April 4. And there is no provision of law whatever that would give the command to General D, notwithstanding the fact that he is senior to General A, for he is junior to both General B and General C, hence the combined force can have no commander unless it be General A. I think, therefore, it is clear that the law of April 4, 1862, in giving through the President's order an officer command over his seniors by commission, abrogates the sixty-second Article of War so far as it relates to himself and other officers of the same grade who are not commanding under the law of April 4.

The second question is not so clear. There is an apparent conflict between the sixty-second Article of War and the act of April 4, 1862, which seems to leave a combined force such as I have supposed without a commander provided for it by law. But in my opinion this conflict is not real. The Article of War itself gives the President the power to direct otherwise than according to the general rule, which I understand to mean simply that he may direct the senior not to assume command of all the forces but leave each under its own commander, and the act of April 4 gives him the additional power to assign a junior officer to the command whenever military operations may require the presence of two or more officers of the same grade in the same field. The President, in pursuance of this law, has assigned a commander to each of three armies or departments (the armies consisting simply of the troops serving in those departments and determined not by the President but by the General-in-Chief of all the armies, or other superior officer having direction of military operations in the three departments), and has assigned a general to command the three departments, combined under the name of a military division, and to direct the operations of the combined armies as general-in-chief. Under the authority conferred by the act of Congress, and the discretion given him in the Article of War, he has provided in advance for the very case in point by naming three army commanders to be next in authority and responsibility to the general-in-chief in the order of their rank, and superior in both authority and responsibility to all other officers; and has given to the general-in-chief authority to combine or separate, detach or unite, his three armies, or any part of them, on any field, as in his judgment "military operations may require." The President has assigned in advance the commanders of the forces which military operations may require to be united on any field, and has left it to his generals-in-chief to judge when, whose, and what forces shall be united. The evident object of the law of April 4, 1862, was to give the President the power to select from all the major-generals of the army those in his judgment most competent to direct the operations of the separate armies, and the power thus given has been habitually exercised. If, when the exigencies of the service require a temporary increase of one of these armies, which is likely to occur only at the most critical periods of a campaign, the army commander selected by the President can be superseded by an officer who has never been intrusted with more than a subordinate command, the object of the law is defeated and the President's selection is of no avail at the most critical moment. It must be observed that, if the sixty-second Article of War was alone taken as the law, a major-general commanding a division in one army might assume command of another army whenever the accidents of a battle should separate him from his own army and throw him in contact with another.

Finally, it is my opinion that the act of April 4, 1862, must be construed as creating, in effect, an additional grade in the army, viz, that of department or army commander superior to that determined by commission alone.

Very respectfully, your obedient servant,
J. M. SCHOFIELD,
Major-General, Commanding.

HEADQUARTERS ARMY OF THE OHIO,
In the Field, September 4, 1864—3.50 p. m.

Brig. Gen. J. D. Cox,
Commanding Third Division:

GENERAL: The commanding general directs me to inform you that the signal officer reports that the enemy is in line of battle behind his works on his right, with battle-flags flying from the parapets, and he has thrown out about fifty skirmishers in his front and a company on his flank.

Very respectfully, your obedient servant,
J. A. CAMPBELL,
Major and Assistant Adjutant-General.

HEADQUARTERS,
In the Field, four miles south of Columbia,
September 4, 1864—12.30 p. m.

Brig. Gen. J. D. WEBSTER:

Wheeler crossed Duck River below this, and, joining Roddey, is again menacing the railroad. General Steedman should be telegraphed to come around by Huntsville as promptly as possible. Please telegraph him at once to this effect.

LOVELL H. ROUSSEAU,
Major-General.

NASHVILLE, *September 4, 1864—8 p. m.*

General STEEDMAN:

Push your force forward rapidly as possible to Huntsville and Pulaski. Johnson has joined Wheeler south of Duck River and menaces Alabama railroad.

By order:
J. D. WEBSTER.

FRANKLIN, *September 4, 1864.*

Maj. B. H. POLK,
Assistant Adjutant-General:

Reliable information from General Rousseau is that Wheeler has crossed Duck River near Columbia and Roddey formed a junction with him. Couriers say Rousseau captured 500 horses in a skirmish where Wheeler dismounted men to fight on foot. General Kelly's friends have asked me to furnish a small escort to bury him. Shall I do it?

J. B. PARK,
Lieutenant-Colonel Fourth Michigan Cavalry, Comdg. Post.

THREE MILES EAST OF TRIUNE,
September 4, 1864.

Major-General ROUSSEAU:

GENERAL: Since yesterday morning we have been chasing a rebel cavalry force of two brigades, under General Williams. We passed five miles around Murfreesborough yesterday. We charged in town and [drove] the rebels four miles from town on the Shelby pike. They have a force of between 1,500 and 2,000. We have been skirmishing with them since 8 o'clock this morning. They have three pieces of artillery. We have killed and captured some 20, and lost about 10 killed and wounded. Lieutenant-Colonel Eifort, Second Kentucky, was killed in a charge. If you can detach a force to head them, their whole force can be bagged. I have Colonel Spalding's old brigade here; you know what it is and what it can do. I left General Steedman at Murfreesborough this morning with a large infantry force.

Yours, in haste,

R. H. MILROY,
Major-General.

ATLANTA, GA., *September 4, 1864—5 p. m.*
(Received 5 p. m. 5th.)

Major ECKERT:

The events of the last ten days may be succinctly stated thus: Hood, losing us from his front, looked two ways for the next blow, and leaving Stewart's corps and the militia here, sent Hardee and Lee down the Macon road to be ready. General Sherman found them there, and before the fight all of Stewart's corps, except one division, joined. On the 1st the Army of the Tennessee threatened Jonesborough on the west, Schofield on the east, and the Fourteenth Corps assaulted from the north, driving the enemy, capturing 2 batteries and 1,000 prisoners. No fighting since of importance, and Sherman will bring the entire army here to refit and rest. Altogether we have fought a battle, occupied Atlanta, got 3,000 prisoners and 12 guns. Probably lost 1,000 men, killed, wounded, and missing. May possibly catch the troops that were left here, but not probable.

J. C. VAN DUZER.

NASHVILLE, TENN., *September 4, 1864.*
(Received 4 p. m.)

Major ECKERT,
   Washington:

Have nothing more from Captain Van Duzer. Have just asked him to send something. A cipher just received here, dated 3d, says: "Atlanta is ours." No particulars. Wheeler is moving down toward Florence, our forces in close pursuit. My repair men were attacked yesterday near La Vergne. Advance again to-day. Think will work to Chattanooga direct by this evening.

SAM. BRUCH,
Captain and Assistant Superintendent Telegraph.

SPECIAL }   HDQRS. MIL. DIV. OF THE MISSISSIPPI,
FIELD ORDERS, }   *In the Field, near Lovejoy's,*
No. 64. }   *September 4, 1864.*

The army having accomplished its undertaking in the complete reduction and occupation of Atlanta will occupy the place and the country near it until a new campaign is planned in concert with the other grand armies of the United States.

I. The Army of the Cumberland will occupy the city and its communications with Chattanooga, the Army of the Tennessee will occupy East Point and the right flank, and the Army of the Ohio the town of Decatur and the left flank; the cavalry will occupy Sandtown, Roswell, and other points on the flanks and along our line of communication.

II. To withdraw to the posts herein designated, the Army of the Cumberland will withdraw, first, to Jonesborough; second, to Rough and Ready, and third, to Atlanta, leaving the cavalry to bring up the rear in the manner herein prescribed.

III. The Army of the Tennessee will move in concert with that of the Cumberland, first, to its old position near Jonesborough; second, across the Flint River to about Morrow's Mill, and third, to East Point and the head of Camp Creek.

IV. The Army of the Ohio will also move in concert with that of the Cumberland, first, to a point near Jonesborough; second, to some point within two miles and east of Rough and Ready, and last to Decatur.

V. General Kilpatrick's cavalry will cover the left rear of the Army of the Tennessee, and that of General Garrard the right rear of the Army of the Ohio until they reach the positions assigned in this order, when the cavalry commands will move to the points designated, viz, Sandtown and Roswell.

VI. The general-in-chief will give notice when the movement will begin, and after reaching Atlanta will establish headquarters in Atlanta, and afford the army an opportunity to have a full month's rest, with every chance to organize, receive pay, replenish clothing, and prepare for a fine winter's campaign.

By order of Maj. Gen. W. T. Sherman:

L. M. DAYTON,
Aide-de-Camp.

SPECIAL }   HEADQUARTERS DEPARTMENT
FIELD ORDERS, }   AND ARMY OF THE TENNESSEE,
No. 117. }   *Near Lovejoy's Station, Ga., September 4, 1864.*

*   *   *   *   *   *   *

VI. Corps commanders will cause their commands to be particularly watchful to-morrow morning at daylight, prepared for any attack of the enemy, or to discover if he has evacuated his works.

By order of Maj. Gen. O. O. Howard:

WM. T. CLARK,
Assistant Adjutant-General.

SPECIAL FIELD ORDERS, ⎫   HDQRS. FIFTEENTH ARMY CORPS,
          No. 93.   ⎬   *Near Lovejoy's, Ga., September 4, 1864.*

I. Brig. Gen. W. B. Hazen, commanding Second Division, will commence the construction of a barricade on the most defensible position north of the cotton-gin, with the left resting on the railroad, and extending to a point on the right to be designated by Capt. C. B. Reese, engineer officer of department staff.

*   *   *   *   *   *   *

By order of Maj. Gen. John A. Logan:

R. R. TOWNES,
Assistant Adjutant-General.

WAR DEPARTMENT,
September 5, 1864—3 p. m.

Major-General SHERMAN,
          Atlanta:

The following-named volunteer officers from the State of Indiana, to wit, General Nathan Kimball, First Division, Fourth Army Corps; Lieut. Col. W. T. B. McIntire, Forty-second Indiana Volunteers; Dr. R. M. Welman, Ninth Indiana Cavalry, Pulaski, Tenn.; Col. Benjamin Harrison, Seventieth Indiana; Col. Edward Anderson, Twelfth Indiana Cavalry, and Chaplain W. W. Curry, Fifty-third Indiana, all under your command, can render valuable service within that State if they can have leave of absence until the 15th of October. In view of the armed organizations against the Government of the United States that have been made throughout the State of Indiana, and are now in active operation in the campaign for Jefferson Davis, this Department deems it expedient that the officers named should have leave to go home, provided they can be spared without injury to the service. This question is submitted to your judgment, with the request that you shall grant them a leave, if it can be done any time before the 1st of October without prejudice to the service; the longer leave the better service they can render. You will please answer by telegraph.

EDWIN M. STANTON,
Secretary of War.

[SEPTEMBER 5, 1864.—For Stanton to Sherman, transmitting thanks from the President, &c., see Part I, p. 86.]

HDQRS. CAVALRY DIVISION, ARMY OF THE OHIO,
September 5, 1864.

Maj. J. A. CAMPBELL,
          Assistant Adjutant-General, Army of the Ohio:

MAJOR: I have the honor to report that the scout to the Fayetteville road, at the point I struck it yesterday, found a rebel picket posted there. This was driven off, but no further information of the rebel position was ascertained. The scout toward McDonough was made by the First Ohio Squadron, under Major Rice. He has just returned bringing with him 15 prisoners. He reached a point within three miles of McDonough, where he came onto a camp of a cavalry regiment. He drove the pickets in so rapidly as to surprise the camp, but they rallied in force sufficient to check him. He lost 1 man killed, the sergeant who led the advance guard. The information he obtained from citizens was, that the enemy is holding all the roads leading south from the Fayetteville and McDonough road, and that there are some troops—cavalry probably—at McDonough; this is not corroborated by the cavalrymen captured. They say that the troops marched from McDonough at daylight this morning, and that there is nothing there now but the provost guard.

Very respectfully, your obedient servant,

ISRAEL GARRARD,
Colonel, Commanding Division.

HEADQUARTERS SEVENTEENTH ARMY CORPS,
Near Lovejoy's Station, Ga., September 5, 1864.

Lieut. Col. WILLIAM T. CLARK,
Asst. Adjt. Gen., Department and Army of the Tennessee:

COLONEL: I have the honor to report that the skirmish firing along my front was unusually heavy during the whole of last night. This morning General Woods reports that the enemy constructed last night a flank work in front of General Logan's right center, through an open field and perpendicular to the main line. The impression prevails that our position on the right flanks the enemy's.

Very respectfully, your obedient servant,

FRANK P. BLAIR, JR.,
Major-General.

HDQRS. SECOND DIVISION, SIXTEENTH ARMY CORPS,
Near Lovejoy's Station, Ga., September 5, 1864.

Col. R. N. ADAMS,
Commanding Second Brigade:

COLONEL: In riding through the camps this morning I was very much grieved to find in the Twelfth Illinois Infantry, lying shamelessly exposed to the whole command, a lot of male and female clothing and wearing apparel, shirts, bed-quilts, &c., evidently recently pillaged from some of the neighboring helpless citizens. I directed Colonel Van Sellar to investigate the matter, and ascertain who the guilty parties are and have them brought to punishment. I neglected to tell him to find out the name of the officer in command of the company where the things were exposed to view, and now order you to ascertain the same and prefer charges against him for conduct prejudicial to good order and military discipline, in permitting the thing to be done under his eyes and not taking steps to punish his men. Pillaging, at all times disgraceful and demoralizing, will not be countenanced or tolerated under any circumstances in this command. While brigade commanders can appropriate properly any articles of provision or forage necessary, they are expected to use every exertion to enforce all orders against marauding and lawlessness of any character.

I am, colonel, very respectfully, your obedient servant,

JNO. M. CORSE,
Brigadier-General, Commanding.

NASHVILLE, *September 5, 1864.*
(Received 9.50 p. m.)

Major CRAVENS, *Assistant Adjutant-General:*

General Milroy is at Franklin, and will go on south. Williams' brigade rebel cavalry went south from Triune last night toward Shelbyville, and may be on your road again. He is cut off from Wheeler, but may attack General Rousseau in the rear.

B. H. POLK,
Major and Assistant Adjutant-General.

HUNTSVILLE, *September 5, 1864.*

Col. E. ANDERSON, *Brownsborough:*

Keep a sharp watch on Johnson's movement. Should he threaten the railroad notify me; concentrate on him as much of your force as is practicable, and I will soon be with you. Patrol the road frequently.

W.M. P. LYON,
Colonel, Commanding.

FRANKLIN, TENN., *September 5, 1864.*

Maj. B. H. POLK,
Assistant Adjutant-General:

Just arrived here with the Fifth, Tenth, and Twelfth Tennessee Cavalry. Fought the rebel General Williams, 2,000 strong, all day; last fight at Triune. Lieutenant-Colonel Eifort, of the Second Kentucky, killed in one of our charges. Rebels turned south at Triune. Our ammunition gave out, and, supposing that Williams joined Wheeler, we came in here for ammunition, provisions, and information. A detachment of the Sixth Indiana has just arrived. We will shoe our horses, get supplies, and go ahead. Can you communicate with Murfreesborough yet?

R. H. MILROY,
Major-General.

FRANKLIN, *September 5, 1864—1.05 p. m.*

Maj. J. O. CRAVENS,
Assistant Adjutant-General:

Arrived here this morning with the Tennessee regiment of cavalry; pursued a rebel division of cavalry under General Williams around Murfreesborough day before yesterday, and pursued from that place yesterday, fighting inch [by inch] to Triune. Rebels turned south from there on pike that runs to Shelbyville. I learned that they are trying to join Wheeler, but they find that they are cut off by General Rousseau. I pass on to Shelbyville and strike Duck River bridge and other points. They are about 2,000 strong. Keep a sharp lookout for them. Inform all the stations along the railroad, that they may be ready for them, and if General Steedman is still on the line, inform him I am in the hunt and don't know when I will get back. Colonel Eifort, Second Kentucky, mortally wounded yesterday; since died. Some 10 or 15 of our boys killed and wounded. We captured 11 rebels and killed and wounded 20.

R. H. MILROY,
Brigadier-General.

SPECIAL FIELD ORDERS, } HDQRS. DEPT. OF THE CUMBERLAND,
    No. 245.   } *Near Lovejoy's Station, September 5, 1864.*

In execution of Special Field Orders, No. 64, from headquarters Military Division of the Mississippi, the following will be the movements of the Army of the Cumberland:

1. The Fourth Army Corps will withdraw at 8 o'clock to-night by the road running east of the railroad, encamping the first night at Jonesborough, the second at Rough and Ready, the third day marching by Hutchins' to the east of Atlanta, and taking up a position near that occupied by the corps at the commencement of the movement which has terminated here, facing south, with two divisions in line and one in reserve.

2. The Fourteenth Army Corps will march on the second day from Jonesborough to Rough and Ready by roads running on the west of the railroad, and encamping on that side of the railroad at Rough and Ready. On the third day the corps will march by the road running past Tomlinson's, Cash's, Mount Zion Church, to White Hall, and take up a position at that place, facing south, with two divisions in line and one in reserve.

3. The Twentieth Army Corps will remain as at present located until further orders, and Major-General Slocum will command the town of Atlanta.

*   *   *   *   *   *   *

By command of Major-General Thomas:
                          WM. D. WHIPPLE,
                          Assistant Adjutant-General.

HEADQUARTERS FOURTH ARMY CORPS,
        Near Lovejoy's Station, Ga., September 5, 1864.

Orders of the day for the Fourth Army Corps for to-day, September 5, 1864: In accordance with instructions received from headquarters the troops of this corps will withdraw to-night to the position they occupied on the night of the first instant, just beyond Jonesborough. After withdrawing to the field to the rear of the one in which corps headquarters is situated, the route of march will be along the east side of the railroad. The order of march will be, first, General Newton's division; second, General Kimball's; third, General Wood's. The troops will be drawn off at 8 p. m. exactly by headquarters time, and the pickets will be drawn off at exactly 12 p. m. Col. I. C. B. Suman, Ninth Indiana Infantry, is hereby detailed as special field officer of the day for to-day. He will report at these headquarters for orders at 5 p. m., and division commanders will send their picket officers to report to him for instructions at the same time and place. All headquarters wagons, ambulances, except six to a division, artillery wagons, ammunition wagons, except five to a division, and such artillery as can be withdrawn without attracting the attention of the enemy, will at once be sent beyond Jonesborough just to the rear of the position to be occupied by the troops to-night.

By order of Major-General Stanley:
                          J. S. FULLERTON,
                          Assistant Adjutant-General.

CIRCULAR.]   HEADQUARTERS FOURTEENTH ARMY CORPS,
                        Jonesborough, Ga., September 5, 1864.

Your command will be held in readiness to move to-morrow morning at daylight. In case the corps does not move immediately toward Atlanta the position of the line will be changed to front southward, and all trains, headquarters, &c., will be moved to the rear. Further orders will be given to-night or in the morning.

By order of Bvt. Maj. Gen. Jef. C. Davis:

                                A. C. McCLURG,
                Assistant Adjutant-General and Chief of Staff.

(To division commanders.)

SPECIAL FIELD ORDERS, }   HDQRS. ARMY OF THE OHIO,
        No. 101.   }   *Near Jonesborough, Ga., September 5, 1864.*

I. The army will move from its present position, in concert with the Army of the Cumberland, in the following manner: The trains will move to the rear, first the baggage and then the ordnance trains, taking the new road leading north from present headquarters. General Cox will send a regiment of infantry to guard the trains. General Cox will place his division on the ridge immediately in rear of headquarters. General Hascall will then withdraw his division to the rear of General Cox, taking care to conceal the movement as much as possible from the enemy, and keeping his men under cover from the enemy's artillery. If the enemy follow, General Hascall will form his division in rear of General Cox, prepared to support him or cover his flank. Otherwise General Hascall will continue his march in rear of the trains. General Cox will follow as rear guard. Colonel Garrard will cover the flank of the infantry and trains during the march, using the road on which the infantry moved on the 2d instant. The first march will be to the position near Jonesborough occupied on the 1st instant, where orders will be given for further movements. The commanding general will give notice when the movement will begin.

By command of Major-General Schofield:

                                J. A. CAMPBELL,
                    Major and Assistant Adjutant-General.

SPECIAL }   HEADQUARTERS DEPARTMENT
FIELD ORDERS, }   AND ARMY OF THE TENNESSEE,
    No. 118. }   *Near Lovejoy's Station, Ga., September 5, 1864.*

In accordance with Special Field Orders, No. 64, Military Division of the Mississippi, and Special Field Orders, No. 116, extract VI, from these headquarters, this army will draw out from its present position at 8 o'clock this evening.

The Fifteenth and Sixteenth Corps, with the exception of the divisions to form the rear guard, will march to Jonesborough, occupying their old positions in the works.

The Seventeenth Corps will cross Flint River and take up the position occupied by it on the evening of September 1. The rear guard and skirmish line will be withdrawn at 12 o'clock to-night and rejoin their respective commands.

Corps commanders will give such directions as will secure the simultaneous withdrawal of the pickets. All reserve artillery, trains, and ambulances, except the ammunition required for the reserve division will at 12 o'clock this p. m. be sent across Flint River into park with the trains already there in charge of Capt. J. T. Conklin, chief quarter-master. Brigadier-General Kilpatrick will throw out a sufficient force to picket the front and right of the army, and, with the remainder of his command, will move back and occupy the same position held by him when this army was at Jonesborough. Lieutenant-Colonel Strong will superintend the withdrawal of the pickets, and corps commanders are requested to instruct one of their staff officers to report to him at these headquarters at 2.30 o'clock this afternoon.

  *   *   *   *   *   *   *

By order of Maj. Gen. O. O. Howard:

WM. T. CLARK,
Assistant Adjutant-General.

SPECIAL FIELD ORDERS, } HDQRS. FIFTEENTH ARMY CORPS,
          Near Lovejoy's Station, Ga.,
   No. 94. }   *September 5, 1864.*

  *   *   *   *   *   *   *

II. In accordance with Special Field Orders, No. 118, from depart-ment headquarters of this date, this corps will draw out from its present position, as follows: The First Division, Major-General Osterhaus com-manding, and the Fourth Division, Brigadier-General Harrow command-ing, will withdraw their main lines at 8 p. m. to-day and march to Jonesborough and occupy their old position in the works. The First Division will move in advance. Brig. Gen. W. B. Hazen's division will act as rear guard to this command, and will at once occupy the works erected by it in rear of the cotton-gin. At 12 o'clock to-night the division and skirmishers of the First and Fourth Divisions will be withdrawn, the division to the works occupied by it at Jonesborough on the 1st instant and the skirmishers to their respective commands. Captain Hoover will superintend the withdrawal of the pickets, and division commanders are requested to instruct one of their staff officers to report to him at these headquarters at 3.30 p. m. to-day. The chief ordnance officer of the corps will limit that five wagons of ammunition be left with each division, and will send the remainder at 2 p. m. across Flint River, on the road advanced on by this command, and parked with the train already there in charge of Capt. J. T. Conklin, chief quartermaster, Department of the Tennessee. The movements must be made with the least possible noise, so as not to attract the attention of the enemy. Brigadier-General Hazen, if he so desires, can send De Gress' [battery] to Jonesborough this evening before dark, and direct it to go into posi-tion on some part of the line to be occupied by him.

By order of Maj. Gen. John A. Logan:

R. R. TOWNES,
Assistant Adjutant-General.

SPECIAL }   HEADQUARTERS LEFT WING,
FIELD ORDERS, }   SIXTEENTH ARMY CORPS,
 No. 76. }   *Near Lovejoy's Station, Ga., September 5, 1864.*

I. This command will withdraw from its present position, in pursu-ance of instructions from military division and department headquar-ters, in the following order:

First. The entire train of wagons and ambulances belonging to this command, except one ambulance to each regiment, will, two hours before the time fixed for the movement of the troops, move by the road to Turner's, and will follow the train of the Seventeenth Corps to Jonesborough, when they will be parked on the west side of Flint Creek, in rear of the position occupied by this corps on the 1st instant.

Second. Brig. Gen. J. W. Fuller, commanding Fourth Division, will, at an hour to be hereafter designated, move his command into the new works at Turner's, and will hold that position until the Seventeenth Corps, and Second Division, Sixteenth Army Corps, have passed, when he will follow in rear of the Second Division, and act as rear guard to the left column, keeping out a strong line of skirmishers and flankers on his rear and left, and taking care to bring up all stragglers.

Third. Brig. Gen. J. M. Corse, commanding Second Division, will, at an hour to be hereafter designated, withdraw his command, including skirmishers, simultaneously with the Seventeenth Corps, and will move toward Jonesborough, on the road leading past Fitzgerald's and Turner's. He will halt in rear of the new works of the Fourth Division, to allow the Seventeenth Corps to pass, when he will follow the Seventeenth Corps into Jonesborough, keeping always within supporting distance of the Fourth Division.

Fourth. Major Hughes, commanding Ninth Illinois Mounted Infantry, will, at an hour to be hereafter designated, move his command to the forks of the road near Fitzgerald's and throw out a line of skirmishers to Hebron Church. He will hold this position until the skirmishers of the Second Division have passed him, when he will fall back toward Jonesborough, keeping in rear of the infantry column, holding his reserves in the main road, and maintaining a strong line of skirmishers and flankers in his rear and on the left of the column.

Fifth. On arriving at Jonesborough the command will move into and occupy their old works of the 1st instant, near Flint Creek.

II. So much of Special Field Orders, No. 76, extract I, from these headquarters, as conflicts with Special Field Orders, No. 118, Department and Army of the Tennessee, is hereby revoked.

By order of Brig. Gen. T. E. G. Ransom:

J. W. BARNES,
Assistant Adjutant-General.

IN THE FIELD,
Near Jonesborough, Ga., September 6, 1864—3 p. m.
(Received 8th.)

Lieut. Gen. U. S. GRANT,
    City Point, Va.:

I have your dispatch* and will announce it to the troops in general orders. We are gradually falling back to Atlanta, feeding high on the corn-fields of the Confederacy. I will be in Atlanta in a day or two and will communicate fully with you. I always felt that you would personally take more pleasure in my success than in your own, and I appreciate the feeling to its fullest extent.

W. T. SHERMAN,
Major-General.

---

* See Part I, p. 87.

IN THE FIELD,
Near Jonesborough, Ga., September 6, 1864—3 p. m.
(Received 11.05 p. m. 8th.)

Hon. E. M. STANTON,
   Secretary of War:

I have just received your telegram,* and shall announce it to the whole army, preceded by the expression, "The general commanding announces to the army with pride and satisfaction," and followed by "All corps, regiments, and batteries may, without further notice, inscribe 'Atlanta' on their colors." We are moving back to Atlanta slowly, making good use of the corn-fields, which our animals needed, and to prevent a boast of the enemy that we were in a hurry. I have burned a good deal of cotton, but will save enough to pay the expenses of the salute.

                                   W. T. SHERMAN,
                                         Major-General.

NEAR JONESBOROUGH, GA., *September 6, 1864—3.30 p. m.*
(Received 10.30 p. m. 8th.)

Hon. E. M. STANTON,
   Secretary of War:

The officers named in your dispatch of the 5th will be ordered to report to the Governor of Indiana, for special duty, as soon as I return to Atlanta, which will be in a day or two, unless the enemy shows fight, which I am willing to accept on his own terms, if he will come outside of his cursed rifle trenches.

                                   W. T. SHERMAN,
                                         Major-General.

HEADQUARTERS DEPARTMENT OF THE CUMBERLAND,
   Near Jonesborough, Ga., September 6, 1864.

Maj. Gen. D. S. STANLEY,
   Commanding Fourth Army Corps:

GENERAL: The general commanding directs that you move with your command to-morrow morning (7th instant) at 7 o'clock precisely, without fail. You will please have a staff officer at these headquarters at 6 a. m. to-morrow, to accompany General Whipple to Rough and Ready to select the ground for the encampment of your troops at that point. This officer must be here punctually at 6 o'clock, as the general commanding will move precisely at that hour.

   I am, general, very respectfully, your obedient servant,
                                   HENRY STONE,
                           Captain and Assistant Adjutant-General.

HEADQUARTERS DEPARTMENT OF THE CUMBERLAND,
   In the Field, September 6, 1864.

Maj. Gen. D. S. STANLEY,
   Commanding Fourth Army Corps:

GENERAL: The major-general commanding directs that Special Field Orders, No. 245, of the 5th instant, be so modified as to change the road

---
* See Part I, p. 86.

by which your column is to march, from one leading all the way to Atlanta, on the east of the railroad, to what is called the Flat Shoal road, which runs from Jonesborough, on the west side of the railroad and very near it, until near the new station south of Rough and Ready, where it crosses the railroad. You will then march by a route, which will be pointed out to you by the guide which I send with this, to the Decatur and Fayetteville road, at Sykes' house, about a mile beyond which the right of your column will rest to-morrow night, forming with the Fourteenth Corps a line of battle facing southward. If you will send a staff officer to go with me in the morning I will point out to him the direction of your line for to-morrow night. We break camp at 6 a. m. to-morrow.

Yours, respectfully,

WM. D. WHIPPLE,
Assistant Adjutant-General.

HEADQUARTERS FOURTH ARMY CORPS,
Near Jonesborough, September 6, 1864—5 p. m.

General KIMBALL:

GENERAL: The troops of this corps will move at 7 a. m. to-morrow precisely. They will be drawn out ready to start at that hour. The leading division will draw out along the railroad, with the head of column resting opposite the present corps headquarters.

By order of Major-General Stanley:

J. S. FULLERTON,
Assistant Adjutant-General.

(Same to General Newton and Colonel Post.)

HEADQUARTERS FOURTEENTH ARMY CORPS,
At Smith's House, September 6, 1864.

[Brig. Gen. WILLIAM D. WHIPPLE:]

GENERAL: I have the honor to report that in pursuance of orders my troops were withdrawn during this morning from their position near Jonesborough, and are now in line of battle facing southward upon a ridge just north of the battle-field of the 1st instant. Colonel Taylor's brigade, forming my rear guard, was quite heavily pressed by the enemy when falling back from its position on the south side of the town, and lost some officers and men killed and wounded. The enemy's skirmishers entered the town before Colonel Taylor had withdrawn from it. Colonel Taylor's brigade now occupies the rebel works on my front as an outlying picket, supported on the right by a regiment of General Morgan and on the left by a regiment of General Baird's division. I have to-day received four deserters from the enemy and captured 12 prisoners of war.

I am, very respectfully,

JEF. C. DAVIS,
Brevet Major-General, Commanding.

HDQRS. FIRST DIVISION, FOURTEENTH ARMY CORPS,
Near McPeak's House, Ga., September 6, 1864.

Capt. A. C. McCLURG,
Asst. Adjt. Gen. and Chief of Staff, Fourteenth Army Corps:

SIR: I have the honor to report that my lines were changed to face southward this morning. In the afternoon the Second and Third Brigades were withdrawn. The First Brigade, Col. M. C. Taylor commanding, covered the approaches to the village of Jonesborough, holding a position about a mile and a half south of the town. About 2.30 p. m., the picket-lines being withdrawn on Colonel Taylor's left, that flank was exposed, and the enemy approaching to turn it, he fell back by my order. Some skirmishing took place between his rear and the enemy's advance. The First Brigade now holds the position assaulted by General Morgan's command on the 1st instant. The Second and Third Brigades, with the batteries, are in position on the ground occupied by the division just before advancing to the assault on the 1st instant. The casualties reported are one officer killed and several enlisted men wounded, number not accurately ascertained.

I am, sir, very respectfully, your obedient servant,
W. P. CARLIN,
Brigadier-General, Commanding.

HEADQUARTERS ARMY OF THE OHIO,
September 6, 1864.

General SHERMAN:

I find I can take the Flat Rock road to a point about three miles from this place (where it leaves the railroad) and then have a good road to Rough and Ready. But I will have to pass two extremely bad hills on the Flat Rock road. On this account, unless you think the presence of my troops necessary with the other armies, I think it would be better for me to move back this evening to Rough and Ready or far enough to clear General Thomas' column along the railroad. Please inform me this morning if this proposition meets your approval.

Very respectfully,
J. M. SCHOFIELD,
Major-General.

HDQRS. MILITARY DIVISION OF THE MISSISSIPPI,
In the Field, near Jonesborough, September 6, 1864—11.20 [a. m.].

General SCHOFIELD:

I have your note of to-day. I have no objection to your going toward Rough and Ready to-day, but prefer you should not more than pass Stanley's flank a mile or so, so as to be in supporting distance. We have gained too much [to lose it] by scattering now and risking anything. You may move so as to clear Stanley's road, which is the one following the railroad west and near it. Stanley day after to-morrow takes the road from Rough and Ready across to about McPherson's battle-ground of July 22. Our map gives a great many roads in that angle toward Decatur.

Yours,
W. T. SHERMAN,
Major-General.

HEADQUARTERS ARMY OF THE OHIO,
September 6, 1864.

Major-General SHERMAN,
Commanding Military Division of the Mississippi:

GENERAL: The following gratifying intelligence is respectfully forwarded for your information:

KNOXVILLE, TENN., *September 5, 1864.*

Major-General SCHOFIELD:

The following has just been received from General Gillem, at Bull's Gap, 4th:
"I surprised, defeated, and killed John Morgan at Greeneville this morning. The killed are scattered for miles, and have not yet been counted; probably number from 50 to 100; prisoners 70, among them Morgan's staff. Captured 1 piece artillery and caisson. The enemy's force outnumbered mine, but the surprise was complete.
"ALVAN C. GILLEM."

DAVIS TILLSON.

Very respectfully,

J. M. SCHOFIELD,
Major-General.

HDQRS. MILITARY DIVISION OF THE MISSISSIPPI,
In the Field, September 6, 1864.

Maj. Gen. J. M. SCHOFIELD:

Yours, with dispatch, is received. Good. I hear from Granger, at Pulaski, that he drove Wheeler from the railroad from Nashville to Decatur, and that he moved east. He also says that Roddey has gone across the Tennessee. Granger, Rousseau, and Steedman are all after Wheeler. Telegraph Ammen to try and stop Wheeler's exit to the east by blocking roads and intrenching gaps. You know how easily 200 or 300 men can close absolutely some of those narrow defiles.

Yours,

W. T. SHERMAN,
Major-General, Commanding.

HDQRS. MILITARY DIVISION OF THE MISSISSIPPI,
In the Field, September 6, 1864.

General HOWARD:

General Thomas had given orders to move out at 7 a. m. I would prefer we should not leave too early, as the enemy would crow over it. I wish you would modify your orders, and assure yourself that the enemy has no heavy force of infantry at Jonesborough, before you leave his old trenches; 7 o'clock will be early enough; you only have seven miles to make to-morrow.

W. T. SHERMAN,
Major-General.

HEADQUARTERS SEVENTEENTH ARMY CORPS,
Near Jonesborough, Ga., September 6, 1864.

Lieut. Col. WILLIAM T. CLARK,
Asst. Adjt. Gen., Department and Army of the Tennessee:

COLONEL: In answer to a communication of this date from headquarters Department and Army of the Tennessee, I have the honor to state that the Special Field Orders, No. 118, did not reach these headquarters until after 1 p. m. yesterday; that it was published to the command as soon as copies could be made, and that the wagons moved out as soon thereafter as possible, the majority of them reaching the point designated as soon as could be expected from the character of the weather and the roads. The remainder were detained in consequence of the road having become impassable at one point, and subsequently taken possession of by other commands. Notwithstanding the extreme darkness of the night, and the terrible condition of the roads, I should have brought my command in in good season and condition but for the fact that the road which had been assigned to me was taken possession of by General Kilpatrick for several hours, who stated to one of my staff officers that he did it by order. By this movement of General Kilpatrick I consider that my command would have been seriously endangered had the enemy chosen to use either of the main roads on my flanks for the purpose of intercepting me. The corduroy bridge over a swamp, which my pioneers had constructed during the day, was swept away by the freshet in the afternoon, and although every exertion was made to repair it, from the nature of the ground it was found impossible to do it hastily in such a manner as to prevent many accidents and serious delays.

Very respectfully, your obedient servant,

FRANK P. BLAIR, JR.,
Major-General, Commanding.

[Indorsement.]

HDQRS. DEPARTMENT AND ARMY OF THE TENNESSEE,
Near Jonesborough, Ga., September 6, 1864.

Maj. Gen. F. P. BLAIR, Jr., *Commanding Seventeenth Corps:*

GENERAL: On referring to the receipt of the order at your headquarters, it is marked 12.35 p. m. I have not the least doubt, general, but that you are as anxious as I am to prevent disaster, but I still think some of your officers have been lax and careless either in the transmission or execution of orders, for I passed a reserve battery at 5.30 o'clock just hitching up, and some hospitals of your corps did not begin to move till dark. General Kilpatrick had no authority to intercept your road. His orders were clear to move to the rear and right. I will communicate with him and prevent any future clogging from his command.

Respectfully,

O. O. HOWARD,
Major-General.

HEADQUARTERS SEVENTEENTH ARMY CORPS,
Near Jonesborough, September 6, 1864.

Brig. Gen. CHARLES R. WOODS, *Commanding Third Division:*

GENERAL : I am directed to inform you that this corps follows the Sixteenth to-morrow, which moves at 5 a. m. The major-general desires you to be in readiness to follow it closely with your division. It will probably pass you about 6.30 or 7 a. m. He also desires you to comply strictly with the order from department headquarters in relation to trains, as some complaint was made to-day about our apparent non-compliance with the orders on that subject last night.

I have the honor to be, very respectfully, your obedient servant,

A. J. ALEXANDER,
Assistant Adjutant-General.

HEADQUARTERS THIRD CAVALRY DIVISION,
Near Jonesborough, Ga., September 6, 1864.

Lieutenant-Colonel CLARK,
  Assistant Adjutant-General, Army of the Tennessee:

In order that there may be no misunderstanding, and that you may be fully advised of my operations of last evening, when acting as rear guard to the Army of the Tennessee, I beg leave to submit the following statement: Major Young's brigade of cavalry was ordered to take post at 7 p. m. yesterday in rear of the center of your line of battle, to cover the front and flanks with vedettes, outposts, and reserves, and after the pickets of the army relieved at 12 had passed his line of vedettes he was to move back as rear guard to the army; that after the army had gone into position at Jonesborough and General Blair's column had recrossed the river, Major Young was to follow him and destroy the bridge. From Major Young's report I believe he carried out the above orders as well as could be expected. I had intended to move back with a portion of my command at 8 p. m., as directed, leaving my picket-line in front, but owing to the continued rapid, and, as I believe, unnecessary firing on the part of the infantry picket-line from 8 p. m. until near midnight, I deemed it best to remain and did not move from my position until 10.30 p. m., and then moved out and took up position in rear of the infantry fortifications immediately on my left and remained until 11 p. m. I then moved back expecting to find the entire army gone and the roads open. I had moved back about a mile and a half when I came upon the wagon trains of the Sixteenth and Seventeenth Army Corps all halted in the road. I immediately rode to the front, overtook Lieutenant-Colonel Alexander, assistant adjutant-general, Seventeenth Army Corps, moving also to the front to ascertain the difficulty. We found the road at one point almost impassable and the wagon train stalled, and little or nothing being done to remedy the evil. The pioneer corps of my entire command was ordered immediately to the front, and after a great deal of trouble, with little or no assistance rendered by those whose duty it was to have rendered such assistance, the train was moved forward. Deeming it to be of the greatest importance to throw a cavalry force across the river at Anthony's Bridge, to protect the wagon train moving in that direction, I rapidly pushed forward one brigade of cavalry; three regiments had passed when I learned that my artillery and another regiment in the rear was stopped by some officer riding at the head of two companies of infantry, followed by another wagon train. This section of artillery and regiment was ordered by one of my staff officers, having my authority, to break the wagon train at any point and hurry it forward to join the command in advance. The wagon train was not delayed, nor was the column of infantry in the rear delayed ten minutes by the break; upon the contrary, had it not been for the pioneer corps of my division, and the exertion of Lieutenant-Colonel Alexander and officers of my command, to repair the road and hurry forward the train, the infantry in the rear would at a late hour this morning have been marching upon the opposite side of the river. I have no knowledge that any portion of my command cut a column of infantry last evening, or delayed for one moment the retrograde movement of the Army of the Tennessee.

I make this statement over my official signature, and if any officer of the infantry thinks that he is better informed than myself he can make such statement officially, and his veracity and mine can then be officially brought into question, and the responsibility for and the cause of the unnecessary delay, and very considerable confusion of last evening, can be traced to and thrown upon the officer or officers deserving.

Very respectfully, your obedient servant,

J. KILPATRICK,
Brigadier-General of Volunteers.

HDQRS. DEPARTMENT AND ARMY OF THE TENNESSEE,
Near Jonesborough, Ga., September 6, 1864.

Brig. Gen. J. KILPATRICK, *Commanding Cavalry Division:*

I received your message through your own aide-de-camp and also through Captain Conn, of my staff. As no ill consequences grew out of last night's operations I do not wish to investigate, except in so far as is necessary to prevent future disaster. I did not contemplate that you would move on the same road with the Sixteenth and Seventeenth Corps, except in so far as was necessary to cover the rear of those columns with cavalry. Cavalry cannot move across an infantry column or along the same road with it without unpleasant collisions. I have already called General Blair's attention to the matter of the trains. I appreciate, general, and so do the officers of my command, the great service that you have rendered us during the late operations, and through you thank your officers and men. Please to scout thoroughly toward Fayetteville, so as to be apprised if the enemy throw any considerable force across Flint River, either cavalry or infantry, or both, during the night.

Respectfully,

O. O. HOWARD,
Major-General.

LAWRENCEBURG, *September 6, 1864—7.40 a. m.*

Maj. Gen. L. H. ROUSSEAU:

GENERAL: I have arrived in town; enemy have gone; I am pushing on after them as fast as possible.

R. S. GRANGER,
Brigadier-General.

ON LAMB'S FERRY ROAD,
Thirteen and a half miles from Lawrenceburg,
[*September 6, 1864*]—*2.40 o'clock.*

Major-General ROUSSEAU:

GENERAL: I am now thirteen miles and a half from Lawrenceburg. I suppose when you wrote you must have thought me only a short distance in front of you. I have halted my command where I received your dispatch, and await further orders. I have been unwell all the morning. It will be impossible for me to ride back to you and return here and be a particle of service in the farther pursuit of Wheeler. The enemy is about an hour in advance of us. I have very little doubt but he will go to the river to-night and attempt to cross. As Roddey's command has been up the road he will keep Roddey as a shield to him while he crosses the river. Roddey will probably be fresh enough to get away.

R. S. GRANGER,
Brigadier-General, Commanding.

THIRTEEN MILES AND A HALF SOUTH OF LAWRENCEBURG,
[September 6, 1864.]

Maj. Gen. L. H. ROUSSEAU:

GENERAL: On consulting with my guide I find the road suggested by you impracticable. As you simply suggest this and seem to leave it to my discretion I will take the much better one from this to Lexington, from Lexington to Rogersville, and from Rogersville to Athens. The road from Rogersville to Athens is, I think, the one Williams will pursue, if he is as low down as you think them to be. It will have the advantage, too, of keeping the detached regiment with me and covering it if Williams should go out by way of Lamb's Ferry or Florence. I have already ordered a move for 5 a. m.

Very respectfully, your obedient servant,
R. S. GRANGER,
Brigadier-General, Commanding.

This movement, too, will look as though we were still after Wheeler. I will endeavor to keep you advised of everything.

HEADQUARTERS U. S. FORCES,
Pulaski, September 6, 1864.

Major-General STEEDMAN,
Larkinsville, or on line of road:

General Granger, with all the mounted command, left here at 2 p. m. to join Major-General Rousseau at Lawrenceburg. Have dispatched him of your movements. I have trains here and shall move forward to repair railroad. General Milroy fought at Triune yesterday. Rebels toward Shelbyville. Williams' command, 2,000, trying to join Wheeler. Wheeler moving toward Florence; had passed by Major-General Rousseau; General Granger gone to the assistance of General R. Crame's [Crews'] rebel brigade passed Lewisburg at 1 p. m. yesterday. Biffle has 300 strong; gone to Swan Creek near Duck River.

JOHN C. STARKWEATHER,
Brigadier-General, Commanding.

HEADQUARTERS U. S. FORCES,
Pulaski, Tenn., September 6, 1864.

Capt. ALFRED MATTHIAS,
Acting Assistant Adjutant-General:

SIR: Your dispatch as to retiring to this point is just received. I went north to Lynnville with troops; found the enemy there and drove them away; left two regiments to rebuild railroad track and put up telegraph wire; returned to this point; found lines down south and the enemy destroying railroad; went down, repaired, and communicated with all points south. Major-General Steedman is twelve miles below here with five trains of troops. Gave him full and complete information. He will probably be here in the morning. Cannot inform you where Williams' command is. Bodies of troops all around me demonstrating against the road. Scouting party just in from mouth Elk River. Roddey has recrossed his entire force, reported by citizens at 3,000 strong, part at mouth Elk River and balance crossing at Lamb's Ferry. Dispatch just received to this effect from Col. John W. Horner, Eighteenth Michigan, at Athens. Scouts sent to find Williams not yet returned; think they are captured. One outpost here captured to-day. We are all on half rations. Have sent to find out what is here and will send you what I can.

 Yours, truly,
       JOHN C. STARKWEATHER,
         Brigadier-General.

        COLUMBIA, *September 6, 1864.*

Major POLK:

 General Rousseau left here on Sunday at 4 p. m.; camped that night near Lynnville. Wheeler had crossed to the east of railroad same day, destroying some five miles track near Campbell's Station; re-crossed to west side Sunday night; was attacked near Campbellsville by Rousseau on Monday; result of fight not known. Report is that Wheeler burned his train and continued his retreat toward Florence; expected to join Roddey to-day. Rousseau met Granger and Stark-weather at Lynnville. Williams moved through Shelbyville yester-day; is thought will join Wheeler south of Pulaski. All rebels making for Tennessee River, pursued by our forces. Milroy passed here this afternoon, going to Pulaski.

        W. B. SIPES,
          Colonel.

      DUCK RIVER, *September 6, 1864.*
        (Received 7.30 p. m.)

Maj. J. O. CRAVENS,
 Assistant Adjutant-General:

 Rebels in considerable numbers have entered Shelbyville by the Unionville and Richmond pikes. Now occupy the place.

      JAS. WARTHAM,
    Captain, Fourth Tennessee Mounted Infantry.

     MURFREESBOROUGH, *September 6, 1864.*

Major-General ROUSSEAU:

 At daylight this morning Colonel Jordan, Ninth Pennsylvania Cav-alry, with 550 men, attacked Dibrell with 1,200 men at Readyville, ut-terly routing him, killing about 25, and bringing in 130 prisoners. Col-onel Jordan's loss is 1 killed, 3 or 4 wounded. The charge was made with sabers.

      H. P. VAN CLEVE,
        Brigadier-General.

 [SEPTEMBER 6, 1864.—For Special Field Orders, No. 66, headquarters Military Division of the Mississippi, communicating the congratulatory orders of the President and telegram of Lieutenant-General Grant, &c., see Part I, p. 87.]

 52 R R—VOL XXXVIII, PT V

HEADQUARTERS FOURTH ARMY CORPS,
Near Jonesborough, September 6, 1864.

Orders of the day for the Fourth Army Corps for to-morrow, September 7: The troops of this corps will remain in their present position to-day, and they will move to Rough and Ready to-morrow morning at daylight in the order: First, General Wood; second, General Newton; third, General Kimball. One battery of rifle guns will accompany General Kimball's division. The rest of the artillery will accompany and follow the trains. One ammunition wagon will accompany each brigade, and ten ambulances will accompany each division. All of the rest of the trains and wagons will move to Rough and Ready at 10 a. m. to-morrow. Division commanders will have all stragglers collected for the purpose of forming a police guard of them. Headquarters trains will accompany the divisions to which they are attached.

By command of Major-General Stanley:

J. S. FULLERTON,
Assistant Adjutant-General.

CIRCULAR.]   HEADQUARTERS FOURTEENTH ARMY CORPS,
Near Jonesborough, Ga., September 6, 1864.

The troops of the corps will remain in their present position during the day and to-night, prepared to repel any attack. Colonel Taylor's brigade will occupy the rebel breast-works as an outlying picket. General Morgan and General Baird will respectively place a regiment on the right and left of Colonel Taylor, in the rebel works, as pickets, to remain during the night. All sick and wounded unable to travel will be moved immediately to the hospital, where empty wagons will be in waiting to-morrow morning to transport them to the rear. All surplus wagons and artillery will be moved to the rear across Flint River to-night.

By order of Bvt. Maj. Gen. Jef. C. Davis:

A. C. McCLURG,
Assistant Adjutant-General and Chief of Staff.

(To division commanders.)

SPECIAL FIELD ORDERS, }   HDQRS. 14TH ARMY CORPS,
No. 5.   }   *Near Smith's House, September 6, 1864.*

The following will be the movements of the Fourteenth Corps to-morrow, September 7:

General Baird will move his division at 6.30 a. m. upon the road leading past McPeak's house, and intersecting the Rough and Ready road near Mrs. Smith's. He will form his division in line of battle on the rising ground immediately on this side of the creek which intervenes between those points, and will cover the retiring of the remainder of the corps, until all the troops are in motion on the Rough and Ready road in his rear, when he will withdraw and form the rear guard. General Carlin, leaving Colonel Taylor's brigade in its present position, will withdraw at 7 a. m., following General Baird, and passing through General Baird's lines, when formed, will move northward upon the Rough and Ready road, forming the advance of the corps. General Morgan will withdraw his division at 7 a. m. by the shortest route to the Rough and Ready road, and will follow General Carlin upon that road. Colonel Taylor will draw in his skirmishers and withdraw his brigade as soon as the remainder of the troops are across the creek, and gaining the Rough and Ready road he will rejoin his division. The rear guard will arrest all stragglers and men without arms found upon the road, place them under guard, and upon reaching Atlanta will turn them over to the provost-marshal-general of the department.

*   *   *   *   *   *   *

By order of Bvt. Maj. Gen. J. C. Davis:

A. C. McCLURG,
Assistant Adjutant-General and Chief of Staff.

SPECIAL FIELD ORDERS, }   HDQRS. ARMY OF THE OHIO,
  No. 102.   }   *Near Atlanta, Ga., September 6, 1864.*

*   *   *   *   *   *   *

II. The trains of the army will be prepared to move at 4 a. m. to-morrow, and will take the road along the railroad in rear of the trains of the Fourth Army Corps, moving to Rough and Ready. (The trains of the Fourth Corps will move at 2 a. m.) The troops will be prepared to move at 7 a. m., the Third Division in advance, and will advance on the Flat Shoal road into the main Atlanta road leading to McDonough. The order to move will be given in the morning.

*   *   *   *   *   *   *

By command of Major-General Schofield:

J. A. CAMPBELL,
Major and Assistant Adjutant-General.

SPECIAL   }   HEADQUARTERS DEPARTMENT
FIELD ORDERS, }   AND ARMY OF THE TENNESSEE,
 No. 119.   }   *Near Jonesborough, Ga., September 6, 1864.*

In accordance with Special Field Orders, No. 64, Military Division of the Mississippi, this army will move back to the vicinity of Morrow's Mill to-morrow, and the following will be observed as the order of march:

1. The trains and train guard in charge of Captain Conklin, chief quartermaster, will move at 3 a. m. precisely on a road to the right which will be designated by Captain Reese, chief engineer. All wagons emptied by the issue of rations to-day will accompany their respective divisions for the transportation of the sick.

2. Maj. Gen. John A. Logan, commanding Fifteenth Army Corps, will withdraw his command from its present position at 5 a. m., cross Flint River, and proceed on the road to the right taken by the train in charge of Captain Conklin.

3. Brig. Gen. T. E. G. Ransom, commanding Left Wing, Sixteenth Army Corps, will withdraw his command at 5 a. m., cross Flint River, and proceed on the Renfroe road, followed by the Seventeenth Corps, Major-General Blair commanding. Each column will have a strong rear guard.

4. Brigadier-General Kilpatrick will keep the Renfroe road clear, and will cover the left and rear of the army as heretofore directed. The position to be taken by the troops on their arrival at Morrow's Mill will be indicated. Brigade commanders will be enjoined to keep their men well in hand and their columns well closed up and to prevent straggling.

    *   *   *   *   *   *   *

V. In accordance with instructions from headquarters Military Division of the Mississippi, the movement of this army to-morrow, indicated in Special Field Orders, No. 119, from these headquarters, will be delayed two hours beyond the time specified therein, the train in charge of Captain Conklin, chief quartermaster, starting at 5 a. m. instead of 3 a. m. and the troops at 7 instead of 5 a. m. Corps commanders will at 7 a. m. simultaneously withdraw their skirmishers and pickets, first assuring themselves that the enemy has no heavy infantry force in his old trenches at Jonesborough.

By order of Maj. Gen. O. O. Howard:

WM. T. CLARK,
Assistant Adjutant-General.

SPECIAL FIELD ORDERS, }   HDQRS. FIFTEENTH ARMY CORPS,
      No. 95.   }   *Near Flint River, Ga., September 6, 1864.*

I. In accordance with Special Field Orders, No. 119, from department headquarters, herewith inclosed,* this command will move forward to-morrow morning at 5 o'clock, with the division of Major-General Osterhaus in advance, to the vicinity of Morrow's Mill. The divisions of Brig. Gens. W. B. Hazen and William Harrow will follow, respectively, that of Major-General Osterhaus. Division commanders will cause each regiment and brigade to detail a rear guard to keep up stragglers. Under no circumstances will men be allowed to fall to the rear of their respective commands. Brigadier-General Harrow's division being the rear guard, he will be required to use every precaution to prevent the enemy from falling suddenly on his rear. His rear guard must receive the most positive and peremptory instructions to prevent straggling, and will be instructed to bring forward all soldiers of whatever command.

II. The artillery will resume its proper place in the column to-morrow, and all wagons, except those necessary for division, brigade, and regimental headquarters, and for the transportation of the sick and wounded, and the ammunition train, will proceed with the general train in charge of Captain Conklin, at 3 o'clock to-morrow morning. All wagons emptied by the issue of rations to-day will accompany their respective divisions for the transportation of the sick. Ten wagons of ammunition will accompany each division; the rest will follow the general train. The wagons mentioned will precede respective commands. Maj. Gen. P. Jos. Osterhaus, commanding First Division, will cause one regiment of his command to report forthwith to Capt. J. T. Conklin, chief quartermaster, for train guard, at or near department headquarters. A copy of the order detailing the regiment will be sent to Captain Conklin through these headquarters.

III. In accordance with Special Field Orders, No. 119, paragraph V, from department headquarters, herewith inclosed, the movements of

---

* See p. 819.

troops indicated in paragraphs I and II, of Special Field Orders, No. 95, from these headquarters, will be delayed until 7 o'clock to-morrow morning, when the movements will commence, as ordered heretofore.

IV. Division commanders will not withdraw their pickets until the troops shall have made the crossing of the river, when they will be withdrawn simultaneously. To this end division picket officers will communicate with each other.

By order of Maj. Gen. John A. Logan:

R. R. TOWNES,
Assistant Adjutant-General.

SPECIAL ⎫　　　　HEADQUARTERS LEFT WING,
FIELD ORDERS, ⎬　　　　SIXTEENTH ARMY CORPS,
No. 77. ⎭　　*Near Jonesborough, Ga., September 6, 1864.*

I. On the march to-morrow the Ninth Illinois (mounted) Volunteers will move in advance at 5 a. m., followed by the Fourth Division; one brigade of the Second Division will immediately follow the Fourth Division. In rear of this brigade the trains will move in their regular order. Brig. Gen. J. M. Corse, commanding Second Division, will designate one brigade to act as rear guard, with full instructions to pick up all stragglers.

By order of Brig. Gen. T. E. G. Ransom:

J. W. BARNES,
Assistant Adjutant-General.

HDQRS. MILITARY DIVISION OF THE MISSISSIPPI,
In the Field, Atlanta, Ga., September 7, 1864.

TYLER,
Louisville:

On the 25th of August, pursuant to a plan of which the War Department had been fully advised, I left the Twentieth Corps at the Chattahoochee bridge, and, with the balance of the army, I drew off from the siege, and using some considerable artifice to mislead the enemy I moved rapidly south, and reached the West Point railroad, near Fairburn, on the 27th, and broke up twelve miles of it; then moving east my right approached the Macon railroad near Jonesborough, and my left near Rough and Ready. The enemy attacked the right, Army of the Tennessee, and was completely beaten on the 31st, and during the combat I pushed the left and center rapidly on the railroad above between Rough and Ready and Jonesborough. On the 1st of September we broke up about eight miles of the Macon road, and turned on the enemy at Jonesborough, assaulting him in his lines, and carried them, capturing Brigadier-General Govan and about 2,000 prisoners, with 8 guns and much plunder. Night alone prevented our capturing all of Hardee's corps, which escaped south that night. That same night Hood, in Atlanta, finding all his railroads broken or in our possession, blew up his ammunition, 7 locomotives, and 80 cars, and evacuated Atlanta, which, on the next day, September 2, was occupied by the corps left for that purpose, Major-General Slocum commanding. We followed the retreating rebel army to near Lovejoy's Station, thirty miles south of Atlanta, when, finding him strongly intrenched, I concluded it would not pay to assault, as we had already gained the great object of the campaign, viz, Atlanta. Accordingly, the army gradually and leisurely returned to Atlanta, and it is now camped eight miles south of the city, and tomorrow will move to the camps appointed. I am now writing in Atlanta, so you need not be uneasy. We have as the result of this quick and, as I think, well-executed movement 27 guns, over 3,000 prisoners; have buried over 400 rebel dead, and left as many wounded that could not be moved. The rebels have lost, besides the important city of Atlanta, immense stores, at least 500 dead, 2,500 wounded, and 3,000 prisoners, whereas our aggregate [loss] will not foot up 1,500. If that is not success, I don't know what is.

Your friend,

W. T. SHERMAN,
Major-General, Commanding.

Hdqrs. Military Division of the Mississippi,
In the Field, Atlanta, Ga., September 7, 1864.

General Hood,
Commanding Confederate Army:

General: I have deemed it to the interest of the United States that the citizens now residing in Atlanta should remove, those who prefer it to go South and the rest North. For the latter I can provide food and transportation to points of their election in Tennessee, Kentucky, or farther north. For the former I can provide transportation by cars as far as Rough and Ready, and also wagons; but that their removal may be made with as little discomfort as possible it will be necessary for you to help the families from Rough and Ready to the cars at Lovejoy's. If you consent I will undertake to remove all families in Atlanta who prefer to go South to Rough and Ready, with all their movable effects, viz, clothing, trunks, reasonable furniture, bedding, &c., with their servants, white and black, with the proviso that no force shall be used toward the blacks one way or the other. If they want to go with their masters or mistresses they may do so, otherwise they will be sent away, unless they be men, when they may be employed by our quartermaster. Atlanta is no place for families or non-combatants and I have no desire to send them North if you will assist in conveying them South. If this proposition meets your views I will consent to a truce in the neighborhood of Rough and Ready, stipulating that any wagons, horses, or animals, or persons sent there for the purposes herein stated shall in no manner be harmed or molested, you in your turn agreeing that any cars, wagons, carriages, persons, or animals sent to the same point shall not be interfered with. Each of us might send a guard of, say, 100 men to maintain order, and limit the truce to, say, two days after a certain time appointed. I have authorized the mayor to choose two citizens to convey to you this letter and such documents as the mayor may forward in explanation, and shall await your reply.

I have the honor to be, your obedient servant,

W. T. SHERMAN,
Major-General, Commanding.

(Sent by Messrs. Ball and Crew.)

[Note.—For subsequent correspondence on this subject, see Vol. XXXIX, Part II.]

'HEADQUARTERS FOURTH ARMY CORPS,
Near Sykes' House and Rough and Ready, Ga.,
September 7, 1864—4 p. m.

Brigadier-General WHIPPLE,
     Chief of Staff, &c.:

GENERAL: I have the honor to report that my command left the camp one mile and a half this side of Jonesborough at 7 o'clock this morning. We marched along the road just on the left side of the railroad to J. Cook's house, where we arrived at 9 a. m. From this point we left the railroad and marched on a road leading direct to Sykes' house, where the head of column arrived at 11 a. m. The Third and Second Divisions of my command are in line, the Third on the right, the Second on the left. The right of this line connects with the left of the Fourteenth Corps about half a mile beyond Sykes' house, and the left rests on the creek, the whole line facing nearly south. The First Division is in reserve in the rear of the Second Division. The enemy did not make his appearance to-day. Our position is good for grass and water, but forage is scarce.

D. S. STANLEY,
Major-General.

HEADQUARTERS DEPARTMENT OF THE CUMBERLAND,
Near Taliaferro's, Ga., September 7, 1864.

Maj. Gen. D. S. STANLEY,
     Commanding Fourth Army Corps:

GENERAL: The general commanding directs that you commence your march to-morrow morning, 8th instant, at 7 o'clock punctually.

I am, general, very respectfully, your obedient servant,
HENRY STONE,
Assistant Adjutant-General.

HEADQUARTERS FOURTEENTH ARMY CORPS,
Near Rough and Ready, Ga., September 7, 1864.

Brig. Gen. W. D. WHIPPLE,
     Chief of Staff, Department of the Cumberland:

I have the honor to report that, in accordance with orders, my corps withdrew from its position north of the battle-field of the 1st instant at an early hour this morning, and marching upon the Rough and Ready road went into position a little north of that point, where it now is. The enemy made no attempt to molest our withdrawal.

I am, very respectfully, your obedient servant,
JEF. C. DAVIS,
Brevet Major-General, Commanding.

HEADQUARTERS ARMY OF THE OHIO,
September 7, 1864.

Brigadier-General AMMEN:

I am informed that Wheeler has been driven from the Nashville and Decatur road, and is retreating eastward. Try to intercept and delay him by blocking roads and intrenching the mountain gaps. Granger, Rousseau, and Steedman are all after him. The destruction of Morgan is very gratifying.

J. M. SCHOFIELD.

HDQRS. MILITARY DIVISION OF THE MISSISSIPPI,
In the Field, Atlanta, Ga., September 7, 1864.

COMMANDING OFFICERS,
Nashville and Chattanooga:

Telegraph me all the news of Wheeler. My army is now within ten miles of Atlanta, all well; and, if necessary, I can send infantry to Chattanooga or Cleveland, to head Wheeler off.

W. T. SHERMAN,
Major-General, Commanding.

ROGERSVILLE, *September 7, 1864—7.30 p. m.*

Major-General ROUSSEAU,
Bethel or Gilbertsborough:

GENERAL: We are now at Rogersville. On the way here I ascertained the enemy, 500 or 600 strong, were coming from the direction of the railroad. Came into the Lexington and Lawrenceburg road one mile and a half from Lexington; passed on and joined Wheeler at that place about 11 p. m. The men of this force stated that they had been cut off from their command for five or six days. About the same hour last night * * * crossed the road from Lexington to this place about five miles this side of Lexington. The men said they were going to join Wheeler. The country is undoubtedly swarming with rebels. Roddey and Johnson are undoubtedly there supporting Wheeler. We fired on their men this a. m. I feel considerable apprehension for the regiment detached to watch Wheeler, as I conceive he has done all it is possible for him to do. I have recalled him, if it is possible for a courier to get to him. It occurred to me that the force which passed down as above stated * * * command. Of this, however, you can judge better than I. Sent a scout to Lamb's Ferry. They have returned; report having "watered their horses in the Tennessee River," and no enemy there. There are evident indications of a train having been there, then turned down the river toward Bainbridge. Lieutenant Prosser, of Second Tennessee, came in at 4 p. m. Colonel Prosser met enemy's pickets about three miles from Lexington, and drove them into Centre Star, about eight miles from Lexington, on Florence road. Wheeler is unquestionably there with his whole force, except 400 or 500, which * * * in charge of sick and wounded, who have crossed the river. Wheeler does not seem to be in a hurry, and citizens say he will not leave until Williams comes up or he hears from him. I shall start for Athens at 5 a. m. to-morrow. Shall move slowly, as I think possibly the enemy may come into this road from some of the cross-roads.

Very respectfully, your obedient servant,

R. S. GRANGER,
Brigadier-General.

P. S.—Your dispatch of 5 p. m. September 6 is just received. Your indorsement on General Milroy's communication is 7.10 p. m. September 6. I shall obey the one of latest date.

R. S. G.,
Brigadier-General.

[NOTE.—Original mutilated; parts missing represented by stars.]

PULASKI, TENN., *September 7, 1864.*

Major-General ROUSSEAU:

GENERAL: I arrived here with the Fifth, Tenth, and Twelfth Tennessee Cavalry and a detachment of the Second Kentucky Cavalry at noon to-day. A detachment of the Sixth Indiana Cavalry came with me from Franklin to this place. Not receiving any communication from you, and fearing lest my being away so long from that portion of the Nashville and Chattanooga Railroad, of which I am boss guard, without orders, might not be acceptable, and fearing that Williams with all or a portion of his forces may have gone southeast (as reported by one of my sergeants captured in one of our charges last Sunday and who was paroled yesterday and came in this morning) and strike the Nashville and Chattanooga Railroad again, I have concluded to take the Fifth Tennessee Cavalry and the detachment of the Second Kentucky Cavalry and cut across to Tullahoma, and leave Colonel Spalding and the detachment of the Sixth Indiana Cavalry and the Tenth and Twelfth Tennessee Cavalry to go on and join you as ordered by you. I hope, general, that my having detained the Tennessee troops and chased Williams as I have will meet your approbation, and I hope that my taking back the Tenth Tennessee Cavalry to Tullahoma will meet your approbation, as I understand that regiment was stationed there by order of General Thomas. My little chase after Williams has been a pleasant episode in the dreary monotony of life at Tullahoma.

Hoping you may bag him yet, I am, very truly, yours, &c.,

R. H. MILROY,
Major-General.

P. S.—I leave here at 6 p. m. this evening, which will be in twenty minutes. Spalding goes on to you at the same time.

R. H. M.,
Major-General.

TULLAHOMA, *September 7, 1864—6.30 p. m.*

Maj. S. B. MOE,
Assistant Adjutant-General:

General Rousseau just heard from. He is driving the enemy. We move on by rail immediately, hoping to strike him in the rear.

By command of Major-General Steedman:

E. B. KIRK,
Captain and Assistant Quartermaster.

JOHNSONVILLE, *September 7, 1864.*

Maj. B. H. POLK,
Assistant Adjutant-General, District of Tennessee:

Colonel Matzdorff, commanding at Waverly, says 1,500 of Wheeler's men are marching toward this place (Johnsonville) with the intention of procuring provisions and crossing the Tennessee River. I feel confident that I can keep off double the number, but the First Kansas Battery has no reliable ammunition. Can you send some for 10-pounder Parrott guns? The ammunition on hand is all condemned. One gunboat remains here.

THEO. TRAUERNICHT,
Lieutenant-Colonel, Commanding Post.

NASHVILLE, TENN., *September 7, 1864.*

Lieut. Col. T. TRAUERNICHT,
          Johnsonville:

Where are the 1,500 men of Wheeler's command? What are Colonel Matzdorff's sources of information? The last we heard of Wheeler, he was making his way rapidly toward Florence, closely pursued by the combined forces of Generals Rousseau, Milroy, Granger, and Starkweather. Wheeler attacks no fortified places, and in his entire raid has been able to take only one block-house, where the garrison disgracefully surrendered without resistance. If he should come your way, of which there is small probability, you can easily use him up.

                    B. H. POLK,
               Major and Assistant Adjutant-General.

COLUMBIA, *September 7, 1864.*

Maj. B. H. POLK,
          Assistant Adjutant-General:

Officers from below report that Wheeler has divided his command and is making for the river at different points. Rousseau is pursuing with effect, and is said to have taken many prisoners. Hundreds of Wheeler's men are deserting. No enemy can be heard of near here. Telegraph is operating south of Pulaski.

                    WM. B. SIPES,
               Colonel, Commanding.

HEADQUARTERS U. S. FORCES,
          Pulaski, September 7, 1864.

Maj. Gen. J. B. STEEDMAN,
          Athens:

Major-General Milroy is here; will move to Elkton this afternoon. Major-General Rousseau is moving toward Athens by way of Bethel. General Granger is moving toward Florence, sixteen miles south of Lawrenceburg. Enemy is in fact everywhere all around me. Roddey is reported on south side Tennessee River again. Wheeler is also trying to cross at or near Florence. Williams is on east side of railroad, supposed to be moving toward Lamb's Ferry. I think he will strike the other road and move out as he came in.

                    JOHN C. STARKWEATHER,
               Brigadier-General, Commanding.

SEPTEMBER 7, 1864.

Major-General STEEDMAN,
          Athens:

At 11 a. m. to-day General Rousseau left Sugar Creek, on Lamb's Ferry road, in the direction of Gordonsville or Gilbertsborough, in search of Williams, and thence above or below Athens as circumstances may require. Seven hundred Wheeler's men passed down Lamb's Ferry road to-day.

                    JOHN C. STARKWEATHER,
               Brigadier-General, Commanding.

LOUDON, *September 7, 1864.*

Brigadier-General AMMEN:

By dispatch by courier from Major Reeves I learn that he is advised of Wheeler's movements. He says Wheeler's force was met and whipped by Rousseau near Manchester, Tenn., and the rebels disbanded. However, a portion of them was reported to be in the Sequatchie Valley, trying to make their way out, and that five regiments had been sent from Chattanooga to intercept them. Major Reeves says he will be ready for them. I will send courier and instructions to Major Reeves, as directed by your telegram this p. m.

M. L. PATTERSON,
Lieutenant-Colonel.

HEADQUARTERS FOURTH ARMY CORPS,
Near Rough and Ready, Ga., September 7, 1864.

Orders of the day for the Fourth Army Corps:

The troops of this corps will march for Atlanta to-morrow. General Kimball's division will lead, followed by General Wood's, then General Newton's. The head of the column will start at 7 a. m. precisely. A section of rifled guns will accompany General Newton's division.* The trains will start at 4 a. m., and they will be conducted by Captain Schoeninger, assistant chief quartermaster. First, will move the supply train, then hospital train and ambulances, then the ammunition. The artillery of the corps will follow the trains. Headquarters trains will accompany the divisions to which they are attached.

By order of Major-General Stanley:

J. S. FULLERTON,
Assistant Adjutant-General.

SPECIAL FIELD ORDERS, }   HDQRS. 14TH ARMY CORPS,
                       }   *Near Rough and Ready, Ga.,*
     No. 6.   }   *September 7, 1864.*

The general supply trains of the corps will move northward on the road leading past Tomlinson's, Cash's, and Mount Zion Church to White Hall, starting promptly at daylight. It will be parked in some convenient position a little beyond White Hall. Colonel Walker's brigade, of General Baird's division, will move at 4 a. m., and, preceding the supply trains, will repair any bad places in the road. It will take position beyond the trains while being parked, and will arrest all stragglers attempting to go through to the city, of whatever command, put them under guard, and report them to the provost-marshal of the corps. General Baird will move his division at 7 a. m., and follow the trains upon the same road. General Carlin will move his division immediately in the rear of General Baird and upon the same road. General Morgan will move a brigade at 6.30 a. m., and place it in position upon the advanced picket-line, in order to cover the withdrawal of the remainder of the corps. When the road is clear he will withdraw his pickets and march his division in the rear of General Carlin upon the same road, and will form the rear guard of the corps. The ammunition, hospital, and headquarters trains and the artillery will move in advan e of their respective

---

*Fullerton's journal, Part I, p. 936, says Wood's division.

divisions. When the troops are in motion a staff officer from each division commander will report to the general commanding the corps and accompany him in advance of the troops to receive instructions in regard to the positions which their respective divisions will occupy.

By order of Bvt. Maj. Gen. J. C. Davis:

A. C. McCLURG,
Assistant Adjutant-General and Chief of Staff.

SPECIAL FIELD ORDERS, }   HDQRS. ARMY OF THE OHIO,
No. 103.   }   *Near Atlanta, Ga., September 7, 1864.*

I. The troops will march to Decatur to-morrow, General Cox's division in advance. The trains will move between the two divisions. The cavalry will cover the movement. The march will begin at 5 a. m. General Cox will take position a short distance out of town, commanding the approaches from the east. General Hascall will take position immediately south of town, covering the roads from the south. Colonel Garrard will encamp between Decatur and Stone Mountain, connecting pickets with General Cox, also with General Garrard at Stone Mountain. General Hascall will connect pickets with the Army of the the Cumberland toward Atlanta. Headquarters of the army in the field will, until further orders, be in Decatur.

II. Until further orders only half rations of grain will be issued to the public animals of this command.

*   *   *   *   *   *   *

By command of Major-General Schofield:

J. A. CAMPBELL,
Major and Assistant Adjutant-General.

SPECIAL FIELD ORDERS, } HEADQUARTERS DEPARTMENT
                       }   AND ARMY OF THE TENNESSEE,
No. 120.   } *Morrow's Mill, Ga., September 7, 1864.*

This army will move back to the vicinity of East Point to-morrow, in the following order:

1. The general train and train guard, in charge of Captain Conklin, chief quartermaster, will move out upon the main East Point road at 3 a. m., and will be followed by the Fifteenth Corps, Major-General Logan commanding, marching at 8 a. m.

2. Brigadier-General Ransom will move out his command at 7 a. m., taking the road on which he marched to-day, and will be followed at 8.30 o'clock by the Seventeenth Corps, Major-General Blair commanding.

3. At East Point the Seventeenth Corps will occupy the right, the Fifteenth Corps the left, and the Sixteenth Corps the center and reserve of the army.

4. Brigadier-General Kilpatrick will continue to cover the rear and right, as heretofore.

By order of Maj. Gen. O. O. Howard:

WM. T. CLARK,
Assistant Adjutant-General.

SPECIAL FIELD ORDERS,)   HDQRS. 15TH ARMY CORPS,
    No. 96.   )   *Morrow's Mill, Ga., September 7, 1864.*

In accordance with Special Field Orders, No. 120, from department headquarters, herewith inclosed, this command will move forward at 8 a. m. to-morrow, with Brig. Gen. W. B. Hazen's division in advance, to the vicinity of East Point. The divisions of Brig. Gen. William Harrow and Maj. Gen. P. J. Osterhaus will follow, respectively, that of Brigadier-General Hazen. The movement will be conducted in the same manner as to-day. The wagons will move in the same relative order described in Special Field Orders, No. 95, of date September 6, from these headquarters. The positions to be taken by the several divisions will be designated upon their arrival at East Point. The division of Major-General Osterhaus, being the rear guard, will cause all stragglers, of whatever command, to be brought forward.

By order of Maj. Gen. John A. Logan:

R. R. TOWNES,
Assistant Adjutant-General.

SPECIAL   )   HEADQUARTERS LEFT WING,
FIELD ORDERS, }   SIXTEENTH ARMY CORPS,
    No. 78.   )   *In the Field, near East Point, September 7, 1864.*

I. On the march to-morrow the Ninth Illinois Infantry Volunteers (mounted) will take the advance, moving on the main East Point road at 7 a. m. The Second Division will take the advance of the infantry column, moving at the same hour. Two brigades of the Fourth Division will immediately follow the Second Division. After these two brigades the trains will move in their regular order. Brig. Gen. J. W. Fuller, commanding Fourth Division, will designate one brigade of his command to bring up the rear.

By order of Brig. Gen. T. E. G. Ransom:

J. W. BARNES,
Assistant Adjutant-General.

SPECIAL ORDERS,)   HDQRS. SEVENTEENTH ARMY CORPS,
    No. 221.   )   *Near East Point, Ga., September 7, 1864.*

I. Brig. Gen. Giles A. Smith, commanding Fourth Division, will have the advance to-morrow, and will move his command at 8.30 a. m., following the Left Wing, Sixteenth Army Corps.

II. The Third Division, Brig. Gen. Charles R. Woods, will follow the Fourth Division.

By command of Maj. Gen. F. P. Blair:

ROWLAND COX,
Assistant Adjutant-General.

ATLANTA, GA., *September 8, 1864—8 a. m.*
(Received 10.45 p. m.)

Hon. E. M. STANTON,
        Secretary of War:

My whole army will be encamped round about Atlanta during to-day, and I have promised them some rest and pay. All the army has eight months' pay due, and the paymaster now tells me the money is not on hand. This army should be paid at once, and it would create discontent if others were preferred to them. I believe and shall assure all that the money will be here as soon as the rolls are made up and it is safe to bring it.

W. T. SHERMAN,
Major-General.

ATLANTA, GA., *September 8, 1864.*
(Received 10.40 p. m.)

Maj. Gen. H. W. HALLECK,
Washington, D. C.:

General Thomas is in, and his troops are now grouping about Atlanta. General Schofield has also arrived, and has gone to place his troops at Decatur. I have not yet heard from General Howard, but suppose him to be at East Point. I have just ridden to see a portion of the enemy's line, which is very strong, and demonstrates the wisdom of our mode and manner of attack. I have but little news of Wheeler, except that last night General Steedman was at Athens, Ala., and Wheeler was supposed to be crossing the Tennessee toward the south about Lamb's Ferry. Rousseau, Granger, and Steedman have enough troops to handle Wheeler, and I suppose the railroad will soon be repaired. We have enough stores for a month, and I feel no uneasiness on that score. Yet, if necessary, I can send some troops to the rear. I telegraphed you yesterday that you could use General A. J. Smith, as proposed, to act against Price in Missouri. We are all well, and have no doubt, after a short rest, will be impatient again to sally forth in search of adventure.

W. T. SHERMAN,
Major-General.

HDQRS. MILITARY DIVISION OF THE MISSISSIPPI,
In the Field, Atlanta, Ga., September 8, 1864.

General WEBSTER,
Nashville:

Don't let any citizens come to Atlanta, not one. I won't allow trade or manufactures of any kind, but will remove all the present population and make Atlanta a pure military town. Give public notice to this effect. General Thomas' army is now in and around Atlanta, General Howard's at East Point, and General Schofield's at Decatur. I want Wheeler cleaned out, the roads repaired, and everything to the rear made right. Send forward paymasters. If the Sanitary Commission have stores let them be sent to the agent at Chattanooga, whence we can draw as fast as we need. Hood's army retreated toward Macon, but will, I suppose, halt about Griffin. I was unprepared to follow below Lovejoy's, twenty-eight miles south of Atlanta, for we have been fighting constantly since about the 7th of May, and the men need rest and quiet. Our last move was beautiful and perfectly successful, as you observe from our occupation of the famous Atlanta. We have already found nineteen guns and others are being found daily. At Jonesborough, at the battle, we took 2 four-gun batteries, and in the whole move have near 3,000 prisoners. We killed about 500 at Jonesborough and wounded about 2,500. Our entire loss since beginning the movement will not exceed 1,500.

W. T. SHERMAN,
Major-General, Commanding.

[SEPTEMBER 8, 1864.—For J. B. Hood to W. T. Sherman, proposing an exchange of prisoners, and Sherman's reply, see Second Series.]

NASHVILLE, *September 8, 1864.*

Major-General SHERMAN,
  Atlanta:

Your dispatch of this date received. I suppose you do not mean to exclude sutlers from Atlanta. Cannot get particulars from General Rousseau. He fought Wheeler thirteen miles below Columbia and beat him on Monday. He is following him and must now be near the Tennessee River. Williams' rebel force is below, south of Wheeler's, followed by Milroy. Granger and Starkweather are moving and the rebels must be pressed if they cannot get over the river. We have so little cavalry that it is difficult to follow them. The railroad to Chattanooga will be open again on Saturday, we hope, when Donaldson will push forward supplies. Accept my hearty congratulations on the glorious success of your successful campaign. All well.

J. D. WEBSTER,
Brigadier-General.

EAST POINT, GA., *September 8, 1864.*

Maj. Gen. JOHN A. LOGAN,
  Commanding Fifteenth Army Corps:

The major-general commanding directs me to say that he has decided to place the Seventeenth Corps upon the left flank of this army and the Sixteenth on the right flank, and that your command will therefore occupy the center.

Very respectfully, your obedient servant,

WM. T. CLARK,
Assistant Adjutant-General.

EAST POINT, GA., *September 8, 1864.*

Brig. Gen. T. E. G. RANSOM,
  Commanding Left Wing, Sixteenth Army Corps:

The major-general commanding directs me to inform you that the Seventeenth Army Corps will to-morrow morning move around to the left, and your command will accordingly occupy and protect the right flank of this army.

Very respectfully, your obedient servant,

SAML. L. TAGGART,
Assistant Adjutant-General.

NASHVILLE, TENN., *September 8, 1864—11.30 p. m.*

Major-General SHERMAN:

Dispatches from General Rousseau, at Athens, received this evening, state that Wheeler with all his force, excepting Williams' division, is west of Tennessee and Alabama Railroad, in vicinity of Rogersville, near Tennessee River. Monday Rousseau defeated Wheeler badly at Campbellsville, from whence he retreated to Lawrenceburg, where part of Rousseau's force attacked him on Tuesday morning, routing him again. Colonel Streight has gone toward Rogersville with 2,500 infantry and two pieces of artillery. Granger is also moving against Wheeler with infantry. General Rousseau this afternoon, with cavalry and artillery, moved toward Rogersville from Athens. General Steedman is said to be at Pulaski with 3,000 infantry. Rousseau's dispatch states that Roddey has joined Wheeler. Doolittle telegraphs from Decatur, Roddey has returned to Courtland. Milroy is pursuing Williams with about 1,600 cavalry, a force equal to Williams'. Nothing heard from Milroy or Williams for two days. Milroy was then moving on Williams from Columbia, Williams going eastward after failing to join Wheeler. Milroy whipped Williams at Triune, and can do it again anywhere. Everything seems to be working well. Great joy over the capture of Atlanta.

JNO. F. MILLER,
Brigadier-General, Commanding Post.

MURFREESBOROUGH, *September 8, 1864.*

Maj. J. O. CRAVENS,
        Assistant Adjutant-General:

The rebel force referred to in your telegram of the 7th passed through Beech Grove yesterday in the direction of McMinnville. We think Dibrell has gone in the same direction.

H. P. VAN CLEVE,
Brigadier-General.

MURFREESBOROUGH, *September 8, 1864.*

Maj. B. H. POLK,
        Assistant Adjutant-General:

Col. Thomas J. Jordan, Ninth Pennsylvania Cavalry, with 550 men, surprised, attacked, and routed Dibrell's brigade of 2,000 men at Readyville, killing 25, wounding many, capturing 130; our loss, 1 killed, 5 wounded, 4 missing. To-day the railroad was torn up near Bell Buckle; damage trifling. The bridge across Stewart's Creek, the only one injured by Wheeler, is rebuilt. The road will be repaired to-day. If Wheeler should start direct for Chattanooga he would be outstripped by a train from Nashville.

H. P. VAN CLEVE,
Brigadier-General.

MURFREESBOROUGH, *September 8, 1864.*

Maj. B. H. POLK:

A rebel force, estimated at 2,000, with five pieces of artillery, passed Beech Grove yesterday, going toward McMinnville from Shelbyville;

name of commander not known. They will doubtless join Dibrell, who
has collected his scattered forces. My scouts do not bring any reliable
information of Dibrell's movements.

> H. P. VAN CLEVE,
> *Brigadier-General.*

MURFREESBOROUGH, *September 8, 1864.*

Maj. B. H. POLK,
> *Assistant Adjutant-General:*

The rebel force I reported this morning going toward McMinnville is
said to be that of General Williams.

> H. P. VAN CLEVE,
> *Brigadier-General.*

DECATUR, ALA., *September 8, 1864.*

Maj. B. H. POLK,
> *Assistant Adjutant-General:*

Have heard nothing from General Granger for two days; was down
between Sulphur trestle and Pulaski; the last I heard General Granger
was skirmishing with Wheeler near Lynnville. General Steedman went
to Pulaski yesterday a. m. with 3,000 men. Roddey returned to Courtland on the 3d.

> CHAS. C. DOOLITTLE,
> *Colonel, Commanding Post.*

NASHVILLE, *September 8, 1864.*

Maj. S. B. MOE,
> *Chattanooga:*

The rebels were yesterday west of Pulaski, making for the Tennessee
River, closely pursued by our forces. There are no rebels between this
place and Murfreesborough, and the road will likely be repaired to-morrow or next day; by Monday at the outside.

> B. H. POLK,
> *Major and Assistant Adjutant-General.*

PULASKI, *September 8, 1864—3 a. m.*

General ROUSSEAU:

Dispatch from General Steedman by my courier line says:

Roddey and Wheeler are on west side Tennessee at mouth Elk River. My infantry, 2,200, have [been] sent to Rogersville.

Have informed General Milroy of this. He is at Elkton, and General Granger also. Wire is again cut. Will move down the road at
daylight toward Athens.

> JOHN C. STARKWEATHER,
> *Brigadier-General.*

ELK RIVER BRIDGE, *September 8, 1864—10.30 a. m.*

Major-General ROUSSEAU, *Commanding:*

DEAR GENERAL: Have just arrived to repair telegraph line; same all O. K.; in good order south, and in good order north to Columbia. Was all right from there to Nashville this morning, but since I have arrived here a break has occurred north of Columbia. I send herewith dispatch from General Milroy, just received at this post by my courier, who carried dispatches last night to General Milroy. Track is repaired to Campbell's Station. Commenced work there at 10 a. m. Have informed General Steedman of your whereabouts. He is at Athens; has sent 2,200 men to Rogersville. No news from General Granger. Have couriers trying to find him. Three hundred cavalry arrived at Pulaski this morning, searching for you. I will send them forward by way of Gourdsville.

Yours, very truly,

JOHN C. STARKWEATHER,
Brigadier-General.

HEADQUARTERS U. S. FORCES,
Pulaski, September 8, 1864.

Major-General STEEDMAN, *Athens:*

Major-General Rousseau is now on the road from Duck Island Ford, on Elk River, to Athens, waiting to hear from you. Just received the following news from Major-General Milroy: He was at 10 a. m. within ten miles of Fayetteville, and had heard that Williams' command was concentrating there; also heard from citizens that Williams would concentrate to-day at or near Lynnville. A rebel officer, with forty men, stated that he would join him there, passing in that direction just prior to the arrival of his (General Steedman's) command. Inform General Rousseau of this. I have scouts out in every direction. Small bodies of enemy all around me; cut wires south this morning, which I immediately repaired. Road north is fixed to Campbell's Station and still pressing on. Inform Colonel Spalding at Elkton.

JOHN C. STARKWEATHER,
Brigadier-General, Commanding.

CHATTANOOGA, *September 8, 1864.*

Brigadier-General AMMEN:

General Milroy reports rebels under Williams moving from Nashville and Chattanooga Railroad toward McMinnville this morning, saying they were ordered by Wheeler to get out of the country. They will probably move up toward Kingston. Cannot General Gillem intercept them?

JAS. B. STEEDMAN,
Major-General.

LOUDON, *September 8, 1864—3 p. m.*

Capt. W. P. AMMEN, *Assistant Adjutant-General:*

By courier just in from Kingston Major Reeves reports the rebels moving up Sequatchie Valley. He, Reeves, is at work obstructing roads, &c. His information is from citizens. Will hear from him again soon as scouts come in. Will keep you posted.

M. L. PATTERSON,
Lieutenant-Colonel.

TULLAHOMA, *September 8, 1864—1 p. m.*

Maj. S. B. MOE, *Assistant Adjutant-General:*

Just received information from a reliable man who was among the rebels under Robertson and Williams. He says they are badly scared, and says they have received an order from Wheeler to get out of this country as fast as possible, and that they are going toward McMinnville this morning. He says only stragglers are left along the railroad now. Can you get this information to General Gillem? We have but one company as cavalry here.

JNO. O. CRAVENS,
Major and Assistant Adjutant-General.

TULLAHOMA, *September 8, 1864.*

Maj. S. B. MOE, *Assistant Adjutant-General:*

The road from here to Wartrace was intact yesterday; don't know how it is this morning. Robertson and Wheeler passed from Shelbyville to Bell Buckle with 2,000 men and four pieces of artillery. Yesterday evening a part of this force was at Haley's water-tank. At dusk yesterday, and last night, small parties were prowling about Duck River bridge; did no damage. Have scouts out, but have not heard from them this morning.

JNO. O. CRAVENS,
Major.

HEADQUARTERS U. S. FORCES,
Murfreesborough, Tenn., September 8, 1864

Maj. B. H. POLK,
Assistant Adjutant-General, District of Tennessee:

MAJOR: A rebel force, variously estimated, but amounting probably to about 2,000, under Generals Williams and Robertson, passed through Shelbyville on the 6th, crossed the railroad between Bell Buckle and Wartrace, tearing up a few rails and burning a few ties. The slight damage is an evidence of haste. Yesterday, the 7th, passed through Beech Grove on the road to McMinnville, to which point they professed to be aiming. My scouts have not been able to learn anything definite respecting Dibrell since his rout by Colonel Jordan, of the Ninth Pennsylvania Cavalry, on the 6th. After collecting his scattered forces at Woodbury it is reported that he marched toward McMinnville. It is my impression that all these forces are aiming to make a speedy exit through East Tennessee. The road south is repaired. A train will leave here this morning for Chattanooga with the mail.

Very respectfully, your obedient servant,
H. P. VAN CLEVE,
Brigadier-General.

NASHVILLE, TENN., *September 8, 1864.*

Major-General BURBRIDGE, *Lexington, Ky.:*

Our latest information places Wheeler southwest of Columbia and making for the Tennessee River. Dibrell and Williams, with a force estimated at 1,200 to 2,000, have turned back, and are said to be going toward McMinnville; probably trying to get out the way they came. There is a report of some rebel force being at Lebanon, but I do not think it is looking toward Kentucky. The Tennessee River is in good stage and rising. They cannot cross the ford opposite Lebanon.

J. D. WEBSTER,
Brigadier-General.

NASHVILLE, TENN., *September 8, 1864—1 p. m.*
(Received 10.30 p. m.)

Maj. Gen. M. C. MEIGS,
   Quartermaster-General:

We expect to have the Chattanooga road open by night of 10th. General Sherman in the mean time will have plenty of subsistence. Forage will be a trifle short. I went over the broken part of the road yesterday. The damage was considerable.

J. L. DONALDSON,
Chief Quartermaster.

ATHENS, *September 8, 1864.*

Brigadier-General WHIPPLE:

Have just returned from the pursuit of Wheeler with 1,300 cavalry and two pieces of artillery. I left Wheeler at Lexington, sending a regiment of cavalry six miles below to look after him. I engaged his rear guard as often and severely as he would permit. The woods were continuous for about nine miles. As he had ten miles start of me that morning we were not able to press him sufficiently to bring on a general engagement. While pressing I was halted by General Rousseau for the purpose of joining with him. General Rousseau, however, did not come up, but changed his direction toward railroad, and ordered me to leave Wheeler and proceed in direction of Athens to intercept General Williams, who, it was supposed, at that time was trying to join Wheeler. Wheeler last night was at Centre Star, two or three miles from the river, with all his force except Williams and some Tennessee troops. From the best information I could get he was about 3,500 strong. He has probably crossed his wagons and artillery over the river. He gave it out, however, that he was not going to cross until he heard from Williams. At 11 a. m. to-day I met Colonel Streight at Elk River; [his force,] from what he said, was 2,500 infantry and two pieces of artillery. In consulting me what he should do, being at liberty, as he said, to do as he pleased, I advised him to move down and attack Wheeler, and gave him one of my best regiments of cavalry, about 450 strong, and ordered the Tenth Michigan Infantry, 300 strong, which had marched down with him, to report to him. General Rousseau, having received report of this, left here this p. m. with all his own cavalry and about 400 of mine; all that were able to travel. Major-General Steedman and Brigadier-Generals McCook and Croxton accompanied him. I would mention that I advised Streight that if Wheeler had crossed the river, or if he forced him over the river, to destroy the ferries and guard the fords, all of which are within a space of sixteen miles, which I concluded will effectually shut in Williams north of the river. I would have remained with Streight, and believed it was proper to have done so, but I had received two dispatches from General Rousseau to leave Wheeler and return to this point immediately to assist in the capture of Williams, who was supposed to be coming toward the rail-road with a view to effect a junction with Wheeler. Williams' whereabouts now is unknown. Before joining in the pursuit of Wheeler I was fortunate enough to have met Roddey and Johnson just as each party struck the railroad—one party at Athens; after short skirmish, in which we killed 3 and wounded 7 of the enemy, including one major, this party turned back; the next at Sulphur trestle, which party was pursued so vigorously by Colonel Prosser that they turned back; third, at Elk River, where enemy were met by Ninth Indiana Cavalry, and driven back. We did not meet them again, and I am informed they returned to Tennessee River and crossed in haste. I understand railroad will be opened to Nashville to-morrow. I repaired all the damage done this side of Lynnville myself. This was as far as I could go with my command.

R. S. GRANGER,
Brigadier-General.

SPECIAL }   HDQRS. MIL. DIV. OF THE MISSISSIPPI,
FIELD ORDERS, }   *In the Field, Atlanta, Ga.,*
No. 67. }   *September 8, 1864.*

I. The city of Atlanta, being exclusively required for warlike purposes, will at once be vacated by all except the armies of the United States and such civilian employés as may be retained by the proper departments of government.

II. The chief quartermaster, Colonel Easton, will at once take possession of buildings of all kinds, and of all staple articles, such as cotton, tobacco, &c., and will make such disposition of them as is required by existing regulations, or such orders as he may receive from time to time from the proper authorities.

III. The chief engineer will promptly reconnoiter the city and suburbs, and indicate the sites needed for the permanent defense of the place, together with any houses, sheds, or shanties that stand in his way, that they may be set apart for destruction. Colonel Easton will then, on consultation with the proper officers of the ordnance, quartermaster, commissary, medical, and railroad departments, set aside such buildings and lots of ground as will be needed for them, and have them suitably marked and set apart. He will then, on consultation with Generals Thomas and Slocum, set apart such as may be necessary to the proper administration of the military duties of the Department of the Cumberland and of the post of Atlanta, and all buildings and materials not thus embraced will be held subject to the use of the Government as may hereafter arise, according to the just rules of the quartermaster's department.

IV. No general, staff, or other officers, or any soldier will on any pretense occupy any house or shanty, unless it be embraced in the limits assigned as the camp of the troops to which such general or staff belongs, but the chief quartermaster may allow the troops to use boards, shingles, or materials of buildings, barns, sheds, warehouses, and shanties, not needed by the proper departments of government, to be used in the reconstruction of such shanties and bivouacs as the troops and officers serving with them require, and he will also provide as early as practicable the proper allowance of tents for the use of the officers and men in their encampments.

V. In proper time just arrangements will be made for the supply to the troops of all articles they may need over and above the clothing, provisions, &c., furnished by Government, and on no pretense whatever will traders, manufacturers, or sutlers be allowed to settle in the limits of fortified places, and if these manage to come in spite of this notice, the quartermaster will seize their stores and appropriate them to the use of the troops, and deliver the parties or other unauthorized citizens who thus place their individual interests above that of the United States, in the hands of some provost-marshal, to be put to labor on the forts or conscripted into one of the regiments or batteries already in service.

VI. The same general principles will apply to all military posts south of Chattanooga.

By order of Maj. Gen. W. T. Sherman:

L. M. DAYTON,
Aide-de-Camp.

[SEPTEMBER 8, 1864.—For Special Field Orders, No. 68, headquarters Military Division of the Mississippi, conveying thanks of the commanding general, &c., see Part I, p. 87.]

SPECIAL FIELD ORDERS,   HDQRS. DEPT. OF THE TENNESSEE,
No. 121.   *East Point, Ga., September 8, 1864.*

*   *   *   */   *   *   *

III. Maj. Gen. F. P. Blair, commanding Seventeenth Army Corps, will, to-morrow morning at 8 o'clock, move his command from the right to the left of this army, and occupy a position selected, with which Captain Hickenlooper, of his staff, is acquainted, and which will be by him indicated.

By order of Maj. Gen. O. O. Howard:

WM. T. CLARK,
Assistant Adjutant-General.

[SEPTEMBER 8, 1864.—For Special Field Orders, No. 104, headquarters Army of the Ohio (congratulatory, &c.), see Part II, p. 521.]

NOTICE.]   ATLANTA, GA., *September 8, 1864.*
To the Citizens of Atlanta:

Major-General Sherman instructs me to say to you that you must all leave Atlanta; that as many of you as want to go North can do so, and that as many as want to go South can do so, and that all can take with them their movable property, servants included, if they want to go, but that no force is to be used, and that he will furnish transportation for persons and property as far as Rough and Ready, from whence it is expected General Hood will assist in carrying it on. Like transportation will be furnished for people and property going North, and it is required that all things contemplated by this notice will be carried into execution as soon as possible.

All persons are requested to leave their names and number in their families with the undersigned as early as possible, that estimates may be made of the quantity of transportation required.

JAMES M. CALHOUN,
Mayor.

WAR DEPARTMENT,
Washington, September 9, 1864—9 p. m.

Major-General SHERMAN:

Last night your dispatches of the following dates were received: To General Halleck, August 31, 8 a. m.; to same, September 6, 3.30 p. m.; to Secretary of War, September 6, 3 p. m.; to General Grant, September 6, 3 p. m.; to General Halleck, September 7, 4 p. m.; to General Halleck, September 8 (hour not stated); to Secretary of War, September 8, 8 a. m. Requisitions for the pay of your army have been in the Treasury for more than a month. It is believed that adequate funds will now be speedily provided, so that payment will be made promptly. The operations of your army and the condition of your lines of communication rendered the transmission of funds insecure, even if they could have been had. The first object of the Department will be the payment of your forces, and the most strenuous efforts will be employed to that end. You will please advise me when you think it safe to forward funds.

EDWIN M. STANTON,
Secretary of War.

ATLANTA, GA., *September 9, 1864—10 a. m.*
(Received 8 p. m.)

Maj. Gen. H. W. HALLECK,
Washington, D. C.:

All our troops are now in position, comfortable and well. In a day or two I will have telegraphic communication from Roswell round to Sandtown, and can act promptly. A few of the enemy's cavalry followed us as far as Rough and Ready, and last evening General Hood sent in a flag of truce asking to exchange prisoners. I have about 2,000 in hand, and will exchange if he will make a fair deal. I have sent out my inspector-general to confer and agree, and to make arrangements for the exodus of citizens. I am not willing to have Atlanta encumbered by the families of our enemies. I want it a pure Gibraltar, and will have it so by October 1. I think Generals Rousseau and Steedman are stirring Wheeler up pretty well, and hope they will make an end of him, as Gillem has of Morgan. I have ordered renewed activity, and to show no mercy to guerrillas or railroad breakers. It makes a world of difference if "my bull gores your ox, or yours mine." Weather beautiful and all things seem bright.

W. T. SHERMAN,
Major-General.

HDQRS. MILITARY DIVISION OF THE MISSISSIPPI,
In the Field, Atlanta, Ga., September 9, 1864.

General WEBSTER:

Your dispatch is received. Even sutlers must be prohibited from coming to Atlanta. I will as soon as the railroad is open make arrangements for opening and supplying three stores, one at Atlanta, one at Decatur, and one at East Point, and allow them jointly one car a day. Telegraph all parties to push Wheeler and his bands to the death. Now is the time to strike them hard, and to wipe out all guerrilla bands.

Show them no mercy. I will exchange with Hood about 2,000 prisoners that I have in hand. Our success has been very complete, and I want to make it thorough from the Ohio River to Atlanta, so that we may use Atlanta hereafter as a base.

W. T. SHERMAN,
Major-General, Commanding.

HEADQUARTERS FOURTH ARMY CORPS,
Near Atlanta, Ga., September 9, 1864.

Brigadier-General WHIPPLE,
Assistant Adjutant-General:

GENERAL: I have the honor to report that my command left camp near Sykes' house at 7 a. m. and marched for Atlanta via the direct road leading there. At 10.30 a. m. my head of column reached the city; then, without halting we marched through it and out the Decatur road to the place designated for our present camp. At this place the head of column arrived at 11.30 a. m. Two of my divisions (First and Third) are in line of battle, facing southward, a short distance south of the Decatur railroad, the right about two miles from Atlanta. Kimball's division is on the right and Wood's on the left. My Second Division (Newton's) is in reserve, in close supporting distance. The ground we occupy is a very good defensible position. Part of it was occupied by the Seventeenth Army Corps on August 22. Our left has not yet made connection with the Army of the Ohio, though the right of said army is not far from it.

D. S. STANLEY,
Major-General.

NASHVILLE, *September 9, 1864.*

General WHIPPLE:

The three brigades of rebel cavalry now retreating toward East Tennessee are commanded by Brigadier-Generals Cerro Gordo [John S.] Williams, and Robertson, and Colonel Dibrell. General Milroy has sent out after them, through McMinnville, the Ninth Pennsylvania and Fifth Tennessee Cavalry. Hon. Edmund Cooper, of Shelbyville, reports Williams' and Robertson's force out of ammunition, only partially armed, and the men and horses much worn. General Starkweather just telegraphs from Pulaski that he has news that General Taylor has crossed into Mississippi, and is concentrating with Forrest to enter West Tennessee and cross the river.

B. H. POLK,
Major and Assistant Adjutant-General.
(In the absence of General Rousseau.)

PULASKI, *September 9, 1864.*

Maj. B. H. POLK,
Assistant Adjutant-General:

Major-General Rousseau concentrated all forces of Generals Steedman and Granger with his own at Athens, and has moved on toward Tennessee River again to-day. Major-General Milroy has returned to Tullahoma. Cars will reach Columbia to-morrow going north. All right south. Country is filled with strolling bands of the enemy, who have been lost from their commands, as also those who were part of a Tennessee brigade of enemy which was disbanded for thirty days. We have news that General Taylor has crossed into Mississippi, and is concentrating with Forrest to enter West Tennessee and cross river. Enemy surrounded Clifton last Thursday. My scout arrived direct from Savannah yesterday. All from fifteen to fifty-five have been conscripted in Mississippi. The country there is full of stragglers. Have our hands more than full here. Losses on our part small.

JOHN C. STARKWEATHER,
Brigadier-General.

ATHENS, ALA., September 9, 1864.

Major-General ROUSSEAU:

SIR : The accompanying dispatch just received from Brigadier-General Starkweather. I have ordered Colonel Lyon, at Huntsville, to concentrate all the mounted force along the railroad at Woodville, and the infantry at his disposal to be ready with three days' rations to move to any point by rail. Have directed him to instruct all his forces, however small, to retard the enemy's progress by every means in their power, and to attack him wherever found.

I have the honor to be, general, very respectfully, your obedient servant,

R. S. GRANGER.

While writing this a second telegram was received from Milroy to you. I took the liberty to open it, as it might determine my movements. I have accordingly recalled the order for Colonel Lyon to concentrate. I conceive there can be no necessity of my going now to Woodville.

R. S. GRANGER,
Brigadier-General.

[Inclosure.]

PULASKI, September 9, 1864.

Brigadier-General GRANGER,
Athens :

My scouts just in report that Williams' command was near Shelbyville yesterday, moving south. Dispatch by my courier-line just received from Major-General Milroy, in which he states his arrival at Fayetteville at 2 p. m. yesterday; had captured 3 rebel soldiers, 2 of Williams' and 1 of Wheeler's commands. Williams was going south through Winchester, he thinks, and will either cross the railroad at Decherd or go on to the river and cross at some place above Huntsville. He, General Milroy, moved toward Tullahoma last night. Enemy in small bands infesting the whole country; cannot do much against them, as I have no cavalry to spare. The One hundred and second Ohio all patrolling the road north.

JOHN C. STARKWEATHER,
Brigadier-General.

TULLAHOMA, September 9, 1864—8 a. m.

Major-General ROUSSEAU:

I arrived here this morning at 6.30. I find that Williams passed through Wartrace yesterday with his whole force, in the direction of

McMinnville. He crossed the railroad in a hurry without interrupting
track or wire. Raid over. Railroad and telegraph all right to Chattanooga from Murfreesborough.

R. H. MILROY,
Major-General.

LEXINGTON, *September 9, 1864.*

Brig. Gen. J. D. WEBSTER,
   Nashville, Tenn.:

Information just received from Knoxville reports Wheeler moving
toward Gallatin. Please give me the latest news. I can move against
him if he is heading for Kentucky. My troops are all in hand ready
for a move in any direction.

S. G. BURBRIDGE,
Brevet Major-General, Commanding.

SHELBYVILLE, *September 9, 1864.*

[General MILROY:]

The enemy passed through this place Wednesday night, traveling
east. They camped Thursday at Fairfield. They have but little ammunition, and will try to get back the way they came. I arrived at this
place at 12 o'clock last night.

JOHN WORTHAM,
Major Fifth Tennessee Cavalry.

SHELBYVILLE, *September 9, 1864.*

Major-General MILROY:

The enemy camped seven miles northeast of this place last night.
They have but one or two rounds ammunition to the man, and we can
capture them if we push on them.

JNO. WORTHAM,
Major, Commanding.

ATHENS, ALA., *September 9, 1864.*

Brig. Gen. W. D. WHIPPLE:

General Milroy telegraphs 8 a. m. this date that rebel General Williams with his whole force crossed railroad yesterday p. m. near Wartrace, moving in direction of McMinnville, without disturbing railroad or
telegraph wire. Nothing heard from General Rousseau since leaving
here yesterday p. m.

R. S. GRANGER,
Brigadier-General.

MURFREESBOROUGH, *September 9, 1864.*

Maj. B. H. POLK,
  Assistant Adjutant-General:

Rebel Generals Williams and Robertson passed Beech Grove on the
7th with about 2,000 men and three pieces of artillery, hastening toward
McMinnville. I think Dibrell is moving in the same direction.

H. P. VAN CLEVE,
Brigadier-General.

GENERAL ORDERS, }   HDQRS. DEPT. OF THE CUMBERLAND,
    No. 134.   }   *Atlanta, Ga., September 9, 1864.*

SOLDIERS OF THE ARMY OF THE CUMBERLAND:

The major-general commanding, with pride and pleasure, congratulates you upon the fact that your achievements during the campaign which has just closed, in connection with those of the Armies of the Tennessee and Ohio, have received such distinguished marks of appreciation as the thanks of the President of the United States and of the major-general commanding the Military Division of the Mississippi.

Your commander now desires to add his thanks to those you have already received, for the tenacity of purpose, unmurmuring endurance, cheerful obedience, brilliant heroism, and all those high qualities which you have displayed to an eminent degree, in attacking and defeating the cohorts of treason, driving them from position after position, each of their own choosing, cutting their communications, and in harassing their flanks and rear, during the many marches, battles, and sieges of this long and eventful campaign.

It is impossible, within the limits of an order like this, to enumerate the many instances in which your gallantry has been conspicuous, but among them may be mentioned the actions of Rocky Face Mountain and before Dalton, fought between the 8th and 13th of May, of Resaca on the 14th and 15th, of Adairsville on the 17th, and of New Hope Church on the 25th of the same month, of Kolb's Farm June 22, Peach Tree Creek July 20, and the crowning one of Jonesborough, fought September 1, which secured the capture of the city of Atlanta, the goal for which we set out more than four months ago, and furnished a brilliant termination to your struggles for that long period.

Let these successes encourage you to the continued exercise of those same high qualities, and to renewed exertions in the cause of our country and humanity when you shall again be called upon to meet the foe, and be assured the time is not far distant when your prowess will conquer what territory now remains within the circumscribed limits of the rebellion. A few more fields like those whose names now crowd your standards and we can dictate the terms of a peace alike honorable to yourselves and our country. You can then retire to your homes amid the plaudits of your friends and with the proud consciousness that you have deserved well of the country.

Our rejoicings are not unmixed with a proud regret for our brave comrades who have fallen. Their graves mark the spots where they went down amid the din and roar of battle, dotting every field and hillside, or lying beneath the spreading boughs of the forest along our route; they will in future days serve like finger boards to point out to the traveler the march of your victorious columns. Those silent mounds appeal to us to remain true to ourselves and the country, and to so discharge the high duty devolving upon us that their lives, which they so freely offered up, may not prove a useless sacrifice.

By command of Major-General Thomas:

WM. D. WHIPPLE,
Assistant Adjutant-General.

NASHVILLE, TENN., *September 10, 1864.*

Major-General SHERMAN, *Atlanta:*

Telegram just received from quartermaster at Athens, Ala., that Generals Rousseau, Steedman, and Granger formed junction there on the 8th, and left immediately for mouth of Elk River, where Wheeler was reported to be. Two regiments left by General Steedman had been ordered forward, which looks as if they had found the enemy.

J. D. WEBSTER,
Brigadier-General.

NASHVILLE, TENN., *September 10, 1864.*

Brigadier-General WHIPPLE:

General Rousseau not been heard from since the 8th, on which day he left Athens with his cavalry and infantry in pursuit of Wheeler's main force, joined by Roddey, toward Lamb's Ferry, near Rogersville, on the Tennessee River. General Milroy, with Spalding's brigade of Tennessee cavalry and small fragments of other regiments, has been occupied during the raid with a force of two brigades under the rebel General Williams, about 2,000 strong, which crossed the Chattanooga road, going west, some three days ago, after Wheeler. His force has been so closely pressed by General Milroy that it has done no damage of consequence, and was unable to form a junction with Wheeler, so it recrossed the railroad on the 7th, going east in the direction of McMinnville. On the 6th the Ninth Pennsylvania Cavalry attacked Dibrell's forces, variously estimated at from 1,000 to 2,000 strong, near Readyville, killing 25, wounding many, and capturing 130 prisoners. Dibrell has joined Williams, and the two will likely endeavor to go out through East Tennessee. In all this raid of Wheeler's only one bridge has been destroyed, that at Stewart's Creek, this side of Murfreesborough, where the block-house surrendered without loss of blood; all the damage done will be repaired in a day or two. A train left Murfreesborough for Atlanta with mail this a. m.; the regular trains on the Nashville and Chattanooga road have up steam to leave here at 2 p. m. to-day. There are still straggling bands of the enemy in the vicinity of the railroads, but not sufficient force to do material damage.

B. H. POLK,
Major and Assistant Adjutant-General.
(In the absence of General Rousseau.)

ATHENS, *September 10, 1864.*

Brigadier-General WHIPPLE:

Major-General Rousseau was at Shoal Creek with his command 8 a. m. to-day. He informs me that Wheeler has sent his broken-down horses to the west side of Tennessee River and has shod up the rest, and is moving, together with a part or all of Roddey's command, below Florence. The latest report is that he is on the Savannah road. The major-general requests me to telegraph General Thomas to send a brigade of infantry to the Nashville and Chattanooga Railroad between Tullahoma and Nashville. It is believed the road will be opened to-morrow.

R. S. GRANGER,
Brigadier-General.

NASHVILLE, *September 10, 1864.*

Brigadier-General WHIPPLE, *Chief of Staff:*

One hundred and eight rebel cavalry were moving west near Shelbyville this a. m. General Milroy telegraphs that a guide, who was pressed by this party, reports that they were sent by Williams to meet Wheeler at Muscle Shoals and report to him that Williams was out of ammunition, and if attacked would have to surrender, and asked that Wheeler would make a diversion in his favor south of the Tennessee River above Chattanooga.

B. H. POLK,
Major and Assistant Adjutant-General.

ATHENS, *September 10, 1864—1.30 p. m.*

Brigadier-General WEBSTER:

Generals Rousseau, Steedman, and Granger formed a junction at this place on the 8th, and left immediately for the mouth of Elk River, where Wheeler was reported to be. We have no news from them, but yesterday two regiments left here by General Steedman were ordered up, which looks as if they had found the enemy.

E. B. KIRK,
Captain and Assistant Quartermaster.

NASHVILLE, *September 10, 1864.*

Maj. S. B. MOE:

The brigades of Generals Williams, Robertson, and Dibrell are retreating eastward through McMinnville, followed by the Ninth Pennsylvania and Fifth Tennessee Cavalry. These troops are about out of ammunition, and have sent a party of 100 men to meet Wheeler at Muscle Shoals to notify him of this fact, and to ask that Wheeler make a diversion in their favor south of the Tennessee River above Chattanooga. The fact that these forces going eastward are out of ammunition came from two or three sources. Nothing has been heard from General Rousseau since the 8th.

B. H. POLK,
Major and Assistant Adjutant-General.

NASHVILLE, TENN., *September 10, 1864.*

Brigadier-General STARKWEATHER,
Pulaski, Tenn.:

Williams has sent 100 men to overtake Wheeler at Muscle Shoals, to report that the former was out of ammunition, and desired a diversion made in his favor by Wheeler south of the river above Chattanooga. This party will likely cross the railroad about fifteen miles south of Columbia. If you have any cavalry please look after this party.

B. H. POLK,
Major and Assistant Adjutant-General.

HEADQUARTERS U. S. FORCES,
Pulaski, September 10, 1864.

Colonel CAMPBELL,
Athens:

Inform Generals Rousseau and Granger that statement as to movements of Williams' command is correct—moved through Cornersville toward Shelbyville and then in direction of Wartrace. After Colonel Spalding left Elkton a body of the enemy, reported 500 strong, were reported there; 300 passed this side of Lynnville yesterday going south. Two hundred passed south of this post going south. No cavalry here more than enough to keep up patrols and follow small bodies.

JOHN C. STARKWEATHER,
Brigadier-General, Commanding.

CAMP ON SHOAL CREEK, *September 10, 1864.*

Maj. Gen. L. H. ROUSSEAU:

GENERAL: I would join you at once but for the information contained in the dispatch of Colonel Jackson herewith forwarded. I have no confidence in the information from Starkweather, for I am satisfied he transmits every idle rumor that reaches him as information. Wheeler is beyond all doubt trying to cross the river, and will do so as soon as we permit him. I think we ought to press him. If you hear a few discharges of artillery you * * * getting the boats of the enemy from the south side of the river. My other brigade reached Elk River at daylight this morning. Will send you further information from Jackson as soon as I receive it.

With esteem, truly yours,

JAMES B. STEEDMAN,
Major-General.

[NOTE.—Original mutilated; part missing represented by stars.]

HUNTSVILLE, [*September 10, 1864.*]

Maj. B. H. POLK,
Assistant Adjutant-General, District of Tennessee:

General Granger directs me to say "that I have information from Whitesburg that Roddey, with 1,000 men, camped last night twelve miles from there, on the opposite side of the river, en route to cross the river at some point near Guntersville. A scout of seventy-five men has been sent to Claysville, and the gun-boat is to patrol the river in the neighborhood."

W. P. LYON,
Colonel Thirteenth Wisconsin, Commanding Railroad Defenses.

HDQRS. FIRST BRIGADE, FIRST DIVISION CAVALRY,
In the Field, September 10, 1864.

Captain MATTHIAS:
Acting Assistant Adjutant-General:

SIR: Say to the general that if he desires I can be in Florence by daybreak, or sooner if he desires it. In the event he will not need my brigade longer, I am anxious to return to where I can resume the arming and equipment of it, and wish to leave for Columbia early in the morning unless you order to the contrary. In the event the general does not need us longer, and is willing I should go, I desire to know what to do with the battery and Colonel Roper's detachments.

I am, very respectfully,

JNO. T. CROXTON,
Brigadier-General, Commanding.

TULLAHOMA, *September 10, 1864.*

Maj. B. H. POLK,
    Assistant Adjutant-General:

I have learned from a man who was pressed for a guide by that party of rebels seen northwest of Shelbyville yesterday morning that they were 108 strong, and were sent by Williams to meet Wheeler at Muscle Shoals, on the Tennessee River, and were to cross the railroad fifteen miles south of Columbia, and were to report to Wheeler that Williams was out of ammunition, and if attacked would have to surrender, and asked Wheeler to try to make a diversion in their favor south of the Tennessee River and above Chattanooga.

R. H. MILROY,
Major-General.

FLORENCE, ALA., *September 10, 1864—11 a. m.*

Capt. EDWIN E. WOODMAN:

SIR: We met the enemy one mile east of this place, drove them into the town, where they took cover, from which we drove them. The enemy is said to be under command of Johnson, and to be two regiments and one battalion strong. Mrs. Boddeker reports that the enemy were crossing at the mouth of Cypress Creek, one mile and a half below here. All last night they were crossing by ferry. As soon as possible I will report the facts.

Respectfully,

GEO. W. JACKSON,
Colonel Ninth Indiana Cavalry.

HEADQUARTERS INDIANA BRIGADE,
Three miles and a half from Florence, on Military Road,
[*September 10, 1864.*]

Capt. EDWIN E. WOODMAN,
    Aide-de-Camp:

SIR: I sent a battalion of the Tenth Indiana Cavalry to Kennedy's Ford and below. They report no enemy seen and the boats removed from ferry. Just as I reached this place three men, belonging to a detachment of twenty-six men sent out by Colonel Spalding in direction of Pride's Ferry, caught up with the command, and report that they were attacked by a force variously estimated at from 100 to 600 men near Cheatham's Ford. Learning this, I sent one battalion of the Tenth Indiana in direction of Florence to assist them and save those whose horses were exhausted, if possible, and to hold the advance of the enemy in check until I could communicate with you. I don't suppose the force is a large one. I will wait here until I hear from the battalion sent to Florence. It will be late before I can get in. If you have any orders that I have not received, please send them by bearer. Since writing the above twelve of the twenty-six men from Colonel Spalding's command have reported. From all the information I can gather the force that attacked them is the same that I drove down the river this morning.

Respectfully,

GEO. W. JACKSON,
Colonel, Commanding Brigade.

FLORENCE, ALA., *September 10, 1864—12 m.*

Capt. EDWIN E. WOODMAN:

SIR: I arrived here at 11 o'clock, after driving the rear guard of Johnson's army, about 150 strong, in and through the town, and dispatched to that effect.   Since then from reports that I have learned and all the information I can gather the enemy were busy crossing the river by ferry at the mouth of Cypress Creek all last night.   I have scouted the country above and below, and am confident that Johnson's entire force has crossed the river.   Citizens report that Wheeler has crossed a portion of his force, and is now crossing the remainder of his men at two different fords below the mouth of Cypress Creek.   Colonel Spalding having reached this place with orders to halt and feed, I have done the same, and am now waiting further orders.   I have just sent a scouting party out to go as far as Cypress Ferry with orders, if possible, to take possession of boats.   Will be governed by circumstances.

Respectfully, yours,

GEO. W. JACKSON,
Colonel, Commanding Brigade.

———

FLORENCE, ALA., *September 10, 1864—2.30 p. m.*

Brig. Gen. EDWARD McCOOK:

The enemy cannot be found; they are supposed to be at Pride's Ferry, ten miles below Florence.   I will send flag of truce if I can find the whereabouts of Wheeler.

Very respectfully, your obedient servant,

GEO. SPALDING,
Commanding Division.

———

FLORENCE, *September 10, 1864.*

Brig. Gen. EDWARD McCOOK,
Commanding Cavalry Forces:

Will send dispatch with flag of truce by Captain Davis, of my staff. I am feeding my command at Florence.   Wheeler did not pass through Florence, but was crossing at Pride's Ferry yesterday afternoon and last night.   This is the information received from citizens.   Shall I move my command back by the military road?

Very respectfully, your obedient servant,

GEO. SPALDING,
Col., Comdg. 4th Cavalry Division, Army of the Cumberland.

———

HDQRS. FOURTH CAV. DIV., ARMY OF THE CUMBERLAND,
Two miles from Florence, on Military Road,
September 10, 1864—7.25 p. m.

Brig. Gen. EDWARD McCOOK,
Commanding Cavalry Forces:

There is no enemy this side of the river in the vicinity of Florence; cannonading was on the other side of the river, and fired at a party of mine.   Colonel Jackson is moving in rear of my column.   I have sent Captain Davis, of my staff, to report all information.

Very respectfully, your obedient servant,

GEO. SPALDING,
Colonel, Commanding.

HEADQUARTERS DEPARTMENT OF THE CUMBERLAND,
Atlanta, Ga., September 11, 1864.

Col. T. R. STANLEY:

If you can fit two of the steam-boats at Chattanooga, putting on board of each some artillery and a sufficient force of infantry to make them secure, I wish you to do so, and have them patrol the river, if possible, as far up as Loudon bridge, and between that point and Chattanooga, keeping a good watch for any attempt at crossing on the part of the enemy, destroying all ferry-boats found along the river, and arresting the parties owning them or having them in possession, as all such boats have been prohibited by my order some time since.

GEO. H. THOMAS,
Major-General, U. S. Volunteers, Commanding.

HEADQUARTERS DEPARTMENT OF THE CUMBERLAND,
Atlanta, Ga., September 11, 1864.

Brig. Gen. R. S. GRANGER, *Decatur, Ala., or Athens:*

Send dispatch to Major-General Rousseau that Williams is trying to escape through East Tennessee, and that the railroad is no longer in danger. That he is to press Wheeler with all his might and try to destroy him.

WM. D. WHIPPLE,
Assistant Adjutant-General.

NASHVILLE, *September 11, 1864—11.35 v. m.*

Major-General MILROY:

General Thomas telegraphed that he wants Colonel Spalding to continue the pursuit of Williams and destroy him entirely, if possible; let the pursuit be kept up. Please telegraph me how much force you have sent out.

B. H. POLK,
Major and Assistant Adjutant-General.

TULLAHOMA, *September 11, 1864—10.30 p. m.*

Maj. B. H. POLK, *Assistant Adjutant-General:*

Colonel Spalding does not belong to my command. I left him with the Tenth and Twelfth Tennessee at Pulaski on the 7th instant. Don't know where he is now. I only have the Fifth Tennessee Cavalry, and they have but 300 mounted men for duty. On my return here General Van Cleve informed me that the Ninth Pennsylvania had arrived at Murfreesborough, and I dispatched him to order that regiment to McMinnville on the 10th instant, and I ordered the Fifth Tennessee to meet the Ninth Pennsylvania there, and to proceed in pursuit of Williams. The Fifth Tennessee went to McMinnville in obedience of order, but finding that the Ninth Pennsylvania had not arrived, returned here to-day. These regiments united are too small to pursue Williams, who is 2,000 strong, but if they are placed at my disposal I will pursue the enemy. The Fifth reports to me that Williams is at Sparta. Spalding is not the man to carry out General Thomas' orders.

R. H. MILROY,
Major-General,

MURFREESBOROUGH, *September 11, 1864.*
(Received 10.50 p. m.)

Major CRAVENS, *Assistant Adjutant-General:*

Colonel Jordan, Ninth Pennsylvania Cavalry, camps to-night two miles from Woodbury. He met a scouting party of 150 men from Williams' rebel division at Woodbury, and drove them toward Lebanon. The prisoners report Williams at Sparta, and that they were sent to communicate with Wheeler. Colonel Jordan marches in the morning for McMinnville.

H. P. VAN CLEVE,
Brigadier-General.

NASHVILLE, TENN., *September 11, 1864.*

Major-General BURBRIDGE:

No late news from Wheeler. He is trying to get across the Tennessee at the Shoals. From 200 to 300 of his forces have turned back eastward, are out of ammunition, and only anxious to get away. The country below is full of stragglers. Our roads are but little injured, and will be repaired in a day or two.

J. D. WEBSTER,
Brigadier-General.

PULASKI, TENN., *September 12, 1864.*

Brigadier-General WHIPPLE:

I telegraphed you this morning of my return from the Tennessee River, after having driven Wheeler across. Am now in receipt of your dispatch of yesterday sent to General Granger, in which I am directed to cross the river and press Wheeler and destroy him if possible. General Croxton's brigade of cavalry is marching on the military road to Columbia, and will reach there this evening. Another portion of the cavalry is here and rest at Athens or on way there. I have no doubt you expected your dispatch to reach me when the command was together and near the river. As matters now stand I deem it proper to await further orders.

LOVELL H. ROUSSEAU,
Major-General.

PULASKI, *September 12, 1864.*

Maj. B. H. POLK, *Assistant Adjutant-General:*

General Rousseau and staff arrived here last night, having left Florence yesterday morning, where [Wheeler] crossed to the west side of the Tennessee River, with the main part of his command, at and below Florence on the 10th. A portion of Roddey's command is supposed to be yet on this side of the river. Nothing positive known about the reported crossing of some of Forrest's forces at Clifton. General Steedman is returning to Athens with his infantry. Colonel Spalding's command of cavalry will be here to-day, and General Croxton's brigade will be at Columbia this evening. General Rousseau will start for Nashville as soon as a train can be obtained, and wishes to have one sent out from Nashville as far as the break in the road to meet him.

ALFRED MATTHIAS,
Captain and Acting Assistant Adjutant-General.

MURFREESBOROUGH, *September 12, 1864.*

Major CRAVENS,
    Assistant Adjutant-General:

From information received from White County I am satisfied that Dibrell and Williams are there with about 3,000 men, many without arms, some without horses, many horses crippled and lame, men demoralized, awaiting further orders from Wheeler.

H. P. VAN CLEVE,
Brigadier-General.

TULLAHOMA, *September 12, 1864.*

Maj. B. H. POLK,
    Assistant Adjutant-General:

Just received dispatch from General Van Cleve, stating that 3,000 rebels are in White County, under Dibrell and Williams; many without arms, some without horses, many horses crippled, and men generally demoralized, awaiting orders from Wheeler. If you will send me an adequate force of cavalry I will guarantee that these rebels are captured or driven clear out of the country in short order.

R. H. MILROY,
Major-General.

COLUMBIA, *September 12, 1864.*

Maj. B. H. POLK,
    Assistant Adjutant-General:

Rousseau, Steedman, McCook, Granger, and Colonel Streight were at Athens last Friday. Streight moved with a column of infantry to Rogersville; Rousseau followed with cavalry. Have heard of no fighting, and can learn nothing of Wheeler; presume he has crossed river near Florence. Milroy moved from Pulaski to Chattanooga railroad; cars run here from below.

W. B. SIPES,
Colonel, Commanding Post.

ATHENS, *September 12, 1864.*

General WHIPPLE,
    Assistant Adjutant-General:

I ascertained yesterday that 108 men of General Williams' command had been detached to join General Wheeler, with the request that he make a diversion so that he (Williams) might get across Tennessee River. I immediately telegraphed General Starkweather, at Pulaski, and Colonel Sipes, at Columbia, to use every means to intercept party. Have just received following telegram from Colonel Sipes:

COLUMBIA, *September 12, 1864.*

Captain Lamson, with 100 men, sent after the party you notified me of yesterday, has just come in, bringing 2 officers and 32 men prisoners. He surprised them on Swan Creek, and met with complete success. No loss on our side.

W. B. SIPES,
Colonel, Commanding.

Your telegram of yesterday giving information of whereabouts [sent] to Major-General Rousseau at Pulaski to-day.

R. S. GRANGER,
Brigadier-General.

NASHVILLE, TENN., *September 12, 1864.*
Brigadier-General WHIPPLE,
　　　　Atlanta:

The order of Major-General Thomas for Colonel Spalding to continue the pursuit of Williams was telegraphed to General Milroy, at Tullahoma. He replies that Colonel Spalding with the Tenth and Twelfth Tennessee Cavalry were left by him at Pulaski on the 7th. I presume by General Rousseau's order that only the Fifth Tennessee went back with him to Tullahoma. He at once started the Fifth Tennessee after Williams, and gave orders for the Ninth Pennsylvania Cavalry, then at Murfreesborough, to follow also and meet the Fifth at McMinnville. The latter went to that place, but returned to Tullahoma last night, not having heard of the Ninth Pennsylvania. Williams they report at Sparta. I have telegraphed to General Starkweather to know if Colonel Spalding is at Pulaski. If there, shall he still be ordered after Williams? Not a word from General Rousseau since the 8th.

[B. H. POLK,]
Major and Assistant Adjutant-General.

———

CHATTANOOGA, *September 12, 1864.*
Brigadier-General AMMEN:

Dibrell's brigade rebel cavalry are reported as being near Sparta on the 10th instant, nearly out of ammunition, and on their way out of Tennessee by the route they came in. The Ninth Pennsylvania Cavalry attacked and routed them on the 6th, inflicting a loss on them of 260 killed and wounded and captured.

Respectfully,

S. B. MOE,
Major and Assistant Adjutant-General.

———

CHATTANOOGA, *September 12, 1864.*
Capt. L. M. DAYTON,
　　　　Aide-de-Camp:

Colonel Jordan reports that on the 6th instant he engaged General Dibrell's command, 1,800 strong, near Readyville; killed 25, wounded 100, and captured 130 men, 200 horses and horse equipments.

Respectfully,

S. B. MOE,
Major and Assistant Adjutant-General.

———

SEPTEMBER 12, 1864.
Major-General ROUSSEAU,
　　　　On line of railroad north:

Twenty-two men of Third Tennessee Cavalry just arrived from Cheatham's Ford, on Tennessee River, charged through a rebel portion of troops—missing, 4 men; captain supposed to be killed; 1 was made prisoner and escaped; he was at General Wheeler's headquarters; reports him and Roddey with a very large force at that place, with trains, &c.; he estimates their force as high as 6,000 strong. All the men coincide with the statement so far as they know it; person seems a reliable boy; have examined him thoroughly, and am satisfied myself of his statement. Have sent this information to General Granger, at Athens. These troops were followed to Lawrenceburg and charged upon there.

JOHN C. STARKWEATHER,
Brigadier-General.

CHATTANOOGA, September 12, 1864.

Brigadier-General AMMEN:

Dibrell's rebel cavalry arrived at Sparta on the 9th, and were reported as having left on the 10th, moving toward Kingston. The Fifth Tennessee and Ninth Pennsylvania Cavalry are on their track. The river is being patrolled as far as Loudon by boats.

Respectfully,

J. B. STEEDMAN,
Major-General.

CALHOUN, September 12, 1864.

General STEEDMAN:

I am ordered by General Elliott, chief of cavalry, to march to intercept Williams' rebel cavalry, and to keep him and yourself informed of any movements of the enemy. I propose to start to-morrow for the Hiwassee River. Can you give me the latest information concerning whereabouts and condition of Williams' and Dibrell's brigades, and where the Ninth Pennsylvania and Fifth Tennessee Regiments are, and what course they will pursue?

WM. J. PALMER,
Colonel, Commanding Fifteenth Pennsylvania Cavalry.

HUNTSVILLE, September 12, 1864.

Major-General ROUSSEAU,
Pulaski:

I have received the following from Brigadier-General Whipple:

ATLANTA, September 11, 1864.

Brigadier-General GRANGER:

Send dispatch to Major-General Rousseau that Williams is trying to escape through East Tennessee; that the railroad is no longer in danger; that he is to cross with all his command, press Wheeler, and try to destroy him.

WM. D. WHIPPLE,
Assistant Adjutant-General.

I will be at Athens 11.30 a. m. to-day.

R. S. GRANGER,
Brigadier-General, Commanding.

HEADQUARTERS DEPARTMENT OF THE CUMBERLAND,
Atlanta, Ga., September 12, 1864.

Maj. B. H. POLK,
Asst. Adjt. Gen., Hdqrs. Dist. of Tennessee, Nashville, Tenn.:

If you can get the Fifth Tennessee and Ninth Pennsylvania together, or sufficient other force to cope with Williams, send them after him as quickly as possible. He should be given no rest.

WM. D. WHIPPLE,
Assistant Adjutant-General.

NASHVILLE, TENN., *September 13, 1864—3.30 p. m.*

Major-General SHERMAN, *Atlanta:*

General Rousseau has just arrived. Wheeler and his main force crossed the Tennessee River at the Shoals on the 10th. Parties of them have been crossing also at Savannah, as I learn from Captain Shirk, of the Navy. Another force of from 2,000 to 3,000 rebels, under Williams, reported to be much demoralized and out of ammunition, is in White County, east of Murfreesborough. General Burbridge is about starting to destroy the salt-works near Abingdon, Va., taking Gillem along. Illumination and a really great congratulatory meeting here last night to celebrate fall of Atlanta, &c.

J. D. WEBSTER,
Brigadier-General.

NASHVILLE, TENN., *September 13, 1864.*

Major-General BURBRIDGE, *Lexington, Ky.:*

There is said to be a rebel force of 2,000 to 3,000 under Williams in White County. They are crippled and demoralized. We have a complete force after them. They will hardly trouble Kentucky. I hear of no other force in that direction.

J. D. WEBSTER,
Brigadier-General.

NASHVILLE, *September 13, 1864.*

Brig. Gen. W. D. WHIPPLE:

The Ninth Pennsylvania Cavalry is at McMinnville. Fifth Tennessee started from Tullahoma this morning, with rations and horseshoes for both regiments, and they will pursue Williams there this evening.

B. H. POLK,
Assistant Adjutant-General.

HDQRS. DEFENSES NASHVILLE AND CHATTANOOGA R. R.,
Tullahoma, Tenn., September 13, 1864.

Major ARMSTRONG, *Fifth Tennessee Cavalry:*

MAJOR: You will immediately proceed with your command to McMinnville, Tenn., and report to Col. Thomas J. Jordan, of the Ninth Regiment Pennsylvania Volunteer Cavalry, for duty in pursuing the rebels under Williams. When this pursuit shall have ended you will return to this post with your regiment.

By command of Major-General Milroy:

JNO. O. CRAVENS,
Assistant Adjutant-General.

CHATTANOOGA, TENN., *September 13, 1864.*

Maj. S. B. MOE,
Assistant Adjutant-General, District of the Etowah:

MAJOR: In obedience to the desire of the general commanding the district, I beg leave to submit the following report of the dates and hours of the occurrences of the expedition under his command:

The troops were loaded upon the trains, and the trains left the depot at this place at 7.30 a. m. September 1, and reached Whiteside's Station at 10 a. m. the same day. Here, in obedience to the orders of the railroad authorities, the command was delayed two hours and forty-five minutes, awaiting the arrival of three engines and the cabooses. We left Whiteside's Station about 12.50 p. m., arrived at Bridgeport, taking on the train at that point the Thirty-ninth Iowa Regiment, and reached Stevenson at 1.10 p. m. At this point the command was again delayed one hour and forty-five minutes by the local agent, Mr. Irish, for the purpose of changing engines and conductors. Mr. Irish also took the responsibility of cutting up one of the sections of the train and joining the cars belonging to it on the other four sections. By this some of the regiments were scattered upon three or four trains, and the horses of the artillery separated from the pieces. The expedition reached Murfreesborough at 10.30 p. m., and was disembarked from the train at that point. After several hour's rest, to give the troops an opportunity to cook their rations, the command moved out upon the La Vergne pike at 2.30 p. m. [a. m.] and marched to that point, reaching there at 9 a. m. Here a messenger was dispatched to General Rousseau, and awaiting his reply the command rested in camp. At 5 p. m., no word having been received from General Rousseau, the command was got in readiness to move, when it was reported to the general commanding that a column of the enemy was moving down the Lebanon pike in the direction of the town. The command was immediately moved into position, and the Eighteenth Ohio Volunteer Infantry deployed as skirmishers. The enemy advanced within sight of the skirmish line, but seeing or learning our force from the inhabitants, fell back, refusing attack. The command then moved up the pike toward Murfreesborough, crossing Stewart's Creek, and taking up position at the church two miles from the creek. Here on the next morning, the 3d of September, the enemy again tried to cross, but finding us in their front again retired and moved up toward Lebanon. At the time the enemy fired upon our pickets, General Milroy had sent word of his coming up with his cavalry, and the command waited until his arrival before moving. At 9 a. m. General Milroy arrived, and line was formed. The command moved forward in line for one mile, when it was found that the enemy had left our front. Pursuit was commenced and kept up as far as old Jefferson Crossing of Stone's River. The command then halted and rested, and then moved over to the railroad, where it had been destroyed by Wheeler. The trains arrived here during the night, and at daylight of the 4th of September the command was again embarked upon the train and moved to Murfreesborough. At 9 a. m. General Milroy sent word that the enemy was crossing the Salem pike five miles from town, and the command was at once moved in that direction. While upon the march word was received that the enemy had gone in full retreat, and General Milroy was in pursuit. The command was moved back to Murfreesborough, where it remained until 10 a. m. September 5, when we moved upon the trains toward Tullahoma, repairing some 300 feet of track near Christiana. Upon arriving at Tullahoma a request was received that the general should move his command to Huntsville and Pulaski. Arrangements were made to comply with this request, and the expedition arrived in Huntsville upon the trains at 8.30 a. m. of the 6th of September. Rations were drawn here by the men, and the expedition proceeded to Pulaski, arriving there at 8.30 p. m., where it remained all night. On the morning of the 7th the command was moved to Athens, and disembarked about 12 m. Here word was received that Generals Rousseau and Granger were making for the same point, and we awaited their arrival. In the mean time Colonel Streight, commanding First Brigade, was sent with his own and the Third Brigade to Rogersville.

Generals Rousseau and Granger arrived at Athens September 8, at 4 p. m., and about 6 p. m., at the earnest solicitation of General Steedman, the whole command of cavalry was set in motion to support Colonel Streight. The cavalry camped at Elk River on the night of the 8th of September. At 4 a. m. September 9 that command moved and overtook the infantry under Colonel Streight's command at Shoal Creek about 3.30 p. m. Colonel Streight had overtaken General Wheeler's rear guard and skirmished with it, driving the enemy and crossing the creek, where he awaited the arrival of the cavalry. At this point it was determined by General Rousseau to remain for the night. On the morning of the 10th of September, after a long delay, the cavalry started in pursuit, and the infantry of this command awaited developments. In the mean time foraging parties were sent out, and meat sufficient for two days' rations collected from the rebel citizens of the country. A portion of the command was moved down to ——— Ferry, where some of the boats of the enemy were concealed. Some skirmishing was had and the guards of the boats driven from their cover, 1 being killed and several wounded. Orders to move up to Florence prevented any attempt to gain possession of the boats. These orders were afterward countermanded, and the troops moved back to their camps. General Rousseau here announced that Wheeler had crossed the Tennessee River at 4 p. m. On the morning of the 11th the command started for Athens, reaching Elk River at dark, and Athens at 9 a. m. on the 12th of September. The command started at 11 a. m. September 12 for Chattanooga, arriving there at 11.30 p. m.

Accompanying this please find the telegrams received during the expedition. The organization of the command was as follows: First Brigade, Colonel Streight commanding—Fifty-first Indiana, Eleventh Michigan, Fourteenth U. S. Colored, Second Ohio Volunteer Infantry. Second Brigade, Lieutenant-Colonel Dunn commanding—Twenty-ninth Indiana Infantry, Eighteenth Ohio Volunteer Infantry, Sixty-eighth Indiana Infantry, and detachments of Fifth and Tenth Iowa. Third Brigade, Lieutenant-Colonel Hurlbut commanding—Thirty-ninth Iowa, Fifty-seventh Illinois.

I have the honor to be, major, very respectfully, your obedient servant,

H. E. STANSBURY,
Capt., 19th Infantry, and Acting Assistant Adjutant-General.

HEADQUARTERS OF THE ARMY,
Washington, September 16, 1864.

General W. T. SHERMAN,
Atlanta, Ga.:

MY DEAR GENERAL: Your very interesting letter of the 4th is just received. Its perusal has given me the greatest pleasure. I have not written before to congratulate you on the capture of Atlanta, the objective point of your brilliant campaign, for the reason that I have been suffering from my annual attack of "coryza," or hay cold. It affects my eyes so much that I can hardly see to write.

As you suppose, I have watched your movements most attentively and critically, and I do not hesitate to say that your campaign has been the most brilliant of the war. Its results are less striking and less complete than those of General Grant at Vicksburg, but then you have had greater difficulties to encounter, a longer line of communication to keep up, and a longer and more continuous strain upon yourself and upon your army. You must have been very considerably annoyed by the State negro recruiting agents.

Your letter was a capital one and did much good. The law was a ridiculous one; it was opposed by the War Department, but passed through the influence of Eastern manufacturers who hoped to escape the draft in that way. They were making immense fortunes out of the war, and could well afford to purchase negro recruits, and thus save their employés at home.

I fully agree with you in regard to the policy of a stringent draft, but, unfortunately, political influences are against us, and I fear it will not amount to much. Mr. Seward's foolish speech at Auburn, again prophesying for the twentieth time that the rebellion would be crushed in a few months, and saying that there would be no draft, as we now had soldiers enough to end the war, &c., has done much harm in a military point of view. But these infernal old political humbugs cannot tell the truth even when it is for their interest to do so. I have seen enough of politics here to last me for life. You are right in avoiding them. McClellan may possibly reach the White House, but he will lose the respect of all honest, high-minded patriots by his association with such traitors and copperheads as Belmont, Vallandigham, Wood, Seymour, and Co. He could not stand upon the traitorous Chicago platform, but he had not the manliness to oppose it. A major-general in the United States service, and yet not one word to utter against rebels or the rebellion! I had much respect for McClellan before he became a politician, but very little after reading his sneaking and cowardly letter accepting the nomination.

Hooker certainly made a mistake in leaving before the capture of Atlanta. I understand that when here he said that you would fail, your army was discouraged and dissatisfied, &c. He is most unmeasured in his abuse of me. I inclose you a specimen of what he publishes in Northern papers wherever he goes.* They are dictated by himself, and written by Wilkes, Butterfield, and such worthies. The funny part of the business is that I had nothing whatever to do with his being relieved on either occasion. Moreover, I have never said anything to the President or Secretary of War to injure him in the slightest degree, and he knows that perfectly well. His animosity arises from another source. He is aware that I know something about his character and conduct in California, and fearing that I may use that information against him, he seeks to ward off its effects by making it appear that I am his personal enemy, am jealous of him, &c. I know of no other reason for his hostility to me. He is welcome to abuse as much as he pleases; I don't think it will do him much good or me much harm.

I know very little of General Howard, but believe him to be a true, honorable man. Thomas is also a noble old war horse. It is true that he is slow, but he is always sure.

I have not seen General Grant since the fall of Atlanta, and do not know what instructions he has sent you.

I fear that Canby has not the means to do much by way of Mobile.

The military effects of Banks' disaster are now showing themselves by the threatened operations of Price and Co. toward Missouri, thus keeping in check our armies west of the Mississippi.

With many thanks for your kind letter and wishes for your future success,

Yours, truly,

H. W. HALLECK.

---

* Not found.

CONFEDERATE CORRESPONDENCE, ETC.

HEADQUARTERS MARTIN'S DIVISION,
July 1, 1864.

Major BURFORD,
Assistant Adjutant-General:

MAJOR: Lieutenant Buice, scout, has just returned from the rear of the enemy on the Bell's Ferry road, and reports that Garrard's division moved camp on Tuesday to the neighborhood of Robert McAfee's. Garrard's headquarters are at McAfee's house. He saw a pass dated from there to-day, 9 a. m.

Very respectfully, your obedient servant,

ALFRED IVERSON,
Brigadier-General.

ATHENS, GA., *July 1, 1864.*

Hon. JAMES A. SEDDON,
Secretary of War, Richmond, Va.:

MY DEAR SIR: I am here for two days only, to organize the local force for the defense of this place against threatened raids. I think I shall have sufficient force for its protection, but I would again urge the appointment or assignment of a suitable officer as commandant of this post. The public interest here in the way of factories, the armory, &c., justifies and requires that arrangements for the defense of the place should be made. All that is now wanting is a proper commandant of the post. I have heretofore approved the application made by the citizens for the appointment of Colonel Mell, of this place. He would be an acceptable and good appointment. I have suggested in former letters other names, and am personally indifferent as to the man, but feel anxious for the appointment of some suitable officer.

Allow me, in this unofficial letter, to express to you an opinion which I feel so strongly that I desire to express it to yourself and the President. While I know too little of the condition of our different armies in the field to express an opinion worthy of much consideration, yet there is a conviction upon my mind so strong and overwhelming that I cannot throw it off, that the defense of Atlanta and Georgia, and the certain defeat and destruction of Sherman's army, are involved in some movement to be made by Forrest (if possible) or some other cavalry on Sherman's line of communication. Unless it is done, I see no end to the slow process of Sherman's advance through Georgia. If his communication was cut for ten days his army would be destroyed, and Georgia, as well as Alabama and Mississippi, saved, and Tennessee recovered. To effect such a result could we not afford to uncover for a short time the country protected by Forrest? It does seem to me that the object to be accomplished makes the proposition worthy of consideration. It is proper I should say that our people are in the best spirits, hopeful and confident. They have the utmost confidence in General Johnston, which has not been shaken by his falling back, and they believe that the President will do all that any man can do. I trust you will pardon the liberty I take in making these suggestions, and be assured that I only do so because I feel a conviction that impressed me with the idea that it is the only certain solution of the present impending danger.

With the assurance of my continued sincere regard,

I am, very truly, yours, &c.,

HOWELL COBB.

[Indorsement.]

JULY 16, 1864.

ADJUTANT-GENERAL:

Is Colonel Mell in active service? If not, assign him as commandant at Athens.

J. A. S.

HDQRS. ROSS' BRIGADE, JACKSON'S CAVALRY DIVISION,
In the Field, Ga., July 1, 1864—2 p. m.

Brigadier-General JACKSON,
Commanding Division:

GENERAL: The enemy are flanking me on my left, and already have possession of the road leading from Moss' house to General Armstrong's position. General G. W. Smith has retired with his command toward Armstrong's position.

I am, general, very respectfully, &c.,

L. S. ROSS,
Brigadier-General.

HDQRS. ROSS' BRIGADE, JACKSON'S CAVALRY DIVISION,
In the Field, Ga., July 1, 1864—3 p. m.

General JACKSON,
Commanding Division:

GENERAL: The force under General Smith have left their position and gone down to Armstrong. The enemy are advancing on the road I fell back on. Their force is not yet known. I can hear firing in the direction of Armstrong.

I am, general, very respectfully, &c.,

L. S. ROSS,
Brigadier-General.

HDQRS. ROSS' BRIGADE, JACKSON'S CAVALRY DIVISION,
In the Field, Ga., July 1, 1864—5 p. m.

Brigadier-General JACKSON,
Commanding Division:

GENERAL: Colonel Boyles, on my right, reports a heavy column of infantry moving on his right. There is an interval between his right and Ferguson's brigade. A heavy line advancing on me from the Sand-town road. Their right extends as far west as the first house from Moss'. There can be no doubt but that the enemy have at least one corps.

I am, general, very respectfully, &c.,

L. S. ROSS,
Brigadier-General.

NEAR MARIETTA, *July 2, 1864.*

General BRAXTON BRAGG,
Richmond:

Scouts report the arrival in the Federal army of another division of the Seventeenth Corps within a few days.

J. E. JOHNSTON.

HEADQUARTERS KELLY'S DIVISION,
July 2, 1864.

Maj. E. S. BURFORD:

I have the honor to state that scout just returned states that it found the enemy's pickets at Roberts' house, on the Bell's Ferry road, about a quarter of a mile this side of McAfee's house. Their line extended both to the right and left of the road at this point.

Very respectfully,

J. H. KELLY,
Brigadier-General, Commanding.

CIRCULAR.]   HEADQUARTERS ARMY OF TENNESSEE,
July 2, 1864—1.30 p. m.

The army will change position to-night.

1. The Army of Mississippi will withdraw its artillery at dark and its infantry at 10 p. m.
2. Hardee's and Hood's corps will move their artillery at dark, their infantry at 11 p. m.
3. Each corps commander will leave on the lines such rear guard as he may think proper until 1 a. m., then to be withdrawn and followed by the skirmish line.
4. The corps will move by routes already indicated to the commanders of each, and take position in two lines on the new line indicated.
5. The reserve artillery will be protected by the corps in whose line it is serving and take the route of the corps.
6. Wheeler's cavalry will cover the infantry from General Hood's left to General Loring's right.
7. Corps commanders will send their spare carriages of every description to the rear at or before sunset.
8. General Johnston will move with the center column.

W. W. MACKALL,
Chief of Staff.

SMYRNA CHURCH, *July 3, 1864.*

General BRAXTON BRAGG:

The extension of the enemy's intrenched line several miles nearer the Chattahoochee than our left has compelled us to fall back about six miles.

J. E. JOHNSTON.

HDQRS. ROSS' BRIGADE, JACKSON'S CAVALRY DIVISION,
In the Field, Ga., July 3, 1864—9.20 a. m.

Brigadier-General JACKSON, *Commanding Division:*

GENERAL: My scouts report the enemy with infantry and cavalry near Sweet Water bridge, but could not ascertain their force. They think they camped there last night. The enemy in front of my position on the Sandtown road remain quiet; no movements made by them this morning. I have made no change in my line, but have detached the Third Texas and sent them to guard the road, which my dispatch of yesterday informed you came into my rear.

I am, general, very respectfully, &c.,

L. S. ROSS,
Brigadier-General.

HDQRS. ROSS' BRIGADE, JACKSON'S CAVALRY DIVISION,
In the Field, Ga., July 3, 1864—10.15 a. m.

Brigadier-General JACKSON,
Commanding Division:

GENERAL: A body of Yankee cavalry is now moving down the road on my left, one regiment, all that has yet been discovered. The skirmishers in my front are still advancing; are now but a little distance from my line.

I am, general, very respectfully, &c.,

L. S. ROSS,
Brigadier-General.

HDQRS. ROSS' BRIGADE, JACKSON'S CAVALRY DIVISION,
In the Field, Ga., July 3, 1864—4.50 p. m.

Brigadier-General JACKSON,
Commanding Division:

GENERAL: The Yankee infantry is moving across my front in the direction of Sweet Water bridge in front of General Armstrong. Their line of skirmishers, which appears to be out merely for the protection of their flanks while moving, are in full view of my pickets, who report that their knapsacks are plainly visible. What amount of force is moving I cannot discover. You may be able to form some estimate of the force from the length of time they may be passing, which I will report as soon as it is done moving by.

I am, general. very respectfully, &c.,

L. S. ROSS,
Brigadier-General, &c.

HDQRS. ROSS' BRIGADE, JACKSON'S CAVALRY DIVISION,
In the Field, Ga., July 3, 1864—7.15 p. m

Brigadier-General JACKSON,
Commanding Division:

GENERAL: The enemy are advancing in my front once more with heavy line of skirmishers, before which my line is being slowly driven back. I cannot decide how large the force is in rear of the skirmish line, but it is at least a brigade of infantry. The line of skirmishers extends to my left beyond my farthest vedettes, and I suppose to General Armstrong's front, as they can be heard that far. At this moment their advance is checked. My skirmishers are, however, not more than 100 yards in advance of my line.

I am, general, very respectfully, &c.,

L. S. ROSS,
Brigadier-General.

JULY 4, 1864—7.10 a. m.

Major-General WHEELER,
Commanding Cavalry:

GENERAL: Please ascertain as soon as possible what force is before you, and where the left of the enemy's infantry is, and as well as you can what force is in our front here.

Respectfully,

J. E. JOHNSTON.

MASON AND TURNER'S FERRY, *East Bank, July 4, 1864.*

[General J. E. JOHNSTON:]

GENERAL: The following are the ferries and crossings between this point and Gorman's Ferry, twelve miles southwest:

Green's (private) Ferry: A mile and a half southwest of this point. Hills on the west side command the ferry; ferry not fortified or guarded, and ferry-boat still there.

Green and Howell's Ferry: Three miles southwest of this point. Ferry fortified on east side; redan with one piece of artillery, and rifle-pits for 100 or 150 men. Two companies (seventy-five men) guard the ferry. Boat on the east side river.

Howell's (old) Ferry (now disused): One mile southwest of Green and Howell's, is fordable in dry weather. Ferry not fortified or guarded. No ferry-boat at this point now.

Wilson and Baker's Ferry: Three miles southwest of Green and Howell's; fortified on east side for 100 men.

Sandtown: Two miles southwest from Wilson and Baker's; fortified on east side by rifle-pits for 100 or 150 men. Ferry-boat on east side of river.

Adaholt's: Two miles southwest from Sandtown Ferry; fortified on east bank of river, with rifle-pits for 100 or 150 men.

Gorman's: Two miles southwest of Sandtown; fortified on east side, and guarded by one company.

At most, if not all, the ferries mentioned above as now in use the ascent and descent to and from the river on either side is good for artillery or wagons. The highest ground and most commanding positions for artillery, in my judgment, are found on the west bank of the river—that is the bank from Atlanta. On our (the east) side, in some instances, pretty fair positions for artillery a little back from the river can be obtained.

Brigadier-General Humes' division of cavalry (two brigades) has just passed down the river for the purpose of re-enforcing the State troops at the crossings mentioned above. I have furnished the commanding officer with a guide and all information I had. On yesterday evening at 4 o'clock the enemy were moving bodies of infantry, number not known, to and around Sweet Water Factory. A portion of this cavalry, evidently on a reconnaissance, appeared opposite to Adaholt's Ferry, but on being fired upon by the State troops retired.

I am, general, respectfully, your obedient servant,

W. CLARE,
Major and Assistant Inspector-General.

HEADQUARTERS HARDEE'S CORPS,
July 4, 1864—8.30 p. m.

Major-General CLEBURNE,
            Commanding Division:

GENERAL: By direction of General Johnston your reserve brigade will be sent to-morrow morning to report to Lieutenant-General Hood, at the Eden house. General Hood will send a guide to conduct it.

Respectfully,

T. B. ROY,
Assistant Adjutant-General.

(Same to General Bate.)

HEADQUARTERS HARDEE'S CORPS,
July 4, 1864—6 p. m.

Major-General BATE:

GENERAL: General Hardee directs that your reserve brigade be sent to report without delay to General Cheatham at Bowie's house. A guide will be sent you to conduct the brigade as soon as possible: meantime let it be ready to move.

Respectfully,

T. B. ROY,
Assistant Adjutant-General.

[Indorsement.]

General Lewis will be ready to move as soon as he can, and report to General Cheatham as directed within. The guide will be on hand directly.

WM. B. BATE,
Major-General.

———

HEADQUARTERS LORING'S DIVISION,
In the Field, July 4, 1864—3 p. m.

Major-General WHEELER,
Commanding Cavalry:

GENERAL: My scouts have just returned from the front, and report three regiments of the enemy's infantry moving to our right in the direction of the Pace's Ferry road. Since I saw you this morning one of my regiments has been put in the trenches, extending my line farther to the right. If you are attacked in force I will give you further assistance if you will communicate with me. Would it not be advisable to put as much artillery in position on your line as possible? Should any further disposition be made of the troops on my line, so as to prevent me from giving you assistance in the event of your being attacked, I will immediately advise you of the fact.

Respectfully, your obedient servant,

W. S. FEATHERSTON,
Brigadier-General, Commanding Division.

———

HDQRS. ROSS' BRIGADE, JACKSON'S CAVALRY DIVISION,
In the Field, Ga., July 4, 1864—3 p. m.

Brigadier-General JACKSON,
Commanding Division:

GENERAL: My command has just repulsed, and then charged in brilliant style, a heavy column of infantry at least one brigade strong, driving them pell-mell for half a mile, running them back on their battery, and forcing them to draw off to keep it from falling into our hands. The flag-bearers of two of my regiments were shot down. My loss is not very heavy.

I am, general, very respectfully, &c.,

L. S. ROSS,
Brigadier-General, &c.

Hdqrs. Ross' Brigade, Jackson's Cavalry Division,
In the Field, Ga., July 4, 1864—4.10 p. m.

Brigadier-General JACKSON,
Commanding Division:

GENERAL: The enemy is moving around my left flank, and are now very near the road leading to General Armstrong's headquarters. I have not learned what force is thus flanking me. My skirmishers are being forced back by cavalry, and cannot discover what is in its rear. My position here is now no longer tenable, as I have no protection either on the right or left. I am moving back.

I am, general, very respectfully, &c.,

L. S. ROSS,
Brigadier-General, &c.

SPECIAL ORDERS, }   ADJT. AND INSP. GENERAL'S OFFICE,
No. 155.   *Richmond, July 4, 1864.*

*   *   *   *   *   *   *

XIII. Maj. G. W. Crane, quartermaster, will report to General Joseph E. Johnston, commanding, &c., for assignment to duty with Brig. Gen. L. E. Polk's brigade.

*   *   *   *   *   *   *

By command of the Secretary of War:

SAML. W. MELTON,
Assistant Adjutant-General.

ORDNANCE OFFICE,
Vining's Station, July 4, 1864.

Brigadier-General MACKALL,
Chief of Staff, Army of Tennessee, Hdqrs. of the Army:

GENERAL: I have the honor herewith to transmit to you statement of ammunition:

Articles.	On cars at Vining's.	In Atlanta.	Total.
Cartridges:			
Caliber .57	33,000	30,000	63,000
Caliber .54	225,000	122,000	347,000
Caliber .69	108,000	68,000	176,000
Musket-caps	115,000	100,000	215,000
Pistol-caps	110,000	....	110,000
Whitworth rifle cartridges	1,250	1,250	2,500
Pistol army cartridges	6,134	....	6,134
Pistol navy cartridges	3,040	....	3,040
12-pounder gun, rounds	300	1,140	1,440
12-pounder howitzer, rounds	202	1,450	1,652
10-pounder Parrott, rounds	256	204	460
3-inch rifled, rounds	266	326	592

Besides the above, invoices from Selma were received; that on the 1st instant, 200,000 cartridges, caliber .57, were forwarded to Atlanta. Thirty thousand cartridges, caliber .57, I was informed by Colonel Wright, was to be finished yesterday evening, and every day the same number will be manufactured. Five thousand rounds of ammunition is in progress of manufacturing at Augusta, and is daily, parts of it, forwarded to Atlanta. The 20-pounder Parrott ammunition, 400 rounds, is preparing at Atlanta, and I am informed will be ready this evening.

I have also to report that the corps under command of Lieutenant-Generals Hardee and Hood are supplied this morning with 80 rounds to each arm.

The Army of Mississippi requires 50,000 cartridges, caliber .57; 34,000 cartridges, caliber .54. It will be supplied as soon as the wagons will arrive, except 17,000, caliber .57.

To-day all supplies for field guns will be issued from the cars at this place. I shall go to-night to Atlanta and return with new supplies without delay.

Very respectfully, your obedient servant,

H. OLADOWSKI,
Lieutenant-Colonel.

NEAR CHATTAHOOCHEE BRIDGE, *July 5, 1864.*
General BRAXTON BRAGG,
　　　Richmond:

In consequence of the enemy's advance toward the river below our left we this morning took this position, which is slightly intrenched. A division of cavalry on the southeast side of the river is guarding the ferries below. The gallant Brigadier-General Vaughan lost his left foot yesterday by a shell. We greatly need the general officers asked for.

J. E. JOHNSTON.

JULY 5, 1864.

Major-General WHEELER:

General Johnston wishes you to destroy all the boats on the river that you can find.

Respectfully,

W. W. MACKALL,
Chief of Staff.

HEADQUARTERS HARDEE'S CORPS,
July 5, 1864.

[General P. R. CLEBURNE:]

GENERAL: It has been determined to withdraw Strahl's old picket-line to the line of works thrown up by his command, near the Marietta road. General Hardee wishes your picket-line adjusted accordingly. I met your division officer of the day, Colonel Robison, on the line, and indicated it to him, and gave him the necessary instructions and the dividing point between your division and General Bate's division.

Respectfully,

W. D. PICKETT,
Lieutenant-Colonel and Assistant Adjutant-General.

HEADQUARTERS KELLY'S CAVALRY DIVISION,
In the Field, July 5, 1864—7 a. m.
Maj. E. S. BURFORD,
　Assistant Adjutant-General, Wheeler's Corps:

MAJOR: I have the honor to state that my pickets are all in, and I am about to move toward the Pace's Ferry road, leaving two regiments at the point designated by the major-general commanding.   Everything quiet in front.   No enemy reported on this, the Powers' Ferry, or Paper-Mill road.

Very respectfully,

J. H. KELLY,
Brigadier-General, Commanding.

HEADQUARTERS KELLY'S CAVALRY DIVISION,
July 5, 1864.

Maj. E. S. BURFORD,
Assistant Adjutant-General, Wheeler's Corps:

MAJOR: I have the honor to report that the enemy, in addition to the fortifications reported near the houses on opposite side of the river, have dug trenches opposite to Colonel Dibrell's line so as to command the river-bank and to make it impossible to retire our skirmishers in the daylight without much exposure and probable loss of life.   We have no rifle-pits or other cover.   Can tools be procured for the purpose of intrenching?   Colonel Gaines, commanding Hannon's brigade, reports that the same thing has been done in his immediate front.

Very respectfully,

M. W. HANNON,
Colonel, Commanding.

HEADQUARTERS,
Chattahoochee Bridge, July 5, 1864—8.30 a. m.

Maj. Gen. SAMUEL JONES, *Charleston, S. C.:*

I sent Brigadier-General Jackson, with the Fifth and Forty-seventh Georgia Regiments.   It is not possible to send more.*

J. E. JOHNSTON.

HDQRS. ROSS' BRIGADE, JACKSON'S CAVALRY DIVISION,
Militia Trenches, Ga., July 5, 1864—6.10 a. m.

Brigadier-General JACKSON, *Commanding Division:*

GENERAL: At daylight this morning I advanced a line of skirmishers, and finding the enemy gone from my immediate front, sent forward scouts afoot and on horseback to ascertain what had become of them. I will inform you as soon as these scouts report back.

I am, general, very respectfully, &c.,

L. S. ROSS,
Brigadier-General, &c.

HDQRS. ROSS' BRIGADE, JACKSON'S CAVALRY DIVISION,
Militia Trenches, Ga., July 5, 1864—9 a. m.

Brigadier-General JACKSON, *Commanding Division:*

GENERAL : The enemy is again advancing in my front, his skirmish line now crossing the field in advance of our breast-works.   A battery is in position at or near the same position it occupied yesterday evening. The advancing line extends to the right and left, far beyond my flanks.

I am, general, very respectfully, &c.,

L. S. ROSS,
Brigadier-General.

---

* This in answer to Jones to Johnston, Vol. XXXV, Part II, p. 556.

RICHMOND, *July 6, 1864.*

General J. E. JOHNSTON:

Yours of 1st received 3d; 4th received after President had acted on the request for officers in yours of 5th, which was received earliest through some bad management at telegraph office.

BRAXTON BRAGG.

———

JULY 6, 1864.

General WHEELER:

General Johnston wishes you to observe the river closely from Pace's Ferry to a point opposite our right. What was the fate of the bridge?
Respectfully,

W. W. MACKALL,
Chief of Staff.

CIRCULAR.]	HEADQUARTERS, &C.,
Chattahoochee, July 6, 1864.

Lieutenant-General HOOD:

Corps commanders will send and keep on the south bank of the river the ordnance wagons and caissons and all the wagons they can possibly spare from the headquarters of their regiments, brigades, and divisions. The expenditure of ammunition will be supplied every morning by drawing from the trains on the south bank. The importance of keeping the bridges free is apparent.

By order of General Johnston:

W. W. MACKALL,
Chief of Staff.

(Same to Lieutenant-General Hardee and Major-General Loring.)

———

RICHMOND, *July 7, 1864.*

General J. E. JOHNSTON:

The announcement that your army has fallen back to the Chattahoochee renders me more apprehensive for the future. That river, if not fordable, should not be immediately in your rear, and if you cross, it will enable the enemy without danger to send a detachment to cut your communications with Alabama, and, in the absence of the troops of that department, to capture the cities, destroy the mines and manufactories, and separate the States by a new line of occupation. At this distance I cannot judge of your condition or the best method of averting calamity. Hopeful of results in Northern Georgia, other places have been stripped to re-enforce your army until we are unable to make further additions, and are dependent on your success. Efforts have been made and are still making to organize the reserves as an auxiliary force for State defense. You well know what progress has been made in Georgia and Alabama.

JEFFERSON DAVIS.

———

NEAR CHATTAHOOCHEE, *July 7, 1864.*

To His Excellency J. E. BROWN, *Governor:*

I have the pleasure to inform you that the State troops promise well, and have already done good service. While the army was near Marietta they were employed to support the cavalry on the extreme left, and occupied a position quite distinct from any other infantry of ours. According to all accounts their conduct in the presence of the enemy was firm and creditable. Such Federal parties as approached the crossing-places of the Chattahoochee guarded by them have been driven back. These proofs of their valor make me anxious that their number be increased. Is it possible? You know that the distinguished officer at their head is competent to high command.

Most respectfully, your obedient servant,

J. E. JOHNSTON.

JULY 7, 1864.

General WHEELER:

General Johnston informs you that a battery for five guns has been completed on the east side of the river opposite to our right flank. He wishes you to observe closely, and if the enemy should bring forward his left flank to put the guns in position at once and open on him.

Respectfully,

W. W. MACKALL,
Chief of Staff.

There has been sharp cannonading on Hood's line this evening. Nothing else of interest.

HEADQUARTERS HARDEE'S CORPS,
July 7, 1864.

[General P. R. CLEBURNE:]

GENERAL: In case of a movement across the Chattahoochee, yours and General Walker's divisions will cross at the second pontoon bridge below the railroad bridge. A corps inspector will show your inspector the route to it, and Lieutenant-General Hardee directs that you cause the road to be opened or repaired as may be necessary.

Respectfully, general, your obedient servant,

T. B. ROY,
Assistant Adjutant-General.

SPECIAL ORDERS, }   HEADQUARTERS HOOD'S CORPS,
    No. 86.   }   *In the Field, July 7, 1864.*

I. Pursuant to instructions from army headquarters, Lieut. Gen. A. P. Stewart is relieved from duty with this corps, and will comply with orders of the army commander heretofore sent him.

II. Brig. Gen. John C. Brown is relieved from duty in command of Hindman's division, and will at once assume command of Stewart's division.

By command of J. B. Hood, lieutenant-general, commanding:

J. W. RATCHFORD,
Assistant Adjutant-General.

NEAR CHATTAHOOCHEE RAILROAD BRIDGE,
July 8, 1864.

His Excellency the PRESIDENT, *Richmond:*

SIR: I have received your dispatch of yesterday. Our falling back was slow. Every change of position has been reported to General

Bragg. We have been forced back by the operations of a siege, which the enemy's extreme caution and greatly superior numbers have made me unable to prevent. I have found no opportunity for battle except by attacking intrenchments. It is supposed in the army that Sherman's immediate object is the capture of Atlanta. A part of our troops is on the north side of the river intrenched, and, having six bridges behind it, so that we do not think it exposed. It is believed here that there are 16,000 cavalry for defense of Mississippi and Alabama, and, therefore, that the enemy cannot make a detachment able to invade that department. Might not 4,000 of this cavalry prevent the danger by breaking up the railroad between the enemy and Dalton, thus compelling Sherman to withdraw?

J. E. JOHNSTON.

JULY 8, 1864.

Major-General WHEELER, *Commanding Cavalry Corps:*

GENERAL: Please watch the force you mention as on this side of the river, and whenever it moves impede its march as much as you can, destroying bridges after you. Give notice of all the roads by which they move also.

Respectfully,

J. E. JOHNSTON.

JULY 8, 1864.

Major-General WHEELER, *Commanding Cavalry:*

General Johnston intends Walthall's division for a reserve to the cavalry, and does wish it spread out along the river, in positions.

Respectfully,

W. W. MACKALL,
Chief of Staff.

JULY 8, 1864.

Colonel ANDERSON, *Commanding Brigade:*

SIR: I am requested by Captain Bettis, of the First Confederate, who is picketing at Powers' Ferry, to write you that owing to the advance of the enemy on the road leading from Shallow Ford, at Mr. Isham's, to Atlanta, he will withdraw his pickets from the river and place them on the road upon which the Yankees are moving. The situation of country is such that he would be in danger of being cut off should he stay at the ferry. The Yankees are supposed to be in considerable force and of all arms.

I am, colonel, very respectfully,

B. FRANK BURKETT,
Lieut., Comdg. Company I, Ninth Tennessee Cavalry.

HEADQUARTERS HANNON'S BRIGADE,
July 8, 1864—about 5 p. m.

Captain TERRETT,
Assistant Adjutant-General, Kelly's Division:

CAPTAIN: Scouting parties of the enemy have made their appearance all along my front to-day as far up as McAfee's Bridge. I think very likely they are reconnoitering for the purpose of attempting a crossing at some point. I have sent another scout across the river on foot, with instructions to go in the rear of the enemy, and advise me of their movements.

Very respectfully,

J. F. GAINES,
Lieutenant-Colonel, Commanding.

P. S.—I am picketing and scouting about five miles above McAfee's Bridge, and have about 200 men on the line below the bridge.

J. F. G.

I inclose you dispatch* just received from Captain Mastin; have ordered the ford picketed which he describes.

Yours,

J. F. GAINES,
Lieutenant-Colonel.

———

BURNT BRIDGE, *July 8, 1864.*

Captain TERRETT,
Kelly's Headquarters:

CAPTAIN: In accordance with report sent in by Lieutenant Cotton, commanding picket, first post above burnt bridge, the enemy is moving with considerable force up the river in the direction of McAfee's Bridge; they have with them four or six pieces of artillery. He reports they have a good many wagons, supposed to be pontoon bridges. They have been quite busy during this afternoon, just opposite us on the river, at work on timber. Their move commenced about dark.

Very respectfully,

J. F. GAINES,
Lieutenant-Colonel, Commanding.

———

NEAR CAVALRY FORD, *July 8, 1864—9 o'clock.*

Col. B. J. HILL:

COLONEL: The advance of the enemy is about a mile and a quarter from the river, on this side. There is no doubt they are crossing infantry and artillery. They can be plainly heard laying a pontoon bridge at Cavalry Ford. One of my men who was at the point late this evening says he saw about two brigades of infantry this side of the river, with fixed bayonets, marching by fours. They can be heard crossing to-night. There is no doubt but there is a considerable force crossing at that point. Cannot tell their number.

Very respectfully,

. C. Y. WILSON.

P. S. There is no mistake about the pontoon, for I was close to the river and could hear them at work on it. A good many of their force waded the river.

C. Y. W.

———

* Not found.

[Indorsement.]

1 a. m.

Inclosed for General Wheeler.

How high above your present position did the enemy's infantry line extend?

Respectfully,

W. W. MACKALL.

HEADQUARTERS HOOD'S CORPS,
In the Field, July 8, 1864.

Major-General STEVENSON,
    Commanding Division:

GENERAL: The lieutenant-general commanding directs me to say that he wishes you to relieve those detached parties, on duty with you, of General G. W. Smith's command, and order them to report back. He also directs me to inform you that the brigade of your division on the other side of the river is not on duty at present, and will be sent to you whenever it is needed; but as the enemy is threatening Generals Clayton's and Brown's positions he desires to keep it there until it is necessary to send it to you. Major-General Cheatham with his division is lying near Turner's Ferry, and will be sent to your support whenever it is necessary.

Very respectfully, your obedient servant,

J. W. RATCHFORD,
    Assistant Adjutant-General.

OFFICE CHIEF QUARTERMASTER, CAVALRY CORPS,
July 8, 1864.

Major-General WHEELER:

I have the honor to report that for the last three days I have received but 13 pounds of corn for this command: On the 5th we received 5 pounds per horse; on the 6th, 6 pounds, and on the 7th, 2 pounds; total, 13 pounds.

Respectfully, general, your obedient servant,

S. E. NORTON,
    Assistant Quartermaster, Wheeler's Corps.

RICHMOND, *July 9, 1864.*
(Received 11th.)

General J. E. JOHNSTON:

My telegram of 7th was marked to be put in cipher.* I only learned that it had not been done after the dispatch had been forwarded.

JEFFERSON DAVIS.

HEADQUARTERS,
July 9, 1864—5 a. m.

Major-General WHEELER,
    Commanding Cavalry Corps:

GENERAL: General Johnston is very anxious to receive your report as to the character of the force which crossed at Isham's Ford. If it

---

* See p. 867.

is a large force you will be supported by at least a division of infantry (Walthall's). In taking your troops to oppose it, leave the necessary parties in observation on the river with artillery.

Very respectfully, &c.,

T. B. MACKALL,
Aide-de-Camp.

CONFIDENTIAL.]   JULY 9, 1864.

General WHEELER:

General Johnston informs you that the army will be withdrawn to the south side of the river to-night, the movement commencing at dark. It will be formed about three miles south of the river.

Respectfully,

W. W. MACKALL,
Chief of Staff.

JULY 9, 1864—7.15 p. m.

Major-General WHEELER:

GENERAL: General Johnston informs you that he will continue to hold the river by infantry from Green's Ferry to Howell's Ferry—that is, by detached brigades in advance of the line. He wishes you to connect with this line of detached brigades on your left, and then to observe as high up the river as practicable, particularly in front of any force that has crossed or may cross. Keep the reserve artillery if you need it; if not, send it back to the main line.

W. W. MACKALL,
Chief of Staff.

HDQRS. ROSS' BRIGADE, JACKSON'S CAVALRY DIVISION,
Howell's Ferry, Ga., July 9, 1864—8.30 a. m.

Brigadier-General JACKSON,
Commanding Division:

GENERAL: The only perceptible change in the enemy's line in my front since yesterday is that their battery on the hill is now intrenched, and their skirmishers advanced to the river-bank, from whence they are shooting this morning.

I am, general, very respectfully, &c.,

L. S. ROSS,
Brigadier-General, &c.

Memoranda.

CONFIDENTIAL.]   HEADQUARTERS HARDEE'S CORPS,
July 9, 1864.

The corps will move across the Chattahoochee to-night, and, wherever precedence is necessary, in the following succession: Cheatham, Bate, Walker, Cleburne.

First. The artillery will be withdrawn across the river at dusk.

Second. The infantry will be withdrawn from the intrenchments at 10 p. m.

Third. The skirmishers will be withdrawn at 1 a. m.

Fourth. Bate's division will cross at the upper of the two pontoon bridges assigned this corps, and Walker and Cleburne at the lower one.

Fifth. All the skirmishers of this corps will cross at the upper pontoon bridge.

Sixth. The divisions of this corps will move on the road southwest of the railroad, and will halt at the place indicated to division commanders.

Seventh. Major-General Cleburne will leave Polk's brigade and a battery of artillery, and Major-General Walker will leave Mercer's brigade and a battery at points to be indicated by the lieutenant-general.

Eighth. The lower pontoon bridge will be taken up by the engineer corps as soon as the rear of Cleburne's infantry has passed, notification of which will be given by a staff officer of Lieutenant-General Hardee. Major-General Cleburne will leave detail of seventy-five men to assist in taking up the bridge.

Ninth. The skirmishers of this corps, after having passed the upper pontoon bridge, will be formed to protect the bridge until it is burned.

By command of Lieutenant-General Hardee:

T. B. ROY,
Assistant Adjutant-General.

ATLANTA, *July 10, 1864.*

General B. BRAGG:

On the night of the 8th the enemy crossed at Isham's, or Cavalry Ford; intrenched. In consequence we crossed at and below the railroad, and are now about two miles from the river, guarding the crossings.

J. E. JOHNSTON.

———

HEADQUARTERS WILLIAMS' CAVALRY BRIGADE,
July 10, 1864—2 p. m.

Maj. E. S. BURFORD,
Assistant Adjutant-General, Wheeler's Corps:

MAJOR: I am to the right of Colonel Dibrell, on a road that leads from Buck Head to Roswell (called the river road). My pickets connect with Colonel Dibrell's to my left, and I scout across to Colonel Gaines', on my right. To my front two roads turn off to the left, one going to Isham's and the other to Stephens' Ford. I am picketing these three roads. General Kelly, in accordance with the instructions of Lieutenant Pointer, will move Dibrell's brigade over to the right. I sent scouts through the enemy's lines last night, but they have not returned. The force at Isham's is not large. The Yankees have not advanced to-day from any point between Roswell and Powers' Ferry. If our infantry all fall back the cavalry on this road will be in danger of being cut off. The Yankee force that crossed between Roswell and Pace's Ferry in advancing will move by concentric roads to Buck Head, which is five miles in my rear, and not more than four or five miles from Pace's Ferry. The road from Pace's Ferry should be held until the troops from this road can move out. I think it would have been better to have moved me to the right of Colonel Gaines, which would have left General Kelly's division together; as it is, I am between Anderson and the balance of Kelly's command.

Very respectfully,

JOHN S. WILLIAMS,
Brigadier-General, Commanding.

HEADQUARTERS KELLY'S DIVISION,
Near Cross Keys, July 10, 1864—6 p. m.

Maj. E. S. BURFORD,
    Assistant Adjutant-General:

MAJOR: I have the honor to inform you that I have just arrived at this point with Dibrell's brigade. Colonel Hannon reports all quiet in his front; he also reports the force which crossed at McAfee's Bridge to have withdrawn to within half a mile of the bridge, leaving only a small force this side of the river. Colonel Gaines reports the enemy in the vicinity of Roswell to have erected fortifications. Their force is cavalry. I am establishing a courier line from this point to corps head-quarters, passing by way of Buck Head.
    Very respectfully,
                                        J. H. KELLY,
                                Brigadier-General, Commanding.

HEADQUARTERS ANDERSON'S BRIGADE,
July 10, 1864.

Maj. E. S. BURFORD,
    Assistant Adjutant-General:

MAJOR: I have the honor very respectfully to report, for the informa-tion of the major-general commanding, that I have just received a com-munication from Captain Irwin, commanding my picket-line, telling me that in order to conform his line to that of General Williams and Colonel Dibrell he has been compelled to retire his line. The right of my present line is at Mrs. Gorman's, on the south bank of Long Island Creek, my left resting on the river about half a mile above the creek, which is about four miles above Pace's Ferry.
    I am, major, very respectfully, your obedient servant,
                                        R. H. ANDERSON,
                                        Colonel, Commanding.

[JULY 10, 1864.—For the organization and strength of Johnston's army, see Part III, pp. 654, 679.]

EXECUTIVE DEPARTMENT, C. S. A.,
Richmond, Va., July 11, 1864.

General S. COOPER,
    Adjutant and Inspector General:

GENERAL: I am directed by the President to request that you will furnish him at once with official information in reply to the following questions: What re-enforcements have been sent to General J. E. John-ston since he took command of the army in Georgia, and at what times have they been sent? What force had he when he assumed command? What force has he now of infantry, what of cavalry, what of artillery? What force is there in General S. D. Lee's department, specifying in-fantry, artillery, and cavalry, and dividing into the commands of Gen-eral Maury, of General Forrest, of General Roddey, &c.?
    Very respectfully, your obedient servant,
                                        BURTON N. HARRISON,
                                        Private Secretary.

RICHMOND, VA., *July 11, 1864.*

General J. E. JOHNSTON:

Your telegram of the 8th received. You know what force you left in Alabama and Mississippi, and what part of it has, since you left that department, been transferred to re-enforce you in Georgia. You were, therefore, in condition to judge of the value of the belief that there are now for the defense of those States 16,000 cavalry, and of the conclusion drawn from that belief. The proposition to send 4,000 cavalry from that department to break up the railroad between the enemy and Dalton suggests the inquiry, Why not so employ those already sent to you from that department, or others of equal number, for the proposed operation, the importance of which has long been recognized, and the immediate execution of which has become a necessity? If it be practicable for distant cavalry, it must be more so for that which is near, and former experiences have taught you the difference there would be in time, which is now of such pressing importance. Will write to you and give information in relation to the condition of General S. D. Lee's department, which, I perceive, you cannot possess.

JEFFERSON DAVIS.

RICHMOND, VA., *July 11, 1864.*

General J. E. JOHNSTON,
  Commanding Army in Georgia:

SIR: In a telegram of this date I promised to give you by letter some information in relation to the department of General S. D. Lee, which your dispatch indicated you did not possess. General Lee telegraphed on the 8th instant from Tupelo:

Enemy advanced to Ripley yesterday evening; is exceedingly cautious and careful. His force about 15,000, mostly veteran troops. Ninety-days' men left on railroad. My force 7,500 cavalry, 1,500 dismounted men, 20 pieces of artillery.*

On the 9th, from same place, he telegraphed:

Troops left Morganza [July] 6th for New Orleans. Canby is no doubt now moving on Mobile with 20,000 men. Column of enemy south of Ripley, reported 12,000 to 15,000 strong, advancing slowly. I deem it of vital importance that an infantry force be put in Mobile at once. I can only put a part of my cavalry there, dismounted.*

On the same day (9th instant) General Maury, at Mobile, telegraphed:

Just heard from New Orleans. Canby preparing to come here with about 20,000 men. Expedition seems almost ready.*

The enemy had made movements from Vicksburg and Natchez. The first was met by General Adams, commanding the brigade of General Lee's division which remained in Mississippi when the other three brigades were sent to Alabama, and thence, I am informed, to re-enforce your army in Georgia, and the expedition, after getting as far as Jackson, was abandoned, and the enemy, it is said, returned to Vicksburg severely punished. Of that which started from Natchez no report has reached me. The recent movement of General Pillow and its results are, I suppose, known to you. I have no official information in regard to it, or of the troops under his command.

If the force confronting the enemy at Ripley were withdrawn a detachment might lay waste the stored and growing supplies of the Tombigbee Valley, and the main body, liberated from the protection of Memphis and free from flank attack, could (and probably would) move rapidly

---

* For full text of dispatches, see Vol. XXXIX, Part II.

on to re-enforce Sherman or cover his line of communication, as the one or the other should be most necessary to counteract or overcome the operation against him.   If General Adams and the fragmentary organizations in Southern Mississippi be withdrawn, there will [be] little difficulty in a movement by the enemy from Vicksburg and the points below it to Selma for the destruction of the valuable machinery and material collected there, as well as the large supplies in that part of Alabama. I have heretofore expressed my estimate of the value of the supplies in the localities named in connection with the maintenance of your army.

Senator Hill has arrived, and after conversing with him I have called for exact statements from the War Department, after the receipt of which I will endeavor to reply to the various propositions and reflections which have been presented to me.

Very respectfully, yours, &c.,

JEFFERSON DAVIS.

[Indorsement.]

MACON, *July 24, 1864—8.30 a. m.*

This letter just received by a messenger, who reports that he left Richmond with Colonel Waddell on the 20th instant.   The colonel stopped on the way and directed him to deliver the letter.

J. E. JOHNSTON.

NEAR ATLANTA, *July 11, 1864.*

General BRAGG:

I strongly recommend the distribution of the U. S. prisoners, now at Andersonville, immediately.

J. E. JOHNSTON,
General.

NEAR ATLANTA, *July 11, 1864.*

General B. BRAGG:

GENERAL: Can I get the two Louisiana regiments in Quarles' brigade for Gibson?   And can I have Brig. Gen. J. C. Brown promoted to command Hindman's division?   It is very important.

J. B. HOOD,
Lieutenant-General.

GENERAL FIELD ORDERS, ⟩   HDQRS. ARMY OF TENNESSEE,
         No. 3.   ⟨   *July 11, 1864.*

Intercourse between the pickets of the enemy and our own is strictly and positively prohibited.   Officers of all grades are required to watch over the enforcement of this order, and to punish every infraction. General Johnston appeals to the good sense of the army to put an end to a practice so dangerous.   Yesterday the enemy had a great interest in finding the fords in the Chattahcochee, and easily attained their object, the pickets by mutual agreement bathing in the river together. The engineers of the enemy most probably mingle with the bathers.

By command of General Johnston:

A. P. MASON,
Assistant Adjutant-General.

NEAR ATLANTA, *July 12, 1864.*

General BRAXTON BRAGG,
          Richmond:

The enemy holds several fords from eight to twelve miles above, where he has troops intrenched on this side. Elsewhere everything quiet, except a little occasional skirmishing at long range across the river, and artillery firing by the enemy, principally near railroad, ineffective.

                                        J. E. JOHNSTON.

RICHMOND, *July 12, 1864.*
                              (Received 13th.)

General J. E. JOHNSTON:

Your telegram received. You have all the force that can be employed to distribute or guard prisoners; know the condition of the country and prospects of military operations. I must rely on you to advise General Winder as to the proper and practicable action in relation to U. S. prisoners.

                                        JEFFN. DAVIS.

HEADQUARTERS,
                              July 12, 1864.

Major-General WHEELER,
          Commanding Cavalry:

GENERAL: General Johnston directs that you will send to Brigadier-General Jackson, commanding cavalry, Captain Waties' battery of artillery, now with Brigadier-General Ferguson.

Very respectfully, your obedient servant,

                                        A. P. MASON,
                              Major and Assistant Adjutant-General.

HEADQUARTERS CAVALRY BRIGADE,
                    July 12, 1864—4.20 p. m.

Maj. E. S. BURFORD,
          Assistant Adjutant-General, Wheeler's Corps:

MAJOR: I am just in receipt of your note of this evening. The enemy are in statu quo in my front. This force is small and chiefly of infantry. Two hundred or 300 mounted men came up the Isham's Ferry road about two hours ago, but after a few shots from my pickets went back. Some scouts who went some days ago with Captain Humber across the Etowah have returned. They killed and wounded 12 Yankees and got their horses. The captain is badly wounded himself.

Respectfully,

                                        JNO. S. WILLIAMS.

P. S.—I will send out my remaining scouts at once.

                                        J. S. W.

HEADQUARTERS WILLIAMS' BRIGADE,
Four miles north of Buck Head, July 12, 1864.

Maj. E. S. BURFORD,
  Assistant Adjutant-General:

MAJOR: There has been a perceptible movement of the enemy on this side of the river in my front in the last twenty-four hours, and that which is in my front I think is small and mostly infantry. It extends but a short distance above Isham's Ford. I am picketing the road picketed by Colonel Dibrell, as well as the Atlanta and Roswell road, the road I picketed when I first moved out here. The pickets on the Isham's Ford road are infantry, and only about half a mile from mine. The enemy has fortified around Isham's Ford.

  Very respectfully,

JNO. S. WILLIAMS,
Brigadier-General, Commanding.

RICHMOND, VA., *July 12, 1864.*

General MARCUS J. WRIGHT, *Atlanta, Ga.:*

Governor Brown proposes to furnish 5,000 old men and boys for the emergency. You will receive such numbers as are tendered, mustering them into service for local defense, and issue arms to them from the ordnance stores, on which you are authorized to draw as required from the depot at Macon.

S. COOPER,
Adjutant and Inspector General.

ATLANTA, *July 13, 1864.*

His Excellency JEFFERSON DAVIS, *Richmond:*

Have just arrived without detention. Our army all south of the Chattahoochee, and indications seem to favor an entire evacuation of this place. Shall see General Johnston immediately.

BRAXTON BRAGG.

ATLANTA, *July 13, 1864—1 p. m.*

His Excellency JEFFERSON DAVIS:

The enemy are reported by General Wheeler as having crossed two corps to this side of the river about nine miles above the railroad bridge. An official report has just reached General Wright that the enemy's cavalry, accompanied by artillery, crossed the Chattahoochee this evening nine miles from Newnan. Were at last accounts advancing on that place. Our army is sadly depleted, and now reports 10,000 less than the return of 10th June. I find but little encouraging.

B. BRAGG.

ATLANTA, *July 13, 1864.*

General S. COOPER:

Brigadier-General Jackson commands three brigades, which are severally under Brigadier-Generals Armstrong, Ferguson, and Ross. Effective total, 3,574. Total present, 5,370.

J. E. JOHNSTON.

JULY 13, 1864.

Major-General WHEELER:

GENERAL: Please watch the force you mention as on this side of the river, and whenever it moves forward impede its march as much as you can, destroying bridges after you. Give notice of all the roads by which they march, also.

Respectfully,

J. E. JOHNSTON.

[Indorsement.]

JULY 13, 1864.

Maj. E. S. BURFORD,
      Assistant Adjutant-General:

MAJOR: General Wheeler says send copy of this to General Kelly and General Williams, and tell them to comply with it.

Respectfully,

W. E. WAILES,
      Acting Assistant Adjutant-General.

NEAR ATLANTA, *July 13, 1864.*

Maj. Gen. D. H. MAURY,
      Commanding, &c., Mobile, Ala.:

It is not possible for me to detach eleven companies. Alabama reserves which I had at West Point are ordered to Mobile.

J. E. JOHNSTON.

NEAR ATLANTA, *July 14, 1864.*

General S. COOPER,
      Richmond:

General Wheeler reports Dodge's corps, with two brigades of cavalry, on this side of the river near Roswell, and Howard's and Schofield's corps also on this side, intrenched midway between Roswell and the railroad. A body of Federal cavalry crossed the river last night opposite Newnan, but was driven back by Brigadier-General Armstrong. All quiet elsewhere.

J. E. JOHNSTON.

RICHMOND, *July 14, 1864.*
(Received 15th.)

General JOHNSTON:

You must do the work with your present force. For God's sake do it.

B. H. HILL.

NEAR ATLANTA, GA., *July 14, 1864.*

General BRAXTON BRAGG,
      Commanding Armies Confederate States, Richmond, Va.:

GENERAL: During the campaign from Dalton to the Chattahoochee River it is natural to suppose that we have had several chances to strike the enemy a decisive blow. We have failed to take advantage of such opportunities, and find our army south of the Chattahoochee, very much decreased in strength. Our loss cannot be less than 20,000, without having fought a decisive battle. I deem it of the greatest importance that General Kirby Smith should be ordered at once, with at least half, if not a larger portion, of his army, on this side of the Mississippi River. Our success west of the Mississippi River has proven a disadvantage to us, since the enemy has re-enforced his army on this side, and we have failed to do so. The strength of the Army of Tennessee is such at this time as to render it necessary to have aid from General Kirby Smith— allowing that we should gain a victory over Sherman—to follow up our success and regain our lost territory. Our present position is a very difficult one, and we should not, under any circumstances, allow the enemy to gain possession of Atlanta, and deem it excessively important, should we find the enemy intends establishing the Chattahoochee as their line, relying upon interrupting our communications and again virtually dividing our country, that we should attack him, even if we should have to recross the river to do so. I have, general, so often urged that we should force the enemy to give us battle as to almost be regarded reckless by the officers high in rank in this army, since their views have been so directly opposite. I regard it as a great misfortune to our country that we failed to give battle to the enemy many miles north of our present position. Please say to the President that I shall continue to do my duty cheerfully and faithfully, and strive to do what I think is best for our country, as my constant prayer is for our success.

  Respectfully,

            J. B. HOOD,
            Lieutenant-General.

        MOORE'S BRIDGE, *July 14, 1864.*
               (Via Newnan.)

General MACKALL:

 I arrived here at 4 a. m. Found the enemy in possession of the bridge where General Humes' pickets had been surprised. I have a small portion of my brigade; ordered the remainder to follow. I think I can hold them in check until my troops get up. They are working on the bridge. The abutment was knocked down. They have an excellent position and have made breast-works. It is a division of cavalry, with artillery. I have heard of no infantry. Scouts report a cavalry column gone below.

  With respect,

         FRANK C. ARMSTRONG,
            Brigadier-General.

    HEADQUARTERS WILLIAMS' CAVALRY BRIGADE,
               July 14, 1864.

Maj. E. S. BURFORD,
  Assistant Adjutant-General, Wheeler's Corps:

 MAJOR: Scouts from beyond the river report heavy masses of the enemy's infantry lying between the railroad and the Johnson's Ferry road. They say there is no infantry above the Johnson's Ferry road. The enemy seems to be resting. Some cavalry in the neighborhood of Roswell. A little skirmishing along my front last night and this morning. The pickets of the command to my immediate left are too weak;

they fell back last night more than a mile, which left my camp exposed. I sent my officer of the day, who aided the captain of these pickets in re-establishing his line, but unless they are strengthened they will give way again.

Respectfully,

JNO. S. WILLIAMS,
Brigadier-General, Commanding.

ATLANTA, *July 15, 1864.*

His Excellency JEFFERSON DAVIS, *Richmond, Va.:*

The enemy were driven back across the Chattahoochee near Newnan this morning by our cavalry before they reached the West Point railroad. Another corps of infantry has crossed above. Nearly all available stores and machinery are removed, and the people have mostly evacuated the town.

BRAXTON BRAGG.

ATLANTA, *July 15, 1864.*

His Excellency JEFFERSON DAVIS, *Richmond:*

I have made General Johnston two visits, and been received courteously and kindly. He has not sought my advice, and it was not volunteered. I cannot learn that he has any more plan for the future than he has had in the past. It is expected that he will await the enemy on a line some three miles from here, and the impression prevails that he is now more inclined to fight. The enemy is very cautious, and intrenches immediately on taking a new position. His force, like our own, is greatly reduced by the hard campaign. His infantry now very little over 60,000. The morale of our army is still reported good.

BRAXTON BRAGG.

JULY 15, 1864.

General BRAGG:

GENERAL: General Wheeler reported only this morning that the enemy's corps at Isham's Ferry advanced eastwardly three or four miles in the afternoon and intrenched. I did not give you this information sooner because I expected to see you here. I have not visited you because absolutely afraid to leave my quarters.

Respectfully and truly, yours,

J. E. JOHNSTON.

HEADQUARTERS MARTIN'S DIVISION,
July 15, 1864.

Maj. E. S. BURFORD,
Assistant Adjutant-General:

MAJOR: I have the honor to report that I am on duty in command of Martin's division.

Very respectfully, your obedient servant,

ALFRED IVERSON,
Brigadier-General.

Headquarters a quarter of a mile outside breast-works on old Decatur road.

A. I.

ATLANTA, GA., *July 15, 1864.*

General S. COOPER,
    Adjutant and Inspector General, Richmond, Va.:

Lieutenant-General Polk asked the President to order me to command the Mississippi reserve forces. No reply received. This service don't meet my wishes. I am still awaiting orders. Please answer immediately.

DANIEL RUGGLES,
    Brigadier-General.

ATLANTA, GA., *July 15, 1864.*

General BRAXTON BRAGG:

I have the honor to state that in conformity to orders (see copies A and B, inclosed*), I reported to Lieutenant-General Polk, commanding the Army of Mississippi in the field, in advance of Marietta, on the 2d day of June. Lieutenant-General Polk stated that he had only the reserve forces of the State of Mississippi, which he wished me to organize and command in the field. Thus deprived of an alternative I found myself virtually assigned to a service not in accordance with my wishes. The general stated that he would immediately telegraph and write to the President, recommending my assignment to that service, and he afterward informed me that he had done so. The general instructed me to await orders, at such convenient place in the vicinity of the army as I might select. Being without guards for my horses and baggage (after having been plundered once to a small extent), and unable for the want of transportation to conform to the developments of the campaign, I applied for and obtained authority to come to Atlanta, where I could watch both with greater certainty. After the fall of Lieutenant-General Polk, in the field, I addressed a communication to Major-General Loring, commanding the Army of the Mississippi (see copies C and D, inclosed*), and subsequently referred the subject to Lieutenant-General Stewart, his successor in command, who instructs me to await a reply from the War Department to Lieutenant-General Polk's recommendation. These circumstances will explain the necessity which has deprived me of active participation for a brief period in the prosecution of the present active campaigns against the enemy.

Very respectfully, your obedient servant,

DANIEL RUGGLES,
    Brigadier-General.

RICHMOND, *July 16, 1864.*

General J. E. JOHNSTON:

A telegram from Atlanta of yesterday announces that the enemy is extending intrenchments from river toward railroad to Augusta. I wish to hear from you as to present situation, and your plan of operations so specifically as will enable me to anticipate events.

JEFFERSON DAVIS.

---

* Not found.

NEAR ATLANTA, *July 16, 1864.*

His Excellency the PRESIDENT,
         Richmond:

Your dispatch of to-day received.   The slight change in the enemy's dispositions made since my dispatch of the 14th to General Cooper was reported to General Bragg yesterday.   It was a report from General Wheeler that Schofield's corps had advanced eastwardly about three miles from Isham's Ford and intrenched.   As the enemy has double our number, we must be on the defensive.   My plan of operations must, therefore, depend upon that of the enemy.   It is mainly to watch for an opportunity to fight to advantage.   We are trying to put Atlanta in condition to be held for a day or two by the Georgia militia, that army movements may be freer and wider.

                                        J. E. JOHNSTON.

NEAR ATLANTA, *July 16, 1864.*

His Excellency the PRESIDENT,
         Richmond:

Our scouts on the Tennessee report on the 6th that a division of the Seventeenth Army Corps passed Shellmound the week before.   It had been relieved at Decatur and Huntsville by 100-days' men, and that from one to three regiments of these 100-days' men had passed up during that week.

                                        J. E. JOHNSTON.

JULY 16, 1864—1 p. m.

Major-General WHEELER,
         Commanding Cavalry:

GENERAL: General Johnston asks if you have ascertained the truth in regard to the reported advance of Schofield yesterday.   We have scout reports which seem to contradict it.

         Respectfully,

                                        W. W. MACKALL,
                                             Chief of Staff.

JULY 16, 1864—9 p. m.

General WHEELER:

GENERAL: The enemy disappeared this evening from their works in front of Green's, and from Turner's Ferry.   A spy reported this evening that their right rested on the railroad—Hooker's corps—and that Palmer, Schofield, and McPherson were on the upper river.

         Respectfully,

                                        W. W. MACKALL,
                                             Chief of Staff.

MOBILE, *July 16, 1864.*
                                        (Received 17th.)

General J. E. JOHNSTON:

Have ordered seven companies reserve troops to General Withers, at Montgomery, to meet raid coming from Talladega.

                                        D. H. MAURY,
                                             Major-General.

Tupelo, *July 16, 1864.*
(Via Meridian 17th.)

Brigadier-General Pillow,
          Montevallo:
Lieutenant-Colonel Polk has been ordered with 400 infantry to Selma
to await your orders.

S. D. LEE,
Lieutenant-General.

Tupelo, *July 16, 1864.*
(Via Meridian 17th.)

Brigadier-General Pillow,
          Montevallo:
If the enemy move for Montgomery or West Point you will dismount
your men and move by rail to meet them at threatened point.

S. D. LEE,
Lieutenant-General.

Hdqrs. Ross' Brigade, Jackson's Cavalry Division,
          Donahue's, Ga., July 16, 1864—11 a. m.

Brigadier-General Jackson,
          Commanding Division:

General: Some of my scouts from the rear of Sherman's army inform me that he is collecting supplies as rapidly as possible at Big
Shanty. One division of cavalry is there as guard, and recruiting their
horses for the purpose of pursuing any cavalry sent from this army to
operate on the railroad. The force in my front on the river, I think,
has retired, passing up the river toward Turner's Ferry. Scouts have
crossed to learn more definitely of their movements. The right of their
infantry is reported to be east of the road leading to Green's Ferry, or
rather above that ferry.

I am, general, very respectfully, &c.,

L. S. ROSS,
Brigadier-General, &c.

Hdqrs. Ross' Brigade, Jackson's Cavalry Division,
          Near Baker's Ferry, Ga., July 16, 1864—8.10 p. m.

Brig. Gen. W. H. Jackson,
          Commanding Division:

General: My scouts crossed the river near Baker's Ferry this
p. m. and found no Federal infantry this side of Ruff's Station. Citizens informed them that it moved off last night in the direction of Roswell Factory. One cavalry brigade is camped about three miles from
Baker's Ferry. Two regiments of cavalry passed down the river this
evening in the direction of Sweet Water.

I am, general, very respectfully, &c.,

L. S. ROSS,
Brigadier-General.

SPECIAL ORDERS, } ADJT. AND INSP. GENERAL'S OFFICE,
No. 167.   }   *Richmond, July 16, 1864.*

* * * * * * *

V. Maj. J. E. McElrath, quartermaster, will relieve Maj. E. H. Ewing, quartermaster of Major-General Stevenson's division. Major Ewing on being relieved will report for duty with Lieut. Col. A. H. Cole, inspector-general field transportation.

VI. Maj. E. W. Baylor, quartermaster, is relieved from duty with General Strahl's brigade, and is assigned to duty with the brigade commanded by Brigadier-General Pettus.

* * * * * * *

By command of the Secretary of War:
SAML. W. MELTON,
Assistant Adjutant-General.

RICHMOND, *July 17, 1864.*
General J. E. JOHNSTON:
Lieut. Gen. J. B. Hood has been commissioned to the temporary rank of general under the late law of Congress. I am directed by the Secretary of War to inform you that as you have failed to arrest the advance of the enemy to the vicinity of Atlanta, far in the interior of Georgia, and express no confidence that you can defeat or repel him, you are hereby relieved from the command of the Army and Department of Tennessee, which you will immediately turn over to General Hood.
S. COOPER,
Adjutant and Inspector General.

[Indorsement.]

Received night of July 17, 1864. Headquarters three miles from Atlanta, at Nelson's house, on Marietta road.

RICHMOND, *July 17, 1864.*
General JOHN B. HOOD:
You are charged with a great trust. You will, I know, test to the utmost your capacities to discharge it. Be wary no less than bold. It may yet be practicable to cut the communication of the enemy or find or make an opportunity of equal encounter whether he moves east or west. God be with you.
JAMES A. SEDDON.

JULY 17, 1864—6.30.
Major-General WHEELER, *Commanding:*
GENERAL: The enemy seemed disposed to pass me by and move down the river. They have skirmished with me but slightly, but the firing below has been lively. Having gained the cross-road where my line first was they ceased all movement to my right, as far as I can ascertain. There is a wide interval between General Williams and myself.
Respectfully,
S. W. FERGUSON,
Brigadier-General.

JULY 17, 1864—6.40.

Maj. Gen. J. WHEELER,
        Commanding Cavalry:

GENERAL: General Allen has just reported that the enemy have crossed Nancy's Creek, about half a mile below me, with infantry and cavalry. The report was made him by Colonel Hart. I am sending to meet them at once.

Respectfully,

S. W. FERGUSON,
Brigadier-General.

———

JULY 17, 1864.

Maj. E. S. BURFORD,
        Assistant Adjutant-General, Wheeler's Corps:

I have just received dispatch (verbal) from officer commanding mounted picket that the enemy had turned his left flank and were driving him back.

Respectfully,

S. W. FERGUSON,
Brigadier-General.

———

HEADQUARTERS BRIGADE,
July 17, 1864.

Capt. J. W. LABOUISSE,
        Acting Assistant Adjutant-General:

CAPTAIN: I have the honor to acknowledge receipt of your last dispatch, and to say in reply thereto that my mounted pickets were driven in this morning. The left of the mounted pickets rested on the river about one mile and a half above where the dismounted men are posted, and their right connects with General Williams. Their left was turned. The enemy's pickets were doubled during the night, and drove in mine this morning. I am not sufficiently acquainted with the localities picketed to answer the general's question definitely. Will ascertain, however, and report more definitely as soon as practicable.

Very respectfully, your obedient servant,

S. W. FERGUSON,
Brigadier-General.

———

HDQRS. ROSS' BRIGADE, JACKSON'S CAVALRY DIVISION,
Glenn's House, Ga., July 17, 1864—7.45 p. m.

Brigadier-General JACKSON,
        Commanding Division:

GENERAL: All is quiet along my position of this line, except occasional picket-firing across the river at and above Green's Ferry. I think the force in my front must be mounted infantry. Their guns are of the longest range, but their men show no knapsacks nor anything that indicates regular infantry.

I am, general, very respectfully, &c.,

L. S. ROSS,
Brigadier-General.

MONTGOMERY, *July 17, 1864.*

Col. J. B. SALE:

General Lee having driven the enemy back in Mississippi will meet me here on 19th. A raiding party, reported at 1,500, has moved down through Talladega, and is now threatening the West Point road. It will be impossible for General Lee to hold this road for General Johnston, and this will require a good garrison to make it safe.

BRAXTON BRAGG,
General.

MONTGOMERY, *July 17, 1864.*

General GIDEON J. PILLOW:

Pursue the raiders vigorously and rapidly in whatever direction they go. They are reported making for Opelika. You will be required hereafter near that point.

BRAXTON BRAGG,
General.

MONTGOMERY, *July 17, 1864.*

General GIDEON J. PILLOW:

Move your horses and train by direct road on south side of river. Indeed it would be as well for all your command to march by that route, as the city is now safe; move with all possible expedition.

BRAXTON BRAGG.

CIRCULAR.]   HEADQUARTERS HARDEE'S CORPS,
July 17, 1864—10.30.

By direction of General Johnston, the command will be held in readiness to move, if necessary, at a moment's notice.

By command of Lieutenant-General Hardee:

T. B. ROY,
Assistant Adjutant-General.

GENERAL ORDERS, }   HEADQUARTERS ARMY OF TENNESSEE,
    No. 4.   }   *July 17, 1864.*

In obedience to orders of the War Department, I turn over to General Hood the command of the Army and Department of Tennessee. I cannot leave this noble army without expressing my admiration of the high military qualities it has displayed. A long and arduous campaign has made conspicuous every soldierly virtue, endurance of toil, obedience to orders, brilliant courage. The enemy has never attacked but to be repulsed and severely punished. You, soldiers, have never argued but from your courage, and never counted your foes. No longer your leader, I will still watch your career, and will rejoice in your victories. To one and all I offer assurances of my friendship, and bid an affectionate farewell.

J. E. JOHNSTON,
General.

ATLANTA, *July 18, 1864.*

General S. COOPER:

GENERAL: I have the honor to acknowledge the receipt of my appointment as general of the Army of Tennessee. There is now heavy skirmishing and indications of a general advance. I deem it dangerous to change the commanders of this army at this particular time, and to be to the interest of the service that no change should be made until the fate of Atlanta is decided.

Respectfully,

J. B. HOOD,
General.

RICHMOND, *July 18, 1864.*

General HOOD:

Your telegram of this date received. A change of commanders, under existing circumstances, was regarded as so objectionable that I only accepted it as the alternative of continuing in a policy which had proved so disastrous. Reluctance to make the change induced me to send a telegram of inquiry to the commanding general on the 16th instant. His reply but confirmed previous apprehensions. There can be but one question which you and I can entertain—that is, what will best promote the public good; and to each of you I confidently look for the sacrifice of every personal consideration in conflict with that object. The order has been executed, and I cannot suspend it without making the case worse than it was before the order was issued.

JEFFERSON DAVIS.

(Same to Generals Hardee and Stewart.)

MONTGOMERY, *July 18, 1864.*

Col. JOHN B. SALE:

The enemy cut the West Point railroad last night above Loachapoka, and are supposed to have gone east. There is no cavalry here to pursue them. This is but a reconnaissance, to be followed up. General S. D. Lee is sending some few troops, and will meet me here to-morrow. The situation is most unsatisfactory, and the only remedy is action by the army at Atlanta.

B. BRAGG.

NEAR ATLANTA, *July 18, 1864.*

General S. COOPER,
       Richmond:

Your dispatch of yesterday received and obeyed. Command of the Army and Department of Tennessee has been transferred to General Hood. As to the alleged cause of my removal, I assert that Sherman's army is much stronger compared with that of Tennessee than Grant's compared with that of Northern Virginia. Yet the enemy has been compelled to advance much more slowly to the vicinity of Atlanta than to that of Richmond and Petersburg, and has penetrated much deeper into Virginia than into Georgia. Confident language by a military commander is not usually regarded as evidence of competency.

J. E. JOHNSTON.

ATLANTA, *July 18, 1864.*

General SAMUEL COOPER,
    Adjutant and Inspector General:

I have assumed command of the Army and Department of Tennessee.

J. B. HOOD.

(Same to President Davis.)

NEAR ATLANTA, *July 18, 1864.*
(Received 19th.)

Hon. SECRETARY OF WAR:

The enemy advanced to-day on all the roads leading from Isham's Ford and Roswell, and established his line on Peach Tree Creek, his right resting on the Chattahoochee in the vicinity of the railroad, his left at Buck Head; our army about four miles from Atlanta, the creek intervening between the armies.

J. B. HOOD,
    General.

JULY 18, 1864—1 a. m.

General J. E. JOHNSTON:

GENERAL: Much to my surprise I received the appointment you refer to. I accept your congratulations and without its concomitants it would have been more agreeable. I desire to have a conversation with you, and for that purpose will be over early in the morning.

Respectfully,

J. B. HOOD.

HEADQUARTERS ARMY OF TENNESSEE,
    In the Field, July 18, 1864.

SOLDIERS: In obedience to orders from the War Department I assume command of this army and department. I feel the weight of the responsibility so suddenly and unexpectedly devolved upon me by this position, and shall bend all my energies and employ all my skill to meet its requirements. I look with confidence to your patriotism to stand by me, and rely upon your prowess to wrest your country from the grasp of the invader, entitling yourselves to the proud distinction of being called the deliverers of an oppressed people.

Respectfully,

J. B. HOOD,
    General.

JULY 18, 1864—11.45 o'clock.

Major-General WHEELER,
    Commanding Cavalry Corps:

The commanding general informs you that the infantry at each bridge on Peach Tree Creek has been ordered to prepare it for burning, and he wishes you if forced back to require a body of cavalry to cross at each

bridge, and the last that crosses at each bridge have orders to burn the
bridge over which it crosses. Please communicate with the infantry
commander at each bridge and have no confusion in the arrangements.
    Respectfully,
                                    W. W. MACKALL,
                                            Chief of Staff.

————

                                    HEADQUARTERS,
                                July 18, 1864—9.30 p. m.
Major-General WHEELER:
    GENERAL: General Mackall requests you to communicate with the
infantry, and learn from them where their right rests to-night.
    Respectfully, &c.,
                                    T. B. MACKALL,
                                            Aide-de-Camp.

————

                            HEADQUARTERS HARDEE'S CORPS,
                                July 18, 1864—12.05.
General CLEBURNE:
    Put your division in motion at once on the road indicated to your
division inspector. Move to woods.
    By command of Lieutenant-General Hardee:
                                    T. B. ROY,
                                    Assistant Adjutant-General.

————

                            HEADQUARTERS HARDEE'S CORPS,
                                    July 18, 1864.
Major-General CLEBURNE,
        Commanding Division:
    GENERAL: General Hardee says commence fortifying as soon as you
get on your line in the morning.
    Very respectfully,
                                    T. B. ROY,
                                    Assistant Adjutant-General.

————

                            HEADQUARTERS STEVENS' BRIGADE,
                                In the Field, July 18, 1864.
General J. E. JOHNSTON, C. S. Army:
    GENERAL: Your order turning over the command of this army to
General Hood has been read to the troops of this brigade. The announcement that you are no longer to be our leader was received by
officers and men in silence and deep sorrow. I have the fullest assurance that I express the undivided sentiment of this brigade when I say
that the abiding and unlimited confidence which we have felt in the
wisdom of your judgment and leadership, has sustained us in the many
trying hours of our very arduous campaign. We have ever felt that
the best was being done that could be, and have looked confidently forward to the day of triumph, when with you as our leader we should
surely march to a glorious victory. This confidence and implicit trust

has been in no way impaired, and we are to-day ready, as we ever have been, to obey your orders, whether they be to retire before a largely outnumbering foe, or to spend our last drop of blood in the fiercest conflict. We feel that in parting with you as our commanding general our loss is irreparable, and that this army and our country loses one of its ablest, most zealous, and patriotic defenders. Our most sincere well wishes will accompany you in your future career, and you carry with you the love, respect, esteem, and confidence of the officers and men of this brigade. We would hail with joy your return to command us.

I have the honor to be, very respectfully, your obedient servant,

C. H. STEVENS,
Brigadier-General, Provisional Army, C. S.

ATLANTA, *July 18, 1864.*
(Received 19th.) ·

General S. COOPER:

Telegraph communication with Montgomery interrupted. A force of the enemy's cavalry, estimated at 3,000, reported moving on Opelika. The enemy in our front concentrating on the right.

MARCUS J. WRIGHT,
Brigadier-General.

SPECIAL ORDERS, }   ADJT. AND INSP. GENERAL'S OFFICE,
No. 168.   }   *Richmond, July 18, 1864.*

*   *   *   *   *   *   *

V. General Joseph E. Johnston, C. S. Army, is hereby relieved from the command of the Army and Department of Tennessee, and will turn over the same to General John B. Hood, Provisional Army, C. S.

*   *   *   *   *   *   *

By command of the Secretary of War:

SAML. W. MELTON,
Assistant Adjutant-General.

GENERAL ORDERS, }   HDQRS. ARMY OF THE MISSISSIPPI,
No. 4.   }   *In the Field, July 18, 1864.*

The troops of this command, excepting the brigades and batteries on picket, will without delay be placed in line of battle on the line adopted by the engineers, the left resting for the present near the church on the Atlanta and Marietta road. The engineer officers will indicate the line to division commanders, and also the positions selected for artillery. Loring's division will occupy the right, French's the left, Walthall's the center. The brigades on picket, if forced back by the enemy, will retire to unite with their respective divisions, communicating their movements to the brigades on their right and left, and halting to check the enemy whenever practicable. The formation will be two brigades front and one brigade in reserve in each division. It is not desired that the line be intrenched for the present.

By command of Lieutenant-General Stewart:

DOUGLAS WEST,
Acting Assistant Adjutant-General.

CIRCULAR.]   HEADQUARTERS HARDEE'S CORPS,
                                          July 18, 1864.

Division commanders will each throw out 100 men to Peach Tree Creek, and deploy them to picket the creek on his front. Bate will picket at the point opposite the brigade of his own outpost. Cleburne will connect with the right of Bate's pickets, and Walker with their left. Cheatham will connect with the left of Walker's pickets.

By command of Lieutenant-General Hardee:

                                          T. B. ROY,
                                Assistant Adjutant-General.

GENERAL ORDERS, }   HEADQUARTERS HOOD'S CORPS,
    No. 57.   }   *In the Field, July 18, 1864.*

Being the senior officer present with it, the undersigned hereby assumes command of Hood's corps.

                                          C. L. STEVENSON,
                                          Major-General.

                        HEADQUARTERS ARMY OF TENNESSEE,
                                          July 19, 1864.

Hon. JAMES A. SEDDON,
    Secretary of War, Richmond, Va.:

I thank you for your kind expressions in your dispatch of the 17th. If General S. D. Lee can co-operate with me by breaking the enemy's communication, I ask that it may be done with the least possible delay. I shall at all times be glad to receive any advice or suggestions from the authorities at Richmond.

                                          J. B. HOOD,
                                          General.

                                          ATLANTA, *July 19, 1864.*

JAMES A. SEDDON,
    Secretary of War:

I need a commander for my old corps. I have assigned Major-General Cheatham to it, although he did not desire it. I have no major-general in that corps whom I deem suitable for the position, and it was Hardee's opinion that Cheatham was the best man at my disposal, my corps commanders concurring also. It is my opinion that if the Department has no more fitting person in view and no strong objection thereto, that Major-General Mansfield Lovell might be assigned here for the purpose, to the great advantage of this army. If a lieutenant-general is to be appointed and sent to me, I know of no one that I would prefer to Maj. Gen. Wade Hampton or S. D. Lee.

                                          J. B. HOOD,
                                          General.

CONFIDENTIAL.]   HEADQUARTERS ARMY OF TENNESSEE,
                                          July 19, 1864—11 a. m.

General WHEELER:

GENERAL: General Hood directs me to inform you that unless circumstances now not seen should prevent, Generals Hardee and Stewart have been ordered to attack the enemy at 1 p. m. to-day. General Cheatham, on the right, is ordered to hold in check any force of the enemy that may advance in that direction, and you are desired to give all the aid in your power to General Cheatham to carry out this part.

Very respectfully, your obedient servant.

A. P. MASON,
Major and Assistant Adjutant-General.

HEADQUARTERS ARMY OF TENNESSEE,
Near Atlanta, July 19, 1864—2.15 p. m.

Major-General WHEELER,
Commanding Cavalry, &c.:

GENERAL: General Hood directs me to acknowledge the receipt of your note (hour not given) in which you express the opinion that the extreme left of the enemy's infantry is moving toward Decatur. It is important to get exact information of the state of affairs in that vicinity at night-fall. He therefore requests you to send your best scouts close in, so as to ascertain whether the left of the enemy's infantry crosses Peach Tree Creek, where it rests, and what is its strength, and notify him of the result.

Very respectfully, your obedient servant,

T. B. MACKALL,
Aide-de-Camp.

HEADQUARTERS ARMY OF TENNESSEE,
July 19, 1864—3.30 p. m.

Major-General WHEELER,
Commanding Cavalry:

GENERAL: Your dispatch about the force pressing Ferguson is received. General Hood directs that you will hold the enemy in check as much as possible, and strike him as you think best.

Yours, most respectfully,

A. P. MASON,
Major and Assistant Adjutant-General.

Please put the hour to your dispatches.

HEADQUARTERS,
July 19, 1864—7.15 p. m.

Major-General WHEELER:

GENERAL: Your dispatch of 5.45 is received. General Hood directs me to say that Cleburne's division is moving to your support. Communicate this to the men and urge them to hold on. General Hood desires to see you as soon as you can safely leave your command. We are now at General Stewart's, but will go presently to our own headquarters.

Yours,

A. P. MASON,
Major and Assistant Adjutant-General.

MONTGOMERY, *July 19, 1864.*
(Via Columbus.)

Col. J. B. SALE:

The enemy still hold West Point railroad. Forces are moving forward to dislodge them. General S. D. Lee informs me 5,000 Thirteenth Army Corps passed Vicksburg on 16th, supposed going to White River, but reported Memphis. Nineteenth Army Corps (Franklin's) left New Orleans the 4th for Fort Monroe, 13,000 strong. Ought not Taylor's forces to cross Mississippi ? I hear nothing from Johnston. Telegraph me to Columbus, Ga.

BRAXTON BRAGG.

———

CIRCULAR.]   HEADQUARTERS HARDEE'S CORPS,
July 19, 1864.

By direction of General Hood you will cause the banks of Peach Tree Creek to be thoroughly examined in front of your division; place a strong skirmish line there, and cause the best defenses that can be made to be placed there. The object is to enable a small force to resist the enemy's crossing for some time. General Hood considers this of great importance, and Lieutenant-General Hardee wishes you to give it your prompt attention.

Respectfully,

T. B. ROY,
Assistant Adjutant-General.

———

NEAR ATLANTA, *July 20, 1864.*

Hon. J. A. SEDDON, *Richmond, Va.:*

Late yesterday evening a force of the enemy, supposed to be a brigade, crossed Peach Tree Creek and attacked Reynolds' brigade, Walthall's division, Stewart's corps. That brigade charged them handsomely, drove them back, capturing about 150 prisoners and 2 stand of colors. The enemy still crossing Peach Tree Creek in our front.

J. B. HOOD,
General.

———

ATLANTA, *July 20, 1864—11 p. m.*
(Received 21st.)

Hon. J. A. SEDDON:

At 3 o'clock to-day a portion of Hardee's and Stewart's corps drove the enemy into his breast-works, but did not gain possession of them. Our loss slight. Brigadier-General Stevens severely wounded. On our extreme right the enemy attacked Wheeler's cavalry with infantry, and were handsomely repulsed.

J. B. HOOD,
General.

———

HEADQUARTERS,
July 20, 1864—10.20 a. m.

Major-General WHEELER, *Commanding Cavalry:*

GENERAL: General Hood directs me to say that you must retard the enemy as much as possible; that General Jackson has been ordered to send 1,000 cavalry to your assistance. Should you finally be forced back, form and strengthen yourself upon the right of our infantry, which is now being extended to the railroad.

Very respectfully,

A. P. MASON,
Major and Assistant Adjutant-General.

HEADQUARTERS ARMY OF TENNESSEE,
July 20, 1864—11 a. m.

Major-General WHEELER,
Commanding Cavalry Corps:

GENERAL: General Hood desires you to form a portion of your cavalry on the right of the infantry, holding the remainder in readiness to strike the enemy in flank in case they should attack General Cheatham. He sent you a note to this effect, and sends this to say that he does not wish your entire command formed on the right. He also desires you to keep them from General Cheatham's front as long as possible, and use every precaution to keep them from our flank. He wishes me to say also that your own judgment will prompt you when it may be best and at what point to strike the enemy in case they should attack General Cheatham.

Very respectfully, general, your obedient servant,

E. B. WADE,
Aide-de-Camp.

JULY 20, 1864—1.10 [p. m.]

General WHEELER:

Are you driven back or have you only fallen back to find a good position? What is your estimate of the enemy? Hold at all hazards. General Smith, with all the reserve artillery, occupies the works behind you.

Respectfully,

W. W. MACKALL,
Brigadier-General.

GEORGIA RAILROAD FORTIFICATIONS,
Atlanta, July 20, 1864—4.35 p. m.

Major-General WHEELER,
Commanding Cavalry:

GENERAL: I have 700 men here in the trenches upon the right and left of the railroad, supporting the reserve artillery. There is nothing to my right. Where is your right and left, and how far are the enemy from this position. Please notify me of anything of moment in regard to your position, that of the enemy, &c., and oblige,

Very truly, yours,

G. W. SMITH,
Major-General.

JULY 20, 1864—6.30 p. m.

General WHEELER:

General Cheatham has been ordered to send you a brigade. Hold on as long as you can, but if forced back you must go into the fortifications with General Smith, who is now behind you, and hold them, says General Hood.

Respectfully,

W. W. MACKALL,
Brigadier-General.

IN THE FIELD, [*July 20,*] *1864.*

Major-General FRENCH, *Commanding Division:*

If your left is not threatened, General Stewart wishes you to move forward and attack the enemy, looking well to your left.

Respectfully,

THOMAS M. JACK,
Assistant Adjutant-General.

IN THE FIELD, *July 20, 1864—7 p. m.*

Major-General FRENCH:

GENERAL: Lieutenant-General Stewart directs, that after securing any wounded you may have on the field and burying your dead, that you withdraw your troops back to the trenches, taking position on the left and connect with Walthall, leaving pickets on the skirmish line. General Ector has instructions in regard to locating the pickets, and has had an understanding with General Walthall.

Respectfully,

D. WEST,
Acting Assistant Adjutant-General.

JULY 20, 1864.

General WHEELER:

General Brown has been ordered to extend to the railroad. You will please keep in communication with him and support him. I am now on the left of my line, which is a long one. If you should find the enemy moving to my left you will please inform me. My skirmishers on my left are now heavily engaged.

B. F. CHEATHAM,
Major-General.

JULY 20, 1864—5.30 p. m.

Major-General WHEELER, *Commanding Cavalry:*

GENERAL: I have 1,000 yards in my center, with the troops deployed in single line, and have been compelled to take a brigade from my left, which is now not protected. I need 2,000 men to fill my line. General G. W. Smith is near you; call on him.

B. F. CHEATHAM,
Major-General.

Hold until night if possible and keep me posted.

B. F. CHEATHAM,
Major-General.

JULY 20, 1864——6.45 [p. m.]

General WHEELER:

The enemy are pressing my center, which is only a single line for one mile. I am afraid it will not sustain itself. I have weakened my entire line to fill up the gap of one mile. I have sent word to General Brown to assist you if he can; you will communicate with him.

B. F. CHEATHAM,
Major-General.

BATE'S DIVISION, *July 20, 1864——6 o'clock.*

[General HARDEE:]

GENERAL: On reaching General Bate, I found that he had swung his division around, and was moving in a direction to strike the enemy's flank. Under the circumstances I thought his movement the best, and did not change it. He is now moving slowly onward, but it is necessarily slow, as the undergrowth is in places dense. I fear he will not be able to strike the enemy's flank much before dark. I sent Captain —— with an order to Walker to swing around, and thought it best to come to Bate.

W. D. PICKETT.

HDQRS. ROSS' BRIGADE, JACKSON'S CAVALRY DIVISION,
Glenn's House, Ga., July 20, 1864——9.30 a. m.

Brig. Gen. W. H. JACKSON, *Commanding Cavalry Division:*

GENERAL: The enemy's cavalry in some force have appeared in the vicinity of Howell's Ferry, and also in front of Green's. There are about two regiments, scouts report, now near Howell's Ferry. The force in front of Green's and between the two ferries is not yet known. I think there is one brigade in all.

Very respectfully, your obedient servant,

L. S. ROSS,
Brigadier-General.

MONTGOMERY, *July 20, 1864.*
(Via Columbus 21st.)

Col. J. B. SALE:

Such forces as could hastily be collected here, mostly infantry, are moving on the line of railroad and driving the enemy. The road is badly damaged, like the Danville, and will require much time for repairs, even if not disturbed. Another large raiding party is reported moving down from Talladega, and they will be constant. The road will be reconstructed and guarded as far as possible, but it cannot be relied on with the enemy in his present position. General S. D. Lee will be here to-day. He reports the enemy's whole force in Arkansas coming down the Arkansas and White Rivers in a fleet convoyed heavily by gun-boats. Destination not yet fully developed, but no doubt to operate in Mississippi or to re-enforce Sherman. Prompt, decided, and expeditious measures should be taken to bring our forces over to meet the emergency. Reply at Columbus.

BRAXTON BRAGG.

SPECIAL ORDERS, }   ADJT. AND INSP. GENERAL'S OFFICE,
    No. 170.   }   *Richmond, July 20, 1864.*
    *   *   *   *   *   *   *

LIII. Maj. Gen. M. L. Smith is assigned as chief engineer to the Army of Tennessee. He will immediately repair to Atlanta, Ga., and report to General J. B. Hood.
    *   *   *   *   *   *

By command of the Secretary of War:

> SAML. W. MELTON,
> *Assistant Adjutant-General.*

NEAR ATLANTA, *July 21, 1864.*

Hon. J. A. SEDDON, *Richmond, Va.:*

This morning the enemy attacked Cleburne's division, of Hardee's corps, and a portion of General Wheeler's cavalry, upon our extreme right, but were handsomely repulsed. Colonel Adams, Thirty-third Alabama, was killed.

> J. B. HOOD.

ATLANTA, *July 21, 1864.*

General CLANTON,
    West Point:

Bragg heard from; said to be 4,000 on new raid; be as active as heretofore to destroy it. Armstrong is in your vicinity; correspond with him. Boats on the river should be destroyed.

> W. W. MACKALL,
> *Chief of Staff.*

HEADQUARTERS,
July 21, 1864—9 a. m.

[General CLEBURNE:]

GENERAL: General Hood directs me to inform you that Cheatham's division, commanded by Maney, is ordered to report to you.

Yours, respectfully,

> A. P. MASON,
> *Major and Assistant Adjutant-General.*

HEADQUARTERS GEORGIA MILITIA,
July 21, 1864—10.55 a. m.

General WHEELER,
    Commanding Cavalry:

A battery of artillery from Colonel Hallonquist's reserves has just come up, and is being placed in position. Immediately on receipt of your request for re-enforcements I sent a staff officer to you with request that you would send one of your staff to conduct them. The troops are ready and waiting; say 300 men.

Yours, truly,

> G. W. SMITH,
> *Major-General.*

HEADQUARTERS ARMY OF TENNESSEE,
July 21, 1864.

Major-General CLEBURNE,
     Commanding Division:

GENERAL: The general commanding desires to call your attention to the importance of sending a regiment from each division, in case the enemy should attack yourself and General Maney, to the support of the cavalry in the gap between yourself and General Maney.

Very respectfully, general, your obedient servant,

E. B. WADE,
Aide-de-Camp.

ARMY HEADQUARTERS,
July 21, 1864—2.30 p. m.

Major-General WHEELER,
     Commanding Cavalry:

GENERAL: The general commanding directs me to say that he will to-night fill the vacancy between Generals Cleburne and Maney with infantry; also, to request that you come to his quarters as soon as you can leave your line this evening.

I am, general, very respectfully, your obedient servant,

JOHN S. SMITH,
Aide-de-Camp.

HEADQUARTERS ARMY OF TENNESSEE,
July 21, 1864.

Major-General WHEELER,
     Commanding Cavalry:

GENERAL: The general commanding directs me to send the inclosure for your information, and to say he wishes you to hold the gap between Generals Cleburne and Maney.*

I am, general, very respectfully, your obedient servant,

JOHN S. SMITH,
Aide-de-Camp.

HEADQUARTERS HARDEE'S CORPS,
July 21, 1864—7.30 p. m.

Major-General CLEBURNE:

GENERAL: At dark you will withdraw your division within the city defenses. You will not take position on the line, but will bivouac your troops, with your left to the right (looking from Atlanta) of the rail road. Your skirmishers will be left out, and will accompany your present line of defenses. It is proper to inform you that Cheatham's corps will also withdraw into the city defenses. The general enjoins watchfulness upon your skirmishers.

By command of Lieutenant-General Hardee:

T. B. ROY,
Assistant Adjutant-General.

---

* Inclosure not found.

HEADQUARTERS HARDEE'S CORPS,
July 21, 1864—11 p. m.

General CLEBURNE:

By direction of Lieutenant-General Hardee, your division will move at 1 o'clock to-night on the road which will be indicated by the guide. Your skirmishers will be left on the line you occupied to-day.

Respectfully,

T. B. ROY,
Assistant Adjutant-General.

Your division follows Walker's.

Respectfully,

T. B. ROY,
Assistant Adjutant-General.

Your skirmishers [will] remain out until driven in.

By order of Lieutenant-General Hardee:

T. B. ROY.

———

HEADQUARTERS, *July 21, 1864.*

Brigadier-General WRIGHT, *Commanding, Atlanta, Ga.:*

GENERAL: I am directed to inform you that you must be prepared to-night for an evacuation of Atlanta, should it become necessary. You will, therefore, without saying anything about it, be prepared to move when Lieutenant-General Stewart's troops move into town, should the evacuation take place.

Most respectfully, your obedient servant,

A. P. MASON,
Major and Assistant Adjutant-General.

———

NEAR ATLANTA, *July 22, 1864—10.30 p. m.*

Hon. J. A. SEDDON, *Richmond:*

The army shifted its position last night, fronting Peach Tree Creek, and formed line of battle around the city with Stewart's and Cheatham's corps. General Hardee, with his corps, made a night march and attacked the enemy's extreme left at 1 o'clock to-day; drove him from his works, capturing 16 pieces of artillery and 5 stand of colors. Major-General Cheatham attacked the enemy at 4 p. m. with a portion of his command; drove the enemy, capturing 6 pieces of artillery. During the engagements we captured about 2,000 prisoners, but loss not fully ascertained. Major-General Walker killed; Brigadier-Generals Smith, Gist, and Mercer wounded. Our troops fought with great gallantry.

J. B. HOOD,
General.

———

HEADQUARTERS CAVALRY CORPS, *July 22, 1864.*

Lieutenant-General HARDEE:

Several more of my scouts have come in, all corroborating the report I sent you this morning that General Garrard had moved toward Covington with his division. Shall I pursue and break up Garrard, or shall I detach a force to follow him?

Very respectfully, your obedient servant,

J. WHEELER,
Major-General.

JULY 22, 1864.

Major-General WHEELER,
    Commanding Cavalry:

GENERAL: I cannot spare you or any force to pursue Garrard now. We must attack, as we arranged, with all our force. I think our attack will bring Garrard back. You had best report the facts to General Hood.

Respectfully,

W. J. HARDEE,
    Lieutenant-General.

HDQRS. ROSS' BRIGADE, JACKSON'S CAVALRY DIVISION,
    Church on Turner's Ferry Road, July 22, 1864—1 p. m.

Brigadier-General JACKSON,
    Commanding Division:

GENERAL: The enemy has been checked. Prisoner informs me that it is McCook's cavalry division, of Stoneman's corps. Some infantry in rear of cavalry, but doubtless turned toward Atlanta. They have a high bridge across the river above the railroad crossing. I have just sent my artillery to Lick Skillet, and will keep two regiments here to hold the place until night, if possible.

I am, general, very respectfully, &c.,

L. S. ROSS,
    Brigadier-General.

HDQRS. ROSS' BRIGADE, JACKSON'S CAVALRY DIVISION,
    Church on Turner's Ferry Road, July 22, 1864—5 p. m.

Brigadier-General JACKSON,
    Commanding, &c.:

GENERAL: Your note to move back to Lick Skillet road just received. The enemy are driving my skirmishers steadily back to this point. One regiment (Ninth Texas) is skirmishing with them. Their line is a long one, and moves forward without firing a shot, paying no attention to Colonel Jones. I have two pieces in position, and will feel of them a little, and try and determine whether the force is infantry or dismounted cavalry.

I am, general, very respectfully, &c.,

L. S. ROSS,
    Brigadier-General.

HDQRS. ROSS' BRIGADE, JACKSON'S CAVALRY DIVISION,
    July 22, 1864—9.11 p. m.

Brigadier-General JACKSON,
    Commanding Division:

GENERAL: My picket, one regiment strong, holds the church on Turner's Ferry road. Yankee cavalry encamped on creek one mile from church on the road leading to railroad bridge. I think I damaged them some this evening. I have one intelligent prisoner (a Dutchman), who says Stoneman's corps is on this side of the river, and will confront your cavalry in the morning. McCook's division came down this evening, as his advance, to clear out the road to this point, and did not anticipate serious opposition.   Scouts inform me a column (could not tell whether cavalry or infantry, but think the latter), with artillery, marched from the railroad crossing in the direction of Atlanta.   The prisoner says infantry was to cross after McCook's division, and Stoneman to follow with all his cavalry.   I did not give up Turner's Ferry road, because I thought General Humes' line [was] on that road, and I would thus have left [it] exposed.   As it seems he does not hold it, I can see nothing to be accomplished by keeping it longer, and with your consent will withdraw the regiment to-night or early to-morrow morning.   From the position assigned me here, I am too far to support the regiment.   The enemy have a fine bridge at the first white house above the railroad crossing, and about two miles from the latter place.   It is fifteen feet above water.   Please send me all the reliable news from our lines by my couriers as they pass.

I am, general, very respectfully, &c.,

L. S. ROSS,
Brigadier-General.

MONTGOMERY, *July 22, 1864.*

General J. B. HOOD:

The order for General E. K. Smith not received by me.   If you know what it is let me know, so it can be transmitted without delay.   Several dispatches here for General Bragg alluding to order, but order itself not received.   General Bragg left here yesterday for Columbus.

S. D. LEE,
Lieutenant-General.

WEST POINT, *July 22, 1864.*

General HOOD:

Have you information from General Bragg of a second raid passing through Talladega to Opelika?

JAS. H. CLANTON,
Brigadier-General.

CIRCULAR.]   HEADQUARTERS,
July 22, 1864—6.20 a. m.

Lieutenant-General Stewart directs that you have everything ready for action, everything hitched up and ready to move should the contingency arise.   Should a flag of truce be sent to your lines let it be fully understood that no intercourse must be permitted, and no want of preparedness for continued action on the part of the command.   Continue work actively on your trenches.   The flag will be sent to General Hood's headquarters, and the bearer sent back with notice that an answer will be returned.

By command of Lieutenant-General Stewart:

DOUGLAS WEST,
Acting Assistant Adjutant-General.

ATLANTA, *July 23, 1864.*

Hon. J. A. SEDDON,
    Richmond:

In the engagement of yesterday we captured 18 stand of colors instead of 5, and 13 guns instead of 22, as previously reported. Brigadier-General Mercer not wounded. All quiet to-day except skirmishing, and the enemy occasionally throwing shell into the city. The army is in good spirits.

                                        J. B. HOOD,
                                            General.

PETERSBURG, *July 23, 1864.*

His Excellency JEFFERSON DAVIS:

Mr. PRESIDENT: I have had the honor to receive your letter of yesterday relative to our supply of corn. If the news of the glorious victory at Atlanta, reported this morning, prove true it will again open to us Alabama and East Mississippi, and remove a part of the great weight pressing upon us. But as far as I am informed there is still a large supply of corn in East Georgia, and with what could be collected in South and North Carolina there would be enough to support us till the new crop is available. That which is now in Richmond should be reserved if possible, and every effort made to increase the supply. The destruction of the railroad bridges beyond Greensborough is a serious evil. I understand it was done by incendiaries, which makes it more lamentable. Those bridges will therefore have to be guarded by the reserves, like those exposed to the enemy. The trains arrived last night from Weldon, but brought only sufficient corn for the cavalry. That was some relief, but obliges us still to diminish our reserve.

With great respect, your obedient servant,

                                        R. E. LEE,
                                            General.

HEADQUARTERS,
    July 23, 1864.

His Excellency Governor BROWN:

The State troops under Major-General Smith fought with great gallantry in the action of yesterday.

                                        J. B. HOOD,
                                            General.

HEADQUARTERS,
    Macon, July 23, 1864.

General J. B. HOOD, *Atlanta:*

I am proud to hear of the gallant conduct of the State troops. Thousands of others have now assembled in response to my call, and will be armed and sent forward as rapidly as possible, who upon the soil of their beloved State will strike with equal valor for the defense of their wives and their children, their homes and their altars. I assure you of the most energetic co-operation with all the aid in my power. May God grant you success and aid to drive the invaders from the soil of the Confederacy.

                                        JOSEPH E. BROWN.

RICHMOND, *July 23, 1864.*

General J. B. HOOD:

Maj. Gen. M. L. Smith has been sent to report to you as chief engineer of your army. He has been serving in that capacity with General R. E. Lee throughout the present campaign in Virginia, and has won the highest reputation, and has the entire confidence both of the general and the army. You will find him an able counsellor and gallant soldier, and he is commended to your special regard.

JEFFERSON DAVIS.

COLUMBUS, *July 23, 1864.*

General S. COOPER,
    Adjutant and Inspector General:

Major-General Hindman is absent from his command sick, and will most probably never rejoin. I suggest that Maj. Gen. Patton Anderson, its old commander, be sent back. Should Hindman return Anderson will still be needed. His present command is unimportant and may well be held by a brigadier from General Sam. Jones' department. This arrangement will give great satisfaction to General Hood and the troops.

BRAXTON BRAGG.

COLUMBUS, *July 23, 1864.*

General S. COOPER:

After learning the result of yesterday's operations at Atlanta, I have ordered Maj. Gen. Patton Anderson to report to General Hood. It is important he should go immediately.

BRAXTON BRAGG.

COLUMBUS, *July 23, 1864.*

Col. JOHN B. SALE:

In view of present condition I suggest the immediate completion of the railroad from this point direct to Montgomery, via Union Springs. About forty miles remain to be completed. Nearly all of this is graded ready for track. Iron can be had from unimportant roads in Florida, Alabama, and Georgia, and the work completed in three or four months. Its great advantage would be in affording means of running rolling-stock east and west of Montgomery by giving us a uniform gauge all the way from Richmond. I leave this evening for Atlanta, having sent forward a large brigade of good troops from this place.

BRAXTON BRAGG.

[First indorsement.]

To Secretary of War, for his information.

[Second indorsement.]

To Engineer Bureau, for consideration and report.

J. A. S.

[Third indorsement.]

ENGINEER BUREAU,
July 26, 1864.

Respectfully returned to the honorable Secretary of War.

The greatest difficulty in making this connection will be the want of iron. I have just ordered Lieutenant-Colonel Meriwether to proceed to Montgomery, Ala., to assist in repairing the Montgomery and West Point Road, and to report upon practicability of making the connection between Columbus and Montgomery, via Union Springs. I have also ordered Capt. L. P. Grant from Atlanta to Montgomery, to assist in pressing forward the work on the West Point road.

J. F. GILMER,
Major-General and Chief of Engineer Bureau.

JULY 23, 1864—4.10.

Major-General WHEELER,
Commanding Cavalry Corps:

GENERAL: Where are the two brigades which you say are on my right flank? The two regiments you sent me were taken away by General Iverson. I must have two regiments of cavalry at once for my left flank.

Respectfully,

W. J. HARDEE,
Lieutenant-General.

HEADQUARTERS HARDEE'S CORPS,
July 23, 1864.

Major-General WHEELER,
Commanding Cavalry Corps:

GENERAL: Lieutenant-General Hardee directs me to say that the three regiments under Colonel Hagan will be sufficient to protect his flank.

Very respectfully, your obedient servant,

SAML. L. BLACK,
Assistant Inspector-General.

JULY 23, 1864.

General WHEELER:

General Hood wishes you to take what you think a sufficient force and pursue the raiding party you report as moving on the Covington road. You must leave a small force to observe General Hardee's right, and if necessary recall the brigade you were ordered to send to East Point.

Respectfully,

W. W. MACKALL,
Chief of Staff.

ATLANTA, *July 23, 1864—10 a. m.*

Col. G. W. RAINS,
        Commanding Post, Augusta:

Night before last a body of enemy's cavalry, estimated at about three brigades, was reported moving toward Covington and Augusta. Our cavalry is pursuing, but the information is sent you that you take measures for defense.

                                J. B. HOOD,
                                        General.

SPECIAL ORDERS, }   ADJT. AND INSP. GENERAL'S OFFICE,
      No. 173.   }   *Richmond, July 23, 1864.*

*   *   *   *   *   *   *

XXXII. The superintendent of the army intelligence office is authorized to send an agent to the Army of Tennessee to prepare a list of casualties occurring in said army. The agent will be governed by instructions received from the superintendent of the army intelligence office.

*   *   *   *   *   *   *

By command of the Secretary of War:
                                SAML. W. MELTON,
                                Assistant Adjutant-General.

ATLANTA, *July 24, 1864.*

Hon. J. A. SEDDON,
        Richmond, Va.:

All has been quiet to-day except a little picket-firing and occasional shells thrown into the city.

                                J. B. HOOD,
                                        General.

ATLANTA, *July 24, 1864.*

Governor BROWN,
        Macon, Ga.:

Your dispatch of yesterday received. I need all the aid Georgia can furnish. Please send me men with muskets as fast as possible.

                                J. B. HOOD,
                                        General.

ATLANTA, *July 24, 1864.*

Maj. Gen. SAMUEL JONES,
        Charleston:

Your dispatch in reference to Maj. Gen. Patton Anderson is received, but cavalry is in pursuit of the forces reported moving on Augusta via Covington. I have communicated the information to Colonel Rains.

                                J. B. HOOD,
                                        General.

ATLANTA, *July 24, 1864.*

Col. JOHN B. SALE:

Considerations of expediency and efficiency induced General Hood to advise the distributing of the three brigades in Walker's division to the other divisions in the same corps. The corps commander also urged it, and I have authorized it. Brigadier-General Mercer, whose age and physical inability unfit him for active service, I propose to order to Savannah.

BRAXTON BRAGG.

HDQRS. ROSS' BRIGADE, JACKSON'S CAVALRY DIVISION,
McGhee's, Ga., July 24, 1864—8 a. m.

Brigadier-General JACKSON,
Commanding Division:

GENERAL: A large train of wagons can be seen from the hills near Baker's Ferry on opposite side the river, between that point and Green's, and a woman has just come to my headquarters from that side the river. Says she left the Baker's Ferry road, about half a mile from ferry, yesterday evening, walking several miles down the river, where she crossed. She saw Colonel Adams' brigade cavalry and some infantry, but could not tell the number. The infantry had stopped and stacked arms on the Baker's Ferry road. She saw two of my men taken before Colonel Adams, and saw the boats in which the party crossed the river yesterday below Baker's (two only of Captain Norsworthy's men were captured), and says the boats looked like cloth. They placed the boats in wagons on their return, and she saw many others in wagons along with this force. My scouts confirm the statements in reference to the brigade of cavalry, wagon train, &c., but have not discovered infantry. There can be no doubt, I think, of this being a pontoon train, and the enemy in all probability intend crossing with a formidable force to strike the road below Atlanta. I have strengthened my pickets on that line. I belive the statement of the woman about the infantry. The cavalry that crossed the river the other evening are in the vicinity of the church at Turner's Ferry. Bands playing, &c. All quiet at present.

I am, general, very respectfully, &c.,

L. S. ROSS,
Brigadier-General.

SPECIAL FIELD ORDERS, }   HDQRS. ARMY OF TENNESSEE,
No. 56.   }   *In the Field, July 24, 1864.*

*   *   *   *   *   *   *

V. Brigadier-General Mackall, Provisional Army, is relieved from duty as chief of staff at his own request.

VI. Brig. Gen. F. A. Shoup, Provisional Army, is assigned to duty as chief of staff, and will be obeyed and respected accordingly.

*   *   *   *   *   *   *

By command of General Hood:

KINLOCH FALCONER,
Assistant Adjutant-General.

GENERAL FIELD ORDERS, ┊   HDQRS. ARMY OF TENNESSEE,
          No. 5.   ┊   *July 24, 1864.*

I. Detailed men employed as clerks in the staff departments of the army able to perform a soldier's duty in the field, and all other employés in those departments whose services can possibly be dispensed with, will be promptly returned to their commands, and remain with them till further orders. The interests of the public service require this in the present emergency, and officers are expected to perform their clerical duties in person.

II. Commanding officers and chiefs of departments are required to see that this order is faithfully executed, and corps commanders will report the number of men in their respective corps returned to ranks under its provisions.

By order of General Hood:

A. P. MASON,
Major and Assistant Adjutant-General.

ATLANTA, *July 25, 1864.*

Hon. J. A. SEDDON,
          Secretary of War:

I respectfully urge the completion of the railroad from Columbus, Ga., to Montgomery, Ala., via Union Springs.

J. B. HOOD,
General.

[Indorsement.]

ENGINEER BUREAU,
July 26, 1864.

Lieutenant-Colonel Meriwether, engineer, has been ordered to report on this connection at once. The want of iron will be the difficulty.

J. F. GILMER,
Major-General and Chief of Bureau.

ATLANTA, GA., *July 25, 1864.*

His Excellency JEFFERSON DAVIS,
          Richmond, Va.:

The moral effect of our brilliant affair of the 22d has been admirable on our troops, and I am happy to say our loss was small in comparison to the enemy's. He was badly defeated and completely failed in one of his bold flank movements, heretofore so successful. Lieutenant-General Lee will probably arrive to-morrow, when I may return to Montgomery to see General Maury and hear from General Smith.

BRAXTON BRAGG.

HEADQUARTERS GEORGIA MILITIA,
July 25, 1864.

Brig. Gen. M. J. WRIGHT,
          Commanding, Atlanta:

GENERAL: Please inform me how many men there are for duty in Stiles' battalion of artillery, and how many there are in the Fulton County militia present for duty, armed. I would be glad, too, if you will inform me how many other men you have for duty. Colonel Anderson, of my staff, will hand you this, and I have requested him to communicate freely with you in regard to affairs in Atlanta.

Yours, very truly,

G. W. SMITH,
Major-General.

GENERAL FIELD ORDERS, }   HDQRS. ARMY OF TENNESSEE,
No. 7.   }   *In the Field, July 25, 1864.*

SOLDIERS: Experience has proved to you that safety in time of battle consists in getting into close quarters with your enemy. Guns and colors are the only unerring indications of victory. The valor of troops is easily estimated, too, by the number of these secured. If your enemy be allowed to continue the operation of flanking you out of position, our cause is in great peril. Your recent brilliant success proves the ability to prevent it. You have but to will it, and God will grant us the victory your commander and your country expect.

J. B. HOOD,
General.

GENERAL FIELD ORDERS, }   HDQRS. ARMY OF TENNESSEE,
No. 8.   }   *In the Field, July 25, 1864.*

I. No communications by flag of truce will be received by any officer of this army, unless it is clear that the communication is from the general officer commanding the U. S. forces and addressed to the officer commanding the Confederate forces. All other flags of truce will be promptly returned with their communications.

II. The attention of the army is earnestly called to General Field Orders, No. 3, from these headquarters, forbidding intercourse between the pickets of the enemy and our own.

By command of General Hood:

A. P. MASON,
Colonel and Assistant Adjutant-General.

GENERAL FIELD ORDERS, }   HDQRS. ARMY OF TENNESSEE,
No. 9.   }   *In the Field, July 25, 1864.*

A provost guard will at once be established in each division of the army, to consist of sixty men, and to be placed under the command of an energetic and competent officer. The duties of the guard will be to prevent straggling and to receive prisoners.

By command of General Hood:

KINLOCH FALCONER,
Assistant Adjutant-General.

SPECIAL ORDERS, }   HDQRS. ROSS' BRIG., JACKSON'S CAV. DIV.,
No. 15.   }   *McGhee's Farm, Ga., July 25, 1864.*

I. Officers on duty in front should not content themselves with merely observing if the enemy advance, but keep themselves informed of his movements, and report promptly whatever changes in his position or line occur during their tour of service. To this end, a few scouts should be kept constantly in front of the advanced vedettes and sufficiently near the enemy to observe his movements. The first duty of a picket commander, after his vedettes have been established, is to inform himself of the exact position of the enemy's vedettes and pickets, and to observe frequently during the day if they have been moved. Especially is it important to know early in the morning what changes may have taken place during the preceding night. It is therefore made the duty of each picket commander to forward very early each morning a report in writing of the exact position of the enemy, and what if any changes may have occurred since the evening before, and to report in person as soon as relieved at the expiration of his tour of service.

II. The officers and men are enjoined to arrest all persons attempting to pass through or about our lines, unless shielded by the proper written authority. It has been but a day or two since some members of the Legion, by their vigilance and prompt discharge of duty, did a most valuable service to our army and country by arresting one, who proved to be a Federal officer, escaped from prison and attempting to make his way to Yankee lines, with information which would have been of great importance to the enemy and might have injured us irreparably. We cannot be too vigilant. Uniforms and badges of rank are not sufficent passports, but all officers, as well as men, will be required to show their papers, and whenever the least doubt exists as to their authority to pass they will be arrested and sent to these headquarters.

By order of Brigadier-General Ross:

> D. R. GURLEY,
> *Assistant Adjutant-General.*

ATLANTA, *July 26, 1864.*

Hon. J. A. SEDDON, *Richmond:*

No material change in affairs to-day. Lieut. Gen. S. D. Lee has reported and been assigned as ordered.

> J. B. HOOD.

ATLANTA, *July 26, 1864.*

General COOPER:

I have assigned Brigadier-General Shoup to duty as chief of staff and Col. R. F. Beckham as chief of artillery. I desire your approval and that Colonel Beckham be appointed brigadier-general.

> J. B. HOOD.

HEADQUARTERS ARMY OF TENNESSEE,
July 26, 1864—12 p. m.

Major-General WHEELER,
    Commanding Cavalry:

GENERAL: General Hood desires you to relieve General Hardee with your command, taking his position. You will move without delay, putting yourself in communication with him at once. You will leave a sufficient force on your right to give you certain information of the movements of the enemy, in case he should make any in that quarter, and to conceal, if possible, your withdrawal. General Hardee waits your movements.

Very respectfully,

> F. A. SHOUP,
> *Chief of Staff.*

CONFIDENTIAL.]   HEADQUARTERS, &C.,
                                                  July 26, 1864—10 a. m.
Major-General WHEELER,
          Commanding, &c.:

General Hood directs that you put Kelly's division in motion toward
Campbellton alone, and that you and General Kelly report in person at
these headquarters without delay.

          Very respectfully,

                                                  F. A. SHOUP,
                                                      Chief of Staff.

———

                                          ATLANTA, *July 26, 1864.*
Col. JOHN B. SALE:

Leave to-morrow to confer with Major-General Maury, in Montgomery,
and urge matters beyond.   Lieutenant-General Lee arrived and goes on
duty to-day.   He is most favorably received.   Tone of army fine, and
strength increasing daily.   The death of Brigadier-General Stevens, the
wounding of Gist, and inability and sickness of Mercer and Stovall leave
four brigadiers vacant, and the material to select from inferior.   Accordingly, ordered Henry R. Jackson from Savannah.   All is quiet to-
day.

                                          BRAXTON BRAGG,
                                                      General.

———

HDQRS. ROSS' BRIGADE, JACKSON'S CAVALRY DIVISION,
                                          July 26, 1864—10.45 a. m.
Brigadier-General JACKSON,
          Commanding Division:

GENERAL: The enemy have advanced to the church at Turner's Ferry
and drove my pickets back to within half a mile of Lick Skillet.   They
seem desirous of extending their line down the river.   They are as far
down as the Green's Ferry road.   Their pickets hold Green's Ferry road
at Glenn's house.   Some cavalry still in sight on the opposite side of
the river.

I am, general, very respectfully, &c.,

                                                  L. S. ROSS,
                                                      Brigadier-General.

———

HDQRS. ROSS' BRIGADE, JACKSON'S CAVALRY DIVISION,
                              Lick Skillet, Ga., July 26, 1864—8 p. m.
Brigadier-General JACKSON,
          Commanding Division:

GENERAL: Captain Wright and Lieutenant McClatchey, who charged
on one of the roads this evening with their companies, inform me that
they ran over and captured within 200 yards of the enemy's works more
of the enemy trying to escape on foot than they could take care of.
Captain Wright turned them back to the rear as rapidly as possible,
but they showed much reluctance to going, and just then the enemy
opened with canister from their works, regardless of their own men
in Captain W[right]'s possession, and all the prisoners fell on the ground
and refused to run, whereupon Captain Wright and his men commenced
killing them.   They fired all their loads from pistols and guns into them

and then retired for shelter from the artillery. Captain W[right] killed 2 and Lieutenant McClatchey fired six rounds at them. A column of cavalry passed up the river on the opposite side this evening just before dark, going in direction of Turner's Ferry. My scouts think it a brigade. The enemy did not advance from their works. My pickets are where they stood this morning.

I am, general, very respectfully, &c.,

L. S. ROSS,
Brigadier-General.

GENERAL FIELD ORDERS, }   HDQRS. ARMY OF TENNESSEE,
No. 10.   }   *In the Field, July 26, 1864.*

I. The attention of commanding officers is especially called to the importance of securing the arms and accouterments of our wounded, and those captured in all engagements with the enemy.

II. Corps ordnance officers will appoint a place in rear of the line, where the arms and accouterments gathered on the field shall be sent. The brigade wagons for carrying arms shall be placed in charge of a sergeant, who shall use them for hauling them to the place appointed. All empty ordnance wagons will also be used for this purpose. Should these prove insufficient, the corps ordnance officer will procure wagons from whatever source he can.

III. Artillery ordnance officers are directed to give their special attention to the removal of artillery.

By command of General Hood:

KINLOCH FALCONER,
Assistant Adjutant-General.

SPECIAL FIELD ORDERS, }   HDQRS. ARMY OF TENNESSEE,
No. 58.   }   *In the Field, July 26, 1864.*

*   *   *   *   *   *   *

III. The divisions of Major-Generals Loring, French, and Walthall, and Preston's, Myrick's, and Storrs' artillery battalions, commanded by Lieut. Gen. A. P. Stewart, will in future be known as " Stewart's corps."

IV. The cavalry division commanded by Brig. Gen. W. H. Jackson will in future report direct to army headquarters.

*   *   *   *   *   *   *

VI. Lieut. Gen. S. D. Lee, Provisional Army, is assigned to the command of the corps heretofore known as " Hood's."

*   *   *   *   *   *   *

By command of General Hood:

KINLOCH FALCONER,
Assistant Adjutant-General.

ATLANTA, GA., *July 27, 1864.*

Hon. J. A. SEDDON,
Richmond, Va.:

Last night the enemy drew back his left, abandoning some of his works, and has extended his right somewhat. A raid has started in the direction of Covington on the Georgia railroad. Our cavalry in pursuit.

J. B. HOOD,
General.

ATLANTA, *July 27, 1864—5.30 p. m.*

General BRAXTON BRAGG,
    Macon and Columbus:
(Post commander will find him on train and deliver.)

There is a raid moving toward Covington. Considerable force. Ten pieces of artillery. Wheeler in pursuit. Destination unknown. Please give such attention as you can.

        [J. B. HOOD,
             General.]

ARMY HEADQUARTERS,
July 27, 1864—4.15 a. m.

Major-General WHEELER:

GENERAL: I am directed by the general commanding to say that the indications are that the enemy will attack our left, and he wishes you to be on the lookout and hold fast your end of the line.

I am, general, very respectfully, your obedient servant,

        JNO. S. SMITH,
           Aide-de-Camp.

HEADQUARTERS,
July 27, 1864—daylight.

General WHEELER,
    Commanding, &c.:

General Hood directs me to say that he desires to hold General Hardee's line, if possible, and wishes you to do all in your power to do so.

Very respectfully, &c.,

        F. A. SHOUP,
           Chief of Staff.

HEADQUARTERS ARMY OF TENNESSEE,
July 27, 1864—11 a. m.

Major-General WHEELER,
    Commanding Cavalry:

In reply to your dispatches regarding movement of enemy's cavalry, General Hood directs that you detach what force you can spare to follow this raid and keep it in observation. They will endeavor to bring the enemy to a stand.

Very respectfully,

        JOHN S. SMITH,
           Aide-de-Camp.

HEADQUARTERS, &C.,
July 27, 1864—1.30 p. m.

General WHEELER,
    Commanding, &c.:

General Hood directs that you dispatch such force as you may deem sufficient to bring the raid you speak of to bay. The force you leave on the line direct to keep in communication with the right of General Hardee. From the time in passing it should not seem to be a heavy force. Have sent to Jackson to know if he can send Humes to join you. Come in the evening, if not too much engaged. Let your attention be directed to the Macon railroad in your movements.

Very respectfully,

F. A. SHOUP.

P. S.—You must not go in person, unless you think it important.

HEADQUARTERS, &c.,
July 27, 1864—5 p. m.

General WHEELER,
Commanding, &c.:

If you decide to go against the raiders please come to headquarters first. You can start Humes to Flat Rock to-night, as you suggest. The enemy seems about to attack our left. He is now pressing Humes back.

Very respectfully, &c.,

F. A. SHOUP,
Brigadier-General.

HEADQUARTERS, &c.,
July 27, 1864—5.40 p. m.

General WHEELER:

You can send forward a part of Kelly's command, and the general will send Humes to-night to Flat Rock. He thinks you will have artillery enough with Humes'. If it be not too much out of your way, ride by this before you go.

Very respectfully, &c.,

F. A. SHOUP,
Chief of Staff.

HEADQUARTERS ARMY OF TENNESSEE,
July 27, 1864—9 p. m.

Major-General WHEELER,
Commanding Cavalry:

General Hood directs that you go yourself in pursuit of the enemy. Direct whoever you leave in command to report to General Hardee. Humes' division starts for Flat Rock to-night, and will there await your orders. General Ferguson's brigade will move to the right to-night.

Very respectfully,

F. A. SHOUP,
Chief of Staff.

HEADQUARTERS ARMY OF TENNESSEE,
July 27, 1864—9.30 p. m.

General WHEELER,
Commanding Cavalry:

General Hood directs that in pursuing the enemy you take the smallest number of troops possible. Should the enemy's force prove such as not to require the greater part of your command, you will detach an officer to continue the pursuit and return with the balance, as he needs you here with all the cavalry we can concentrate. He, however, leaves the general management in your hands, relying on your judgment, in which he has full confidence.

Very respectfully,

F. A. SHOUP,
Chief of Staff.

HEADQUARTERS HARDEE'S CORPS,
July 27, 1864.

Major-General WHEELER,
Commanding, &c.:

GENERAL : Lieutenant-General Hardee directs me to say he has left a brigade on the left of our line, from which he has directed that skirmishers shall be thrown out to cover the front to the angle of the line. He would like to have this skirmish line relieved as soon as you have men sufficient.

Respectfully,

T. B. ROY,
Assistant Adjutant-General.

HDQRS. ROSS' BRIGADE, JACKSON'S CAVALRY DIVISION,
Lick Skillet, Ga., July 27, 1864—8.30 a. m.

Brigadier-General JACKSON,
Commanding Division:

GENERAL: The enemy recrossed the river at Howell's Ferry. No report from Colonel Ross of the force that came to this side. It was doubtless an attempt to capture my pickets watching that point. No advance of the force from the church.

I am, general, very respectfully, &c.,

L. S. ROSS,
Brigadier-General.

HEADQUARTERS, &C.,
July 27, 1864—daylight.

General HARDEE,
Commanding, &c.:

General Hood desires you not to withdraw your skirmishers, as directed last night. They will be relieved to-night.

Very respectfully,

F. A. SHOUP,
Chief of Staff.

JULY 27, 1864—1.30 p. m.

General STEWART :

General Hood directs that you supply your troops with sixty rounds of ammunition, if practicable, and hold them in readiness to move at a moment's notice.

Yours, respectfully, &c.,

F. A. SHOUP,
Brigadier-General.

JULY 27, 1864—1.30 p. m.

Lieutenant-General LEE:

As soon as relieved by General Hardee, General Hood directs that you move Brown's and Clayton's divisions to the left, under cover, so that the movement may not be observed by the enemy. Let these divisions rest in rear of the line between the Peach Tree and Marietta roads, and be in readiness to move at any moment. Supply them with sixty rounds of ammunition, if practicable. After making these dispositions please report in person to these headquarters.

F. A. SHOUP.

P. S.—That part of Stevenson's division to the left of the Peach Tree road will not be withdrawn. Your left will rest near the Marietta road.

F. A. S.

———

JULY 27, 1864—4 p. m.

Lieutenant-General STEWART:

From present appearances the enemy is preparing to attack our left. Please have everybody on the alert and in readiness. As soon as Lee gets into position in your rear the general thinks you had better move Walthall's division a little farther to the left.

[F. A. SHOUP,
Chief of Staff.]

———

JULY 27, 1864—4.15 p. m.

Colonel BECKHAM:

From present appearances the enemy intends to attack our left. Order everybody to the lines. Drivers will support their own guns.

[F. A. SHOUP,
Chief of Staff.]

———

JULY 27, 1864—5.10 p. m.

Lieutenant-General LEE:

General Hood directs that you send support to General Stewart should he send to you for troops.

[F. A. SHOUP,
Chief of Staff.]

———

ATLANTA, *July 27, 1864—5.30 p. m.*

General WINDER,
 Andersonville, Ga.:

The raid toward Covington is stronger than at first reported. Destination still unknown. We have a heavy force in pursuit.

[J. B. HOOD,
General.]

———

JULY 27, 1864—6.40 p. m.

Lieutenant-General STEWART:

Hold command in readiness to move to-night. Come to headquarters if all is quiet.

[F. A. SHOUP,
Chief of Staff.]

JULY 27, 1864—6.45 p. m.

Lieutenant-General LEE:

Hold command in readiness to move to-night. Come to headquarters. General Hardee ordered to relieve skirmishers. Send officers to conduct them with certainty.

[J. B. HOOD,
General.]

————

ATLANTA, *July 27, 1864—7.20 p. m.*

Major-General COBB,
      Macon, Ga.:

The destination of the raiding party is still unknown. Prepare for it.

[J. B. HOOD,
General.]

————

GENERAL ORDERS, }   HEADQUARTERS HOOD'S CORPS,
      No. 58.   }   *In the Field, July 27, 1864.*

In obedience to orders from headquarters Army of Tennessee, the undersigned hereby assumes command of this corps.

S. D. LEE,
Lieutenant-General.

————

GENERAL ORDERS, }   HEADQUARTERS LEE'S CORPS,
      No. 59.   }   *In the Field, July 27, 1864.*

In addition to the staff already with the corps, the following-named officers are announced on the staff of the lieutenant-general commanding: Maj. William Elliott, assistant adjutant-general; Lieut. Henry B. Lee, aide-de-camp; Lieut. Samuel Hunter, aide-de-camp; Lieut. J. D. McFarland, acting aide-de-camp; Lieut. W. S. Farish, acting aide-de-camp.

By command of Lieutenant-General Lee:

J. W. RATCHFORD,
Assistant Adjutant-General.

————

ATLANTA, *July 28, 1864.*

Hon. J. A. SEDDON,
      Richmond:

The enemy commenced extending his right about 8 this morning, driving in our cavalry. Lieutenant-Generals Stewart and Lee were directed to hold the Lick Skillet road for the day with a portion of their commands. About 1.30 o'clock a sharp engagement ensued with no decided advantage to either side. We still occupy the Lick Skillet road. I regret to say that Lieutenant-General Stewart and Major-General Loring were wounded. In my dispatch of yesterday I should have mentioned that Brigadier-General Ector was severely wounded during that day.

J. B. HOOD,
General.

JULY 28, 1864—9 a. m.
(Received 9.45 a. m.)

Lieutenant-General HARDEE:

The militia did not quite reach the Peach Tree road. If it be possible for you to fill it and relieve Lee's troops, the general will be greatly pleased.

[F. A. SHOUP,
Chief of Staff.|

JULY 28, 1864—9 a. m.
(Received 9.45 a. m.)

Lieutenant-General HARDEE,
Commanding, &c.:

The chief of artillery has instructions to open fire upon the enemy in certain contingencies. Please instruct your skirmishers in front to prepare cover, so that they may retain their positions. They must remain at all hazards.

[F. A. SHOUP,
Chief of Staff.|

(Same to Stewart.)

JULY 28, 1864—10.30 a. m.
(Received 11 a. m.)

Lieutenant-General HARDEE:

General Lee·is now moving against the enemy to our left.

[F. A. SHOUP,
Chief of Staff.|

JULY 28, 1864—10.30 a. m.
(Received 11 a. m.)

Lieutenant-General HARDEE:

General Hood directs me to again impress upon you the importance of relieving the troops of General Lee on the left of Peach Tree road.

[F. A. SHOUP,
Chief of Staff.]

JULY 28, 1864—12 o'clock.

Lieutenant-General HARDEE:

GENERAL: General Hood has written twice to know if you can relieve the detachment of Lee's corps west of Peach Tree road. He also wrote you that he was moving on the enemy. I have sent to both generals to know how many men they can spare, and General Cheatham, who is here, has sent to see whether he can draw out a brigade and place it on the road to await your order.

Respectfully,

T. B. ROY,
Assistant Adjutant-General.

JULY 28, 1864—12.30 p. m.
(Received 1.10 p. m.)

Lieutenant-General HARDEE,
    Commanding Corps:

General Lee is directed to prevent the enemy from gaining the Lick Skillet road, and not to attack unless the enemy exposes himself in attacking us. Please inform your officers that all indications are that the enemy intends to attack us to-day or to-morrow.

[F. A. SHOUP,
    Chief of Staff.]

JULY 28, 1864—11.50 p. m.

Lieutenant-General HARDEE :

Inclosed please find communication from Major-General Stevenson.* The general desires that you order the co-operation, and arrange with General Stevenson that the movement may be simultaneous. He also directs me to acknowledge the receipt of your communication of 10.45 p. m., referring to the proposed night attack.

[F. A. SHOUP,
    Chief of Staff.]

JULY 28, 1864—12 m.
(Received 1.05 p. m.)

Lieutenant-General LEE,
    Commanding Corps:

Inclosed please find dispatch* from General Jackson. If the enemy should make an assault upon our left the general directs you to strike him in flank.

[F. A. SHOUP,
    Chief of Staff.]

JULY 28, 1864—2.20 p. m.
(Received 3.45 p. m.)

Lieutenant-General LEE :

General Hood directs that you hold the enemy in check. The object is to prevent him from gaining the Lick Skillet road.

[F. A. SHOUP,
    Chief of Staff.]

JULY 28, 1864—4 p. m.

Lieutenant-General LEE :

General Hood directs me to inform you that he desires you not to allow the enemy to gain upon you any more than possible, and that General Stewart has directions to support you fully.

[F. A. SHOUP,
    Chief of Staff.]

---

*Not found.

JULY 28, 1864—7 p. m.
(Received 7.40 p. m.)

Lieutenant-General LEE,
        Commanding, &c.:

Your dispatch of 6.10 received.   The general says it will be necessary to change our lines to-night.   Please ride in and bring General Bate with you, if all is quiet.

[F. A. SHOUP,
    Chief of Staff.]

JULY 28, 1864—3.25 p. m.
(Returned to headquarters 5.15 p. m.)

Lieutenant-General STEWART:

General Hood directs me to say that if you are pressed you can draw a brigade or so from Bate, but he does not want you to weaken his line more than you can help.   He desires you to hold the enemy, but not to do more fighting than necessary, unless you should get a decided advantage.   It may be well for you to cause Bate's skirmishers to threaten the enemy in your favor.

[F. A. SHOUP,
    Chief of Staff.]

JULY 28, 1864—5 p. m.

Major-General CHEATHAM:

Please ride to headquarters.   General Stewart is wounded.

[F. A. SHOUP,
    Chief of Staff.]

CONFIDENTIAL.]   HEADQUARTERS HARDEE'S CORPS,
                                    July 28, 1864.

Major-General CLEBURNE:

GENERAL: General Hood desires Lieutenant-General Hardee to inform his division commanders that all the indications are that the enemy intends to attack us to-day or to-morrow.

Very respectfully, your obedient servant,

T. B. ROY,
    Assistant Adjutant-General.

JULY, 28, 1864—5.15 p. m.
(Received 5.25 p. m.)

Major-General CLEBURNE:

In the absence of General Hardee, General Hood desires you to hold your division in readiness to change position to-night, should it become necessary.

[F. A. SHOUP,
    Chief of Staff.]

(Same to Brigadier-General Strahl.)

HEADQUARTERS ARMY OF TENNESSEE,
July 28, 1864—3.35 p. m.

[General WALTHALL:]

GENERAL: The general commanding requests me to say that you know the position of General French, and can send to him for a brigade if you should need it. He desires you to send orders to General French to open his artillery on them; you can judge whether such will assist you any or not.

Very respectfully, your obedient servant,

E. B. WADE,
Aide-de-Camp.

[Indorsement.]

HEADQUARTERS,
In the Field, July 28, 1864.

Respectfully referred to Major-General French, who will send a brigade at once to the Lick Skillet road. The courier will conduct you. You will please open fire, if in your judgment it is advisable.

For Major-General Walthall:

DOUGLAS WEST,
Acting Assistant Adjutant-General.

JULY 28, 1864—5 p. m.

Major-General WALTHALL:

The general directs that you call upon Generals Bate and French to support, if you require it. The object is to hold the enemy in check. The general desires not to lose Bate's position, however.

[F. A. SHOUP,
Chief of Staff.]

HEADQUARTERS, &c.,
July 28, 1864—11.20 a. m.

General WHEELER,
Commanding Cavalry:

Your dispatches of 5.35 and 7.05 a. m. received. The general approves your determination to guard the railroad. Take such steps as your best judgment prompts.

Very respectfully,

F. A. SHOUP,
Chief of Staff.

HEADQUARTERS ARMY OF TENNESSEE,
July 28, 1864—6.20 p. m.

General WHEELER:

Your dispatches of 10.45 and 11.05 received and approved. The enemy reported to be attempting a raid on our left, and crossing at Campbellton. If you can spare Humes, send him back. Use your discretion.

Very respectfully,

F. A. SHOUP,
Chief of Staff.

HEADQUARTERS,
July 28, 1864.

Major-General WHEELER,
    Commanding Cavalry Corps:

GENERAL: The enemy advanced from Decatur to Courtland yesterday. Left this morning on Moulton road—a raid somewhere. The force they had at Courtland was four pretty large regiments infantry, three cavalry regiments. I send some papers; refer you to orders in the Nashville paper of the 17th of General Milroy, at the head of the last column, first page. Please give me a general order for scouting, &c.

N. W. CARTER,
Commanding Scouts.

I am just starting in pursuit of enemy.

JULY 28, 1864—12 m.

Major-General WHEELER,
    Commanding Cavalry Corps:

GENERAL: I have with me parts of four regiments, numbering in all about 500 men. I have left on picket on the left four regiments and parts of other regiments. By General Jackson's order I left my pickets, to be relieved by him to-day, when they could rejoin their commands. I send General Jackson's order,* in virtue of which I moved, for the purpose of showing you why the command with me is so small.

Respectfully, general, your obedient servant,

W. Y. C. HUMES,
Brigadier-General.

JULY 28, 1864—1 p. m.

Maj. E. S. BURFORD,
    Assistant Adjutant-General:

MAJOR: Your dispatch of 10.10 a. m. just received. I have halted my command on the McDonough road, three miles from Doctor Avery's, where it will await orders.

Respectfully, &c.,

W. Y. C. HUMES,
Brigadier-General.

JULY 28, 1864—1.20 p. m.

Maj. E. S. BURFORD,
    Assistant Adjutant-General, Wheeler's Corps:

MAJOR: I have just received the inclosed note* from Colonel Harrison, in reply to which I have ordered him to move at once to this point with the rest of my division, regardless of any orders he may receive from General Jackson. I also send Jackson's orders,* by virtue of which I moved, which I intended but failed to send by last courier.

Respectfully, &c.,

W. Y. C. HUMES,
Brigadier-General.

---

* Not found.

JULY 28, 1864——9.30 a. m.
(Received 10.45 a. m.)

Brigadier-General JACKSON,
          Commanding, &c.:

The general directs me to inform you that he wishes the enemy resisted to the best of your power, and that he desires to hear what is passing on your line.

[F. A. SHOUP,
          Chief of Staff.]

———

JULY 28, 1864——11.20 a. m.
(Received 12.10 p. m.)

Brig. Gen. W. H. JACKSON:

Draw out Ross and Harrison, as you suggest, leaving only sufficient men to keep a good lookout and communication with our flank.

[F. A. SHOUP,
          Chief of Staff.]

———

JULY 28, 1864——11.45 a. m.

Brigadier-General JACKSON,
          Commanding, &c.:

The general prefers you do not go yourself to Campbellton; but if you think it necessary for you to go he desires that you will direct General Armstrong to come to headquarters this evening.

[F. A. SHOUP,
          Chief of Staff.]

———

JULY 28, 1864——2 p. m.
(Received 2.30 p. m.)

Brig. Gen. W. H. JACKSON:

The general approves your proposition to go with the brigades to the left.

[F. A. SHOUP,
          Chief of Staff.]

———

HDQRS. ROSS' BRIGADE, JACKSON'S CAVALRY DIVISION,
          In the Field, Ga., July 28, 1864——3 o'clock.

Brigadier-General JACKSON,
          Commanding Division:

GENERAL: Lieutenant-Colonel Boggess, who is on picket duty near the church, reports infantry advancing in his front. Only their line of skirmishers are yet in sight. I have a prisoner who belongs to Logan's corps. He says that three corps marched from their left last night, and are now flanking around to strike the railroad this side of Atlanta. I have sent Colonel Jones with Ninth Texas to re-enforce Colonel Boggess.

I am, general, very respectfully, &c.,

L. S. ROSS,
          Brigadier-General.

JULY 28, 1864—9.45 a. m.
Surg. A. J. FOARD,
    Medical Director, Army of Tennessee:

The commanding general desires you to thank the proper authorities of the several relief associations for the valuable assistance they have rendered the sick and wounded of this army. He highly appreciates their efforts, and is glad to assure them they are rendering vast service.

[F. A. SHOUP,
    Chief of Staff.]

JULY 28, 1864—4.40 p. m.
Doctor FOARD,
    Medical Director, Army of Tennessee:

You will please cause the wounded to be shipped to the rear as rapidly as possible to-night. As soon as you ascertain what can be accomplished, report the facts.

[F. A. SHOUP,
    Chief of Staff.]

JULY 28, 1864—3.30 p. m.
(Received 4 p. m.)
Major-General SMITH:

General Hood directs me to say that Stewart's troops are supporting you. The skirmishers are from Lee and Stewart. Colonel Beckham commands the artillery, assisted by the several field officers on the line— Myrick, Hoxton, Storrs, and Cobb. Lee had a pretty sharp engagement on the left to save the Lick Skillet road.

[F. A. SHOUP,
    Chief of Staff.]

ATLANTA, *July 28, 1864—5.10 p. m.*
General HOWELL COBB, *Macon, Ga.:*

Let the militia remain at Andersonville for the present. Raiders reported across South River; one column moving toward McDonough.

[J. B. HOOD,
    General.]

ATLANTA, *July 28, 1864—6.20 p. m.*
Governor JOSEPH E. BROWN, *Macon, Ga.:*

Raid on our right checked at Flat Rock. Enemy reported as crossing at Campbellton and at Varner's for raid. Cavalry sent to meet it. Send troops to Griffin.

[J. B. HOOD,
    General.]

ATLANTA, *July 29, 1864.*
His Excellency the PRESIDENT, *Richmond, Va.:*

Major-General Loring having been wounded yesterday it is highly important that temporary rank of major-general should be given Brig.

Gen. John C. Brown, that he may command Loring's division. Maj. Gen. Patton Anderson, having reported for duty, has been assigned to command Hindman's division.

> J. B. HOOD,
> *General.*

JULY 29, 1864—3.25 p. m.

Lieutenant-General HARDEE:

The supply of ammunition is very small. General Hood appeals to you to use every means to reduce its expenditure. Skirmishers, even, must not fire except in cases of necessity. This is important.

> [F. A. SHOUP,
> *Chief of Staff.*]

(Same to Generals Lee and Cheatham.)

JULY 29, 1864—9.20 p. m.

General HARDEE, *Commanding, &c.:*

Please cause scouts to be kept out on your flank, to gather any information that may be obtained. If the enemy should shift troops, the general is anxious to know the fact.

> [F. A. SHOUP,
> *Chief of Staff.*]

JULY 29, 1864—9.20 p. m.
(Received 10.55 p. m.)

Lieutenant-General LEE,
> *Commanding Corps:*

General Hood directs that you complete your works before moving farther to the left. When complete continue to move brigades to extend the works as far as Baugh's house without, however, too far weakening your lines.

> [F. A. SHOUP,
> *Chief of Staff.*]

JULY 29, 1864—9.30 a. m.

General CHEATHAM:

The general desires me to say that it is not necessary to regain the road.

> [F. A. SHOUP,
> *Chief of Staff.*]

JULY 29, 1864—3 p. m.

Major-General CHEATHAM,
> *Commanding Stewart's Corps:*

General Hood desires you to co-operate with General Lee, and to extend the line to the left just before dark, so that works may be erected by the men.

> [F. A. SHOUP,
> *Chief of Staff.*]

(Same to Lieutenant-General Lee.)

JULY 29, 1864—8.40 a. m.
(Received 9.25 a. m.)

General BROWN, *Commanding, &c.:*

General Anderson will be assigned to command of Hindman's division. Upon being relieved by him the general desires you to report here in person.

[F. A. SHOUP,
Chief of Staff.]

————

JULY 29, 1864—9.45 a. m.
(Received 10 a. m.)

Major-General STEVENSON, *Commanding Division:*

Communicate with General Maney, and arrange your picket-line as you best can, holding as much ground as possible.

[F. A. SHOUP,
Chief of Staff.]

————

WAR DEPARTMENT, C. S. A.,
Richmond, Va., July 29, 1864.

Maj. Gen. T. C. HINDMAN, *Atlanta, Ga.:*

GENERAL: Your letter making application for transfer to the Trans-Mississippi Department, addressed to General Cooper, has been referred to me. On conference with the President on the subject, he made the following indorsement:

A transfer and assignment to the Trans-Mississippi Department requires a previous inquiry as to a command there to which he can be consistently assigned. I would be pleased to relieve General Hindman of the embarrassment described in any practicable and proper manner. Physical disability for immediate service would justify a leave of absence.

I regret to say I know, and, upon inquiry, can receive intelligence of no command in the Trans-Mississippi Department to which you could be appropriately assigned. Indeed, there are already in that department more major-generals than divisions to be commanded, and appointments warmly recommended have been declined by the President because he did not deem that suitable employment could be found for the appointees. Very serious regret is felt by the Department at the physical disability and other causes that induce you to desire a transfer, but it is hoped that they may be removed without involving your permanent severance from the army with which you are connected. You will note the intimation of the President as to a leave of absence, and exercise your own choice with regard to making application for it.

Very respectfully,

JAMES A. SEDDON,
Secretary of War.

————

MONTGOMERY, *July 29, 1864.*

Col. JOHN B. SALE:

Have received your several dispatches. I did not know of the movement of Roddey's command in time to stop it. As soon as it can be assembled General Maury will return it to Blue Mountain and Gadsden. The move through that country will be good.

BRAXTON BRAGG.

HEADQUARTERS ARMY OF TENNESSEE,
July 29, 1864—4.30 a. m.

General JOSEPH WHEELER, *Commanding Cavalry:*

Your dispatch of yesterday, 6.30 p. m., just received. At same time one from General Jackson, dated near Campbellton, 28th, 9 p. m., stating that the force which crossed the river near that point was McCook's cavalry division. They were evidently making for the Macon and Western Railroad, moving via Fairburn. The commanding general directs that you send a force to co-operate with General Jackson, moving across to such point as you may deem best calculated to intercept the enemy. Use your own discretion in selecting force, and in general instructions given them. It is intended that you should exercise your own judgment in detaching this force from your command. General Jackson says:

I move in an hour to Fairburn, thence below to intercept or strike them in flank, and shall endeavor to protect railroad.

He has two brigades—Harrison's and Ross'—and will probably require assistance.

Very respectfully,

L. P. DODGE,
Aide-de-Camp.
(For Brigadier-General Shoup.)

HEADQUARTERS ARMY OF TENNESSEE,
July 29, 1864—2 p. m.

General WHEELER:

A raid from the left has struck the Macon railroad below Jonesborough about six miles. Troops have gone from here by rail. Important to prevent damage as far as possible. There is armed militia below on the road; should be advanced to prevent destruction north. Take such steps as your judgment suggests. Force unknown.

Very respectfully,

F. A. SHOUP,
Chief of Staff.

P. S.—Have not heard from Jackson this evening.

JULY 29, 1864—3.45 p. m.

Major-General WHEELER, *Commanding:*

Your dispatch of 9.20 a. m. received. The raid from our left has cut the Macon road below Jonesborough, as I have already informed you. The general thinks it is best not to order Humes or Ferguson direct, as you may have taken such steps as to produce a conflict of orders. Do what you think best. It is of great importance to prevent the destruction of the road. If you gain any information of moment send it toward Griffin and Macon. General Hood desires your return very much as soon as you can get through with those fellows in rear. He has most important service for you.

[F. A. SHOUP,
Chief of Staff.]

HEADQUARTERS ARMY OF TENNESSEE,
July 29, 1864—6.20 p. m.

General WHEELER, *Commanding Cavalry:*

Your dispatch of 1.15 p. m. just received. Jackson engaged the raid from the west at 3 p. m. Enemy said to be 3,000 strong. Infantry sent; 3,000 militia at Macon; some directed to be sent to Griffin. Send information south when important to them.

Very respectfully,

F. A. SHOUP,
Chief of Staff.

TWO MILES AND A HALF FROM FAYETTEVILLE,
July 29, 1864—10 p. m.

General WHEELER,
Commanding Cavalry Corps:

GENERAL: The latest reports represent the enemy moving toward Fayetteville. I am quite certain they are moving back to cross the Chattahoochee. I have Harrison's brigade in their front at Fayetteville, and am moving now with Ross' brigade to that place. Should enemy attempt to pass round the place I will gain their front or flank about Newnan. If you can follow and push them in rear it would be well.

Very respectfully,

W. H. JACKSON,
Brigadier-General.

HEADQUARTERS HUMES' CAVALRY DIVISION,
In the Field, July 29, 1864.

Maj. E. S. BURFORD,
Assistant Adjutant-General:

MAJOR: Mr. Bond, a soldier of the C. S. Army, under General Cobb, now on furlough, reports that about forty Yankees were seen this morning near Brushy Knob, about four miles from this place. They were going in the direction of Jonesborough. This fact he says was reported to him by reliable parties, but he did not see the Yankees himself. They took everything they could find from Mr. Martin, a citizen who lives near Brushy Knob, and left this morning.

I am, major, very respectfully, your obedient servant,

W. Y. C. HUMES,
Brigadier-General, Commanding.

P. S.—I have just sent a scout of 100 men, with orders to go four or five miles to reconnoiter.

HUMES.

JULY 29, 1864—6.45 p. m.

General ARMSTRONG, *Commanding, &c.:*

General Hood desires you to keep your scouts active about the Etowah. Send some of them across the river. He wants to know what is going on about Sweet Water and in that region.

[F. A. SHOUP,
Chief of Staff.]

ATLANTA, *July 29, 1864—5.45 p. m.*

General W. H. JACKSON,
    Commanding Cavalry, between Jonesborough and Lovejoy's:

An infantry brigade (700) went down by rail several hours ago. Humes' cavalry also ordered against your raiders should you need more force.

[J. B. HOOD,
    General.]

HDQRS. CAVALRY CORPS, ARMY OF TENNESSEE,
    Fayetteville, July 29, 1864—12 p. m.

Brigadier-General JACKSON:

GENERAL: Major-General Wheeler directs me, in reply to your dispatch of 10 p. m., to say that he finds the enemy have moved on through the town of Fayetteville and on the Newnan road; that he will press on rapidly on this road in pursuit of them, and desires you, as you suggested, to gain their front on the upper Fayetteville and Newnan road. He cannot hear of Harrison's brigade.

Respectfully, your obedient servant,

W. E. WAILES,
    Assistant Adjutant-General.

JULY 29, 1864—12.30 p. m.

Brigadier-General LEWIS,
    Commanding, &c.:

You will proceed by rail to Jonesborough, or that vicinity, with your brigade, to intercept raid in that quarter. You will control the movement of your train through its proper officers.

[F. A. SHOUP,
    Chief of Staff.]

JULY 29, 1864—1 p. m.

Colonel McMICKEN:

Is the railroad intercepted? Give the railroad authorities directions to give preference to General Lewis' train.

[F. A. SHOUP,
    Chief of Staff.]

P. S.—The enemy has struck the road about six miles below Jonesborough.

JULY 29, 1864—2.45 p. m.

Lieutenant-Colonel McMICKEN,
    Chief Quartermaster:

General Shoup directs that you use the utmost caution in issuing and consuming the corn now on hand, and that you instruct your quartermasters to this effect.

[L. P. DODGE,
    Aide-de-Camp.]

JULY 29, 1864—1.12 p. m.

Governor JOSEPH E. BROWN, *Macon, Ga.:*

Just have information that the enemy have struck the Macon road six miles below Jonesborough. General Hood desires you to give all possible assistance to repair the damage. Troops have been sent from here to prevent its destruction as far as possible. Please communicate with Captain Hazlehurst, who is somewhere below, gathering railroad iron. I send this letter by Captain Shoup, my aide-de-camp.

[F. A. SHOUP,
Chief of Staff.]

JULY 29, 1864—9.20 a. m.

TELEGRAPH OPERATOR:

Please use every exertion to have line to Macon repaired. It cannot be seriously interrupted. Ascertain cause, and let me know. Keep me informed of whatever you learn.

[F. A. SHOUP,
Chief of Staff.]

JULY 29, 1864.

To Conscript Authorities at Macon, Ga.:

It is of great importance to recruit the battalion of engineer troops serving with this army. General Hood desires you to give whatever aid you can, and, if possible, to turn over 200 men to Lieutenant-Colonel Presstman, commanding battalion.

[F. A. SHOUP,
Chief of Staff.]

SPECIAL FIELD ORDERS, }   HDQRS. ARMY OF TENNESSEE,
          No. 61.   }   *In the Field, July 29, 1864.*

*   *   *   *   *   *   *

II. Maj. Gen. B. F. Cheatham is assigned to the command of Stewart's corps.

III. Maj. Gen. Patton Anderson is assigned to the command of Hindman's division, Lee's corps.

IV. Brig. Gen. Henry R. Jackson is assigned to the command of Stevens' brigade, Bate's division.

By command of General Hood:

KINLOCH FALCONER,
Assistant Adjutant-General.

ATLANTA, GA., *July 30, 1864.*

Hon. JAMES A. SEDDON,
     Secretary of War, Richmond:

As soon as I can get the dismounted cavalry General Bragg is to send and the militia here I hope to strike the enemy with my main force. The recent raids have caused delay in receiving the re-enforcements referred to. I hope in a few days to send Wheeler, with his cavalry, to break Sherman's communications. The two recent engagements have checked his extension on both flanks.

J. B. HOOD,
General.

JULY 30, 1864—9.45 a. m.

Lieutenant-General HARDEE,
            Commanding, &c. :

Please furnish Captain Hill, the bearer, with thirty brave and intelligent men, with at least one lieutenant, for special service. Captain H. will explain confidentially.

[F. A. SHOUP,
                    Chief of Staff.]

(Same to Generals Lee and Cheatham.)

JULY 30, 1864—9.30 p. m.

Lieut. Gen. S. D. LEE:

The general commanding directs me to inform you that he does not consider it necessary to extend the line any farther to the left.

[F. A. SHOUP,
                    Chief of Staff.]

JULY 30, 1864—8.45 a. m.

Major-General STEVENSON,
            Commanding, &c. :

The general directs me to say that the engineers have been ordered to give special attention to the works on the Marietta road. Please give them whatever details they may require.

[F. A. SHOUP,
                    Chief of Staff.]

JULY 30, 1864—1 p. m.

Major-General STEVENSON:

General Hood directs that you make such disposition from the Peach Tree road to your left as you see proper. Please report direct.

[F. A. SHOUP,
                    Chief of Staff.]

JULY 30, 1864—11 a. m.

General WALTHALL:

Your dispatch of 8.30 received. Colonel Beckham, commanding artillery, has gone to look to that arm. Engineers have also been sent to assist at that point. If your skirmish line be driven back, please make the connection complete with General Stevenson's line.

[F. A. SHOUP,
                    Chief of Staff.]

JULY 30, 1864—1.30 p. m.

Colonel BECKHAM,
            Commanding Artillery :

The general desires you to use all the guns against the enemy's working parties on the Marietta road that can do execution. It is of great importance that the enemy do not gain a lodgment in front of that point.

[F. A. SHOUP,
                    Chief of Staff.]

HEADQUARTERS CAVALRY DIVISION,
Three miles and a half from Fayetteville, July 30, 1864—3 a. m.

Major-General WHEELER,
          Commanding Cavalry:

GENERAL: Since arrival of your courier, I received notice from Colonel Harrison that he is opposite the enemy at Shakerag, three miles from here. The enemy has gone into camp there. I move on at once with Ross' brigade.

          Very respectfully, your obedient servant,
                              W. H. JACKSON,
                                   Brigadier-General.

———

JULY 30, 1864—12.30 p. m.
(Received 2 p. m.)

Brigadier-General ARMSTRONG,
          Commanding, &c.:

Your dispatch of 10.45 a. m. received. The general desires you to hold the crossing at Herring's Mill, if possible. He thinks you may be able to do so by a dismounted force on the east side of the creek. It is important to hold it. If the enemy attempts to cross the Utoy Creek, give them stout resistance.

                              [F. A. SHOUP,
                                   Chief of Staff.]

———

JULY 30, 1864—11.10 p. m.

Brigadier-General KELLY,
          Commanding Cavalry, &c.:

The general directs me to acknowledge the receipt of your dispatch of to-day from Flat Shoals. There has been no information of General Wheeler since he passed through Jonesborough in pursuit of Yankee raid. The present whereabouts of the raid itself is unknown. The damage by it on Macon road was slight; it will, in fact, be repaired to-morrow. The telegraph communication, however, between the break and Macon has to-day been interrupted, and vague rumors report that a raid has gone to Macon itself. The general directs that you rely upon and act according to your best judgment, and keep him informed as to your movements and whereabouts.

                              [F. A. SHOUP,
                                   Chief of Staff.]

———

SPECIAL ORDERS, }   ADJT. AND INSP. GENERAL'S OFFICE,
     No. 179.   }   *Richmond, July 30, 1864.*

*   *   *   *   *   *   *

II. The following-named officers are assigned to duty with the cavalry command of Maj. Gen. W. T. Martin, Provisional Army, C. S., and will report accordingly: Majs. S. J. Shortt, R. W. Memminger, assistant adjutants-general.

*   *   *   *   *   *   *

VIII. Maj. J. H. F. Mayo, commissary of subsistence, is assigned to duty as chief commissary of Maj. Gen. T. C. Hindman's division, and will report accordingly.

*   *   *   *   *   *   *

XXVI. The following-named officers are assigned to duty with General J. B. Hood, Provisional Army, C. S., commanding, &c., and will report accordingly: Maj. James Hamilton, Provisional Army, C. S.; Cadets E. B. Wade, F. H. Wigfall, C. S. Army.

*   *   *   *   *   *   *

By command of the Secretary of War:

> SAML. W. MELTON,
> *Assistant Adjutant-General.*

JULY 31, 1864—2 a. m.

Major-General STEVENSON,
        Commanding &c.:

General Hood directs me to say that your troops should not be in the trenches with the militia, your place being in rear, within supporting distance, that in the event of the State troops failing you can hold the position. The State troops cannot be relieved before to-morrow night. General Hood thinks that the militia are able and will hold the position. He also directs that a slow constant fire be kept up on the enemy to annoy his working parties, and that your works be so improved as to protect you from any fire that may be opened upon your position after daylight.

> [F. A. SHOUP,
> *Chief of Staff.*]

P. S.—General Hood directs that for the present you report to Major-General Cheatham, who has been notified to take command as far around as Peach Tree street.

HEADQUARTERS HARDEE'S CORPS,
July 31, 1864.

Major-General CLEBURNE:

GENERAL: Cavalry report the enemy moving all night last, from your front to their right (our left). Lieutenant-General Hardee desires you to send out scouts to get information and report promptly.

Respectfully,

> T. B. ROY,
> *Assistant Adjutant-General.*

JULY 31, 1864—10.30 a. m.
(Received 12 m.)

Major-General MARTIN, *Commanding, &c.:*

The general directs that you at once push out your scouts and find positively where the enemy's left is resting, and also what he is doing.

> [F. A. SHOUP,
> *Chief of Staff.*]

JULY 31, 1864—4.15 p. m.

Lieutenant-General HARDEE, *Commanding Corps:*

The following dispatch just received from General Wheeler:

We fought the enemy from last night until to-night, killing and capturing many. We have thus far succeeded in keeping between them and the river, and they are showing evident signs of demoralization, having abandoned all their artillery, ambulance train, a large number of horses and mules, strewing the road with their arms and accouterments, and releasing some 300 of our people, whom they captured with the wagon trains at Fayetteville.

[F. A. SHOUP,
Chief of Staff.]

JULY 31, 1864—4.15 p. m.

Maj. Gen. W. B. BATE,
        Commanding Division:

General Hood directed General Lee to call upon you, if he thought proper. Please receive orders from him.

[F. A. SHOUP,
Chief of Staff.]

JULY 31, 1864—4.40 p. m.

Lieutenant-General LEE,
        Commanding Corps:

The general thinks you had better put enough of Bate in the line to extend to Baugh's house, so that he can strengthen it to-night. Your dispatch of 3.40 p. m. received.

[F. A. SHOUP,
Chief of Staff.]

JULY 31, 1864—2.30 p. m.

Lieutenant-General LEE:

Your movement will throw Bate in reserve. The general directs that you send to him for assistance, if necessary.

[F. A. SHOUP,
Chief of Staff.]

JULY 31, 1864—5.25 p. m.

Lieut. Gen. S. D. LEE, *Commanding Corps:*

The general directs me to inform you that two batteries have been ordered to report to you, to be placed in position near Baugh's house.

[F. A. SHOUP,
Chief of Staff.]

JULY 31, 1864—4.45 p. m.
(Received 6.50 p. m.)

Major-General CHEATHAM, *Commanding Corps:*

The general directs me to acknowledge the receipt of your dispatch of 3.45 p. m., and to say that he has referred it to General Smith for his information, so that he may co-operate with you. He thinks it well to have a regiment of each brigade about the Marietta road, formed in two ranks. The general will arrange about the picketing of the militia. General Bate has been put subject to the orders of Lieutenant-General Lee. General Lee has already ordered General Bate to move to his left.

[F. A. SHOUP,
Chief of Staff.]

JULY 31, 1864—5.35 p. m.
(Received 6.30 p. m.)

Major-General CHEATHAM,
        Commanding Corps:

General Hood directs that you fell the timber, large and small, in your front as far as practicable, leaving immediately about the works an amount sufficient for shade, the object being to form an impassable abatis.

[F. A. SHOUP,
        Chief of Staff.]

(Same to General S. D. Lee.)

ATLANTA, *July 31*, 1864—8.55 p. m.

General HOWELL COBB:

Wheeler has overtaken the raiders who cut the Macon road near Lovejoy's. He says, "We fought them from last night till to-night, killing and capturing many. They have abandoned all their artillery, ambulance train, a number of horses and mules, strewing the road with their accouterments, and releasing some 300 of our people." He is still in pursuit. Please send news of raid in your quarter.

[J. B. HOOD,
        General.]

ATLANTA, *July 31*, 1864—9.15 p. m.

Governor BROWN,
        Macon, Ga.:

Wheeler has been fighting the Jonesborough raiders. Has captured many prisoners, their artillery, ambulances, many horses and mules, and is still pursuing them. They passed back by way of Newnan.

[J. B. HOOD,
        General.]

JULY 31, 1864—12 m.

Major-General MAURY,
        Commanding, &c., Montgomery, Ala.:

General Hood begs you to send him as much ammunition as you can possibly spare. Please forward it by Capt. Charles Swett, who will deliver this. Captain S. is an excellent officer, and will faithfully execute any directions you may give.

[F. A. SHOUP,
        Chief of Staff.]

ATLANTA, *July 31*, 1864—10.10 p. m.

Major-General MAURY,
        Montgomery, Ala.:

Can you not send me some artillery and small-arm ammunition? I dispatch an officer to you on this business. We have killed, captured, or dispersed the raid that struck the Macon road. Have their artillery, horses, &c.

[J. B. HOOD,
        General.]

CIRCULAR.]   HEADQUARTERS LEE'S CORPS,
                                    In the Field, July 31, 1864.

I am directed by the lieutenant-general commanding to call the attention of brigade, regimental, and company commanders to the great importance of prompt and energetic action upon the part of all officers whenever the occasion arises that any part of their command should be rallied. Whenever the point for rallying the troops is indicated then every officer in the command should exert all of his influence and energy in rallying and forming the men upon the line indicated. This line will be indicated by the senior officer present. It then becomes the duty of every officer present to exert himself to the utmost to reform the line as quickly as possible. The issuing of this circular is deemed necessary from what came under his own observation on the evening of the 28th. He further desires to call the attention of brigade and division commanders to the necessity, when moving their men forward in line of battle, that they should move forward slowly and steadily until they become well engaged with the enemy before they are commanded to charge. By adopting this course, when it becomes necessary to charge, your command will be well aligned and your men not fatigued.

Very respectfully, your obedient servant,
J. W. RATCHFORD,
Assistant Adjutant-General.

ADDRESS.]   HDQRS. ROSS' BRIG., JACKSON'S CAVALRY DIV.,
                               In the Field, Ga., July 31, 1864.

SOLDIERS: You have nobly done your duty during the arduous service of the last four days, and by your gallantry added new laurels to the already wide-extended reputation of the brigade. Through your brigadier-general you were highly complimented on the battle-field yesterday by Major-General Wheeler, who acknowledged that his success was due chiefly to your good fighting. Your brigadier-general is proud of you; proud to command such soldiers, and hereby tenders to officers and men his thanks for their gallant services.

L. S. ROSS,
Brigadier-General.

[JULY 31, 1864.—For the organization and strength of Hood's army, see Part III, pp. 661, 680.]

ATLANTA, GA., *August 1, 1864.*
Hon. J. A. SEDDON,
Secretary of War, Richmond:

On yesterday and the day before our cavalry, under Generals Wheeler and Jackson, fought near Newnan the raiding party of the enemy which had intercepted our communication with Macon, completely routing them, killing a large number, capturing all their artillery, ambulances, most of their arms and equipments, with a large number of prisoners, including 2 brigade commanders and 12 surgeons, and recapturing all property and prisoners previously taken from us. Major-General Wheeler reports the expedition entirely broken up.

J. B. HOOD,
General.

ATLANTA, GA., *August 1, 1864.*

Hon. JAMES A. SEDDON,
    Secretary of War, Richmond:

The following dispatch is just received from Brigadier-General Iverson, through Major-General Cobb, at Macon, concerning the party of raiders who struck the Macon and Savannah road:

General Stoneman, after having his force routed, yesterday surrendered with 500 men. The rest of his command are scattered and fleeing toward Eatonton. Many have already been killed and captured. I shall be in Macon to-day, and wish rations for my men and prisoners.

A. IVERSON,
    Brigadier-General.

J. B. HOOD,
    General.

ATLANTA, *August 1, 1864—12.30 p. m.*

General BRAXTON BRAGG,
    Columbus, Ga.:

Have done all in my power to send iron. Captain Hazlehurst, of the engineers, was sent to the rear some time ago with full power.

J. B. HOOD,
    General.

AUGUST 1, 1864—5 p. m.

Lieutenant-General HARDEE,
    Commanding Corps:

The following dispatch just received from Maj. Gen. Howell Cobb, Macon:

General Iverson sends me the following dispatch: General Stoneman, after having his force routed, yesterday surrendered with 500 men. The rest of his command are scattered and flying toward Eatonton. Many have been already killed and captured.

[F. A. SHOUP,
    Chief of Staff.]

AUGUST 1, 1864—8.40 a. m.
(Received 9.30 a. m.)

Lieut. Gen. S. D. LEE,
    Commanding Corps:

The general directs me to say to you that it is all-important to have our line of battle continuous, also that every means be used to make an impassable abatis in front of your lines.

[F. A. SHOUP,
    Chief of Staff.]

ATLANTA, *August 1, 1864—10.10 a. m.*

General HOWELL COBB,
    Macon, Ga.:

Use the duplicate bridges constructed by Colonel Maxwell for repairing Central road.

J. B. HOOD,
    General.

August 1, 1864—10.45 a. m.

Isaac Scott, Esq.,
  President Macon and Western Railroad, Macon, Ga.:

General Shoup desires me to ask your attention to a matter of great
importance. Great suffering and loss of life is occasioned by the delay
of trains in transporting the wounded to the rear. Instances have
been reported where the trains have been seventy hours in making the
run from Atlanta to Macon. He is well aware that the road is doing a
large amount of business, and perhaps with inadequate means, but he
desires, if possible, that you so arrange your schedule that this evil
may be, as far as possible, remedied. Cannot the road be cleared, giving these trains the preference? He relies upon you to give this matter your special attention. Humanity asks it.

                                        L. P. DODGE,
                                            Aide-de-Camp.

August 1, 1864—11.10 a. m.

Colonel Presstman, *Chief Engineer:*

General Hood directs that you cause the line in rear of the salient on
the Marietta road to be staked off, so that the work can be done to-night.
Let General Cheatham know where it is.

                                        [F. A. SHOUP,
                                            Chief of Staff.]

Atlanta, *August 1, 1864—5 p. m.*

Major-General Wheeler, *Newnan, Ga.:*

General Iverson telegraphs to Macon that Stoneman, after being
routed, surrendered with 500 men to him; that the balance of his command are dispersed and flying through the country.

                                        [J. B. HOOD,
                                            General.]

August 1, 1864—5.15 p. m.

Brigadier-General Kelly, *Commanding, &c.:*

The general directs me to call your attention to the following information just received from a scout: He reports that a column of three
regiments of Yankee cavalry passed around Decatur on the north side
of town, about 10 p. m. yesterday, taking the old Covington road in
the direction of Flat Rock Shoals. They were under command of
Colonel Garrard (brother of the general), and have just arrived from
Chattanooga. They say they are going to aid Stoneman and Garrard
in their raid; that they allowed Wheeler would follow Stoneman and
Garrard, and that they would follow in Wheeler's rear to harass and
delay him as much as possible, while Stoneman could get to Macon and
Andersonville and release the prisoners; that Stoneman had 1,000
muskets and ammunition in his ambulances for the prisoners. We are
just informed by telegraph from Macon that General Stoneman, after
being routed, surrendered to General Iverson with 500 of his men; the
balance of his command are dispersed through the country. The general desires you to make such disposition of your force as you shall
think best under the circumstances.

                                        [F. A. SHOUP,
                                            Chief of Staff.]

AUGUST 1, 1864—10.30 a. m.

Brig. Gen. JOHN H. KELLY,
    Commanding, &c.:

The general directs me to say that there is no news of importance here. Wheeler dispatches from Newnan that he has completed the killing, capturing, and breaking up of the raiding party under McCook. Yours of 9.40 received.

           L. P. DODGE,
             Aide-de-Camp.

ATLANTA, *August 1, 1864—9.50 p. m.*

Brig. Gen. W. H. JACKSON,
    Commanding, &c., Newnan, Ga.:

Stoneman's raiders have come to grief. Stoneman and 500 of his braves surrendered to General Iverson yesterday near Clinton; balance of his command routed and being captured hourly.

           J. B. HOOD,
             General.

ATLANTA, *August 1, 1864—8 p. m.*

Capt. J. C. SHOUP,
    Macon, Ga.:

Use all material. Push everything forward. Let there be no delay.

           [J. B. HOOD,
             General.]

ATLANTA, *August 1, 1864—9 p. m.*

Colonel CUYLER and
Major MALLETT,
    Ordnance Officers, Macon, Ga.:

General Bragg directs that you send me at once all the negroes employed on public buildings at your post.

           J. B. HOOD,
             General.

COLUMBUS, *August 1, 1864.*

Col. JOHN B. SALE:

Roddey's command will reassemble at Opelika and march to North Alabama. The withdrawal was most unfortunate. The raid upon Macon is driven back, and railroad and telegraphic communication will soon be restored; but we are reaping the bitter fruits of seed long since sown. Many of Hood's brigades are so reduced in numbers, some as low as 500, and the material for commanders so exhausted, that I suggest to the President the expediency of consolidation when the commanding general deems it best.

           BRAXTON BRAGG.

MACON, GA., *August 1, 1864.*
(Received 2d.)
General S. COOPER,
   Adjutant and Inspector General:

General Stoneman, with a cavalry force estimated at 2,800, with artillery, was met two miles from this city by our forces, composed of Georgia reserves, citizens, local companies, and the militia, which Governor Brown is organizing here. The enemy's assault was repulsed and his force held in check along our entire line all day. Retiring toward Clinton, he was attacked next morning by General Iverson, who, having routed the main body, captured General Stoneman and 500 prisoners. His men are still capturing stragglers.

HOWELL COBB,
Major-General.

SPECIAL FIELD ORDERS, }   HDQRS. ARMY OF TENNESSEE,
     No. 64.   }   *In the Field, August 1, 1864.*

*   *   *   *   *   *   *

II. In obedience to paragraph LIII, Special Orders, No. 170, Adjutant and Inspector General's Office, dated Richmond, July 20, 1864, Maj. Gen. M. L. Smith is assigned as chief engineer to the Army of Tennessee. He will be obeyed and respected accordingly.

*   *   *   *   *   *   *

By command of General Hood:

KINLOCH FALCONER,
Assistant Adjutant-General.

ATLANTA, GA., *August 2, 1864.*
His Excellency President DAVIS,
   Richmond, Va.:

Since our late success over the enemy's cavalry I hope now to be able, by interrupting Sherman's communications, either to force him to fight me in position or to retreat. Please give me your advice freely at all times.

J. B. HOOD,
General.

ATLANTA, *August 2, 1864.*
General S. COOPER:

I suggest that pardon be offered all soldiers in the Trans-Mississippi Department if they will rejoin their commands on this side of the river. I am informed that many men can thus be had.

J. B. HOOD,
General.

AUGUST 2, 1864—10 p. m.
Lieutenant-General HARDEE:

The enemy is reported marching to our left in considerable force. Armstrong says he has large camps on Utoy Creek. General Smith is

directed to move his command to the right in the morning, so as to relieve as much of yours as possible. The general desires you to be in
readiness to go to the left if necessary.

[F. A. SHOUP,
Chief of Staff.]

AUGUST 2, 1864—10 p. m.

Lieutenant-General LEE:

General Armstrong's dispatch of 7 p. m. received. The general
thinks you had better move Bate to the Sandtown road, to be in readiness.

[F. A. SHOUP,
Chief of Staff.]

HEADQUARTERS HARDEE'S CORPS,
August 2, 1864.

Major-General CLEBURNE:

GENERAL: General Hardee wishes you to continue to send out scouts.
He directs me to say that although your troops are to be withdrawn
from the trenches they are to be held in readiness to return and repel
any assault that may be made by the enemy.

Yours, respectfully, &c.,

T. B. ROY,
Assistant Adjutant-General.

AUGUST 2, 1864—10 a. m.
(Received 11 a. m.)

Brig. Gen. F. C. ARMSTRONG, *Commanding, &c.:*

The general directs that you destroy the bridge at Bankston's.

[F. A. SHOUP,
Chief of Staff.]

AUGUST 2, 1864—11.30 a. m.

Maj. Gen. G. W. SMITH, *Commanding, &c.:*

General Hood directs me to say that he will place your left to the
right of the Peach Tree road as soon as possible. He does not desire
these men placed in the trenches to-night, but those now arriving he
wishes organized and made to relieve those now in trenches. Stoneman & Co. are really in our possession; have a telegram from General
Stoneman to his wife, sent from Macon. More when you come over.

[F. A. SHOUP,
Chief of Staff.]

ATLANTA, GA., *August 2, 1864.*

Maj. Gen. D. H. MAURY, *Montgomery, Ala.:*

If you can possibly spare some of your cavalry send it upon Sherman's railroad. Small parties could do great service.

J. B. HOOD,
General.

AUGUST 3, 1864—9.45 a. m.
(Received 10.25 a. m.)

General WHEELER, *Commanding, &c.* :

The general wants more specific information touching the position and strength of the enemy's left. Have sent the same information to General Martin.

[F. A. SHOUP,
Chief of Staff.]

AUGUST 3, 1864—9.45 a. m.
(Received 11.14 a. m.)

General MARTIN, *Commanding, &c.*:

General Hood is in want of definite information of the enemy's left. He wants to know not only where it is, but what forces are there. Use every means in your power to ascertain.

[F. A. SHOUP,
Chief of Staff.]

ATLANTA, *August 3, 1864—8.30 p. m.*

Brig. Gen. DANIEL W. ADAMS, *Opelika:*

Roddey's command will return to you to-morrow.

[J. B. HOOD,
General.]

MACON, *August 3, 1864.*

Col. JOHN B. SALE:

General Hood's command should include the whole State of Georgia, west of a line due south from Augusta. Confusion and conflicts now exist here, at his main depots, and at other points where he has stores and hospitals, and he is powerless to correct them. Great irregularities, drunkenness, and consequent demoralization, are too apparent at this place. I am detained by the condition of the railroad east. It will take several days yet for the track and four weeks for the Oconee bridge.

BRAXTON BRAGG.

[Indorsements.]

Submitted to the President.

SECRETARY OF WAR:

A modification of limits is no doubt desirable, but I doubt the advisability of the one proposed. Please consider, inquire, and confer.

J. D.

SPECIAL ORDERS, }   ADJT. AND INSP. GENERAL'S OFFICE,
      No. 182.   }   *Richmond, August 3, 1864.*
      *   *   *   *   *   *   *

IX. Maj. Gen. Patton Anderson, Provisional Army, C. S., is relieved from service in the Department of South Carolina, Georgia, and Florida, and is assigned to duty with the Army of Tennessee. He will report to General John B. Hood, commanding, &c., Atlanta, Ga.
      *   *   *   *   *   *   *

XXXIX. Lieut. Col. J. M. Kennard, artillery, Provisional Army, C. S., is relieved from service with the Department of Alabama, Mississippi, and East Louisiana, and is assigned to duty as chief ordnance officer of Army of Tennessee. He will report to General John B. Hood, commanding, &c.

*   *   *   *   *   *   *

By command of the Secretary of War:

SAML. W. MELTON,
Assistant Adjutant-General.

GENERAL FIELD ORDERS, }   HDQRS. ARMY OF TENNESSEE,
No. 10.   }   *In the Field, August 3, 1864.*

I. Hereafter the allowance of couriers will be as follows: For corps headquarters, twenty men, under a commissioned officer; for division headquarters, ten men, under a non-commissioned officer; for brigade headquarters, four men, under a non-commissioned officer.

II. As far as practicable these couriers will be furnished from the unattached companies of cavalry now serving with the army, in order that companies belonging to regular organizations may be returned to them entire.

III. Infantry soldiers at present detailed as couriers will be permitted to remain, within the number above allowed. All in excess will be promptly returned to their commands, and their horses, if public, turned in; if private, disposed of.

By command of General Hood:

KINLOCH FALCONER,
Assistant Adjutant-General.

ATLANTA, *August 4, 1864.*

Hon. J. A. SEDDON:

No important change in the past two days. Some skirmishing and a little shelling from the enemy.

J. B. HOOD,
General.

AUGUST 4, 1864—9.15 a. m.

Lieutenant-General LEE,
       Commanding, &c.:

The general desires to call your attention to the urgent necessity of economy in the expenditure of ammunition, even upon the picket-line. He desires that the firing be discontinued, except in cases of necessity.

[F. A. SHOUP,
Chief of Staff.]

AUGUST 4, 1864—12 m.

Lieutenant-General LEE,
       Commanding, &c.:

The general desires you to increase the force of General Lewis on the Sandtown road by about 300 men.

[F. A. SHOUP,
Chief of Staff.]

AUGUST 4, 1864—12 m.
(Received 2.15 p. m.)

General W. H. JACKSON,
        Commanding, &c.:

The general desires you to resist the crossing of the east fork of the Utoy Creek; it is important to hold it.

[F. A. SHOUP,
                Chief of Staff.]

———

AUGUST 4, 1864—1.20 p. m.

General JACKSON,
        Commanding, &c.:

Please issue imperative orders to your command to gather together all captured horses, and hold them ready to be turned over. It is of the last importance that they shall not be scattered and lost.

[F. A. SHOUP,
                Chief of Staff.]

———

AUGUST 4, 1864—9.40 p. m.

Brigadier-General FERGUSON,
        Commanding, &c.:

The general directs me to say that in a short time he will place you permanently under the orders of General Wheeler. For a few days General W. will probably be absent, and, in the mean time, it will be necessary for you to be under the general command of General Jackson. When General W. returns, your affairs can be, it is hoped, satisfactorily arranged.

[F. A. SHOUP,
                Chief of Staff.]

———

AUGUST 4, 1864—9 a. m.

Brig. Gen. M. J. WRIGHT,
        Commanding, &c.:

General Shoup directs me to inform you that you have been assigned to command of post at Macon. He desires that you will lose no time in reporting for duty, as your services are very much needed.

[L. P. DODGE,
                Aide-de-Camp.]

———

MACON, August 4, 1864.

Col. JOHN B. SALE,
        Military Secretary:

The question of subsisting the Georgia militia is becoming serious and embarrassing. So far none of them have been mustered into the Confederate service, but under the orders of local commanders and others subsistence and forage are being issued to all from the time they report at the rendezvous. If the evil increases or is continued much longer our ability to feed the main army in front, with communications so limited, is very questionable.

BRAXTON BRAGG.

[First indorsement.]

Respectfully submitted to His Excellency the President.

JOHN B. SALE,
Colonel and Military Secretary.

[Second indorsement.]

AUGUST 5, 1864.

SECRETARY OF WAR:

Public supplies can only be issued to militia who have been received into the service of the Confederate States. Of the particular case I have no other knowledge than that contained within.

J. D.

[Third indorsement.]

AUGUST 6, 1864.

ADJUTANT-GENERAL:

Instruct General Hood, in conformity with the President's indorsement. Also refer this to the Commissary-General, that he may give instructions to his officers conforming to the same.

J. A. S.,
Secretary.

[Fourth indorsement.]

ADJUTANT AND INSPECTOR GENERAL'S OFFICE,
August 10, 1864.

Respectfully referred to the Commissary-General.
By command of the Secretary of War:

H. L. CLAY,
Assistant Adjutant-General.

[Fifth indorsement.]

OFFICE COMMISSARY-GENERAL OF SUBSISTENCE,
August 13, 1864.

Respectfully returned to Adjutant and Inspector General.
Instructions have been given in accordance with the President's indorsement.

L. B. NORTHROP,
Commissary-General of Subsistence.

SPECIAL ORDERS, ⎰   ADJT. AND INSP. GENERAL'S OFFICE,
No. 183.   ⎱   *Richmond, August 4, 1864.*

*   *   *   *   *   *   *

XL. Lieut. Col. B. W. Frobel, artillery, Provisional Army, C. S., is relieved from duty at Wilmington and is temporarily assigned to engineer duty with the Army of Tennessee. He will report to General J. B. Hood.

*   *   *   *   *   *   *

By command of the Secretary of War:

SAML. W. MELTON,
Assistant Adjutant-General.

GENERAL ORDERS, ⎱ HDQRS. GOVERNMENT WORKS, ORDNANCE,
No. 1.   ⎰   *Macon, Ga., August 4, 1864.*

I. In obedience to instructions from the Chief of Ordnance, C. S. Army, Richmond, Va., I assume command of the ordnance department in this city, embracing the arsenal, armory, and laboratories.

M. H. WRIGHT,
Colonel, Commanding Government Works.

RICHMOND, *August 5, 1864.*
General J. B. HOOD:

Yours of August 2 received. I concur in your plan, and hope your cavalry will be able to destroy the railroad bridges and depots of the enemy on the line to Bridgeport, so as to compel the enemy to attack you in position or to retreat. The loss consequent upon attacking him in his intrenchments requires you to avoid that if practicable. The enemy have now reached a country where supplies can be gathered by foraging expeditions, and a part of your cavalry will be required to prevent that. If he can be forced to retreat for want of supplies, he will be in the worst condition to escape or resist your pursuing army. General Hardee's minute knowledge of the country, and his extensive acquaintance with the officers and men of the command, must render his large professional knowledge and experience peculiarly valuable in such a campaign as I hope is before you.

JEFFERSON DAVIS.

ATLANTA, GA., *August 5, 1864.*
His Excellency President DAVIS,
Richmond, Va.:

Your cipher dispatch of to-day received. There is no material change in the enemy's position. He is endeavoring gradually to extend his right.

J. B. HOOD,
General.

HEADQUARTERS ARMY,
[*August 5, 1864*]—*10.15 p. m.*
General CHEATHAM:

General Hood thinks it will assist General Lee if you will cause General French to make a demonstration of attack to-morrow about 7 a. m. He does not wish, however, that there shall be any great sacrifice of life.

F. A. SHOUP,
Chief of Staff.

[Indorsement.]

General FRENCH:

I will call to see you in reference to the within. Hold your command in hand.

B. F. CHEATHAM,
Major-General.

AUGUST 5, 1864—2 p. m.

General MARTIN, *Commanding, &c.*:

If the enemy should attempt to move around our right resist him to the full extent of your ability. He is pressing our picket-line with some vigor.

[F. A. SHOUP,
Chief of Staff.]

MACON, *August 5, 1864.*
(Received 6th.)

General S. COOPER:

General Wright relieves me of command by order of General Hood. I await orders. Officers at Columbus have asked that I be ordered to command that post.

GEO. C. GIBBS,
Colonel.

ATLANTA, *August 6, 1864.*

Hon. J. A. SEDDON:

The enemy made two assaults to-day on Finley's and Lewis' brigades, of Bate's division, in Lee's corps, both of which were handsomely repulsed, with loss to them.

J. B. HOOD,
General.

AUGUST 6, 1864—11.30 a. m.

General CHEATHAM:

The general is pleased to know that General French has succeeded so well. Let him be careful not to too far commit himself.

[F. A. SHOUP,
Chief of Staff.]

AUGUST 6, 1864—5.50 p. m.

General LEE, *Commanding, &c.*:

General Cleburne is moving to your assistance with two brigades. Please hold them to support any part of your line that may be in most danger.

[F. A. SHOUP,
Chief of Staff.]

AUGUST 6, 1864—6.30 p. m.

Lieutenant-General LEE, *Commanding, &c.*:

If you find Bate too much exposed to a flank attack to-night the general thinks you had [better] fall back into the line at Baugh's. You must judge of the necessity, getting all the information you can from Jackson. Should you fall back, try to carry off whatever arms, &c., there may be in your front.

[F. A. SHOUP,
Chief of Staff.]

AUGUST 6, 1864—6.15 p. m.

General JACKSON,
    Commanding Cavalry:

The general directs that Armstrong form so as best to protect Bate's left.

[F. A. SHOUP,
        Chief of Staff.]

AUGUSTA, *August 6, 1864.*

Col. J. B. SALE:

Just arrived after much difficulty. Found the repairs on Georgia Central Railroad progressing slowly and unsatisfactorily. Gave such orders as ought to expedite them. The command should be transferred to Hood's department. He is now embarrassed for want of ammunition, which I shall force through from here. The unfortunate withdrawal of the guard to Savannah a few hours before the raiding party arrived, caused the loss of the Oconee bridge, burned by only fifty men. I shall leave for Charleston this evening or to-morrow morning, thence to Richmond, unless otherwise ordered. Have no dispatches for over a week.

BRAXTON BRAGG.

AUGUSTA, *August 6, 1864.*

Col. J. B. SALE:

The newspapers announced the exchange of Maj. Gen. Frank Gardner at Charleston. He should go to Hood immediately to replace Stewart or Loring, now disabled by wounds. The corps needs a commander badly.

BRAXTON BRAGG.

SPECIAL ORDERS, }   HDQRS. CAV. CORPS, ARMY OF TENN.,
    No. 92.   }   *August 6, 1864.*

I. Pursuant to instructions from army headquarters, Maj. James Hamilton, Provisional Army, C. S., is assigned to the command of the artillery of this corps.

    *   *   *   *   *   *   *

By order of Maj. Gen. Joseph Wheeler:

E. S. BURFORD,
        Assistant Adjutant-General.

AUGUST 7, 1864—1.30 p. m.

Lieutenant-General LEE,
        Commanding, &c.:

The general approves your action in strengthening the advanced position held by General Bate. It is important to hold it, if possible.

[F. A. SHOUP,
        Chief of Staff.]

August 7, 1864—2.40 p. m.

Lieutenant-General LEE, *Commanding, &c.:*

General Jackson's note* of 1.30, with your indorsement, received. The general says you must exercise your best judgment.

[F. A. SHOUP,
Chief of Staff.|

———

HEADQUARTERS LEE'S CORPS,
Phillips' House, August 7, 1864.

Maj. Gen. W. B. BATE, *Commanding Division:*

GENERAL: General Lee directs me to say that he wishes you to strain every effort to strengthen your line to-night, as General Armstrong reports that a large force of the enemy, over a corps, came into the Sandtown road at Doctor Gilbert's this evening, from the direction of Bankston's, and were at last accounts moving in this direction. The general thinks there is no doubt that these troops are intended for your front, and wishes you to provide accordingly.

Very respectfully, your obedient servant,

W. RATCHFORD,
Assistant Adjutant-General.

———

HEADQUARTERS HARDEE'S CORPS,
Richards' House, August 7, 1864.

[Maj. Gen. P. R. CLEBURNE:]

GENERAL: Lieutenant-General Hardee desires me to say that by direction of General Hood he resumes command of Cleburne's and Bate's divisions. Your reports will be made to these headquarters, and he wishes you to inform him at dark this evening how nearly your works are completed.

Respectfully, general, your obedient servant,

D. H. POOLE.

———

HEADQUARTERS CLEBURNE'S DIVISION,
August 7, 1864.

Lieutenant-Colonel ROY:

COLONEL: My line is anything but a good one. Three of my brigades, Mercer's, Granbury's, and Lowrey's, have nearly completed their works. If General Hardee expects Mercer's brigade to do any good a brigade commander is immediately necessary. Its present commander is not efficient.

Very respectfully,

P. R. CLEBURNE,
Major-General.

———

HEADQUARTERS HARDEE'S CORPS,
August 7, 1864—10 p. m.

Major-General CLEBURNE, *Commanding Division:*

GENERAL: General Hood directs that your whole division be held in reserve, two brigades in rear of Lee and two in rear of Bate. Your

———
* Not found.

command will accordingly move at 3 a. m. to-morrow and take position as above indicated. Your present line will be occupied by a force of one man in every two yards, which you will leave for that purpose, or about one-third of your command. General Hardee would like to see you at his quarters about 7.30 o'clock in the morning. General Hood has ordered two batteries sent you. General Hardee wishes you to lend them to General Bate in case he needs them.

By direction of Lieutenant-General Hardee:

> T. B. ROY,
> *Assistant Adjutant-General.*

GENERAL ORDERS,   HEADQUARTERS LEE'S CORPS,
    No. 62.   *In the Field, August 7, 1864.*

The lieutenant-general commanding takes pleasure in announcing to the officers and men of this corps the splendid conduct of a portion of Bate's division, particularly Tyler's brigade, in sustaining and repulsing on yesterday three assaults of the enemy, in which his loss in killed, wounded, and prisoners was from 800 to 1,000 men, 2 colors, and 300 or 400 stand small-arms, and all of his intrenching tools. Our loss was from 15 to 20 killed and wounded. Soldiers who fight with the coolness and determination that these men did will always be victorious over any reasonable number.

By command of Lieutenant-General Lee:

> J. W. RATCHFORD,
> *Assistant Adjutant-General.*

ATLANTA, *August 8, 1864.*
(Received 9th.)

Hon. J. A. SEDDON, *Secretary:*

There is no material change to report yesterday or to-day in the enemy's position. He still evinces a desire to extend his right.

> J. B. HOOD,
> *General.*

HEADQUARTERS ARMY OF TENNESSEE,
August 8, 1864—11 p. m.

Maj. Gen. P. R. CLEBURNE, *Commanding Division, &c.:*

GENERAL: The general commanding directs me to inform you that General Hardee wrote you a note a little after dark, which he supposes you to have received ere this, authorizing you to move Lowrey's brigade on your left.

I am, very respectfully, your obedient servant,

> JAMES D. HILL,
> *Aide-de-Camp.*

AUGUST 8, 1864—9 a. m.

Major-General WHEELER, *Commanding Cavalry:*

The general commanding directs me to state that you are so far off from all supplies that he thinks it would be better to move your command nearer to this place, so as to get yourself in readiness. General Shoup informs him that Captain Norton did not come to these head-quarters in reference to the horseshoes; also a good portion of those collected by Colonel Beckham have been left here untouched. It will not be well for you to take up your line of march without being fairly equipped for it. He thinks you will save time by moving nearer to the main body of the army. You will please order Colonel Clinch's regi-ment to report to General Morgan.

[L. P. DODGE,
Aide-de-Camp.]

P. S.—The general desires me to say that he is not disappointed in the least, and directs as above in case you cannot make effective prep-aration where you now are. He thinks your preparations will be facilitated by a nearer approach to the main body. He doubts being able to send Ross, even if you should move on the enemy at once. You will, therefore, make your plans, not counting upon General Ross' co-operation. If the general is able to send him it will be a piece of good fortune. A telegram has been received stating that the salt had been sent to Social Circle by a special messenger.

SPECIAL FIELD ORDERS, }
No. 71.   }

HDQRS. ARMY OF TENNESSEE,
In the Field, August 8, 1864.

*   *   *   *   *   *   *

III. Brig. Gen. Z. C. Deas, Provisional Army, C. S., will report to Maj. Gen. Patton Anderson, for assignment to a brigade in his division.

*   *   *   *   *   *   *

By command of General Hood:

KINLOCH FALCONER,
Assistant Adjutant-General.

ATLANTA, GA., *August 9, 1864.*

His Excellency President DAVIS, *Richmond, Va.:*

The Nineteenth Army Corps having gone to Virginia or Washington City, the infantry force threatening Mobile cannot be more than 7,000 at the most, after leaving a garrison at New Orleans and in Louisiana. All that is necessary at Mobile is 7,000 men, as 6,000 will man the trenches. The reserve and militia of Alabama are thought to be am-ple. None but small boats can get near to Mobile, and the heaviest batteries are near the city. This information in regard to Mobile I got from Lieutenant-General Lee. The force at Holly Springs is the same or less than Lee compelled to retreat. I suggest that the Trans-Missis-sippi troops come here. If they, or a part of them, are retained in Mis-sissippi Forrest should go to Middle Tennessee, as the force at Holly Springs cannot march to Mobile with Forrest or a part of the Trans-Mississippi troops to oppose them. To march the Trans-Mississippi troops to Middle Tennessee may be too late, as they have to equip themselves with transportation. To hold Atlanta I have to hold East Point. The enemy are gradually extending to East Point, and hope to force me to give up Atlanta or to fight him at great disadvantage to us. I am making dispositions which will, I hope, enable me to hold both East Point and Atlanta.

J. B. HOOD,
General.

ATLANTA, *August 9, 1864.*

General S. COOPER:

General Wright was ordered to the command of Macon by the direction of General Bragg.

J. B. HOOD,
General.

AUGUST 9, 1864—2 p. m.
(Received 3.05 p. m.)

Lieutenant-General LEE, *Commanding Corps:*

In the next official dispatch the error spoken of by General Bate in his communication of the 8th instant will be corrected. The general regrets very much that it occurred.

[F. A. SHOUP,
Chief of Staff.]

HEADQUARTERS LEE'S CORPS,
Phillips' House, August 9, 1864.

Maj. Gen. P. R. CLEBURNE:

GENERAL: General Lee does not wish Govan's brigade to be returned to him, as it was his intention to have ordered it back to you. He thinks, however, it would be well to make the inquiry as to what orders General Govan acted under.

I am, general, very respectfully, your obedient servant,

WILLIAM ELLIOTT,
Assistant Adjutant-General.

AUGUST 9, 1864—4.45 p. m.

General FERGUSON, *Commanding, &c.:*

Your note of 3.30 received. The general desires you to take sufficient force and ascertain what the movement means. Leave a regiment on the right, and report your departure to the officer commanding the infantry. Keep us informed of your movements. Send certain information to General Wheeler of this movement. Say that we have some information which rather leads to the belief that the enemy has a cavalry force intended to pursue him or make another raid.

[F. A. SHOUP,
Chief of Staff.]

Above dispatch duplicated at 5.50 p. m., with instructions to leave General Morgan in command of cavalry on right.

AUGUST 9, 1864—8 p. m.

Brigadier-General FERGUSON, *Commanding, &c.:*

Your dispatch of 6.30 received. Please send to General Wheeler, Covington, any information you may have. It is important that his movements shall not be unnecessarily checked. Do not trust to one messenger.

[F. A. SHOUP,
Chief of Staff.]

SPECIAL ORDERS, }   ADJT. AND INSP. GENERAL'S OFFICE,
   No. 187.   }   *Richmond, Va., August 9, 1864.*

*   *   *   *   *   *   *

III. Brig. Gen. A. R. Wright, Provisional Army, C. S., is assigned to duty in the Army of Tennessee. He will report to General J. B. Hood, commanding, &c., Atlanta, Ga.

*   *   *   *   *   *   *

X. Maj. Gen. Edward Johnson, Provisional Army, C. S., is assigned to duty in the Army of Tennessee. He will report without delay to General John B. Hood, commanding, &c., Atlanta, Ga.

*   *   *   *   *   *   *

XIII. Brig. Gen. St. John R. Liddell, Provisional, Army, C. S., is assigned to duty in the District of the Gulf, and will report for orders to Major-General Maury, commanding, &c. If no appropriate duty can be found there, General Liddell will proceed to the Army of Tennessee, and report for orders to General J. B. Hood, commanding, &c.

XIV. Brig. Gen. J. J. Archer, Provisional Army, C. S., is assigned to duty in the Army of Tennessee. He will report for orders to General John B. Hood, commanding, &c., Atlanta, Ga.

*   *   *   *   *   *   *

By command of the Secretary of War:

SAML. W. MELTON,
Assistant Adjutant-General.

———

CIRCULAR.]   HEADQUARTERS CAVALRY CORPS,
                                   August 9, 1864.

I. In the march about to commence no soldier or officer of any grade whatever will be permitted to carry any article of private property, except one single blanket and one oil-cloth.

II. The troops will be inspected daily while en route, and any additional article found upon the person or horse of any trooper or officer will be immediately destroyed.

III. The ordnance wagons, ambulances, limber-boxes, and caissons will be inspected twice each day, and the officer controlling them will be arrested, and, if practicable, immediately punished if the smallest article of private property is found being thus transported.

J. WHEELER,
Major-General.

———

                                ATLANTA, GA., *August 10, 1864.*
Hon. J. A. SEDDON:

When your telegram of July 23 was received, ordering Brigadier-General Deas' case before an examining board, it was impracticable to execute the order, General Deas being absent sick and Major-General Hindman having left for the Trans-Mississippi Department. On the 6th of August General Deas reported, and I have placed him on duty, hoping it will meet your approval.

J. B. HOOD.

———

                                         AUGUST 10, 1864.
General M. L. SMITH, *Chief Engineer, Army of Tennessee:*

General Hood desires you to take immediate steps to prepare bridge timbers to reconstruct the bridges on the railroads leading from this place to Tennessee, and also to prepare duplicate bridges for all bridges in our rear that are liable to be destroyed by the enemy. He desires you to take the whole matter in charge, and trusts that in the event that there shall be occasion to rapidly rebuild any of these structures you will be prepared for the emergency.

> [F. A. SHOUP,
> *Chief of Staff.*]

> HEADQUARTERS HARDEE'S CORPS,
> *August 10, 1864—11 p. m.*

General CLEBURNE:

GENERAL: General Hardee directs me to say he wishes your artillery to open upon any force of the enemy that may attempt to intrench in the open ground in front of your line.

Respectfully,

> T. B. ROY,
> *Assistant Adjutant-General.*

> ATLANTA, *August 10, 1864—12.15 p. m.*

General HOWELL COBB, *Macon, Ga.:*

General Hood desires to know the strength of your garrison at Andersonville, exclusive of the militia; also the number of men you can depend upon to defend Macon in case of emergency.

> [F. A. SHOUP,
> *Chief of Staff.*]

> HDQRS. DEPARTMENT OF ALA., MISS., AND EAST LA.,
> *Meridian, August 10, 1864.*

Brig. Gen. D. W. ADAMS, *Childersville:*

GENERAL: I am directed by Major-General Maury to say that since his telegram to you relative to Brigadier-General Roddey's brigade he has received from General Bragg a letter so strongly insisting upon that command being kept in North Alabama that he does not feel at liberty to remove it at the present time. General Maury has a communication from General Hood urging him to send small parties of cavalry to Sherman's rear for the purpose of operating against his communications. He intrusts you with organizing such expeditions out of Brigadier-General Roddey's command, and hopes that you will lose no unnecessary time in inaugurating such a system of raids upon Sherman's communications as would prove most beneficial to the grand result. You have been ordered by telegraph to send any mounted troops, other than General Roddey's command, that you may have to Artesia, to report to Major-General Forrest; also to send the Tuscaloosa Cadets, to report to Col. H. Maury, at Pollard, Ala. Please forward to General Maury the reports of new companies as fast as they are organized.

Very respectfully, your obedient servant,

> W. F. BULLOCK,
> *Assistant Adjutant-General.*

[AUGUST 10, 1864.—For the strength of Hood's army, see Part III, p. 681.]

ATLANTA, GA., *August 11, 1864.*

Hon. J. A. SEDDON:

There was no material change in affairs yesterday.   I regret to report Major-General Bate was wounded.

J. B. HOOD.

———

ATLANTA, *August 11, 1864.*

Hon. J. A. SEDDON:

Your telegram of yesterday is received.   When I assumed command of this army General Johnston had accepted the services of the Georgia militia.   Since that time they have been under my orders as much as any other troops in the army.   Rations and forage have and are now being issued to them.   They furnish now about 5,000 muskets in the trenches here.   If it be required of the State to ration and forage these troops it is important that officers of the Confederate States should continue to issue such supplies now, and that the State return the supplies hereafter to the Confederate Government, either in kind or value.

J. B. HOOD,
General.

[First indorsement.]

AUGUST 12, 1864.

Respectfully submitted for the information of the President.

JAMES A. SEDDON,
Secretary of War.

[Second indorsement.]

Referred to General Bragg.

Militia when mustered into service are entitled to the pay and allowance of other troops, and are also to be exchanged, if captured, as other prisoners of war.   They are to be received with their State organization, officers, &c., the only restriction being that the organization shall conform to the laws of the Confederate States.

J. D.

[Third indorsement.]

HDQRS. ARMIES OF THE CONFEDERATE STATES,
August 16, 1864.

Respectfully returned to His Excellency the President.

When I was in Atlanta the Georgia militia had not been mustered into the Confederate service, and were not so organized as to admit of such musters.   The greatest evil of their supply, however, existed in the rear of the army where they were assembling, and where they were being subsisted without any apparent authority, and before they were at all prepared for any service.

BRAXTON BRAGG,
General.

[Fourth indorsement.]

SECRETARY OF WAR:

The case is not sufficiently understood for action.   It would be well to correspond with General Hood.   It is desirable to get every aid which can be obtained, but to make it efficient the force should be under military law.

J. D.

ATLANTA, *August 11, 1864.*

General S. COOPER:

General Loring will be able for duty in a few days. Have assigned Major-General Brown to command of Bate's division. Bate's wounds will, I fear, cause him to be absent some time. I desire your approval.

J. B. HOOD,
General.

AUGUST 11, 1864—1.45 p. m.
(Received 3.45 p. m.)

Lieut. Gen. S. D. LEE,
Commanding Corps:

The general directs me to say that he thinks you had better build traverses, every ten paces if necessary, to protect your men from the artillery fire of the enemy.

[F. A. SHOUP,
Chief of Staff.]

AUGUST 11, 1864—12 m.

Brig. Gen. W. H. JACKSON,
Commanding Cavalry Division:

As yet, only a small portion of General Morgan's command has arrived on the right. As soon as the entire command arrives the First Mississippi Regiment will be ordered back to you. For fear the matter may escape me, however, please repeat the application in a few days.

[F. A. SHOUP,
Chief of Staff.]

AUGUST 11, 1864.

Colonel COLE,
Inspector-General Field Transportation, C. S. Army:

The general commanding requires the services of 4,000 negroes for teamsters and other services in this army. He requests you to undertake the duty of having them procured, and, to accomplish it with as little delay as possible, he has directed as many officers detailed from this army to report to you as you may require for that purpose. He further delegates to you all power vested in him by law to order impressment of negroes.

[F. A. SHOUP,
Chief of Staff.]

HEADQUARTERS ARMY OF TENNESSEE,
INSPECTOR-GENERAL'S OFFICE,
Near Atlanta, Ga., August 11, 1864.

General R. H. CHILTON,
Assistant Adjutant and Inspector General, Richmond, Va.:

GENERAL: I have the honor to acknowledge the receipt of your communication of the 31st ultimo, calling my attention to General Orders, No. 42,* the requirements of which have not as yet been complied with.

---

*Of April 14, 1864, requiring monthly inspection reports from the different Confederate States armies.

In explanation of this apparent neglect of duty on my part I beg leave, respectfully, to state that since the reception of this order at these headquarters this army has been constantly in motion, undergoing the most tedious and harassing campaign that has been experienced since the war commened. Commanding generals and inspectors both united in urging me to suspend carrying into effect the paragraphs of this order, stating that it was impossible to make the inspections called for. Believing this to be the case myself, the order was not complied with. I should have written you to this effect, and would have done so but for the care and trouble attendant upon my position. I beg to assure you, general, that I did not intentionally fail to comply with the provisions of this order, and to assure you further that the reports called for shall be forwarded without any unnecessary delay.

Very respectfully, your obedient servant,

E. J. HARVIE,
Colonel and Assistant Inspector-General, Army of Tennessee.

GENERAL FIELD ORDERS, }   HDQRS. ARMY OF TENNESSEE,
No. 13.   }   *In the Field, August 11, 1864.*

Capt. James Cooper, First Louisiana Infantry [Regulars], is assigned to duty at army headquarters as acting assistant adjutant-general. He will be obeyed and respected as such.

By command of General Hood:

A. P. MASON,
Major and Assistant Adjutant-General.

ATLANTA, *August 12, 1864.*

Hon. J. A. SEDDON:

There was no material change in affairs yesterday. Wheeler, with his command, left on the 10th for Sherman's rear.

J. B. HOOD,
General.

ATLANTA, *August 12, 1864—2 p. m.*

General S. COOPER,
Richmond, Va.:

I desire that Col. Joseph B. Palmer, Eighteenth Tennessee Regiment, be given temporary rank to command Brown's brigade; also the appointment of Col. Robert J. Henderson, Forty-second Georgia, to command Stovall's brigade. General Wright is not able to take the field.

J. B. HOOD,
General.

AUGUST 12, 1864—1.15 a. m.
(Received 2 a. m.)

Major-General CHEATHAM:

The general commanding directs that you cause General Scott's brigade to move by daylight to occupy the strong work at East Point. You will also please send a battery from that part of your line where it can be best spared to follow General Scott. Please fill vacancy thus created by a section from some other battery. General S., when in position, will report to General Cleburne.

[F. A. SHOUP,
Chief of Staff.]

AUGUST 12, 1864—2.45 p. m.

Brigadier-General MANEY,
    Commanding, &c.:

General Hood directs me to say that Vaughan's brigade is ready to go to your support if you think it necessary. He thinks you had better move some of your batteries farther to the right, but use your best judgment. The general thinks the movement on the right is intended to deceive. Please watch it closely.

[F. A. SHOUP,
Chief of Staff.]

HEADQUARTERS HARDEE'S CORPS,
August 12, 1864.

General CLEBURNE:

GENERAL: A report from the cavalry, and which General Jackson thinks entitled to some consideration, is as follows: The Fourteenth Corps moved up behind Schofield's corps last evening, and deserters say will, in conjunction with that, attack and attempt to force a way to the railroad to-day (12th).

Respectfully,

T. B. ROY,
Assistant Adjutant-General.

HEADQUARTERS HARDEE'S CORPS,
August 12, 1864.

[Maj. Gen. P. R. CLEBURNE:]

GENERAL: General Hardee desires you, wherever it is practicable, to keep one regiment of each brigade in reserve behind that brigade. General Hood thinks the enemy will attack to-morrow. General Hardee directs me to say he has found that the picket duty has been done very neglectfully on some parts of Bate's line; he takes it for granted that you have your picket-line regularly inspected.

Respectfully,

T. B. ROY,
Assistant Adjutant-General.

AUGUST 12, 1864—4 o'clock.

Maj. E. S. BURFORD,
    Assistant Adjutant-General, Wheeler's Corps:

SIR: I am moving my command to Frogtown in obedience to orders from General Wheeler, received at Brown's Bridge. This order, however, stated that General Kelly would cross Etowah River above Frogtown, and General Martin would cross at Frogtown. We find that General Martin's command has taken the road leading to the river above Frogtown, while General Kelly takes the road to Frogtown.

Very respectfully, your obedient servant,

W. Y. C. HUMES,
Brigadier-General.

AUGUST 12, 1864—10.45 a. m.

General MORGAN,
Commanding Cavalry:

Let the wagons of General Wheeler's command go to some point below Griffin. Direct a careful lookout for raids, and that in the event of the approach of raiders the train shall move out of the way. Let the troops and artillery come to you at once.

[F. A. SHOUP,
Chief of Staff.]

AUGUST 12, 1864—10 p. m.

Brig. Gen. W. H. JACKSON,
Commanding Cavalry Division:

If you are driven back to-morrow General Hood desires you to leave at least one good regiment to garrison the redoubt at East Point in the event that General Hardee has not troops there for that purpose.

[F. A. SHOUP,
Chief of Staff.]

AUGUST 12, 1864.

Maj. Gen. D. H. MAURY,
Enterprise, Miss.:

Who are you sending; to what point; and what strength to operate on Sherman's rear?

J. B. HOOD,
General.

AUGUST 12, 1864.

Maj. Gen. D. H. MAURY,
Mobile, Ala.:

I have sent strong cavalry force to operate on railroads in Sherman's rear. Better inform your cavalry.

J. B. HOOD,
General.

MOBILE, *August 12, 1864.*

General D. W. ADAMS,
Commanding Northern and Central Alabama:

MY DEAR GENERAL: I have just seen General Roddey's recently-received orders from General Bragg prohibiting me from removing him from his allotted sphere of action in Alabama. Forrest reports yesterday enemy not pressing forward in Mississippi. I am exceedingly anxious to aid in cutting Sherman's communication. Roddey thinks he can do it. I hope you will be able to send him and others on that service without interfering with other objects of your command. Things are very exciting here, but I believe all will come out right; the people are at last aroused to a sense of duty and danger, except the non-combatants, who will not go away. How does the railroad work go on? Push it forward.

Yours,

DABNEY H. MAURY.

GENERAL FIELD ORDERS, }   HDQRS. ARMY OF TENNESSEE,
       No. 14.   }   *In the Field, August 12, 1864.*

I. The lawless seizure and destruction of private property by straggling soldiers in the rear and on the flanks of this army has become intolerable. It must come to an end. It is believed to be chargeable to worthless men, especially from mounted commands, who are odious alike to the citizen and the well-disposed soldier. Citizens and soldiers are, therefore, called upon to arrest and forward to the provost-marshal-general all persons guilty of wanton destruction or illegal seizure of property, that examples may be immediately made. The laws of war justify the execution of such offenders, and those laws shall govern.

II. Officers are held responsible that their men conduct themselves properly. In any case where it is shown that an officer, high or low, has permitted or failed to take proper steps to prevent such depredations as those complained of herein, he shall be deprived of his commission.

III. Hereafter all cavalry horses must be branded. Division and brigade commanders will determine the manner so as to best designate the commands to which they belong. No purchase or exchange of horses will be permitted except by authority of the company and regimental commanders. In each case of such purchase or exchange the soldier must receive a written statement of the transaction. Any soldier otherwise introducing a horse into any command will be immediately arrested. General, field, and company officers are expected, and, are earnestly requested, to give this matter their attention. Officers failing must be arrested. In procuring forage, the least possible damage must be done the farmer. Too much attention cannot be given this. At best he is compelled to suffer.

IV. Citizens are warned not to purchase from or exchange horses with soldiers, except when the authority for the transaction is previously had from the company and regimental commanders. Otherwise they may lose their property and will fail to receive the support of the military authorities.

By command of General Hood:

A. P. MASON,
Major and Assistant Adjutant-General.

GENERAL ORDERS, }   HEADQUARTERS LEE'S CORPS,
     No. 63.   }   *Phillips' House, August 12, 1864.*

The lieutenant-general commanding is gratified with the gallantry and determination displayed by the skirmishers of this corps in resisting the numerous attacks upon them. In one of the charges of the enemy some of Deas' and Brantly's skirmishers allowed themselves to be bayoneted in the pits rather than be driven back. The skirmishers of Gibson's brigade on the 5th, and of Baker's on the 7th, permitted half of their number to be killed, wounded, and captured before the others would leave their position. These few instances of heroism out of many are mentioned with the hope that they may be imitated rather than permit the enemy to approach our main line.

By command of Lieutenant-General Lee:

J. W. RATCHFORD,
Assistant Adjutant-General.

CIRCULAR.] HEADQUARTERS LEE'S CORPS,
Phillips' House, August 12, 1864.

Hereafter, instead of arousing the men in the trenches at 3 a. m., it will not be done until 3.45, when only half of them will be awakened. The other half will be allowed to sleep unless movements of the enemy make it necessary to awaken them. The attention of commanding officers is called to the number of men killed and wounded in the trenches.

Every effort will be taken to prevent the loss of life by building traverses and using every means that may suggest themselves.

By command of Lieutenant-General Lee:

J. W. RATCHFORD,
Assistant Adjutant-General.

AUGUST 13, 1864.

Hon. J. A. SEDDON,
Richmond, Va.:

The enemy extended his right a little yesterday.

J. B. HOOD,
General.

AUGUST 13, 1864.

Hon. J. A. SEDDON,
Richmond, Va.:

The enemy's extension to their right reported yesterday is withdrawn. Lieutenant-General Stewart returned to duty to-day.

J. B. HOOD,
General.

AUGUST 13, 1864—11.40 a. m.
(Received 1.45 p. m.)

Lieutenant-General HARDEE,
Commanding Corps:

General Jackson has been directed to occupy the redoubts at East Point with at least one good regiment in the event that he is driven back, and you cannot furnish troops for that purpose. Colonel Presstman's regiment engineer troops, say 600 strong, is also instructed to occupy that work.

[F. A. SHOUP,
Chief of Staff.]

AUGUST 13, 1864—6.30 p. m.

General HARDEE, *Commanding, &c.:*

General Hood desires you to send the brigade you now have of Cheatham's to report back to its command. If all is quiet, please ride in this evening.

[F. A. SHOUP,
Chief of Staff.]

HEADQUARTERS LEE'S CORPS,
Phillips' House, August 13, 1864.

[Maj. Gen. H. D. CLAYTON:]

GENERAL: The lieutenant-general commanding directs me to inform you that the truce still exists between your pickets and the enemy, and he desires that a reliable officer be placed in command of them who will see that they do their duty. It is also reported by a prisoner there is an understanding between Stovall's pickets and those of the enemy that when they do fire they are not to fire to take effect, but to shoot over each others' heads. He wishes this matter looked into, and if any man is found firing intentionally too high, he will be sent under guard to these headquarters.

He wishes all intercourse whatever stopped at once.

Respectfully, your obedient servant,
J. W. RATCHFORD,
Assistant Adjutant-General.

AUGUST 13, 1864—6 p. m.

General JACKSON, *Commanding Cavalry:*

The general desires you to push your scouts well in rear of the enemy to night, to try to ascertain what has become of the corps on the right, and what the enemy is doing.

[F. A. SHOUP,
Chief of Staff.]

CIRCULAR.]   AUGUST 13, 1864—11.30 a. m.

General Hood desires that you impress upon your officers and men the absolute necessity of holding the lines they occupy, to the very last. He feels perfectly confident that, with the obstructions in their front, and the artillery to break his masses, the enemy cannot carry our works, however many lines he may advance against them, and however determined may be his assaults, so long as the men occupy the trenches, and use their rifles. Let every man remember that he is individually responsible for his few feet of line, and that the destiny of Atlanta hangs upon the issue.

[F. A. SHOUP,
Chief of Staff.]

CIRCULAR.]   HEADQUARTERS LEE'S CORPS,
Phillips' House, August 13, 1864.

It has been reported to these headquarters that, contrary to orders, intercourse between our pickets and those of the enemy is still kept up, and in some instances it has been agreed that they shall not fire at each other with intent to kill, but to shoot over each others' heads. A stop must be put to these proceedings, and any one found so offending will be sent to these headquarters. Artillery officers and men in the trenches are directed to fire upon any man, or group of men, who are discovered holding communication with the enemy.

By command of Lieutenant-General Lee:

J. W. RATCHFORD,
Assistant Adjutant-General.

AUGUST 14, 1864—7.30 p. m.

Lieutenant-General HARDEE,
        Commanding Corps:

General Hood desires me to thank you for your note touching the probable movement of the enemy.

He has directed all parties to keep an unusually sharp lookout to-night. He thinks the lines about equally strong. Has directed Scott's brigade to support Featherston's and French's lines, to which the enemy is nearest. Probably the enemy would try to maintain his skirmishers in the position taken to-night to protect him where his line now is.

[F. A. SHOUP,
Chief of Staff.]

AUGUST 14, 1864—10 p. m.

Lieutenant-General HARDEE,
        Commanding Corps:

Your dispatch of — p. m. received. General Hood says he can send you force enough to occupy the position you indicate for Jackson. Jackson is ordered to take the position until he can be relieved. Please find inclosed* the last information from Jackson.

[F. A. SHOUP,
Chief of Staff.]

AUGUST 14, 1864—10 p. m.
(Received 12.50 a. m. 15th.)

General JACKSON,
        Commanding, &c.:

General Hood desires you to occupy, in the event that the enemy attempt to turn our left, as much of the line to the right and left of the Newnan road as possible, till he can send troops to take your place.

[F. A. SHOUP,
Chief of Staff.]

GENERAL ORDERS, ⎰ HDQRS. ROSS' BRIG., JACKSON'S CAV. DIV.,
    No. 16.   ⎱   *In the Field, Ga., August 14, 1864.*

I. The men and officers of this brigade are hereby warned that henceforth the general orders from Army Headquarters and from the War Department, forbidding depredations will be most rigidly enforced in this command. Under existing regulations a cavalryman may be trans-

---

* Inclosure not found.

ferred to infantry upon the request of his company, regiment, or brigade commander, accompanied by the simple statement that said soldier has been guilty of committing depredations upon private property or is "inefficient as a cavalryman." It is determined, therefore, that no excuse will hereafter be accepted from any one caught invading unpurchased corn-fields, or interfering with private property of any kind whatever, but the offender will be transferred direct to the infantry and his horse and equipments reserved for the use of some more worthy soldier.

II. When forage is to be procured in the country regular details must go for it, accompanied by an officer, who will be responsible for the conduct and behavior of his men. Individuals are prohibited from bringing forage into camps except when properly detailed for such duty and accompanied by an officer as herein provided.

III. Commanding officers are required to publish orders received to all the members of their respective commands. If, therefore, any one caught infringing upon the rights of citizens should plead ignorance of this order, his company commander will be held accountable unless he can make it appear that he himself has not heard it, in which case the regimental commander must bear the consequences of having failed to make known an important general order to his command.

IV. The provost-marshal of brigade will endeavor to detect and arrest all offenders henceforth against the rights of citizens with a view to the prompt punishment by transfer to infantry.

By order of Brigadier-General Ross:

> D. R. GURLEY,
> *Assistant Adjutant-General.*

AUGUST 15, 1864—4.45 p. m.

Brigadier-General FERGUSON,
   Commanding, &c.:

Your dispatch 3.10 p. m. received. General Hood directs that you oppose the enemy's cavalry if he advances on your position. At Cobb's Mill you have a good position to hold him in check if he advances that far; if he retires, follow him up with your scouts and watch his movements closely to-night. Keep General Hood advised.

> [F. A. SHOUP,
> *Chief of Staff.*]

ATLANTA, *August 15, 1864—8.05 p. m.*

COMMANDING OFFICER,
   Jonesborough:

Send out small parties in the direction of Fairburn. Let them picket all the roads leading from Fairburn in the direction of Jonesborough and Fayetteville. Let them start to-night and go as near Fairburn as possible. I desire information of a force of the enemy moving in that direction. Let part of the pickets remain in observation of the enemy, while others bear dispatches to you. Captain Carey will use his signal corps for this purpose.

> J. B. HOOD,
> *General.*

ATLANTA, *August 15, 1864—8.15 p. m.*

Brig. Gen. M. J. WRIGHT,
    Macon, Ga.:

A force of the enemy moved this evening from Sandtown in the direction of Fairburn. Its strength and destination have not yet been ascertained. Retain whatever militia there may be at Macon until we know further.

[J. B. HOOD,
General.]

SPECIAL ORDERS, }   ADJT. AND INSP. GENERAL'S OFFICE,
    No. 192.   }   *Richmond, Va., August 15, 1864.*

*   *   *   *   *   *

XIII. The Department of Tennessee* commanded by General John B. Hood, Provisional Army, C. S., is extended to include all the State of Georgia north and west of the following line: Commencing at Augusta and running along the line of the Augusta and Savannah Railroad to Millen, thence along the western boundary lines of the counties of Bulloch and Tattnall, thence along the south bank of the Ocmulgee River to the northeast corner of Irwin County, thence south to the Florida line, thence along the Florida line to the Appalachicola River. The command will hereafter be known as the Department of Tennessee and Georgia.

*   *   *   *   *   *   *

By command of the Secretary of War:

SAML. W. MELTON,
Assistant Adjutant-General.

GENERAL FIELD ORDERS, }   HDQRS. ARMY OF TENNESSEE,
        No. 15.   }   *In the Field, August 15, 1864.*

Notwithstanding reiterated orders forbidding communication with the enemy, it is reported that certain commands have been guilty of this offense on the picket-line. The commanding general is persuaded that this arises from no desire on the part of the soldiers to injure our cause, but from ignorance of the consequences. He, therefore, reluctantly, but most positively, orders that all parties, friends or foes, who shall in any way communicate or attempt to communicate with the enemy without authority, be fired upon by all parties in reach, and further that any officer so offending, or in any manner permitting such offense, shall be immediately sent to the rear in charge of a guard for immediate trial. If the officer in command of pickets finds it necessary at night, he may keep up such fire as he deems expedient to prevent this evil, always informing his immediate superior of the occasion of his fire.

By command of General Hood:

KINLOCH FALCONER,
Assistant Adjutant-General.

---

* See Special Orders, No. 71, Adjutant and Inspector General's Office, Richmond, March 25, 1864, Vol. XXXII, Part III, p. 673.

ATLANTA, *August 16, 1864.*

Hon. J. A. SEDDON:

No change in affairs in the past few days. Yesterday evening a small party of the enemy's cavalry made a dash in Fairburn, on the West Point railroad, and burned the depot, but retreated immediately.

J. B. HOOD,
General.

ATLANTA, GA., *August 16, 1864.*

General BRAXTON BRAGG, *Richmond, Va.:*

Major-General French having applied to be relieved from duty with this army, Lieutenant-General Stewart and myself respectfully request that his application be granted, and that Maj. Gen. Edward Johnson, who is now ordered here, may command his division.

J. B. HOOD,
General.

HEADQUARTERS DEPARTMENT OF TENNESSEE,
Near Atlanta, Ga., August 16, 1864.

General S. COOPER,
Adjutant and Inspector General, Richmond, Va.:

GENERAL: I have had the honor to receive your letter of July 28 in regard to the recommendation for the promotion of Brig. Gen. W. H. Jackson to the rank of major-general. Inclosed I send the organization of his command.* The cavalry commanded by Brigadier-General Jackson came here with Lieutenant-General Polk, as a part of the Army of the Mississippi. As all the troops which came at that time, however, have been decided by the War Department to belong to this army, I think that Major-General Wheeler (as the commander of all the cavalry of this army) should now designate who of those available should be selected to be major-generals of cavalry. The matter will receive attention on the return of General Wheeler.

I am, sir, very respectfully, your obedient servant,

J. B. HOOD,
General.

AUGUST 16, 1864—11.25 a. m.

Lieutenant-General HARDEE, *Commanding:*

GENERAL: The report of picket officers in Armstrong's front this morning is that the enemy have extended their works last night along the Campbellton road to Holbrook's. The infantry picket three or four miles lower down that road. The enemy, as you will see, is now in position to turn our left by a rapid advance. I would, therefore, suggest that the left of our infantry line be extended at once to cover East Point, as it will certainly be necessary for me to draw out Armstrong to look after that force opposing Ross in the vicinity of Fairburn.

Respectfully,

W. H. JACKSON,
Brigadier-General, Commanding Cavalry.

I have made the same suggestions to General Hood.

W. H. J.

---

* Not found.

AUGUST 16, 1864—8.30 p. m.

Lieutenant-General HARDEE,
       Commanding Corps, &c.:

The pioneer parties have already gone to you. If you have not done so, please inform General Cleburne that they are to report to him.

[F. A. SHOUP,
Chief of Staff.]

AUGUST 16, 1864—2.10 p. m.
(Received 2.30 p. m.)

Lieut. Gen. A. P. STEWART,
       Commanding Corps, &c.:

General Hood directs me to say that he has ordered Scott's brigade to East Point to form on the left of Lieutenant-General Hardee. The enemy are reported to be advancing in that direction.

[F. A. SHOUP,
Chief of Staff.]

AUGUST 16, 1864—2.10 p. m.
(Received 2.35 p. m.)

Lieutenant-General LEE,
       Commanding Corps, &c.:

If General Hardee should call upon you for your reserve regiments, please send them to him. The enemy is apparently moving upon our left.

[F. A. SHOUP,
Chief of Staff.]

HEADQUARTERS CAVALRY CORPS,
Near Spring Place, August 16, 1864.

General F. A. SHOUP,
       Chief of Staff:

GENERAL: Colonel Thompson destroyed railroad near Big Shanty for one mile on Friday night. Colonel Hannon, commanding brigade, destroyed the railroad near Calhoun on Saturday night, capturing 1,020 beef-cattle and a few wagons. Allen's brigade and Humes' and Kelly's divisions destroyed the railroad for several miles between Resaca and Tunnel Hill, and Kelly's and parts of Humes' commands captured Dalton Sunday evening with a considerable amount of stores, 3 trains of cars, and 200 fine mules. The train and part of the stores were destroyed and the remainder appropriated.

Prisoners report re-enforcements at Chattanooga, said to be part of A. J. Smith's troops. On Monday morning we were attacked by General Steedman with about 4,000 infantry, and obliged to leave Dalton. Our entire loss up to this time about 30, most of them still with the command.

The most violent rains have embarrassed me very much, and made some of the roads very bad. The large force sent from Chattanooga prevented our working at the tunnel. I have several parties still working at the railroad.

Respectfully, your obedient servant,

JOS. WHEELER,
Major-General.

AUGUST 16, 1864—1.40 p. m.

Brig. Gen. W. H. JACKSON,
          Commanding, &c.:

Your dispatch of 11.25 received. The general says he will send you Pinson's regiment when clearly necessary. To-morrow he hopes to send them any way, as General Iverson will probably bring up some of Wheeler's people from Griffin. He thinks the force you speak of over-estimated; that Ross, with the regiment you sent him last night, can take care of them. Let him look to them closely, and hold yourself in readiness to move to his assistance; in case you do so move the general would like to see you here while your command is preparing to move.

                              [F. A. SHOUP,
                                   Chief of Staff.]

          HDQRS. ROSS' BRIGADE, JACKSON'S CAVALRY DIVISION,
                    Wolf Creek, Ga., August 16, 1864—5.20 p. m.

Brigadier-General JACKSON, *Commanding Division:*

GENERAL: The force in my front is cavalry so far as developed. The principal part of it has gone in direction of Fairburn. I think the force here only intended to attract attention. I shall, therefore, leave only a squadron to skirmish with it, and move with the balance of my command to join Colonel Jones, between the enemy and Fairburn. I have directed the regiment left at Mount Gilead Church to join me at Fairburn, leaving a company of thirty men at the church subject to your orders. I would be pleased to have that company relieved and ordered to overtake me to-night, should the enemy be intending a raid.

I am, general, very respectfully, your obedient servant,
                              L. S. ROSS,
                                   Brigadier-General, &c.

          HDQRS. ROSS' BRIGADE, JACKSON'S CAVALRY DIVISION,
                    Fairburn, Ga., August 16, 1864—9.30 p. m.

Brigadier-General JACKSON, *Commanding Division:*

GENERAL: The enemy have gone back, being closely pursued by a portion of my command which entered this place soon after the enemy retired. They burnt the depot buildings, but did little damage to the road. The force is estimated at two regiments. About 200 came to this place in a sweeping gallop, while the remainder made demonstrations on all the flanking roads. They certainly had an infantry force that came as far as Owl Rock Church, but no farther. The enemy's advance was so rapid that my scouts in their rear could not get to the front in time to report, and those who kept in their immediate front were overrun, hence my difficulty and delay in ascertaining their force, &c. Upon my arrival at this place I was led to believe that this force was only a flanking party, and I sent forward a portion of my command to Palmetto to prevent any move upon the road at that point. Colonel Jones, who had been ordered to intercept the enemy at this place, got within a mile or two and found the enemy occupying it, and he turned to the left with intention of gaining their supposed front on the Fayetteville road. I have no report from him.

I am, general, very respectfully, your obedient servant,
                              L. S. ROSS,
                                   Brigadier-General.

AUGUST 16, 1864—10 a. m.

Brigadier-General FERGUSON,
　　　Commanding, &c.:

General Hood desires that you send out scouts as far to your right and rear as possible, and that you watch all small parties moving in the direction of Monticello. He is exceedingly anxious to obtain information of the enemy's movements in that quarter. Your dispatch of this morning received.

　　　　　　　　　　　　[F. A. SHOUP,
　　　　　　　　　　　　　　Chief of Staff.]

———

ATLANTA, *August 16, 1864—2 p. m.*

Governor J. E. BROWN,
　　　Milledgeville:

General Wright has been directed to hold the militia at present, as the enemy seems to be threatening a raid on our left from the direction of Campbellton. Can you not replace the men at Andersonville with militia from some quarter of the State other than that?

　　　　　　　　　　　　[J. B. HOOD,
　　　　　　　　　　　　　　General.]

———

ATLANTA, *August 16, 1864—7 p. m.*

Governor J. E. BROWN,
　　　Milledgeville, Ga.:

Fairburn raid amounted to nothing, but the enemy's cavalry still hover in that direction. Retain the militia until further orders.

　　　　　　　　　　　　[J. B. HOOD,
　　　　　　　　　　　　　　General.]

———

AUGUST 16, 1864—2 p. m.
(Received 2.15 p. m.)

Maj. Gen. G. W. SMITH,
　　　Commanding Georgia Militia, &c.:

General Hood desires me to say that he has information that the enemy has withdrawn his dismounted cavalry on our left in front of General Strahl, replacing it with a small division of infantry.

　　　　　　　　　　　　[F. A. SHOUP,
　　　　　　　　　　　　　　Chief of Staff.]

———

HEADQUARTERS PICKET,
August 16, 1864.

Captain MOORE:

This morning the enemy's fortifications are plainly visible on the Campbellton road as far down as the house next below Herron's. Their skirmish line was advanced in the night to the hollow and woods this side Campbellton road. Their works are well built, and regular fortifications with rifle-pits in front. No movement in front.

　　　Respectfully,

　　　　　　　　　　　　J. J. PERRY,
　　　　　　　　　　　　　　Major.

HEADQUARTERS ARMY OF TENNESSEE,
August 17, 1864—10.20 [p. m.].

General HARDEE, *Commanding, &c.:*

It is reported that the enemy is moving on our right; that twenty-seven flags have been seen to pass in that direction. General Hood desires you to notify Scott's brigade to be in readiness to move by rail at dawn, if it should prove necessary. Cars will be prepared; also that you hold all the rest of your disposable force ready to move if need be.

Very respectfully, &c.,

F. A. SHOUP,
Chief of Staff.

[Indorsement.]

Have Scott's brigade under arms at daylight so that it may move at a moment's notice.

W. J. HARDEE,
Lieutenant-General, &c.

———

AUGUST 17, 1864—10.50 p. m.

Lieutenant-General LEE, *Commanding Corps, &c.:*

General Stewart is directed to open fire on the enemy at daylight. It is reported that the enemy are moving on our right; that twenty-seven flags have passed in that direction. The general desires that you hold all your reserves ready to move at dawn.

[F. A. SHOUP,
Chief of Staff.]

———

HEADQUARTERS STEWART'S CORPS,
Atlanta, August 17, 1864—11 p. m.

Major-General FRENCH, *Commanding Division:*

GENERAL: The lieutenant-general commanding directs me to inform you that the artillery on your line has been ordered to open fire on the enemy to-morrow morning at sunrise, and to fire four rounds from each piece at intervals of ten minutes. You will notify your officers on the skirmish line, and direct them to observe closely the effect of the fire, and report the result, which you will communicate to these headquarters.

Respectfully, your obedient servant,

DOUGLAS WEST,
Acting Assistant Adjutant-General.

———

AUGUST 17, 1864.
(Received 12.30 p. m.)

Brigadier-General JACKSON, *Commanding Cavalry, &c.:*

General Ferguson reports that the enemy on our right is engaged in gathering bacon, &c. The general thinks they are now doing or may do the same thing on the left. It is important to prevent them from gathering supplies. Please watch them closely and prevent it as far as possible, without too much risk to yourself.

[F. A. SHOUP,
Chief of Staff.]

AUGUST 17, 1864—3.20 p. m.

Brigadier-General JACKSON,
    Commanding Cavalry, &c.:

General Hood is anxious to know what the enemy means by fortifying on the other side of the river—on the Sweet Water. Please instruct your scouts to give their attention to this.

                                        [F. A. SHOUP,
                                            Chief of Staff.]

HDQRS. ROSS' BRIGADE, JACKSON'S CAVALRY DIVISION,
    Fairburn, Ga., August 17, 1864—5.30 a. m.

Brigadier-General JACKSON,
    Commanding Division:

GENERAL: Scouts from the vicinity of Bethel Church reported the enemy about 9 p. m. in camps or halted, and building fires, and that drums were heard among them. I left scouts on all the roads by which they could approach East Point, and have sent scouts this morning in every direction. The force following the cavalry which came here became divided; only a few scouts followed in rear, and they reported about 2.30 a. m. that the enemy had halted. I will move back toward East Point three or four miles, as it may be possible that a force in the vicinity of Bethel Church may move in that direction this morning. None of my scouts from the rear of the enemy have reported to me, and I know nothing as to his strength farther than has been developed and reported by me. I suppose they have been reporting to you.

I am, general, very respectfully, your obedient servant,

                                        L. S. ROSS,
                                            Brigadier-General.

HEADQUARTERS HUMES' CAVALRY DIVISION,
    Savannah Farm, August 17, 1864—9.15 a. m.

Maj. W. E. WAILES,
    Assistant Adjutant-General:

MAJOR: I regret very much that by my march to this place, which was made in obedience to orders, I have incurred the displeasure of the major-general commanding. I regret also that neither your dispatch nor the courier who bore it gives me any information of the whereabouts of General Wheeler. A scout from Athens reports thirty-seven men at that place. Citizens report a small force at Charleston, and a concentration of forces from Knoxville and Chattanooga at Cleveland. I would be glad to be informed how long I am to wait here for General Wheeler, and if driven from here where I may be able probably to join him. I have been most anxious to join him.

Very respectfully, &c.,

                                        W. Y. C. HUMES,
                                            Brigadier-General.

HEADQUARTERS ARMY OF TENNESSEE,
    Atlanta, Ga., August 17, 1864.

Maj. Gen. SAMUEL JONES,
    Commanding, &c., Charleston, S. C.:

If the enemy again attempt to release the prisoners at Andersonville it will be a determined effort. In such an event I request that you send whatever troops you can spare for the occasion to defeat it. I desire you also to assist me against any movement toward Augusta. The enemy has shown some signs of undertaking another raid. I send this lest the lines should be cut at any time.

J. B. HOOD,
General.

ATLANTA, August 17, 1864.

Brig. Gen. JOHN H. WINDER,
                Andersonville:

General Hood desires to know how the fortifications for the safety of the prisoners are progressing. Do you feel secure, and can the 500 militia there be spared?

[F. A. SHOUP,
Chief of Staff.]

ATLANTA, August 18, 1864.

Hon. J. A. SEDDON:

Exaggerated statements of the losses of this army since I assumed command having been made in reports of Federal commanders, I send the following statement: The effective strength of the army when I assumed command was, of all arms, 49,012; effective strength by last report, 43,091; decrease, 5,921. Re-enforcements proper since I assumed command have been sent back.

J. B. HOOD,
General.

ATLANTA, August 18, 1864—10.10 p. m.

General B. BRAGG,
                Richmond, Va.:

Gholson's brigade, which ought to be 1,200 or 1,500 strong, has less than 300 men. I desire the remainder with the horses of the command ordered here.

[J. B. HOOD,
General.]

HEADQUARTERS HARDEE'S CORPS,
August 18, 1864—12.30 [a. m.].

[General CLEBURNE:]

GENERAL: In consequence of a movement of the enemy on our right, General Hood directs that Scott's brigade be put under arms at daylight in the morning, and held in readiness to move to-morrow. General Hardee suggests that you put yourself in communication with the telegraph office at East Point. We have a courier there who can be used. General Hood has been requested to communicate direct with you.

Respectfully, yours,

T. B. ROY,
Assistant Adjutant-General.

HEADQUARTERS JACKSON'S CAVALRY DIVISION,
August 18, 1864—2.30 p. m.

Major-General CLEBURNE:

GENERAL: General Armstrong reports at 12 m. that the enemy had driven Colonel Pinson, First Mississippi, back to the forks of the road, and were still pressing him in strong force. General Ross' scouts report the enemy, both infantry and cavalry, to be at Sandtown and Campbellton, and fortified, but no demonstrations of an advance visible.

By order of Brig. Gen. W. H. Jackson:

E. T. SYKES,
Assistant Adjutant-General.

HEADQUARTERS HARDEE'S CORPS,
August 18, 1864.

General CLEBURNE:

GENERAL: General Hardee says, as there seems to be no prospect of an immediate call for Scott's brigade, you had as well use it to push your work.

Yours, respectfully,

T. B. ROY,
Assistant Adjutant-General.

HEADQUARTERS HARDEE'S CORPS,
August 18, 1864.

General CLEBURNE:

GENERAL: General Hardee directs me to say that General Hood wishes you to be ready to move your entire division, leaving your skirmish line in position. He wishes you not to move Govan until his place is supplied by Lewis' brigade, which he thinks he can do.

Respectfully,

THOMAS S. HARDEE,
Aide-de-Camp.

HEADQUARTERS LEE'S CORPS,
In the Field, August 18, 1864.

Maj. Gen. P. ANDERSON,
Commanding Division:

GENERAL: The lieutenant-general commanding directs me to inform you that he does not deem it proper to recall your regiments until he hears something more definite, as the point they are now at is considered very important by General Hood. One regiment from General Clayton's division has been ordered to report to you; if this is not enough to make you feel safe, he suggests that you take some of your Mississippians out of the trenches, and hold them at a point where they can re-enforce General Deas or be sent back to their own line if it is attacked. He also suggests that you take a section of one of the batteries on your line that can best be spared and place it in rear of your line at the weak point, in a concealed position, so that if the enemy advance the guns can be run up by hand and used on them.

Very respectfully, your obedient servant,

J. W. RATCHFORD,
Assistant Adjutant-General.

HEADQUARTERS PICKET,
August 18, 1864.

General ARMSTRONG:

GENERAL: About 100 cavalry, all but one mounted on white horses, have just passed through enemy's breast-works, and have moved off to their right; a thin line of skirmishers is slowly advancing on me; a shell occasionally comes over. I have ordered all my reserve up and one company with it is at the church.

Respectfully,

R. A. PINSON,
Colonel First Mississippi.

———

HEADQUARTERS ARMSTRONG'S BRIGADE,
August 18, 1864—10.35 a. m.

Brigadier-General ARMSTRONG:

GENERAL: Colonel Pinson has just sent in a verbal message by Adjutant Johnson that a brigade of infantry had advanced on Captain Taylor, who is on the left, and had driven him about 200 yards. I have ordered Colonel Maxwell's regiment to the front, and the balance of the brigade to saddle.

Respectfully,

VIRGIL V. MOORE,
Acting Assistant Adjutant-General.

———

ATLANTA, *August 18, 1864—1 p. m.*

Brigadier-General JACKSON,
East Point, Ga.:

Detain the enemy's line of skirmishers advancing against Armstrong as much as possible by giving them what resistance you can. Report force of line skirmishers, if possible.

[J. B. HOOD,
General.]

———

AUGUST 18, 1864.

Brig. Gen. ALFRED IVERSON,
Commanding, &c.:

General Hood desires you to proceed to Griffin, Ga., and there establish a rendezvous for all the cavalry absent and unable to reach their commands at this time. You will take such steps as you may deem necessary to assemble these men. Such officers as may in like manner be absent will report to you.

[F. A. SHOUP,
Chief of Staff.]

———

SPECIAL ORDERS, }   ADJT. AND INSP. GENERAL'S OFFICE,
No. 195.   }   *Richmond, August 18, 1864.*

*   *   *   *   *   *   *

XIV. The following-named officers are assigned to duty with Maj. Gen. Patton Anderson, commanding division, Army of Tennessee, and will report without delay: Capt. W. G. Barth, assistant adjutant-general, Provisional Army, C. S.; Surg. C. B. Gamble, Provisional Army, C. S.

*   *   *   *   *   *   *

By command of the Secretary of War:

JNO. WITHERS,
Assistant Adjutant-General.

CIRCULAR.]   HEADQUARTERS CAVALRY CORPS,
August 18, 1864.

Division and brigade commanders with their entire staff will stand on the banks of the river and not permit a man to attempt to cross until they are satisfied that his cartridge and cap boxes and ammunition are so arranged as not to get wet in crossing the river.

By order of Major-General Wheeler:

WM. E. WAILES,
Assistant Adjutant-General.

AUGUST 19, 1864—8 a. m.

Lieutenant-General HARDEE,
Commanding Corps, &c.:

General Ferguson reports line of skirmishers advancing against him and Strahl; thought to be a heavy line of battle supporting. Am sending one brigade to Jonesborough; have sent Ferguson also. Don't think it safe to send you more troops, except in case of necessity. Call upon General Lee for all of his reserves if necessary. General Walthall has two brigades in reserve.

[F. A. SHOUP,
Chief of Staff.]

ATLANTA, *August 19, 1864.*

Lieutenant-General HARDEE and
Major-General CLEBURNE:

A train of cars ready to send a brigade to your assistance when necessary.

F. A. SHOUP,
Chief of Staff.

HEADQUARTERS HARDEE'S CORPS,
August 19, 1864—7.15.

Major-General CLEBURNE:

GENERAL: General Hardee had written to General Hood for additional force before the receipt of your note.

Very respectfully, your obedient servant,

T. B. ROY,
Assistant Adjutant-General.

ATLANTA, *August 19, 1864—11.50 a. m.*

Major-General CLEBURNE, *East Point, Ga.:*

General Hood thinks the enemy will hardly giv you battle to-day. Better block all the roads leading from Camp Creek Church toward East Point if not already done. Keep an infantry picket at Hornsby's. Use pioneers to push forward works. He will send you troops if pressed.

T. B. ROY,
Assistant Adjutant-General.

ATLANTA, *[August] 19, 1864—4. p. m.*

Maj. Gen. P. R. CLEBURNE:

Has the enemy made any further demonstration since General Hood left you?

F. A. SHOUP,
Chief of Staff.

ATLANTA, *August 19, 1864—5.40 p. m.*

Major-General CLEBURNE:

General Walthall is moving to your support; use him if you find it necessary. Please duplicate all important dispatches by courier.

F. A. SHOUP,
Chief of Staff.

ATLANTA, *August 19, 1864—9 p. m.*

Maj. Gen. P. R. CLEBURNE, *East Point:*

General Hood desires one brigade of Walthall's division to remain at East Point, with a train of cars, with steam up from daylight to dark, ready to carry up the other brigade or bring down the one already there, as the case may require. Please establish your headquarters near East Point.

[F. A. SHOUP,
Chief of Staff.]

ATLANTA, *August 19, 1864—9 p. m.*

Maj. Gen. E. C. WALTHALL, *East Point:*

Keep one brigade at East Point, and establish your headquarters near there. Have a train of cars, with steam up from daylight to dark, ready to carry the other brigade up or bring the one there down, as the case may require.

F. A. SHOUP,
Chief of Staff.

JONESBOROUGH, *August 19, 1864—12 m.*

General HOOD:

I am moving down toward Lovejoy's Station. General Ross is between here and Fairburn. Ferguson is behind me.

F. C. ARMSTRONG,
Brigadier-General.

JONESBOROUGH, *August 19, 1864.*

General HOOD:

I will move on below Lovejoy's Station and in direction of Griffin. A scout from Fayetteville reports that 500 of the enemy passed through that place en route to Griffin one hour after sunrise.

F. C. ARMSTRONG,
Brigadier-General.

AUGUST 19, 1864—6 a. m.

General JACKSON,
Commanding Cavalry:

Ferguson has been ordered to you at Rough and Ready. The general has a brigade of infantry to send at any moment. Keep us constantly advised.

[F. A. SHOUP,
Chief of Staff.]

ATLANTA, *August 19, 1864—8 a. m.*

Brigadier-General JACKSON,
Cavalry, East Point:

Brigade of infantry will start to Jonesborough without delay. Ferguson has been ordered to Rough and Ready. Go ahead with your force.

[J. B. HOOD,
General.]

ATLANTA, *August 19, 1864—12.15 p. m.*

General W. H. JACKSON, *East Point:*

A cavalry force of the enemy is reported moving on the Fayetteville road from Decatur, and also on the McDonough road. On the former road their advance at Mrs. Alston's. On the McDonough road their advance at Ousley Chapel. Look out for them and use your discretion.

[J. B. HOOD,
General.]

ATLANTA, *August 19, 1864—3.50 p. m.*

Brig. Gen. W. H. JACKSON, *Jonesborough:*

General Hood desires me to say that a great deal depends upon your exertions. You must beat the enemy, if possible.

[F. A. SHOUP,
Chief of Staff.]

ATLANTA, *August 19, 1864—5.20 p. m.*

Brig. Gen. W. H. JACKSON, *Jonesborough:*

The forces reported to be moving out from Decatur gone back. The general desires you to be careful not to divide your force too much; better make sure of one party.

[F. A. SHOUP,
Chief of Staff.] .

HDQRS. ROSS' BRIGADE, JACKSON'S·CAVALRY DIVISION,
Sewell's House, Ga., August 19, 1864—1.30 a. m.

Brigadier-General JACKSON,
Commanding Division:

GENERAL: The enemy is advancing on Sandtown and Fairburn road in force. Scouts from their flanks and rear report at least a brigade of cavalry, followed closely by infantry. My pickets are now fighting them between Bethel and Enon Church.

I am, general, very respectfully, &c.,

L. S. ROSS,
Brigadier-General.

HDQRS. ROSS' BRIGADE, JACKSON'S CAVALRY DIVISION,
Sewell's, Ga., August 19, 1864—2 a. m.

Brigadier-General JACKSON,
Commanding Division:

GENERAL: I am convinced the enemy I have been fighting is Kilpatrick's division on a raid. It has passed our flank and gone on in the direction of Fairburn. Scouts from their rear now report the column two miles and a half long and all cavalry. I have sent the Third Texas across to get in their front, and will move on after with the rest of my command at once. We had a severe skirmish with the enemy's advance and have lost several men.

I am, very respectfully, &c.,

L. S. ROSS,
Brigadier-General.

HDQRS. ROSS' BRIGADE, JACKSON'S CAVALRY DIVISION,
On the Road, August 19, 1864—9 a. m.

Brigadier-General JACKSON,
Commanding Division:

GENERAL: I am again moving on the flank of the enemy on Fairburn and Jonesborough road. Their force has been divided. One column, the largest, is moving rapidly on the Fairburn and Jonesborough, and the other column on the Fairburn and Fayetteville road. My supply of ammunition has been nearly exhausted. Some companies of my command have only a few rounds left. Cannot you hurry forward to me a wagon lightly loaded with ammunition?

I am, general, very respectfully, &c.,

L. S. ROSS,
Brigadier-General.

ATLANTA, *August 19, 1864—6 a. m.*

Brigadier-General WRIGHT, *Macon, Ga.:*

A raid has been started this morning from our left in the direction of Fairburn; will probably strike Macon road. Look out for it. Take means to ascertain the point of attack and report.

[J. B. HOOD,
General.]

(Same to Brigadier-General Iverson, Griffin, Ga., and to post commanders at intermediate stations.)

ATLANTA, *August 19, 1864—10.35 a. m.*

Governor JOSEPH E. BROWN, *Milledgeville, Ga.:*

General Winder has been instructed to send the militia at Andersonville to Macon.

[J. B. HOOD,
General.]

(Line broken before dispatch could be sent.)

ATLANTA, *August 20, 1864.*

General BRAXTON BRAGG:

Your dispatch in regard to a small Alabama brigade for Mobile just received. I am ready to send it if the necessity is great. Cannot, however, do so till day after to-morrow owing to the break in the road. Have telegraphed General Maury to know the condition of affairs at Mobile. The brigade ought not to leave here except in case of great emergency. Please answer.

J. B. HOOD.

ATLANTA, *August 20, 1864.*

Lieutenant-General HARDEE, *East Point:*

General Hood has directed General Cleburne to have Scott and Granbury in readiness to move to the right in case the demonstration should prove to be serious.

[F. A. SHOUP,
Chief of Staff.]

ATLANTA, *August 20, 1864.*

General CLEBURNE:

General Walthall is ordered to move with his brigade here at once. Enemy moving on our right.

F. A. SHOUP,
Chief of Staff.

ATLANTA, *August 20, 1864.*

Major-General CLEBURNE, *East Point:*

Have Scott and Granbury in readiness to move to the right in case of necessity.

[J. B. HOOD,
General.]

ATLANTA, *August 20, 1864.*

Major-General CLEBURNE,
    East Point:

Movement on the right seems to be foraging party. Let Walthall move down, however, and be ready here for you if needed. Will not send for Granbury and Scott unless absolutely necessary.

[J. B. HOOD,
General.]

BACON'S HOUSE, *August 20, 1864.*

Major-General CLEBURNE:

In the absence of Captain McDowell I report that a scout is just in. He reports that he saw four Federal scouts about three miles below here on the railroad, and heard that the enemy's infantry and cavalry are on the railroad (both sides), about four miles below here. I have just sent out a reliable scout to find out by actual sight the truth of the matter. Since writing the above two scouts have come in who report a pretty heavy force of infantry at Trimble's Mill. I send this by one of the last-named scouts, so that you can question him yourself. He is a reliable scout.

Respectfully,

J. A. ANDERSON,
Capt., Comdg. Camp of Detach. of Cav. from Armstrong's Brig.

ATLANTA, *August 20, 1864.*

Maj. Gen. E. C. WALTHALL,
        East Point:

Put your brigade on the cars and move here at once.

J. B. HOOD,
General.

AUGUST 20, 1864—8.30 p. m.

Brigadier-General MORGAN,
        Commanding Cavalry, &c.:

The raiders were dispersed at Lovejoy's (reported by scouts) this evening. Our cavalry said to be in their front and rear. Keep a sharp lookout and report often.

[F. A. SHOUP,
Chief of Staff.]

HEADQUARTERS ARMY OF TENNESSEE,
        August 20, 1864.

Captain McDowell is hereby authorized to collect and take command of all men of Ross' and Armstrong's brigades, Jackson's division, not on duty, who may be found fit for service.

By command of General Hood:

F. H. WIGFALL,
Aide-de-Camp.

HEADQUARTERS,
In front of Widow Trimble's, August 20, 1864—4 p. m.

[Captain BUCK:]

CAPTAIN: I have dismounted a picket and pushed them forward to the edge of this in rear of the church, and find the enemy's skirmish line about 300 yards this side of Camp Creek Church in the middle of the field just this side of the church.

Very respectfully,

W. W. McDOWELL,
Captain, Commanding.

MACON, *August 20, 1864.*
(Received 21st.)

General S. COOPER:

The damage on road to Atlanta much less than supposed. The road now clear, and will be repaired in few days at furthest.

HOWELL COBB.

HDQRS. ROSS' BRIGADE, JACKSON'S CAVALRY DIVISION,
August 20, 1864—8.30 a. m.

Brigadier-General JACKSON,
Commanding Division:

GENERAL: We came upon the enemy halted to feed, and have driven his rear guard from two lines of rail works. He is now formed, a brigade strong, on the hill at the far side of an open field some three quarters of a mile in my front, and has artillery in position and at work. We are on the road leading toward McDonough, and from the direction the enemy has chosen I infer his raid will be continued on farther down the country.

I am, general, very respectfully, &c.,

L. S. ROSS,
Brigadier-General.

HDQRS. ROSS' BRIGADE, JACKSON'S CAVALRY DIVISION,
Mrs. Carnes' Gin-House, Ga., August 20, 1864—10 a. m.

Brigadier-General JACKSON,
Commanding Division:

GENERAL: The enemy's whole force has been formed near Lee's Mill, on the south side of Cotton Indian Creek, and is now just commencing to withdraw. The direction they are moving will lead them into the Jonesborough and McDonough road, about half a mile from Lee's Mill, but whether they will continue straight across that road to Lovejoy's Station, or will go on through McDonough, is yet undecided. Their force is large. I have had a plain view of at least 4,000 formed in line. The road they are moving on intersects the Jonesborough and McDonough road at Noah's Ark Church.

I am, general, very respectfully, &c.,

L. S. ROSS,
Brigadier-General.

[AUGUST 20, 1864.—For the strength of Hood's army, see Part III, p. 682.]

ATLANTA, GA., *August 21, 1864.*

Hon. J. A. SEDDON,
Richmond, Va.:

In the evening of the 19th the enemy's cavalry struck the Macon railroad near Jonesborough, tearing up the track a short distance. Brigadier-General Jackson's cavalry command and Brig. Gen. D. H. Reynolds' infantry brigade met the enemy at Lovejoy's Station yesterday evening, routed them, capturing a number of prisoners, 2 stand of colors, and 1 piece of artillery.

J. B. HOOD,
General.

ATLANTA, *August 21, 1864.*
(Received 8.40 a. m.)

Major-General CLEBURNE:

GENERAL: With Scott and Granbury, where does your left rest? Keep your scouts close up to enemy day and night and well down West Point road.

J. B. HOOD,
General.

ATLANTA, *August 21, 1864—2.30 p. m.*

Major-General CLEBURNE,
East Point, Ga.:

Jackson says there are four guns on the left reporting to you, two 3-inch at Armstrong's wagon train. Please send order to Lieutenant Young at Ross' wagon train near East Point to proceed at once to Jonesborough with two steel guns and one caisson.

[F. A. SHOUP,
Chief of Staff.]

ATLANTA, *August 21, 1864.*

Brigadier-General JACKSON,
Jonesborough, Ga.:

Do you think you have broken the enemy sufficiently to spare a regiment for our left? The cavalry serving with the several corps probably annoy us. What has become of the raiders?

[J. B. HOOD,
General.]

ATLANTA, *August 21, 1864—3 p. m.*

Brigadier-General JACKSON,
Jonesborough:

A report has just been received that a raid is moving on Opelika—probably the brigade heretofore on Sweet Water. Also a scout reports that the cavalry on our right left yesterday, saying that they were going after Wheeler. The general thinks the force you are after is the only one you have to fear.

[F. A. SHOUP,
Chief of Staff.]

ATLANTA, *August 21, 1864—2.30 p. m.*

Maj. Gen. HOWELL COBB,
Macon, Ga.:

If there be any force moving down Tallapoosa River it must be small. Have no news to send.

J. B. HOOD.

MERIDIAN, MISS., *August 21, 1864.*

Brig. Gen. S. W. FERGUSON,
  Cavalry Brigade, Atlanta, Ga.:

Lose no time in procuring and executing orders for transfer of your brigade. I want you immediately; answer.

D. H. MAURY,
Major-General, Commanding.

ATLANTA, *August 21, 1864—7.30 p. m.*

Maj. Gen. D. H. MAURY,
  Meridian, Miss.:

Ferguson on raid. Don't know when he will return. I had no intimation that the exchange of Pillow for Ferguson was contemplated until receipt of your former dispatch consenting thereto. What news from Mobile? Have you enough troops to hold it?

[J. B. HOOD,
General.]

HEADQUARTERS LEE'S CORPS,
  Phillips' House, August 21, 1864.

TO DIVISION COMMANDERS:

Sunday night is a favorite time with the enemy to make changes on his line. The lieutenant-general commanding directs that you keep your scouts up to his line to-night, and impress upon your officers the importance of working every day.

Very respectfully, your obedient servant,

J. W. RATCHFORD,
Assistant Adjutant-General.

AUGUST 22, 1864.

Hon. JAMES A. SEDDON,
  Richmond, Va.:

No change in enemy's position to-day.

J. B. HOOD,
General.

AUGUST 22, 1864.

General BRAXTON BRAGG,
  Richmond, Va.:

Maj. Gen. Edward Johnson reported for duty here to-day. I am daily expecting Major-General Loring to return, and would, therefore, respectfully suggest that as Major-General French has applied to be relieved from duty with this army, his wishes be complied with, and Major-General Johnson assigned to his division. The application of Major-General French was forwarded August 11, by mail.

J. B. HOOD,
General.

WAR DEPARTMENT, C. S. A.,
Richmond, Va., August 22, 1864.

Lieut. Gen. S. D. LEE,
Army of Tennessee:

GENERAL: Brig. Gen. W. H. Jackson, of the cavalry, has been recommended by Lieutenant-General Hardee for promotion as major-general of cavalry. As the Department has but imperfect information of the services and qualifications of this officer, and is informed that he has been under your command, and is probably well known to you, I take the liberty of asking from you a frank communication in regard to his merits and adaptation to such command. If you prefer, your reply may be addressed to me personally, and will be regarded as confidential.

Very respectfully,

JAMES A. SEDDON,
Secretary of War.

————

ATLANTA, *August 22, 1864—9 a. m.*

General WRIGHT,
Macon, Ga.:

Have militia come from Andersonville? General Hood wants them sent forward. Anything of reported raid on Opelika? Is Oconee bridge down?

[F. A. SHOUP,
Chief of Staff.]

————

MACON, *August 22, 1864.*
(Received 23d.)

General S. COOPER:

Trains running as usual.

HOWELL COBB.

————

CAMP OF SCOUTS,
Near Camp Creek Church, August 22, 1864—12 m.

Captain BUCK:

CAPTAIN: My scouts from the neighborhood of Mount Gilead Church report they saw a small body of enemy's cavalry on road between Oliver's and Baker's; also a small body of infantry about 10.30 o'clock at Heathcote's, and that their camp is near Mount Gilead Church. The infantry that were at Heathcote's say that they were ordered back to the trenches this morning. Their pickets are stationed at Mr. Biggs', about 400 yards west from Camp Creek Church. My pickets near the church report five or six just appearing a few hundred yards from Newnan road. Scouts report that enemy give as a reason for taking citizens' provisions, that Wheeler had made theirs scarce.

J. A. ANDERSON,
Captain, Commanding McDowell's Scouts.

[Indorsement.]

Capt. I. A. BUCK,
          Assistant Adjutant-General :

The within note is a report of Captain Anderson, on duty at the church. The word " west," succeeding "400 yards," should be "northwest."

Very respectfully,

W. W. McDOWELL.

P. S.—My scouts reported all quiet down about Fairburn at 6 o'clock this morning.

W. W. McD.

HEADQUARTERS ARMY OF TENNESSEE,
                              August 23, 1864.

General CLEBURNE,
          Commanding, &c. :

General Jackson is directed to hold at least a regiment on the left of your line, his vedettes connecting with yours at Camp Creek Church. This regiment can be effective to-morrow.

Very respectfully,

F. A. SHOUP.

ATLANTA, *August 23, 1864—3.30 p. m.*

General CLEBURNE,
          East Point :

General Hood thinks you may keep a thin line of skirmishers along the Newnan road to the Widow Lee's or Camp Creek Church, connecting with the cavalry; also that it will be well to block the road leading from Camp Creek Church by Hornsby's.

[F. A. SHOUP,
          Chief of Staff.]

ATLANTA, *August 23, 1864—10.30 a. m.*

General WINDER,
          Andersonville :

Governor Brown desires the militia to come here. The Third Georgia Reserves will be returned you. Please send the militia.

[F. A. SHOUP,
          Chief of Staff.]

ATLANTA, *August 23, 1864—11.45 a. m.*

General WRIGHT,
          Macon :

You are ordered to take command at Augusta. Send you instructions by mail. Colonel Cofer will relieve you.

[F. A. SHOUP,
          Chief of Staff.]

HEADQUARTERS,
Bacon's House, August 23, 1864—6.30 o'clock.

[Captain Buck:]

CAPTAIN: General Armstrong's brigade crossed last night one mile and a half east of here, and I will be relieved this morning. None of my scouts have reported to-day. If they get any information I will forward it to you. I will call in my scouts at Fairburn and Milam's (four miles down the railroad) to-day.

Very respectfully, yours,

W. W. McDOWELL,
Chief of Scouts.

HEADQUARTERS GOVAN'S BRIGADE,
August 23, 1864.

[Captain Buck:]

CAPTAIN: My scouts sent out last night to see if there had been any change in the enemy's position report that they could observe none. Their infantry seems to reach Pratt's house, and they have cavalry at Trimble's Mill.

Respectfully, your obedient servant,

D. C. GOVAN,
Brigadier-General.

ATLANTA, *August 24, 1864.*

General BRAGG, *Richmond:*

Have letter from General Maury, 19th; expected troops from Arkansas to cross river next night; has gone to Meridian to see General Taylor. Will this not relieve me from sending troops? Will do so gladly if you think best. Have a brigade in readiness.

J. B. HOOD,
General.

AUGUST 24, 1864—6.30 p. m.

Lieut. Gen. S. D. LEE, *Commanding Corps:*

General Hardee has been directed to put Lewis' brigade in the line to relieve a sufficient number of regiments to enable you to take out Baker's brigade. Direct that brigade to bivouac near these headquarters and General Baker to report in person.

[F. A. SHOUP,
Chief of Staff.]

AUGUST 24, 1864—7.10 p. m.

Brigadier-General FERGUSON, *Commanding Cavalry:*

A scout reports that the enemy has a brigade of cavalry on the road below Decatur, tearing up and burning. The general directs that you attend to the matter. Better send General Morgan with such force as you can spare to drive them, if possible. You should keep your scouts well out in that direction to give you notice of such doings.

[F. A. SHOUP,
Chief of Staff.]

ATLANTA, *August 24, 1864.*

General MAURY, *Meridian:*

Send you a brigade, though I cannot spare it. It goes at daylight.

J. B. HOOD,
General.

———

AUGUST 24, 1864—4 p. m.

Major BURFORD, *Assistant Adjutant-General:*

MAJOR: We have driven the enemy across the river, and have possession of the fortification on College Hill, which commands the bridge, but with the guns we have I do not think we could inflict such serious damage to the bridge as would warrant the expenditure of ammunition. There are 216 tents visible on the opposite side of the river, which I think accommodate two regiments. I cannot advance farther without crossing the foot bridge, which is completely enfiladed by the enemy's works, and is within rifle range of the redoubt and pits in which all his forces seem to have assembled. I desire to know whether you design attacking on the opposite side, so that I may govern myself accordingly.

I am, major, respectfully,

JOHN S. WILLIAMS,
Brigadier-General.

———

HEADQUARTERS,
Near Atlanta, August 24, 1864.

[General W. W. MACKALL:]

DEAR GENERAL: Your favor of the 19th did not reach me till yesterday. I have a corps paymaster, Major Malone, who was wounded on the 22d ultimo, but writes me that he will soon be fit for duty. I know Captain Wickham slightly, and would be glad to oblige him on your account as well as his own. I suppose many reports are in circulation respecting my position in this army. The President is endeavoring to create the impression that in declining the command at Dalton, I declined it for all future time. You are entirely correct in saying that Hood was, of all others, in favor of retreating. If General Johnston had followed his advice he would have crossed the Chattahoochee two or three weeks before he did. This can be proved beyond all controversy. I inclose you, for your own eyes solely, a copy of my correspondence with the President. I saw Tom yesterday; he was at my headquarters, and is in fine health but not so spruce looking as when with you. Remember me kindly to the members of your household.

Truly, yours,

W. J. HARDEE.

[Inclosure No. 1.]

ATLANTA, GA., *August 3, 1864.*

His Excellency President DAVIS, *Richmond, Va.:*

I applied to General Bragg to be relieved from duty with this army. His proposition to substitute Lieutenant-General Taylor for me and to send me to the Mississippi Department, will, I hope, meet your approval. I rely upon your kindness to relieve me from an unpleasant position.

W. J. HARDEE,
Lieutenant-General.

[Inclosure No. 2.]

RICHMOND, VA., *August 4, 1864.*

Lieutenant-General HARDEE:

I regret that your position is felt to be unpleasant. You need no assurance that no wound was intended. Your letters, when commanding-in-chief, created the belief that the course adopted would be satisfactory to you. The country needs every effort of all her sons. You can most aid our cause in your present position; other motives will not be necessary to you.

JEFFERSON DAVIS.

[Inclosure No. 3.]

ATLANTA, *August 6, 1864.*

His Excellency President DAVIS,
        Richmond, Va.:

No letter of mine while commanding-in-chief was intended to convey the impression that the appointment of a junior to command me would be satisfactory. The justice or propriety of that appointment I do not propose to question. I only ask to be relieved from a position which is personally humiliating. This I think due to an old soldier who has faithfully endeavored to perform his duty, and who is still willing to make any sacrifice for the cause except his self-respect. I respectfully renew my request to be relieved. General Hood approves my application.

W. J. HARDEE,
Lieutenant-General.

[Inclosure No. 4.]

RICHMOND, *August 7, 1864.*

Lieutenant-General HARDEE:

Your telegram of yesterday received with regret and disappointment. I will look for your letters to send you by mail extracts showing what you said, and from which your intention was inferred. I now ask, is this a time to weigh professional or personal pride against the needs of the country, or for an old soldier to withdraw the support he can give the public defense from the place where it is most wanted? Let your patriotic instincts answer, rejecting all other advices.

JEFFERSON DAVIS.

SPECIAL FIELD ORDERS, }   HDQRS. ARMY OF TENNESSEE,
        No. 87.   }   *In the Field, August 24, 1864.*
*   *   *   *   *   *   *

X. Col. B. J. Hill, Thirty-fifth Tennessee Regiment, is relieved from duty as provost-marshal-general of the army.

XI. Lieut. Col. Gustavus A. Henry, jr., assistant inspector-general, will assume the duties of provost-marshal-general (under the inspector-general) until a successor to Colonel Hill can be appointed.

*   *   *   *   *   *   *

By command of General Hood:

KINLOCH FALCONER,
Assistant Adjutant-General.

ATLANTA, GA., *August 25, 1864.*

Hon. JAMES A. SEDDON,
   Secretary of War, Richmond:

No material change in lines of enemy during the past two days.

J. B. HOOD,
General.

_____

ATLANTA, *August 25, 1864—7.45 a. m.*

Major-General CLEBURNE,
   East Point:

General Hood desires you to have the citizens move their hogs and cattle from the immediate flanks of the army. He does not wish to take the stock if the citizens are willing to drive them from the enemy's reach.

[F. A. SHOUP,
Chief of Staff.]

_____

AUGUST 25, 1864—7.35 a. m.

Brig. Gen. W. H. JACKSON,
   Commanding Cavalry:

The general commanding requests me to say that any cattle or hogs found in reach of the enemy he desires you to have the citizens move from the immediate flanks of the army. It is not his desire to take the stock from the citizens if they are willing to drive them inside of our lines.

[F. A. SHOUP,
Chief of Staff.]

_____

AUGUST 25, 1864—1.35 p. m.

Brig. Gen. W. H. JACKSON,
   Commanding Cavalry Division:

Brigadier-General Ferguson has been directed to make all reports directly to you during the absence of General Wheeler. You will please send couriers to inform him of the whereabouts of your headquarters.

[F. A. SHOUP,
Chief of Staff.]

_____

Report of the condition of the works and obstructions on the main line occupied by Stewart's corps, August 25, 1864.

GENERAL FRENCH'S FRONT.

The only work required in front of this line is in strengthening and extending the obstructions. On portions of this line the abatis is well constructed of large timber, thickly placed. In front of Ward's and Hoskins' batteries particularly the obstructions are weak. Chevaux-de-frise can be placed throughout the line with advantage.

W. F. FOSTER,
Major and Senior Engineer, Stewart's Corps.

[Indorsement.]

HEADQUARTERS STEWART'S CORPS,
Atlanta, August 25, 1864.

The within report of an examination of the lines of this corps, made by the senior engineer of the corps, at the request of the lieutenant-general commanding, is respectfully referred to Major-General French, who will carry out Major Foster's suggestions and report them to these headquarters.

By command of Lieutenant-General Stewart:

DOUGLAS WEST,
Acting Assistant Adjutant-General.

ATLANTA, GA., *August 26, 1864.*

Hon. JAMES A. SEDDON,
Richmond:

Last night the enemy abandoned the Augusta railroad and all the country between that road and the Dalton railroad. His left now rests on the Dalton railroad. He has not extended his right at all. We received to-day 1,000 head of cattle, captured by a portion of Major-General Wheeler's command.

J. B. HOOD,
General.

AUGUST 26, 1864—8 a. m.

Lieutenant-General STEWART,
Commanding Corps:

General Hood desires me to say that there is no news of the enemy's massing this morning. They have disappeared from Stevenson's and Maney's fronts, but thus far their whereabouts has not been ascertained.

[F. A. SHOUP,
Chief of Staff.]

AUGUST 26, 1864—9.25 a. m.

Lieutenant-General STEWART,
Commanding Corps:

General Hood desires that you should not move your main body from the trenches.

[F. A. SHOUP,
Chief of Staff.]

AUGUST 26, 1864—3 p. m.

Lieut. Gen. A. P. STEWART,
Commanding Corps:

Maj. Gen. G. W. Smith has been directed to occupy the position now occupied by Major-General Stevenson at dark. Please direct General Stevenson to withdraw his command to enable him to do so, and hold it at convenient point in rear.

[F. A. SHOUP,
Chief of Staff.]

HEADQUARTERS STEVENSON'S DIVISION,
August 26, 1864—daybreak.

Maj. DOUGLAS WEST,
    Acting Assistant Adjutant-General:

MAJOR: I occupy the picket-line of the enemy, and am moving to their main line. Will ascertain by scouts where they have gone.

I am, major, &c.,

C. L. STEVENSON,
Major-General.

[First indorsement.]

HEADQUARTERS FRENCH'S DIVISION,
August 26, 1864.

Brigadier-General YOUNG:

The general wishes to know if you have any information of the enemy on your front and right.

D. W. SANDERS,
Assistant Adjutant-General.

[Second indorsement.]

HEADQUARTERS ECTOR'S BRIGADE,
August 26, 1864.

MAJOR: My picket-officer has just reported. He thinks the enemy have only a few scattering men in our front, and as soon as he can secure concert of action with command on the right will feel of the enemy's line. I will keep you informed.

WM. H. YOUNG,
Brigadier-General, Commanding.

HEADQUARTERS STEWART'S CORPS,
Atlanta, August 26, 1864—10 a. m.

Major-General FRENCH,
    Commanding Division:

GENERAL: Lieutenant-General Stewart desires that you should not move your main body from the trenches.

Very respectfully,

DOUGLAS WEST,
Acting Assistant Adjutant-General.

N. B.—Please read and return the inclosed note* forwarded by General Hood. The lieutenant-general desires that you push your scouts carefully forward.

Respectfully,

DOUGLAS WEST,
Acting Assistant Adjutant-General.

AUGUST 26, 1864—7.10 a. m.

Maj. Gen. E. C. WALTHALL,
    Commanding, &c.:

General Hood desires you to keep your command under arms, ready to move at a moment's notice.

[F. A. SHOUP,
Chief of Staff.]

---

*Not found.

AUGUST 26, 1864—7.45 a. m.

Brigadier-General MANEY, *Commanding, &c.:*

General Hood desires you to have your command under arms and in readiness to move at a moment's notice. He has ordered the cavalry to move down Peach Tree Creek. General Stevenson reports that he now occupies the enemy's works, and is pressing forward his scouts.

[F. A. SHOUP,
Chief of Staff.]

AUGUST 26, 1864—8.15 a. m.

Major-General SMITH,
Commanding First Division Militia:

General Hood desires you to hold your command in readiness to move by the left flank at a moment's notice.

[F. A. SHOUP,
Chief of Staff.]

AUGUST 26, 1864—3 p. m.
(Received 3.50 p. m.)

Maj. Gen. G. W. SMITH,
Commanding Georgia Militia:

You will please move your command at dark, by the left flank, to to occupy the position now occupied by General Stevenson.

[F. A. SHOUP,
Chief of Staff.]

AUGUST 26, 1864—8.15 a. m.

General FERGUSON, *Commanding Cavalry:*

The enemy are reported to have withdrawn on the Marietta road. General Hood desires you to push your cavalry down Peach Tree Creek, and report such information as you may procure.

[F. A. SHOUP,
Chief of Staff.]

AUGUST 26, 1864—8.20 a. m.

Brigadier-General JACKSON, *Commanding Cavalry:*

General Hood directs me to say that the enemy have disappeared from the front of the militia and Stewart's right. He desires your command to be on the alert, and if attacked at any point to make as stubborn resistance as possible.

[F. A. SHOUP,
Chief of Staff.]

AUGUST 26, 1864—9 a. m.

Brigadier-General JACKSON, *Commanding Cavalry:*

General Hood desires you to direct Armstrong to press forward his cavalry in on the enemy's right, to ascertain what is going on. Enemy has given up his works on our right.

[F. A. SHOUP,
Chief of Staff.]

ATLANTA, *August 26, 1864—2.50 p. m.*

Brig. Gen. A. R. WRIGHT,
       Augusta, Ga.:

If General Marcus J. Wright should arrive at Augusta, you will inform him that the order assigning him to command of Augusta has been rescinded, and that he will return to Macon.

[F. A. SHOUP,
Chief of Staff.]

ROGERSVILLE, *August 26, 1864.*
(Via Carter's Depot 27th.)

Hon. JAMES A. SEDDON,
       Secretary of War, Richmond :

General Wheeler on the 24th instant was crossing to north side of French Broad River, within fifteen miles of Strawberry Plains.

JNO. H. MORGAN,
Brigadier-General, Commanding.

ATLANTA, *August 27, 1864.*

Hon. J. A. SEDDON,
       Secretary of War:

Last night the enemy continued [to] change their position by their left and center. They have drawn back so that their left is now on the Chattahoochee at the railroad bridge; their right is unchanged, and they appear to be moving troops in that direction. They have no troops nearer than four miles of Atlanta.

J. B. HOOD.

HEADQUARTERS ARMY OF TENNESSEE,
August 27, 1864—7.40 a. m.

Lieutenant-General STEWART,
       Commanding, &c. :

GENERAL : General Hood desires me to inform you that General Hardee reports the enemy still in his front. He desires you to move forward with extreme caution if you try to develop their position.
       Respectfully,

L. P. DODGE,
Aide-de-Camp.

AUGUST 27, 1864—7.30 a. m.

Lieutenant-General LEE,
       Commanding Corps:

General Hood directs me to inform you that General Hardee reports the enemy still in his front. He desires you to move with caution as you go forward.

[F. A. SHOUP,
Chief of Staff.]

AUGUST 27, 1864—10.50 a. m.
(Received 11.05 a. m.)

Lieutenant-General LEE,
  Commanding Corps:

The general is of the opinion that the enemy has taken up a new line. Please establish strong picket on all roads leading to your works. Co-operate with General Stewart. Let your troops remain in the works heretofore occupied. Please cause your engineer to make a thorough reconnaissance of the enemy's line.

[F. A. SHOUP,
  Chief of Staff.]

(Duplicate sent Lieutenant-General Stewart, commanding corps.)

ATLANTA, *August 27, 1864—dawn.*

General CLEBURNE:

Generals Lee and Stewart report enemy gone from their fronts. Send some of Scott's men to ascertain facts in your front. Keep your own division well in hand, however.

[J. B. HOOD,
  General.]

AUGUST 27, 1864—9.55 p. m.
(Received 10 p. m.)

Col. E. J. HARVIE,
  Assistant Inspector-General, &c.:

General Hood desires you to order the destruction of the bridge referred to in scout report of this p. m.

[F. A. SHOUP,
  Chief of Staff.]

AUGUST 27, 1864—10.30 a. m.

Brigadier-General FERGUSON,
  Commanding Cavalry:

Your dispatch of 7.30 a. m. received. General Hood desires you to connect your pickets with the infantry across Peach Tree Creek.

[F. A. SHOUP,
  Chief of Staff.]

ATLANTA, *August 27, 1864—4.30 p. m.*

Brigadier-General JACKSON,
  East Point:

Direct General Armstrong to oppose stoutly the enemy should he attempt to cross the creek at Trimble's; also to keep General Cleburne advised of the enemy's movements.

[J. B. HOOD,
  General.]

HDQRS. ROSS' BRIGADE, JACKSON'S CAVALRY DIVISION,
William Baker's, Ga., August 27, 1864—12 m.

Brigadier-General JACKSON,
Commanding Division:

GENERAL: The force reported advancing on the Sandtown and Fairburn road has halted at Milam's, this side of Camp Creek. The enemy is now advancing from the direction of Redwine's and Mount Gilead Church.

I am, general, very respectfully, &c.,

L. S. ROSS,
Brigadier-General.

HDQRS. ROSS' BRIGADE, JACKSON'S CAVALRY DIVISION,
William Baker's, Ga., August 27, 1864—12.30 p. m.

Brigadier-General ARMSTRONG,
Commanding Division:

GENERAL: A force of infantry is moving in this direction on a country road leading from Owl Rock Church across to the Atlanta and Campbellton road at Sewell's. About 100 men have been seen.

I am, general, very respectfully,

L. S. ROSS,
Brigadier-General.

HDQRS. ROSS' BRIGADE, JACKSON'S CAVALRY DIVISION,
In the Field, Ga., August 27, 1864—2.15 p. m.

Brigadier-General ARMSTRONG,
Commanding Division:

GENERAL: The right of the enemy's infantry so far as developed rests near old man Sewell's. They are fortifying on the hill near Sewell's house.

I am, general, very respectfully,

L. S. ROSS,
Brigadier-General.

HDQRS. ROSS' BRIGADE, JACKSON'S CAVALRY DIVISION,
Baker's House, Ga., August 27, 1864—3 p. m.

Brigadier-General ARMSTRONG,
Commanding Division:

GENERAL: The right of the infantry in position near Redwine's and Mount Gilead Church rests on Camp Creek, near old man Sewell's. They are constructing works rapidly. The infantry force from Sandtown came to Enon Church, and thence up Wolf Creek to Widow Parker's, and have gone into camp. Large wagon trains, tents, &c., can be seen from commanding positions near Griffin's or Dave Smith's. I have not been satisfied by reports from scouts as to the strength of the infantry force on Wolf Creek.

Very respectfully,

L. S. ROSS,
Brigadier-General.

HDQRS. ROSS' BRIGADE, JACKSON'S CAVALRY DIVISION,
Isaac Cook's, Ga., August 27, 1864—6 p. m.

Brigadier-General ARMSTRONG,
   Commanding Division:

GENERAL: My scouts have just reported from the north side of the Chattahoochee. Kilpatrick's cavalry is encamped along Sweet Water from Sandtown up. They finished the bridge over the river at Sandtown Monday and took out their pontoons. The advance of enemy on Sandtown and Fayetteville road is one mile this side of Stephens' house. No farther advance on part of the force on Camp Creek. They are now shelling my pickets.

I am, general, very respectfully, &c.,

          L. S. ROSS,
          Brigadier-General.

SPECIAL ORDERS,   ADJT. AND INSP. GENERAL'S OFFICE,
 No. 203.   *Richmond, August 27, 1864.*

 *   *   *   *   *   *   *

XXVIII. Capt. W. W. Gordon, assistant adjutant-general, Provisional Army, C. S., is relieved from service with the brigade lately commanded by Brig. Gen. H. W. Mercer, and is assigned to duty with the brigade commanded by Brig. Gen. R. H. Anderson, Army of Tennessee.

 *   *   *   *   *   *   *

By command of the Secretary of War:

         JNO. WITHERS,
         Assistant Adjutant-General.

GENERAL ORDERS,   HDQRS. ROSS' BRIG., JACKSON'S CAV. DIV.,
 No. 19.   *Baker's House, Ga., August 27, 1864.*

I. With a view of promoting the efficiency of the brigade, the policy of a "union on duty" of companies as practiced in other portions of the army will be adopted in this. Regimental commanders will therefore proceed at once to organize their respective commands each into five companies, uniting for this purpose two into one, and will assign to each new company thus formed three officers (captain and two lieutenants), provided said officers shall be selected for each company from the number of those belonging to the two companies before united.

II. All the surplus or unassigned officers remaining in the brigade, after the completion of the organization, required in paragraph I of this order, will constitute a company of "brigade scouts" until their services as officers are needed or can be made available. A report of names therefore of all such officers will be forwarded promptly from each regiment.

III. The precedent for this mode of procedure has been established in other brigades of cavalry and found to do well. It is hoped therefore that officers and men will not only acquiesce readily in its adoption here, but will zealously co-operate with the brigade commander in his efforts to render available the services of each individual in the command. The duty upon which the unassigned officers are to be employed will, it is believed, be as pleasant and agreeable as it will no doubt be efficient.

IV. It is not intended that this policy of "union on duty" shall in any manner affect the rendition of returns. All reports, musters, &c., will continue to be made by the companies as now organized.

V. Regimental commanders will report the organization of their new companies, as above provided, as soon as completed.

By order of Brigadier-General Ross:

D. R. GURLEY,
Assistant Adjutant-General.

ATLANTA, GA., *August 28, 1864.*

Hon. J. A. SEDDON, *Richmond, Va.:*

The enemy have changed their entire position, the left of their line resting near the Chattahoochee about Sandtown, and their right extending to a point opposite and near the West Point railroad between East Point and Fairburn. They hold all the crossings on the Chattahoochee from Pace's Ferry down to Sandtown, but not with a continuous line. Dispatches from General Wheeler of the 19th, in which he reports the capture of Dalton, with large quantity of stores, about 200 prisoners and 200 mules, destroying 3 trains of cars and 25 miles of railroad. His command is in good condition.

J. B. HOOD,
General.

(Same to General Bragg.)

AUGUST 28, 1864—7 p. m.

Lieutenant-General STEWART, *Commanding Corps:*

Upon inquiring again, I find that General Hood mistook this command for the other Reynolds. He desires you to order them to the railroad at Bartimeus Hospital, if that be nearer than these headquarters; if not, send them here to bivouac for the night, and be in readiness for the train to Jonesborough in the morning. Direct the officer in command to report in person at these headquarters when he shall have made the above dispositions.

[F. A. SHOUP,
Chief of Staff.]

AUGUST 28, 1864—12 m.

Lieutenant-General LEE, *Commanding Corps:*

General Hood desires you to relieve General Brown's division (Hardee's corps) with General Stevenson's division. General Brown is directed to march to East Point.

[F. A. SHOUP,
Chief of Staff.]

ATLANTA, *August 28, 1864—12.20 p. m.*

General ARMSTRONG:

Keep your main force well in hand till you find where the enemy's principal force is, so that you can fall upon him with effect.

[J. B. HOOD,
General.]

ATLANTA, *August 28, 1864—6 p. m.*
(Via East Point.)

Brigadier-General ARMSTRONG:

Reynolds' brigade already sent to Jonesborough; Lewis' to go; Brown's division ordered to Rough and Ready; all to co-operate with you in repelling raids.

F. A. SHOUP;
Chief of Staff.

————

AUGUST 28, 1864—12.55 p. m.

Brigadier-General FERGUSON:

General Hood desires you to send one of your regiments to the left to report to Major-General Cleburne. Leave some officer in command on the right, and please report here in person.

[F. A. SHOUP,
Chief of Staff.]

————

HEADQUARTERS HUMES' CAVALRY DIVISION,
Officer's Farm, August 28, 1864—5.45 p. m.

Maj. Gen. JOSEPH WHEELER, *Cavalry Corps:*

GENERAL: My command has just arrived here. I shall camp here to-night and move between daylight and sunrise for the ford designated in your order. No instructions were sent for the artillery, and I do not know what road it has taken, whether to Sparta or this place.

Respectfully, your obedient servant,

W. Y. C. HUMES,
Brigadier-General.

Where will you be to-morrow ?

————

ATLANTA, *August 28, 1864—6 p. m.*

Maj. Gen. JOHN C. BROWN, *East Point:*

General Hood directs that you send Lewis' brigade to Jonesborough by rail. Cars that carried Reynolds' brigade to that point ordered to return for that purpose. This force is intended to co-operate with General Armstrong in repelling raids. March the rest of your division to Rough and Ready to repel raids from the direction of West Point railroad. Acquaint yourself with the approaches in that quarter. Keep couriers at telegraph office at East Point. It may be well to fortify your position, and also direct General Lewis to do the same. Look to movements upon the Fayetteville road. You will probably find good position with right at Rough and Ready and line along Mud Creek.

[F. A. SHOUP,
Chief of Staff.]

————

ATLANTA, *August 28, 1864—10.50 a. m.*

Maj. Gen. HOWELL COBB, *Macon:*

General Hood desires the militia to come up. If necessary organized troops had better be sent to General Winder.

[F. A. SHOUP,
Chief of Staff.]

ATLANTA, *August 28, 1864—9.40 p. m.*

Brig. Gen. M. J. WRIGHT, *Macon:*

Send Colonel Hannon, with his command, to Jonesborough. No immediate danger of raid. Yankees have not left West Point railroad.

[J. B. HOOD,
General.]

ATLANTA, *August 29, 1864—3 p. m.*

Lieutenant-General HARDEE, *Commanding Corps, East Point:*

General Lee is instructed to ascertain position of the enemy, as suggested; also to relieve an additional brigade, if necessary.

[J. B. HOOD,
General.]

ATLANTA, *August 29, 1864—5 p. m.*

Lieutenant-General HARDEE, *East Point:*

General Hood desires you to send copy of dispatch received from General Armstrong at 2 p. m. to Maj. Gen. John C. Brown. He also directs that all parties approaching from direction of the enemy shall be halted and not suffered to enter our lines without permission from these headquarters.

[F. A. SHOUP,
Chief of Staff.]

HEADQUARTERS ARMY OF TENNESSEE,
August 29, 1864.

Lieutenant-General STEWART, *Commanding Corps:*

General Hood directs that you use rails as far as possible in the construction of stockades, they being easily procured.

Respectfully, &c.,

L. P. DODGE,
Aide-de-Camp.

ATLANTA, *August 29, 1864.*

Maj. Gen. D. H. MAURY, *Enterprise, Miss.:*

It is of the last importance that you assist me to protect my communications at Opelika. Sherman has changed his position so that he faces east, thus putting that road to his back. What forces can I rely upon to defend it?

J. B. HOOD,
General.

ATLANTA, *August 29, 1864—9.10 p. m.*

General DANIEL W. ADAMS, *Opelika, care Post Commander:*

General Hood desires you to look well to the defenses of Opelika and that quarter against raids. What force can you rely upon for such purpose?

[F. A. SHOUP,
Chief of Staff.]

Special Field Orders, }   Hdqrs. Army of Tennessee,
         No. 92.   }   *In the Field, August 29, 1864.*

*   *   *   *   *   *   *

X. Col. M. H. Cofer, Sixth Kentucky Regiment, will relieve Lieut. Col. Gustavus A. Henry, jr., assistant inspector-general, temporarily acting provost-marshal-general of the army.

*   *   *   *   *   *   *

By command of General Hood:

A. P. MASON,
Major and Assistant Adjutant-General.

ATLANTA, *August 30, 1864—12.40 p. m.*

General BRAXTON BRAGG, *Richmond, Va.:*

General Maury telegraphs following dispatch:

FORREST'S, *Grenada, August 29, 1864.*

Enemy left Holly Springs at 2 a. m. yesterday, moving rapidly in direction of Memphis and La Grange. They say they are ordered to re-enforce Sherman.

[J. B. HOOD,
General.]

ATLANTA, *August 30, 1864—1 p. m.*

Lieutenant-General HARDEE, *East Point:*

General Hood does not think the necessity will arise to send any more troops to Jonesborough to-day. Will send you a map soon as one can be procured. General Lee is instructed to move Patton Anderson's division near the railroad to assist you if need be. Please place yourself in communication with General Anderson.

[F. A. SHOUP,
Chief of Staff.]

ATLANTA, *August 30, 1864—1.45 p. m.*

Lieutenant-General HARDEE, *Rough and Ready:*

I start map to you at once. General Lee has ordered Anderson's division to East Point. It may become necessary for you to send another brigade and battery to Jonesborough. General Lee's headquarters at East Point. General Anderson's division can go into line in place of Maney's. Use judgment, and communicate with General Lee at East Point.

[J. B. HOOD,
General.]

ATLANTA, *August 30, 1864—2 p. m.*

General HARDEE, *Rough and Ready:*

General Hood desires you to take whatever measures you may think necessary to prevent the enemy from gaining Jonesborough or Rough and Ready this afternoon, so that he may make other dispositions to-night. He does not think they will attack Jonesborough to-day.

[F. A. SHOUP,
Chief of Staff.]

ATLANTA, *August 30, 1864—3.15 p. m.*

Lieutenant-General HARDEE, *Rough and Ready:*

Will send engine for you; had anticipated it before your dispatch was received.

[J. B. HOOD,
General.]

———

ATLANTA, *August 30, 1864—3.20 p. m.*

General HARDEE, *Rough and Ready:*

Please have your command under arms at sunset. Leave a staff officer at your headquarters to receive dispatches for you. An engine will be at East Point for you at sunset. Please come to headquarters.

[J. B. HOOD,
General.]

———

ATLANTA, *August 30, 1864—6 p. m.*

Lieutenant-General HARDEE, *East Point:*

General Armstrong telegraphs that there is a probability of the enemy striking the railroad to-night between Jonesborough and the left of our army. Please prevent it if possible.

[J. B. HOOD,
General.]

———

ATLANTA, *August 30, 1864—6.10 p. m.*

Lieutenant-General HARDEE, *Rough and Ready:*

Your corps will move to Jonesborough to-night. Put it in motion at once if necessary to protect the railroad. General Lee will follow up the movement. Inform Lee if you move and what force. Please come in to-night.

[J. B. HOOD,
General.]

———

ATLANTA, *August 30, 1864.*

Lieutenant-General HARDEE, *Rough and Ready:*

When you move let Scott's brigade go to East Point. General Lee is directed to confer with you touching skirmishers, and such other matters as may be necessary.

[J. B. HOOD,
General.]

———

AUGUST 30, 1864—11.30 a. m.
(Received 12 m.)

Lieutenant-General LEE, *Commanding Corps:*

General Jackson has been directed to send regiment to East Point to make a reconnaissance on Campbellton road. Please send a staff officer to meet this command. See the commanding officer and personally give him such instructions as may be necessary to procure the required information.

[F. A. SHOUP,
Chief of Staff.]

AUGUST 30, 1864—11.30 a. m.
Lieutenant-General LEE:

General Hood calls attention to the necessity of using the greatest exertion to procure a sufficient supply of forage. The wagons of the command, whether appropriated to that use or not, should be used to gather green corn from the country between the Macon and Augusta railroads. The matter requires the attention of the commanding officers.

[F. A. SHOUP,
Chief of Staff.]

(Same as above to Lieutenant-Generals Stewart and Hardee.)

———

AUGUST 30, 1864—1.10 p. m.
Lieutenant-General LEE,
Commanding Corps:

General Hardee reports the enemy moving upon him. General Hood directs that you move Anderson's division to your left, near the rail-road, to support him. Please keep your command under arms.

[F. A. SHOUP,
Chief of Staff.]

———

AUGUST 30, 1864—1.25 p. m.
(Received 2.30 p. m.)
Lieutenant-General LEE,
Commanding Corps:

General Hardee's headquarters are now at Rough and Ready. General Hood desires you to move to East Point as soon as possible.

[F. A. SHOUP,
Chief of Staff.]

———

ATLANTA, *August 30, 1864—2.40 p. m.*
General LEE,
East Point:

Please send Anderson's division to Mount Gilead Church, as requested by General Hardee.

[F. A. SHOUP,
Chief of Staff.]

———

ATLANTA, *August 30, 1864—3.15 p. m.*
Lieutenant-General LEE,
East Point:

General Hood directs me to say that Scott's brigade will be relieved to-night as soon as may be. He desires you to move Anderson's division to the vicinity of Mount Gilead Church.

[F. A. SHOUP,
Chief of Staff.]

ATLANTA, *August 30, 1864—3.25 p. m.*

Lieutenant-General LEE,
    East Point:

Place Anderson's division on the right of Maney's instead of sending it to Mount Gilead Church. It will take the place of Maney's if General Hardee moves to the left.

[J. B. HOOD,
General.]

ATLANTA, *August 30, 1864—3.45 p. m.*

General LEE,
    East Point:

An engine will be at East Point to bring you and General Hardee to headquarters at sunset. Leave a staff officer at your headquarters to receive dispatches for you. Have your command under arms. Acknowledge receipt of this by telegraph.

[J. B. HOOD,
General.]

ATLANTA, *August 30, 1864—5.45 p. m.*

Lieut. Gen. S. D. LEE,
    East Point:

General Hood desires you to hold your command under arms and ready to move at a moment's warning.

[F. A. SHOUP,
Chief of Staff.]

ATLANTA, *August* [*30, 1864—6.35 p. m.*].

Lieutenant-General LEE,
    East Point:

General Hardee is directed to move if need be in direction of Jonesborough to protect railroad. If he moves he will inform you, and you will follow up the movement. If you should move come in as directed to headquarters. Communicate with General Hardee touching skirmishers, &c.

[J. B. HOOD,
General.]

ATLANTA, *August 30, 1864—8.45 p. m.*

Lieutenant-General LEE,
    East Point:

Follow up movement of General Hardee. Take brigade from Sandtown road. Leave staff officers and courier at telegraph office to carry any order you may desire to send after your arrival here. Let your trains move on road to the east of railroad.

[J. B. HOOD,
General.]

CONFIDENTIAL.]   AUGUST 30, 1864—12 m.

Brigadier-General LEWIS, *Commanding, &c.:*

General Hood desires you to send some of your most discreet officers
to such point as you may think best to procure horse equipments for
your command, to be held ready to use at any moment. It may become
necessary to mount you very soon, but he desires that you shall not
inform your command of the fact, so that they may not feel useless
anxiety on the subject. Direct your officers to consult with chief of
ordnance of this army, who has been instructed to assist you.

[F. A. SHOUP,
Chief of Staff.]

ATLANTA, *August 30, 1864—5.15 p. m.*

Brigadier-General LEWIS, *Jonesborough:*

You will co-operate with General Armstrong in preventing the enemy
crossing Flint River to-night.

[J. B. HOOD,
General.]

ATLANTA, *August 30, 1864—6.35 p. m.*

General LEWIS, *Jonesborough:*

Hold your position at all hazards. Help is ordered to you.

[J. B. HOOD,
General.]

HEADQUARTERS,
In the Field, August 30, 1864.

TENNESSEEANS: Confederate troops again press the soil of your noble
State. The opportunity for which you have so long asked is now given
you. The brave men, who, in this hour of your country's peril, still
cling to your country's standard, appeal to you for aid. Shall they call
in vain? Georgia has called her last available citizens between the
ages of seventeen and fifty years. They are now fighting beside your
chivalrous sons before Atlanta. Other States are also throwing their
entire male population into the field.

Citizens of Tennessee! You who have always been ready to respond
to your country's call, every one of you must rise to duty. If all who
should come will now join us, we pledge the honor of those States whose
sons compose the Western army of the Confederacy that Tennessee
shall be redeemed.

J. WHEELER,
Major-General.

ATLANTA, *August 30, 1864—8 a. m.*

General JACKSON, *Commanding, &c.:*

Should the enemy move to the railroad you must detain them as long
as possible. Flint River gives us great advantages in protecting the
Macon railroad.

[J. B. HOOD,
General.]

ATLANTA, *August 30, 1864—10 a. m.*

Brigadier-General JACKSON,
    Rough and Ready:

Should the enemy detach raiding party do not send all your cavairy in pursuit. Enemy's cavalry remaining with his corps might cause us considerable annoyance. Retain at least one regiment.

        [J. B. HOOD,
            General.]

ATLANTA, *August 30, 1864—10.30 a. m.*

Brigadier-General JACKSON,
    Rough and Ready:

Can you send a regiment under a "dashing" colonel to make reconnaissance on Campbellton road? If so, send them at once to East Point, and telegraph to these headquarters their arrival there.

        [J. B. HOOD,
            General.]

ATLANTA, *August 30, 1864—1.20 p. m.*

General JACKSON,
    Rough and Ready:

General Hood does not think there can be a large force advancing upon Jonesborough. Please ascertain from Armstrong what infantry it is, if possible.

        [F. A. SHOUP,
            Chief of Staff.]

ATLANTA, *August 30, 1864—6.55 p. m.*

General JACKSON,
    Rough and Ready:

Have your command saddled before you start for headquarters, so that you can send orders to your staff officer to move if need be.

        [J. B. HOOD,
            General.]

ATLANTA, *August 30, 1864—5.15 p. m.*

Brigadier-General ARMSTRONG,
    Jonesborough:

General Hood directs that you prevent the enemy crossing Flint River to-night. General Lewis will assist you.

        [F. A. SHOUP,
            Chief of Staff.]

ATLANTA, *August 30, 1864—7.20 p. m.*

Brigadier-General ARMSTRONG,
    Jonesborough:

Look out for enemy's cavalry. Has Hannon reached you? If not, stop him at such point as you may think best.

        [F. A. SHOUP,
            Chief of Staff.]

ATLANTA, *August 30, 1864—11 a. m.*

Major-General MAURY,
  Enterprise:

General Bragg informs me that he has ordered the remainder of
Gholson's brigade to me. I have ordered this brigade to Opelika, and
desire his horses, transportation, and absent men ordered to join him
there.

            J. B. HOOD,
               General.

[AUGUST 31, 1864.—For Hardee to Jefferson Davis, reporting engagement at Jonesborough, see Part III, p. 696.]

ATLANTA, *August 31, 1864—3 a. m.*

Lieutenant-General HARDEE,
  Jonesborough:

Have dispatch from Pickett. He says Cleburne and Brown are within
three miles of Jonesborough. Have directed him to push them forward.
As soon as you can get your troops in position the general says you
must attack and drive the enemy across the river.

            [F. A. SHOUP,
              Chief of Staff.]

ATLANTA, *August 31, 1864—3.10 a. m.*

Lieutenant-General HARDEE,
  Jonesborough:

You must not fail to attack the enemy so soon as you can get your
troops up.   I trust that God will give us victory.

            [J. B. HOOD,
              General.]

ATLANTA, *August 31, 1864—3.20 a. m.*

Lieutenant-General HARDEE,
  Jonesborough:

General Hood desires you to say to your officers and men that the
necessity is imperative.   The enemy must be driven into and across the
river.

            [F. A. SHOUP,
              Chief of Staff.]

ATLANTA, *August 31, 1864—9.10 a. m.*

Lieutenant-General HARDEE,
  Jonesborough:

There are about 600 horses east of Griffin to mount the Kentucky brigade if it becomes necessary. General Hood desires you to use your
best judgment.

            [F. A. SHOUP,
              Chief of Staff.]

ATLANTA, *August 31, 1864—10 a. m.*

General HARDEE,
   Jonesborough:

General Hood desires the men to go at the enemy with bayonets fixed, determined to drive everything they may come against.

[F. A. SHOUP,
Chief of Staff.]

ATLANTA, *August 31, 1864—12.15 p. m.*

General HARDEE,
   Jonesborough:

General Morgan reports enemy in strong force advancing against Clinch at Mount Gilead Church.

[F. A. SHOUP,
Chief of Staff.]

ATLANTA, *August 31, 1864—2 p. m.*

General HARDEE,
   Jonesborough:

General Morgan says enemy drove Clinch from breast-works at Mount Gilead Church about 11 a. m.; were in considerable force. This sent you to show that enemy have not all his troops in your front.

[F. A. SHOUP,
Chief of Staff.]

HEADQUARTERS ARMY OF TENNESSEE,
OFFICE CHIEF OF STAFF,
August 31, 1864—6 p. m.

Lieutenant-General HARDEE,
   Commanding, &c.:

General Hood directs that you return Lee's corps to this place. Let it march by 2 o'clock to-morrow morning. Remain with your corps and the cavalry, and so dispose your force as to best protect Macon and communications in rear. Retain provision and ordnance trains. Please return Reynolds' brigade, and, if you think you can do so and still accomplish your object, send back a brigade or so of your corps also. There are some indications that the enemy may make an attempt on Atlanta to-morrow.

Very respectfully, &c.,

F. A. SHOUP,
Chief of Staff.

HEADQUARTERS ARMY OF TENNESSEE,
OFFICE CHIEF OF STAFF,
August 31, 1864.

Lieutenant-General HARDEE,
   Commanding Corps:

General Hood directs that you return Lee's corps to this place. Let it march by 2 o'clock to-morrow morning. Remain with your corps and the cavalry, and so dispose of your force as to best protect the Macon railroad and communications in rear. Retain provision and ordnance trains. Please return Reynolds' brigade. Should Lee have been badly cut up to-day, and you think you can spare them, send back some of the troops of your own corps. There are indications that the enemy may make an attempt on Atlanta to-morrow.

Very respectfully, &c.,

F. A. SHOUP,
Chief of Staff.

Enemy at Rough and Ready in considerable force. Morgan thinks that they will attack East Point to-morrow. Send back Lieutenant-Colonel McMicken, chief quartermaster.

Respectfully, &c.,

F. A. S.

(Duplicate of dispatch sent at 6 p. m.*)

ATLANTA, *August 31, 1864.*

General J. T. MORGAN,
East Point:

Move the ordnance train to this place at once.

[J. B. HOOD,
General.]

ATLANTA, *August 31, 1864—9.10 a. m.*

Brigadier-General MORGAN,
East Point:

Keep up vedettes in the direction of Jonesborough as far as possible.

[J. B. HOOD,
General.]

ATLANTA, *August 31, 1864—12.15 p. m.*

General MORGAN,
East Point:

Let Clinch offer the last resistance in his power. If beaten back, and they move in this direction, keep us thoroughly informed.

[F. A. SHOUP,
Chief of Staff.]

ATLANTA, *August 31, 1864—5 p. m.*

Brigadier-General MORGAN,
East Point:

Notify General Scott of all the enemy's movements. He is on your right. What force is it that has driven in Clinch? Try to ascertain.

[F. A. SHOUP,
Chief of Staff.]

---

* So indorsed in same handwriting as that of the dispatch. It, however, differs somewhat from that first sent.

ATLANTA, *August 31, 1864—5,05 p. m.*

Brigadier-General MORGAN,
    East Point:

Send scouts around the enemy to report the facts to General Hardee. Try and get his strength.

[J. B. HOOD,
    General.]

ATLANTA, *August 31, 1864—6 p. m.*

General MORGAN, *East Point:*

Please give the position of the enemy on the Macon railroad and else-where at dark. Watch him closely to-night, and send information.

[F. A. SHOUP,
    Chief of Staff.]

ATLANTA, *August 31, 1864—8.30 p. m.*

Brigadier-General MORGAN,
    East Point:

Make the best resistance you can. It is not expected that you should hold your position against a movement in force. Keep General Scott fully informed. If pushed back retire fighting, giving timely notice. Have you heard much firing in direction of Jonesborough since 2 p. m.?

[J. B. HOOD,
    General.]

ATLANTA, *August 31, 1864—9.30 a. m.*

General SCOTT, *East Point:*

Take position with right on Newnan wagon road and left on railroad Keep us fully advised. If driven back retire on this place.

[J. B. HOOD,
    General.]

ATLANTA, *August 31, 1864—11.30 a. m.*

Brigadier-General SCOTT,
    East Point:

Some cavalry covering Campbellton road. You had better, however, keep a lookout for yourself.

[F. A. SHOUP,
    Chief of Staff.]

ATLANTA, *August 31, 1864—9.15 p. m.*

Brigadier-General SCOTT,
    East Point:

Keep yourself in constant communication with General Morgan. He is instructed to keep you advised of all movements of the enemy. Be careful not to allow yourself to be cut off. If forced to fall back retire skirmishing. Use sound judgment. Keep us informed.

[J. B. HOOD,
    General.]

ATLANTA, *August 31, 1864—3 a. m.*

Colonel PICKETT,
      Rough and Ready:

Hasten forward the troops to Jonesborough.   General Hardee is there.

[J. B. HOOD,
                          General.]

———

ATLANTA, *August 31, 1864—12.35 p. m.*

POST COMMANDER,
      Jonesborough:

There is said to be a train of cars at Rough and Ready.   It must be moved down the road; it has no engine.   Take measures to get it down; be careful, however.   Colonel McMicken has started down the road on engine.

[F. A. SHOUP,
                          Chief of Staff.]

———

HEADQUARTERS SEARS' BRIGADE,
                          August 31, 1864.

Maj. D. W. SANDERS,
      Assistant Adjutant-General:

MAJOR: The report rendered regarding the strength of the enemy in our front has been greatly exaggerated.   It was brought in by our cavalry scouts.   Not more than ten of the enemy were seen in one body. The report about their deploying was not sustained.   It amounts to a few cavalry scouts.   We have extended our line to the right, connecting with the militia, so that we now cover the whole of General Walthall's front.   I sent a staff officer to our right.   He has just come in; reports our scouts in front as having lost sight of the enemy.   The report of having killed a man was incorrect; his horse fell, and evidence of blood shows that horse or man was badly wounded.   On visiting the ground the men were a good deal disappointed in finding horse and man both gone.

Very respectfully, your obedient servant,

C. W. SEARS,
                          Brigadier-General.

———

AUGUST 31, 1864.

Major-General WHEELER,
      Commanding Cavalry:

Sherman faces Atlanta from the west, crossing the Chattahoochee at Sandtown.   His wagon trains must be greatly exposed.   General Hood thinks you had better move this way, destroying as you come, to operate upon them.

[F. A. SHOUP,
                          Chief of Staff.]

———

[AUGUST 31, 1864.—For the organization and strength of Hood's army, see Part III, pp. 668, 683.]

JONESBOROUGH, *September 1, 1864.*

His Excellency JEFFERSON DAVIS, *Richmond, Va.:*

Last night Lee's corps was ordered back to Atlanta by General Hood. I recommended that he should evacuate Atlanta while it was practicable. He will be compelled to contract his lines, and the enemy has force enough to invest him. My instructions are to protect Macon.

W. J. HARDEE,
Lieutenant-General.

RICHMOND, *September 1, 1864.*
(Received Lovejoy's 2d.)

Lieut. Gen. W. J. HARDEE:

The enemy's movement is to gain Atlanta; we must endeavor to defeat his purpose. I have called on General Cobb with the hope that he will be able to re-enforce you. If you can beat the detachment in front of you, and then march to join Hood, entire success might be hoped to result from the division which the enemy have made of his force. I hope General Cobb may increase your cavalry to enable you more effectually to deprive the enemy of supplies and impede his movements.

JEFFERSON DAVIS.

HEADQUARTERS STEWART'S CORPS,
September 1, 1864.

Major-General FRENCH, *Commanding Division:*

GENERAL: A brigade is reported as advancing on the Marietta road. Major-General Walthall has been ordered to take his division out and drive them away. In case the enemy advance on the East Point road it may become necessary for you to move on Brigadier-General Featherston.

Respectfully, general, your obedient servant,
DOUGLAS WEST,
Acting Assistant Adjutant-General.

HEADQUARTERS STEWART'S CORPS,
September 1, 1864—7.30 p. m.
(Received 8.10 p. m.)

Major-General FRENCH, *Commanding Division:*

GENERAL: The lieutenant-general commanding directs that you put your troops in motion immediately in the order of march indicated in the previous order this evening.*

Respectfully, general, your obedient servant,
D. WEST,
Acting Assistant Adjutant-General.

HEADQUARTERS STEWART'S CORPS,
September 1, 1864—8 p. m.

Major-General FRENCH, *Commanding Division:*

GENERAL: The lieutenant-general commanding directs that you leave a staff officer to withdraw all your pickets at 11 o'clock to-night

---

* See circular, p. 1014.

and bring them on by the route you will march. Direct them to pick up all stragglers as they pass through town. Impress on all your commanders to prevent straggling by all means in their power.

I am, general,

D. WEST,
Acting Assistant Adjutant-General.

ATLANTA, *September 1, 1864—8.25 a. m.*

General MORGAN,
        East Point:

Keep some of your cavalry between Rough and Ready and Decatur, as well as between enemy and this place. Send situation this morning.

[J. B. HOOD,
General.]

ATLANTA, *September 1, 1864—9.30 a. m.*

Brigadier-General MORGAN,
        East Point:

Make the stoutest possible resistance, and keep us informed of result.

[J. B. HOOD,
General.]

ATLANTA, *September 1, 1864—12.15 p. m.*

Brigadier-General MORGAN,
        East Point:

Has there been any change in the enemy's position? Have they moved from Rough and Ready toward East Point?

[J. B. HOOD,
General.]

ATLANTA, *September 1, 1864—12.30 p. m.*

Brigadier-General MORGAN,
        East Point:

Watch your left. Be careful to report any movement in direction of Decatur. Please send in staff officer to report to these headquarters.

J. B. HOOD,
General.

ATLANTA, GA., *September 1, 1864—3.40 p. m.*

Brigadier-General MORGAN,
        East Point:

Look well to your left and see that enemy does not move on any other than the railroad. Keep General Hood advised. Remove the telegraph office from East Point. Place the telegraph instrument somewhere near you so as you can be in constant [communication] with me.

[F. A. SHOUP,
Chief of Staff.]

ATLANTA, GA., *September 1, 1864—3.40 p. m.*

General MORGAN,
        East Point:

General Lee is moving up the McDonough road. Send scout to see
if it is him.

[J. B. HOOD,
        General.]

———

ATLANTA, *September 1, 1864—12.40 p. m.*

Brigadier-General SCOTT,
        East Point:

If you have not already done so, assemble your command at East
Point. Keep in communication with General Morgan, and between the
enemy and Atlanta.

[J. B. HOOD,
        General.]

———

ATLANTA, GA., *September 1, 1864—1 p. m.*

Brigadier-General SCOTT,
        East Point:

General Hood desires you not to let the enemy get between you and
Atlanta.

[F. A. SHOUP,
        Chief of Staff.]

———

FOUR MILES SOUTHWEST OF ROGERSVILLE,
        Friday morning, September 1, 1864.

General WHEELER:

The enemy passed through Rogersville at 1 p. m. yesterday on the
Florence road from the direction of Athens, the force between 2,000
and 2,500, consisting of four regiments of white infantry and one negro
regiment, one regiment of cavalry, about 250 men, two pieces of artillery, commanded by General Streight. General Rousseau reported in
Athens with two brigades of cavalry. The Yankees expect him to re-
enforce them to-day.

Most respectfully,

JOHN H. LESTER,
Captain, Commanding Company E, Seventh Alabama Cavalry.

———

SPECIAL FIELD ORDERS, }   HDQRS. ARMY OF TENNESSEE,
        No. 95.   }   *In the Field, September 1, 1864.*

I. Maj. Gen. Edward Johnson, Provisional Army, C. S., is assigned to
the command of Anderson's division, Lee's corps.

*   *   *   *   *   *   *

By command of General Hood:

KINLOCH FALCONER,
Assistant Adjutant-General.

CIRCULAR.] HEADQUARTERS STEWART'S CORPS,
                                           September 1, 1864.

I. When the order to march is given the order of march will be left in front.

II. In the following order: Walthall's division, Featherston's division, French's division. The battalions of artillery will, in each division, precede the infantry.

III. French's division will bring up the rear, and will have one brigade as a rear guard with one battery of artillery.

IV. The battalions of artillery will be under the orders of the division commanders on this march.

By order of Lieutenant-General Stewart:

                                           DOUGLAS WEST,
                                   Acting Assistant Adjutant-General.

                               HEADQUARTERS LEE'S CORPS,
                                           September 1, 1864.

The lieutenant-general commanding directs that you have your troops under arms and ready to move at daylight to-morrow morning. Send to the McDonough and Jonesborough road, half way between the two points, all trains now with the command, except brigade ordnance trains and ambulances, starting at 10 o'clock to-morrow morning, taking the first plain, left-hand road leading from the road traveled to-day. Send at once to your trains which went in the direction of Decatur, and order them to the point above specified. The order of march will be: Clayton's division, with the battalion of artillery; Stevenson's division, with battalion of artillery; Johnson's division, with battalion of artillery. Each division will march prepared to fight if necessary.

I remain, general, very respectfully, your obedient servant,

                                           J. W. RATCHFORD,
                                   Assistant Adjutant-General.

(To division commanders.)

           OFFICE INSPECTOR OF FIELD TRANSPORTATION,
                                   ARMY OF TENNESSEE,
                                   Atlanta, September 1, 1864.

Lieut. Col. A. H. COLE,
       Chief of Field Transportation, C. S. Army:

COLONEL: I respectfully call your attention to the following statements, and ask that you will please forward to the proper officials with such remarks as you may see fit:

The policy adopted at the beginning of the war by the Government of making cavalrymen mount themselves is, in my opinion, the most extravagant to the Government, and has done more to demoralize the troops of this branch of the service than any other cause. When a soldier is dismounted, whether by general or special orders I do not know, he is entitled to a furlough of thirty days to go home and remount himself. This makes every cavalry soldier, or at least all that desire to be, mere horse traders, selling their animals whenever they desire to go home. Many even go further than this; they steal every animal, whether public or private, when it can be done with any show of success in retaining him for a few days, until they can sell or swap him. Some stations through which the army has passed have in this way been entirely swept of animals, thereby taking from the people their only means of support. They do not hesitate to take possession of all public animals captured from the enemy, wherever to be found, and dispose of them as private property, thus depriving the Government of all benefit of such capture.

I do not think it any exaggeration when I make the assertion that had the cavalry been mounted on public animals at the beginning of the war, and captured animals been used to remount those "by the chances of war dismounted," a fair valuation having been paid for all purchased, less money would have been expended, and a large number of animals been secured to the Government, than has already been paid out for animals killed in action or lost through carelessness of owner, not to say anything of public animals that have been taken possession of by dismounted men. I respectfully suggest that all private animals now ridden by cavalrymen be taken possession of by the Government and paid for either with money or by certificate of purchase, and when a soldier is dismounted, if it can be shown that it was through no carelessness of his, let him be remounted by the Government. If through his negligence let him at once be sent to an infantry command. This mode of mounting troops will, in my opinion, be beneficial to the service and do away with much of the odium now attached to the cavalry arm.

I am, colonel, very respectfully,

E. H. EWING,
Major and Inspector of Field Transportation; Army of Tennessee.

[SEPTEMBER 2, 1864.—For Hardee to Jefferson Davis, reporting engagement at Jonesborough (September 1), see Part III, p. 696.]

SEPTEMBER 2, 1864—6.50 p. m.

Lieutenant-General HARDEE,
Commanding Corps:

General Hood directs me to say that Stewart and Lee are in supporting distance of you. Stewart is within nine miles. If you can hold your position they will reach you at an early hour to-morrow. Stewart is ordered to join you as early as possible in the morning. If you should be driven from your present position the general thinks the several corps are so placed that they can be united at some point not far south of your position to-morrow night.

[F. A. SHOUP,
Chief of Staff.]

SEPTEMBER 2, 1864—6.30 p. m.

Lieutenant-General STEWART,
Commanding Corps:

From information recently received from General Hardee, and the artillery firing now going on, General Hood thinks it important that you take a very early start in the morning and move to his assistance. Be certain you have good guides, well informed. Do not bear too far north, as it is reported the enemy moved out on the McDonough road from Jonesborough to-day. General Hardee's line of battle crosses the railroad, running east and west, about half a mile in front of Lovejoy's Station. From your present position you should come into the road leading to Lovejoy's at or near Mount Carmel Church, approaching Hardee's position rather from the north. Should he be driven from his position to-night I hope to inform you in time. That would make it necessary for you to move south on the Griffin road.

[F. A. SHOUP,
Chief of Staff.]

SEPTEMBER 2, 1864—6.50 p. m.

Lieutenant-General LEE,
Commanding Corps:

General Hood desires you to leave a brigade in your rear as a vanguard, if there be any wagons or artillery not yet come up, if you think necessary.

[F. A. SHOUP,
Chief of Staff.]

LOVEJOY'S STATION, *September 3, 1864.*

General BRAXTON BRAGG, *Richmond:*

On the evening of the 30th the enemy made a lodgment across Flint River, near Jonesborough. We attacked them on the evening of the 31st with two corps, failing to dislodge them. This made it necessary to abandon Atlanta, which was done on the night of September 1. Our loss on the evening of the 31st was so small that it is evident that our effort was not a vigorous one. On the evening of September 1 General Hardee's corps, in position at Jonesborough, was assaulted by a superior force of the enemy, and being outflanked was forced to withdraw during the night to this point, with the loss of 8 pieces of artillery. The enemy's prisoners report their loss very severe. I send a bearer of dispatches to-morrow.

J. B. HOOD,
General.

LOVEJOY'S STATION, *September 3, 1864.*

General BRAXTON BRAGG, *Richmond:*

Maj. Gen. Edward Johnson has been assigned to command General P. Anderson's division.

J. B. HOOD,
General.

LOVEJOY'S STATION, GA., *September 3, 1864—1.45 p. m.*

General BRAXTON BRAGG,
Richmond, Va.:

For the offensive, my troops at present are not more than equal to their own numbers. To prevent this country from being overrun reenforcements are absolutely necessary.

J. B. HOOD.

LOVEJOY'S STATION, GA., *September 3, 1864—6.10 p. m.*

General BRAXTON BRAGG,
     Richmond, Va.:

My telegram in cipher this morning is based upon the supposition that the enemy will not content himself with Atlanta, but will continue offensive movements. All the lieutenant-generals agree with me.

                                        J. B. HOOD.

LOVEJOY'S STATION, GA., *September 3, 1864.*

General BRAGG,
     Richmond:

I again urge the importance of removing the prisoners from Andersonville.

                                        J. B. HOOD,
                                             General.

[SEPTEMBER 3, 1864.—For Hardee to Jefferson Davis, reporting action at Lovejoy's Station (September 2), see Part III, p. 697.]

SEPTEMBER 3, 1864—2.05 p. m.

Major-General SMITH,
     Commanding Georgia State Troops:

Let your command move quietly and steadily to Griffin, covering the artillery. In case of a raid against that place, or any other point within its vicinity, make such disposition as you may think expedient to resist it.

                                   [F. A. SHOUP,
                                        Chief of Staff.]

SEPTEMBER 3, 1864.

Brigadier-General JACKSON,
     Commanding Cavalry, Bear Creek Station:

Keep scouts out in the direction of Greenville, to give information of the approach of any force of the enemy on the Macon and Columbus Railroad. Burn the bridge at Flat Shoals Factory.

                                   [F. A. SHOUP,
                                        Chief of Staff.]

LOVEJOY'S STATION, GA., *September 3, 1864—6.10 p. m.*

Brigadier-General JACKSON,
     Bear Creek Station:

Colonel Hannon reports a brigade of enemy's cavalry moving between his pickets and the left of the infantry. My headquarters will be where you were last night. Will be glad to see you to-night.

                                   [J. B. HOOD,
                                        General.]

AUGUSTA, *September 3, 1864.*

General BRAGG:

I have sent 1,000 volunteers and detailed men this day to General Hardee, and will send some 300 more to-night. This stops all the Government works here.

A. R. WRIGHT,
Brigadier-General.

LOVEJOY'S STATION, GA., *September 4, 1864—1 p. m.*

General BRAXTON BRAGG, *Richmond, Va.:*

Should the enemy move to the east or west I shall endeavor to strike him with my entire force on his flank and rear. I think his move will be down and west of Flint River.

J. B. HOOD.

LOVEJOY'S STATION, GA., *September 4, 1864.*

General B. BRAGG, *Richmond, Va.:*

Owing to the wanton neglect of the chief quartermaster of this army a large amount of ammunition and railroad stock had to be destroyed at Atlanta. He had more than ample time to remove the whole and had repeated instructions. I am reliably informed that he is too much addicted to drink of late to attend to his duties. Am greatly in want of an officer to take his place. Can you not send one?

J. B. HOOD.

LOVEJOY'S STATION, *September 4, 1864.*

General BRAXTON BRAGG:

I think the officers and men of this army feel that every effort was made to hold Atlanta to the last. I do not think the army is discouraged.

J. B. HOOD,
General.

LOVEJOY'S STATION, GA., *September 4, 1864—11.30 a. m.*

His Excellency President DAVIS, *Richmond, Va.:*

Unless this army is speedily and heavily re-enforced Georgia and Alabama will be overrun. I see no other means to avert this calamity. Never in my opinion was our liberty in such danger. What can you do for us?

W. J. HARDEE,
Lieutenant-General.

SEPTEMBER 4, 1864.

Lieutenant-General LEE, *Commanding Corps:*

General Hood desires you to relieve Colonel Presstman's regiment engineer troops on the right. Please direct Colonel P. when relieved to report with his command to these headquarters. If you can spare him, please let Captain Coleman report to General Hood.

[F. A. SHOUP,
Chief of Staff.]

LOVEJOY'S STATION, *September 4, 1864—7.50 p. m.*

Maj. Gen. G. W. SMITH,
  Commanding Georgia State Troops, Griffin:

General Hood desires you to dispose of your forces so as to cover the approaches from Flint River.

[F. A. SHOUP,
Chief of Staff.]

SEPTEMBER 4, 1864.

General M. L. SMITH.
  Griffin:

General Hood is much in want of a map of this country. Please have one made. He desires you to return with as little delay as possible.

[F. A. SHOUP,
Chief of Staff.]

SEPTEMBER 4, 1864—12 m.

Brigadier-General LEWIS,
  Commanding, &c.:

General Hood directs that you mount your men at once, using blankets, if need be, in place of saddles.

[F. A. SHOUP,
Chief of Staff.]

LOVEJOY'S STATION, GA., *September 4, 1864.*

Lieutenant-Colonel COLE,
  Inspector Field Transportation, Montgomery:

Send the horses impressed for General Roddey's cavalry to General Maury.

[F. A. SHOUP,
Chief of Staff.]

SEPTEMBER 4, 1864.

Maj. W. E. MOORE,
  Chief of Subsistence:

General Hood desires you to procure, if possible, five days' supply of hard bread, and keep on hand.

[F. A. SHOUP,
Chief of Staff.]

LOVEJOY'S STATION, GA., *September 4, 1864.*

Colonel VON ZINKEN,
  Macon:

You are to assume command of post at Columbus. Orders will be sent you, care of General Wright, Macon.

[F. A. SHOUP,
Chief of Staff.]

SEPTEMBER 4, 1864—11.15 a. m.

Brigadier-General JACKSON, *Commanding Cavalry:*

General G. W. Smith will arrive at Griffin to-night, where he will remain with his command. General Lewis has been ordered to mount his brigade and report to you. While making his preparations, you can place him at Barnesville, or such other point as you may think best. Put yourself in communication with him. General Ferguson's command is at McDonough and this side. Morgan is ordered to report to you at Griffin.

[F. A. SHOUP,
Chief of Staff.]

SEPTEMBER 4, 1864—9.15 a. m.

Brigadier-General FERGUSON, *Commanding Cavalry:*

General Hood directs me to inform you that the right of his infantry rests on the McDonough and Jonesborough road, which is the same as the McDonough and Lovejoy road. Extend well out to the right, covering the roads thoroughly. You will please place yourself in communication with the infantry commands on the right. You will draw your supplies from Griffin.

F. A. SHOUP,
Chief of Staff.

SEPTEMBER 4, 1864—11.30 a. m.

Brigadier-General FERGUSON, *Commanding, &c.:*

General Hood directs that you send Morgan to Griffin, to report to General Jackson. He will retain Colonel Clinch's regiment and Colonel Miller's, who has heretofore been reporting to General Cleburne.

[F. A. SHOUP,
Chief of Staff.]

LOVEJOY'S STATION, GA., *September 4, 1864.*

Brigadier-General IVERSON, *Commanding Cavalry:*

Move with all your available force across Flint River to Rocky Mount, Meriwether County, and take position at Rocky Mount to observe the enemy between Flint River and West Point railroad. You will please keep General Jackson informed of all movements of the enemy, as well as these headquarters.

[J. B. HOOD,
General.]

SPECIAL FIELD ORDERS, }   HDQRS. ARMY OF TENNESSEE,
No. 96.   }   *In the Field, September 4, 1864.*

I. Lewis' brigade, Hardee's corps, will proceed to Griffin, Ga., and report to Brig. Gen. A. Iverson for the purpose of being mounted.

*   *   *   *   *   *   *

By command of General Hood:

KINLOCH FALCONER,
Assistant Adjutant-General.

RICHMOND, *September 5, 1864.*
(Received 6th.)

General J. B. HOOD:

Your dispatch to General Bragg of the 3d instant has been referred. To re-enforce your army all available troops were sent, and realizing the necessity for a further increase, the reserves, detailed men, and militia were called out. General Cobb informs me that you have ordered the troops sent from Augusta and other points to Macon to return to their posts. I cannot reconcile this with your declaration that re-enforcements are absolutely necessary, or with the necessity for a prompt and vigorous movement upon the enemy before his divided forces could make a junction, or re-enforcements be sent him from Tennessee or Mississippi.

JEFFERSON DAVIS.

RICHMOND, *September 5, 1864.*

General W. J. HARDEE:

Your dispatch of yesterday received. The necessity for re-enforcements was realized, and every effort was made to bring forward reserves, militia, and detailed men for the purpose. Polk, Maury, S. D. Lee, and Jones had been drawn on to fullest extent; E. K. Smith had been called on. No other resource remains. It is now requisite that absentees be brought back, the addition required from the surrounding country be promptly made available, and that the means in hand be used with energy proportionate to the country's need.

JEFFERSON DAVIS.

LOVEJOY'S STATION, *September 5, 1864—7.30 p. m.*

General BRAXTON BRAGG,
        Richmond:

No change in position to-day.

J. B. HOOD,
General.

LOVEJOY'S STATION, GA., *September 5, 1864.*

General B. BRAGG,
        Richmond, Va.:

To let you know what a disgraceful effort was made by our men in the engagement of August 31, I give you the wounded in the two corps: Hardee's corps, 539; Lee's, 946; killed, a very small number.

J. B. HOOD.

LOVEJOY'S STATION, GA., *September 5, 1864—10.45 a. m.*

General BRAXTON BRAGG,
        Richmond:

I think the operatives had better remain. They are a protection to their shops against raids and would be of better service to me. If re-enforcements are sent, should be organized bodies. Every effort is being made to gather absentees.

J. B. HOOD,
General.

LOVEJOY'S STATION, GA., *September 5, 1864.*

Generai B. BRAGG, *Richmond, Va.:*

In my dispatch in regard to operatives this morning it is for the authorities to decide what troops shall be sent here. Whatever forces are sent, I shall use them in the best manner possible to defeat our enemy. You may feel assured that I know the necessity of troops at different points, and will co-operate thoroughly with you in doing the best that can be done. It is necessary for me to give battle should the enemy continue to advance. Let me know what forces I can have.

J. B. HOOD.

LOVEJOY'S STATION, GA., *September 5, 1864.*

Brigadier-General MORGAN, *Griffin:*

Return Colonel Miller at once to General Ferguson.

[F. A. SHOUP,
Chief of Staff.]

LOVEJOY'S STATION, GA., *September 5, 1864—10.45 a. m.*

Brigadier-General JACKSON, *Bear Creek Station:*

Order General Morgan and command to return to the right, General M. to assume command. Please ride to headquarters.

[J. B. HOOD,
General.]

SEPTEMBER 5, 1864.

Major-General WHEELER, *Commanding, &c.:*

GENERAL: The division in my front has detained the column very much this morning, and now the entire wagon train has been halted to allow that division to pass forward. Colonel Harrison reports that the enemy are still in his front on the fields at Campbellsville, though they have made no demonstrations on him.

Respectfully, your obedient servant,

W. Y. C. HUMES,
Brigadier-General.

Later: Colonel Harrison has information that the enemy are moving on a road nearly parallel and to the right of the one we travel.

Very respectfully,

W. Y. C. HUMES,
Brigadier-General.

LOVEJOY'S STATION, GA., *September 5, 1864.*

Governor BROWN, *Milledgeville:*

We are greatly in need of cars to transport sick and wounded. Can you not allow me to use the cars you have sent to Griffin for your purposes?

J. B. HOOD,
General.

LOVEJOY'S STATION, GA., *September 6, 1864.*
His Excellency JEFFERSON DAVIS,
   Richmond, Va.:

Your dispatches of the 5th instant received. I ordered General Cobb to have these troops returned to Augusta and Columbus, as the information through scouts was that the enemy was about making another raid in that direction, and I could easily bring them up when I was ready to give battle. The enemy have now withdrawn in the direction of Jonesborough, and I think will take position at East Point, Atlanta, and Decatur to recruit his army and prepare for another campaign. I am making, and shall still make, every possible effort to gather the absentees of this army. Shoes and clothing are very much needed. Detailed men I think had better for the present remain in the workshops, as they cannot march and fight. I shall continue to interrupt as much as possible the communications of the enemy, and hope that Taylor's forces will soon cross the river. I would be glad if yourself or General Bragg would visit the army.

               J. B. HOOD.

LOVEJOY'S STATION, GA., *September 6, 1864—7 a. m.*
General BRAXTON BRAGG,
   Richmond:

The enemy withdrew from my front in the direction of Jonesborough last night.

               J. B. HOOD,
                 General.

HEADQUARTERS ARMY OF TENNESSEE,
             September 6, 1864.
Hon. J. A. SEDDON,
   Secretary of War:

Sherman continues his retreat beyond Jonesborough.

               J. B. HOOD,
                 General.

(Same to General Bragg.)

LOVEJOY'S STATION, GA., *September 6, 1864*
His Excellency JEFFERSON DAVIS,
   Richmond, Va.:

I shall make dispositions to prevent the enemy, as far as possible, from foraging south of Atlanta, and at the same time endeavor to prevent his massing supplies at that place. I deem it important that the prisoners at Andersonville should be so disposed of as not to prevent this army from moving in any direction it may be thought best. According to all human calculations we should have saved Atlanta had the officers and men of the army done what was expected of them. It has been God's will for it to be otherwise. I am of good heart and feel that we shall yet succeed. The army is much in need of a little rest. After removing the prisoners from Andersonville, I think we should, as soon as practicable, place our army upon the communications of the enemy, drawing our supplies from the West Point and Montgomery Railroad.

Looking to this, I shall at once proceed to strongly fortify Macon. Please do not fail to give me advice at all times. It is my desire to do the best for you and my country. May God be with you and us.

J. B. HOOD.

[SEPTEMBER 6, 1864.—For Hood to Bragg, relating to exchange of prisoners with Sherman, see Second Series.]

HEADQUARTERS LEE'S CORPS,
In the Field, September [6], *1864.*

Maj. Gen. H. D. CLAYTON,
Commanding Division:

GENERAL: The lieutenant-general commanding desires that you discontinue the work on your main line, but complete the picket-line. He wishes you to place a strong picket a mile and a half out on each road, leading to your position, with vedettes two miles farther out than your pickets. You can drop back a short distance into bivouac, but resume your position on the line should the enemy approach.

I am, general, very respectfully, your obedient servant,

J. W. RATCHFORD,
Assistant Adjutant-General.

LOVEJOY'S STATION, GA., *September 6, 1864—9.25 a. m.*

Brigadier-General IVERSON:
(Care General Armstrong, Bear Creek Station.)

Move up with your command to some point between Fayetteville and the river, arranging your pickets on the right so as to connect with General Jackson on the left.

[J. B. HOOD,
General.]

LOVEJOY'S STATION, GA., *September 6, 1864.*

Major-General MAURY,
Mobile:

Have you any news from Taylor? When will he be over?

[F. A. SHOUP,
Chief of Staff.]

LOVEJOY'S STATION, GA., *September 6, 1864.*

Brigadier-General JACKSON,
Bear Creek Station:

The enemy has withdrawn from the immediate front. Please push up cavalry toward Flint River and ascertain what he is doing.

[J. B. HOOD,
General.]

Lovejoy's Station, Ga., *September 6, 1864—3.45 p. m.*

Brigadier-General Cobb,
     Macon:

Send all the reserves at Macon to Andersonville at once, to report to General Winder.

[J. B. HOOD,
     General.]

September 6, 1864—7 p. m.

Brigadier-General Morgan,
     McDonough:

Our infantry occupy Jonesborough. Unless you receive counter instructions from General Jackson you will early to-morrow place your troops on a line between Tucker's cabin and Flat Rock. We are informed that the enemy are under orders to occupy Decatur, Atlanta, and East Point.

[F. A. SHOUP,
     Chief of Staff.]

Headquarters Roddey's Cavalry,
Courtland, Ala., September 6, 1864—10 a. m.

[General Wheeler:]

General: Brigadier-General Roddey directs me to say that your two favors of the 5th and 6th are just to hand. The general is very much indisposed, but will take the saddle and join you, and will be at Lamb's Ferry by daylight. He has ordered Colonel Johnson to report to you. Colonel Patterson's brigade is to-night at Gilchrist's, ready to cross. He has been ordered to communicate with you. (Gilchrist's is opposite mouth of Elk, your former crossing.)

There are three good boats at Lamb's Ferry that will carry artillery; there are four boats at Bainbridge, which is the best crossing. Any of these will carry artillery. There are a number of other boats below Bainbridge, the location of which Colonel Johnson knows better than he does, and can give you more information about them than I can.

The general directs me to say that he believes that the enemy can be defeated without hazard north of the river, between Chattanooga and Pulaski; that the mounted force does not exceed 2,000, and that the infantry force at each garrison has not left their stockades for several days, and that they are mostly negroes, and feebly garrisoned. Colonel Patterson's orders from General Roddey were to cross the river at mouth of Elk, passing between Athens and the river, strike the road and destroy as far as practicable in the direction of Decatur; then to pass across, striking the road between Decatur and Huntsville, destroying as much as possible, and then passing across, leaving Huntsville to the left, and striking the road between that place and Stevenson. The general directs me to say that you may exercise your own judgment; that you can order him to carry out these orders or to come to your support. He is subject to your orders, and he requests me to say that you will communicate with him. To carry out the orders would prevent the enemy from re-enforcing the party in your front and create a diversion in your favor, and, besides, the road can be badly damaged in the mean time. The general also directs me to say that if you choose to fight to-morrow that he thinks there is very little difficulty in crossing below Florence, if, after fighting, you should think it best to cross.

I am, general, very respectfully, your obedient servant,

J. T. PARRISH,
Assistant Adjutant-General.

Since writing above General Roddey directs me to say that he will most probably cross the river in person at Green's Bluff, two miles and a half of Centre Star, but will have couriers at Lamb's Ferry also, where he has one section of artillery.

J. T. PARRISH,
Assistant Adjutant-General.

LOVEJOY'S STATION, GA., *September 6, 1864.*

Col. F. R. LUBBOCK :

DEAR SIR : My attention has just been directed to the announcement of your arrival in Macon, en route to Richmond, to take position on President Davis' staff. I rejoice very much over this intelligence, for the Texas troops recognize in you a friend, freely sympathizing with them in their sufferings, and fully appreciating the sacrifices they have made in their long separation from home and families, and I feel assured of your deep and abiding interest in whatever pertains to the honor of our State or the success of the great cause, dear alike to us all; and I do not, therefore, hesitate to inform you of the true condition of my command, trusting in securing your influence in its behalf. While in Mississippi an order was obtained, through Lieutenant-General Polk, permitting the regiments of my brigade to go home on furlough to recruit their depleted ranks. Before the order was carried into effect, another was received suspending the privilege upon the ground that our services were just then much needed, and we started to General Forrest's assistance in Tennessee. At Grenada, however, we were informed that we were no longer required in that quarter and were directed to Columbus, Miss. There Lieutenant-General Polk received the brigade and informed the men that his word was pledged to furlough them, and his promises should be fulfilled so soon as the emergency demanding their services should be over. There had been no murmuring and all were satisfied. From Columbus we came to this department, and since our arrival the brigade has lost in battle one-fourth its effective strength, and it would scarcely make one regiment now.

During the campaign it has received the special commendation and complimentary orders from superior officers after almost every engagement. You are aware that their original term of service and enlistment was twelve months, and in leaving their families and property they did not anticipate a more protracted absence, and hence did not make preparation for the wants of their families or protection of property, but by an act of Congress they were continued in service for a term of three years, and now that term has expired. Lieutenant-General Polk has been killed, and they have despaired of receiving furloughs, and I am convinced beyond the shadow of a doubt that the greater portion of them, if not all, will go to the Trans-Mississippi Department as soon as the enemy ceases to advance in Georgia. When in Mississippi one man of every twenty-five effective was furloughed, and thus all could communicate with their homes, and our duties on the Mississippi River were the most agreeable to the brigade of any to which it has before or since been assigned, and it rendered valuable service to the Confederacy. I feel sensibly that it is no part of a good soldier to say where he should serve his country, but a desire to preserve the brilliant, but hard-earned, reputation of my command from the disgrace which it now threatens to bring upon itself, induces me to solicit your influence in obtaining the transfer of my brigade to Mississippi, and, if compatible with the interests of the service, have it assigned for awhile to operate on the river, subject to the orders of any commander, no matter whom, for I am confident the influence and representations of my men will bring the brigade many recruits from the Trans-Mississippi Department, and many could, I think, be obtained from independent squads now in the swamps, who would otherwise continue to avoid the service.

Above all, after these men had heard from home, and while there existed even a remote prospect of their getting home on furlough, under the system in force before they came to this department, I think they would no longer entertain the idea of desertion. I hope you will render all the assistance you can. I could not make an application and forward it through the regular channels, for I know it would not meet the approval of Brigadier-General Jackson, commanding division, and most likely General Hood would be unwilling to give his approval. Do not think I seek a different field from the present for myself; however, to me, the attractions of the change consist altogether in the fact that I think that the only plan by which I can detain my command on this side the Mississippi River. Please let me know at once if anything can be done.

Very respectfully, your obedient servant,

L. S. ROSS.

LOVEJOY'S STATION, GA., *September 7, 1864—8 a. m.*
General B. BRAGG,
    Richmond:

Think that General Dan. Adams should remain in Northeast Alabama. Am sending an additional brigade to Opelika to protect the railroad.

[J. B. HOOD,
    General.]

LOVEJOY'S STATION, GA., *September 7, 1864.*
General B. BRAGG,
    Richmond:

It would be of vast benefit to have this army paid, a good portion of which has not been paid for ten months.

J. B. HOOD,
    General.

HEADQUARTERS,
    September 7, 1864.
General BRAGG:

Will make every effort to reduce extra-duty lists.

J. B. HOOD,
    General.

HEADQUARTERS,
September 7, 1864.

General BRAGG:

Sherman still occupies his works one mile and a half beyond Jonesborough. He visited our wounded in hospital at that place, stating he was going to Atlanta to rest, and then he was going to Andersonville. I give you this for what it is worth. Is it not of the first importance to remove the prisoners and get as soon as possible all the troops we can from Kirby Smith?

J. B. HOOD,
General.

LOVEJOY'S, *September 7, 1864.*

General BRAGG:

Enemy has left Jonesborough. Has gone in direction of Atlanta.

J. B. HOOD,
General.

SEPTEMBER 7, 1864.

General HARDEE,
Commanding Corps :

General Hood desires you to use all diligence in reorganizing and recuperating your commands. Please hand in without delay all recommendations for promotions to fill vacancies.

[F. A. SHOUP,
Chief of Staff.]

(Same as above to the corps commanders, Generals Lee and Stewart.)

SEPTEMBER 7, 1864—7 p. m.

Lieutenant-General HARDEE,
Commanding Corps :

General Hood directs that you move your corps to Jonesborough tomorrow. You are at liberty to move at such hour as you may select.

[F. A. SHOUP,
Chief of Staff.]

SEPTEMBER 7, 1864—10.50 p. m.

General LEE,
Commanding Corps :

General Hood desires that you select some convenient place near your present lines and bivouac your corps. Let your artillery go into regular park under its senior officer. Establish such police regulations as shall secure the presence of the men.

[F. A. SHOUP,
Chief of Staff.]

(Same to General Stewart, commanding corps.)

SEPTEMBER 7, 1864.

Maj. Gen. M. L. SMITH,
        Chief Engineer :

You will proceed to Macon with a view to taking immediate steps for placing it in a state of defense.   As soon as may be, you will then visit Augusta, and afterward Columbus, Ga., to see what works or changes in the works are required at these last points.   The commanding officers of the places named will afford you all possible facilities to enable these instructions to be carried into effect.

[F. A. SHOUP,
        Chief of Staff.]

SEPTEMBER 7, 1864.

General IVERSON,
        Commanding Cavalry :

General Hood directs that you move your command to Stockbridge, and take position at or near that place.   You will exercise command of all of the cavalry east of the railroad.   Your command will consist of General Morgan's and Colonel Hannon's forces, in addition to your present command.   Your line will extend from the railroad to such point to the east as may be necessary to thoroughly observe the enemy and to prevent him, as far as possible, from getting supplies in the country.

[F. A. SHOUP,
        Chief of Staff.]

MACON, *September 7, 1864.*

General BRAGG:

Dispatch received.   Vigorous measures have already been taken here to arrest stragglers, and orders issued requiring every man to be in some organization.   Your orders will be strictly enforced, and weekly reports made.   Accounts of stragglers from Army of Tennessee are much exaggerated.   Governor Harris and other reliable parties from there report the army in good condition.

MARCUS J. WRIGHT,
        Brigadier-General, Commanding.

HEADQUARTERS ARMY OF TENNESSEE,
        September 7, 1864.

Major-General WHEELER,
        Commanding Cavalry :

GENERAL: The order for your moving back to the army is repeated. The destruction as you return of railroad and wagon trains is important, if not attended with too much risk.

Very respectfully, your obedient servant,

F. A. SHOUP,
        Chief of Staff.

HEADQUARTERS HUMES' DIVISION,
September 7, 1864.

Major-General WHEELER,
    Commanding Cavalry:

GENERAL: Colonel Russell, who is in front on the road we came in on, reports that a scout he sent out only saw three or four of the enemy. A lady told the scout that about fifty Federals advanced on that road, and that they had gone back about an hour ago.

    Respectfully,

W. Y. C. HUMES,
Brigadier-General.

2.20 P. M.

Nothing further has been heard from the enemy on the Athens road.
W. Y. C. HUMES.

WAR DEPARTMENT, C. S. A.,
Richmond, Va., September 7, 1864.

Governor M. L. BONHAM,
    Columbia, S. C.:

Movement by Sherman toward your State not anticipated. Should it occur, General Hood's army, still intact, will operate to prevent and defend. General Jones' needs do not allow withdrawal of reserves from Charleston. Instead, as many prisoners have to be temporarily sent to that city, more of the reserves are needed as indispensable guards.

J. A. SEDDON,
Secretary of War.

LOVEJOY'S STATION, GA., *September 8, 1864—2.30 p. m.*

General BRAXTON BRAGG:

I suggest that all the reserves of Georgia, under General Cobb, be ordered to this army and the prisoners removed; that Lieutenant-General Taylor be ordered to relieve General Hardee, bringing with him all the troops he can.

J. B. HOOD,
General.

LOVEJOY'S STATION, GA., *September 8, 1864—2.30 p. m.*

Maj. Gen. F. GARDNER,
    Mobile, Ala.:

I send the following dispatch to Lieutenant-General Taylor; if not there please answer. "Have any your troops crossed the river as yet? If not, when will they be over?"

[J. B. HOOD,
General.]

MOBILE, *September 8, 1864.*

General J. B. HOOD:

Your telegram received. None crossed; believe no effort is being made to cross any.

R. TAYLOR,
Lieutenant-General.

MOBILE, *September 8, 1864.*

General J. B. HOOD:

None; expect none.

R. TAYLOR,
Lieutenant-General.

SPECIAL ORDERS, }   ADJT. AND INSP. GENERAL'S OFFICE,
No. 213. }   *Richmond, Va., September 8, 1864.*

*   *   *   *   *   *   *

XVI. Maj. Gen. Arnold Elzey, Provisional Army, C. S., is assigned to duty as chief of artillery in the Army of Tennessee, and will report in person to General John B. Hood, commanding, &c.

*   *   *   *   *   *   *

By command of the Secretary of War:

JNO. WITHERS,
Assistant Adjutant-General.

HEADQUARTERS ARMY OF TENNESSEE,
September 10, 1864.

Hon. J. A. SEDDON,
Secretary of War:

The following dispatch has just been received from Major-General Wheeler, dated between Lawrenceburg, Tenn., and Athens, Ala., 6th, via Corinth and Mobile September 9:

We destroyed the railroad and bridge on the Nashville railroad, and then worked down on the Alabama and Tennessee Railroad. We destroyed fifty miles of the two railroads and destroyed several trains and much property. Every fight thus far with the enemy successful, capturing and damaging large numbers. Our loss about 100 killed and wounded. No prisoners captured in action from us.

J. B. HOOD.

ALTERNATE DESIGNATIONS

OF

ORGANIZATIONS MENTIONED IN THIS VOLUME.*

Allen's (Hiram) **Artillery.** See *Indiana Troops, 24th Battery.*
Anderson's (Edward) **Cavalry.** See *Indiana Troops, 12th Regiment.*
Armstrong's (John F.) **Cavalry.** See *Tennessee Troops, Union, 5th Regiment.*
Austin's (John H.) **Infantry.** See *Illinois Troops, 20th Regiment.*
Avery's (Isaac W.) **Cavalry.** See *Georgia Troops, 4th Regiment.*
Baldwin's (Oliver L.) **Cavalry.** See *Kentucky Troops, Union, 5th Regiment.*
Ballentine's (John G.) **Cavalry.** See *Mississippi Troops.*
Beebe's (Yates V.) **Artillery.** See *Wisconsin Troops, 10th Battery.*
Bridges' (Lyman) **Artillery.** See *Illinois Troops.*
Brookhaven Artillery. See *Mississippi Troops.*
Brown's Home Guards. (Official designation not of record.) See ——— *Brown.*
Brownlow's (James P.) **Cavalry.** See *Tennessee Troops, Union, 1st Regiment.*
Buell's (George P.) **Infantry.** See *Indiana Troops, 58th Regiment.*
Burnett's (Henry S.) **Infantry.** See *Michigan Troops, 10th Regiment.*
Byrd's (Robert K.) **Infantry.** See *Tennessee Troops, Union, 1st Regiment.*
Clinch's (Duncan L.) **Cavalry.** See *Georgia Troops, 4th Regiment.*
Cockerill's (Giles J.) **Artillery.** See *Ohio Troops, 1st Regiment, Battery D.*
Croxton's (John T.) **Infantry.** See *Kentucky Troops, Union, 4th Regiment.*
Cummings' (John P.) **Cavalry.** See *Kentucky Troops, Union, 3d Regiment.*
Dean's (Benjamin D.) **Infantry.** See *Missouri Troops, Union, 26th Regiment.*
De Gress' (Francis) **Artillery.** See *Illinois Troops, 1st Regiment, Battery H.*
Deimling's (Francis C.) **Infantry.** See *Missouri Troops, Union, 10th Regiment.*
Fulton County Militia. See *Georgia Troops.*
Gallagher's (Andrew P.) **Cavalry.** See *Indiana Troops, 4th Regiment.*
Garrard's (Israel) **Cavalry.** See *Ohio Troops, 7th Regiment.*
Gaw's (William B.) **Infantry.** See *Union Troops, Colored, 16th Regiment.*
Hall's (John P.) **Infantry.** See *Illinois Troops, 56th Regiment.*
Hamilton's (William D.) **Cavalry.** See *Ohio Troops, 9th Regiment.*
Hart's (John R.) **Cavalry.** See *Georgia Troops, 6th Regiment.*
Heath's (Thomas T.) **Cavalry.** See *Ohio Troops, 5th Regiment.*
Hoskins' (James A.) **Artillery.** See *Brookhaven Artillery, ante.*
Hughes' (Samuel T.) **Infantry.** See *Illinois Troops, 9th Regiment.*
Hurlbut's (Frederick J.) **Infantry.** See *Illinois Troops, 57th Regiment.*
Innes' (William P.) **Engineers.** See *Michigan Troops, 1st Regiment.*
Jones' (Dudley W.) **Cavalry.** See *Texas Troops, 9th Regiment.*
Jordan's (Ben.) **Guerrillas.** (Official designation not of record.) See *Ben. Jordan.*
Kennard's (George W.) **Infantry.** See *Illinois Troops, 20th Regiment.*
Lilly's (Eli) **Artillery.** See *Indiana Troops, 18th Battery.*
McClatchey's (W. T.) **Cavalry.** See *Texas Troops, 9th Regiment.*
McLaughlin's (William) **Cavalry.** See *Ohio Troops.*
Maxwell's (William L.) **Cavalry.** See *John G. Ballentine's Cavalry, ante.*

---

* References, unless otherwise indicated, are to index following.

Merrill's (William E.) **Engineers.** See *Union Troops, Volunteers, 1st Regiment, Veteran.*

Metham's (Pren.) **Infantry.** See *Ohio Troops, 80th Regiment.*

Miller's (Horace H.) **Cavalry.** See *Mississippi Troops.*

Morgan's (Thomas J.) **Infantry.** See *Union Troops, Colored, 14th Regiment.*

Murray's (Albert M.) **Artillery.** See *Union Troops, Regulars, 2d Regiment, Battery F.*

Norsworthy's (Benjamin H.) **Cavalry.** See *Texas Troops, 27th Regiment.*

Palmer's (William J.) **Cavalry.** See *Pennsylvania Troops, 15th Regiment.*

Palmetto Battalion, Artillery. See *South Carolina Troops.*

Phillips' (Jesse J.) **Infantry.** See *Illinois Troops, 9th Regiment.*

Pinson's (R. A.) **Cavalry.** See *Mississippi Troops, 1st Regiment.*

Post's (P. Sidney) **Infantry.** See *Illinois Troops, 59th Regiment.*

Presstman's (Stephen W.) **Engineers.** See *Confederate Troops, Regulars, 3d Regiment.*

Pugh's (Isaac C.) **Infantry.** See *Illinois Troops, 41st Regiment.*

Reeves' (Thomas H.) **Infantry.** See *Tennessee Troops, Union, 4th Regiment.*

Rice's (Richard) **Cavalry.** See *William McLaughlin's Cavalry, ante.*

Rippetoe's (William B.) **Artillery.** See *Indiana Troops, 18th Battery.*

Star's (Owen) **Cavalry.** See *Kentucky Troops, Union, 2d Regiment.*

Stark's (Charles W.) **Infantry.** See *Wisconsin Troops, 33d Regiment.*

Stephens' (Meshack) **Cavalry.** See *Tennessee Troops, Union, 4th Regiment.*

Stiles' (Robert A.) **Artillery.** See *Georgia Troops.*

Sutermeister's (Arnold) **Artillery.** See *Indiana Troops, 11th Battery.*

Tennessee (Confederate) **First [Sixth] Cavalry.** See *James T. Wheeler's Cavalry, post.*

Thomas' Artillery.* See *Indiana Troops, 18th Battery.*

Tuscaloosa Cadets, Infantry. See *Alabama Troops, Confederate.*

Ward's (John J.) **Artillery.** See *Alabama Troops, Confederate.*

Waties' (John) **Artillery.** See *Palmetto Battalion, Artillery, ante, Battery B.*

Welker's (Frederick) **Artillery.** See *Missouri Troops, Union, 1st Regiment, Battery H.*

Wever's (Clark R.) **Infantry.** See *Iowa Troops, 17th Regiment.*

Wheeler's (James T.) **Cavalry.** See *Tennessee Troops, Confederate.*

Windsor's (John S.) **Infantry.** See *Illinois Troops, 116th Regiment.*

Wright's (E. M.) **Cavalry.** See *Texas Troops, 9th Regiment.*

Youngblood's Battalion. (Official designation not of record.) See *Major Youngblood.*

---

* Temporarily commanding.

INDEX.

Brigades, Divisions, Corps, Armies, and improvised organizations are "Mentioned" under name of commanding officer; State and other organizations under their official designation. (See Alternate Designations, pp. 1033, 1034.)

(1035)

Page.

Page.

Page.

○